MEMOIRS OF LOUIS XIV AND HIS COURT AND OF THE REGENCY —— COMPLETE

BY

duc de Louis de Rouvroy Saint-Simon

MEMOIRS OF LOUIS XIV AND HIS COURT AND OF THE REGENCY — COMPLETE

Published by Wallachia Publishers

New York City, NY

First published circa 1755

ABOUT WALLACHIA PUBLISHERS

<u>**Wallachia Publishers**</u> mission is to publish the world's finest European history texts. More information on our recent publications and catalog can be found on our website.

MEMOIRS OF LOUIS XIV: AND HIS COURT AND OF THE REGENCY: BY THE DUKE OF SAINT-SIMON

front1 (122K)

INTRODUCTION

ILLUSTRATIONS

INTRODUCTION

No library of Court documents could pretend to be representative which ignored the famous "Memoirs" of the Duc de Saint-Simon. They stand, by universal consent, at the head of French historical papers, and are the one great source from which all historians derive their insight into the closing years of the reign of the "Grand Monarch," Louis XIV: whom the author shows to be anything but grand—and of the Regency. The opinion of the French critic, Sainte-Beuve, is fairly typical. "With the Memoirs of De Retz, it seemed that perfection had been attained, in interest, in movement, in moral analysis, in pictorial vivacity, and that there was no reason for expecting they could be surpassed. But the 'Memoirs' of Saint-Simon came; and they offer merits . . . which make them the most precious body of Memoirs that as yet exist."

Villemain declared their author to be "the most original of geniuses in French literature, the foremost of prose satirists; inexhaustible in details of manners and customs, a word-painter like Tacitus; the author of a language of his own, lacking in accuracy, system, and art, yet an admirable writer." Leon Vallee reinforces this by saying: "Saint-Simon can not be compared to any of his contemporaries. He has an individuality, a style, and a language solely his own.... Language he treated like an abject slave. When he had gone to its farthest limit, when it failed to express his ideas or feelings, he forced it—the result was a new term, or a change in the ordinary meaning of words sprang forth from has pen. With this was joined a vigour and breadth of style, very pronounced, which makes up the originality of the works of Saint-Simon and contributes toward placing their author in the foremost rank of French writers."

Louis de Rouvroy, who later became the Duc de Saint-Simon, was born in Paris, January 16, 1675. He claimed descent from Charlemagne, but the story goes that his father, as a young page of Louis XIII., gained favour with his royal master by his skill in holding the stirrup, and was finally made a duke and peer of France. The boy Louis had no lesser persons than the King and Queen Marie Therese as godparents, and made his first formal appearance at Court when seventeen. He tells us that he was not a studious boy, but was fond of reading history; and that if he had been given rein to read all he desired of it, he might have made "some figure in the world." At nineteen, like D'Artagnan, he entered the King's Musketeers. At twenty he was made a captain in the cavalry; and the same year he married the beautiful daughter of the Marechal de Larges. This marriage, which was purely political in its inception, finally turned into a genuine love match—a pleasant exception to the majority of such affairs. He became devoted to his wife, saying: "she exceeded all that was promised of her, and all that I myself had hoped." Partly because of this marriage, and also because he felt himself slighted in certain army appointments, he resigned his commissim after five years' service, and retired for a time to private life.

Upon his return to Court, taking up apartments which the royal favour had reserved for him at Versailles, Saint-Simon secretly entered upon the self-appointed task for which he is now known to fame—a task which the proud King of a vainglorious Court would have lost no time in terminating had it been discovered—the task of judge, spy, critic, portraitist, and historian, rolled into one. Day by day, henceforth for many years, he was to set down upon his private "Memoirs" the results of his personal observations, supplemented by the gossip brought to him by his unsuspecting friends; for neither courtier, statesman, minister, nor friend ever looked upon those notes which this "little Duke with his cruel, piercing, unsatisfied eyes" was so busily penning. Says Vallee: "He filled a unique position at Court, being accepted by all, even by the King himself, as a cynic, personally liked for his disposition, enjoying consideration on account of the prestige of his social connections, inspiring fear in the more timid by the severity and fearlessness of his criticism." Yet Louis XIV. never seems to have liked him, and Saint- Simon owed his influence chiefly to his friendly relations with the Dauphin's family. During the Regency, he tried to restrain the profligate Duke of Orleans, and in return was offered the position of governor of the boy, Louis XV., which he refused. Soon after, he retired to private life, and devoted his remaining years largely to revising his beloved "Memoirs." The autograph manuscript, still in existence, reveals the immense labour which he put into it. The writing is remarkable for its legibility and freedom from erasure. It comprises no less than 2,300 pages in folio.

After the author's death, in 1755, the secret of his lifelong labour was revealed; and the Duc de Choiseul, fearing the result of these frank revelations, confiscated them and placed them among the state archives. For sixty years they remained under lock and key, being seen by only a few privileged persons, among them Marmontel, Duclos, and Voltaire. A garbled version of extracts appeared in 1789, possibly being used as a Revolutionary text. Finally, in 1819, a descendant of the analyst, bearing the same name, obtained permission from Louis XVIII. to set this "prisoner of the Bastille" at liberty; and in 1829 an authoritative edition, revised and arranged by chapters, appeared. It created a tremendous stir. Saint-Simon had been merciless, from King down to lady's maid, in depicting the daily life of a famous Court. He had stripped it of all its tinsel and pretension, and laid the ragged framework bare. "He wrote like the Devil for posterity!" exclaimed Chateaubriand. But the work at once became universally read and quoted, both in France and England. Macaulay made frequent use of it in his historical essays. It was, in a word, recognised as the chief authority upon an important period of thirty years (1694-1723).

Since then it has passed through many editions, finally receiving an adequate English translation at the hands of Bayle St. John, who has been careful to adhere to the peculiarities of Saint-Simon's style. It is this version which is now presented in full, giving us not only many vivid pictures of the author's time, but of the author himself. "I do not pride myself upon my freedom from prejudice—impartiality," he confesses—"it would be useless to attempt it. But I have tried at all times to tell the truth."

VOLUME 1.: CHAPTER I

I was born on the night of the 15th of January, 1675, of Claude Duc de Saint-Simon, Peer of France, and of his second wife Charlotte de l'Aubepine. I was the only child of that marriage. By his first wife, Diana de Budos, my father had had only a daughter. He married her to the Duc de Brissac, Peer of France, only brother of the Duchesse de Villeroy. She died in 1684, without children,—having been long before separated from a husband who was unworthy of her— leaving me heir of all her property.

I bore the name of the Vidame de Chartres; and was educated with great care and attention. My mother, who was remarkable for virtue, perseverance, and sense, busied herself continually in forming my mind and body. She feared for me the usual fate of young men, who believe their fortunes made, and who find themselves their own masters early in life. It was not likely that my father, born in 1606, would live long enough to ward off from me this danger; and my mother repeatedly impressed on, me how necessary it was for a young man, the son of the favourite of a King long dead,—with no new friends at Court,—to acquire some personal value of his own. She succeeded in stimulating my courage; and in exciting in me the desire to make the acquisitions she laid stress on; but my aptitude for study and the sciences did not come up to my desire to succeed in them. However, I had an innate inclination for reading, especially works of history; and thus was inspired with ambition to emulate the examples presented to my imagination,—to do something and become somebody, which partly made amends for my coldness for letters. In fact, I have always thought that if I had been allowed to read history more constantly, instead of losing my time in studies for which I had no aptness, I might have made some figure in the world.

What I read of my own accord, of history, and, above all, of the personal memoirs of the times since Francis I., bred in me the desire to write down what I might myself see. The hope of advancement, and of becoming familiar with the affairs of my time, stirred me. The annoyances I might thus bring upon myself did not fail to present themselves to my mind; but the firm resolution I made to keep my writings secret from everybody, appeared to me to remedy all evils. I commenced my memoirs then in July, 1694, being at that time colonel of a cavalry regiment bearing my name, in the camp of Guinsheim, upon the old Rhine, in the army commanded by the Marechal Duc de Lorges.

In 1691 I was studying my philosophy and beginning to learn to ride at an academy at Rochefort, getting mightily tired of masters and books, and anxious to join the army. The siege of Mons, formed by the King in person, at the commencement of the spring, had drawn away all the young men of my age to commence their first campaign; and, what piqued me most, the Duc de Chartres was there, too. I had been, as it were, educated with him. I was younger than he by eight months; and if the expression be allowed in speaking of young people, so unequal in position, friendship had united us. I made up my mind, therefore, to escape from my leading-strings; but pass lightly over the artifices I used in order to attain success. I addressed myself to my mother. I soon saw that she trifled with me. I had recourse to my father, whom I made believe that the King, having led a great siege this year, would rest the next. I said nothing of this to my mother, who did not discover my plot until it was just upon the point, of execution.

The King had determined rigidly to adhere to a rule he had laid down— namely, that none who entered the service, except his illegitimate children, and the Princes of the blood royal, should be exempt from serving for a year in one of his two companies of musketeers; and passing afterwards through the ordeal of being private or subaltern in one of the regiments of cavalry or infantry, before receiving permission to purchase a regiment. My father took me, therefore, to Versailles, where he had not been for many years, and begged of the King admission for me into the Musketeers. It was on the day of St. Simon and St. Jude, at half-past twelve, and just as his Majesty came out of the council.

The King did my father the honour of embracing him three times, and then turned towards me. Finding that I was little and of delicate appearance, he said I was still very young; to which my father replied, that I should be able in consequence to serve longer. Thereupon the King demanded in which of the two companies he wished to put me; and my father named that commanded by Maupertuis, who was one of his friends. The King relied much upon the information given him by the captains of the two companies of Musketeers, as to the young men who served in them. I have reason for believing, that I owe to Maupertuis the first good opinion that his Majesty had of me.

Three months after entering the Musketeers, that is to say, in the March of the following year, the King held a review of his guards, and of the gendarmerie, at Compiegne, and I mounted guard once at the palace. During this little journey there was talk of a much more important one. My joy was extreme; but my father, who had not counted upon this, repented of having believed me, when I told him that the King would no doubt rest at Paris this year. My mother, after a little vexation and pouting at finding me enrolled by my father against her will, did not fail to bring him to reason, and to make him provide me with an equipment of thirty-five horses or mules, and means to live honourably.

A grievous annoyance happened in our house about three weeks before my departure. A steward of my father named Tesse, who had been with him many years, disappeared all at once with fifty thousand francs due to various tradesfolk. He had written out false receipts from these people, and put them in his accounts. He was a little man, gentle, affable, and clever; who had shown some probity, and who had many friends.

The King set out on the 10th of May, 1692, with the ladies; and I performed the journey on horseback with the soldiers and all the attendants, like the other Musketeers, and continued to do so through the whole campaign. I was accompanied by two gentlemen; the one had been my tutor, the other was my mother's squire. The King's army was formed at the camp of Gevries; that of M. de Luxembourg almost joined it: The ladies were at Mons, two leagues distant. The King made them come into his camp, where he entertained them; and then showed them, perhaps; the most superb review which had ever been seen. The two armies were ranged in two lines, the right of M. de Luxembourg's touching the left of the King's,—the whole extending over three leagues of ground.

After stopping ten days at Gevries, the two armies separated and marched. Two days afterwards the seige of Namur was declared. The King arrived there in five days. Monseigneur (son of the King); Monsieur (Duc d'Orleans, brother of the King); M. le Prince (de Conde) and Marechal d'Humieres; all four, the one under the other, commanded in the King's army under the King himself. The Duc de Luxembourg, sole general of his own army, covered the siege operations, and observed the enemy. The ladies went away to Dinant. On the third day of the march M. le Prince went forward to invest the place.

The celebrated Vauban, the life and soul of all the sieges the King made, was of opinion that the town should be attacked separately from the castle; and his advice was acted upon. The Baron de Bresse, however, who had fortified the place, was for attacking town and castle together. He was a humble down-looking man, whose physiognomy promised nothing, but who soon acquired the confidence of the King, and the esteem of the army.

The Prince de Conde, Marechal d'Humieres, and the Marquis de Boufflers each led an attack. There was nothing worthy of note during the ten days the siege lasted. On the eleventh day, after the trenches had been opened, a parley was beaten and a capitulation made almost as the besieged desired it. They withdrew to the castle; and it was agreed that it should not be attacked from the town-side, and that the town was not to be battered by it. During the siege the King was almost always in his tent; and the weather remained constantly warm and serene. We lost scarcely anybody of consequence. The Comte de Toulouse received a slight wound in the arm while quite close to the King, who from a prominent place was witnessing the attack of a half-moon, which was carried in broad daylight by a detachment of the oldest of the two companies of Musketeers.

The siege of the castle next commenced. The position of the camp was changed. The King's tents and those of all the Court were pitched in a beautiful meadow about five hundred paces from the monastery of Marlaigne. The fine weather changed to rain, which fell with an abundance and perseverance never before known by any one in the army. This circumstance increased the reputation of Saint Medard, whose fete falls on the 8th of June. It rained in torrents that day, and it is said that when such is the case it will rain for forty days afterwards. By chance it happened so this year. The soldiers in despair at this deluge uttered many imprecations against the Saint; and looked for images of him, burning and breaking as many as they could find. The rains sadly interfered with the progress of the siege. The tents of the King could only be communicated with by paths laid with fascines which required to be renewed every day, as they sank down into the soil. The camps and quarters were no longer accessible; the trenches were full of mud and water, and it took often three days to remove cannon from one battery to another. The waggons became useless, too, so that the transport of bombs, shot, and so forth, could not be performed except upon the backs of mules and of horses taken from the equipages of the Court and the army. The state of the roads deprived the Duc de Luxembourg of the use of waggons and other vehicles. His army was perishing for want of grain. To remedy this inconvenience the King ordered all his household troops to mount every day on horseback by detachments, and to take sacks of grain upon their cruppers to a village where they were to be received and counted by the officers of the Duc de Luxembourg. Although the household of the King had scarcely any repose during this siege, what with carrying fascines, furnishing guards, and other daily services, this increase of duty was given to it because the cavalry served continually also, and was reduced almost entirely to leaves of trees for provender.

The household of the King, accustomed to all sorts of distinctions, complained bitterly of this task. But the King turned a deaf ear to them, and would be obeyed. On the first day some of the Gendarmes and of the light horse of the guard arrived early in the morning at the depot of the sacks, and commenced murmuring and exciting each other by their discourses. They threw down the sacks at last and flatly refused to carry them. I had been asked very politely if I would be of the detachment for the sacks or of some other. I decided for the sacks, because I felt that I might thereby advance myself, the subject having already made much noise. I arrived with the detachment of the Musketeers at the moment of the refusal of the others; and I loaded my sack before their eyes. Marin, a brigadier of cavalry and lieutenant of the body guards, who was there to superintend the operation, noticed me, and full of anger at the refusal he had just met with, exclaimed that as I did not think such work beneath me, the rest would do well to imitate my example. Without a word being spoken each took up his sack; and from that time forward no further difficulty occurred in the matter. As soon as the detachment had gone, Marin went straight to the King and told him what had occurred. This was a service which procured for me several obliging discourses from his Majesty, who during the rest of the siege always sought to say something agreeable every time he met me.

The twenty-seventh day after opening the trenches, that is, the first of July, 1692, a parley was sounded by the Prince de Barbançon, governor of the place,—a fortunate circumstance for the besiegers, who were worn out with fatigue; and destitute of means, on account of the wretched weather which still continued, and which had turned the whole country round into a quagmire. Even the horses of the King lived upon leaves, and not a horse of all our numerous cavalry ever thoroughly recovered from the effects of such sorry fare. It is certain that without the presence of the King the siege might never have been successful; but he being there, everybody was stimulated. Yet had the place held out ten days longer, there is no saying what might have happened. Before the end of the siege the King was so much fatigued with his exertions, that a new attack of gout came on, with more pain than ever, and compelled him to keep his bed, where, however, he thought of everything, and laid out his plans as though he had been at Versailles.

During the entire siege, the Prince of Orange (William III. of England) had unavailingly used all his science to dislodge the Duc de Luxembourg; but he had to do with a man who in matters of war was his superior, and who continued so all his life. Namur, which, by the surrender of the castle, was now entirely in our power, was one of the strongest places in the Low Countries, and had hitherto boasted of having never changed masters. The inhabitants could not restrain their tears of sorrow. Even the monks of Marlaigne were profoundly moved, so much so, that they could not disguise their grief. The King, feeling for the loss of their corn that they had sent for safety into Namur, gave them double the quantity, and abundant alms. He incommoded them as little as possible, and would not permit the passage of cannon across their park, until it was found impossible to transport it by any other road. Notwithstanding these acts of goodness, they could scarcely look upon a Frenchman after the taking of the place; and one actually refused to give a bottle of beer to an usher of the King's antechamber, although offered a bottle of champagne in exchange for it!

A circumstance happened just after the taking of Namur, which might have led to the saddest results, under any other prince than the King. Before he entered the town, a strict examination of every place was made, although by the capitulation all the mines, magazines, &c., had to be shown. At a visit paid to the Jesuits, they pretended to show everything, expressing, however, surprise and something more, that their bare word was not enough. But on examining here and there, where they did not expect search would be made, their cellars were found to be stored with gunpowder, of which they had taken good care to say no word. What they meant to do with it is uncertain. It was carried away, and as they were Jesuits nothing was done.

During the course of this siege, the King suffered a cruel disappointment. James II. of England, then a refugee in France, had advised the King to give battle to the English fleet. Joined to that of Holland it was very superior to the sea forces of France. Tourville, our admiral, so famous for his valour and skill, pointed this circumstance out to the King. But it was all to no effect. He was ordered to attack the enemy. He did so. Many of his ships were burnt, and the victory was won by the English. A courier entrusted with this sad intelligence was despatched to the King. On his way he was joined by another courier, who pressed him for his news. The first courier knew that if he gave up his news, the other, who was better mounted, would outstrip him, and be the first to carry it to the King. He told his companion, therefore, an idle tale, very different indeed from the truth, for he changed the defeat into a great victory. Having gained this wonderful intelligence, the second courier put spurs to his horse, and hurried away to the King's camp, eager to be the bearer of good tidings. He reached the camp first, and was received with delight. While his Majesty was still in great joy at his happy victory, the other courier arrived with the real details. The Court appeared prostrated. The King was much afflicted. Nevertheless he found means to appear to retain his self-possession, and I saw, for the first time, that Courts are not long in affliction or occupied with sadness. I must mention that the (exiled) King of England looked on at this naval battle from the shore; and was accused of allowing expressions of partiality to escape him in favour of his countrymen, although none had kept their promises to him.

Two days after the defeated garrison had marched out, the King went to Dinant, to join the ladies, with whom he returned to Versailles. I had hoped that Monseigneur would finish the campaign, and that I should be with him, and it was not without regret that I returned towards Paris. On the way a little circumstance happened. One of our halting-places was Marienburgh, where we camped for the night. I had become united in friendship with Comte de Coetquen, who was in the same company with myself. He was well instructed and full of wit; was exceedingly rich, and even more idle than rich. That evening he had invited several of us to supper in his tent. I went there early, and found him stretched out upon his bed, from which I dislodged him playfully and laid myself down in his place, several of our officers standing by. Coetquen, sporting with me in return, took his gun, which he thought to be unloaded, and pointed it at me. But to our great surprise the weapon went off. Fortunately for me, I was at that moment lying flat upon the bed. Three balls passed just above my head, and then just above the heads of our two tutors, who were walking outside the tent. Coetquen fainted at thought of the mischief he might have done, and we had all the pains in the world to bring him to himself again. Indeed, he did not thoroughly recover for several days. I relate this as a lesson which ought to teach us never to play with fire-arms.

The poor lad,—to finish at once all that concerns him,—did not long survive this incident. He entered the King's regiment, and when just upon the point of joining it in the following spring, came to me and said he had had his fortune told by a woman named Du Perehoir, who practised her trade secretly at Paris, and that she had predicted he would be soon drowned. I rated him soundly for indulging a curiosity so dangerous and so foolish. A few days after he set out for Amiens. He found another fortune-teller there, a man, who made the same prediction. In marching afterwards with the regiment of the King to join the army, he wished to water his horse in the Escaut, and was drowned there, in the presence of the whole regiment, without it being possible to give him any aid. I felt extreme regret for his loss, which for his friends and his family was irreparable.

But I must go back a little, and speak of two marriages that took place at the commencement of this year the first (most extraordinary) on the 18th February the other a month after.

CHAPTER II.

The King was very anxious to establish his illegitimate children, whom he advanced day by day; and had married two of them, daughters, to Princes of the blood. One of these, the Princesse de Conti, only daughter of the King and Madame de la Valliere, was a widow without children; the other, eldest daughter of the King and Madame de Montespan, had married Monsieur le Duc (Louis de Bourbon, eldest son of the Prince de Conde). For some time past Madame de Maintenon, even more than the King, had thought of nothing else than how to raise the remaining illegitimate children, and wished to marry Mademoiselle de Blois (second daughter of the King and of Madame de Montespan) to Monsieur the Duc de Chartres. The Duc de Chartres was the sole nephew of the King, and was much above the Princes of the blood by his rank of Grandson of France, and by the Court that Monsieur his father kept up.

The marriages of the two Princes of the blood, of which I have just spoken, had scandalised all the world. The King was not ignorant of this; and he could thus judge of the effect of a marriage even more startling; such as was this proposed one. But for four years he had turned it over in his mind and had even taken the first steps to bring it about. It was the more difficult because the father of the Duc de Chartres was infinitely proud of his rank, and the mother belonged to a nation which abhorred illegitimacy and, misalliances, and was indeed of a character to forbid all hope of her ever relishing this marriage.

In order to vanquish all these obstacles, the King applied to M. le Grand (Louis de Lorraine). This person was brother of the Chevalier de Lorraine, the favourite, by disgraceful means, of Monsieur, father of the Duc de Chartres. The two brothers, unscrupulous and corrupt, entered willingly into the scheme, but demanded as a reward, paid in advance, to be made "Chevaliers of the Order." This was done, although somewhat against the inclination of the King, and success was promised.

The young Duc de Chartres had at that time for teacher Dubois (afterwards the famous Cardinal Dubois), whose history was singular. He had formerly been a valet; but displaying unusual aptitude for learning, had been instructed by his master in literature and history, and in due time passed into the service of Saint Laurent, who was the Duc de Chartres' first instructor. He became so useful and showed so much skill, that Saint Laurent made him become an abbe. Thus raised in position, he passed much time with the Duc de Chartres, assisting him to prepare his lessons, to write his exercises, and to look out words in the dictionary. I have seen him thus engaged over and over again, when I used to go and play with the Duc de Chartres. As Saint Laurent grew infirm, Dubois little by little supplied his place; supplied it well too, and yet pleased the young Duke. When Saint Laurent died Dubois aspired to succeed him. He had paid his court to the Chevalier de Lorraine, by whose influence he was much aided in obtaining his wish. When at last appointed successor to Saint Laurent, I never saw a man so glad, nor with more reason. The extreme obligation he was under to the Chevalier de Lorraine, and still more the difficulty of maintaining himself in his new position, attached him more and more to his protector.

It was, then, Dubois that the Chevalier de Lorraine made use of to gain the consent of the young Duc de Chartres to the marriage proposed by the King. Dubois had, in fact, gained the Duke's confidence, which it was easy to do at that age; had made him afraid of his father and of the King; and, on the other hand, had filled him with fine hopes and expectations. All that Dubois could do, however, when he broke the matter of the marriage to the young Duke, was to ward off a direct refusal; but that was sufficient for the success of the enterprise. Monsieur was already gained, and as soon as the King had a reply from Dubois he hastened to broach the affair. A day or two before this, however, Madame (mother of the Duc de Chartres) had scent of what was going on. She spoke to her son of the indignity of this marriage with that force in which she was never wanting, and drew from him a promise that he would not consent to it. Thus, he was feeble towards his teacher, feeble towards his mother, and there was aversion on the one hand and fear on the other, and great embarrassment on all sides.

One day early after dinner I saw M. de Chartres, with a very sad air, come out of his apartment and enter the closet of the King. He found his Majesty alone with Monsieur. The King spoke very obligingly to the Duc de Chartres, said that he wished to see him married; that he offered him his daughter, but that he did not intend to constrain him in the matter, but left him quite at liberty. This discourse, however, pronounced with that terrifying majesty so natural to the King, and addressed to a timid young prince, took away his voice, and quite unnerved him. He, thought to escape from his slippery position by throwing himself upon Monsieur and Madame, and stammeringly replied that the King was master, but that a son's will depended upon that of his parents. "What you say is very proper," replied the King; "but as soon as you consent to my proposition your father and mother will not oppose it." And then turning to Monsieur he said, "Is this not true, my brother?" Monsieur consented, as he had already done, and the only person remaining to consult was Madame, who was immediately sent for.

As soon as she came, the King, making her acquainted with his project, said that he reckoned she would not oppose what her husband and her son had already agreed to. Madame, who had counted upon the refusal of her son, was tongue-tied. She threw two furious glances upon Monsieur and upon the Duc de Chartres, and then said that, as they wished it, she had nothing to say, made a slight reverence, and went away. Her son immediately followed her to explain his conduct; but railing against him, with tears in her eyes, she would not listen, and drove him from her room. Her husband, who shortly afterwards joined her, met with almost the same treatment.

That evening an "Apartment" was held at the palace, as was customary three times a week during the winter; the other three evenings being set apart for comedy, and the Sunday being free. An Apartment as it was called, was an assemblage of all the Court in the grand saloon, from seven o'clock in the evening until ten, when the King sat down to table; and, after ten, in one of the saloons at the end of the grand gallery towards the tribune of the chapel. In the first place there was some music; then tables were placed all about for all kinds of gambling; there was a 'lansquenet'; at which Monsieur and Monseigneur always played; also a billiard-table; in a word, every one was free to play with every one, and allowed to ask for fresh tables as all the others were occupied. Beyond the billiards was a refreshment-room. All was perfectly lighted. At the outset, the King went to the "apartments" very often and played, but lately he had ceased to do so. He spent the evening with Madame de Maintenon, working with different ministers one after the other. But still he wished his courtiers to attend assiduously.

This evening, directly after the music had finished, the King sent for Monseigneur and Monsieur, who were already playing at 'lansquenet'; Madame, who scarcely looked at a party of 'hombre' at which she had seated herself; the Duc de Chartres, who, with a rueful visage, was playing at chess; and Mademoiselle de Blois, who had scarcely begun to appear in society, but who this evening was extraordinarily decked out, and who, as yet, knew nothing and suspected nothing; and therefore, being naturally very timid, and horribly afraid of the King, believed herself sent for in order to be reprimanded, and trembled so that Madame de Maintenon took her upon her knees, where she held her, but was scarcely able to reassure her. The fact of these royal persons being sent for by the King at once made people think that a marriage was in contemplation. In a few minutes they returned, and then the announcement was made public. I arrived at that moment. I found everybody in clusters, and great astonishment expressed upon every face. Madame was walking in the gallery with Chateauthiers—her favourite, and worthy of being so. She took long strides, her handkerchief in her hand, weeping without constraint, speaking pretty loudly, gesticulating; and looking like Ceres after the rape of her daughter Proserpine, seeking her in fury, and demanding her back from Jupiter. Every one respectfully made way to let her pass. Monsieur, who had returned to 'lansquenet', seemed overwhelmed with shame, and his son appeared in despair; and the bride-elect was marvellously embarrassed and sad. Though very young, and likely to be dazzled by such a marriage, she understood what was passing, and feared the consequences. Most people appeared full of consternation.

The Apartment, which, however heavy in appearance, was full of interest to, me, seemed quite short. It finished by the supper of the King. His Majesty appeared quite at ease. Madame's eyes were full of tears, which fell from time to time as she looked into every face around, as if in search of all our thoughts. Her son, whose eyes too were red, she would not give a glance to; nor to Monsieur: all three ate scarcely anything. I remarked that the King offered Madame nearly all the dishes that were before him, and that she refused with an air of rudeness which did not, however, check his politeness. It was furthermore noticeable that, after leaving the table, he made to Madame a very marked and very low reverence, during which she performed so complete a pirouette, that the King on raising his head found nothing but her back before him, removed about a step further towards the door.

On the morrow we went as usual to wait in the gallery for the breaking-up of the council, and for the King's Mass. Madame came there. Her son approached her, as he did every day, to kiss her hand. At that very moment she gave him a box on the ear, so sonorous that it was heard several steps distant. Such treatment in presence of all the Court covered with confusion this unfortunate prince, and overwhelmed the infinite number of spectators, of whom I was one, with prodigious astonishment.

That day the immense dowry was declared; and on Sunday there was a grand ball, that is, a ball opened by a 'branle' which settled the order of the dancing throughout the evening. Monseigneur the Duc de Bourgogne danced on this occasion for the first time; and led off the 'branle' with Mademoiselle. I danced also for the first time at Court. My partner was Mademoiselle de Sourches, daughter of the Grand Prevot; she danced excellently. I had been that morning to wait on Madame, who could not refrain from saying, in a sharp and angry voice, that I was doubtless very glad of the promise of so many balls—that this was natural at my age; but that, for her part, she was old, and wished they were well over. A few days after, the contract of marriage was signed in the closet of the King, and in the presence of all the Court. The same day the household of the future Duchesse de Chartres was declared. The King gave her a first gentleman usher and a Dame d'Atours, until then reserved to the daughters of France, and a lady of honour, in order to carry out completely so strange a novelty. I must say something about the persons who composed this household.

M. de Villars was gentleman usher; he was grandson of a recorder of Coindrieu, and one of the best made men in France. There was a great deal of fighting in his young days, and he had acquired a reputation for courage and skill. To these qualities he owed his fortune. M. de Nemours was his first patron, and, in a duel which he had with M. de Beaufort, took Villars for second. M. de Nemours was killed; but Villars was victorious against his adversary, and passed into the service of the Prince de Conti as one of his gentlemen. He succeeded in gaining confidence in his new employment; so much so, that the marriage which afterwards took place between the Prince de Conti and the niece of Cardinal Mazarin was brought about in part by his assistance. He became the confidant of the married pair, and their bond: of union with the Cardinal. His position gave him an opportunity of mixing in society much above him; but on this he never presumed. His face was his, passport with the ladies: he was gallant, even discreet; and this means was not unuseful to him. He pleased Madame Scarron, who upon the throne never forgot the friendships of this kind, so freely intimate, which she had formed as a private person. Villars was employed in diplomacy; and from honour to honour, at last reached the order of the Saint Esprit, in 1698. His wife was full of wit, and scandalously inclined. Both were very poor— and always dangled about the Court, where they had many powerful friends.

The Marechale de Rochefort was lady of honour. She was of the house of Montmorency—a widow—handsome—sprightly; formed by nature to live at Court—apt for gallantry and intrigues; full of worldly cleverness, from living much in the world, with little cleverness of any other kind, nearly enough for any post and any business. M. de Louvois found her suited to his taste, and she accommodated herself very well to his purse, and to the display she made by this intimacy. She always became the friend of every new mistress of the King; and when he favoured Madame de Soubise, it was at the Marechale's house that she waited, with closed doors, for Bontems, the King's valet, who led her by private ways to his Majesty. The Marechale herself has related to me how one day she was embarrassed to get rid of the people that Madame de Soubise (who had not had time to announce her arrival) found at her house; and how she most died of fright lest Bontems should return and the interview be broken off if he arrived before the company had departed. The Marechale de Rochefort was in this way the friend of Mesdames de la Valliere, de Montespan, and de Soubise; and she became the friend of Madame de Maintenon, to whom she attached herself in proportion as she saw her favour increase. She had, at the marriage of Monseigneur, been made Dame d'Atours to the new Dauphiness; and, if people were astonished at that, they were also astonished to see her lady of honour to an "illegitimate grand-daughter of France."

The Comtesse de Mailly was Dame d'Atours. She was related to Madame de Maintenon, to whose favour she owed her marriage with the Comte de Mailly. She had come to Paris with all her provincial awkwardness, and, from want of wit, had never been able to get rid of it. On the contrary, she grafted thereon an immense conceit, caused by the favour of Madame de Maintenon. To complete the household, came M. de Fontaine-Martel, poor and gouty, who was first master of the horse.

On the Monday before Shrove Tuesday, all the marriage party and the bride and bridegroom, superbly dressed, repaired, a little before mid-day, to the closet of the King, and afterwards to the chapel. It was arranged, as usual, for the Mass of the King, excepting that between his place and the altar were two cushions for the bride and bridegroom, who turned their backs to the King. Cardinal de Bouillon, in full robes, married them, and said Mass. From the chapel all the company went to table: it was of horse-shoe shape. The Princes and Princesses of the blood were placed at the right and at the left, according to their rank, terminated by the two illegitimate children of the King, and, for the first time, after them, the Duchesse de Verneuil; so that M. de Verneuil, illegitimate son of Henry IV., became thus "Prince of the blood" so many years after his death, without having ever suspected it. The Duc d'Uzes thought this so amusing that he marched in front of the Duchess, crying out, as loud as he could—"Place, place for Madame Charlotte Seguier!" In the afternoon the King and Queen of England came to Versailles with their Court. There was a great concert; and the play-tables were set out. The supper was similar to the dinner. Afterwards the married couple were led into the apartment of the new Duchesse de Chartres. The Queen of England gave the Duchess her chemise; and the shirt of the Duke was given to him by the King, who had at first refused on the plea that he was in too unhappy circumstances. The benediction of the bed was pronounced by the Cardinal de Bouillon, who kept us all waiting for a quarter of an hour; which made people say that such airs little became a man returned as he was from a long exile, to which he had been sent because he had had the madness to refuse the nuptial benediction to Madame la Duchesse unless admitted to the royal banquet.

On Shrove Tuesday, there was a grand toilette of the Duchesse de Chartres, to which the King and all the Court came; and in the evening a grand ball, similar to that which had just taken place, except that the new Duchesse de Chartres was led out by the Duc de Bourgogne. Every one wore the same dress, and had the same partner as before.

I cannot pass over in silence a very ridiculous adventure which occurred at both of these balls. A son of Montbron, no more made to dance at Court than his father was to be chevalier of the order (to which however, he was promoted in 1688), was among the company. He had been asked if he danced well; and he had replied with a confidence which made every one hope that the contrary was the case. Every one was satisfied. From the very first bow, he became confused, and he lost step at once. He tried to divert attention from his mistake by affected attitudes, and carrying his arms high; but this made him only more ridiculous, and excited bursts of laughter, which, in despite of the respect due to the person of the King (who likewise had great difficulty to hinder himself from laughing), degenerated at length into regular hooting. On the morrow, instead of flying the Court or holding his tongue, he excused himself by saying that the presence of the King had disconcerted him; and promised marvels for the ball which was to follow. He was one of my friends, and I felt for him, I should even have warned him against a second attempt, if the very indifferent success I had met with had not made me fear that my advice would be taken in ill part. As soon as he began to dance at the second ball, those who were near stood up, those who were far off climbed wherever they could get a sight; and the shouts of laughter were mingled with clapping of hands. Every one, even the King himself, laughed heartily, and most of us quite loud, so that I do not think any one was ever treated so before. Montbron disappeared immediately afterwards, and did not show himself again for a long time, It was a pity he exposed himself to this defeat, for he was an honourable and brave man.

Ash Wednesday put an end to all these sad rejoicings by command, and only the expected rejoicings were spoken of. M. du Maine wished to marry. The King tried to turn him from it, and said frankly to him, that it was not for such as he to make a lineage. But pressed M. by Madame de Maintenon, who had educated Maine; and who felt for him as a nurse the King resolved to marry him to a daughter of the Prince de Conde. The Prince was greatly pleased at the project. He had three daughters for M. du Maine to choose from: all three were extremely little. An inch of height, that the second had above the others, procured for her the preference, much to the grief of the eldest, who was beautiful and clever, and who dearly wished to escape from the slavery in which her father kept her. The dignity with which she bore her disappointment was admired by every one, but it cost her an effort that ruined her health. The marriage once arranged, was celebrated on the 19th of March; much in the same manner as had been that of the Duc de Chartres. Madame de Saint-Vallery was appointed lady of honour to Madame du Maine, and M. de Montchevreuil gentleman of the chamber. This last had been one of the friends of Madame de Maintenon when she was Madame Scarron. Montchevreuil was a very honest man, modest, brave, but thick-headed. His wife was a tall creature, meagre, and yellow, who laughed sillily, and showed long and ugly teeth; who was extremely devout, of a compassed mien, and who only wanted a broomstick to be a perfect witch. Without possessing any wit, she had so captivated Madame de Maintenon, that the latter saw only with her eyes. All the ladies of the Court were under her surveillance: they depended upon her for their distinctions, and often for their fortunes. Everybody, from the ministers to the daughters of the King, trembled before her. The King himself showed her the most marked consideration. She was of all the Court journeys, and always with Madame de Maintenon.

The marriage of M. du Maine caused a rupture between the Princess de Conde and the Duchess of Hanover her sister, who had strongly desired M. du Maine for one of her daughters, and who pretended that the Prince de Conde had cut the grass from under her feet. She lived in Paris, making a display quite unsuited to her rank, and had even carried it so far as to go about with two coaches and many liveried servants. With this state one day she met in the streets the coach of Madame de Bouillon, which the servants of the German woman forced to give way to their mistress's. The Bouillons, piqued to excess, resolved to be revenged. One day, when they knew the Duchess was going to the play, they went there attended by a numerous livery. Their servants had orders to pick a quarrel with those of the Duchess. They executed these orders completely; the servants of the Duchess were thoroughly thrashed—the harness of her horses cut—her coaches maltreated. The Duchess made a great fuss, and complained to the King, but he would not mix himself in the matter. She was so outraged, that she resolved to retire into Germany, and in a very few months did so.

My year of service in the Musketeers being over, the King, after a time, gave me, without purchase, a company of cavalry in the Royal Roussillon, in garrison at Mons, and just then very incomplete. I thanked the King, who replied to me very obligingly. The company was entirely made up in a fortnight. This was towards the middle of April.

A little before, that is, on the 27th of March, the King made seven new marechals of France. They were the Comte de Choiseul, the Duc de Villeroy, the Marquis de Joyeuse, Tourville, the Duc de Noailles, the Marquis de Boufllers, and Catinat. These promotions caused very great discontent. Complaint was more especially made that the Duc de Choiseul had not been named. The cause of his exclusion is curious. His wife, beautiful, with the form of a goddess—notorious for the number of her gallantries—was very intimate with the Princess de Conti. The King, not liking such a companion for his daughter, gave the Duc de Choiseul to understand that the public disorders of the Duchess offended him. If the Duke would send her into a convent, the Marechal's baton would be his. The Duc de Choiseul, indignant that the reward of his services in the war was attached to a domestic affair which concerned himself alone, refused promotion on such terms. He thus lost the baton; and, what was worse for him, the Duchess soon after was driven from Court, and so misbehaved herself, that at last he could endure her no longer, drove her away himself, and separated from her for ever.

Mademoiselle la grande Mademoiselle, as she was called, to distinguish her from the daughter of Monsieur—or to call her by her name, Mademoiselle de Montpensier, died on Sunday the 5th of April, at her palace in the Luxembourg, sixty-three years of age, and the richest private princess in Europe. She interested herself much in those who were related to her, even to the lowest degree, and wore mourning for them, however far removed. It is well known, from all the memoirs of the time, that she was greatly in love with M. de Lauzun, and that she suffered much when the King withheld his permission to their marriage. M. de Lauzun was so enraged, that he could not contain himself, and at last went so far beyond bounds, that he was sent prisoner to Pignerol, where he remained, extremely ill-treated, for ten years. The affection of Mademoiselle did not grow cold by separation. The King profited by it, to make M. de Lauzun buy his liberty at her expense, and thus enriched M. du Maine. He always gave out that he had married Mademoiselle, and appeared before the King, after her death, in a long cloak, which gave great displeasure. He also assumed ever afterwards a dark brown livery, as an external expression of his grief for Mademoiselle, of whom he had portraits everywhere. As for Mademoiselle, the

King never quite forgave her the day of Saint Antoine; and I heard him once at supper reproach her in jest, for having fired the cannons of the Bastille upon his troops. She was a little embarrassed, but she got out of the difficulty very well.

Her body was laid out with great state, watched for several days, two hours at a time, by a duchess or a princess, and by two ladies of quality. The Comtesse de Soissons refused to take part in this watching, and would not obey until the King threatened to dismiss her from the Court. A very ridiculous accident happened in the midst of this ceremony. The urn containing the entrails fell over, with a frightful noise and a stink sudden and intolerable. The ladies, the heralds, the psalmodists, everybody present fled, in confusion. Every one tried to gain the door first. The entrails had been badly embalmed, and it was their fermentation which caused the accident. They were soon perfumed and put in order, and everybody laughed at this mishap. These entrails were in the end carried to the Celestins, the heart to Val de Grace, and the body to the Cathedral of Saint Denis, followed by a numerous company.

CHAPTER III

On May 3d 1693, the King announced his intention of placing himself at the head of his army in Flanders, and, having made certain alterations in the rule of precedence of the marechale of France, soon after began the campaign. I have here, however, to draw attention to my private affairs, for on the above-mentioned day, at ten o'clock in the morning, I had the misfortune to lose my father. He was eighty-seven years of age, and had been in bad health for some time, with a touch of gout during the last three weeks. On the day in question he had dined as usual with his friends, had retired to bed, and, while talking to those around him there, all at once gave three violent sighs. He was dead almost before it was perceived that he was ill; there was no more oil in the lamp.

I learned this sad news after seeing the King to bed; his Majesty was to purge himself on the morrow. The night was given to the just sentiments of nature; but the next day I went early to visit Bontems, and then the Duc de Beauvilliers, who promised to ask the King, as soon as his curtains were opened, to grant me the—offices my father had held. The King very graciously complied with his request, and in the afternoon said many obliging things to me, particularly expressing his regret that my father had not been able to receive the last sacraments. I was able to say that a very short time before, my father had retired for several days to Saint Lazare, where was his confessor, and added something on the piety of his life. The King exhorted me to behave well, and promised to take care of me. When my father was first taken ill; several persons, amongst others, D'Aubigne, brother of Madame de Maintenon, had asked for the governorship of Blaye. But the King refused them all, and said very bluntly to D'Aubigne, "Is there not a son?" He had, in fact, always given my father to understand I should succeed him, although generally he did not allow offices to descend from father to son.

Let me say a few words about my father. Our family in my grandfather's time had become impoverished; and my father was early sent to the Court as page to Louis XIII. It was very customary then for the sons of reduced gentlemen to accept this occupation. The King was passionately fond of hunting, an amusement that was carried on with far less state, without that abundance of dogs, and followers, and convenience of all kinds which his successor introduced, and especially without roads through the forests. My father, who noticed the impatience of the King at the delays that occurred in changing horses, thought of turning the head of the horse he brought towards the crupper of that which the King quitted. By this means, without putting his feet to the ground, his Majesty, who was active, jumped from one horse to another. He was so pleased that whenever he changed horses he asked for this same page. From that time my father grew day by day in favour. The King made him Chief Ecuyer, and in course of years bestowed other rewards upon him, created him Duke and peer of France, and gave him the Government of Blaye. My father, much attached to the King, followed him in all his expeditions, several times commanded the cavalry of the army, was commander-in-chief of all the arrierebans of the kingdom, and acquired great reputation in the field for his valour and skill. With Cardinal Richelieu he was intimate without sympathy, and more than once, but notably on the famous

Day of the Dupes, rendered signal service to that minister. My father used often to be startled out of his sleep in the middle of the night by a valet, with a taper in his hand, drawing the curtain—having behind him the Cardinal de Richelieu, who would often take the taper and sit down upon the bed and exclaim that he was a lost man, and ask my father's advice upon news that he had received or on quarrels he had had with the King. When all Paris was in consternation at the success of the Spaniards, who had crossed the frontier, taken Corbie, and seized all the country as far as Compiegne, the King insisted on my father being present at the council which was then held. The Cardinal de Richelieu maintained that the King should retreat beyond the Seine, and all the assembly seemed of that opinion. But the King in a speech which lasted a quarter of an hour opposed this, and said that to retreat at such a moment would be to increase the general disorder. Then turning to my father he ordered him to be prepared to depart for Corbie on the morrow, with as many of his men as he could get ready. The histories and the memoirs of the time show that this bold step saved the state. The Cardinal, great man as he was, trembled, until the first appearance of success, when he grew bold enough to join the King. This is a specimen of the conduct of that weak King governed by that first minister to whom poets and historians have given the glory they have stripped from his master; as, for instance, all the works of the siege of Rochelle, and the invention and unheard-of success of the celebrated dyke, all solely due to the late King!

Louis XIII. loved my father; but he could scold him at times. On two occasions he did so. The first, as my father has related to me, was on account of the Duc de Bellegarde. The Duke was in disgrace, and had been exiled. My father, who was a friend of his, wished to write to him one day, and for want of other leisure, being then much occupied, took the opportunity of the King's momentary absence to carry out his desire. Just as he was finishing his letter, the King came in; my father tried to hide the paper, but the eyes of the King were too quick for him. "What is that paper?" said he. My father, embarrassed, admitted that it was a few words he had written to M. de Bellegarde.

"Let me see it," said the King; and he took the paper and read it. "I don't find fault with you," said he, "for writing to your friends, although in disgrace, for I know you will write nothing improper; but what displeases me is, that you should fail in the respect you owe to a duke and peer, in that, because he is exiled, you should omit to address him as Monseigneur;" and then tearing the letter in two, he added, "Write it again after the hunt, and put, Monseigneur, as you ought." My father was very glad to be let off so easily.

The other reprimand was upon a more serious subject. The King was really enamoured of Mademoiselle d'Hautefort. My father, young and gallant, could not comprehend why he did not gratify his love. He believed his reserve to arise from timidity, and under this impression proposed one day to the King to be his ambassador and to bring the affair to a satisfactory conclusion. The King allowed him to speak to the end, and then assumed a severe air. "It is true," said he, "that I am enamoured of her, that I feel it, that I seek her, that I speak of her willingly, and think of her still more willingly; it is true also that I act thus in spite of myself, because I am mortal and have this weakness; but the more facility I have as King to gratify myself, the more I ought to be on my guard against sin and scandal. I pardon you this time, but never address to me a similar discourse again if you wish that I should continue to love you." This was a thunderbolt for my father; the scales fell from his eyes; the idea of the King's timidity in love disappeared before the display of a virtue so pure and so triumphant.

My father's career was for a long time very successful, but unfortunately he had an enemy who brought it to an end. This enemy was M. de Chavigny: he was secretary of state, and had also the war department. Either from stupidity or malice he had left all the towns in Picardy badly supported; a circumstance the Spaniards knew well how to profit by when they took Corbie in 1636. My father had an uncle who commanded in one of these towns, La Capelle, and who had several times asked for ammunition and stores without success. My father spoke upon this subject to Chavigny, to the Cardinal de Richelieu, and to the King, but with no good effect. La Capelle, left without resources, fell like the places around. As I have said before, Louis XIII. did not long allow the Spaniards to enjoy the advantages they had gained. All the towns in Picardy were soon retaken, and the King, urged on by Chavigny, determined to punish the governors of these places for surrendering them so easily. My father's uncle was included with the others. This injustice was not to be borne. My father represented the real state of the case and used every effort, to save his uncle, but it was in vain. Stung to the quick he demanded permission to retire, and was allowed to do so. Accordingly, at the commencement of 1637, he left for Blaye; and remained there until the death of Cardinal Richelieu. During this retirement the King frequently wrote to him, in a language they had composed so as to speak before people without being understood; and I possess still many of these letters, with much regret that I am ignorant of their contents.

Chavigny served my father another ill turn. At the Cardinal's death my father had returned to the Court and was in greater favour than ever. Just before Louis XIII. died he gave my father the place of first master of the horse, but left his name blank in the paper fixing the appointment. The paper was given into the hands of Chavigny. At the King's death he had the villainy, in concert with the Queen-regent, to fill in the name of Comte d'Harcourt, instead of that the King had instructed him of. The indignation of my father was great, but, as he could obtain no redress, he retired once again to his Government of Blaye. Notwithstanding the manner in which he had been treated by the Queen-regent, he stoutly defended her cause when the civil war broke out, led by M. le Prince. He garrisoned Blaye at his own expense, incurring thereby debts which hung upon him all his life, and which I feel the effects of still, and repulsed all attempts of friends to corrupt his loyalty. The Queen and Mazarin could not close their eyes to his devotion, and offered him, while the war was still going on, a marechal's baton, or the title of foreign prince. But he refused both, and the offer was not renewed when the war ended. These disturbances over, and Louis XIV. being married, my father came again to Paris, where he had many friends. He had married in 1644, and had had, as I have said, one only daughter. His wife dying in 1670, and leaving him without male children, he determined, however much he might be afflicted at the loss he had sustained, to marry again, although old. He carried out his resolution in October of the same year, and was very pleased with the choice he had made. He liked his new wife so much, in fact, that when Madame de Montespan obtained for her a place at the Court, he declined it at once. At his age—it was thus he wrote to Madame de Montespan, he had taken a wife not for the Court, but for himself. My mother, who was absent when the letter announcing the appointment was sent, felt much regret, but never showed it.

Before I finish this account of my father, I will here relate adventures which happened to him, and which I ought to have placed before his second marriage. A disagreement arose between my father and M. de Vardes, and still existed long after everybody thought they were reconciled. It was ultimately agreed that upon an early day, at about twelve o'clock, they should meet at the Porte St. Honore, then a very deserted spot, and that the coach of M. de Vardes should run against my father's, and a general quarrel arise between masters and servants. Under cover of this quarrel, a duel could easily take place, and would seem simply to arise out of the broil there and then occasioned. On the morning appointed, my father called as usual upon several of his friends, and, taking one of them for second, went to the Porte St. Honore. There everything fell out just as had been arranged. The coach of M. de Vardes struck against the other. My father leaped out, M. de Vardes did the same, and the duel took place. M. de Vardes fell, and was disarmed. My father wished to make him beg for his life; he would not do this, but confessed himself vanquished. My father's coach being the nearest, M. de Vardes got into it. He fainted on the road. They separated afterwards like brave people, and went their way. Madame de Chatillon, since of Mecklenburg, lodged in one of the last houses near the Porte St. Honore, and at the noise made by the coaches, put, her head to the window, and coolly looked at the whole of the combat. It soon made a great noise. My father was complimented everywhere. M. de Vardes was sent for ten or twelve days to the Bastille. My father and he afterwards became completely reconciled to each other.

The other adventure was of gentler ending. The Memoirs of M. de la Rochefoucauld appeared. They contained certain atrocious and false statements against my father, who so severely resented the calumny, that he seized a pen, and wrote upon the margin of the book, "The author has told a lie." Not content with this, he went to the bookseller, whom he discovered with some difficulty, for the book was not sold publicly at first. He asked to see all the copies of the work, prayed, promised, threatened, and at last succeeded in obtaining them. Then he took a pen and wrote in all of them the same marginal note. The astonishment of the bookseller may be imagined. He was not long in letting M. de la Rochefoucauld know what had happened to his books: it may well be believed that he also was astonished. This affair made great noise. My father, having truth on his side, wished to obtain public satisfaction from M. de la Rochefoucauld. Friends, however, interposed, and the matter was allowed to drop. But M. de la Rochefoucauld never pardoned my father; so true it is that we less easily forget the injuries we inflict than those that we receive.

My father passed the rest of his long life surrounded by friends, and held in high esteem by the King and his ministers. His advice was often sought for by them, and was always acted upon. He never consoled himself for the loss of Louis XIII., to whom he owed his advancement and his fortune. Every year he kept sacred the day of his death, going to Saint-Denis, or holding solemnities in his own house if at Blaye. Veneration, gratitude, tenderness, ever adorned his lips every time he spoke of that monarch.

CHAPTER IV

After having paid the last duties to my father I betook myself to Mons to join the Royal Roussillon cavalry regiment, in which I was captain. The King, after stopping eight or ten days with the ladies at Quesnoy, sent them to Namur, and put himself at the head of the army of M. de Boufflers, and camped at Gembloux, so that his left was only half a league distant from the right of M. de Luxembourg. The Prince of Orange was encamped at the Abbey of Pure, was unable to receive supplies, and could not leave his position without having the two armies of the King to grapple with: he entrenched himself in haste, and bitterly repented having allowed himself to be thus driven into a corner. We knew afterwards that he wrote several times to his intimate friend the Prince de Vaudemont, saying that he was lost, and that nothing short of a miracle could save him.

We were in this position, with an army in every way infinitely superior to that of the Prince of Orange, and with four whole months before us to profit by our strength, when the King declared on the 8th of June that he should return to Versailles, and sent off a large detachment of the army into Germany. The surprise of the Marechal de Luxembourg was without bounds. He represented the facility with which the Prince of Orange might now be beaten with one army and pursued by another; and how important it was to draw off detachments of the Imperial forces from Germany into Flanders, and how, by sending an army into Flanders instead of Germany, the whole of the Low Countries would be in our power. But the King would not change his plans, although M. de Luxembourg went down on his knees and begged him not to allow such a glorious opportunity to escape. Madame de Maintenon, by her tears when she parted from his Majesty, and by her letters since, had brought about this resolution.

The news had not spread on the morrow, June 9th. I chanced to go alone to the quarters of M. de Luxembourg, and was surprised to find not a soul there; every one had gone to the King's army. Pensively bringing my horse to a stand, I was ruminating on a fact so strange, and debating whether I should return to my tent or push on to the royal camp, when up came M. le Prince de Conti with a single page and a groom leading a horse. "What are you doing there?" cried he, laughing at my surprise. Thereupon he told me he was going to say adieu to the King, and advised me to do likewise. "What do you mean by saying Adieu?" answered I. He sent his servants to a little distance, and begged me to do the same, and with shouts of laughter told me about the King's retreat, making tremendous fun of him, despite my youth, for he had confidence in me. I was astonished. We soon after met the whole company coming back; and the great people went aside to talk and sneer. I then proceeded to pay my respects to the King, by whom I was honourably received. Surprise, however, was expressed by all faces, and indignation by some.

The effect of the King's retreat, indeed, was incredible, even amongst the soldiers and the people. The general officers could not keep silent upon it, and the inferior officers spoke loudly, with a license that could not be restrained. All through the army, in the towns, and even at Court, it was talked about openly. The courtiers, generally so glad to find themselves again at

Versailles, now declared that they were ashamed to be there; as for the enemy, they could not contain their surprise and joy. The Prince of Orange said that the retreat was a miracle he could not have hoped for; that he could scarcely believe in it, but that it had saved his army, and the whole of the Low Countries. In the midst of all this excitement the King arrived with the ladies, on the 25th of June, at Versailles.

We gained some successes, however, this year. Marechal de Villeroy took Huy in three days, losing only a sub-engineer and some soldiers. On the 29th of July we attacked at dawn the Prince of Orange at Neerwinden, and after twelve hours of hard fighting, under a blazing sun, entirely routed him. I was of the third squadron of the Royal Roussillon, and made five charges. One of the gold ornaments of my coat was torn away, but I received no wound. During the battle our brigadier, Quoadt, was killed before my eyes. The Duc de Feuillade became thus commander of the brigade. We missed him immediately, and for more than half an hour saw nothing of him; he had gone to make his toilette. When he returned he was powdered and decked out in a fine red surtotxt, embroidered with silver, and all his trappings and those of his horse were magnificent; he acquitted himself with distinction.

Our cavalry stood so well against the fire from the enemy's guns, that the Prince of Orange lost all patience, and turning away, exclaimed— "Oh, the insolent nation!" He fought until the last, and retired with the Elector of Hanover only when he saw there was no longer any hope. After the battle my people brought us a leg of mutton and a bottle of wine, which they had wisely saved from the previous evening, and we attacked them in good earnest, as may be believed.

The enemy lost about twenty thousand men, including a large number of officers; our loss was not more than half that number. We took all their cannon, eight mortars, many artillery waggons, a quantity of standards, and some pairs of kettle-drums. The victory was complete.

Meanwhile, the army which had been sent to Germany under the command of Monseigneur and of the Marechal de Lorges, did little or nothing. The Marechal wished to attack Heilbronn, but Monseigneur was opposed to it; and, to the great regret of the principal generals and of the troops, the attack was not made. Monseigneur returned early to Versailles.

At sea we were more active. The rich merchant fleet of Smyrna was attacked by Tourville; fifty vessels were burnt or sunk, and twenty-seven taken, all richly freighted. This campaign cost the English and Dutch dear. It is believed their loss was more than thirty millions of ecus.

The season finished with the taking of Charleroy. On the 16th of September the Marechal de Villeroy, supported by M. de Luxembourg, laid siege to it, and on the 11th of October, after a good defence, the place capitulated. Our loss was very slight. Charleroy taken, our troops went into winter-quarters, and I returned to Court, like the rest. The roads and the posting service were in great disorder. Amongst other adventures I met with, I was driven by a deaf and dumb postillion, who stuck me fast in the mud when near Quesnoy. At Pont Saint-Maxence all the horses were retained by M. de Luxembourg. Fearing I might be left behind, I told the postmaster that I was governor (which was true), and that I would put him in jail if he did not give me horses. I should have been sadly puzzled how to do it; but he was simple enough to believe me, and gave the horses. I arrived, however, at last at Paris, and found a change at the Court, which surprised me.

Daquin—first doctor of the King and creature of Madame de Montespan—had lost nothing of his credit by her removal, but had never been able to get on well with Madame de Maintenon, who looked coldly upon all the friends of her predecessor. Daquin had a son, an abbe, and wearied the King with solicitations on his behalf. Madame de Maintenon seized the opportunity, when the King was more than usually angry with Daquin, to obtain his dismissal: it came upon him like a thunderbolt. On the previous evening the King had spoken to him for a long time as usual, and had never treated him better. All the Court was astonished also. Fagon, a very skilful and learned man, was appointed in his place at the instance of Madame de Maintenon.

Another event excited less surprise than interest. On Sunday, the 29th of November, the King learned that La Vauguyon had killed himself in his bed, that morning, by firing twice into his throat. I must say a few words about this Vauguyon. He was one of the pettiest and poorest gentlemen of France: he was well-made, but very swarthy, with Spanish features, had a charming voice, played the guitar and lute very well, and was skilled in the arts of gallantry. By these talents he had succeeded, in finding favour with Madame de Beauvais, much regarded at the Court as having been the King's first mistress. I have seen her—old, blear-eyed, and half blind,— at the toilette of the Dauphiness of Bavaria, where everybody courted her, because she was still much considered by the King. Under this protection La Vauguyon succeeded well; was several times sent as ambassador to foreign countries; was made councillor of state, and to the scandal of everybody, was raised to the Order in 1688. Of late years, having no appointments, he had scarcely the means of living, and endeavoured, but without success, to improve his condition.

Poverty by degrees turned his brain; but a long time passed before it was perceived. The first proof that he gave of it was at the house of Madame Pelot, widow of the Chief President of the Rouen parliament. Playing at brelan one evening, she offered him a stake, and because he would not accept it bantered him, and playfully called him a poltroon. He said nothing, but waited until all the rest of the company had left the room; and when he found himself alone with Madame Pelot, he bolted the door, clapped his hat on his head, drove her up against the chimney, and holding her head between his two fists, said he knew no reason why he should not pound it into a jelly, in order to teach her to call him poltroon again. The poor woman was horribly frightened, and made perpendicular curtseys between his two fists, and all sorts of excuses. At last he let her go, more dead than alive. She had the generosity to say no syllable of this occurrence until after his death; she even allowed him to come to the house as usual, but took care never to be alone with him.

One day, a long time after this, meeting, in a gallery, at Fontainebleau, M. de Courtenay, La Vauguyon drew his sword, and compelled the other to draw also, although there had never been the slightest quarrel between them. They were soon separated and La Vauguyon immediately fled to the King, who was just then in his private closet, where nobody ever entered unless expressly summoned. But La Vauguyon turned the key, and, in spite of the usher on guard, forced his way in. The King in great emotion asked him what was the matter. La Vauguyon on his knees said he had been insulted by M. de Courtenay and demanded pardon for having drawn his sword in the palace. His Majesty, promising to examine the matter, with great trouble got rid of La Vauguyon. As nothing could be made of it, M. de Courtenay declaring he had been insulted by La Vauguyon and forced to draw his sword, and the other telling the same tale, both were sent to the Bastille. After a short imprisonment they were released, and appeared at the Court as usual.

Another adventure, which succeeded this, threw some light upon the state of affairs. Going to Versailles, one day, La Vauguyon met a groom of the Prince de Conde leading a saddled horse, he stopped the man, descended from his coach, asked whom the horse belonged to, said that the Prince would not object to his riding it, and leaping upon the animal's back, galloped off. The groom, all amazed, followed him. La Vauguyon rode on until he reached the Bastille, descended there, gave a gratuity to the man, and dismissed him: he then went straight to the governor of the prison, said he had had the misfortune to displease the King, and begged to be confined there. The governor, having no orders to do so, refused; and sent off an express for instructions how to act. In reply he was told not to receive La Vauguyon, whom at last, after great difficulty, he prevailed upon to go away. This occurrence made great noise. Yet even afterwards the King continued to receive La Vauguyon at the Court, and to affect to treat him well, although everybody else avoided him and was afraid of him. His poor wife became so affected by these public derangements, that she retired from Paris, and shortly afterwards died. This completed her husband's madness; he survived her only a month, dying by his own hand, as I have mentioned. During the last two years of his life he carried pistols in his carriage, and frequently pointed them at his coachman and postilion. It is certain that without the assistance of M. de Beauvais he would often have been brought to the last extremities. Beauvais frequently spoke of him to the King; and it is inconceivable that having raised this man to such a point; and having always shown him particular kindness, his Majesty should perseveringly have left him to die of hunger and become mad from misery.

The year finished without any remarkable occurrence.

My mother; who had been much disquieted for me during the campaign, desired strongly that I should not make another without being married. Although very young, I had no repugnance to marry, but wished to do so according to my own inclinations. With a large establishment I felt very lonely in a country where credit and consideration do more than all the rest. Without uncle, aunt, cousins-German, or near relatives, I found myself, I say, extremely solitary.

Among my best friends, as he had been the friend of my father; was the Duc de Beauvilliers. He had always shown me much affection, and I felt a great desire to unite myself to his family: My mother approved of my inclination, and gave me an exact account of my estates and possessions. I carried it to Versailles, and sought a private interview with M. de Beauvilliers. At eight o'clock the same evening he received me alone in the cabinet of Madame de Beauvilliers. After making my compliments to him, I told him my wish, showed him the state of my affairs, and said that all I demanded of him was one of his daughters in marriage, and that whatever contract he thought fit to draw up would be signed by my mother and myself without examination.

The Duke, who had fixed his eyes upon me all this time, replied like a man penetrated with gratitude by the offer I had made. He said, that of his eight daughters the eldest was between fourteen and fifteen years old; the second much deformed, and in no way marriageable; the third between twelve and thirteen years of age, and the rest were children: the eldest wished to enter a convent, and had shown herself firm upon that point. He seemed inclined to make a difficulty of his want of fortune; but, reminding him of the proposition I had made, I said that it was not for fortune I had come to him, not even for his daughter, whom I had never seen; that it was he and Madame de Beauvilliers who had charmed me, and whom I wished to marry!

"But," said he, "if my eldest daughter wishes absolutely to enter a convent?"

"Then," replied I, "I ask the third of you." To this he objected, on the ground that if he gave the dowry of the first to the third daughter, and the first afterwards changed her mind and wished to marry, he should be thrown into an embarrassment. I replied that I would take the third as though the first were to be married, and that if she were not, the difference between what he destined for her and what he destined for the third, should be given to me. The Duke, raising his eyes to heaven, protested that he had never been combated in this manner, and that he was obliged to gather up all his forces in order to prevent himself yielding to me that very instant.

On the next day, at half-past three, I had another interview with M. de Beauvilliers. With much tenderness he declined my proposal, resting his refusal upon the inclination his daughter had displayed for the convent, upon his little wealth, if, the marriage of the third being made, she should change her mind—and upon other reasons. He spoke to me with much regret and friendship, and I to him in the same manner; and we separated, unable any longer to speak to each other. Two days after, however, I had another interview with him by his appointment. I endeavoured to overcome the objections that he made, but all in vain. He could not give me his third daughter with the first unmarried, and he would not force her, he said, to change her wish of retiring from the world. His words, pious and elevated, augmented my respect for him, and my desire for the marriage. In the evening, at the breaking up of the appointment, I could not prevent myself whispering in his ear that I should never live happily with anybody but his daughter, and without waiting for a reply hastened away. I had the next evening, at eight o'clock, an interview with Madame de Beauvilliers. I argued with her with such prodigious ardor that she was surprised, and, although she did not give way, she said she would be inconsolable for the loss of me, repeating the same tender and flattering things her husband had said before, and with the same effusion of feeling.

I had yet another interview with M. de Beauvilliers. He showed even more affection for me than before, but I could not succeed in putting aside his scruples. He unbosomed himself afterwards to one of our friends, and in his bitterness said he could only console himself by hoping that his children and mine might some day intermarry, and he prayed me to go and pass some days at Paris, in order to allow him to seek a truce to his grief in my absence. We both were in want of it. I have judged it fitting to give these details, for they afford a key to my exceeding intimacy with M. de Beauvilliers, which otherwise, considering the difference in our ages, might appear incomprehensible.

There was nothing left for me but to look out for another marriage. One soon presented itself, but as soon fell to the ground; and I went to La Trappe to console myself for the impossibility of making an alliance with the Duc de Beauvilliers.

La Trappe is a place so celebrated and so well known, and its reformer so famous, that I shall say but little about it. I will, however, mention that this abbey is five leagues from La Ferme-au-Vidame, or Arnold, which is the real distinctive name of this Ferme among so many other Fetes in France, which have preserved the generic name of what they have been, that is to say, forts or fortresses ('freitas'). My father had been very intimate with M. de la Trappe, and had taken me to him.

Although I was very young then, M. de la Trappe charmed me, and the sanctity of the place enchanted me. Every year I stayed some days there, sometimes a week at a time, and was never tired of admiring this great and distinguished man. He loved me as a son, and I respected him as though he were any father. This intimacy, singular at my age, I kept secret from everybody, and only went to the convent clandestinely.

CHAPTER V

On my return from La Trappe, I became engaged in an affair which made a great noise, and which had many results for me.

M. de Luxembourg, proud of his successes, and of the applause of the world at his victories, believed himself sufficiently strong to claim precedence over seventeen dukes, myself among the number; to step, in fact, from the eighteenth rank, that he held amongst the peers, to the second. The following are the names and the order in precedence of the dukes he wished to supersede:

The Duc d'Elboeuf; the Duc de Montbazon; the Duc de Ventadour; the Duc de Vendome; the Duc de la Tremoille; the Duc de Sully; the Duc de Chevreuse, the son (minor) of the Duchesse de Lesdiguieres-Gondi; the Duc de Brissac; Charles d'Albert, called d'Ailly; the Duc de Richelieu; the Duc de Saint-Simon; the Duc de la Rochefoucauld; the Duc de la Force; the Duc de Valentinois; the Duc de Rohan; the Duc de Bouillon.

To explain this pretension of M. de Luxembourg, I must give some details respecting him and the family whose name he bore. He was the only son of M. de Bouteville, and had married a descendant of Francois de Luxembourg, Duke of Piney, created Peer of France in 1581. It was a peerage which, in default of male successors, went to the female, but this descendant was not heir to it. She was the child of a second marriage, and by a first marriage her mother had given birth to a son and a daughter, who were the inheritors of the peerage, both of whom were still living. The son was, however, an idiot, had been declared incapable of attending to his affairs, and was shut up in Saint Lazare, at Paris. The daughter had taken the veil, and was mistress of the novices at the Abbaye-aux-Bois. The peerage had thus, it might almost be said, become extinct, for it was vested in an idiot, who could not marry (to prevent him doing so, he had been made a deacon, and he was bound in consequence to remain single), and in a nun, who was equally bound by her vows to the same state of celibacy.

When M. de Bouteville, for that was his only title then, married, he took the arms and the name of Luxembourg. He did more. By powerful influence—notably that of his patron the Prince de Conde—he released the idiot deacon from his asylum, and the nun from her convent, and induced them both to surrender to him their possessions and their titles. This done, he commenced proceedings at once in order to obtain legal recognition of his right to the dignities he had thus got possession of. He claimed to be acknowledged Duc de Piney, with all the privileges attached to that title as a creation of 1581. Foremost among these privileges was that of taking precedence of all dukes whose title did not go back so far as that year. Before any decision was given either for or against this claim, he was made Duc de Piney by new letters patent, dating from 1662, with a clause which left his pretensions to the title of 1581 by no means affected by this new creation. M. de Luxembourg, however, seemed satisfied with what he had obtained, and was apparently disposed to pursue his claim no further. He was received as Duke and Peer in the Parliament, took his seat in the last rank after all the other peers, and allowed his suit to drop. Since then he had tried successfully to gain it by stealth, but for several years nothing more had been heard of it. Now, however, he recommenced it, and with every intention, as we soon found, to stop at no intrigue or baseness in order to carry his point.

Nearly everybody was in his favour. The Court, though not the King, was almost entirely for him; and the town, dazzled by the splendour of his exploits, was devoted to him. The young men regarded him as the protector of their debauches; for, notwithstanding his age, his conduct was as free as theirs. He had captivated the troops and the general officers.

In the Parliament he had a staunch supporter in Harlay, the Chief President, who led that great body at his will, and whose devotion he had acquired to such a degree, that he believed that to undertake and succeed were only the same things, and that this grand affair would scarcely cost him a winter to carry.

Let me say something more of this Harlay.

Descended from two celebrated magistrates, Achille d'Harlay and Christopher De Thou, Harlay imitated their gravity, but carried it to a cynical extent, affected their disinterestedness and modesty, but dishonoured the first by his conduct, and the second by a refined pride which he endeavoured without success to conceal. He piqued himself, above all things, upon his probity and justice, but the mask soon fell. Between Peter and Paul he maintained the strictest fairness, but as soon as he perceived interest or favour to be acquired, he sold himself. This trial will show him stripped of all disguise. He was learned in the law; in letters he was second to no one; he was well acquainted with history, and knew how, above all, to govern his company with an authority which suffered no reply, and which no other chief president had ever attained.

A pharisaical austerity rendered him redoubtable by the license he assumed in his public reprimands, whether to plaintiffs, or defendants, advocates or magistrates; so that there was not a single person who did not tremble to have to do with him. Besides this, sustained in all by the Court (of which he was the slave, and the very humble servant of those who were really in favour), a subtle courtier, a singularly crafty politician, he used all those talents solely to further his ambition, his desire of domination and his thirst of the reputation of a great man. He was without real honour, secretly of corrupt manners, with only outside probity, without humanity even; in one word, a perfect hypocrite; without faith, without law, without a God, and without a soul; a cruel husband, a barbarous father, a tyrannical brother, a friend of himself alone, wicked by nature—taking pleasure in insulting, outraging, and overwhelming others, and never in his life having lost an occasion to do so. His wit was great, but was always subservient to his wickedness. He was small, vigorous, and thin, with a lozenge-shaped face, a long aquiline nose—fine, speaking, keen eyes, that usually looked furtively at you, but which, if fixed on a client or a magistrate, were fit to make him sink into the earth. He wore narrow robes, an almost ecclesiastical collar and wristband to match, a brown wig mimed with white, thickly furnished but short, and with a great cap over it. He affected a bending attitude, and walked so, with a false air, more humble than modest, and always shaved along the walls, to make people make way for him with greater noise; and at Versailles worked his way on by a series of respectful and, as it were, shame-faced bows to the right and left. He held to the King and to Madame de Maintenon by knowing their weak side; and it was he who, being consulted upon the unheard-of legitimation of children without naming the mother, had sanctioned that illegality in favour of the King.

Such was the man whose influence was given entirely to our opponent.

To assist M. de Luxembourg's case as much as possible, the celebrated Racine, so known by his plays, and by the order he had received at that time to write the history of the King, was employed to polish and ornament his pleas. Nothing was left undone by M. de Luxembourg in order to gain this cause.

I cannot give all the details of the case, the statements made on both sides, and the defences; they would occupy entire volumes. We maintained that M. de Luxembourg was in no way entitled to the precedence he claimed, and we had both law and justice on our side. To give instructions to our counsel, and to follow the progress of the case, we met once a week, seven or eight of us at least, those best disposed to give our time to the matter. Among the most punctual was M. de la Rochefoucauld. I had been solicited from the commencement to take part in the proceedings, and I complied most willingly, apologising for so doing to M. de Luxembourg, who replied with all the politeness and gallantry possible, that I could not do less than follow an example my father had set me.

The trial having commenced, we soon saw how badly disposed the Chief President was towards us. He obstructed us in every way, and acted against all rules. There seemed no other means of defeating his evident intention of judging against us than by gaining time, first of all; and to do this we determined to get the case adjourned, There were, however, only two days at our disposal, and that was not enough in order to comply with the forms required for such a step. We were all in the greatest embarrassment, when it fortunately came into the head of one of our lawyers to remind us of a privilege we possessed, by which, without much difficulty, we could obtain what we required. I was the only one who could, at that moment, make use of this privilege. I hastened home, at once, to obtain the necessary papers, deposited them with the procureur of M. de Luxembourg, and the adjournment was obtained. The rage of M. de Luxembourg was without bounds. When we met he would not salute me, and in consequence I discontinued to salute him; by which he lost more than I, in his position and at his age, and furnished in the rooms and the galleries of Versailles a sufficiently ridiculous spectacle. In addition to this he quarrelled openly with M. de Richelieu, and made a bitter attack upon him in one of his pleas. But M. de Richelieu, meeting him soon after in the Salle des Gardes at Versailles, told him to his face that he should soon have a reply; and said that he feared him neither on horseback nor on foot—neither him nor his crew—neither in town nor at the Court, nor even in the army, nor in any place in the world; and without allowing time for a reply he turned on his heel. In the end, M. de Luxembourg found himself so closely pressed that he was glad to apologise to M. de Richelieu.

After a time our cause, sent back again to the Parliament, was argued there with the same vigour, the same partiality, and the same injustice as before: seeing this, we felt that the only course left open to us was to get the case sent before the Assembly of all the Chambers, where the judges, from their number, could not be corrupted by M. de Luxembourg, and where the authority of Harlay was feeble, while over the Grand Chambre, in which the case was at present, it was absolute. The difficulty was to obtain an assembly of all the Chambers, for the power of summoning them was vested solely in Harlay. However, we determined to try and gain his consent. M. de Chaulnes undertook to go upon this delicate errand, and acquitted himself well of his mission. He pointed out to Harlay that everybody was convinced of his leaning towards M. de Luxembourg, and that the only way to efface the conviction that had gone abroad was to comply with our request; in fine, he used so many arguments, and with such address, that Harlay, confused and thrown off his guard, and repenting of the manner in which he had acted towards us as being likely to injure his interests, gave a positive assurance to M. de Chaulnes that what we asked should be granted.

We had scarcely finished congratulating ourselves upon this unhoped-for success, when we found that we had to do with a man whose word was a very sorry support to rest upon. M. de Luxembourg, affrighted at the promise Harlay had given, made him resolve to break it. Suspecting this, M. de Chaulnes paid another visit to the Chief President, who admitted, with much confusion, that he had changed his views, and that it was impossible to carry out what he had agreed to. After this we felt that to treat any longer with a man so perfidious would be time lost; and we determined, therefore, to put it out of his power to judge the case at all.

According to the received maxim, whoever is at law with the son cannot be judged by the father. Harlay had a son who was Advocate-General. We resolved that one among us should bring an action against him.

After trying in vain to induce the Duc de Rohan, who was the only one of our number who could readily have done it, to commence a suit against Harlay's sort, we began to despair of arriving at our aim. Fortunately for us, the vexation of Harlay became so great at this time, in consequence of the disdain with which we treated him, and which we openly published, that he extricated us himself from our difficulty. We had only to supplicate the Duc de Gesvres in the cause (he said to some of our people), and we should obtain what we wanted; for the Duc de Gesvres was his relative. We took him at his word. The Duc de Gesvres received in two days a summons on our part. Harlay, annoyed with himself for the advice he had given, relented of it: but it was too late; he was declared unable to judge the cause, and the case itself was postponed until the next year.

Meanwhile, let me mention a circumstance which should have found a place before, and then state what occurred in the interval which followed until the trial recommenced.

It was while our proceedings were making some little stir that fresh favours were heaped upon the King's illegitimate sons, at the instance of the King himself, and with the connivance of Harlay, who, for the part he took in the affair, was promised the chancellorship when it should become vacant. The rank of these illegitimate sons was placed just below that of the princes, of the blood, and just above that of the peers even of the oldest creation. This gave us all exceeding annoyance: it was the greatest injury the peerage could have received, and became its leprosy and sore. All the peers who could, kept themselves aloof from the parliament, when M. du Maine, M. de Vendome, and the Comte de Toulouse, for whom this arrangement was specially made, were received there.

There were several marriages at the Court this winter and many very fine balls, at which latter I danced. By the spring, preparations were ready for fresh campaigns. My regiment (I had bought one at the close of the last season) was ordered to join the army of M. de Luxembourg; but, as I had no desire to be under him, I wrote to the King, begging to be exchanged. In a short time, to the great vexation, as I know, of M. de Luxembourg, my request was granted. The Chevalier de Sully went to Flanders in my place, and I to Germany in his. I went first to Soissons to see my regiment, and in consequence of the recommendation of the King, was more severe with it than I should otherwise have been. I set out afterwards for Strasbourg, where I was surprised with the magnificence of the town, and with the number, beauty, and grandeur of its fortifications. As from my youth I knew and spoke German perfectly, I sought out one of my early German acquaintances, who gave me much pleasure. I stopped six days at Strasbourg and then went by the Rhine to Philipsburg. On the next day after arriving there, I joined the cavalry, which was encamped at Obersheim.

After several movements—in which we passed and repassed the Rhine—but which led to no effective result, we encamped for forty days at Gaw- Boecklheim, one of the best and most beautiful positions in the world, and where we had charming weather, although a little disposed to cold. It was in the leisure of that long camp that I commenced these memoirs, incited by the pleasure I took in reading those of Marshal Bassompierre, which invited me thus to write what I should see in my own time.

During this season M. de Noailles took Palamos, Girone, and the fortress of Castel-Follit in Catalonia. This last was taken by the daring of a soldier, who led on a small number of his comrades, and carried the place by assault. Nothing was done in Italy; and in Flanders M. de Luxembourg came to no engagement with the Prince of Orange.

CHAPTER VI

After our long rest at the camp of Gaw-Boecklheim we again put ourselves in movement, but without doing much against the enemy, and on the 16th of October I received permission to return to Paris. Upon my arrival there I learnt that many things had occurred since I left. During that time some adventures had happened to the Princesses, as the three illegitimate daughters of the King were called for distinction sake. Monsieur wished that the Duchesse de Chartres should always call the others "sister," but that the others should never address her except as "Madame." The Princesse de Conti submitted to this; but the other (Madame la Duchesse, being the produce of the same love) set herself to call the Duchesse de Chartres "mignonne." But nothing was less a mignonne than her face and her figure; and Monsieur, feeling the ridicule, complained to the King. The King prohibited very severely this familiarity.

While at Trianon these Princesses took it into their heads to walk out at night and divert themselves with crackers. Either from malice or imprudence they let off some one night under the windows of Monsieur, rousing him thereby out of his sleep. He was so displeased, that he complained to the King, who made him many excuses (scolding the Princesses), but had great trouble to appease him. His anger lasted a long time, and the Duchesse de Chartres felt it. I do not know if the other two were very sorry. Madame la Duchesse was accused of writing some songs upon the Duchesse de Chartres.

The Princesse de Conti had another adventure, which made considerable noise, and which had great results. She had taken into her favour Clermont, ensign of the gensdarmes and of the Guard. He had pretended to be enamoured of her, and had not been repelled, for she soon became in love with him. Clermont had attached himself to the service of M. de Luxembourg, and was the merest creature in his hands. At the instigation of M. de Luxembourg, he turned away his regards from the Princesse de Conti, and fixed them upon one of her maids of honour— Mademoiselle Choin, a great, ugly, brown, thick-set girl, upon whom Monseigneur had lately bestowed his affection. Monseigneur made no secret of this, nor did she. Such being the case, it occurred to M. de Luxembourg (who knew he was no favourite with the King, and who built all his hopes of the future upon Monseigneur) that Clermont, by marrying La Choin, might thus secure the favour of Monseigneur, whose entire confidence she possessed. Clermont was easily persuaded that this would be for him a royal road to fortune, and he accordingly entered willingly into the scheme, which had just begun to move, when the campaign commenced, and everybody went away to join the armies.

The King, who partly saw this intrigue, soon made himself entirely master of it, by intercepting the letters which passed between the various parties. He read there the project of Clermont and La Choin to marry, and thus govern Monseigneur; he saw how M. de Luxembourg was the soul of this scheme, and the marvels to himself he expected from it. The letters Clermont had received from the Princesse de Conti he now sent to Mademoiselle la Choin, and always spoke to her of Monseigneur as their "fat friend." With this correspondence in his hands, the King one day sent for the Princesse de Conti, said in a severe tone that he knew of her weakness for Clermont; and, to prove to her how badly she had placed her affection, showed her her own letters to Clermont, and letters in which he had spoken most contemptuously of her to La Choin. Then, as a cruel punishment, he made her read aloud to him the whole of those letters. At this she almost died, and threw herself, bathed in tears, at the feet of the King, scarcely able to articulate. Then came sobs, entreaty, despair, and rage, and cries for justice and revenge. This was soon obtained. Mademoiselle la Choin was driven away the next day; and M. de Luxembourg had orders to strip Clermont of his office, and send him to the most distant part of the kingdom. The terror of M. de Luxembourg and the Prince de Conti at this discovery may be imagined. Songs increased the notoriety of this strange adventure between the Princess and her confidant.

M. de Noyon had furnished on my return another subject for the song- writers, and felt it the more sensibly because everybody was diverted at his expense, M. de Noyon was extremely vain, and afforded thereby much amusement to the King. A Chair was vacant at the Academic Francaise. The King wished it to be given to M. de Noyon, and expressed himself to that effect to Dangeau, who was a member. As may be believed, the prelate was elected without difficulty. His Majesty testified to the Prince de Conde, and to the most distinguished persons of the Court, that he should be glad to see them at the reception. Thus M. de Noyon was the first member of the Academia chosen by the King, and the first at whose reception he had taken the trouble to invite his courtiers to attend.

The Abbe de Caumartin was at that time Director of the Academie. He knew the vanity of M. de Noyon, and determined to divert the public at his expense. He had many friends in power, and judged that his pleasantry would be overlooked, and even approved. He composed, therefore, a confused and bombastic discourse in the style of M. de Noyon, full of pompous phrases, turning the prelate into ridicule, while they seemed to praise him. After finishing this work, he was afraid lest it should be thought out of all measure, and, to reassure himself, carried it to M. de Noyon himself, as a scholar might to his master, in order to see whether it fully met with his approval. M. de Noyon, so far from suspecting anything, was charmed by the discourse, and simply made a few corrections in the style. The Abbe de Caumartin rejoiced at the success of the snare he had laid, and felt quite bold enough to deliver his harangue.

The day came. The Academie was crowded. The King and the Court were there, all expecting to be diverted. M. de Noyon, saluting everybody with a satisfaction he did not dissimulate, made his speech with his usual confidence, and in his usual style. The Abbe replied with a modest air, and with a gravity and slowness that gave great effect to his ridiculous discourse. The surprise and pleasure were general, and each person strove to intoxicate M. de Noyon more and more, making him believe that the speech of the Abbe was relished solely because it had so worthily praised him. The prelate was delighted with the Abbe and the public, and conceived not the slightest mistrust.

The noise which this occurrence made may be imagined, and the praises M. de Noyon gave himself in relating everywhere what he had said, and what had been replied to him. M. de Paris, to whose house he went, thus triumphing, did not like him, and endeavoured to open his eyes to the humiliation he had received. For some time M. de Noyon would not be convinced of the truth; it was not until he had consulted with Pere la Chaise that he believed it. The excess of rage and vexation succeeded then to the excess of rapture he had felt. In this state he returned to his house, and went the next day to Versailles. There he made the most bitter complaints to the King, of the Abbe de Caumartin, by whose means he had become the sport and laughing-stock of all the world.

The King, who had learned what had passed, was himself displeased. He ordered Pontchartrain (who was related to Caumartin) to rebuke the Abbe, and to send him a lettre de cachet, in order that he might go and ripen his brain in his Abbey of Busay, in Brittany, and better learn there how to speak and write. Pontchartrain executed the first part of his commission, but not the second. He pointed out to the King that the speech of the Abbe de Caumartin had been revised and corrected by M. de Noyon, and that, therefore, this latter had only himself to blame in the matter. He declared, too, that the Abbe was very sorry for what he had done, and was most willing to beg pardon of M. de Noyon. The lettre de cachet thus fell to the ground, but not the anger of the prelate. He was so outraged that he would not see the Abbe, retired into his diocese to hide his shame, and remained there a long time.

Upon his return to Paris, however, being taken ill, before consenting to receive the sacraments, he sent for the Abbe, embraced him, pardoned him, and gave him a diamond ring, that he drew from his finger, and that he begged him to keep in memory of him. Nay, more, when he was cured, he used all his influence to reinstate the Abbe in the esteem of the King. But the King could never forgive what had taken place, and M. de Noyon, by this grand action, gained only the favour of God and the honour of the world.

I must finish the account of the war of this year with a strange incident. M. de Noailles, who had been so successful in Catalonia, was on very bad terms with Barbezieux, secretary of state for the war department. Both were in good favour with the King; both high in power, both spoiled. The successes in Catalonia had annoyed Barbezieux. They smoothed the way for the siege of Barcelona, and that place once taken, the very heart of Spain would have been exposed, and M. de Noailles would have gained fresh honours and glory. M. de Noailles felt this so completely that he had pressed upon the King the siege of Barcelona; and when the fitting time came for undertaking it, sent a messenger to him with full information of the forces and supplies he required. Fearing that if he wrote out this information it might fall into the hands of Barbezieux, and never reach the King, he simply gave his messenger instructions by word of mouth, and charged him to deliver them so. But the very means he had taken to ensure success brought about failure. Barbezieux, informed by his spies of the departure of the messenger, waylaid him, bribed him, and induced him to act with the blackest perfidy, by telling the King quite a different story to that he was charged with. In this way, the project for the siege of Barcelona was entirely broken, at the moment for its execution, and with the most reasonable hopes of success; and upon M. de Noailles rested all the blame. What a thunderbolt this was for him may easily be imagined. But the trick had been so well played, that he could not clear himself with the King; and all through this winter he remained out of favour.

At last he thought of a means by which he might regain his position. He saw the inclination of the King for his illegitimate children; and determined to make a sacrifice in favour of one of them; rightly judging that this would be a sure means to step back into the confidence he had been so craftily driven from. His scheme, which he caused to be placed before the King, was to go into Catalonia at the commencement of the next campaign, to make a semblance of falling ill immediately upon arriving, to send to Versailles a request that he might be recalled, and at the same time a suggestion that M. de Vendome (who would then be near Nice, under Marechal Catinat) should succeed him. In order that no time might be lost, nor the army left without a general, he proposed to carry with him the letters patent; appointing M. de Vendome, and to send them to him at the same time that he sent to be recalled.

It is impossible to express the relief and satisfaction with which this proposition was received. The King was delighted with it, as with everything tending to advance his illegitimate children and to put a slight upon the Princes of the blood. He could not openly have made this promotion without embroiling himself with the latter; but coming as it would from M. de Noailles, he had nothing to fear. M. de Vendome, once general of an army, could no longer serve in any other quality; and would act as a stepping-stone for M. du Maine.

From this moment M. de Noailles returned more than ever into the good graces of the King. Everything happened as it had been arranged. But the secret was betrayed in the execution. Surprise was felt that at the same moment M. de Noailles sent a request to be recalled, he also sent, and without waiting for a reply, to call M. de Vendame to the command. What completely raised the veil were the letters patent that he sent immediately after to M. de Vendome, and that it was known he could not have received from the King in the time that had elapsed. M. de Noailles returned from Catalonia, and was received as his address merited. He feigned being lame with rheumatism, and played the part for a long time, but forgot himself occasionally, and made his company smile. He fixed himself at the Court, and gained there much more favour than he could have gained by the war; to the great vexation of Barbezieux.

M. de Luxembourg very strangely married his daughter at this time to the Chevalier de Soissons (an illegitimate son of the Comte de Soissons), brought out from the greatest obscurity by the Comtesse de Nemours, and adopted by her to spite her family: M. de Luxembourg did not long survive this fine marriage. At sixty-seven years of age he believed himself twenty-five, and lived accordingly. The want of genuine intrigues, from which his age and his face excluded him, he supplied by money-power; and his intimacy, and that of his son, with the Prince de Conti and Albergotti was kept up almost entirely by the community of their habits, and the secret parties of pleasure they concocted together. All the burden of marches, of orders of subsistence, fell upon a subordinate. Nothing could be more exact than the coup d'oeil of M. de Luxembourg— nobody could be more brilliant, more sagacious, more penetrating than he before the enemy or in battle, and this, too, with an audacity, an ease, and at the same time a coolness, which allowed him to see all and foresee all under the hottest fire, and in the most imminent danger: It was at such times that he was great. For the rest he was idleness itself. He rarely walked unless absolutely obliged, spent his time in gaming, or in conversation With his familiars; and had every evening a supper with a chosen few (nearly always the same); and if near a town, the other sex were always agreeably mingled with them. When thus occupied, he was inaccessible to everybody, and if anything pressing happened, it was his subordinate who attended to it. Such was at the army the life of this great general, and such it was at Paris, except that the Court and the great world occupied his days, and his pleasures the evenings. At last, age, temperament, and constitution betrayed him. He fell ill at Versailles. Given over by Fagon, the King's physician, Coretti, an Italian, who had secrets of his own, undertook his cure, and relieved him, but only for a short time. His door during this illness was besieged by all the Court. The King sent to inquire after him, but it was more for appearance' sake than from sympathy, for I have already remarked that the King did not like him. The brilliancy of his campaigns, and the difficulty of replacing him, caused all the disquietude. Becoming worse, M. de Luxembourg received the sacraments, showed some religion and firmness, and died on the morning of the 4th of January, 1695, the fifth day of his illness, much regretted by many people, but personally esteemed by none, and loved by very few.

Not one of the Dukes M. de Luxembourg had attacked went to see him during his illness. I neither went nor sent, although at Versailles; and I must admit that I felt my deliverance from such an enemy.

Here, perhaps, I may as well relate the result of the trial in which we were engaged, and which, after the death of M. de Luxembourg, was continued by his son. It was not judged until the following year. I have shown that by our implicating the Duc de Gesvres, the Chief President had been declared incapable of trying the case. The rage he conceived against us cannot be expressed, and, great actor that he was, he could not hide it. All his endeavour afterwards was to do what he could against us; the rest of the mask fell, and the deformity of the judge appeared in the man, stripped of all disguise.

We immediately signified to M. de Luxembourg that he must choose between the letters patent of 1581 and those of 1662. If he abandoned the first the case fell through; in repudiating the last he renounced the certainty of being duke and peer after us; and ran the risk of being reduced to an inferior title previously granted to him. The position was a delicate one; he was affrighted; but after much consultation he resolved to run all risks and maintain his pretensions. It thus simply became a question of his right to the title of Duc de Piney, with the privilege attached to it as a creation of 1581.

In the spring of 1696 the case was at last brought on, before the Assembly of all the Chambers. Myself and the other Dukes seated ourselves in court to hear the proceedings. The trial commenced. All the facts and particulars of the cause were brought forward. Our advocates spoke, and then few doubted but that we should gain the victory. M. de Luxembourg's advocate, Dumont, was next heard. He was very audacious, and spoke so insolently of us, saying, in Scripture phraseology, that we honoured the King with our lips, whilst our hearts were far from him, that I could not contain myself. I was seated between the Duc de la Rochefoucauld and the Duc d'Estrees. I stood up, crying out against the imposture of this knave, and calling for justice on him. M. de la Rochefoucauld pulled me back, made me keep silent, and I plunged down into my seat more from anger against him than against the advocate. My movement excited a murmur. We might on the instant have had justice against Dumont, but the opportunity had passed for us to ask for it, and the President de Maisons made a slight excuse for him. We complained, however, afterwards to the King, who expressed his surprise that Dumont had not been stopped in the midst of his speech.

The summing up was made by D'Aguesseau, who acquitted himself of the task with much eloquence and impartiality. His speech lasted two days. This being over, the court was cleared, and the judges were left alone to deliberate upon their verdict. Some time after we were called in to hear that verdict given. It was in favour of M. de Luxembourg in so far as the title dating from 1662 was concerned; but the consideration of his claim to the title of 1581 was adjourned indefinitely, so that he remained exactly in the same position as his father.

It was with difficulty we could believe in a decree so unjust and so novel, and which decided a question that was not under dispute. I was outraged, but I endeavoured to contain myself. I spoke to M. de la Rochefoucauld; I tried to make him listen to me, and to agree that we should complain to the King, but I spoke to a man furious, incapable of understanding anything or of doing anything. Returning to my own house, I wrote a letter to the King, in which I complained of the opinion of the judges. I also pointed out, that when everybody had been ordered to retire from the council chamber, Harlay and his secretary had been allowed to remain. On these and other grounds I begged the King to grant a new trial.

I carried this letter to the Duc de la Tremoille, but I could not get him to look at it. I returned home more vexed if possible than when I left. The King, nevertheless, was exceedingly dissatisfied with the judgment. He explained himself to that effect at his dinner, and in a manner but little advantageous to the Parliament, and prepared himself to receive the complaints he expected would be laid before him. But the obstinacy of M. de la Rochefoucauld, which turned into vexation against himself, rendered it impossible for us to take any steps in the matter, and so overwhelmed me with displeasure, that I retired to La Trappe during Passion Week in order to recover myself.

At my return I learned that the King had spoken of this judgment to the Chief President, and that that magistrate had blamed it, saying the cause was indubitably ours, and that he had always thought so! If he thought so, why oppose us so long? and if he did not think so, what a prevaricator was he to reply with this flattery, so as to be in accord with the King? The judges themselves were ashamed of their verdict, and excused themselves for it on the ground of their compassion for the state in which M. de Luxembourg would have been placed had he lost the title of 1662, and upon its being impossible that he should gain the one of 1581, of which they had left him the chimera. M. de Luxembourg was accordingly received at the Parliament on the 4th of the following May, with the rank of 1662. He came and visited all of us, but we would have no intercourse with him or with his judges. To the Advocate-General, D'Aguesseau, we carried our thanks.

CHAPTER VII

Thus ended this long and important case; and now let me go back again to the events of the previous year.

Towards the end of the summer and the commencement of the winter of 1695, negotiations for peace were set on foot by the King. Harlay, son-in-law of our enemy, was sent to Maestricht to sound the Dutch. But in proportion as they saw peace desired were they less inclined to listen to terms. They had even the impudence to insinuate to Harlay, whose paleness and thinness were extraordinary, that they took him for a sample of the reduced state of France! He, without getting angry, replied pleasantly, that if they would give him the time to send for his wife, they would, perhaps, conceive another opinion of the position of the realm. In effect, she was extremely fat, and of a very high colour. He was rather roughly dismissed, and hastened to regain our frontier.

Two events followed each other very closely this winter. The first was the death of the Princess of Orange, in London, at the end of January. The King of England prayed our King to allow the Court to wear no mourning, and it was even prohibited to M. de Bouillon and M. de Duras, who were both related to the Prince of Orange. The order was obeyed, and no word was said; but this sort of vengeance was thought petty. Hopes were held out of a change in England, but they vanished immediately, and the Prince of Orange appeared more accredited there and stronger than ever. The Princess was much regretted, and the Prince of Orange, who loved her and gave her his entire confidence, and even most marked respect, was for some days ill with grief.

The other event was strange. The Duke of Hanover, who, in consequence of the Revolution, was destined to the throne of England after the Prince and Princess of Orange and the Princess of Denmark, had married his cousin-german, a daughter of the Duke of Zell. She was beautiful, and he lived happily with her for some time. The Count of Koenigsmarck, young and very well made, came to the Court, and gave him some umbrage. The Duke of Hanover became jealous; he watched his wife and the Count, and at length believed himself fully assured of what he would have wished to remain ignorant of all his life. Fury seized him: he had the Count arrested and thrown into a hot oven. Immediately afterwards he sent his wife to her father, who shut her up in one of his castles, where she was strictly guarded by the people of the Duke of Hanover. An assembly of the Consistory was held in order to break off his marriage. It was decided, very singularly, that the marriage was annulled so far as the Duke was concerned, and that he could marry another woman; but that it remained binding on the Duchess, and that she could not marry. The children she had had during her marriage were declared legitimate. The Duke of Hanover did not remain persuaded as to this last article.

The King, entirely occupied with the aggrandisement of his natural children, had heaped upon the Comte de Toulouse every possible favour. He now (in order to evade a promise he had made to his brother, that the first vacant government should be given to the Duc de Chartres) forced M. de Chaulnes to give up the government of Brittany, which he had long held, and conferred it upon the Comte de Toulouse, giving to the friend and heir of the former the successorship to the government of Guyenne, by way of recompense.

M. de Chaulnes was old and fat, but much loved by the people of Brittany. He was overwhelmed by this determination of the King, and his wife, who had long been accustomed to play the little Queen, still more so; yet there was nothing for them but to obey. They did obey, but it was with a sorrow and chagrin they could not hide.

The appointment was announced one morning at the rising of the King. Monsieur, who awoke later, heard of it at the drawing of his curtains, and was extremely piqued. The Comte de Toulouse came shortly afterwards, and announced it himself. Monsieur interrupted him, and before everybody assembled there said, "The King has given you a good present; but I know not if what he has done is good policy." Monsieur went shortly afterwards to the King, and reproached him for giving, under cover of a trick, the government of Brittany to the Comte de Toulouse, having promised it to the Duc de Chartres. The King heard him in silence: he knew well how to appease him. Some money for play and to embellish Saint Cloud, soon effaced Monsieur's chagrin.

All this winter my mother was solely occupied in finding a good match for me. Some attempt was made to marry me to Mademoiselle de Royan. It would have been a noble and rich marriage; but I was alone, Mademoiselle de Royan was an orphan, and I wished a father-in-law and a family upon whom I could lean. During the preceding year there had been some talk of the eldest daughter of Marechal de Lorges for me. The affair had fallen through, almost as soon as suggested, and now, on both sides, there was a desire to recommence negotiations. The probity, integrity, the freedom of Marechal de Lorges pleased me infinitely, and everything tended to give me an extreme desire for this marriage. Madame de Lorges by her virtue and good sense was all I could wish for as the mother of my future wife. Mademoiselle de Lorges was a blonde, with a complexion and figure perfect, a very amiable face, an extremely noble and modest deportment, and with I know not what of majesty derived from her air of virtue, and of natural gentleness. The Marechal had five other daughters, but I liked this one best without comparison, and hoped to find with her that happiness which she since has given me. As she has become my wife, I will abstain here from saying more about her, unless it be that she has exceeded all that was promised of her, and all that I myself had hoped.

My marriage being agreed upon and arranged the Marechal de Lorges spoke of it to the King, who had the goodness to reply to him that he could not do better, and to speak of me very obligingly. The marriage accordingly took place at the Hotel de Lorges, on the 8th of April, 1695, which I have always regarded, and with good reason, as the happiest day of my life. My mother treated me like the best mother in the world. On the Thursday before Quasimodo the contract was signed; a grand repast followed; at midnight the cure of Saint Roch said mass, and married us in the chapel of the house. On the eve, my mother had sent forty thousand livres' worth of precious stones to Mademoiselle de Lorges, and I six hundred Louis in a corbeille filled with all the knick-knacks that are given on these occasions.

We slept in the grand apartment of the Hotel des Lorges. On the morrow, after dinner, my wife went to bed, and received a crowd of visitors, who came to pay their respects and to gratify their curiosity. The next evening we went to Versailles, and were received by Madame de Maintenon and the King. On arriving at the supper-table, the King said to the new Duchess:—"Madame, will you be pleased to seat yourself?"

His napkin being unfolded, he saw all the duchesses and princesses still standing; and rising in his chair, he said to Madame de Saint-Simon— "Madame, I have already begged you to be seated;" and all immediately seated themselves. On the morrow, Madame de Saint-Simon received all the Court in her bed in the apartment of the Duchesse d'Arpajon, as being more handy, being on the ground floor. Our festivities finished by a supper that I gave to the former friends of my father, whose acquaintance I had always cultivated with great care.

Almost immediately after my marriage the second daughter of the Marechal de Lorges followed in the footsteps of her sister. She was fifteen years of age, and at the reception of Madame de Saint-Simon had attracted the admiration of M. de Lauzun, who was then sixty-three. Since his return to the Court he had been reinstated in the dignity he had previously held. He flattered himself that by marrying the daughter of a General he should re-open a path to himself for command in the army. Full of this idea he spoke to M. de Lorges, who was by no means inclined towards the marriage. M. de Lauzun offered, however, to marry without dowry; and M. de Lorges, moved by this consideration, assented to his wish. The affair concluded, M. de Lorges spoke of it to the King. "You are bold," said his Majesty, "to take Lauzun into your family. I hope you may not repent of it."

The contract was soon after signed. M. de Lorges gave no dowry with his daughter, but she was to inherit something upon the death of M. Fremont. We carried this contract to the King, who smiled and bantered M. de Lauzun. M. de Lauzun replied, that he was only too happy, since it was the first time since his return that he had seen the King smile at him. The marriage took place without delay: there were only seven or eight persons present at the ceremony. M. de Lauzun would undress himself alone with his valet de chambre, and did not enter the apartment of his wife until after everybody had left it, and she was in bed with the curtains closed, and nobody to meet him on his passage. His wife received company in bed, as mine had done. Nobody was able to understand this marriage; and all foresaw that a rupture would speedily be brought about by the well-known temper of M. de Lauzun. In effect, this is what soon happened. The Marechal de Lorges, remaining still in weak health, was deemed by the King unable to take the field again, and his army given over to the command of another General. M. de Lauzun thus saw all his hopes of advancement at an end, and, discontented that the Marechal had done nothing for him, broke off all connection with the family, took away Madame de Lauzun from her mother (to the great grief of the latter; who doted upon this daughter), and established her in a house of his own adjoining the Assumption, in the Faubourg Saint-Honore. There she had to endure her husband's continual caprices, but little removed in their manifestation from madness. Everybody cast blame upon him, and strongly pitied her and her father and mother; but nobody was surprised.

A few days after the marriage of M. de Lauzun, as the King was being wheeled in his easy chair in the gardens at Versailles, he asked me for many minute particulars concerning the family of the Marechal de Lorges. He then set himself to joke with me upon the marriage of M. de

Lauzun— and upon mine. He said to me, in spite of that gravity which never quitted him, that he had learnt from the Marechal I had well acquitted myself, but that he believed the Marechal had still better news.

The loss of two illustrious men about this time, made more noise than that of two of our grand ladies. The first of these men was La Fontaine, so well known by his "Fables" and stories, and who, nevertheless, was so heavy in conversation. The other was Mignard—so illustrious by his pencil: he had an only daughter—perfectly beautiful: she is repeated in several of those magnificent historical pictures which adorn the grand gallery of Versailles and its two salons, and which have had no slight share in irritating all Europe against the King, and in leaguing it still more against his person than his realm.

At the usual time the armies were got ready for active service, and everybody set out to join them. That of the Rhine, in which I was, was commanded by the Marechal de Lorges. No sooner had we crossed the river and come upon the enemy, than the Marechal fell ill. Although we were in want of forage and were badly encamped, nobody complained—nobody wished to move. Never did an army show so much interest in the life of its chief, or so much love for him. M. de Lorges was, in truth, at the last extremity, and the doctors that had been sent for from Strasbourg gave him up entirely. I took upon myself to administer to him some "English Drops." One hundred and thirty were given him in three doses: the effect was astonishing; an eruption burst out upon the Marechal's body, and saved his life. His illness was not, however, at an end; and the army, although suffering considerably, would not hear of moving until he was quite ready to move also. There was no extremity it would not undergo rather than endanger the life of its chief.

Prince Louis of Baden offered by trumpets all sorts of assistance— doctors and remedies, and gave his word that if the army removed from its General, he and those who remained with him should be provided with forage and provisions—should be unmolested and allowed to rejoin the main body in perfect safety, or go whithersoever they pleased. He was thanked, as he merited, for those very kind offers, which we did not wish, however, to profit by.

Little by little the health of the General was reestablished, and the army demonstrated its joy by bonfire's all over the camp, and by salvos, which it was impossible to prevent. Never was seen testimony of love so universal or so flattering. The King was much concerned at the illness of the Marechal; all the Court was infinitely touched by it. M. de Lorges was not less loved by it than by the troops. When able to support the fatigues of the journey, he was removed in a coach to Philipsburg, where he was joined by the Marechal, who had come there to meet him. The next day he went to Landau, and I, who formed one of his numerous and distinguished escort, accompanied him there, and then returned to the army, which was placed under the command of the Marechal de Joyeuse.

We found it at about three leagues from Ketsch, its right at Roth, and its left at Waldsdorff. We learned that the Marechal de Joyeuse had lost a good occasion of fighting the enemy; but as I was not in camp at the time, I will say no more of the matter. Our position was not good: Schwartz was on our left, and the Prince of Baden on our right, hemming us in, as it were, between them. We had no forage, whilst they had abundance of everything, and were able to procure all they wanted. There was a contest who should decamp the last. All our communications were cut off with Philipsburg, so that we could not repass the Rhine under the protection of that place. To get out of our position, it was necessary to defile before our enemies into the plain of Hockenun, and this was a delicate operation. The most annoying circumstance was, that M. de Joyeuse would communicate with nobody, and was so ill-tempered that none dared to speak to him. At last he determined upon his plans, and I was of the detachment by which they were to be carried out. We were sent to Manheim to see if out of the ruins of that place (burned in 1688 by M. de Louvois) sufficient, materials could be found to construct bridges, by which we might cross the Rhine there. We found that the bridges could be made, and returned to announce this to M. de Joyeuse. Accordingly, on the 20th of July, the army put itself in movement. The march was made in the utmost confusion. Everything was in disorder; the infantry and cavalry were huddled together pell-mell; no commands could be acted upon, and indeed the whole army was so disorganised that it could have been easily beaten by a handful of men. In effect, the enemy at last tried to take advantage of our confusion, by sending a few troops to harass us. But it was too late; we had sufficiently rallied to be able to turn upon them, and they narrowly escaped falling into our hands. We encamped that night in the plain on the banks of the Necker—our rear at Manheim, and our left at Seckenheim, while waiting for the remainder of the army, still very distant. Indeed, so great had been the confusion, that the first troops arrived at one o'clock at night, and the last late in the morning of the next day.

I thought that our headquarters were to be in this village of Seckenheim, and, in company with several officers took possession of a large house and prepared to pass the night there. While we were resting from the fatigues of the day we heard a great noise, and soon after a frightful uproar. It was caused by a body of our men, who, searching for water, had discovered this village, and after having quenched their thirst had, under the cover of thick darkness, set themselves to pillage, to violate, to massacre, and to commit all the horrors inspired by the most unbridled licence: La Bretesche, a lieutenant-general, declared to me that he had never seen anything like it, although he had several times been at pillages and sackings. He was very grateful that he had not yielded to my advice, and taken off his wooden leg to be more at ease; for in a short time we ourselves were invaded, and had some trouble to defend ourselves. As we bore the livery of M. de Lorges, we were respected, but those who bore that of M. de Joyeuse were in some cases severely maltreated. We passed the rest of the night as well as we could in this unhappy place, which was not abandoned by our soldiers until long after there was nothing more to find. At daylight we went to the camp.

We found the army beginning to move: it had passed the night as well as it could without order, the troops constantly arriving, and the last comers simply joining themselves on to the rest. Our camp was soon, however, properly formed, and on the 24th July, the bridges being ready, all the army crossed the Rhine, without any attempt being made by the enemy to follow us. On the day after, the Marechal de Joyeuse permitted me to go to Landau, where I remained with the Marechal and the Marechale de Lorges until the General was again able to place himself at the head of his army.

Nothing of importance was done by our other armies; but in Flanders an interesting adventure occurred. The Prince of Orange, after playing a fine game of chess with our army, suddenly invested Namur with a large force, leaving the rest of his troops under the command of M. de Vaudemont. The Marechal de Villeroy, who had the command of our army in Flanders, at once pressed upon M. de Vaudemont, who, being much the weaker of the two, tried hard to escape. Both felt that everything was in their hands: Vaudemont, that upon his safety depended the success of the siege of Namur; and Villeroy, that to his victory was attached the fate of the Low Countries, and very likely a glorious peace, with all the personal results of such an event. He took his measures so well that on the evening of the 13th of July it was impossible for M. de Vaudemont to escape falling into his hands on the 14th, and he wrote thus to the King. At daybreak on the 14th M. de Villeroy sent word to M. du Maine to commence the action. Impatient that his orders were not obeyed, he sent again five or six times. M. du Maine wished in the first instance to reconnoitre, then to confess himself, and delayed in effect so long that M. de Vaudemont was able to commence his retreat. The general officers cried out at this. One of them came to M. du Maine and reminded him of the repeated orders of the Marechal de Villeroy, represented the importance of victory, and the ease with which it could be obtained: with tears in his eyes he begged M. du Maine to commence the attack. It was all in vain; M. du Maine stammered, and could not be prevailed upon to charge, and so allowed M. de Vaudemont's army to escape, when by a single movement it might have been entirely defeated.

All our army was in despair, and officers and soldiers made no scruple of expressing their anger and contempt. M. de Villeroy, more outraged than anybody else, was yet too good a courtier to excuse himself at the expense of M. du Maine. He simply wrote to the King, that he had been deceived in those hopes of success which appeared certain the day before, entered into no further details, and resigned himself to all that might happen. The King, who had counted the hours until news of a great and decisive victory should reach him, was very much surprised when this letter came: he saw at once that something strange had happened of which no intelligence had been sent: he searched the gazettes of Holland; in one he read of a great action said to have been fought, and in which M. du Maine had been grievously wounded; in the next the news of the action was contradicted, and M. du Maine was declared to have received no wounds at all. In order to learn what had really taken place, the King sent for Lavienne, a man he was in the habit of consulting when he wanted to learn things no one else dared to tell him.

This Lavienne had been a bath-keeper much in vogue in Paris, and had become bath-keeper to the King at the time of his amours. He had pleased by his drugs, which had frequently put the King in a state to enjoy himself more, and this road had led Lavienne to become one of the four chief valets de chambre. He was a very honest man, but coarse, rough, and free-spoken; it was this last quality which made him useful in the manner I have before mentioned. From Lavienne the King, but not without difficulty, learned the truth: it threw him into despair. The other illegitimate children were favourites with him, but it was upon M. du Maine that all his hopes were placed. They now fell to the ground, and the grief of the King was insupportable: he felt deeply for that dear son whose troops had become the laughing stock of the army; he felt the railleries that, as the gazettes showed him, foreigners were heaping upon his forces; and his vexation was inconceivable.

This Prince, so equal in his manners, so thoroughly master of his lightest movements, even upon the gravest occasions, succumbed under this event. On rising from the table at Marly he saw a servant who, while taking away the dessert, helped himself to a biscuit, which he put in his pocket. On the instant, the King forgets his dignity, and cane in hand runs to this valet (who little suspected what was in store for him), strikes him; abuses him, and breaks the cane upon his body! The truth is, 'twas only a reed, and snapped easily. However, the stump in his hand, he walked away like a man quite beside himself, continuing to abuse this valet, and entered Madame de Maintenon's room, where he remained nearly an hour. Upon coming out he met Father la Chaise. "My father," said the King to him, in a very loud voice, "I have beaten a knave and broken my cane over his shoulders, but I do not think I have offended God." Everybody around trembled at this public confession, and the poor priest muttered a semblance of approval between his teeth, to avoid irritating the King more. The noise that the affair made and the terror it inspired may be imagined; for nobody could divine for some time the cause; and everybody easily understood that that which had appeared could not be the real one. To finish with this matter, once for all, let us add here the saying of M. d'Elboeuf. Courtier though he was, the upward flight of the illegitimate children weighed upon his heart. As the campaign was at its close and the Princes were about to depart, he begged M. du Maine before everybody to say where he expected to serve during the next campaign, because wherever it might be he should like to be there also.

After being pressed to say why, he replied that "with him one's life was safe." This pointed remark made much noise. M. du Maine lowered his eyes, and did not reply one word. As for the Marechal de Villeroy he grew more and more in favour with the King and with Madame de Maintenon. The bitter fruit of M. du Maine's act was the taking of Namur, which capitulated on August 4th (1695). The Marechal de Villeroy in turn bombarded Brussels, which was sorely maltreated. The Marechal de Boufflers, who had defended Namur, was made Duke, and those who had served under him were variously rewarded. This gave occasion for the Prince of Orange to say, that the King recompensed more liberally the loss of a place than he could the conquest of one. The army retired into winter-quarters at the end of October, and the Generals went to Paris.

As for me, I remained six weeks at Landau with M. and Madame de Lorges. At the end of that time, the Marechal, having regained his health, returned to the army, where he was welcomed with the utmost joy: he soon after had an attack of apoplexy, and, by not attending to his malady in time, became seriously ill again. When a little recovered, he and Madame de Lorges set out for Vichy, and I went to Paris.

CHAPTER VIII

Before speaking of what happened at Court after my return, it will be necessary to record what had occurred there during the campaign.

M. de Brias, Archbishop of Cambrai, had died, and the King had given that valuable preferment to the Abbe de Fenelon, preceptor of the children of France. Fenelon was a man of quality, without fortune, whom the consciousness of wit—of the insinuating and captivating kind—united with much ability, gracefulness of intellect, and learning, inspired with ambition. He had been long going about from door to door, knocking for admission, but without success. Piqued against the Jesuits, to whom he had addressed himself at first, as holding all favours in their hands, and discouraged because unable to succeed in that quarter, he turned next to the Jansenists, to console himself by the reputation he hoped he should derive from them, for the loss of those gifts of fortune which hitherto had despised him.

He remained a considerable time undergoing the process of initiation, and succeeded at last in being of the private parties that some of the important Jansenists then held once or twice a week at the house of the Duchesse de Brancas. I know not if he appeared too clever for them, or if he hoped elsewhere for better things than he could get among people who had only sores to share; but little by little his intimacy with them cooled; and by dint of turning around Saint Sulpice, he succeeded in forming another connection there, upon which he built greater expectations. This society of priests was beginning to distinguish itself, and from a seminary of a Paris parish to extend abroad. Ignorance, the minuteness of their practices, the absence of all patrons and of members at all distinguished in any way, inspired them with a blind obedience to Rome and to all its maxims; with a great aversion for everything that passed for Jansenism, and made them so dependent upon the bishops that they began to be considered an acquisition in many dioceses. They appeared a middle party, very useful to the prelates; who equally feared the Court, on account of suspicions of doctrine, and the Jesuits for as soon as the latter had insinuated themselves into the good graces of the prelates, they imposed their yoke upon them, or ruined them hopelessly;—thus the Sulpicians grew apace. None amongst them could compare in any way with the Abbe de Fenelon; so that he was able easily to play first fiddle, and to make for himself protectors who were interested in advancing him, in order that they might be protected in turn.

His piety, which was all things to all men, and his doctrine that he formed upon theirs (abjuring, as it were, in whispers, the impurities he might have contracted amongst those he had abandoned)—the charms, the graces, the sweetness, the insinuation of his mind, rendered him a dear friend to this new congregation, and procured for him what he had long sought, people upon whom he could lean, and who could and would serve. Whilst waiting opportunities, he carefully courted these people, without thinking, however, of positively joining them, his views being more ambitious; so that he ever sought to make new acquaintances and friends. His was a coquettish mind, which from people the most influential down to the workman and the lackey sought appreciation and was determined to please; and his talents for this work perfectly seconded his desires.

At this time, and while still obscure, he heard speak of Madame Guyon, who has since made so much noise in the world, and who is too well known to need that I should dwell upon her here. He saw her. There was an interchange of pleasure between their minds. Their sublimes amalgamated. I know not if they understood each other very clearly in that system, and that new tongue which they hatched subsequently, but they persuaded themselves they did, and friendship grew up between them. Although more known than he, Madame Guyon was nevertheless not much known, and their intimacy was not perceived, because nobody thought of them; Saint Sulpice even was ignorant of what was going on.

The Duc de Beauvilliers became Governor of the children of France almost in spite of himself, without having thought of it. He had to choose a preceptor for Monseigneur le Duc de Bourgogne. He addressed himself to Saint Sulpice, where for a long time he had confessed, for he liked and protected it. He had heard speak of Fenelon with eulogy: the Sulpicians vaunted his piety, his intelligence, his knowledge, his talents; at last they proposed him for preceptor. The Duc de Beauvilliers saw him, was charmed with him, and appointed him to the office.

As soon as installed, Fenelon saw of what importance it would be to gain the entire favour of the Duc de Beauvilliers, and of his brother-in-law the Duc de Chevreuse, both very intimate friends, and both in the highest confidence of the King and Madame de Maintenon. This was his first care, and he succeeded beyond his hopes, becoming the master of their hearts and minds, and the director of their consciences.

Madame de Maintenon dined regularly once a week at the house of one or other of the two Dukes, fifth of a little party, composed of the two sisters and the two husbands,—with a bell upon the table, in order to dispense with servants in waiting, and to be able to talk without restraint. Fenelon was at last admitted to this sanctuary, at foot of which all the Court was prostrated. He was almost as successful with Madame de Maintenon as he had been with the two Dukes. His spirituality enchanted her: the Court soon perceived the giant strides of the fortunate Abbe, and eagerly courted him. But, desiring to be free and entirely devoted to his great object, he kept himself aloof from their flatteries—made for himself a shield with his modesty and his duties of preceptor—and thus rendered himself still more dear to the persons he had captivated, and that he had so much interest in retaining in that attachment.

Among these cares he forgot not his dear Madame Guyon; he had already vaunted her to the two Dukes and to Madame de Maintenon. He had even introduced her to them, but as though with difficulty and for a few moments, as a woman all in God, whose humility and whose love of contemplation and solitude kept her within the strictest limits, and whose fear, above all, was that she should become known. The tone of her mind pleased Madame de Maintenon extremely; her reserve, mixed with delicate flatteries, won upon her. Madame de Maintenon wished to hear her talk upon matters of piety; with difficulty she consented to speak. She seemed to surrender herself to the charms and to the virtue of Madame de Maintenon, and Madame de Maintenon fell into the nets so skilfully prepared for her.

Such was the situation of Fenelon when he became Archbishop of Cambrai; increasing the admiration in which he was held by taking no step to gain that great benefice. He had taken care not to seek to procure himself Cambrai; the least spark of ambition would have destroyed all his edifice; and, moreover, it was not Cambrai that he coveted.

Little by little he appropriated to himself some distinguished sheep of the small flock Madame Guyon had gathered together. He only conducted them, however, under the direction of that prophetess, and, everything passed with a secrecy and mystery that gave additional relish to the manna distributed.

Cambrai was a thunderbolt for this little flock. It was the archbishopric of Paris they wished. Cambrai they looked upon with disdain as a country diocese, the residence in which (impossible to avoid from time to time) would deprive them of their pastor. Their grief was then profound at what the rest of the world took for a piece of amazing luck, and the Countess of Guiche was so affected as to be unable to hide her tears. The new prelate had not neglected such of his brethren as made the most figure; they, in turn, considered it a distinction to command his regard. Saint Cyr, that spot so valuable and so inaccessible, was the place chosen for his consecration; and M. de Meaux, dictator then of the episcopacy and or doctrine, consecrated him. The children of France were among the spectators, and Madame de Maintenon was present with her little court of familiars. No others were invited; the doors were closed to those who sought to pay their court.

The new Archbishop of Cambrai, gratified with his influence over Madame de Maintenon and with the advantages it had brought him, felt that unless he became completely master of her, the hopes he still entertained could not be satisfied. But there was a rival in his way—Godet, Bishop of Chartres, who was much in the confidence of Madame de Maintenon, and had long discourses with her at Saint Cyr. As he was, however, of a very ill figure, had but little support at Court, and appeared exceedingly simple, M. de Cambrai believed he could easily overthrow him. To do this, he determined to make use of Madame Guyon, whose new spirituality had already been so highly relished by Madame de Maintenon. He persuaded this latter to allow Madame Guyon to enter Saint Cyr, where they could discourse together much more at their ease than at the Hotel de Chevreuse or Beauvilliers. Madame Guyon went accordingly to Saint Cyr two or three times. Soon after, Madame de Maintenon, who relished her more and more, made her sleep there, and their meetings grew longer. Madame Guyon admitted that she sought persons proper to become her disciples, and in a short time she formed a little flock, whose maxims and language appeared very strange to all the rest of the house, and, above all, to M. de Chartres. That prelate was not so simple as M. de Cambrai imagined. Profound theologian and scholar, pious, disinterested, and of rare probity, he could be, if necessary, a most skilful courtier; but he rarely exerted this power, for the favour of Madame de Maintenon sufficed him of itself. As soon as he got scent of this strange doctrine, he caused two ladies, upon whom he could count, to be admitted to Saint Cyr, as if to become disciples of Madame Guyon. He gave them full instructions, and they played their parts to perfection. In the first place they appeared to be ravished, and by degrees enchanted, with the new doctrine. Madame Guyon, pleased with this fresh conquest, took the ladies into her most intimate confidence in order to gain them entirely. They communicated everything to M. de Chartres, who quietly looked on, allowed things to take their course, and, when he believed the right moment had arrived, disclosed all he had learnt to Madame de Maintenon. She was strangely surprised when she saw the extraordinary drift of the new doctrine. Troubled and uncertain, she consulted with M. de Cambrai, who, not suspecting she had been so well instructed, became, when he discovered it, embarrassed, and thus augmented her suspicions.

Suddenly Madame Guyon was driven away from Saint Cyr, and prohibited from spreading her doctrine elsewhere. But the admiring disciples she had made still gathered round her in secret, and this becoming known, she was ordered to leave Paris. She feigned obedience, but in effect went no further than the Faubourg Saint Antoine, where, with great secrecy, she continued to receive her flock. But being again detected, she was sent, without further parley, to the Bastille, well treated there, but allowed to see nobody, not even to write. Before being arrested, however, she had been put into the hands of M. de Meaux, who used all his endeavours to change her sentiments. Tired at last of his sermons, she feigned conviction, signed a recantation of her opinions, and was set at liberty. Yet, directly after, she held her secret assemblies in the Faubourg Saint Antoine, and it was in consequence of this abuse of freedom that she was arrested. These adventures bring me far into the year 1696, and the sequel extends into the following year. Let us finish this history at once, and return afterwards to what happened meanwhile.

Monsieur de Cambrai, stunned but not overpowered by the reverse he had sustained, and by his loss of favour with Madame de Maintenon, stood firm in his stirrups. After Madame Guyon's abuse of her liberty, and the conferences of Issy, he bethought himself of confessing to M. de Meaux, by which celebrated trick he hoped to close that prelate's mouth. These circumstances induced M. de Meaux to take pen in hand, in order to expose to the public the full account of his affair, and of Madame Guyon's doctrine; and he did so in a work under the title of 'Instruction sur les Etats d'Oyaison'.

While the book was yet unpublished, M. de Cambrai was shown a copy. He saw at once the necessity of writing another to ward off the effect of such a blow. He must have had a great deal of matter already prepared, otherwise the diligence he used would be incredible. Before M. de Meaux's book was ready, M. de Cambrai's, entitled 'Maximes des Saints', was published and distributed. M. de Chevreuse, who corrected the proofs, installed himself at the printer's, so as to see every sheet as soon as printed.

This book, written in the strangest manner, did M. de Cambrai little service. If people were offended to find it supported upon no authority, they were much more so with its confused and embarrassed style, its precision so restrained and so decided, its barbarous terms which seemed as though taken from a foreign tongue, above all, its high-flown and far- fetched thoughts, which took one's breath away, as in the too subtle air of the middle region. Nobody, except the theologians, understood it, and even they not without reading it three or four times. Connoisseurs found in it a pure Quietism, which, although wrapped up in fine language, was clearly visible. I do not give my own judgment of things so much beyond me, but repeat what was said everywhere. Nothing else was talked about, even by the ladies; and a propos of this, the saying of Madame de Sevigne was revived: "Make religion a little more palpable; it evaporates by dint of being over-refined."

Not a word was heard in praise of the book; everybody was opposed to it, and it was the means of making Madame de Maintenon more unfavourable to M. de Cambrai than ever. He sent the King a copy, without informing her. This completed her annoyance against him. M. de Cambrai, finding his book so ill-received by the Court and by the prelates, determined to try and support it on the authority of Rome, a step quite opposed to our manners. In the mean time, M. de Meaux's book appeared in two volumes octavo, well written, clear, modest, and supported upon the authority of the Scriptures. It was received with avidity, and absolutely devoured. There was not a person at the Court who did not take a pleasure in reading it, so that for a long time it was the common subject of conversation of the Court and of the town.

These two books, so opposed in doctrine and in style, made such a stir on every side that the King interposed, and forced M. de Cambrai to submit his work to an examination by a council of prelates, whom he named. M. de Cambrai asked permission to go to Rome to defend his cause in person, but this the King refused. He sent his book, therefore, to the Pope, and had the annoyance to receive a dry, cold reply, and to see M. de Meaux's book triumph. His good fortune was in effect at an end. He remained at Court some little time, but the King was soon irritated against him, sent him off post-haste to Paris, and from there to his diocese, whence he has never returned. He left behind him a letter for one of his friends, M. de Chevreuse it was generally believed, which immediately after became public. It appeared like the manifesto of a man who disgorges his bile and restrains himself no more, because he has nothing more to hope. The letter, bold and bitter in style, was besides so full of ability and artifice, that it was extremely pleasant to read, without finding approvers; so true it is that a wise and disdainful silence is difficult to keep under reverses.

VOLUME 2.: CHAPTER IX

To return now to the date from which I started. On the 6th of August, 1695, Harlay, Archbishop of Paris, died of epilepsy at Conflans. He was a prelate of profound knowledge and ability, very amiable, and of most gallant manners. For some time past he had lost favour with the King and with Madame de Maintenon, for opposing the declaration of her marriage— of which marriage he had been one of the three witnesses. The clergy, who perceived his fall, and to whom envy is not unfamiliar, took pleasure in revenging themselves upon M. de Paris, for the domination, although gentle and kindly, he had exercised. Unaccustomed to this decay of his power, all the graces of his mind and body withered. He could find no resource but to shut himself up with his dear friend the Duchesse de Lesdiguieres, whom he saw every day of his life, either at her own house or at Conflans, where he had laid out a delicious garden, kept so strictly clean, that as the two walked, gardeners followed at a distance, and effaced their footprints with rakes. The vapours seized the Archbishop, and turned themselves into slight attacks of epilepsy. He felt this, but prohibited his servants to send for help, when they should see him attacked; and he was only too well obeyed. The Duchesse de Lesdiguieres never slept at Conflans, but she went there every afternoon, and was always alone with him. On the 6th of August, he passed the morning, as usual, until dinner-time; his steward came there to him, and found him in his cabinet, fallen back upon a sofa; he was dead. The celebrated Jesuit-Father Gaillard preached his funeral sermon, and carefully eluded pointing the moral of the event. The King and Madame de Maintenon were much relieved by the loss of M. de Paris. Various places he had held were at once distributed. His archbishopric and his nomination to the cardinalship required more discussion. The King learnt the news of the death of M. de Paris on the 6th. On the 8th, in going as usual to his cabinet, he went straight up to the Bishop of Orleans, led him to the Cardinals de Bouillon and de Fursternberg, and said to them:- "Gentlemen, I think you will thank me for giving you an associate like M. d'Orleans, to whom I give my nomination to the cardinalship." At this word the Bishop, who little expected such a scene, fell at the King's feet and embraced his knees. He was a man whose face spoke at once of the virtue and benignity he possessed. In youth he was so pious, that young and old were afraid to say afoul word in his presence. Although very rich, he appropriated scarcely any of his wealth to himself, but gave it away for good works. The modesty and the simplicity with which M. d'Orleans sustained his nomination, increased the universal esteem in which he was held.

The archbishopric of Paris was given to a brother of the Duc de Noailles- the Bishop of Chalons-sur-Marne—M. de Noailles thus reaping the fruit of his wise sacrifice to M. de Vendome, before related. M. de Chalons was of singular goodness and modesty. He did not wish for this preferment, and seeing from far the prospect of its being given to him, hastened to declare himself against the Jesuits, in the expectation that Pere la Chaise, who was of them, and who was always consulted upon these occasions, might oppose him. But it happened, perhaps for the first time, that Madame de Maintenon, who felt restrained by the Jesuits, did not consult Pere la Chaise, and the preferment was made without his knowledge, and without that of M. de

Chalons. The affront was a violent one, and the Jesuits never forgave the new Archbishop: he was, however, so little anxious for the office, that it was only after repeated orders he could be made to accept it.

The Bishop of Langres also died about this time. He was a true gentleman, much liked, and called "the good Langres." There was nothing bad about him, except his manners; he was not made for a bishop—gambled very much, and staked high. M. de Vendome and others won largely at billiards of him, two or three times. He said no word, but, on returning to Langres, did nothing but practise billiards in secret for six months. When next in Paris, he was again asked to play, and his adversaries, who thought him as unskilful as before, expected an easy victory but, to their astonishment, he gained almost every game, won back much more than he had lost, and then laughed in the faces of his companions.

I paid about this time, my first journey to Marly, and a singular scene happened there. The King at dinner, setting aside his usual gravity, laughed and joked very much with Madame la Duchesse, eating olives with her in sport, and thereby causing her to drink more than usual—which he also pretended to do. Upon rising from the table the King, seeing the Princesse de Conti look extremely serious, said, dryly, that her gravity did not accommodate itself to their drunkenness. The Princess, piqued, allowed the King to pass without saying anything; and then, turning to Madame de Chatillon, said, in the midst of the noise, whilst everybody was washing his mouth, "that she would rather be grave than be a wine- sack" (alluding to some bouts a little prolonged that her sister had recently had).

The saying was heard by the Duchesse de Chartres, who replied, loud enough to be heard, in her slow and trembling voice, that she preferred to be a "winesack" rather than a "rag-sack" (sac d'guenilles) by which she alluded to the Clermont and La Choin adventure I have related before.

This remark was so cruel that it met with no reply; it spread through Marly, and thence to Paris; and Madame la Duchesse, who had the art of writing witty songs, made one upon this theme. The Princesse de Conti was in despair, for she had not the same weapon at her disposal. Monsieur tried to reconcile them gave them a dinner at Meudon—but they returned from it as they went.

The end of the year was stormy at Marly. One evening, after the King had gone to bed, and while Monseigneur was playing in the saloon, the Duchesse de Chartres and Madame la Duchesse (who were bound together by their mutual aversion to the Princesse de Conti) sat down to a supper in the chamber of the first-named. Monseigneur, upon retiring late to his own room, found them smoking with pipes, which they had sent for from the Swiss Guards! Knowing what would happen if the smell were discovered, he made them leave off, but the smoke had betrayed them. The King next day severely scolded them, at which the Princesse de Conti triumphed. Nevertheless, these broils multiplied, and the King at last grew so weary of them that one evening he called the Princesses before him, and threatened that if they did not improve he would banish them all from the Court. The measure had its effect; calm and decorum returned, and supplied the place of friendship.

There were many marriages this winter, and amongst them one very strange —a marriage of love, between a brother of Feuquiere's, who had never done much, and the daughter of the celebrated Mignard, first painter of his time. This daughter was still so beautiful, that Bloin, chief valet of the King, had kept her for some time, with the knowledge of every one, and used his influence to make the King sign the marriage-contract.

There are in all Courts persons who, without wit and without distinguished birth, without patrons, or service rendered, pierce into the intimacy of the most brilliant, and succeed at last, I know not how, in forcing the world to look upon them as somebody. Such a person was Cavoye. Rising from nothing, he became Grand Marechal des Logis in the royal household: he arrived at that office by a perfect romance. He was one of the best made men in France, and was much in favour with the ladies. He first appeared at the Court at a time when much duelling was taking place, in spite of the edicts. Cavoye, brave and skilful, acquired so much reputation m this particular, that the name of "Brave Cavoye" has stuck to him ever since. An ugly but very good creature, Mademoiselle de Coetlogon, one of the Queen's waiting-women, fill in love with him, even to madness. She made all the advances; but Cavoye treated her so cruelly, nay, sometimes so brutally, that (wonderful to say) everybody pitied her, and the King at last interfered, and commanded him to be more humane. Cavoye went to the army; the poor Coetlogon was in tears until his return. In the winter, for being second in a duel, he was sent to the Bastille. Then the grief of Coetlogon knew no bounds: she threw aside all ornaments, and clad herself as meanly as possible; she begged the King to grant Cavoye his liberty, and, upon the King's refusing, quarrelled with him violently, and when in return he laughed at her, became so furious, that she would have used her nails, had he not been too wise to expose himself to them. Then she refused to attend to her duties, would not serve the King, saying, that he did not deserve it, and grew so yellow and ill, that at last she was allowed to visit her lover at the Bastille. When he was liberated, her joy was extreme, she decked herself out anon, but it was with difficulty that she consented to be reconciled to the King.

Cavoye had many times been promised an appointment, but had never received one such as he wished. The office of Grand Marechal des Logis had just become vacant: the King offered it to Cavoye, but on condition that he should marry Mademoiselle Coetlogon. Cavoye sniffed a little longer, but was obliged to submit to this condition at last. They were married, and she has still the same admiration for him, and it is sometimes fine fun to see the caresses she gives him before all the world, and the constrained gravity with which he receives them. The history of Cavoye would fill a volume, but this I have selected suffices for its singularity, which assuredly is without example.

About this time the King of England thought matters were ripe for an attempt to reinstate himself upon the throne. The Duke of Berwick had been secretly into England, where he narrowly escaped being arrested, and upon his report these hopes were built. Great preparations were made, but they came to nothing, as was always the case with the projects of this unhappy prince.

Madame de Guise died at this time. Her father was the brother of Louis XIII., and she, humpbacked and deformed to excess, had married the last Duc de Guise, rather than not marry at all. During all their lives, she compelled him to pay her all the deference due to her rank. At table he stood while she unfolded her napkin and seated herself, and did not sit until she told him to do so, and then at the end of the table. This form was observed every day of their lives. She was equally severe in such matters of etiquette with all the rest of the world. She would keep her diocesan, the Bishop of Seez, standing for entire hours, while she was seated in her arm-chair and never once offered him a seat even in the corner. She was in other things an entirely good and sensible woman. Not until after her death was it discovered that she had been afflicted for a long time with a cancer, which appeared as though about to burst. God spared her this pain.

We lost, in the month of March, Madame de Miramion, aged sixty-six. She was a bourgeoise, married, and in the same year became a widow very rich, young, and beautiful. Bussy Rabutin, so known by his 'Histoire Amoureuse des Gaules', and by the profound disgrace it drew upon him, and still more by the vanity of his mind and the baseness of his heart, wished absolutely to marry her, and actually carried her off to a chateau. Upon arriving at the place, she pronounced before everybody assembled there a vow of chastity, and then dared Bussy to do his worst. He, strangely discomfited by this action, at once set her at liberty, and tried to accommodate the affair. From that moment she devoted herself entirely, to works of piety, and was much esteemed by the King. She was the first woman of her condition who wrote above her door, "Hotel de Nesmond." Everybody cried out, and was scandalised, but the writing remained, and became the example and the father of those of all kinds which little by little have inundated Paris.

Madame de Sevigne, so amiable and of such excellent company, died some time after at Grignan, at the house of her daughter, her idol, but who merited little to be so. I was very intimate with the young Marquis de Grignan, her grandson. This woman, by her natural graces, the sweetness of her wit, communicated these qualities to those who had them not; she was besides extremely good, and knew thoroughly many things without ever wishing to appear as though she knew anything.

Father Seraphin preached during Lent this year at the Court. His sermons, in which he often repeated twice running the same phrase, were much in vogue. It was from him that came the saying, "Without God there is no wit." The King was much pleased with him, and reproached M. de Vendome and M. de la Rochefoucauld because they never went to hear his sermons. M. de Vendome replied off-hand, that he did not care to go to hear a man who said whatever he pleased without allowing anybody to reply to him, and made the King smile by this sally. But M. de la Rochefoucauld treated the matter in another manner he said that he could not induce himself to go like the merest hanger-on about the Court, and beg a seat of the officer who distributed them, and then betake himself early to church in order to have a good one, and wait about in order to put himself where it might please that officer to place him. Whereupon the King immediately gave him a fourth seat behind him, by the side of the Grand Chamberlain, so that everywhere he is thus placed. M. d'Orleans had been in the habit of seating himself there (although his right place was on the prie-Dieu), and little by little had accustomed himself to consider it as his proper place. When he found himself driven away, he made a great ado, and, not daring to complain to the King, quarrelled with M. de la Rochefoucauld, who, until then, had been one of his particular friends. The affair soon made a great stir; the friends of both parties mixed themselves up in it. The King tried in vain to make M. d'Orleans listen to reason; the prelate was inflexible, and when he found he could gain nothing by clamour and complaint, he retired in high dudgeon into his diocese: he remained there some time, and upon his return resumed his complaints with more determination than ever; he fell at the feet of the King, protesting that he would rather die than see his office degraded. M. de la Rochefoucauld entreated the King to be allowed to surrender the seat in favour of M. d'Orleans. But the King would not change his decision; he said that if the matter were to be decided between M. d'Orleans and a lackey, he would give the seat to the lackey rather than to M. d'Orleans. Upon this the prelate returned to his diocese, which he would have been wiser never to have quitted in order to obtain a place which did not belong to him.

As the King really esteemed M. d'Orleans, he determined to appease his anger; and to put an end to this dispute he gave therefore the bishopric of Metz to the nephew of M. d'Orleans; and by this means a reconciliation was established. M. d'Orleans and M. de la Rochefoucauld joined hands again, and the King looked on delighted.

The public lost soon after a man illustrious by his genius, by his style, and by his knowledge of men, I mean La Bruyere, who died of apoplexy at Versailles, after having surpassed Theophrastus in his own manner, and after painting, in the new characters, the men of our days in a manner inimitable. He was besides a very honest man, of excellent breeding, simple, very disinterested, and without anything of the pedant. I had sufficiently known him to regret his death, and the works that might have been hoped from him.

The command of the armies was distributed in the same manner as before, with the exception that M. de Choiseul had the army of the Rhine in place of M. de Lorges. Every one set out to take the field. The Duc de la Feuillade in passing by Metz, to join the army in Germany, called upon his uncle, who was very rich and in his second childhood. La Feuillade thought fit to make sure of his uncle's money beforehand, demanded the key of the cabinet and of the coffers, broke them open upon being refused by the servants, and took away thirty thousand crowns in gold, and many jewels, leaving untouched the silver. The King, who for a long time had been much discontented with La Feuillade for his debauches and his negligence, spoke very strongly and very openly upon this strange forestalling of inheritance. It was only with great difficulty he could be persuaded not to strip La Feuillade of his rank.

Our campaign was undistinguished by any striking event. From June to September of this year (1696), we did little but subsist and observe, after which we recrossed the Rhine at Philipsburg, where our rear guard was slightly inconvenienced by the enemy. In Italy there was more movement. The King sought to bring about peace by dividing the forces of his enemies, and secretly entered into a treaty with Savoy. The conditions were, that every place belonging to Savoy which had been taken by our troops should be restored, and that a marriage should take place between Monseigneur the Duc de Bourgogne and the daughter of the Duke of Savoy, when she became twelve years of age. In the mean time she was to be sent to the Court of France, and preparations were at once made there to provide her with a suitable establishment.

The King was ill with an anthrax in the throat. The eyes of all Europe were turned towards him, for his malady was not without danger; nevertheless in his bed he affected to attend to affairs as usual; and he arranged there with Madame de Maintenon, who scarcely ever quitted his side, the household of the Savoy Princess. The persons selected for the offices in that household were either entirely devoted to Madame de Maintenon, or possessed of so little wit that she had nothing to fear from them. A selection which excited much envy and great surprise was that of the Duchesse de Lude to be lady of honour. The day before she was appointed, Monsieur had mentioned her name in sport to the King. "Yes," said the King, "she would be the best woman in the world to teach the Princess to put rouge and patches on her cheek;" and then, being more devout than usual, he said other things as bitter and marking strong aversion on his part to the Duchess. In fact, she was no favourite of his nor of Madame de Maintenon; and this was so well understood that the surprise of Monsieur and of everybody else was great, upon finding, the day after this discourse, that she had been appointed to the place.

The cause of this was soon learnt. The Duchesse de Lude coveted much to be made lady of honour to the Princess, but knew she had but little chance, so many others more in favour than herself being in the field. Madame de Maintenon had an old servant named Nanon, who had been with her from the time of her early days of misery, and who had such influence with her, that this servant was made much of by everybody at Court, even by the ministers and the daughters of the King. The Duchesse de Lude had also an old servant who was on good terms with the other. The affair therefore was not difficult. The Duchesse de Lude sent twenty thousand crowns to Nanon, and on the very evening of the day on which the King had spoken to Monsieur, she had the place. Thus it is! A Nanon sells the most important and the most brilliant offices, and a Duchess of high birth is silly enough to buy herself into servitude!

This appointment excited much envy. The Marechal de Rochefort, who had expected to be named, made a great ado. Madame de Maintenon, who despised her, was piqued, and said that she should have had it but for the conduct of her daughter. This was a mere artifice; but the daughter was, in truth, no sample of purity. She had acted in such a manner with Blansac that he was sent for from the army to marry her, and on the very night of their wedding she gave birth to a daughter. She was full of wit, vivacity, intrigue, and sweetness; yet most wicked, false, and artificial, and all this with a simplicity of manner, that imposed even upon those who knew her best. More than gallant while her face lasted, she afterwards was easier of access, and at last ruined herself for the meanest valets. Yet, notwithstanding her vices, she was the prettiest flower of the Court bunch, and had her chamber always full of the best company: she was also much sought after by the three daughters of the King. Driven away from the Court, she was after much supplication recalled, and pleased the King so much that Madame de Maintenon, in fear of her, sent her away again. But to go back again to the household of the Princess of Savoy.

Dangeau was made chevalier d'honneur. He owed his success to his good looks, to the court he paid to the King's mistresses, to his skilfulness at play, and to a lucky stroke of fortune. The King had oftentimes been importuned to give him a lodging, and one day, joking with him upon his fancy of versifying; proposed to him some very hard rhymes, and promised him a lodging if he filled them up upon the spot. Dangeau accepted, thought but for a moment, performed the task, and thus gained his lodging. He was an old friend of Madame de Maintenon, and it was to her he was indebted for his post of chevalier d'honneur in the new household.

Madame d'O was appointed lady of the palace. Her father, named Guilleragues, a gluttonous Gascon, had been one of the intimate friends of Madame Scarron, who, as Madame de Maintenon, did not forget her old acquaintance, but procured him the embassy to Constantinople. Dying there, he left an only daughter, who, on the voyage home to France, gained the heart of Villers, lieutenant of the vessel, and became his wife in Asia-Minor, near the ruins of Troy. Villers claimed to be of the house of d'O; hence the name his wife bore.

Established at the Court, the newly-married couple quickly worked themselves into the favour of Madame de Maintenon, both being very clever in intrigue. M. d'O was made governor of the Comte de Toulouse, and soon gained his entire confidence. Madame d'O, too, infinitely pleased the young Count, just then entering upon manhood, by her gallantry, her wit, and the facilities she allowed him. Both, in consequence, grew in great esteem with the King. Had they been attendants upon Princes of the blood, he would assuredly have slighted them. But he always showed great indulgence to those who served his illegitimate children. Hence the appointment of Madame d'O to be lady of the palace.

The household of the Princess of Savoy being completed, the members of it were sent to the Pont Beauvosin to meet their young mistress. She arrived early on the 16th of October, slept at the Pont Beauvosin that night, and on the morrow parted with her Italian attendants without shedding a single tear. On the 4th of November she arrived at Montargis, and was received by the King, Monseigneur, and Monsieur. The King handed her down from her coach, and conducted her to the apartment he had prepared for her. Her respectful and flattering manners pleased him highly. Her cajoleries, too, soon bewitched Madame de Maintenon, whom she never addressed except as "Aunt;" whom she treated with a respect, and yet with a freedom, that ravished everybody. She became the doll of Madame de Maintenon and the King, pleased them infinitely by her insinuating spirit, and took greater liberties with them than the children of the King had ever dared to attempt.

CHAPTER X

Meanwhile our campaign upon the Rhine proceeded, and the enemy, having had all their grand projects of victory defeated by the firmness and the capacity of the Marechal de Choiseul, retired into winter-quarters, and we prepared to do the same. The month of October was almost over when Madame de Saint-Simon lost M. Fremont, father of the Marechal de Lorges. She had happily given birth to a daughter on the 8th of September. I was desirous accordingly to go to Paris, and having obtained permission from the Marechal de Choiseul, who had treated me throughout the campaign with much politeness and attention, I set out. Upon arriving at Paris I found the Court at Fontainebleau. I had arrived from the army a little before the rest, and did not wish that the King should know it without seeing me, lest he might think I had returned in secret. I hastened at once therefore to Fontainebleau, where the King received me with his usual goodness,-saying, nevertheless, that I had returned a little too early, but that it was of no consequence.

I had not long left his presence when I learned a report that made my face burn again. It was affirmed that when the King remarked upon my arriving a little early, I had replied that I preferred arriving at once to see him, as my sole mistress, than to remain some days in Paris, as did the other young men with their mistresses. I went at once to the King, who had a numerous company around him; and I openly denied what had been reported, offering a reward for the discovery of the knave who had thus calumniated me, in order that I might give him a sound thrashing. All day I sought to discover the scoundrel. My speech to the King and my choler were the topic of the day, and I was blamed for having spoken so loudly and in such terms. But of two evils I had chosen the least,—a reprimand from the King, or a few days in the Bastille; and I had avoided the greatest, which was to allow myself to be believed an infamous libeller of our young men, in order to basely and miserably curry favour at the Court. The course I took succeeded. The King said nothing of the matter, and I went upon a little journey I wished particularly to take, for reasons I will now relate.

I had, as I have already mentioned, conceived a strong attachment and admiration for M. de La Trappe. I wished to secure a portrait of him, but such was his modesty and humility that I feared to ask him to allow himself to be painted. I went therefore to Rigault, then the first portrait-painter in Europe. In consideration of a sum of a thousand crowns, and all his expenses paid, he agreed to accompany me to La Trappe, and to make a portrait of him from memory. The whole affair was to be kept a profound secret, and only one copy of the picture was to be made, and that for the artist himself.

My plan being fully arranged, I and Rigault set out. As soon as we arrived at our journey's end, I sought M. de La Trappe, and begged to be allowed to introduce to him a friend of mine, an officer, who much wished to see him: I added, that my friend was a stammerer, and that therefore he would be importuned merely with looks and not words. M. de La Trappe smiled with goodness, thought the officer curious about little, and consented to see him. The interview took place. Rigault excusing himself on the ground of his infirmity, did little during three-quarters of an hour but keep his eyes upon M. de La Trappe, and at the end went into a room where materials were already provided for him, and covered his canvas with the images and the ideas he had filled himself with. On the morrow the same thing was repeated, although M. de La Trappe, thinking that a man whom he knew not, and who could take no part in conversation, had sufficiently seen him, agreed to the interview only out of complaisance to me. Another sitting was needed in order to finish the work; but it was with great difficulty M. de La Trappe could be persuaded to consent to it. When the third and last interview was at an end, M. de La Trappe testified to me his surprise at having been so much and so long looked at by a species of mute. I made the best excuses I could, and hastened to turn the conversation.

The portrait was at length finished, and was a most perfect likeness of my venerable friend. Rigault admitted to me that he had worked so hard to produce it from memory, that for several months afterwards he had been unable to do anything to his other portraits. Notwithstanding the thousand crowns I had paid him, he broke the engagement he had made by showing the portrait before giving it up to me. Then, solicited for copies, he made several, gaining thereby, according to his own admission, more than twenty-five thousand francs, and thus gave publicity to the affair.

I was very much annoyed at this, and with the noise it made in the world; and I wrote to M. de La Trappe, relating the deception I had practised upon him, and sued for pardon. He was pained to excess, hurt, and afflicted; nevertheless he showed no anger. He wrote in return to me, and said, I was not ignorant that a Roman Emperor had said, "I love treason but not traitors;" but that, as for himself, he felt on the contrary that he loved the traitor but could only hate his treason. I made presents of three copies of the picture to the monastery of La Trappe. On the back of the original I described the circumstance under which the portrait had been taken, in order to show that M. de La Trappe had not consented to it, and I pointed out that for some years he had been unable to use his right hand, to acknowledge thus the error which had been made in representing him as writing.

The King, about this time, set on foot negotiations for peace in Holland, sending there two plenipotentiaries, Courtin and Harlay, and acknowledging one of his agents, Caillieres, who had been for some little time secretly in that country.

The year finished with the disgrace of Madame de Saint Geran. She was on the best of terms with the Princesses, and as much a lover of good cheer as Madame de Chartres and Madame la Duchesse. This latter had in the park of Versailles a little house that she called the "Desert." There she had received very doubtful company, giving such gay repasts that the King, informed of her doings, was angry, and forbade her to continue these parties or to receive certain guests. Madame de Saint Geran was then in the first year of her mourning, so that the King did not think it necessary to include her among the interdicted; but he intimated that he did not approve of her. In spite of this, Madame la Duchesse invited her to an early supper at the Desert a short time after, and the meal was prolonged so far into the night, and with so much gaiety, that it came to the ears of the King. He was in great anger, and learning that Madame de Saint Geran had been of the party, sentenced her to be banished twenty leagues from the Court. Like a clever woman, she retired into a convent at Rouen, saying that as she had been unfortunate enough to displease the King, a convent was the only place for her; and this was much approved.

At the commencement of the next year (1697) the eldest son of the Comte d'Auvergne completed his dishonour by a duel he fought with the Chevalier de Caylus, on account of a tavern broil, and a dispute about some wenches. Caylus, who had fought well, fled from the kingdom; the other, who had used his sword like a poltroon, and had run away dismayed into the streets, was disinherited by his father, sent out of the country, and returned no more. He was in every respect a wretch, who, on account of his disgraceful adventures, was forced to allow himself to be disinherited and to take the cross of Malta; he was hanged in effigy at the Greve, to the great regret of his family, not on account of the sentence, but because, in spite of every entreaty, he had been proceeded against like the most obscure gentleman. The exile of Caylus afterwards made his fortune.

We had another instance, about this time, of the perfidy of Harlay. He had been entrusted with a valuable deposit by Ruvigny, a Huguenot officer, who, quitting France, had entered the service of the Prince of Orange, and who was, with the exception of Marshal Schomberg, the only Huguenot to whom the King offered the permission of remaining at Court with full liberty to practise his religion in secret. This, Ruvigny, like Marshal Schomberg, refused. He was, nevertheless, allowed to retain the property he possessed in France; but after his death his son, not showing himself at all grateful for this favour, the King at last confiscated the property, and publicly testified his anger. This was the moment that Harlay seized to tell the King of the deposit he had. As a recompense the King gave it to him as confiscated, and this hypocrite of justice, of virtue, of disinterestedness, and of rigorism was not ashamed to appropriate it to himself, and to close his ears and his eyes to the noise this perfidy excited.

M. de Monaco, who had obtained for himself the title of foreign prince by the marriage of his son with the Duchesse de Valentinois, daughter of M. le Grand, and who enjoyed, as it were, the sovereignty of a rock—beyond whose narrow limits anybody might spit, so to speak, whilst standing in the middle—soon found, and his son still more so, that they had bought the title very dearly. The Duchess was charming, gallant, and was spoiled by the homage of the Court, in a house open night and day, and to which her beauty attracted all that was young and brilliant. Her husband, with much intelligence, was diffident; his face and figure had acquired for him the name of Goliath; he suffered for a long time the haughtiness and the disdain of his wife and her family. At last he and his father grew tired and took away Madame de Valentinois to Monaco. She grieved, and her parents also, as though she had been carried off to the Indies. After two years of absence and repentance, she promised marvels, and was allowed to return to Paris. I know not who counselled her, but, without changing her conduct, she thought only how to prevent a return to Monaco; and to insure herself against this, she accused her father-in-law of having made vile proposals to her, and of attempting to take her by force. This charge made a most scandalous uproar, but was believed by nobody. M. de Monaco was no longer young; he was a very honest man, and had always passed for such; besides, he was almost blind in both eyes, and had a huge pointed belly, which absolutely excited fear, it jutted out so far!

After some time, as Madame de Valentinois still continued to swim in the pleasures of the Court under the shelter of her family, her husband redemanded her; and though he was laughed at at first, she was at last given up to him.

A marriage took place at this time between the son of Pontchartrain and the daughter of the Comte de Roye. The Comte de Roye was a Huguenot, and, at the revocation of the edict of Nantes, had taken refuge, with his wife, in Denmark, where he had been made grand marshal and commander of all the troops. One day, as the Comte de Roye was dining with his wife and daughter at the King's table, the Comtesse de Roye asked her daughter if she did not think the Queen of Denmark and Madame Panache resembled each other like two drops of water? Although she spoke in French and in a low tone, the Queen both heard and understood her, and inquired at once who was Madame Panache. The Countess in her surprise replied, that she was a very amiable woman at the French Court. The Queen, who had noticed the surprise of the Countess, was not satisfied with this reply. She wrote to the Danish minister at Paris, desiring to be informed of every particular respecting Madame Panache, her face, her age, her condition, and upon what footing she was at the French Court. The minister, all astonished that the Queen should have heard of Madame Panache, wrote word that she was a little and very old creature, with lips and eyes so disfigured that they were painful to look upon; a species of beggar who had obtained a footing at Court from being half-witted, who was now at the supper of the King, now at the dinner of Monseigneur, or at other places, where everybody amused themselves by tormenting her: She in turn abused the company at these parties, in order to cause diversion, but sometimes rated them very seriously and with strong words, which delighted still more those princes and princesses, who emptied into her pockets meat and ragouts, the sauces of which ran all down her petticoats: at these parties some gave her a pistole or a crown, and others a filip or a smack in the face, which put her in a fury, because with her bleared eyes not being able to see the end of her nose, she could not tell who had struck her;—she was, in a word, the pastime of the Court!

Upon learning this, the Queen of Denmark was so piqued, that she could no longer suffer the Comtesse de Roye near her; she complained to the King: he was much offended that foreigners, whom he had loaded with favour, should so repay him. The Comte de Roye was unable to stand up against the storm, and withdrew to England, where he died a few years after.

The King at this time drove away the company of Italian actors, and would not permit another in its place. So long as the Italians had simply allowed their stage to overflow with filth or impiety they only caused laughter; but they set about playing a piece called "The False Prude," in which Madame de Maintenon was easily recognised. Everybody ran to see the piece; but after three or four representations, given consecutively on account of the gain it brought, the Italians received orders to close their theatre and to quit the realm in a month. This affair made a great noise; and if the comedians lost an establishment by their boldness and folly, they who drove them away gained nothing—such was the licence with which this ridiculous event was spoken of!

CHAPTER XI

The disposition of the armies was the same this year as last, except that the Princes did not serve. Towards the end of May I joined the army of the Rhine, under the Marechal de Choiseul, as before. We made some skilful manoeuvres, but did little in the way of fighting. For sixteen days we encamped at Nieder-buhl, where we obtained a good supply of forage. At the end of that time the Marechal de Choiseul determined to change his position. Our army was so placed, that the enemy could see almost all of it quite distinctly; yet, nevertheless, we succeeded in decamping so quickly, that we disappeared from under their very eyes in open daylight, and in a moment as it were. Such of the Imperial Generals as were out riding ran from all parts to the banks of the Murg, to see our retreat, but it was so promptly executed that there was no time for them, to attempt to hinder us. When the Prince of Baden was told of our departure he could not credit it. He had seen us so lately, quietly resting in our position, that it seemed impossible to him we had left it in such a short space of time. When his own eyes assured him of the fact, he was filled with such astonishment and admiration, that he asked those around him if they had ever seen such a retreat, adding, that he could not have believed, until then, that an army so numerous and so considerable should have been able to disappear thus in an instant. This honourable and bold retreat was attended by a sad accident. One of our officers, named Blansac, while leading a column of infantry through the wood, was overtaken by night. A small party of his men heard some cavalry near them. The cavalry belonged to the enemy, and had lost their way. Instead of replying when challenged, they said to each other in German, "Let us run for it." Nothing more was wanting to draw upon them a discharge from the small body of our men, by whom they had been heard. To this they replied with their pistols. Immediately, and without orders, the whole column of infantry fired in that direction, and, before Blansac could inquire the cause, fired again. Fortunately he was not wounded; but five unhappy captains were killed, and some subalterns wounded.

Our campaign was brought to an end by the peace of Ryswick. The first news of that event arrived at Fontainebleau on the 22nd of September. Celi, son of Harlay, had been despatched with the intelligence; but he did not arrive until five o'clock in the morning of the 26th of September. He had amused himself by the way with a young girl who had struck his fancy, and with some wine that he equally relished. He had committed all the absurdities and impertinences which might be expected of a debauched, hare-brained young fellow, completely spoiled by his father, and he crowned all by this fine delay.

A little time before the signing of peace, the Prince de Conti, having been elected King of Poland, set out to take possession of his throne. The King, ravished with joy to see himself delivered from a Prince whom he disliked, could not hide his satisfaction—his eagerness—to get rid of a Prince whose only faults were that he had no bastard blood in his veins, and that he was so much liked by all the nation that they wished him at the head of the army, and murmured at the little favour he received, as compared with that showered down upon the illegitimate children.

The King made all haste to treat the Prince to royal honours. After an interview in the cabinet of Madame de Maintenon, he presented him to a number of ladies, saying, "I bring you a king." The Prince was all along doubtful of the validity of his election, and begged that the Princess might not be treated as a queen, until he should have been crowned. He received two millions in cash from the King, and other assistances. Samuel Bernard undertook to make the necessary payments in Poland. The Prince started by way of Dunkerque, and went to that place at such speed, that an ill-closed chest opened, and two thousand Louis were scattered on the road, a portion only of which was brought back to the Hotel Conti. The celebrated Jean Bart pledged himself to take him safely, despite the enemy's fleet; and kept his word. The convoy was of five frigates. The Chevalier de Sillery, before starting, married Mademoiselle Bigot, rich and witty, with whom he had been living for some time. Meanwhile the best news arrived from our ambassador, the Abbe de Polignac, to the King; but all answers were intercepted at Dantzic by the retired Queen of Poland, who sent on only the envelopes! However, the Prince de Conti passed up the Sound; and the King and Queen of Denmark watched them from the windows of the Chateau de Cronenbourg. Jean Bart, against custom, ordered a salute to be fired. It was returned; and as some light vessels passing near the frigates said that the King and Queen were looking on, the Prince ordered another salvo.

There was, however, another claimant to the throne of Poland; I mean the Elector of Saxony, who had also been elected, and who had many partisans; so many, indeed, that when the Prince de Conti arrived at Dantzic, he found himself almost entirely unsupported. The people even refused provision to his frigates. However, the Prince's partisans at length arrived to salute him. The Bishop of Plosko gave him a grand repast, near the Abbey of Oliva. Marege, a Gascon gentleman of the Prince's suite, was present, but had been ill. There was drinking in the Polish fashion, and he tried to be let off. The Prince pleaded for him; but these Poles, who, in order to make themselves understood, spoke Latin— and very bad Latin indeed—would not accept such an excuse, and forcing him to drink, howled furiously 'Bibat et Moriatur! Marege, who was very jocular and yet very choleric; used to tell this story in the same spirit, and made everyone who heard it laugh.

However, the party of the Prince de Conti made no way, and at length he was fain to make his way back to France with all speed. The King received him very graciously, although at heart exceeding sorry to see him again. A short time after, the Elector of Saxony mounted the throne of Poland without opposition, and was publicly recognised by the King, towards the commencement of August.

By the above-mentioned peace of Ryswick, the King acknowledged the Prince of Orange as King of England. It was, however, a bitter draught for him to swallow, and for these reasons: Some years before, the King had offered his illegitimate daughter, the Princesse de Conti, in marriage to the Prince of Orange, believing he did that Prince great honour by the proposal. The Prince did not think in the same manner, and flatly refused; saying, that the House of Orange was accustomed to marry the legitimate daughters of great kings, and not their bastards. These words sank so deeply into the heart of the King, that he never forgot them; and often, against even his most palpable interest, showed how firmly the indignation he felt at them had taken possession of his mind: Since then, the Prince of Orange had done all in his power to efface the effect his words had made, but every attempt was rejected with disdain. The King's ministers in Holland had orders to do all they could to thwart the projects of the Prince of Orange, to excite people against him, to protect openly those opposed to him, and to be in no way niggard of money in order to secure the election of magistrates unfavourable to him. The Prince never ceased, until the breaking-out of this war, to use every effort to appease the anger of the King. At last, growing tired, and hoping soon to make his invasion into England, he said publicly, that he had uselessly laboured all his life to gain the favours of the King, but that he hoped to be more fortunate in meriting his esteem. It may be imagined, therefore, what a triumph it was for him when he forced the King to recognise him as monarch of England, and what that recognition cost the King.

M. le Duc presided this year over the Assembly of the States of Burgundy, in place of his father M. le Prince, who did not wish to go there. The Duke gave on that occasion a striking example of the friendship of princes, and a fine lesson to those who seek it. Santeuil, Canon of Saint Victor, and the greatest Latin poet who has appeared for many centuries, accompanied him. Santeuil was an excellent fellow, full of wit and of life, and of pleasantries, which rendered him an admirable boon-companion. Fond of wine and of good cheer, he was not debauched; and with a disposition and talents so little fitted for the cloister, was nevertheless, at bottom, as good a churchman as with such a character he could be. He was a great favourite with all the house of Conde, and was invited to their parties, where his witticisms, his verses, and his pleasantries had afforded infinite amusement for many years.

M. le Duc wished to take him to Dijon. Santeuil tried to excuse himself, but without effect; he was obliged to go, and was established at the house of the Duke while the States were held. Every evening there was a supper, and Santeuil was always the life of the company. One evening M. le Duc diverted himself by forcing Santeuil to drink champagne, and passing from pleasantry to pleasantry, thought it would be a good joke to empty his snuff-box, full of Spanish snuff, into a large glass of wine, and to make Santeuil drink it, in order to see what would happen. It was not long before he was enlightened upon this point. Santeuil was seized with vomiting and with fever, and in twice twenty-four hours the unhappy man died-suffering the tortures of the damned, but with sentiments of extreme penitence, in which he received the sacrament, and edified a company little disposed towards edification, but who detested such a cruel joke.

In consequence of the peace just concluded at Ryswick, many fresh arrangements were made about this time in our embassies abroad. This allusion to our foreign appointments brings to my mind an anecdote which deserves to be remembered. When M. de Vendome took Barcelona, the Montjoui (which is as it were its citadel) was commanded by the Prince of Darmstadt. He was of the house of Hesse, and had gone into Spain to seek employment; he was a relative of the Queen of Spain, and, being a very well-made man, had not, it was said, displeased her. It was said also, and by people whose word was not without weight, that the same council of Vienna, which for reasons of state had made no scruple of poisoning the late Queen of Spain (daughter of

Monsieur), because she had no children, and because she had, also, too much ascendancy over the heart of her husband; it was said, I say, that this same council had no scruples upon another point. After poisoning the first Queen, it had remarried the King of Spain to a sister of the Empress. She was tall, majestic, not without beauty and capacity, and, guided by the ministers of the Emperor, soon acquired much influence over the King her husband. So far all was well, but the most important thing was wanting—she had no children. The council had hoped some from this second marriage, because it had lured itself into the belief that previously the fault rested with the late Queen. After some years, this same council, being no longer able to disguise the fact that the King could have no children, sent the Prince of Darmstadt into Spain, for the purpose of establishing himself there, and of ingratiating himself into the favour of the Queen to such an extent that this defect might be remedied. The Prince of Darmstadt was well received; he obtained command in the army; defended, as I have said, Barcelona; and obtained a good footing at the Court. But the object for which he had been more especially sent he could not accomplish. I will not say whether the Queen was inaccessible from her own fault or that of others. Nor will I say, although I have been assured, but I believe by persons without good knowledge of the subject, that naturally it was impossible for her to become a mother. I will simply say that the Prince of Darmstadt was on the best terms with the King and the Queen, and had opportunities very rare in that country, without any fruit which could put the succession of the monarchy in safety against the different pretensions afloat, or reassure on that head the politic council of Vienna.

But to return to France.

Madame de Maintenon, despite the height to which her insignificance had risen, had yet her troubles. Her brother, who was called the Comte d'Aubigne, was of but little worth, yet always spoke as though no man were his equal, complained that he had not been made Marechal of France —sometimes said that he had taken his baton in money, and constantly bullied Madame de Maintenon because she did not make him a duke and a peer. He spent his time running after girls in the Tuileries, always had several on his hands, and lived and spent his money with their families and friends of the same kidney. He was just fit for a strait-waistcoat, but comical, full of wit and unexpected repartees. A good, humorous fellow, and honest-polite, and not too impertinent on account of his sister's fortune. Yet it was a pleasure to hear him talk of the time of Scarron and the Hotel d'Albret, and of the gallantries and adventures of his sister, which he contrasted with her present position and devotion. He would talk in this manner, not before one or two, but in a compromising manner, quite openly in the Tuileries gardens, or in the galleries of Versailles, before everybody, and would often drolly speak of the King as "the brother-in-law." I have frequently heard him talk in this manner; above all, when he came (more often than was desired) to dine with my father and mother, who were much embarrassed with him; at which I used to laugh in my sleeve.

A brother like this was a great annoyance to Madame de Maintenon. His wife, an obscure creature, more obscure, if possible, than her birth; —foolish to the last degree, and of humble mien, was almost equally so. Madame de Maintenon determined to rid herself of both. She persuaded her brother to enter a society that had been established by a M. Doyen, at St. Sulpice, for decayed gentlemen. His wife at the same time was induced to retire into another community, where, however, she did not fail to say to her companions that her fate was very hard, and that she wished to be free. As for d'Aubigne he concealed from nobody that his sister was putting a joke on him by trying to persuade him that he was devout, declared that he was pestered by priests, and that he should give up the ghost in M. Doyen's house. He could not stand it long, and went back to his girls and to the Tuileries, and wherever he could; but they caught him again, and placed him under the guardianship of one of the stupidest priests of St. Sulpice, who followed him everywhere like his shadow, and made him miserable. The fellow's name was Madot: he was good for no other employment, but gained his pay in this one by an assiduity of which perhaps no one else would have been capable. The only child of this Comte d'Aubigne was a daughter, taken care of by Madame de Maintenon, and educated under her eyes as though her own child.

Towards the end of the year, and not long after my return from the army, the King fixed the day for the marriage of the Duc de Bourgogne to the young Princesse de Savoy. He announced that on that occasion he should be glad to see a magnificent Court; and he himself, who for a long time had worn only the most simple habits, ordered the most superb. This was enough; no one thought of consulting his purse or his state; everyone tried to surpass his neighbour in richness and invention. Gold and silver scarcely sufficed: the shops of the dealers were emptied in a few days; in a word luxury the most unbridled reigned over Court and city, for the fete had a huge crowd of spectators. Things went to such a point, that the King almost repented of what he had said, and remarked, that he could not understand how husbands could be such fools as to ruin themselves by dresses for their wives; he might have added, by dresses for themselves. But the impulse had been given; there was now no time to remedy it, and I believe the King at heart was glad; for it pleased him during the fetes to look at all the dresses. He loved passionately all kinds of sumptuosity at his Court; and he who should have held only to what had been said, as to the folly of expense, would have grown little in favour. There was no means, therefore, of being wise among so many fools. Several dresses were necessary. Those for Madame Saint-Simon and myself cost us twenty thousand francs. Workmen were wanting to make up so many rich habits. Madame la Duchesse actually sent her people to take some by force who were working at the Duc de Rohan's! The King heard of it, did not like it, and had the workmen sent back immediately to the Hotel de Rohan, although the Duc de Rohan was one of the men he liked the least in all France. The King did another thing, which showed that he desired everybody to be magnificent: he himself chose the design for the embroidery of the Princess. The embroiderer said he would leave all his other designs for that. The King would not permit this, but caused him to finish the work he had in hand, and to set himself afterwards at the other; adding, that if it was not ready in time, the Princess could do without it.

The marriage was fixed for Saturday, the 7th of December; and, to avoid disputes and difficulties, the King suppressed all ceremonies. The day arrived. At an early hour all the Court went to Monseigneur the Duc de Bourgogne, who went afterwards to the Princess. A little before mid-day the procession started from the salon, and proceeded to the chapel.

Cardinal de Coislin performed the marriage service.

As soon as the ceremony was finished, a courier, ready at the door of the chapel, started for Turin. The day passed wearily. The King and Queen of England came about seven o'clock in the evening, and some time afterwards supper was served. Upon rising from the table, the Princess was shown to her bed, none but ladies being allowed to remain in the chamber. Her chemise was given her by the Queen of England through the Duchesse de Lude. The Duc de Bourgogne undressed in another room, in the midst of all the Court, and seated upon a folding-chair. The King of England gave him his shirt, which was presented by the Duc de Beauvilliers. As soon as the Duchesse de Bourgogne was in bed, the Duc de Bourgogne entered, and placed himself at her side, in the presence of all the Court. Immediately afterwards everybody went away from the nuptial chamber, except Monseigneur, the ladies of the Princess, and the Duc de Beauvilliers, who remained at the pillow by the side of his pupil, with the Duchesse de Lude on the other side. Monseigneur stopped a quarter of an hour talking with the newly-married couple, then he made his son get up, after having told him to kiss the Princess, in spite of the opposition of the Duchesse de Lude. As it proved, too, her opposition was not wrong. The King said he did not wish that his grandson should kiss the end of the Princess's finger until they were completely on the footing of man and wife. Monsieur le Duc de Bourgogne after this re-dressed himself in the ante-chamber, and went to his own bed as usual. The little Duc de Berry, spirited and resolute, did not approve of the docility of his brother, and declared that he would have remained in bed. The young couple were not, indeed, allowed to live together as man and wife until nearly two years afterwards. The first night that this privilege was granted them, the King repaired to their chamber hoping to surprise them as they went to bed; but he found the doors closed, and would not allow them to be opened. The marriage-fetes spread over several days. On the Sunday there was an assembly in the apartments of the new Duchesse de Bourgogne. It was magnificent by the prodigious number of ladies seated in a circle, or standing behind the stools, gentlemen in turn behind them, and the dresses of all beautiful. It commenced at six o'clock. The King came at the end, and led all the ladies into the saloon near the chapel, where was a fine collation, and the music. At nine o'clock he conducted Monsieur and Madame la Duchesse de Bourgogne to the apartment of the latter, and all was finished for the day. The Princess continued to live just as before, and the ladies had strict orders never to leave her alone with her husband.

On the Wednesday there was a grand ball in the gallery, superbly ornamented for the occasion. There was such a crowd, and such disorder, that even the King was inconvenienced, and Monsieur was pushed and knocked about in the crush. How other people fared may be imagined. No place was kept—strength or chance decided everything—people squeezed in where they could. This spoiled all the fete. About nine o'clock refreshments were handed round, and at half-past ten supper was served. Only the Princesses of the blood and the royal family were admitted to it. On the following Sunday there was another ball, but this time matters were so arranged that no crowding or inconvenience occurred. The ball commenced at seven o'clock and was admirable; everybody appeared in dresses that had not previously been seen. The King found that of Madame de Saint-Simon much to his taste, and gave it the palm over all the others.

Madame de Maintenon did not appear at these balls, at least only for half an hour at each. On the following Tuesday all the Court went at four o'clock in the afternoon to Trianon, where all gambled until the arrival of the King and Queen of England. The King took them into the theatre, where Destouches's opera of Isse was very well performed. The opera being finished, everybody went his way, and thus these marriage-fetes were brought to an end.

Tesse had married his eldest daughter to La Varenne last year, and now married his second daughter to Maulevrier, son of a brother of Colbert. This mention of La Varenne brings to my recollection a very pleasant anecdote of his ancestor, the La Varenne so known in all the memoirs of the time as having risen from the position of scullion to that of cook, and then to that of cloak-bearer to Henry IV., whom he served in his pleasures, and afterwards in his state-affairs. At the death of the King, La Varenne retired, very old and very rich, into the country. Birds were much in vogue at that time, and he often amused himself with falconry. One day a magpie perched on one of his trees, and neither sticks nor stones could dislodge it. La Varenne and a number of sportsmen gathered around the tree and tried to drive away the magpie. Importuned with all this noise, the bird at last began to cry repeatedly with all its might, "Pandar! Pandar!"

Now La Varenne had gained all he possessed by that trade. Hearing the magpie repeat again and again the same word, he took it into his head that by a miracle, like the observation Balaam's ass made to his master, the bird was reproaching him for his sins. He was so troubled that he could not help showing it; then, more and more agitated, he told the cause of his disturbance to the company, who laughed at him in the first place, but, upon finding that he was growing really ill, they endeavoured to convince him that the magpie belonged to a neighbouring village, where it had learned the word. It was all in vain: La Varenne was so ill that he was obliged to be carried home; fever seized him and in four days he died.

CHAPTER XII

Here perhaps is the place to speak of Charles IV., Duc de Lorraine, so well known by his genius, and the extremities to which he was urged. He was married in 1621 to the Duchesse Nicole, his cousin-german, but after a time ceased to live with her. Being at Brussels he fell in love with Madame de Cantecroix, a widow. He bribed a courier to bring him news of the death of the Duchesse Nicole; he circulated the report throughout the town, wore mourning, and fourteen days afterwards, in April, 1637, married Madame de Cantecroix. In a short time it was discovered that the Duchesse Nicole was full of life and health, and had not even been ill. Madame de Cantecroix made believe that she had been duped, but still lived with the Duke. They continued to repute the Duchesse Nicole as dead, and lived together in the face of the world as though effectually married, although there had never been any question either before or since of dissolving the first marriage. The Duc Charles had by this fine marriage a daughter and then a son, both perfectly illegitimate, and universally regarded as such. Of these the daughter married Comte de Lislebonne, by whom she had four children. The son, educated under his father's eye as legitimate, was called Prince de Vaudemont, and by that name has ever since been known. He entered the service of Spain, distinguished himself in the army, obtained the support of the Prince of Orange, and ultimately rose to the very highest influence and prosperity. People were astonished this year, that while the Princess of Savoy was at Fontainebleau, just before her marriage, she was taken several times by Madame de Maintenon to a little unknown convent at Moret, where there was nothing to amuse her, and no nuns who were known. Madame de Maintenon often went there, and Monseigneur with his children sometimes; the late Queen used to go also. This awakened much curiosity and gave rise to many reports. It seems that in this convent there was a woman of colour, a Moorish woman, who had been placed there very young by Bontems, valet of the King. She received the utmost care and attention, but never was shown to anybody. When the late Queen or Madame de Maintenon went, they did not always see her, but always watched over her welfare. She was treated with more consideration than people the most distinguished; and herself made much of the care that was taken of her, and the mystery by which she was surrounded. Although she lived regularly, it was easy to see she was not too contented with her position. Hearing Monseigneur hunt in the forest one day, she forgot herself so far as to exclaim, "My brother is hunting!" It was pretended that she was a daughter of the King and Queen, but that she had been hidden away on account of her colour; and the report was spread that the Queen had had a miscarriage. Many people believed this story; but whether it was true or not has remained an enigma.

The year 1698 commenced by a reconciliation between the Jesuits and the Archbishop of Rheims. That prelate upon the occasion of an ordinance had expressed himself upon matters of doctrine and morality in a manner that displeased the Jesuits. They acted towards him in their usual manner, by writing an attack upon him, which appeared without any author's name. But the Archbishop complained to the King, and altogether stood his ground so firmly, that in the end the Jesuits were glad to give way, disavow the book, and arrange the reconciliation which took place.

The Czar, Peter the Great, Emperor of Russia, had at this time already commenced his voyages; he was in Holland, learning ship-building. Although incognito, he wished to be recognised, but after his own fashion; and was annoyed that, being so near to England, no embassy was sent to him from that country, which he wished to ally himself with for commercial reasons.

At last an embassy arrived; he delayed for some time to give it an audience, but in the end fixed the day and hour at which he would see it. The reception, however, was to take place on board a large Dutch vessel that he was going to examine. There were two ambassadors; they thought the meeting-place rather an odd one, but were obliged to go there. When they arrived on board the Czar sent word that he was in the "top," and that it was there he would see them. The ambassadors, whose feet were unaccustomed to rope-ladders, tried to excuse themselves from mounting; but it was all in vain. The Czar would receive them in the "top" or not at all. At last they were compelled to ascend, and the meeting took place on that narrow place high up in the air. The Czar received them there with as much majesty as though he had been upon his throne, listened to their harangue, replied very graciously, and then laughed at the fear painted upon their faces, and good-humouredly gave them to understand that he had punished them thus for arriving so late.

After this the Czar passed into England, curious to see and learn as much as possible; and, having well fulfilled his views, repaired into Holland. He wished to visit France, but the King civilly declined to receive him. He went, therefore, much mortified, to Vienna instead. Three weeks after his arrival he was informed of a conspiracy that had been formed against him in Moscow. He hastened there at once, and found that it was headed by his own sister; he put her in prison, and hanged her most guilty accomplices to the bars of his windows, as many each day as the bars would hold. I have related at once all that regards the Czar for this year, in order not to leap without ceasing from one matter to another; I shall do this, and for the same reason, with that which follows.

The King of England was, as I have before said, at the height of satisfaction at having been recognised by the King (Louis XIV.), and at finding himself secure upon the throne. But a usurper is never tranquil and content. William was annoyed by the residence of the legitimate King and his family at Saint Germains. It was too close to the King (of France), and too near England to leave him without disquietude. He had tried hard at Ryswick to obtain the dismissal of James II. from the realm, or at least from the Court of France, but without effect. Afterwards he sent the Duke of St. Albans to our King openly, in order to compliment him upon the marriage of the Duc de Bourgogne, but in reality to obtain the dismissal.

The Duke of St. Albans meeting with no success, the Duke of Portland was sent to succeed him. The Duke of Portland came over with a numerous and superb suite; he kept up a magnificent table, and had horses, liveries, furniture, and dresses of the most tasteful and costly kind. He was on his way when a fire destroyed Whitehall, the largest and ugliest palace in Europe, and which has not since been rebuilt; so that the kings are lodged, and very badly, at St.

James's Palace.

Portland had his first audience of the King on the 4th of February, and remained four months in France. His politeness, his courtly and gallant manners, and the good cheer he gave, charmed everybody, and made him universally popular. It became the fashion to give fetes in his honour; and the astonishing fact is, that the King, who at heart was more offended than ever with William of Orange, treated this ambassador with the most marked distinction. One evening he even gave Portland his bedroom candlestick, a favour only accorded to the most considerable persons, and always regarded as a special mark of the King's bounty.

Notwithstanding all these attentions, Portland was as unsuccessful as his predecessor. The King had firmly resolved to continue his protection to James II., and nothing could shake this determination. Portland was warned from the first, that if he attempted to speak to the King upon the point, his labour would be thrown away; he wisely therefore kept silence, and went home again without in any way having fulfilled the mission upon which he had been sent.

We had another distinguished foreigner arrive in France about this time, —I mean, the Prince of Parma, respecting whom I remember a pleasing adventure. At Fontainebleau more great dancing-parties are given than elsewhere, and Cardinal d'Estrees wished to give one there in honour of this Prince. I and many others were invited to the banquet; but the Prince himself, for whom the invitation was specially provided, was forgotten. The Cardinal had given invitations right and left, but by some omission the Prince had not had one sent to him. On the morning of the dinner this discovery was made. The Prince was at once sent to, but he was engaged, and for several days. The dinner therefore took place without him; the Cardinal was much laughed at for his absence of mind. He was often similarly forgetful.

The Bishop of Poitiers died at the commencement of this year, and his bishopric was given at Easter to the Abbe de Caudelet. The Abbe was a very good man, but made himself an enemy, who circulated the blackest calumnies against him. Amongst other impostures it was said that the Abbe had gambled all Good Friday; the truth being, that in the evening, after all the services were over, he went to see the Marechale de Crequi, who prevailed upon him to amuse her for an hour by playing at piquet. But the calumny had such effect, that the bishopric of Poitiers was taken from him, and he retired into Brittany, where he passed the rest of his life in solitude and piety. His brother in the meantime fully proved to Pere de la Chaise the falsehood of this accusation; and he, who was upright and good, did all he could to bestow some other living upon the Abbe, in recompense for that he had been stripped of. But the King would not consent, although often importuned, and even reproached for his cruelty.

It was known, too, who was the author of the calumny. It was the Abbe de la Chatre, who for a long time had been chaplain to the King, and who was enraged against everyone who was made bishop before him. He was a man not wanting in intelligence, but bitter, disagreeable, punctilious; very ignorant, because he would never study, and so destitute of morality, that I saw him say mass in the chapel on Ash Wednesday, after having passed a night, masked at a ball, where he said and did the most filthy things, as seen and heard by M. de La Vrilliere, before whom he unmasked, and who related this to me: half an hour after, I met the Abbe de la Chatre, dressed and going to the altar. Other adventures had already deprived him of all chance of being made bishop by the King.

The old Villars died at this time. I have already mentioned him as having been made chevalier d'honneur to the Duchesse de Chartres at her marriage. I mention him now, because I omitted to say before the origin of his name of Orondat, by which he was generally known, and which did not displease him. This is the circumstance that gave rise to it. Madame de Choisy, a lady of the fashionable world, went one day to see the Comtesse de Fiesque, and found there a large company. The Countess had a young girl living with her, whose name was Mademoiselle d'Outrelaise, but who was called the Divine. Madame de Choisy, wishing to go into the bedroom, said she would go there, and see the Divine. Mounting rapidly, she found in the chamber a young and very pretty girl, Mademoiselle Bellefonds, and a man, who escaped immediately upon seeing her. The face of this man being perfectly well made, so struck her, that, upon coming down again, she said it could only be that of Orondat. Now that romances are happily no longer read, it is necessary to say that Orondat is a character in Cyrus, celebrated by his figure and his good looks, and who charmed all the heroines of that romance, which was then much in vogue. The greater part of the company knew that Villars was upstairs to see Mademoiselle de Bellefonds, with whom he was much in love, and whom he soon afterwards married. Everybody therefore smiled at this adventure of Orondat, and the name clung ever afterwards to Villars.

The Prince de Conti lost, before this time, his son, Prince la Roche-sur-Yon, who was only four years old. The King wore mourning for him, although it was the custom not to do so for children under seven years of age. But the King had already departed from this custom for one of the children of M. du Maine, and he dared not afterwards act differently towards the children of a prince of the blood. Just at the end of September, M. du Maine lost another child, his only son. The King wept very much, and, although the child was considerably under seven years of age, wore mourning for it. The marriage of Mademoiselle to M. de Lorraine was then just upon the point of taking place; and Monsieur (father of Mademoiselle) begged that this mourning might be laid aside when the marriage was celebrated. The King agreed, but Madame la Duchesse and the Princesse de Conti believed it apparently beneath them to render this respect to Monsieur, and refused to comply. The King commanded them to do so, but they pushed the matter so far as to say that they had no other clothes. Upon this, the King ordered them to send and get some directly. They were obliged to obey, and admit themselves vanquished; but they did so not without great vexation. M. de Cambrai's affairs still continued to make a great stir among the prelates and at the Court. Madame Guyon was transferred from the Vincennes to the Bastille, and it was believed she would remain there all her life. The Ducs de Chevreuse and Beauvilliers lost all favour with M. de Maintenon, and narrowly escaped losing the favour of the King. An attempt was in fact made, which Madame de Maintenon strongly supported, to get them disgraced; and, but for the Archbishop of Paris, this would have taken place. But this prelate, thoroughly upright and conscientious, counselled the King against such a step, to the great vexation of his relations, who were the chief plotters in the conspiracy to overthrow the two Dukes. As for M. de Cambrai's book 'Les Maxinies des Saints', it was as little liked as ever, and underwent rather a strong criticism at this time from M. de La Trappe, which did not do much to improve its reputation. At the commencement of the dispute M. de Meaux had sent a copy of 'Les Maximes des Saints' to M. de La Trappe, asking as a friend for his opinion of the work. M. de La Trappe read it, and was much scandalized. The more he studied it, the more this sentiment penetrated him. At last, after having well examined the book, he sent his opinion to M. de Meaux, believing it would be considered as private, and not be shown to anybody. He did not measure his words, therefore, but wrote openly, that if M. de Cambrai was right he might burn the Evangelists, and complain of Jesus Christ, who could have come into the world only to deceive us. The frightful force of this phrase was so terrifying, that M. de Meaux thought it worthy of being shown to Madame de Maintenon; and she, seeking only to crush M. de Cambrai with all the authorities possible, would insist upon this opinion of M. de La Trappe being printed.

It may be imagined what triumphing there was on the one side, and what piercing cries on the other. The friends of M. de Cambrai complained most bitterly that M. de La Trappe had mixed himself up in the matter, and had passed such a violent and cruel sentence upon a book then under the consideration of the Pope. M. de La Trappe on his side was much afflicted that his letter had been published. He wrote to M. de Meaux protesting against this breach of confidence; and said that, although he had only expressed what he really thought, he should have been careful to use more measured language, had he supposed his letter would have seen the light. He said all he could to heal the wounds his words had caused, but M. de Cambrai and his friends never forgave him for having written them.

This circumstance caused much discussion, and M. de La Trappe, to whom I was passionately attached, was frequently spoken of in a manner that caused me much annoyance. Riding out one day in a coach with some of my friends, the conversation took this turn. I listened in silence for some time, and then, feeling no longer able to support the discourse, desired to be set down, so that my friends might talk at their ease, without pain to me. They tried to retain me, but I insisted and carried my point. Another time, Charost, one of my friends, spoke so disdainfully of M. de La Trappe, and I replied to him with such warmth, that on the instant he was seized with a fit, tottered, stammered, his throat swelled, his eyes seemed starting from his head, and his tongue from his mouth. Madame de Saint-Simon and the other ladies who were present flew to his assistance; one unfastened his cravat and his shirt-collar, another threw a jug of water over him and made him drink something; but as for me, I was struck motionless at the sudden change brought about by an excess of anger and infatuation. Charost was soon restored, and when he left I was taken to task by the ladies. In reply I simply smiled. I gained this by the occurrence, that Charost never committed himself again upon the subject of M. de La Trappe.

Before quitting this theme, I will relate an anecdote which has found belief. It has been said, that when M. de La Trappe was the Abbe de Rance he was much in love with the beautiful Madame de Montbazon, and that he was well treated by her. On one occasion after leaving her, in perfect health, in order to go into the country, he learnt that she had fallen ill. He hastened back, entered hurriedly into her chamber, and the first sight he saw there was her head, that the surgeons, in opening her, had separated from her body. It was the first intimation he had had that she was dead, and the surprise and horror of the sight so converted him that immediately afterwards he retired from the world. There is nothing true in all this except the foundation upon which the fiction arose. I have frankly asked M. de La Trappe upon this matter, and from him I have learned that he was one of the friends of Madame de Montbazon, but that so far from being ignorant of the time of her death, he was by her side at the time, administered the sacrament to her, and had never quitted her during the few days she was ill. The truth is, her sudden death so touched him, that it made him carry out his intention of retiring from the world—an intention, however, he had formed for many years.

The affair of M. de Cambrai was not finally settled until the commencement of the following year, 1699, but went on making more noise day by day. At the date I have named the verdict from Rome arrived Twenty-three propositions of the 'Maximes des Saints' were declared rash, dangerous, erroneous—'in globo'—and the Pope excommunicated those who read the book or kept it in their houses. The King was much pleased with this condemnation, and openly expressed his satisfaction. Madame de Maintenon appeared at the summit of joy. As for M. de Cambrai, he learnt his fate in a moment which would have overwhelmed a man with less resources in himself. He was on the point of mounting into the pulpit: he was by no means troubled; put aside the sermon he had prepared, and, without delaying a moment, took for subject the submission due to the Church; he treated this theme in a powerful and touching manner; announced the condemnation of his book; retracted the opinions he had professed; and concluded his sermon by a perfect acquiescence and submission to the judgment the Pope had just pronounced. Two days afterwards he published his retraction, condemned his book, prohibited the reading of it, acquiesced and submitted himself anew to his condemnation, and in the clearest terms took away from himself all means of returning to his opinions. A submission so prompt, so clear, so perfect, was generally admired, although there were not wanting censors who wished he had shown less readiness in giving way. His friends believed the submission would be so flattering to the Pope, that M. de Cambrai might rely upon advancement to a cardinalship, and steps were taken, but without any good result, to bring about that event.

CHAPTER XIII

About this time the King caused Charnace to be arrested in a province to which he had been banished. He was accused of many wicked things, and; amongst others, of coining. Charnace was a lad of spirit, who had been page to the King and officer in the body-guard. Having retired to his own house, he often played off many a prank. One of these I will mention, as being full of wit and very laughable.

He had a very long and perfectly beautiful avenue before his house in Anjou, but in the midst of it were the cottage and garden of a peasant; and neither Charnace, nor his father before him, could prevail upon him to remove, although they offered him large sums. Charnace at last determined to gain his point by stratagem. The peasant was a tailor, and lived all alone, without wife or child. One day Charnace sent for him, said he wanted a Court suit in all haste, and, agreeing to lodge and feed him, stipulated that he should not leave the house until it was done. The tailor agreed, and set himself to the work. While he was thus occupied, Charnace had the dimensions of his house and garden taken with the utmost exactitude; made a plan of the interior, showing the precise position of the furniture and the utensils; and, when all was done, pulled down the house and removed it a short distance off.

Then it was arranged as before with a similar looking garden, and at the same time the spot on which it had previously stood was smoothed and levelled. All this was done before the suit was finished. The work being at length over on both sides, Charnace amused the tailor until it was quite dark, paid him, and dismissed him content. The man went on his way down the avenue; but, finding the distance longer than usual, looked about, and perceived he had gone too far. Returning, he searched diligently for his house, but without being able to find it. The night passed in this exercise. When the day came, he rubbed his eyes, thinking they might have been in fault; but as he found them as clear as usual, began to believe that the devil had carried away his house, garden and all. By dint of wandering to and fro, and casting his eyes in every direction, he saw at last a house which was as like to his as are two drops of water to each other. Curiosity tempted him to go and examine it. He did so, and became convinced it was his own. He entered, found everything inside as he had left it, and then became quite persuaded he had been tricked by a sorcerer. The day was not, however, very far advanced before he learned the truth through the banter of his neighbours. In fury he talked of going to law, or demanding justice, but was laughed at everywhere. The King when he heard of it laughed also; and Charnace had his avenue free. If he had never done anything worse than this, he would have preserved his reputation and his liberty.

A strange scene happened at Meudon after supper one evening, towards the end of July. The Prince de Conti and the Grand Prieur were playing, and a dispute arose respecting the game. The Grand Prieur, inflated by pride on account of the favours the King had showered upon him, and rendered audacious by being placed almost on a level with the Princes of the blood, used words which would have been too strong even towards an equal. The Prince de Conti answered by a repartee, in which the other's honesty at play and his courage in war—both, in truth, little to boast about— were attacked. Upon this the Grand Prieur flew into a passion, flung away the cards, and demanded satisfaction, sword in hand. The Prince de Conti, with a smile of contempt, reminded him that he was wanting in respect, and at the same time said he could have the satisfaction he asked for whenever he pleased. The arrival of Monseigneur, in his dressing-gown, put an end to the fray. He ordered the Marquis de Gesvres, who was one of the courtiers present, to report the whole affair to the King, and that every one should go to bed. On the morrow the King was informed of what had taken place, and immediately ordered the Grand Prieur to go to the Bastille. He was obliged to obey, and remained in confinement several days. The affair made a great stir at Court. The Princes of the blood took a very high tone, and the illegitimates were much embarrassed. At last, on the 7th of August, the affair was finally accommodated through the intercession of Monseigneur. The Grand Prieur demanded pardon of the Prince de Conti in the presence of his brother, M. de Vendome, who was obliged to swallow this bitter draught, although against his will, in order to appease the Princes of the blood, who were extremely excited.

Nearly at the same time, that is to say, on the 29th of May, in the morning Madame de Saint-Simon was happily delivered of a child. God did us the grace to give us a son. He bore, as I had, the name of Vidame of Chartres. I do not know why people have the fancy for these odd names, but they seduce in all nations, and they who feel the triviality of them, imitate them. It is true that the titles of Count and Marquis have fallen into the dust because of the quantity of people without wealth, and even without land, who usurp them; and that they have become so worthless, that people of quality who are Marquises or Counts (if they will permit me to say it) are silly enough to be annoyed if those titles are given to them in conversation. It is certain, however, that these titles emanated from landed creations, and that in their origin they had functions attached to them, which, they have since outlived. The vidames, on the contrary, were only principal officers of certain bishops, with authority to lead all the rest of their seigneurs' vassals to the field, either to fight against other lords, or in the armies that our kings used to assemble to combat their enemies before the creation of a standing army put an end to the employment of vassals (there being no further need for them), and to all the power and authority of the seigneurs. There is thus no comparison between the title of vidame, which only marks a vassal, and the titles which by fief emanate from the King. Yet because the few Vidames who have been known were illustrious, the name has appeared grand, and for this reason was given to me, and afterwards by me to my son:

Some little time before this, the King resolved to show all Europe, which believed his resources exhausted by a long war, that in the midst of profound peace, he was as fully prepared as ever for arms. He wished at the same time, to present a superb spectacle to Madame de Maintenon, under pretext of teaching the young Duc de Bourgogne his first lesson in war. He gave all the necessary orders, therefore, for forming a camp at Compiegne, to be commanded by the Marechal de Boufflers under the young Duke. On Thursday, the 28th of August, all the Court set out for the camp. Sixty thousand men were assembled there. The King, as at the marriage of the Duc de Bourgogne, had announced that he counted upon seeing the troops look their best.

The consequence of this was to excite the army to an emulation that was repented of afterwards. Not only were the troops in such beautiful order that it was impossible to give the palm to any one corps, but their commanders added the finery and magnificence of the Court to the majestic and warlike beauty of the men, of the arms, and of the horses; and the officers exhausted their means in uniforms which would have graced a fete.

Colonels, and even simple captains, kept open table; but the Marechal de Boufflers outstripped everybody by his expenditure, by his magnificence, and his good taste. Never was seen a spectacle so transcendent—so dazzling—and (it must be said) so terrifying. At all hours, day or night, the Marechal's table was open to every comer—whether officer, courtier, or spectator. All were welcomed and invited, with the utmost civility and attention, to partake of the good things provided. There was every kind of hot and cold liquors; everything which can be the most widely and the most splendidly comprehended under the term refreshment: French and foreign wines, and the rarest liqueurs in the utmost abundance. Measures were so well taken that quantities of game and venison arrived from all sides; and the seas of Normandy, of Holland, of England, of Brittany, even the Mediterranean, furnished all they contained—the most unheard-of, extraordinary, and most exquisite—at a given day and hour with inimitable order, and by a prodigious number of horsemen and little express carriages. Even the water was fetched from Sainte Reine, from the Seine, and from sources the most esteemed; and it is impossible to imagine anything of any kind which was not at once ready for the obscurest as for the most distinguished visitor, the guest most expected, and the guest not expected at all. Wooden houses and magnificent tents stretched all around, in number sufficient to form a camp of themselves, and were furnished in the most superb manner, like the houses in Paris. Kitchens and rooms for every purpose were there, and the whole was marked by an order and cleanliness that excited surprise and admiration. The King, wishing that the magnificence of this camp should be seen by the ambassadors, invited them there, and prepared lodgings for them. But the ambassadors claimed a silly distinction, which the King would not grant, and they refused his invitation. This distinction I call silly because it brings no advantage with it of any kind. I am ignorant of its origin, but this is what it consists in. When, as upon such an occasion as this, lodgings are allotted to the Court, the quartermaster writes in chalk, "for Monsieur Such-a-one," upon those intended for Princes of the blood, cardinals, and foreign princes; but for none other. The King would not allow the "for" to be written upon the lodgings of the ambassadors; and the ambassadors, therefore, kept away. The King was much piqued at this, and I heard him say at supper, that if he treated them as they deserved, he should only allow them to come to Court at audience times, as was the custom everywhere else.

The King arrived at the camp on Saturday, the 30th of August, and went with the Duc and Duchesse de Bourgogne and others to the quarters of Marechal de Boufflers, where a magnificent collation was served up to them—so magnificent that when the King returned, he said it would be useless for the Duc de Bourgogne to attempt anything so splendid; and that whenever he went to the camp he ought to dine with Marechal de Boufflers. In effect, the King himself soon after dined there, and led to the Marechal's table the King of England, who was passing three or four days in the camp.

On these occasions the King pressed Marechal de Boufflers to be seated. He would never comply, but waited upon the King while the Duc de Grammont, his brother-in-law, waited upon Monseigneur.

The King amused himself much in pointing out the disposition of the troops to the ladies of the Court, and in the evening showed them a grand review.

A very pleasant adventure happened at this review to Count Tesse, colonel of dragoons. Two days previously M. de Lauzun, in the course of chit- chat, asked him how he intended to dress at the review; and persuaded him that, it being the custom, he must appear at the head of his troops in a grey hat, or that he would assuredly displease the King. Tesse, grateful for this information, and ashamed of his ignorance, thanked M. de Lauzun, and sent off for a hat in all haste to Paris. The King, as M. de Lauzun well knew, had an aversion to grey, and nobody had worn it for several years. When, therefore, on the day of the review he saw Tesse in a hat of that colour, with a black feather, and a huge cockade dangling and flaunting above, he called to him, and asked him why he wore it. Tesse replied that it was the privilege of the colonel-general to wear that day a grey hat. "A grey hat," replied the King; "where the devil did you learn that?"

"From M. de, Lauzun, Sire, for whom you created the charge," said Tesse, all embarrassment. On the instant, the good Lauzun vanished, bursting with laughter, and the King assured Tesse that M. de Lauzun had merely been joking with him. I never saw a man so confounded as Tesse at this. He remained with downcast eyes, looking at his hat, with a sadness and confusion that rendered the scene perfect. He was obliged to treat the matter as a joke, but was for a long time much tormented about it, and much ashamed of it.

Nearly every day the Princes dined with Marechal de Boufflers, whose splendour and abundance knew no end. Everybody who visited him, even the humblest, was served with liberality and attention. All the villages and farms for four leagues round Compiegne were filled with people, French, and foreigners, yet there was no disorder. The gentlemen and valets at the Marechal's quarters were of themselves quite a world, each more polite than his neighbour, and all incessantly engaged from five o'clock in the morning until ten and eleven o'clock at night, doing the honours to various guests. I return in spite of myself to the Marechal's liberality; because, who ever saw it, cannot forget, or ever cease to be in a state of astonishment and admiration at its abundance and sumptuousness, or at the order, never deranged for a moment at a single point, that prevailed.

The King wished to show the Court all the manoeuvres of war; the siege of Compiegne was therefore undertaken, according to due form, with lines, trenches, batteries, mines, &c. On Saturday, the 13th of September, the assault took place. To witness it, the King, Madame de Maintenon, all the ladies of the Court, and a number of gentlemen, stationed themselves upon an old rampart, from which the plain and all the disposition of the troops could be seen. I was in the half circle very close to the King. It was the most beautiful sight that can be imagined, to see all that army, and the prodigious number of spectators on horse and foot, and that game of attack and defence so cleverly conducted.

But a spectacle of another sort, that I could paint forty years hence as well as to-day, so strongly did it strike me, was that which from the summit of this rampart the King gave to all his army, and to the innumerable crowd of spectators of all kinds in the plain below. Madame de Maintenon faced the plain and the troops in her sedan-chair-alone, between its three windows drawn up-her porters having retired to a distance. On the left pole in front sat Madame la Duchesse de Bourgogne; and on the same side in a semicircle, standing, were Madame la Duchesse, Madame la Princesse de Conti, and all the ladies, and behind them again, many men. At the right window was the King, standing, and a little in the rear, a semicircle of the most distinguished men of the Court. The King was nearly always uncovered; and every now and then stooped to speak to Madame de Maintenon, and explain to her what she saw, and the reason of each movement. Each time that he did so she was obliging enough to open the window four or five inches, but never half way; for I noticed particularly, and I admit that I was more attentive to this spectacle than to that of the troops. Sometimes she opened of her own accord to ask some question of him, but generally it was he who, without waiting for her, stooped down to instruct her of what was passing; and sometimes, if she did not notice him, he tapped at the glass to make her open it. He never spoke, save to her, except when he gave a few brief orders, or just answered Madame la Duchesse de Bourgogne, who wanted to make him speak, and with whom Madame de Maintenon carried on a conversation by signs, without opening the front window, through which the young Princess screamed to her from time to time. I watched the countenance of every one carefully; all expressed surprise tempered with prudence and shame, that was, as it were, ashamed of itself: every one behind the chair and in the semicircle watched this scene more than what was going on in the army. The King often put his hat on the top of the chair in order to get his head in to speak; and this continual exercise tired his loins very much. Monseigneur was on horseback in the plain with the young Princes. It was about five o'clock in the afternoon, and the weather was as brilliant as could be desired.

Opposite the sedan-chair was an opening with some steps cut through the wall, and communicating with the plain below. It had been made for the purpose of fetching orders from the King, should they be necessary. The case happened. Crenan, who commanded, sent Conillac, an officer in one of the defending regiments, to ask for some instructions from the King. Conillac had been stationed at the foot of the rampart, where what was passing above could not be seen. He mounted the steps; and as soon as his head and shoulders were at the top, caught sight of the chair, the King, and all the assembled company. He was not prepared for such a scene, and it struck him with such astonishment, that he stopped short, with mouth and eyes wide open-surprise painted upon every feature. I see him now as distinctly as I did then. The King, as well as all the rest of the company, remarked the agitation of Conillac, and said to him with emotion, "Well, Conillac! come up." Conillac remained motionless, and the King continued, "Come up. What is the matter?" Conillac, thus addressed, finished his ascent, and came towards the King with slow and trembling steps, rolling his eyes from right to left like one deranged. Then he stammered something, but in a tone so low that it could not be heard. "What do you say?" cried the King. "Speak up." But Conillac was unable; and the King, finding he could get nothing out of him, told him to go away. He did not need to be told twice, but disappeared at once. As soon as he was gone, the King, looking round, said, "I don't know what is the matter with Conillac. He has lost his wits; he did not remember what he had to say to me." No one answered.

Towards the moment of the capitulation, Madame de Maintenon apparently asked permission to go away, for the King cried, "The chairmen of Madame!" They came and took her away; in less than a quarter of an hour afterwards the King retired also, and nearly everybody else. There was much interchange of glances, nudging with elbows, and then whisperings in the ear. Everybody was full of what had taken place on the ramparts between the King and Madame de Maintenon. Even the soldiers asked what meant that sedan-chair and the King every moment stooping to put his head inside of it. It became necessary gently to silence these questions of the troops. What effect this sight had upon foreigners present, and what they said of it, may be imagined. All over Europe it was as much talked of as the camp of Compiegne itself, with all its pomp and prodigious splendour.

The last act of this great drama was a sham fight. The execution was perfect; but the commander, Rose, who was supposed to be beaten, would not yield. Marechal de Boufflers sent and told him more than once that it was time. Rose flew into a passion, and would not obey. The King laughed much at this, and said, "Rose does not like to be beaten." At last he himself sent the order for retreat. Rose was forced then to comply; but he did it with a very bad grace, and abused the bearer of the order.

The King left the camp on Monday the 22d of September, much pleased with the troops. He gave, in parting, six hundred francs to each cavalry captain, and three hundred francs to each captain of infantry. He gave as much to the majors of all the regiments, and distributed some favours to his household. To Marechal de Boufflers he presented one hundred thousand francs. All these gifts together amounted to something: but separately were as mere drops of water. There was not a single regiment that was not ruined, officers and men, for several years. As for Marechal de Boufflers, I leave it to be imagined what a hundred thousand francs were to him whose magnificence astounded all Europe, described as it was by foreigners who were witnesses of it, and who day after day could scarcely believe their own eyes.

CHAPTER XIV

Here I will relate an adventure, which shows that, however wise and enlightened a man may be, he is never infallible. M. de La Trappe had selected from amongst his brethren one who was to be his successor. The name of this monk was D. Francois Gervaise. He had been in the monastery for some years, had lived regularly during that time, and had gained the confidence of M. de La Trappe. As soon, however, as he received this appointment, his manners began to change. He acted as though he were already master, brought disorder and ill-feeling into the monastery, and sorely grieved M. de La Trapp; who, however, looked upon this affliction as the work of Heaven, and meekly resigned him self to it. At last, Francois Gervaise was by the merest chance detected openly, under circumstances which blasted his character for ever. His companion in guilt was brought before M. de La Trappe, to leave no doubt upon the matter. D. Francois Gervaise, utterly prostrated, resigned his office, and left La Trappe. Yet, even after this, he had the hardihood to show himself in the world, and to try and work himself into the favour of Pere la Chaise. A discovery that was made, effectually stopped short his hopes in this direction. A letter of his was found, written to a nun with whom he had been intimate, whom he loved, and by whom he was passionately loved. It was a tissue of filthiness and stark indecency, enough to make the most abandoned tremble. The pleasures, the regrets, the desires, the hopes of this precious pair, were all expressed in the boldest language, and with the utmost licence. I believe that so many abominations are not uttered in several days, even in the worst places. For this offence Gervaise might have been confined in a dungeon all his life, but he was allowed to go at large. He wandered from monastery to monastery for five or six years, and always caused so much disorder wherever he stopped, that at last the superiors thought it best to let him live as he liked in a curacy of his brother's. He never ceased troubling La Trappe, to which he wished to return; so that at last I obtained a 'lettre de cachet', which prohibited him from approaching within thirty leagues of the abbey, and within twenty of Paris. It was I who made known to him that his abominations had been discovered. He was in no way disturbed, declared he was glad to be free, and assured me with the hypocrisy which never left him, that in his solitude he was going to occupy himself in studying the Holy Scriptures.

Bonnceil, introducer of the ambassadors, being dead, Breteuil obtained his post. Breteuil was not without intellect, but aped courtly manners, called himself Baron de Breteuil, and was much tormented and laughed at by his friends. One day, dining at the house of Madame de Pontchartrain, and, speaking very authoritatively, Madame de Pontchartrain disputed with him, and, to test his knowledge, offered to make a bet that he did not know who wrote the Lord's Prayer. He defended himself as well as he was able, and succeeded in leaving the table without being called upon to decide the point. Caumartin, who saw his embarrassment, ran to him, and kindly whispered in his ear that Moses was the author of the Lord's Prayer. Thus strengthened, Breteuil returned to the attack, brought, while taking coffee, the conversation back again to the bet; and, after reproaching Madame de Pontchartrain for supposing him ignorant upon such a point, and declaring he was ashamed of being obliged to say such a trivial thing, pronounced emphatically that it was Moses who had written the Lord's Prayer. The burst of laughter that, of course, followed this, overwhelmed him with confusion. Poor Breteuil was for a long time at loggerheads with his friend, and the Lord's Prayer became a standing reproach to him.

He had a friend, the Marquis de Gesvres, who, upon some points, was not much better informed. Talking one day in the cabinet of the King, and admiring in the tone of a connoisseur some fine paintings of the Crucifixion by the first masters, he remarked that they were all by one hand.

He was laughed at, and the different painters were named, as recognized by their style.

"Not at all," said the Marquis, "the painter is called INRI; do you not see his name upon all the pictures?" What followed after such gross stupidity and ignorance may be imagined.

At the end of this year the King resolved to undertake three grand projects, which ought to have been carried out long before: the chapel of Versailles, the Church of the Invalides, and the altar of Notre-Dame de Paris. This last was a vow of Louis XIII., made when, he no longer was able to accomplish it, and which he had left to his successor, who had been more than fifty years without thinking of it.

On the 6th of January, upon the reception of the ambassadors at the house of the Duchesse de Bourogogne, an adventure happened which I will here relate. M. de Lorraine belonged to a family which had been noted for its pretensions, and for the disputes of precedency in which it engaged. He was as prone to this absurdity as the rest, and on this occasion incited the Princesse d'Harcourt, one of his relations, to act in a manner that scandalised all the Court. Entering the room in which the ambassadors were to be received and where a large number of ladies were already collected, she glided behind the Duchesse de Rohan, and told her to pass to the left. The Duchesse de Rohan, much surprised, replied that she was very well placed already. Whereupon, the Princesse d'Harcourt, who was tall and strong, made no further ado, but with her two arms seized the Duchesse de Rohan, turned her round, and sat down in her place. All the ladies were strangely scandalised at this, but none dared say a word, not even Madame de Lude, lady in waiting on the Duchesse de Bourgogne, who, for her part also, felt the insolence of the act, but dared not speak, being so young. As for the Duchesse de Rohan, feeling that opposition must lead to fisticuffs, she curtseyed to the Duchess, and quietly retired to another place. A few minutes after this, Madame de Saint- Simon, who was then with child, feeling herself unwell, and tired of standing, seated herself upon the first cushion she could find. It so happened, that in the position she thus occupied, she had taken precedence of Madame d'Armagnac by two degrees. Madame d'Armagnac, perceiving it, spoke to her upon the subject. Madame de Saint-Simon, who had only placed herself there for a moment, did not reply, but went elsewhere.

As soon as I learnt of the first adventure, I thought it important that such an insult should not be borne, and I went and conferred with M. de la Rochefoucauld upon the subject, at the same time that Marechal de Boufflers spoke of it to M. de Noailles. I called upon other of my friends, and the opinion was that the Duc de Rohan should complain to the King on the morrow of the treatment his wife had received.

In the evening while I was at the King's supper, I was sent for by Madame de Saint-Simon, who informed me that the Lorraines, afraid of the complaints that would probably be addressed to the King upon what had taken place between the Princesse d'Harcourt and the Duchesse de Rohan, had availed themselves of what happened between Madame de Saint-Simon and Madame d'Armagnac, in order to be the first to complain, so that one might balance the other. Here was a specimen of the artifice of these gentlemen, which much enraged me. On the instant I determined to lose no time in speaking to the King; and that very evening I related what had occurred, in so far as Madame de Saint-Simon was concerned, but made no allusion to M. de Rohan's affair, thinking it best to leave that to be settled by itself on the morrow. The King replied to me very graciously, and I retired, after assuring him that all I had said was true from beginning to end.

The next day the Duc de Rohan made his complaint. The King, who had already been fully informed of the matter, received him well, praised the respect and moderation of Madame de Rohan, declared Madame d'Harcourt to have been very impertinent, and said some very hard words upon the Lorraines.

I found afterwards, that Madame de Maintenon, who much favoured Madame d'Harcourt, had all the trouble in the world to persuade the King not to exclude her from the next journey to Marly. She received a severe reprimand from the King, a good scolding from Madame de Maintenon, and was compelled publicly to ask pardon of the Duchesse de Rohan. This she did; but with a crawling baseness equal to her previous audacity. Such was the end of this strange history.

There appeared at this time a book entitled "Probleme," but without name of author, and directed against M. de Paris, declaring that he had uttered sentiments favourable to the Jansenists being at Chalons, and unfavourable being at Paris. The book came from the Jesuits, who could not pardon M. de Paris for having become archbishop without their assistance. It was condemned and burnt by decree of the Parliament, and the Jesuits had to swallow all the shame of it. The author was soon after discovered. He was named Boileau; not the friend of Bontems, who so often preached before the King, and still less the celebrated poet and author of the 'Flagellants', but a doctor of much wit and learning whom M. de Paris had taken into his favour and treated like a brother. Who would have believed that "Probleme" could spring from such a man? M. de Paris was much hurt; but instead of imprisoning Boileau for the rest of his days, as he might have done, he acted the part of a great bishop, and gave him a good canonical of Saint Honore, which became vacant a few days afterwards. Boileau, who was quite without means, completed his dishonour by accepting it.

The honest people of the Court regretted a cynic who died at this time, I mean the Chevalier de Coislin. He was a most extraordinary man, very splenetic, and very difficult to deal with. He rarely left Versailles, and never went to see the king. I have seen him get out of the way not to meet him. He lived with Cardinal Coislin, his brother. If anybody displeased him, he would go and sulk in his own room; and if, whilst at table, any one came whom he did not like, he would throw away his plate, go off to sulk, or to finish his dinner all alone. One circumstance will paint him completely. Being on a journey once with his brothers, the Duc de Coislin and the Cardinal de Coislin, the party rested for the night at the house of a vivacious and very pretty bourgeoise.

The Duc de Coislin was an exceedingly polite man, and bestowed amiable compliments and civilities upon their hostess, much to the disgust of the Chevalier. At parting, the Duke renewed the politeness he had displayed so abundantly the previous evening, and delayed the others by his long-winded flatteries. When, at last, they left the house, and were two or three leagues away from it, the Chevalier de Coislin said, that, in spite of all this politeness, he had reason to believe that their pretty hostess would not long be pleased with the Duke. The Duke, disturbed, asked his reason for thinking so. "Do you wish to learn it?" said the Chevalier; "well, then, you must know that, disgusted by your compliments, I went up into the bedroom in which you slept, and made a filthy mess on the floor, which the landlady will no doubt attribute to you, despite all your fine speeches."

At this there was loud laughter, but the Duke was in fury, and wished to return in order to clear up his character. Although it rained hard, they had all the pains in the world to hinder him, and still more to bring about a reconciliation. Nothing was more pleasant than to hear the brothers relate this adventure each in his own way.

Two cruel effects of gambling were noticed at this time. Reineville, a lieutenant of the body-guard, a general officer distinguished in war, very well treated by the King, and much esteemed by the captain of the Guards, suddenly disappeared, and could not be found anywhere, although the utmost care was taken to search for him. He loved gaming. He had lost what he could not pay. He was a man of honour, and could not sustain his misfortune. Twelve or fifteen years afterwards he was recognised among the Bavarian troops, in which he was serving in order to gain his bread and to live unknown. The other case was still worse. Permillac, a man of much intelligence and talent, had lost more than he possessed, and blew his brains out one morning in bed. He was much liked throughout the army; had taken a friendship for me, and I for him. Everybody pitied him, and I much regretted him.

Nearly at the same time we lost the celebrated Racine, so known by his beautiful plays. No one possessed a greater talent or a more agreeable mien. There was nothing of the poet in his manners: he had the air of a well-bred and modest man, and at last that of a good man. He had friends, the most illustrious, at the Court as well as among men of letters. I leave it to the latter to speak of him in a better way than I can. He wrote, for the amusement of the King and Madame de Maintenon, and to exercise the young ladies of Saint Cyr, two dramatic masterpieces, Esther and Athalie. They were very difficult to write, because there could be no love in them, and because they are sacred tragedies, in which, from respect to the Holy Scriptures, it was necessary rigidly to keep to the historical truth. They were several times played at Saint Cyr before a select Court. Racine was charged with the history of the King, conjointly with Despreaux, his friend. This employment, the pieces I have just spoken of, and his friends, gained for Racine some special favours: It sometimes happened that the King had no ministers with him, as on Fridays, and, above all, when the bad weather of winter rendered the sittings very long; then he would send for Racine to amuse him and Madame de Maintenon. Unfortunately the poet was oftentimes very absent. It happened one evening that, talking with Racine upon the theatre, the King asked why comedy was so much out of fashion. Racine gave several reasons, and concluded by naming the principal,—namely, that for want of new pieces the comedians gave old ones, and, amongst others, those of Scarron, which were worth nothing, and which found no favour with anybody. At this the poor widow blushed, not for the reputation of the cripple attacked, but at hearing his name uttered in presence of his successor! The King was also embarrassed, and the unhappy Racine, by the silence which followed, felt what a slip he had made. He remained the most confounded of the three, without daring to raise his eyes or to open his mouth. This silence did not terminate for several moments, so heavy and profound was the surprise. The end was that the King sent away Racine, saying he was going to work. The poet never afterwards recovered his position. Neither the King nor Madame de Maintenon ever spoke to him again, or even looked at him; and he conceived so much sorrow at this, that he fell into a languor, and died two years afterwards. At his death, Valincourt was chosen to work in his place with Despreaux upon the history of the King.

The King, who had just paid the heavy gaming and tradesmen's debts of Madame la Duchesse, paid also those of Monseigneur, which amounted to fifty thousand francs, undertook the payment of the buildings at Meudon, and, in lieu of fifteen hundred pistoles a month which he had allowed Monseigneur, gave him fifty thousand crowns. M. de la Rochefoucauld, always necessitous and pitiful in the midst of riches, a prey to his servants, obtained an increase of forty-two thousand francs a-year upon the salary he received as Grand Veneur, although it was but a short time since the King had paid his debts. The King gave also, but in secret, twenty thousand francs a-year to M. de Chartres, who had spent so much in journeys and building that he feared he should be unable to pay his debts. He had asked for an abbey; but as he had already one, the King did not like to give him another, lest it should be thought too much.

M. de Vendome began at last to think about his health, which his debauches had thrown into a very bad state. He took public leave of the King and of all the Court before going away, to put himself in the hands of the doctors. It was the first and only example of such impudence. From this time he lost ground. The King said, at parting, that he hoped he would come back in such a state that people might kiss him without danger! His going in triumph, where another would have gone in shame and secrecy, was startling and disgusting. He was nearly three months under the most skilful treatment-and returned to the Court with half his nose, his teeth out, and a physiognomy entirely changed, almost idiotic. The King was so much struck by this change, that he recommended the courtiers not to appear to notice it, for fear of afflicting M. de Vendome. That was taking much interest in him assuredly. As, moreover, he had departed in triumph upon this medical expedition, so he returned triumphant by the reception of the King, which was imitated by all the Court. He remained only a few days, and then, his mirror telling sad tales, went away to Anet, to see if nose and teeth would come back to him with his hair.

A strange adventure, which happened at this time, terrified everybody, and gave rise to many surmises. Savary was found assassinated in his house at Paris he kept only a valet and a maid-servant, and they were discovered murdered at the same time, quite dressed, like their master, and in different parts of the house. It appeared by writings found there, that the crime was one of revenge: it was supposed to have been committed in broad daylight. Savary was a citizen of

Paris, very rich, without occupation, and lived like an epicurean. He had some friends of the highest rank, and gave parties, of all kinds of pleasure, at his house, politics sometimes being discussed. The cause of this assassination was never known; but so much of it was found out, that no one dared to search for more. Few doubted but that the deed had been done by a very ugly little man, but of a blood so highly respected, that all forms were dispensed with, in the fear lest it should be brought home to him; and, after the first excitement, everybody ceased to speak of this tragic history.

On the night between the 3rd and 4th of June, a daring robbery was effected at the grand stables of Versailles. All the horse-cloths and trappings, worth at least fifty thousand crowns, were carried off, and so cleverly and with such speed, although the night was short, that no traces of them could ever afterwards be found. This theft reminds me of another which took place a little before the commencement of these memoirs. The grand apartment at Versailles, that is to say, from the gallery to the tribune, was hung with crimson velvet, trimmed and fringed with gold. One fine morning the fringe and trimmings were all found to have been cut away. This appeared extraordinary in a place so frequented all day, so well closed at night, and so well guarded at all times. Bontems, the King's valet, was in despair, and did his utmost to discover the thieves, but without success.

Five or six days afterwards, I was at the King's supper, with nobody but Daqum, chief physician, between the King and me, and nobody at all between one and the table. Suddenly I perceived a large black form in the air, but before I could tell what it was, it fell upon the end of the King's table just before the cover which had been laid for Monseigneur and Madame. By the noise it made in falling, and the weight of the thing itself, it seemed as though the table must be broken. The plates jumped up, but none were upset, and the thing, as luck would have it, did not fall upon any of them, but simply upon the cloth. The King moved his head half round, and without being moved in any way said, "I think that is my fringe!"

It was indeed a bundle, larger than a flat-brimmed priest's hat, about two feet in height, and shaped like a pyramid. It had come from behind me, from towards the middle door of the two ante-chambers, and a piece of fringe getting loose in the air, had fallen upon the King's wig, from which it was removed by Livry, a gentleman-in-waiting. Livry also opened the bundle, and saw that it did indeed contain the fringes all twisted up, and everybody saw likewise. A murmur was heard. Livry wishing to take away the bundle found a paper attached to it. He took the paper and left the bundle. The King stretched out his hand and said, "Let us see." Livry, and with reason, would not give up the paper, but stepped back, read it, and then passed it to Daquin, in whose hands I read it. The writing, counterfeited and long like that of a woman, was in these words:—
"Take back your fringes, Bontems; they are not worth the trouble of keeping—my compliments to the King."

The paper was rolled up, not folded: the King wished to take it from Daquin, who, after much hesitation, allowed him to read it, but did not let it out of his hands. "Well, that is very insolent!" said the King, but in quite a placid unmoved tone—as it were, an historical tone. Afterwards he ordered the bundle to be taken away. Livry found it so heavy that he could scarcely lift it from the table, and gave it to an attendant who presented himself. The King spoke no more of this matter, nobody else dared to do so; and the supper finished as though nothing had happened.

Besides the excess of insolence and impudence of this act, it was so perilous as to be scarcely understood. How could any one, without being seconded by accomplices, throw a bundle of this weight and volume in the midst of a crowd such as was always present at the supper of the King, so dense that it could with difficulty be passed through? How, in spite of a circle of accomplices, could a movement of the arms necessary for such a throw escape all eyes? The Duc de Gesvres was in waiting. Neither he nor anybody else thought of closing the doors until the King had left the table. It may be guessed whether the guilty parties remained until then, having had more than three-quarters of an hour to escape, and every issue being free. Only one person was discovered, who was not known, but he proved to be a very honest man, and was dismissed after a short detention. Nothing has since been discovered respecting this theft or its bold restitution.

CHAPTER XV

On the 12th August, Madame de Saint-Simon was happily delivered of a second son, who bore the name of Marquis de Ruffec. A singular event which happened soon after, made all the world marvel.

There arrived at Versailles a farrier, from the little town of Salon, in Provence, who asked to see the King in private. In spite of the rebuffs he met with, he persisted in his request, so that at last it got to the ears of the King. The King sent word that he was not accustomed to grant such audiences to whoever liked to ask for them. Thereupon the farrier declared that if he was allowed to see the King he would tell him things so secret and so unknown to everybody else that he would be persuaded of their importance, demanding, if the King would not see him, to be sent to a minister of state. Upon this the King allowed him to have an interview with one of his secretaries, Barbezieux. But Barbezieux was not a minister of state, and to the great surprise of everybody, the farrier, who had only just arrived from the country, and who had never before left it or his trade, replied, that not being a minister of state he would not speak with him. Upon this he was allowed to see Pomponne, and converse with him; and this is the story he told:

He said, that returning home late one evening he found himself surrounded by a great light, close against a tree and near Salon. A woman clad in white—but altogether in a royal manner, and beautiful, fair, and very dazzling—called him by his name, commanded him to listen to her, and spake to him more than half-an-hour. She told him she was the Queen, who had been the wife of the King; to whom she ordered him to go and say what she had communicated; assuring him that God would assist him through all the journey, and that upon a secret thing he should say, the King, who alone knew that secret, would recognise the truth of all he uttered. She said that in case he could not see the King he was to speak with a minister of state, telling him certain things, but reserving certain others for the King alone. She told him, moreover, to set out at once, assuring him he would be punished with death if he neglected to acquit himself of his commission. The farrier promised to obey her in everything, and the queen then disappeared. He found himself in darkness near the tree. He lay down and passed the night there, scarcely knowing whether he was awake or asleep. In the morning he went home, persuaded that what he had seen was a mere delusion and folly, and said nothing about it to a living soul.

Two days afterwards he was passing by the same place when the same vision appeared to him, and he was addressed in the same terms. Fresh threats of punishment were uttered if he did not comply, and he was ordered to go at once to the Intendant of the province, who would assuredly furnish him with money, after saying what he had seen. This time the farrier was convinced there was no delusion in the matter; but, halting between his fears and doubts, knew not what to do, told no one what had passed, and was in great perplexity. He remained thus eight days, and at last had resolved not to make the journey; when, passing by the same spot, he saw and heard the same vision, which bestowed upon him so many dreadful menaces that he no longer thought of anything but setting out immediately. In two days from that time he presented himself, at Aix, to the Intendant of the province, who, without a moment's hesitation, urged him to pursue his journey, and gave him sufficient money to travel by a public conveyance. Nothing more of the story was ever known.

The farrier had three interviews with M. de Pomponne, each of two hours' length. M. de Pomponne rendered, in private, an account of these to the King, who desired him to speak more fully upon the point in a council composed of the Ducs de Beauvilliers, Pontchartrain, Torcy, and Pomponne himself; Monseigneur to be excluded. This council sat very long, perhaps because other things were spoken of. Be that as it may, the King after this wished to converse with the farrier, and did so in his cabinet. Two days afterwards he saw the man again; at each time was nearly an hour with him, and was careful that no one was within hearing.

The day after the first interview, as the King was descending the staircase, to go a-hunting, M. de Duras, who was in waiting, and who was upon such a footing that he said almost what he liked, began to speak of this farrier with contempt, and, quoting the bad proverb, said, "The man was mad, or the King was not noble." At this the King stopped, and, turning round, a thing he scarcely ever did in walking, replied, "If that be so, I am not noble, for I have discoursed with him long, he has spoken to me with much good sense, and I assure you he is far from being mad."

These last words were pronounced with a sustained gravity which greatly surprised those near, and which in the midst of deep silence opened all eyes and ears. After the second interview the King felt persuaded that one circumstance had been related to him by the farrier, which he alone knew, and which had happened more than twenty years before. It was that he had seen a phantom in the forest of Saint Germains. Of this phantom he had never breathed a syllable to anybody.

The King on several other occasions spoke favourably of the farrier; moreover, he paid all the expenses the man had been put to, gave him a gratuity, sent him back free, and wrote to the Intendant of the province to take particular care of him, and never to let him want for anything all his life.

The most surprising thing of all this is, that none of the ministers could be induced to speak a word upon the occurrence. Their most intimate friends continually questioned them, but without being able to draw forth a syllable. The ministers either affected to laugh at the matter or answered evasively. This was the case whenever I questioned M. de Beauvilliers or M. de Pontchartrain, and I knew from their most intimate friends that nothing more could ever be obtained from M. de Pomponne or M. de Torcy. As for the farrier himself, he was equally reserved. He was a simple, honest, and modest man, about fifty years of age. Whenever addressed upon this subject, he cut short all discourse by saying, "I am not allowed to speak," and nothing more could be extracted from him. When he returned to his home he conducted himself just as before, gave himself no airs, and never boasted of the interview he had had with the King and his ministers. He went back to his trade, and worked at it as usual.

Such is the singular story which filled everybody with astonishment, but which nobody could understand. It is true that some people persuaded themselves, and tried to persuade others, that the whole affair was a clever trick, of which the simple farrier had been the dupe. They said that a certain Madame Arnoul, who passed for a witch, and who, having known Madame de Maintenon when she was Madame Scarron, still kept up a secret intimacy with her, had caused the three visions to appear to the farrier, in order to oblige the King to declare Madame de Maintenon queen. But the truth of the matter was never known.

The King bestowed at this time some more distinctions on his illegitimate children. M. du Maine, as grand-master of the artillery, had to be received at the Chambre des Comptes; and his place ought to have been, according to custom, immediately above that of the senior member. But the King wished him to be put between the first and second presidents; and this was done. The King accorded also to the Princesse de Conti that her two ladies of honour should be allowed to sit at the Duchesse de Bourgogne's table. It was a privilege that no lady of honour to a Princess of the blood had ever been allowed. But the King gave these distinctions to the ladies of his illegitimate children, and refused it to those of the Princesses of the blood.

In thus according honours, the King seemed to merit some new ones himself. But nothing fresh could be thought of. What had been done therefore at his statue in the Place des Victoires, was done over again in the Place Vendome on the 13th August, after midday. Another statue which had been erected there was uncovered. The Duc de Gesvres, Governor of Paris, was in attendance on horseback, at the head of the city troops, and made turns, and reverences, and other ceremonies, imitated from those in use at the consecration of the Roman Emperors. There were, it is true, no incense and no victims: something more in harmony with the title of Christian King was necessary. In the evening, there was upon the river a fine illumination, which Monsieur and Madame went to see.

A difficulty arose soon after this with Denmark. The Prince Royal had become King, and announced the circumstance to our King, but would not receive the reply sent him because he was not styled in it "Majesty." We had never accorded to the Kings of Denmark this title, and they had always been contented with that of "Serenity." The King in his turn would not wear mourning for the King of Denmark, just dead, although he always did so for any crowned head, whether related to him or not. This state of things lasted some months; until, in the end, the new King of Denmark gave way, received the reply as it had been first sent, and our King wore mourning as if the time for it had not long since passed.

Boucherat, chancellor and keeper of the seals, died on the 2nd of September. Harlay, as I have previously said, had been promised this appointment when it became vacant. But the part he had taken in our case with M. de Luxembourg had made him so lose ground, that the appointment was not given to him. M. de la Rochefoucauld, above all, had undermined him in the favour of the King; and none of us had lost an opportunity of assisting in this work. Our joy, therefore, was extreme when we saw all Harlay's hopes frustrated, and we did not fail to let it burst forth. The vexation that Harlay conceived was so great, that he became absolutely intractable, and often cried out with a bitterness he could not contain, that he should be left to die in the dust of the palace. His weakness was such, that he could not prevent himself six weeks after from complaining to the King at Fontainebleau, where he was playing the valet with his accustomed suppleness and deceit. The King put him off with fine speeches, and by appointing him to take part in a commission then sitting for the purpose of bringing about a reduction in the price of corn in Paris and the suburbs, where it had become very dear. Harlay made a semblance of being contented, but remained not the less annoyed. His health and his head were at last so much attacked that he was forced to quit his post: he then fell into contempt after having excited so much hatred. The chancellorship was given to Pontchartrain, and the office of comptroller-general, which became vacant at the same time, was given to Chamillart; a very honest man, who owed his first advancement to his skill at billiards, of which game the King was formerly very fond. It was while Chamillart was accustomed to play billiards with the King, at least three times a week, that an incident happened which ought not to be forgotten. Chamillart was Counsellor of the Parliament at that time. He had just reported on a case that had been submitted to him. The losing party came to him, and complained that he had omitted to bring forward a document that had been given into his hands, and that would assuredly have turned the verdict. Chamillart searched for the document, found it, and saw that the complainer was right. He said so, and added, —"I do not know how the document escaped me, but it decides in your favour. You claimed twenty thousand francs, and it is my fault you did not get them. Come to-morrow, and I will pay you." Chamillart, although then by no means rich, scraped together all the money he had, borrowing the rest, and paid the man as he had promised, only demanding that the matter should be kept a secret. But after this, feeling that billiards three times a week interfered with his legal duties, he surrendered part of them, and thus left himself more free for other charges he was obliged to attend to.

The Comtesse de Fiesque died very aged, while the Court was at Fontainebleau this year. She had passed her life with the most frivolous of the great world. Two incidents amongst a thousand will characterise her. She was very straitened in means, because she had frittered away all her substance, or allowed herself to be pillaged by her business people. When those beautiful mirrors were first introduced she obtained one, although they were then very dear and very rare. "Ah, Countess!" said her friends, "where did you find that?"

"Oh!" replied she, "I had a miserable piece of land, which only yielded me corn; I have sold it, and I have this mirror instead. Is not this excellent? Who would hesitate between corn and this beautiful mirror?"

On another occasion she harangued with her son, who was as poor as a rat, for the purpose of persuading him to make a good match and thus enrich himself. Her son, who had no desire to marry, allowed her to talk on, and pretended to listen to her reasons: She was delighted—entered into a description of the wife she destined for him, painting her as young, rich, an only child, beautiful, well-educated, and with parents who would be delighted to agree to the marriage. When she had finished, he pressed her for the name of this charming and desirable person. The Countess said she was the daughter of Jacquier, a man well known to everybody, and who had been a contractor of provisions to the armies of M. de Turenne. Upon this, her son burst out into a hearty laugh, and she in anger demanded why he did so and what he found so ridiculous in the match.

The truth was, Jacquier had no children, as the Countess soon remembered. At which she said it was a great pity, since no marriage would have better suited all parties. She was full of such oddities, which she persisted in for some time with anger, but at which she was the first to laugh. People said of her that she had never been more than eighteen years old. The memoirs of Mademoiselle paint her well. She lived with Mademoiselle, and passed all her life in quarrels about trifles.

It was immediately after leaving Fontainebleau that the marriage between the Duc and Duchesse de Bourgogne was consummated. It was upon this occasion that the King named four gentlemen to wait upon the Duke,— four who in truth could not have been more badly chosen. One of them, Gamaches, was a gossip; who never knew what he was doing or saying— who knew nothing of the world, or the Court, or of war, although he had always been in the army. D'O was another; but of him I have spoken. Cheverny was the third, and Saumery the fourth. Saumery had been raised out of obscurity by M. de Beauvilliers. Never was man so intriguing, so truckling, so mean, so boastful, so ambitious, so intent upon fortune, and all this without disguise, without veil, without shame! Saumery had been wounded, and no man ever made so much of such a mishap. I used to say of him that he limped audaciously, and it was true. He would speak of personages the most distinguished, whose ante-chambers even he had scarcely seen, as though he spoke of his equals or of his particular friends. He related what he had heard, and was not ashamed to say before people who at least had common sense, "Poor Mons. Turenne said to me," M. de Turenne never having probably heard of his existence. With Monsieur in full he honoured nobody. It was Mons. de Beauvilliers, Mons. de Chevreuse, and so on; except with those whose names he clipped off short, as he frequently would even with Princes of the blood. I have heard him say many times, "the Princesse de Conti," in speaking of the daughter of the King; and "the Prince de Conti," in speaking of Monsieur her brother-in-law! As for the chief nobles of the Court, it was rare for him to give them the Monsieur or the Mons. It was Marechal d'Humieres, and so on with the others. Fatuity and insolence were united in him, and by dint of mounting a hundred staircases a day, and bowing and scraping everywhere, he had gained the ear of I know not how many people. His wife was a tall creature, as impertinent as he, who wore the breeches, and before whom he dared not breathe. Her effrontery blushed at nothing, and after many gallantries she had linked herself on to M. de Duras, whom she governed, and of whom she was publicly and absolutely the mistress, living at his expense. Children, friends, servants, all were at her mercy; even Madame de Duras herself when she came, which was but seldom, from the country.

Such were the people whom the King placed near M. le Duc de Bourgogne.

The Duc de Gesvres, a malicious old man, a cruel husband and unnatural father, sadly annoyed Marechal de Villeroy towards the end of this year, having previously treated me very scurvily for some advice I gave him respecting the ceremonies to be observed at the reception by the King of M. de Lorraine as Duc de Bar. M. de Gesvres and M. de Villeroy had both had fathers who made large fortunes and who became secretaries of state. One morning M. de Gesvres was waiting for the King, with a number of other courtiers, when M. de Villeroy arrived, with all that noise and those airs he had long assumed, and which his favour and his appointments rendered more superb. I know not whether this annoyed De Gesvres, more than usual, but as soon as the other had placed himself, he said, "Monsieur le Marechal, it must be admitted that you and I are very lucky." The Marechal, surprised at a remark which seemed to be suggested by nothing, assented with a modest air, and, shaking his head and his wig, began to talk to some one else. But M. de Gesvres had not commenced without a purpose. He went on, addressed M. de Villeroy point-blank, admiring their mutual good fortune, but when he came to speak of the father of each, "Let us go no further," said he, "for what did our fathers spring from? From tradesmen; even tradesmen they were themselves. Yours was the son of a dealer in fresh fish at the markets, and mine of a pedlar, or, perhaps, worse. Gentlemen," said he, addressing the company, "have we not reason to think our fortune prodigious—the Marechal and I?" The Marechal would have liked to strangle M. de Gesvres, or to see him dead—but what can be done with a man who, in order to say something cutting to you, says it to himself first? Everybody was silent, and all eyes were lowered. Many, however, were not sorry to see M. de Villeroy so pleasantly humiliated. The King came and put an end to the scene, which was the talk of the Court for several days.

Omissions must be repaired as soon as they are perceived. Other matters have carried me away. At the commencement of April, Ticquet, Counsellor at the Parliament, was assassinated in his own house; and if he did not die, it was not the fault of his porter, or of the soldier who had attempted to kill him, and who left him for dead, disturbed by a noise they heard. This councillor, who was a very poor man, had complained to the King, the preceding year, of the conduct of his wife with Montgeorges, captain in the Guards, and much esteemed. The King prohibited Montgeorges from seeing the wife of the councillor again.

Such having been the case, when the crime was attempted, suspicion fell upon Montgeorges and the wife of Ticquet, a beautiful, gallant, and bold woman, who took a very high tone in the matter. She was advised to fly, and one of my friends offered to assist her to do so, maintaining that in all such cases it is safer to be far off than close at hand. The woman would listen to no such advice, and in a few days she was no longer able. The porter and the soldier were arrested and tortured, and Madame Ticquet, who was foolish enough to allow herself to be arrested, also underwent the same examination, and avowed all. She was condemned to lose her head, and her accomplice to be broken on the wheel. Montgeorges managed so well, that he was not legally criminated. When Ticquet heard the sentence, he came with all his family to the King, and sued for mercy. But the King would not listen to him, and the execution took place on Wednesday, the 17th of June, after mid-day, at the Greve. All the windows of the Hotel de Ville, and of the houses in the Place de Greve, in the streets that lead to it from the Conciergerie of the palace where Madame Ticquet was confined, were filled with spectators, men and women, many of title and distinction. There were even friends of both sexes of this unhappy woman, who felt no shame or horror in going there. In the streets the crowd was so great that it could not be passed through. In general, pity was felt for the culprit; people hoped she would be pardoned, and it was because they hoped so, that they went to see her die. But such is the world; so unreasoning, and so little in accord with itself.

CHAPTER XVI

The year 1700 commenced by a reform. The King declared that he would no longer bear the expense of the changes that the courtiers introduced into their apartments. It had cost him more than sixty thousand francs since the Court left Fontainebleau. It is believed that Madame de Mailly was the cause of this determination of the King; for during the last two or three years she had made changes in her apartments every year.

A difficulty occurred at this time which much mortified the King. Little by little he had taken all the ambassadors to visit Messieurs du Maine and de Toulouse, as though they were Princes of the blood. The nuncio, Cavallerini, visited them thus, but upon his return to Rome was so taken to task for it, that his successor, Delfini, did not dare to imitate him. The cardinals considered that they had lowered themselves, since Richelieu and Mazarm, by treating even the Princes of the blood on terms of equality, and giving them their hand, which had not been customary m the time of the two first ministers just named. To do so to the illegitimate offspring of the King, and on occasions of ceremony, appeared to them monstrous. Negotiations were carried on for a month, but Delfini would not bend, and although in every other respect he had afforded great satisfaction during his nunciature, no farewell audience was given to him; nor even a secret audience. He was deprived of the gift of a silver vessel worth eighteen hundred francs, that it was customary to present to the cardinal nuncios at their departure: and he went away without saying adieu to anybody.

Some time before, M. de Monaco had been sent as ambassador to Rome. He claimed to be addressed by the title of "Highness," and persisted in it with so much obstinacy that he isolated, himself from almost everybody, and brought the affairs of his embassy nearly to a standstill by the fetters he imposed upon them in the most necessary transactions. Tired at last of the resistance he met with, he determined to refuse the title of "Excellence," although it might fairly belong to them, to all who refused to address him as "Highness." This finished his affair; for after that determination no one would see him, and the business of the embassy suffered even more than before. It is difficult to comprehend why the King permitted such a man to remain as his representative at a foreign Court.

Madame de Navailles died on the 14th of February: Her mother, Madame de Neuillant, who became a widow, was avarice itself. I cannot say by what accident or chance it was that Madame de Maintenon in returning young and poor from America, where she had lost her father and mother, fell in landing at Rochelle into the hands of Madame de Neuillant, who lived in Poitou. Madame de Neuillant took home Madame de Maintenon, but could not resolve to feed her without making her do something in return. Madame de Maintenon was charged therefore with the key of the granary, had to measure out the corn and to see that it was given to the horses. It was Madame de Neuillant who brought Madame de Maintenon to Paris, and to get rid of her married her to Scarron, and then retired into Poitou.

Madame de Navailles was the eldest daughter of this Madame de Neuillant, and it was her husband, M. de Navailles, who, serving under M. le Prince in Flanders, received from that

General a strong reprimand for his ignorance. M. le Prince wanted to find the exact position of a little brook which his maps did not mark. To assist him in the search, M. de Navailles brought a map of the world! On another occasion, visiting M. Colbert, at Sceaux, the only thing M. de Navailles could find to praise was the endive of the kitchen garden: and when on the occasion of the Huguenots the difficulty of changing religion was spoken of, he declared that if God had been good enough to make him a Turk, he should have remained so.

Madame de Navailles had been lady of honour to the Queen-mother, and lost that place by a strange adventure.

She was a woman of spirit and of virtue, and the young ladies of honour were put under her charge. The King was at this time young and gallant. So long as he held aloof from the chamber of the young ladies, Madame de Navailles meddled not, but she kept her eye fixed upon all that she controlled. She soon perceived that the King was beginning to amuse himself, and immediately after she found that a door had secretly been made into the chamber of the young ladies; that this door communicated with a staircase by which the King mounted into the room at night, and was hidden during the day by the back of a bed placed against it. Upon this Madame de Navailles held counsel with her husband. On one side was virtue and honour, on the other, the King's anger, disgrace, and exile. The husband and wife did not long hesitate. Madame de Navailles at once took her measures, and so well, that in a few hours one evening the door was entirely closed up. During the same night the King, thinking to enter as usual by the little staircase, was much surprised to no longer find a door. He groped, he searched, he could not comprehend the disappearance of the door, or by what means it had become wall again. Anger seized him; he doubted not that the door had been closed by Madame de Navailles and her husband. He soon found that such was the case, and on the instant stripped them of almost all their offices, and exiled them from the Court. The exile was not long; the Queen-mother on her death- bed implored him to receive back Monsieur and Madame de Navailles, and he could not refuse. They returned, and M. de Navailles nine years afterwards was made Marechal of France. After this Madame de Navailles rarely appeared at the Court. Madame de Maintenon could not refuse her distinctions and special favours, but they were accorded rarely and by moments. The King always remembered his door; Madame de Maintenon always remembered the hay and barley of Madame de Neuillant, and neither years nor devotion could deaden the bitterness of the recollection.

From just before Candlemas-day to Easter of this year, nothing was heard of but balls and pleasures of the Court. The King gave at Versailles and at Marly several masquerades, by which he was much amused, under pretext of amusing the Duchesse de Bourgogne. At one of these balls at Marly a ridiculous scene occurred. Dancers were wanting and Madame de Luxembourg on account of this obtained an invitation, but with great difficulty, for she lived in such a fashion that no woman would see her. Monsieur de Luxembourg was perhaps the only person in France who was ignorant of Madame de Luxembourg's conduct. He lived with his wife on apparently good terms and as though he had not the slightest mistrust of her. On this occasion, because of the want of dancers, the King made older people dance than was customary, and among others

M. de Luxembourg. Everybody was compelled to be masked. M. de Luxembourg spoke on this subject to M. le Prince, who, malicious as any monkey, determined to divert all the Court and himself at the Duke's expense. He invited M. de Luxembourg to supper, and after that meal was over, masked him according to his fancy.

Soon after my arrival at the ball, I saw a figure strangely clad in long flowing muslin, and with a headdress on which was fixed the horns of a stag, so high that they became entangled in the chandelier. Of course everybody was much astonished at so strange a sight, and all thought that that mask must be very sure of his wife to deck himself so. Suddenly the mask turned round and showed us M. de Luxembourg. The burst of laughter at this was scandalous. Good M. de Luxembourg, who never was very remarkable for wit, benignly took all this laughter as having been excited simply by the singularity of his costume, and to the questions addressed him, replied quite simply that his dress had been arranged by M. le Prince; then, turning to the right and to the left, he admired himself and strutted with pleasure at having been masked by M. le Prince. In a moment more the ladies arrived, and the King immediately after them. The laughter commenced anew as loudly as ever, and M. de Luxembourg presented himself to the company with a confidence that was ravishing. His wife had heard nothing of this masquerading, and when she saw it, lost countenance, brazen as she was. Everybody stared at her and her husband, and seemed dying of laughter. M. le Prince looked at the scene from behind the King, and inwardly laughed at his malicious trick. This amusement lasted throughout all the ball, and the King, self-contained as he usually was, laughed also; people were never tired of admiring an invention so, cruelly ridiculous, and spoke of it for several days.

No evening passed on which there was not a ball. The chancellor's wife gave one which was a fete the most gallant and the most magnificent possible. There were different rooms for the fancy-dress ball, for the masqueraders, for a superb collation, for shops of all countries, Chinese, Japanese, &c., where many singular and beautiful things were sold, but no money taken; they were presents for the Duchesse de Bourgogne and the ladies. Everybody was especially diverted at this entertainment, which did not finish until eight o'clock in the morning. Madame de Saint-Simon and I passed the last three weeks of this time without ever seeing the day. Certain dancers were only allowed to leave off dancing at the same time as the Duchesse de Bourgogne. One morning, at Marty, wishing to escape too early, the Duchess caused me to be forbidden to pass the doors of the salon; several of us had the same fate. I was delighted when Ash Wednesday arrived; and I remained a day or two dead beat, and Madame de Saint-Simon could not get over Shrove Tuesday.

La Bourlie, brother of Guiscard, after having quitted the service, had retired to his estate near Cevennes, where he led a life of much licence. About this time a robbery was committed in his house; he suspected one of the servants, and on his own authority put the man to the torture. This circumstance could not remain so secret but that complaints spread abroad. The offence was a capital one. La Bourlie fled from the realm, and did many strange things until his death, which was still more strange; but of which it is not yet time to speak.

Madame la Duchesse, whose heavy tradesmen's debts the King had paid not long since, had not dared to speak of her gambling debts, also very heavy. They increased, and, entirely unable to pay them, she found herself in the greatest embarrassment. She feared, above all things, lest M. le Prince or M. le Duc should hear of this. In this extremity she addressed herself to Madame de Maintenon, laying bare the state of her finances, without the slightest disguise. Madame de Maintenon had pity on her situation, and arranged that the King should pay her debts, abstain from scolding her, and keep her secret. Thus, in a few weeks, Madame la Duchesse found herself free of debts, without anybody whom she feared having known even of their existence.

Langlee was entrusted with the payment and arrangement of these debts. He was a singular kind of man at the Court, and deserves a word. Born of obscure parents, who had enriched themselves, he had early been introduced into the great world, and had devoted himself to play, gaining an immense fortune; but without being accused of the least unfairness. With but little or no wit, but much knowledge of the world, he had succeeded in securing many friends, and in making his way at the Court. He joined in all the King's parties, at the time of his mistresses. Similarity of tastes attached Langlee to Monsieur, but he never lost sight of the King. At all the fetes Langlee was present, he took part in the journeys, he was invited to Marly, was intimate with all the King's mistresses; then with all the daughters of the King, with whom indeed he was so familiar that he often spoke to them with the utmost freedom. He had become such a master of fashions and of fetes that none of the latter were given, even by Princes of the blood, except under his directions; and no houses were bought, built, furnished, or ornamented, without his taste being consulted. There were no marriages of which the dresses and the presents were not chosen, or at least approved, by him. He was on intimate terms with the most distinguished people of the Court; and often took improper advantage of his position. To the daughters of the King and to a number of female friends he said horribly filthy things, and that too in their own houses, at St. Cloud or at Marly. He was often made a confidant in matters of gallantry, and continued to be made so all his life. For he was a sure man, had nothing disagreeable about him, was obliging, always ready to serve others with his purse or his influence, and was on bad terms with no one.

While everybody, during all this winter, was at balls and amusements, the beautiful Madame de Soubise—for she was so still—employed herself with more serious matters. She had just bought, very cheap, the immense Hotel de Guise, that the King assisted her to pay for. Assisted also by the King, she took steps to make her bastard son canon of Strasbourg; intrigued so well that his birth was made to pass muster, although among Germans there is a great horror of illegitimacy, and he was received into the chapter. This point gained, she laid her plans for carrying out another, and a higher one, nothing less than that of making her son Archbishop of Strasbourg.

But there was an obstacle, in the way. This obstacle was the Abbe d'Auvergne (nephew of Cardinal de Bouillon), who had the highest position in the chapter, that of Grand Prevot, had been there much longer than the Abbe de Soubise, was older, and of more consequence. His reputation, however, was against him; his habits were publicly known to be those of the Greeks, whilst his intellect resembled theirs in no way. By his stupidity he published his bad conduct, his perfect ignorance, his dissipation, his ambition; and to sustain himself he had only a low, stinking, continual vanity, which drew upon him as much disdain as did his habits, alienated him from all the world, and constantly subjected him to ridicule.

The Abbe de Soubise had, on the contrary, everything smiling in his favour, even his exterior, which showed that he was born of the tenderest amours. Upon the farms of the Sorbonne he had much distinguished himself. He had been made Prior of Sorbonne, and had shone conspicuously in that position, gaining eulogies of the most flattering kind from everybody, and highly pleasing the King. After this, he entered the seminary of Saint Magloire, then much in vogue, and gained the good graces of the Archbishop of Paris, by whom that seminary was favoured. On every side the Abbe de Soubise was regarded, either as a marvel of learning, or a miracle of piety and purity of manners. He had made himself loved everywhere, and his gentleness, his politeness, his intelligence, his graces, and his talent for securing friends, confirmed more and more the reputation he had established.

The Abbe d'Auvergne had a relative, the Cardinal de Furstenberg, who also had two nephews, canons of Strasbourg, and in a position to become claimants to the bishopric. Madame de Soubise rightly thought that her first step must be to gain over the Cardinal to her side. There was a channel through which this could be done which at once suggested itself to her mind. Cardinal Furstenberg, it was said, had been much enamoured of the Comtesse de La Marck, and had married her to one of his nephews, in order that he might thus see her more easily. It was also said that he had been well treated, and it is certain that nothing was so striking as the resemblance, feature for feature, of the Comte de La Marck to Cardinal de Furstenberg. If the Count was not the son of the Cardinal he was nothing to him. The attachment of Cardinal Furstenberg for the Comtesse de La Marck did not abate when she became by her marriage Comtesse de Furstenberg; indeed he could not exist without her; she lived and reigned in his house. Her son, the Comte de La Marck, lived there also, and her dominion over the Cardinal was so public, that whoever had affairs with him spoke to the Countess, if he wished to succeed. She had been very beautiful, and at fifty-two years of age, still showed it, although tall, stout, and coarse featured as a Swiss guard in woman's clothes. She was, moreover, bold, audacious, talking loudly and always with authority; was polished, however, and of good manners when she pleased. Being the most imperious woman in the world, the Cardinal was fairly tied to her apron-strings, and scarcely dared to breathe in her presence. In dress and finery she spent like a prodigal, played every night, and lost large sums, oftentimes staking her jewels and her various ornaments. She was a woman who loved herself alone, who wished for everything, and who refused herself nothing, not even, it was said, certain gallantries which the poor Cardinal was obliged to pay for, as for everything else. Her extravagance was such, that she was obliged to pass six or seven months of the year in the country, in order to have enough to spend in Paris during the remainder of the year.

It was to the Comtesse de Furstenberg, therefore, that Madame de Soubise addressed herself in order to gain over the support of Cardinal de Furstenberg, in behalf of her son. Rumour said, and it was never contradicted, that Madame de Soubise paid much money to the Cardinal through the

Countess, in order to carry this point. It is certain that in addition to the prodigious pensions the Cardinal drew from the King, he touched at this time a gratification of forty thousand crowns, that it was pretended had been long promised him.

Madame de Soubise having thus assured herself of the Countess and the Cardinal (and they having been privately thanked by the King), she caused an order to be sent to Cardinal de Bouillon, who was then at Rome, requesting him to ask the Pope in the name of the King, for a bull summoning the Chapter of Strasbourg to meet and elect a coadjutor and a declaration of the eligibility of the Abbe de Soubise.

But here a new obstacle arose in the path of Madame de Soubise. Cardinal de Bouillon, a man of excessive pride and pretension, who upon reaching Rome claimed to be addressed as "Most Eminent Highness," and obtaining this title from nobody except his servants, set himself at loggerheads with all the city—Cardinal de Bouillon, I say, was himself canon of Strasbourg, and uncle of the Abbe d'Auvergne. So anxious was the Cardinal to secure the advancement of the Abbe d'Auvergne, that he had already made a daring and fraudulent attempt to procure for him a cardinalship. But the false representations which he made in order to carry his point, having been seen through, his attempt came to nothing, and he himself lost all favour with the King for his deceit. He, however; hoped to make the Abbe d'Auvergne bishop of Strasbourg, and was overpowered, therefore, when he saw this magnificent prey about to escape him. The news came upon him like a thunderbolt. It was bad enough to see his hopes trampled under foot; it was insupportable to be obliged to aid in crushing them. Vexation so transported and blinded him, that he forgot the relative positions of himself and of Madame de Soubise, and imagined that he should be able to make the King break a resolution he had taken, and an engagement he had entered into. He sent therefore, as though he had been a great man, a letter to the King, telling him that he had not thought sufficiently upon this matter, and raising scruples against it. At the same time he despatched a letter to the canons of Strasbourg, full of gall and compliments, trying to persuade them that the Abbe de Soubise was too young for the honour intended him, and plainly intimating that the Cardinal de Furstenberg had been gained over by a heavy bribe paid to the Comtesse de Furstenberg. These letters. made a terrible uproar.

I was at the palace on Tuesday, March 30th, and after supper I saw Madame de Soubise arrive, leading the Comtesse de Furstenberg, both of whom posted themselves at the door of the King's cabinet. It was not that Madame de Soubise had not the privilege of entering if she pleased, but she preferred making her complaint as public as the charges made against her by Cardinal de Bouillon had become. I approached in order to witness the scene. Madame de Soubise appeared scarcely able to contain herself, and the Countess seemed furious. As the King passed, they stopped him. Madame de Soubise said two words in a low tone. The Countess in a louder strain demanded justice against the Cardinal de Bouillon, who, she said, not content in his pride and ambition with disregarding the orders of the King, had calumniated her and Cardinal de Furstenberg in the most atrocious manner, and had not even spared Madame de Soubise herself. The King replied to her with much politeness, assured her she should be contented, and passed on.

Madame de Soubise was so much the more piqued because Cardinal de Bouillon had acquainted the King with the simony she had committed, and assuredly if he had not been ignorant of this he would never have supported her in the affair. She hastened therefore to secure the success of her son, and was so well served by the whispered authority of the King, and the money she had spent, that the Abbe de Soubise was elected by unanimity Coadjutor of Strasbourg.

As for the Cardinal de Bouillon, foiled in all his attempts to prevent the election, he wrote a second letter to the King, more foolish than the first. This filled the cup to overflowing. For reply, he received orders, by a courier, to quit Rome immediately and to retire to Cluni or to Tournus, at his choice, until further orders. This order appeared so cruel to him that he could not make up his mind to obey. He was underdoyen of the sacred college. Cibo, the doyen, was no longer able to leave his bed. To become doyen, it was necessary to be in Rome when the appointment became vacant. Cardinal de Bouillon wrote therefore to the King, begging to be allowed to stay a short time, in order to pray the Pope to set aside this rule, and give him permission to succeed to the doyenship, even although absent from Rome when it became vacant. He knew he should not obtain this permission, but he asked for it in order to gain time, hoping that in the meanwhile Cardinal Cibo might die, or even the Pope himself, whose health had been threatened with ruin for some time. This request of the Cardinal de Bouillon was refused. There seemed nothing for him but to comply with the orders he had received. But he had evaded them so long that he thought he might continue to do so. He wrote to Pere la Chaise, begging him to ask the King for permission to remain at Rome until the death of Cardinal Cibo, adding that he would wait for a reply at Caprarole, a magnificent house of the Duke of Parma, at eight leagues from Rome. He addressed himself to Pere la Chaise, because M. de Torcy, to whom he had previously written, had been forbidden to open his letters, and had sent him word to that effect. Having, too, been always on the best of terms with the Jesuits, he hoped for good assistance from Pere la Chaise. But he found this door closed like that of M. de Torcy. Pere la Chaise wrote to Cardinal de Bouillon that he too was prohibited from opening his letters. At the same time a new order was sent to the Cardinal to set out immediately. Just after he had read it Cardinal Cibo died, and the Cardinal de Bouillon hastened at once to Rome to secure the doyenship, writing to the King to say that he had done so, that he would depart in twenty-four hours, and expressing a hope that this delay would not be refused him. This was laughing at the King and his orders, and becoming doyen in spite of him. The King, therefore, displayed his anger immediately he learnt this last act of disobedience. He sent word immediately to M. de Monaco to command the Cardinal de Bouillon to surrender his charge of grand chaplain, to give up his cordon bleu, and to take down the arms of France from the door of his palace; M. de Monaco was also ordered to prohibit all French people in Rome from seeing Cardinal de Bouillon, or from having any communication with him. M. de Monaco, who hated the Cardinal, hastened willingly to obey these instructions. The Cardinal appeared overwhelmed, but he did not even then give in. He pretended that his charge of grand chaplain was a crown office, of which he could not be dispossessed, without resigning. The King, out of all patience with a disobedience so stubborn and so marked, ordered, by a decree in council, on the 12th September, the seizure of all the Cardinal's estates, laical and ecclesiastical, the latter to be confiscated to the state, the former to be divided into three portions, and applied to various uses. The same day the charge of grand chaplain was given to Cardinal Coislin, and that of chief chaplain to the Bishop of Metz. The despair of the Cardinal de Bouillon, on hearing of this decree, was extreme. Pride had hitherto hindered him from believing that matters would be pushed so far against him. He sent in his resignation only when it was no longer needed of him. His order he would not give up. M. de Monaco warned him that, in case of refusal, he had orders to snatch it from his neck. Upon this the Cardinal saw the folly of holding out against the orders of the King. He quitted then the marks of the order, but he was pitiful enough to wear a narrow blue ribbon, with a cross of gold attached, under his cassock, and tried from time to time to show a little of the blue. A short time afterwards, to make the best of a bad bargain, he tried to persuade himself and others, that no cardinal was at liberty to wear the orders of any prince. But it was rather late in the day to think of this, after having worn the order of the King for thirty years, as grand chaplain; and everybody thought so, and laughed at the idea.

CHAPTER XVII

Chateauneuf, Secretary of State, died about this time. He had asked that his son, La Vrilliere, might be allowed to succeed him, and was much vexed that the King refused this favour. The news of Chateauneuf's death was brought to La Vrilliere by a courier, at five o'clock in the morning. He did not lose his wits at the news, but at once sent and woke up the Princesse d'Harcourt, and begged her to come and see him instantly. Opening his purse, he prayed her to go and see Madame de Maintenon as soon as she got up, and propose his marriage with Mademoiselle de Mailly, whom he would take without dowry, if the King gave him his father's appointments. The Princesse d'Harcourt, whose habit it was to accept any sum, from a crown upwards, willingly undertook this strange business. She went upon her errand immediately, and then repaired to Madame de Mailly, who without property, and burdened with a troop of children—sons and daughters, was in no way averse to the marriage.

The King, upon getting up, was duly made acquainted with La Vrilliere's proposal, and at once agreed to it. There was only one person opposed to the marriage, and that was Mademoiselle de Mailly. She was not quite twelve years of age. She burst out a-crying, and declared she was very unhappy, that she would not mind marrying a poor man, if necessary, provided he was a gentleman, but that to marry a paltry bourgeois, in order to make his fortune, was odious to her. She was furious against her mother and against Madame de Maintenon. She could not be kept quiet or appeased, or hindered from making grimaces at La Vrilliere and all his family, who came to see her and her mother.

They felt it; but the bargain was made, and was too good to be broken. They thought Mademoiselle de Mailly's annoyance would pass with her youth—but they were mistaken. Mademoiselle de Mailly always was sore at having been made Madame de la Vrilliere, and people often observed it.

At the marriage of Monseigneur the Duc de Bourgogne, the King had offered to augment considerably his monthly income. The young Prince, who found it sufficient, replied with thanks, and said that if money failed him at any time he would take the liberty, of asking the King for more. Finding himself short just now, he was as good as his word. The King praised him highly, and told him to ask whenever he wanted money, not through a third person, but direct, as he had done in this instance. The King, moreover, told the Duc de Bourgogne to play without fear, for it was of no consequence how much such persons as he might lose. The King was pleased with confidence, but liked not less to see himself feared; and when timid people who spoke to him discovered themselves, and grew embarrassed in their discourse, nothing better made their court, or advanced their interests.

The Archbishop of Rheims presided this year over the assembly of the clergy, which was held every five years. It took place on this occasion at Saint Germains, although the King of England occupied the chateau. M. de Rheims kept open table there, and had some champagne that was much vaunted. The King of England, who drank scarcely any other wine, heard of this and asked for some. The Archbishop sent him six bottles. Some time after, the King of England, who had much relished the wine, sent and asked for more. The Archbishop, more sparing of his wine than of his money, bluntly sent word that his wine was not mad, and did not run through the streets; and sent none. However accustomed people might be to the rudeness of the Archbishop, this appeared so strange that it was much spoken of: but that was all.

M. de Vendome took another public leave of the King, the Princes, and the Princesses, in order to place himself again under the doctor's hands. He perceived at last that he was not cured, and that it would be long before he was; so went to Anet to try and recover his health, but without success better than before. He brought back a face upon which his state was still more plainly printed than at first. Madame d'Uzes, only daughter of the Prince de Monaco, died of this disease. She was a woman of merit—very virtuous and unhappy—who merited a better fate. M. d'Uzes was an obscure man, who frequented the lowest society, and suffered less from its effects than his wife, who was much pitied and regretted. Her children perished of the same disease, and she left none behind her.—[Syphilis. D.W.]

Soon after this the King ordered the Comtes d'Uzes and d'Albert to go to the Conciergerie for having fought a duel against the Comtes de Rontzau, a Dane, and Schwartzenberg, an Austrian. Uzes gave himself up, but the Comte d'Albert did not do so for a long Time, and was broken for his disobedience. He had been on more than good terms with Madame de Luxembourg—the Comte de Rontzau also: hence the quarrel; the cause of which was known by everybody, and made a great stir. Everybody knew it, at least, except M. de Luxembourg, and said nothing, but was glad of it; and yet in every direction he asked the reason; but, as may be imagined, could find nobody to tell him, so that he went over and over again to M. le Prince de Conti, his most intimate friend, praying him for information upon the subject. M. de Conti related to me that on one occasion, coming from Meudon, he was so solicited by M. de Luxembourg on this account, that he was completely embarrassed, and never suffered to such an extent in all his life. He contrived to put off M. de Luxembourg, and said nothing, but was glad indeed to get away from him at the end of the journey.

Le Notre died about this time, after having been eighty-eight years in perfect health, and with all his faculties and good taste to the very last. He was illustrious, as having been the first designer of those beautiful gardens which adorn France, and which, indeed, have so surpassed the gardens of Italy, that the most famous masters of that country come here to admire and learn. Le Notre had a probity, an exactitude, and an uprightness which made him esteemed and loved by everybody. He never forgot his position, and was always perfectly disinterested. He worked for private people as for the King, and with the same application—seeking only to aid nature, and to attain the beautiful by the shortest road. He was of a charming simplicity and truthfulness. The Pope, upon one occasion, begged the King to lend him Le Notre for some months. On entering the Pope's chamber, instead of going down upon his knees, Le Notre ran to the Holy Father, clasped him round the neck, kissed him on the two cheeks, and said—"Good morning, Reverend Father; how well you look, and how glad I am to see you in such good health."

The Pope, who was Clement X., Altieri, burst out laughing with all his might. He was delighted with this odd salutation, and showed his friendship towards the gardener in a thousand ways. Upon Le Notre's return, the King led him into the gardens of Versailles, and showed him what had been done in his absence. About the Colonnade he said nothing. The King pressed him to give his opinion thereupon.

"Why, sire," said Le Notre, "what can I say? Of a mason you have made a gardener, and he has given you a sample of his trade."

The King kept silence and everybody laughed; and it was true that this morsel of architecture, which was anything but a fountain, and yet which was intended to be one, was much out of place in a garden. A month before Le Notre's death, the King, who liked to see him and to make him talk, led him into the gardens, and on account of his great age, placed him in a wheeled chair, by the side of his own. Upon this Le Notre said, "Ah, my poor father, if you were living and could see a simple gardener like me, your son, wheeled along in a chair by the side of the greatest King in the world, nothing would be wanting to my joy!"

Le Notre was Overseer of the Public Buildings, and lodged at the Tuileries, the garden of which (his design), together with the Palace, being under his charge. All that he did is still much superior to everything that has been done since, whatever care may have been taken to imitate and follow him as closely as possible. He used to say of flower- beds that they were only good for nurses, who, not being able to quit the children, walked on them with their eyes, and admired them from the second floor. He excelled, nevertheless, in flowerbeds, as in everything concerning gardens; but he made little account of them, and he was right, for they are the spots upon which people never walk.

The King of England (William III.) lost the Duke of Gloucester, heir- presumptive to the crown. He was eleven years of age, and was the only son of the Princess of Denmark, sister of the defunct Queen Mary, wife of William. His preceptor was Doctor Burnet, Bishop of Salisbury, who was in the secret of the invasion, and who passed into England with the Prince of Orange at the Revolution, of which Revolution he has left a very fraudulent history, and many other works of as little truth and good faith. The underpreceptor was the famous Vassor, author of the "History of Louis XIII.," which would be read with more pleasure if there were less spite against the Catholic religion, and less passion against the King. With those exceptions it is excellent and true. Vassor must have been singularly well informed of the anecdotes that he relates, and which escape almost all historians. I have found there, for instance, the Day of the Dupes related precisely as my father has related it to me, and several other curious things not less exact. This author has made such a stir that it is worth while to say something about him. He was a priest of the Oratory, and in much estimation as a man whose manners were without reproach. After a time, however, he was found to have disclosed a secret that had been entrusted to him, and to have acted the spy on behalf of the Jesuits. The proofs of his treason were found upon his table, and were so conclusive that there was nothing for him but to leave the Oratory. He did so, and being deserted by his Jesuit employers, threw himself into La Trappe. But he did not enter the place in a proper spirit, and in a few days withdrew. After this he went to the Abbey of Perseigne, hired a lodging there, and remained several months. But he was continually at loggerheads with the monks. Their garden was separate from his only by a thick hedge; their fowls could jump over it. He laid the blame upon the monks, and one day caught as many of their fowls as he could; cut off their beaks and their spurs with a cleaver, and threw them back again over the hedge. This was cruelty so marked that I could not refrain from relating it.

Vassor did not long remain in this retreat, but returned to Paris, and still being unable to gain a living, passed into Holland, from rage and hunger became a Protestant, and set himself to work to live by his pen. His knowledge, talent, and intelligence procured him many friends, and his reputation reached England, into which country he passed, hoping to gain there more fortune than in Holland. Burnet received him with open arms, and obtained for him the post of under-preceptor to the Duke of Gloucester. It would have been difficult to have found two instructors so opposed to the Catholics and to France, or so well suited to the King as teachers of his successor.

Among so many things which paved the way for the greatest events, a very strange one happened, which from its singularity merits a short recital. For many years the Comtesse de Verrue lived at Turin, mistress, publicly, of M. de Savoie. The Comtesse de Verrue was daughter of the Duc de Luynes, and had been married in Piedmont, when she was only fourteen years of age, to the Comte de Verrue, young, handsome, rich, and honest; whose mother was lady of honour to Madame de Savoie.

M. de Savoie often met the Comtesse de Verrue, and soon found her much to his taste. She saw this, and said so to her husband and her mother-in- law. They praised her, but took no further notice of the matter. M. de Savoie redoubled his attentions, and, contrary to his usual custom, gave fetes, which the Comtesse de Verrue felt were for her. She did all she could not to attend them, but her mother-in-law quarrelled with her, said she wished to play the important, and that it was her vanity which gave her these ideas. Her husband, more gentle, desired her to attend these fetes, saying that even if M. de Savoie were really in love with her, it would not do to fail in anything towards him. Soon after M. de Savoie spoke to the Comtesse de Verrue. She told her husband and her mother-in- law, and used every entreaty in order to prevail upon them to let her go and pass some time in the country. They would not listen to her, and seeing no other course open, she feigned to be ill, and had herself sent to the waters of Bourbon. She wrote to her father, the Duc de Luynes, to meet her there, and set out under the charge of the Abbe de Verrue; uncle of her husband. As soon as the Duc de Luynes arrived at Bourbon, and became acquainted with the danger which threatened his daughter; he conferred with the Abbe as to the best course to adopt, and agreed with him that the Countess should remain away from Turin some time, in order that M. de Savoie might get cured of his passion. M. de Luynes little thought that he had conferred with a wolf who wished to carry off his lamb. The Abbe de Verrue, it seems, was himself violently in love with the Countess, and directly her father had gone declared the state of his heart. Finding himself only repulsed, the miserable old man turned his love into hate; ill-treated the Countess, and upon her return to Turin, lost no opportunity of injuring her in the eyes of her husband and her mother-in-law.

The Comtesse de Verrue suffered this for some time, but at last her virtue yielded to the bad treatment she received. She listened to M. de Savoie, and delivered herself up to him in order to free herself from persecution. Is not this a real romance? But it happened in our own time, under the eyes and to the knowledge of everybody.

When the truth became known, the Verrues were in despair, although they had only themselves to blame for what had happened. Soon the new mistress ruled all the Court of Savoy, whose sovereign was at her feet as before a goddess. She disposed of the favours of her lover, and was feared and courted by the ministry. Her haughtiness made her hated; she was poisoned; M. de Savoie gave her a subtle antidote, which fortunately cured her, and without injury to her beauty. Her reign still lasted. After a while she had the small-pox. M. de Savoie tended her during this illness, as though he had been a nurse; and although her face suffered a little by it, he loved her not the less. But he loved her after his own fashion. He kept her shut up from view, and at last she grew so tired of her restraint that she determined to fly. She conferred with her brother, the Chevalier de Luynes, who served with much distinction in the navy, and together they arranged the matter.

They seized an opportunity when M. de Savoie had gone on a tour to Chambery, and departed furtively. Crossing our frontier, they arrived m Paris, where the Comtesse de Verrue, who had grown very rich, took a house, and by degrees succeeded in getting people to come and see her, though, at first, owing to the scandal of her life, this was difficult. In the end, her opulence gained her a large number of friends, and she availed herself so well of her opportunities, that she became of much importance, and influenced strongly the government. But that time goes beyond my memoirs. She left in Turin a son and a daughter, both recognised by M. de Savoie, after the manner of our King. He loved passionately these, illegitimate children, and married the daughter to the Prince de Carignan.

Mademoiselle de Conde died at Paris on October 24th, after a long illness, from a disease in the chest, which consumed her less than the torments she experienced without end from M. le Prince, her father, whose continual caprices were the plague of all those over whom he could exercise them. Almost all the children of M. le Prince were little bigger than dwarfs, which caused M. le Prince, who was tall, to say in pleasantry, that if his race went on always thus diminishing it would come to nothing. People attributed the cause to a dwarf that Madame la Princesse had had for a long time near her.

At the funeral of Mademoiselle de Conde, a very indecorous incident happened. My mother, who was invited to take part in the ceremony, went to the Hotel de Conde, in a coach and six horses, to join Mademoiselle d'Enghien. When the procession was about to start the Duchesse de Chatillon tried to take precedence of my mother. But my mother called upon Mademoiselle d'Enghien to prevent this, or else to allow her to return. Madame de Chatillon persisted in her attempt, saying that relationship decided the question of precedence on these occasions, and that she was a nearer relative to the deceased than my mother. My mother, in a cold but haughty tone, replied that she could pardon this mistake on account of the youth and ignorance of Madame de Chatillon; but that in all such cases it was rank and not relationship which decided the point. The dispute was at last put to an end by Madame de Chatillon giving way. But when the procession started an attempt was made by her coachman to drive before the coach of my mother, and one of the company had to descend and decide the dispute. On the morrow M. le Prince sent to apologise to my mother for the occurrence that had taken place, and came himself shortly afterwards full of compliments and excuses. I never could understand what induced Madame de Chatillon to take this fancy into her head; but she was much ashamed of it afterwards, and made many excuses to my mother.

I experienced, shortly after this, at Fontainebleau, one of the greatest afflictions I had ever endured. I mean the loss of M. de La Trappe, These Memoirs are too profane to treat slightly of a life so sublimely holy, and of a death so glorious and precious before God. I will content myself with saying here that praises of M. de La Trappe were so much the more great and prolonged because the King eulogised him in public; that he wished to see narrations of his death; and that he spoke more than once of it to his grandsons by way of instruction. In every part of Europe this great loss was severely felt. The Church wept for him, and the world even rendered him justice. His death, so happy for him and so sad for his friends, happened on the 26th of October, towards half-past twelve, in the arms of his bishop, and in presence of his community, at the age of nearly seventy-seven years, and after nearly forty years of the most prodigious penance. I cannot omit, however, the most touching and the most honourable mark of his friendship. Lying upon the ground, on straw and ashes, in order to die like all the brethren of La Trappe, he deigned, of his own accord, to recollect me, and charged the Abbe La Trappe to send word to me, on his part, that as he was quite sure of my affection for him, he reckoned that I should not doubt of his tenderness for me. I check myself at this point; everything I could add would be too much out of place here.

VOLUME 3.: CHAPTER XVIII

For the last two or three years the King of Spain had been in very weak health, and in danger of his life several times. He had no children, and no hope of having any. The question, therefore, of the succession to his vast empire began now to agitate every European Court. The King of England (William III.), who since his usurpation had much augmented his credit by the grand alliance he had formed against France, and of which he had been the soul and the chief up to the Peace of Ryswick, undertook to arrange this question in a manner that should prevent war when the King of Spain died. His plan was to give Spain, the Indies, the Low Countries, and the title of King of Spain to the Archduke, second son of the Emperor; Guipuscoa, Naples, Sicily, and Lorraine to France; and the Milanese to M. de Lorraine, as compensation for taking away from him his territory.

The King of England made this proposition first of all to our King; who, tired of war, and anxious for repose, as was natural at his age, made few difficulties, and soon accepted. M. de Lorraine was not in a position to refuse his consent to a change recommended by England, France, and Holland. Thus much being settled, the Emperor was next applied to. But he was not so easy to persuade: he wished to inherit the entire succession, and would not brook the idea of seeing the House of Austria driven from Italy, as it would have been if the King of England's proposal had been carried out. He therefore declared it was altogether unheard of and unnatural to divide a succession under such circumstances, and that he would hear nothing upon the subject until after the death of the King of Spain. The resistance he made caused the whole scheme to come to the ears of the King of Spain, instead of remaining a secret, as was intended.

The King of Spain made a great stir in consequence of what had taken place, as though the project had been formed to strip him, during his lifetime, of his realm. His ambassador in England spoke so insolently that he was ordered to leave the country by William, and retired to Flanders. The Emperor, who did not wish to quarrel with England, intervened at this point, and brought about a reconciliation between the two powers. The Spanish ambassador returned to London.

The Emperor next endeavoured to strengthen his party in Spain. The reigning Queen was his sister-in-law and was all-powerful. Such of the nobility and of the ministers who would not bend before her she caused to be dismissed; and none were favoured by her who were not partisans of the House of Austria. The Emperor had, therefore, a powerful ally at the Court of Madrid to aid him in carrying out his plans; and the King was so much in his favour, that he had made a will bequeathing his succession to the Archduke. Everything therefore seemed to promise success to the Emperor.

But just at this time, a small party arose in Spain, equally opposed to the Emperor, and to the propositions of the King of England. This party consisted at first of only five persons: namely, Villafranca, Medina- Sidonia, Villagarcias, Villena, and San Estevan, all of them nobles, and well instructed in the affairs of government. Their wish was to prevent the dismemberment of the Spanish kingdom by conferring the whole succession upon the son of the only son of the Queen of France, Maria Theresa, sister of the King of Spain. There were, however, two great obstacles in their path. Maria Theresa, upon her marriage with our King, had solemnly renounced all claim to the Spanish throne, and these renunciations had been repeated at the Peace of the Pyrenees. The other obstacle was the affection the King of Spain bore to the House of Austria,—an affection which naturally would render him opposed to any project by which a rival house would be aggrandised at its expense.

As to the first obstacle, these politicians were of opinion that the renunciations made by Maria Theresa held good only as far as they applied to the object for which they were made. That object was to prevent the crowns of France and Spain from being united upon one head, as might have happened in the person of the Dauphin. But now that the Dauphin had three sons, the second of whom could be called to the throne of Spain, the renunciations of the Queen became of no import. As to the second obstacle, it was only to be removed by great perseverance and exertions; but they determined to leave no stone unturned to achieve their ends.

One of the first resolutions of this little party was to bind one another to secrecy. Their next was to admit into their confidence Cardinal Portocarrero, a determined enemy to the Queen. Then they commenced an attack upon the Queen in the council; and being supported by the popular voice, succeeded in driving out of the country Madame Berlips, a German favourite of hers, who was much hated on account of the undue influence she exerted, and the rapacity she displayed. The next measure was of equal importance. Madrid and its environs groaned under the weight of a regiment of Germans commanded by the Prince of Darmstadt. The council decreed that this regiment should be disbanded, and the Prince thanked for his assistance. These two blows following upon each other so closely, frightened the Queen, isolated her, and put it out of her power to act during the rest of the life of the King.

There was yet one of the preliminary steps to take, without which it was thought that success would not be certain. This was to dismiss the King's Confessor, who had been given to him by the Queen, and who was a zealous Austrian.

Cardinal Portocarrero was charged with this duty, and he succeeded so well, that two birds were killed with one stone. The Confessor was dismissed, and another was put in his place, who could be relied upon to do and say exactly as he was requested. Thus, the King of Spain was influenced in his conscience, which had over him so much the more power, because he was beginning to look upon the things of this world by the glare of that terrible flambeau that is lighted for the dying. The Confessor and the Cardinal, after a short time, began unceasingly to attack the King upon the subject of the succession. The King, enfeebled by illness, and by a lifetime of weak health, had little power of resistance. Pressed by the many temporal, and affrighted by the many spiritual reasons which were brought forward by the two ecclesiastics, with no friend near whose opinion he could consult, no Austrian at hand to confer with, and no Spaniard who was not opposed to Austria;—the King fell into a profound perplexity, and in this strait, proposed to consult the Pope, as an authority whose decision would be infallible. The Cardinal, who felt persuaded that the Pope was sufficiently enlightened and sufficiently impartial to declare in favour of France, assented to this step; and the King of Spain accordingly wrote a long letter to Rome, feeling much relieved by the course he had adopted.

The Pope replied at once and in the most decided manner. He said he saw clearly that the children of the Dauphin were the next heirs to the Spanish throne, and that the House of Austria had not the smallest right to it. He recommended therefore the King of Spain to render justice to whom justice was due, and to assign the succession of his monarchy to a son of France. This reply, and the letter which had given rise to it, were kept so profoundly secret that they were not known in Spain until after the King's death.

Directly the Pope's answer had been received the King was pressed to make a fresh will, and to destroy that which he had previously made in favour of the Archduke. The new will accordingly was at once drawn up and signed; and the old one burned in the presence, of several witnesses. Matters having arrived at this point, it was thought opportune to admit others to the knowledge of what had taken place. The council of state, consisting of eight members, four of whom were already in the secret, was made acquainted with the movements of the new party; and, after a little hesitation, were gained over.

The King, meantime, was drawing near to his end. A few days after he had signed the new will he was at the last extremity, and in a few days more he died. In his last moments the Queen had been kept from him as much as possible, and was unable in any way to interfere with the plans that had been so deeply laid. As soon as the King was dead the first thing to be done was to open his will. The council of state assembled for that purpose, and all the grandees of Spain who were in the capital took part in it, The singularity and the importance of such an event, interesting many millions of men, drew all Madrid to the palace, and the rooms adjoining that in which the council assembled were filled to suffocation. All the foreign ministers besieged the door. Every one sought to be the first to know the choice of the King who had just died, in order to be the first to inform his court. Blecourt, our ambassador, was there with the others, without knowing more than they; and Count d'Harrach, ambassador from the Emperor, who counted upon the will in favour of the Archduke, was there also, with a triumphant look, just opposite the door, and close by it.

At last the door opened, and immediately closed again. The Duc d'Abrantes, a man of much wit and humour, but not to be trifled with, came out. He wished to have the pleasure of announcing upon whom the successorship had fallen, and was surrounded as soon as he appeared. Keeping silence, and turning his eyes on all sides, he fixed them for a moment on Blecourt, then looked in another direction, as if seeking some one else. Blecourt interpreted this action as a bad omen. The Duc d'Abrantes feigning at last to discover the Count d'Harrach, assumed a gratified look, flew to him, embraced him, and said aloud in Spanish, "Sir, it is with much pleasure;" then pausing, as though to embrace him better, he added: "Yes, sir, it is with an extreme joy that for all my life," here the embraces were redoubled as an excuse for a second pause, after which he went on—"and with the greatest contentment that I part from you, and take leave of the very august House of Austria." So saying he clove the crowd, and every one ran after him to know the name of the real heir.

The astonishment and indignation of Count d'Harrach disabled him from speaking, but showed themselves upon his face in all their extent. He remained motionless some moments, and then went away in the greatest confusion at the manner in which he had been duped.

Blecourt, on the other hand, ran home without asking other information, and at once despatched to the King a courier, who fell ill at Bayonne, and was replaced by one named by Harcourt, then at Bayonne getting ready for the occupation of Guipuscoa. The news arrived at Court (Fontainebleau) in the month of November. The King was going out shooting that day; but, upon learning what had taken place, at once countermanded the sport, announced the death of the King of Spain, and at three o'clock held a council of the ministers in the apartments of Madame de Maintenon. This council lasted until past seven o'clock in the evening. Monseigneur, who had been out wolf-hunting, returned in time to attend it. On the next morning, Wednesday, another council was held, and in the evening a third, in the apartments of Madame de Maintenon. However accustomed persons were at the Court to the favour Madame de Maintenon enjoyed there, they were extremely surprised to see two councils assembled in her rooms for the greatest and most important deliberation that had taken place during this long reign, or indeed during many others.

The King, Monseigneur, the Chancellor, the Duc de Brinvilliers, Torcy, and Madame de Maintenon, were the only persons who deliberated upon this affair. Madame de Maintenon preserved at first a modest silence; but the King forced her to give her opinion after everybody had spoken except herself. The council was divided. Two were for keeping to the treaty that had been signed with King William, two for accepting the will. Monseigneur, drowned as he was in fat and sloth, appeared in quite another character from his usual ones at these councils. To the great surprise of the King and his assistants, when it was his turn to speak he expressed himself with force in favour of accepting the testament. Then, turning towards the King in a respectful but firm manner, he said that he took the liberty of asking for his inheritance, that the monarchy of Spain belonged to the Queen his mother, and consequently to him; that he surrendered it willingly to his second son for the tranquillity of Europe; but that to none other would he yield an inch of ground. These words, spoken with an inflamed countenance, caused excessive surprise, The King listened very attentively, and then said to Madame de Maintenon, "And you, Madame, what do you think upon all this?" She began by affecting modesty; but pressed, and even commanded to speak, she expressed herself with becoming confusion; briefly sang the praises of Monseigneur, whom she feared and liked but little—sentiments perfectly reciprocated—and at last was for accepting the will.

Madame Maintenon in Conferance--painted by Sir John Gilbert

The King did not yet declare himself. He said that the affair might well be allowed to sleep for four-and-twenty hours, in order that they might ascertain if the Spaniards approved the choice of their King. He dismissed the council, but ordered it to meet again the next evening at the same hour and place. Next day, several couriers arrived from Spain, and the news they brought left no doubt upon the King's mind as to the wishes of the Spanish nobles and people upon the subject of the will. When therefore the council reassembled in the apartments of Madame de Maintenon, the King, after fully discussing the matter, resolved to accept the will.

At the first receipt of the news the King and his ministers had been overwhelmed with a surprise that they could not recover from for several days. When the news was spread abroad, the Court was equally surprised. The foreign ministers passed whole nights deliberating upon the course the King would adopt. Nothing else was spoken of but this matter. The King one evening, to divert himself, asked the princesses their opinion. They replied that he should send M. le Duc d'Anjou (the second son of Monseigneur), into Spain, and that this was the general sentiment. "I am sure," replied the King, "that whatever course I adopt many people will condemn me."

At last, on Tuesday, the 16th of November, the King publicly declared himself. The Spanish ambassador had received intelligence which proved the eagerness of Spain to welcome the Duc d'Anjou as its King. There seemed to be no doubt of the matter. The King, immediately after getting up, called the ambassador into his cabinet, where M. le Duc d'Anjou had already arrived. Then, pointing to the Duke, he told the ambassador he might salute him as King of Spain. The ambassador threw himself upon his knees after the fashion of his country, and addressed to the Duke a tolerably long compliment in the Spanish language. Immediately afterwards, the King, contrary to all custom, opened the two folding doors of his cabinet, and commanded everybody to enter. It was a very full Court that day. The King, majestically turning his eyes towards the numerous company, and showing them M. le Duc d'Anjou said—"Gentlemen, behold the King of Spain. His birth called him to that crown: the late King also has called him to it by his will; the whole nation wished for him, and has asked me for him eagerly; it is the will of heaven: I have obeyed it with pleasure." And then, turning towards his grandson, he said, "Be a good Spaniard, that is your first duty; but remember that you are a Frenchman born, in order that the union between the two nations may be preserved; it will be the means of rendering both happy, and of preserving the peace of Europe." Pointing afterwards with his finger to the Duc d'Anjou, to indicate him to the ambassador, the King added, "If he follows my counsels you will be a grandee, and soon; he cannot do better than follow your advice."

When the hubbub of the courtiers had subsided, the two other sons of France, brothers of M. d'Anjou, arrived, and all three embraced one another tenderly several times, with tears in their eyes. The ambassador of the Emperor immediately entered, little suspecting what had taken place, and was confounded when he learned the news. The King afterwards went to mass, during which at his right hand was the new King of Spain, who during the rest of his stay in France, was publicly treated in every respect as a sovereign, by the King and all the Court.

The joy of Monseigneur at all this was very great. He seemed beside himself, and continually repeated that no man had ever found himself in a condition to say as he could, "The King my father, and the King my son." If he had known the prophecy which from his birth had been said of him, "A King's son, a King's father, and never a King," which everybody had heard repeated a thousand times, I think he would not have so much rejoiced, however vain may be such prophecies. The King himself was so overcome, that at supper he turned to the Spanish ambassador and said that the whole affair seemed to him like a dream. In public, as I have observed, the new King of Spain was treated in every respect as a sovereign, but in private he was still the Duc d'Anjou. He passed his evenings in the apartments of Madame de Maintenon, where he played at all sorts of children's games, scampering to and fro with Messeigneurs his brothers, with Madame la Duchesse de Bourgogne, and with the few ladies to whom access was permitted.

On Friday, the 19th of November, the new King of Spain put on mourning. Two days after, the King did the same. On Monday, the 22nd, letters were received from the Elector of Bavaria, stating that the King of Spain had been proclaimed at Brussels with much rejoicing and illuminations. On Sunday, the 28th, M. Vaudemont, governor of the Milanese, sent word that he had been proclaimed in that territory, and with the same demonstrations of joy as at Brussels.

On Saturday, the 4th of December, the King of Spain set out for his dominions. The King rode with him in his coach as far as Sceaux, surrounded in pomp by many more guards than usual, gendarmes and light horse, all the road covered with coaches and people; and Sceaux, where they arrived a little after midday, full of ladies and courtiers, guarded by two companies of Musketeers. There was a good deal of leave-taking, and all the family was collected alone in the last room of the apartment; but as the doors were left open, the tears they shed so bitterly could be seen. In presenting the King of Spain to the Princes of the blood, the King said—"Behold the Princes of my blood and of yours; the two nations from this time ought to regard themselves as one nation; they ought to have the same interests; therefore I wish these Princes to be attached to you as to me; you cannot have friends more faithful or more certain." All this lasted a good hour and a half. But the time of separation at last came. The King conducted the King of Spain to the end of the apartment, and embraced him several times, holding him a long while in. his arms. Monseigneur did the same. The spectacle was extremely touching.

The King returned into the palace for some time, in order to recover himself. Monseigneur got into a caleche alone, and went to Meudon; and the King of Spain, with his brother, M. de Noailles, and a large number of courtiers, set out on his journey. The King gave to his grandson twenty-one purses of a thousand louis each, for pocket-money, and much money besides for presents. Let us leave them on their journey, and admire the Providence which sports with the thoughts of men and disposes of states. What would have said Ferdinand and Isabella, Charles V. and Philip II., who so many times attempted to conquer France, and who have been so frequently accused of aspiring to universal monarchy, and Philip IV., even, with all his precautions at the marriage of the King and at the Peace of the Pyrenees,—what would they have said, to see a son of France become King of Spain, by the will and testament of the last of their blood in Spain, and by the universal wish of all the Spaniards— without plot, without intrigue, without a shot being fired on our part, and without the sanction of our King, nay even to his extreme surprise and that of all his ministers, who had only the trouble of making up their minds and of accepting? What great and wise reflections might be made thereon! But they would be out of place in these Memoirs.

The King of Spain arrived in Madrid on the 19th February. From his first entrance into the country he had everywhere been most warmly welcomed. Acclamations were uttered when he appeared; fetes and bull-fights were given in his honour; the nobles and ladies pressed around him. He had been proclaimed in Madrid some time before, in the midst of demonstrations of joy.

Now that he had arrived among his subjects there, that joy burst out anew. There was such a crowd in the streets that sixty people were stifled! All along the line of route were an infinity of coaches filled with ladies richly decked. The streets through which he passed were hung in the Spanish fashion; stands were placed, adorned with fine pictures and a vast number of silver vessels; triumphal arches were built from side to side. It is impossible to conceive a greater or more general demonstration of joy. The Buen-Retiro, where the new King took up his quarters, was filled with the Court and the nobility. The junta and a number of great men received him at the door, and the Cardinal Portocarrero, who was there, threw himself on his knees, and wished to kiss the King's hand. But the King would not permit this; raised the Cardinal, embraced him, and treated him as his father. The Cardinal wept with joy, and could not take his eyes off the King. He was just then in the flower of his first youth—fair like the late King Charles, and the Queen his grandmother; grave, silent, measured, self- contained, formed exactly to live among Spaniards. With all this, very attentive in his demeanour, and paying everybody the attention due to him, having taken lessons from d'Harcourt on the way. Indeed he took off his hat or raised it to nearly everybody, so that the Spaniards spoke on the subject to the Duc d'Harcourt, who replied to them that the King in all essential things would conform himself to usage, but that in others he must be allowed to act according to French politeness. It cannot be imagined how much these trifling external attentions attached all hearts to this Prince.

He was, indeed, completely triumphant in Spain, and the Austrian party as completely routed. The Queen of Spain was sent away from Madrid, and banished to Toledo, where she remained with but a small suite, and still less consideration. Each day the nobles, the citizens, and the people had given fresh proof of their hatred against the Germans and against the Queen. She had been almost entirely abandoned, and was refused the most ordinary necessaries of her state.

CHAPTER XIX

Shortly after his arrival in Madrid, the new King of Spain began to look about him for a wife, and his marriage with the second daughter of M. de Savoie (younger sister of Madame de Bourgogne) was decided upon as an alliance of much honour and importance to M. de Savoie, and, by binding him to her interest, of much utility to France. An extraordinary ambassador (Homodei, brother of the Cardinal of that name) was sent to Turin to sign the contract of marriage, and bring back the new Queen into Spain. He was also appointed her Ecuyer, and the Princesse des Ursins was selected as her 'Camarera Mayor', a very important office. The Princesse des Ursins seemed just adapted for it. A Spanish lady could not have been relied upon: a lady of our court would not have been fit for the post. The Princesse des Ursins was, as it were, both French and Spanish—French by birth, Spanish by marriage. She had passed the greater part of her life in Rome and Italy, and was a widow without children. I shall have more hereafter to say of this celebrated woman, who so long and so publicly governed the Court and Crown of Spain, and who has made so much stir in the world by her reign and by her fall; at present let me finish with the new Queen of Spain.

She was married, then, at Turin, on the 11th of September, with but little display, the King being represented by procuration, and set out on the 13th for Nice, where she was to embark on board the Spanish galleys for Barcelona. The King of Spain, meanwhile, after hearing news that he had been proclaimed with much unanimity and rejoicing in Peru and Mexico, left Madrid on the 5th of September, to journey through Aragon and Catalonia to Barcelona to meet his wife. He was much welcomed on his route, above all by Saragossa, which received him magnificently.

The new Queen of Spain, brought by the French galleys to Nice, was so fatigued with the sea when she arrived there, that she determined to finish the rest of the journey by land, through Provence and Languedoc. Her graces, her presence of mind, the aptness and the politeness of her short replies, and her judicious curiosity, remarkable at her age, surprised everybody, and gave great hopes to the Princesse des Ursins.

When within two days' journey of Barcelona, the Queen was met by a messenger, bearing presents and compliments from the King. All her household joined her at the same time, being sent on in advance for that purpose, and her Piedmontese attendants were dismissed. She appeared more affected by this separation than Madame de Bourgogne had been when parting from her attendants. She wept bitterly, and seemed quite lost in the midst of so many new faces, the most familiar of which (that of Madame des Ursins) was quite fresh to her. Upon arriving at Figueras, the King, impatient to see her, went on before on horseback. In this first embarrassment Madame des Ursins, although completely unknown to the King, and but little known to the Queen, was of great service to both.

Upon arriving at Figueras, the bishop diocesan married them anew, with little ceremony, and soon after they sat down to supper, waited upon by the Princesse des Ursins and the ladies of the palace, half the dishes being French, half Spanish. This mixture displeased the ladies of the palace and several of the Spanish grandees, who plotted with the ladies openly to mark their displeasure; and they did so in a scandalous manner. Under one pretext or another—such as the weight or heat of the dishes— not one of the French dishes arrived upon the table; all were upset; while the Spanish dishes, on the contrary, were served without any accident. The affectation and air of chagrin, to say the least of it, of the ladies of the palace, were too visible not to be perceived. But the King and Queen were wise enough to appear not to notice this; and Madame des Ursins, much astonished, said not a word.

After a long and disagreeable supper, the King and Queen withdrew. Then feelings which had been kept in during supper overflowed. The Queen wept for her Piedmontese women. Like a child, as she was, she thought herself lost in the hands of ladies so insolent; and when it was time to go to bed, she said flatly that she would not go, and that she wished to return home. Everything was done to console her; but the astonishment and embarrassment were great indeed when it was found that all was of no avail. The King had undressed, and was awaiting her. Madame des Ursins was at length obliged to go and tell him the resolution the Queen had taken. He was piqued and annoyed. He had until that time lived with the completest regularity; which had contributed to make him find the Princess more to his taste than he might otherwise have done. He was therefore affected by her 'fantaisie', and by the same reason easily persuaded that she would not keep to it beyond the first night. They did not see each other therefore until the morrow, and after they were dressed. It was lucky that by the Spanish custom no one was permitted to be present when the newly-married pair went to bed; or this affair, which went no further than the young couple, Madame des Ursins, and one or two domestics, might have made a very unpleasant noise.

Madame des Ursins consulted with two of the courtiers, as to the best measures to be adopted with a child who showed so much force and resolution. The night was passed in exhortations and in promises upon what had occurred at the supper; and the Queen consented at last to remain Queen. The Duke of Medina-Sidonia and Count San Estevan were consulted on the morrow. They were of opinion that in his turn the King, in order to mortify her and reduce her to terms, should not visit the Queen on the following night. This opinion was acted upon. The King and Queen did not see each other in private that day. In the evening the Queen was very sorry. Her pride and her little vanity were wounded; perhaps also she had found the King to her taste.

The ladies and the grand seigneurs who had attended at the supper were lectured for what had occurred there. Excuses, promises, demands for pardon, followed; all was put right; the third day was tranquil, and the third night still more agreeable to the young people. On the fourth day they went to Barcelona, where only fetes and pleasures awaited them. Soon after they set out for Madrid.

At the commencement of the following year (1702), it was resolved, after much debate, at our court, that Philip V. should make a journey to Italy, and on Easter-day he set out. He went to Naples, Leghorn, Milan, and Alessandria. While at the first-named place a conspiracy which had been hatching against his life was discovered, and put down. But other things which previously occurred in Italy ought to have been related before. I must therefore return to them now.

From the moment that Philip V. ascended the Spanish throne it was seen that a war was certain.

England maintained for some time an obstinate silence, refusing to acknowledge the new King; the Dutch secretly murmured against him, and the Emperor openly prepared for battle. Italy, it was evident at once, would be the spot on which hostilities would commence, and our King lost no time in taking measures to be ready for events. By land and by sea every preparation was made for the struggle about to take place.

After some time the war, waited for and expected by all Europe, at last broke out, by some Imperialist troops firing upon a handful of men near Albaredo. One Spaniard was killed, and all the rest of the men were taken prisoners. The Imperialists would not give them up until a cartel was arranged. The King, upon hearing this, at once despatched the general officers to Italy. Our troops were to be commanded by Catinat, under M. de Savoie; and the Spanish troops by Vaudemont, who was Governor-General of the Milanese, and to whom, and his dislike to our King, I have before alluded.

Vaudemont at once began to plot to overthrow Catinat, in conjunction with Tesse, who had expected the command, and who was irritated because it had not been given to him. They were in communication with Chamillart, Minister of War, who aided them, as did other friends at Court, to be hereafter named, in carrying out their object. It was all the more easy because they had to do with a man who depended for support solely upon his own talent, and whose virtue and simplicity raised him above all intrigue and scheming; and who, with much ability and intelligence, was severe in command, very laconic, disinterested, and of exceeding pure life.

Prince Eugene commanded the army of the Emperor in Italy. The first two generals under him, in order of rank, were allied with Vaudemont: one, in fact, was his only son; the other was the son of a friend of his. The least reflection ought to have opened all eyes to the conduct of Vaudemont, and to have discerned it to be more than suspicious. Catinat soon found it out. He could plan nothing against the enemy that they did not learn immediately; and he never attempted any movement without finding himself opposed by a force more than double his own; so gross was this treachery.

Catinat often complained of this: he sent word of it to the Court, but without daring to draw any conclusion from what happened. Nobody sustained him at Court, for Vaudemont had everybody in his favour. He captured our general officers by his politeness, his magnificence, and, above all, by presenting them with abundant supplies. All the useful, and the agreeable, came from his side; all the dryness, all the exactitude, came from Catinat. It need not be asked which of the two had all hearts. In fine, Tesse and Vaudemont carried out their schemes so well that Catinat could do nothing.

While these schemes were going on, the Imperialists were enabled to gain time, to strengthen themselves, to cross the rivers without obstacle, to, approach us; and, acquainted with everything as they were, to attack a portion of our army on the 9th July, at Capri, with five regiments of cavalry and dragoons. Prince Eugene led this attack without his coming being in the least degree suspected, and fell suddenly upon our troops. Tesse, who was in the immediate neighbourhood with some dragoons, advanced rapidly upon hearing this, but only with a few dragoons. A long resistance was made, but at last retreat became necessary. It was accomplished in excellent order, and without disturbance from the enemy; but our loss was very great, many officers of rank being among the dead.

Such was our first exploit in Italy; all the fault of which was attributed to Catinat. Tesse and Vaudemont did everything in their power to secure his disgrace. The King, indeed, thus prejudiced against Catinat, determined to take from him the command, and appointed the Marechal de Villeroy as his successor. The surprise of everybody at this was very great, for no one expected that the Marechal de Villeroy would repair the fault of Catinat. On the evening of his appointment, this general was exposed in a very straightforward and public manner by M. de Duras. He did not like the Marechal de Villeroy; and, while everybody else was applauding, took the Marechal by the arm, and said, "Monsieur le Marechal, everybody is paying you compliments upon your departure to Italy, I keep mine until you return;" and then, bursting out laughing, he looked round upon the company. Villeroy remained confounded, without offering a word. Everybody smiled and looked down. The King took no notice.

Catinat, when the command was taken out of his hands by the Marechal de Villeroy, made himself admired on every side by the moderation and tranquillity with which he conducted himself. If Vaudemont was satisfied with the success of his schemes, it was far otherwise with Tesse, who had merely intrigued against Catinat for the purpose of obtaining the command of the army. He did all in his power to ingratiate himself into the favour of the Marechal de Villeroy; but the Marechal received these advances very coldly. Tesse's schemes against Catinat were beginning to be scented out; he was accused of having wished the Imperialists to succeed at Capri, and of indirectly aiding them by keeping back his troops; his tirades against Catinat, too, made him suspected. The Marechal de Villeroy would have nothing to do with him. His conduct was contrasted with that of Catinat, who, free after his fall to retire from the army, continued to remain there, with rare modesty, interfering in nothing.

The first campaign passed without notable incident, except an unsuccessful attack upon Chiari, by our troops on the 1st of September. M. de Savoie led the attack; but was so firmly met by Prince Eugene, who was in an excellent position for defence, that he could do nothing, and in the end was compelled to retire disgracefully. We lost five or six colonels and many men, and had a large number wounded. This action much astonished our army, and encouraged that of the enemy, who did almost as they wished during the rest of the campaign.

Towards the end of this campaign, the grand airs of familiarity which the Marechal de Villeroy gave himself with M. de Savoie drew upon him a cruel rebuke, not to say an affront. M. de Savoie being in the midst of all the generals and of the flower of the army, opened, while talking, his snuff-box, and was about to take a pinch of snuff, when M. de Villeroy, who was standing near, stretched out his hand and put it into the box without saying a word. M. de Savoie flushed up, and instantly threw all the snuff upon the ground, gave the box to one of his attendants, and told him to fill it again. The Marechal, not knowing what to do with himself, swallowed his shame without daring to say a word, M. de Savoie continuing the conversation that he had not interrupted, except to ask for the fresh snuff.

The campaign passed away, our troops always retreating, the Imperialists always gaining ground; they continually increasing in numbers; we diminishing little by little every day. The Marechal de Villeroy and Prince Eugene each took up his winter quarters and crossed the frontier: M. de Savoie returned to Turin, and Catinat went to Paris. The King received him well, but spoke of nothing but unimportant matters, and gave him no private audience, nor did he ask for one.

Prince Eugene, who was more knowing than the Marechal de Villeroy, had obliged him to winter in the midst of the Milanese, and kept him closely pressed there, while his own troops enjoyed perfect liberty, by means of which they much disturbed ours. In this advantageous situation, Prince Eugene conceived the design of surprising the centre of our quarters, and by that blow to make himself master of our positions, and afterwards of Milan, and other places of the country, all in very bad order; thus finishing effectively and suddenly his conquest.

Cremona was our centre, and it was defended by a strong garrison. Prince Eugene ascertained that there was at Cremona an ancient aqueduct which extended far out into the country, and which started from the town in the vault of a house occupied by a priest. He also learnt that this aqueduct had been recently cleaned, but that it carried very little water, and that in former times the town had been surprised by means of it. He caused the entrance of the aqueduct, in the country, to be reconnoitred, he gained over the priest in whose vault it ended, and who lived close to one of the gates of the city, which was walled up and but little guarded; he sent into Cremona as many chosen soldiers as he could, disguised as priests or peasants, and these hiding themselves in the house of the friendly priest, obtained secretly as many axes as they could. Then the Prince despatched five hundred picked men and officers to march by the aqueduct to the priest's vault; he put Thomas de Vaudemont, son of the Governor General of the Milanese, at the head of a large detachment of troops, with orders to occupy a redoubt that defended the Po, and to come by the bridge to his assistance, when the struggle commenced in the town; and he charged the soldiers secreted in the priest's house to break down the walled-up gate, so as to admit the troops whom he would lead there.

Everything, thus concerted with exactness, was executed with precision, and with all possible secrecy and success. It was on the 1st of February, 1702, at break of day, that the surprise was attempted. The Marechal de Villeroy had only arrived in the town on the previous night. The first person who got scent of what was going forward was the cook of the Lieutenant-General Crenan, who going out in the early morning to buy provisions, saw the streets full of soldiers, whose uniforms were unknown to him. He ran back and awakened his master. Neither he nor his valets would believe what the cook said, but nevertheless Crenan hurriedly dressed himself, went out, and was only too soon convinced that it was true.

At the same time, by a piece of good luck, which proved the saving of Cremona, a regiment under the command of D'Entragues, drew up in battle array in one of the public places. D'Entragues was a bold and skilful soldier, with a great desire to distinguish himself. He wished to review this regiment, and had commenced business before the dawn. While the light was still uncertain and feeble, and his battalions were under arms, he indistinctly perceived infantry troops forming at the end of the street, in front of him. He knew by the order's given on the previous evening that no other review was to take place except his own. He immediately feared, therefore, some surprise, marched at once to these troops, whom he found to be Imperialists, charged them, overthrew them, sustained the shock of the fresh troops which arrived, and kept up a defence so obstinate, that he gave time to all the town to awake, and to the majority of the troops to take up arms. Without him, all would have been slaughtered as they slept.

Just at dawn the Marechal de Villeroy, already up and dressed, was writing in his chamber. He heard a noise, called for a horse, and followed by a single aide-de-camp and a page, threaded his way through the streets to the grand place, which is always the rendezvous in case of alarm. At the turning of one of the streets he fell into the midst of an Imperialist corps de garde, who surrounded him and arrested him. Feeling that it was impossible to defend himself, the Marechal de Villeroy whispered his name to the officer, and promised him ten thousand pistoles, a regiment, and the grandest recompenses from the King, to be allowed to escape. The officer was, however, above all bribes, said he had not served the Emperor so long in order to end by betraying him, and conducted the Marechal de Villeroy to Prince Eugene, who did not receive him so well as he himself would have been received, under similar circumstances, by the Marechal. While in the suite of Prince Eugene, Villeroy saw Crenan led in prisoner, and wounded to the death, and exclaimed that he should like to be in his place. A moment after they were both sent out of the town, and passed the day, guarded, in the coach of Prince Eugene.

Revel, become commander-in-chief by the capture of the Marechal de Villeroy, tried to rally the troops. There was a fight in every street; the troops dispersed about, some in detachments, several scarcely armed; some only in their shirts fought with the greatest bravery. They were driven at last to the ramparts, where they had time to look about them, to rally and form themselves. If the enemy had not allowed our troops time to gain the ramparts, or if they had driven them beyond this position, when they reached it, the town could never have held out. But the imperialists kept themselves entirely towards the centre of the town, and made no effort to fall upon our men, or to drive them from the ramparts.

Praslin, who had the command of our cavalry, put himself at the head of some Irish battalions which under him did wonders. Although continually occupied in defending and attacking, Praslin conceived the idea that the safety of Cremona depended upon the destruction of the bridge of the Po, so that the Imperialists could not receive reinforcements from that point. He repeated this so many times, that Revel was informed of it, and ordered Praslin to do what he thought most advisable in the matter. Thereupon, Praslin instantly commanded the bridge to be broken down: There was not a moment to lose. Thomas de Vaudemont was already approaching the bridge at the head of his troops. But the bridge, nevertheless, was destroyed before his eyes, and with all his musketeers he was not able to prevent it.

It was now three o'clock in the afternoon. Prince Eugene was at the Hotel de Ville, swearing in the magistrates. Leaving that place, and finding that his troops were giving way, he ascended the cathedral steeple to see what was passing in different parts of the town, and to discover why the troops of Thomas de Vaudemont did not arrive. He had scarcely reached the top of the steeple, when he saw his detachments on the banks of the Po, and the bridge broken, thus rendering their assistance useless. He was not more satisfied with what he discovered in every other direction. Furious at seeing his enterprise in such bad case, after having been so nearly successful, he descended, tearing his hair and yelling. From that time, although superior in force, he thought of nothing but retreat.

Revel, who saw that his troops were overwhelmed by hunger, fatigue, and wounds, for since the break of day they had had no repose or leisure, thought on his side of withdrawing his men into the castle of Cremona, in order, at least, to defend himself under cover, and to obtain a capitulation. So that the two opposing chiefs each thought at one and the same time of retreat.

Towards the evening therefore the combat slackened on both sides, until our troops made a last effort to drive the enemy from one of the gates of the town; so as to have that gate free and open during the night to let in assistance. The Irish seconded so well this attack, that it was at length successful. A tolerably long calm succeeded this last struggle. Revel, nevertheless, thought of withdrawing his troops to the castle, when Mahony, an Irish officer who had fought bravely as a lion all day, proposed to go and see what was passing all around. It was already growing dark; the reconnoiterers profited by this. They saw that everything was tranquil, and understood that the enemy had retreated. This grand news was carried to Revel, who, with many around him, was a long time in believing it. Persuaded at last, he left everything as it was then, until broad daylight, when he found that the enemy had gone, and that the streets and public places were filled with the wounded, the dying, and the dead. He made arrangements for everything, and dispatched Mahony to the King.

Prince Eugene retreated all that night with the detachment he had led, and made the Marechal de Villeroy, disarmed and badly mounted, follow him, very indecently. The Marechal was afterwards sent to Gratz in Styria. Crenan died in the coach of the Marechal de Villeroy. D'Entragues, to whose valour the safety of Cremona was owing, did not survive this glorious day. Our loss was great; that of the enemy greater.

The news of this, the most surprising event that has been heard of in recent ages, was brought to the King at Marly on the 9th of February, 1702, by Mahony. Soon after it arrived I heard of it, and at once hastened to the chateau, where I found a great buzzing and several groups of people talking. Mahony was closeted a long time with the King. At the end of an hour the King came out of his cabinet, and spoke strongly in praise of what had occurred. He took pleasure in dwelling at great length upon Mahony, and declared that he had never heard anybody give such a clear and good account of an occurrence as he. The King kindly added that he should bestow a thousand francs a year upon Mahony, and a brevet of Colonel.

In the evening M. le Prince de Conti told me that the King had decorated Revel, and made Praslin Lieutenant-General. As the latter was one of my particular friends, this intelligence gave me much joy. I asked again to be more sure of the news. The other principal officers were advanced in proportion to their grades, and many received pensions.

As for the Marechal de Villeroy he was treated as those who excite envy and then become unfortunate are always treated. The King, however, openly took his part; and in truth it was no fault of the Marechal, who had arrived at Cremona the day before the surprise, that he was taken prisoner directly he set his foot in the street.—How could he know of the aqueduct, the barred-up gate, and the concealed soldiers? Nevertheless, his friends were plunged into the greatest grief, and his wife, who had not been duped by the eclat which accompanied her husband upon his departure for Italy, but who feared for the result, was completely overwhelmed, and for a long time could not be prevailed upon to see anybody.

M. de Vendome was appointed successor to M. de Villeroy, in command of the army in Italy.

CHAPTER XX

But it is time now for me to go back to other matters, and to start again from the commencement of 1701, from which I have been led by reciting, in a continuous story, the particulars of our first campaign in Italy.

Barbezieux had viewed with discontent the elevation of Chamillart. His pride and presumption rose in arms against it; but as there was no remedy he gave himself up to debauch, to dissipate his annoyance. He had built between Versailles and Vaucresson, at the end of the park of Saint Cloud, a house in the open fields, called l'Etang, which though in the dismalest position in the world had cost him millions. He went there to feast and riot with his friends; and committing excesses above his strength, was seized with a fever, and died in a few days, looking death steadily in the face. He was told of his approaching end by the Archbishop of Rheims; for he would not believe Fagon.

He was thirty-three years of age, with a striking and expressive countenance, and much wit and aptitude for labour. He was remarkable for grace, fine manners, and winning ways; but his pride and ambition were excessive, and when his fits of ill-temper came, nothing could repress them. Resistance always excited and irritated him. He had accustomed the King—whenever he had drunk too much, or when a party of pleasure was toward—to put off work to another time. It was a great question, whether the State gained or lost most by his death?

As soon as he was dead, Saint-Pouange went to Marly to tell the news to the King, who was so prepared for it that two hours before, starting from Versailles, he had left La Vrilliere behind to put the seals everywhere. Fagon, who had condemned him at once, had never loved him or his father, and was accused of over-bleeding him on purpose. At any rate he allowed, at one of his last visits, expressions of joy to escape him because recovery was impossible. Barbezieux used to annoy people very much by answering aloud when they spoke to him in whispers, and by keeping visitors waiting whilst he was playing with his dogs or some base parasite.

Many people, especially divers beautiful ladies, lost much by his death. Some of the latter looked very disconsolate in the salon at Marly; but when they had gone to table, and the cake had been cut (it was Twelfth Night), the King manifested a joy which seemed to command imitation. He was not content with exclaiming "The Queen drinks," but as in a common wine-shop, he clattered his spoon and fork on his plate, and made others do so likewise, which caused a strange din, that lasted at intervals all through the supper. The snivellers made more noise than the others, and uttered louder screams of laughter; and the nearest relatives and best friends were still more riotous. On the morrow all signs of grief had disappeared.

Chamillart was appointed in the place of Barbezieux, as Secretary of State; and wanted to give up the Finance, but the King, remembering the disputes of Louvois and Colbert, insisted on his occupying both posts. Chamillart was a very worthy man, with clean hands and the best intentions; polite, patient, obliging, a good friend, and a moderate enemy, loving his country, but his King better; and on very good terms with him and Madame de Maintenon. His mind was limited and; like all persons of little wit and knowledge, he was obstinate and pig-headed—

smiling affectedly with a gentle compassion on whoever opposed reasons to his, but utterly incapable of understanding them—consequently a dupe in friendship, in business, in everything; governed by all who could manage to win his admiration, or on very slight grounds could claim his affection. His capacity was small, and yet he believed he knew everything, which was the more pitiable, as all this came to him with his places, and arose more from stupidity than presumption—not at all from vanity, of which he was divested. The most remarkable thing is that the chief origin of the King's tender regard for him was this very incapacity. He used to confess it to the King at every opportunity; and the King took pleasure in directing and instructing him, so that he was interested in his successes as if they had been his own, and always excused him. The world and the Court excused him also, charmed by the facility with which he received people, the pleasure he felt in granting requests and rendering services, the gentleness and regretfulness of his refusals, and his indefatigable patience as a listener. His memory was so great that he remembered all matters submitted to him, which gave pleasure to people who were afraid of being forgotten. He wrote excellently; and his clear, flowing, and precise style was extremely pleasing to the King and Madame de Maintenon, who were never weary of praising him, encouraging him, and congratulating themselves for having placed upon such weak shoulders two burdens, each of which was sufficient to overwhelm the most sturdy.

Rose, secretary in the King's cabinet, died, aged about eighty-six, at the commencement of the year 1701. For nearly fifty years he had held the office of the "pen," as it is called. To have the "pen," is to be a public forger, and to do what would cost anybody else his life. This office consists in imitating so exactly the handwriting of the King; that the real cannot be distinguished from the counterfeit. In this manner are written all the letters that the King ought or wishes to write with his own hand, but which, nevertheless, he will not take the trouble to write. Sovereigns and people of high rank, even generals and others of importance, employ a secretary of this kind. It is not possible to make a great King speak with more dignity than did Rose; nor with more fitness to each person, and upon every subject. The King signed all the letters Rose wrote, and the characters were so alike it was impossible to find the smallest difference. Many important things had passed through the hands of Rose: He was extremely faithful and secret, and the King put entire trust in him.

Rose was artful, scheming, adroit, and dangerous. There are stories without number of him; and I will relate one or two solely because they characterise him, and those to whom they also relate.

He had, near Chantilly, a nice house and grounds that he much liked, and that he often visited. This little property bordered the estate of M. le Prince, who, not liking so close a neighbour, wished to get rid of him. M. le Prince endeavoured to induce Rose to give up his house and grounds, but all to no effect; and at last tried to annoy him in various ways into acquiescence. Among other of his tricks, he put about four hundred foxes, old and young, into Rose's park. It may be imagined what disorder this company made there, and the surprise of Rose and his servants at an inexhaustible ant-hill of foxes come to one night!

The worthy fellow, who was anger and vehemence itself, knew only too well who had treated him thus scurvily, and straightway went to the King, requesting to be allowed to ask him rather a rough question. The King, quite accustomed to him and to his jokes,—for he was pleasant and very witty, demanded what was the matter.

"What is the matter, Sire?" replied Rose, with a face all flushed. "Why, I beg you will tell me if we have two Kings in France?"

"What do you mean?" said the King, surprised, and flushing in his turn.

"What I mean, Sire, is, that if M. le Prince is King like you, folks must weep and lower their heads before that tyrant. If he is only Prince of the blood, I ask justice from you, Sire, for you owe it to all your subjects, and you ought not to suffer them to be the prey of M. le Prince," said Rose; and he related everything that had taken place, concluding with the adventure of the foxes.

The King promised that he would speak to M. le Prince in a manner to insure the future repose of Rose; and, indeed, he ordered all the foxes to be removed from the worthy man's park, all the damages they had made to be repaired, and all the expenses incurred to be paid by M. le Prince. M. le Prince was too good a courtier to fail in obeying this order, and never afterwards troubled Rose in the least thing; but, on the contrary, made all the advances towards a reconciliation. Rose was obliged to receive them, but held himself aloof, nevertheless, and continually let slip some raillery against M. le Prince. I and fifty others were one day witnesses of this.

M. le Prince was accustomed to pay his court to the ministers as they stood waiting to attend the council in the King's chamber; and although he had nothing to say, spoke to them with the mien of a client obliged to fawn. One morning, when there was a large assembly of the Court in this chamber, and M. le Prince had been cajoling the ministers with much suppleness and flattery, Secretary Rose, who saw what had been going on, went up to him on a sudden, and said aloud, putting one finger under his closed eye, as was sometimes his habit, "Sir, I have seen your scheming here with all these gentlemen, and for several days; it is not for nothing. I have known the Court and mankind many years; and am not to be imposed upon: I see clearly where matters point:" and this with turns and inflections of voice which thoroughly embarrassed M. le Prince, who defended himself as he could. Every one crowded to hear what was going on; and at last Rose, taking M. le Prince respectfully by his arm, said, with a cunning and meaning smile; "Is it not that you wish to be made first Prince of the blood royal?" Then he turned on his heel, and slipped off. The Prince was stupefied; and all present tried in vain to restrain their laughter.

Rose had never pardoned M. de Duras an ill turn the latter had served him. During one of the Court journeys, the carriage in which Rose was riding broke down. He took a horse; but, not being a good equestrian, was very soon pitched into a hole full of mud. While there M. de Duras passed, and Rose from the midst of the mire cried for help. But M. de Duras, instead of giving assistance, looked from his coach-window, burst out laughing, and cried out: "What a luxurious horse thus to roll upon Roses!"—and with this witticism passed gently on through the mud. The next comer, the Duc de Coislin, was more charitable; he picked up the worthy man, who was so furious, so carried away by anger, that it was some time before he could say who he was. But the worst was to come; for M. de Duras, who feared nobody, and whose tongue was accustomed to wag as freely as that of Rose, told the story to the King and to all the Court, who much laughed at it. This outraged Rose to such a point, that he never afterwards approached M. de Duras, and only spoke of him in fury. Whenever he hazarded some joke upon M. de Duras, the King began to laugh, and reminded him of the mud-ducking he had received.

Towards the end of his life, Rose married his granddaughter, who was to be his heiress, to Portail, since Chief President of the Parliament. The marriage was not a happy one; the young spouse despised her husband; and said that instead of entering into a good house, she had remained at the portal. At last her husband and his father complained to Rose. He paid no attention at first; but, tired out at last, said if his granddaughter persisted in her bad conduct, he would disinherit her. There were no complaints after this.

Rose was a little man, neither fat nor lean, with a tolerably handsome face, keen expression, piercing eyes sparkling with cleverness; a little cloak, a satin skull-cap over his grey hairs, a smooth collar, almost like an Abbe's, and his pocket-handkerchief always between his coat and his vest. He used to say that it was nearer his nose there. He had taken me into his friendship. He laughed very freely at the foreign princes; and always called the Dukes with whom he was familiar, "Your Ducal Highness," in ridicule of the sham Highnesses. He was extremely neat and brisk, and full of sense to the last; he was a sort of personage.

CHAPTER XXI

On Saturday, the 19th of March, in the evening, the King was about to undress himself, when he heard cries in his chamber, which was full of courtiers; everybody calling for Fagon and Felix. Monseigneur had been taken very ill. He had passed the day at Meudon, where he had eaten only a collation; at the King's supper he had made amends by gorging himself nigh to bursting with fish. He was a great eater, like the King, and like the Queens his mother and grandmother. He had not appeared after supper, but had jest gone down to his own room from the King's cabinet, and was about to undress himself, when all at once he lost consciousness. His valets, frightened out of their wits, and some courtiers who were near, ran to the King's chambers, to his chief physician and his chief surgeon with the hubbub which I have mentioned above. The King, all unbuttoned, started to his feet immediately, and descended by a little dark, narrow, and steep staircase towards the chamber of Monseigneur. Madame la Duchesse de Bourgogne arrived at the same time, and in an instant the chamber, which was vast, was filled.

They found Monseigneur half naked: his servants endeavouring to make him walk erect, and dragging rather than leading him about. He did not know the King, who spoke to him, nor anybody else; and defended himself as long as he could against Felix, who, in this pressing necessity, hazarded bleeding him, and succeeded. Consciousness returned. Monseigneur asked for a confessor; the King had already sent for, the cure. Many emetics were given to him: but two hours passed before they operated. At half- past two in the morning, no further danger appearing, the King, who had shed tears, went to bed, leaving orders that he was to be awakened if any fresh accident happened. At five o'clock, however, all the effect having passed, the doctors went away, and made everybody leave the sick chamber. During the night all Paris hastened hither. Monseigneur was compelled to keep his room for eight or ten days; and took care in future not to gorge himself so much with food. Had this accident happened a quarter of an hour later, the chief valet de chambre, who slept in his room, would have found him dead in his bed.

Paris loved Monseigneur, perhaps because he often went to the opera. The fish-fags of the Halles thought it would be proper to exhibit their affection, and deputed four stout gossips to wait upon him: they were admitted. One of them took him round the neck and kissed him on both cheeks; the others kissed his hand. They were all very well received. Bontems showed them over the apartments, and treated them to a dinner. Monseigneur gave them some money, and the King did so also. They determined not to remain in debt, and had a fine Te Deum sung at Saint Eustache, and then feasted.

For some time past Monsieur had been sorely grieved that his son, M. le Duc de Chartres, had not been appointed to the command of an army. When M. de Chartres married, the King, who had converted his nephew by force into a son-in-law, promised him all kinds of favours; but except those which were written down in black and white had not given him any. M. de Chartres, annoyed at this, and at the manner m which the illegitimate children were promoted over his head, had given himself up to all kinds of youthful follies and excesses. The King was surprised to find Monsieur agree with his son's ambition; but gave a flat refusal when overtures were made to him on the subject. All hope of rising to a high command was thus forbidden to the Duc de Chartres; so that Madame had a fine excuse for sneering at the weakness which had been shown by Monsieur, who, on his part, had long before repented of it. He winked, therefore, at all the escapades performed or threatened by his son, and said nothing, not being sorry that the King should become uneasy, which was soon the case.

The King at last spoke to Monsieur; and being coldly received, reproached him for not knowing how to exercise authority over his son. Upon this Monsieur fired up; and, quite as much from foregone decision as from anger, in his turn asked the King what was to be done with a son at such an age: who was sick of treading the galleries of Versailles and the pavement of the Court; of being married as he was, and of remaining, as it were, naked, whilst his brothers-in-law were clothed in dignities, governments, establishments, and offices,—against all policy and all example. His son, he said, was worse off than any one in the King's service, for all others could earn distinction; added, that idleness was the mother of all vice, and that it gave him much pain to see his only son abandon himself to debauchery and bad company; but that it would be cruel to blame a young man, forced as it were into these follies, and to say nothing against him by whom he was thus forced.

Who was astonished to hear this straightforward language? Why, the King. Monsieur had never let out to within a thousand leagues of this tone, which was only the more annoying because supported by unanswerable reasons that did not convince. Mastering his embarrassments however, the King answered as a brother rather than as a sovereign; endeavouring, by gentle words, to calm the excitement of Monsieur. But Monsieur was stung to the quick by the King's neglect of M. de Chartres, and would not be pacified; yet the real subject of the annoyance was never once alluded to, whilst the one kept it steadily in his mind; and the other was determined not to yield. The conversation lasted very long, and was pushed very far; Monsieur throughout taking the high tone, the King very gentle. They separated in this manner,—Monsieur frowning, but not daring to burst out; the King annoyed, but not wishing to estrange his brother, much less to let their squabble be known.

As Monsieur passed most of his summers at Saint Cloud, the separation which this occasioned put them at their ease whilst waiting for a reconciliation; and Monsieur came less often than before, but when he did filled all their private interviews with bitter talk. In public little or nothing appeared, except that familiar people remarked politeness and attention on the King's part, coldness on that of Monsieur—moods not common to either. Nevertheless, being advised not to push matters too far, he read a lecture to his son, and made him change his conduct by degrees. But Monsieur still remained irritated against the King; and this completely upset him, accustomed as he always had been to live on the best of terms with his brother, and to be treated by him in every respect as such—except that the King would not allow Monsieur to become a great personage.

Ordinarily, whenever Monsieur or Madame were unwell, even if their little finger ached, the King visited them at once; and continued his visits if the sickness lasted. But now, Madame had been laid up for six weeks with a tertian fever, for which she would do nothing, because she treated herself in her German fashion, and despised physic and doctors. The King, who, besides the affair of M. le Duc de Chartres, was secretly angered with her, as will presently be seen, had not been to see her, although Monsieur had urged him to do so during those flying visits which he made to Versailles without sleeping there. This was taken by Monsieur, who was ignorant of the private cause of indignation alluded to, for a public mark of extreme disrespect; and being proud and sensitive he was piqued thereby to the last degree.

He had other mental troubles to torment him. For some time past he had had a confessor who, although a Jesuit, kept as tight a hand over him as he could. He was a gentleman of good birth, and of Brittany, by name le Pere du Trevoux. He forbade Monsieur not only certain strange pleasures, but many which he thought he could innocently indulge in as a penance for his past life. He often told him that he had no mind to be damned on his account; and that if he was thought too harsh let another confessor be appointed. He also told him to take great care of himself, as he was old, worn out with debauchery, fat, short-necked, and, according to all appearance, likely to die soon of apoplexy. These were terrible words to a prince the most voluptuous and the most attached to life that had been seen for a long time; who had always passed his days in the most luxurious idleness and who was the most incapable by nature of all serious application, of all serious reading, and of all self-examination. He was afraid of the devil; and he remembered that his former confessor had resigned for similar reasons as this new one was actuated by. He was forced now, therefore, to look a little into himself, and to live in a manner that, for him, might be considered rigid. From time to time he said many prayers; he obeyed his confessor, and rendered an account to him of the conduct he had prescribed in respect to play and many other things, and patiently suffered his confessor's long discourses. He became sad, dejected, and spoke less than usual—that is to say, only about as much as three or four women—so that everybody soon saw this great change. It would have been strange if all these troubles together had not made a great revolution in a man like Monsieur, full-bodied, and a great eater, not only at meals, but all the day.

On Thursday, the 8th of June, he went from Saint Cloud to dine with the King at Marly; and, as was his custom, entered the cabinet as soon as the Council of State went out. He found the King angry with M. de Chartres for neglecting his wife, and allowing her to seek consolation for this neglect in the society of others. M. de Chartres was at that time enamoured of Mademoiselle de Sary, maid of honour to Madame, and carried on his suit in the most open and flagrant manner. The King took this for his theme, and very stiffly reproached Monsieur for the conduct of his son. Monsieur, who needed little to exasperate him, tartly replied, that fathers who had led certain lives had little authority over their children, and little right to blame them. The King, who felt the point of the answer, fell back on the patience of his daughter, and said that at least she ought not to be allowed to see the truth so clearly. But Monsieur was resolved to have his fling, and recalled, in the most aggravating manner, the conduct the King had adopted towards his Queen, with respect to his mistresses, even allowing the latter to accompany him in his journeys—the Queen at his side, and all in the same coach. This last remark drove the King beyond all patience, and he redoubled his reproaches, so that presently both were shouting to each other at the top of their voices. The door of the room in which they wrangled was open, and only covered by a curtain, as was the custom at Marly, and the adjoining room was full of courtiers, waiting to see the King go by to dinner. On the other side was a little salon, devoted to very private purposes, and filled with valets, who could hear distinctly every word of what passed. The attendant without, upon hearing this noise, entered, and told the King how many people were within hearing, and immediately retired. The conversation did not stop, however; it was simply carried on in a lower tone. Monsieur continued his reproaches; said that the King, in marrying his daughter to M. de Chartres, had promised marvels, and had done nothing; that for his part he had wished his son to serve, to keep him out of the way of these intrigues, but that his demands had been vain; that it was no wonder M. de Chartres amused himself, by way of consolation, for the neglect he had been treated with. Monsieur added, that he saw only too plainly the truth of what had been predicted, namely, that he would have all the shame and dishonour of the marriage without ever deriving any profit from it. The King, more and more carried away by anger, replied, that the war would soon oblige him to make some retrenchments, and that he would commence by cutting down the pensions of Monsieur, since he showed himself so little accommodating.

At this moment the King was informed that his dinner was ready, and both he and Monsieur left the room and went to table, Monsieur, all fury, flushed, and with eyes inflamed by anger. His face thus crimsoned induced some ladies who were at table, and some courtiers behind—but more for the purpose of saying something than anything else—to make the remark, that Monsieur, by his appearance, had great need of bleeding. The same thing had been said some time before at Saint Cloud; he was absolutely too full; and, indeed, he had himself admitted that it was true. Even the King, in spite of their squabbles, had more than once pressed him to consent. But Tancrede, his head surgeon, was old, and an unskilful bleeder: he had missed fire once. Monsieur would not be bled by him; and not to vex him was good enough to refuse being bled by another, and to die in consequence.

Upon hearing this observation about bleeding, the King spoke to him again on the subject; and said that he did not know what prevented him from having him at once taken to his room, and bled by force. The dinner passed in the ordinary manner; and Monsieur ate extremely, as he did at all his meals, to say nothing of an abundant supply of chocolate in the morning, and what he swallowed all day in the shape of fruit, pastry, preserves, and every kind of dainties, with which indeed the tables of his cabinets and his pockets were always filled.

Upon rising from the table, the King, in his carriage, alone went to Saint Germain, to visit the King and Queen of England. Other members of the family went there likewise separately; and Monsieur, after going there also, returned to Saint Cloud.

In the evening, after supper, the King was in his cabinet, with Monseigneur and the Princesses, as at Versailles, when a messenger came from Saint Cloud, and asked to see the King in the name of the Duc de Chartres. He was admitted into the cabinet, and said that Monsieur had been taken very ill while at supper; that he had been bled, that he was better, but that an emetic had been given to him. The fact was, Monsieur had supped as usual with the ladies, who were at

Saint Cloud. During the meal, as he poured out a glass of liqueur for Madame de Bouillon, it was perceived that he stammered, and pointed at something with his hand. As it was customary with him sometimes to speak Spanish, some of the ladies asked what he said, others cried aloud. All this was the work of an instant, and immediately afterwards Monsieur fell in a fit of apoplexy upon M. de Chartres, who supported him. He was taken into his room, shaken, moved about, bled considerably, and had strong emetics administered to him, but scarcely any signs of life did he show.

Upon hearing this news, the King, who had been accustomed to fly to visit Monsieur for a mere nothing, went to Madame de Maintenon's, and had her waked up. He passed a quarter of an hour with her, and then, towards midnight, returning to his room, ordered his coach to be got ready, and sent the Marquis de Gesvres to Saint Cloud, to see if Monsieur was worse, in which case he was to return and wake him; and they went quickly to bed. Besides the particular relations in which they were at that time, I think that the King suspected some artifice; that he went in consequence to consult Madame de Maintenon, and preferred sinning against all laws of propriety to running the chance of being duped. Madame de Maintenon did not like Monsieur. She feared him. He paid her very little court, and despite all his timidity and his more than deference, observations escaped him at times, when he was with the King, which marked his disdain of her, and the shame that he felt of public opinion. She was not eager, therefore, to advise the King to go and visit him, still less to commence a journey by night, the loss of rest, and the witnessing a spectacle so sad, and so likely to touch him, and make him make reflections on himself; for she hoped that if things went quietly he might be spared the trouble altogether.

A moment after the King had got into bed, a page came to say that Monsieur was better, and that he had just asked for some Schaffhausen water, which is excellent for apoplexy. An hour and a half later, another messenger came, awakened the King, and told him that the emetic had no effect, and that Monsieur was very ill. At this the King rose and set out at once. On the way he met the Marquis de Gesvres, who was coming to fetch him, and brought similar news. It may be imagined what a hubbub and disorder there was this night at Marly, and what horror at Saint Cloud, that palace of delight! Everybody who was at Marly hastened as he was best able to Saint Cloud. Whoever was first ready started together. Men and women jostled each other, and then threw themselves into the coaches without order and without regard to etiquette. Monseigneur was with Madame la Duchesse. He was so struck by what had occurred, and its resemblance to what he himself had experienced, that he could scarcely stand, and was dragged, almost carried, to the carriage, all trembling.

The King arrived at Saint Cloud before three o'clock in the morning. Monsieur had not had a moment's consciousness since his attack. A ray of intelligence came to him for an instant, while his confessor, Pere du Trevoux, went to say mass, but it returned no more. The most horrible sights have often ridiculous contrasts. When the said confessor came back, he cried, "Monsieur, do you not know your confessor? Do you not know the good little Pere du Trevoux, who is speaking to you?" and thus caused the less afflicted to laugh indecently.

The King appeared much moved; naturally he wept with great facility; he was, therefore, all tears. He had never had cause not to love his brother tenderly; although on bad terms with him for the last two months, these sad moments recalled all his tenderness; perhaps, too, he reproached himself for having hastened death by the scene of the morning. And finally, Monsieur was younger than he by two years, and all his life had enjoyed as good health as he, and better! The King heard mass at Saint Cloud; and, towards eight o'clock in the morning, Monsieur being past all hope, Madame de Maintenon and Madame la Duchesse de Bourgogne persuaded the King to stay no longer, and accordingly returned with him in his carriage to Marly. As he was going out and was showing some sign of affection to M. de Chartres—both weeping very much—that young Prince did not fail to take advantage of the opportunity. "Oh Sire!" he exclaimed, embracing the King's thighs, "what will become of me? I lose Monsieur, and I know that you do not like me." The King, surprised and much touched, embraced him, and said all the tender things he could.

On arriving at Marly, the King went with the Duchesse de Bourgogne to Madame de Maintenon. Three hours after came M. Fagon, who had been ordered not to leave Monsieur until he was dead or better—which could not be but by miracle. The King said, as soon as he saw him: "Well! M. Fagon, my brother is dead?"—"Yes, Sire," said Fagon, "no remedy has taken effect."

The King wept a good deal. He was pressed to dine with Madame de Maintenon; but he would not do so, and had his dinner, as usual, with the ladies. The tears often ran down his cheek, during the meal, which was short. After this, he shut himself up in Madame de Maintenon's rooms until seven o'clock, and then took a turn in his garden. Afterwards he worked with Chamillart and Pontchartrain; and arranged all the funeral ceremonies of Monsieur. He supped an hour before his customary time, and went to bed soon afterwards.

At the departure from St. Cloud of the King, all the crowd assembled there little by little withdrew, so that Monsieur dying, stretched upon a couch in his cabinet, remained exposed to the scullions and the lower officers of the household, the majority of whom, either by affection or interest, were much afflicted. The chief officers and others who lost posts and pensions filled the air with their cries; whilst all the women who were at Saint Cloud, and who lost their consideration and their amusement, ran here and there, crying, with dishevelled hair, like Bacchantes. The Duchesse de la Ferme, who had basely married her daughter to one of Monsieur's minions, named La Carte, came into the cabinet; and, whilst gazing on the Prince, who still palpitated there, exclaimed, giving vent to her profound reflections, "Pardi! Here is a daughter well married!"

"A very important matter!" cried Chatillon, who himself lost everything by this death. "Is this a moment to consider whether your daughter is well married or not?"

Madame, who had never had great affection or great esteem for Monsieur, but who felt her loss and her fall, meanwhile remained in her cabinet, and in the midst of her grief cried out, with all her might, "No convent! Let no one talk of a convent! I will have nothing to do with a convent!" The good Princess had not lost her judgment. She knew that, by her compact of marriage, she had to choose, on becoming a widow, between a convent and the chateau of Montargis. She liked neither alternative; but she had greater fear of the convent than of Montargis; and perhaps thought it would be easier to escape from the latter than the former. She knew she had much to fear from the King, although she did not yet know all, and although he had been properly polite to her, considering the occasion.

Next morning, Friday, M. de Chartres, came to the King, who was still in bed, and who spoke to him in a very friendly manner. He said that the Duke must for the future regard him as his father; that he would take care of his position and his interests; that he had forgotten all the little causes of anger he had had against him; that he hoped the Duke would also forget them; that he begged that the advances of friendship he made, might serve to attach him to him, and make their two hearts belong to one another again. It may easily be conceived how well M. de Chartres answered all this.

CHAPTER XXII

After such a frightful spectacle as had been witnessed, so many tears and so much tenderness, nobody doubted that the three, days which remained of the stay at Marly would be exceedingly sad. But, on the very morrow of the day on which Monsieur died, some ladies of the palace, upon entering the apartments of Madame de Maintenon, where was the King with the Duchesse de Bourgogne, about twelve o'clock, heard her from the chamber where they were, next to hers, singing opera tunes. A little while after, the King, seeing the Duchesse de Bourgogne very sad in a corner of the room, asked Madame de Maintenon, with surprise, why the said Duchess was so melancholy; set himself to work to rouse her; then played with her and some ladies of the palace he had called in to join in the sport. This was not all. Before rising from the dinner table, at a little after two o'clock, and twenty-six hours after the death of Monsieur, Monseigneur the Duc de Bourgogne asked the Duc de Montfort if he would play at brelan.

"At brelan!" cried Montfort, in extreme astonishment; "you cannot mean it! Monsieur is still warm."

"Pardon me," replied the Prince, "I do mean it though. The King does not wish that we should be dull here at Marly, and has ordered me to make everybody play; and, for fear that nobody should dare to begin, to set, myself, the example;" and with this he began to play at brelan; and the salon was soon filled with gaming tables.

Such was the affection of the King: such that of Madame de Maintenon! She felt the loss of Monsieur as a deliverance, and could scarcely restrain her joy; and it was with the greatest difficulty she succeeded in putting on a mournful countenance. She saw that the King was already consoled; nothing could therefore be more becoming than for her to divert him, and nothing suited her better than to bring things back into their usual course, so that there might be no more talk of Monsieur nor of affliction. For propriety of appearance she cared nothing. The thing could not fail, however, to be scandalous; and in whispers was found so. Monseigneur, though he had appeared to like Monsieur, who had given him all sorts of balls and amusements, and shown him every kind of attention and complaisance, went out wolf hunting the very day after his death; and, upon his return, finding play going on in the salons, went without hesitation and played himself like the rest. Monseigneur le Duc de Bourgogne and M. le Duc de Berry only saw Monsieur on public occasions, and therefore could not be much moved by his loss. But Madame la Duchesse was extremely touched by this event. He was her grandfather; and she tenderly loved her mother, who loved Monsieur; and Monsieur had always been very kind to her, and provided all kinds of diversion for her. Although not very loving to anybody, she loved Monsieur; and was much affected not to dare to show her grief, which she indulged a long time in private. What the grief of Madame was has already been seen.

As for M. de Chartres, he was much affected by his loss. The father and son loved each other extremely. Monsieur was a gentle and indulgent parent, who had never constrained his son. But if the Duke's heart was touched, his reason also was. Besides the great assistance it was to him to have a father, brother of the King, that father was, as it were, a barrier between him and the King, under whose hand he now found himself directly placed. His greatness, his consideration, the comfort of his house and his life, would, therefore, depend on him alone. Assiduity, propriety of conduct, a certain manner, and, above all, a very different deportment towards his wife, would now become the price of everything he could expect to obtain from the King. Madame la Duchesse de Chartres, although well treated by Monsieur, was glad to be delivered from him; for he was a barrier betwixt her and the King, that left her at the mercy of her husband. She was charmed to be quit of the duty of following Monsieur to Paris or Saint Cloud, where she found herself, as it were, in a foreign country, with faces which she never saw anywhere else, which did not make her welcome; and where she was exposed to the contempt and humour of Madame, who little spared her. She expected for the future never to leave the Court, and to be not only exempt from paying her court to Monsieur, but that Madame and her husband would for the future be obliged to treat her in quite another manner.

The bulk of the Court regretted Monsieur, for it was he who set all pleasure a-going; and when he left it, life and merriment seemed to have disappeared likewise. Setting aside his obstinacy with regard to the Princes, he loved the order of rank; preferences, and distinctions: he caused them to be observed as much as possible, and himself set the example. He loved great people; and was so affable and polite, that crowds came to him. The difference which he knew how to make, and which he never failed to make, between every one according to his position, contributed greatly to his popularity. In his receptions, by his greater or less, or more neglectful attention, and by his words, he always marked in a flattering manner the differences made by birth and dignity, by age and merit, and by profession; and all this with a dignity natural to him, and a constant facility which he had acquired. His familiarity obliged, and yet no rash people ever ventured to take advantage of it. He visited or sent exactly when it was proper; and under his roof he allowed a complete liberty, without injury to the respect shown him, or to a perfect court air.

He had learned from the Queen his mother, and well remembered this art. The crowd, therefore, constantly flocked towards the Palais Royal.

At Saint Cloud, where all his numerous household used to assemble, there were many ladies who, to speak the truth, would scarcely have been received elsewhere, but many also of a higher set, and great store of gamblers. The pleasures of all kinds of games, and the singular beauty of the place, where a thousand caleches were always ready to whirl even the most lazy ladies through the walks, soft music and good cheer, made it a palace of delight, grace, and magnificence.

All this without any assistance from Madame, who dined and supped with the ladies and Monsieur, rode out sometimes in a caleche with one of them, often sulked with the company, made herself feared for her harsh and surly temper—frequently even for her words; and passed her days in a little cabinet she had chosen, where the windows were ten feet from the ground, gazing perpetually on the portraits of Paladins and other German princes, with which she had tapestried the walls; and writing every day with her own hand whole volumes of letters, of which she always kept autograph copies. Monsieur had never been able to bend her to a more human way of life; and lived decently with her, without caring for her person in any way.

For his part, Monsieur, who had very gallantly won the battle of Cassel, and who had always shown courage in the sieges where he had served, had only the bad qualities that distinguish women. With more knowledge of the world than wit, with no reading, though he had a vast and exact acquaintance with noble houses, their births and marriages, he was good for nothing. Nobody was so flabby in body and mind, no one so weak, so timid, so open to deception, so led by the nose, so despised by his favourites, often so roughly treated by them. He was quarrelsome in small matters, incapable of keeping any secret, suspicious, mistrustful; fond of spreading reports in his Court to make mischief, to learn what was really going on or just to amuse himself: he fetched and carried from one to the other. With so many defects, unrelated to any virtue, he had such an abominable taste, that his gifts and the fortunes that he gave to those he took into favour had rendered him publicly scandalous. He neither respected times nor places. His minions, who owed him everything, sometimes treated him most insolently; and he had often much to do to appease horrible jealousies. He lived in continual hot water with his favourites, to say nothing of the quarrels of that troop of ladies of a very decided character—many of whom were very malicious, and, most, more than malicious—with whom Monsieur used to divert himself, entering into all their wretched squabbles.

The Chevaliers de Lorraine and Chatillon had both made a large fortune by their good looks, with which he was more smitten than with those of any other of his favourites. Chatillon, who had neither head, nor sense, nor wit, got on in this way, and acquired fortune. The other behaved like a Guisard, who blushes at nothing provided he succeeds; and governed Monsieur with a high hand all his life, was overwhelmed with money and benefices, did what he liked for his family, lived always publicly as the master with Monsieur; and as he had, with the pride of the Guises, their art and cleverness, he contrived to get between the King and Monsieur, to be dealt with gingerly, if not feared by both, and was almost as important a man with the one as with the other. He had the finest apartments in the Palais Royal and Saint Cloud, and a pension of ten thousand crowns. He remained in his apartments after the death of Monsieur, but would not from pride continue to receive the pension, which from pride was offered him. Although it would have been difficult to be more timid and submissive than was Monsieur with the King—for he flattered both his ministers and his mistresses—he, nevertheless, mingled with his respectful demeanour the demeanour of a brother, and the free and easy ways of one. In private, he was yet more unconstrained; always taking an armed chair, and never waiting until the King told him to sit. In the Cabinet, after the King appeared, no other Prince sat besides him, not even Monseigneur. But in what regarded his service, and his manner of approaching and leaving the King, no private person could behave with more respect; and he naturally did everything with grace and dignity. He never, however, was able to bend to Madame de Maintenon completely, nor avoid making small attacks on her to the King, nor avoid satirising her pretty broadly in person. It was not her success that annoyed him; but simply the idea that La Scarron had become his sister-in-law; this was insupportable to him. Monsieur was extremely vain, but not haughty, very sensitive, and a great stickler for what was due to him. Upon one occasion he complained to the King that M. le

Duc had for some time neglected to attend upon him, as he was bound, and had boasted that he would not do it. The King replied, that it was not a thing to be angry about, that he ought to seek an opportunity to be served by M. le Duc, and if he would not, to affront him. Accordingly, one morning at Marly, as he was dressing, seeing M. le Duc walking in the garden, Monsieur opened the window and called to him. Monsieur le Duc came up, and entered the room. Then, while one remark was leading to another, Monsieur slipped off his dressing-gown, and then his shirt. A valet de chambre standing by, at once slipped a clean shirt into the hands of M. le Duc, who, caught thus in a trap, was compelled to offer the garment to Monsieur, as it was his duty to do. As soon as Monsieur had received it, he burst out laughing, and said—"Good-bye, cousin, go away. I do not want to delay you longer." M. le Duc felt the point of this, and went away very angry, and continued so in consequence of the high tone Monsieur afterwards kept up on the subject.

Monsieur was a little round-bellied man, who wore such high-heeled shoes that he seemed mounted always upon stilts; was always decked out like a woman, covered everywhere with rings, bracelets, jewels; with a long black wig, powdered, and curled in front; with ribbons wherever he could put them; steeped in perfumes, and in fine a model of cleanliness. He was accused of putting on an imperceptible touch of rouge. He had a long nose, good eyes and mouth, a full but very long face. All his portraits resembled him. I was piqued to see that his features recalled those of Louis XIII., to whom; except in matters of courage, he was so completely dissimilar.

On Saturday, the 11th of June, the Court returned to Versailles. On arriving there the King went to visit Madame and her son and daughter-in- law separately. Madame, very much troubled by reflection on her position with regard to the King, had sent the Duchesse de Ventadour to Madame de Maintenon. The latter replied to the message only in general terms; said she would visit Madame after dinner, and requested that the Duchess might be present at the interview. It was Sunday, the morning after the return from Marly. After the first compliments, every one went out except Madame de Ventadour. Then Madame requested Madame de Maintenon to sit down; and she must have felt her position keenly to bring her to this.

She began the conversation by complaining of the indifference with which the King had treated her during her illness. Madame de Maintenon allowed her to talk on; and when she had finished, said that the King had commanded her to say that their common loss effaced all the past, provided that he had reason to be better satisfied for the future, not only as regarded M. le Duc de Chartres, but other matters also. Upon this Madame exclaimed and protested that, except in as far as regarded her son, she had never given cause for displeasure; and went on alternating complaints and justifications. Precisely at the point when she was most emphatic, Madame de Maintenon drew forth a letter from her pocket and asked if the handwriting was known to her. It was a letter from Madame to the Duchess of Hanover, in which she said, after giving news of the Court, that no one knew what to say of the intercourse between the King and Madame de Maintenon, whether it was that of marriage or of concubinage; and then, touching upon other matters, launched out upon the misery of the realm: that, she said, was too great to be relieved.

This letter had been opened at the post—as almost all letters were at that time, and are indeed still—and sent to the King. It may be imagined that this was a thunderstroke to Madame: it nearly killed her. She burst into tears; and Madame de Maintenon very quietly and demurely began to represent to her the contents of the letter in all its parts, especially as it was addressed to a foreign country. Madame de Ventadour interposed with some twaddle, to give Madame time to breathe and recover sufficiently to say something. The best excuse was the admission of what could not be denied, with supplications for pardon, expressions of repentance, prayers, promises. But Madame de Maintenon had not finished yet. Having got rid of the commission she had been charged with by the King, she next turned to her own business: she asked Madame how it was, that after being so friendly with her a long time ago, she had suddenly ceased to bestow any regard upon her, and had continued to treat her with coldness ever since. At this, Madame thinking herself quite safe, said that the coldness was on the part of Madame de Maintenon, who had all on a sudden discontinued the friendly intercourse which formerly existed between them. As before, Madame de Maintenon allowed Madame to talk her fill before she replied. She then said she was about to divulge a secret which had never escaped her mouth, although she had for ten years been at liberty to tell it; and she forthwith related a thousand most offensive things which had been uttered against her by Madame to the late Madame la Dauphine. This latter, falling out with Madame, had related all these things to Madame de Maintenon, who now brought them forward triumphantly.

At this new blow, Madame was thunderstruck, and stood like a statue. There was nothing for it but to behave as before—that is to say, shed tears, cry, ask pardon, humble herself, and beg for mercy. Madame de Maintenon triumphed coldly over her for a long time,—allowing her to excite herself in talking, and weeping, and taking her hands, which she did with increasing energy and humility. This was a terrible humiliation for such a haughty German. Madame de Maintenon at last gave way, as she had always meant to do after having satiated her vengeance. They embraced, promised forgetfulness on both sides, and a new friendship from that time. The King, who was not ignorant of what had occurred, took back Madame into favour. She went neither to a convent nor to Montargis, but was allowed to remain in Paris, and her pension was augmented. As for M. le Duc de Chartres, he was prodigiously well treated. The King gave him all the pensions Monsieur had enjoyed, besides allowing him to retain his own; so that he had one million eight hundred thousand livres a year; added to the Palais Royal, Saint Cloud, and other mansions. He had a Swiss guard, which none but the sons of France had ever had before; in fact he retained all the privileges his father had enjoyed, and he took the name of Duc d'Orleans. The pensions of Madame de Chartres were augmented. All these honours so great and so unheard of bestowed on M. de Chartres, and an income of a hundred thousand crowns more than his father, were due solely to the quarrel which had recently taken place between Monsieur and the King, as to the marriage M. de Chartres had made. People accustom themselves to everything, but this prodigious good fortune infinitely surprised everybody. The Princes of the blood were extremely mortified. To console them, the King immediately gave to M. le Prince all the advantages of a first Prince of the blood, and added ten thousand crowns to his pension.

Madame wore deep mourning for forty days, after which she threw it almost entirely aside, with the King's permission. He did not like to see such sad-looking things before his eyes every day. Madame went about in public, and with the Court, in her half-mourning, under pretence that being with the King, and living under his roof, she was of the family. But her conduct was not the less thought strange in spite of this excuse. During the winter, as the King could not well go to the theatre, the theatre cane to him, in the apartments of Madame de Maintenon, where comedies with music were played. The King wore mourning for six months, and paid all the expenses of the superb funeral which took place on the 13th of June.

While upon the subject of Monsieur, I will relate an anecdote known to but few people, concerning the death of his first wife, Henriette d'Angleterre, whom nobody doubts was poisoned. Her gallantries made Monsieur jealous; and his tastes made her furious. His favourites, whom she hated, did all in their power to sow discord between them, in order to dispose of Monsieur at their will. The Chevalier de Lorraine, then in the prime of his first youth (having been born in 1643) completely ruled over Monsieur, and made Madame feel that he had this power. She, charming and young, could not suffer this, and complained to the King, so that M. de Lorraine was exiled. When Monsieur heard this, he swooned, then melted into tears, and throwing himself at the feet of the King, implored him to recall M. de Lorraine. But his prayers were useless, and, rushing away in fury, he retired into the country and remained there until, ashamed of a thing so publicly disgraceful, he returned to Paris and lived with Madame as before.

Although M. de Lorraine was banished, two of his intimate friends, D'Effiat and the Count de Beuvron, remained in the household of Monsieur. The absence of M. de Lorraine nipped all their hopes of success, and made them fear that some other favourite might arrive from whom they could hope for nothing. They saw no chance that M. de Lorraine's exile would speedily terminate; for Madame (Henriette d'Angleterre) was in greater favour with the King than ever, and had just been sent by him into England on a mysterious errand in which she had perfectly succeeded. She returned triumphant and very well in health. This gave the last blow to the hopes of D'Effiat and Beuvron, as to the return of M. de Lorraine, who had gone to Italy to try to get rid of his vexation. I know not which of the three thought of it first, but the Chevalier de Lorraine sent a sure and rapid poison to his two friends by a messenger who did not probably know what he carried.

At Saint Cloud, Madame was in the habit of taking a glass of endive- water, at about seven o'clock in the evening. A servant of hers used to make it, and then put it away in a cupboard where there was some ordinary water for the use of Madame if she found the other too bitter. The cupboard was in an antechamber which served as the public passage by which the apartments of Madame were reached. D'Effiat took notice of all these things, and on the 29th of June, 1670, he went to the ante-chamber; saw that he was unobserved and that nobody was near, and threw the poison into the endive-water; then hearing some one approaching, he seized the jug of common water and feigned to be putting it back in its place just as the servant, before alluded to, entered and asked him sharply what he was doing in that cupboard. D'Effiat, without losing countenance, asked his pardon, and said, that being thirsty, and knowing there was some water in the cupboard, he could not resist drinking. The servant grumbled; and D'Effiat, trying to appease him, entered the apartments of Madame, like the other courtiers, and began talking without the slightest emotion.

What followed an hour afterwards does not belong to my subject, and has made only too much stir throughout all Europe. Madame died on the morrow, June 30, at three o'clock in the morning; and the King was profoundly prostrated with grief. Apparently during the day, some indications showed him that Purnon, chief steward of Madame, was in the secret of her decease. Purnon was brought before him privately, and was threatened with instant death, unless he disclosed all; full pardon being on the contrary promised him if he did. Purnon, thus pressed, admitted that Madame had been poisoned, and under the circumstance I have just related. "And my brother," said the King, "did he know of this?"— "No, Sire, not one of us was stupid enough to tell him; he has no secrecy, he would have betrayed us." On hearing this answer the King uttered a great "ah!" like a man oppressed, who suddenly breathes again.

Purnon was immediately set at liberty; and years afterwards related this narrative to M. Joly de Fleury, procureur-general of the Parliament, by which magistrate it was related to me. From this same magistrate I learned that, a few days before the second marriage of Monsieur, the King took Madame aside and told her that circumstance, assuring her that he was too honest a man to wish her to marry his brother, if that brother could be capable of such a crime. Madame profited by what she heard. Purnon remained in her service; but after a time she pretended to find faults in him, and made him resign; he sold his post accordingly, towards the end of 1674, to Maurel de Vaulonne, and quitted her service.

CHAPTER XXIII

A the breaking out of the war in Italy this year Segur bought the government of the Foix country from Tallard, one of the generals called away to serve in that war. Segur had been in his youth a very handsome fellow; he was at that time in the Black Musketeers, and this company was always quartered at Nemours while the Court was at Fontainebleau. Segur played very well upon the lute; but found life dull, nevertheless, at Nemours, made the acquaintance of the Abbesse de la Joye, a place hard by, and charmed her ears and eyes so much that she became with child by him. After some months the Abbess pleaded illness, left the convent, and set out for the waters, as she said. Putting off her journey too long, she was obliged to stop a night at Fontainebleau; and in consequence of the Court being there, could find no accommodation, except in a wretched little inn already full of company. She had delayed so long that the pangs of labour seized her in the night, and the cries she uttered brought all the house to her assistance. She was delivered of a child then and there; and the next morning this fact was the talk of the town.

The Duc de Saint Aignan, one of the first of the courtiers who learned it, went straight to the King, who was brisk and free enough in those days, and related to him what had occurred; the King laughed heartily at the poor Abbess, who, while trying to hide her shame, had come into the very midst of the Court. Nobody knew then that her abbey was only four leagues distant, but everybody learned it soon, and the Duc de Saint Aignan among the first.

When he returned to his house, he found long faces on every side. His servants made signs one to another, but nobody said a word. He perceived this, and asked what was the matter; but, for some time, no one dared to reply. At last a valet-de-chambre grew bold enough to say to Saint Aignan, that the Abbess, whose adventure had afforded so much mirth, was his own daughter; and that, after he had gone to the King, she had sent for assistance, in order to get out of the place where she was staying.

It was now the Duke's turn to be confused. After having made the King and all the Court laugh at this adventure, he became himself the laughing-stock of everybody. He bore the affair as well as he could; carried away the Abbess and her baggage; and, as the scandal was public, made her send in her resignation and hide herself in another convent, where she lived more than forty years.

That worthy man, Saint-Herem, died this year at his house in Auvergne, to which he had retired. Everybody liked him; and M. de Rochefoucauld had reproached the King for not making him Chevalier of the Order. The King had confounded him with Courtine, his brother-in-law, for they had married two sisters; but when put right had not given the favour.

Madame de Saint-Herem was the most singular creature in the world, not only in face but in manners. She half boiled her thigh one day in the Seine, near Fontainebleau, where she was bathing. The river was too cold; she wished to warm it, and had a quantity of water heated and thrown into the stream just above her. The water reaching her before it could grow cold, scalded her so much that she was forced to keep her bed.

When it thundered, she used to squat herself under a couch and make all her servants lie above, one upon the other, so that if the thunderbolt fell, it might have its effect upon them before penetrating to her. She had ruined herself and her husband, though they were rich, through sheer imbecility; and it is incredible the amount of money she spent in her absurdities.

The best adventure which happened to her, among a thousand others, was at her house in the Place Royale, where she was one day attacked by a madman, who, finding her alone in her chamber, was very enterprising. The good lady, hideous at eighteen, but who was at this time eighty and a widow, cried aloud as well as she could. Her servants heard her at last, ran to her assistance, and found her all disordered, struggling in the hands of this raging madman. The man was found to be really out of his senses when brought before the tribunal, and the story amused everybody.

The health of the King of England (James II.), which had for some time been very languishing, grew weaker towards the middle of August of this year, and by the 8th of September completely gave way. There was no longer any hope. The King, Madame de Maintenon, and all the royal persons, visited him often. He received the last sacrament with a piety in keeping with his past life, and his death was expected every instant. In this conjuncture the King made a resolve more worthy of Louis XII., or Francis I., than of his own wisdom. On Tuesday, the 13th of September, he went from Marly to Saint Germain. The King of England was so ill that when the King was announced to him he scarcely opened his eyes for an instant. The King told him that he might die in peace respecting the Prince of Wales, whom he would recognise as King of England, Scotland, and Ireland.

The few English who were there threw themselves upon their knees, but the King of England gave no signs of life. The gratitude of the Prince of Wales and of his mother, when they heard what the King had said, may be imagined. Returned to Marly, the King repeated to all the Court what he had said. Nothing was heard but praises and applause.

Yet reflections did not fail to be made promptly, if not publicly. It was seen, that to recognise the Prince of Wales was to act in direct opposition to the recognition of the Prince of Orange as King of England, that the King had declared at the Peace of Ryswick. It was to wound the Prince of Orange in the tenderest point, and to invite England and Holland to become allies of the Emperor against France. As for the Prince of Wales, this recognition was no solid advantage to him, but was calculated to make the party opposed to him in England only more bitter and vigilant in their opposition.

The King of England, in the few intervals of intelligence he had, appeared much impressed by what the King had done. He died about three o'clock in the afternoon of the 16th September of this year, 1701. He had requested that there might be no display at his funeral, and his wish was faithfully observed. He was buried on the Saturday, at seven o'clock in the evening, in the church of the English Benedictines at Paris, Rue St. Jacques, without pomp, and attended by but few mourners. His body rests in the chapel, like that of the simplest private person, until the time, apparently very distant, when it shall be transported to England. His heart is at the Filles de Sainte Marie, of Chaillot.

Immediately afterwards, the Prince of Wales was received by the King as King of England, with all the formalities and state with which his father before him had been received. Soon afterwards he was recognised by the new King of Spain.

The Count of Manchester, English ambassador in France, ceased to appear at Versailles after this recognition of the Prince of Wales by the King, and immediately quitted his post and left the country without any leave- taking. King William heard, while in Holland, of the death of James II. and of this recognition. He was at table with some German princes and other lords when the news arrived; did not utter a word, except to announce the death; but blushed, pulled down his hat, and could not keep his countenance. He sent orders to London, to drive out Poussin, acting as French ambassador, immediately; and Poussin directly crossed the sea and arrived at Calais.

This event was itself followed by the signing of the great treaty of alliance, offensive and defensive, against France and Spain, by Austria, England, and Holland; in which they afterwards succeeded in engaging other powers, which compelled the King to increase the number of his troops.

Just after the return of the Court from Fontainebleau, a strange scene happened at St. Maur, in a pretty house there which M. le Duc possessed. He was at this house one night with five or six intimate friends, whom he had invited to pass the night there. One of these friends was the Comte de Fiesque. At table, and before the wine had begun to circulate, a dispute upon some historical point arose between him and M. le Duc. The Comte de Fiesque, who had some intellect and learning, strongly sustained his opinion. M. le Duc sustained his; and for want of better reasons, threw a plate at the head of Fiesque, drove him from the table and out of the house. So sudden and strange a scene frightened the guests. The Comte de Fiesque, who had gone to M. le Duc's house with the intention of passing the night there, had not retained a carriage, went to ask shelter of the cure, and got back to Paris the next day as early in the morning as he could. It may be imagined that the rest of the supper and of the evening was terribly dull. M. le Duc remained fuming (perhaps against himself, but without saying so), and could not be induced to apologise for the affront. It made a great stir in society, and things remained thus several months. After a while, friends mixed themselves in the matter; M. le Duc, completely himself again, made all the advances towards a reconciliation. The Comte de Fiesque received them, and the reconciliation took place. The most surprising thing is, that after this they continued on as good terms as though nothing had passed between them.

The year 1702 commenced with balls at Versailles, many of which were masquerades. Madame du Maine gave several in her chamber, always keeping her bed because she was in the family-way; which made rather a singular spectacle. There were several balls at Marly, but the majority were not masquerades. The King often witnessed, but in strict privacy, and always in the apartments of Madame de Maintenon, sacred dramas such as "Absalon," "Athalie," &c. Madame la Duchesse de Bourgogne, M. le Duc d'Orleans, the Comte and Comtesse d'Anjou, the young Comte de Noailles, Mademoiselle de Melun, urged by the Noailles, played the principal characters in very magnificent stage dresses. Baron, the excellent old actor, instructed them and played with them. M. de Noailles and his clever wife were the inventors and promoters of these interior pleasures, for the purpose of intruding themselves more and more into the society of the King, in support of the alliance of Madame de Maintenon.

Only forty spectators were admitted to the representations. Madame was sometimes invited by the King, because she liked plays. This favour was much sought after. Madame de Maintenon wished to show that she had forgotten the past.

Longepierre had written a very singular piece called "Electra," which was played on a magnificent stage erected in Madame de Conti's house, and all the Court flocked several times to see it. This piece was without love, but full of other passions and of most interesting situations. I think it had been written in the hopes that the King would go and see it. But he contented himself with hearing it talked about, and the representation was confined to the Hotel de Conti. Longepierre would not allow it to be given elsewhere. He was an intriguing fellow of much wit, gentle, insinuating, and who, under a tranquillity and indifference and a very deceitful philosophy, thrust himself everywhere, and meddled with everything in order to make his fortune. He succeeded in intruding himself into favour with the Duc d'Orleans, but behaved so badly that he was driven away.

The death of the Abbe de Vatteville occurred at the commencement of this year, and made some noise, on account of the prodigies of the Abbe's life. This Vatteville was the younger son of a Franche-Comte family; early in life he joined the Order of the Chartreux monks, and was ordained priest. He had much intellect, but was of an impetuous spirit, and soon began to chafe under the yoke of a religious life. He determined, therefore, to set himself free from it, and procured some secular habits, pistols, and a horse. Just as he was about to escape over the walls of the monastery by means of a ladder, the prior entered his cell.

Vatteville made no to-do, but at once drew a pistol, shot the prior dead, and effected his escape.

Two or three days afterwards, travelling over the country and avoiding as much as possible the frequented places, he arrived at a wretched roadside inn, and asked what there was in the house. The landlord replied—"A leg of mutton and a capon."—"Good!" replied our unfrocked monk; "put them down to roast."

The landlord replied that they were too much for a single person, and that he had nothing else for the whole house. The monk upon this flew into a passion, and declared that the least the landlord could do was to give him what he would pay for; and that he had sufficient appetite to eat both leg of mutton and capon. They were accordingly put down to the fire, the landlord not daring to say another word. While they were cooking, a traveller on horseback arrived at the inn, and learning that they were for one person, was much astonished. He offered to pay his share to be allowed to dine off them with the stranger who had ordered this dinner; but the landlord told him he was afraid the gentleman would not consent to the arrangement. Thereupon the traveller went upstairs, and civilly asked Vatteville if he might dine with him on paying half of the expense. Vatteville would not consent, and a dispute soon arose between the two; to be brief, the monk served this traveller as he had served the prior, killed him with a pistol shot. After this he went downstairs tranquilly, and in the midst of the fright of the landlord and of the whole house, had the leg of mutton and capon served up to him, picked both to the very bone, paid his score, remounted his horse, and went his way.

Not knowing what course to take, he went to Turkey, and in order to succeed there, had himself circumcised, put on the turban, and entered into the militia. His blasphemy advanced him, his talents and his colour distinguished him; he became Bacha, and the confidential man in the Morea, where the Turks were making war against the Venetians. He determined to make use of this position in order to advance his own interests, and entering into communication with the generalissimo of the Republic, promised to betray into his hands several secret places belonging to the Turks, but on certain conditions. These were, absolution from the Pope for all crimes of his life, his murders and his apostasy included; security against the Chartreux and against being placed in any other Order; full restitution of his civil rights, and liberty to exercise his profession of priest with the right of possessing all benefices of every kind. The Venetians thought the bargain too good to be refused, and the Pope, in the interest of the Church, accorded all the demands of the Bacha. When Vatteville was quite assured that his conditions would be complied with, he took his measures so well that he executed perfectly all he had undertaken. Immediately after he threw himself into the Venetian army, and passed into Italy. He was well received at Rome by the Pope, and returned to his family in Franche- Comte, and amused himself by braving the Chartreux.

At the first conquest of the Franche-Comte, he intrigued so well with the Queen-mother and the ministry, that he was promised the Archbishopric of Besancon; but the Pope cried out against this on account of his murders, circumcision, and apostasy. The King sided with the Pope, and Vatteville was obliged to be contented with the abbey of Baume, another good abbey in Picardy, and divers other advantages.

Except when he came to the Court, where he was always received with great distinction, he remained at his abbey of Baume, living there like a grand seigneur, keeping a fine pack of hounds, a good table, entertaining jovial company, keeping mistresses very freely; tyrannising over his tenants and his neighbours in the most absolute manner. The intendants gave way to him, and by express orders of the Court allowed him to act much as he pleased, even with the taxes, which he regulated at his will, and in his conduct was oftentimes very violent. With these manners and this bearing, which caused him to be both feared and respected, he would often amuse himself by going to see the Chartreux, in order to plume himself on having quitted their frock. He played much at hombre, and frequently gained 'codille' (a term of the game), so that the name of the Abbe Codille was given to him. He lived in this manner always with the same licence and in the same consideration, until nearly ninety years of age.

CHAPTER XXIV

The changes which took place in the army after the Peace of Ryswick, were very great and very strange. The excellence of the regiments, the merits of the officers, those who commanded, all were forgotten by Barbezieux, young and impetuous, whom the King allowed to act as he liked. My regiment was disbanded, and my company was incorporated with that of Count d'Uzes, brother-in-law of Duras, who looked well after the interests of his relative. I was thus deprived of command, without regiment, without company, and the only opportunity offered me was to serve in a regiment commanded by Saint Morris, where I should have been, as it were, at the lowest step of the ladder, with my whole military career to begin over again.

I had served at the head of my regiment during four campaigns, with applause and reputation, I am bold enough to say it. I thought therefore I was entitled to better treatment than this. Promotions were made; five officers, all my juniors, were placed over my head. I resolved then to leave the service, but not to take a rash step. I consulted first with several friends before sending in my resignation. All whom I consulted advised me to quit the service, but for a long time I could not resolve to do so. Nearly three months passed, during which I suffered cruel anguish of mind from my irresolution. I knew that if I left the army I should be certain to incur the anger of the King, and I do not hesitate to say that this was not a matter of indifference to me. The King was always annoyed when anybody ceased to serve; he called it "quitting him;" and made his anger felt for a long time. At last, however, I determined on my course of action.

I wrote a short letter to the King, in which, without making any complaints, I said that as my health was not good (it had given me some trouble on different occasions) I begged to be allowed to quit his service, and said that I hoped I should be permitted to console myself for leaving the army by assiduously attending upon him at the Court: After despatching this letter I went away immediately to Paris.

I learnt afterwards from my friends, that upon receiving my letter the King called Chamillart to him, and said with emotion: "Well! Monsieur, here is another man who quits us!—" and he read my letter word for word. I did not learn that anything else escaped him.

As for me, I did not return to Versailles for a whole week, or see the King again until Easter Monday. After his supper that evening, and when about to undress himself, he paid me a distinction, a mere trifle I admit, and which I should be ashamed to mention if it did not under the circumstances serve as a characteristic of him.

Although the place he undressed in was very well illuminated, the chaplain at the evening prayers there held in his hand a lighted candle, which he gave afterwards to the chief valet-de-chambre, who carried it before the King until he reached his arm-chair, and then handed it to whomever the King ordered him to give it to. On this evening the King, glancing all around him, cast his eye upon me, and told the valet to give the candle to me. It was an honour which he bestowed sometimes upon one, sometimes upon another, according to his whim, but which, by his manner of bestowing it, was always coveted, as a great distinction. My surprise may be imagined when I heard myself named aloud for this office, not only on this but on many other occasions. It was not that there was any lack of people of consideration to hold the candle; but the King was sufficiently piqued by my retirement not to wish everybody to see that he was so.

For three years he failed not to make me feel to what extent he was angry with me. He spoke to me no longer; he scarcely bestowed a glance upon me, and never once alluded to my letter. To show that his annoyance did not extend to my wife, but that it was solely and wholly directed against me, he bestowed, about eight months after, several marks of favour upon Madame de Saint-Simon. She was continually invited to the suppers at Trianon—an honour which had never before been granted her. I only laughed at this. Madame de Saint-Simon was not invited to Marly; because the husbands always, by right, accompanied their wives there, apartments being given for both. At Trianon it was different. Nobody was allowed to sleep there except those absolutely in attendance. The King wished, therefore, the better to mark by this distinction that the exclusion was intended for me alone, and that my wife had no part in it.

Notwithstanding this; I persevered in my ordinary assiduity, without ever asking to be invited to Marly, and lived agreeably with my wife and my friends. I have thought it best to finish with this subject at once—now I must go back to my starting point.

At the commencement of this year (1702) it seemed as though the flatterers of the King foresaw that the prosperity of his reign was at an end, and that henceforth they would only have to praise him for his constancy. The great number of medals that had been struck on all occasions—the most ordinary not having been forgotten—were collected, engraved, and destined for a medallic history. The Abbes Tallemant, Toureil, and Dacier, three learned members of the Academy, were charged with the explanation to be placed opposite each of these medals, in a large volume of the most magnificent impression of the Louvre. As the history commenced at the death of Louis XIII., his medal was placed at the head of the book, and thus it became necessary to say something of him in the preface.

As it was known that I had a correct knowledge of Louis XIII., I was asked to write that portion of the preface which related to him. I consented to this, but on condition that I should be spared the ridicule of it in society, and that the matter should be faithfully kept secret. I wrote my theme then, which cost me little more than a morning, being of small extent. I had the fate of authors: my writing was praised, and appeared to answer all expectations. I congratulated myself, delighted at having devoted two or three hours to a grateful duty—for so I considered it.

But when my essay was examined, the three gentlemen above-named were affrighted. There are truths the unstudied simplicity of which emits a lustre which obscures all the results of an eloquence which exaggerates or extenuates; Louis XIII. furnished such proofs in abundance. I had contented myself by showing them forth; but this picture tarnished those which followed— so at least it appeared to those who had gilded the latter. They applied themselves, therefore, to cut out, or weaken, everything that might, by comparison, obscure their hero. But as they found at last that it was not me they had to correct, but the thing itself, they gave up the task altogether, threw aside my writing, and printed the history without any notice whatever of Louis XIII. under his portrait—except to note that his death caused his son to ascend the throne.

Reflections upon this kind of iniquity would carry me too far.

In the early part of this year (1702), King William (of England), worn out before his time with labours and business, in which he had been engaged all his life, and which he had carried on with a capacity, an address, a superiority of genius that acquired for him supreme authority in Holland, the crown of England, the confidence, and, to speak the truth, the complete dictatorship of all Europe—except France;—King William, I say, had fallen into a wasting of strength and of health which, without attacking or diminishing his intellect, or causing him to relax the infinite labours of his cabinet, was accompanied by a deficiency of breath, which aggravated the asthma he had had for several years. He felt his condition, and his powerful genius did not disavow it. Under forged names he consulted the most eminent physicians of Europe, among others, Fagon; who, having to do, as he thought, with a cure, replied in all sincerity, and with out dissimulation, that he must prepare for a speedy death. His illness increasing, William consulted Fagon, anew, but this time openly. The physician recognised the malady of the cure—he did not change his opinion, but expressed it in a less decided manner, and prescribed with much feeling the remedies most likely if not to cure, at least to prolong. These remedies were followed and gave relief; but at last the time had arrived when William was to feel that the greatest men finish like the humblest and to see the nothingness of what the world calls great destinies.

He rode out as often as he could; but no longer having the strength to hold himself on horseback, received a fall, which hastened his end by the shock it gave him. He occupied himself with religion as little as he had all his life. He ordered everything, and spoke to his ministers and his familiars with a surprising tranquillity, which did not abandon him until the last moment. Although crushed with pain, he had the satisfaction of thinking that he had consummated a great alliance, which would last after his death, and that it would strike the great blow against France, which he had projected. This thought, which flattered him even in the hour of death, stood in place of all other consolation,—a consolation frivolous and cruelly deceitful, which left him soon the prey to eternal truths! For two days he was sustained by strong waters and spirituous liquors. His last nourishment was a cup of chocolate. He died the 19th March, 1702, at ten o'clock in the morning.

The Princess Anne, his sister-in-law, wife of Prince George of Denmark, was at the same time proclaimed queen. A few days after, she declared her husband Grand Admiral and Commander-in-Chief (generalissimo), recalled the Earl of Rochester, her maternal uncle, and the Earl of Sunderland, and sent the Count of Marlborough, afterwards so well known, to Holland to follow out there all the plans of his predecessor.

The King did not learn this death until the Saturday morning following, by a courier from Calais. A boat had escaped, in spite of the vigilance which had closed the ports. The King was silent upon the news, except to Monseigneur and to Madame de Maintenon. On the next day confirmation of the intelligence arrived from all parts. The King no longer made a secret of it, but spoke little on the subject, and affected much indifference respecting it. With the recollection of all the indecent follies committed in Paris during the last war, when it was believed that William had been killed at the battle of the Boyne in Ireland, the necessary precautions against falling into the same error were taken by the King's orders.

The King simply declared that he would not wear mourning, and prohibited the Duc de Bouillon, the Marechal de Duras and the Marechal de Lorges, who were all related to William, from doing so—an act probably without example. Nearly all England and the United Provinces mourned the loss of William. Some good republicans alone breathed again with joy in secret, at having recovered their liberty. The grand alliance was very sensibly touched by this loss, but found itself so well cemented, that the spirit of William continued to animate it; and Heinsius, his confidant, perpetuated it, and inspired all the chiefs of the republic, their allies and their generals, with it, so that it scarcely appeared that William was no more.

I have related, in its proper place, all that happened to Catinat in Italy, when the schemes of Tesse and M. de Vaudemont caused him to be dismissed from the command of the army. After the signing of the alliance against France by the Emperor, England, and Holland, the war took a more extended field. It became necessary to send an army to the Rhine. There was nothing for it but to have recourse to Catinat.

Since his return from Italy, he had almost always lived at his little house of Saint Gratien, beyond Saint Denis, where he bore with wisdom the injury that had been done him and the neglect he had experienced upon his return, surrounded by his family and a small number of friends. Chamillart one day sent for him, saying that he had the King's order to talk with him. Catinat went accordingly to Chamillart, from whom he learned that he was destined for the Rhine; he refused the command, and only accepted it after a long dispute, by the necessity of obedience.

On the morrow, the 11th of March, the King called Catinat into his cabinet. The conversation was amiable on the part of the King, serious and respectful on the part of Catinat. The King, who perceived this, wished to make him speak about Italy, and pressed him to explain what had really passed there. Catinat excused himself, saying that everything belonged to the past, and that it was useless now to rake up matters which would give him a bad opinion of the people who served him, and nourish eternal enmity. The King admired the sagacity and virtue of Catinat, but, wishing to sound the depths of certain things, and discover who was really to blame, pressed him more and more to speak out; mentioning certain things which Catinat had not rendered an account of, and others he had been silent upon, all of which had come to him from other sources.

Catinat, who, by his conversation of the previous evening with Chamillart, suspected that the King would say something to him, had brought his papers to Versailles. Sure of his position, he declared that he had not in any way failed to render account to Chamillart or to the King, and detailed the very things that had just been mentioned to him. He begged that a messenger might be despatched in order to search his cassette, in which the proofs of what he had advanced could be seen, truths that Chamillart, if present, he said, would not dare to disavow. The King took him at his word, and sent in search of Chamillart.

When he arrived, the King related to him the conversation that had just taken place. Chamillart replied with an embarrassed voice, that there was no necessity to wait for the cassette of Catinat, for he admitted that the accusation against him was true in every respect. The King, much astonished, reproved him for his infidelity in keeping silence upon these comments, whereby

Catinat had lost his favour.

Chamillart, his eyes lowered, allowed the King to say on; but as he felt that his anger was rising; said. "Sire, you are right; but it is not my fault."

"And whose is it, then?" replied the King warmly. "Is it mine?"

"Certainly not, Sire," said Chamillart, trembling; "but I am bold enough to tell you, with the most exact truth, that it is not mine."

The King insisting, Chamillart was obliged to explain, that having shown the letters of Catinat to Madame de Maintenon, she had commanded him to keep them from his Majesty, and to say not a syllable about them. Chamillart added, that Madame de Maintenon was not far off, and supplicated the King to ask her the truth of this matter.

In his turn, the King was now more embarrassed than Chamillart; lowering his voice, he said that it was inconceivable how Madame de Maintenon felt interested in his comfort, and endeavoured to keep from him everything that might vex him, and without showing any more displeasure, turned to Marshal Catinat, said he was delighted with an explanation which showed that nobody was wrong; addressed several gracious remarks to the Marshal; begged him to remain on good terms with Chamillart, and hastened to quit them and enter into his private cabinet.

Catinat, more ashamed of what he had just heard and seen than pleased with a justification so complete, paid some compliments to Chamillart, who, out of his wits at the perilous explanation he had given, received them, and returned them as well as he could. They left the cabinet soon after, and the selection of Catinat by the King for the command of the army of the Rhine was declared.

Reflections upon this affair present themselves of their own accord. The King verified what had been said that very evening with Madame de Maintenon. They were only on better terms than ever in consequence. She approved of Chamillart for avowing all; and this minister was only the better treated afterwards by the King and by Madame de Maintenon.

As for Catinat, he took the command he had been called to, but did not remain long in it. The explanations that had passed, all the more dangerous because in his favour, were not of a kind to prove otherwise than hurtful to him. He soon resigned his command, finding himself too much obstructed to do anything, and retired to his house of Saint Gratien, near Saint Denis, which he scarcely ever left, and where he saw only a few private friends, sorry that he had ever left it, and that he had listened to the cajoleries of the King.

Canaples, brother of the Marechal de Crequi, wished to marry Mademoiselle de Vivonne who was no longer young, but was distinguished by talent, virtue and high birth; she had not a penny. The Cardinal de Coislin, thinking Canaples too old to marry, told him so. Canaples said he wanted to have children. "Children!" exclaimed the Cardinal. "But she is so virtuous!" Everybody burst out laughing; and the more willingly, as the Cardinal, very pure in his manners, was still more so in his language. His saying was verified by the event: the marriage proved sterile.

The Duc de Coislin died about this time. I have related in its proper place an adventure that happened to him and his brother, the Chevalier de Coislin: now I will say something more of the Duke. He was a very little man, of much humour and virtue, but of a politeness that was unendurable, and that passed all bounds, though not incompatible with dignity. He had been lieutenant-general in the army. Upon one occasion, after a battle in which he had taken part, one of the Rhingraves who had been made prisoner, fell to his lot. The Duc de Coislin wished to give up to the other his bed, which consisted indeed of but a mattress. They complimented each other so much, the one pressing, the other refusing, that in the end they both slept upon the ground, leaving the mattress between them. The Rhingrave in due time came to Paris and called on the Duc de Coislin. When he was going, there was such a profusion of compliments, and the Duke insisted so much on seeing him out, that the Rhingrave, as a last resource, ran out of the room, and double locked the door outside. M. de Coislin was not thus to be outdone. His apartments were only a few feet above the ground. He opened the window accordingly, leaped out into the court, and arrived thus at the entrance-door before the Rhingrave, who thought the devil must have carried him there. The Duc de Coislin, however, had managed to put his thumb out of joint by this leap. He called in Felix, chief surgeon of the King, who soon put the thumb to rights. Soon afterwards Felix made a call upon M. de Coislin to see how he was, and found that the cure was perfect. As he was about to leave, M. de Coislin must needs open the door for him. Felix, with a shower of bows, tried hard to prevent this, and while they were thus vying in politeness, each with a hand upon the door, the Duke suddenly drew back; he had put his thumb out of joint again, and Felix was obliged to attend to it on the spot! It may be imagined what laughter this story caused the King, and everybody else, when it became known.

There was no end to the outrageous civilities of M. de Coislin. On returning from Fontainebleau one day, we, that is Madame de Saint-Simon and myself, encountered M. de Coislin and his son, M. de Metz, on foot upon the pavement of Ponthierry, where their coach had broken down. We sent word, accordingly, that we should be glad to accommodate them in ours. But message followed message on both sides; and at last I was compelled to alight and to walk through the mud, begging them to mount into my coach. M. de Coislin, yielding to my prayers, consented to this. M. de Metz was furious with him for his compliments, and at last prevailed on him. When M. de Coislin had accepted my offer and we had nothing more to do than to gain the coach, he began to capitulate, and to protest that he would not displace the two young ladies he saw seated in the vehicle. I told him that the two young ladies were chambermaids, who could well afford to wait until the other carriage was mended, and then continue their journey in that. But he would not hear of this; and at last all that M. de Metz and I could do was to compromise the matter, by agreeing to take one of the chambermaids with us. When we arrived at the coach, they both descended, in order to allow us to mount. During the compliments that passed—and they were not short—I told the servant who held the coach-door open, to close it as soon as I was inside, and to order the coachman to drive on at once. This was done; but M. de Coislin immediately began to cry aloud that he would jump out if we did not stop for the young ladies; and he set himself to do so in such an odd manner, that I had only time to catch hold of the belt of his breeches and hold him back; but he still, with his head hanging out of the window, exclaimed that he would leap out, and pulled against me. At this absurdity I called to the coachman to stop; the Duke with difficulty recovered himself, and persisted that he would have thrown himself out. The chambermaid was ordered to mount, and mount she did, all covered with mud, which daubed us; and she nearly crushed M. de Metz and me in this carriage fit only for four.

M. de Coislin could not bear that at parting anybody should give him the "last touch;" a piece of sport, rarely cared for except in early youth, and out of which arises a chase by the person touched, in order to catch him by whom he has been touched. One evening, when the Court was at Nancy, and just as everybody was going to bed, M. de Longueville spoke a few words in private to two of his torch-bearers, and then touching the Duc de Coislin, said he had given him the last touch, and scampered away, the Duke hotly pursuing him. Once a little in advance, M. de Longueville hid himself in a doorway, allowed M. de Coislin to pass on, and then went quietly home to bed. Meanwhile the Duke, lighted by the torch-bearers, searched for M. de Longueville all over the town, but meeting with no success, was obliged to give up the chase, and went home all in a sweat. He was obliged of course to laugh a good deal at this joke, but he evidently did not like it over much.

With all his politeness, which was in no way put on, M. de Coislin could, when he pleased, show a great deal of firmness, and a resolution to maintain his proper dignity worthy of much praise. At Nancy, on this same occasion, the Duc de Crequi, not finding apartments provided for him to his taste on arriving in town, went, in his brutal manner, and seized upon those allotted to the Duc de Coislin. The Duke, arriving a moment after, found his servants turned into the street, and soon learned who had sent them there. M. de Crequi had precedence of him in rank; he said not a word, therefore, but went to the apartments provided for the Marechal de Crequi (brother of the other), served him exactly as he himself had just been served, and took up his quarters there. The Marechal de Crequi arrived in his turn, learned what had occurred, and immediately seized upon the apartments of Cavoye, in order to teach him how to provide quarters in future so as to avoid all disputes.

On another occasion, M. de Coislin went to the Sorbonne to listen to a thesis sustained by the second son of M. de Bouillon. When persons of distinction gave these discourses, it was customary for the Princes of the blood, and for many of the Court, to go and hear them. M. de

Coislin was at that time almost last in order of precedence among the Dukes. When he took his seat, therefore, knowing that a number of them would probably arrive, he left several rows of vacant places in front of him, and sat himself down. Immediately afterwards, Novion, Chief President of the Parliament, arrived, and seated himself in front of M. de Coislin. Astonished at this act of madness, M. de Coislin said not a word, but took an arm-chair, and, while Novion turned his head to speak to Cardinal de Bouillon, placed that arm-chair in front of the Chief President in such a manner that he was as it were imprisoned, and unable to stir. M. de Coislin then sat down. This was done so rapidly, that nobody saw it until it was finished. When once it was observed, a great stir arose. Cardinal de Bouillon tried to intervene. M. de Coislin replied, that since the Chief President had forgotten his position he must be taught it, and would not budge. The other presidents were in a fright, and Novion, enraged by the offence put on him, knew not what to do. It was in vain that Cardinal de Bouillon on one side, and his brother on the other, tried to persuade M. de Coislin to give way. He would not listen to them. They sent a message to him to say that somebody wanted to see him at the door on most important business. But this had no effect. "There is no business so important," replied M. de Coislin, "as that of teaching M. le Premier President what he owes me, and nothing will make me go from this place unless M. le President, whom you see behind me, goes away first."

At last M. le Prince was sent for, and he with much persuasion endeavoured to induce M. de Coislin to release the Chief President from his prison. But for some time M. de Coislin would listen as little to M. le Prince as he had listened to the others, and threatened to keep Novion thus shut up during all the thesis. At length, he consented to set the Chief President free, but only on condition that he left the building immediately; that M. le Prince should guarantee this; and that no "juggling tricks" (that was the term he made use of), should be played off to defeat the agreement. M. le Prince at once gave his word that everything should be as he required, and M. de Coislin then rose, moved away his arm-chair, and said to the Chief President, "Go away, sir! go away, sir!" Novion did on the instant go away, in the utmost confusion, and jumped into his coach. M. de Coislin thereupon took back his chair to its former position and composed himself to listen again.

On every side M. de Coislin was praised for the firmness he had shown. The Princes of the blood called upon him the same evening, and complimented him for the course he had adopted; and so many other visitors came during the evening that his house was quite full until a late hour. On the morrow the King also praised him for his conduct, and severely blamed the Chief President. Nay more, he commanded the latter to go to M. de Coislin, at his house, and beg pardon of him. It is easy to comprehend the shame and despair of Novion at being ordered to take so humiliating a step, especially after what had already happened to him. He prevailed upon M. le Coislin, through the mediation of friends, to spare him this pain, and M. de Coislin had the generosity to do so. He agreed therefore that when Novion called upon him he would pretend to be out, and this was done. The King, when he heard of it, praised very highly the forbearance of the Duke.

He was not an old man when he died, but was eaten up with the gout, which he sometimes had in his eyes, in his nose, and in his tongue. When in this state, his room was filled with the best company. He was very generally liked, was truth itself in his dealings and his words, and was one of my friends, as he had been the friend of my father before me.

The President de Novion, above alluded to, was a man given up to iniquity, whom money and obscure mistresses alone influenced. Lawyers complained of his caprices, and pleaders of his injustice. At last, he went so far as to change decisions of the court when they were given him to sign, which was not found out for some time, but which led to his disgrace. He was replaced by Harlay in 1689; and lived in ignominy for four years more.

About this time died Petit, a great physician, who had wit, knowledge, experience, and probity; and yet lived to the last without being ever brought to admit the circulation of the blood.

A rather strange novelty was observed at Fontainebleau: Madame publicly at the play, in the second year of her mourning for Monsieur! She made some objections at first, but the King persuaded her, saying that what took place in his palace ought not to be considered as public.

On Saturday, the 22nd of October of this year (1702), at about ten in the morning, I had the misfortune to lose my father-in-law, the Marechal de Lorges, who died from the effects of an unskilful operation performed upon him for the stone. He had been brought up as a Protestant, and had practised that religion. But he had consulted on the one hand with Bossuet, and on the other hand with M. Claude, (Protestant) minister of Charenton, without acquainting them that he was thus in communication with both. In the end the arguments of Bossuet so convinced him that he lost from that time all his doubts, became steadfastly attached to the Catholic religion, and strove hard to convert to it all the Protestants with whom he spoke. M. de Turenne, with whom he was intimately allied, was in a similar state of mind, and, singularly enough, his doubts were resolved at the same time, and in exactly the same manner, as those of M. de Lorges. The joy of the two friends, who had both feared they should be estranged from each other when they announced their conversion, was very great. The Comtesse de Roye, sister to M. de Lorges, was sorely affected at this change, and she would not consent to see him except on condition that he never spoke of it.

M. de Lorges commanded with great distinction in Holland and elsewhere, and at the death of M. de Turenne, took for the time, and with great honour, his place. He was made Marshal of France on the 21st of February, 1676, not before he had fairly won that distinction. The remainder of his career showed his capacity in many ways, and acquired for him the esteem of all. His family were affected beyond measure at his loss. That house was in truth terrible to see. Never was man so tenderly or so universally regretted, or so worthy of being so. Besides my own grief, I had to sustain that of Madame de Saint-Simon, whom many times I thought I should lose. Nothing was comparable to the attachment she had for her father, or the tenderness he had for her; nothing more perfectly alike than their hearts and their dispositions. As for me, I loved him as a father, and he loved me as a son, with the most entire and sweetest confidence.

About the same time died the Duchesse de Gesvres, separated from a husband who had been the scourge of his family, and had dissipated millions of her fortune. She was a sort of witch, tall and lean, who walked like an ostrich. She sometimes came to Court, with the odd look and famished expression to which her husband had brought her. Virtue, wit, and dignity distinguished her. I remember that one summer the King took to going very often in the evening to Trianon, and that once for all he gave permission to all the Court, men and women, to follow him. There was a grand collation for the Princesses, his daughters, who took their friends there, and indeed all the women went to it if they pleased. One day the Duchesse de Gesvres took it into her head to go to Trianon and partake of this meal; her age, her rarity at Court, her accoutrements, and her face, provoked the Princesses to make fun of her in whispers with their fair visitors. She perceived this, and without being embarrassed, took them up so sharply, that they were silenced, and looked down. But this was not all: after the collation she began to talk so freely and yet so humorously about them that they were frightened, and went and made their excuses, and very frankly asked for quarter. Madame de Gesvres was good enough to grant them this, but said it was only on condition that they learned how to behave. Never afterwards did they venture to look at her impertinently. Nothing was ever so magnificent as these soirees of Trianon. All the flowers of the parterres were renewed every day; and I have seen the King and all the Court obliged to go away because of the tuberoses, the odour of which perfumed the air, but so powerfully, on account of their quantity, that nobody could remain in the garden, although very vast, and stretching like a terrace all along the canal.

CHAPTER XXVI

The Prince d'Harcourt at last obtained permission to wait on the King, after having never appeared at Court for seventeen years. He had followed the King in all his conquests in the Low Countries and Franche- Comte; but he had remained little at the Court since his voyage to Spain, whither he had accompanied the daughter of Monsieur to the King, Charles II., her husband. The Prince d'Harcourt took service with Venice, and fought in the Morea until the Republic made peace with the Turks. He was tall, well made; and, although he looked like a nobleman and had wit, reminded one at the same time of a country actor. He was a great liar, and a libertine in body and mind; a great spendthrift, a great and impudent swindler, with a tendency to low debauchery, that cursed him all his life. Having fluttered about a long time after his return, and found it impossible either to live with his wife—which is not surprising—or accommodate himself to the Court or to Paris, he set up his rest at Lyons with wine, street-walkers, a society to match, a pack of hounds, and a gaming-table to support his extravagance and enable him to live at the expense of the dupes, the imbeciles, and the sons of fat tradesmen, whom he could lure into his nets. Thus he spent many years, and seemed to forget that there existed in the world another country besides Lyons. At last he got tired, and returned to Paris. The King, who despised him, let him alone, but would not see him; and it was only after two months of begging for him by the Lorraines, that he received permission to present himself. His wife, the Princesse d'Harcourt, was a favourite of Madame de Maintenon. The origin of their friendship is traced to the fact that Brancas, the father of the Princess, had been one of the lovers of Madame de Maintenon. No claim less powerful could have induced the latter to take into her favour a person who was so little worthy. Like all women who know nothing but what chance has taught them, and who have long languished in obscurity before arriving at splendour, Madame de Maintenon was dazzled by the very name of Princess, even if assumed: as to a real Princess, nothing equalled her in her opinion. The Princess then tried hard to get the Prince invited to Marly, but without success. Upon this she pretended to sulk, in hopes that Madame de Maintenon would exert all her influence; but in this she was mistaken. The Prince accordingly by degrees got disgusted with the Court, and retired into the provinces for a time.

The Princesse d'Harcourt was a sort of personage whom it is good to make known, in order better to lay bare a Court which did not scruple to receive such as she. She had once been beautiful and gay; but though not old, all her grace and beauty had vanished. The rose had become an ugly thorn. At the time I speak of she was a tall, fat creature, mightily brisk in her movements, with a complexion like milk-porridge; great, ugly, thick lips, and hair like tow, always sticking out and hanging down in disorder, like all the rest of her fittings out. Dirty, slatternly, always intriguing, pretending, enterprising, quarrelling—always low as the grass or high as the rainbow, according to the person with whom she had to deal: she was a blonde Fury, nay more, a harpy: she had all the effrontery of one, and the deceit and violence; all the avarice and the audacity; moreover, all the gluttony, and all the promptitude to relieve herself from the effects thereof; so that she drove out of their wits those at whose house she dined; was often a victim of her confidence; and was many a time sent to the devil by the servants of M. du Maine and M. le Grand. She, however, was never in the least embarrassed, tucked up her petticoats and went her way; then returned, saying she had been unwell. People were accustomed to it.

Whenever money was to be made by scheming and bribery, she was there to make it. At play she always cheated, and if found out stormed and raged; but pocketed what she had won. People looked upon her as they would have looked upon a fish-fag, and did not like to commit themselves by quarrelling with her. At the end of every game she used to say that she gave whatever might have been unfairly gained to those who had gained it, and hoped that others would do likewise. For she was very devout by profession, and thought by so doing to put her conscience in safety; because, she used to add, in play there is always some mistake. She went to church always, and constantly took the sacrament, very often after having played until four o'clock in the morning.

One day, when there was a grand fete at Fontainebleau, Madame la Marechale de Villeroy persuaded her, out of malice, to sit down and play, instead of going to evening prayers. She resisted some time, saying that Madame de Maintenon was going; but the Marechale laughed at her for believing that her patron could see who was and who was not at the chapel: so down they sat to play. When the prayers were over, Madame de Maintenon, by the merest accident—for she scarcely ever visited any one —went to the apartments of the Marechale de Villeroy. The door was flung back, and she was announced. This was a thunderbolt for the Princesse d'Harcourt. "I am ruined," cried she, unable to restrain herself; "she will see me playing, and I ought to have been at chapel!" Down fell the cards from her hands, and down fell she all abroad in her chair. The Marechale laughed most heartily at so complete an adventure. Madame de Maintenon entered slowly, and found the Princess in this state, with five or six persons. The Marechale de Villeroy, who was full of wit, began to say that, whilst doing her a great honour, Madame was the cause of great disorder; and showed her the Princesse d'Harcourt in her state of discomfiture. Madame de Maintenon smiled with majestic kindness, and addressing the Princesse d'Harcourt, "Is this the way," said she; "that you go to prayers?" Thereupon the Princess flew out of her half-faint into a sort of fury; said that this was the kind of trick that was played off upon her; that no doubt the Marechale knew that Madame de Maintenon was coming, and for that reason had persecuted her to play. "Persecuted!" exclaimed the Marechale, "I thought I could not receive you better than by proposing a game; it is true you were for a moment troubled at missing the chapel, but your tastes carried the day. —This, Madame, is my whole crime," continued she, addressing Madame de Maintenon. Upon this, everybody laughed louder than before: Madame de Maintenon, in order to stop the quarrel; commanded them both to continue their game; and they continued accordingly, the Princesse d'Harcourt, still grumbling, quite beside herself, blinded with fury, so as to commit fresh mistakes every minute. So ridiculous an adventure diverted the Court for several days; for this beautiful Princess was equally feared, hated, and despised.

Monseigneur le Duc and Madame la Duchesse de Bourgogne continually played off pranks upon her. They put, one day, crackers all along the avenue of the chateau at Marly, that led to the

Perspective where she lodged. She was horribly afraid of everything. The Duke and Duchess bribed two porters to be ready to take her into the mischief. When she was right in the middle of the avenue the crackers began to go off; and she to cry aloud for mercy; the chairman set her down and ran for it. There she was, then, struggling in her chair, furiously enough to upset it, and yelling like a demon. At this the company, which had gathered at the door of the chateau to see the fun, ran to her assistance, in order to have the pleasure of enjoying the scene more fully. Thereupon she set to abusing everybody right and left, commencing with Monseigneur and Madame la Duchesse de Bourgogne. At another time M. de Bourgogne put a cracker under her chair in the salon, where she was playing at piquet. As he was about to set fire to this cracker, some charitable soul warned him that it would maim her, and he desisted.

Sometimes they used to send about twenty Swiss guards, with drums, into her chamber, who roused her from her first sleep by their horrid din. Another time—and these scenes were always at Marly—they waited until very late for her to go to bed and sleep. She lodged not far from the post of the captain of the guards, who was at that time the Marechal de Lorges. It had snowed very hard, and had frozen. Madame la Duchesse de Bourgogne and her suite gathered snow from the terrace which is on a level with their lodgings; and, in order to be better supplied, waked up, to assist them, the Marechal's people, who did not let them want for ammunition. Then, with a false key, and lights, they gently slipped into the chamber of the Princesse d'Harcourt; and, suddenly drawing the curtains of her bed, pelted her amain with snowballs. The filthy creature, waking up with a start, bruised and stifled in snow, with which even her ears were filled, with dishevelled hair, yelling at the top of her voice, and wriggling like an eel, without knowing where to hide, formed a spectacle that diverted people more than half an hour: so that at last the nymph swam in her bed, from which the water flowed everywhere, slushing all the chamber. It was enough to make one die of laughter. On the morrow she sulked, and was more than ever laughed at for her pains.

Her fits of sulkiness came over her either when the tricks played were too violent, or when M. le Grand abused her. He thought, very properly, that a person who bore the name of Lorraine should not put herself so much on the footing of a buffoon; and, as he was a rough speaker, he sometimes said the most abominable things to her at table; upon which the Princess would burst out crying, and then, being enraged, would sulk. The Duchesse de Bourgogne used then to pretend to sulk, too; but the other did not hold out long, and came crawling back to her, crying, begging pardon for having sulked, and praying that she might not cease to be a source of amusement! After some time the Duchess would allow herself to be melted, and the Princess was more villainously treated than ever, for the Duchesse de Bourgogne had her own way in everything. Neither the King nor Madame de Maintenon found fault with what she did, so that the Princesse d'Harcourt had no resource; she did not even dare to complain of those who aided in tormenting her; yet it would not have been prudent in any one to make her an enemy.

The Princesse d'Harcourt paid her servants so badly that they concocted a plan, and one fine day drew up on the Pont Neuf. The coachman and footmen got down, and came and spoke to her at the door, in language she was not used to hear. Her ladies and chambermaid got down, and went away, leaving her to shift as she might. Upon this she set herself to harangue the blackguards who collected, and was only too happy to find a man, who mounted upon the seat and drove her home. Another time, Madame de Saint-Simon, returning from Versailles, overtook her, walking in full dress in the street, and with her train under her arms. Madame de Saint-Simon stopped, offered her assistance, and found that she had been left by her servants, as on the Pont Neuf. It was volume the second of that story; and even when she came back she found her house deserted, every one having gone away at once by agreement. She was very violent with her servants, beat them, and changed diem every day.

Upon one occasion, she took into her service a strong and robust chambermaid, to whom, from the first day of her arrival, she gave many slaps and boxes on the ear. The chambermaid said nothing, but after submitting to this treatment for five or six days, conferred with the other servants; and one morning, while in her mistress's room, locked the door without being perceived, said something to bring down punishment upon her, and at the first box on the ear she received, flew upon the Princesse d'Harcourt, gave her no end of thumps and slaps, knocked her down, kicked her, mauled her from her head to her feet, and when she was tired of this exercise, left her on the ground, all torn and dishevelled, howling like a devil. The chambermaid then quitted the room, double- locked the door on the outside, gained the staircase, and fled the house.

Every day the Princess was fighting, or mixed up in some adventures. Her neighbours at Marly said they could not sleep for the riot she made at night; and I remember that, after one of these scenes, everybody went to see the room of the Duchesse de Villeroy and that of Madame d'Espinoy, who had put their bed in the middle of their room, and who related their night vigils to every one.

Such was this favourite of Madame de Maintenon; so insolent and so insupportable to every one, but who had favours and preferences for those who brought her over, and who had raised so many young men, amassed their wealth, and made herself feared even by the Prince and minister.

CHAPTER XXVII

In a previous page I have alluded to the Princesse des Ursins, when she was appointed 'Camerera Mayor' to the Queen of Spain on her marriage. As I have now to occupy myself more particularly with her, it may be as well to give a description of this extraordinary woman, which I omitted when I first spoke of her.

Anne Marie de la Tremoille, was daughter of M. de Noirmoutiers, who figured sufficiently in the troubles of the minority to be made a 'Duc a brevet'. She first married M. Talleyrand, who called himself Prince de Chalais, and who was obliged to quit the kingdom for engaging in the famous duel against Messieurs de la Frette. She followed her husband to Spain, where he died. Having gone to Rome, she got into favour with the Cardinals de Bouillon and d'Estrees, first on account of her name and nation, and afterwards for more tender reasons. In order to detain her at Rome, these dignitaries thought of obtaining her an establishment. She had no children, and almost no fortune, they wrote to Court that so important a man as the Duc de Bracciano, Prince des Ursins, was worth gaining; and that the way to arrive at this result was to have him married to Madame de Chalais. The Duke was persuaded by the two Cardinals that he was in love with Madame de Chalais: and so the affair was arranged. Madame des Ursins displayed all her wit and charms at Rome; and soon her palace became a sort of court, where all the best company assembled. It grew to be the fashion to go there.

The husband amidst all this counts for not much. There was sometimes a little disagreement between the two, without open rupture; yet they were now and then glad to separate. This is why the Duchesse de Bracciano made two journeys to France: the second time she spent four or five years there. It was then I knew her, or rather formed a particular friendship with her. My mother had made her acquaintance during her previous visit. She lodged near us. Her wit, her grace, her manners enchanted me: she received me with tenderness and I was always at her house. It was she who proposed to me a marriage with Mlle. de Royan, which I rejected for the reason already given.

When Madame des Ursins was appointed 'Camerera Mayor', she was a widow, without children. No one could have been better suited for the post. A lady of our court would not have done: a Spanish lady was not to be depended on, and might have easily disgusted the Queen. The Princesse des Ursins appeared to be a middle term. She was French, had been in Spain, and she passed a great part of her life at Rome, and in Italy. She was of the house of La Tremoille: her husband was chief of the house of Ursins, a grandee of Spain, and Prince of the Soglio. She was also on very good terms with the Duchess of Savoy, and with the Queen of Portugal. The Cardinal d'Estrees, also, was known to have remained her friend, after having been something more in their youth; and he gave information that the Cardinal Portocarrero had been much in love with her at Rome, and that they were then on very good terms. As it was through the latter Cardinal that it was necessary to govern everything, this circumstance was considered very important.

Age and health were also appropriate; and likewise her appearance. She was rather tall than otherwise, a brunette, with blue eyes of the most varied expression, in figure perfect, with a most exquisite bosom; her face, without being beautiful, was charming; she was extremely noble in air, very majestic in demeanour, full of graces so natural and so continual in everything, that I have never seen any one approach her, either in form or mind. Her wit was copious and of all kinds: she was flattering, caressing, insinuating, moderate, wishing to please for pleasing's sake, with charms irresistible when she strove to persuade and win over; accompanying all this, she had a grandeur that encouraged instead of frightening; a delicious conversation, inexhaustible and very amusing, for she had seen many countries and persons; a voice and way of speaking extremely agreeable, and full of sweetness. She had read much, and reflected much. She knew how to choose the best society, how to receive them, and could even have held a court; was polite, distinguished; and above all was careful never to take a step in advance without dignity and discretion. She was eminently fitted for intrigue, in which, from taste; she had passed her time at Rome; with much ambition, but of that vast kind, far above her sex, and the common run of men—a desire to occupy a great position and to govern. A love for gallantry and personal vanity were her foibles, and these clung to her until her latest day; consequently, she dressed in a way that no longer became her, and as she advanced in life, removed further from propriety in this particular. She was an ardent and excellent friend—of a friendship that time and absence never enfeebled; and, consequently, an implacable enemy, pursuing her hatred to the infernal regions. While caring little for the means by which she gained her ends, she tried as much as possible to reach them by honest means. Secret, not only for herself, but for her friends, she was yet, of a decorous gaiety, and so governed her humours, that at all times and in everything she was mistress of herself. Such was the Princesse des Ursins.

From the first moment on which she entered the service of the Queen of Spain, it became her desire to govern not only the Queen, but the King; and by this means the realm itself. Such a grand project had need of support from our King, who, at the commencement, ruled the Court of Spain as much as his own Court, with entire influence over all matters.

The young Queen of Spain had been not less carefully educated than her sister, the Duchesse de Bourgogne. She had even when so young much intelligence and firmness, without being incapable of restraint; and as time went on, improved still further, and displayed a constancy and courage which were admirably set off by her meekness and natural graces. According to everything I have heard said in France and in Spain, she possessed all qualities that were necessary to make her adored. Indeed she became a divinity among the Spaniards, and to their affection for her, Philip V. was more than once indebted for his crown. Lords, ladies, soldiers, and the people still remember her with tears in their eyes; and even after the lapse of so many years, are not yet consoled for her loss.

Madame des Ursins soon managed to obtain the entire confidence of this Queen; and during the absence of Philip V. in Italy, assisted her in the administration of all public offices. She even accompanied her to the junta, it not being thought proper that the Queen should be alone amid such an assemblage of men. In this way she became acquainted with everything that was passing, and knew all the affairs of the Government.

This step gained, it will be imagined that the Princesse des Ursins did not forget to pay her court most assiduously to our King and to Madame de Maintenon. She continually sent them an exact account of everything relating to the Queen—making her appear in the most favourable light possible. Little by little she introduced into her letters details respecting public events; without, however, conveying a suspicion of her own ambition, or that she wished to meddle in these matters. Anchored in this way, she next began to flatter Madame de Maintenon, and by degrees to hint that she might rule over Spain, even more firmly than she ruled over France, if she would entrust her commands to Madame des Ursins. Madame des Ursins offered, in fact, to be the instrument of Madame de Maintenon; representing how much better it would be to rule affairs in this manner, than through the instrumentality of the ministers of either country.

Madame de Maintenon, whose passion it was to know everything, to mix herself in everything, and to govern everything, was, enchanted by the siren. This method of governing Spain without ministers appeared to her an admirable idea. She embraced it with avidity, without reflecting that she would govern only in appearance, since she would know nothing except through the Princesse des Ursins, see nothing except in the light in which she presented it. From that time dates the intimate union which existed between these two important women, the unbounded authority of Madame des Ursins, the fall of all those who had placed Philip V. upon the throne, and of all our ministers in Spain who stood in the way of the new power.

Such an alliance being made between the two women, it was necessary to draw the King of Spain into the same net. This was not a very arduous task. Nature and art indeed had combined to make it easy.

Younger brother of an excitable, violent, and robust Prince, Philip V, had been bred up in a submission and dependence that were necessary for the repose of the Royal family. Until the testament of Charles II., the Duc d'Anjou was necessarily regarded as destined to be a subject all his life; and therefore could not be too much abased by education, and trained to patience and obedience: That supreme law, the reason of state, demanded this preference, for the safety and happiness of the kingdom, of the elder over the younger brother. His mind for this reason was purposely narrowed and beaten down, and his natural docility and gentleness greatly assisted in the process, He was quite formed to be led, although he had enough judgment left to choose the better of two courses proposed to him, and even to express himself in good phrase, when the slowness, not to say the laziness, of his mind did not prevent him from speaking at all. His great piety contributed to weaken his mind; and, being joined to very lively passions, made it disagreeable and even dangerous for him to be separated from his Queen. It may easily be conceived, therefore, how he loved her; and that he allowed himself to be guided by her in all things. As the Queen herself was guided in all things by Madame des Ursins, the influence of this latter was all- powerful.

Soon, indeed, the junta became a mere show. Everything was brought before the King in private, and he gave no decision until the Queen and Madame des Ursins had passed theirs. This conduct met with no opposition from our Court, but our ministers at the Court of Spain and the Spanish ministers here soon began to complain of it. The first to do so were Cardinals d'Estrees and Portocarrero. Madame de Maintenon laughed at them, and Madame des Ursins, of whom they were old friends, soon showed them that she did not mean to abate one jot of her power. She first endeavoured to bring about a coldness between the two, and this succeeded so well, that in consequence of the quarrels that resulted, the Spanish Cardinal, Portocarrero (who, it will be remembered, had played an important part in bringing Philip to the Spanish throne) wished to quit the junta. But Madame des Ursins, who thought that the time had not yet arrived for this step, persuaded him to remain, and endeavoured to flatter his vanity by an expedient altogether ridiculous. She gave him the command of a regiment of guards, and he, priest, archbishop, primate and cardinal, accepted it, and was, of course, well laughed at by everybody for his pains. The two cardinals soon after became reconciled to each other, feeling, perhaps, the necessity of uniting against the common enemy. But they could come to no better understanding with her. Disagreements continued, so that at last, feeling her position perfectly secure, the Princesse des Ursins begged permission to retire into Italy, knowing full well that she would not be taken at her word, and hoping by this means to deliver herself of these stumbling-blocks in her path.

Our ministers, who felt they would lose all control over Spanish affairs if Madame des Ursins was allowed to remain mistress, did all in their power to support the D'Estrees. But Madame de Maintenon pleaded so well with the King, representing the good policy of allowing a woman so much attached to him, and to the Spanish Queen, as was Madame des Ursins, to remain where she was, that he entirely swallowed the bait; the D'Estrees were left without support; the French ambassador at Madrid was virtually deprived of all power: the Spanish ministers were fettered in their every movement, and the authority of Madame des Ursins became stronger than ever. All public affairs passed through her hands. The King decided nothing without conferring with the Queen and her.

While excluding almost all the ministers from public offices, Madame des Ursins admitted a few favourites into her confidence. Amongst them was D'Harcourt, who stood well with Madame de Maintenon, and who cared little for the means by which he obtained consideration; Orry, who had the management of the finances; and D'Aubigny, son of a Procureur in Paris. The last was a tall, handsome fellow, well made, and active in mind and body; who for many years had been with the Princess, as a sort of squire, and on very intimate terms with her. One day, when, followed by some of the ministers, she entered a room in which he was writing, he burst out into exclamations against her, without being aware that she was not alone, swore at her, asked her why she could not leave him an hour in peace, called her by the strangest names, and all this with so much impetuosity that she had no time to show him who were behind her. When he found it out, he ran from the room, leaving Madame des Ursins so confused that the ministers looked for two or three minutes upon the walls of the room in order to give her time to recover herself. Soon after this, D'Aubigny had a splendid suite of apartments, that had formerly been occupied by Maria Theresa (afterwards wife of Louis XIV.), placed at his disposal, with some rooms added, in despite of the murmurs that arose at a distinction so strange accorded to this favourite.

At length, Cardinal d'Estrees, continually in arms against Madame des Ursins, and continually defeated, could not bear his position any longer, but asked to be immediately recalled. All that the ministry could do was to obtain permission for the Abbe d'Estrees (nephew of the Cardinal) to remain as Ambassador of France at Madrid. As for Portocarrero, seeing the step his associate had taken, he resolved to quit public business also, and resigned his place accordingly. Several others who stood in the way of the Princesse des Ursins were got rid of at the same time, so that she was now left mistress of the field. She governed absolutely in all things; the ministers became instruments in her hands; the King and Queen agents to work out her will. She was at the highest pinnacle of power. Together with Orry she enjoyed a power such as no one had ever attained since the time of the Duke of Lerma and of Olivares.

In the mean time the Archduke was declared King of Spain by the Emperor, who made no mystery of his intention of attacking Spain by way of Portugal. The Archduke soon afterwards was recognised by Holland, England, Portugal, Brandenburg, Savoy, and Hanover, as King of Spain, under the title of Charles III., and soon after by the other powers of Europe. The Duke of Savoy had been treacherous to us, had shown that he was in league with the Emperor. The King accordingly had broken off all relations with him, and sent an army to invade his territory. It need be no cause of surprise, therefore, that the Archduke was recognised by Savoy. While our armies were fighting with varied fortune those of the Emperor and his allies, in different parts of Europe, notably upon the Rhine, Madame des Ursins was pressing matters to extremities in Spain. Dazzled by her success in expelling the two cardinals from public affairs, and all the ministers who had assisted in placing Philip V. upon the throne, she committed a blunder of which she soon had cause to repent.

I have said, that when Cardinal d'Estrees quitted Spain, the Abbe d'Estrees was left behind, so that France should not be altogether unrepresented in an official manner at the Court of Madrid. Madame des Ursins did not like this arrangement, but as Madame de Maintenon insisted upon it, she was obliged to accept it with as good grace as possible. The Abbe, vain of his family and of his position, was not a man much to be feared as it seemed. Madame des Ursins accordingly laughed at and despised him. He was admitted to the council, but was quite without influence there, and when he attempted to make any representations to Madame des Ursins or to Orry, they listened to him without attending in the least to what he said. The Princess reigned supreme, and thought of nothing but getting rid of all who attempted to divide her authority. At last she obtained such a command over the poor Abbe d'Estrees, so teased and hampered him, that he consented to the hitherto unheard-of arrangement, that the Ambassador of France should not write to the King without first concerting his letter with her, and then show her its contents before he despatched it. But such restraint as this became, in a short time, so fettering, that the Abbe determined to break away from it. He wrote a letter to the King, without showing it to Madame des Ursins. She soon had scent of what he had done; seized the letter as it passed through the post, opened it, and, as she expected, found its contents were not of a kind to give her much satisfaction. But what piqued her most was, to find details exaggerating the authority of D'Aubigny, and a statement to the effect that it was generally believed she had married him. Beside herself with rage and vexation, she wrote with her own hand upon the margin of the letter, 'Pour mariee non' ("At any rate, not married"), showed it in this state to the King and Queen of Spain, to a number of other people, always with strange clamouring, and finally crowned her folly by sending it to the King (Louis XIV.), with furious complaints against the Abbe for writing it without her knowledge, and for inflicting upon her such an atrocious injury as to mention this pretended marriage. Her letter and its enclosure reached the King at a very inopportune moment. Just before, he had received a letter, which, taken in connection with this of the Princesse des Ursins, struck a blow at her power of the most decisive kind.

CHAPTER XXVIII

Some little time previously it had been thought necessary to send an army to the frontiers of Portugal to oppose the Archduke. A French general was wanted to command this army. Madame des Ursins, who had been very intimate with the King of England (James II.) and his Queen, thought she would please them if she gave this post to the Duke of Berwick, illegitimate son of King James. She proposed this therefore; and our King, out of regard for his brother monarch, and from a natural affection for bastards, consented to the appointment; but as the Duke of Berwick had never before commanded an army, he stipulated that Pursegur, known to be a skilful officer, should go with him and assist him with his counsels and advice.

Pursegur set out before the Duke of Berwick. From the Pyrenees as far as Madrid, he found every provision made for the subsistence of the French troops, and sent a very advantageous account to the King of this circumstance. Arrived at Madrid, he had interviews with Orry (who, as I have already mentioned, had the finances under his control, and who was a mere instrument in the hands of Madame des Ursins), and was assured by the minister that all the magazines along the line of route to the frontiers of Portugal were abundantly filled with supplies for the French troops, that all the money necessary was ready; and that nothing, in fact, should fail in the course of the campaign. Pursegur, who had found nothing wanting up to that time, never doubted but that these statements were perfectly correct; and had no suspicion that a minister would have the effrontery to show him in detail all these precautions if he had taken none. Pleased, then, to the utmost degree, he wrote to the King in praise of Orry, and consequently of Madame des Ursins and her wise government. Full of these ideas, he set out for the frontier of Portugal to reconnoitre the ground himself, and arrange everything for the arrival of the army and its general. What was his surprise, when he found that from Madrid to the frontier not a single preparation had been made for the troops, and that in consequence all that Orry had shown him, drawn out upon paper, was utterly fictitious. His vexation upon finding that nothing upon which he had reckoned was provided, may be imagined. He at once wrote to the King, in order to contradict all that he had recently written.

This conduct of Orry—his impudence, I may say—in deceiving a man who immediately after would have under his eyes the proof of his deceit, is a thing past all comprehension. It is easy to understand that rogues should steal, but not that they should have the audacity to do so in the face of facts which so quickly and so easily could prove their villainy.

It was Pursegur's letter then, detailing this rascality on the part of Orry, that had reached the King just before that respecting the Abbe d'Estrees. The two disclosed a state of things that could not be allowed any longer to exist. Our ministers, who, step by step, had been deprived of all control over the affairs of Spain, profited by the discontentment of the King to reclaim their functions. Harcourt and Madame de Maintenon did all they could to ward off the blow from Madame des Ursins, but without effect. The King determined to banish her to Rome and to dismiss Orry from his post.

It was felt, however, that these steps must be taken cautiously, to avoid offending too deeply the King and Queen of Spain, who supported their favourite through every emergency.

In the first place, then, a simple reprimand was sent to the Princesse des Ursins for the violation of the respect due to the King, by opening a letter addressed to him by one of his ambassadors. The Abbe d'Estrees, who expected that Madame des Ursins would be at once disgraced, and who had made a great outcry when his letter was opened, fell into such despair when he saw how lightly she was let off, that he asked for his dismissal. He was taken at his word; and this was a new triumph for Madame des Ursins, who thought herself more secure than ever. Her triumph was of but short duration. The King wrote to Philip, recommending him to head in person the army for the frontiers of Portugal, which, in spite of Orry's deception, it was still determined to send. No sooner was Philip fairly away, separated from the Queen and Madame des Ursins, and no longer under their influence, than the King wrote to the Queen of Spain, requesting her, in terms that could not be disputed, to dismiss at once and for ever her favourite 'Camerera Mayor'. The Queen, in despair at the idea of losing a friend and adviser to whom she had been so much attached, believed herself lost. At the same time that the King wrote to the Queen of Spain, he also wrote to the Princesse des Ursins, ordering her to quit Madrid immediately, to leave Spain, and to retire into Italy.

At this conjuncture of affairs, when the Queen was in despair, Madame des Ursins did not lose her composure. She opened her eyes to all that had passed since she had violated D'Estrees' letter, and saw the vanity of the triumph she had recently enjoyed. She felt at once that for the present all was lost, that her only hope was to be allowed to remain in France. She made all her arrangements, therefore, so that affairs might proceed in her absence as much as possible as though she were present, and then prepared to set out. Dawdling day by day, she put off her departure as long as could be, and when at length she left Madrid only went to Alcala, a few leagues distant. She stopped there under various pretexts, and at length, after five weeks of delay, set out for Bayonne, journeying as slowly as she could and stopping as often as she dared.

She lost no opportunity of demanding an audience at Versailles, in order to clear herself of the charge which weighed upon her, and her importunities at length were not without effect. The most terrible storms at Court soon blow over. The King (Louis XIV.) was satisfied with the success of his plans. He had been revenged in every way, and had humbled the pride of the Princesse des Ursins. It was not necessary to excite the anger of the Queen and King of Spain by too great harshness against their fallen friend. Madame de Maintenon took advantage of this change in the temper of the King, and by dint of persuasion and scheming succeeded in obtaining from him the permission for Madame des Ursins to remain in France. Toulouse was fixed upon for her residence. It was a place that just suited her, and from which communication with Spain was easy. Here accordingly she took up her residence, determined to watch well the course of events, and to avail herself of every opportunity that could bring about her complete reconciliation with the King (Louis XIV.), and obtain for her in consequence the permission to return to Madrid.

In the mean time, the King and Queen of Spain, distressed beyond measure at the loss of their favourite, thought only of the best means of obtaining her recall. They plotted with such ministers as were favourable to her; they openly quarrelled with and thwarted those who were her opponents, so that the most important matters perished in their hands. Nay more, upon the King of Spain's return, the Queen persuaded him to oppose in all things the wishes of the King (Louis XIV.), his grandfather, and to neglect his counsels with studied care. Our King complained of this with bitterness. The aim of it was to tire him out, and to make him understand that it was only Madame des Ursins, well treated and sent back, who could restore Spanish affairs to their original state, and cause his authority to be respected. Madame de Maintenon, on her side, neglected no opportunity of pressing the King to allow Madame des Ursins, not to return into Spain—that would have been to spoil all by asking too much but simply to come to Versailles in order to have the opportunity of justifying herself for her past conduct. From other quarters the King was similarly importuned. Tired at last of the obstinate opposition he met with in Spain from the Queen; who governed completely her husband, he gave permission to Madame des Ursins to come to Versailles to plead her own cause. Self-imprisoned as he was in seclusion, the truth never approached him, and he was the only man in the two kingdoms who had no suspicion that the arrival of Madame ales Ursins at the Court was the certain sign of her speedy return to Spain more powerful than ever. But he was fatigued with the constant resistance he met with; with the disorder which this occasioned in public affairs at a time too when, as I will afterwards explain, the closest union was necessary between the two crowns in order to repel the common enemy, and these motives induced him, to the astonishment of his ministers, to grant the favour requested of him.

However well informed Madame des Ursins might be of all that was being done on her account, this permission surpassed her hopes. Her joy accordingly was very great; but it did not at all carry her away. She saw that her return to Spain would now depend upon herself. She determined to put on the air of one who is disgraced, but who hopes, and yet is humiliated. She instructed all her friends to assume the same manner; took all measures with infinite presence of mind; did not hurry her departure, and yet set out with sufficient promptness to prevent any coldness springing up, and to show with what eagerness she profited by the favour accorded to her, and which she had so much wished.

No sooner was the courier gone who carried this news to her, than the rumour of her return was whispered all over the Court, and became publicly confirmed a few days afterwards. The movement that it produced at Court was inconceivable. Only the friends of Madame des Ursins were able to remain in a tolerably tranquil state. Everybody opened his eyes and comprehended that the return of such an important personage was a fact that could not be insignificant. People prepared themselves for a sort of rising sun that was going to change and renew many things in nature. On every side were seen people who had scarcely ever uttered her name, and who now boasted of their intimacy with her and of her friendship for them. Other people were seen, who, although openly allied with her enemies, had the baseness to affect transports of joy at her forthcoming return, and to flatter those whom they thought likely to favour them with her.

She reached Paris on Sunday, the 4th of January, 1705. The Duc d'Albe met her several miles out of the city, escorted her to his house, and gave a fete in her honour there. Several persons of distinction went out to meet her. Madame des Ursins had reason to be surprised at an entry so triumphant: she would not, however, stay with the Duc and Duchesse d'Albe, but took up her quarters with the Comtesse d'Egmont, niece of the Archbishop of Aix; the said Archbishop having been instrumental in obtaining her recall. The King was at Marly. I was there with Madame de Saint-Simon. During the remainder of the stay at Marly everybody flocked to the house of Madame des Ursins, anxious to pay her their court. However flattered she may have been by this concourse, she had matters to occupy her, pleaded want of repose, and shut her door to three people out of four who called upon her. Curiosity, perhaps fashion, drew this great crowd to her. The ministers were startled by it. Torcy had orders from the King to go, and see her: he did so; and from that moment Madame des Ursins changed her tone. Until then her manner had been modest, supplicating, nearly timid. She now saw and heard so much that from defendant, which she had intended to be, she thought herself in a condition to become accuser; and to demand justice of those who, abusing the confidence of the King, had drawn upon her such a long and cruel punishment, and made her a show for the two kingdoms. All that happened to her surpassed her hopes. Several times when with me she has expressed her astonishment; and with me has laughed at many people, often of much consideration, whom she scarcely knew, or who had been strongly opposed to her, and who basely crouched at her feet.

The King returned to Versailles on Saturday, the 10th of January. Madame des Ursins arrived there the same day. I went immediately to see her, not having been able to do so before, because I could not quit Marly. My mother had seen a great deal of Madame des Ursins at Paris. I had always been on good terms with her, and had received on all occasions proofs of her friendship. She received me very well, spoke with much freedom, and said she promised herself the pleasure of seeing me again, and of talking with me more at her ease. On, the morrow, Sunday, she dined at home alone, dressed herself in grand style, and went to the King, with whom she remained alone two hours and a half conversing in his cabinet. From there she went to the Duchesse de Bourgogne, with whom she also conversed a long time alone. In the evening, the King said, while in Madame de Maintenon's apartments, that there were still many things upon which he had not yet spoken to Madame des Ursins. The next day she saw Madame de Maintenon in private for a long time, and much at her ease. She had an interview soon after with the King and Madame de Maintenon, which was also very long.

A month after this a special courier arrived from the King and Queen of Spain, to thank the King (Louis XIV.) for his conduct towards the Princesse des Ursins. From that moment it was announced that she would remain at Court until the month of April, in order to attend to her affairs and her health. It was already to have made a grand step to be mistress enough to announce thus her stay. Nobody in truth doubted of her return to Spain, but the word was not yet said. She avoided all explanations, and it may be believed did not have many indiscreet questions put to her upon the subject.

So many and such long audiences with the King, followed by so much serenity, had a great effect upon the world, and the crowd that flocked to see Madame des Ursins was greater than ever; but under various pretences she shut herself up and would see only a few intimate friends, foremost among which were Madame de Saint-Simon and myself. Whilst triumphant beyond all her hopes in Paris, she was at work in Spain, and with equal success. Rivas, who had drawn up the will of the late King Charles II., was disgraced, and never afterwards rose to favour. The Duc de Grammont, our ambassador at Madrid, was so overwhelmed with annoyance, that he asked for his recall. Amelot, whom Madame des Ursins favoured, was appointed in his place, and many who had been disgraced were reinstated in office; everything was ordered according to her wishes.

We returned to Marly, where many balls took place. It need not be doubted that Madame des Ursins was among the invited. Apartments were given her, and nothing could equal the triumphant air with which she took possession of them, the continual attentions of the King to her, as though she were some little foreign queen just arrived at his Court, or the majestic fashion in which she received them, mingled with grace and respectful politeness, then almost out of date, and which recalled the stately old dames of the Queen-mother. She never came without the King, who appeared to be completely occupied with her, talking with her, pointing out objects for her inspection, seeking her opinion and her approbation with an air of gallantry, even of flattery, which never ceased. The frequent private conversations that she had with him in the apartment of Madame de Maintenon, and which lasted an hour, and sometimes double that time; those that she very often had in the morning alone with Madame de Maintenon, rendered her the divinity of the Court. The Princesses encircled her the moment she appeared anywhere, and went to see her in her chamber. Nothing was more surprising than the servile eagerness with which the greatest people, the highest in power and the most in favour, clustered around her. Her very glances were counted, and her words, addressed even to ladies of the highest rank, imprinted upon them a look of ravishment.

I went nearly every morning to her house: she always rose very early, dressed herself at once, so that she was never seen at her toilette. I was in advance of the hour fixed for the most important visitors, and we talked with the same liberty as of yore. I learnt from her many details, and the opinion of the King and of Madame de Maintenon upon many people. We often used to laugh in concert at the truckling to her of persons the most considerable, and of the disdain they drew upon themselves, although she did not testify it to them. We laughed too at the falsehood of others, who after having done her all the injury in their power ever since her arrival, lavished upon her all kinds of flatteries, and boasted of their affection for her and of zeal in her cause. I was flattered with this confidence of the dictatress of the Court. It drew upon me a sudden consideration; for people of the greatest distinction often found me alone with her in the morning, and the messengers who rained down at that time reported that they had found me with her, and that they had not been able to speak to her. Oftentimes in the salon she called me to her, or at other times I went to her and whispered a word in her ear, with an air of ease and liberty much envied but little imitated. She never met Madame de Saint-Simon without going to her, praising her, making her join in the conversation that was passing around; oftentimes leading her to the glass and adjusting her head-dress or her robe as she might have done in private to a daughter. People asked with surprise and much annoyance whence came such a great friendship which had never been suspected by anybody? What completed the torment of the majority, was to see Madame des Ursins, as soon as she quitted the chamber of Madame de Maintenon, go immediately to Madame de Saint-Simon, lead her aside, and speak to her in a low tone. This opened the eyes of everybody and drew upon us many civilities.

A more solid gratification to us were the kind things Madame des Ursins said in our behalf to the King and Madame de Maintenon. She spoke in the highest praise of Madame de Saint-Simon, and declared that there was no woman at Court so fitting as she, so expressly made by her virtue, good conduct, and ability, to be lady of the Palace, or even lady-of-honour to Madame la Duchesse de Bourgogne, should the post become vacant. Madame des Ursins did not forget me; but a woman was more susceptible of her praise. It made, therefore, all the more impression. This kind manner towards us did not change during all her stay at Court.

At all the balls which Madame des Ursins attended, she was treated with much distinction, and at one she obtained permission for the Duc and Duchesse d'Albe to be present, but with some little trouble. I say with some little trouble, because no ambassador, no foreigner, had ever, with one exception, been admitted to Marly. It was a great favour, therefore, for Madame des Ursins to obtain. The King, too, treated the Duc and Duchesse d'Albe, throughout the evening with marked respect, and placed the latter in the most distinguished position, not only in the ball-room but at supper. When he went to bed, too, he gave the Duc d'Albe his candlestick; an honour the importance of which I have already described.

At the other balls Madame des Ursins seated herself near the Grand Chamberlain, and looked at everybody with her lorgnette. At every moment the King turned round to speak to her and Madame de Maintenon, who came for half an hour or so to these balls, and on her account displaced the Grand Chamberlain, who put himself behind her. In this manner she joined Madame des Ursins, and was close to the King—the conversation between the three being continual. What appeared extremely singular was to see Madame des Ursins in the salon with a little spaniel in her arms, as though she had been in her own house. People could not sufficiently express their astonishment at a familiarity which even Madame la Duchesse de Bourgogne would not have dared to venture; still less could they do so when they saw the King caress this little dog over and over again. In fine, such a high flight has never been seen. People could not accustom themselves to it, and those who knew the King and his Court are surprised still, when they think of it, after so many years. There was no longer any doubt that Madame des Ursins would return into Spain. All her frequent private conversations with the King and Madame de Maintenon were upon that country. I will only add here that her return took place in due time; and that her influence became more paramount than ever.

CHAPTER XXIX

In relating what happened to Madame des Ursins upon her return to Spain, I have carried the narrative into the year 1705. It is not necessary to retrace our steps. Towards the end of 1703 Courtin died. He had early shone at the Council, and had been made Intendant of Picardy. M. de Chaulnes, whose estates were there, begged him to tax them as lightly as possible. Courtin, who was a very intimate friend of M. de Chaulnes, complied with his request; but the next year, in going over his accounts, he found that to do a good turn to M. de Chaulnes he had done an ill turn to many others—that is to say, he had relieved M. de Chaulnes at the expense of other parishes, which he had overcharged. The trouble this caused him made him search deeply into the matter, and he found that the wrong he had done amounted to forty thousand francs. Without a second thought he paid back this money, and asked to be recalled. As he was much esteemed, his request was not at once complied with, but he represented so well that he could not pass his life doing wrong, and unable to serve his friends, that at last what he asked was granted. He afterwards had several embassies, went to England as ambassador, and was very successful in that capacity. I cannot quit Courtin without relating an adventure he had one day with Fieubet, a Councillor of State like himself. As they were going to Saint Germain they were stopped by several men and robbed; robbery was common in those days, and Fieubet lost all he had in his pockets. When the thieves had left them, and while Fieubet was complaining of his misfortune, Courtin began to applaud himself for having saved his watch and fifty pistoles that he had time to slip into his trowsers. Immediately on hearing this, Fieubet put his head out of the coach window, and called back the thieves, who came sure enough to see what he wanted.

"Gentlemen," said he, "you appear to be honest folks in distress; it is not reasonable that you should be the dupes of this gentleman, who his swindled you out of fifty pistoles and his watch." And then turning to Courtin, he smilingly said: "You told me so yourself, monsieur; so give the things up like a man, without being searched."

The astonishment and indignation of Courtin were such that he allowed money and watch to be taken from him without uttering a single word; but when the thieves were gone away, he would have strangled Fieubet had not this latter been the stronger of the two. Fieubet only laughed at him; and upon arriving at Saint Germain told the adventure to everybody he met. Their friends had all the trouble in the world to reconcile them.

The year finished with an affair in which I was not a little interested. During the year there were several grand fetes, at which the King went to High Mass and vespers. On these occasions a lady of the Court, named by the Queen, or when there was none, by the Dauphiness, made a collection for the poor. The house of Lorraine, always anxious to increase its importance, shirked impudently this duty, in order thereby to give itself a new distinction, and assimilate its rank to that of the Princes of the blood. It was a long time before this was perceived. At last the Duchesse de Noailles, the Duchesse de Guiche, her daughter, the Marechal de Boufflers, and others, took notice of it; and I was soon after informed of it. I determined that the matter should be arranged, and that justice should be done.

The Duchesse de Lude was first spoken to on the subject; she, weak and timid, did not dare to do anything; but at last was induced to speak to Madame la Duchesse de Bourgogne, who, wishing to judge for herself as to the truth of the matter, ordered Madame de Montbazon to make the collection for the poor at the next fete that took place. Although very well, Madame de Montbazon pretended to be ill, stopped in bed half a day, and excused herself on this ground from performing the duty. Madame de Bourgogne was annoyed, but she did not dare to push matters farther; and, in consequence of this refusal, none of the Duchesses would make the collection. Other ladies of quality soon perceived this, and they also refused to serve; so that the collection fell into all sorts of hands, and sometimes was not made at all. Matters went on so far, indeed, that the King at last grew angry, and threatened to make Madame de Bourgogne herself take this office. But refusals still followed upon refusals, and the bomb thus at length was ready to burst.

The King, who at last ordered the daughter of M. le Grand to take the plate on New Year's Day, 1704., had, it seems, got scent of the part I was taking in this matter, and expressed himself to Madame de Maintenon, as I learnt, as very discontented with me and one or two other Dukes. He said that the Dukes were much less obedient to him than the Princes; and that although many Duchesses had refused to make the collection, the moment he had proposed that the daughter of M. le Grand should take it, M. le Grand consented. On the next day, early in the morning, I saw Chamillart, who related to me that on the previous evening, before he had had time to open his business, the King had burst out in anger against me, saying it was very strange, but that since I had quitted the army I did nothing but meddle in matters of rank and bring actions against everybody; finishing, by declaring that if he acted well he should send me so far away that I should be unable to importune him any more. Chamillart added, that he had done all in his power to appease the King, but with little effect.

After consulting with my friends, I determined to go up to the King and boldly ask to speak to him in his cabinet, believing that to be the wisest course I could pursue. He was not yet so reconciled to me as he afterwards became, and, in fact, was sorely out of humour with me. This step did not seem, therefore, altogether unattended with danger; but, as I have said, I resolved to take it. As he passed, therefore, from his dinner that same day, I asked permission to follow him into his cabinet. Without replying to me, he made a sign that I might enter, and went into the embrasure of the window.

When we were quite alone I explained, at considerable length, my reasons for acting in this matter, declaring that it was from no disrespect to his Majesty that I had requested Madame de Saint-Simon and the other Duchesses to refuse to collect for the poor, but simply to bring those to account who had claimed without reason to be exempt from this duty. I added, keeping my eyes fixed upon the King all the time, that I begged him to believe that none of his subjects were more submissive to his will or more willing to acknowledge the supremacy of his authority in all things than the Dukes. Until this his tone and manner had been very severe; but now they both softened, and he said, with much goodness and familiarity, that "that was how it was proper to speak and think," and other remarks equally gracious. I took then the opportunity of expressing the sorrow I felt at seeing, that while my sole endeavour was to please him, my enemies did all they could to blacken me in his eyes, indicating that I suspected M. le Grand, who had never pardoned me for the part I took in the affair of the Princesse d'Harcourt, was one of the number. After I had finished the King remained still a moment, as if ready to hear if I had anything more to say, and then quitted me with a bow, slight but very gracious, saying it was well, and that he was pleased with me.

I learnt afterwards that he said the same thing of me in the evening to Chamillart, but, nevertheless, that he did not seem at all shaken in his prejudice in favour of M. le Grand. The King was in fact very easy to prejudice, difficult to lead back, and most unwilling to seek enlightenment, or to listen to any explanations, if authority was in the slightest degree at stake. Whoever had the address to make a question take this shape, might be assured that the King would throw aside all consideration of justice, right, and reason, and dismiss all evidence. It was by playing on this chord that his ministers knew how to manage him with so much art, and to make themselves despotic masters, causing him to believe all they wished, while at the same time they rendered him inaccessible to explanation, and to those who might have explained.

I have, perhaps, too much expanded an affair which might have been more compressed. But in addition to the fact that I was mixed up in it, it is by these little private details, as it seems to me, that the characters of the Court and King are best made known.

In the early part of the next year, 1704., the King made La Queue, who was a captain of cavalry, campmaster. This La Queue was seigneur of the place of which he bore the name, distant six leagues from Versailles, and as much from Dreux. He had married a girl that the King had had by a gardener's wife. Bontems, the confidential valet of the King, had brought about the marriage without declaring the names of the father or the mother of the girl; but La Queue knew it, and promised himself a fortune. The girl herself was tall and strongly resembled the King. Unfortunately for her, she knew the secret of her birth, and much envied her three sisters— recognised, and so grandly married. She lived on very good terms with her husband—always, however, in the greatest privacy— and had several children by him. La Queue himself, although by this marriage son-in-law of the King, seldom appeared at the Court, and, when there, was on the same footing as the simplest soldier. Bontems did not fail from time to time to give him money. The wife of La Queue lived very melancholily for twenty years in her village, never left it, and scarcely ever went abroad for fear of betraying herself.

On Wednesday, the 25th of June, Monseigneur le Duc de Bourgogne had a son born to him. This event caused great joy to the King and the Court. The town shared their delight, and carried their enthusiasm almost to madness, by the excess of their demonstration and their fetes. The King gave a fete at Marly, and made the most magnificent presents to Madame la Duchesse de Bourgogne when she left her bed. But we soon had reason to repent of so much joy, for the child died in less than a year—and of so much money unwisely spent, in fetes when it was wanted for more pressing purposes. Even while these rejoicings were being celebrated, news reached us which spread consternation in every family, and cast a gloom over the whole city.

I have already said that a grand alliance, with the Emperor at its head, had been formed against

France, and that our troops were opposing the Allies in various parts of Europe. The Elector of Bavaria had joined his forces to ours, and had already done us some service. On the 12th of August he led his men into the plain of Hochstedt, where, during the previous year, he had gained a victory over the Imperialists. In this plain he was joined by our troops, who took up positions right and left of him, under the command of Tallard and Marsin. The Elector himself had command of all. Soon after their arrival at Hochstedt, they received intelligence that Prince Eugene, with the Imperialist forces, and the Duke of Marlborough with the English were coming to meet them. Our generals had, however, all the day before them to choose their ground, and to make their dispositions. It would have been difficult to succeed worse, both with the one and the other. A brook, by no means of a miry kind, ran parallel to our army; and in front of it a spring, which formed a long and large quagmire, nearly separated the two lines of Marshal Tallard. It was a strange situation for a general to take up, who is master of a vast plain; and it became, as will be seen, a very sad one. At his extreme right was the large village of Blenheim, in which, by a blindness without example, he had placed twenty-six battalions of infantry, six regiments of dragoons, and a brigade of cavalry. It was an entire army merely for the purpose of holding this village, and supporting his right, and of course he had all these troops the less to aid him in the battle which took place. The first battle of Hochstedt afforded a lesson which ought to have been studied on this occasion. There were many officers present, too, who had been at that battle; but they were not consulted. One of two courses was open, either to take up a position behind the brook, and parallel to it, so as to dispute its passage with the enemies, or to take advantage of the disorder they would be thrown into in crossing it by attacking them then. Both these plans were good; the second was the better; but neither was adopted. What was done was, to leave a large space between our troops and the brook, that the enemy might pass at their ease, and be overthrown afterwards, as was said. With such dispositions it is impossible to doubt but that our chiefs were struck with blindness. The Danube flowed near enough to Blenheim to be of sufficient support to our right, better indeed than that village, which consequently there was no necessity to hold.

The enemies arrived on the 13th of August at the dawn, and at once took up their position on the banks of the brook. Their surprise must have been great to see our army so far off, drawn up in battle array. They profited by the extent of ground left to them, crossed the brook at nearly every point, formed themselves in several lines on the side to which they crossed, and then extended themselves at their ease, without receiving the slightest opposition. This is exact truth, but without any appearance of being so; and posterity will with difficulty believe it. It was nearly eight o'clock before all these dispositions, which our troops saw made without moving, were completed. Prince Eugene with his army had the right; the Duke of Marlborough the left. The latter thus opposed to the forces of Tallard, and Prince Eugene to those of Marsin.

The battle commenced; and in one part was so far favourable to us that the attack of Prince Eugene was repulsed by Marsin, who might have profited by this circumstance but for the unfortunate position of our right. Two things contributed to place us at a disadvantage. The second line, separated by the quagmire I have alluded to from the first line, could not sustain it properly; and in consequence of the long bend it was necessary to make round this quagmire, neither line, after receiving or making a charge, could retire quickly to rally and return again to the attack. As for the infantry, the twenty-six battalions shut up in Blenheim left a great gap in it that could not fail to, be felt. The English, who soon perceived the advantage they might obtain from this want of infantry, and from the difficulty with which our cavalry of the right was rallied, profited by these circumstances with the readiness of people who have plenty of ground at their disposal. They redoubled their charges, and to say all in one word, they defeated at their first attack all this army, notwithstanding the efforts of our general officers and of several regiments to repel them. The army of the Elector, entirely unsupported, and taken in flank by the English, wavered in its turn. All the valour of the Bavarians, all the prodigies of the Elector, were unable to remedy the effects of this wavering. Thus was seen, at one and the same time, the army of Tallard beaten and thrown into the utmost disorder; that of the Elector sustaining itself with great intrepidity, but already in retreat; and that of Marsin charging and gaining ground upon Prince Eugene. It was not until Marsin learnt of the defeat of Tallard and of the Elector, that he ceased to pursue his advantages, and commenced his retreat. This retreat he was able to make without being pursued.

After the Battle of Blenheim--painted by R. Canton Woodville

In the mean time the troops in Blenheim had been twice attacked, and had twice repulsed the enemy. Tallard had given orders to these troops on no account to leave their positions, nor to allow a single man even to quit them. Now, seeing his army defeated and in flight, he wished to countermand these orders. He was riding in hot haste to Blenheim to do so, with only two attendants, when all three were surrounded, recognised, and taken prisoners.

These troops shut up in Blenheim had been left under the command of Blansac, camp-marshal, and Clerembault, lieutenant-general. During the battle this latter was missed, and could nowhere be found. It was known afterwards that, for fear of being killed, he had endeavoured to escape across the Danube on horseback attended by a single valet. The valet passed over the river in safety, but his master went to the bottom. Blansac, thus left alone in command, was much troubled by the disorders he saw and heard, and by the want which he felt of fresh orders. He sent a messenger to Tallard for instructions how to act, but his messenger was stopped on the road, and taken prisoner. I only repeat what Blansac himself reported in his defence, which was equally ill-received by the King and the public, but which had no contradictors, for nobody was witness of what took place at Blenheim except those actually there, and they all, the principals at least, agreed in their story. What some of the soldiers said was not of a kind that could altogether be relied upon.

While Blansac was in this trouble, he saw Denonville, one of our officers who had been taken prisoner, coming towards the village, accompanied by an officer who waved a handkerchief in the air and demanded a parley. Denonville was a young man, very handsome and well made, who being a great favourite with Monseigneur le Duc de Bourgogne had become presumptuous and somewhat audacious. Instead of speaking in private to Blansac and the other principal officers—since he had undertaken so strange a mission—Denonville, who had some intellect, plenty of fine talk, and a mighty opinion of himself, set to work haranguing the troops, trying to persuade them to surrender themselves prisoners of war, so that they might preserve themselves for the service of the King. Blansac, who saw the wavering this caused among the troops, sharply told Denonville to hold his tongue, and began himself to harangue the troops in a contrary spirit. But it was to late. The mischief was done. Only one regiment, that of Navarre, applauded him, all the rest maintained a dull silence. I remind my readers that it is Blansac's version of the story I am giving.

Soon after Denonville and his companion had returned to the enemy, an English lord came, demanding a parley with the commandant. He was admitted to Blansac, to whom he said that the Duke of Marlborough had sent him to say that he had forty battalions and sixty pieces of cannon at his disposal, with reinforcements to any extent at command; that he should surround the village on all sides; that the army of Tallard was in flight, and the remains of that of the Elector in retreat; that Tallard and many general officers were prisoners; that Blansac could hope for no reinforcements; and that, therefore, he had better at once make an honourable capitulation, and surrender, himself with all his men prisoners of war, than attempt a struggle in which he was sure to be worsted with great loss. Blansac wanted to dismiss this messenger at once, but the Englishman pressed him to advance a few steps out of the village, and see with his own eyes the defeat of the Electoral army, and the preparations that were made on the other side to continue the battle. Blansac accordingly, attended by one of his officers, followed this lord, and was astounded to see with his own eyes that all he had just heard was true. Returned into Bleinheim, Blansac assembled all his principal officers, made them acquainted with the proposition that had been made, and told them what he had himself seen. Every one comprehended what a frightful shock it would be for the country when it learnt that they had surrendered themselves prisoners of war; but all things well considered, it was thought best to accept these terms, and so preserve to the King the twenty-six battalions and the twelve squadrons of dragoons who were there. This terrible capitulation was at once, therefore, drawn up and signed by Blansac, the general officers, and the heads of every corps except that of Navarre, which was thus the sole one which refused.

The number of prisoners that fell to the enemy in this battle was infinite. The Duke of Marlborough took charge of the most distinguished, until he could carry them away to England, to grace his triumph there. He treated them all, even the humblest, with the utmost attention, consideration, and politeness, and with a modesty that did him even more honour than his victory. Those that came under the charge of Prince Louis of Baden were much less kindly treated.

The King received the cruel news of this battle on the 21st of August, by a courier from the Marechal de Villeroy. By this courier the King learnt that a battle had taken place on the 13th; had lasted from eight o'clock in the morning until evening; that the entire army of Tallard was killed or taken prisoners; that it was not known what had become of Tallard himself, or whether the Elector and Marsin had been at the action. The private letters that arrived were all opened to see what news they contained, but no fresh information could be got from them. For six days the King remained in this uncertainty as to the real losses that had been sustained. Everybody was afraid to write bad news; all the letters which from time to time arrived, gave, therefore, but an unsatisfactory account of what had taken place. The King used every means in his power to obtain some news. Every post that came in was examined by him, but there was little found to satisfy him. Neither the King nor anybody else could understand, from what had reached them, how it was that an entire army had been placed inside a village, and had surrendered itself by a signed capitulation. It puzzled every brain. At last the details, that had oozed out little by little, augmented to a perfect stream, by the arrival of one of our officers, who, taken prisoner, had been allowed by the Duke of Marlborough to go to Paris to relate to the King the misfortune that had happened to him.

We were not accustomed to misfortunes. This one, very reasonably, was utterly unexpected. It seemed in every way the result of bad generalship, of an unjustifiable disposition of troops, and of a series of gross and incredible errors. The commotion was general. There was scarcely an illustrious family that had not had one of its members killed, wounded, or taken prisoner. Other families were in the same case. The public sorrow and indignation burst out without restraint. Nobody who had taken part in this humiliation was spared; the generals and the private soldiers alike came in for blame. Denonville was ignominiously broken for the speech he had made at Blenheim. The generals, however, were entirely let off. All the punishment fell upon certain regiments, which were broken, and upon certain unimportant officers—the guilty and innocent mixed together. The outcry was universal. The grief of the King at this ignominy and this loss, at the moment when he imagined that the fate of the Emperor was in his hands, may be imagined. At a time when he might have counted upon striking a decisive blow, he saw himself reduced to act simply on the defensive, in order to preserve his troops; and had to repair the loss of an entire army, killed or taken prisoners. The sequel showed not less that the hand of God was weighty upon us. All judgment was lost. We trembled even in the midst of Alsace.

In the midst of all this public sorrow, the rejoicing and the fetes for the birth of the Duc de Bretagne son of Monseigneur le Duc de Bourgogne, were not discontinued. The city gave a firework fete upon the river, that Monseigneur, the Princes, his sons, and Madame la Duchesse de Bourgogne, with many ladies and courtiers, came to see from the windows of the Louvre, magnificent cheer and refreshments being provided for them. This was a contrast which irritated the people, who would not understand that it was meant for magnanimity. A few days afterwards the King gave an illumination and a fete at Marly, to which the Court of Saint Germain was invited; and which was all in honour of Madame la Duchesse de Bourgogne. He thanked the Prevot des Marchand for the fireworks upon the river, and said that Monseigneur and Madame had found them very beautiful.

Shortly after this, I received a letter from one of my friends, the Duc de Montfort, who had always been in the army of the Marechal de Villeroy. He sent word to me, that upon his return he intended to break his sword, and retire from the army. His letter was written in such a despairing tone that, fearing lest with his burning courage he might commit some martial folly, I conjured him not to throw himself into danger for the sake of being killed. It seemed that I had anticipated his intentions. A convoy of money was to be sent to Landau. Twice he asked to be allowed to take charge of this convoy, and twice he was told it was too insignificant a charge for a camp-marshal to undertake. The third time that he asked this favour, he obtained it by pure importunity. He carried the money safely into Landau, without meeting with any obstacle. On his return he saw some hussars roving about. Without a moment's hesitation he resolved to give chase to them. He was with difficulty restrained for some time, and a last, breaking away, he set off to attack them, followed by only two officers. The hussars dispersed themselves, and retreated; the Duc de Montfort followed them, rode into the midst of them, was surrounded on all sides, and soon received a blow which overturned him. In a few moments after, being carried off by his men, he died, having only had time to confess himself, and to arrive at his quarters. He was infinitely regretted by everybody who had known him. The grief of his family may be imagined.

CHAPTER XXX

The King did not long remain without some consolation for the loss of the battle of Hochstedt (Blenheim). The Comte de Toulouse—very different in every respect from his brother, the Duc du Maine—was wearied with cruising in the Mediterranean, without daring to attack enemies that were too strong for him. He had, therefore, obtained reinforcements this year, so that he was in a state to measure his forces with any opponent. The English fleet was under the command of Admiral Rooks. The Comte de Toulouse wished above all things to attack. He asked permission to do so, and, the permission being granted, he set about his enterprise. He met the fleet of Admiral Rooks near Malaga, on the 24th of September of this year, and fought with it from ten o'clock in the morning until eight o'clock in the evening. The fleets, as far as the number of vessels was concerned, were nearly equal. So furious or so obstinate a sea-fight had not been seen for a long time. They had always the wind upon our fleet, yet all the advantage was on the side of the Comte de Toulouse, who could boast that he had obtained the victory, and whose vessel fought that of Rooks, dismasted it, and pursued it all next day towards the coast of Barbary, where the Admiral retired. The enemy lost six thousand men; the ship of the Dutch Vice-Admiral was blown up; several others were sunk, and some dismasted. Our fleet lost neither ship nor mast, but the victory cost the lives of many distinguished people, in addition to those of fifteen hundred soldiers or sailors killed or wounded.

Towards evening on the 25th, by dint of maneuvers, aided by the wind, our fleet came up again with that of Rooks. The Comte de Toulouse was for attacking it again on the morrow, and showed that if the attack were successful, Gibraltar would be the first result of the victory. That famous place, which commands the important strait of the same name, had been allowed to fall into neglect, and was defended by a miserable garrison of forty men. In this state it had of course easily fallen into the hands of the enemies. But they had not yet had time to man it with a much superior force, and Admiral Rooks once defeated, it must have surrendered to us.

The Comte de Toulouse urged his advice with all the energy of which he was capable, and he was supported in opinion by others of more experience than himself. But D'O, the mentor of the fleet, against whose counsel he had been expressly ordered by the King never to act, opposed the project of another attack with such disdainful determination, that the Comte had no course open but to give way. The annoyance which this caused throughout the fleet was very great. It soon was known what would have become of the enemy's fleet had it been attacked, and that Gibraltar would have been found in exactly the same state as when abandoned. The Comte de Toulouse acquired great honour in this campaign, and his stupid teacher lost little, because he had little to lose.

M. de Mantua having surrendered his state to the King, thereby rendering us a most important service in Italy, found himself ill at ease in his territory, which had become the theatre of war, and had come incognito to Paris. He had apartments provided for him in the Luxembourg, furnished magnificently with the Crown furniture, and was very graciously received by the King. The principal object of his journey was to marry some French lady; and as he made no secret of this intention, more than one plot was laid in order to provide him with a wife. M. de Vaudemont, intent upon aggrandizing the house of Lorraine, wished. M de Mantua to marry a member of that family, and fixed upon Mademoiselle d'Elboeuf for his bride. The Lorraines did all in their power to induce M. de Mantua to accept her. But M. le Prince had also his designs in this matter. He had a daughter; whom he knew not how to get off his hands, and he thought that in more ways than one it would be to his advantage to marry her to the Duke of Mantua. He explained his views to the King, who gave him permission to follow them out, and promised to serve him with all his protection. But when the subject was broached to M. de Mantua, he declined this match in such a respectful, yet firm, manner that M. le Prince felt he must abandon all hope of carrying it out. The Lorraines were not more successful in their designs. When M. de Vaudemont had first spoken of Mademoiselle d'Elboeuf, M. de Mantua had appeared to listen favourably. This was in Italy. Now that he was in Paris he acted very differently. It was in vain that Mademoiselle d'Elboeuf was thrust in his way, as though by chance, at the promenades, in the churches; her beauty, which might have touched many others, made no impression upon him. The fact was that M. de Mantua, even long before leaving his state, had fixed upon a wife.

Supping one evening with the Duc de Lesdiguieres, a little before the death of the latter, he saw a ring with a portrait in it; upon the Duke's finger. He begged to be allowed to look at the portrait, was charmed with it, and said he should be very happy to have such a beautiful mistress. The Duke at this burst out laughing, and said it was the portrait of his wife. As soon as the Duc de Lesdiguieres was dead, de Mantua thought only of marrying the young widowed Duchess. He sought her everywhere when he arrived in Paris, but without being able to find her; because she was in the first year of her widowhood. He therefore unbosomed himself to Torcy, who reported the matter to the King. The King approved of the design of M. de Mantua, and charged the Marechal de Duras to speak to the Duchesse de Lesdiguieres, who was his daughter. The Duchess was equally surprised and afflicted when she learned what was in progress. She testified to her father her repugnance to abandon herself to the caprices and the jealousy of an old Italian 'debauche' the horror she felt at the idea of being left alone with him in Italy; and the reasonable fear she had of her health, with a man whose own could not be good.

I was promptly made acquainted with this affair; for Madame de Lesdiguieres and Madame de Saint-Simon were on the most intimate terms. I did everything in my power to persuade Madame de Lesdirguieres to content to the match, insisting at once on her family position, on the reason of state, and on the pleasure of ousting Madame d'Elboeuf,—but it was all in vain. I never saw such firmness. Pontchartrain, who came and reasoned with her, was even less successful than I, for he excited her by threats and menaces. M. le Prince himself supported us—having no longer any hope for himself, and fearing, above all things, M. de Mantua's marriage with a Lorraine— and did all he could to persuade Madame de Lesdiguieres to give in. I renewed my efforts in the same direction, but with no better success than before. Nevertheless, M. de Mantua, irritated by not being able to see Madame de Lesdirguieres, resolved to go and wait for her on a Sunday at the Minimes. He found her shut up in a chapel, and drew near the door in order to see her as she went out. He was not much gratified; her thick crape veil was lowered; it was with difficulty he could get a glance at her. Resolved to succeed, he spoke to Torcy, intimating that Madame de Lesdiguieres ought not to refuse such a slight favour as to allow herself to be seen in a church. Torcy communicated this to the King, who sent word to Madame de Lesdiguieres that she must consent to the favour M. de Mantua demanded. She could not refuse after this. M. de Mantua went accordingly, and waited for her in the same place, where he had once already so badly seen her. He found her, in the chapel, and drew near the door, as before. She came out, her veil raised, passed lightly before him, made him a sliding courtesy as she glided by, in reply to his bow, and reached her coach.

M. de Mantua was charmed; he redoubled his efforts with the King and M. de Duras; the matter was discussed in full council, like an affair of state—indeed it was one; and it was resolved to amuse M. de Mantua, and yet at the same time to do everything to vanquish this resistance of Madame de Lesdiguieres, except employing the full authority of the King, which the King himself did not wish to exert. Everything was promised to her on the part of the King: that it should be his Majesty who would make the stipulations of the marriage contract; that it should be his Majesty who would give her a dowry, and would guarantee her return to France if she became a widow, and assure her his protection while she remained a wife; in one word, everything was tried, and in the gentlest and most honourable manner, to persuade her. Her mother lent us her house one afternoon, in order that we might speak more at length and more at our ease there to Madame de Lesdiguieres than we could at the Hotel de Duras. We only gained a torrent of tears for our pains.

A few days after this, I was very much astonished to hear Chamillart relate to me all that had passed at this interview. I learnt afterwards that Madame de Lesdiguieres, fearing that if, entirely unsupported, she persisted in her refusal, it might draw upon her the anger of the King, had begged Chamillart to implore his Majesty not to insist upon this marriage. M. de Mantua hearing this, turned his thoughts elsewhere; and she was at last delivered of a pursuit which had become a painful persecution to her. Chamillart served her so well that the affair came to an end; and the King, flattered perhaps by the desire this young Duchess showed to remain his subject instead of becoming a sovereign, passed a eulogium upon her the same evening in his cabinet to his family and to the Princesses, by whom it was spread abroad through society.

I may as well finish this matter at once. The Lorraines, who had watched very closely the affair up to this point, took hope again directly they heard of the resolution M. de Mantua had formed to abandon his pursuit of Madame de Lesdiguieres. They, in their turn, were closely watched by M. le Prince, who so excited the King against them, that Madame d'Elboeuf received orders from him not to continue pressing her suit upon M. de Mantua. That did not stop them. They felt that the King would not interfere with them by an express prohibition, and sure, by past experience, of being on better terms with him afterwards than before, they pursued their object with obstinacy. By dint of much plotting and scheming, and by the aid of their creatures, they contrived to overcome the repugnance of M. de Mantua to Mademoiselle d'Elboeuf, which at bottom could be only caprice—her beauty, her figure, and her birth taken into account. But Mademoiselle d'Elboeuf, in her turn, was as opposed to marriage with M. de Mantua as Madame de Lesdiguieres had been. She was, however, brought round ere long, and then the consent of the King was the only thing left to be obtained. The Lorraines made use of their usual suppleness in order to gain that. They represented the impolicy of interfering with the selection of a sovereign who was the ally of France, and who wished to select a wife from among her subjects, and succeeded so well, that the King determined to become neutral; that is to say, neither to prohibit nor to sanction this match. M. le Prince was instrumental in inducing the King to take this neutral position; and he furthermore caused the stipulation to be made, that it should not be celebrated in France, but at Mantua.

After parting with the King, M. de Mantua, on the 21st of September, went to Nemours, slept there, and then set out for Italy. At the same time Madame and Mademoiselle d'Elboeuf, with Madame de Pompadour, sister of the former, passed through Fontainebleau without going to see a soul, and followed their prey lest he should change his mind and escape them until the road he was to take branched off from that they were to go by; he in fact intending to travel by sea and they by land. On the way their fears redoubled. Arrived at Nevers, and lodged in a hostelrie, they thought it would not be well to commit themselves further without more certain security: Madame de Pompadour therefore proposed to M. de Mantua not to delay his happiness any longer, but to celebrate his marriage at once. He defended himself as well as he could, but was at last obliged to give in. During this indecent dispute, the Bishop was sent to. He had just died, and the Grand Vicar, not knowing what might be the wishes of the King upon this marriage, refused to celebrate it. The chaplain was therefore appealed to, and he at once married Mademoiselle d'Elboeuf to M. de Mantua in the hotel. As soon as the ceremony was over, Madame d'Elboeuf wished to leave her daughter alone with M. de Mantua, and although he strongly objected to this, everybody quitted the room, leaving only the newly married couple there, and Madame de Pompadour outside upon the step listening to what passed between them. But finding after a while that both were very much embarrassed, and that M. de Mantua did little but cry out for the company to return, she conferred with her sister, and they agreed to give him his liberty. Immediately he had obtained it, he mounted his horse, though it was not early, and did not see them again until they reached Italy—though all went the same road as far as Lyons. The news of this strange celebration of marriage was soon spread abroad with all the ridicule which attached to it.

The King was very much annoyed when he learnt that his orders had been thus disobeyed. The Lorraines plastered over the affair by representing that they feared an affront from M. de Mantua, and indeed it did not seem at all unlikely that M. de Mantua, forced as it were into compliance with their wishes, might have liked nothing better than to reach Italy and then laugh at them. Meanwhile, Madame d'Elboeuf and her daughter embarked on board the royal galleys and started for Italy. On the way they were fiercely chased by some African corsairs, and it is a great pity they were not taken to finish the romance.

However, upon arriving in Italy, the marriage was again celebrated, this time with all the forms necessary for the occasion. But Madame d'Elboeuf had no cause to rejoice that she had succeeded in thus disposing of her daughter. The new Duchesse de Mantua was guarded by her husband with the utmost jealousy. She was not allowed to see anybody except her mother, and that only for an hour each day. Her women entered her apartment only to dress and undress her. The Duke walled up very high all the windows of his house, and caused his wife to, be guarded by old women. She passed her days thus in a cruel prison. This treatment, which I did not expect, and the little consideration, not to say contempt, shown here for M. de Mantua since his departure, consoled me much for the invincible obstinacy of Madame de Lesdiguieres. Six months after, Madame d'Elboeuf returned, beside herself with vexation, but too vain to show it. She disguised the misfortune of her daughter, and appeared to be offended if it was spoken of; but all our letters from the army showed that the news was true. The strangest thing of all is, that the Lorraines after this journey were as well treated by the King as if they had never undertaken it; a fact which shows their art and ascendency.

I have dwelt too long perhaps upon this matter. It appeared to me to merit attention by its singularity, and still more so because it is by facts of this sort that is shown what was the composition of the Court of the King.

About this time the Comtesse d'Auvergne finished a short life by an illness very strange and uncommon. When she married the Comte d'Auvergne she was a Huguenot, and he much wanted to make her turn Catholic. A famous advocate of that time, who was named Chardon, had been a Huguenot, and his wife also; they had made a semblance, however, of abjuring, but made no open profession of Catholicism. Chardon was sustained by his great reputation, and by the number of protectors he had made for himself.

One morning he and his wife were in their coach before the Hotel-Dieu, waiting for a reply that their lackey was a very long time in bringing them. Madame Chardon glanced by chance upon the grand portal of Notre Dame, and little by little fell into a profound reverie, which might be better called reflection. Her husband, who at last perceived this, asked her what had sent her into such deep thought, and pushed her elbow even to draw a reply from her. She told him then what she was thinking about. Pointing to Notre Dame, she said that it was many centuries before Luther and Calvin that those images of saints had been sculptured over that portal; that this proved that saints had long since been invoked; the opposition of the reformers to this ancient opinion was a novelty; that this novelty rendered suspicious other dogmas against the antiquity of Catholicism that they taught; that these reflections, which she had never before made, gave her much disquietude, and made her form the resolution to seek to enlighten herself.

Chardon thought his wife right, and from that day they laid themselves out to seek the truth, then to consult, then to be instructed. This lasted a year, and then they made a new abjuration, and both ever afterwards passed their lives in zeal and good works. Madame Chardon converted many Huguenots. The Comte d'Auvergne took his wife to her. The Countess was converted by her, and became a very good Catholic. When she died she was extremely regretted by all the relatives of her husband, although at first they had looked upon her coldly.

In the month of this September, a strange attempt at assassination occurred. Vervins had been forced into many suits against his relatives, and was upon the point of gaining them all, when one of his cousins- german, who called himself the Abbe de Pre, caused him to be attacked as he passed in his coach along the Quai de la Tournelle, before the community of Madame de Miramion. Vervins was wounded with several sword cuts, and also his coachman, who wished to defend him. In consequence of the complaint Vervins made, the Abbe escaped abroad, whence he never returned, and soon after, his crime being proved, was condemned to be broken alive on the wheel. Vervins had long been menaced with an attack by the Abbe. Vervins was an agreeable, well-made man, but very idle. He had entered the army; but quitted it soon, and retired to his estates in Picardy. There he shut himself up without any cause of disgust or of displeasure, without being in any embarrassment, for on the contrary he was well to do, and all his affairs were in good order, and he never married; without motives of piety, for piety was not at all in his vein; without being in bad health, for his health was always perfect; without a taste for improvement, for no workmen were ever seen in his house; still less on account of the chase, for he never went to it. Yet he stayed in his house for several years, without intercourse with a soul, and, what is most incomprehensible, without budging from his bed, except to allow it to be made. He dined there, and often all alone; he transacted what little business he had to do there, and received while there the few people he could not refuse admission to; and each day, from the moment he opened his eyes until he closed them again, worked at tapestry, or read a little; he persevered until his death in this strange fashion of existence; so uniquely singular, that I have wished to describe it.

CHAPTER XXXI

There presents itself to my memory an anecdote which it would be very prudent perhaps to be silent upon, and which is very curious for anybody who has seen things so closely as I have, to describe. What determines me to relate it is that the fact is not altogether unknown, and that every Court swarms with similar adventures. Must it be said then? We had amongst us a charming young Princess who, by her graces, her attentions, and her original manners, had taken possession of the hearts of the King, of Madame de Maintenon, and of her husband, Monseigneur le Duc de Bourgogne. The extreme discontent so justly felt against her father, M. de Savoie, had not made the slightest alteration in their tenderness for her. The King, who hid nothing from her, who worked with his ministers in her presence whenever she liked to enter, took care not to say a word in her hearing against her father. In private, she clasped the King round the neck at all hours, jumped upon his knees, tormented him with all sorts of sportiveness, rummaged among his papers, opened his letters end read them in his presence, sometimes in spite of him; and acted in the same manner with Madame de Maintenon. Despite this extreme liberty, she never spoke against any one: gracious to all, she endeavoured to ward off blows from all whenever she could; was attentive to the private comforts of the King, even the humblest: kind to all who served her, and living with her ladies, as with friends, in complete liberty, old and young; she was the darling of the Court, adored by all; everybody, great and small, was anxious to please her; everybody missed her when she was away; when she reappeared the void was filled up; in a word, she had attached all hearts to her; but while in this brilliant situation she lost her own.

Nangis, now a very commonplace Marshal of France, was at that time in full bloom. He had an agreeable but not an uncommon face; was well made, without anything marvellous; and had been educated in intrigue by the Marechale de Rochefort, his grandmother, and Madame de Blansac, his mother, who were skilled mistresses of that art. Early introduced by them into the great world of which they were, so to speak, the centre, he had no talent but that of pleasing women, of speaking their language, and of monopolising the most desirable by a discretion beyond his years, and which did not belong to his time. Nobody was more in vogue than he. He had had the command of a regiment when he was quite a child. He had shown firmness, application, and brilliant valour in war, that the ladies had made the most of, and they sufficed at his age; he was of the Court of Monseigneur le Duc de Bourgogne, about the same age, and well treated by him.

The Duc de Bourgogne, passionately in love with his wife, was not so well made as Nangis; but the Princess reciprocated his ardor so perfectly that up to his death he never suspected that her glances had wandered to any one else. They fell, however, upon Nangis, and soon redoubled. Nangis was not ungrateful, but he feared the thunderbolt; and his heart, too, was already engaged. Madame de la Vrilliere, who, without beauty, was pretty and grateful as Love, had made this conquest. She was, as I have said, daughter of Madame de Mailly, Dame d'Atours of Madame la Duchesse de Bourgogne; and was always near her. Jealousy soon enlightened her as to what was taking place. Far from yielding her conquest to the Duchess; she made a point of preserving it, of disputing its possession, and carrying it off. This struggle threw Nangis into a terrible embarrassment. He feared the fury of Madame de la Vrilliere, who affected to be more ready to break out than in reality she was. Besides his love for her, he feared the result of an outburst, and already saw his fortune lost. On the other hand, any reserve of his towards the Duchess, who had so much power in her hands—and seemed destined to have more—and who he knew was not likely to suffer a rival —might, he felt, be his ruin. This perplexity, for those who were aware of it, gave rise to continual scenes. I was then a constant visitor of Madame de Blansac, at Paris, and of the Marechale de Rochefort, at Versailles; and, through them and several other ladies of the Court, with whom I was intimate, I learnt, day by day, everything that passed. In addition to the fact that nothing diverted me more, the results of this affair might be great; and it was my especial ambition to be well informed of everything. At length, all members of the Court who were assiduous and enlightened understood the state of affairs; but either through fear or from love to the Duchess, the whole Court was silent, saw everything, whispered discreetly, and actually kept the secret that was not entrusted to it. The struggle between the two ladies, not without bitterness, and sometimes insolence on the part of Madame de la Vrilliere, nor without suffering and displeasure gently manifested on the part of Madame de Bourgogne, was for a long time a singular sight.

Whether Nangis, too faithful to his first love, needed some grains of jealousy to excite him, or whether things fell out naturally, it happened that he found a rival. Maulevrier, son of a brother of Colbert who had died of grief at not being named Marshal of France, was this rival. He had married a daughter of the Marechal de Tesse, and was not very agreeable in appearance—his face, indeed, was very commonplace. He was by no means framed for gallantry; but he had wit, and a mind fertile in intrigues, with a measureless ambition that was sometimes pushed to madness. His wife was pretty, not clever, quarrelsome, and under a virginal appearance; mischievous to the last degree. As daughter of a man for whom Madame de Bourgogne had much gratitude for the part he had taken in negotiating her marriage, and the Peace of Savoy, she was easily enabled to make her way at Court, and her husband with her. He soon sniffed what was passing in respect to Nangis, and obtained means of access to Madame de Bourgogne, through the influence of his father-in- law; was assiduous in his attentions; and at length, excited by example, dared to sigh. Tired of not being understood, he ventured to write. It is pretended that he sent his letters through one of the Court ladies, who thought they came from Tesse, delivered them, and handed him back the answers, as though for delivery by him. I will not add what more was believed. I will simply say that this affair was as soon perceived as had been the other, and was treated, with the same silence.

Under pretext of friendship, Madame de Bourgogne went more than once—on account of the speedy departure of her husband (for the army), attended some, times by La Maintenon,—to the house of Madame de Maulevrier, to weep with her. The Court smiled. Whether the tears were for Madame de Maulevrier or for Nangis, was doubtful. But Nangis, nevertheless, aroused by this rivalry, threw Madame de la Vrilliere into terrible grief, and into a humour over which she was not mistress.

This tocsin made itself heard by Maulevrier. What will not a man think of doing when possessed to excess by love or ambition? He pretended to have something the matter with his chest, put himself on a milk diet, made believe that he had lost his voice, and was sufficiently master of himself to refrain from uttering an intelligible word during a whole year; by these means evading the campaign and remaining at the Court. He was mad enough to relate this project, and many others, to his friend the Duc de Lorges, from whom, in turn, I learnt it. The fact was, that bringing himself thus to the necessity of never speaking to anybody except in their ear, he had the liberty of speaking low to—Madame la Duchesse de Bourgogne before all the Court without impropriety and without suspicion. In this manner he said to her whatever he wished day by day, and was never overheard. He also contrived to say things the short answers to which were equally unheard. He so accustomed people to this manner of speaking that they took no more notice of it than was expressed in pity for such a sad state; but it happened that those who approached the nearest to Madame la Duchesse de Bourgogne when Maulevrier was at her side, soon knew enough not to be eager to draw near her again when she was thus situated. This trick lasted more than a year: his conversation was principally composed of reproaches— but reproaches rarely succeed in love. Maulevrier, judging by the ill-humour of Madame de la Vrilliere, believed Nangis to be happy. Jealousy and rage transported him at last to the extremity of folly.

One day, as Madame de Bourgogne was coming from mass and he knew that Dangeau, her chevalier d'honneur, was absent, he gave her his hand. The attendants had accustomed themselves to let him have this honour, on account of his distinguished voice, so as to allow him to speak by the way, and retired respectfully so as not to hear what he said. The ladies always followed far behind, so that, in the midst of all the Court, he had, from the chapel to the apartments of Madame de Bourgogne, the full advantages of a private interview—advantages that he had availed himself of several times. On this day he railed against Nangis to Madame de Bourgogne, called him by all sorts of names, threatened to tell everything to the King and to Madame de Maintenon, and to the Duc de Bourgogne, squeezed her fingers as if he would break them, and led her in this manner, like a madman as he was, to her apartments. Upon entering them she was ready to swoon. Trembling all over she entered her wardrobe, called one of her favourite ladies, Madame de Nogaret, to her, related what had occurred, saying she knew not how she had reached her rooms, or how it was she had not sunk beneath the floor, or died. She had never been so dismayed. The same day Madame de Nogaret related this to Madame de Saint-Simon and to me, in the strictest confidence. She counselled the Duchess to behave gently with such a dangerous madman, and to avoid committing herself in any way with him. The worst was, that after this he threatened and said many things against Nangis, as a man with whom he was deeply offended, and whom he meant to call to account. Although he gave no reason for this, the reason was only too evident. The fear of Madame de Bourgogne at this may be imagined, and also that of Nangis. He was brave and cared for nobody; but to be mixed up in such an affair as this made him quake with fright. He beheld his fortune and his happiness in the hands of a furious madman. He shunned Maulevrier from that time as much as possible, showed himself but little, and held his peace.

For six weeks Madame de Bourgogne lived in the most measured manner, and in mortal tremors of fear, without, however, anything happening. I know not who warned Tesse of what was going on. But when he learnt it he acted like a man of ability. He persuaded his son-in-law, Maulevrier, to follow him to Spain, as to a place where his fortune was assured to him. He spoke to Fagon, who saw all and knew all. He understood matters in a moment, and at once said, that as so many remedies had been tried ineffectually for Maulevrier, he must go to a warmer climate, as a winter in France would inevitably kill him. It was then as a remedy, and as people go to the waters, that he went to Spain. The King and all the Court believed this, and neither the King nor Madame de Maintenon offered any objections. As soon as Tesse knew this he hurried his son-in-law out of the realm, and so put a stop to his follies and the mortal fear they had caused. To finish this adventure at once, although it will lead me far beyond the date of other matters to be spoken of after, let me say what became of Maulevrier after this point of the narrative.

He went first to Spain with Tesse. On the way they had an interview with Madame des Ursins, and succeeded in gaining her favour so completely, that, upon arriving at Madrid, the King and Queen of Spain, informed of this, welcomed them with much cordiality. Maulevrier soon became a great favourite with the Queen of Spain. It has been said, that he wished to please her, and that he succeeded. At all events he often had long interviews with her in private, and these made people think and talk.

Maulevrier began to believe it time to reap after having so well sown. He counted upon nothing less than being made grandee of Spain, and would have obtained this favour but for his indiscretion. News of what was in store for him was noised abroad. The Duc de Grammont, then our ambassador at Madrid, wrote word to the King of the rumours that were in circulation of Maulevrier's audacious conduct towards the Queen of Spain, and of the reward it was to meet with. The King at once sent a very strong letter to the King of Spain about Maulevrier, who, by the same courier, was prohibited from accepting any favour that might be offered him. He was ordered at the same time to join Tesse at Gibraltar. He had already done so at the instance of Tesse himself; so the courier went from Madrid to Gibraltar to find him. His rage and vexation upon seeing himself deprived of the recompense he had considered certain were very great. But they yielded in time to the hopes he formed of success, and he determined to set off for Madrid and thence to Versailles. His father-in-law tried to retain him at the siege, but in vain. His representations and his authority were alike useless. Maulevrier hoped to gain over the King and Queen of Spain so completely, that our King would be forced, as it were, to range himself on their side; but the Duc de Grammont at once wrote word that Maulevrier had left the siege of Gibraltar and returned to Madrid. This disobedience was at once chastised. A courier was immediately despatched to Maulevrier, commanding him to set out for France. He took leave of the King and Queen of Spain like a man without hope, and left Spain. The most remarkable thing is, that upon arriving at Paris, and finding the Court at Marly, and his wife there also, he asked permission to go too, the husbands being allowed by right to accompany their wives there, and the King, to avoid a disturbance, did not refuse him.

At first everything seemed to smile upon Maulervrier. He had, as I have said, made friends with Madame des Ursins when he was on the road to Spain. He had done so chiefly by vaunting his intimacy with Madame de Bourgogne, and by showing to Madame des Ursins that he was in many of the secrets of the Court. Accordingly, upon his return, she took him by the hand and showed a disposition towards him which could not fail to reinstate him in favour. She spoke well of him to Madame de Maintenon, who, always much smitten with new friends, received him well, and often had conversations with him which lasted more than three hours. Madame de Maintenon mentioned him to the King, and Maulevrier, who had returned out of all hope, now saw himself in a more favourable position than ever.

But the old cause of trouble still existed, and with fresh complications. Nangis was still in favour, and his appearance made Maulevrier miserable. There was a new rival too in the field, the Abbe de Polignac.

Pleasing, nay most fascinating in manner, the Abbe was a man to gain all hearts. He stopped at no flattery to succeed in this. One day when following the King through the gardens of Marly, it came on to rain. The King considerately noticed the Abbe's dress, little calculated to keep off rain. "It is no matter, Sire," said De Polignac, "the rain of Marly does not wet." People laughed much at this, and these words were a standing reproach to the soft-spoken Abbe.

One of the means by which the Abbe gained the favour of the King was by being the lover of Madame du Maine. His success at length was great in every direction. He even envied the situations of Nangis and Maulevrier; and sought to participate in the same happiness. He took the same road. Madame d'O and the Marechale de Coeuvres became his friends.

He sought to be heard, and was heard. At last he faced the danger of the Swiss, and on fine nights was seen with the Duchess in the gardens. Nangis diminished in favour. Maulevrier on his return increased in fury. The Abbe met with the same fate as they: everything was perceived: people talked about the matter in whispers, but silence was kept. This triumph, in spite of his age, did not satisfy the Abbe: he aimed at something more solid. He wished to arrive at the cardinalship, and to further his views he thought it advisable to ingratiate himself into the favour of Monsieur de Bourgogne. He sought introduction to them through friends of mine, whom I warned against him as a man without scruple, and intent only upon advancing himself. My warnings were in vain. My friends would not heed me, and the Abbe de Polignac succeeded in gaining the confidence of Monsieur de Bourgogne, as well as the favour of Madame de Bourgogne.

Maulevrier had thus two sources of annoyance—the Abbe de Polignac and Nangis. Of the latter he showed himself so jealous, that Madame de Maulevrier, out of pique, made advances to him. Nangis, to screen himself the better, replied to her. Maulevrier perceived this. He knew his wife to be sufficiently wicked to make him fear her. So many troubles of heart and brain transported him. He lost his head.

One day the Marechale de Coeuvres came to see him, apparently on some message of reconciliation. He shut the door upon her; barricaded her within, and through the door quarrelled with her, even to abuse, for an hour, during which she had the patience to remain there without being able to see him. After this he went rarely to Court, but generally kept himself shut up at home.

Sometimes he would go out all alone at the strangest hours, take a fiacre and drive away to the back of the Chartreux or to other remote spots. Alighting there, he would whistle, and a grey-headed old man would advance and give him a packet, or one would be thrown to him from a window, or he would pick up a box filled with despatches, hidden behind a post. I heard of these mysterious doings from people to whom he was vain and indiscreet enough to boast of them. He continually wrote letters to Madame de Bourgogne, and to Madame de Maintenon, but more frequently to the former. Madame Cantin was their agent; and I know people who have seen letters of hers in which she assured Maulevrier, in the strongest terms, that he might ever reckon on the Duchess.

He made a last journey to Versailles, where he saw his mistress in private, and quarrelled with her cruelly. After dining with Torcy he returned to Paris. There, torn by a thousand storms of love, of jealousy, of ambition, his head was so troubled that doctors were obliged to be called in, and he was forbidden to see any but the most indispensable persons, and those at the hours when he was least ill. A hundred visions passed through his brain. Now like a madman he would speak only of Spain, of Madame de Bourgogne, of Nangis, whom he wished to kill or to have assassinated; now full of remorse towards M. de Bourgogne, he made reflections so curious to hear, that no one dared to remain with him, and he was left alone. At other times, recalling his early days, he had nothing but ideas of retreat and penitence. Then a confession was necessary in order to banish his despair as to the mercy of God. Often he thought himself very ill and upon the point of death.

The world, however, and even his nearest friends persuaded themselves that he was only playing a part; and hoping to put an end to it, they declared to him that he passed for mad in society, and that it behoved him to rise out of such a strange state and show himself. This was the last blow and it overwhelmed him. Furious at finding that this opinion was ruining all the designs of his ambition, he delivered himself up to despair. Although watched with extreme care by his wife, by particular friends, and by his servants, he took his measures so well, that on the Good Friday of the year 1706, at about eight o'clock in the morning, he slipped away from them all, entered a passage behind his room, opened the window, threw himself into the court below, and dashed out his brains upon the pavement. Such was the end of an ambitious man, who, by his wild and dangerous passions, lost his wits, and then his life, a tragic victim of himself.

Madame de Bourgogne learnt the news at night. In public she showed no emotion, but in private some tears escaped her. They might have been of pity, but were not so charitably interpreted. Soon after, it was noticed that Madame de Maintenon seemed embarrassed and harsh towards Madame de Bourgogne. It was no longer doubted that Madame de Maintenon had heard the whole story. She often had long interviews with Madame de Bourgogne, who always left them in tears. Her sadness grew so much, and her eyes were so often red, that Monsieur de Bourgogne at last became alarmed. But he had no suspicion of the truth, and was easily satisfied with the explanation he received. Madame de Bourgogne felt the necessity, however, of appearing gayer, and showed herself so. As for the Abbe de Polignac, it was felt that that dangerous person was best away. He received therefore a post which called him away, as it were, into exile; and though he delayed his departure as long as possible, was at length obliged to go. Madame de Bourgogne took leave of him in a manner that showed how much she was affected. Some rather insolent verses were written upon this event; and were found written on a balustrade by Madame, who was not discreet enough or good enough to forget them. But they made little noise; everybody loved Madame de Bourgogne, and hid these verses as much as possible.

CHAPTER XXXII

At the beginning of October, news reached the Court, which was at Fontainebleau, that M. de Duras was at the point of death. Upon hearing this, Madame de Saint-Simon and Madame de Lauzun, who were both related to M. Duras, wished to absent themselves from the Court performances that were to take place in the palace that evening. They expressed this wish to Madame de Bourgogne, who approved of it, but said she was afraid the King would not do the same. He had been very angry lately because the ladies had neglected to go full dressed to the Court performances. A few words he had spoken made everybody take good care not to rouse his anger on this point again. He expected so much accordingly from everybody who attended the Court, that Madame de Bourgogne was afraid he would not consent to dispense with the attendance of Madame de Saint-Simon and Madame de Lauzun on this occasion. They compromised the matter, therefore, by dressing themselves, going to the room where the performance was held, and, under pretext of not finding places, going away; Madame de Bourgogne agreeing to explain their absence in this way to the King. I notice this very insignificant bagatelle to show how the King thought only of himself, and how much he wished to be obeyed; and that that which would not have been pardoned to the nieces of a dying man, except at the Court, was a duty there, and one which it needed great address to escape from, without seriously infringing the etiquette established.

After the return of the Court from Fontainebleau this year, Puysieux came back from Switzerland, having been sent there as ambassador. Puysieux was a little fat man, very agreeable, pleasant, and witty, one of the best fellows in the world, in fact. As he had much wit, and thoroughly knew the King, he bethought himself of making the best of his position; and as his Majesty testified much friendship for him on his return, and declared himself satisfied with his mission in Switzerland, Puysieux asked if what he heard was not mere compliment, and whether he could count upon it. As the King assured him that he might do so, Puysieux assumed a brisk air, and said that he was not so sure of that, and that he was not pleased with his Majesty.

"And why not?" said the King.

"Why not?" replied Puysieux; "why, because although the most honest man in your realm, you have not kept to a promise you made me more than fifty years ago."

"What promise?" asked the King.

"What promise, Sire?" said Puysieux; "you have a good memory, you cannot have forgotten it. Does not your Majesty remember that one day, having the honour to play at blindman's buff with you at my grandmother's, you put your cordon bleu on my back, the better to hide yourself; and that when, after the game, I restored it to you, you promised to give it me when you became master; you have long been so, thoroughly master, and nevertheless that cordon bleu is still to come."

The King, who recollected the circumstance, here burst out laughing, and told Puysieux he was in the right, and that a chapter should be held on the first day of the new year expressly for the purpose of receiving him into the order. And so in fact it was, and Puysieux received the cordon bleu on the day the King had named. This fact is not important, but it is amusing. It is altogether singular in connection with a prince as serious and as imposing as Louis XIV.; and it is one of those little Court anecdotes which are curious.

Here is another more important fact, the consequences of which are still felt by the State. Pontchartrain, Secretary of State for the Navy, was the plague of it, as of all those who were under his cruel dependence. He was a man who, with some-amount of ability, was disagreeable and pedantic to an excess; who loved evil for its own sake; who was jealous even of his father; who was a cruel tyrant towards his wife, a woman all docility and goodness; who was in one word a monster, whom the King kept in office only because he feared him. An admiral was the abhorrence of Pontchartrain, and an admiral who was an illegitimate son of the King, he loathed. There was nothing, therefore, that he had not done during the war to thwart the Comte de Toulouse; he laid some obstacles everywhere in his path; he had tried to keep him out of the command of the fleet, and failing this, had done everything to render the fleet useless.

These were bold strokes against a person the King so much loved, but Pontchartrain knew the weak side of the King; he knew how to balance the father against the master, to bring forward the admiral and set aside the son. In this manner the Secretary of State was able to put obstacles in the way of the Comte de Toulouse that threw him almost into despair, and the Count could do little to defend himself. It was a well-known fact at sea and in the ports where the ships touched, and it angered all the fleet. Pontchartrain accordingly was abhorred there, while the Comte de Toulouse, by his amiability and other good qualities, was adored.

At last, the annoyance he caused became so unendurable, that the Comte de Toulouse, at the end of his cruise in the Mediterranean, returned to Court and determined to expose the doings of Pontchartrain to the King.

The very day he had made up his mind to do this, and just before he intended to have his interview with the King, Madame Pontchartrain, casting aside her natural timidity and modesty, came to him, and with tears in her eyes begged him not to bring about the ruin of her husband. The Comte de Toulouse was softened. He admitted afterwards that he could not resist the sweetness and sorrow of Madame de Pontchartrain, and that all his resolutions, his weapons, fell from his hands at the thought of the sorrow which the poor woman would undergo, after the fall of her brutal husband, left entirely in the hands of such a furious Cyclops. In this manner Pontchartrain was saved, but it cost dear to the State. The fear he was in of succumbing under the glory or under the vengeance of an admiral who was son of the King determined him to ruin the fleet itself, so as to render it incapable of receiving the admiral again. He determined to do this, and kept to his word, as was afterwards only too clearly verified by the facts. The Comte de Toulouse saw no more either ports or vessels, and from that time only very feeble squadrons went out, and even those very seldom. Pontchartrain, had the impudence to boast of this before my face.

When I last spoke of Madame des Ursins, I described her as living in the midst of the Court, flattered and caressed by all, and on the highest terms of favour with the King and Madame de Maintenon. She found her position, indeed, so far above her hopes, that she began to waver in her intention of returning to Spain. The age and the health of Madame de Maintenon tempted her. She would have preferred to govern here rather than in Spain. Flattered by the attentions paid her, she thought those attentions, or, I may say, rather those servile adorations, would continue for ever, and that in time she might arrive at the highest point of power. The Archbishop of Aix and her brother divined her thoughts, for she did not dare to avow them, and showed her in the clearest way that those thoughts were calculated to lead her astray. They explained to her that the only interest Madame de Maintenon had in favouring her was on account of Spain. Madame des Ursins—once back in that country, Madame de Maintenon looked forward to a recommencement of those relations which had formerly existed between them, by which the government of Spain in appearance, if not in reality, passed through her hands. They therefore advised Madame des Ursins on no account to think of remaining in France, at the same time suggesting that it would not be amiss to stop there long enough to cause some inquietude to Madame de Maintenon, so as to gain as much advantage as possible from it.

The solidity of these reasons persuaded Madame des Ursins to follow the advice given her. She resolved to depart, but not until after a delay by which she meant to profit to the utmost. We shall soon see what success attended her schemes. The terms upon which I stood with her enabled me to have knowledge of all the sentiments that had passed through her mind: her extreme desire, upon arriving in Paris, to return to Spain; the intoxication which seized her in consequence of the treatment she received, and which made her balance this desire; and her final resolution. It was not until afterwards, however, that I learnt all the details I have just related.

It was not long before Madame de Maintenon began to feel impatient at the long-delayed departure of Madame des Ursins. She spoke at last upon the subject, and pressed Madame des Ursins to set out for Spain. This was just what the other wanted. She said that as she had been driven out of Spain like a criminal, she must go back with honour, if Madame de Maintenon wished her to gain the confidence and esteem of the Spaniards. That although she had been treated by the King with every consideration and goodness, many people in Spain were, and would be, ignorant of it, and that, therefore, her return to favour ought to be made known in as public and convincing a manner as was her disgrace. This was said with all that eloquence and persuasiveness for which Madame des Ursins was remarkable. The effect of it exceeded her hopes.

The favours she obtained were prodigious. Twenty thousand livres by way of annual pension, and thirty thousand for her journey. One of her brothers, M. de Noirmoutiers, blind since the age of eighteen or twenty, was made hereditary duke; another, the Abbe de la Tremoille, of exceeding bad life, and much despised in Rome, where he lived, was made cardinal. What a success was this! How many obstacles had to be overcome in order to attain it! Yet this was what Madame des Ursins obtained, so anxious was Madame de Maintenon to get rid of her and to send her to reign in Spain, that she might reign there herself. Pleased and loaded with favour as never subject was before, Madame des Ursins set out towards the middle of July, and was nearly a month on the road. It may be imagined what sort of a reception awaited her in Spain. The King and the Queen went a day's journey out of Madrid to meet her. Here, then, we see again at the height of power this woman, whose fall the King but a short time since had so ardently desired, and whose separation from the King and Queen of Spain he had applauded himself for bringing about with so much tact. What a change in a few months!

The war continued this year, but without bringing any great success to our arms. Villars, at Circk, outmanoeuvred Marlborough in a manner that would have done credit to the greatest general. Marlborough, compelled to change the plan of campaign he had determined on, returned into Flanders, where the Marechal de Villeroy was stationed with his forces. Nothing of importance occurred during the campaign, and the two armies went into winter quarters at the end of October.

I cannot quit Flanders without relating another instance of the pleasant malignity of M. de Lauzun. In marrying a daughter of the Marechal de Lorges, he had hoped, as I have already said, to return into the confidence of the King by means of the Marechal, and so be again entrusted with military command. Finding these hopes frustrated, he thought of another means of reinstating himself in favour. He determined to go to the waters of Aix-la-Chapelle, not, as may be believed, for his health, but in order to ingratiate himself with the important foreigners whom he thought to find there, learn some of the enemy's plans, and come back with an account of them to the King, who would, no doubt, reward him for his zeal. But he was deceived in his calculation. Aix-la-Chapelle, generally so full of foreigners of rank, was this year, owing to the war, almost empty. M. de Lauzun found, therefore, nobody of consequence from whom he could obtain any useful information. Before his return, he visited the Marechal de Villeroy, who received him with all military honours, and conducted him all over the army, pointing out to him the enemy's post; for the two armies were then quite close to each other. His extreme anxiety, however, to get information, and the multitude of his questions, irritated the officers who were ordered to do the honours to him; and, in going about, they actually, at their own risk, exposed him often to be shot or taken. They did not know that his courage was extreme; and were quite taken aback by his calmness, and, his evident readiness to push on even farther than they chose to venture.

On returning to Court, M. de Lauzun was of course pressed by everybody to relate all he knew of the position of the two armies. But he held himself aloof from all questioners, and would not answer. On the day after his arrival he went to pay his court to Monseigneur, who did not like him, but who also was no friend to the Marechal de Villeroy. Monseigneur put many questions to him upon the situation of the two armies, and upon the reasons which had prevented them from engaging each other. M. de Lauzun shirked reply, like a man who wished to be pressed; did not deny that he had well inspected the position of the two armies, but instead of answering Monseigneur, dwelt upon the beauty of our troops, their gaiety at finding themselves so near an enemy, and their eagerness to fight. Pushed at last to the point at which he wished to arrive, "I will tell you, Monseigneur," said he, "since you absolutely command me; I scanned most minutely the front of the two armies to the right and to the left, and all the ground between them. It is true there is no brook, and that I saw; neither are there any ravines, nor hollow roads ascending or descending; but it is true that there were other hindrances which I particularly remarked."

"But what hindrance could there be," said Monseigneur, "since there was nothing between the two armies?"

M. de Lauzun allowed himself to be pressed upon this point, constantly repeating the list of hindrances that did not exist, but keeping silent upon the others. At last, driven into a corner, he took his snuff-box from his pocket.

"You see," said he, to Monseigneur, "there is one thing which much embarrasses the feet, the furze that grows upon the ground, where M. le Marechal de Villeroy is encamped. The furze, it is true, is not mixed with any other plant, either hard or thorny; but it is a high furze, as high, as high, let me see, what shall I say?"—and he looked all around to find some object of comparison—"as high, I assure you, as this snuffbox!"

Monseigneur burst out laughing at this sally, and all the company followed his example, in the midst of which M. de Lauzun turned on his heel and left the room. His joke soon spread all over the Court and the town, and in the evening was told to the King. This was all the thanks M. de Villeroy obtained from M. de Lauzun for the honours he had paid him; and this was M. de Lauzun's consolation for his ill-success at Aix- la-Chapelle.

In Italy our armies were not more successful than elsewhere. From time to time, M. de Vendome attacked some unimportant post, and, having carried it, despatched couriers to the King, magnifying the importance of the exploit. But the fact was, all these successes led to nothing. On one occasion, at Cassano, M. de Vendome was so vigorously attacked by Prince Louis of Baden that, in spite of his contempt and his audacity, he gave himself up for lost. When danger was most imminent, instead of remaining at his post, he retired from the field of battle to a distant country-house, and began to consider how a retreat might be managed. The Grand Prieur, his brother, was in command under him, and was ordered to remain upon the field; but he was more intent upon saving his skin than on obeying orders, and so, at the very outset of the fight, ran away to a country-house hard by. M. de Vendome strangely enough had sat down to eat at the country-house whither he had retired, and was in the midst of his meal when news was brought him that, owing to the prodigies performed by one of his officers, Le Guerchois, the fortunes of the day had changed, and Prince Louis of Baden was retiring. M. Vendome had great difficulty to believe this, but ordered his horse, mounted, and, pushing on, concluded the combat gloriously. He did not fail, of course, to claim all the honours of this victory, which in reality was a barren one; and sent word of his triumph to the King. He dared to say that the loss of the enemy was more than thirteen thousand; and our loss less than three thousand—whereas, the loss was at least equal. This exploit, nevertheless, resounded at the Court and through the town as an advantage the most complete and the most decisive, and due entirely to the vigilance, valour, and capacity of Vendome. Not a word was said of his country-house, or the interrupted meal. These facts were only known after the return of the general officers. As for the Grand Prieur, his poltroonery had been so public, his flight so disgraceful—for he had taken troops with him to protect the country-house in which he sought shelter—that he could not be pardoned. The two brothers quarrelled upon these points, and in the end the Grand Prieur was obliged to give up his command. He retired to his house at Clichy, near Paris; but, tiring of that place, he went to Rome, made the acquaintance there of the Marquise de Richelieu, a wanderer like himself, and passed some time with her at Genoa. Leaving that city, he went to Chalons-sur-Saone, which had been fixed upon as the place of his a exile, and there gave himself up to the debaucheries in which he usually lived. From this time until the Regency we shall see nothing more of him. I shall only add, therefore, that he never went sober to bed during thirty years, but was always carried thither dead drunk: was a liar, swindler, and thief; a rogue to the marrow of his bones, rotted with vile diseases; the most contemptible and yet most dangerous fellow in the world.

One day-I am speaking of a time many years previous to the date of the occurrences just related-one day there was a great hunting party at Saint Germain. The chase was pursued so long, that the King gave up, and returned to Saint Germain. A number of courtiers, among whom was M. de Lauzun, who related this story to me, continued their sport; and just as darkness was coming on, discovered that they had lost their way. After a time, they espied a light, by which they guided their steps, and at length reached the door of a kind of castle. They knocked, they called aloud, they named themselves, and asked for hospitality. It was then between ten and eleven at night, and towards the end of autumn. The door was opened to them. The master of the house came forth. He made them take their boots off, and warm themselves; he put their horses into his stables; and at the same time had a supper prepared for his guests, who stood much in need of it. They did not wait long for the meal; yet when served it proved excellent; the wines served with it, too, were of several kinds, and excellent likewise: as for the master of the house, he was so polite and respectful, yet without being ceremonious or eager,

VOLUME 5.: CHAPTER XXXIII

Two very different persons died towards the latter part of this year. The first was Lamoignon, Chief President; the second, Ninon, known by the name of Mademoiselle de l'Enclos. Of Lamoignon I will relate a single anecdote, curious and instructive, which will show the corruption of which he was capable.

One day—I am speaking of a time many years previous to the date of the occurrences just related—one day there was a great hunting party at Saint Germain. The chase was pursued so long, that the King gave up, and returned to Saint Germain. A number of courtiers, among whom was M. de Lauzun, who related this story to me, continued their sport; and just as darkness was coming on, discovered that they had lost their way. After a time, they espied a light, by which they guided their steps, and at length reached the door of a kind of castle. They knocked, they called aloud, they named themselves, and asked for hospitality. It was then between ten and eleven at night, and towards the end of autumn. The door was opened to them. The master of the house came forth. He made them take their boots off, and warm themselves; he put their horses into his stables; and at the same time had a supper prepared for his guests, who stood much in need of it. They did not wait long for the meal; yet when served it proved excellent; the wines served with it, too, were of several kinds, and excellent likewise: as for the master of the house, he was so polite and respectful, yet without being ceremonious or eager, that it was evident he had frequented the best company. The courtiers soon learnt that his name vitas Fargues, that the place was called Courson, and that he had lived there in retirement several years. After having supped, Fargues showed each of them into a separate bedroom, where they were waited upon by his valets with every proper attention. In the morning, as soon as the courtiers had dressed themselves, they found an excellent breakfast awaiting them; and upon leaving the table they saw their horses ready for them, and as thoroughly attended to as they had been themselves. Charmed with the politeness and with the manners of Fargues, and touched by his hospitable reception of them, they made him many offers of service, and made their way back to Saint Germain. Their non-appearance on the previous night had been the common talk, their return and the adventure they had met with was no less so.

These gentlemen were then the very flower of the Court, and all of them very intimate with the King. They related to him, therefore, their story, the manner of their reception, and highly praised the master of the house and his good cheer. The King asked his name, and, as soon as he heard it, exclaimed, "What, Fargues! is he so near here, then?" The courtiers redoubled their praises, and the King said no more; but soon after, went to the Queen-mother, and told her what had happened.

Fargues, indeed, was no stranger, either to her or to the King. He had taken a prominent part in the movements of Paris against the Court and Cardinal Mazarin. If he had not been hanged, it was because he was well supported by his party, who had him included in the amnesty granted to those who had been engaged in these troubles. Fearing, however, that the hatred of his enemies might place his life in danger if he remained in Paris, he retired from the capital to this country-house which has just been mentioned, where he continued to live in strict privacy, even when the death of Cardinal Mazarin seemed to render such seclusion no longer necessary.

The King and the Queen-mother, who had pardoned Fargues in spite of themselves, were much annoyed at finding that he was living in opulence and tranquillity so near the Court; thought him extremely bold to do so; and determined to punish him for this and for his former insolence. They directed Lamoignon, therefore, to find out something in the past life of Fargues for which punishment might be awarded; and Lamoignon, eager to please, and make a profit out of his eagerness, was not long in satisfying them. He made researches, and found means to implicate Fargues in a murder that had been committed in Paris at the height of the troubles. Officers were accordingly sent to Courson, and its owner was arrested.

Fargues was much astonished when he learnt of what he was accused. He exculpated himself, nevertheless, completely; alleging, moreover, that as the murder of which he was accused had been committed during the troubles, the amnesty in which he was included effaced all memory of the deed, according to law and usage, which had never been contested until this occasion. The courtiers who had been so well treated by the unhappy man, did everything they could with the judges and the King to obtain the release of the accused. It was all in vain. Fargues was decapitated at once, and all his wealth was given by way of recompense to the Chief- President Lamoignon, who had no scruple thus to enrich himself with the blood of the innocent.

The other person who died at the same time was, as I have said, Ninon, the famous courtesan, known, since age had compelled her to quit that trade, as Mademoiselle de l'Enclos. She was a new example of the triumph of vice carried on cleverly and repaired by some virtue. The stir that she made, and still more the disorder that she caused among the highest and most brilliant youth, overcame the extreme indulgence that, not without cause, the Queen-mother entertained for persons whose conduct was gallant, and more than gallant, and made her send her an order to retire into a convent. But Ninon, observing that no especial convent was named, said, with a great courtesy, to the officer who brought the order, that, as the option was left to her, she would choose "the convent of the Cordeliers at Paris;" which impudent joke so diverted the Queen that she left her alone for the future. Ninon never had but one lover at a time— but her admirers were numberless—so that when wearied of one incumbent she told him so frankly, and took another: The abandoned one might groan and complain; her decree was without appeal; and this creature had acquired such an influence, that the deserted lovers never dared to take revenge on the favoured one, and were too happy to remain on the footing of friend of the house. She sometimes kept faithful to one, when he pleased her very much, during an entire campaign.

Ninon had illustrious friends of all sorts, and had so much wit that she preserved them all and kept them on good terms with each other; or, at least, no quarrels ever came to light. There was an external respect and decency about everything that passed in her house, such as princesses of the highest rank have rarely been able to preserve in their intrigues.

In this way she had among her friends a selection of the best members of the Court; so that it became the fashion to be received by her, and it was useful to be so, on account of the connections that were thus formed.

There was never any gambling there, nor loud laughing, nor disputes, nor talk about religion or politics; but much and elegant wit, ancient and modern stories, news of gallantries, yet without scandal. All was delicate, light, measured; and she herself maintained the conversation by her wit and her great knowledge of facts. The respect which, strange to say, she had acquired, and the number and distinction of her friends and acquaintances, continued when her charms ceased to attract; and when propriety and fashion compelled her to use only intellectual baits. She knew all the intrigues of the old and the new Court, serious and otherwise; her conversation was charming; she was disinterested, faithful, secret, safe to the last degree; and, setting aside her frailty, virtuous and full of probity. She frequently succoured her friends with money and influence; constantly did them the most important services, and very faithfully kept the secrets or the money deposits that were confided to her.

She had been intimate with Madame de Maintenon during the whole of her residence at Paris; but Madame de Maintenon, although not daring to disavow this friendship, did not like to hear her spoken about.

She wrote to Ninon with amity from time to time, even until her death; and Ninon in like manner, when she wanted to serve any friend in whom she took great interest, wrote to Madame de Maintenon, who did her what service she required efficaciously and with promptness.

But since Madame de Maintenon came to power, they had only seen each other two or three times, and then in secret.

Ninon was remarkable for her repartees. One that she made to the last Marechal de Choiseul is worth repeating. The Marechal was virtue itself, but not fond of company or blessed with much wit. One day, after a long visit he had paid her, Ninon gaped, looked at the Marechal, and cried:

"Oh, my lord! how many virtues you make me detest!"

A line from I know not what play. The laughter at this may be imagined. L'Enclos lived, long beyond her eightieth year, always healthy, visited, respected. She gave her last years to God, and her death was the news of the day. The singularity of this personage has made me extend my observations upon her.

A short time after the death of Mademoiselle de l'Enclos, a terrible adventure happened to Courtenvaux, eldest son of M. de Louvois. Courtenvaux was commander of the Cent-Suisses, fond of obscure debauches; with a ridiculous voice, miserly, quarrelsome, though modest and respectful; and in fine a very stupid fellow. The King, more eager to know all that was passing than most people believed, although they gave him credit for not a little curiosity in this respect, had authorised Bontems to engage a number of Swiss in addition to those posted at the doors, and in the parks and gardens. These attendants had orders to stroll morning, noon, and night, along the corridors, the passages, the staircases, even into the private places, and, when it was fine, in the court-yards and gardens; and in secret to watch people, to follow them, to notice where they went, to notice who was there, to listen to all the conversation they could hear, and to make reports of their discoveries. This was assiduously done at Versailles, at Marly, at Trianon, at Fontainebleau, and in all the places where the King was. These new attendants vexed Courtenvaux considerably, for over such new-comers he had no sort of authority. This season, at

Fontainebleau, a room, which had formerly been occupied by a party of the Cent-Suisses and of the body-guard, was given up entirely to the new corps. The room was in a public passage of communication indispensable to all in the chateau, and in consequence, excellently well adapted for watching those who passed through it. Courtenvaux, more than ever vexed by this new arrangement, regarded it as a fresh encroachment upon his authority, and flew into a violent rage with the new-comers, and railed at them in good set terms. They allowed him to fume as he would; they had their orders, and were too wise to be disturbed by his rage. The King, who heard of all this, sent at once for Courtenvaux. As soon as he appeared in the cabinet, the King called to him from the other end of the room, without giving him time to approach, and in a rage so terrible, and for him so novel, that not only Courtenvaux, but Princes, Princesses, and everybody in the chamber, trembled. Menaces that his post should be taken away from him, terms the most severe and the most unusual, rained upon Courtenvaux, who, fainting with fright, and ready to sink under the ground, had neither the time nor the means to prefer a word. The reprimand finished by the King saying, "Get out." He had scarcely the strength to obey.

The cause of this strange scene was that Courtenvaux, by the fuss he had made, had drawn the attention of the whole Court to the change effected by the King, and that, when once seen, its object was clear to all eyes. The King, who hid his spy system with the greatest care, had counted upon this change passing unperceived, and was beside himself with anger when he found it made apparent to everybody by Courtenvaux's noise. He never regained the King's favour during the rest of his life; and but for his family he would certainly have been driven away, and his office taken from him.

Let me speak now of something of more moment.

The war, as I have said, still continued, but without bringing us any advantages. On the contrary, our losses in Germany and Italy by sickness, rather than by the sword, were so great that it was resolved to augment each company by five men; and, at the same time, twenty-five thousand militia were raised, thus causing great ruin and great desolation in the provinces. The King was rocked into the belief that the people were all anxious to enter this militia, and, from time to time, at Marly, specimens of those enlisted were shown to him, and their joy and eagerness to serve made much of. I have heard this often; while, at the same time, I knew from my own tenantry, and from everything that was said, that the raising of this militia carried despair everywhere, and that many people mutilated themselves in order to exempt themselves from serving. Nobody at the Court was ignorant of this. People lowered their eyes when they saw the deceit practised upon the King, and the credulity he displayed, and afterwards whispered one to another what they thought of flattery so ruinous. Fresh regiments, too, were raised at this time, and a crowd of new colonels and staffs created, instead of giving a new battalion or a squadron additional to regiments already in existence. I saw quite plainly towards what rock we were drifting. We had met losses at Hochstedt, Gibraltar, and Barcelona; Catalonia and the neighbouring countries were in revolt; Italy yielding us nothing but miserable successes; Spain exhausted; France, failing in men and money, and with incapable generals, protected by the Court against their faults. I saw all these things so plainly that I could not avoid making reflections, or reporting them to my friends in office. I thought that it was time to finish the war before we sank still lower, and that it might be finished by giving to the Archduke what we could not defend, and making a division of the rest. My plan was to leave Philip V. possession of all Italy, except those parts which belonged to the Grand Duke, the republics of Venice and Genoa, and the ecclesiastical states of Naples and Sicily; our King to have Lorraine and some other slight additions of territory; and to place elsewhere the Dukes of Savoy, of Lorraine, of Parma, and of Modem. I related this plan to the Chancellor and to Chamillart, amongst others. The contrast between their replies was striking. The Chancellor, after having listened to me very attentively, said, if my plan were adopted, he would most willingly kiss my toe for joy. Chamillart, with gravity replied, that the King would not give up a single mill of all the Spanish succession. Then I felt the blindness which had fallen upon us, and how much the results of it were to be dreaded.

Nevertheless, the King, as if to mock at misfortune and to show his enemies the little uneasiness he felt, determined, at the commencement of the new year, 1706, that the Court should be gayer than ever. He announced that there would be balls at Marly every time he was there this winter, and he named those who were to dance there; and said he should be very glad to see balls given to Madame de Bourgogne at Versailles. Accordingly, many took place there, and also at Marly, and from time to time there were masquerades. One day, the King wished that everybody, even the most aged, who were at Marly, should go to the ball masked; and, to avoid all distinction, he went there himself with a gauze robe above his habit; but such a slight disguise was for himself alone; everybody else was completely disguised. M. and Madame de Beauvilliers were there perfectly disguised. When I say they were there, those who knew the Court will admit that I have said more than enough. I had the pleasure of seeing them, and of quietly laughing with them. At all these balls the King made people dance who had long since passed the age for doing so. As for the Comte de Brionne and the Chevalier de Sully, their dancing was so perfect that there was no age for them.

CHAPTER XXXIV

In the midst of all this gaiety, that is to say on the 12th of February, 1706, one of our generals, of whom I have often spoken, I mean M. de Vendome, arrived at Marly. He had not quitted Italy since succeeding to Marechal de Villeroy, after the affair of Cremona. His battles, such as they were, the places he had taken, the authority he had assumed, the reputation he had usurped, his incomprehensible successes with the King, the certainty of the support he leaned on,—all this inspired him with the desire to come and enjoy at Court a situation so brilliant, and which so far surpassed what he had a right to expect. But before speaking of the reception which was given him, and of the incredible ascendancy he took, let me paint him from the life a little more completely than I have yet done.

Vendome was of ordinary height, rather stout, but vigorous and active: with a very noble countenance and lofty mien. There was much natural grace in his carriage and words; he had a good deal of innate wit, which he had not cultivated, and spoke easily, supported by a natural boldness, which afterwards turned to the wildest audacity; he knew the world and the Court; was above all things an admirable courtier; was polite when necessary, but insolent when he dared—familiar with common people—in reality, full of the most ravenous pride. As his rank rose and his favour increased, his obstinacy, and pig-headedness increased too, so that at last he would listen to no advice whatever, and was inaccessible to all, except a small number of familiars and valets. No one better than he knew the subserviency of the French character, or took more advantage of it. Little by little he accustomed his subalterns, and then from one to the other all his army, to call him nothing but "Monseigneur," and "Your Highness." In time the gangrene spread, and even lieutenant-generals and the most distinguished people did not dare to address him in any other manner.

The most wonderful thing to whoever knew the King—so gallant to the ladies during a long part of his life, so devout the other, and often importunate to make others do as he did—was that the said King had always a singular horror of the inhabitants of the Cities of the Plain; and yet M. de Vendome, though most odiously stained with that vice—so publicly that he treated it as an ordinary gallantry—never found his favour diminished on that account. The Court, Anet, the army, knew of these abominations. Valets and subaltern officers soon found the way to promotion. I have already mentioned how publicly he placed himself in the doctor's hands, and how basely the Court acted, imitating the King, who would never have pardoned a legitimate prince what he indulged so strangely in Vendome.

The idleness of M. de Vendome was equally matter of notoriety. More than once he ran the risk of being taken prisoner from mere indolence. He rarely himself saw anything at the army, trusting to his familiars when ready to trust anybody. The way he employed his day prevented any real attention to business. He was filthy in the extreme, and proud of it. Fools called it simplicity. His bed was always full of dogs and bitches, who littered at his side, the pops rolling in the clothes. He himself was under constraint in nothing. One of his theses was, that everybody resembled him, but was not honest enough to confess it as he was. He mentioned this once to the

Princesse de Conti—the cleanest person in the world, and the most delicate in her cleanliness.

He rose rather late when at the army. In this situation he wrote his letters, and gave his morning orders. Whoever had business with him, general officers and distinguished persons, could speak to him then. He had accustomed the army to this infamy. At the same time he gobbled his breakfast; and whilst he ate, listened, or gave orders, many spectators always standing round.... (I must be excused these disgraceful details, in order better to make him known).... On shaving days he used the same vessel to lather his chin in. This, according to him, was a simplicity of manner worthy of the ancient Romans, and which condemned the splendour and superfluity of the others. When all was over, he dressed; then played high at piquet or hombre; or rode out, if it was absolutely necessary. All was now over for the day. He supped copiously with his familiars: was a great eater, of wonderful gluttony; a connoisseur in no dish, liked fish much, but the stale and stinking better than the good. The meal prolonged itself in theses and disputes, and above all in praise and flattery.

He would never have forgiven the slightest blame from any one. He wanted to pass for the first captain of his age, and spoke with indecent contempt of Prince Eugene and all the others. The faintest contradiction would have been a crime. The soldier and the subaltern adored him for his familiarity with them, and the licence he allowed in order to gain their hearts; for all which he made up by excessive haughtiness towards whoever was elevated by rank or birth.

On one occasion the Duke of Parma sent the bishop of that place to negotiate some affair with him; but M. de Vendome took such disgusting liberties in his presence, that the ecclesiastic, though without saying a word, returned to Parma, and declared to his master that never would he undertake such an embassy again. In his place another envoy was sent, the famous Alberoni. He was the son of a gardener, who became an Abbe in order to get on. He was full of buffoonery; and pleased M. de Parma as might a valet who amused him, but he soon showed talent and capacity for affairs. The Duke thought that the night-chair of M. de Vendome required no other ambassador than Alberoni, who was accordingly sent to conclude what the bishop had left undone. The Abbe determined to please, and was not proud. M. de Vendome exhibited himself as before; and Alberoni, by an infamous act of personal adoration, gained his heart. He was thenceforth much with him, made cheese-soup and other odd messes for him; and finally worked his way. It is true he was cudgelled by some one he had offended, for a thousand paces, in sight of the whole army, but this did not prevent his advancement. Vendome liked such an unscrupulous flatterer; and yet as we have seen, he was not in want of praise. The extraordinary favour shown him by the King—the credulity with which his accounts of victories were received—showed to every one in what direction their laudation was to be sent.

Such was the man whom the King and the whole Court hastened to caress and flatter from the first moment of his arrival amongst us. There was a terrible hubbub: boys, porters, and valets rallied round his postchaise when he reached Marly. Scarcely had he ascended into his chamber, than everybody, princes, bastards and all the rest, ran after him. The ministers followed: so that in a short time nobody was left in the salon but the ladies. M. de Beauvilliers was at Vaucresson. As for me, I remained spectator, and did not go and adore this idol.

In a few minutes Vendome was sent for by the King and Monseigneur. As soon as he could dress himself, surrounded as he was by such a crowd, he went to the salon, carried by it rather than environed. Monseigneur stopped the music that was playing, in order to embrace him. The King left the cabinet where he was at work, and came out to meet him, embracing him several times. Chamillart on the morrow gave a fete in his honour at L'Etang, which lasted two days. Following his example, Pontchartrain, Torcy, and the most distinguished lords of the Court, did the same. People begged and entreated to give him fetes; people begged and entreated to be invited to them. Never was triumph equal to his; each step he took procured him a new one. It is not too much to say, that everybody disappeared before him; Princes of the blood, ministers, the grandest seigneurs, all appeared only to show how high he was above them; even the King seemed only to remain King to elevate him more.

The people joined in this enthusiasm, both in Versailles and at Paris, where he went under pretence of going to the opera. As he passed along the streets crowds collected to cheer him; they billed him at the doors, and every seat was taken in advance; people pushed and squeezed everywhere, and the price of admission was doubled, as on the nights of first performances. Vendome, who received all these homages with extreme ease, was yet internally surprised by a folly so universal. He feared that all this heat would not last out even the short stay he intended to make. To keep himself more in reserve, he asked and obtained permission to go to Anet, in the intervals between the journeys to Marly. All the Court, however, followed him there, and the King was pleased rather than otherwise, at seeing Versailles half deserted for Anet, actually asking some if they had been, others, when they intended to go.

It was evident that every one had resolved to raise M. de Vendome to the rank of a hero. He determined to profit by the resolution. If they made him Mars, why should he not act as such? He claimed to be appointed commander of the Marechals of France, and although the King refused him this favour, he accorded him one which was but the stepping-stone to it. M. de Vendome went away towards the middle of March to command the army in Italy, with a letter signed by the King himself, promising him that if a Marechal of France were sent to Italy, that Marechal was to take commands from him. M. de Vendome was content, and determined to obtain all he asked on a future day. The disposition of the armies had been arranged just before. Tesse, for Catalonia and Spain; Berwick, for the frontier of Portugal; Marechal Villars, for Alsace; Marsin, for the Moselle; Marechal de Villeroy, for Flanders; and M. de Vendome, as I have said, for Italy.

Now that I am speaking of the armies, let me give here an account of all our military operations this year, so as to complete that subject at once.

M. de Vendome commenced his Italian campaign by a victory. He attacked the troops of Prince Eugene upon the heights of Calcinato, drove them before him, killed three thousand men, took twenty standards, ten pieces of cannon, and eight thousand prisoners. It was a rout rather than a combat. The enemy was much inferior in force to us, and was without its general, Prince Eugene, he not having returned to open the campaign. He came back, however, the day after this engagement, soon re-established order among his troops, and M. de Vendome from that time, far from being able to recommence the attack, was obliged to keep strictly on the defensive while he remained in Italy. He did not fail to make the most of his victory, which, however, to say the truth, led to nothing.

Our armies just now were, it must be admitted, in by no means a good condition. The generals owed their promotion to favour and fantasy. The King thought he gave them capacity when he gave them their patents. Under M. de Turenne the army had afforded, as in a school, opportunities for young officers to learn the art of warfare, and to qualify themselves step by step to take command. They were promoted as they showed signs of their capacity, and gave proof of their talent. Now, however, it was very different. Promotion was granted according to length of service, thus rendering all application and diligence unnecessary, except when M. de Louvois suggested to the King such officers as he had private reasons for being favourable to, and whose actions he could control. He persuaded the King that it was he himself who ought to direct the armies from his cabinet. The King, flattered by this, swallowed the bait, and Louvois himself was thus enabled to govern in the name of the King, to keep the generals in leading-strings, and to fetter their every movement. In consequence of the way in which promotions were made, the greatest ignorance prevailed amongst all grades of officers. None knew scarcely anything more than mere routine duties, and sometimes not even so much as that. The luxury which had inundated the army, too, where everybody wished to live as delicately as at Paris, hindered the general officers from associating with the other officers, and in consequence from knowing and appreciating them. As a matter of course, there were no longer any deliberations upon the state of affairs, in which the young might profit by the counsels of the old, and the army profit by the discussions of all. The young officers talked only of pay and women; the old, of forage and equipages; the generals spent half their time in writing costly despatches, often useless, and sending them away by couriers. The luxury of the Court and city had spread into the army, so that delicacies were carried there unknown formerly. Nothing was spoken of but hot dishes in the marches and in the detachments; and the repasts that were carried to the trenches, during sieges, were not only well served, but ices and fruits were partaken of as at a fete, and a profusion of all sorts of liqueurs. Expense ruined the officers, who vied with one another in their endeavours to appear magnificent; and the things to be carried, the work to be done, quadrupled the number of domestics and grooms, who often starved. For a long time, people had complained of all this; even those who were put to the expenses, which ruined them; but none dared to spend less. At last, that is to say, in the spring of the following year, the King made severe rules, with the object of bringing about a reform in this particular. There is no country in Europe where there are so many fine laws, or where the observance of them is of shorter duration. It often happens, that in the first year all are infringed, and in the second, forgotten. Such was the army at this time, and we soon had abundant opportunities to note its incapacity to overcome the enemies with whom we had to contend.

The King wished to open this campaign with two battles; one in Italy, the other in Flanders. His desire was to some extent gratified in the former case; but in the other he met with a sad and cruel disappointment. Since the departure of Marechal de Villeroy for Flanders, the King had more than once pressed him to engage the enemy. The Marechal, piqued with these reiterated orders, which he considered as reflections upon his courage, determined to risk anything in order to satisfy the desire of the King. But the King did not wish this. At the same time that he wished for a battle in Flanders, he wished to place Villeroy in a state to fight it. He sent orders, therefore, to Marsin to take eighteen battalions and twenty squadrons of his army, to proceed to the Moselle, where he would find twenty others, and then to march with the whole into Flanders, and join Marechal de Villeroy. At the same time he prohibited the latter from doing anything until this reinforcement reached him. Four couriers, one after the other, carried this prohibition to the Marechal; but he had determined to give battle without assistance, and he did so, with what result will be seen.

On the 24th of May he posted himself between the villages of Taviers and Ramillies. He was superior in force to the Duke of Marlborough, who was opposed to him, and this fact gave him confidence. Yet the position which he had taken up was one which was well known to be bad. The late M. de Luxembourg had declared it so, and had avoided it. M. de Villeroy had been a witness of this, but it was his destiny and that of France that he should forget it. Before he took up this position he announced that it was his intention to do so to M. d'Orleans. M. d'Orleans said publicly to all who came to listen, that if M. de Villeroy did so he would be beaten. M. d'Orleans proved to be only too good a prophet.

Just as M. de Villeroy had taken up his position and made his arrangements, the Elector arrived in hot haste from Brussels. It was too late now to blame what had been done. There was nothing for it but to complete what had been already begun, and await the result.

It was about two hours after midday when the enemy arrived within range, and came under our fire from Ramillies. It forced them to halt until their cannon could be brought into play, which was soon done. The cannonade lasted a good hour. At the end of that time they marched to Taviers, where a part of our army was posted, found but little resistance, and made themselves masters of that place. From that moment they brought their cavalry to bear. They perceived that there was a marsh which covered our left, but which hindered our two wings from joining. They made good use of the advantage this gave them. We were taken in the rear at more than one point, and Taviers being no longer able to assist us, Ramillies itself fell, after a prodigious fire and an obstinate resistance. The Comte de Guiche at the head of the regiment of Guards defended it for four hours, and performed prodigies, but in the end he was obliged to give way. All this time our left had been utterly useless with its nose in the marsh, no enemy in front of it, and with strict orders not to budge from its position.

Marlborough at Ramillies--painted by R. Canton Woodville

Our retreat commenced in good order, but soon the night came and threw us into confusion. The defile of Judoigne became so gorged with baggage and with the wrecks of the artillery we had been able to save, that everything was taken from us there. Nevertheless, we arrived at Louvain, and then not feeling in safety, passed the canal of Wilworde without being very closely followed by the enemy.

We lost in this battle four thousand men, and many prisoners of rank, all of whom were treated with much politeness by Marlborough. Brussels was one of the first-fruits he gathered of this victory, which had such grave and important results.

The King did not learn this disaster until Wednesday, the 26th of May, at his waking. I was at Versailles. Never was such trouble or such consternation. The worst was, that only the broad fact was known; for six days we were without a courier to give us details. Even the post was stopped. Days seemed like years in the ignorance of everybody as to details, and in the inquietude of everybody for relatives and friends. The King was forced to ask one and another for news; but nobody could tell him any. Worn out at last by the silence, he determined to despatch Chamillart to Flanders to ascertain the real state of affairs. Chamillart accordingly left Versailles on Sunday, the 30th of May, to the astonishment of all the Court, at seeing a man charged with the war and the finance department sent on such an errand. He astonished no less the army when he arrived at Courtrai, where it had stationed itself. Having gained all the information he sought, Chamillart returned to Versailles on Friday, the 4th of June, at about eight o'clock in the evening, and at once went to the King, who was in the apartments of Madame de Maintenon. It was known then that the army, after several hasty marches, finding itself at Ghent, the Elector of Bavaria had insisted that it ought at least to remain there. A council of war was held, the Marechal de Villeroy, who was quite discouraged by the loss he had sustained, opposed the advice of the Elector. Ghent was abandoned, so was the open country. The army was separated and distributed here and there, under the command of the general officers. In this way, with the exception of Namur, Mons, and a very few other places, all the Spanish Low Countries were lost, and a part of ours, even. Never was rapidity equal to this. The enemies were as much astonished as we.

However tranquilly the King sustained in appearance this misfortune, he felt it to the quick. He was so affected by what was said of his body- guards, that he spoke of them himself with bitterness. Court warriors testified in their favour, but persuaded nobody. But the King seized these testimonies with joy, and sent word to the Guards that he was well contended with them. Others, however, were not so easily satisfied.

This sad reverse and the discontent of the Elector made the King feel at last that his favourites must give way to those better able to fill their places. Villeroy, who, since his defeat, had quite lost his head, and who, if he had been a general of the Empire, would have lost it in reality in another manner, received several strong hints from the King that he ought to give up his command. But he either could not or would not understand them, and so tired out the King's patience, at length. But he was informed in language which admitted of no misapprehension that he must return. Even then, the King was so kindly disposed towards him, that he said the Marechal had begged to be recalled with such obstinacy that he could not refuse him. But M. de Villeroy was absurd enough to reject this salve for his honour; which led to his disgrace. M. de Vendome had orders to leave Italy, and succeed to the command in Flanders, where the enemies had very promptly taken Ostend and Nieuport.

CHAPTER XXXV

Meanwhile, as I have promised to relate, in a continuous narrative, all our military operations of this year, let me say what passed in other directions. The siege of Barcelona made no progress. Our engineers were so slow and so ignorant, that they did next to nothing. They were so venal, too, that they aided the enemy rather than us by their movements. According to a new rule made by the King, whenever they changed the position of their guns, they were entitled to a pecuniary recompense. Accordingly, they passed all their time in uselessly changing about from place to place, in order to receive the recompense which thus became due to them.

Our fleet, too, hearing that a much superior naval force was coming to the assistance of the enemy, and being, thanks to Pontchartrain, utterly unable to meet it, was obliged to weigh anchor, and sailed away to Toulon. The enemy's fleet arrived, and the besieged at once took new courage. Tesse, who had joined the siege, saw at once that it was useless to continue it. We had for some time depended upon the open sea for supplies. Now that the English fleet had arrived, we could depend upon the sea no longer. The King of Spain saw, at last, that there was no help for it but to raise the siege.

It was raised accordingly on the night between the 10th and 11th of May, after fourteen days' bombardment. We abandoned one hundred pieces of artillery; one hundred and fifty thousand pounds of powder; thirty thousand sacks of flour; twenty thousand sacks of sevade, a kind of oats; and a great number of bombs, cannon-balls, and implements. As Catalonia was in revolt, it was felt that retreat could not take place in that direction; it was determined, therefore, to retire by the way of the French frontier. For eight days, however, our troops were harassed in flank and rear by Miquelets, who followed us from mountain to mountain. It was not until the Duc de Noailles, whose father had done some service to the chiefs of these Miquelets, had parleyed with them, and made terms with them, that our troops were relieved from these cruel wasps. We suffered much loss in our retreat, which, with the siege, cost us full four thousand men. The army stopped at Roussillon, and the King of Spain, escorted by two regiments of dragoons, made the best of his way to Madrid. That city was itself in danger from the Portuguese, and, indeed, fell into their hands soon after. The Queen, who, with her children, had left it in time to avoid capture, felt matters to be in such extremity, that she despatched all the jewels belonging to herself and her husband to France. They were placed in the custody of the King. Among them was that famous pear-shaped pearl called the Peregrine, which, for its weight, its form, its size, and its water, is beyond all price and all comparison.

The King of Spain effected a junction with the army of Berwick, and both set to work to reconquer the places the Portuguese had taken from them. In this they were successful. The Portuguese, much harassed by the people of Castille, were forced to abandon all they had gained; and the King of Spain was enabled to enter Madrid towards the end of September, where he was received with much rejoicing.

In Italy we experienced the most disastrous misfortunes. M. de Vendome, having been called from the command to go into Flanders, M. d'Orleans, after some deliberation, was appointed to take his place. M. d'Orleans set out from Paris on the 1st of July, with twenty-eight horses and five chaises, to arrive in three days at Lyons, and then to hasten on into Italy. La Feuillade was besieging Turin. M. d'Orleans went to the siege. He was magnificently received by La Feuillade, and shown all over the works. He found everything defective. La Feuillade was very young, and very inexperienced. I have already related an adventure of his, that of his seizing upon the coffers of his uncle, and so forestalling his inheritance. To recover from the disgrace this occurrence brought upon him, he had married a daughter of Chamillart. Favoured by this minister, but coldly looked upon by the King, he had succeeded in obtaining command in the army, and had been appointed to conduct this siege. Inflated by the importance of his position, and by the support of Chamillart, he would listen to no advice from any one. M. d'Orleans attempted to bring about some changes, and gave orders to that effect, but as soon as he was gone, La Feuillade countermanded those orders and had everything his own way. The siege accordingly went on with the same ill-success as before.

M. d'Orleans joined M. de Vendome on the 17th of July, upon the Mincio. The pretended hero had just made some irreparable faults. He had allowed Prince Eugene to pass the Po, nearly in front of him, and nobody knew what had become of twelve of our battalions posted near the place where this passage had been made. Prince Eugene had taken all the boats that we had upon the river. We could not cross it, therefore, and follow the enemy without making a bridge. Vendome feared lest his faults should be perceived. He wished that his successor should remain charged with them. M. d'Orleans, indeed, soon saw all the faults that M. de Vendome had committed, and tried hard to induce the latter to aid him to repair them. But M. de Vendome would not listen to his representations, and started away almost immediately to take the command of the army in Flanders, leaving M. d'Orleans to get out of the difficulty as he might.

M. d'Orleans, abandoned to himself (except when interfered with by Marechal de Marsin, under whose tutelage he was), could do nothing. He found as much opposition to his plans from Marsin as he had found from M. de Vendome. Marsin wished to keep in the good graces of La Feuillade, son-in-law of the all-powerful minister, and would not adopt the views of M. d'Orleans. This latter had proposed to dispute the passage of the Tanaro, a confluent of the Po, with the enemy, or compel them to accept battle. An intercepted letter, in cypher, from Prince Eugene to the Emperor, which fell into our hands, proved, subsequently, that this course would have been the right one to adopt; but the proof came too late; the decyphering table having been forgotten at Versailles! M. d'Orleans had in the mean time been forced to lead his army to Turin, to assist the besiegers, instead of waiting to stop the passage of the troops that were destined for the aid of the besieged. He arrived at Turin on the 28th of August, in the evening. La Feuillade, now under two masters, grew, it might be imagined, more docile. But no! He allied himself with Marsin (without whom M. d'Orleans could do nothing), and so gained him over that they acted completely in accord. When M. d'Orleans was convinced, soon after his arrival, that the enemy was approaching to succour Turin, he suggested that they should be opposed as they attempted the passage of the Dora.

But his advice was not listened to. He was displeased with everything. He found that all the orders he had given had been disregarded. He found the siege works bad, imperfect, very wet, and very ill-guarded. He tried to remedy all these defects, but he was opposed at every step. A council of war was held. M. d'Orleans stated his views, but all the officers present, with one honourable exception, servilely chimed in with the views of Marsin and La Feuillade, and things remained as they were. M. d'Orleans, thereupon, protested that he washed his hands of all the misfortunes that might happen in consequence of his advice being neglected. He declared that as he was no longer master over anything, it was not just that he should bear any part of the blame which would entail to those in command. He asked, therefore, for his post-chaise, and wished immediately to quit the army. La Feuillade and Marsin, however, begged him to remain, and upon second thoughts he thought it better to do so. The simple reason of all this opposition was, that La Feuillade, being very young and very vain, wished to have all the honours of the siege. He was afraid that if the counsel of M. d'Orleans prevailed, some of that honour would be taken from him. This was the real reason, and to this France owes the disastrous failure of the siege of Turin.

After the council of war, M. d'Orleans ceased to take any share in the command, walked about or stopped at home, like a man who had nothing to do with what was passing around him. On the night of the 6th to the 7th of September, he rose from his bed alarmed by information sent to him in a letter, that Prince Eugene was about to attack the castle of Pianezza, in order to cross the Dora, and so proceed to attack the besiegers. He hastened at once to Marsin, showed him the letter, and recommended that troops should at once be sent to dispute the passage of a brook that the enemies had yet to cross, even supposing them to be masters of Pianezza. Even as he was speaking, confirmation of the intelligence he had received was brought by one of our officers. But it was resolved, in the Eternal decrees, that France should be struck to the heart that day.

Marsin would listen to none of the arguments of M. d'Orleans. He maintained that it would be unsafe to leave the lines; that the news was false; that Prince Eugene could not possibly arrive so promptly; he would give no orders; and he counselled M. d'Orleans to go back to bed. The Prince, more piqued and more disgusted than ever, retired to his quarters fully resolved to abandon everything to the blind and deaf, who would neither see nor hear.

Soon after entering his chamber the news spread from all parts of the arrival of Prince Eugene. He did not stir. Some general officers came, and forced him to mount his horse. He went forth negligently at a walking pace. What had taken place during the previous days had made so much noise that even the common soldiers were ashamed of it. They liked him, and murmured because he would no longer command them. One of them called him by his name, and asked him if he refused them his sword. This question did more than all that the general officers had been able to do. M. d'Orleans replied to the soldier, that he would not refuse to serve them, and at once resolved to lend all his aid to Marsin and La Feuillade.

But it was no longer possible to leave the lines. The enemy was in sight, and advanced so diligently, that there was no time to make arrangements. Marsin, more dead than alive, was incapable of giving any order or any advice. But La Feuillade still persevered in his obstinacy. He disputed the orders of the Duc d'Orleans, and prevented their execution, possessed by I know not what demon.

The attack was commenced about ten o'clock in the morning, was pushed with incredible vigour, and sustained, at first, in the same manner. Prince Eugene poured his troops into those places which the smallness of our forces had compelled us to leave open. Marsin, towards the middle of the battle, received a wound which incapacitated him from further service, end was taken prisoner immediately after. Le Feuillade ran about like a madman, tearing his hair, and incapable of giving any order. The Duc d'Orleans preserved his coolness, and did wonders to save the day. Finding our men beginning to waver, he called the officers by their names, aroused the soldiers by his voice, and himself led the squadrons and battalions to the charge. Vanquished at last by pain, and weakened by the blood he had lost, he was constrained to retire a little, to have his wounds dressed. He scarcely gave himself time for this, however, but returned at once where the fire was hottest. Three times the enemy had been repulsed and their guns spiked by one of our officers, Le Guerchois, with his brigade of the old marine, when, enfeebled by the losses he had sustained, he called upon a neighbouring brigade to advance with him to oppose a number of fresh battalions the enemy had sent against him. This brigade and its brigadier refused bluntly to aid him. It was positively known afterwards, that had Le Guerchois sustained this fourth charge, Prince Eugene would have retreated.

This was the last moment of the little order that there had been at this battle. All that followed was only trouble, confusion, disorder, flight, discomfiture. The most terrible thing is, that the general officers, with but few exceptions, more intent upon their equipage and upon what they had saved by pillage, added to the confusion instead of diminishing it, and were worse than useless.

M. d'Orleans, convinced at last that it was impossible to re-establish the day, thought only how to retire as advantageously as possible. He withdrew his light artillery, his ammunition, everything that was at the siege, even at the most advanced of its works, and attended to everything with a presence of mind that allowed nothing to escape him. Then, gathering round him all the officers he could collect, he explained to them that nothing but retreat was open to them, and that the road to Italy was that which they ought to pursue. By this means they would leave the victorious army of the enemy in a country entirely ruined and desolate, and hinder it from returning into Italy, where the army of the King, on the contrary, would have abundance, and where it would cut off all succour from the others.

This proposition dismayed to the last degree our officers, who hoped at least to reap the fruit of this disaster by returning to France with the money with which they were gorged. La Feuillade opposed it with so much impatience, that the Prince, exasperated by an effrontery so sustained, told him to hold his peace and let others speak. Others did speak, but only one was for following the counsel of M. d'Orleans. Feeling himself now, however, the master, he stopped all further discussion, and gave orders that the retreat to Italy should commence. This was all he could do. His body and his brain were equally exhausted. After having waited some little time, he was compelled to throw himself into a post-chaise, and in that to continue the journey.

The officers obeyed his orders most unwillingly. They murmured amongst each other so loudly that the Duc d'Orleans, justly irritated by so much opposition to his will, made them hold their peace. The retreat continued. But it was decreed that the spirit of error and vertigo should ruin us and save the allies. As the army was about to cross the bridge over the Ticino, and march into Italy, information was brought to M. d'Orleans, that the enemy occupied the roads by which it was indispensable to pass. M. d'Orleans, not believing this intelligence, persisted in going forward. Our officers, thus foiled, for it was known afterwards that the story was their invention, and that the passes were entirely free, hit upon another expedient. They declared there were no more provisions or ammunition, and that it was accordingly impossible to go into Italy. M. d'Orleans, worn out by so much criminal disobedience, and weakened by his wound, could hold out no longer. He threw himself back in the chaise, and said they might go where they would. The army therefore turned about, and directed itself towards Pignerol, losing many equipages from our rear-guard during the night in the mountains, although that rear-guard was protected by Albergotti, and was not annoyed by the enemy.

The joy of the enemy at their success was unbounded. They could scarcely believe in it. Their army was just at its last gasp. They had not more than four days' supply of powder left in the place. After the victory, M. de Savoie and Prince Eugene lost no time in idle rejoicings. They thought only how to profit by a success so unheard of and so unexpected. They retook rapidly all the places in Piedmont and Lombardy that we occupied, and we had no power to prevent them.

Never battle cost fewer soldiers than that of Turin; never was retreat more undisturbed than ours; yet never were results more frightful or more rapid. Ramillies, with a light loss, cost the Spanish Low Countries and part of ours: Turin cost all Italy by the ambition of La Feuillade, the incapacity of Marsin, the avarice, the trickery, the disobedience of the general officers opposed to M. d'Orleans. So complete was the rout of our army, that it was found impossible to restore it sufficiently to send it back to Italy, not at least before the following spring. M. d'Orleans returned therefore to Versailles, on Monday, the 8th of November, and was well received by the King. La Feuillade arrived on Monday, the 13th of December, having remained several days at Paris without daring to go to Versailles. He was taken to the King by Chamillart. As soon as the King saw them enter he rose, went to the door, and without giving them time to utter a word, said to La Feuillade, "Monsieur, we are both very unfortunate!" and instantly turned his back upon him. La Feuillade, on the threshold of the door that he had not had time to cross, left the place immediately, without having dared to say a single word. The King always afterwards turned his eye from La Feuillade, and would never speak to him. Such was the fall of this Phaeton. He saw that he had no more hope, and retired from the army; although there was no baseness that he did not afterwards employ to return to command. I think there never was a more wrong-headed man or a man more radically dishonest, even to the marrow of his bones. As for Marsin, he died soon after his capture, from the effect of his wounds.

CHAPTER XXXVI

Such was our military history of the year 1706—history of losses and dishonour. It may be imagined in what condition was the exchequer with so many demands upon its treasures. For the last two or three years the King had been obliged, on account of the expenses of the war, and the losses we had sustained, to cut down the presents that he made at the commencement of the year. Thirty-five thousand louis in gold was the sum he ordinarily spent in this manner. This year, 1707, he diminished it by ten thousand Louis. It was upon Madame de Montespan that the blow fell. Since she had quitted the Court the King gave her twelve thousand Louis of gold each year. This year he sent word to her that he could only give her eight. Madame de Montespan testified not the least surprise. She replied, that she was only sorry for the poor, to whom indeed she gave with profusion. A short time after the King had made this reduction, that is, on the 8th of January, Madame la Duchesse de Bourgogne gave birth to a son. The joy was great, but the King prohibited all those expenses which had been made at the birth of the first-born of Madame de Bourgogne, and which had amounted to a large sum. The want of money indeed made itself felt so much at this time, that the King was obliged to seek for resources as a private person might have done. A mining speculator, named Rodes, having pretended that he had discovered many veins of gold in the Pyrenees, assistance was given him in order that he might bring these treasures to light.

He declared that with eighteen hundred workmen he would furnish a million (francs' worth of gold) each week. Fifty-two millions a-year would have been a fine increase of revenue. However, after waiting some little time, no gold was forthcoming, and the money that had been spent to assist this enterprise was found to be pure loss.

The difficulty of finding money to carry on the affairs of the nation continued to grow so irksome that Chamillart, who had both the finance and the war departments under his control, was unable to stand against the increased trouble and vexation which this state of things brought him. More than once he had represented that this double work was too much for him. But the King had in former times expressed so much annoyance from the troubles that arose between the finance and war departments, that he would not separate them, after having once joined them together. At last, Chamillart could bear up against his heavy load no longer. The vapours seized him: he had attacks of giddiness in the head; his digestion was obstructed; he grew thin as a lath. He wrote again to the King, begging to be released from his duties, and frankly stated that, in the state he was, if some relief was not afforded him, everything would go wrong and perish. He always left a large margin to his letters, and upon this the King generally wrote his reply. Chamillart showed me this letter when it came back to him, and I saw upon it with great surprise, in the handwriting of the King, this short note: "Well! let us perish together."

The necessity for money had now become so great, that all sorts of means were adopted to obtain it. Amongst other things, a tax was established upon baptisms and marriages. This tax was extremely onerous and odious. The result of it was a strange confusion. Poor people, and many of humble means, baptised their children themselves, without carrying them to the church, and were married at home by reciprocal consent and before witnesses, when they could find no priest who would marry them without formality. In consequence of this there were no longer any baptismal extracts; no longer any certainty as to baptisms or births; and the children of the marriages solemnised in the way I have stated above were illegitimate in the eyes of the law. Researches and rigours in respect to abuses so prejudicial were redoubled therefore; that is to say, they were redoubled for the purpose of collecting the tax.

From public cries and murmurs the people in some places passed to sedition. Matters went so far at Cahors, that two battalions which were there had great difficulty in holding the town against the armed peasants; and troops intended for Spain were obliged to be sent there. It was found necessary to suspend the operation of the tax, but it was with great trouble that the movement of Quercy was put down, and the peasants, who had armed and collected together, induced to retire into their villages. In Perigord they rose, pillaged the bureaux, and rendered themselves masters of a little town and some castles, and forced some gentlemen to put themselves at their head. They declared publicly that they would pay the old taxes to King, curate, and lord, but that they would pay no more, or hear a word of any other taxes or vexation. In the end it was found necessary to drop this tax upon baptism and marriages, to the great regret of the tax-gatherers, who, by all manner of vexations and rogueries, had enriched themselves cruelly.

It was at this time, and in consequence, to some extent, of these events, that a man who had acquired the highest distinction in France was brought to the tomb in bitterness and grief, for that which in any other country would have covered him with honour. Vauban, for it is to him that I allude, patriot as he was, had all his life been touched with the misery of the people and the vexations they suffered. The knowledge that his offices gave him of the necessity for expense, the little hope he had that the King would retrench in matters of splendour and amusement, made him groan to see no remedy to an oppression which increased in weight from day to day. Feeling this, he made no journey that he did not collect information upon the value and produce of the land, upon the trade and industry of the towns and provinces, on the nature of the imposts, and the manner of collecting them. Not content with this, he secretly sent to such places as he could not visit himself, or even to those he had visited, to instruct him in everything, and compare the reports he received with those he had himself made. The last twenty years of his life were spent in these researches, and at considerable cost to himself. In, the end, he convinced himself that the land was the only real wealth, and he set himself to work to form a new system.

He had already made much progress, when several little books appeared by Boisguilbert, lieutenant-general at Rouen, who long since had had the same views as Vauban, and had wanted to make them known. From this labour had resulted a learned and profound book, in which a system was explained by which the people could be relieved of all the expenses they supported, and from every tax, and by which the revenue collected would go at once into the treasury of the King, instead of enriching, first the traitants, the intendants, and the finance ministers. These latter, therefore, were opposed to the system, and their opposition, as will be seen, was of no slight consequence.

Vauban read this book with much attention. He differed on some points with the author, but agreed with him in the main. Boisguilbert wished to preserve some imposts upon foreign commerce and upon provisions. Vauban wished to abolish all imposts, and to substitute for them two taxes, one upon the land, the other upon trade and industry. His book, in which he put forth these ideas, was full of information and figures, all arranged with the utmost clearness, simplicity, and exactitude.

But it had a grand fault. It described a course which, if followed, would have ruined an army of financiers, of clerks, of functionaries of all kinds; it would have forced them to live at their own expense, instead of at the expense of the people; and it would have sapped the foundations of those immense fortunes that are seen to grow up in such a short time. This was enough to cause its failure.

All the people interested in opposing the work set up a cry. They saw place, power, everything, about to fly from their grasp, if the counsels of Vauban were acted upon. What wonder, then, that the King, who was surrounded by these people, listened to their reasons, and received with a very ill grace Marechal Vauban when he presented his book to him. The ministers, it may well be believed, did not give him a better welcome. From that moment his services, his military capacity (unique of its kind), his virtues, the affection the King had had for him, all were forgotten. The King saw only in Marechal Vauban a man led astray by love for the people, a criminal who attacked the authority of the ministers, and consequently that of the King. He explained himself to this effect without scruple.

The unhappy Marechal could not survive the loss of his royal master's favour, or stand up against the enmity the King's explanations had created against him; he died a few months after consumed with grief, and with an affliction nothing could soften, and to which the King was insensible to such a point, that he made semblance of not perceiving that he had lost a servitor so useful and so illustrious. Vauban, justly celebrated over all Europe, was regretted in France by all who were not financiers or their supporters.

Boisguilbert, whom this event ought to have rendered wise, could not contain himself. One of the objections which had been urged against his theories, was the difficulty of carrying out changes in the midst of a great war. He now published a book refuting this point, and describing such a number of abuses then existing, to abolish which, he asked, was it necessary to wait for peace, that the ministers were outraged. Boisguilbert was exiled to Auvergne. I did all in my power to revoke this sentence, having known Boisguilbert at Rouen, but did not succeed until the end of two months. He was then allowed to return to Rouen, but was severely reprimanded, and stripped of his functions for some little time. He was amply indemnified, however, for this by the crowd of people, and the acclamations with which he was received.

It is due to Chamillart to say, that he was the only minister who had listened with any attention to these new systems of Vauban and Boisguilbert. He indeed made trial of the plans suggested by the former, but the circumstances were not favourable to his success, and they of course failed. Some time after, instead of following the system of Vauban, and reducing the imposts, fresh ones were added. Who would have said to the Marechal that all his labours for the relief of the people of France would lead to new imposts, more harsh, more permanent, and more heavy than he protested against? It is a terrible lesson against all improvements in matters of taxation and finance.

But it is time, now, that I should retrace my steps to other matters, which, if related in due order of time, should have found a place ere this. And first, let me relate the particulars concerning a trial in which I was engaged, and which I have deferred allusion to until now, so as not to entangle the thread of my narrative.

My sister, as I have said in its proper place, had married the Duc de Brissac, and the marriage had not been a happy one. After a time, in fact, they separated. My sister at her death left me her universal legatee; and shortly after this, M. de Brissac brought an action against me on her account for five hundred thousand francs. After his death, his representatives continued the action, which I resisted, not only maintaining that I owed none of the five hundred thousand francs, but claiming to have two hundred thousand owing to me, out of six hundred thousand which had formed the dowry of my sister.

When M. de Brissac died, there seemed some probability that his peerage would become extinct; for the Comte de Cosse, who claimed to succeed him, was opposed by a number of peers, and but for me might have failed to establish his pretensions. I, however, as his claim was just, interested myself in him, supported him with all my influence, and gained for him the support of several influential peers: so that in the end he was recognised as Duc de Brissac, and received as such at the parliament on the 6th of May, 1700.

Having succeeded thus to the titles and estates of his predecessor, he succeeded also to his liabilities, debts, and engagements. Among these was the trial against me for five hundred thousand francs. Cosse felt so thoroughly that he owed his rank to me, that he offered to give me five hundred thousand francs, so as to indemnify me against an adverse decision in the cause. Now, as I have said, I not only resisted this demand made upon me for five hundred thousand francs, but I, in my turn, claimed two hundred thousand francs, and my claim, once admitted, all the personal creditors of the late Duc de Brissac (creditors who, of course, had to be paid by the new Duke) would have been forced to stand aside until my debt was settled.

I, therefore, refused this offer of Cosse, lest other creditors should hear of the arrangement, and force him to make a similar one with them. He was overwhelmed with a generosity so little expected, and we became more intimately connected from that day.

Cosse, once received as Duc de Brissac, I no longer feared to push forward the action I had commenced for the recovery of the two hundred thousand francs due to me, and which I had interrupted only on his account. I had gained it twice running against the late Duc de Brissac, at the parliament of Rouen; but the Duchesse d'Aumont, who in the last years of his life had lent him money, and whose debt was in danger, succeeded in getting this cause sent up for appeal to the parliament at Paris, where she threw obstacle upon obstacle in its path, and caused judgment to be delayed month after month. When I came to take active steps in the matter, my surprise—to use no stronger word—was great, to find Cosse, after all I had done for him, favouring the pretensions of the Duchesse d'Aumont, and lending her his aid to establish them. However, he and the Duchesse d'Aumont lost their cause, for when it was submitted to the judges of the council at Paris, it was sent back to Rouen, and they had to pay damages and expenses.

For years the affair had been ready to be judged at Rouen, but M. d'Aumont every year, by means of his letters of state, obtained a postponement. At last, however, M. d'Aumont died, and I was assured that the letters of state should not be again produced, and that in consequence no further adjournment should take place. I and Madame de Saint-Simon at once set out, therefore, for Rouen, where we were exceedingly well received, fetes and entertainments being continually given in our honour.

After we had been there but eight or ten days, I received a letter from Pontchartrain, who sent me word that the King had learnt with surprise I was at Rouen, and had charged him to ask me why I was there: so attentive was the King as to what became of the people of mark, he was accustomed to see around him! My reply was not difficult.

Meanwhile our cause proceeded. The parliament, that is to say, the Grand Chamber, suspended all other business in order to finish ours. The affair was already far advanced, when it was interrupted by an obstacle, of all obstacles the least possible to foresee. The letters of state had again been put in, for the purpose of obtaining another adjournment.

My design is not to weary by recitals, which interest only myself; but I must explain this matter fully. It was Monday evening. The parliament of Rouen ended on the following Saturday. If we waited until the opening of the next parliament, we should have to begin our cause from the beginning, and with new presidents and judges, who would know nothing of the facts. What was to be done? To appeal to the King seemed impossible, for he was at Marly, and, while there, never listened to such matters. By the time he left Marly, it would be too late to apply to him.

Madame de Saint-Simon and others advised me, however, at all hazards, to go straight to the King, instead of sending a courier, as I thought of doing, and to keep my journey secret. I followed their advice, and setting out at once, arrived at Marly on Tuesday morning, the 8th of August, at eight of the clock. The Chancellor and Chamillart, to whom I told my errand, pitied me, but gave me no hope of success. Nevertheless, a council of state was to be held on the following morning, presided over by the King, and my petition was laid before it. The letters of state were thrown out by every voice. This information was brought to me at mid-day. I partook of a hasty dinner, and turned back to Rouen, where I arrived on Thursday, at eight o'clock in the morning, three hours after a courier, by whom I had sent this unhoped-for news.

I brought with me, besides the order respecting the letters of state, an order to the parliament to proceed to judgment at once. It was laid before the judges very early on Saturday, the 11th of August, the last day of the parliament. From four o'clock in the morning we had an infinite number of visitors, wanting to accompany us to the palace. The parliament had been much irritated against these letters of state, after having suspended all other business for us. The withdrawal of these letters was now announced. We gained our cause, with penalties and expenses, amid acclamations which resounded through the court, and which followed us into the streets. We could scarcely enter our street, so full was it with the crowd, or our house, which was equally crowded. Our kitchen chimney soon after took fire, and it was only a marvel that it was extinguished, without damage, after having strongly warned us, and turned our joy into bitterness. There was only the master of the house who was unmoved. We dined, however, with a grand company; and after stopping one or two days more to thank our friends, we went to see the sea at Dieppe, and then to Cani, to a beautiful house belonging to our host at Rouen.

As for Madame d'Aumont, she was furious at the ill-success of her affair. It was she who had obtained the letters of state from the steward of her son-in-law. Her son-in-law had promised me that they should not be used, and wrote at once to say he had had no hand in their production. M. de Brissac, who had been afraid to look me in the face ever since he had taken part in this matter, and with whom I had openly broken, was now so much ashamed that he avoided me everywhere.

CHAPTER XXXVII

It was just at the commencement of the year 1706, that I received a piece of news which almost took away my breath by its suddenness, and by the surprise it caused me. I was on very intimate terms with Gualterio, the nuncio of the Pope. Just about this time we were without an ambassador at Rome. The nuncio spoke to me about this post; but at my age—I was but thirty— and knowing the unwillingness of the King to employ young men in public affairs, I paid no attention to his words. Eight days afterwards he entered my chamber-one Tuesday, about an hour after mid- day-his arms open, joy painted upon his face, and embracing me, told me to shut my door, and even that of my antechamber, so that he should not be seen. I was to go to Rome as ambassador. I made him repeat this twice over: it seemed so impossible. If one of the portraits in my chamber had spoken to me, I could not have been more surprised. Gualterio begged me to keep the matter secret, saying, that the appointment would be officially announced to me ere long.

I went immediately and sought out Chamillart, reproaching him for not having apprised me of this good news. He smiled at my anger, and said that the King had ordered the news to be kept secret. I admit that I was flattered at being chosen at my age for an embassy so important. I was advised on every side to accept it, and this I determined to do. I could not understand, however, how it was I had been selected. Torcy, years afterwards, when the King was dead, related to me how it came about. At this time I had no relations with Torcy; it was not until long afterwards that friendship grew up between us.

He said, then, that the embassy being vacant, the King wished to fill up that appointment, and wished also that a Duke should be ambassador. He took an almanack and began reading the names of the Dukes, commencing with M. de Uzes. He made no stop until he came to my name. Then he said (to Torcy), "What do you think of him? He is young, but he is good," &c. The King, after hearing a few opinions expressed by those around him, shut up the almanack, and said it was not worth while to go farther, determined that I should be ambassador, but ordered the appointment to be kept secret. I learnt this, more than ten years after its occurrence, from a true man, who had no longer any interest or reason to disguise anything from me.

Advised on all sides by my friends to accept the post offered to me, I did not long hesitate to do so. Madame de Saint-Simon gave me the same advice, although she herself was pained at the idea of quitting her family. I cannot refuse myself the pleasure of relating here what the three ministers each said of my wife, a woman then of only twenty-seven years of age. All three, unknown to each other, and without solicitation on my part, counselled me to keep none of the affairs of my embassy secret from her, but to give her a place at the end of the table when I read or wrote my despatches, and to consult her with deference upon everything. I have rarely so much relished advice as I did in this case. Although, as things fell out, I could not follow it at Rome, I had followed it long before, and continued to do so all my life. I kept nothing secret from her, and I had good reason to be pleased that I did not. Her counsel was always wise, judicious, and useful, and oftentimes she warded off from me many inconveniences.

But to continue the narrative of this embassy. It was soon so generally known that I was going to Rome, that as we danced at Marly, we heard people say, "Look! M. l'Ambassadeur and Madame l'Ambassadrice are dancing." After this I wished the announcement to be made public as soon as possible, but the King was not to be hurried. Day after day passed by, and still I was kept in suspense. At last, about the middle of April, I had an interview with Chamillart one day, just after he came out of the council at which I knew my fate had been decided. I learnt then that the King had determined to send no ambassador to Rome. The Abbe de La Tremoille was already there; he had been made Cardinal, and was to remain and attend to the affairs of the embassy. I found out afterwards that I had reason to attribute to Madame de Maintenon and M. du Maine the change in the King's intention towards me. Madame de Saint-Simon was delighted. It seemed as though she foresaw the strange discredit in which the affairs of the King were going to fall in Italy, the embarrassment and the disorder that public misfortunes would cause the finances, and the cruel situation to which all things would have reduced us at Rome. As for me, I had had so much leisure to console myself beforehand, that I had need of no more. I felt, however, that I had now lost all favour with the King, and, indeed, he estranged himself from me more and more each day. By what means I recovered myself it is not yet time to tell.

On the night between the 3rd and 4th of February, Cardinal Coislin, Bishop of Orleans, died. He was a little man, very fat, who looked like a village curate. His purity of manners and his virtues caused him to be much loved. Two good actions of his life deserve to be remembered.

When, after the revocation of the edict of Nantes, the King determined to convert the Huguenots by means of dragoons and torture, a regiment was sent to Orleans, to be spread abroad in the diocese. As soon as it arrived, M. d'Orleans sent word to the officers that they might make his house their home; that their horses should be lodged in his stables. He begged them not to allow a single one of their men to leave the town, to make the slightest disorder; to say no word to the Huguenots, and not to lodge in their houses. He resolved to be obeyed, and he was. The regiment stayed a month; and cost him a good deal. At the end of that time he so managed matters that the soldiers were sent away, and none came again. This conduct, so full of charity, so opposed to that of nearly all the other dioceses, gained as many Huguenots as were gained by the barbarities they suffered elsewhere. It needed some courage, to say nothing of generosity, to act thus, and to silently blame, as it were, the conduct of the King.

The other action of M. d'Orleans was less public and less dangerous, but was not less good. He secretly gave away many alms to the poor, in addition to those he gave publicly. Among those whom he succoured was a poor, broken-down gentleman, without wife or child, to whom he gave four hundred livres of pension, and a place at his table whenever he was at Orleans. One morning the servants of M. d'Orleans told their master that ten pieces of plate were missing, and that suspicion fell upon the gentleman. M. d'Orleans could not believe him guilty, but as he did not make his appearance at the house for several days, was forced at last to imagine he was so. Upon this he sent for the gentleman, who admitted himself to be the offender.

M. d'Orleans said he must have been strangely pressed to commit an action of this nature, and reproached him for not having mentioned his wants. Then, drawing twenty Louis from his pocket, he gave them to the gentleman, told him to forget what had occurred, and to use his table as before. M. d'Orleans prohibited his servants to mention their suspicions, and this anecdote would never have been known, had it not been told by the gentleman himself, penetrated with confusion and gratitude.

M. d'Orleans, after he became cardinal, was often pressed by his friends to give up his bishopric. But this he would not listen to. The King had for him a respect that was almost devotion. When Madame de Bourgogne was about to be delivered of her first child, the King sent a courier to M. d'Orleans requesting him to come to Court immediately, and to remain there until after the delivery. When the child was born, the King would not allow it to be sprinkled by any other hand than that of M. d'Orleans. The poor man, very fat, as I have said, always sweated very much;—on this occasion, wrapped up in his cloak and his lawn, his body ran with sweat in such abundance, that in the antechamber the floor was wet all round where he stood. All the Court was much afflicted at his death; the King more than anybody spoke his praises. It was known after his death, from his valet de chambre, that he mortified himself continually with instruments of penitence, and that he rose every night and passed an hour on his knees in prayer. He received the sacraments with great piety, and died the night following as he had lived.

Heudicourt the younger, a species of very mischievous satyr, and much mixed up in grand intrigues of gallantry, made, about this time, a song upon the grand 'prevot' and his family. It was so simple, so true to nature, withal so pleasant, that some one having whispered it in the ear of the Marechal de Boufflers at chapel, he could not refrain from bursting into laughter, although he was in attendance at the mass of the King. The Marechal was the gravest and most serious man in all France; the greatest slave to decorum. The King turned round therefore, in surprise, which augmented considerably when he saw the Marechal de Boufflers nigh to bursting with laughter, and the tears running down his cheeks. On turning into his cabinet, he called the Marechal, and asked what had got him in that state at the mass. The Marechal repeated the song to him. Thereupon the King burst out louder than the Marechal had, and for a whole fortnight afterwards could not help smiling whenever he saw the grand 'prevot' or any of his family. The song soon spread about, and much diverted the Court and the town.

I should particularly avoid soiling this page with an account of the operation for fistula which Courcillon, only son of Dangeau, had performed upon him, but for the extreme ridicule with which it was accompanied. Courcillon was a dashing young fellow, much given to witty sayings, to mischief, to impiety, and to the filthiest debauchery, of which latter, indeed, this operation passed publicly as the fruit. His mother, Madams Dangeau, was in the strictest intimacy with Madame de Maintenon. They two alone, of all the Court, were ignorant of the life Courcillon led. Madame was much afflicted; and quitted his bed-side, even for a moment, with pain. Madame de Maintenon entered into her sorrow, and went every day to bear her company at the pillow of Courcillon. Madame d'Heudicourt, another intimate friend of Madame de Maintenon, was admitted there also, but scarcely anybody else. Courcillon listened to them, spoke devotionally to them, and uttered the reflections suggested by his state. They, all admiration, published everywhere that he was a saint. Madame d'Heudicourt and a few others who listened to these discourses, and who knew the pilgrim well, and saw him loll out his tongue at them on the sly, knew not what to do to prevent their laughter, and as soon as they could get away went and related all they had heard to their friends. Courcillon, who thought it a mighty honour to have Madame de Maintenon every day for nurse, but who, nevertheless, was dying of weariness, used to see his friends in the evening (when Madame de Maintenon and his mother were gone), and would relate to them, with burlesque exaggeration, all the miseries he had suffered during the day, and ridicule the devotional discourses he had listened to. All the time his illness lasted, Madame de Maintenon came every day to see him, so that her credulity, which no one dared to enlighten, was the laughing-stock of the Court. She conceived such a high opinion of the virtue of Courcillon, that she cited him always as an example, and the King also formed the same opinion. Courcillon took good care not to try and cultivate it when he became cured; yet neither the King nor Madame de Maintenon opened their eyes, or changed their conduct towards him. Madame de Maintenon, it must be said, except in the sublime intrigue of her government and with the King, was always the queen of dupes.

It would seem that there are, at certain times, fashions in crimes as in clothes. At the period of the Voysins and the Brinvilliers, there were nothing but poisoners abroad; and against these, a court was expressly instituted, called ardente, because it condemned them to the flames. At the time of which I am now speaking, 1703, for I forgot to relate what follows in its proper place, forgers of writings were in the ascendant, and became so common, that a chamber was established composed of councillors of state and others, solely to judge the accusations which this sort of criminals gave rise to.

The Bouillons wished to be recognised as descended, by male issue, of the Counts of Auvergne, and to claim all kinds of distinctions and honours in consequence. They had, however, no proofs of this, but, on the contrary, their genealogy proved it to be false. All on a sudden, an old document that had been interred in the obscurity of ages in the church of Brioude, was presented to Cardinal Bouillon. It had all the marks of antiquity, and contained a triumphant proof of the descent of the house of La Tour, to which the Bouillons belonged, from the ancient Counts of Auvergne. The Cardinal was delighted to have in his hands this precious document. But to avoid all suspicion, he affected modesty, and hesitated to give faith to evidence so decisive. He spoke in confidence to all the learned men he knew, and begged them to examine the document with care, so that he might not be the dupe of a too easy belief in it.

Whether the examiners were deceived by the document, or whether they allowed themselves to be seduced into believing it, as is more than probable, from fear of giving offence to the Cardinal, need not be discussed. It is enough to say that they pronounced in favour of the deed, and that Father Mabillon, that Benedictine so well known throughout all Europe by his sense and his candour, was led by the others to share their opinion.

After this, Cardinal de Bouillon no longer affected any doubt about the authenticity of the discovery. All his friends complimented him upon it, the majority to see how he would receive their congratulations. It was a chaos rather than a mixture, of vanity the most outrageous, modesty the most affected, and joy the most immoderate which he could not restrain.

Unfortunately, De Bar, who had found the precious document, and who had presented it to Cardinal de Bouillon, was arrested and put in prison a short time after this, charged with many forgeries. This event made some stir, and caused suspicion to fall upon the document, which was now attentively examined through many new spectacles. Learned men unacquainted with the Bouillons contested it, and De Bar was so pushed upon this point, that he made many delicate admissions. Alarm at once spread among the Bouillons. They did all in their power to ward off the blow that was about to fall. Seeing the tribunal firm, and fully resolved to follow the affair to the end, they openly solicited for De Bar, and employed all their credit to gain his liberation. At last, finding the tribunal inflexible, they were reduced to take an extreme resolution. M. de Bouillon admitted to the King, that his brother, Cardinal de Bouillon, might, unknown to all of them, have brought forward facts he could not prove. He added, that putting himself in the King's hands, he begged that the affair might be stopped at once, out of consideration for those whose only guilt was too great credulity, and too much confidence in a brother who had deceived them. The King, with more of friendship for M. de Bouillon than of reflection as to what he owed by way of reparation for a public offence, agreed to this course.

De Bar, convicted of having fabricated this document, by his own admission before the public tribunal, was not condemned to death, but to perpetual imprisonment. As may be believed, this adventure made a great stir; but what cannot be believed so easily is, the conduct of the Messieurs Bouillon about fifteen months afterwards.

At the time when the false document above referred to was discovered, Cardinal de Bouillon had commissioned Baluze, a man much given to genealogical studies, to write the history of the house of Auvergne. In this history, the descent, by male issue; of the Bouillons from the Counts of Auvergne, was established upon the evidence supplied by this document. At least, nobody doubted that such was the case, and the world was strangely scandalised to see the work appear after that document had been pronounced to be a forgery. Many learned men and friends of Baluze considered him so dishonoured by it, that they broke off all relations with him, and this put the finishing touch to the confusion of this affair.

On Thursday, the 7th of March, 1707, a strange event troubled the King, and filled the Court and the town with rumours. Beringhen, first master of the horse, left Versailles at seven o'clock in the evening of that day, to go to Paris, alone in one of the King's coaches, two of the royal footmen behind, and a groom carrying a torch before him on the seventh horse. The carriage had reached the plain of Bissancourt, and was passing between a farm on the road near Sevres bridge and a cabaret, called the "Dawn of Day," when it was stopped by fifteen or sixteen men on horseback, who seized on Beringhen, hurried him into a post-chaise in waiting, and drove off with him. The King's carriage, with the coachman, footmen, and groom, was allowed to go back to Versailles. As soon as it reached Versailles the King was informed of what had taken place. He sent immediately to his four Secretaries of State, ordering them to send couriers everywhere to the frontiers, with instructions to the governors to guard all the passages, so that if these horsemen were foreign enemies, as was suspected, they would be caught in attempting to pass out of the kingdom. It was known that a party of the enemy had entered Artois, that they had committed no disorders, but that they were there still. Although people found it difficult, at first, to believe that Beringhen had been carried off by a party such as this, yet as it was known that he had no enemies, that he was not reputed sufficiently rich to afford hope of a large ransom, and that not one of our wealthiest financiers had been seized in this manner, this explanation was at last accepted as the right one.

So in fact it proved. A certain Guetem, a fiddler of the Elector of Bavaria, had entered the service of Holland, had taken part in her war against France, and had become a colonel. Chatting one evening with his comrades, he laid a wager that he would carry off some one of mark between Paris and Versailles. He obtained a passport, and thirty chosen men, nearly all of whom were officers. They passed the rivers disguised as traders, by which means they were enabled to post their relays [of horses]. Several of them had remained seven or eight days at Sevres, Saint Cloud, and Boulogne, from which they had the hardihood to go to Versailles and see the King sup. One of these was caught on the day after the disappearance of Beringhen, and when interrogated by Chamillart, replied with a tolerable amount of impudence. Another was caught in the forest of Chantilly by one of the servants of M. le Prince. From him it became known that relays of horses and a post-chaise had been provided at Morliere for the prisoner when he should arrive there, and that he had already passed the Oise.

As I have said, couriers were despatched to the governors of the frontiers; in addition to this, information of what had taken place was sent to all the intendants of the frontier, to all the troops in quarters there. Several of the King's guards, too, and the grooms of the stable, went in pursuit of the captors of Beringhen. Notwithstanding the diligence used, the horsemen had traversed the Somme and had gone four leagues beyond Ham-Beringhen, guarded by the officers, and pledged to offer no resistance—when the party was stopped by a quartermaster and two detachments of the Livry regiment. Beringhen was at once set at liberty. Guetem and his companion were made prisoners.

The grand fault they had committed was to allow the King's carriage and the footmen to go back to Versailles so soon after the abduction. Had they led away the coach under cover of the night, and so kept the King in ignorance of their doings until the next day, they would have had more time for their retreat. Instead of doing this they fatigued themselves by too much haste. They had grown tired of waiting for a carriage that seemed likely to contain somebody of mark. The Chancellor had passed, but in broad daylight, and they were afraid in consequence to stop him. M. le Duc d'Orleans had passed, but in a post-chaise, which they mistrusted. At last Beringhen appeared in one of the King's coaches, attended by servants in the King's livery, and wearing his cordon Neu, as was his custom. They thought they had found a prize indeed. They soon learnt with whom they had to deal, and told him also who they were. Guetem bestowed upon Beringhen all kinds of attention, and testified a great desire to spare him as much as possible all fatigue. He pushed his attentions so far that they caused his failure. He allowed Beringhen to stop and rest on two occasions. The party missed one of their relays, and that delayed them very much.

Beringhen, delighted with his rescue, and very grateful for the good treatment he had received, changed places with Guetem and his companions, led them to Ham, and in his turn treated them well. He wrote to his wife and to Charnillart announcing his release, and these letters were read with much satisfaction by the King.

On Tuesday, the 29th of March, Beringhen arrived at Versailles, about eight o'clock in the evening, and went at once to the King, who was in the apartments of Madame de Maintenon, and who received him well, and made him relate all his adventures. But the King was not pleased when he found the officers of the stable in a state of great delight, and preparing fireworks to welcome Beringhen back. He prohibited all these marks of rejoicing, and would not allow the fireworks to be let off. He had these little jealousies. He wished that all should be devoted to him alone, without reserve and without division. All the Court, however, showed interest in this return, and Beringhen was consoled by the public welcome he received for his fatigue.

Guetem and his officers, while waiting the pleasure of the King, were lodged in Beringhen's house in Paris, where they were treated above their deserts. Beringhen obtained permission for Guetem to see the King. He did more; he presented Guetem to the King, who praised him for having so well treated his prisoner, and said that war always ought to be conducted properly. Guetem, who was not without wit, replied, that he was so astonished to find himself before the greatest King in the world, and to find that King doing him the honour of speaking to him, that he had not power enough to answer. He remained ten or twelve days in Beringhen's house to see Paris, the Opera and the Comedy, and became the talk of the town. People ran after him everywhere, and the most distinguished were not ashamed to do likewise. On all sides he was applauded for an act of temerity, which might have passed for insolence. Beringhen regaled him, furnished him with carriages and servants to accompany him, and, at parting, with money and considerable presents. Guetem went on his parole to Rheims to rejoin his comrades until exchanged, and had the town for prison. Nearly all the others had escaped. The project was nothing less than to carry off Monseigneur, or one of the princes, his sons.

This ridiculous adventure gave rise to precautions, excessive in the first place, and which caused sad obstructions of bridges and gates. It caused, too, a number of people to be arrested. The hunting parties of the princes were for some time interfered with, until matters resumed their usual course. But it was not bad fun to see, during some time, the terror of ladies, and even of men, of the Court, who no longer dared go abroad except in broad daylight, even then with little assurance, and imagining themselves everywhere in marvellous danger of capture.

I have related in its proper place the adventure of Madame la Princesse de Conti with Mademoiselle Choin and the attachment of Monseigneur for the latter. This attachment was only augmented by the difficulty of seeing each other.

Mademoiselle Choin retired to the house of Lacroix, one of her relatives at Paris, where she lived quite hidden. She was informed of the rare days when Monseigneur dined alone at Meudon, without sleeping there. She went there the day before in a fiacre, passed through the courts on foot, ill clad, like a common sort of woman going to see some officer at Meudon, and, by a back staircase, was admitted to Monseigneur who passed some hours with her in a little apartment on the first floor. In time she came there with a lady's-maid, her parcel in her pocket, on the evenings of the days that Monseigneur slept there.

She remained in this apartment without seeing anybody, attended by her lady's-maid, and waited upon by a servant who alone was in the secret.

Little by little the friends of Monseigneur were allowed to see her; and amongst these were M. le Prince de Conti, Monseigneur le Duc de Bourgogne, Madame la Duchesse de Bourgogne, and M. le Duc de Berry. There was always, however, an air of mystery about the matter. The parties that took place were kept secret, although frequent, and were called parvulos.

Mademoiselle Choin remained in her little apartment only for the convenience of Monseigneur. She slept in the bed and in the grand apartment where Madame la Duchesse de Bourgogne lodged when the King was at Meudon. She always sat in an arm-chair before Monseigneur; Madame de Bourgogne sat on a stool. Mademoiselle Choin never rose for her; in speaking of her, even before Monseigneur and the company, she used to say "the Duchesse de Bourgogne," and lived with her as Madame de Maintenon did excepting that "darling" and "my aunt," were terms not exchanged between them, and that Madame de Bourgogne was not nearly so free, or so much at her ease, as with the King and Madame de Maintenon. Monsieur de Bourgogne was much in restraint. His manners did not agree with those of that world. Monseigneur le Duc de Berry, who was more free, was quite at home.

Mademoiselle Choin went on fete-days to hear mass in the chapel at six o'clock in the morning, well wrapped up, and took her meals alone, when Monseigneur did not eat with her. When he was alone with her, the doors were all guarded and barricaded to keep out intruders. People regarded her as being to Monseigneur, what Madame de Maintenon was to the King. All the batteries for the future were directed and pointed towards her. People schemed to gain permission to visit her at Paris; people paid court to her friends and acquaintances, Monseigneur le Duc de Bourgogne sought to please her, was respectful to her, attentive to her friends, not always with success. She acted towards Monseigneur le Duc de Bourgogne like a mother-in-law, and sometimes spoke with such authority and bluntness to Madame de Bourgogne as to make her cry.

The King and Madame de Maintenon were in no way ignorant of all this, but they held their tongues, and all the Court who knew it, spoke only in whispers of it. This is enough for the present; it will serve to explain many things, of which I shall speak anon.

CHAPTER XXXVIII

On Wednesday, the 27th of May, 1707, at three o'clock in the morning, Madame de Montespan, aged sixty, died very suddenly at the waters of Bourbon. Her death made much stir, although she had long retired from the Court and from the world, and preserved no trace of the commanding influence she had so long possessed. I need not go back beyond my own experience, and to the time of her reign as mistress of the King. I will simply say, because the anecdote is little known, that her conduct was more the fault of her husband than her own. She warned him as soon as she suspected the King to be in love with her; and told him when there was no longer any doubt upon her mind. She assured him that a great entertainment that the King gave was in her honour. She pressed him, she entreated him in the most eloquent manner, to take her away to his estates of Guyenne, and leave her there until the King had forgotten her or chosen another mistress. It was all to no purpose; and Montespan was not long before repentance seized him; for his torment was that he loved her all his life, and died still in love with her— although he would never consent to see her again after the first scandal.

Nor will I speak of the divers degrees which the fear of the devil at various times put to her separation from the Court; and I will elsewhere speak of Madame de Maintenon, who owed her everything, who fed her on serpents, and who at last ousted her from the Court. What no one dared to say, what the King himself dared not, M. du Maine, her son, dared. M. de Meaux (Bossuet) did the rest. She went in tears and fury, and never forgave M. du Maine, who by his strange service gained over for ever to his interests the heart and the mighty influence of Madame de Maintenon.

The mistress, retired amongst the Community of Saint Joseph, which she had built, was long in accustoming herself to it. She carried about her idleness and unhappiness to Bourbon, to Fontevrault, to D'Antin; she was many years without succeeding in obtaining mastery over herself. At last God touched her. Her sin had never been accompanied by forgetfulness; she used often to leave the King to go and pray in her cabinet; nothing could ever make her evade any fast day or meagre day; her austerity in fasting continued amidst all her dissipation. She gave alms, was esteemed by good people, never gave way to doubt of impiety; but she was imperious, haughty and overbearing, full of mockery, and of all the qualities by which beauty with the power it bestows is naturally accompanied. Being resolved at last to take advantage of an opportunity which had been given her against her will, she put herself in the hands of Pere de la Tour, that famous General of the Oratory. From that moment to the time of her death her conversion continued steadily, and her penitence augmented. She had first to get rid of the secret fondness she still entertained for the Court, even of the hopes which, however chimerical, had always flattered her. She was persuaded that nothing but the fear of the devil had forced the King to separate himself from her, that it was nothing but this fear that had raised Madame de Maintenon to the height she had attained; that age and ill-health, which she was pleased to imagine, would soon clear the way; that when the King was a widower, she being a widow, nothing would oppose their reunion, which might easily be brought about by their affection for their children. These children entertained similar hopes, and were therefore assiduous in their attention to her for some time.

Pere de la Tour made her perform a terrible act of penitence. It was to ask pardon of her husband, and to submit herself to his commands. To all who knew Madame de Montespan this will seem the most heroic sacrifice. M. de Montespan, however, imposed no restraint upon his wife. He sent word that he wished in no way to interfere with her, or even to see her. She experienced no further trouble, therefore, on this score.

Little by little she gave almost all she had to the poor. She worked for them several hours a day, making stout shirts and such things for them. Her table, that she had loved to excess, became the most frugal; her fasts multiplied; she would interrupt her meals in order to go and pray. Her mortifications were continued; her chemises and her sheets were of rough linen, of the hardest and thickest kind, but hidden under others of ordinary kind. She unceasingly wore bracelets, garters, and a girdle, all armed with iron points, which oftentimes inflicted wounds upon her; and her tongue, formerly so dangerous, had also its peculiar penance imposed on it. She was, moreover, so tormented with the fear of death, that she employed several women, whose sole occupation was to watch her. She went to sleep with all the curtains of her bed open, many lights in her chamber, and her women around her. Whenever she awoke she wished to find them chatting, playing, or enjoying themselves, so as to re-assure herself against their drowsiness.

With all this she could never throw off the manners of a queen. She had an arm-chair in her chamber with its back turned to the foot of the bed. There was no other in the chamber, not even when her natural children came to see her, not even for Madame la Duchesse d'Orleans. She was oftentimes visited by the most distinguished people of the Court, and she spoke like a queen to all. She treated everybody with much respect, and was treated so in turn. I have mentioned in its proper place, that a short time before her death, the King gave her a hundred thousand francs to buy an estate; but this present was not gratis, for she had to send back a necklace worth a hundred and fifty thousand, to which the King made additions, and bestowed it on the Duchesse de Bourgogne.

The last time Madame de Montespan went to Bourbon she paid all her charitable pensions and gratuities two years in advance and doubled her alms. Although in good health she had a presentiment that she should return no more. This presentiment, in effect, proved correct. She felt herself so ill one night, although she had been very well just before, that she confessed herself, and received the sacrament. Previous to this she called all her servants into her room and made a public confession of her public sins, asking pardon for the scandal she had caused with a humility so decent, so profound, so penitent, that nothing could be more edifying. She received the last sacrament with an ardent piety. The fear of death which all her life had so continually troubled her, disappeared suddenly, and disturbed her no more. She died, without regret, occupied only with thoughts of eternity, and with a sweetness and tranquillity that accompanied all her actions.

Her only son by Monsieur de Montespan, whom she had treated like a mother-in-law, until her separation from the King, but who had since returned to her affection, D'Antin, arrived just before her death. She looked at him, and only said that he saw her in a very different state to what he had seen her at Bellegarde. As soon as she was dead he set out for Paris, leaving orders for her obsequies, which were strange, or were strangely executed. Her body, formerly so perfect, became the prey of the unskilfulness and the ignorance of a surgeon. The obsequies were at the discretion of the commonest valets, all the rest of the house having suddenly deserted. The body remained a long time at the door of the house, whilst the canons of the Sainte Chapelle and the priests of the parish disputed about the order of precedence with more than indecency. It was put in keeping under care of the parish, like the corpse of the meanest citizen of the place, and not until a long time afterwards was it sent to Poitiers to be placed in the family tomb, and then with an unworthy parsimony. Madame de Montespan was bitterly regretted by all the poor of the province, amongst whom she spread an infinity of alms, as well as amongst others of different degree.

As for the King, his perfect insensibility at the death of a mistress he had so passionately loved, and for so many years, was so extreme, that Madame de Bourgogne could not keep her surprise from him. He replied, tranquilly, that since he had dismissed her he had reckoned upon never seeing her again, and that thus she was from that time dead to him. It is easy to believe that the grief of the children he had had by her did not please him. Those children did not dare to wear mourning for a mother not recognised. Their appearance, therefore, contrasted with that of the children of Madame de la Valliere, who had just died, and for whom they were wearing mourning. Nothing could equal the grief which Madame la Duchesse d'Orleans, Madame la Duchesse, and the Comte de Toulouse exhibited. The grief of Madame la Duchesse especially was astonishing, for she always prided herself on loving nobody; still more astonishing was the grief of M. le Duc, so inaccessible to friendship. We must remember, however, that this death put an end to many hopes. M. du Maine, for his part, could scarcely repress his joy at the death of his mother, and after having stopped away from Marly two days, returned and caused the Comte de Toulouse to be recalled likewise. Madame de Maintenon, delivered of a former rival, whose place she had taken, ought, it might have been thought, to have felt relieved. It was otherwise; remorse for the benefits she had received from Madame de Montespan, and for the manner in which those benefits had been repaid, overwhelmed her. Tears stole down her cheeks, and she went into a strange privacy to hide them. Madame de Bourgogne, who followed, was speechless with astonishment.

The life and conduct of so famous a mistress, subsequent to her forced retirement, have appeared to me sufficiently curious to describe at length; and what happened at her death was equally characteristic of the Court.

The death of the Duchesse de Nemours, which followed quickly upon that of Madame de Montespart, made still more stir in the world, but of another kind. Madame de Nemours was daughter, by a first marriage, of the last Duc de Longueville. She was extremely rich, and lived in great splendour. She had a strange look, and a droll way of dressing, big eyes, with which she could scarcely see, a shoulder that constantly twitched, grey hairs that she wore flowing, and a very imposing air. She had a very bad temper, and could not forgive. When somebody asked her if she said the Pater, she replied, yes, but that she passed by without saying it the clause respecting pardon for our enemies. She did not like her kinsfolk, the Matignons, and would never see nor speak to any of them. One day talking to the King at a window of his cabinet, she saw Matignon passing in the court below. Whereupon she set to spitting five or six times running, and then turned to the King and begged his pardon, saying, that she could never see a Matignon without spitting in that manner. It may be imagined that devotion did not incommode her. She herself used to tell a story, that having entered one day a confessional, without being followed into the church, neither her appearance nor her dress gave her confessor an idea of her rank. She spoke of her great wealth, and said much about the Princes de Conde and de Conti. The confessor told her to pass by all that. She, feeling that the case was a serious one, insisted upon explaining and made allusion to her large estates and her millions. The good priest believed her mad, and told her to calm herself; to get rid of such ideas; to think no more of them; and above all to eat good soups, if she had the means to procure them. Seized with anger she rose and left the place. The confessor out of curiosity followed her to the door. When he saw the good lady, whom he thought mad, received by grooms, waiting women, and so on, he had like to have fallen backwards; but he ran to the coach door and asked her pardon. It was now her turn to laugh at him, and she got off scot-free that day from the confessional.

Madame de Nemours had amongst other possessions the sovereignty of Neufchatel. As soon as she was dead, various claimants arose to dispute the succession. Madame de Mailly laid claim to it, as to the succession to the principality of Orange, upon the strength of a very doubtful alliance with the house of Chalons, and hoped to be supported by Madame de Maintenon. But Madame de Maintenon laughed at her chimeras, as they were laughed at in Switzerland.

M. le Prince de Conti was another claimant. He based his right upon the will of the last Duc de Longueville, by which he had been called to all the Duke's wealth, after the Comte de Saint Paul, his brother, and his posterity. In addition to these, there were Matignon and the dowager Duchesse de Lesdiguieres, who claimed Neufchatel by right of their relationship to Madame de Nemours.

Matignon was an intimate friend of Chamillart, who did not like the Prince de Conti, and was the declared enemy of the Marechal de Villeroy, the representative of Madame de Lesdiguieres, in this affair. Chamillart, therefore, persuaded the King to remain neutral, and aided Matignon by money and influence to get the start of the other claimants.

The haughty citizens of Neufchatel saw then all these suitors begging for their suffrages, when a minister of the Elector of Brandenbourg appeared amongst them, and disputed the pretensions of the Prince de Conti in favour of his master, the Elector of Brandenbourg (King of Prussia), who drew his claim from the family of Chalons. It was more distant; more entangled if possible, than that of Madame de Mailly. He only made use of it, therefore, as a pretext. His reasons were his religion, in conformity with that of the country; the support of the neighbouring Protestant cantons, allies, and protectors of Neufchatel; the pressing reflection that the principality of Orange having fallen by the death of William III. to M. le Prince de Conti, the King (Louis XIV.)

had appropriated it and recompensed him for it: and that he might act similarly if Neufchatel fell to one of his subjects; lastly, a treaty produced in good form, by which, in the event of the death of Madame de Nemours, England and Holland agreed to declare for the Elector of Brandenbourg, and to assist him by force in procuring this little state. This minister of the Elector was in concert with the Protestant cantons, who upon his declaration at once sided with him; and who, by the money spent, the conformity of religion, the power of the Elector, the reflection of what had happened at Orange, found nearly all the suffrages favourable. So striking while the iron was hot, they obtained a provisional judgment from Neufchatel, which adjudged their state to the Elector until the peace; and in consequence of this, his minister was put into actual possession, and M. le Prince de Conti saw himself constrained to return more shamefully than he had returned once before, and was followed by the other claimants.

Madame de Mailly made such an uproar at the news of this intrusion of the Elector, that at last the attention of our ministers was awakened. They found, with her, that it was the duty of the King not to allow this morsel to be carried off from his subjects; and that there was danger in leaving it in the hands of such a powerful Protestant prince, capable of making a fortified place of it so close to the county of Burgundy, and on a frontier so little protected. Thereupon, the King despatched a courier to our minister in Switzerland, with orders to go to Neufchatel, and employ every means, even menaces, to exclude the Elector, and to promise that the neutrality of France should be maintained if one of her subjects was selected, no matter which one. It was too late. The affair was finished; the cantons were engaged, without means of withdrawing. They, moreover, were piqued into resistance, by an appeal to their honour by the electoral minister, who insisted on the menaces of Puysieux, our representative, to whose memoir the ministers of England and Holland printed a violent reply. The provisional judgment received no alteration. Shame was felt; and resentment was testified during six weeks; after which, for lack of being able to do better, this resentment was appeased of itself. It may be imagined what hope remained to the claimants of reversing at the peace this provisional judgment, and of struggling against a prince so powerful and so solidly supported. No mention of it was afterwards made, and Neufchatel has remained ever since fully and peaceably to this prince, who was even expressly confirmed in his possession at the peace by France.

The armies assembled this year towards the end of May, and the campaign commenced. The Duc de Vendome was in command in Flanders, under the Elector of Bavaria, and by his slothfulness and inattention, allowed Marlborough to steal a march upon him, which, but for the failure of some of the arrangements, might have caused serious loss to our troops. The enemy was content to keep simply on the defensive after this, having projects of attack in hand elsewhere to which I shall soon allude.

On the Rhine, the Marechal de Villars was in command, and was opposed by the Marquis of Bayreuth, and afterwards by the Duke of Hanover, since King of England. Villars was so far successful, that finding himself feebly opposed by the Imperials, he penetrated into Germany, after having made himself master of Heidelberg, Mannheim, and all the Palatinate, and seized upon a number of cannons, provisions, and munitions of war. He did not forget to tax the enemy wherever he went. He gathered immense sums—treasures beyond all his hopes. Thus gorged, he could not hope that his brigandage would remain unknown. He put on a bold face and wrote to the King, that the army would cost him nothing this year. Villars begged at the same time to be allowed to appropriate some of the money he had acquired to the levelling of a hill on his estate which displeased him. Another than he would have been dishonoured by such a request. But it made no difference in his respect, except with the public, with whom, however, he occupied himself but little. His booty clutched, he thought of withdrawing from the enemy's country, and passing the Rhine.

He crossed it tranquilly, with his army and his immense booty, despite the attempts of the Duke of Hanover to prevent him, and as soon as he was on this side, had no care but how to terminate the campaign in repose. Thus finished a campaign tolerably brilliant, if the sordid and prodigious gain of the general had not soiled it. Yet that general, on his return, was not less well received by the King.

At sea we had successes. Frobin, with vessels more feeble than the four English ones of seventy guns, which convoyed a fleet of eighteen ships loaded with provisions and articles of war, took two of those vessels of war and the eighteen merchantmen, after four hours' fighting, and set fire to one of the two others. Three months after he took at the mouth of the Dwiria seven richly-loaded Dutch merchant-ships, bound for Muscovy. He took or sunk more than fifty during this campaign. Afterwards he took three large English ships of war that he led to Brest, and sank another of a hundred guns. The English of New England and of New York were not more successful in Acadia; they attacked our colony twelve days running, without success, and were obliged to retire with much loss.

The maritime year finished by a terrible tempest upon the coast of Holland, which caused many vessels to perish in the Texel, and submerged a large number of districts and villages. France had also its share of these catastrophes. The Loire overflowed in a manner hitherto unheard of, broke down the embankments, inundated and covered with sand many parts of the country, carried away villages, drowned numbers of people and a quantity of cattle, and caused damage to the amount of above eight millions. This was another of our obligations to M. de la Feuillade—an obligation which we have not yet escaped from. Nature, wiser than man, had placed rocks in the Loire above Roanne, which prevented navigation to that place, the principal in the duchy of M. de la Feuillade. His father, tempted by the profit of this navigation, wished to get rid of the rocks. Orleans, Blois, Tours, in one word, all the places on the Loire, opposed this. They represented the danger of inundations; they were listened to, and although the M. de la Feuillade of that day was a favourite, and on good terms with M. Colbert, he was not allowed to carry out his wishes with respect to these rocks. His son, the M. de la Feuillade whom we have seen figuring with so little distinction at the siege of Turin, had more credit. Without listening to anybody, he blew up the rocks, and the navigation was rendered free in his favour; the inundations that they used to prevent have overflowed since at immense loss to the King and private individuals. The cause was clearly seen afterwards, but then it was too late.

The little effort made by the enemy in Flanders and Germany, had a cause, which began to be perceived towards the middle of July. We had been forced to abandon Italy. By a shameful treaty that was made, all our troops had retired from that country into Savoy. We had given up everything. Prince Eugene, who had had the glory of driving us out of Italy, remained there some time, and then entered the county of Nice.

Forty of the enemy's vessels arrived at Nice shortly afterwards, and landed artillery. M. de Savoie arrived there also, with six or seven thousand men. It was now no longer hidden that the siege of Toulon was determined on. Every preparation was at once made to defend the place. Tesse was in command. The delay of a day on the part of the enemy saved Toulon, and it may be said, France. M. de Savoie had been promised money by the English. They disputed a whole day about the payment, and so retarded the departure of the fleet from Nice. In the end, seeing M. de Savoie firm, they paid him a million, which he received himself. But in the mean time twenty-one of our battalions had had time to arrive at Toulon. They decided the fortune of the siege. After several unsuccessful attempts to take the place, the enemy gave up the siege and retired in the night, between the 22nd and 23rd of August, in good order, and without being disturbed. Our troops could obtain no sort of assistance from the people of Provence, so as to harass M. de Savoie in his passage of the Var. They refused money, militia, and provisions bluntly, saying that it was no matter to them who came, and that M. de Savoie could not torment them more than they were tormented already.

The important news of a deliverance so desired arrived at Marly on Friday, the 26th of August, and overwhelmed all the Court with joy. A scandalous fuss arose, however, out of this event. The first courier who brought the intelligence of it, had been despatched by the commander of the fleet, and had been conducted to the King by Pontchartrain, who had the affairs of the navy under his control. The courier sent by Tesse, who commanded the land forces, did not arrive until some hours after the other. Chamillart, who received this second courier, was piqued to excess that Pontchartrain had outstripped him with the news. He declared that the news did not belong to the navy, and consequently Pontchartrain had no right to carry it to the King. The public, strangely enough, sided with Chamillart, and on every side Pontchartrain was treated as a greedy usurper. Nobody had sufficient sense to reflect upon the anger which a master would feel against a servant who, having the information by which that master could be relieved from extreme anxiety, should yet withhold the information for six or eight hours, on the ground that to tell it was the duty of another servant!

The strangest thing is, that the King, who was the most interested, had not the force to declare himself on either side, but kept silent. The torrent was so impetuous that Pontchartrain had only to lower his head, keep silent, and let the waters pass. Such was the weakness of the King for his ministers. I recollect that, in 1702, the Duc de Villeroy brought to Marly the important news of the battle of Luzzara. But, because Chamillart was not there, he hid himself, left the King and the Court in the utmost anxiety, and did not announce his news until long after, when Chamillart, hearing of his arrival, hastened to join him and present him to the King. The King was so far from being displeased, that he made the Duc de Villeroy Lieutenant-General before dismissing him.

There is another odd thing that I must relate before quitting this affair. Tesse, as I have said, was charged with the defence of Toulon by land. It was a charge of no slight importance. He was in a country where nothing was prepared, and where everything was wanting; the fleet of the enemy and their army were near at hand, commanded by two of the most skilful captains of the day: if they succeeded, the kingdom itself was in danger, and the road open to the enemy even to Paris. A general thus situated would have been in no humour for jesting, it might have been thought. But this was not the case with Tesse. He found time to write to Pontchartrain all the details of the war and all that passed amongst our troops in the style of Don Quixote, of whom he called himself the wretched squire and the Sancho; and everything he wrote he adapted to the adventures of that romance. Pontchartrain showed me these letters; they made him die with laughing, he admired them so; and in truth they were very comical, and he imitated that romance with more wit than I believed him to possess. It appeared to me incredible, however, that a man should write thus, at such a critical time, to curry, favour with a secretary of state. I could not have believed it had I not seen it.

VOLUME 6.: CHAPTER XXXIX

I went this summer to Forges, to try, by means of the waters there, to get rid of a tertian fever that quinquina only suspended. While there I heard of a new enterprise on the part of the Princes of the blood, who, in the discredit in which the King held them, profited without measure by his desire for the grandeur of the illegitimate children, to acquire new advantages which were suffered because the others shared them. This was the case in question.

After the elevation of the mass—at the King's communion—a folding-chair was pushed to the foot of the altar, was covered with a piece of stuff, and then with a large cloth, which hung down before and behind. At the Pater the chaplain rose and whispered in the King's ear the names of all the Dukes who were in the chapel. The King named two, always the oldest, to each of whom the chaplain advanced and made a reverence. During the communion of the priest the King rose, and went and knelt down on the bare floor behind this folding seat, and took hold of the cloth; at the same time the two Dukes, the elder on the right, the other on the left, each took hold of a corner of the cloth; the two chaplains took hold of the other two corners of the same cloth, on the side of the altar, all four kneeling, and the captain of the guards also kneeling and behind the King. The communion received and the oblation taken some moments afterwards, the King remained a little while in the same place, then returned to his own, followed by the two Dukes and the captain of the guards, who took theirs. If a son of France happened to be there alone, he alone held the right corner of the cloth, and nobody the other; and when M. le Duc d'Orleans was there, and no son of France was present, M. le Duc d'Orleans held the cloth in like manner. If a Prince of the blood were alone present, however, he held the cloth, but a Duke was called forward to assist him. He was not privileged to act without the Duke.

The Princes of the blood wanted to change this; they were envious of the distinction accorded to M. d'Orleans, and wished to put themselves on the same footing. Accordingly, at the Assumption of this year, they managed so well that M. le Duc served alone at the altar at the King's communion, no Duke being called upon to come and join him. The surprise at this was very great. The Duc de la Force and the Marechal de Boufflers, who ought to have served, were both present. I wrote to this last to say that such a thing had never happened before, and that it was contrary to all precedent. I wrote, too, to M. d'Orleans, who was then in Spain, informing him of the circumstance. When he returned he complained to the King. But the King merely said that the Dukes ought to have presented themselves and taken hold of the cloth. But how could they have done so, without being requested, as was customary, to come forward? What would the king have thought of them if they had? To conclude, nothing could be made of the matter, and it remained thus. Never then, since that time, did I go to the communions of the King.

An incident occurred at Marly about the same time, which made much stir. The ladies who were invited to Marly had the privilege of dining with the King. Tables were placed for them, and they took up positions according to their rank. The non-titled ladies had also their special place. It so happened one day; that Madame de Torcy (an untitled lady) placed herself above the Duchesse de Duras, who arrived at table a moment after her. Madame de Torcy offered to give up her place, but it was a little late, and the offer passed away in compliments. The King entered, and put himself at table. As soon as he sat down, he saw the place Madame de Torcy had taken, and fixed such a serious and surprised look upon her, that she again offered to give up her place to the Duchesse de Duras; but the offer was again declined. All through the dinner the King scarcely ever took his eyes off Madame de Torcy, said hardly a word, and bore a look of anger that rendered everybody very attentive, and even troubled the Duchesse de Duras.

Upon rising from the table, the King passed, according to custom, into the apartments of Madame de Maintenon, followed by the Princesses of the blood, who grouped themselves around him upon stools; the others who entered, kept at a distance. Almost before he had seated himself in his chair, he said to Madame de Maintenon, that he had just been witness of an act of "incredible insolence" (that was the term he used) which had thrown him into such a rage that he had been unable to eat: that such an enterprise would have been insupportable in a woman of the highest quality; but coming, as it did, from a mere bourgeoise, it had so affected him, that ten times he had been upon the point of making her leave the table, and that he was only restrained by consideration for her husband. After this outbreak he made a long discourse upon the genealogy of Madame de Torcy's family, and other matters; and then, to the astonishment of all present, grew as angry as ever against Madame de Torcy. He went off then into a discourse upon the dignity of the Dukes, and in conclusion, he charged the Princesses to tell Madame de Torcy to what extent he had found her conduct impertinent. The Princesses looked at each other, and not one seemed to like this commission; whereupon the King, growing more angry, said; that it must be undertaken however, and left the robes; The news of what had taken place, and of the King's choler, soon spread all over the Court. It was believed, however, that all was over, and that no more would be heard of the matter. Yet the very same evening the King broke out again with even more bitterness than before. On the morrow, too, surprise was great indeed, when it was found that the King, immediately after dinner, could talk of nothing but this subject, and that, too, without any softening of tone. At last he was assured that Madame de Torcy had been spoken to, and this appeased him a little. Torcy was obliged to write him a letter, apologising for the fault of Madame de Torcy; and the King at this grew content. It may be imagined what a sensation this adventure produced all through the Court.

While upon the subject of the King, let me relate an anecdote of him, which should have found a place ere this. When M. d'Orleans was about to start for Spain, he named the officers who were to be of his suite. Amongst others was Fontpertius. At that name the King put on a serious look.

"What! my nephew," he said. "Fontpertius! the son of a Jansenist—of that silly woman who ran everywhere after M. Arnould! I do not wish that man to go with you."

"By my faith, Sire," replied the Duc d'Orleans, "I know not what the mother has done; but as for the son, he is far enough from being a Jansenist, I'll answer for it; for he does not believe in God."

"Is it possible, my nephew?" said the King, softening.

"Nothing more certain, Sire, I assure you."

"Well, since it is so," said the King, "there is no harm: you can take him with you."

This scene—for it can be called by no other name—took place in the morning. After dinner M. d'Orleans repeated it to me, bursting with laughter, word for word, just as I have written it. When we had both well laughed at this, we admired the profound instruction of a discreet and religious King, who considered it better not to believe in God than to be a Jansenist, and who thought there was less danger to his nephew from the impiety of an unbeliever than from the doctrines of a sectarian. M. d'Orleans could not contain himself while he told the story, and never spoke of it without laughing until the tears came into his eyes. It ran all through the Court and all over the town, and the marvellous thing was, that the King was not angry at this. It was a testimony of his attachment to the good doctrine which withdrew him further and further from Jansenism. The majority of people laughed with all their heart. Others, more wise, felt rather disposed to weep than to laugh, in considering to what excess of blindness the King had reached.

For a long time a most important project had knocked at every door, without being able to obtain a hearing anywhere. The project was this:— Hough, an English gentleman full of talent and knowledge, and who, above all, knew profoundly the laws of his country, had filled various posts in England. As first a minister by profession, and furious against King James; afterwards a Catholic and King James's spy, he had been delivered up to King William, who pardoned him. He profited by this only to continue his services to James. He was taken several times, and always escaped from the Tower of London and other prisons. Being no longer able to dwell in England he came to France, where he occupied himself always with the same line of business, and was paid for that by the King (Louis XIV.) and by King James, the latter of whom he unceasingly sought to re- establish. The union of Scotland with England appeared to him a favourable conjuncture, by the despair of that ancient kingdom at seeing itself reduced into a province under the yoke of the English. The Jacobite party remained there; the vexation caused by this forced union had increased it, by the desire felt to break that union with the aid of a King that they would have reestablished. Hough, who was aware of the fermentation going on, made several secret journeys to Scotland, and planned an invasion of that country; but, as I have said, for a long time could get no one to listen to him.

The King, indeed, was so tired of such enterprises, that nobody dared to speak to him upon this. All drew back. No one liked to bell the cat. At last, however, Madame de Maintenon being gained over, the King was induced to listen to the project. As soon as his consent was gained to it, another scheme was added to the first. This was to profit by the disorder in which the Spanish Low Countries were thrown, and to make them revolt against the Imperialists at the very moment when the affair of Scotland would bewilder the allies, and deprive them of all support from England. Bergheyck, a man well acquainted with the state of those countries, was consulted, and thought the scheme good. He and the Duc de Vendome conferred upon it in presence of the King.

After talking over various matters, the discussion fell, upon the Meuse, and its position with reference to Maastricht. Vendome held that the Meuse flowed in a certain direction. Bergheyck opposed him. Vendome, indignant that a civilian should dare to dispute military movements with him, grew warm. The other remained respectful and cool, but firm. Vendome laughed at

Bergheyck, as at an ignorant fellow who did not know the position of places. Bergheyck maintained his point. Vendome grew more and more hot. If he was right, what he proposed was easy enough; if wrong, it was impossible. It was in vain that Vendome pretended to treat with disdain his opponent; Bergheyck was not to be put down, and the King, tired out at last with a discussion upon a simple question of fact, examined the maps. He found at once that Bergheyck was right. Any other than the King would have felt by this what manner of man was this general of his taste, of his heart, and of his confidence; any other than Vendome would have been confounded; but it was Bergheyck in reality who was so, to see the army in such hands and the blindness of the King for him! He was immediately sent into Flanders to work up a revolt, and he did it so well, that success seemed certain, dependent, of course, upon success in Scotland.

The preparations for the invasion of that country were at once commenced. Thirty vessels were armed at Dunkerque and in the neighbouring ports. The Chevalier de Forbin was chosen to command the squadron. Four thousand men were brought from Flanders to Dunkerque; and it was given out that this movement was a mere change of garrison. The secret of the expedition was well kept; but the misfortune was that things were done too slowly. The fleet, which depended upon Pontchartrain, was not ready in time, and that which depended upon Chamillart, was still more behindhand. The two ministers threw the fault upon each other; but the truth is, both were to blame. Pontchartrain was more than accused of delaying matters from unwillingness; the other from powerlessness.

Great care was taken that no movement should be seen at Saint Germain. The affair, however, began in time to get noised abroad. A prodigious quantity of arms and clothing for the Scotch had been embarked; the movements by sea and land became only too visible upon the coast. At last, on Wednesday, the 6th of March, the King of England set out from Saint Germain. He was attended by the Duke of Perth, who had been his sub-preceptor; by the two Hamiltons, by Middleton, and a very few others. But his departure had been postponed too long. At the moment when all were ready to start, people learned with surprise that the English fleet had appeared in sight, and was blockading Dunkerque. Our troops, who were already on board ship, were at once landed. The King of England cried out so loudly against this, and proposed so eagerly that an attempt should be made to pass the enemy at all risks, that a fleet was sent out to reconnoitre the enemy, and the troops were re-embarked. But then a fresh mischance happened. The Princess of England had had the measles, and was barely growing convalescent at the time of the departure of the King, her brother. She had been prevented from seeing him, lest he should be attacked by the same complaint. In spite of this precaution, however, it declared itself upon him at Dunkerque, just as the troops were re-embarked. He was in despair, and wished to be wrapped up in blankets and carried on board. The doctors said that it would kill him; and he was obliged to remain. The worst of it was, that two of five Scotch deputies who had been hidden at Montrouge near Paris, had been sent into Scotland a fortnight before, to announce the immediate arrival of the King with arms and troops. The movement which it was felt this announcement would create, increased the impatience for departure. At last, on Saturday, the 19th of March, the King of England, half cured and very weak, determined to embark in spite of his physicians, and did so. The enemy's vessels hats retired; so, at six o'clock in the morning, our ships set sail with a good breeze, and in the midst of a mist, which hid them from view in about an hour.

Forty-eight hours after the departure of our squadron, twenty-seven English ships of war appeared before Dunkerque. But our fleet was away. The very first night it experienced a furious tempest. The ship in which was the King of England took shelter afterwards behind the works of Ostend. During the storm, another ship was separated from the squadron, and was obliged to take refuge on the coast of Picardy. This vessel, a frigate, was commanded by Rambure, a lieutenant. As, soon as he was able he sailed after the squadron that he believed already in Scotland. He directed his course towards Edinburgh, and found no vessel during all the voyage. As he approached the mouth of the river, he saw around him a number of barques and small vessels that he could not avoid, and that he determined in consequence to approach with as good a grace as possible. The masters of these ships' told him that the King was expected with impatience, but that they had no news of him, that they had come out to meet him, and that they would send pilots to Rambure, to conduct him up the river to Edinburgh, where all was hope and joy. Rambure, equally surprised that the squadron which bore the King of England had not appeared, and by the publicity of his forthcoming arrival, went up towards Edinburgh more and more surrounded by barques, which addressed to him the same language. A gentleman of the country passed from one of these barques upon the frigate. He told Rambure that the principal noblemen of Scotland had resolved to act together, that these noblemen could count upon more than twenty thousand men ready to take up arms, and that all the towns awaited only the arrival of the King to proclaim him.

More and more troubled that the squadron did not appear, Rambure, after a time, turned back and went in search of it. As he approached the mouth of the river, which he had so lately entered, he heard a great noise of cannon out at sea, and a short time afterwards he saw many vessels of war there. Approaching more and more, and quitting the river, he distinguished our squadron, chased by twenty-six large ships of war and a number of other vessels, all of which he soon lost sight of, so much was our squadron in advance. He continued on his course in order to join them; but he could not do so until all had passed by the mouth of the river. Then steering clear of the rear-guard of the English ships, he remarked that the English fleet was hotly chasing the ship of the King of England, which ran along the coast, however, amid the fire of cannon and oftentimes of musketry. Rambure tried, for a long time, to profit by the lightness of his frigate to get ahead; but, always cut off by the enemy's vessels, and continually in danger of being taken, he returned to Dunkerque, where he immediately despatched to the Court this sad and disturbing news. He was followed, five or six days after, by the King of England, who returned to Dunkerque on the 7th of April, with his vessels badly knocked about.

It seems that the ship in which was the Prince, after experiencing the storm I have already alluded to, set sail again with its squadron, but twice got out of its reckoning within forty-eight hours; a fact not easy to understand in a voyage from Ostend to Edinburgh. This circumstance gave time to the English to join them; thereupon the King held a council, and much time was lost in deliberations. When the squadron drew near the river, the enemy was so close upon us, that to enter, without fighting either inside or out, seemed impossible. In this emergency it was suggested that our ships should go on to Inverness, about eighteen or twenty leagues further off. But this was objected to by Middleton and the Chevalier Forbin, who declared that the King of England was expected only at Edinburgh, and that it was useless to go elsewhere; and accordingly the project was given up, and the ships returned to France.

This return, however, was not accomplished without some difficulty. The enemy's fleet attacked the rear guard of ours, and after an obstinate combat, took two vessels of war and some other vessels. Among the prisoners made by the English were the Marquis de Levi, Lord Griffin, and the two sons of Middleton; who all, after suffering some little bad treatment, were conducted to London.

Lord Griffin was an old Englishman, who deserves a word of special mention. A firm Protestant, but much attached to the King of England, he knew nothing of this expedition until after the King's departure. He went immediately in quest of the Queen. With English freedom he reproached her for the little confidence she had had in him, in spite of his services and his constant fidelity, and finished by assuring her that neither his age nor his religion would hinder him from serving the King to the last drop of his blood. He spoke so feelingly that the Queen was ashamed. After this he went to Versailles, asked M. de Toulouse for a hundred Louis and a horse, and without delay rode off to Dunkerque, where he embarked with the others. In London he was condemned to death; but he showed so much firmness and such disdain of death, that his judges were too much ashamed to avow the execution to be carried out. The Queen sent him one respite, then another, although he had never asked for either, and finally he was allowed to remain at liberty in London on parole. He always received fresh respites, and lived in London as if it his own country, well received everywhere. Being informed that these respites would never cease, he lived thus several years, and died very old, a natural death. The other prisoners were equally well treated. It was in this expedition that the King of England first assumed the title of the Chevalier de Saint George, and that his enemies gave him that of the Pretender; both of which have remained to him. He showed much will and firmness, which he spoiled by a docility, the result of a bad education, austere and confined, that devotion, ill understood, together with the desire of maintaining him in fear and dependence, caused the Queen (who, with all her sanctity, always wished to dominate) to give him. He asked to serve in the next campaign in Flanders, and wished to go there at once, or remain near Dunkerque. Service was promised him, but he was made to return to Saint Germain. Hough, who had been made a peer of Ireland before starting, preceded him with the journals of the voyage, and that of Forbin, to whom the King gave a thousand crowns pension and ten thousand as a recompense.

The King of England arrived at Saint Germain on Friday, the 20th of April, and came with the Queen, the following Sunday, to Marly, where our King was. The two Kings embraced each other several times, in the presence of the two Courts. But the visit altogether was a sad one. The Courts, which met in the garden, returned towards the Chateau, exchanging indifferent words in an indifferent way.

Middleton was strongly suspected of having acquainted the English with our project. They acted, at all events, as if they had been informed of everything, and wished to appear to know nothing. They made a semblance of sending their fleet to escort a convoy to Portugal; they got in readiness the few troops they had in England and sent them towards Scotland; and the Queen, under various pretexts, detained in London, until the affair had failed, the Duke of Hamilton, the most powerful Scotch lord; and the life and soul of the expedition. When all was over, she made no arrests, and wisely avoided throwing Scotland into despair. This conduct much augmented her authority in England, attached all hearts to her, and took away all desire of stirring again by taking away all hope of success. Thus failed a project so well and so secretly conducted until the end, which was pitiable; and with this project failed that of the Low Countries, which was no longer thought of.

The allies uttered loud cries against this attempt on the part of a power they believed at its last gasp, and which, while pretending to seek peace, thought of nothing less than the invasion of Great Britain. The effect of our failure was to bind closer, and to irritate more and more this formidable alliance.

CHAPTER XL

Brissac, Major of the Body-guards, died of age and ennui about this time, more than eighty years old, at his country-house, to which he had not long retired. The King had made use of him to put the Guards upon that grand military footing they have reached. He had acquired the confidence of the King by his inexorable exactitude, his honesty, and his aptitude. He was a sort of wild boar, who had all the appearance of a bad man, without being so in reality; but his manners were, it must be admitted, harsh and disagreeable. The King, speaking one day of the majors of the troops, said that if they were good, they were sure to be hated.

"If it is necessary to be perfectly hated in order to be a good major," replied M. de Duras, who was behind the King with the baton, "behold, Sire, the best major in France!" and he took Brissac, all confusion, by the arm. The King laughed, though he would have thought such a sally very bad in any other; but M. de Duras had put himself on such a free footing, that he stopped at nothing before the King, and often said the sharpest things. This major had very robust health, and laughed at the doctors—very often, even before the King, at Fagon, whom nobody else would have dared to attack. Fagon replied by disdain, often by anger, and with all his wit was embarrassed. These short scenes were sometimes very amusing.

Brissac, a few years before his retirement, served the Court ladies a nice turn. All through the winter they attended evening prayers on Thursdays and Sundays, because the King went there; and, under the pretence of reading their prayer-books, had little tapers before them, which cast a light on their faces, and enabled the King to recognise them as he passed. On the evenings when they knew he would not go, scarcely one of them went. One evening, when the King was expected, all the ladies had arrived, and were in their places, and the guards were at their doors. Suddenly, Brissac appeared in the King's place, lifted his baton, and cried aloud, "Guards of the King, withdraw, return to your quarters; the King is not coming this evening." The guards withdrew; but after they had proceeded a short distance, were stopped by brigadiers posted for the purpose, and told to return in a few minutes. What Brissac had said was a joke. The ladies at once began to murmur one to another. In a moment or two all the candles were put out, and the ladies, with but few exceptions, left the chapel. Soon after the King arrived, and, much astonished to see so few ladies present, asked how it was that nobody was there. At the conclusion of the prayers Brissac related what he had done, not without dwelling on the piety of the Court ladies. The King and all who accompanied him laughed heartily. The story soon spread, and these ladies would have strangled Brissac if they had been able.

The Duchesse de Bourgogne being in the family way this spring, was much inconvenienced. The King wished to go to Fontainebleau at the commencement of the fine season, contrary to his usual custom; and had declared this wish. In the mean time he desired to pay visits to Marly. Madame de Bourgogne much amused him; he could not do without her, yet so much movement was not suitable to her state. Madame de Maintenon was uneasy, and Fagon gently intimated his opinion. This annoyed the King, accustomed to restrain himself for nothing, and spoiled by having seen his mistresses travel when big with child, or when just recovering from their confinement, and always in full dress. The hints against going to Marly bothered him, but did not make him give them up. All he would consent to was, that the journey should put off from the day after Quasimodo to the Wednesday of the following week; but nothing could make him delay his amusement, beyond that time, or induce him to allow the Princess to remain at Versailles.

The King's Walk at Versailles--painted by J. L. Jerome

On the following Saturday, as the King was taking a walk after mass, and amusing himself at the carp basin between the Chateau and the Perspective, we saw the Duchesse de Lude coming towards him on foot and all alone, which, as no lady was with the King, was a rarity in the morning. We understood that she had something important to say to him, and when he was a short distance from her, we stopped so as to allow him to join her alone. The interview was not long. She went away again, and the King came back towards us and near the carps without saying a word. Each saw clearly what was in the wind, and nobody was eager to speak. At last the King, when quite close to the basin, looked at the principal people around, and without addressing anybody, said, with an air of vexation, these few words:

"The Duchesse de Bourgogne is hurt."

M. de la Rochefoucauld at once uttered an exclamation. M. de Bouillon, the Duc de Tresmes, and Marechal de Boufflers repeated in a low tone the words I have named; and M. de la Rochefoucauld returning to the charge, declared emphatically that it was the greatest misfortune in the world, and that as she had already wounded herself on other occasions, she might never, perhaps, have any more children.

"And if so," interrupted the King all on a sudden, with anger, "what is that to me? Has she not already a son; and if he should die, is not the Duc de Berry old enough to marry and have one? What matters it to the who succeeds me,—the one or the other? Are the not all equally my grandchildren?" And immediately, with impetuosity he added, "Thank God, she is wounded, since she was to be so; and I shall no longer be annoyed in my journeys and in everything I wish to do, by the representations of doctors, and the reasonings of matrons. I shall go and come at my pleasure, and shall be left in peace."

A silence so deep that an ant might be heard to walk, succeeded this strange outburst. All eyes were lowered; no one hardly dared to breathe. All remained stupefied. Even the domestics and the gardeners stood motionless.

This silence lasted more than a quarter of an hour. The King broke it as he leaned upon a balustrade to speak of a carp. Nobody replied. He addressed himself afterwards on the subject of these carps to domestics, who did not ordinarily join in the conversation. Nothing but carps was spoken of with them. All was languishing, and the King went away some time after. As soon as we dared look at each other—out of his sight, our eyes met and told all. Everybody there was for the moment the confidant of his neighbour. We admired—we marvelled—we grieved, we shrugged our shoulders. However distant may be that scene, it is always equally present to me. M. de la Rochefoucauld was in a fury, and this time without being wrong. The chief ecuyer was ready to faint with affright; I myself examined everybody with my eyes and ears, and was satisfied with myself for having long since thought that the King loved and cared for himself alone, and was himself his only object in life.

This strange discourse sounded far and wide-much beyond Marly.

Let me here relate another anecdote of the King—a trifle I was witness of. It was on the 7th of May, of this year, and at Marly. The King walking round the gardens, showing them to Bergheyck, and talking with him upon the approaching campaign in Flanders, stopped before one of the pavilions. It was that occupied by Desmarets, who had recently succeeded Chamillart in the direction of the finances, and who was at work within with Samuel Bernard, the famous banker, the richest man in Europe, and whose money dealings were the largest. The King observed to Desmarets that he was very glad to see him with M. Bernard; then immediately said to this latter:

"You are just the man never to have seen Marly—come and see it now; I will give you up afterwards to Desmarets."

Bernard followed, and while the walk lasted the King spoke only to Bergheyck and to Bernard, leading them everywhere, and showing them everything with the grace he so well knew how to employ when he desired to overwhelm. I admired, and I was not the only one, this species of prostitution of the King, so niggard of his words, to a man of Bernard's degree. I was not long in learning the cause of it, and I admired to see how low the greatest kings sometimes find themselves reduced.

Our finances just then were exhausted. Desmarets no longer knew of what wood to make a crutch. He had been to Paris knocking at every door. But the most exact engagements had been so often broken that he found nothing but excuses and closed doors. Bernard, like the rest, would advance nothing. Much was due to him. In vain Desmarets represented to him the pressing necessity for money, and the enormous gains he had made out of the King. Bernard remained unshakeable. The King and the minister were cruelly embarrassed. Desmarets said to the King that, after all was said and done, only Samuel Bernard could draw them out of the mess, because it was not doubtful that he had plenty of money everywhere; that the only thing needed was to vanquish his determination and the obstinacy—even insolence—he had shown; that he was a man crazy with vanity, and capable of opening his purse if the King deigned to flatter him.

It was agreed, therefore, that Desmarets should invite Bernard to dinner —should walk with him—and that the King should come and disturb them as I have related. Bernard was the dupe of this scheme; he returned from his walk with the King enchanted to such an extent that he said he would prefer ruining himself rather than leave in embarrassment a Prince who had just treated him so graciously, and whose eulogiums he uttered with enthusiasm! Desmarets profited by this trick immediately, and drew much more from it than he had proposed to himself..

The Prince de Leon had an adventure just about this time, which made much noise. He was a great, ugly, idle, mischievous fellow, son of the Duc de Rohan, who had given him the title I have just named. He had served in one campaign very indolently, and then quitted the army, under pretence of ill-health, to serve no more. Glib in speech, and with the manners of the great world, he was full of caprices and fancies; although a great gambler and spendthrift, he was miserly, and cared only for himself. He had been enamoured of Florence, an actress, whom M. d'Orleans had for a long time kept, and by whom he had children, one of whom is now Archbishop of Cambrai. M. de Leon also had several children by this creature, and spent large sums upon her. When he went in place of his father to open the States of Brittany, she accompanied him in a coach and six horses, with a ridiculous scandal. His father was in agony lest he should marry her. He offered to insure her five thousand francs a-year pension, and to take care of their children, if M. de Leon would quit her. But M. de Leon would not hear of this, and his father accordingly complained to the King. The King summoned M. de Leon into his cabinet; but the young man pleaded his cause so well there, that he gained pity rather than condemnation. Nevertheless, La Florence was carried away from a pretty little house at the Ternes, near Paris, where M. de Leon kept her, and was put in a convent. M. de Leon became furious; for some time he would neither see nor speak of his father or mother, and repulsed all idea of marriage.

At last, however, no longer hoping to see his actress, he not only consented, but wished to marry. His parents were delighted at this, and at once looked about for a wife for him. Their choice, fell upon the eldest daughter of the Duc de Roquelaure, who, although humpbacked and extremely ugly, she was to be very rich some day, and was, in fact, a very good match. The affair had been arranged and concluded up to a certain point, when all was broken off, in consequence of the haughty obstinacy with which the Duchesse de Roquelaure demanded a larger sum with M. de Leon than M. de Rohan chose to give.

The young couple were in despair: M. de Leon, lest his father should always act in this way, as an excuse for giving him nothing; the young lady, because she, feared she should rot in a convent, through the avarice of her mother, and never marry. She was more than twenty-four years, of age; he was more than eight-and-twenty. She was in the convent of the Daughters of the Cross in the Faubourg Saint Antoine.

As soon as M. de Leon learnt that the marriage was broken off, he hastened to the convent; and told all to Mademoiselle de Roquelaure; played the passionate, the despairing; said that if they waited for their parents' consent they would never marry; and that she would rot in her convent. He proposed, therefore, that, in spite of their parents, they should marry and be their own guardians. She agreed to this project; and he went away in order to execute it.

One of the most intimate friends of Madame de Roquelaure was Madame de la Vieuville, and she was the only person (excepting Madame de Roquelaure herself) to whom the Superior of the convent had permission to confide Mademoiselle de Roquelaure. Madame de la Vieuville often came to see Mademoiselle de Roquelaure to take her out, and sometimes sent for her. M. de Leon was made acquainted with this, and took his measures accordingly. He procured a coach of the same size, shape, and fittings as that of Madame de la Vieuville, with her arms upon it, and with three servants in her livery; he counterfeited a letter in her handwriting and with her seal, and sent this coach with a lackey well instructed to carry the letter to the convent, on Tuesday morning, the 29th of May, at the hour Madame de la Vieuville was accustomed to send for her.

Mademoiselle de Roquelaure, who had been let into the scheme, carried the letter to the

Superior of the convent, and said Madame de la Vieuville had sent for her. Had the Superior any message to send?

The Superior, accustomed to these invitations; did not even look at the letter, but gave her consent at once. Mademoiselle de Roquelaure, accompanied solely by her governess, left the convent immediately, and entered the coach, which drove off directly. At the first turning it stopped, and the Prince de Leon, who had been in waiting, jumped-in. The governess at this began to cry out with all her might; but at the very first sound M. de Leon thrust a handkerchief into her mouth and stifled the noise. The coachman meanwhile lashed his horses, and the vehicle went off at full speed to Bruyeres near Menilmontant, the country-house of the Duc de Lorges, my brother-in-law, and friend of the Prince de Leon, and who, with the Comte de Rieux, awaited the runaway pair.

An interdicted and wandering priest was in waiting, and as soon as they arrived married them. My brother-in-law then led these nice young people into a fine chamber, where they were undressed, put to bed, and left alone for two or three hours. A good meal was then given to them, after which the bride was put into the coach, with her attendant, who was in despair, and driven back to the convent.

Mademoiselle de Roquelaure at once went deliberately to the Superior, told her all that happened, and then calmly went into her chamber, and wrote a fine letter to her mother, giving her an account of her marriage, and asking for pardon; the Superior of the convent, the attendants, and all the household being, meanwhile, in the utmost emotion at what had occurred.

The rage of the Duchesse de Roquelaure at this incident may be imagined. In her first unreasoning fury, she went to Madame de la Vieuville, who, all in ignorance of what had happened, was utterly at a loss to understand her stormy and insulting reproaches. At last Madame de Roquelaure saw that her friend was innocent of all connection with the matter; and turned the current of her wrath upon M. de Leon, against whom she felt the more indignant, inasmuch as he had treated her with much respect and attention since the rupture, and had thus, to some extent, gained her heart. Against her daughter she was also indignant, not only for what she had done, but because she had exhibited much gaiety and freedom of spirit at the marriage repast, and had diverted the company by some songs.

The Duc and Duchesse de Rohan were on their side equally furious, although less to be pitied, and made a strange uproar. Their son, troubled to know how to extricate himself from this affair, had recourse to his aunt, Soubise, so as to assure himself of the King. She sent him to Pontchartrain to see the chancellor. M. de Leon saw him the day after this fine marriage, at five o'clock in the morning, as he was dressing. The chancellor advised him to do all he could to gain the pardon of his father and of Madame de Roquelaure. But he had scarcely begun to speak, when Madame de Roquelaure sent word to say, that she was close at hand, and wished the chancellor to come and see her. He did so, and she immediately poured out all her griefs to him, saying that she came not to ask, his advice, but to state her complaint as to a friend (they were very intimate), and as to the chief officer of justice to demand justice of him. When he attempted to put in a word on behalf of M. de Leon, her fury burst out anew; she would not listen to his words, but drove off to Marly, where she had an interview with Madame de Maintenon, and by her was presented to the King.

As soon as she was in his presence, she fell down on her knees before him, and demanded justice in its fullest extent against M. de Leon. The King raised her with the gallantry of a prince to whom she had not been indifferent, and sought to console her; but as she still insisted upon justice, he asked her if she knew fully what she asked for, which was nothing less than the head of M. de Leon. She redoubled her entreaties notwithstanding this information, so that the King at last promised her that she should have complete justice. With that, and many compliments, he quitted her, and passed into his own rooms with a very serious air, and without stopping for anybody.

The news of this interview, and of what had taken place, soon spread through the chamber. Scarcely had people begun to pity Madame de Roquelaure, than some, by aversion for the grand imperial airs of this poor mother,—the majority, seized by mirth at the idea of a creature, well known to be very ugly and humpbacked, being carried off by such an ugly gallant,—burst out laughing, even to tears, and with an uproar completely scandalous. Madame de Maintenon abandoned herself to mirth, like the rest, and corrected the others at last, by saying it was not very charitable, in a tone that could impose upon no one.

Madame de Saint-Simon and I were at Paris. We knew with all Paris of this affair, but were ignorant of the place of the marriage and the part M. de Lorges had had in it, when the third day after the adventure I was startled out of my sleep at five o'clock in the morning, and saw my curtains and my windows open at the same time, and Madame de Saint-Simon and her brother (M. de Lorges) before me. They related to me all that had occurred, and then went away to consult with a skilful person what course to adopt, leaving me to dress. I never saw a man so crestfallen as M. de Lorges. He had confessed what he had done to a clever lawyer, who had much frightened him. After quitting him, he had hastened to us to make us go and see Pontchartrain. The most serious things are sometimes accompanied with the most ridiculous. M. de Lorges upon arriving knocked at the door of a little room which preceded the chamber of Madame de Saint-Simon. My daughter was rather unwell. Madame de Saint-Simon thought she was worse, and supposing it was I who had knocked, ran and opened the door. At the sight of her brother she ran back to her bed, to which he followed her, in order to relate his disaster. She rang for the windows to be opened, in order that she might see better. It so happened that she had taken the evening before a new servant, a country girl of sixteen, who slept in the little room. M. de Lorges, in a hurry to be off, told this girl to make haste in opening the windows, and then to go away and close the door. At this, the simple girl, all amazed, took her robe and her cotillon, and went upstairs to an old chambermaid, awoke her, and with much hesitation told her what had just happened, and that she had left by the bedside of Madame de Saint Simon a fine gentleman, very young, all powdered, curled, and decorated, who had driven her very quickly out of the chamber. She was all of a tremble, and much astonished. She soon learnt who he was. The story was told to us, and in spite of our disquietude, much diverted us.

We hurried away to the chancellor, and he advised the priest, the witnesses to the signatures of the marriage, and, in fact, all concerned, to keep out of the way, except M. de Lorges, who he assured us had nothing to fear. We went afterwards to Chamillart, whom we found much displeased, but in little alarm. The King had ordered an account to be drawn up of the whole affair. Nevertheless, in spite of the uproar made on all sides, people began to see that the King would not abandon to public dishonour the daughter of Madame de Roquelaure, nor doom to the scaffold or to civil death in foreign countries the nephew of Madame de Soubise.

Friends of M. and Madame de Roquelaure tried to arrange matters. They represented that it would be better to accept the marriage as it was than to expose a daughter to cruel dishonour. Strange enough, the Duc and Duchesse de Rohan were the most stormy. They wished to drive a very hard bargain in the matter, and made proposals so out of the way, that nothing could have been arranged but for the King. He did what he had never done before in all his life; he entered into all the details; he begged, then commanded as master; he had separate interviews with the parties concerned; and finally appointed the Duc d'Aumont and the chancellor to draw up the conditions of the marriage.

As Madame de Rohan, even after this, still refused to give her consent, the King sent for her, and said that if she and her husband did not at once give in, he would make the marriage valid by his own sovereign authority. Finally, after so much noise, anguish, and trouble, the contract was signed by the two families, assembled at the house of the Duchesse de Roquelaure. The banns were published, and the marriage took place at the church of the Convent of the Cross, where Mademoiselle de Roquelaure had been confined since her beautiful marriage, guarded night and day by five or six nuns. She entered the church by one door, Prince de Leon by another; not a compliment or a word passed between them; the curate said mass; married them; they mounted a coach, and drove off to the house of a friend some leagues from Paris. They paid for their folly by a cruel indigence which lasted all their lives, neither of them having survived the Duc de Rohan, Monsieur de Roquelaure, or Madame de Roquelaure. They left several children.

CHAPTER XLI

The war this year proceeded much as before. M. d'Orleans went to Spain again. Before taking the field he stopped at Madrid to arrange matters. There he found nothing prepared, and every thing in disorder. He was compelled to work day after day, for many hours, in order to obtain the most necessary supplies. This is what accounted for a delay which was maliciously interpreted at Paris into love for the Queen. M. le Duc was angry at the idleness in which he was kept; even Madame la Duchesse, who hated him, because she had formerly loved him too well, industriously circulated this report, which was believed at Court, in the city, even in foreign countries, everywhere, save in Spain, where the truth was too well known. It was while he was thus engaged that he gave utterance to a pleasantry that made Madame de Maintenon and Madame des Ursins his two most bitter enemies for ever afterwards.

One evening he was at table with several French and Spanish gentlemen, all occupied with his vexation against Madame des Ursins, who governed everything, and who had not thought of even the smallest thing for the campaign. The supper and the wine somewhat affected M. d'Orleans. Still full of his vexation, he took a glass, and, looking at the company, made an allusion in a toast to the two women, one the captain, the other the lieutenant, who governed France and Spain, and that in so coarse and yet humorous a manner, that it struck at once the imagination of the guests.

No comment was made, but everybody burst out laughing, sense of drollery overcoming prudence, for it was well known that the she-captain was Madame de Maintenon, and the she-lieutenant Madame des Ursins. The health was drunk, although the words were not repeated, and the scandal was strange.

Half an hour at most after this, Madame des Ursins was informed of what had taken place. She knew well who were meant by the toast, and was transported with rage. She at once wrote an account of the circumstance to Madame de Maintenon, who, for her part, was quite as furious. 'Inde ira'. They never pardoned M. d'Orleans, and we shall see how very nearly they succeeded in compassing his death. Until then, Madame de Maintenon had neither liked nor disliked M. d'Orleans. Madame des Ursins had omitted nothing in order to please him. From that moment they swore the ruin of this prince. All the rest of the King's life M. d'Orleans did not fail to find that Madame de Maintenon was an implacable and cruel enemy. The sad state to which she succeeded in reducing him influenced him during all the rest of his life. As for Madame des Ursins, he soon found a change in her manner. She endeavoured that everything should fail that passed through his hands. There are some wounds that can never be healed; and it must be admitted that the Duke's toast inflicted one especially of that sort. He felt this; did not attempt any reconciliation; and followed his usual course. I know not if he ever, repented of what he had said, whatever cause he may have had, so droll did it seem to him, but he has many times spoken of it since to me, laughing with all his might. I saw all the sad results which might arise from his speech, and nevertheless, while reproaching M. d'Orleans, I could not help laughing myself, so well, so simply; and so wittily expressed was his ridicule of the government on this and the other side of the Pyrenees.

At last, M. le Duc d'Orleans found means to enter upon his campaign, but was so ill-provided, that he never was supplied with more than a fortnight's subsistence in advance. He obtained several small successes; but these were more than swallowed up by a fatal loss in another direction. The island of Sardinia, which was then under the Spanish Crown, was lost through the misconduct of the viceroy, the Duke of Veragua, and taken possession of by the troops of the Archduke. In the month of October, the island of Minorca also fell into the hands of the Archduke. Port Mahon made but little resistance; so that with this conquest and Gibraltar, the English found themselves able to rule in the Mediterranean, to winter entire fleets there, and to blockade all the ports of Spain upon that sea. Leaving Spain in this situation, let us turn to Flanders.

Early in July, we took Ghent and Bruges by surprise, and the news of these successes was received with the most unbridled joy at Fontainebleau. It appeared easy to profit by these two conquests, obtained without difficulty, by passing the Escaut, burning Oudenarde, closing the country to the enemies, and cutting them off from all supplies. Ours were very abundant, and came by water, with a camp that could not be attacked. M. de Vendome agreed to all this; and alleged nothing against it. There was only one difficulty in the way; his idleness and unwillingness to move from quarters where he was comfortable. He wished to enjoy those quarters as long as possible, and maintained, therefore, that these movements would be just as good if delayed. Monseigneur le Duc de Bourgogne maintained on the contrary, with all the army—even the favourites of M. de Vendome—that it would be better to execute the operation at once, that there was no reason for delay, and that delay might prove disastrous. He argued in vain. Vendome disliked fatigue and change of quarters. They interfered with the daily life he was accustomed to lead, and which I have elsewhere described. He would not move.

Marlborough clearly seeing that M. de Vendome did not at once take advantage of his position, determined to put it out of his power to do so. To reach Oudenarde, Marlborough had a journey to make of twenty-five leagues. Vendome was so placed that he could have gained it in six leagues at the most. Marlborough put himself in motion with so much diligence that he stole three forced marches before Vendome had the slightest suspicion or information of them. The news reached him in time, but he treated it with contempt according to his custom, assuring himself that he should outstrip the enemy by setting out the next morning. Monseigneur le Duc de Bourgogne pressed him to start that evening; such as dared represented to him the necessity and the importance of doing so. All was vain—in spite of repeated information of the enemy's march. The neglect was such that bridges had not been thought of for a little brook at the head of the camp, which it was necessary to cross.

On the next day, Wednesday, the 11th of July, a party of our troops, under the command of Biron, which had been sent on in advance to the Escaut, discovered, after passing it as they could, for the bridges were not yet made, all the army of the enemy bending round towards them, the rear of their columns touching at Oudenarde, where they also had crossed. Biron at once despatched a messenger to the Princes and to M. de Vendome to inform them of this, and to ask for orders. Vendome, annoyed by information so different to what he expected, maintained that it could not be true. As he was disputing, an officer arrived from Biron to confirm the news; but this only irritated Vendome anew, and made him more obstinate. A third messenger arrived, and then M. de Vendome, still affecting disbelief of the news sent him, flew in a passion, but nevertheless mounted his horse, saying that all this was the work of the devil, and that such diligence was impossible. He sent orders to Biron to attack the enemy, promising to support him immediately. He told the Princes, at the same time, to gently follow with the whole of the army, while he placed himself at the head of his columns, and pushed on briskly to Biron.

Biron meanwhile placed his troops as well as he could, on ground very unequal and much cut up. He wished to execute the order he had received, less from any hopes of success in a combat so vastly disproportioned than to secure himself from the blame of a general so ready to censure those who did not follow his instructions. But he was advised so strongly not to take so hazardous a step, that he refrained. Marechal Matignon, who arrived soon after, indeed specially prohibited him from acting.

While this was passing, Biron heard sharp firing on his left, beyond the village. He hastened there, and found an encounter of infantry going on. He sustained it as well as he could, whilst the enemy were gaining ground on the left, and, the ground being difficult (there was a ravine there), the enemy were kept at bay until M. de Vendome came up. The troops he brought were all out of breath. As soon as they arrived, they threw themselves amidst the hedges, nearly all in columns, and sustained thus the attacks of the enemies, and an engagement which every moment grew hotter, without having the means to arranging themselves in any order. The columns that arrived from time to time to the relief of these were as out of breath as the others; and were at once sharply charged by the enemies; who, being extended in lines and in order, knew well how to profit by our disorder. The confusion was very great: the new-comers had no time to rally; there was a long interval between the platoons engaged and those meant to sustain them; the cavalry and the household troops were mixed up pell-mell with the infantry, which increased the disorder to such a point that our troops no longer recognised each other. This enabled the enemy to fill up the ravine with fascines sufficient to enable them to pass it, and allowed the rear of their army to make a grand tour by our right to gain the head of the ravine, and take us in flank there.

Towards this same right were the Princes, who for some time had been looking from a mill at so strange a combat, so disadvantageously commenced. As soon as our troops saw pouring down upon them others much more numerous, they gave way towards their left with so much promptitude that the attendants of the Princes became mixed up with their masters,— and all were hurried away towards the thick of the fight, with a rapidity and confusion that were indecent. The Princes showed themselves everywhere, and in places the most exposed, displaying much valour and coolness, encouraging the men, praising the officers, asking the principal officers what was to be done, and telling M. de Vendome what they thought.

The inequality of the ground that the enemies found in advancing, after having driven in our right, enabled our them to rally and to resist. But this resistance was of short duration. Every one had been engaged in hand-to-hand combats; every one was worn out with lassitude and despair of success, and a confusion so general and so unheard-of. The household troops owed their escape to the mistake of one of the enemy's officers, who carried an order to the red coats, thinking them his own men. He was taken, and seeing that he was about to share the peril with our troops, warned them that they were going to be surrounded. They retired in some disorder, and so avoided this.

The disorder increased, however, every moment. Nobody recognised his troop. All were pell-mell, cavalry, infantry, dragoons; not a battalion, not a squadron together, and all in confusion, one upon the other.

Night came. We had lost much ground, one-half of the army had not finished arriving. In this sad situation the Princes consulted with M. de Vendome as to what was to be done. He, furious at being so terribly out of his reckoning, affronted everybody. Monseigneur le Duc de Bourgogne wished to speak; but Vendome intoxicated with choler and authority; closed his mouth, by saying to him in an imperious voice before everybody, "That he came to the army only on condition of obeying him." These enormous words, pronounced at a moment in which everybody felt so terribly the weight of the obedience rendered to his idleness and obstinacy, made everybody tremble with indignation. The young Prince to whom they were addressed, hesitated, mastered himself, and kept silence. Vendome went on declaring that the battle was not lost—that it could be recommenced the next morning, when the rest of the army had arrived, and so on. No one of consequence cared to reply.

From every side soon came information, however, that the disorder was extreme. Pursegur, Matignon, Sousternon, Cheladet, Purguyon, all brought the same news. Vendome, seeing that it was useless to resist, all this testimony, and beside himself with rage, cried, "Oh, very well, gentlemen! I see clearly what you wish. We must retire, then;" and looking at Monseigneur le Duc de Bourgogne, he added, "I know you have long wished to do so, Monseigneur."

These words, which could not fail to be taken in a double sense, were pronounced exactly as I relate them, and were emphasized in a manner to leave no doubt as to their signification. Monseigneur le Duc de Bourgogne remained silent as before, and for some time the silence was unbroken. At last, Pursegur interrupted it, by asking how the retreat was to be executed. Each, then, spoke confusedly. Vendome, in his turn, kept silence from vexation or embarrassment; then he said they must march to Ghent, without adding how, or anything else.

The day had been very fatiguing; the retreat was long and perilous. The Princes mounted their horses, and took the road to Ghent. Vendome set out without giving any orders, or seeing to anything. The general officers returned to their posts, and of themselves gave the order to retreat. Yet so great was the confusion, that the Chevalier Rosel, lieutenant-general, at the head of a hundred squadrons, received no orders. In the morning he found himself with his hundred squadrons, which had been utterly forgotten. He at once commenced his march; but to retreat in full daylight was very difficult, as he soon found. He had to sustain the attacks of the enemy during several hours of his march.

Elsewhere, also, the difficulty of retreating was great. Fighting went on at various points all night, and the enemy were on the alert. Some of the troops of our right, while debating as to the means of retreat, found they were about to be surrounded by the enemy. The Vidame of Amiens saw that not a moment was to be lost. He cried to the light horse, of which he was captain, "Follow me," and pierced his way through a line of the enemy's cavalry. He then found himself in front of a line of infantry, which fired upon him, but opened to give him passage. At the same moment, the household troops and others, profiting by a movement so bold, followed the Vidame and his men, and all escaped together to Ghent, led on by the Vidame, to whose sense and courage the safety of these troops was owing.

M. de Vendome arrived at Ghent, between seven and eight o'clock in the morning. Even at this moment he did not forget his disgusting habits, and as soon as he set foot to ground.... in sight of all the troops as they came by,—then at once went to bed, without giving any orders, or seeing to anything, and remained more than thirty hours without rising, in order to repose himself after his fatigues. He learnt that Monseigneur de Bourgogne and the army had pushed on to Lawendeghem; but he paid no attention to it, and continued to sup and to sleep at Ghent several days running, without attending to anything.

CHAPTER XLII

As soon as Monseigneur le Duc de Bourgogne arrived at Lawendeghem, he wrote a short letter to the King, and referred him for details to M. de Vendome. But at the same time he wrote to the Duchess, very clearly expressing to her where the fault lay. M. de Vendome, on his side, wrote to the King, and tried to persuade him that the battle had not been disadvantageous to us. A short time afterwards, he wrote again, telling the King that he could have beaten the enemies had he been sustained; and that, if, contrary to his advice, retreat had not been determined on, he would certainly have beaten them the next day. For the details he referred to Monseigneur le Duc de Bourgogne.

I had always feared that some ill-fortune would fall to the lot of Monseigneur, le Duc de Bourgogne if he served under M. de Vendome at the army. When I first learned that he was going to Flanders with M. de Vendome, I expressed my apprehensions to M. de Beauvilliers, who treated them as unreasonable and ridiculous. He soon had good cause to admit that I had not spoken without justice. Our disasters at Oudenarde were very great. We had many men and officers killed and wounded, four thousand men and seven hundred officers taken prisoners, and a prodigious quantity missing and dispersed. All these losses were, as I have shown, entirely due to the laziness and inattention of M. de Vendome. Yet the friends of that general—and he had many at the Court and in the army— actually had the audacity to lay the blame upon Monseigneur le Duc de Bourgogne. This was what I had foreseen, viz., M. de Vendome, in case any misfortune occurred, would be sure to throw the burden of it upon Monseigneur le Duc de Bourgogne.

Alberoni, who, as I have said, was one of M. de Vendome's creatures, published a deceitful and impudent letter, in which he endeavoured to prove that M. de Vendome had acted throughout like a good general, but that he had been thwarted by Monseigneur le Duc de Bourgogne. This letter was distributed everywhere, and well served the purpose for which it was intended. Another writer, Campistron—-a poor, starving poet, ready to do anything to live—went further. He wrote a letter, in which Monseigneur le Duc de Bourgogne was personally attacked in the tenderest points, and in which Marechal Matignon was said to merit a court-martial for having counselled retreat. This letter, like the other, although circulated with more precaution, was shown even in the cafes and in the theatres; in the public places of gambling and debauchery; on the promenades, and amongst the news-vendors. Copies of it were even shown in the provinces, and in foreign countries; but always with much circumspection. Another letter soon afterwards appeared, apologising for M. de Vendome. This was written by Comte d'Evreux, and was of much the same tone as the two others.

A powerful cabal was in fact got up against Monseigneur de Bourgogne. Vaudeville, verses, atrocious songs against him, ran all over Paris and the provinces with a licence and a rapidity that no one checked; while at the Court, the libertines and the fashionables applauded; so that in six days it was thought disgraceful to speak with any measure of this Prince, even in his father's house.

Madame de Bourgogne could not witness all this uproar against her husband, without feeling sensibly affected by it. She had been made acquainted by Monseigneur de Bourgogne with the true state of the case. She saw her own happiness and reputation at stake. Though very gentle, and still more timid, the grandeur of the occasion raised her above herself. She was cruelly wounded by the insults of Vendome to her husband, and by all the atrocities and falsehoods his emissaries published. She gained Madame de Maintenon, and the first result of this step was, that the King censured Chamillart for not speaking of the letters in circulation, and ordered him to write to Alberoni and D'Evreux (Campistron, strangely enough, was forgotten), commanding them to keep silence for the future.

The cabal was amazed to see Madame de Maintenon on the side of Madame de Bourgogne, while M. du Maine (who was generally in accord with Madame de Maintenon) was for M. de Vendome. They concluded that the King had been led away, but that if they held firm, his partiality for M. de Vendome, for M. du Maine, and for bastardy in general, would bring him round to them. In point of fact, the King was led now one way, and now another, with a leaning always towards M. de Vendome.

Soon after this, Chamillart, who was completely of the party of M. de Vendome, thought fit to write a letter to Monseigneur le Duc de Bourgogne, in which he counselled him to live on good terms with his general. Madame de Bourgogne never forgave Chamillart this letter, and was always annoyed with her husband that he acted upon it. His religious sentiments induced him to do so. Vendome so profited by the advances made to him by the young Prince, that he audaciously brought Alberoni with him when he visited Monseigneur de Bourgogne. This weakness of Monseigneur de Bourgogne lost him many friends, and made his enemies more bold than ever: Madame de Bourgogne, however, did not despair. She wrote to her husband that for M. de Vendome she had more aversion and contempt than for any one else in the world, and that nothing would make her forget what he had done. We shall see with what courage she knew how to keep her word.

While the discussions upon the battle of Oudenarde were yet proceeding, a league was formed with France against the Emperor by all the states of Italy. The King (Louis XIV.) accepted, however, too late, a project he himself ought to have proposed and executed. He lost perhaps the most precious opportunity he had had during all his reign. The step he at last took was so apparent that it alarmed the allies, and put them on their guard. Except Flanders, they did nothing in any other spot, and turned all their attention to Italy.

Let us return, however, to Flanders.

Prince Eugene, with a large booty gathered in Artois and elsewhere, had fixed himself at Brussels. He wished to bear off his spoils, which required more than five thousand waggons to carry it, and which consisted in great part of provisions, worth three million five hundred thousand francs, and set out with them to join the army of the Duke of Marlborough. Our troops could not, of course, be in ignorance of this. M. de Vendome wished to attack the convoy with half his troops. The project seemed good, and, in case of success, would have brought results equally honourable and useful. Monseigneur de Bourgogne, however, opposed the attack, I know not why; and M. de Vendome, so obstinate until then, gave in to him in this case. His object was to ruin the Prince utterly, for allowing such a good chance to escape, the blame resting entirely upon him. Obstinacy and audacity had served M. de Vendome at Oudenarde: he expected no less a success now from his deference.

Some anxiety was felt just about this time for Lille, which it was feared the enemy would lay siege to. Boufflers went to command there, at his own request, end found the place very ill-garrisoned with raw troops, many of whom had never smelt powder. M. de Vendome, however, laughed at the idea of the siege of Lille, as something mad and ridiculous. Nevertheless, the town was invested on the 12th of August, as the King duly learned on the 14th. Even then, flattery did its work. The friends of Vendome declared that such an enterprise was the best, thing that could happen to France, as the besiegers, inferior in numbers to our army, were sure to be miserably beaten. M. de Vendome, in the mean time, did not budge from the post he had taken up near Ghent. The King wrote to him to go with his army to the relief of Lille. M. de Vendome still delayed; another courier was sent, with the same result. At this, the King, losing temper, despatched another courier, with orders to Monseigneur de Bourgogne, to lead the army to Lille, if M. de Vendome refused to do so. At this, M. de Vendome awoke from his lethargy. He set out for Lille, but took the longest road, and dawdled as long as he could on the way, stopping five days at Mons Puenelle, amongst other places.

The agitation, meanwhile, in Paris, was extreme. The King demanded news of the siege from his courtiers, and could not understand why no couriers arrived. It was generally expected that some decisive battle had been fought. Each day increased the uneasiness. The Princes and the principal noblemen of the Court were at the army. Every one at Versailles feared for the safety of a relative or friend. Prayers were offered everywhere. Madame de Bourgogne passed whole nights in the chapel, when people thought her in bed, and drove her women to despair. Following her example, ladies who had husbands at the army stirred not from the churches. Gaming, conversation ceased. Fear was painted upon every face, and seen in every speech, without shame. If a horse passed a little quickly, everybody ran without knowing where. The apartments of Chamillart were crowded with lackeys, even into the street, sent by people desiring to be informed of the moment that a courier arrived; and this terror and uncertainty lasted nearly a month. The provinces were even more troubled than Paris. The King wrote to the Bishop, in order that they should offer up prayers in terms which suited with the danger of the time. It may be judged what was the general impression and alarm.

It is true, that in the midst of this trepidation, the partisans of M. de Vendome affected to pity that poor Prince Eugene, and to declare that he must inevitably fail in his undertaking; but these discourses did not impose upon me. I knew what kind of enemies we had to deal with, and I foresaw the worst results from the idleness and inattention of M. de Vendome. One evening, in the presence of Chamillart and five or six others, annoyed by the conversation which passed, I offered to bet four pistoles that there would be no general battle, and that Lille would be taken without being relieved. This strange proposition excited much surprise, and caused many questions to be addressed to me. I would explain nothing at all; but sustained my proposal in the

English manner, and my bet was taken; Cani, who accepted it, thanking me for the present of four pistoles I was making him, as he said. The stakes were placed in the hand of Chamillart.

By the next day, the news of my bet had spread a frightful uproar. The partisans of M. de Vendome, knowing I was no friend to them, took this opportunity to damage me in the eyes of the King. They so far succeeded that I entirely lost favour with him, without however suspecting it, for more than two months. All that I could do then, was to let the storm pass over my head and keep silent, so as not to make matters worse. Meanwhile, M. de Vendome continued the inactive policy he had hitherto followed. In despite of reiterated advice from the King, he took no steps to attack the enemy. Monseigneur de Bourgogne was for doing so, but Vendome would make no movement. As before, too, he contrived to throw all the blame of his inactivity upon Monseigneur de Bourgogne. He succeeded so well in making this believed, that his followers in the army cried out against the followers of Monseigneur de Bourgogne wherever they appeared. Chamillart was sent by the King to report upon the state and position of our troops, and if a battle had taken place and proved unfavourable to us, to prevent such sad results as had taken place after Ramillies. Chamillart came back on the 18th of September. No battle had been fought, but M. de Vendome felt sure, he said, of cutting off all supplies from the enemy, and thus compelling them to raise the siege. The King had need of these intervals of consolation and hope. Master as he might be of his words and of his features, he profoundly felt the powerlessness to resist his enemies that he fell into day by day. What I have related, about Samuel Bernard, the banker, to whom he almost did the honours of his gardens at Marly, in order to draw from him the assistance he had refused, is a great proof of this. It was much remarked at Fontainebleau, just as Lille was invested, that, the city of Paris coming to harangue him on the occasion of the oath taken by Bignon, new Prevot des Marchand, he replied, not only with kindness, but that he made use of the term "gratitude for his good city," and that in doing so he lost countenance,— two things which during all his reign had never escaped him. On the other hand, he sometimes had intervals of firmness which edified less than they surprised. When everybody at the Court was in the anxiety I have already described, he offended them by going out every day hunting or walking, so that they could not know, until after his return, the news which might arrive when he was out.

As for Monseigneur, he seemed altogether exempt from anxiety. After Ramillies, when everybody was waiting for the return of Chamillart, to learn the truth, Monseigneur went away to dine at Meudon, saying he should learn the news soon enough. From this time he showed no more interest in what was passing. When news was brought that Lille was invested, he turned on his heel before the letter announcing it had been read to the end. The King called him back to hear the rest. He returned and heard it. The reading finished, he went away, without offering a word. Entering the apartments of the Princesse de Conti, he found there Madame d'Espinoy, who had much property in Flanders, and who had wished to take a trip there.

"Madame," said he, smiling, as he arrived, "how would you do just now to get to Lille?" And at once made them acquainted with the investment. These things really wounded the Princesse de Conti. Arriving at Fontainebleau one day, during the movements of the army, Monseigneur set to work reciting, for amusement, a long list of strange names of places in the forest.

"Dear me, Monseigneur," cried she, "what a good memory you have. What a pity it is loaded with such things only!" If he felt the reproach, he did not profit by it.

As for Monseigneur le Duc de Bourgogne, Monseigneur (his father) was ill- disposed towards him, and readily swallowed all that was said in his dispraise. Monseigneur had no sympathy with the piety of his son; it constrained and bothered him. The cabal well profited by this. They succeeded to such an extent in alienating the father from the son, that it is only strict truth to say that no one dared to speak well of Monseigneur le Duc de Bourgogne in the presence of Monseigneur. From this it may be imagined what was the licence and freedom of speech elsewhere against this Prince. They reached such a point, indeed, that the King, not daring to complain publicly against the Prince de Conti, who hated Vendome, for speaking in favour of Monseigneur de Bourgogne, reprimanded him sharply in reality for having done so, but ostensibly because he had talked about the affairs of Flanders at his sister's. Madame de Bourgogne did all she could to turn the current that was setting in against her husband; and in this she was assisted by Madame de Maintenon, who was annoyed to the last degree to see that other people had more influence over the King than she had.

The siege of Lille meanwhile continued, and at last it began to be seen that, instead of attempting to fight a grand battle, the wisest course would be to throw assistance into the place. An attempt was made to do so, but it was now too late.

The besieged, under the guidance of Marechal Boufflers, who watched over all, and attended to all, in a manner that gained him all hearts, made a gallant and determined resistance. A volume would be necessary in order to relate all the marvels of capacity and valour displayed in this defence. Our troops disputed the ground inch by inch. They repulsed, three times running, the enemy from a mill, took it the third time, and burnt it. They sustained an attack, in three places at once, of ten thousand men, from nine o'clock in the evening to three o'clock in the morning, without giving way. They re-captured the sole traverse the enemy had been able to take from them. They drove out the besiegers from the projecting angles of the counterscarp, which they had kept possession of for eight days. They twice repulsed seven thousand men who attacked their covered way and an outwork; at the third attack they lost an angle of the outwork; but remained masters of all the rest.

So many attacks and engagements terribly weakened the garrison. On the 28th of September some assistance was sent to the besieged by the daring of the Chevalier de Luxembourg. It enabled them to sustain with vigour the fresh attacks that were directed against them, to repulse the enemy, and, by a grand sortie, to damage some of their works, and kill many of their men. But all was in vain. The enemy returned again and again to the attack. Every attempt to cut off their supplies failed. Finally, on the 23rd of October, a capitulation was signed. The place had become untenable; three new breaches had been made on the 20th and 21st; powder and ammunition were failing; the provisions were almost all eaten up there was nothing for it but to give in.

Marechal Boufflers obtained all he asked, and retired into the citadel with all the prisoners of war, after two months of resistance. He offered discharge to all the soldiers who did not wish to enter the citadel. But not one of the six thousand he had left to him accepted it. They were all ready for a new resistance, and when their chief appeared among them their joy burst out in the most flattering praises of him. It was on Friday, the 26th of October, that they shut themselves up in the citadel.

The enemy opened their trenches before the citadel on the 29th of October. On the 7th of November they made a grand attack, but were repulsed with considerable loss. But they did not flinch from their work, and Boufflers began to see that he could not long hold out. By the commencement of December he had only twenty thousand pounds of powder left; very little of other munitions, and still less food. In the town and the citadel they had eaten eight hundred horses. Boufflers, as soon as the others were reduced to this food, had it served upon his own table, and ate of it like the rest. The King, learning in what state these soldiers were, personally sent word to Boufflers to surrender, but the Marechal, even after he had received this order, delayed many days to obey it.

At last, in want of the commonest necessaries, and able to protract his defence no longer, he beat a parley, signed a capitulation on the 9th of December, obtaining all he asked, and retired from Lille. Prince Eugene, to whom he surrendered, treated him with much distinction and friendship, invited him to dinner several times,—overwhelmed him, in fact, with attention and civilities. The Prince was glad indeed to have brought to a successful issue such a difficult siege.

CHAPTER XLIII

The position of Monseigneur le Duc de Bourgogne at the army continued to be equivocal. He was constantly in collision with M. de Vendome. The latter, after the loss of Lille, wished to defend the Escaut, without any regard to its extent of forty miles. The Duc de Bourgogne, as far as he dared, took the part of Berwick, who maintained that the defence was impossible. The King, hearing of all these disputes, actually sent Chamillart to the army to compose them; and it was a curious sight to behold this penman, this financier, acting as arbiter between generals on the most delicate operations of war. Chamillart continued to admire Vendome, and treated the Duc de Bourgogne with little respect, both at the army, and, after his return, in conversation with the King. His report was given in presence of Madame de Maintenon, who listened without daring to say a word, and repeated everything to the Duchesse de Bourgogne. We may imagine what passed between them, and the anger of the Princess against the minister. For the present, however, nothing could be done. Berwick was soon afterwards almost disgraced. As soon as he was gone, M. de Vendome wrote to the King, saying, that he was sure of preventing the enemy from passing the Escaut—that he answered for it on his head. With such a guarantee from a man in such favour at Court, who could doubt? Yet, shortly after, Marlborough crossed the Escaut in four places, and Vendome actually wrote to the King, begging him to remember that he had always declared the defence of the Escaut to be, impossible!

The cabal made a great noise to cover this monstrous audacity, and endeavoured to renew the attack against the Duc de Bourgogne. We shall see what success attended their efforts. The army was at Soissons, near Tournai, in a profound tranquillity, the opium of which had gained the Duc de Bourgogne when news of the approach of the enemy was brought. M. de Vendome advanced in that direction, and sent word to the Duke, that he thought he ought to advance on the morrow with all his army. The Duke was going to bed when he received the letter; and although it was too late to repulse the enemy, was much blamed for continuing to undress himself, and putting off action till the morrow.

To this fault he added another. He had eaten; it was very early; and it was no longer proper to march. It was necessary to wait fresh orders from M. de Vendome. Tournai was near. The Duc de Bourgogne went there to have a game at tennis. This sudden party of pleasure strongly scandalized the army, and raised all manner of unpleasant talk. Advantage was taken of the young Prince's imprudence to throw upon him the blame of what was caused by the negligence of M. de Vendome.

A serious and disastrous action that took place during these operations was actually kept a secret from the King, until the Duc de la Tremoille, whose son was engaged there, let out the truth. Annoyed that the King said nothing to him on the way in which his son had distinguished himself, he took the opportunity, whilst he was serving the King, to talk of the passage of the Escaut, and said that his son's regiment had much suffered. "How, suffered?" cried the King; "nothing has happened." Whereupon the Duke related all to him. The King listened with the greatest attention, and questioned him, and admitted before everybody that he knew nothing of all this. His surprise, and the surprise it occasioned, may be imagined. It happened that when the King left table, Chamillart unexpectedly came into his cabinet. He was soon asked about the action of the Escaut, and why it had not been reported. The minister, embarrassed, said that it was a thing of no consequence. The king continued to press him, mentioned details, and talked of the regiment of the Prince of Tarento. Chamillart then admitted that what happened at the passage was so disagreeable, and the combat so disagreeable, but so little important, that Madame de Maintenon, to whom he had reported all, had thought it best not to trouble the King upon the matter, and it had accordingly been agreed not to trouble him. Upon this singular answer the King stopped short in his questions, and said not a word more.

The Escaut being forced, the citadel of Lille on the point of being taken, our army exhausted with fatigue was at last dispersed, to the scandal of everybody; for it was known that Ghent was about to be besieged. The Princes received orders to return to Court, but they insisted on the propriety of remaining with the army. M. de Vendome, who began to fear the effect of his rashness and insolence, tried to obtain permission to pass the winter with the army on the frontier.

He was not listened to. The Princes received orders most positively to return to Court, and accordingly set out.

The Duchesse de Bourgogne was very anxious about the way in which the Duke was to be received, and eager to talk to him and explain how matters stood, before he saw the King or anybody else. I sent a message to him that he ought to contrive to arrive after midnight, in order to pass two or three hours with the Duchess, and perhaps see Madame de Maintenon early in the morning. My message was not received; at any rate not followed. The Duc de Bourgogne arrived on the 11th of December, a little after seven o'clock in the evening, just as Monseigneur had gone to the play, whither the Duchess had not gone, in order to wait for her husband. I know not why he alighted in the Cour des Princes, instead of the Great Court. I was put then in the apartments of the Comtesse de Roncy, from which I could see all that passed. I came down, and saw the Prince ascending the steps between the Ducs de Beauvilliers and De la Rocheguyon, who happened to be there. He looked quite satisfied, was gay, and laughing, and spoke right and left. I bowed to him. He did me the honour to embrace me in a way that showed me he knew better what was going on than how to maintain his dignity. He then talked only to me, and whispered that he knew what I had said. A troop of courtiers met him. In their midst he passed the Great Hall of the Guards, and instead of going to Madame de Maintenon's by the private door, though the nearest way, went to the great public entrance. There was no one there but the King and Madame de Maintenon, with Pontchartrain; for I do not count the Duchesse de Bourgogne. Pontchartrain noted well what passed at the interview, and related it all to me that very evening.

As soon as in Madame de Maintenon's apartment was heard the rumour which usually precedes such an arrival, the King became sufficiently embarrassed to change countenance several times. The Duchesse de Bourgogne appeared somewhat tremulous, and fluttered about the room to hide her trouble, pretending not to know exactly by which door the Prince would arrive. Madame de

Maintenon was thoughtful. Suddenly all the doors flew open: the young Prince advanced towards the King, who, master of himself, more than any one ever was, lost at once all embarrassment, took two or three steps towards his grandson, embraced him with some demonstration of tenderness, spoke of his voyage, and then pointing to the Princess, said, with a smiling countenance: "Do you say nothing to her?" The Prince turned a moment towards her, and answered respectfully, as if he dared not turn away from the King, and did not move. He then saluted Madame de Maintenon, who received him well. Talk of travel, beds, roads, and so forth, lasted, all standing, some half-quarter of an hour; then the King said it would not be fair to deprive him any longer of the pleasure of being alone with Madame la Duchesse de Bourgogne, and that they would have time enough to see each other. The Prince made a bow to the King, another to Madame de Maintenon, passed before the few ladies of the palace who had taken courage to put their heads into the room, entered the neighbouring cabinet, where he embraced the Duchess, saluted the ladies who were there, that is, kissed them; remained a few moments, and then went into his apartment, where he shut himself up with the Duchesse de Bourgogne.

Their tete-a-tete lasted two hours and more: just towards the end, Madame d'O was let in; soon after the Marechal d'Estrees entered, and soon after that the Duchesse de Bourgogne came out with them, and returned into the great cabinet of Madame de Maintenon. Monseigneur came there as usual, on returning from the comedy. Madame la Duchesse de Bourgogne, troubled that the Duke did not hurry himself to come and salute his father, went to fetch him, and came back saying that he was putting on his powder; but observing that Monseigneur was little satisfied with this want of eagerness, sent again to hurry him. Just then the Marechale d'Estrees, hair-brained and light, and free to say just what came into her head, began to attack Monseigneur for waiting so tranquilly for his son, instead of going himself to embrace him. This random expression did not succeed. Monseigneur replied stiffly that it was not for him to seek the Duc de Bourgogne; but the duty of the Duc de Bourgogne to seek him. He came at last. The reception was pretty good, but did not by any means equal that of the King. Almost immediately the King rang, and everybody went to the supper-room.

During the supper, M. le Duc de Berry arrived, and came to salute the King at table. To greet him all hearts opened. The King embraced him very tenderly. Monseigneur only looked at him tenderly, not daring to embrace his (youngest) son in presence of the King. All present courted him. He remained standing near the King all the rest of the supper, and there was no talk save of post-horses, of roads, and such like trifles. The King spoke sufficiently at table to Monseigneur le Duc de Bourgogne; but to the Duc de Berry, he assumed a very different air. Afterwards, there was a supper for the Duc de Berry in the apartments of the Duchesse de Bourgogne; but the conjugal impatience of the Duc de Bourgogne cut it rather too short.

I expressed to the Duc de Beauvilliers, with my accustomed freedom, that the Duc de Bourgogne seemed to me very gay on returning from so sad a campaign. He could not deny this, and made up his mind to give a hint on the subject. Everybody indeed blamed so misplaced a gaiety. Two or three days after his arrival the Duc de Bourgogne passed three hours with the King in the apartments of Madame de Maintenon. I was afraid that, his piety would withhold him from letting out on the subject of M. de Vendome, but I heard that he spoke on that subject without restraint, impelled by the advice of the Duchesse de Bourgogne, and also by the Duc de Beauvilliers, who set his conscience at ease. His account of the campaign, of affairs, of things, of advices, of proceedings, was complete. Another, perhaps, less virtuous, might have used weightier terms; but at any rate everything was said with a completeness beyond all hope, if we consider who spoke and who listened. The Duke concluded with an eager prayer to be given an army in the next campaign, and with the promise of the King to that effect. Soon after an explanation took place with Monseigneur at Meudon, Mademoiselle Choin being present. With the latter he spoke much more in private: she had taken his part with Monseigneur. The Duchesse de Bourgogne had gained her over. The connection of this girl with Madame de Maintenon was beginning to grow very close indeed.

Gamaches had been to the army with the Duc do Bourgogne, and being a free-tongued man had often spoken out very sharply on the puerilities in which he indulged in company with the Duc de Berry, influenced by his example. One day returning from mass, in company with the Duke on a critical day, when he would rather have seen him on horseback; he said aloud, "You will certainly win the kingdom of heaven; but as for the kingdom of the earth, Prince Eugene and Marlborough know how to seek it better than you." What he said quite as publicly to the two Princes on their treatment of the King of England, was admirable. That Prince (known as the Chevalier de Saint George) served incognito, with a modesty that the Princes took advantage of to treat him with the greatest indifference and contempt. Towards the end of the campaign, Gamaches, exasperated with their conduct, exclaimed to them in the presence of everybody: "Is this a wager? speak frankly; if so, you have won, there can be no doubt of that; but now, speak a little to the Chevalier de Saint George, and treat him more politely." These sallies, however, were too public to produce any good effect. They were suffered, but not attended to.

The citadel of Lille capitulated as we have seen, with the consent of the King, who was obliged to acknowledge that the Marechal de Boufflers had done all he could, and that further defence was impossible. Prince Eugene treated Boufflers with the greatest possible consideration. The enemy at this time made no secret of their intention to invest Ghent, which made the dispersal of our army the more shameful; but necessity commanded, for no more provisions were to be got.

M. de Vendome arrived at Versailles on the morning of December 15th, and saluted the King as he left table. The King embraced him with a sort of enthusiasm that made his cabal triumph. He monopolised all conversation during the dinner, but only trifles were talked of. The King said he would talk to him next day at Madame de Maintenon's. This delay, which was new to him, did not seem of good augury. He went to pay his respects to M. de Bourgogne, who received him well in spite of all that had passed. Then Vendome went to wait on Monseigneur at the Princesse de Coriti's: here he thought himself in his stronghold. He was received excellently, and the conversation turned on nothings. He wished to take advantage of this, and proposed a visit to Anet. His surprise and that of those present were great at the uncertain reply of Monseigneur, who caused it to be understood, and rather stiffly too, that he would not go. Vendome appeared embarrassed, and abridged his visit. I met him at the end of the gallery of the new wing, as I was coming from M. de Beauvilliers, turning towards the steps in the middle of the gallery. He was alone, without torches or valets, with Alberoni, followed by a man I did not know. I saw him by the light of my torches; we saluted each other politely, though we had not much acquaintance one with the other. He seemed chagrined, and was going to M. du Maine, his counsel and principal support.

Next day he passed an hour with the King at Madame de Maintenon's. He remained eight or ten days at Versailles or at Meudon, and never went to the Duchesse de Bourgogne's. This was nothing new for him. The mixture of grandeur and irregularity which he had long affected seemed to him to have freed him from the most indispensable duties. His Abbe Alberoni showed himself at the King's mass in the character of a courtier with unparalleled effrontery. At last they went to Anet. Even before he went he perceived some diminution in his position, since he lowered himself so far as to invite people to come and see him, he, who in former years made it a favour to receive the most distinguished persons. He soon perceived the falling-off in the number of his visitors. Some excused themselves from going; others promised to go and did not. Every one made a difficulty about a journey of fifteen leagues, which, the year before, was considered as easy and as necessary as that of Marly. Vendome remained at Anet until the first voyage to Marly, when he came; and he always came to Marly and Meudon, never to Versailles, until the change of which I shall soon have occasion to speak.

The Marechal de Boufflers returned to Court from his first but unsuccessful defence of Lille, and was received in a triumphant manner, and overwhelmed with honours and rewards. This contrast with Vendome was remarkable: the one raised by force of trickery, heaping up mountains like the giants, leaning on vice, lies, audacity, on a cabal inimical to the state and its heirs, a factitious hero, made such by will in despite of truth;—the other, without cabal, with no support but virtue and modesty, was inundated with favours, and the applause of enemies was followed by the acclamations of the public, so that the nature of even courtiers changed, and they were happy in the recompenses showered upon him!

Some days after the return of the Duc de Bourgogne Cheverny had an interview with him, on leaving which he told me what I cannot refrain from relating here, though it is necessarily with confusion that I write it. He said that, speaking freely with him on what had been circulated during the campaign, the Prince observed that he knew how and with what vivacity I had expressed myself, and that he was informed of the manner in which the Prince de Conti had given his opinion, and added that with the approval of two such men, that of others might be dispensed with. Cheverny, a very truthful man, came full of this to tell it to me at once. I was filled with confusion at being placed beside a man as superior to me in knowledge of war as he was in rank and birth; but I felt with gratitude how well M. de Beauvilliers had kept his word and spoken in my favour.

The last evening of this year (1708) was very remarkable, because there had not yet been an example of any such thing. The King having retired after supper to his cabinet with his family, as usual, Chamillart came without being sent for. He whispered in the King's ear that he had a long despatch from the Marechal de Boufflers. Immediately the King said good-night to Monseigneur and the Princesses, who went out with every one else; and the King actually worked for an hour with his minister before going to bed, so excited was he by the great project for retaking Lille!

Since the fall of Lille, in fact, Chamillart, impressed with the importance of the place being in our possession, had laid out a plan by which he were to lay siege to it and recapture it. One part of his plan was, that the King should conduct the siege in person. Another was that, as money was so difficult to obtain, the ladies of the Court should not accompany the King, as their presence caused a large increase of expense for carriages, servants, and so on. He confided his project to the King, under a strict promise that it would be kept secret from Madame de Maintenon. He feared, and with reason, that if she heard of it she would object to being separated from the King for such a long time as would be necessary for the siege: Chamillart was warned that if he acted thus, hiding his plant from Madame de Maintenon, to whom he owed everything, she would assuredly ruin him, but he paid no attention to the warning. He felt all the danger he ran, but he was courageous; he loved the State, and, if I may say so, he loved the King as a mistress. He followed his own counsels then, and made the King acquainted with his project.

The King was at once delighted with it. He entered into the details submitted to him by Chamillart with the liveliest interest, and promised to carry out all that was proposed. He sent for Boufflers, who had returned from Lille, and having, as I have said, recompensed him for his brave defence of that place with a peerage and other marks of favour, despatched him privately into Flanders to make preparations for the siege. The abandonment of Ghent by our troop, after a short and miserable defence, made him more than ever anxious to carry out this scheme.

But the King had been so unused to keep a secret from Madame de Maintenon, that he felt himself constrained in attempting to do so now. He confided to her, therefore, the admirable plan of Chamillart. She had the address to hide her surprise, and the strength to dissimulate perfectly her vexation; she praised the project; she appeared charmed with it; she entered into the details; she spoke of them to Chamillart; admired his zeal, his labour, his diligence, and, above all, his ability, in having conceived and rendered possible so fine and grand a project.

From that moment, however, she forgot nothing in order to ensure its failure. The first sight of it had made her tremble. To be separated from the King during a long siege; to abandon him to a minister to whom he would be grateful for all the success of that siege; a minister, too, who, although her creature, had dared to submit this project to the King without informing her; who, moreover, had recently offended her by marrying his son into a family she considered inimical to her, and by supporting M. de Vendome against Monseigneur de Bourgogne! These were considerations that determined her to bring about the failure of Chamillart's project and the disgrace of Chamillart himself.

She employed her art so well, that after a time the project upon Lille did not appear so easy to the King as at first. Soon after, it seemed difficult; then too hazardous and ruinous; so that at last it was abandoned, and Boufflers had orders to cease his preparations and return to France! She succeeded thus in an affair she considered the most important she had undertaken during all her life. Chamillart was much touched, but little surprised: As soon as he knew his secret had been confided to Madame de Maintenon he had feeble hope for it. Now he began to fear for himself.

CHAPTER XLIV.

One of the reasons Madame de Maintenon had brought forward, which much assisted her in opposing the siege of Lille, was the excessive cold of this winter. The winter was, in fact, terrible; the memory of man could find no parallel to it. The frost came suddenly on Twelfth Night, and lasted nearly two months, beyond all recollection. In four days the Seine and all the other rivers were frozen, and,—what had never been seen before,—the sea froze all along the coasts, so as to bear carts, even heavily laden, upon it. Curious observers pretended that this cold surpassed what had ever been felt in Sweden and Denmark. The tribunals were closed a considerable time. The worst thing was, that it completely thawed for seven or eight days, and then froze again as rudely as before. This caused the complete destruction of all kinds of vegetation—even fruit-trees; and others of the most hardy kind, were destroyed. The violence of the cold was such, that the strongest elixirs and the most spirituous liquors broke their bottles in cupboards of rooms with fires in them, and surrounded by chimneys, in several parts of the chateau of Versailles. As I myself was one evening supping with the Duc de Villeroy, in his little bedroom, I saw bottles that had come from a well- heated kitchen, and that had been put on the chimney-piece of this bed- room (which was close to the kitchen), so frozen, that pieces of ice fell into our glasses as we poured out from them. The second frost ruined everything. There were no walnut-trees, no olive-trees, no apple-trees, no vines left, none worth speaking of, at least. The other trees died in great numbers; the gardens perished, and all the grain in the earth. It is impossible to imagine the desolation of this general ruin. Everybody held tight his old grain. The price of bread increased in proportion to the despair for the next harvest. The most knowing resowed barley where there had been wheat, and were imitated by the majority. They were the most successful, and saved all; but the police bethought themselves of prohibiting this, and repented too late! Divers edicts were published respecting grain, researches were made and granaries filled; commissioners were appointed to scour the provinces, and all these steps contributed to increase the general dearness and poverty, and that, too, at a time when, as was afterwards proved, there was enough corn in the country to feed all France for two years, without a fresh ear being reaped.

Many people believed that the finance gentlemen had clutched at this occasion to seize upon all the corn in the kingdom, by emissaries they sent about, in order to sell it at whatever price they wished for the profit of the King, not forgetting their own. The fact that a large quantity of corn that the King had bought, and that had spoiled upon the Loire, was thrown into the water in consequence, did not shake this opinion, as the accident could not be hidden. It is certain that the price of corn was equal in all the markets of the realm; that at Paris, commissioners fixed the price by force, and often obliged the vendors to raise it in spite of themselves; that when people cried out, "How long will this scarcity last?" some commissioners in a market, close to my house, near Saint Germain-des-Pres, replied openly, "As long as you please," moved by compassion and indignation, meaning thereby, as long as the people chose to submit to the regulation, according to which no corn entered Paris, except on an order of D'Argenson.

D'Argenson was the lieutenant of police. The bakers were treated with the utmost rigour in order to keep up the price of bread all over France. In the provinces, officers called intendents did what D'Argenson did at Paris. On all the markets, the corn that was not sold at the hour fixed for closing was forcibly carried off; those who, from pity, sold their corn lower than the fixed rate were punished with cruelty!

Marechal, the King's surgeon, had the courage and the probity to tell all these things to the King, and to state the sinister opinions it gave rise to among all classes, even the most enlightened. The King appeared touched, was not offended with Marechal, but did nothing.

In several places large stores of corn were collected; by the government authorities, but with the greatest possible secrecy. Private people were expressly forbidden to do this, and informers were encouraged to; betray them. A poor fellow, having bethought himself of informing against one of the stores alluded to above, was severely punished for his pains. The Parliament assembled to debate upon these disorders. It came to the resolution of submitting various proposals to the King, which it deemed likely to improve the condition of the country, and offered to send its Conseillers to examine into the conduct of the monopolists. As soon as the King heard of this, he flew into a strange passion, and his first intention was to send a harsh message to the Parliament to attend to law trials, and not to mix with matters that did not concern it. The chancellor did not dare to represent to, the King that what the Parliament wished to do belonged to its province, but calmed him by representing the respect and affection with which the Parliament regarded him, and that he was master either to accept or refuse its offers. No reprimand was given, therefore, to the Parliament, but it was informed that the King prohibited it from meddling with the corn question. However accustomed the Parliament, as well as all the other public bodies, might be to humiliations, it was exceedingly vexed by this treatment, and obeyed with the greatest grief. The public was, nevertheless, much affected by the conduct of the Parliament, and felt that if the Finance Ministry had been innocent in the matter, the King would have been pleased with what had taken place, which was in no respect an attack on the absolute and unbounded authority of which he was so vilely jealous.

In the country a somewhat similar incident occurred. The Parliament of Burgundy, seeing the province in the direst necessity, wrote to the Intendant, who did not bestir himself the least in the world. In this pressing danger of a murderous famine, the members assembled to debate upon the course to adopt. Nothing was said or done more than was necessary, and all with infinite discretion, yet the King was no sooner informed of it than he grew extremely irritated. He sent a severe reprimand to this Parliament; prohibited it from meddling again in the matter; and ordered the President, who had conducted the assembly, to come at once to Court to explain his conduct. He came, and but for the intervention of M. le Duc would have been deprived of his post, irreproachable as his conduct had been. He received a sharp scolding from the King, and was then allowed to depart. At the end of a few weeks he returned to Dijon, where it had been resolved to receive him in triumph; but, like a wise and experienced man, he shunned these attentions, arranging so that he arrived at Dijon at four o'clock in the morning. The other Parliaments, with these examples before them, were afraid to act, and allowed the Intendants and their emissaries to have it all their own way. It was at this time that those commissioners were appointed, to whom I have already alluded, who acted under the authority of the Intendants, and without dependence of any kind upon the Parliaments. True, a court of appeal against their decisions was established, but it was a mere mockery. The members who composed it did not set out to fulfil their duties until three months after having been appointed.

Then, matters had been so arranged that they received no appeals, and found no cases to judge. All this dark work remained, therefore, in the hands of D'Argenson and the Intendants, and it continued to be done with the same harshness as ever.

Without passing a more definite judgment on those who invented and profited by this scheme, it may be said that there has scarcely been a century which has produced one more mysterious, more daring, better arranged, and resulting in an oppression so enduring, so sure, so cruel. The sums it produced were innumerable; and innumerable were the people who died literally of hunger, and those who perished afterwards of the maladies caused by the extremity of misery; innumerable also were the families who were ruined, whose ruin brought down a torrent of other ills.

Despite all this, payments hitherto most strictly made began to cease. Those of the customs, those of the divers loans, the dividends upon the Hotel de Ville—in all times so sacred—all were suspended; these last alone continued, but with delays, then with retrenchments, which desolated nearly all the families of Paris and many others. At the same time the taxes—increased, multiplied, and exacted with the most extreme rigour—completed the devastation of France.

Everything rose incredibly in price, while nothing was left to buy with, even at the cheapest rate; and although—the majority of the cattle had perished for want of food, and by the misery of those who kept them, a new monopoly was established upon, horned beasts. A great number of people who, in preceding years, used to relieve the poor, found, themselves so reduced as to be able to subsist only with great difficulty, and many of them received alms in secret. It is impossible to say how many others laid siege to the hospitals, until then the shame and punishment of the poor; how many ruined hospitals revomited forth their inmates to the public charge—that is to say, sent them away to die actually of hunger; and how many decent families shut themselves up in garrets to die of want.

It is impossible to say, moreover, how all this misery warmed up zeal and charity, or how immense were the alms distributed. But want increasing each instant, an indiscreet and tyrannical charity imagined new taxes for the benefit of the poor. They were imposed, and, added to so many others, vexed numbers of people, who were annoyed at being compelled to pay, who would have preferred giving voluntarily. Thus, these new taxes, instead of helping the poor, really took away assistance from them, and left them worse off than before. The strangest thing of all is, that these taxes in favour of the poor were, perpetuated and appropriated by the King, and are received by the financiers on his account to this day as a branch of the revenue, the name of them not having even been changed. The same thing has happened with respect to the annual tax for keeping up the highways and thoroughfares of the kingdom. The majority of the bridges were broken, and the high roads had become impracticable. Trade, which suffered by this, awakened attention. The Intendant of Champagne determined to mend the roads by parties of men, whom he compelled to work for nothing, not even giving them bread. He was imitated everywhere, and was made Counsellor of State. The people died of hunger and misery at this work, while those who overlooked them made fortunes. In the end the thing was found to be impracticable, and was abandoned, and so were the roads. But the impost for making them and keeping them up did not in the least stop during this experiment or since, nor has it ceased to be appropriated as a branch of the King's revenue.

But to return to the year 1709. People never ceased wondering what had become of all the money of the realm. Nobody could any longer pay, because nobody was paid: the country-people, overwhelmed with exactions and with valueless property, had become insolvent: trade no longer yielded anything—good faith and confidence were at an end. Thus the King had no resources, except in terror and in his unlimited power, which, boundless as it was, failed also for want of having something to take and to exercise itself upon. There was no more circulation, no means of re-establishing it. All was perishing step by step; the realm was entirely exhausted; the troops, even, were not paid, although no one could imagine what was done with the millions that came into the King's coffers. The unfed soldiers, disheartened too at being so badly commanded, were always unsuccessful; there was no capacity in generals or ministers; no appointment except by whim or intrigue; nothing was punished, nothing examined, nothing weighed: there was equal impotence to sustain the war and bring about peace: all suffered, yet none dared to put the hand to this arch, tottering as it was and ready to fall.

This was the frightful state to which we were reduced, when envoys were sent into Holland to try and bring about peace. The picture is exact, faithful, and not overcharged. It was necessary to present it as it was, in order to explain the extremity to which we were reduced, the enormity of the concessions which the King made to obtain peace, and the visible miracle of Him who sets bounds to the seas, by which France was allowed to escape from the hands of Europe, resolved and ready to destroy her.

Meanwhile the money was re-coined; and its increase to a third more than its intrinsic value, brought some profit to the King, but ruin to private people, and a disorder to trade which completed its annihilation.

Samuel Bernard, the banker, overthrew all Lyons by his prodigious bankruptcy, which caused the most terrible results. Desmarets assisted him as much as possible. The discredit into which paper money had fallen, was the cause of his failure. He had issued notes to the amount of twenty millions, and owed almost as much at Lyons. Fourteen millions were given to him in assignats, in order to draw him out of his difficulties. It is pretended that he found means to gain much by his bankruptcy, but this seems doubtful.

The winter at length passed away. In the spring so many disorders took place in the market of Paris, that more guards than usual were kept in the city. At Saint Roch there was a disturbance, on account of a poor fellow who had fallen, and been trampled under foot; and the crowd, which was very large, was very insolent to D'Argenson, Lieutenant of Police, who had hastened there. M. de la Rochefoucauld, who had retired from the Court to Chenil, on account of his loss of sight, received an atrocious letter against the King, in which it was plainly intimated that there were still Ravaillacs left in the world; and to this madness was added an eulogy of Brutus. M. de la Rochefoucauld at once went in all haste to the King with this letter. His sudden appearance showed that something important had occurred, and the object of his visit, of course, soon became known. He was very ill received for coming so publicly on such an errand. The Ducs de Beauvilliers and de Bouillon, it seems, had received similar letters, but had given them to the King privately. The King for some days was much troubled, but after due reflection, he came to the conclusion that people who menace and warn have less intention of committing a crime than of causing alarm.

What annoyed the King more was, the inundation of placards, the most daring and the most unmeasured, against his person, his conduct, and his government—placards, which for a long time were found pasted upon the gates of Paris, the churches, the public places; above all upon the statues; which during the night were insulted in various fashions, the marks being seen the next morning, and the inscriptions erased. There were also, multitudes of verses and songs, in which nothing was spared.

We were in this state until the 16th of May. The procession of Saint Genevieve took place. This procession never takes place except in times of the direst necessity; and then, only in virtue of orders from the King, the Parliament, or the Archbishop of Paris. On the one hand, it was hoped that it would bring succour to the country; on the other, that it would amuse the people.

It was shortly after this, when the news of the arrogant demands of the allies, and the vain attempts of the King to obtain an honourable peace became known, that the Duchesse de Grammont conceived the idea of offering her plate to the King, to replenish his impoverished exchequer, and to afford him means carry on the war. She hoped that her example would be followed by all the Court, and that she alone would have the merit and the profit of suggesting the idea. Unfortunately for this hope, the Duke, her husband, spoke of the project to Marechal Boufflers, who thought it so good, that he noised it abroad, and made such a stir, exhorting everybody to adopt it, that he passed for the inventor, and; no mention was made of the Duke or the old Duchesse de Grammont, the latter of whom was much enraged at this.

The project made a great hubbub at the Court. Nobody dared to refuse to offer his plate, yet each offered it with much regret. Some had been keeping it as a last resource, which they; were very sorry to deprive themselves of; others feared the dirtiness of copper and earthenware; others again were annoyed at being obliged to imitate an ungrateful fashion, all the merit of which would go to the inventor. It was in vain that Pontchartrain objected to the project, as one from which only trifling benefit could be derived, and which would do great injury to France by acting as a proclamation of its embarrassed state to all the world, at home and abroad. The King would not listen to his reasonings, but declared himself willing to receive all the plate that was sent to him as a free-will offering. He announced this; and two means were indicated at the same time, which all good citizens might follow. One was, to send their plate to the King's goldsmith; the other, to send it to the Mint. Those who made an unconditional gift of their plate, sent it to the former, who kept a register of the names and of the number of marks he received. The King regularly looked over this list; at least at first, and promised in general terms to restore to everybody the weight of metal they gave when his affairs permitted—a promise nobody believed in or hoped to see executed. Those who wished to be paid for their plate sent it to the Mint. It was weighed on arrival; the names were written, the marks and the date; payment was made according as money could be found. Many people were not sorry thus to sell, their plate without shame. But the loss and the damage were inestimable in admirable ornaments of all kinds, with which much of the plate of the rich was embellished. When an account came to be drawn up, it was found that not a hundred people were upon the list of Launay, the goldsmith; and the total product of the gift did not amount to three millions. I confess that I was very late in sending any plate. When I found that I was almost the only one of my rank using silver, I sent plate to the value of a thousand pistoles to the Mint, and locked up the rest. All the great people turned to earthenware, exhausted the shops where it was sold, and set the trade in it on fire, while common folks continued to use their silver. Even the King thought of using earthenware, having sent his gold vessels to the Mint, but afterwards decided upon plated metal and silver; the Princes and Princesses of the blood used crockery.

Ere three months were over his head the King felt all the shame and the weakness of having consented to this surrendering of plate, and avowed that he repented of it. The inundations of the Loire, which happened at the same time, and caused the utmost disorder, did not restore the Court or the public to good humour. The losses they caused, and the damage they did, were very considerable, and ruined many private people, and desolated home trade.

Summer came. The dearness of all things, and of bread in particular, continued to cause frequent commotions all over the realm. Although, as I have said, the guards of Paris were much increased, above all in the markets and the suspected places, they were unable to hinder disturbances from breaking out. In many of these D'Argenson nearly lost his life.

Monseigneur arriving and returning from the Opera, was assailed by the populace and by women in great numbers crying, "Bread! Bread!" so that he was afraid, even in the midst of his guards, who did not dare to disperse the crowd for fear of worse happening. He got away by throwing money to the people, and promising wonders; but as the wonders did not follow, he no longer dared to go to Paris.

The King himself from his windows heard the people of Versailles crying aloud in the street. The discourses they held were daring and continual in the streets and public places; they uttered complaints, sharp, and but little measured, against the government, and even against the King's person; and even exhorted each other no longer to be so enduring, saying that nothing worse could happen to them than what they suffered, dying as they were of starvation.

To amuse the people, the idle and the poor were employed to level a rather large hillock which remained upon the Boulevard, between the Portes Saint Denis and Saint Martin; and for all salary, bad bread in small quantities was distributed to these workers. If happened that on Tuesday morning, the 20th of August, there was no bread for a large number of these people. A woman amongst others cried out at this, which excited the rest to do likewise. The archers appointed to watch over these labourers, threatened the woman; she only cried the louder;

thereupon the archers seized her and indiscreetly put her in an adjoining pillory. In a moment all her companions ran to her aid, pulled down the pillory, and scoured the streets, pillaging the bakers and pastrycooks. One by one the shops closed. The disorder increased and spread through the neighbouring streets; no harm was done anybody, but the cry was "Bread! Bread!" and bread was seized everywhere.

It so fell out that Marechal Boufflers, who little thought what was happening, was in the neighbourhood, calling upon his notary. Surprised at the fright he saw everywhere, and learning, the cause, he wished of himself to appease it. Accompanied by the Duc de Gramont, he directed himself towards the scene of the disturbance, although advised not to do so. When he arrived at the top of the Rue Saint Denis, the crowd and the tumult made him judge that it would be best to alight from his coach. He advanced, therefore, on foot with the Duc de Grammont among the furious and infinite crowd of people, of whom he asked the cause of this uproar, promised them bread, spoke his best with gentleness but firmness, and remonstrated with them. He was listened to. Cries, several times repeated, of "Vive M. le Marechal de Boufflers!" burst from the crowd. M. de Boufflers walked thus with M. de Grammont all along the Rue aux Ours and the neighbouring streets, into the very centre of the sedition, in fact. The people begged him to represent their misery to the King, and to obtain for them some food. He promised this, and upon his word being given all were appeased and all dispersed with thanks and fresh acclamations of "Vive M. le Marechal de Boufflers!" He did a real service that day. D'Argenson had marched to the spot with troops; and had it not been for the Marechal, blood would have been spilt, and things might have gone very far.

The Marechal had scarcely reached his own house in the Place Royale than he was informed that the sedition had broken out with even greater force in the Faubourg Saint Antoine. He ran there immediately, with the Duc de Grammont, and appeased it as he had appeased the other. He returned to his own home to eat a mouthful or two, and then set out for Versailles. Scarcely had he left the Place Royale than the people in the streets and the shopkeepers cried to him to have pity on them, and to get them some bread, always with "Vive M. le Marechal de Boufflers!" He was conducted thus as far as the quay of the Louvre.

On arriving at Versailles he went straight to the King, told him what had occurred, and was much thanked. He was even offered by the King the command of Paris,—troops, citizens, police, and all; but this he declined, Paris, as he said, having already a governor and proper officers to conduct its affairs. He afterwards, however, willingly lent his aid to them in office, and the modesty with which he acted brought him new glory.

Immediately after, the supply of bread was carefully looked to. Paris was filled with patrols, perhaps with too many, but they succeeded so well that no fresh disturbances took place.

CHAPTER XLV

After his return from the campaign, M. de Vendome continued to be paid like a general serving in winter, and to enjoy many other advantages. From all this, people inferred that he would serve during the following campaign; nobody dared to doubt as much, and the cabal derived new strength therefrom. But their little triumph was not of long continuance. M. de Vendome came to Versailles for the ceremony of the Order on Candlemas-Day. He then learned that he was not to serve, and that he was no longer to receive general's pay. The blow was violent, and he felt it to its fullest extent; but, with a prudence that equalled his former imprudence, he swallowed the pill without making a face, because he feared other more bitter ones, which he felt he had deserved. This it was that, for the first time in his life, made him moderate. He did not affect to conceal what had taken place, but did not say whether it was in consequence of any request of his, or whether he was glad or sorry,—giving it out as an indifferent piece of news; and changed nothing but his language, the audacity of which he diminished as no longer suited to the times. He sold his equipages.

M. le Prince de Conti died February 22, aged not quite forty-five. His face had been charming; even the defects of his body and mind had infinite graces. His shoulders were too high; his head was a little on one side; his laugh would have seemed a bray in any one else; his mind was strangely absent. He was gallant with the women, in love with many, well treated by several; he was even coquettish with men. He endeavoured to please the cobbler, the lackey, the porter, as well as the Minister of State, the Grand Seigneur, the General, all so naturally that success was certain. He was consequently the constant delight of every one, of the Court, the armies; the divinity of the people, the idol of the soldiers, the hero of the officers, the hope of whatever was most distinguished, the love of the Parliament, the friend of the learned, and often the admiration of the historian, of jurisconsults, of astronomers, and mathematicians, the most profound. He was especially learned in genealogies, and knew their chimeras and their realities. With him the useful and the polite, the agreeable and the deep, all was distinct and in its place. He had friends, knew how to choose them, cultivate them, visit them, live with them, put himself on their level without haughtiness or baseness. But this man, so amiable, so charming, so delicious, loved nothing. He had and desired friends, as other people have and desire articles of furniture. Although with much self-respect he was a humble courtier, and showed too much how greatly he was in want of support and assistance from all sides; he was avaricious, greedy of fortune, ardent and unjust. The King could not bear him, and was grieved with the respect he was obliged to show him, and which he was careful never to trespass over by a single jot. Certain intercepted letters had excited a hatred against him in Madame de Maintenon, and an indignation in the King which nothing could efface. The riches, the talents, the agreeable qualities, the great reputation which this Prince had acquired, the general love of all, became crimes in him. The contrast with M. du Maine excited daily irritation and jealousy. The very purity of his blood was a reproach to him. Even his friends were odious, and felt that this was so. At last, however, various causes made him to be chosen, in the midst of a very marked disgrace, to command the army in

Flanders. He was delighted, and gave himself up to the most agreeable hopes. But it was no longer time: he had sought to drown his sorrow at wearing out his life unoccupied in wine and other pleasures, for which his age and his already enfeebled body were no longer suited. His health gave way. He felt it soon. The tardy return to favour which he had enjoyed made him regret life more. He perished slowly, regretting to have been brought to death's door by disgrace, and the impossibility of being restored by the unexpected opening of a brilliant career.

The Prince, against the custom of those of his rank, had been very well educated. He was full of instruction. The disorders of his life had clouded his knowledge but not extinguished it, and he often read to brush up his learning. He chose M. de la Tour to prepare him, and help him to die well. He was so attached to life that all his courage was required. For three months crowds of visitors filled his palace, and the people even collected in the place before it. The churches echoed with prayers for his life. The members of his family often went to pay for masses for him; and found that others had already done so. All questions were about his health. People stopped each other in the street to inquire; passers- by were called to by shopmen, anxious to know whether the Prince de Conti was to live or to die. Amidst all this, Monseigneur never visited him; and, to the indignation of all Paris, passed along the quay near the Louvre going to the Opera, whilst the sacraments were being carried to the Prince on the other side. He was compelled by public opinion to make a short visit after this. The Prince died at last in his arm-chair, surrounded by a few worthy people. Regrets were universal; but perhaps he gained by his disgrace. His heart was firmer than his head. He might have been timid at the head of an army or in the Council of the King if he had entered it. The King was much relieved by his death; Madame de Maintenon also; M. le Duc much more; for M. du Maine it was a deliverance, and for M. de Vendome a consolation. Monseigneur learned it at Meudon as he was going out to hunt, and showed no feeling of any kind.

The death of M. le Prince de Conti seemed to the Duc de Vendome a considerable advantage, because he was thus delivered from a rival most embarrassing by the superiority of his birth, just when he was about to be placed in a high military position. I have already mentioned Vendome's exclusion from command. The fall of this Prince of the Proud had been begun we have now reached the second step, between which and the third there was a space of between two and three months; but as the third had no connection with any other event, I will relate it at once.

Whatever reasons existed to induce the King to take from M. de Vendome the command of his armies, I know not if all the art and credit of Madame de Maintenon would not have been employed in vain, together with the intrigues of M. du Maine, without an adventure, which I must at once explain, to set before the reader's eyes the issue of the terrible struggle, pushed to such extremes, between Vendome, seconded by his formidable cabal, and the necessary, heir of the Crown, supported by his wife, the favourite of the King, and Madame de Maintenon, which last; to speak clearly, as all the Court saw, for thirty years governed him completely.

When M. de Vendome returned from Flanders, he had a short interview with the King, in which he made many bitter complaints against Pursegur, one of his lieutenant-generals, whose sole offence was that he was much attached to M. de Bourgogne. Pursegur was a great favourite with the King, and often, on account of the business of the infantry regiment, of which the thought himself the private colonel, had private interviews with him, and was held in high estimation for his capacity and virtue. He, in his turn, came back from Flanders, and had a private audience of the King. The complaints that had been made against him by M. de Vendome were repeated to him by the King, who, however, did not mention from whom they came. Pursegur defended himself so well, that the King in his surprise mentioned this latter fact. At the name of Vendome, Pursegur lost all patience. He described, to the King all the faults, the impertinences; the obstinacy, the insolence of M. de Vendome, with a precision and clearness which made his listener very attentive and very fruitful in questions. Pursegur, seeing that he might go on, gave himself rein, unmasked M. de Vendome from top to toe, described his ordinary life at the army, the incapacity of his body, the incapacity of his judgment, the prejudice of his mind, the absurdity and crudity of his maxims, his utter ignorance of the art of war, and showed to demonstration, that it was only by a profusion of miracles France had not been ruined by him—lost a hundred times over.

The conversation lasted more than two hours. The' King, long since convinced of the capacity, fidelity, and truthfulness of Pursegur, at last opened his eyes to the truth respecting this Vendome, hidden with so much art until then, and regarded as a hero and the tutelary genius of France. He was vexed and ashamed of his credulity, and from the date of this conversation Vendome fell at once from his favour.

Pursegur, naturally humble, gentle, and modest, but truthful, and on this occasion piqued, went out into the gallery after his conversation, and made a general report of it to all, virtuously, braving Vendome and all his cabal. This cabal trembled with rage; Vendome still more so. They answered by miserable reasonings, which nobody cared for. This was what led to the suppression of his pay, and his retirement to Anet, where he affected a philosophical indifference.

Crestfallen as he was, he continued to sustain at Meudon and Marly the grand manners he had usurped at the time of his prosperity. After having got over the first embarrassment, he put on again his haughty air, and ruled the roast. To see him at Meudon you would have said he was certainly the master of the saloon, and by his free and easy manner to Monseigneur, and, when he dared, to the King, he would have been thought the principal person there. Monseigneur de Bourgogne supported this—his piety made him do so—but Madame de Bourgogne was grievously offended, and watched her opportunity to get rid of M. de Vendome altogether.

It came, the first journey the King made to Marly after Easter. 'Brelan' was then the fashion. Monseigneur, playing at it one day with Madame de Bourgogne and others, and being in want of a fifth player, sent for M. de Vendome from the other end of the saloon, to come and join the party. That instant Madame de Bourgogne said modestly, but very intelligibly, to Monseigneur, that the presence of M. de Vendome at Marly was sufficiently painful to her, without having him at play with her, and that she begged he might be dispensed with. Monseigneur, who had sent for Vendome without the slightest reflection, looked round the room, and sent for somebody else. When Vendome arrived, his place was taken, and he had to suffer this annoyance before all the company. It may be imagined to what an extent this superb gentleman was stung by the affront.

He served no longer; he commanded no longer; he was no longer the adored idol; he found himself in the paternal mansion of the Prince he had so cruelly offended, and the outraged wife of that Prince was more than a match for him. He turned upon his heel, absented himself from the room as soon as he could, and retired to his own chamber, there to storm at his leisure.

Other and more cruel annoyances were yet in store for him, however. Madame de Bourgogne reflected on what had just taken place. The facility with which she had succeeded in one respect encouraged her, but she was a little troubled to know how the King would take what she had done, and accordingly, whilst playing, she resolved to push matters still further, both to ruin her guest utterly and to get out of her embarrassment; for, despite her extreme familiarity, she was easily embarrassed, being gentle and timid. The 'brelan' over, she ran to Madame de Maintenon; told her what had just occurred; said that the presence of M. de Vendome at Marly was a continual insult to her; and begged her to solicit the King to forbid M. de Vendome to come there. Madame de Maintenon, only too glad. to have an opportunity of revenging herself upon an enemy who had set her at defiance, and against whom all her batteries had at one time failed, consented to this request. She spoke out to the King, who, completely weary of M. de Vendome, and troubled to have under his eyes a man whom he could not doubt was discontented, at once granted what was asked. Before going to bed, he charged one of his valets to tell M. de Vendome the next morning, that henceforth he was to absent himself from Marly, his presence there being disagreeable to Madame de Bourgogne.

It may be imagined into what an excess of despair M. de Vendome fell, at a message so unexpected, and which sapped the foundations of all his hopes. He kept silent, however, for fear of making matters worse, did not venture attempting, to speak to the King, and hastily retired to Clichy to hide his rage and shame. The news of his banishment from Marly soon spread abroad, and made so much stir, that to show it was not worth attention, he returned two days before the end of the visit, and stopped until the end in a continual shame and embarrassment. He set out for Anet at the same time that the King set out for Versailles, and has never since put his foot in Marly.

But another bitter draught was to be mixed for him. Banished from Marly, he had yet the privilege of going to Meudon. He did not fail to avail himself of this every time Monseigneur was there, and stopped as long as he stopped, although in the times of his splendour he had never stayed more than one or two days. It was seldom that Monseigneur visited Meudon without Madame la Duchesse de Bourgogne going to see him. And yet M. de Vendome never failed audaciously to present himself before her, as if to make her feel that at all events in Monseigneur's house he was a match for her. Guided by former experience, the Princess gently suffered this in silence, and watched her opportunity. It soon came.

Two months afterwards it happened that, while Monseigneur was at Meudon, the King, Madame de Maintenon; and Madame de Bourgogne, came to dine with him. Madame de Maintenon wished to talk with Mademoiselle Choin without sending for her to Versailles, and the King, as may be believed, was in the secret. I mention this to account for the King's visit. M. de Vendome, who was at Meudon as usual, was stupid enough to present himself at the coach door as the King and his companions descended. Madame de Bourgogne was much offended, constrained herself less than usual, and turned away her head with affectation, after a sort of sham salute. He felt the sting, but had the folly to approach her again after dinner, while she was playing. He experienced the same treatment, but this time in a still more marked manner. Stung to the quick and out of countenance, he went up to his chamber, and did not descend until very late. During this time Madame de Bourgogne spoke to Monseigneur of the conduct of M. de Vendorne, and the same evening she addressed herself to Madame de Maintenon, and openly complained to the King. She represented to him how hard it was to her to be treated by Monseigneur with less respect than by the King: for while the latter had banished M. de Vendome from Marly, the former continued to grant him an asylum at Meudon.

M. de Vendome, on his side, complained bitterly to Monseigneur of the strange persecution that he suffered everywhere from Madame de Bourgogne; but Monseigneur replied to him so coldly that he withdrew with tears in his eyes, determined, however, not to give up until he had obtained some sort of satisfaction. He set his friends to work to speak to Monseigneur; all they could draw from him was, that M. de Vendome must avoid Madame de Bourgogne whenever she came to Meudon, and that it was the smallest respect he owed her until she was reconciled to him. A reply so dry and so precise was cruelly felt; but M. de Vendome was not at the end of the chastisement he had more than merited. The next day put an end to all discussion upon the matter.

He was card-playing after dinner in a private cabinet, when D'Antin arrived from Versailles. He approached the players, and asked what was the position of the game, with an eagerness which made M. de Vendome inquire the reason. D'Antin said he had to render an account to him of the matter he had entrusted him with.

"I!" exclaimed Vendome, with surprise, "I have entrusted you with nothing."

"Pardon me," replied D'Antin; "you do not recollect, then, that I have an answer to make to you?"

From this perseverance M. de Vendome comprehended that something was amiss, quitted his game, and went into an obscure wardrobe with D'Antin, who told him that he had been ordered by the King to beg Monseigneur not to invite M. de Vendome to Meudon any more; that his presence there was as unpleasant to Madame de Bourgogne as it had been at Marly. Upon this, Vendome, transported with fury, vomited forth all that his rage inspired him with. He spoke to Monseigneur in the evening, but was listened to as coldly as before. Vendome passed the rest of his visit in a rage and embarrassment easy to conceive, and on the day Monseigneur returned to Versailles he hurried straight to Anet.

But he was unable to remain quiet anywhere; so went off with his dogs, under pretence of going a hunting, to pass a month in his estate of La Ferme-Aleps, where he had no proper lodging and no society, and gave there free vent to his rage. Thence he returned again to Anet, where he remained abandoned by every one. Into this solitude, into this startling and public seclusion, incapable of sustaining a fall so complete, after a long habit of attaining everything, and doing everything he pleased, of being the idol of the world, of the Court, of the armies, of making his very vices adored, and his greatest faults admired, his defects commended, so that he dared to conceive the prodigious design of ruining and destroying the necessary heir of the Crown, though he had never received anything but evidences of tenderness from him, and triumphed over him for eight months with the most scandalous success; it was, I say, thus that this Colossus was overthrown by the breath of a prudent and courageous princess, who earned by this act merited applause. All who were concerned with her, were charmed to see of what she was capable; and all who were opposed to her and her husband trembled. The cabal, so formidable, so lofty, so accredited, so closely united to overthrow them, and reign, after the King, under Monseigneur in their place—these chiefs, male and female, so enterprising and audacious, fell now into mortal discouragement and fear. It was a pleasure to see them work their way back with art and extreme humility, and turn round those of the opposite party who remained influential, and whom they had hitherto despised; and especially to see with what embarrassment, what fear, what terror, they began to crawl before the young Princess, and wretchedly court the Duc de Bourgogne and his friends, and bend to them in the most extraordinary manner.

As for M. de Vendome, without any resource, save what he found in his vices and his valets, he did not refrain from bragging among them of the friendship of Monseigneur for him, of which he said he was well assured. Violence had been done to Monseigneur's feelings. He was reduced to this misery of hoping that his words would be spread about by these valets, and would procure him some consideration from those who thought of the future. But the present was insupportable to him. To escape from it, he thought of serving in Spain, and wrote to Madame des Ursins asking employment. The King was annoyed at this step, and flatly refused to let him go to Spain. His intrigue, therefore, came to an end at once.

Nobody gained more by the fall of M. de Vendome than Madame de Maintenon. Besides the joy she felt in overthrowing a man who, through M. du Maine, owed everything to her, and yet dared to resist her so long and successfully, she felt, also, that her credit became still more the terror of the Court; for no one doubted that what had occurred was a great example of her power. We shall presently see how she furnished another, which startled no less.

CHAPTER XLVI.

It is time now to retrace my steps to the point from which I have been led away in relating all the incidents which arose out of the terrible winter and the scarcity it caused.

The Court at that time beheld the renewal of a ministry; which from the time it had lasted was worn down to its very roots, and which was on that account only the more agreeable to the King. On the 20th of January, the Pere La Chaise, the confessor of the King, died at a very advanced age. He was of good family, and his father would have been rich had he not had a dozen children. Pere La Chaise succeeded in 1675 to Pere Ferrier as confessor of the King, and occupied that post thirty-two years. The festival of Easter often caused him politic absences during the attachment of the King for Madame de Montespan. On one occasion he sent in his place the Pere Deschamps, who bravely refused absolution. The Pere La Chaise was of mediocre mind but of good character, just, upright, sensible, prudent, gentle, and moderate, an enemy of informers, and of violence of every kind. He kept clear of many scandalous transactions, befriended the Archbishop of Cambrai as much as he could, refused to push the Port Royal des Champs to its destruction, and always had on his table a copy of the New Testament of Pere Quesnel, saying that he liked what was good wherever he found it. When near his eightieth year, with his head and his health still good, he wished to retire, but the King would not hear of it. Soon after, his faculties became worn out, and feeling this, he repeated his wish. The Jesuits, who perceived his failing more than he did himself, and felt the diminution of his credit, exhorted him to make way for another who should have the grace and zeal of novelty. For his part he sincerely desired repose, and he pressed the King to allow him to take it, but all in vain. He was obliged to bear his burthen to the very end. Even the infirmities and the decrepitude that afflicted could not deliver him. Decaying legs, memory extinguished, judgment collapsed, all his faculties confused, strange inconveniences for a confessor—nothing could disgust the King, and he persisted in having this corpse brought to him and carrying on customary business with it. At last, two days after a return from Versailles, he grew much weaker, received the sacrament, wrote with his own hand a long letter to the King, received a very rapid and hurried one in reply, and soon after died at five o'clock in the morning very peaceably. His confessor asked him two things, whether he had acted according to his conscience, and whether he had thought of the interests and honour of the company of Jesuits; and to both these questions he answered satisfactorily.

The news was brought to the King as he came out of his cabinet. He received it like a Prince accustomed to losses, praised the Pere La Chaise for his goodness, and then said smilingly, before all the courtiers, and quite aloud, to the two fathers who had come to announce the death: "He was so good that I sometimes reproached him for it, and he used to reply to me: 'It is not I who am good; it is you who are hard.'"

Truly the fathers and all the auditors were so surprised at this that they lowered their eyes. The remark spread directly; nobody was able to blame the Pere La Chaise. He was generally regretted, for he had done much good and never harm except in self-defence. Marechal, first surgeon of the King, and possessed of his confidence, related once to me and Madame de Saint-Simon, a very important anecdote referring to this time. He said that the King, talking to him privately of the Pere La Chaise, and praising him for his attachment, related one of the great proofs he had given of it. A few years before his death the Pere said that he felt getting old, and that the King might soon have to choose a new confessor; he begged that that confessor might be chosen from among the Jesuits, that he knew them well, that they were far from deserving all that had been said against them, but still—he knew them well—and that attachment for the King and desire for his safety induced him to conjure him to act as he requested; because the company contained many sorts of minds and characters which could not be answered for, and must not be reduced to despair, and that the King must not incur a risk—that in fact an unlucky blow is soon given, and had been given before then. Marechal turned pale at this recital of the King, and concealed as well as he could the disorder it caused in him. We must remember that Henry IV. recalled the Jesuits, and loaded them with gifts merely from fear of them. The King was not superior to Henry IV. He took care not to forget the communication of the Pere La Chaise, or expose himself to the vengeance of the company by choosing a confessor out of their limits. He wanted to live, and to live in safety. He requested the Ducs de Chevreuse and de Beauvilliers to make secret inquiries for a proper person. They fell into a trap made, were dupes themselves, and the Church and State the victims.

The Pere Tellier, in fact, was chosen as successor of Pere La Chaise, and a terrible successor he made. Harsh, exact, laborious, enemy of all dissipation, of all amusement, of all society, incapable of associating even with his colleagues, he demanded no leniency for himself and accorded none to others. His brain and his health were of iron; his conduct was so also; his nature was savage and cruel. He was profoundly false, deceitful, hidden under a thousand folds; and when he could show himself and make himself feared, he yielded nothing, laughed at the most express promises when he no longer cared to keep to them, and pursued with fury those who had trusted to them. He was the terror even of the Jesuits, and was so violent to them that they scarcely dared approach him. His exterior kept faith with his interior. He would have been terrible to meet in a dark lane. His physiognomy was cloudy, false, terrible; his eyes were burning, evil, extremely squinting; his aspect struck all with dismay. The whole aim of his life was to advance the interests of his Society; that was his god; his life had been absorbed in that study: surprisingly ignorant, insolent, impudent, impetuous, without measure and without discretion, all means were good that furthered his designs.

The first time Pere Tellier saw the King in his cabinet, after having been presented to him, there was nobody but Bloin and Fagon in a corner. Fagon, bent double and leaning on his stick, watched the interview and studied the physiognomy of this new personage his duckings, and scrapings, and his words. The King asked him if he were a relation of MM. le Tellier. The good father humbled himself in the dust. "I, Sire!" answered he, "a relative of MM. le Tellier! I am very different from that. I am a poor peasant of Lower Normandy, where my father was a farmer." Fagon, who watched him in every movement, twisted himself up to look at Bloin, and said, pointing to the Jesuit: "Monsieur, what a cursed ————!" Then shrugging his shoulders, he curved over his stick again.

It turned out that he was not mistaken in his strange judgment of a confessor. This Tellier made all the grimaces, not to say the hypocritical monkey-tricks of a man who was afraid of his place, and only took it out of, deference to his company.

I have dwelt thus upon this new confessor, because from him have come the incredible tempests under, which the Church, the State, knowledge, and doctrine, and many good people of all kinds, are still groaning; and, because I had a more intimate acquaintance with this terrible personage than had any man at the Court. He introduced himself to me in fact, to my surprise; and although I did all in my power to shun his acquaintance, I could not succeed. He was too dangerous a man to be treated with anything but great prudence.

During the autumn of this year, he gave a sample of his quality in the part he took in the destruction of the celebrated monastery of Port Royal des Champs. I need not dwell at any great length upon the origin and progress of the two religious parties, the Jansenists and the Molinists; enough has been written on both sides to form a whole library. It is enough for me to say that the Molinists were so called because they adopted the views expounded by, the Pere Molina in a book he wrote against the doctrines of St. Augustine and of the Church of Rome, upon the subject of spiritual grace. The Pere Molina was a Jesuit, and it was by the Jesuits his book was brought forward and supported. Finding, however, that the views it expounded met with general opposition, not only throughout France, but at Rome, they had recourse to their usual artifices on feeling themselves embarrassed, turned themselves into accusers instead of defendants, and invented a heresy that had neither author nor follower, which they attributed to Cornelius Jansenius, Bishop of Ypres. Many and long were the discussions at Rome upon this ideal heresy, invented by the Jesuits solely for the purpose of weakening the adversaries of Molina. To oppose his doctrines was to be a Jansenist. That in substance was what was meant by Jansenism.

At the monastery of Port Royal des Champs, a number of holy and learned personages lived in retirement. Some wrote, some gathered youths around them, and instructed them in science and piety. The finest moral works, works which have thrown the most light upon the science and practice, of religion, and have been found so by everybody, issued from their hands. These men entered into the quarrel against Molinism. This was enough to excite against them the hatred of the Jesuits and to determine that body to attempt their destruction.

They were accused of Jansenism, and defended themselves perfectly; but at the same time they carried the war into the enemy's camp, especially by the ingenious "Provincial Letters" of the famous Pascal.

The quarrel grew more hot between the Jesuits and Port Royal, and was telling against the former, when the Pere Tellier brought all his influence to bear, to change the current of success. He was, as I have said, an ardent man, whose divinity was his Molinism, and the company to which he belonged. Confessor to the King, he saw himself in a good position to exercise unlimited authority. He saw that the King was very ignorant, and prejudiced upon all religious matters; that he was surrounded by people as ignorant and as prejudiced as himself, Madame de Maintenon, M. de Beauvilliers, M. de Chevreuse, and others, and he determined to take good advantage of this state of things.

Step by step he gained over the King to his views, and convinced him that the destruction of the monastery of Port Royal des Champs was a duty which he owed to his conscience, and the cause of religion. This point gained, the means to destroy the establishment were soon resolved on.

There was another monastery called Port Royal, at Paws, in addition to the one in question. It was now pretended that the latter had only been allowed to exist by tolerance, and that it was necessary one should cease to exist. Of the two, it was alleged that it was better to preserve the one, at Paris. A decree in council was, therefore, rendered, in virtue of which, on the night from the 28th to the 29th of October, the abbey of Port Royal des Champs was secretly invested by troops, and, on the next morning, the officer in command made all the inmates assemble, showed them a 'lettre de cachet', and, without giving them more than a quarter of an hour's warning, carried off everybody and everything. He had brought with him many coaches, with an elderly woman in each; he put the nuns in these coaches, and sent them away to their destinations, which were different monasteries, at ten, twenty, thirty, forty, and even fifty leagues distant, each coach accompanied by mounted archers, just as public women are carried away from a house of ill-fame! I pass in silence all the accompaniments of this scene, so touching and so strangely new. There have been entire volumes written upon it.

The treatment that these nuns received in their various prisons, in order to force them to sign a condemnation of themselves, is the matter of other volumes, which, in spite of the vigilance of the oppressors, were soon in everybody's hands; public indignation so burst out, that the Court and the Jesuits even were embarrassed with it. But the Pere Tellier was not a man to stop half-way anywhere. He finished this matter directly; decree followed decree, 'Lettres de cachet' followed 'lettres de cachet'. The families who had relatives buried in the cemetery of Port Royal des Champs were ordered to exhume and carry them elsewhere. All the others were thrown into the cemetery of an adjoining parish, with the indecency that may: be imagined. Afterwards, the house, the church, and all the buildings were razed to the ground, so that not one stone was left upon another. All the materials were sold, the ground was ploughed up, and sown—not with salt, it is true, but that was all the favour it received! The scandal at this reached even to Rome. I have restricted myself to this simple and short recital of an expedition so military and so odious.

The death of D'Avaux, who had formerly been our ambassador in Holland, occurred in the early part of this year (1709). D'Avaux was one of the first to hear of the project of William of Orange upon England, when that project was still only in embryo, and kept profoundly secret. He apprised the King (Louis XIV.) of it, but was laughed at. Barillon, then our ambassador in England, was listened to in preference. He, deceived by Sunderland and the other perfidious ministers of James II.; assured our Court that D'Avaux's reports were mere chimeras. It was not until it was impossible any longer to doubt that credit was given to them. The steps that we then took, instead of disconcerting all the measures of the conspirators, as we could have done, did not interfere with the working out of any one of their plans. All liberty was left, in fact, to William to carry out his scheme. The anecdote which explains how this happened is so curious, that it deserves to be mentioned here.

Louvois, who was then Minister of War, was also superintendent of the buildings. The King, who liked building, and who had cast off all his mistresses, had pulled down the little porcelain Trianon he had made for Madame de Montespan, and was rebuilding it in the form it still retains. One day he perceived, for his glance was most searching, that one window was a trifle narrower than the others. He showed it to Louvois, in order that it might be altered, which, as it was not then finished, was easy to do. Louvois sustained that the window was all right. The King insisted then, and on the morrow also, but Louvois, pigheaded and inflated with his authority, would not yield.

The next day the King saw Le Notre in the gallery. Although his trade was gardens rather than houses, the King did not fail to consult him upon the latter. He asked him if he had been to Trianon. Le Notre replied that he had not. The King ordered him to go. On the morrow he saw Le Notre again; same question, same answer. The King comprehended the reason of this, and a little annoyed, commanded him to be there that afternoon at a given time. Le Notre did not dare to disobey this time. The King arrived, and Louvois being present, they returned to the subject of the window, which Louvois obstinately said was as broad as the rest. The King wished Le Notre to measure it, for he knew that, upright and true, he would openly say what he found. Louvois, piqued, grew angry. The King, who was not less so, allowed him to say his say. Le Notre, meanwhile, did not stir. At last, the King made him go, Louvois still grumbling, and maintaining his assertion with audacity and little measure. Le Notre measured the window, and said that the King was right by several inches. Louvois still wished to argue, but the King silenced him, and commanded him to see that the window was altered at once, contrary to custom abusing him most harshly.

What annoyed Louvois most was, that this scene passed not only before all the officers of the buildings, but in presence of all who followed the King in his promenades, nobles, courtiers, officers of the guard, and others, even all the rolete. The dressing given to Louvois was smart and long, mixed with reflections upon the fault of this window, which, not noticed so soon, might have spoiled all the facade, and compelled it to be re-built.

Louvois, who was not accustomed to be thus treated, returned home in fury, and like a man in despair. His familiars were frightened, and in their disquietude angled to learn what had happened. At last he told them, said he was lost, and that for a few inches the King forgot all his services, which had led to so many conquests; he declared that henceforth he would leave the trowel to the King, bring about a war, and so arrange matters that the King should have good need of him!

He soon kept his word. He caused a war to grow out of the affair of the double election of Cologne, of the Prince of Bavaria, and of the Cardinal of Furstenberg; he confirmed it in carrying the flames into the Palatinate, and in leaving, as I have said, all liberty to the project upon England; he put the finishing touch to his work by forcing the Duke of Savoy into the arms of his enemies, and making him become, by the position of his country, our enemy, the most difficult and the most ruinous. All that I have here related was clearly brought to light in due time.

Boisseuil died shortly after D'Avaux. He was a tall, big man, warm and violent, a great gambler, bad tempered,—who often treated M. le Grand and Madame d'Armagnac, great people as they were, so that the company were ashamed,—and who swore in the saloon of Marly as if he had been in a tap-room. He was feared; and he said to women whatever came uppermost when the fury of a cut-throat seized him. During a journey the King and Court made to Nancy, Boisseuil one evening sat down to play in the house of one of the courtiers. A player happened to be there who played very high. Boisseuil lost a good deal, and was very angry. He thought he perceived that this gentleman, who was only permitted on account of his play, was cheating, and made such good use of his eyes that he soon found this was the case, and all on a sudden stretched across the table and seized the gambler's hand, which he held upon the table, with the cards he was going to deal. The gentleman, very much astonished, wished to withdraw his hand, and was angry. Boisseuil, stronger than he, said that he was a rogue, and that the company should see it, and immediately shaking his hand with fury put in evidence his deceit. The player, confounded, rose and went away. The game went on, and lasted long into the night. When finished, Boisseuil went away. As he was leaving the door he found a man stuck against the wall—it was the player—who called him to account for the insult he had received. Boisseuil replied that he should give him no satisfaction, and that he was a rogue.

"That may be," said the player, "but I don't like to be told so."

They went away directly and fought. Boisseuil received two wounds, from one of which he was like to die. The other escaped without injury.

I have said, that after the affair of M. de Cambrai, Madame de Maintenon had taken a rooted dislike to M. de Beauvilliers. She had become reconciled to him in appearance during the time that Monseigneur de Bourgogne was a victim to the calumnies of M. de Vendome, because she had need of him. Now that Monseigneur de Bourgogne was brought back to favour, and M. de Vendome was disgraced, her antipathy for M, de Beauvilliers burst out anew, and she set her wits to work to get rid of him from the Council of State, of which he was a member. The witch wished to introduce her favourite Harcourt there in his place, and worked so well to bring about this result that the King promised he should be received.

His word given, or rather snatched from him, the King was embarrassed as to how, to keep it, for he did not wish openly to proclaim Harcourt minister. It was agreed, therefore, that at the next Council Harcourt should be present, as though by accident, in the King's ante-chamber; that, Spanish matters being brought up, the King should propose to consult Harcourt, and immediately after should direct search to be made far him, to see if, by chance, he was close at hand; that upon finding him, he should be conducted to the Council, made to enter and seat himself, and ever afterwards be regarded as a Minister of State.

This arrangement was kept extremely secret, according to the express commands of the King: I knew it, however, just before it was to be executed, and I saw at once that the day of Harcourt's entry into the Council would be the day of M. de Beauvilliers' disgrace. I sent, therefore, at once for M. de Beauvilliers, begging him to come to my house immediately, and that I would then tell him why I could not come to him. Without great precaution everything becomes known at Court.

In less than half an hour M. de Beauvilliers arrived, tolerably disturbed at my message. I asked him if he knew anything, and I turned him about, less to pump him than to make him ashamed of his ignorance, and to persuade him the better afterwards to do what I wished. When I had well trotted out his ignorance, I apprised him of what I had just learnt. He was astounded; he so little expected it! I had not much trouble to persuade him that, although his expulsion might not yet be determined on, the intrusion of Harcourt must pave the way for it. He admitted to me that for some days he had found, the King cold and embarrassed with him, but that he had paid little attention to the circumstance, the reason of which was now clear. There was no time to lose. In twenty-four hours all would be over. I therefore took the liberty in the first instance of scolding him for his profound ignorance of what passed at the Court, and was bold enough to say to him that he had only to thank himself for the situation he found himself in. He let me say to the end without growing angry, then smiled, and said, "Well! what do you think I ought to do?"

That was just what I wanted. I replied that there was only one course open to him, and that was to have an interview with the King early the next morning; to say to him, that he had been informed Harcourt was about to enter the Council; that he thought the affairs of State would suffer rather than otherwise if Harcourt did so; and finally, to allude to the change that had taken place in the King's manner towards him lately, and to say, with all respect, affection, and submission, that he was equally ready to continue serving the King or to give up his appointments, as his Majesty might desire.

M. de Beauvilliers took pleasure in listening to me. He embraced me closely, and promised to follow the course I had marked out.

The next morning I went straight to him, and learned that he had perfectly succeeded. He had spoken exactly as I had suggested. The King appeared astonished and piqued that the secret of Harcourt's entry into the Council was discovered. He would not hear a word as to resignation of office on the part of M. de Beauvilliers, and appeared more satisfied with him than ever. Whether, without this interview, he would have been lost, I know not, but by the coldness and embarrassment of the King before that interview, and during the first part of it, I am nearly persuaded that he would. M. de Beauvilliers embraced me again very tenderly—more than once.

As for Harcourt, sure of his good fortune, and scarcely able to contain his joy, he arrived at the meeting place. Time ran on. During the Council there are only the most subaltern people in the antechambers and a few courtiers who pass that way to go from one wing to another. Each of these subalterns eagerly asked M. d'Harcourt what he wanted, if he wished for anything, and importuned him strongly. He was obliged to remain there, although he had no pretext. He went and came, limping with his stick, not knowing what to reply to the passers-by, or the attendants by whom he was remarked. At last, after waiting long, he returned as he came, much disturbed at not having been called. He sent word so to Madame de Maintenon, who, in her turn, was as much disturbed, the King not having said a word to her, and she not having dared to say a word to him. She consoled Harcourt, hoping that at the next Council he would be called. At her wish he waited again, as before, during another Council, but with as little success. He was very much annoyed, comprehending that the affair had fallen through.

Madame de Maintenon did not, however, like to be defeated in this way. After waiting some time she spoke to the King, reminding him what he had promised to do. The King replied in confusion that he had thought better of it; that Harcourt was on bad terms with all the Ministers, and might, if admitted to the Council, cause them much embarrassment; he preferred, therefore, things to remain as they were. This was said in a manner that admitted of no reply.

Madame de Maintenon felt herself beaten; Harcourt was in despair. M. de Beauvilliers was quite reestablished in the favour of the King. I pretended to have known nothing of this affair, and innocent asked many questions about it when all was over. I was happy to the last degree that everything had turned out so well.

M. le Prince, who for more than two years had not appeared at the Court, died at Paris a little after midnight on the night between Easter Sunday and Monday, the last of March and first of April, and in his seventy- sixth year. No man had ever more ability of all kinds, extending even to the arts and mechanics more valour, and, when it pleased him, more discernment, grace, politeness, and nobility. But then no man had ever before so many useless talents, so much genius of no avail, or an imagination so calculated to be a bugbear to itself and a plague to others. Abjectly and vilely servile even to lackeys, he scrupled not to use the lowest and paltriest means to gain his ends. Unnatural son, cruel father, terrible husband, detestable master, pernicious neighbour; without friendship, without friends—incapable of having any jealous, suspicious, ever restless, full of slyness and artifices to discover and to scrutinise all, (in which he was unceasingly occupied, aided by an extreme vivacity and a surprising penetration,) choleric and headstrong to excess even for trifles, difficult of access, never in accord with himself, and keeping all around him in a tremble; to conclude, impetuosity and avarice were his masters, which monopolised him always. With all this he was a man difficult to be proof against when he put in play the pleasing qualities he possessed.

Madame la Princesse, his wife, was his continual victim. She was disgustingly ugly, virtuous, and foolish, a little humpbacked, and stunk like a skunk, even from a distance. All these things did not hinder M. le Prince from being jealous of her even to fury up to the very last. The piety, the indefatigable attention of Madame la Princesse, her sweetness, her novice-like submission, could not guarantee her from frequent injuries, or from kicks, and blows with the fist, which were not rare. She was not mistress even of the most trifling things; she did not dare to propose or ask anything. He made her set out from one place to another the moment the fancy took him. Often when seated in their coach he made her descend, or return from the end of the street, then recommence the journey after dinner, or the next day. This see-sawing lasted once fifteen days running, before a trip to Fontainebleau. At other times he sent for her from church, made her quit high mass, and sometimes sent for her the moment she was going to receive the sacrament; she was obliged to return at once and put off her communion to another occasion. It was not that he wanted her, but it was merely to gratify his whim that he thus troubled her.

He was always of, uncertain habits, and had four dinners ready for him every day; one at Paris, one at Ecouen, one at Chantilly, and one where the Court was. But the expense of this arrangement was not great; he dined on soup, and the half of a fowl roasted upon a crust of bread; the other half serving for the next day. He rarely invited anybody to dinner, but when he did, no man could be more polite or attentive to his guests.

Formerly he had been in love with several ladies of the Court; then, nothing cost too much. He was grace, magnificence, gallantry in person— a Jupiter transformed into a shower of gold. Now he disguised himself as a lackey, another time as a female broker in articles for the toilette; and now in another fashion. He was the most ingenious man in the world. He once gave a grand fete solely for the purpose of retarding the journey into Italy of a lady with whom he was enamoured, with whom he was on good terms, and whose husband he amused by making verses. He hired all the houses on one side of a street near Saint Sulpice, furnished them, and pierced the connecting walls, in order to be able thus to reach the place of rendezvous without being suspected.

Jealous and cruel to his mistresses, he had, amongst others, the Marquise de Richelieu; whom I name, because she is not worth the trouble of being silent upon. He was hopelessly smitten and spent millions upon her and to learn her movements. He knew that the Comte de Roucy shared her favours (it was for her that sagacious Count proposed to put straw before the house in order to guarantee her against the sound of the church bells, of which she complained). M. le Prince reproached her for favouring the Count. She defended herself; but he watched her so closely, that he brought home the offence to her without her being able to deny it. The fear of losing a lover so rich as was M. le Prince furnished her on the spot with an excellent suggestion for putting him at ease. She proposed to make an appointment at her own house with the Comte de Roucy, M. le Prince's people to lie in wait, and when the Count appeared, to make away with him. Instead of the success she expected from a proposition so humane and ingenious, M. le Prince was so horror- struck, that he warned the Comte de Roucy, and never saw the Marquise de Richelieu again all his life.

The most surprising thing was, that with so much ability, penetration, activity, and valour, as had M. le Prince, with the desire to be as great a warrior as the Great Conde, his father, he could never succeed in understanding even the first elements of the military art. Instructed as he was by his father, he never acquired the least aptitude in war. It was a profession was not born for, and for which he could not qualify himself by study. During the last fifteen or twenty years of his life, he was accused of something more than fierceness and ferocity. Wanderings were noticed in his conduct, which were not exhibited in his own house alone. Entering one morning into the apartment of the Marechale de Noailles (she herself has related this to me) as her bed was being made, and there being only the counterpane to put on, he stopped short at the door, crying with transport, "Oh, the nice bed, the nice bed!" took a spring, leaped upon the bed, rolled himself upon it seven or eight times, then descended and made his excuses to the Marechale, saying that her bed was so clean and so well-made, that he could not hinder himself from jumping upon it; and this, although there had never been anything between them; and when the Marechale, who all her life had been above suspicion, was at an age at which she could not give birth to any. Her servants remained stupefied, and she as much as they. She got out of the difficulty by laughing and treating it as a joke. It was whispered that there were times when M. le Prince believed himself a dog, or some other beast, whose manners he imitated; and I have known people very worthy of faith who have assured me they have seen him at the going to bed of the King suddenly throw his head into the air several times running, and open his mouth quite wide, like a dog while barking, yet without making a noise. It is certain, that for a long time nobody saw him except a single valet, who had control over him, and who did not annoy him.

In the latter part of his life he attended in a ridiculously minute manner to his diet and its results, and entered into discussions which drove his doctors to despair. Fever and gout at last attacked him, and he augmented them by the course he pursued. Finot, our physician and his, at times knew not what to do with him. What embarrassed Finot most, as he related to us more than once, was that M. le Prince would eat nothing, for the simple reason, as he alleged, that he was dead, and that dead men did not eat! It was necessary, however, that he should take something, or he would have really died. Finot, and another doctor who attended him, determined to agree with him that he was dead, but to maintain that dead men sometimes eat. They offered to produce dead men of this kind; and, in point of fact, led to M. le Prince some persons unknown to him, who pretended to be dead, but who ate nevertheless. This trick succeeded, but he would never eat except with these men and Finot. On that condition he ate well, and this jealousy lasted a long time, and drove Finot to despair by its duration; who, nevertheless, sometimes nearly died of laughter in relating to us what passed at these repasts, and the conversation from the other world heard there.

M. le Prince's malady augmenting, Madame la Princesse grew bold enough to ask him if he did not wish to think of his conscience, and to see a confessor. He amused himself tolerably long in refusing to do so. Some months before he had seen in secret Pere de la Tour. He had sent to the reverend father asking him to, come by night and disguised. Pere de la Tour, surprised to the last degree at so wild a proposition, replied that the respect he owed to the cloth would prevent him visiting M. le Prince in disguise; but that he would come in his ordinary attire. M. le Prince agreed to this last imposed condition. He made the Pere de la Tour enter at night by a little back door, at which an attendant was in waiting to receive him. He was led by this attendant, who had a lantern in one hand and a key in the other, through many long and obscure passages; and through many doors, which were opened and closed upon him as he passed. Having arrived at last at the sick-chamber, he confessed M. le Prince, and was conducted out of the house in the same manner and by the same way as before. These visits were repeated during several months.

The Prince's malady rapidly increased and became extreme. The doctors found him so ill on the night of Easter Sunday that they proposed to him the sacrament for the next day. He disputed with them, and said that if he was so very bad it would be better to take the sacraments at once, and have done with them. They in their turn opposed this, saying there was no need of so much hurry. At last, for fear of incensing him, they consented, and he received all hurriedly the last sacraments. A little while after he called M. le Duc to him, and spoke of the honours he wished at his funeral, mentioning those which had been omitted at the funeral of his father, but which he did not wish to be omitted from his. He talked of nothing but this and of the sums he had spent at Chantilly, until his reason began to wander.

Not a soul regretted him; neither servants, nor friends, neither child nor wife. Indeed the Princess was so ashamed of her tears that she made excuses for them. This was scarcely to be wondered at.

CHAPTER XLVIII.

It is time now that I should speak of our military operations this year and of the progress of the war. Let me commence by stating the disposition of our armies at the beginning of the campaign.

Marechal Boufflers, having become dangerously ill, was unable to take command in Flanders. Marechal de Villars was accordingly appointed in his stead under Monseigneur, and with him served the King of England, under his incognito of the previous year, and M. le Duc de Berry, as volunteers. The Marechal d'Harcourt was appointed to command upon the Rhine under Monseigneur le Duc de Bourgogne. M. d'Orleans commanded in Spain; Marechal Berwick in Dauphiny; and the Duc de Noailles in Roussillon, as usual. The generals went to their destinations, but the Princes remained at the Court.

Before I relate what we did in war, let me here state the strange opposition of our ministers in their attempts to bring about peace. Since Villars had introduced Chamillart to Court, he had heard it said that M. de Louvois did everybody's business as much as he could; and took it into his head that having succeeded to M. de Louvois he ought to act exactly like him. For some time past, accordingly, Chamillart, with the knowledge of the King, had sent people to Holland and elsewhere to negotiate for peace, although he had no right to do so, Torcy being the minister to whose department this business belonged. Torcy likewise sent people to Holland and elsewhere with a similar object, and these ambassadors of the two ministers, instead of working in common, did all in their power thwart each other. They succeeded so well that it was said they seemed in foreign countries ministers of different powers, whose interests were quite opposed. This manner of conducting business gave a most injurious idea of our government, and tended very much to bring it into ridicule. Those who sincerely wished to treat with us, found themselves so embarrassed between the rival factions, that they did not know what to do; and others made our disagreements a plausible pretext for not listening to our propositions.

At last Torcy was so annoyed with the interference of Chamillart, that he called the latter to account for it, and made him sign an agreement by which he bound himself to enter into no negotiations for peace and to mix himself in no foreign affairs; and so this absurdity came to an end.

In Italy, early this year, we received a check of no small importance. I have mentioned that we were invited to join in an Italian league, having for its object to oppose the Emperor. We joined this league, but not before its existence had been noised abroad, and put the allies on their guard as to the danger they ran of losing Italy. Therefore the Imperialists entered the Papal States, laid them under contribution, ravaged them, lived there in true Tartar style, and snapped their fingers at the Pope, who cried aloud as he could obtain no redress and no assistance. Pushed at last to extremity by the military occupation which desolated his States, he yielded to all the rashes of the Emperor, and recognised the Archduke as King of Spain. Philip V. immediately ceased all intercourse with Rome, and dismissed the nuncio from Madrid. The Imperialists, even after the Pope had ceded to their wishes, treated him with the utmost disdain, and continued to ravage, his territories. The Imperialist minister at Rome actually gave a comedy and a ball in his palace there, contrary to the express orders of the Pope, who had forbidden all kinds of amusement in this period of calamity. When remonstrated with by the Pope, this minister said that he had promised a fete to the ladies, and could not break his word, The strangest thing is, that after this public instance of contempt the nephews of the Pope went to the fete, and the Pope had the weakness to suffer it.

In Spain, everything went wrong, and people began to think it would be best to give up that country to the house of Austria, under the hope that by this means the war would be terminated. It was therefore seriously resolved to recall all our troops from Spain, and to give orders to Madame des Ursins to quit the country. Instructions were accordingly sent to this effect. The King and Queen of Spain, in the greatest alarm at such a violent determination, cried aloud against it, and begged that the execution of it might at least be suspended for a while.

At this, our King paused and called a Council to discuss the subject. It was ultimately agreed to leave sixty-six battalions of our troops to the King of Spain, but to withdraw all the rest. This compromise satisfied nobody. Those who wished to support Spain said this assistance was not enough. The other party said it was too much.

This determination being arrived at, it seemed as though the only thing to be done was to send M. d'Orleans to Spain to take command there. But now will be seen the effect of that mischievous pleasantry of his upon Madame de Maintenon and Madame des Ursins, the "she-captain," and the "she-lieutenant"—as he called them, in the gross language to which I have before alluded. Those two ladies had not forgiven him his witticism, and had determined to accomplish his disgrace. His own thoughtless conduct assisted them it bringing about this result.

The King one day asked him if he had much desire to return into Spain. He replied in a manner evidencing his willingness to serve, marking no eagerness. He did not notice that there might be a secret meaning, hidden under this question. When he related to me what had passed between him and the King, I blamed the feebleness of his reply, and represented to him the ill effect it would create if at such a time he evinced any desire to keep out of the campaign. He appeared convinced by my arguments, and to wish with more eagerness than before to return to Spain.

A few days after, the King asked him, on what terms he believed himself with the Princesse des Ursins; and when M. d'Orleans replied that he believed himself to be on good terms with her, as he had done all in his power to be so, the King said that he feared it was not thus, since she had asked that he should not be again sent to Spain, saying that he had leagued himself with all her enemies there, and that a secretary of his, named Renaut, whom he had left behind him, kept up such strict and secret intercourse with those enemies, that she was obliged to demand his recall lest he might do wrong to the name of his master.

Upon this, M. d'Orleans replied that he was infinitely surprised at these complaints of Madame des Ursins, since he had done nothing to deserve them. The King, after reflecting for a moment, said he thought, all things considered, that M. d'Orleans had better not return to Spain. In a few days it was publicly known that he would not go. The withdrawal of so many of our troops from Spain was the reason alleged. At the same time the King gave orders to M. d'Orleans to send for his equipages from Spain, and added in his ear, that he had better send some one of sense for them, who might be the bearer of a protest, if Philip V. quitted his throne. At least this is what M. d'Orleans told me, although few people believed him in the end.

M. d'Orleans chose for this errand a man named Flotte, very skilful in intrigue, in which he had, so to speak, been always brought up. He went straight to Madrid, and one of his first employments when he arrived there was to look for Renaut, the secretary just alluded to. But Renaut was nowhere to be found, nor could any news be heard of him. Flotte stayed some time in Madrid, and then went to the army, which was still in quarters. He remained there three weeks, idling from quarter to quarter, saluting the Marechal in command, who was much surprised at his long stay, and who pressed him to return into France. At last Flotte took leave of the Marechal, asking him for an escort for himself and a commissary, with whom he meant to go in company across the Pyrenees. Twenty dragoons were given him as escort, and he and the commissary set out in a chaise.

They had not proceeded far before Flotte perceived that they were followed by other troops besides those guarding them. Flotte fearing that something was meant by this, slipped a pocket-book into the hands of the commissary, requesting him to take care of it. Shortly afterwards the chaise was surrounded by troops, and stopped; the two travellers were made to alight. The commissary was ordered to give up the pocket-book, an order that he complied with very rapidly, and Flotte was made prisoner, and escorted back to the spot he had just left.

The news of this occurrence reached the King on the 12th of July, by the ordinary courier from Madrid.

The King informed M. d'Orleans of it, who, having learnt it by a private courier six days before, affected nevertheless surprise, and said it was strange that one of his people should have been thus arrested, and that as his Majesty was concerned, it was for him to demand the reason. The King replied, that in fact the injury regarded him more than M. d'Orleans, and that he would give orders to Torcy to write as was necessary to Spain.

It is not difficult to believe that such an explosion made a great noise, both in France and Spain; but the noise it made at first was nothing to that which followed. A cabal was formed against Monsieur le Duc d'Orleans. It was said that he had plotted to place himself upon the Spanish throne, by driving out Philip V., under pretext of his incapacity, of the domination of Madame des Ursins, and of the abandonment of the country by France; that he had treated with Stanhope, commander of the English troops in Spain, and with whom he was known to be on friendly terms, in order to be protected by the Archduke. This was the report most widely spread. Others went further. In these M. d'Orleans was accused of nothing less than of intending to divorce himself from Madame la Duchesse d'Orleans, as having been married to her by force; of intending to marry the sister of the Empress (widow of Charles II.), and of mounting with her upon the Spanish throne; to marry Madame d'Argenton, as the Queen Dowager was sure to have no children, and finally, to poison Madame d'Orleans.

Meanwhile the reply from Spain came not. The King and Monseigneur treated M. d'Orleans with a coldness which made him sorely ill at ease; the majority of the courtiers, following this example, withdrew from him. He was left almost alone.

I learnt at last from M. d'Orleans how far he was deserving of public censure, and what had given colouring to the reports spread against him. He admitted to me, that several of the Spanish grandees had persuaded him that it was not possible the King of Spain could stand, and had proposed to him to hasten his fall, and take his place; that he had rejected this proposition with indignation, but had been induced to promise, that if Philip V. fell of himself, without hope of rising, he would not object to mounting the vacant throne, believing that by so doing he would be doing good to our King, by preserving Spain to his house.

As soon as I heard this, I advised him to make a clean breast of it to the King, and to ask his pardon for having acted in this matter without his orders and without his knowledge. He thought my advice good, and acted upon it. But the King was too much under the influence of the enemies of M. d'Orleans, to listen favourably to what was said to him. The facts of the case, too, were much against M. d'Orleans. Both Renaut and Flotte had been entrusted with his secret. The former had openly leagued himself with the enemies of Madame des Ursins, and acted with the utmost imprudence. He had been privately arrested just before the arrival of Flotte. When this latter was arrested, papers were found upon him which brought everything to light. The views of M. d'Orleans and of those who supported him were clearly shown. The King would not listen to anything in favour of his nephew.

The whole Court cried out against M. d'Orleans; never was such an uproar heard. He was accused of plotting to overthrow the King of Spain, he, a Prince of the blood, and so closely allied to the two crowns! Monseigneur, usually so plunged in apathy, roused himself to fury against M. d'Orleans, and insisted upon nothing less than a criminal prosecution. He insisted so strongly upon this, that the King at last consented that it should take place, and gave orders to the chancellor to examine the forms requisite in such a case. While the chancellor was about this work, I went to see him one day, and represented to him so strongly, that M. d'Orleans' misdemeanour did not concern us at all, and could only be judged before a Spanish tribunal, that the idea of a criminal trial was altogether abandoned almost immediately after. M. d'Orleans was allowed to remain in peace.

Madame des Ursins and Madame de Maintenon had so far triumphed, however, that M. d'Orleans found himself plunged in the deepest disgrace. He was universally shunned. Whenever he appeared, people flew away, so that they might not be seen in communication with him. His solitude was so great, that for a whole month only one friend entered his house. In the midst of this desertion, he had no resource but debauchery, and the society of his mistress, Madame d'Argenton. The disorder and scandal of his life had for a long time offended the King, the Court, and the public. They now unhappily confirmed everybody in the bad opinion they had formed of him. That the long disgrace he suffered continued to confirm him in his bad habits, and that it explains to some extent his after-conduct, there can be no doubt. But I must leave him now, and return to other matters.

CHAPTER XLIX

But, meanwhile, a great change had taken place at Court. Chamillart had committed the mistake of allowing the advancement of D'Harcourt to the head of an army. The poor man did not see the danger; and when warned of it, thought his cleverness would preserve him. Reports of his fall had already begun to circulate, and D'Antin had been spoken of in his place. I warned his daughter Dreux, the only one of the family to whom it was possible to speak with profit. The mother, with little wit and knowledge of the Court, full of apparent confidence and sham cunning, received all advice ill. The brothers were imbecile, the son was a child and a simpleton, the two other daughters too light-headed. I had often warned Madame de Dreux of the enmity of the Duchesse de Bourgogne; and she had spoken to her on the subject. The Princess had answered very coldly that she was mistaken, that she had no such enmity. At last I succeeded, in this indirect way, in forcing Chamillart to speak to the King on the reports that were abroad; but he did so in a half-and-half way, and committed the capital mistake of not naming the successor which public rumour mentioned. The King appeared touched, and gave him all sorts of assurances of friendship, and made as if he liked him better than ever. I do not know if Chamillart was then near his destruction, and whether this conversation set him up again; but from the day it took place all reports died away, and the Court thought him perfectly re-established.

But his enemies continued to work against him. Madame de Maintenon and the Duchesse de Bourgogne abated not a jot in their enmity. The Marechal d'Harcourt lost no opportunity of pulling him to pieces. One day, among others, he was declaiming violently against him at Madame de Maintenon's, whom he knew he should thus please. She asked him whom he would put in his place. "M. Fagon, Madame," he replied coldly. She laughed, but said this was not a thing to joke about; but he maintained seriously that the old doctor would make a much better minister than Chamillart, for he had some intelligence, which would make up for his ignorance of many matters; but what could be expected of a man who was ignorant and stupid too? The cunning Norman knew well the effect this strange parallel would have; and it is indeed inconceivable how damaging his sarcasm proved. A short time afterwards, D'Antin, wishing also to please, but more imprudent, insulted the son of Chamillart so grossly, and abused the father so publicly, that he was obliged afterwards to excuse himself.

The King held, for the first time in his life, a real council of war. He told the Duc de Bourgogne of it, saying rather sharply: "Come, unless you prefer going to vespers." The council lasted nearly three hours; and was stormy. The Marechals were freer in their language than usual, and complained of the ministers. All fell upon Chamillart, who was accused, among other things, of matters that concerned Desmarets, on whom, he finished by turning off the King's anger. Chamillart defended himself with so much anger that his voice was heard by people outside.

But he had of late heaped fault on fault. Besides setting Madame de Maintenon and the Duchesse de Bourgogne against him, he rather wantonly irritated Monseigneur, at that time more than ever under the government of Mademoiselle Choin. The latter had asked him a favour, and had been refused even with contempt. Various advances at reconciliation she made were also repulsed with contumely. Yet every one, even the Duchesse de Bourgogne, crawled before this creature—the favourite of the heir to the throne. Madame de Maintenon actually caused the King to offer her apartments at Versailles, which she refused, for fear of losing the liberty she enjoyed at Meudon. D'Antin, who saw all that was going on, became the soul of a conspiracy against Chamillart. It was infinitely well managed. Everything moved in order and harmony—always prudently, always knowingly.

The King, quietly attacked on all hands, was shaken; but he had many reasons for sticking to Chamillart. He was his own choice. No minister had stood aside so completely, and allowed the King to receive all the praise of whatever was done. Though the King's reason way, therefore, soon influenced, his heart was not so easily. But Madame de Maintenon was not discouraged. Monseigneur, urged by Mademoiselle Choin, had already spoken out to the King. She laboured to make him speak again; for, on the previous occasion, he had been listened to attentively.

So many machines could not be set in motion without some noise being heard abroad. There rose in the Court, I know not what confused murmurs, the origin of which could not be pointed out, publishing that either the State or Chamillart must perish; that already his ignorance had brought the kingdom within an ace of destruction; that it was a miracle this destruction had not yet come to pass; and that it would be madness to tempt Providence any longer. Some did not blush to abuse him; others praised his intentions, and spoke with moderation of faults that many people reproached him bitterly with. All admitted his rectitude, but maintained that a successor of some kind or other was absolutely necessary. Some, believing or trying to persuade others that they carried friendship to as far a point as was possible, protested that they should ever preserve this friendship, and would never forget the pleasure and the services that they had received from Chamillart; but delicately confessed that they preferred the interests of the State to their own personal advantage and the support they would lose; that, even if Chamillart were their brother, they would sorrowfully admit the necessity of removing him! At last, nobody could understand either how such a man could ever have been chosen, or how he could have remained so long in his place! All his faults and all his ridicules formed the staple of Court conversation. If anybody referred to the great things he had done, to the rapid gathering of armies after our disasters, people turned on their heels and walked away. Such were the presages of the fall of Chamillart.

The Marechal de Boufflers, who had never forgiven the causes that led to the loss of Lille, joined in the attack on Chamillart; and assisted in exciting the King against him. Chamillart has since related to me that up to the last moment he had always been received equally graciously by the King—that is, up to two days before his fall. Then, indeed, he noticed that the King's countenance was embarrassed; and felt inclined to ask if he was displeasing to him, and to offer to retire. Had he done so, he might, if we may judge from what transpired subsequently, have remained in office. But now Madame de Maintenon had come personally into the field, and, believing herself sure of success, only attacked Chamillart. What passed between her and the King was quite private and never related; but there seems reason to believe that she did not succeed without difficulty.

On Sunday morning, November 9, the King, on entering the Council of State, called the Duc de Beauvilliers to him, and requested him to go in the afternoon and tell Chamillart that he was obliged, for motives of public interest, to ask him to resign his office; but that, in order to give him a mark of his esteem and satisfaction with his services, he continued his pension of Minister—that is to say, twenty thousand francs—and added as much more, with one to his son of twenty thousand francs likewise. He added that he should have liked to see Chamillart, but that at first it would grieve him too much: he was not to come till sent for; he might live in Paris, and go where he liked. The Duc de Beauvilliers did all he could to escape from carrying so harsh a message, but could only obtain permission to let the Duc de Chevreuse accompany him.

They went to Chamillart, and found him alone, working in his cabinet. The air of consternation with which they entered, told the unfortunate Minister that something disagreeable had happened; and without giving them time to speak, he said, with a serene and tranquil countenance, "What is the matter, gentlemen? If what you have to say concerns only me, you may speak: I have long been prepared for everything." This gentle firmness touched them still more. They could scarcely explain what they came about. Chamillart listened without any change of countenance, and said, with the same air and tone as at first: "The King is the master. I have endeavoured to serve him to the best of my ability. I hope some one else will please him better, and be more lucky." He then asked if he had been forbidden to write to the King, and being told not, he wrote a letter of respect and thanks, and sent it by the two Dukes, with a memoir which he had just finished. He also wrote to Madame de Maintenon. He sent a verbal message to his wife; and, without complaint, murmur, or sighs, got into his carriage, and drove to L'Etang. Both then and afterwards he showed the greatest magnanimity. Every one went, from a sort of fashion, to visit him. When I went, the house looked as if a death had taken place; and it was frightful to see, in the midst of cries and tears, the dead man walking, speaking with a quiet, gentle air, and serene brow,—unconstrained, unaffected, attentive to every one, not at all or scarcely different from what he was accustomed to be.

Chamillart, as I have said, had received permission to live at Paris, if he liked; but soon afterwards he innocently gave umbrage to Madame de Maintenon, who was annoyed that his disgrace was not followed by general abandonment. She caused him to be threatened secretly, and he prudently left Paris, and went far away, under pretence of seeking for an estate to buy.

Next day after the fall of Chamillart, it became known that the triumph of Madame de Maintenon was completed, and that Voysin, her creature, was the succeeding Secretary of State. This Voysin had the one indispensable quality for admission into the counsels of Louis XIV.— not a drop of noble blood in his veins. He had married, in 1683, the daughter of Trudaine. She had a very agreeable countenance, without any affectation. She appeared simple and modest, and occupied with her household and good works; but in reality, had sense, wit, cleverness, above all, a natural insinuation, and the art of bringing things to pass without being perceived. She kept with great tact a magnificent house. It was she who received Madame de Maintenon at Dinan, when the King was besieging Namur; and, as she had been instructed by M. de Luxembourg in the way to please that lady, succeeded most effectually. Among her arts was her modesty, which led her prudently to avoid pressing herself on Madame de Maintenon, or showing herself more than was absolutely necessary. She was sometimes two whole days without seeing her. A trifle, luckily contrived, finished the conquest of Madame de Maintenon. It happened that the weather passed suddenly from excessive heat to a damp cold, which lasted a long time. Immediately, an excellent dressing-gown, simple, and well lined, appeared in the corner of the chamber. This present, by so much the more agreeable, as Madame de Maintenon had not brought any warm clothing, touched her also by its suddenness, and by its simple appearance, as if of its own accord.

In this way, the taste of Madame de Maintenon for Madame Voysin was formed and increased. Madame Voysin obtained an appointment for her husband, and coming to Paris, at last grew extremely familiar with Madame de Maintenon. Voysin himself had much need of the wife that Providence had given him. He was perfectly ignorant of everything but the duties of an Intendant. He was, moreover, rough and uncivil, as the courtiers soon found. He was never unjust for the sake of being so, nor was he bad naturally; but he knew nothing but authority, the King and Madame de Maintenon, whose will was unanswerable—his sovereign law and reason. The choice was settled between the King and Madame de Maintenon after supper, the day of Chamillart's fall. Voysin was conducted to the King by Bloin, after having received the orders and instructions of his benefactress. In the evening of that day, the King found Madame Voysin with Madame de Maintenon, and kissed her several times to please his lady.

Voysin's first experience of the duties of his office was unpleasant. He was foolish enough, feeling his ignorance, to tell the King, that at the outset he should be obliged to leave everything to his Majesty, but that when he knew better, he would take more on himself. The King, to whom Chamillart used himself to leave everything, was much offended by this language; and drawing himself up, in the tone of a master, told Voysin to learn, once for all, that his duties were to receive, and expedite orders, nothing else. He then took the projects brought to him, examined them, prescribed the measures he thought fit, and very stiffly sent away Voysin, who did not know where he was, and had great want of his wife to set his head to rights, and of Madame de Maintenon to give him completer lessons than she had yet been able to do. Shortly afterwards he was forbidden to send any orders without submitting them to the Marechal de Boufflers. He was supple, and sure of Madame de Maintenon, and through her of the Marechal, waited for time to release him from this state of tutelage and showed nothing of his annoyance, especially to Boufflers himself.

Events soon happened to alter the position of the Marechal de Boufflers.

Flanders, ever since the opening of the campaign, had been the principal object of attention. Prince Eugene and Marlborough, joined together, continued their vast designs, and disdained to hide them. Their prodigious preparations spoke of sieges. Shall I say that we desired them, and that we thought of nothing but how to preserve, not use our army?

Tournai was the first place towards which the enemies directed their arms. After a short resistance it fell into their hands. Villars, as I have said, was coriander in Flanders. Boufflers feeling that, in the position of affairs, such a post must weigh very heavily upon one man, and that in case of his death there was no one to take his place, offered to go to assist him. The King, after some little hesitation, accepted this magnanimous offer, and Boufflers set out. I say magnanimous offer, because Boufflers, loaded with honours and glory, might well have hoped to pass the rest of his life in repose. It was hardly possible, do what he might, that he could add to his reputation; while, on the other hand, it was not unlikely that he might be made answerable for the faults or shortcomings of others, and return to Paris stripped of some of the laurels that adorned his brow. But he thought only of the welfare of the State, and pressed the King to allow him to depart to Flanders. The King, as I have said, at last consented.

The surprise was great in the army when he arrived there. The general impression was that he was the bearer of news of peace. Villars received him with an air of joy and respect, and at once showed every willingness to act in concert with him. The two generals accordingly worked harmoniously together, taking no steps without consulting each other, and showing great deference for each other's opinions. They were like one man.

Marlborough at Malplaquet--painted by R. Canton Woodville

After the fall of Tournai, our army took up position at Malplaquet, the right and the left supported by two woods, with hedges and woods before the centre, so that the plain was, as it were, cut in two. Marlborough and Prince Eugene marched in their turn, fearing lest Villars should embarrass them as they went towards Mons, which place they had resolved to besiege. They sent on a large detachment of their army, under the command of the Prince of Hesse, to watch ours. He arrived in sight of the camp at Malpladuet at the same time that we entered it, and was quickly warned of our existence by, three cannon shots that Villars, out of braggadocio, fired by way of appeal to Marlborough and Prince Eugene. Some little firing took place this day and the next, the 10th of September, but without doing much harm on either side.

Marlborough and Prince Eugene, warned of the perilous state in which the Prince of Hesse was placed—he would have been lost if attacked hastened at once to join him, and arrived in the middle of the morning of the 10th. Their first care was to examine the position of our army, and to do so, while waiting for their rear-guard, they employed a stratagem which succeeded admirably.

They sent several officers, who had the look of subalterns, to our lines, and asked to be allowed to speak to our officers. Their request was granted. Albergotti came down to them, and discoursed with them a long time. They pretended they came to see whether peace could not be arranged, but they, in reality, spoke of little but compliments, which signified nothing. They stayed so long, under various pretexts, that at last we were obliged to threaten them in order to get rid of them. All this time a few of their best general officers on horseback, and a larger number of engineers and designers on foot, profited by these ridiculous colloquies to put upon paper drawings of our position, thus being able to see the best positions for their cannon, and the best mode, in fact, in which all their disposition might be made. We learnt this artifice afterwards from the prisoners.

It was decided that evening to give us battle on the morrow, although the deputies of the States-General, content with the advantages that had been already gained, and not liking to run the risk of failure, were, opposed to an action taking place. They were, however, persuaded to agree, and on the following morning the battle began.

The struggle lasted many hours. But our position had been badly chosen, and, in spite of every effort, we were unable to maintain it. Villars, in the early part of the action, received a wound which incapacitated him from duty. All the burden of command fell upon Boufflers. He bore it well; but after a time finding his army dispersed, his infantry overwhelmed, the ground slipping from under his feet, he thought only of beating a good and honourable retreat. He led away his army in such good order, that the enemy were unable to interfere with it in the slightest degree. During all the march, which lasted until night, we did not lose a hundred stragglers, and carried off all the cannon with the exception of a few pieces. The enemy passed the night upon the battle-field, in the midst of twenty-five thousand dead, and marched towards Mons the next evening. They frankly admitted that in men killed and wounded, in general officers and privates, in flags and standards, they had lost more than we. The battle cost them, in fact, seven lieutenant-generals, five other generals, about eighteen hundred officers killed or wounded, and more than fifteen thousand men killed or rendered unfit for service. They openly avowed, also, how much they had been surprised by the valour of the majority of our troops, above all of the cavalry, and did not dissimulate that we should have gained the day, had we been better led.

Why the Marechal Villars waited ten days to be attacked in a position so disadvantageous, instead of at once marching upon the enemies and overcoming, as he might at first easily have done, it is difficult to understand. He threw all the blame upon his wound, although it was well known that the fate of the day was decided long before he was hurt.

Although forced to retire, our men burned with eagerness to engage the enemies again. Mons had been laid siege to. Boufflers tried to make the besiegers give up the undertaking. But his men were without bread and without pay: the subaltern officers were compelled to eat the regulation bread, the general-officers were reduced to the most miserable shifts, and were like the privates, without pay, oftentimes for seven or eight days running. There was no meat and no bread for the army. The common soldiers were reduced to herbs and roots for all sustenance. Under these circumstances it was found impossible to persevere in trying to save Mons. Nothing but subsistence could be thought of.

The Court had now become so accustomed to defeats that a battle lost as was Malplaquet seemed half a victory. Boufflers sent a courier to the King with an account of the event, and spoke so favourably of Villars, that all the blame of the defeat fell upon himself. Villars was everywhere pitied and applauded, although he had lost an important battle: when it was in his power to beat the enemies in detail, and render them unable to undertake the siege of Mons, or any other siege. If Boufflers was indignant at this, he was still more indignant at what happened afterwards. In the first dispatch he sent to the King he promised to send another as soon as possible giving full details, with propositions as to how the vacancies which had occurred in the army might be filled up. On the very evening he sent off his second dispatch, he received intelligence that the King had already taken his dispositions with respect to these vacancies, without having consulted him upon a single point. This was the first reward Boufflers received for the services he had just rendered, and that, too, from a King who had said in public that without Boufflers all was lost, and that assuredly it was God who had inspired him with the idea of going to the army. From that time Boufflers fell into a disgrace from which he never recovered. He had the courage to appear as usual at the Court; but a worm was gnawing him within and destroyed him. Oftentimes he opened his heart to me without rashness, and without passing the strict limits of his virtue; but the poniard was in his heart, and neither time nor reflection could dull its edge. He did nothing but languish afterwards, yet without being confined to his bed or to his chamber, but did not live more than two years. Villars, on the contrary, was in greater favour than ever. He arrived at Court triumphant. The King made him occupy an apartment at Versailles, so that his wound might be well attended to.

What a contrast! What a difference between the services, the merit, the condition, the virtue, the situation of these two men! What inexhaustible funds of reflection.

CHAPTER L

I have described in its proper place the profound fall of M. le Duc d'Orleans and the neglect in which he lived, out of all favour with the King, hated by Madame de Maintenon and Monseigneur, and regarded with an unfavourable eye by the public, on account of the scandals of his private life. I had long seen that the only way in which he could hope to recover his position would be to give up his mistress, Madame d'Argenton, with whom he had been on terms of intimacy for many years past, to the knowledge and the scandal of all the world. I knew it would be a bold and dangerous game to play, to try to persuade him to separate himself from a woman he had known and loved so long; but I determined to engage in it, nevertheless, and I looked about for some one to assist me in this enterprise. At once I cast my eyes upon the Marechal de Besons, who for many long years had been the bosom friend of M. d'Orleans. He applauded the undertaking, but doubted, he said, its success; nevertheless he promised to aid me to the utmost of his power, and, it will be seen, was as good as his word. For some time I had no opportunity of accosting M. d'Orleans, and was obliged to keep my project in abeyance, but I did not lose sight of it; and when I saw my way clear, I took the matter in hand, determined to strain every nerve in order to succeed.

It was just at the commencement of the year 1710, that I first spoke to M. d'Orleans. I began by extracting from him an admission of the neglect into which he had fallen—the dislike of the King, the hatred of Monseigneur, who accused him of wishing to replace his son in Spain; that of Madame de Maintenon, whom he had offended by his bon mot; the suspicions of the public, who talked of his chemical experiments—and then, throwing off all fear of consequences, I said that before he could hope to draw back his friends and the world to him, he must reinstate himself in the favour of the King. He appeared struck with what I had said, rose after a profound silence, paced to and fro, and then asked, "But how?" Seeing the opportunity so good, I replied in a firm and significant tone, "How? I know well enough, but I will never tell you; and yet it is the only thing to do."—"Ah, I understand you," said he, as though struck with a thunderbolt; "I understand you perfectly;" and he threw himself upon the chair at the end of the room. There he remained some time, without speaking a word, yet agitated and sighing, and with his eyes lowered. I broke silence at last, by saying that the state which he was in had touched me to the quick, and that I had determined in conjunction with the Marechal de Besons to speak to him upon the subject, and to propose the only means by which he could hope to bring about a change in his position. He considered some time, and then giving me encouragement to proceed, I entered at some length upon the proposal I had to make to him and left him evidently affected by what I had said, when I thought I had for the time gone far enough.

The next day, Thursday, January 2nd, Besons, to whom I had written, joined me; and after I had communicated to him what had passed the previous evening, we hastened to M. d'Orleans. He received us well, and we at once commenced an attack. In order to aid my purpose as much as possible, I repeated to M. d'Orleans, at this meeting, the odious reports that were in circulation against him, viz., that he intended to repudiate his wife forced upon him by the King, in order to marry the Queen Dowager of Spain, and by means of her gold to open up a path for himself to the Spanish throne; that he intended to wait for his new wife's death, and then marry Madame D'ARGENSON, to whom the genii had promised a throne; and I added, that it was very fortunate that the Duchesse d'Orleans had safely passed through the dangers of her confinement, for already some wretches had begun to spread the saying, that he was not the son of Monsieur for nothing. (An allusion to the death of Henriette d'Angleterre.)

On hearing these words, the Duke was seized with a terror that cannot be described, and at the same time with a grief that is above expression. I took advantage of the effect my discourse had had upon him to show how necessary it was he should make a great effort in order to win back the favour of the King and of the public. I represented to him that the only way to do this was to give up Madame d'Argenton, at once and for ever, and to announce to the King that he had done so. At first he would not hear of such a step, and I was obliged to employ all my eloquence, and all my firmness too, to make him listen to reason. One great obstacle in our way was the repugnance of M. d'Orleans for his wife. He had been married, as I have described in the early part of these memoirs, against his will, and with no sort of affection for the woman he was given to. It was natural that he should look upon her with dislike ever since she had become his wife. I did what I could to speak in praise of Madame la Duchesse d'Orleans, and Besons aided me; but we did little else than waste our breath for sometime. Our praises in fact irritated M. d'Orleans, and to such a point, that no longer screening things or names, he told us what we should have wished not to hear, but what it was very lucky we did hear. He had suspicions, in fact, of his wife's honour; but fortunately I was able to prove clearly and decisively that those suspicions were unfounded, and I did so. The joy of M. d'Orleans upon finding he had been deceived was great indeed; and when we separated from him after mid-day, in order to go to dinner, I saw that a point was gained.

A little before three o'clock I returned to M. d'Orleans, whom I found alone in his cabinet with Besons. He received me with pleasure, and made me seat myself between him and the Marechal, whom he complimented upon his diligence. Our conversation recommenced. I returned to the attack with all the arguments I could muster, and the Marechal supported me; but I saw with affright that M. d'Orleans was less reduced than when we had quitted him in the morning, and that he had sadly taken breath during our short absence. I saw that, if we were to succeed, we must make the best use we could of our time, and accordingly I brought all my powers into play in order to gain over M. d'Orleans.

Feeling that everything was now to be lost or gained, I spoke out with all the force of which I was capable, surprising and terrifying Marechal Besons to such a point, with my hardihood, that he had not a word to say in order to aid me. When I had finished, M. d'Orleans thanked me in a piteous tone, by which I knew the profound impression I had made upon his mind. I proposed, while he was still shaken, that he should at once send to Madame de Maintenon, to know when she, would grant him an audience; for he had determined to speak to her first of his intention to give up Madame d'Argenton. Besons seconded me; and while we were talking together, not daring to push our point farther, M. d'Orleans much astonished us by rising, running with impetuosity to the door, and calling aloud for his servants. One ran to him, whom he ordered in a whisper to go to Madame de Maintenon, to ask at what hour she would see him on the morrow. He returned immediately, and threw himself into a chair like a man whose strength fails him and who is at his last gasp. Uncertain as to what he had just done, I asked him if he had sent to Madame de Maintenon. "Yes, Monsieur," said he, in a tone of despair. Instantly I started towards him, and thanked him with all the contentment and all the joy imaginable. This terrible interview, for the struggle we had all gone through was very great, was soon after brought to a close, and Besons and myself went our way, congratulating each other on the success of this day's labour.

On the next day, Friday, the 3rd of January, I saw M. d'Orleans as he preceded the King to mass, and in my impatience I approached him, and speaking in a low tone, asked him if he had seen "that woman." I did not dare to mention names just then. He replied "yes," but in so lackadaisical a tone that I feared he had seen her to effect, and I asked him if he had spoken to her. Upon receiving another "yes," like the other, my emotion redoubled. "But have you told her all?" I said. "Yes," he replied, "I have told her all."—"And are you content?" said I. "Nobody could be more so," he replied; "I was nearly an hour with her, she was very much surprised and ravished."

I saw M. d'Orleans under better circumstances at another period of the day, and then I learnt from him that since meeting me he had spoken to the King also, and told him all. "Ah, Monsieur," cried I with transport, "how I love you!" and advancing warmly toward him, I added, "How glad I am to see you at last delivered; how did you bring this to pass?"— "I mistrusted myself so much," replied he, "and was so violently agitated after speaking to Madame de Maintenon, that I feared to run the risk of pausing all the morning; so, immediately after mass I spoke to the King, and—" here, overcome by his grief, his voice faltered, and he burst into sighs, into tears, and into sobs. I retired into a corner. A moment after Besons entered: the spectacle and the profound silence astonished him. He lowered his eyes, and advanced but little. At last we gently approached each other. I told him that M. d'Orleans had conquered himself, and had spoken to the King. The Marechal was so bewildered with surprise and joy that he remained for some moments speechless and motionless: then running towards M. d'Orleans, he thanked him, felicitated him, and wept for very joy. M. d'Orleans was cruelly agitated, now maintaining a ferocious silence, and now bursting into a torrent of sighs, sobs, and tears. He said at last that Madame de Maintenon had been extremely surprised with the resolution he had taken, and at the same time delighted. She assured him that it would put him on better terms than ever with the King, and that Madame d'Argenton should be treated with every consideration. I pressed M. d'Orleans to let us know how the King had received him. He replied that the King had appeared very much surprised, but had spoken coldly. I comforted him for this disappointment by assuring him that the King's coldness arose only from his astonishment, and that in the end all would be well.

It would be impossible to describe the joy felt by Besons and myself at seeing our labours brought to this satisfactory point. I knew I should make many enemies when the part I had taken in influencing M. d'Orleans to give up Madame d'Argenton came to be known, as it necessarily would; but I felt I had done rightly, and left the consequences to Providence. Madame la Duchesse d'Orleans showed me the utmost gratitude for what I had done. She exhibited, too, so much intelligence, good sense, and ability, in the conversation I had with her, that I determined to spare no pains to unite her husband to her more closely; being firmly persuaded that he would nowhere find a better counsellor than in her. The surprise of the whole Court, when it became known that M. d'Orleans had at last separated himself from Madame d'Argenton, was great indeed. It was only equalled by the vexation of those who were opposed to him. Of course in this matter I was not spared. For several days nothing was spoken of but this rupture, and everywhere I was pointed out as the author of it.

Besons being scarcely alluded to. I parried the thrust made at me as well as I could, as much for the purpose of leaving all the honour to M. d'Orleans, as for the purpose of avoiding the anger of those who were annoyed with me; and also from a just fear of showing that I had too much influence over the mind of a Prince not without faults, and who could not always be led.

As for Madame d'Argenton, she received the news that her reign was over with all the consternation, rage, and despair that might have been expected. Mademoiselle de Chausseraye was sent by Madame de Maintenon to announce the ill news to her. When Mademoiselle de Chausseraye arrived at Madame l'Argenton's house, Madame d'Argenton was out she had gone to supper with the Princesse de Rohan. Mademoiselle de Chausseraye waited until she returned, and then broke the matter to her gently, and after much preamble and circumlocution, as though she were about to announce the death of some one.

The tears, the cries, the howlings of Madame d'Argenton filled the house, and announced to all the domestics that the reign of felicity was at an end there. After a long silence on the part of Mademoiselle de Chausseraye, she spoke her best in order to appease the poor lady. She represented to her the delicacy and liberality of the arrangements M. d'Orleans had made in her behalf. In the first place she was free to live in any part of the realm except Paris and its appanages. In the next place he assured to her forty-five thousand livres a year, nearly all the capital of which would belong to the son he had had by her, whom he had recognised and made legitimate, and who has since become Grandee of Spain, Grand Prieur of France, and General of the Galleys (for the best of all conditions in France is to have none at all, and to be a bastard). Lastly he undertook to pay all her debts up to the day of the rupture, so that she should not be importuned by any creditor, and allowed her to retain her jewellery, her plate, her furniture— worth altogether about four hundred thousand livres. His liberality amounted to a total of about two million livres, which I thought prodigious.

Madame d'Argenton, in despair at first, became more tractable as she learnt the provisions which had been made for her, and the delicacy with which she was treated. She remained four days in Paris, and then returned to her father's house near Port-Sainte-Maxence, the Chevalier d'Orleans, her son, remaining at the Palais Royal. The King after his first surprise had worn away, was in the greatest joy at the rupture; and testified his gratification to M. d'Orleans, whom he treated better and better every day. Madame de Maintenon did not dare not to contribute a little at first; and in this the Prince felt the friendship of the Jesuits, whom he had contrived to attach to him.

The Duchesse de Bourgogne did marvels of her own accord; and the Duc de Bourgogne, also, being urged by M. de Beauvilliers. Monseigneur alone remained irritated, on account of the Spanish affair.

I must here mention the death of M. le Duc. He was engaged in a trial which was just about to be pleaded. He had for some time suffered from a strange disease, a mixture of apoplexy and epilepsy, which he concealed so carefully, that he drove away one of his servants for speaking of it to his fellows.

For some time he had had a continual headache. This state troubled the gladness he felt at being delivered from his troublesome father and brother-in-law. One evening he was riding in his carriage, returning from a visit to the Hotel de Coislin, without torches, and with only one servant behind, when he felt so ill that he drew the string, and made his lackey get up to tell him whether his mouth was not all on one side. This was not the case, but he soon lost speech and consciousness after having requested to be taken in privately to the Hotel de Conde. They there put him in bed. Priests and doctors came. But he only made horrible faces, and died about four o'clock in the morning.

Madame la Duchesse did not lose her presence of mind, and, whilst her husband was dying, took steps to secure her future fortune. Meanwhile she managed to cry a little, but nobody believed in her grief. As for M. le Duc, I have already mentioned some anecdotes of him that exhibit his cruel character. He was a marvellously little man, short, without being fat. A dwarf of Madame la Princesse was said to be the cause. He was of a livid yellow, nearly always looked furious, and was ever so proud, so audacious, that it was difficult to get used to him. His cruelty and ferocity were so extreme that people avoided him, and his pretended friends would not invite him to join in any merriment. They avoided him: he ran after them to escape from solitude, and would sometimes burst upon them during their jovial repasts, reproach them with turning a cold shoulder to him, and change their merriment to desolation.

After the death of M. le Duc, a grand discussion on precedence at the After-suppers, set on foot by the proud Duchesse d'Orleans, was,—after an elaborate examination by the King, brought to a close. The King ordered his determination to be kept secret until he formally declared it. It is necessary to set forth in a few words the mechanism of the After-suppers every day. The King, on leaving table, stopped less than a half-quarter of an hour with his back leaning against the balustrade of his chamber. He there found in a circle all the ladies who had been at his supper, and who came there to wait for him a little before he left table, except the ladies who sat, who came out after him, and who, in the suite of the Princes and the Princesses who had supped with him, advanced one by one and made him a courtesy, and filled up the remainder of the standing circle; for a space was always left for them by the other ladies. The men stood behind. The King amused himself by observing the dresses, the countenances, and the gracefulness of the ladies courtesies, said a word to the Princes and Princesses who had supped with him, and who closed the circle near him an either hand, then bowed to the ladies on right and left, bowed once or twice more as he went away, with a grace and majesty unparalleled, spoke sometimes, but very rarely, to some lady in passing, entered the first cabinet, where he gave the order, and then advanced to the second cabinet, the doors from the first to the second always remaining open. There he placed himself in a fauteuil, Monsieur, while he was there, in another; the Duchesse de Bourgogne, Madame (but only after the death of Monsieur), the Duchesse de Berry (after her marriage), the three bastard-daughters, and Madame du Maine (when she was at Versailles), on stools on each side. Monseigneur, the Duc de Bourgogne, the Duc de Berry, the Duc d'Orleans, the two bastards, M. le Duc (as the husband of Madame la Duchesse), and afterwards the two sons of M. du Maine, when they had grown a little, and D'Antin, came afterwards, all standing. It was the object of the Duchesse d'Orleans to change this order, and make her daughters take precedence of the wives of the Princes of the blood; but the King declared against her. When he made the public announcement of his decision, the Duc d'Orleans took the opportunity of alluding to a marriage which would console him for everything. "I should think so," replied the King, dryly, and with a bitter and mocking smile.

CHAPTER LI

It was the desire of the Duc and Duchesse d'Orleans to marry Mademoiselle (their daughter) to the Duc de Berry (third son of Monseigneur, and consequently brother of the Duc de Bourgogne and of the King of Spain). There were many obstacles in the way—partly the state of public affairs —partly the fact that the King, though seemingly, was not really quite reconciled—partly the recollection of that cruel 'bon mot' in Spain— partly the fact that Monseigneur would naturally object to marry his favourite son with the daughter of a man toward whom he always testified hatred in the most indecent manner. The recent union between Madame de Maintenon, Mademoiselle Choin, and Monseigneur was also a great obstacle. In fact after what M. le Duc d'Or leans had been accused of in Spain, with his abilities and talents it seemed dangerous to make him the father-in-law of M. le Duc de Berry.

For my part I passionately desired the marriage of Mademoiselle, although I saw that all tended to the marriage of Mademoiselle de Bourbon, daughter of Madame la Duchesse, in her place. I had many reasons, private and public, for acting against the latter marriage; but it was clear that unless very vigorous steps were taken it would fall like a mill-stone upon my head, crush me, and wound the persons to whom I was attached. M. le Duc d'Orleans and Madame la Duchesse d'Orleans were immersed in the deepest indolence. They desired, but did not act. I went to them and explained the state of the case—pointed out the danger of Madame la Duchesse—excited their pride, their jealousy, their spite. Will it be believed that it was necessary to put all this machinery in motion? At last, by working on them by the most powerful motives, I made them attend to their own interests. The natural but extreme laziness of the Duchesse d'Orleans gave way this time, but less to ambition than to the desire of defeating a sister who was so inimical to her. We next concerted how we should make use of M. d'Orleans himself.

That Prince, with all his wit and his passion for Mademoiselle—which had never weakened since her birth—was like a motionless beam, which stirred only in obedience to our redoubled efforts, and who remained so to the conclusion of this great business. I often reflected on the causes of this incredible conduct, and was led to suppose that the knowledge of the irremediable nature of what had taken place in Spain was the rein that restrained him. However this may have been, I was throughout obliged to use main force to bring him to activity. I determined to form and direct a powerful cabal in order to bring my views to pass. The first person of whom it was necessary to make sure was the Duchesse de Bourgogne. That Princess had many reasons for the preference of Mademoiselle over Mademoiselle de Bourbon (daughter of Madame la Duchesse). She knew the King perfectly; and could not be ignorant of the power of novelty over his mind, of which power she had herself made a happy experiment. What she had to fear was another herself—I mean a Princess on the same terms with the King as she was, who, being younger than she, would amuse him by new childish playfulness no longer suited to her age, and yet which she (the Duchess) was still obliged to employ. The very contrast of her own untimely childishness, with a childishness so much more natural, would injure her. The new favourite would, moreover, not have a husband to support; for the Duc de Berry was already well liked. The Duc de

Bourgogne, on the contrary, since the affair of Flanders, had fallen into disgrace with his father, Monseigneur; and his scruples, his preciseness, his retired life, devoted to literal compliance with the rules of devotion, contrasted unfavourably with the free life of his younger brother.

The present and the future—whatever was important in life—were therefore at stake with Madame la Duchesse de Bourgogne; and yet her great duty to herself was perpetually in danger of being stifled by the fictitious and petty duties of daily life. It was necessary to stimulate her. She felt these things in general; and that it was necessary that her sister-in-law should be a Princess, neither able nor willing to give her umbrage, and over whom she should be mistress. But in spite of her wit and sense, she was not capable of feeling in a sufficiently lively manner of herself all the importance of these things, amidst the effervescence of her youth, the occupation of her successive duties, the private and general favour she seemed to enjoy, the greatness of a rank in expectation of a throne, the round of amusements which dissipated her mind and her days: gentle, light, easy—perhaps too easy. I felt, however, that from the effect of these considerations upon her I should derive the greatest assistance, on account of the influence she could exert upon the King, and still more on Madame de Maintenon, both of whom loved her exceedingly; and I felt also that the Duchesse d'Orleans would have neither the grace nor the fire necessary to stick it in deep enough —on account of her great interest in the matter.

I influenced the Duchesse de Villeroy and Madame de Levi, who could work on the Duchess, and also Madame d'O; obtained the indirect assistance of M. du Maine—and by representing to the Ducs de Chevreuse, and de Beauvilliers, that if M. de Berry married Mademoiselle de Bourbon, hatred would arise between him and his brother, and great danger to the state, enlisted them also on my side. I knew that the Joie de Berry was a fort that could only be carried by mine and assault. Working still further, I obtained the concurrence of the Jesuits; and made the Pere de Trevoux our partisan. Nothing is indifferent to the Jesuits. They became a powerful instrument. As a last ally I obtained the co-operation of the Marechal de Boufflers. Such were the machines that my friendship for those to whom I was attached, my hatred for Madame la Duchesse, my care of my present and future situation, enabled me to discover, to set going, with an exact and compassed movement, a precise agreement, and the strength of a lever—which the space of one Lent commenced and perfected —all whose movements, embarrassments, and progress in their divers lines I knew; and which I regularly wound up in reciprocal cadence every day!

Towards the end of the Lent, the Duchesse de Bourgogne, having sounded the King and Madame de Maintenon, had found the latter well disposed, and the former without any particular objection. One day that Mademoiselle had been taken to see the King at the apartments of Madame de Maintenon, where Monseigneur happened to be, the Duchesse de Bourgogne praised her, and when she had gone away, ventured, with that freedom and that predetermined impulsiveness and gaiety which she sometimes made use of, to say: "What an excellent wife for M. le Duc de Berry!" This expression made Monseigneur redden with anger, and exclaim, "that would be an excellent method of recompensing the Duc d'Orleans for his conduct in Spain!" When he had said these words he hastily left the company, all very much astonished; for no one expected a person seemingly so indifferent and so measured to come out so strongly. The

Duchesse de Bourgogne, who had only spoken so to feel the way with Monseigneur in presence of the King, was bold and clever to the end. Turning with a bewildered look towards Madame de Maintenon, "My Aunt," quoth she to her, "have I said something foolish?" the King, piqued, answered for Madame de Maintenon, and said, warmly, that if Madame la Duchesse was working upon Monseigneur she would have to deal with him. Madame de Maintenon adroitly envenomed the matter by wondering at a vivacity so uncommon with Monseigneur, and said that if Madame la Duchesse had that much of influence, she would soon make him do other things of more consequence. The conversation, interrupted in various ways and renewed, advanced with emotion, and in the midst of reflections that did more injury to Mademoiselle de Bourbon than the friendship of Monseigneur for Madame la Duchesse could serve her.

When I learned this adventure, I saw that it was necessary to attack Monseigneur by piquing the King against Madame la Duchesse, and making him fear the influence of that Princess on Monseigneur and through Monseigneur on himself; that no opportunity should be lost to impress on the King the fear of being governed and kept in pupilage by his children; that it was equally important to frighten Madame de Maintenon, and show her the danger she was in from the influence of Monseigneur. I worked on the fears of the Duchesse de Bourgogne, by Madame de Villeroy and de Levi; on the Duc de Bourgogne, by M. de Beauvilliers; on Madame de Maintenon, by the Marechal de Boufflers; on the King himself, by the Pere Tellier; and all these batteries succeeded.

In order not to hurry matters too much, I took a turn to La Ferme, and then came back to Marly just as the King arrived. Here I had a little alarm, which did not, however, discourage me. I learned, in fact, that one day the Duchesse de Bourgogne, urged perhaps rather too much on the subject of Mademoiselle by Madame d'O, and somewhat annoyed, had shown an inclination for a foreign marriage. Would to God that such a marriage could have been brought about! I should always have preferred it, but there were many reasons to render it impossible.

On my arrival at Marly, I found everything in trouble there: the King so chagrined that he could not hide it—although usually a master of himself and of his face: the Court believing that some new disaster had happened which would unwillingly be declared. Four or five days passed in this way: at last it became known what was in the wind. The King, informed that Paris and all the public were murmuring loudly about the expenses of Marly—at a time when it was impossible to meet the most indispensable claims of a necessary and unfortunate war—was more annoyed this time than on any other occasion, although he had often received the same warnings. Madame de Maintenon had the greatest difficulty to hinder him from returning straight to Versailles. The upshot was that the King declared with a sort of bitter joy, that he would no longer feed the ladies at Marly; that for the future he would dine alone, simply, as at Versailles; that he would sup every day at a table for sixteen with his family, and that the spare places should be occupied by ladies invited in the morning; that the Princesses of his family should each have a table for the ladies they brought with them; and that Mesdames Voysin and Desmarets should each have one for the ladies who did not choose to eat in their own rooms. He added bitterly, that by making retrenchments at Marly he should not spend more there than at

Versailles, so that he could go there when he pleased without being exposed to the blame of any one. He deceived himself from one end of this business to the other, but nobody but himself was deceived, if indeed he was in any other way but in expecting to deceive the world. The truth is, that no change was made at Marly, except in name. The same expenses went on. The enemies insultingly ridiculed these retrenchments. The King's subjects did not cease to complain.

About this time an invitation to Marly having been obtained by Madame la Duchesse for her daughters, Mademoiselles de Bourbon and de Charolois, the King offered one to Mademoiselle. This offer was discussed before the Duc and Duchesse d'Orleans and me. We at last resolved to leave Mademoiselle at Versailles; and not to be troubled by seeing Mademoiselle de Bourbon passing her days in the same salon, often at the same play- table with the Duc de Berry, making herself admired by the Court, fluttering round Monseigneur, and accustoming the eye of the King to her. We knew that these trifles would not bring about a marriage; and it was still more important not to give up Mademoiselle to the malignity of the Court, to exposure, and complaints, from which it might not always be possible to protect her.

But I had felt that it was necessary to act vigorously, and pressed the Duc d'Orleans to speak to the King. To my surprise he suddenly heaped up objections, derived from the public disasters, with which a princely marriage would contrast disagreeably. The Duchesse d'Orleans was strangely staggered by this admission; it only angered me. I answered by repeating all my arguments. At last he gave way, and agreed to write to the King. Here, again, I had many difficulties to overcome, and was obliged, in fact, to write the letter myself, and dictate it to him. He made one or two changes; and at last signed and sealed it. But I had the greatest difficulty yet in inciting him to give it to the King. I had to follow him, to urge him, to pique him, almost to push him into the presence. The King received the letter very graciously; it had its effect; and the marriage was resolved on.

When the preliminaries were settled, the Duc and Duchesse d'Orleans began to show their desire that Madame de Saint-Simon should be lady of honour to their daughter when she had become the Duchesse de Berry. I was far from flattered by this distinction and refused as best I might. Madame de Saint-Simon went to have an audience of the Duchesse de Bourgogne, and asked not to be appointed; but her objections were not listened to, or listened to with astonishment. Meanwhile I endeavoured to bring about a reconciliation of the Duc d'Orleans with La Choin; but utterly failed. La Choin positively refused to have anything to do with the Duke and Duchess. I was much embarrassed to communicate this news to them, to whom I was attached. It was necessary; however, to do so. I hastened to Saint-Cloud, and found the Duc and Duchesse d'Orleans at table with Mademoiselle and some ladies in a most delightful menagerie, adjoining the railing of the avenue near the village, with a charming pleasure- garden attached to it. All this belonged, under the name of Mademoiselle, to Madame de Mare, her governess. I sat down and chatted with them; but the impatience of the Duc d'Orleans to learn the news could not be checked. He asked me if I was very satisfied. "Middling," I replied, not to spoil his dinner; but he rose at once and took me into the garden. He was much affected to hear of the ill-success of my negotiation; and returned downcast to table. I took the first opportunity to blame his impatience, and the facility with which he allowed the impressions he received to appear. Always in extreme, he said he cared not; and talked wildly of planting cabbages—talk in which he indulged often without meaning anything.

Soon after, M. le Duc d'Orleans went aside with Mademoiselle, and I found myself placed accidentally near Madame de Fontaine-Martel. She was a great friend of mine, and much attached to M. d'Orleans; and it was by her means that I had become friendly with the Duke. She felt at once that something was going on; and did not doubt that the marriage of Mademoiselle was on the carpet. She said so, but I did not answer, yet without assuming an air of reserve that would have convinced her. Taking her text from the presence of M. le Duc d'Orleans with Mademoiselle, she said to me confidentially, that it would be well to hasten this marriage if it was possible, because all sorts of horrible things were invented to prevent it; and without waiting to be too much pressed, she told me that the most abominable stories were in circulation as to the friendship of father and daughter. The hair of my head stood on end. I now felt more heavily than ever with what demons we had to do; and how necessary it was to hurry on matters. For this reason, after we had walked about a good deal after dark, I again spoke with M. d'Orleans, and told him that if, before the end of this voyage to Marly, he did not carry the declaration of his daughter's marriage, it would never take place.

I persuaded him; and left him more animated and encouraged than I had seen him. He amused himself I know not in what other part of the house. I then talked a little with Madame de Mare, my relation and friend, until I was told that Madame de Fontaine-Martel wished to speak to me in the chateau. When I went there I was taken to the cabinet of the Duchesse d'Orleans, when I learnt that she had just been made acquainted with the abominable reports spread against her husband and daughter. We deplored together the misfortune of having to do with such furies. The Duchess protested that there was not even any seeming in favour of these calumnies. The Duke had ever tenderly loved his daughter from the age of two years, when he was nearly driven to despair by a serious illness she had, during which he watched her night and day; and this tenderness had gone on increasing day by day, so that he loved her more than his son. We agreed that it would be cruel, wicked, and dangerous to tell M. d'Orleans what was said.

At length the decisive blow was struck. The King had an interview with Monseigneur; and told him he had determined on the marriage, begging him to make up his mind as soon as possible. The declaration was soon made. What must have been the state of Madame la Duchesse! I never knew what took place in her house at this strange moment; and would have dearly paid for a hiding-place behind the tapestry. As for Monseigneur, as soon as his original repugnance was overcome, and he saw that it was necessary to comply, he behaved very well. He received the Duc and Duchesse d'Orleans very well, and kissed her and drank their health and that of all the family cheerfully. They were extremely delighted and surprised.

My next visit to Saint-Cloud was very different from that in which I reported the failure of my endeavours with Mademoiselle Choin. I was received in triumph before a large company. To my surprise, Mademoiselle, as soon as I appeared, ran towards me, kissed me on both cheeks, took me by the hand, and led me into the orangery. Then she thanked me, and admitted that her father had constantly kept her acquainted with all the negotiations as they went on. I could not help blaming his easiness and imprudence. She mingled all with testimonies of the most lively joy; and I was surprised by her grace, her eloquence, the dignity and the propriety of the terms she used. I learned an immense number of things in this half-hour's conversation. Afterwards Mademoiselle took the opportunity to say and do all manner of graceful things to Madame de Saint-Simon.

The Duchesse d'Orleans now returned once more to the charge, in order to persuade my wife to be dame d'honneur to her daughter. I refused as firmly as I could. But soon after the King himself named Madame de Saint-Simon; and when the Duchesse de Bourgogne suggested a doubt of her acceptance, exclaimed, almost piqued: "Refuse! O, no! not when she learns that it is my desire." In fact, I soon received so many menacing warnings that I was obliged to give in; and Madame de Saint-Simon received the appointment. This was made publicly known by the King, who up to that very morning remained doubtful whether he would be met by a refusal or not; and who, as he was about to speak, looked at me with a smile that was meant to please and warn me to be silent. Madame de Saint-Simon learned the news with tears. She was excellently well received by the King, and complimented agreeably by Madame de Maintenon.

The marriage took place with the usual ceremonies. The Duc de Beauvilliers and Madame de Saint-Simon drew the curtains of the couple when they went to bed; and laughed together at being thus employed. The King, who had given a very mediocre present of diamonds to the new Duchesse de Berry, gave nothing to the Duc de Berry. The latter had so little money that he could not play during the first days of the voyage to Marly. The Duchesse de Bourgogne told this to the King, who, feeling the state in which he himself was, said that he had only five hundred pistoles to give him. He gave them with an excuse on the misfortunes of the time, because the Duchesse de Bourgogne thought with reason that a little was better than nothing, and that it was insufferable not to be able to play.

Madame de Mare was now set at liberty. The place of Dame d'Atours was offered to her; but she advanced many reasons for not accepting it, and on being pressed, refused with an obstinacy that surprised every one. We were not long in finding out the cause of her obstinate unwillingness to remain with Madame la Duchesse de Berry. The more that Princess allowed people to see what she was—and she never concealed herself—the more we saw that Madame de Mare was in the right; and the more we admired the miracle of care and prudence which had prevented anything from coming to light; and the more we felt how blindly people act in what they desire with the most eagerness, and achieve with much trouble and much joy; and the more we deplored having succeeded in an affair which, so far from having undertaken and carried out as I did, I should have traversed with still greater zeal, even if Mademoiselle de Bourbon had profited thereby without knowing it, if I had known half a quarter—what do I say? the thousandth part—of what we unhappily witnessed! I shall say no more for the present; and as I go on, I shall only say what cannot be concealed; and I say thus much so soon merely because the strange things that soon happened began to develop themselves a little during this first voyage to Marly.

CHAPTER LII

On Saturday, the 15th of February, the King was waked up at seven o'clock in the morning, an hour earlier than usual, because Madame la Duchesse de Bourgogne was in the pains of labour. He dressed himself diligently in order to go to her. She did not keep him waiting long. At three minutes and three seconds after eight o'clock, she brought into the world a Duc d'Anjou, who is the King Louis XV., at present reigning, which caused a great joy. This Prince was soon after sprinkled by Cardinal de Janson in the chamber where he was born, and then carried upon the knees of the Duchesse de Ventadour in the sedan chair of the King into the King's apartments, accompanied by the Marechal de Boufflers and by the body-guards with officers. A little while after La Villiere carried to him the cordon bleu, and all the Court went to see him, two things which much displeased his brother, who did not scruple to show it. Madame de Saint-Simon, who was in the chamber of Madame la Dauphine, was by chance one of the first who saw this new-born Prince. The accouchement passed over very well.

About this time died the Marechale de la Meilleraye, aged eighty-eight years. She was the paternal aunt of the Marechal de Villeroy and the Duc de Brissac, his brother-in-law. It was she who unwittingly put the cap on MM. de Brissac, which they have ever since worn in their arms, and which has been imitated. She was walking in a picture gallery of her ancestors one day with her niece, a lively, merry person, whom she obliged to salute and be polite to each portrait, and who in pleasant revenge persuaded her that one of the said portraits wore a cap which proved him to be an Italian Prince. She swallowed this, and had the cap introduced into her, arms, despite her family, who are now obliged to keep it, but who always call it, "My Aunt's cap." On another occasion, people were speaking in her presence of the death of the Chevalier de Savoie, brother of the Comte de Soissons, and of the famous Prince Eugene, who died very young, very suddenly, very debauched; and full of benefices. The talk became religious. She listened some time, and then, with a profound look of conviction, said: "For my part, I am persuaded that God will think twice about damning a man of such high birth as that!" This caused a burst of laughter, but nothing could make her change her opinion. Her vanity was cruelly punished. She used to affect to apologise for having married the Marechal de la Meilleraye. After his death, being in love with Saint-Ruth, her page, she married him; but took care not to disclose her marriage for fear of losing her distinction at Court. Saint-Ruth was a very honourable gentleman, very poor, tall, and well made, whom everybody knew; extremely ugly—I don't know whether he became so after his marriage. He was a worthy man and a good soldier. But he was also a rough customer, and when his distinguished wife annoyed him he twirled his cudgel and belaboured her soundly. This went so far that the Marechale, not being able to stand it any longer, demanded an audience of the King, admitted her weakness and her shame, and implored his protection. The King kindly promised to set matters to rights. He soundly rated Saint-Ruth in his cabinet, and forbade him to ill-treat the Marechale. But what is bred in the bone will never get out of the flesh. The Marechale came to make fresh complaints. The King grew angry in earnest, and threatened Saint-Ruth. This kept him quiet for some time. But the habit of the stick was too powerful; and he flourished it again. The Marechale flew as usual to the King, who, seeing that Saint-Ruth was incorrigible, was good enough to send him to Guyenne under pretence, of employment. Afterwards he was sent to Ireland; where he was killed.

The Marechale de la Meilleraye had been perfectly beautiful, and was full of wit. She so turned the head of the Cardinal de Retz, that he wanted to turn everything topsy-turvy in France, in order to make himself, a necessary man and force the King to use his influence at Rome in order to obtain a dispensation by which he (the Cardinal) should be allowed, though a priest—and a consecrated bishop, to marry the Marechale de la Meilleraye while her husband was alive and she on very good terms with him! This madness is inconceivable and yet existed.

I have described in its place the disgrace of Cardinal de Bouillon, and the banishment to which he was sentenced. Exile did not improve him. He languished in weariness and rage, and saw no hope that his position would ever change. Incapable of repose, he had passed all his long enforced leisure in a monastic war. The monks of Cluni were his antagonists. He was constantly bringing actions against them, which they as constantly defended. He accused them of revolt—they accused him of scheming. They profited by his disgrace, and omitted nothing to shake off the yoke which, when in favour, he had imposed on them. These broils went on, until at last a suit, which Cardinal de Bouillon had commenced against the refractory monks, and which had been carried into Grand Council of Paris, was decided against him, notwithstanding all the efforts he made to obtain a contrary verdict. This was the last drop which made the too full cup overflow, and which consummated the resolution that Cardinal had long since had in his head, and which he now executed.

By the terms of his exile, he was allowed to visit, without restraint, his various abbeys, situated in different parts of the realm. He took advantage of this privilege, gave out that he was going to Normandy, but instead of doing so, posted away to Picardy, stopped briefly at Abbeville, gained Arras, where he had the Abbey of Saint-Waast, thence feigning to go and see his abbey of Vigogne, he passed over into the camp of the enemy, and threw himself into the arms of the Duke of Marlborough and Prince Eugene. The Prince d'Auvergne, his nephew, had deserted from France in a similar manner some time before, as I have related in its place, and was in waiting to receive the Cardinal, who was also very graciously welcomed by Prince Eugene and the Duke of Marlborough, who introduced him to the heads of the army, and lavished upon him the greatest honours.

Such a change of condition appeared very sweet to this spirit so haughty and so ulcerated, and marvellously inflated the Cardinal's courage. He recompensed his dear hosts by discourses, which were the most agreeable to them, upon the misery of France (which his frequent journeys through the provinces had placed before his eyes), upon its powerlessness to sustain the war; upon the discontent which reigned among the people; upon the exhaustion of the finances; in fine, he spared nothing that perfidy or ingratitude could suggest to flatter them and gain their favour.

No sooner had the Cardinal had time to turn round among his new friends than he wrote a letter to the King announcing his flight—a letter which was such a monstrous production of insolence, of madness, of felony, and which was written in a style so extravagant and confused that it deserves to be thus specially alluded to. In this letter, as full of absurdities, impudence, and of madness, as of words, the Cardinal, while pretending much devotion for the King, and much submission to the Church, plainly intimated that he cared for neither. Although this was as the sting of a gnat upon an elephant, the King was horribly piqued at it. He received the letter on the 24th of May, gave it the next day to D'Aguesseau, attorney-general, and ordered him to commence a suit against Cardinal de Bouillon, as guilty of felony. At the same time the King wrote to Rome, enclosing a copy of Bouillon's letter, so that it might be laid before the Pope. This letter received little approbation. People considered that the King had forgotten his dignity in writing it, it seemed so much like a justification and so little worthy, of a great monarch. As for the Cardinal de Bouillon, he grew more haughty than ever. He wrote a letter upon the subject of this trial with which he was threatened, even more violent than his previous letter, and proclaimed that cardinals were not in any way amenable to secular justice, and could not be judged except by the Pope and all the sacred college.

So in fact it seemed to, be; for although the Parliament commenced the trial, and issued an order of arrest against the Cardinal, they soon found themselves stopped by difficulties which arose, and by this immunity of the cardinals, which was supported by many examples. After all the fuss made, therefore, this cause fell by its own weakness, and exhaled itself, so to speak, in insensible perspiration. A fine lesson this for the most powerful princes, and calculated to teach them that if they want to be served by Rome they should favour those that are there, instead of raising their own subjects, who, out of Rome, can be of no service to the State; and who are good only to seize three or four hundred thousand livres a year in benefices, with the quarter of which an Italian would be more than recompensed. A French cardinal in France is the friend of the Pope, but the enemy of the King, the Church, and the State; a tyrant very often to the clergy and the ministers, at liberty to do what he likes without ever being punished for anything.

As nothing could be done in this way against the Cardinal, other steps were taken. The fraudulent "Genealogical History of the House of Auvergne," which I have previously alluded to, was suppressed by royal edict, and orders given that all the copies of it should be seized. Baluze, who had written it, was deprived of his chair of Professor of the Royal College, and driven out of the realm. A large quantity of copies of this edict were printed and publicly distributed. The little patrimony that Cardinal de Bouillon had not been able to carry away, was immediately confiscated: the temporality of his benefices had been already seized, and on the 7th of July appeared a declaration from the King, which, depriving the Cardinal of all his advowsons, distributed them to the bishops of the dioceses in which those advowsons were situated.

These blows were very sensibly felt by the other Bouillons, but it was no time for complaint. The Cardinal himself became more enraged than ever. Even up to this time he had kept so little within bounds that he had pontifically officiated in the church of Tournai at the Te Deum for the taking of Douai (by the enemies); and from that town (Tournai), where he had fixed his residence, he wrote a long letter to M. de Beauvais,— bishop of the place, when it yielded, and who would not sing the Te Deum, exhorting him to return to Tournai and submit to the new rule.

Some time after this, that is to say, towards the end of the year, he was guilty of even greater presumption. The Abbey of Saint-Arnaud, in Flanders, had just been given by the King to Cardinal La Tremoille, who had been confirmed in his possession by bulls from the Pope. Since then the abbey had fallen into the power of the enemy. Upon this, Cardinal de Bouillon caused himself to be elected Abbot by a minority of the monks and in spite of the opposition of the others. It was curious to see this dutiful son of Rome, who had declared in his letter to the King, that he thought of nothing except the dignity of the King, and how he could best. serve God and the Church, thus elect him self in spite of the bull of the Pope, in spite of the orders of the King, and enjoy by force the revenues of the abbey, protected solely by heretics!

But I have in the above recital alluded to the taking of Douai: this reminds me that I have got to speak of our military movements, our losses, and our victories, of this year. In Flanders and in Spain they were of some importance, and had better, perhaps, have a chapter or more to themselves.

CHAPTER LIII

The King, who had made numberless promotions, appointed this year the same generals to the same armies. Villars was chosen for Flanders, as before. Having, arrived at the very summit of favour, he thought he might venture, for the first time in his life, to bring a few truths before the King. He did nothing then but represent to the ministers, nay, even to the King and Madame de Maintenon themselves, the wretched state of our magazines and our garrisons; the utter absence of all provision for the campaign, and the piteous condition of the troops and their officers, without money and without pay. This was new language in the mouth of Villars, who hitherto had owed all his success to the smiling, rose-tinted account he had given of everything. It was the frequency and the hardihood of his falsehoods in this respect that made the King and Madame de Maintenon look upon him as their sole resource; for he never said anything disagreeable, and never found difficulties anywhere. Now that he had raised this fatal curtain, the aspect appeared so hideous to them, that they found it easier to fly into a rage than to reply. From that moment they began to regard Villars with other eyes. Finding that he spoke now the language which everybody spoke, they began to look upon him as the world had always looked upon him, to find him ridiculous, silly, impudent, lying, insupportable; to reproach themselves with having elevated him from nothing, so rapidly and so enormously; they began to shun him, to put him aside, to make him perceive what they thought, and to let others perceive it also.

Villars in his turn was frightened. He saw the prospect of losing what he had gained, and of sinking into hopeless disgrace. With the effrontery that was natural to him, he returned therefore to his usual flatteries, artifices, and deceits; laughed at all dangers and inconveniences, as having resources in himself against everything! The coarseness of this variation was as plain as possible; but the difficulty of choosing another general was equally plain, and Villars thus got out of the quagmire. He set forth for the frontier, therefore, in his coach, and travelling easy stages, on account of his wound, arrived in due time at the army.

Neither Prince Eugene nor the Duke of Marlborough wished for peace; their object was, the first, from personal vengeance against the King, and a desire to obtain a still greater reputation; the second, to get rich, for ambition was the prominent passion of one, and avarice of the other— their object was, I say, to enter France, and, profiting by the extreme weakness and straitened state of our troops and of our places, to push their conquests as far as possible.

As for the King, stung by his continual losses, he wished passionately for nothing so much as a victory, which should disturb the plans of the enemies, and deliver him from the necessity of continuing the sad and shameful negotiations for peace he had set an foot at Gertruydemberg. But the enemies were well posted, end Villars had imprudently lost a good opportunity of engaging them. All the army had noticed this fault; he had been warned in time by several general officers, and by the Marechal de Montesquiou, but he would not believe them. He did not dare to attack the enemies, now, after having left them leisure to make all their dispositions. The army cried aloud against so capital a fault. Villars answered with his usual effrontery. He had quarrelled with his second in command, the Marechal de Montesquiou, and now knew not what to do.

In this crisis, no engagement taking place, the King thought it fitting to send Berwick into Flanders to act as mediator, even, to some extent, as dictator to the army. He was ordered to bring back an account of all things, so that it might be seen whether a battle could or could not be fought.

I think I have already stated who Berwick was; but I will here add a few more words about him to signalise his prodigious and rapid advancement.

We were in the golden age of bastards, and Berwick was a man who had reason to think so. Bastard of James II., of England, he had arrived in France, at the age of eighteen, with that monarch, after the Revolution of 1688. At twenty-two he was made lieutenant-general, and served as such in Flanders, without having passed through any other rank. At thirty-three he commanded in chief in Spain with a patent of general. At thirty-four he was made, on account of his victory at Almanza, Grandee of Spain, and Chevalier of the Golden Fleece. He continued to command in chief until February, 1706, when he was made Marshal of France, being then not more than thirty-six years old. He was an English Duke, and although as such he had no rank in France, the King had awarded it to him, as to all who came over with James. This was making a rapid fortune with a vengeance, under a King who regarded people of thirty-odd as children, but who thought no more of the ages of bastards than of those of the gods.

For more than a year past Berwick had coveted to be made Duke and Peer; But he could not obtain his wish. Now, however, that he was to be sent into Flanders for the purpose I have just described, it seemed a good opportunity to try again. He did try, and was successful. He was made Duke and Peer. He had been twice married. By his first wife he had had a son. By his second several sons and daughters. Will it be believed, that he was hardy enough to propose, and that we were weak enough to accord to him, that his son of the first bed should be formally excluded from the letters-patent of Duke and Peer, and that those of the second bed should alone be entered there? Yet so it was. Berwick was, in respect to England, like the Jews, who await the Messiah. He coaxed himself always with the hope of a revolution in England, which should put the Stuarts on the throne again, and reinstate him in his wealth and honours. He was son of the sister of the Duke of Marlborough, by which general he was much loved, and with whom, by permission of the King, and of King James, he kept up a secret intercourse, of which all three were the dupes, but which enabled Berwick to maintain other intercourses in England, and to establish his batteries there, hoping thus for his reinstatement even under the government established. This explains his motive for the arrangement he made in the letters-patent. He wished his eldest son to succeed to his English dukedom and his English estates; to make the second Duke and Peer of France, and the third Grandee of Spain. Three sons hereditarily elevated to the three chief dignities of the three, chief realms in Europe, it must be agreed was not bad work for a man to have achieved at fifty years of age! But Berwick failed in his English projects. Do what he could all his life to court the various ministers who came from England, he never could succeed in reestablishing himself.

The scandal was great at the complaisance of the King in consenting to a family arrangement, by which a cadet was put over the head of his elder brother; but the time of the monsters had arrived. Berwick bought an estate that he created under the name of Fitz-James. The King, who allowed him to do so, was shocked by the name; and, in my presence, asked Berwick the meaning of it; he, without any embarrassment, thus explained it.

The Kings of England, in legitimatising their children gave them a name and arms, which pass to their posterity. The name varies. Thus the Duke of Richmond, bastard of Charles II., had the name of "Lennox;" the Dukes of Cleveland and of Grafton, by the same king, that of "Fitz-Roi," which means "son of the king;" in fine, the Duke of Berwick had the name of "Fitz-James;" so that his family name for his posterity is thus "Son of James;" as a name, it is so ridiculous in French, that nobody could help laughing at it, or being astonished at the scandal of imposing it in English upon France.

Berwick having thus obtained his recompense beforehand, started off for Flanders, but not until he had seen everything signed and sealed and delivered in due form. He found the enemy so advantageously placed, and so well prepared, that he had no difficulty in subscribing to the common opinion of the general officers, that an attack could no longer be thought of. He gathered up all the opinions he could, and then returned to Court, having been only about three weeks absent. His report dismayed the King, and those who penetrated it. Letters from the army soon showed the fault of which Villars had been guilty, and everybody revolted against this wordy bully.

He soon after was the subject of common talk at the Court, and in the army, in consequence of a ridiculous adventure, in which he was the hero. His wound, or the airs that he gave himself in consequence of it, often forced him to hold his leg upon the neck of his horse, almost in the same manner as ladies do. One day, he let slip the remark that he was sick to death of mounting on horseback like those "harlots" in the suite of Madame de Bourgogne. Those "harlots," I will observe parenthetically, were all the young ladies of the Court, and the daughters of Madame la Duchesse! Such a remark uttered by a general not much loved, speedily flew from one end of the camp to the other, and was not long in making its way to the Court and to Paris. The young horsewomen alluded to were offended; their friends took up arms for them, and Madame la Duchesse de Bourgogne could not help showing irritation, or avoid complaining.

Villars was apprised of all, and was much troubled by this increase of enemies so redoubtable, of whom just then he assuredly had no need. He took it into his head to try and discover who had blabbed; and found it was Heudicourt, whom Villars, to advance his own interests, by means of Heudicourt's mother (who was the evil genius of Madame de Maintenon,) had protected; and to whom even, much against his custom, he had actually not lent, but given money.

This Heudicourt (whom I have previously allluded to, 'a propos' of a song he wrote) was a merry wag who excelled in making fun of people, in highly-seasoned pleasantry, and in comic songs. Spoiled by the favour which had always sustained him, he gave full licence to his tongue, and by this audacity had rendered himself redoubtable. He was a scurrilous wretch, a great drunkard, and a debauchee; not at all cowardly, and with a face hideous as that of an ugly satyr. He was not insensible to this; and so, unfitted for intrigues himself, he assisted others in them, and, by this honest trade, had acquired many friends amongst the flower of the courtiers of both sexes—above all with the ladies. By way of contrast to his wickedness, he was called "the good little fellow" and "the good little fellow" was mixed up in all intrigues; the ladies of the Court positively struggled for him; and not one of them, even of the highest ranks, would have dared to fall out with him. Thus protected, he was rather an embarrassing customer for Marechal de Villars, who, nevertheless, falling back as usual upon his effrontery, hit upon a bright project to bring home to Heudicourt the expedient he had against him.

He collected together about fifteen general officers, and Heudicourt with them. When they had all arrived, he left his chamber, and went to them. A number of loiterers had gathered round. This was just what Villars wanted. He asked all the officers in turn, if they remembered hearing him utter the expression attributed to him. Albergotti said he remembered to have heard Villars apply the term "harlots" to the sutlers and the camp creatures, but never to any other woman. All the rest followed in the same track. Then Villars, after letting out against this frightful calumny, and against the impostor who had written and sent it to the Court, addressed himself to Heudicourt, whom he treated in the most cruel fashion. "The good little fellow" was strangely taken aback, and wished to defend himself; but Villars produced proofs that could not be contradicted. Thereupon the ill-favoured dog avowed his turpitude, and had the audacity to approach Villars in order to speak low to him; but the Marechal, drawing back, and repelling him with an air of indignation, said to him, aloud, that with scoundrels like him he wished for no privacy. Gathering up, his pluck at this, Heudicourt gave rein to all his impudence, and declared that they who had been questioned had not dared to own the truth for fear of offending a Marechal; that as for himself he might have been wrong in speaking and writing about it, but he had not imagined that words said before such a numerous company; and in such a public place, could remain secret, or that he had done more harm in writing about them that so, many others who had acted likewise.

The Marechal, outraged upon hearing so bold and so truthful a reply, let out with, greater violence than ever against Heudicourt, accused him of ingratitude and villainy, drove him away, and a few minutes after had him arrested and conducted as a prisoner to the chateau at Calais. This violent scene made as much stir at the Court and in the army as that which had caused it. The consistent and public conduct of Villars was much approved. The King declared that he left Heudicourt in his hands: Madame de Maintenon and, Madame de Bourgogne, that they abandoned him; and his friends avowed that his fault was inexcusable. But the tide soon turned. After the first hubbub, the excuse of "the good little fellow" appeared excellent to the ladies who had their reasons for liking him and for fearing to irritate him; and also to the army, where the Marechal was not liked. Several of the officers who had been publicly interrogated by Villars, now admitted that they had been taken by surprise, and had not wished to compromise themselves. It was even, going into base details, argued that the Marechal's expression could not apply to the vivandieres and the other camp women, as they always rode astride, one leg on this side one leg on the other, like men, a manner very different from that of the ladies of Madame de Bourgogne. People contested the power of a general to deal out justice upon his inferiors for personal matters in which the service was in nowise concerned; in a word, Heudicourt was soon let out of Calais, and remained "the good little fellow" in fashion in spite of the Marechal, who, tormented by so many things this campaign, sought for and obtained permission to go and take the waters; and did so. He was succeeded by Harcourt, who was himself in weak health. Thus one cripple replaced another. One began, the other ended, at Bourbonne. Douai, Saint-Venant, and Aire fell into the hands of the enemy during this 'campaign, who thus gained upon us more and more, while we did little or nothing. This was the last campaign in Flanders of the Duke of Marlborough. On the Rhine our troops observed and subsisted: nothing more; but in Spain there was more movement, and I will therefore turn my glances towards that country, and relate what took place there.

CHAPTER LIV

Before I commence speaking of the affairs of Spain, let me pass lightly over an event which, engrafted upon some others, made much noise, notwithstanding the care taken to stifle it.

Madame la Duchesse de Bourgogne supped at Saint-Cloud one evening with Madame la Duchesse de Berry and others—Madame de Saint-Simon absenting herself from the party. Madame la Duchesse de Berry and M. d'Orleans— but she more than he—got so drunk, that Madame la Duchesse d'Orleans, Madame la Duchesse de Bourgogne, and the rest of the numerous company there assembled, knew not what to do. M. le Duc de Berry was there, and him they talked over as well as they could; and the numerous company was amused by the Grand Duchess as well as she was able. The effect of the wine, in more ways than one, was such, that people were troubled. In spite of all, the Duchesse de Berry could not be sobered, so that it became necessary to carry her, drunk as she was; to Versailles. All the servants saw her state, and did not keep it to themselves; nevertheless, it was hidden from the King, from Monseigneur, and from Madame de Maintenon.

And now, having related this incident, let me turn to Spain.

The events which took place in that country were so important, that I have thought it best to relate them in a continuous narrative without interruption. We must go back to the commencement of the year, and remember the dangerous state which Spain was thrown into, delivered up to her own weakness, France being too feeble to defend her; finding it difficult enough, in fact, to defend herself, and willing to abandon her ally entirely in the hope by this means to obtain peace.

Towards the end of March the King of Spain set out from Madrid to put himself at the head of his army in Aragon. Villadatias, one of his best and oldest general officers, was chosen to command under him. The King of Spain went from Saragossa to Lerida, where he was received with acclamations by the people and his army. He crossed the Segre on the 14th of May, and advanced towards Balaguier; designing to lay siege to it. But heavy rains falling and causing the waters to rise, he was obliged to abandon his project. Joined a month afterwards by troops arrived from Flanders, he sought to attack the enemy, but was obliged to content himself for the moment by scouring the country, and taking some little towns where the Archduke had established stores. All this time the Count of Staremberg, who commanded the forces of the Archduke, was ill; this circumstance the King of Spain was profiting by. But the Count grew well again quicker than was expected; promptly assembled his forces; marched against the army of the King of Spain; engaged it, and obliged it, all astonished, to retire under Saragossa. This ill-success fell entirely on Villadarias, who was accused of imprudence and negligence. The King of Spain was desperately in want of generals, and M. de Vendome, knowing this, and sick to death of banishment, had asked some little time before to be allowed to offer his services. At first he was snubbed. But the King of Spain, who eagerly wished for M. de Vendome, despatched a courier, after this defeat, begging the King to allow him to come and take command. The King held out no longer.

The Duc de Vendome had prepared everything in advance; and having got over a slight attack of gout, hastened to Versailles. M. du Maine had negotiated with Madame de Maintenon to obtain permission to take Vendome to the Duchesse de Bourgogne. The opportunity seemed favourable to them. Vendome was going to Spain to serve the brother and sister of the Duchess; and his departure without seeing her would have had a very disagreeable effect. The Duc du Maine, followed by Vendome, came then that day to the toilette of the Duchesse de Bourgogne. There happened that there was a very large company of men and ladies. The Duchess rose for them, as she always did for the Princes of the blood and others, and for all the Dukes and Duchesses, and sat down again as usual; but after this first glance, which could not be refused, she, though usually very talkative and accustomed to look round, became for once attentive to her adornment, fixed her eyes on her mirror, and spoke no more to any one. M. du Maine, with M. de Vendome stuck by his side, remained very disconcerted; and M. du Maine, usually so free and easy, dared not utter a single word. Nobody went near them or spoke to them. They remained thus about half a quarter of an hour, with an universal silence throughout the chamber—all eyes being fixed on them; and not being able to stand this any longer, slunk away. This reception was not sufficiently agreeable to induce Vendome to pay his respects at parting; for it would have been more embarrassing still if, when according to custom he advanced to kiss the Duchesse de Bourgogne, she had given him the unheard-of affront of a refusal. As for the Duc de Bourgogne, he received Vendome tolerably politely, that is to say, much too well.

Staremberg meanwhile profited by the advantage he had gained; he attacked the Spanish army under Saragossa and totally defeated it. Artillery, baggage, all was lost; and the rout was complete. This misfortune happened on the 20th of August. The King, who had witnessed it from Saragossa, immediately afterwards took the road for Madrid. Bay, one of his generals, gathered together eighteen thousand men, with whom he retired to Tudela, without any impediment on the part of the enemy.

M. de Vendome learnt the news of this defeat while on his way to Spain. Like a prudent man as he was, for his own interests, he stopped at once so as to see what turn affairs were taking, and to know how to act. He waited at Bayonne, gaining time there by sending a courier to the King for instructions how to act, and remaining until the reply came. After its arrival he set out to continue his journey, and joined the King of Spain at Valladolid.

Staremberg, after his victory, was joined by the Archduke, and a debate soon took place as to the steps next to be taken. Staremberg was for giving battle to the army of eighteen thousand men under Bay, which I have just alluded to, beating it, and then advancing little by little into Spain, to make head against the vanquished army of the King. Had this advice been acted on, it could scarcely have failed to ruin the King of Spain, and the whole country must have fallen into the hands of the enemy. But it was not acted on. Stanhope, who commanded the English and Dutch troops, said that his Queen had ordered him to march upon Madrid when possible, in preference to every other place. He therefore proposed that they should go straight to Madrid with the Archduke, proclaim him King there, and thus terrify all Spain by seizing the capital. Staremberg, who admitted that the project was dazzling, sustained, however, that it was of little use, and of great danger. He tried all in his power to shake the inflexibility of Stanhope, but in vain, and at last was obliged to yield as being the feebler of the two. The time lost in this dispute saved the wreck of the army which had just been defeated. What was afterwards done saved the King of Spain.

When the plan of the allies became known, however, the consternation at Madrid, which was already great, was extreme. The King resolved to withdraw from a place which could not defend itself, and to carry away with him the Queen, the Prince, and the Councils. The grandees declared that they would follow the King and his fortune everywhere, and very few failed to do so; the departure succeeded the declaration in twenty-four hours. The Queen, holding the Prince in her arms, at a balcony of the palace, spoke to the people assembled beneath, with so much grace, force, and courage, that the success she had is incredible. The impression that the people received was communicated everywhere, and soon gained all the provinces. The Court thus left Madrid for the second time in the midst of the most lamentable cries, uttered from the bottom of their hearts, by people who came from town and country, and who so wished to follow the King and Queen that considerable effort was required in order to induce them to return, each one to his home.

Valladolid was the retreat of this wretched Court, which in the most terrible trouble it had yet experienced, lost neither judgment nor courage. Meanwhile the grandest and rarest example of attachment and of courage that had ever been heard of or seen was seen in Spain. Prelates and the humblest of the clergy, noblemen and the poorest people, lawyers and artisans all bled themselves of the last drop of their substance, in order to form new troops and magazines, and to provide all kinds of provisions for the Court, and those who had followed it. Never nation made more efforts so surprising, with a unanimity and a concert which acted everywhere at once. The Queen sold off all she possessed, received with her own hands sometimes even as little as ten pistoles, in order to content the zeal of those; who brought, and thanked them with as much affection as they themselves displayed. She would continually say that she should like to put herself at the head of her troops, with her son in her arms. With this language and her conduct, she gained all hearts, and was very useful in such a strange extremity.

The Archduke meanwhile arrived in Madrid with his army. He entered there in triumph, and caused himself to be proclaimed King of Spain, by the violence of his troops, who dragged the trembling Corregidor through the streets, which for the most part were deserted, whilst the majority of the houses were without inhabitants, the few who remained having barricaded their doors and windows, and shut themselves up in the most remote places, where the troops did not dare to break in upon them, for fear of increasing the visible and general despair, and in the hope of gaining by gentleness. The entry of the Archduke was not less sad than his proclamation. A few scarcely audible and feeble acclamations were heard, but were so forced that the Archduke, sensibly astonished, made them cease of himself. He did not dare to lodge in the palace, or in the centre of Madrid, but slept at the extremity of the city, and even there only for two or three nights. Scarcely any damage was inflicted upon the town. Staremberg was careful to gain over the inhabitants by conciliation and clemency; yet his army perished of all kinds of misery.

Not a single person could be found to supply it with subsistence for man or beast—not even when offered money. Prayers, menaces, executions, all were perfectly useless. There was not a Castilian who would not have believed himself dishonourable in selling the least thing to the enemies, or in allowing them to take it. It is thus that this magnanimous people, without any other help than their courage and their fidelity, sustained themselves in the midst of their enemies, whose army they caused to perish; while at the same time; by inconceivable prodigies, they formed a new army for themselves, perfectly equipped and furnished, and put thus, by themselves; alone, and for the second time, the crown upon the head of their King; with a glory for ever an example to all the people of Europe; so true it is that nothing approaches the strength which is found in the heart of a nation for the succour and re-establishment of kings!

Stanhope, who had not failed to see the excellence of Staremberg's advice from the first moment of their dispute, now said insolently, that having executed the orders of his Queen, it was for Staremberg to draw the army out of its embarrassment. As for himself, he had nothing more to do in the matter! When ten or twelve days had elapsed, it was resolved to remove from Madrid towards Toledo. From the former place nothing was taken away, except same of the king's tapestry; which Stanhope was not ashamed to carry off, but which he did not long keep. This act of meanness was blamed even by his own countrymen. Staremberg did not make a long stay at Toledo, but in quitting the town, burnt the superb palace in the Moorish style that Charles Quint had built there, and that, was called the Alcazar. This was an irreparable damage, which he made believe happened accidentally.

As nothing now hindered the King of Spain from going to see his faithful subjects at Madrid, he entered that city on the 2nd of December, in the midst of an infinite crowd and incredible acclamations. He descended at the church of Notre Dame d'Atocha, and was three hours in arriving at the palace, so prodigious was the crowd. The city made a present to him of twenty thousand pistoles. On the fourth day after his arrival at Madrid, the King left, in order to join M. de Vendome and his army.

But a little while before, this monarch was a fugitive wanderer, almost entirely destroyed, without troops, without money, and without subsistence. Now he found himself at the head of ten or fifteen thousand men well armed, well clad, well paid, with provisions, money, and ammunition in abundance; and this magical change was brought about by the sudden universal conspiracy of the unshakable fidelity and attachment— without example, of all the orders of his subjects; by their efforts and their industry, as prodigious the one as the other.

Vendome, in the utmost surprise at a change so little to be hoped for, wished to profit by it by joining the army under Bay, which was too weak itself to appear before Staremberg. Vendome accordingly set about making this junction, which Staremberg thought only how to hinder. He knew well the Duc de Vendome. In Savoy he had gained many a march upon him; had passed five rivers in front of him; and in spite of him had led his troops to M. de Savoie. Staremberg thought only therefore in what manner he could lay a trap for M. de Vendome, in which he, with his army, might fall and break his neck without hope of escape. With this view he put his army into quarters access to which was easy everywhere, which were near each other, and which could assist each other in case of need. He then placed all his English and Dutch, Stanhope at their head, in Brighuega, a little fortified town in good condition for defence. It was at the head of all the quarters of Staremberg's army, and at the entrance of a plain over which M. de Vendome had to pass to join Bay.

Staremberg was on the point of being joined by his army of Estremadura, so that in the event of M. de Vendeme attacking Brighuega, as he hoped, he had a large number of troops to depend upon.

Vendome, meanwhile, set out on his march. He was informed of Staremberg's position, but in a manner just such as Staremberg wished; that is to say, he was led to believe that Stanhope had made a wrong move in occupying Brighuega, that he was too far removed from Staremberg to receive any assistance from him, and that he could be easily overpowered. That is how matters appeared to Vendome. He hastened his march, therefore, made his dispositions, and on the 8th of December, after mid- day, approached Brighuega, called upon it to surrender, and upon its refusal, prepared to attack it.

Immediately afterwards his surprise was great, upon discovering that there were so many troops in the town, and that instead of having to do with a mere outpost, he was engaged against a place of some consequence. He did not wish to retire, and could not have done so with impunity. He set to therefore, storming in his usual manner, and did what he could to excite his troops to make short work, of a conquest so different from what he had imagined, and so dangerous to delay.

Nevertheless, the weight of his mistake pressed upon him as the hours passed and he saw fresh enemies arrive. Two of his assaults had failed: he determined to play at double or quits, and ordered a third assault. While the dispositions were being made, on the 9th of December he learnt that Staremberg was marching against him with four or five thousand men, that is to say, with just about half of what he really led. In this anguish, Vendome did not hesitate to stake even the Crown of Spain upon the hazard of the die. His third attack was made with all the force of which he was capable. Every one of the assailants knew the extremity of the danger, and behaved with so much valour and impetuosity, that the town was carried in spite of an obstinate resistance. The besieged were obliged to yield, and to the number of eight battalions and eight squadrons, surrendered themselves prisoners of war, and with them, Stanhope, their general, who, so triumphant in Madrid, was here obliged to disgorge the King's tapestries that he had taken from the palace.

While the capitulation was being made, various information came to Vendome of Staremberg's march, which it was necessary, above all, to hide from the prisoners, who, had they known their liberator was only a league and a half distant from them, as he was then, would have broken the capitulation; and defended themselves. M. de Vendome's embarrassment was great. He had, at the same time, to march out and meet Staremberg and to get rid of, his numerous prisoners. All was done, however, very successfully. Sufficient troops were left in Brighuega to attend to the evacuation, and when it was at an end, those troops left the place themselves and joined their comrades, who, with M. de Vendome, were waiting for Staremberg outside the town, at

Villaviciosa, a little place that afterwards gave its name to the battle. Only four hundred men were left in Brighuega.

M. de Vendome arranged his army in order of battle in a tolerably open plain, but embarrassed by little knolls in several places; very disadvantageous for the cavalry. Immediately afterwards the cannon began to fire on both sides, and almost immediately the two links of the King of Spain prepared to charge. After the battle had proceeded some time, M. de Vendome perceived that his centre began to give way, and that the left of his cavalry could not break the right of the enemies. He thought all was lost, and gave orders accordingly to his men to retire towards Torija. Straightway, too, he directed himself in that direction, with the King of Spain and a good part of his troops. While thus retreating, he learnt that two of his officers had charged the enemy's infantry with the cavalry they had at their orders, had much knocked it about and had rendered themselves masters, on the field of battle, of a large number of-prisoners, and of the artillery that the enemy had abandoned. News so agreeable and so little expected determined the Duc de Vendome and the King of Spain to return to the battle with the troops that had followed them. The day was, in fact, won just as night came on. The enemies abandoned twenty pieces of cannon, two mortars, their wounded and their equipages; and numbers of them were taken prisoners. But Staremberg, having all the night to himself, succeeded in retiring in good order with seven or eight thousand men. His baggage and the majority of his waggons fell a prey to the vanquisher. Counting the garrison of Brighuega, the loss to the enemy was eleven thousand men killed or taken, their ammunition, artillery, baggage, and a great number of flags and standards.

When we consider the extreme peril the Crown of Spain ran in these engagements, and that this time, if things had gone ill there was no resource, we tremble still. Had a catastrophe happened, there was nothing to hope from France. Its exhaustion and its losses would not have enabled it to lend aid. In its desire for peace, in fact, it would have hailed the loss of the Spanish Crown as a relief. The imprudence, therefore, of M. de Vendome in so readily falling into the snare laid for him, is all the more to be blamed. He takes no trouble to inform himself of the dispositions of the enemy; he comes upon a place which he believes a mere post, but soon sees it contains a numerous garrison, and finds that the principal part of the enemy's army is ready to fall upon him as he makes the attack. Then he begins to see in what ship he has embarked; he sees the double peril of a double action to sustain against Stanhope, whom he must overwhelm by furious assault, and against Staremberg, whom he must meet and defeat; or, leave to the enemies the Crown of Spain, and perhaps the person of Philip V., as price of his folly. Brighuega is gained, but it is without him. Villaviciosa is gained, but it is also without him. This hero is not sharp-sighted enough to see success when it comes. He thinks it defeat, and gives orders for retreat. When informed that the battle is gained, he returns to the field, and as daylight comes perceives the fact to be so. He is quite without shame for his stupid mistake, and cries out that he has vanquished, with an impudence to which the Spaniards were not accustomed; and, to conclude, he allows Staremberg's army to get clean off, instead of destroying it at once, as he might have done, and so finished the war. Such were the exploits of this great warrior, so desired in Spain to resuscitate it, and such, were the first proofs of his capacity upon arriving in that country!

At the moment that the King of Spain was led back to the battle-field by Vendome, and that they could no longer doubt their good fortune, he sent a courier to the Queen. Her mortal anguish was on the instant changed into so great a joy, that she went out immediately on foot into the streets of Vittoria, where all was delight; as it soon was over all Spain. The news of the victory was brought to the King (of France) by Don Gaspard de Zuniga, who gave an exact account of all that had occurred, hiding nothing respecting M. de Vendome, who was thus unmasked and disgraced, in spite of every effort on the part of his cabal to defend him.

Among the allies, all the blame, of this defeat fell upon Stanhope. Seven or eight hours more of resistance on his part at Brighuega would have enabled Staremberg to come up to his assistance, and all the resources of Spain would then have been annihilated. Staremberg, outraged at the ill-success of his undertaking, cried out loudly against Stanhope. Some of the principal officers who had been at Brighuega seconded these complaints. Stanhope even did not dare to deny his fault. He was allowed to demand leave of absence to go home and defend himself. He was badly received, stripped of all military rank in England and Holland, and (as well as the officers under him) was not without fear of his degradation, and was even in danger of his life.

This recital of the events that took place in Spain has led me away from other matters of earlier date. It is time now that I should return to them.

VOLUME 8.: CHAPTER LV

Although, as we have just seen, matters were beginning to brighten a little in Spain, they remained as dull and overcast as ever in France. The impossibility of obtaining peace, and the exhaustion of the realm, threw, the King into the most cruel anguish, and Desmarets into the saddest embarrassment. The paper of all kinds with which trade was inundated, and which had all more or less lost credit, made a chaos for which no remedy could be perceived. State-bills, bank-bills, receiver- general's-bills, title-bills, utensil-bills, were the ruin of private people, who were forced by the King to take them in payment, and who lost half, two-thirds, and sometimes more, by the transaction. This depreciation enriched the money people, at the expense of the public; and the circulation of money ceased, because there was no longer any money; because the King no longer paid anybody, but drew his revenues still; and because all the specie out of his control was locked up in the coffers of the possessors.

The capitation tax was doubled and trebled, at the will of the Intendants of the Provinces; merchandise and all kinds of provision were taxed to the amount of four times their value; new taxes of all kinds and upon all sorts of things were exacted; all this crushed nobles and roturiers, lords and clergy, and yet did not bring enough to the King, who drew the blood of all his subjects, squeezed out their very marrow, without distinction, and who enriched an army of tax-gatherers and officials of all kinds, in whose hands the best part of what was collected remained.

Desmarets, in whom the King had been forced to put all his confidence in finance matters, conceived the idea of establishing, in addition to so many taxes, that Royal Tithe upon all the property of each community and of each private person of the realm, that the Marechal de Vauban, on the one hand, and Boisguilbert on the other, had formerly proposed; but, as I have already described, as a simple and stile tax which would suffice for all, which would all enter the coffers of the King, and by means of which every other impost would be abolished.

We have seen what success this proposition met with; how the fanciers trembled at it; how the ministers blushed at it, with what anathemas it was rejected, and to what extent these two excellent and skilful citizens were disgraced. All this must be recollected here, since Desmarets, who had not lost sight of this system (not as relief and remedy—unpardonable crimes in the financial doctrine), now had recourse to it.

He imparted his project to three friends, Councillors of State, who examined it well, and worked hard to see how to overcome the obstacles which arose in the way of its execution. In the first place, it was necessary, in order to collect this tax, to draw from each person a clear statement of his wealth, of his debts, and so on. It was necessary to demand sure proofs on these points so as not to be deceived. Here was all the difficulty. Nothing was thought of the desolation this extra impost must cause to a prodigious number of men, or of their despair upon finding themselves obliged to disclose their family secrets; to hate a lamp thrown, as it were, upon their most delicate parts; all these things, I say, went for nothing. Less than a month sufficed these humane commissioners to render an account of this gentle project to the Cyclops who had charged them with it. Desmarets thereupon proposed it to the King, who, accustomed as he was to the most ruinous imposts, could not avoid being terrified at this. For a long while he had heard nothing talked of but the most extreme misery; this increase saddened him in a manner so evident, that his valets perceived it several days running, and were so disturbed at it, that Marechal (who related all this curious anecdote to me) made bold to speak to the King upon this sadness, fearing for his health. The King avowed to him that he felt infinite trouble, and threw himself vaguely upon the state of affairs. Eight or ten days. after (during which he continued to feel the same melancholy), the King regained his usual calmness, and called Marechal to explain the cause of his trouble.

The King related to Marechal that the extremity of his affairs had forced him to put on furious imposts; that setting aside compassion, scruples had much tormented him for taking thus the wealth of his subjects; that at last he had unbosomed himself to the Pere Tellier, who had asked for a few days to think upon the matter, and that he had returned after having had a consultation with some of the most skilful doctors of the Sorbonne, who had decided that all the wealth of his subjects was his, and that when he took it he only took what belonged to him! The King added, that this decision had taken away all his scruples, and had restored to him the calm and tranquillity he had lost. Marechal was so astonished, so bewildered to hear, this recital, that he could not offer one word. Happily for him, the King quitted him almost immediately, and Marechal remained some time in the same place, scarcely knowing where he was.

After the King had been thus satisfied by his confessor, no time was lost in establishing the tax. On Tuesday, the 30th of September, Desmarets entered the Finance Council with the necessary edict in his bag.

For some days everybody had known of this bombshell in the air, and had trembled with that remnant of hope which is founded only upon desire; all the Court as well as all Paris waited in a dejected sadness to see what would happen. People whispered to each other, and even when the project was rendered public, no one dared to talk of it aloud.

On the day above-named, the King brought forward this measure in the Council, by saying, that the impossibility of obtaining peace, and the extreme difficulty of sustaining the war, had caused Desmarets to look about in order to discover some means, which should appear good, of raising money; that he had pitched upon this tax; that he (the King), although sorry to adopt such a resource, approved it, and had no doubt the Council would do so likewise, when it was explained to them. Desmarets, in a pathetic discourse, then dwelt upon the reasons which had induced him to propose this tax, and afterwards read the edict through from beginning to end without interruption.

No one spoke, moreover, when it was over, until the King asked D'Aguesseau his opinion. D'Aguesseau replied, that it would be necessary for him to take home the edict and read it through very carefully before expressing an opinion. The King said that D'Aguesseau was right—it would take a long time to examine the edict—but after all, examination was unnecessary, and would only be loss of time. All remained silent again, except the Duc de Beauvilliers, who, seduced by the nephew of Colbert, whom he thought an oracle in finance, said a few words in favour of the project.

Thus was settled this bloody business, and immediately after signed, sealed, and registered, among stifled sobs, and published amidst the most gentle but most piteous complaints. The product of this tax was nothing like so much as had been imagined in this bureau of Cannibals; and the King did not pay a single farthing more to any one than he had previously done. Thus all the fine relief expected by this tax ended in smoke.

The Marechal de Vauban had died of grief at the ill-success of his task and his zeal, as I have related in its place. Poor Boisguilbert, in the exile his zeal had brought him, was terribly afflicted, to find he had innocently given advice which he intended for the relief of the State, but which had been made use of in this frightful manner. Every man, without exception, saw himself a prey to the tax-gatherers: reduced to calculate and discuss with them his own patrimony, to receive their signature and their protection under the most terrible pains; to show in public all the secrets of his family; to bring into the broad open daylight domestic turpitudes enveloped until then in the folds of precautions the wisest and the most multiplied. Many had to convince the tax agents, but vainly, that although proprietors, they did not enjoy the tenth part of them property. All Languedoc offered to give up its entire wealth, if allowed to enjoy, free from every impost, the tenth part of it. The proposition not only was not listened to, but was reputed an insult and severely blamed.

Monseigneur le Duc de Bourgogne spoke openly against this tax; and against the finance people, who lived upon the very marrow of the people; spoke with a just and holy anger that recalled the memory of Saint-Louis, of Louis XII., Father of the People, and of Louis the Just. Monseigneur, too, moved by this indignation, so unusual, of his son, sided with him, and showed anger at so many exactions as injurious as barbarous, and at so many insignificant men so monstrously enriched with the nation's blood. Both father and son infinitely surprised those who heard them, and made themselves looked upon, in some sort as resources from which something might hereafter be hoped for. But the edict was issued, and though there might be some hope in the future, there was none in the present. And no one knew who was to be the real successor of Louis XIV., and how under the next government we were to be still more overwhelmed than under this one.

One result of this tax was, that it enabled the King to augment all his infantry with five men per company.

A tax was also levied upon the usurers, who had much gained by trafficking in the paper of the King, that is to say, had taken advantage of the need of those to whom the King gave this paper in payment. These usurers are called 'agioteurs'. Their mode was, ordinarily, to give, for example, according as the holder of paper was more or less pressed, three or four hundred francs (the greater part often in provisions), for a bill of a thousand francs! This game was called 'agio'. It was said that thirty millions were obtained from this tax. Many people gained much by it; I know not if the King was the better treated.

Soon after this the coin was re-coined, by which much profit was made for the King, and much wrong done to private people and to trade. In all times it has, been regarded as a very great misfortune to meddle with corn and money. Desmarets has accustomed us to tricks with the money; M. le Duc and Cardinal Fleury to interfere with corn and to fictitious famine.

At the commencement of December, the King declared that he wished there should be, contrary to custom, plays and "apartments" at Versailles even when Monseigneur should be at Meudon. He thought apparently he must keep his Court full of amusements, to hide, if it was possible, abroad and at home, the disorder and the extremity of affairs. For the same reason, the carnival was opened early this season, and all through the winter there were many balls of all kinds at the Court, where the wives of the ministers gave very magnificent displays, like fetes, to Madame la Duchesse de Bourgogne and to all the Court.

But Paris did not remain less wretched or the provinces less desolated.

And thus I have arrived at the end of 1710.

At the commencement of the following year, 1711, that is to say, a few days after the middle of March, a cruel misfortune happened to the Marechal de Boufflers. His eldest son was fourteen years of age, handsome, well made, of much promise, and who succeeded marvellously at the Court, when his father presented him there to the King to thank his Majesty for the reversion of the government of Flow and of Lille. He returned afterwards to the College of the Jesuits, where he was being educated. I know not what youthful folly he was guilty of with the two sons of D'Argenson; but the Jesuits, wishing to show that they made no distinction of persons, whipped the little lad, because, to say the truth, they had nothing to fear from the Marechal de Boufflers; but they took good care to left the others off, although equally guilty, because they had to reckon with D'Argenson, lieutenant of the police, of much credit in book matters, Jansenism, and all sorts of things and affairs in which they were interested.

Little Boufflers, who was full of courage, and who had done no more than the two Argensons, and with them, was seized with such despair, that he fell ill that same day. He was carried to the Marechal's house, but it was impossible to save him. The heart was seized, the blood diseased, the purples appeared; in four days all was over. The state of the father and mother may be imagined! The King, who was much touched by it, did not let them ask or wait for him. He sent one of his gentlemen to testify to them the share he had in their loss, and announced that he would give to their remaining son 'what he had already given to the other. As for the Jesuits, the universal cry against them was prodigious; but that was all. This would be the place, now that I am speaking of the Jesuits, to speak of another affair in which they were concerned. But I pass over, for the present, the dissensions that broke out at about this time, and that ultimately led to the famous Papal Bull Unigenitus, so fatal to the Church and to the State, so shameful far Rome, and so injurious to religion; and I proceed to speak of the great event of this year which led to others so memorable and so unexpected.

CHAPTER LVI

But in Order to understand the part I played in the event I have alluded to and the interest I took in it, it is necessary for me to relate some personal matters that occurred in the previous year. Du Mont was one of the confidants of Monseigneur; but also had never forgotten what his father owed to mine. Some days after the commencement of the second voyage to Marly, subsequently to the marriage of the Duchesse de Berry, as I was coming back from the King's mass, the said Du Mont, in the crush at the door of the little salon of the chapel, took an opportunity when he was not perceived, to pull me by my coat, and when I turned round put a finger to his lips, and pointed towards the gardens which are at the bottom of the river, that is to say, of that superb cascade which the Cardinal Fleury has destroyed, and which faced the rear of the chateau. At the same time du Mont whispered in my car: "To the arbours!" That part of the garden was surrounded with arbours palisaded so as to conceal what was inside. It was the least frequented place at Marly, leading to nothing; and in the afternoon even, and the evening, few people within them.

Uneasy to know what Du Mont wished to communicate with so much mystery, I gently went towards the arbours where, without being seen, I looked through one of the openings until I saw him appear. He slipped in by the corner of the chapel, and I went towards him. As he joined me he begged me to return towards the river, so as to be still more out of the way; and then we set ourselves against the thickest palisades, as far as possible from all openings, so as to be still more concealed. All this surprised and frightened me: I was still more so when I learned what was the matter.

Du Mont then told me, on condition that I promised not to show that I knew it, and not to make use of my knowledge in any way without his consent, that two days after the marriage of the Duc de Berry, having entered towards the end of the morning the cabinet of Monseigneur, he found him alone, looking very serious. He followed Monseigneur, through the gardens alone, until he entered by the window the apartments of the Princesse de Conti, who was also alone. As he entered Monseigneur said with an air not natural to him, and very inflamed—as if by way of interrogation—that she "sat very quietly there." This frightened her so, that she asked if there was any news from Flanders, and what had happened. Monseigneur answered, in a tone of great annoyance, that there was no news except that the Duc de Saint-Simon had said, that now that the marriage of the Duc de Berry was brought about, it would be proper to drive away Madame la Duchesse and the Princesse de Conti, after which it would be easy to govern "the great imbecile," meaning himself. This was why he thought she ought not to be so much at her ease. Then, suddenly, as if lashing his sides to get into a greater rage, he spoke in a way such a speech would have deserved, added menaces, said that he would have the Duc de Bourgogne to fear me, to put me aside, and separate himself entirely from me. This sort of soliloquy lasted a long time, and I was not told what the Princesse de Conti said to it; but from the silence of Du Mont, her annoyance at the marriage, I had brought about, and other reasons, it seems to me unlikely that she tried to soften Monseigneur.

Du Mont begged me not, for a long time at least, to show that I knew what had taken place, and to behave with the utmost prudence. Then he fled away by the path he had come by, fearing to be seen. I remained walking up and down in the arbour all the time, reflecting on the wickedness of my enemies, and the gross credulity of Monseigneur. Then I ran away, and escaped to Madame de Saint-Simon, who, as astonished and frightened as I, said not a word of the communication I had received.

I never knew who had served me this ill-turn with Monseigneur, but I always suspected Mademoiselle de Lillebonne. After a long time, having obtained with difficulty the consent of the timid Du Mont, I made Madame de Saint-Simon speak to the Duchesse de Bourgogne, who undertook to arrange the affair as well as it could be arranged. The Duchesse spoke indeed to Monseigneur, and showed him how ridiculously he had been deceived, when he was persuaded that I could ever have entertained the ideas attributed to me. Monseigneur admitted that he had been carried away by anger; and that there was no likelihood that I should have thought of anything so wicked and incredible.

About this time the household of the Duc and Duchesse de Berry was constituted. Racilly obtained the splendid appointment of first surgeon, and was worthy of it; but the Duchesse de Berry wept bitterly, because she did not consider him of high family enough. She was not so delicate about La Haye, whose appointment she rapidly secured. The fellow looked in the glass more complaisantly than ever. He was well made, but stiff, and with a face not at all handsome, and looking as if it had been skinned. He was happy in more ways than one, and was far more attached to his new mistress than to his master. The King was very angry when he learned that the Duc de Berry had supplied himself with such an assistant.

Meantime, I continued on very uneasy terms with Monseigneur, since I had learned his strange credulity with respect to me. I began to feel my position very irksome, not to say painful, on this account. Meudon I would not go to—for me it was a place infested with demons—yet by stopping away I ran great risks of losing the favour and consideration I enjoyed at Court. Monseigneur was a man so easily imposed upon, as I had already experienced, and his intimate friends were so unscrupulous that there was no saying what might be invented on the one side and swallowed on the other, to my discredit. Those friends, too, were, I knew, enraged against me for divers weighty reasons, and would stop at nothing, I was satisfied, to procure my downfall. For want of better support I sustained myself with courage. I said to myself, "We never experience all the evil or all the good that we have apparently the most reason to expect." I hoped, therefore, against hope, terribly troubled it must be confessed on the score of Meudon. At Easter, this year, I went away to La Ferme, far from the Court and the world, to solace myself as I could; but this thorn in my side was cruelly sharp! At the moment the most unlooked-for it pleased God to deliver me from it.

At La Ferme I had but few guests: M. de Saint-Louis, an old brigadier of cavalry, and a Normandy gentleman, who had been in my regiment, and who was much attached to me. On Saturday, the 11th of the month, and the day before Quasimodo, I had been walking with them all the morning, and I had entered all-alone into my cabinet a little before dinner, when a courier sent by Madame de Saint-Simon, gave me a letter from her, in which I was informed that Monseigneur was ill!

I learnt afterwards that this Prince, while on his way to Meudon for the Easter fetes, met at Chaville a priest, who was carrying Our Lord to a sick person. Monseigneur, and Madame de Bourgogne, who was with him, knelt down to adore the Host, and then Monseigneur inquired what was the malady of the patient. "The small-pox," he was told. That disease was very prevalent just then. Monseigneur had had it, but very lightly, and when young. He feared it very much, and was struck with the answer he now received. In the evening he said to Boudin, his chief doctor, "I should not be surprised if I were to have the small-pox." The day, however, passed over as usual.

On the morrow, Thursday, the 9th, Monseigneur rose, and meant to go out wolf-hunting; but as he was dressing, such a fit of weakness seized him, that he fell into his chair. Boudin made him get into bed again; but all the day his pulse was in an alarming state. The King, only half informed by Fagon of what had taken place, believed there was nothing the matter, and went out walking at Marly after dinner, receiving news from time to time. Monseigneur le Duc de Bourgogne and Madame de Bourgogne dined at Meudon, and they would not quit Monseigneur for one moment. The Princess added to the strict duties of a daughter-in-law all that her gracefulness could suggest, and gave everything to Monseigneur with her own hand. Her heart could not have been troubled by what her reason foresaw; but, nevertheless, her care and attention were extreme, without any airs of affectation or acting. The Duc de Bourgogne, simple and holy as he was, and full of the idea of his duty, exaggerated his attention; and although there was a strong suspicion of the small-pox, neither quitted Monseigneur, except for the King's supper.

The next day, Friday, the 10th, in reply to his express demands, the King was informed of the extremely dangerous state of Monseigneur. He had said on the previous evening that he would go on the following morning to Meudon, and remain there during all the illness of Monseigneur whatever its nature might be. He was now as good as his word. Immediately after mass he set out for Meudon. Before doing so, he forbade his children, and all who had not had the small-pox, to go there, which was suggested by a motive of kindness. With Madame de Maintenon and a small suite, he had just taken up his abode in Meudon, when Madame de Saint-Simon sent me the letter of which I have just made mention.

I will continue to speak of myself with the same truthfulness I speak of others, and with as much exactness as possible. According to the terms on which I was with Monseigneur and his intimates, may be imagined the impression made upon me by this news. I felt that one way or other, well or ill, the malady of Monseigneur would soon terminate. I was quite at my ease at La Ferme. I resolved therefore to wait there until I received fresh particulars. I despatched a courier to Madame de Saint-Simon, requesting her to send me another the next day, and I passed the rest of this day, in an ebb and flow of feelings; the man and the Christian struggling against the man and the courtier, and in the midst of a crowd of vague fancies catching glimpses of the future, painted in the most agreeable colours.

The courier I expected so impatiently arrived the next day, Sunday, after dinner. The small-pox had declared itself, I learnt, and was going on as well as could be wished. I believed Monseigneur saved, and wished to remain at my own house; nevertheless I took advice, as I have done all my life, and with great regret set out the next morning. At La queue, about six leagues from Versailles, I met a financier of the name of La Fontaine, whom I knew well. He was coming from Paris and Versailles, and came up to me as I changed horses. Monseigneur, he said, was going on admirably; and he added details which convinced me he was out of all danger. I arrived at Versailles, full of this opinion, which was confirmed by Madame de Saint-Simon and everybody I met, so that nobody any longer feared, except on account of the treacherous nature of this disease in a very fat man of fifty.

The King held his Council, and worked in the evening with his ministers as usual. He saw Monseigneur morning and evening, oftentimes in the afternoon, and always remained long by the bedside. On the Monday I arrived he had dined early, and had driven to Marly, where the Duchesse de Bourgogne joined him. He saw in passing on the outskirts of the garden of Versailles his grandchildren, who had come out to meet him, but he would not let them come near, and said, "good day" from a distance. The Duchesse de Bourgogne had had the small-pox, but no trace was left.

The King only liked his own houses, and could not bear to be anywhere else. This was why his visits to Meudon were few and short, and only made from complaisance. Madame de Maintenon was still more out of her element there. Although her chamber was everywhere a sanctuary, where only ladies entitled to the most extreme familiarity entered, she always wanted another retreat near at hand entirely inaccessible except to the Duchesse de Bourgogne alone, and that only for a few instants at a time. Thus she had Saint-Cyr for Versailles and for Marly; and at Marly also a particular retiring place; at Fontainebleau she had her town house. Seeing therefore that Monseigneur was getting on well, and that a long sojourn it Meudon would be necessary, the upholsterers of the King were ordered to furnish a house in the park which once belonged to the Chancellor le Tellier, but which Monseigneur had bought.

When I arrived at Versailles, I wrote to M. de Beauvilliers at Meudon praying him to apprise the King that I had returned on account of the illness of Monseigneur, and that I would have gone to see him, but that, never having had the small-pox, I was included in the prohibition. M. de Beauvilliers did as I asked, and sent word back to me that my return had been very well timed, and that the King still forbade me as well as Madame de Saint-Simon to go to Meudon. This fresh prohibition did not distress me in the least. I was informed of all that was passing there; and that satisfied me.

There were yet contrasts at Meudon worth noticing. Mademoiselle Choin never appeared while the King was with Monseigneur, but kept close in her loft. When the coast was clear she came out, and took up her position at the sick man's bedside. All sorts of compliments passed between her and Madame de Maintenon, yet the two ladies never met. The King asked Madame de Maintenon if she had seen Mademoiselle Choin, and upon learning that she had not, was but ill-pleased. Therefore Madame de Maintenon sent excuses and apologies to Mademoiselle Choin, and hoped she said to see her soon,—strange compliments from one chamber to another under the same roof. They never saw each other afterwards.

It should be observed, that Pere Tellier was also incognito at Meudon, and dwelt in a retired room from which he issued to see the King, but never approached the apartments of Monseigneur.

Versailles presented another scene. Monseigneur le Duc and Madame la Duchesse de Bourgogne held their Court openly there; and this Court resembled the first gleamings of the dawn. All the Court assembled there; all Paris also; and as discretion and precaution were never French virtues, all Meudon came as well. People were believed on their word when they declared that they had not entered the apartments of Monseigneur that day, and consequently could not bring the infection. When the Prince and Princess rose, when they weft to bed, when they dined and supped with the ladies,—all public conversations—all meals—all assembled—were opportunities of paying court to them. The apartments could not contain the crowd. The characteristic features of the room were many. Couriers arrived every quarter of an hour, and reminded people of the illness of Monseigneur—he was going on as well as could be expected; confidence and hope were easily felt; but there was an extreme desire to please at the new Court. The young Prince and the Princess exhibited majesty and gravity, mixed with gaiety; obligingly received all, continually spoke to every one; the crowd wore an air of complaisance; reciprocal satisfaction showed in every face; the Duc and Duchesse de Berry ware treated almost as nobody. Thus five days fled away in increasing thought of future events—in preparation to be ready for whatever might happen.

On Tuesday, the 14th of April, I went to see the chancellor, and asked for information upon the state of Monseigneur. He assured me it was good, and repeated to me the words Fagon had spoken to him, "that things were going an according to their wishes, and beyond their hopes." The Chancellor appeared to me very confident, and I had faith in him, so much the more, because he was on extremely good footing with Monseigneur. The Prince, indeed, had so much recovered, that the fish-women came in a body the self-same day to congratulate him, as they did after his attack of indigestion. They threw the themselves at the foot of his bed, which they kissed several times, and in their joy said they would go back to Paris and have a Te Deum sung. But Monseigneur, who was not insensible to these marks of popular affection, told them it was not yet time, thanked them, and gave them a dinner and some money.

As I was going home, I saw the Duchesse d'Orleans walking on a terrace. She called to me; but I pretended not to notice her, because La Montauban was with her, and hastened home, my mind filled with this news, and withdrew to my cabinet. Almost immediately afterwards Madame la Duchesse d'Orleans joined me there. We were bursting to speak to each other alone, upon a point on which our thoughts were alike. She had left Meudon not an hour before, and she had the same tale to tell as the Chancellor. Everybody was at ease there she said; and then she extolled the care and capacities of the doctors, exaggerating their success; and, to speak frankly and to our shame, she and I lamented together to see Monseigneur, in spite of his age and his fat, escape from so dangerous an illness. She reflected seriously but wittily, that after an illness of this sort, apoplexy was not to be looked for; that an attack of indigestion was equally unlikely to arise, considering the care Monseigneur had taken not to over-gorge himself since his recent danger; and we concluded more than dolefully, that henceforth we must make up our minds that the Prince would live and reign for a long time. In a word, we let ourselves loose in this rare conversation, although not without an occasional scruple of conscience which disturbed it. Madame de Saint-Simon all devoutly tried what she could to put a drag upon our tongues, but the drag broke, so to speak, and we continued our free discourse, humanly speaking very reasonable on our parts, but which we felt, nevertheless, was not according to religion. Thus two hours passed, seemingly very short. Madame d'Orleans went away, and I repaired with Madame de Saint-Simon to receive a numerous company.

While thus all was tranquillity at Versailles, and even at Meudon, everything had changed its aspect at the chateau. The King had seen Monseigneur several times during the day; but in his after-dinner visit he was so much struck with the extraordinary swelling of the face and of the head, that he shortened his stay, and on leaving the chateau, shed tears. He was reassured as much as possible, and after the council he took a walk in the garden.

Nevertheless Monseigneur had already mistaken Madame la Princesse de Conti for some one else; and Boudin, the doctor, was alarmed. Monseigneur himself had been so from the first, and he admitted, that for a long time before being attacked, he had been very unwell, and so much on Good Friday, that he had been unable to read his prayer-book at chapel.

Towards four o'clock he grew worse, so much so that Boudin proposed to Fagon to call in other doctors, more familiar with the disease than they were. But Fagon flew into a rage at this, and would call in nobody. He declared that it would be better to act for themselves, and to keep Monseigneur's state secret, although it was hourly growing worse, and towards seven o'clock was perceived by several valets and courtiers. But nobody dared to open his mouth before Fagon, and the King was actually allowed to go to supper and to finish it without interruption, believing on the faith of Fagon that Monseigneur was going on well.

While the King supped thus tranquilly, all those who were in the sick- chamber began to lose their wits. Fagon and the others poured down physic on physic, without leaving time for any to work. The Cure, who was accustomed to go and learn the news every evening, found, against all custom, the doors thrown wide open, and the valets in confusion. He entered the chamber, and perceiving what was the matter, ran to the bedside, took the hand of Monseigneur, spoke to him of God, and seeing him full of consciousness, but scarcely able to speak, drew from him a sort of confession, of which nobody had hitherto thought, and suggested some acts of contrition. The poor Prince repeated distinctly several words suggested to him, and confusedly answered others, struck his breast, squeezed the Cure's hand, appeared penetrated with the best sentiments, and received with a contrite and willing air the absolution of the Cure.

As the King rose from the supper-table, he well-nigh fell backward when Fagon, coming forward, cried in great trouble that all was lost. It may be imagined what terror seized all the company at this abrupt passage from perfect security to hopeless despair. The King, scarcely master of himself, at once began to go towards the apartment of Monseigneur, and repelled very stiffly the indiscreet eagerness of some courtiers who wished to prevent him, saying that he would see his son again, and be quite certain that nothing could be done. As he was about to enter the chamber, Madame la Princesse de Conti presented herself before him, and prevented him from going in. She pushed him back with her hands, and said that henceforth he had only to think of himself. Then the King, nearly fainting from a shock so complete and so sudden, fell upon a sofa that stood near. He asked unceasingly for news of all who passed, but scarce anybody dared to reply to him. He had sent for here Tellier, who went into Monseigneur's room; but it was no longer time. It is true the Jesuit, perhaps to console the King, said that he gave him a well-founded absolution. Madame de Maintenon hastened after the King, and sitting down beside him on the same sofa, tried to cry. She endeavoured to lead away the King into the carriage already waiting for him in the courtyard, but he would not go, and sat thus outside the door until Monseigneur had expired.

The agony, without consciousness, of Monseigneur lasted more than an hour after the King had come into the cabinet. Madame la Duchesse and Madame la Princesse de Conti divided their cares between the dying man and the King, to whom they constantly came back; whilst the faculty confounded, the valets bewildered, the courtiers hurrying and murmuring, hustled against each other, and moved unceasingly to and fro, backwards and forwards, in the same narrow space. At last the fatal moment arrived. Fagon came out, and allowed so much to be understood.

The King, much afflicted, and very grieved that Monseigneur's confession had been so tardily made, abused Fagon a little; and went away led by Madame de Maintenon and the two Princesses. He was somewhat struck by finding the vehicle of Monseigneur outside; and made a sign that he would have another coach, for that one made him suffer, and left the chateau. He was not, however, so much occupied with his grief that he could not call Pontchartrain to arrange the hour of the council on the next day. I will not comment on this coolness, and shall merely say it surprised extremely all present; and that if Pontchartrain had not said the council could be put off, no interruption to business would have taken place. The King got into his coach with difficulty, supported on both sides. Madame de Maintenon seated herself beside him. A crowd of officers of Monseigneur lined both sides of the court on their knees, as he passed out, crying to him with strange howlings to have compassion on them, for they had lost all, and must die of hunger.

CHAPTER LVII

While Meudon was filled with horror, all was tranquil at Versailles, without the least suspicion. We had supped. The company some time after had retired, and I was talking with Madame de Saint-Simon, who had nearly finished undressing herself to go to bed, when a servant of Madame la Duchesse de Berry, who had formerly belonged to us, entered, all terrified. He said that there must be some bad news from Meudon, since Monseigneur le Duc de Bourgogne had just whispered in the ear of M. le Duc de Berry, whose eyes had at once become red, that he left the table, and that all the company shortly after him rose with precipitation. So sudden a change rendered my surprise extreme. I ran in hot haste to Madame la Duchesse de Berry's. Nobody was there. Everybody had gone to Madame la Duchesse de Bourgogne. I followed on with all speed.

I found all Versailles assembled on arriving, all the ladies hastily dressed—the majority having been on the point of going to bed—all the doors open, and all in trouble. I learnt that Monseigneur had received the extreme unction, that he was without consciousness and beyond hope, and that the King had sent word to Madame de Bourgogne that he was going to Marly, and that she was to meet him as he passed through the avenue between the two stables.

The spectacle before me attracted all the attention I could bestow. The two Princes and the two Princesses were in the little cabinet behind the bed.

The bed toilette was as usual in the chamber of the Duchesse de Bourgogne, which was filled with all the Court in confusion. She came and went from the cabinet to the chamber, waiting for the moment when she was to meet the King; and her demeanour, always distinguished by the same graces, was one of trouble and compassion, which the trouble and compassion of others induced them to take for grief. Now and then, in passing, she said a few rare words. All present were in truth expressive personages. Whoever had eyes, without any knowledge of the Court, could see the interests of all interested painted on their faces, and the indifference of the indifferent; these tranquil, the former penetrated with grief, or gravely attentive to themselves to, hide their emancipation and their joy.

For my part, my first care was to inform myself thoroughly of the state of affairs, fearing lest there might be too much alarm for too trifling a cause; then, recovering myself, I reflected upon the misery common to all men, and that I myself should find myself some day at the gates of death. Joy, nevertheless, found its way through the momentary reflections of religion and of humanity, by which I tried to master myself. My own private deliverance seemed so great and so unhoped for, that it appeared to me that the State must gain everything by such a loss. And with these thoughts I felt, in spite of myself, a lingering fear lest the sick man should recover, and was extremely ashamed of it.

Wrapped up thus in myself, I did not fail, nevertheless, to cast clandestine looks upon each face, to see what was passing there. I saw Madame la Duchesse d'Orleans arrive, but her countenance, majestic and constrained, said nothing. She went into the little cabinet, whence she presently issued with the Duc d'Orleans, whose activity and turbulent air marked his emotion at the spectacle more than any other sentiment. They went away, and I notice this expressly, on account of what happened afterwards in my presence.

Soon afterwards I caught a distant glimpse of the Duc de Bourgogne, who seemed much moved and troubled; but the glance with which I probed him rapidly, revealed nothing tender, and told merely of a mind profoundly occupied with the bearings of what had taken place.

Valets and chamber-women were already indiscreetly crying out; and their grief showed well that they were about to lose something!

Towards half-past twelve we had news of the King, and immediately after Madame de Bourgogne came out of the little cabinet with the Duke, who seemed more touched than when I first saw him. The Princess took her scarf and her coifs from the toilette, standing with a deliberate air, her eyes scarcely wet—a fact betrayed by inquisitive glances cast rapidly to the right and left—and, followed only by her ladies, went to her coach by the great staircase.

I took the opportunity to go to the Duchesse d'Orleans, where I found many people. Their presence made me very impatient; the Duchess, who was equally impatient, took a light and went in. I whispered in the ear of the Duchesse de Villeroy, who thought as I thought of this event. She nudged me, and said in a very low voice that I must contain myself. I was smothered with silence, amidst the complaints and the narrative surprises of these ladies; but at last M. le Duc d'Orleans appeared at the door of his cabinet, and beckoned me to come to him.

I followed him into the cabinet, where we were alone. What was my surprise, remembering the terms on which he was with Monseigneur, to see the tears streaming from his eyes.

"Sir!" exclaimed I, rising: He understood me at once; and answered in a broken voice, really crying: "You are right to be surprised—I am surprised myself; but such a spectacle touches. He was a man with whom I passed much of my life, and who treated me well when he was uninfluenced. I feel very well that my grief won't last long; in a few days I shall discover motives of joy; at present, blood, relationship, humanity,—all work; and my entrails are moved." I praised his sentiments, but repeated my surprise. He rose, thrust his head into a corner, and with his nose there, wept bitterly and sobbed, which if I had not seen I could not have believed.

After a little silence, however, I exhorted him to calm himself. I represented to him that, everybody knowing on what terms he had been with Monseigneur, he would be laughed at, as playing a part, if his eyes showed that he had been weeping. He did what he could to remove the marks of his tears, and we then went back into the other room.

The interview of the Duchesse de Bourgogne with the King had not been long. She met him in the avenue between the two stables, got down, and went to the door of the carriage. Madame de Maintenon cried out, "Where are you going? We bear the plague about with us." I do not know what the King said or did. The Princess returned to her carriage, and came back to Versailles, bringing in reality the first news of the actual death of Monseigneur.

Acting upon the advice of M. de Beauvilliers, all the company had gone into the salon. The two Princes, Monseigneur de Bourgogne and M. de Berry, were there, seated on one sofa, their Princesses at their sides; all the rest of the company were scattered about in confusion, seated or standing, some of the ladies being on the floor, near the sofa. There could be no doubt of what had happened. It was plainly written on every face in the chamber and throughout the apartment.

Monseigneur was no more: it was known: it was spoken of: constraint with respect to him no longer existed. Amidst the surprise, the confusion, and the movements that prevailed, the sentiments of all were painted to the life in looks and gestures.

In the outside rooms were heard the constrained groans and sighs of the valets—grieving for the master they had lost as well as for the master that had succeeded. Farther on began the crowd of courtiers of all kinds. The greater number—that is to say the fools—pumped up sighs as well as they could, and with wandering but dry eyes, sung the praises of Monseigneur—insisting especially on his goodness. They pitied the King for the loss of so good a son. The keener began already to be uneasy about the health of the King; and admired themselves for preserving so much judgment amidst so much trouble, which could be perceived by the frequency of their repetitions. Others, really afflicted—the discomfited cabal—wept bitterly, and kept themselves under with an effort as easy to notice as sobs. The most strong-minded or the wisest, with eyes fixed on the ground, in corners, meditated on the consequences of such an event—and especially on their own interests. Few words passed in conversation—here and there an exclamation wrung from grief was answered by some neighbouring grief—a word every quarter of an hour — sombre and haggard eyes—movements quite involuntary of the hands— immobility of all other parts of the body. Those who already looked upon the event as favourable in vain exaggerated their gravity so as to make it resemble chagrin and severity; the veil over their faces was transparent and hid not a single feature. They remained as motionless as those who grieved most, fearing opinion, curiosity, their own satisfaction, their every movement; but their eyes made up for their immobility. Indeed they could not refrain from repeatedly changing their attitude like people ill at ease, sitting or standing, from avoiding each other too carefully, even from allowing their eyes to meet—nor repress a manifest air of liberty—nor conceal their increased liveliness— nor put out a sort of brilliancy which distinguished them in spite of themselves.

The two Princes, and the two Princesses who sat by their sides, were more exposed to view than any other. The Duc de Bourgogne wept with tenderness, sincerity, and gentleness, the tears of nature, of religion, and patience. M. le Duc de Berry also sincerely shed abundance of tears, but bloody tears, so to speak, so great appeared their bitterness; and he uttered not only sobs, but cries, nay, even yells. He was silent sometimes, but from suffocation, and then would burst out again with such a noise, such a trumpet sound of despair, that the majority present burst out also at these dolorous repetitions, either impelled by affliction or decorum. He became so bad, in fact, that his people were forced to undress him then and there, put him to bed, and call in the doctor, Madame la Duchesse de Berry was beside herself, and we shall soon see why. The most bitter despair was painted with horror on her face. There was seen written, as it were, a sort of furious grief, based on interest, not affection; now and then came dry lulls deep and sullen, then a torrent of tears and involuntary gestures, yet restrained, which showed extreme bitterness of mind, fruit of the profound meditation that had preceded. Often aroused by the cries of her husband, prompt to assist him, to support him, to embrace him, to give her smelling-bottle, her care for him was evident; but soon came another profound reverie—then a gush of tears assisted to suppress her cries. As for Madame la Duchesse de Bourgogne she consoled her husband with less trouble than she had to appear herself in want of consolation. Without attempting to play a part, it was evident that she did her best to acquit herself of a pressing duty of decorum. But she found extreme difficulty in keeping up appearances. When the Prince her brother-in-law howled, she blew her nose. She had brought some tears along with her and kept them up with care; and these, combined with the art of the handkerchief, enabled her to redden her eyes, and make them swell, and smudge her face; but her glances often wandered on the sly to the countenances of all present.

Madame arrived, in full dress she knew not why, and howling she knew not why, inundated everybody with her tears in embracing them, making the chateau echo with renewed cries, and furnished the odd spectacle of a Princess putting on her robes of ceremony in the dead of night to come and cry among a crowd of women with but little on except their night- dresses,—almost as masqueraders.

In the gallery several ladies, Madame la Duchesse d'Orleans, Madame de Castries, and Madame de Saint-Simon among the rest, finding no one close by, drew near each other by the side of a tent-bedstead, and began to open their hearts to each other, which they did with the more freedom, inasmuch as they had but one sentiment in common upon what had occurred. In this gallery, and in the salon, there were always during the night several beds, in which, for security's sake, certain Swiss guards and servants slept. These beds had been put in their usual place this evening before the bad news came from Meudon. In the midst of the conversation of the ladies, Madame de Castries touched the bed, felt something move, and was much terrified. A moment after they saw a sturdy arm, nearly naked, raise on a sudden the curtains, and thus show them a great brawny Swiss under the sheets, half awake, and wholly amazed. The fellow was a long time in making out his position, fixing his eyes upon every face one after the other; but at last, not judging it advisable to get up in the midst of such a grand company, he reburied himself in his bed, and closed the curtains. Apparently the good man had gone to bed before anything had transpired, and had slept so soundly ever since that he had not been aroused until then. The saddest sights have often the most ridiculous contrasts. This caused some of the ladies to laugh, and Madame d'Orleans to fear lest the conversation should have been overheard. But after reflection, the sleep and the stupidity of the sleeper reassured her.

I had some doubts yet as to the event that had taken place; for I did not like to abandon myself to belief, until the word was pronounced by some one in whom I could have faith. By chance I met D'O, and I asked him. He answered me clearly that Monseigneur was no more. Thus answered, I tried not to be glad. I know not if I succeeded well, but at least it is certain, that neither joy nor sorrow blunted my curiosity, and that while taking due care to preserve all decorum, I did not consider myself in any way forced to play the doleful. I no longer feared any fresh attack from the citadel of Meudon, nor any cruel charges from its implacable garrison. I felt, therefore, under no constraint, and followed every face with my glances, and tried to scrutinise them unobserved.

It must be admitted, that for him who is well acquainted with the privacies of a Court, the first sight of rare events of this nature, so interesting in so many different respects, is extremely satisfactory. Every countenance recalls the cares, the intrigues, the labours employed in the advancement of fortunes—in the overthrow of rivals: the relations, the coldness, the hatreds, the evil offices done, the baseness of all; hope, despair, rage, satisfaction, express themselves in the features. See how all eyes wander to and fro examining what passes around—how some are astonished to find others more mean, or less mean than was expected! Thus this spectacle produced a pleasure, which, hollow as it may be, is one of the greatest a Court can bestow.

The turmoil in this vast apartment lasted about an hour, at the end of which M. de Beauvilliers thought it was high time to deliver the Princes of their company. The rooms were cleared. M. le Duc de Berry went away to his rooms, partly supported by his wife. All through the night he asked, amid tears and cries, for news from Meudon; he would not understand the cause of the King's departure to Marly. When at length the mournful curtain was drawn from before his eyes, the state he fell into cannot be described. The night of Monseigneur and Madame de Bourgogne was more tranquil. Some one having said to the Princess, that having—no real cause to be affected, it would be terrible to play a part, she replied, quite naturally, that without feigning, pity touched her and decorum controlled her; and indeed she kept herself within these bounds with truth and decency. Their chamber, in which they invited several ladies to pass the night in armchairs, became immediately a palace of Morpheus. All quietly fell asleep. The curtains were left open, so that the Prince and Princess could be seen sleeping profoundly. They woke up once or twice for a moment. In the morning the Duke and Duchess rose early, their tears quite dried up. They shed no more for this cause, except on special and rare occasions. The ladies who had watched and slept in their chamber, told their friends how tranquil the night had been. But nobody was surprised, and as there was no longer a Monseigneur, nobody was scandalised. Madame de Saint-Simon and I remained up two hours before going to bed, and then went there without feeling any want of rest. In fact, I slept so little that at seven in the morning I was up; but it must be admitted that such restlessness is sweet, and such re-awakenings are savoury.

Horror reigned at Meudon. As soon as the King left, all the courtiers left also, crowding into the first carriages that came. In an instant Meudon was empty. Mademoiselle Choin remained alone in her garret, and unaware of what had taken place. She learned it only by the cry raised. Nobody thought of telling her. At last some friends went up to her, hurried her into a hired coach, and took her to Paris. The dispersion was general. One or two valets, at the most, remained near the body. La Villiere, to his praise be it said, was the only courtier who, not having abandoned Monseigneur during life, did not abandon him after his death. He had some difficulty to find somebody to go in search of Capuchins to pray over the corpse. The decomposition became so rapid and so great, that the opening of the windows was not enough; the Capuchins, La Vrilliere, and the valets, were compelled to pass the night outside.

At Marly everybody had felt so confident that the King's return there was not dreamt of. Nothing was ready, no keys of the rooms, no fires, scarcely an end of candle. The King was more than an hour thus with Madame de Maintenon and other ladies in one of the ante-chambers. The King retired into a corner, seated between Madame de Maintenon and two other ladies, and wept at long intervals. At last the chamber of Madame de Maintenon was ready. The King entered, remained there an hour, and then 'went to bed at nearly four o'clock in the morning.

Monseigneur was rather tall than short; very fat, but without being bloated; with a very lofty and noble aspect without any harshness; and he would have had a very agreeable face if M. le Prince de Conti had not unfortunately broken his nose in playing while they were both young. He was of a very beautiful fair complexion; he had a face everywhere covered with a healthy red, but without expression; the most beautiful legs in the world; his feet singularly small and delicate. He wavered always in walking, and felt his way with his feet; he was always afraid of falling, and if the path was not perfectly even and straight, he called for assistance. He was a good horseman, and looked well when mounted; but he was not a bold rider. When hunting— they had persuaded him that he liked this amusement—a servant rode before him; if he lost sight of this servant he gave himself up for lost, slicked his pace to a gentle trot, and oftentimes waited under a tree for the hunting party, and returned to it slowly. He was very fond of the table, but always without indecency. Ever since that great attack of indigestion, which was taken at first for apoplexy, he made but one real meal a day, and was content,—although a great eater, like the rest of the royal family. Nearly all his portraits well resemble him.

As for his character he had none; he was without enlightenment or knowledge of any kind, radically incapable of acquiring any; very idle, without imagination or productiveness; without taste, without choice, without discernment; neither seeing the weariness he caused others, nor that he was as a ball moving at hap-hazard by the impulsion of others; obstinate and little to excess in everything; amazingly credulous and accessible to prejudice, keeping himself, always, in the most pernicious hands, yet incapable of seeing his position or of changing it; absorbed in his fat and his ignorance; so that without any desire to do ill he would have made a pernicious King.

His avariciousness, except in certain things, passed all belief. He kept an account of his personal expenditure, and knew to a penny what his smallest and his largest expenses amounted to. He spent large sums in building, in furniture, in jewels, and in hunting, which he made himself believe he was fond of.

It is inconceivable the little he gave to La Choin, whom he so much loved. It never exceeded four hundred Louis a quarter in gold, or sixteen hundred Louis a year, whatever the Louis might be worth. He gave them to her with his own hand, without adding or subtracting a pistole, and, at the most, made her but one present a year, and that he looked at twice before giving. It was said that they were married, and certain circumstances seemed to justify this rumour. As for instance, during the illness of Monseigneur, the King, as I have said, asked Madame de Maintenon if she had seen Mademoiselle Choin, and upon receiving negative reply, was displeased. Instead of driving her away from the chateau he inquired particularly after her! This, to say the least, looked as though Mademoiselle Choin was Monseigneur's Maintenon—but the matter remained incomprehensible to the last. Mademoiselle Choin threw no light upon it, although she spoke on many other things concerning Monseigneur. In the modest home at Paris, to which she had retired for the rest of her days. The King gave her a pension of twelve thousand livres.

Monseigneur was, I have said, ignorant to the last degree, and had a thorough aversion for learning; so that, according to his own admission, ever since he had been released from the hands of teachers he had never read anything except the article in the "Gazette de France," in which deaths and marriages are recorded. His timidity, especially before the King, was equal to his ignorance, which indeed contributed not a little to cause it. The King took advantage of it, and never treated him as a son, but as a subject. He was the monarch always, never the father. Monseigneur had not the slightest influence with the King. If he showed any preference for a person it was enough! That person was sure to be kept back by the King. The King was so anxious to show that Monseigneur could do nothing, that Monseigneur after a time did not even try. He contented himself by complaining occasionally in monosyllables, and by hoping for better times.

The body of Monseigneur so soon grew decomposed; that immediate burial was necessary. At midnight on Wednesday he was carried, with but little ceremony, to Saint-Denis, and deposited in the royal vaults. His funeral services were said at Saint-Denis on the 18th of the following June, and at Notre Dame on the 3rd of July. As the procession passed through Paris nothing but cries, acclamations, and eulogiums of the defunct were heard. Monseigneur had, I know not how, much endeared himself to the common people of Paris, and this sentiment soon gained the provinces; so true it is, that in France it costs little to its Princes to make themselves almost adored!

The King soon got over his affliction for the loss of this son of fifty. Never was a man so ready with tears, so backward with grief, or so promptly restored to his ordinary state. The morning after the death of Monseigneur he rose late, called M. de Beauvilliers into his cabinet, shed some more tears, and then said that from that time Monseigneur le Duc de Bourgogne and Madame la Duchesse de Bourgogne were to enjoy the honours, the rank, and the name of Dauphin and of Dauphine. Henceforth I shall call them by no other names.

My joy at this change may be imagined. In a few days all my causes of disquietude had been removed, and I saw a future opening before me full of light and promise. Monseigneur le Duc de Bourgogne become Dauphin, heir to the throne of France; what favour might I not hope for? I could not conceal or control my satisfaction.

But alas! it was soon followed by sad disappointment and grievous sorrow.

CHAPTER LVIII

The death of Monseigneur, as we have seen, made a great change in the aspect of the Court and in the relative positions of its members. But the two persons to whom I must chiefly direct attention are the Duchesse de Bourgogne and the Duchesse de Berry. The former, on account of her husband's fall in the opinion of his father, had long been out of favour likewise. Although Monseigneur had begun to treat her less well for a long time, and most harshly during the campaign of Lille, and above all after the expulsion of the Duc de Vendome from Marly and Meudon; yet after the marriage of the Duc de Berry his coldness had still further increased. The adroit Princess, it is true, had rowed against the current with a steadiness and grace capable of disarming even a well-founded resentment; but the persons who surrounded him looked upon the meeting of them as dangerous for their projects. The Duc and Duchesse de Bourgogne were every day still further removed in comparative disgrace.

Things even went so far that apropos of an engagement broken off, the Duchesse resolved to exert her power instead of her persuasion, and threatened the two Lillebonnes. A sort of reconciliation was then patched up, but it was neither sincere nor apparently so.

The cabal which laboured to destroy the Duc and Duchesse de Bourgogne was equally assiduous in augmenting the influence of the Duc de Berry, whose wife had at once been admitted without having asked into the sanctuary of the Parvulo. The object was to disunite the two brothers and excite jealousy between then. In this they did not succeed even in the slightest degree. But they found a formidable ally in the Duchesse de Berry, who proved as full of wickedness and ambition as any among them. The Duc d'Orleans often called his Duchess Madame Lucifer, at which she used to smile with complacency. He was right, for she would have been a prodigy of pride had she not, had a daughter who far surpassed her. This is not yet the time to paint their portraits; but I must give a word or two of explanation on the Duchesse de Berry.

That princess was a marvel of wit, of pride, of ingratitude and folly— nay, of debauchery and obstinacy.

Scarcely had she been married a week when she began to exhibit herself in all these lights,— not too manifestly it is true, for one of the qualities of which she was most vain was her falsity and power of concealment, but sufficiently to make an impression on those around her. People soon perceived how annoyed she was to be the daughter of an illegitimate mother, and to have lived under her restraint however mild; how she despised the weakness of her father, the Duc d'Orleans, and how confident she was of her influence over him; and how she had hated all who had interfered in her marriage—merely because she could not bear to be under obligations to any one—a reason she was absurd enough publicly to avow and boast of. Her conduct was now based on those motives. This is an example of how in this world people work with their heads in a sack, and how human prudence and wisdom are sometimes confounded by successes which have been reasonably desired and which turn out to be detestable! We had brought about this marriage to avoid a marriage with Mademoiselle de Bourbon and to cement the union of the two brothers. We now discovered that there was little danger of Mademoiselle de Bourbon, and then instead of her we had a Fury who had no thought but how to ruin those who had established her, to injure her benefactors, to make her husband and her brother quarrel; and to put herself in the power of her enemies because they were the enemies of her natural friends. It never occurred to her that the cabal would not be likely to abandon to her the fruit of so much labour and so many crimes.

It may easily be imagined that she was neither gentle nor docile when Madame la Duchesse began to give her advice. Certain that her father would support her, she played the stranger and the daughter of France with her mother. Estrangement, however, soon came on. She behaved differently in form, but in effect the same with the Duchesse de Bourgogne, who wished to guide her as a daughter, but who soon gave up the attempt. The Duchesse de Berry's object could only be gained by bringing about disunion between the two brothers, and for this purpose she employed as a spring the passion of her husband for herself.

The first night at Versailles after the death of Monseigneur was sleepless. The Dauphin and Dauphine heard mass early next morning. I went to see them. Few persons were present on account of the hour. The Princess wished to be at Marly at the King's waking. Their eyes were wonderfully dry, but carefully managed; and it was easy to see they were more occupied with their new position than with the death of Monseigneur. A smile which they exchanged as they spoke, in whispers convinced me of this. One of their first cares was to endeavour to increase their good relations with the Duc and Duchesse de Berry. They were to see them before they were up. The Duc de Berry showed himself very sensible to this act, and the Duchess was eloquent, clever, and full of tears. But her heart was wrung by these advances of pure generosity. The separation she had planned soon followed: and the two princesses felt relieved at no longer being obliged to dine together.

Thus never was change greater or more marked than that brought about by the death of Monseigneur. That prince had become the centre of all hope and of all fear, a formidable cabal had seized upon him, yet without awakening the jealousy of the King, before whom all trembled, but whose anxieties did not extend beyond his own lifetime, during which, and very reasonably, he feared nothing.

Before I go any further, let me note a circumstance characteristic of the King. Madame la Dauphine went every day to Marly to see him. On the day after the death of Monseigneur she received, not without surprise, easily understood, a hint from Madame de Maintenon. It was to the effect that she should dress herself with some little care, inasmuch as the negligence of her attire displeased the King! The Princess did not think that dress ought to occupy her then; and even if she had thought so, she would have believed, and with good reason, that she was committing a grave fault against decorum, a fault which would have been less readily pardoned, since in every way she had gained too much by what had just occurred not to be very guarded in her behaviour. On the next day she took more pains with her toilette; but what she did not being found sufficient, the day following she carried with her some things and dressed herself secretly in Madame de Maintenon's rooms; and resumed there her ordinary apparel before returning to

Versailles. Thus she avoided offence both to the King and to society. The latter certainly would with difficulty have been persuaded that in this ill-timed adornment of her person, her own tastes went for nothing. The Comtesse de Mailly, who invented the scheme, and Madame de Nogaret, who both liked Monseigneur, related this to me and were piqued by it. From this fact and from the circumstance that all the ordinary pleasures and occupations were resumed immediately after the death of Monseigneur, the King passing his days without any constraint,—it may be assumed that if the royal grief was bitter its evidences were of a kind to promise that it would not be of long duration.

M. le Dauphin, for, as I have said, it is by that title I shall now name Monseigneur le Duc de Bourgogne—M. le Dauphin, I say, soon gained all hearts. In the first days of solitude following upon the death of Monseigneur, the King intimated to M. de Beauvilliers that he should not care to see the new Dauphin go very often to Meudon. This was enough. M. le Dauphin at once declared that he would never set his foot in that palace, and that he would never quit the King. He was as good as his word, and not one single visit did he ever afterwards pay to Meudon. The King wished to give him fifty thousand livres a month, Monseigneur having had that sum. M. le Dauphin would not accept them. He had only six thousand livres per month. He was satisfied with double that amount and would not receive more. This disinterestedness much pleased the public. M. le Dauphin wished for nothing special on his account, and persisted in remaining in nearly everything as he was during the life of Monseigneur. These auguries of a prudent and measured reign, suggested the brightest of hopes.

Aided by his adroit spouse, who already had full possession of the King's heart and of that of Madame de Maintenon, M. le Dauphin redoubled his attentions in order to possess them also. These attentions, addressed to Madame de Maintenon, produced their fruit. She was transported with pleasure at finding a Dauphin upon whom she could rely, instead of one whom she did not like, gave herself up to him accordingly, and by that means secured to him the King's favour. The first fortnight made evident to everybody at Marly the extraordinary change that had come over the King with respect to the Dauphin. His Majesty, generally severe beyond measure with his legitimate children, showed the most marked graciousness for this prince. The effects of this, and of the change that had taken place in his state, were soon most clearly visible in the Dauphin. Instead of being timid and retiring, diffident in speech, and more fond of his study than of the salon, he became on a sudden easy and frank, showing himself in public on all occasions, conversing right and left in a gay, agreeable, and dignified manner; presiding, in fact, over the Salon of Marly, and over the groups gathered round him, like the divinity of a temple, who receives with goodness the homage to which he is accustomed, and recompenses the mortals who offer it with gentle regard.

In a short time hunting became a less usual topic of conversation. History, and even science, were touched upon lightly, pleasantly, and discreetly, in a manner that charmed while it instructed. The Dauphin spoke with an eloquent freedom that opened all eyes, ears and hearts. People sometimes, in gathering near him, were less anxious to make their court than to listen to his natural eloquence, and to draw from it delicious instruction. It is astonishing with what rapidity he gained universal esteem and admiration. The public joy could not keep silent. People asked each other if this was really the same man they had known as the Duc de Bourgogne, whether he was a vision or a reality? One of M. le Dauphin's friends, to whom this question was addressed, gave a keen reply. He answered, that the cause of all this surprise was, that previously the people did not, and would not, know this prince, who, nevertheless, to those who had known him, was the same now as he had ever been; and that this justice would be rendered to him when time had shown how much it was deserved.

From the Court to Paris, and from Paris to the provinces, the reputation of the Dauphin flew on rapid wings. However founded might be this prodigious success, we need not believe it was entirely due to the marvellous qualities of the young prince. It was in a great measure a reaction against the hostile feeling towards him which had been excited by the cabal, whose efforts I have previously spoken of. Now that people saw how unjust was this feeling, their astonishment added to their admiration. Everybody was filled with a sentiment of joy at seeing the first dawn of a new state of things, which promised so much order and happiness after such a long confusion and so much obscurity.

Gracious as the King showed himself to M. le Dauphin, and accustomed as the people grew to his graciousness, all the Court was strangely surprised at a fresh mark of favour that was bestowed one morning by his Majesty on this virtuous prince. The King, after having been closeted alone with him for some time, ordered his ministers to work with the Dauphin whenever sent for, and, whether sent for or not, to make him acquainted with all public affairs; this command being given once for all.

It is not easy to describe the prodigious movement caused at the Court by this order, so directly opposed to the tastes, to the disposition, to the maxims, to the usage of the King, who thus showed a confidence in the Dauphin which was nothing less than tacitly transferring to him a large part of the disposition of public affairs. This was a thunderbolt for the ministers; who, accustomed to have almost everything their own way, to rule over everybody and browbeat everybody at will, to govern the state abroad and at home, in fact, fixing all punishments, all recompenses, and always sheltering themselves behind the royal authority "the King wills it so" being the phrase ever on their lips,—to these officers, I say, it was a thunderbolt which so bewildered them, that they could not hide their astonishment or their confusion. The public joy at an order which reduced these ministers, or rather these kings, to the condition of subjects, which put a curb upon their power, and provided against the abuses they committed, was great indeed! The ministers were compelled to bend their necks, though stiff as iron, to the yoke. They all went, with a hang-dog look, to show the Dauphin a feigned joy and a forced obedience to the order they had received.

Here, perhaps, I may as well speak of the situation in which I soon afterwards found myself with the Dauphin, the confidence as to the present and the future that I enjoyed with him, and the many deliberations we had upon public affairs. The matter is curious and interesting, and need no longer be deferred.

The Court being changed by the death of Monseigneur, I soon began indeed to think of changing my conduct with regard to the new Dauphin. M. de Beauvilliers spoke to me about this matter first, but he judged, and I shared his opinion, that slandered as I had been on previous occasions, and remaining still, as it were, half in disgrace, I must approach the Dauphin only by slow degrees, and not endeavour to shelter myself under him until his authority with the King had become strong enough to afford me a safe asylum. I believed, nevertheless, that it would be well to sound him immediately; and one evening, when he was but thinly accompanied, I joined him in the gardens at Marly and profited by his gracious welcome to say to him, on the sly, that many reasons, of which he was not ignorant, had necessarily kept me until then removed from him, but that now I hoped to be able to follow with less constraint my attachment and my inclination, and that I flattered myself this would be agreeable to him. He replied in a low tone, that there were sometimes reasons which fettered people, but in our case such no longer existed; that he knew of my regard for him, and reckoned with pleasure that we should soon see each other more frequently than before. I am writing the exact words of his reply, on account of the singular politeness of the concluding ones. I regarded that reply as the successful result of a bait that had been taken as I wished. Little by little I became more assiduous at his promenades, but without following them when the crowd or any dangerous people do so; and I spoke more freely. I remained content with seeing the Dauphin in public, and I approached him in the Salon only when if I saw a good opportunity.

Some days after, being in the Salon, I saw the Dauphin and the Dauphine enter together and converse. I approached and heard their last words; they stimulated me to ask the prince what was in debate, not in a straightforward manner, but in a sort of respectful insinuating way which I already adopted. He explained to me that he was going to Saint-Germain to pay an ordinary visit; that on this occasion there would be some change in the ceremonial; explained the matter, and enlarged with eagerness on the necessity of not abandoning legitimate rights.

"How glad I am to see you think thus," I replied, "and how well you act in advocating these forms, the neglect of which tarnishes everything."

He responded with warmth; and I seized the moment to say, that if he, whose rank was so great and so derided, was right to pay attention to these things, how such we dukes had reason to complain of our losses, and to try to sustain ourselves! Thereupon he entered into the question so far as to become the advocate of our cause, and finished by saying that he regarded our restoration as an act of justice important to the state; that he knew I was well instructed in these things, and that I should give him pleasure by talking of them some day. He rejoined at that, moment the Dauphine, and they set off for Saint-Germain.

A few days after this the Dauphin sent for me. I entered by the wardrobe, where a sure and trusty valet was in waiting; he conducted me to a cabinet in which the Dauphin was sitting alone. Our conversation at once commenced. For a full hour we talked upon the state of affairs, the Dauphin listening with much attention to all I said, and expressing himself with infinite modesty, sense, and judgment. His view, I found, were almost entirely in harmony with mine. He was sorry, and touchingly said so, for the ignorance of all things in which the King was kept by his ministers; he was anxious to see the power of those ministers restricted; he looked with dislike upon the incredible elevation of the illegitimate children; he wished to see the order to which I belonged restored to the position it deserved to occupy.

It is difficult to express what I felt in quitting the Dauphin. A magnificent and near future opened out before me. I saw a prince, pious, just, debonnaire, enlightened, and seeking to become more so; with principles completely in accord with my own, and capacity to carry out those principles when the time for doing so arrived. I relished deliciously a confident so precious and so full upon the most momentous matters and at a first interview. I felt all the sweetness of this perspective, and of my deliverance from a servitude which, in spite of myself, I sometimes could not help showing myself impatient of. I felt, too, that I now had an opportunity of elevating myself, and of contributing to those grand works, for the happiness and advantage of the state I so much wished to see accomplished.

A few days after this I had another interview with the Dauphin. I was introduced secretly as before, so that no one perceived either my coming or my departure. The same subjects we had previously touched upon we now entered into again, and more amply than on the former occasion. The Dauphin, in taking leave of me, gave me full permission to see him in private as often as I desired, though in public I was still to be circumspect.

Indeed there was need of great circumspection in carrying on even private intercourse with the Dauphin. From this time I continually saw him in his cabinet, talking with him in all liberty upon the various persons of the Court, and upon the various subjects relating to the state; but always with the same secrecy as at first. This was absolutely necessary; as I have just said, I was still in a sort of half disgrace the King did not regard me with the eyes of favour; Madame de Maintenon was resolutely averse to me. If they two had suspected my strict intimacy with the heir to the throne, I should have been assuredly lost.

To show what need there was of precaution in my private interviews with the Dauphin, let me here recall an incident which one day occurred when we were closeted together, and which might have led to the greatest results. The Prince lodged then in one of the four grand suites of apartments, on the same level as the Salon, the suite that was broken up during an illness of Madame la Princesse de Conti, to make way for a grand stair case, the narrow and crooked one in use annoying the King when he ascended it. The chamber of the Dauphine was there; the bed had its foot towards the window; by the chimney was the door of the obscure wardrobe by which I entered; between the chimney and one of the two windows was a little portable bureau; in front of the ordinary entrance door of the chamber and behind the bureau was the door of one of the Dauphine's rooms; between the two windows was a chest of drawers which was used for papers only.

There were always some moments of conversation before the Dauphin set himself down at his bureau, and ordered me to place myself opposite him. Having become more free with him, I took the liberty to say one day in these first moments of our discourse, that he would do well to bolt the door behind him, the door I mean of the Dauphine's chamber. He said that the Dauphine would not come, it not being her hour. I replied that I did not fear that princess herself, but the crowd that always accompanied her. He was obstinate, and would not bolt the door. I did not dare to press him more. He sat down before his bureau, and ordered me to sit also. Our deliberation was long; afterwards we sorted our papers. Here let me say this—Every time I went to see the Dauphin I garnished all my pockets with papers, and I often smiled within myself passing through the Salon, at seeing there many people who at that moment were in my pockets, and who were far indeed from suspecting the important discussion that was going to take place. To return: the Dauphin gave, me his papers to put in my pockets, and kept mine. He locked up some in his cupboard, and instead of locking up the others in his bureau, kept them out, and began talking to me, his back to the chimney, his papers in one hand, his keys in the other. I was standing at the bureau looking for some other papers, when on a sudden the door in front of me opened, and the Dauphine entered!

The first appearance of all three—for, thank God! she was alone—the astonishment, the countenance of all have never left my memory. Our fixed eyes, our statue-like immobility, and our embarrassment were all alike, and lasted longer than a slow Pater-poster. The Princess spoke first. She said to the Prince in a very ill-assured voice, that she had not imagined him in such good company; smiling upon him and upon me. I had scarce time to smile also and to lower my eyes, before the Dauphin replied.

"Since you find me so," said he, smiling in turn, "leave me so."

For an instant she looked on him, he and she both smiling at each other more; then she looked on me, still smiling with greater liberty than at first, made a pirouette, went away and closed the door, beyond the threshold of which she had not come.

Never have I seen woman so astonished; never man so taken aback, as the Prince after the Dauphine's departure; and never man, to say truth, was so afraid as I was at first, though I quickly reassured myself when I found that our intruder was alone. As soon as she had closed the door, "Well, Monsieur," said I to the Dauphin, "if you had drawn the bolt?"

"You were right," he replied, "and I was wrong. But no harm is done. She was alone fortunately, and I guarantee to you her secrecy."

"I am not troubled," said I to him, (yet I was so mightily) "but it is a miracle she was alone. With her suite you would have escaped with a scolding perhaps but for me, I should have been utterly lost."

He admitted again he had, been wrong, and assure me more and more that our secret was safe. The Dauphine had caught us, not only tete-a-tete— of which no one had the least suspicion—she had caught us in the fact, so to say, our crimes in out hands. I felt that she would not expose the Dauphin, but I feared an after-revelation through some over-easy confidant. Nevertheless our secret was so well kept if confided that it never transpired. We finished, I to pocket, the Prince to lock up, the papers. The rest of the conversation was short, and I withdrew by the wardrobe as usual. M. de Beauvilliers, to whom I related this adventure shortly afterwards, grew pale at first, but recovered when I said the Dauphine was alone. He blamed the imprudence of the Dauphin, but assured me my secret was safe. Ever since that adventure the Dauphine often smiled upon me when we met, as if to remind me of it, and showed marked attention to me.

No sooner did I feel myself pretty firmly established on this footing of delicious intimacy with the Dauphin than I conceived the desire to unite him with M. le Duc d'Orleans through the means of M. de Beauvilliers. At the very outset, however, an obstacle arose in my path.

I have already said, that the friendship of M. d'Orleans for his daughter, Madame la Duchesse de Berry, had given employment to the tongues of Satan, set in Motion by hatred and jealousy. Evil reports even reached M. le Duc de Berry, who on his part, wishing to enjoy the society of his wife in full liberty, was importuned by the continual presence near her, of her father. To ward off a quarrel between son-in- law and father-in-law, based upon so false and so odious a foundation, appeared to Madame de Saint-Simon and myself a pressing duty.

I had already tried to divert M. le Duc d'Orleans from an assiduity which wearied M. le Duc de Berry; but I had not succeeded. I believed it my duty then to return to the charge more hotly; and remembering my previous ill-success, I prefaced properly, and then said what I had to say. M. d'Orleans was astonished; he cried out against the horror of such a vile imputation and the villainy that had carried it to M. le Duc de Berry. He thanked me for having warned him of it, a service few besides myself would have rendered him. I left him to draw the proper and natural conclusion on the conduct he should pursue. This conversation passed one day at Versailles about four o'clock in the afternoon.

On the morrow Madame de Saint-Simon related to me, that returning home the previous evening, from the supper and the cabinet of the King with Madame la Duchesse de Berry, the Duchess had passed straight into the wardrobe and called her there; and then with a cold and angry air, said she was very much astonished that I wished to get up a quarrel between her and M. le Duc d'Orleans. Madame Saint-Simon exhibited surprise, but Madame la Duchesse de Berry declared that nothing was so true; that I wished to estrange M. d'Orleans from her, but that I should not succeed; and immediately related all that I had just said to her father. He had had the goodness to repeat it to her an hour afterwards! Madame de Saint-Simon, still more surprised, listened attentively to the end, and replied that this horrible report was public, that she herself could see what consequences it would have, false and abominable as it might be, and feel whether it was not important that M. le Duc d'Orleans should be informed of it. She added, that I had shown such proofs of my attachment for them and of my desire for their happiness, that I was above all suspicion. Then she curtsied and leaving the Princess went to bed. This scene appeared to me enormous.

For some time after this I ceased entirely to see Duc d'Orleans and Madame la Duchesse de Berry. They cajoled me with all sorts of excuses, apologies, and so forth, but I remained frozen. They redoubled their excuses and their prayers. Friendship, I dare not say compassion, seduced me, and I allowed myself to be led away. In a word, we were reconciled. I kept aloof, however, from Madame la Duchesse de Berry as much as possible, visiting her only for form's sake; and as long as she lived never changed in this respect.

Being reconciled with M. d'Orleans, I again thought of my project of uniting him to the Dauphin through M. de Beauvilliers. He had need of some support, for on all sides he was sadly out of favour. His debauchery and his impiety, which he had quitted for a time after separating himself from Madame d'Argenton, his mistress, had now seized on him again as firmly as ever. It seemed as though there were a wager between him and his daughter, Madame la Duchesse de Berry, which should cast most contempt on religion and good manners.

The King was nothing ignorant of the conduct of his nephew. He had been much shocked with the return to debauchery and low company. The enemies of M. d'Orleans, foremost among whom was M. du Maine, had therefore everything in their favour. As I have said, without some support M. d'Orleans seemed in danger of being utterly lost.

It was no easy matter to persuade M. de Beauvilliers to, fall in with the plan I had concocted, and lend his aid to it. But I worked him hard. I dwelt upon the taste of the Dauphin for history, science, and the arts, and showed what a ripe knowledge of those subjects M. d'Orleans had, and what agreeable conversation thereon they both might enjoy together. In brief I won over M. de Beauvilliers to my scheme. M. D'Orleans, on his side, saw without difficulty the advantage to him of union with the Dauphin. To bring it about I laid before him two conditions. One, that when in the presence of the Prince he should suppress that detestable heroism of impiety he affected more than he felt, and allow no licentious expressions to escape him. The second was to go less often into evil company at Paris, and if he must continue his debauchery, to do so at the least within closed doors, and avoid all public scandal. He promised obedience, and was faithful to his promise. The Dauphin perceived and approved the change; little by little the object of my desire was gained.

As I have already said, it would be impossible for me to express all the joy I felt at my deliverance from the dangers I was threatened with during the lifetime of Monseigneur. My respect, esteem, and admiration for the Dauphin grew more and more day by day, as I saw his noble qualities blossom out in richer luxuriance. My hopes, too, took a brighter colour from the rising dawn of prosperity that was breaking around me. Alas! that I should be compelled to relate the cruel manner in which envious fortune took from me the cup of gladness just as I was raising it to my lips.

CHAPTER LIX

On Monday, the 18th of January, 1712, after a visit to Versailles, the King went to Marly. I mark expressly this journey. No sooner were we settled there than Boudin, chief doctor of the Dauphine, warned her to take care of herself, as he had received sure information that there was a plot to poison her and the Dauphin, to whom he made a similar communication. Not content with this he repeated it with a terrified manner to everybody in the salon, and frightened all who listened to him. The King spoke to him about it in private. Boudin declared that this information was good, and yet that he did not know whence it came; and he stuck to this contradiction. For, if he did not know where the information came from how could he be assured it was trustworthy?

The most singular thing is, that twenty-four hours after Boudin had uttered this warning, the Dauphin received a similar one from the King of Spain, vague, and without mentioning whence obtained, and yet also declared to be of good source. In this only the Dauphin was named distinctly—the Dauphine obscurely and by implication—at least, so the Dauphin explained the matter, and I never heard that he said otherwise. People pretended to despise these stories of origin unknown, but they were struck by them nevertheless, and in the midst of the amusements and occupations of the Court, seriousness, silence, and consternation were spread.

The King, as I have said, went to Marly on Monday, the 18th of January, 1712. The Dauphine came there early with a face very much swelled, and went to bed at once; yet she rose at seven o'clock in the evening because the King wished her to preside in the salon. She played there, in morning-dress, with her head wrapped up, visited the King m the apartment of Madame de Maintenon just before his supper, and then again went to bed, where she supped. On the morrow, the 19th, she rose only to play in the salon, and see the King, returning to her bed and supping there. On the 20th, her swelling diminished, and she was better. She was subject to this complaint, which was caused by her teeth. She passed the following days as usual. On Monday, the 1st of February, the Court returned to Versailles.

On Friday, the 5th of February, the Duc de Noailles gave a very fine box full of excellent Spanish snuff to the Dauphine, who took some, and liked it. This was towards the end of the morning. Upon entering her cabinet (closed to everybody else), she put this box upon the table, and left it there. Towards the evening she was seized with trembling fits of fever. She went to bed, and could not rise again even to go to the King's cabinet after the supper. On Saturday, the 6th of February, the Dauphine, who had had fever all night, did not fail to rise at her ordinary hour, and to pass the day as usual; but in the evening the fever returned. She was but middling all that night, a little worse the next day; but towards ten o'clock at night she was suddenly seized by a sharp pain under the temple. It did not extend to the dimensions of a ten sous piece, but was so violent that she begged the King, who was coming to see her, not to enter. This kind of madness of suffering lasted without intermission until Monday, the 8th, and was proof against tobacco chewed and smoked, a quantity of opium, and two bleedings in the arms. Fever showed itself more then this pain was a little calmed; the Dauphine said she had suffered more than in child-birth.

Such a violent illness filled the chamber with rumours concerning the snuff-box given to the Dauphine by the Duc de Noailles. In going to bed the day she had received it and was seized by fever, she spoke of the snuff to her ladies, highly praising it and the box, which she told one of them to go and look for upon the table in the cabinet, where, as I have said, it had been left. The box could not be found, although looked for high and low. This disappearance had seemed very extraordinary from the first moment it became known. Now, joined to the grave illness with which the Dauphine was so cruelly assailed, it aroused the most sombre suspicions. Nothing, however, was breathed of these suspicions, beyond a very restricted circle; for the Princess took snuff with the knowledge of Madame de Maintenon, but without that of the King, who would have made a fine scene if he had discovered it. This was what was feared, if the singular loss of the box became divulged.

Let me here say, that although one of my friends, the Archbishop of Rheims, believed to his dying day that the Duc de Noailles had poisoned the Dauphine by means of this box of Spanish snuff, I never could induce myself to believe so too. The Archbishop declared that in the manner of the Duc de Noailles, after quitting the chamber of the Princess, there was something which suggested both confusion and contentment. He brought forward other proofs of guilt, but they made no impression upon me. I endeavoured, on the contrary, to shake his belief, but my labour was in vain. I entreated him, however, at least to maintain the most profound silence upon this horrible thought, and he did so.

Those who afterwards knew the history of the box—and they were in good number—were as inaccessible to suspicion as I; and nobody thought of charging the Duc de Noailles with the offence it was said he had committed. As for me, I believed in his guilt so little that our intimacy remained the same; and although that intimacy grew even up to the death of the King, we never spoke of this fatal snuff-box.

During the night, from Monday to Tuesday, the 9th of February, the lethargy was great. During the day the King approached the bed many times: the fever was strong, the awakenings were short; the head was confused, and some marks upon the skin gave tokens of measles, because they extended quickly, and because many people at Versailles and at Paris were known to be, at this time, attacked with that disease. The night from Tuesday to Wednesday passed so much the more badly, because the hope of measles had already vanished. The King came in the morning to see Madame la Dauphine, to whom an emetic had been given. It operated well, but produced no relief. The Dauphin, who scarcely ever left the bedside of his wife, was forced into the garden to take the air, of which he had much need; but his disquiet led him back immediately into the chamber. The malady increased towards the evening, and at eleven o'clock there was a considerable augmentation of fever. The night was very bad. On Thursday, the 11th of February, at nine o'clock in the morning, the King entered the Dauphine's chamber, which Madame de Maintenon scarcely ever left, except when he was in her apartments. The Princess was so ill that it was resolved to speak to her of receiving the sacrament. Prostrated though she was she was surprised at this. She put some questions as to her state; replies as little terrifying as possible were given to her, and little by little she was warned against delay. Grateful for this advice, she said she would prepare herself.

After some time, accidents being feared, Father la Rue, her (Jesuit) confessor, whom she had always appeared to like, approached her to exhort her not to delay confession. She looked at him, replied that she understood him, and then remained silent. Like a sensible man he saw what was the matter, and at once said that if she had any objection to confess to him to have no hesitation in admitting it. Thereupon she indicated that she should like to have M. Bailly, priest of the mission of the parish of Versailles. He was a man much esteemed, but not altogether free from the suspicion of Jansenism. Bailly, as it happened, had gone to Paris. This being told her, the Dauphine asked for Father Noel, who was instantly sent for.

The excitement that this change of confessor made at a moment so critical may be imagined. All the cruelty of the tyranny that the King never ceased to exercise over every member of his family was now apparent. They could not have a confessor not of his choosing! What was his surprise and the surprise of all the Court, to find that in these last terrible moments of life the Dauphine wished to change her confessor, whose order even she repudiated!

Meanwhile the Dauphin had given way. He had hidden his own illness as long as he could, so as not to leave the pillow of his Dauphine. Now the fever he had was too strong to be dissimulated; and the doctors, who wished to spare him the sight of the horrors they foresaw, forgot nothing to induce him to stay in his chamber, where, to sustain him, false news was, from time to time, brought him of the state of his spouse.

The confession of the Dauphine was long. Extreme unction was administered immediately afterwards; and the holy viaticum directly. An hour afterwards the Dauphine desired the prayers for the dying to be said. They told her she was not yet in that state, and with words of consolation exhorted her to try and get to sleep. Seven doctors of the Court and of Paris were sent for. They consulted together in the presence of the King and Madame de Maintenon. All with one voice were in favour of bleeding at the foot; and in case it did not have the effect desired, to give an emetic at the end of the night. The bleeding was executed at seven o'clock in the evening. The return of the fever came and was found less violent than the preceding. The night was cruel. The King came early next morning to see the Dauphine. The emetic she took at about nine o'clock had little effect. The day passed in symptoms each more sad than the other; consciousness only at rare intervals. All at once towards evening, the whole chamber fell into dismay. A number of people were allowed to enter although the King was there. Just before she expired he left, mounted into his coach at the foot of the grand staircase, and with Madame de Maintenon and Madame de Caylus went away to Marly. They were both in the most bitter grief, and had not the courage to go to the Dauphin. Upon arriving at Marly the King supped in his own room; and passed a short time with M. d'Orleans and his natural children. M. le Duc de Berry, entirely occupied with his affliction, which was great and real, had remained at Versailles with Madame la Duchesse de Berry, who, transported with joy upon seeing herself delivered from a powerful rival, to whom, however, she owed all, made her face do duty for her heart.

Monseigneur le Dauphin, ill and agitated by the most bitter grief, kept his chamber; but on Saturday morning the 13th, being pressed to go to Marly to avoid the horror of the noise overhead where the Dauphine was lying dead, he set out for that place at seven o'clock in the morning. Shortly after arriving he heard mass in the chapel, and thence was carried in a chair to the window of one of his rooms. Madame de Maintenon came to see him there afterwards; the anguish of the interview was speedily too much for her, and she went away. Early in the morning I went uninvited to see M. le Dauphin. He showed me that he perceived this with an air of gentleness and of affection which penetrated me. But I was terrified with his looks, constrained, fixed and with something wild about them, with the change in his face and with the marks there, livid rather than red, that I observed in good number and large; marks observed by the others also. The Dauphin was standing. In a few minutes he was apprised that the King had awaked. The tears that he had restrained, now rolled from his eyes; he turned round at the news but said nothing, remaining stock still. His three attendants proposed to him, once or twice, that he should go to the King. He neither spoke nor stirred. I approached and made signs to him to go, then softly spoke to the same effect. Seeing that he still remained speechless and motionless, I made bold to take his arm, representing to him that sooner or later he must see the King, who expected him, and assuredly with the desire to see and embrace him; and pressing him in this manner, I took the liberty to gently push him. He cast upon me a look that pierced my soul and went away: I followed him some few steps and then withdrew to recover breath; I never saw him again. May I, by the mercy of God, see him eternally where God's goodness doubtless has placed him!

The Dauphin reached the chamber of the King, full just then of company. As soon as, he appeared the King called him and embraced him tenderly again and again. These first moments, so touching, passed in words broken by sobs and tears.

Shortly afterwards the King looking at the Dauphin was terrified by the same things that had previously struck me with affright. Everybody around was so, also the doctors more than the others. The King ordered them to feel his pulse; that they found bad, so they said afterwards; for the time they contented themselves with saying it was not regular, and that the Dauphin would do wisely to go to bed. The King embraced him again, recommended him very tenderly to take care of himself, and ordered him to go to bed. He obeyed and rose no more!

It was now late in the morning. The King had passed a cruel night and had a bad headache; he saw at his dinner, the few courtiers who presented themselves, and after dinner went to the Dauphin. The fever had augmented: the pulse was worse than before. The King passed into the apartments of Madame de Maintenon, and the Dauphin was left with his attendants and his doctors. He spent the day in prayers and holy reading.

On the morrow, Sunday, the uneasiness felt on account of the Dauphin augmented. He himself did not conceal his belief that he should never rise again, and that the plot Boudin had warned him of, had been executed. He explained himself to this effect more than once, and always with a disdain of earthly grandeur and an incomparable submission and love of God. It is impossible to describe the general consternation. On Monday the 15th, the King was bled. The Dauphin was no better than before. The King and Madame de Maintenon saw him separately several times during the day, which was passed in prayers and reading.

On Tuesday, the 16th, the Dauphin was worse. He felt himself devoured by a consuming fire, which the external fever did not seem to justify; but the pulse was very extraordinary and exceedingly menacing. This was a deceptive day. The marks on the Dauphin's face extended over all the body. They were regarded as the marks of measles. Hope arose thereon, but the doctors and the most clear-sighted of the Court could not forget that these same marks had shown themselves on the body of the Dauphine; a fact unknown out of her chamber until after death.

On Wednesday, the 17th, the malady considerably increased. I had news at all moments of the Dauphin's state from Cheverny, an excellent apothecary of the King and of my family. He hid nothing from us. He had told us what he thought of the Dauphine's illness; he told us now what he thought of the Dauphin's. I no longer hoped therefore, or rather I hoped to the end, against all hope.

On Wednesday the pains increased. They were like a devouring fire, but more violent than ever. Very late into the evening the Dauphin sent to the King for permission to receive the communion early the next morning, without ceremony and without display, at the mass performed in his chamber. Nobody heard of this, that evening; it was not known until the following morning. I was in extreme desolation; I scarcely saw the King once a day. I did nothing but go in quest of news several times a day, and to the house of M. de Chevreuse, where I was completely free. M. de Chevreuse—always calm, always sanguine—endeavoured to prove to us by his medical reasonings that there was more reason to hope than to fear, but he did so with a tranquillity that roused my impatience. I returned home to pass a cruel night.

On Thursday morning, the 18th of February, I learned that the Dauphin, who had waited for midnight with impatience, had heard mass immediately after the communion, had passed two hours in devout communication with God, and that his reason then became embarrassed. Madame de Saint-Simon told me afterwards that he had received extreme unction: in fine, that he died at half-past eight. These memoirs are not written to describe my private sentiments. But in reading them,—if, long after me, they shall ever appear, my state and that of Madame de Saint-Simon will only too keenly be felt. I will content myself with saying, that the first days after the Dauphin's death scarcely appeared to us more than moments; that I wished to quit all, to withdraw from the Court and the world, and that I was only hindered by the wisdom, conduct, and power over me of Madame de Saint-Simon, who yet had much trouble to subdue my sorrowful desires. Let me say something now of the young prince and his spouse, whom we thus lost in such quick succession.

Never did princess arrive amongst us so young with so much instruction, or with such capacity to profit by instruction. Her skilful father, who thoroughly knew our Court, had painted it to her, and had made her acquainted with the only manner of making herself happy there. From the first moment of her arrival she had acted upon his lessons. Gentle, timid, but adroit, fearing to give the slightest pain to anybody, and though all lightness and vivacity, very capable of far-stretching views; constraint, even to annoyance, cost her nothing, though she felt all its weight. Complacency was natural to her, flowed from her, and was exhibited towards every member of the Court.

Regularly plain, with cheeks hanging, a forehead too prominent, a nose without meaning, thick biting lips, hair and eye-brows of dark chestnut, and well planted; the most speaking and most beautiful eyes in the world; few teeth, and those all rotten, about which she was the first to talk and jest; the most beautiful complexion and skin; not much bosom, but what there was admirable; the throat long, with the suspicion of a goitre, which did not ill become her; her head carried gallantly, majestically, gracefully; her mien noble; her smile most expressive; her figure long, round, slender, easy, perfectly-shaped; her walk that of a goddess upon the clouds: with such qualifications she pleased supremely. Grace accompanied her every step, and shone through her manners and her most ordinary conversation. An air always simple and natural, often naive, but seasoned with wit-this with the ease peculiar to her, charmed all who approached her, and communicated itself to them. She wished to please even the most useless and the most ordinary persons, and yet without making an effort to do so. You were tempted to believe her wholly and solely devoted to those with whom she found herself. Her gaiety—young, quick, and active—animated all; and her nymph-like lightness carried her everywhere, like a whirlwind which fills several places at once, and gives them movement and life. She was the ornament of all diversions, the life and soul of all pleasure, and at balls ravished everybody by the justness and perfection of her dancing. She could be amused by playing for small sums but liked high gambling better, and was an excellent, good-tempered, and bold gamester.

She spared nothing, not even her health, to gain Madame de Maintenon, and through her the King. Her suppleness towards them was without example, and never for a moment was at fault. She accompanied it with all the discretion that her knowledge of them, acquired by study and experience, had given her, and could measure their dispositions to an inch. In this way she had acquired a familiarity with them such as none of the King's children, not even the bastards, had approached.

In public, serious, measured, with the King, and in timid decorum with Madame de Maintenon, whom she never addressed except as my aunt, thus prettily confounding friendship and rank. In private, prattling, skipping, flying around them, now perched upon the sides of their arm- chairs, now playing upon their knees, she clasped them round the neck, embraced them, kissed them, caressed them, rumpled them, tickled them under the chin, tormented them, rummaged their tables, their papers, their letters, broke open the seals, and read the contents in spite of opposition, if she saw that her waggeries were likely to be received in good part. When the King was with his ministers, when he received couriers, when the most important affairs were under discussion, she was present, and with such liberty, that, hearing the King and Madame de Maintenon speak one evening with affection of the Court of England, at the time when peace was hoped for from Queen Anne, "My aunt," she said, "you must admit that in England the queens govern better than the kings, and do you know why, my aunt?" asked she, running about and gambolling all the time, "because under kings it is women who govern, and men under queens." The joke is that they both laughed, and said she was right.

The King really could not do without her. Everything went wrong with him if she was not by; even at his public supper, if she were away an additional cloud of seriousness and silence settled around him. She took great care to see him every day upon arriving and departing; and if some ball in winter, or some pleasure party in summer, made her lose half the night, she nevertheless adjusted things so well that she went and embraced the King the moment he was up, and amused him with a description of the fete.

She was so far removed from the thoughts of death, that on Candlemas-day she talked with Madame de Saint-Simon of people who had died since she had been at Court, and of what she would herself do in old age, of the life she would lead, and of such like matters. Alas! it pleased God, for our misfortune, to dispose of her differently.

With all her coquetry—and she was not wanting in it—never woman seemed to take less heed of her appearance; her toilette was finished in a moment, she cared nothing for finery except at balls and fetes; if she displayed a little at other times it was simply in order to please the king. If the Court subsisted after her it was only to languish. Never was princess so regretted, never one so worthy of it: regrets have not yet passed away, the involuntary and secret bitterness they caused still remain, with a frightful blank not yet filled up.

Let me now turn to the Dauphin.

The youth of this prince made every one tremble. Stern and choleric to the last degree, and even against inanimate objects; impetuous with frenzy, incapable of suffering the slightest resistance even from the hours and the elements, without flying into a passion that threatened to destroy his body; obstinate to excess; passionately fond of all kind of voluptuousness, of women, with even a worse passion strongly developed at the same time; fond not less of wine, good living, hunting, music, and gaming, in which last he could not endure to be beaten; in fine, abandoned to every passion, and transported by every pleasure; oftentimes wild, naturally disposed towards cruelty; barbarous in raillery, and with an all-powerful capacity for ridicule.

He looked down upon all men as from the sky, as atoms with whom he had nothing in common; even his brothers scarcely appeared connecting links between himself and human nature, although all had been educated together in perfect equality. His sense and penetration shone through everything. His replies, even in anger, astonished everybody. He amused himself with the most abstract knowledge. The extent and vivacity of his intellect were prodigious, and rendered him incapable of applying himself to one study at a time.

So much intelligence and of such a kind, joined to such vivacity, sensibility, and passion, rendered his education difficult. But God, who is the master of all hearts, and whose divine spirit breathes where he wishes, worked a miracle on this prince between his eighteenth and twentieth years. From this abyss he came out affable, gentle, humane, moderate, patient, modest, penitent, and humble; and austere, even more than harmonised with his position. Devoted to his duties, feeling them to be immense, he thought only how to unite the duties of son and subject with those he saw to be destined for himself. The shortness of each day was his only sorrow. All his force, all his consolation, was in prayer and pious reading. He clung with joy to the cross of his Saviour, repenting sincerely of his past pride. The King, with his outside devotion, soon saw with secret displeasure his own life censured by that of a prince so young, who refused himself a new desk in order to give the money it would cost to the poor, and who did not care to accept some new gilding with which it was proposed to furnish his little room. Madame la Duchesse de Bourgogne, alarmed at so austere a spouse, left nothing undone in order to soften him. Her charms, with which he was smitten, the cunning and the unbridled importunities of the young ladies of her suite, disguised in a hundred different forms—the attraction of parties and pleasures to which he was far from insensible, all were displayed every day.. But for a long time he behaved not like a prince but like a novice. On one occasion he refused to be present at a ball on Twelfth Night, and in various ways made himself ridiculous at Court. In due time, however, he comprehended that the faithful performance of the duties proper to the state in which he had been placed, would be the conduct most agreeable to God. The bark of the tree, little by little, grew softer without affecting the solidity of the trunk. He applied himself to the studies which were necessary, in order to instruct himself in public affairs, and at the same time he lent himself more to the world, doing so with so much grace, with such a natural air, that everybody soon began to grow reconciled to him.

The discernment of this prince was such, that, like the bee, he gathered the most perfect substance from the best and most beautiful flowers. He tried to fathom men, to draw from them the instruction and the light that he could hope for. He conferred sometimes, but rarely, with others besides his chosen few. I was the only one, not of that number, who had complete access to him; with me he opened his heart upon the present and the future with confidence, with sageness, with discretion. A volume would not describe sufficiently my private interviews with this prince, what love of good! what forgetfulness of self! what researches! what fruit! what purity of purpose!—May I say it? what reflection of the divinity in that mind, candid, simple, strong, which as much as is possible here below had preserved the image of its maker!

If you had business, and thought of opening it to him, say for a quarter of an hour or half an hour, he gave you oftentimes two hours or more, according as he found himself at liberty. Yet he was without verbiage, compliments, prefaces, pleasantries, or other hindrances; went straight to the point, and allowed you to go also.

His undue scruples of devotion diminished every day, as he found himself face to face with the world; above all, he was well cured of the inclination for piety in preference to talent, that is to say, for making a man ambassador, minister, or general, rather on account of his devotedness than of his capacity or experience. He saw the danger of inducing hypocrisy by placing devotion too high as a qualification for employ.

It was he who was not afraid to say publicly, in the Salon of Marly, that "a king is made for his subjects, and not the subjects for him;" a remark that, except under his own reign, which God did not permit, would have been the most frightful blasphemy.

Great God! what a spectacle you gave to us in him. What tender but tranquil views he had! What submission and love of God! What a consciousness of his own nothingness, and of his sins! What a magnificent idea of the infinite mercy! What religious and humble fear! What tempered confidence! What patience!

What constant goodness for all who approached him! France fell, in fine, under this last chastisement. God showed to her a prince she merited not. The earth was not worthy of him; he was ripe already for the blessed eternity!

CHAPTER LX

The consternation at the event that had taken place was real and general; it penetrated to foreign lands and courts. Whilst the people wept for him who thought only of their relief, and all France lamented a prince who only wished to reign in order to render it flourishing and happy, the sovereigns of Europe publicly lamented him whom they regarded as their example, and whose virtues were preparing him to be their arbitrator, and the peaceful and revered moderator of nations. The Pope was so touched that he resolved of himself to set aside all rule and hold expressly a consistory; deplored there the infinite loss the church and all Christianity had sustained, and pronounced a complete eulogium of the prince who caused the just regrets of all Europe.

On Saturday, the 13th, the corpse of the Dauphine was left in its bed with uncovered face, and opened the same evening at eleven in presence of all the faculty. On the 15th it was placed in the grand cabinet, where masses were continually said.

On Friday, the 19th, the corpse of Monseigneur le Dauphin was opened, a little more than twenty-four hours after his death, also in presence of all the faculty. His heart was immediately carried to Versailles, and placed by the side of that of Madame la Dauphine. Both were afterwards taken to the Val de Grace. They arrived at midnight with a numerous cortege. All was finished in two hours. The corpse of Monseigneur le Dauphin was afterwards carried from Marly to Versailles, and placed by the side of Madame la Dauphine on the same estrade.

On Tuesday, the 23rd February, the two bodies were taken from Versailles to Saint-Denis in the same chariot. The procession began to enter Paris by the Porte Saint-Honore at two o'clock in the morning, and arrived between seven and eight o'clock in the morning at Saint-Denis. There was great order in Paris, and no confusion.

On Tuesday, the 8th March, Monseigneur le Duc de Bretagne, eldest son of Monsieur le Dauphin, who had succeeded to the name and rank of his father, being then only five years and some months old, and who had been seized with measles within a few days, expired, in spite of all the remedies given him. His brother, M. le Duc d'Anjou, who still sucked, was taken ill at the same time, but thanks to the care of the Duchesse de Ventadour, whom in after life he never forgot, and who administered an antidote, escaped, and is now King.

Thus three Dauphins died in less than a year, and father, mother, and eldest son in twenty-four days! On Wednesday, the 9th of March, the corpse of the little Dauphin was opened at night, and without any ceremony his heart was taken to the Val de Grace, his body to Saint-Denis, and placed by the side of those of his father and mother. M. le Duc d'Anjou, now, sole remaining child, succeeded to the title and to the rank of Dauphin.

I have said that the bodies of the Dauphin and the Dauphine were opened in presence of all the faculty. The report made upon the opening of the latter was not consolatory. Only one of the doctors declared there were no signs of poison; the rest were of the opposite opinion. When the body of the Dauphin was opened, everybody was terrified. His viscera were all dissolved; his heart had no consistency; its substance flowed through the hands of those who tried to hold it; an intolerable odour, too, filled the apartment. The majority of the doctors declared they saw in all this the effect of a very subtle and very violent poison, which had consumed all the interior of the body, like a burning fire. As before, there was one of their number who held different views, but this was Marechal, who declared that to persuade the King of the existence of secret enemies of his family would be to kill him by degrees.

This medical opinion that the cause of the Dauphin's and the Dauphine's death was poison, soon spread like wildfire over the Court and the city. Public indignation fell upon M. d'Orleans, who was at once pointed out as the poisoner. The rapidity with which this rumour filled the Court, Paris, the provinces, the least frequented places, the most isolated monasteries, the most deserted solitudes, all foreign countries and all the peoples of Europe, recalled to me the efforts of the cabal, which had previously spread such black reports against the honour of him whom all the world now wept, and showed that the cabal, though dispersed, was not dissolved.

In effect M. du Maine, now the head of the cabal, who had all to gain and nothing to lose by the death of the Dauphin and Dauphine, from both of whom he had studiously held aloof, and who thoroughly disliked M. d'Orleans, did all in his power to circulate this odious report. He communicated it to Madame de Maintenon, by whom it reached the King. In a short time all the Court, down to the meanest valets, publicly cried vengeance upon M. d'Orleans, with an air of the most unbridled indignation and of perfect security.

M. d'Orleans, with respect to the two losses that afflicted the public, had an interest the most directly opposite to that of M. du Maine; he had everything to gain by the life of the Dauphin and Dauphine, and unless he had been a monster vomited forth from hell he could not have been guilty of the crime with which he was charged. Nevertheless, the odious accusation flew from mouth to mouth, and took refuge in every breast.

Let us compare the interest M. d'Orleans had in the life of the Dauphin with the interest M. du Maine had in his death, and then look about for the poisoner. But this is not all. Let us remember how M. le Duc d'Orleans was treated by Monseigneur, and yet what genuine grief he displayed at the death of that prince. What a contrast was this conduct with that of M. du Maine at another time, who, after leaving the King (Louis XIV.) at the point of death, delivered over to an ignorant peasant, imitated that peasant so naturally and so pleasantly, that bursts of laughter extended to the gallery, and scandalized the passers-by. This is a celebrated and very characteristic fact, which will find its proper place if I live long enough to carry these memoirs up to the death of the King.

M. d'Orleans was, however, already in such bad odour, that people were ready to believe anything to his discredit. They drank in this new report so rapidly, that on the 17th of February, as he went with Madame to give the holy water to the corpse of the Dauphine, the crowd of the people threw out all sorts of accusations against him, which both he and Madame very distinctly heard, without daring to show it, and were in trouble, embarrassment, and indignation, as may be imagined. There was even ground for fearing worse from an excited and credulous populace when M. d'Orleans went alone to give the holy water to the corpse of the Dauphin. For he had to endure on his passage atrocious insults from a populace which uttered aloud the most frightful observations, which pointed the finger at him with the coarsest epithets, and which believed it was doing him a favour in not falling upon him and tearing him to pieces!

Similar circumstances took place at the funeral procession. The streets resounded more with cries of indignation against M. d'Orleans and abuse of him than with grief. Silent precautions were not forgotten in Paris in order to check the public fury, the boiling over of which was feared at different moments. The people recompensed themselves by gestures, cries, and other atrocities, vomited against M. d'Orleans. Near the Palais Royal, before which the procession passed, the increase of shouts, of cries, of abuse, was so great, that for some minutes everything was to be feared.

It may be imagined what use M. du Maine contrived to make of the public folly, the rumours of the Paris cafes, the feeling of the salon of Marly, that of the Parliament, the reports that arrived from the provinces and foreign countries. In a short time so overpowered was M. d'Orleans by the feeling against him everywhere exhibited, that acting upon very ill- judged advice he spoke to the King upon the subject, and begged to be allowed to surrender himself as a prisoner at the Bastille, until his character was cleared from stain.

I was terribly annoyed when I heard that M. d'Orleans had taken this step, which could not possibly lead to good. I had quite another sort of scheme in my head which I should have proposed to him had I known of his resolve. Fortunately, however, the King was persuaded not to grant M. d'Orleans' request, out of which therefore nothing came. The Duke meanwhile lived more abandoned by everybody than ever; if in the salon he approached a group of courtiers, each, without the least hesitation, turned to the right or to the left and went elsewhere, so that it was impossible for him to accost anybody except by surprise, and if he did so, he was left alone directly after with the most marked indecency. In a word, I was the only person, I say distinctly, the only person, who spoke to M. d'Orleans as before. Whether in his own house or in the palace I conversed with him, seated myself by his side in a corner of the salon, where assuredly we had no third person to fear, and walked with him in the gardens under the very windows of the King and of Madame de Maintenon.

Nevertheless, all my friends warned me that if I pursued this conduct so opposite to that in vogue, I should assuredly fall into disgrace. I held firm. I thought that when we did not believe our friends guilty we ought not to desert them, but, on the contrary, to draw closer to them, as by honour bound, give them the consolation due from us, and show thus to the world our hatred for calumny. My friends insisted; gave me to understand that the King disapproved my conduct, that Madame de Maintenon was annoyed at it: they forgot nothing to awaken my fears. But I was insensible to all they said to me, and did not omit seeing M. d'Orleans a single day; often stopping with him two and three hours at a time.

A few weeks had passed over thus, when one morning M. de Beauvilliers called upon me, and urged me to plead business, and at once withdraw to La Ferme; intimating that if I did not do so of my own accord, I should be compelled by an order from the King. He never explained himself more fully, but I have always remained persuaded that the King or Madame de Maintenon had sent him to me, and had told him that I should be banished if I did not banish myself. Neither my absence nor my departure made any stir; nobody suspected anything. I was carefully informed, without knowing by whom, when my exile was likely to end: and I returned, after a month or five weeks, straight to the Court, where I kept up the same intimacy with M. d'Orleans as before.

But he was not yet at the end of his misfortunes. The Princesse des Ursins had not forgiven him his pleasantry at her expense. Chalais, one of her most useful agents, was despatched by her on a journey so mysterious that its obscurity has never been illuminated. He was eighteen days on the road, unknown, concealing his name, and passing within two leagues of Chalais, where his father and mother lived, without giving them any signs of life, although all were on very good terms. He loitered secretly in Poitou, and at last arrested there a Cordelier monk, of middle age, in the convent of Bressuire, who cried, "Ah! I am lost!" upon being caught. Chalais conducted him to the prison of Poitiers, whence he despatched to Madrid an officer of dragoons he had brought with him, and who knew this Cordelier, whose name has never transpired, although it is certain he was really a Cordelier, and that he was returning from as journey in Italy and Germany that had extended as far as Vienna. Chalais pushed on to Paris, and came to Marly on the 27th of April, a day on which the King had taken medicine. After dinner he was taken by Torcy to the King, with whom he remained half an hour, delaying thus the Council of State for the same time, and then returned immediately to Paris. So much trouble had not been taken for no purpose: and Chalais had not prostituted himself to play the part of prevot to a miserable monk without expecting good winnings from the game. Immediately afterwards the most dreadful rumours were everywhere in circulation against M. d'Orleans, who, it was said, had poisoned the Dauphin and Dauphine by means of this monk, who, nevertheless, was far enough away from our Prince and Princess at the time of their death. In an instant Paris resounded with these horrors; the provinces were inundated with them, and immediately afterwards foreign countries—this too with an incredible rapidity, which plainly showed how well the plot had been prepared—and a publicity that reached the very caverns of the earth. Madame des Ursins was not less served in Spain than M. du Maine and Madame de Maintenon in France. The anger of the public was doubled. The Cordelier was brought, bound hand and foot, to the Bastille, and delivered up to D'Argenson, Lieutenant of Police.

This D'Argenson rendered an account to the King of many things which Pontchartrain, as Secretary of State, considered to belong to his department. Pontchartrain was vexed beyond measure at this, and could not see without despair his subaltern become a kind of minister more feared, more valued, more in consideration than he, and conduct himself always in such manner that he gained many powerful friends, and made but few enemies, and those of but little moment. M. d'Orleans bowed before the storm that he could not avert; it could not increase the general desertion; he had accustomed himself to his solitude, and, as he had never heard this monk spoken of, had not the slightest fear on his account. D'Argenson, who questioned the Cordelier several times, and carried his replies daily to the King, was sufficiently adroit to pay his court to M. d'Orleans, by telling him that the prisoner had uttered nothing which concerned him, and by representing the services he did M. d'Orleans with the King. Like a sagacious man, D'Argenson saw the madness of popular anger devoid of all foundation, and which could not hinder M.

d'Orleans from being a very considerable person in France, during a minority that—the age of the King showed to be pretty near. He took care, therefore, to avail himself of the mystery which surrounded his office, to ingratiate himself more and more with M. d'Orleans, whom he had always carefully though secretly served; and his conduct, as will be seen in due time, procured him a large fortune.

But I have gone too far. I must retrace my steps, to speak of things I have omitted to notice in their proper place.

The two Dauphins and the Dauphine were interred at Saint-Denis, on Monday, the 18th of April. The funeral oration was pronounced by Maboul, Bishop of Aleth, and pleased; M. de Metz, chief chaplain, officiated; the service commenced at about eleven o'clock. As it was very long, it was thought well to have at hand a large vase of vinegar, in case anybody should be ill. M. de Metz having taken the first oblation, and observing that very little wine was left for the second, asked for more. This large vase of vinegar was supposed to be wine, and M. de Metz, who wished to strengthen himself, said, washing his fingers over the chalice, "fill right up." He swallowed all at a draught, and did not perceive until the end that he had drunk vinegar; his grimace and his complaint caused some little laughter round him; and he often related this adventure, which much soured him. On Monday, the 20th of May, the funeral service for the Dauphin and Dauphine was performed at Notre Dame.

Let me here say, that before the Prince and his spouse were buried, that is to say, the 6th of April, the King gave orders for the recommencement of the usual play at Marly; and that M. le Duc de Berry and Madame la Duchesse de Berry presided in the salon at the public lansquenet and brelan; and the different gaming tables for all the Court. In a short time the King dined in Madame de Maintenon's apartments once or twice a week, and had music there. And all this, as I have remarked, with the corpse of the Dauphin and that of the Dauphine still above ground.

The gap left by the death of the Dauphine could not, however, be easily filled up. Some months after her loss, the King began to feel great ennui steal upon him in the hours when he had no work with his ministers. The few ladies admitted into the apartments of Madame de Maintenon when he was there, were unable to entertain him. Music, frequently introduced, languished from that cause. Detached scenes from the comedies of Moliere were thought of, and were played by the King's musicians, comedians for the nonce. Madame de Maintenon introduced, too, the Marechal de Villeroy, to amuse the King by relating their youthful adventures.

Evening amusements became more and more frequent in Madame de Maintenon's apartments, where, however, nothing could fill up the void left by the poor Dauphine.

I have said little of the grief I felt at the loss of the prince whom everybody so deeply regretted. As will be believed, it was bitter and profound. The day of his death, I barricaded myself in my own house, and only left it for one instant in order to join the King at his promenade in the gardens. The vexation I felt upon seeing him followed almost as usual, did not permit me to stop more than an instant. All the rest of the stay at Versailles, I scarcely left my room, except to visit M. de Beauvilliers. I will admit that, to reach M. de Beauvilliers' house, I made a circuit between the canal and the gardens of Versailles, so as to spare myself the sight of the chamber of death, which I had not force enough to approach. I admit that I was weak. I was sustained neither by the piety, superior to all things, of M. de Beauvilliers, nor by that of Madame de Saint-Simon, who nevertheless not the less suffered. The truth is, I was in despair. To those who know my position, this will appear less strange than my being able to support at all so complete a misfortune. I experienced this sadness precisely at the same age as that of my father when he lost Louis XIII.; but he at least had enjoyed the results of favour, whilst I, 'Gustavi paululum mellis, et ecce morior.' Yet this was not all.

In the casket of the Dauphin there were several papers he had asked me for. I had drawn them up in all confidence; he had preserved them in the same manner. There was one, very large, in my hand, which if seen by the King, would have robbed me of his favour for ever; ruined me without hope of return. We do not think in time of such catastrophes. The King knew my handwriting; he did not know my mode of thought, but might pretty well have guessed it. I had sometimes supplied him with means to do so; my good friends of the Court had done the rest. The King when he discovered my paper would also discover on what close terms of intimacy I had been with the Dauphin, of which he had no suspicion. My anguish was then cruel, and there seemed every reason to believe that if my secret was found out, I should be disgraced and exiled during all the rest of the King's reign.

What a contrast between the bright heaven I had so recently gazed upon and the abyss now yawning at my feet! But so it is in the Court and the world! I felt then the nothingness of even the most desirable future, by an inward sentiment, which, nevertheless, indicates how we cling to it. Fear on account of the contents of the casket had scarcely any power over me. I was obliged to reflect in order to return to it from time to time. Regret for this incomparable Dauphin pierced my heart, and suspended all the faculties of my soul. For a long time I wished to fly from the Court, so that I might never again see the deceitful face of the world; and it was some time before prudence and honour got the upper hand.

It so happened that the Duc de Beauvilliers himself was able to carry this casket to the King, who had the key of it. M. de Beauvilliers in fact resolved not to trust it out of his own hands, but to wait until he was well enough to take it to the King, so that he might then try to hide my papers from view. This task was difficult, for he did not know the position in the casket of these dangerous documents, and yet it was our only resource. This terrible uncertainty lasted more than a fortnight.

On Tuesday, the 1st of March, M. de Beauvilliers carried the casket to the King. He came to me shortly after, and before sitting down, indicated by signs that there was no further occasion for fear. He then related to me that he had found the casket full of a mass of documents, finance projects, reports from the provinces, papers of all kinds, that he had read some of them to the King on purpose to weary him, and had succeeded so well that the King soon was satisfied by hearing only the titles; and, at last, tired out by not finding anything important, said it was not worth while to read more, and that there was nothing to do but to throw everything into the fire. The Duke assured me that he did not wait to be told twice, being all the more anxious to comply, because at the bottom of the casket he had seen some of my handwriting, which he had promptly covered up in taking other papers to read their titles to the King; and that immediately the word "fire" was uttered, he confusedly threw all the papers into the casket, and then emptied it near the fire, between the King and Madame de Maintenon, taking good care as he did so that my documents should not be seen,—even cautiously using the tongs in order to prevent any piece flying away, and not quitting the fireplace until he had seen every page consumed. We embraced each other, in the relief we reciprocally felt, relief proportioned to the danger we had run.

VOLUME 9.: CHAPTER LXI

Let me here relate an incident which should have found a place earlier, but which has been omitted in order that what has gone before might be uninterrupted. On the 16th of the previous July the King made a journey to Fontainebleau, where he remained until the 14th of September. I should suppress the bagatelle which happened on the occasion of this journey, if it did not serve more and more to characterize the King.

Madame la Duchesse de Berry was in the family way for the first time, had been so for nearly three months, was much inconvenienced, and had a pretty strong fever. M. Fagon, the doctor, thought it would be imprudent for her not to put off travelling for a day or two. Neither she nor M, d'Orleans dared to speak about it. M. le Duc de Berry timidly hazarded a word, and was ill received. Madame la Duchesse d'Orleans more timid still, addressed herself to Madame, and to Madame de Maintenon, who, indifferent as they might be respecting Madame la Duchesse de Berry, thought her departure so hazardous that, supported by Fagon, they spoke of it to the King. It was useless. They were not daunted, however, and this dispute lasted three or four days. The end of it was, that the King grew thoroughly angry and agreed, by way of capitulation, that the journey should be performed in a boat instead of a coach.

It was arranged that Madame la Duchesse de Berry should leave Marly, where the King then was, on the 13th, sleep at the Palais Royal that night and repose herself there all the next day and night, that on the 15th she should set out for Petit-Bourg, where the King was to halt for the night, and arrive like him, on the 16th, at Fontainebleau, the whole journey to be by the river. M. le Duc de Berry had permission to accompany his wife; but during the two nights they were to rest in Paris the King angrily forbade them to go anywhere, even to the Opera, although that building joined the Palais Royal, and M. d'Orleans' box could be reached without going out of the palace.

On the 14th the King, under pretence of inquiry after them, repeated this prohibition to M. le Duc de Berry and Madame his wife, and also to M. d'Orleans and Madame d'Orleans, who had been included in it. He carried his caution so far as to enjoin Madame de Saint-Simon to see that Madame la Duchesse de Berry obeyed the instructions she had received. As may be believed, his orders were punctually obeyed. Madame de Saint-Simon could not refuse to remain and sleep in the Palais Royal, where the apartment of the queen-mother was given to her. All the while the party was shut up there was a good deal of gaming in order to console M. le Duc de Berry for his confinement.

The provost of the merchants had orders to prepare boats for the trip to Fontainebleau. He had so little time that they were ill chosen. Madame la Duchesse de Berry embarked, however, on the 15th, and arrived, with fever, at ten o'clock at night at Petit-Bourg, where the King appeared rejoiced by an obedience so exact.

On the morrow the journey recommenced. In passing Melun, the boat of Madame la Duchesse de Berry struck against the bridge, was nearly capsized, and almost swamped, so that they were all in great danger. They got off, however, with fear and a delay. Disembarking in great disorder at Valvin, where their equipages were waiting for there, they arrived at Fontainebleau two hours after midnight. The King, pleased beyond measure, went the next morning to see Madame la Duchesse de Berry in the beautiful apartment of the queen-mother that had been given to her. From the moment of her arrival she had been forced to keep her bed, and at six o'clock in the morning of the 21st of July she miscarried and was delivered of a daughter, still-born. Madame de Saint-Simon ran to tell the King; he did not appear much moved; he had been obeyed! The Duchesse de Beauvilliers and the Marquise de Chatillon were named by the King to carry the embryo to Saint-Denis. As it was only a girl, and as the miscarriage had no ill effect, consolation soon came.

It was some little time after this occurrence, that we heard of the defeat of the Czar by the Grand Vizier upon the Pruth. The Czar, annoyed by the protection the Porte had accorded to the King of Sweden (in retirement at Bender), made an appeal to arms, and fell into the same error as that which had occasioned the defeat of the King of Sweden by him. The Turks drew him to the Pruth across deserts supplied with nothing; if he did not risk all, by a very unequal battle, he must perish. The Czar was at the head of sixty thousand men: he lost more than thirty thousand on the Pruth, the rest were dying of hunger and misery; and he, without any resources, could scarcely avoid surrendering himself and his forces to the Turks. In this pressing extremity, a common woman whom he had taken away from her husband, a drummer in the army, and whom he had publicly espoused after having repudiated and confined his own wife in a convent,— proposed that he should try by bribery to induce the Grand Vizier to allow him and the wreck of his forces to retreat The Czar approved of the proposition, without hoping for success from it. He sent to the Grand Vizier and ordered him to be spoken to in secret. The Vizier was dazzled by the gold, the precious stones, and several valuable things that were offered to him. He accepted and received them; and signed a treaty by which the Czar was permitted to retire, with all who accompanied him, into his own states by the shortest road, the Turks to furnish him with provisions, with which he was entirely unprovided. The Czar, on his side, agreed to give up Azof as soon as he returned; destroy all the forts and burn all the vessels that he had upon the Black Sea; allow the King of Sweden to return by Pomerania; and to pay the Turks and their Prince all the expenses of the war.

The Grand Vizier found such an opposition in the Divan to this treaty, and such boldness in the minister of the King of Sweden, who accompanied him, in exciting against him all the chiefs of the army, that it was within an ace of being broken; and the Czar, with every one left to him, of being made prisoner. The latter was in no condition to make even the least resistance. The Grand Vizier had only to will it, in order to execute it on the spot. In addition to the glory of leading captive to Constantinople the Czar, his Court, and his troops, there would have been his ransom, which must have cost not a little. But if he had been thus stripped of his riches, they would have been for the Sultan, and the Grand Vizier preferred having them for himself. He braved it then with authority and menaces, and hastened the Czar's departure and his own. The Swedish minister, charged with protests from the principal Turkish chiefs, hurried to Constantinople, where the Grand Vizier was strangled upon arriving.

The Czar never forgot this service of his wife, by whose courage and presence of mind he had been saved. The esteem he conceived for her, joined to his friendship, induced him to crown her Czarina, and to consult her upon all his affairs and all his schemes. Escaped from danger, he was a long time without giving up Azof, or demolishing his forts on the Black Sea. As for his vessels, he kept them nearly all, and would not allow the King of Sweden to return into Germany, as he had agreed, thus almost lighting up a fresh war with the Turk.

On the 6th of November, 1711, at about eight o'clock in the evening, the shock of an earthquake was felt in Paris and at Versailles; but it was so slight that few people perceived it. In several places towards Touraine and Poitou, in Saxony, and in some of the German towns near, it was very perceptible at the same day and hour. At this date a new tontine was established in Paris.

I have so often spoken of Marshal Catinat, of his virtue, wisdom, modesty, and disinterestedness; of the rare superiority of his sentiments, and of his great qualities as captain, that nothing remains for me to say except that he died at this time very advanced in years, at his little house of Saint-Gratien, near Saint-Denis, where he had retired, and which he seldom quitted, although receiving there but few friends. By his simplicity and frugality, his contempt for worldly distinction, and his uniformity of conduct, he recalled the memory of those great men who, after the best-merited triumphs, peacefully returned to the plough, still loving their country and but little offended by the ingratitude of the Rome they had so well served. Catinat placed his philosophy at the service of his piety. He had intelligence, good sense, ripe reflection; and he never forgot his origin; his dress, his equipages, his furniture, all were of the greatest simplicity. His air and his deportment were so also. He was tall, dark, and thin; had an aspect pensive, slow, and somewhat mean; with very fine and expressive eyes. He deplored the signal faults that he saw succeed each other unceasingly; the gradual extinction of all emulation; the luxury, the emptiness, the ignorance, the confusion of ranks; the inquisition in the place of the police: he saw all the signs of destruction, and he used to say it was only a climax of dangerous disorder that could restore order to the realm.

Vendome was one of the few to whom the death of the Dauphin and the Dauphine brought hope and joy. He had deemed himself expatriated for the rest of his life. He saw, now, good chances before him of returning to our Court, and of playing a part there again. He had obtained some honour in Spain; he aimed at others even higher, and hoped to return to France with all the honours of a Prince of the Blood. His idleness, his free living, his debauchery, had prolonged his stay upon the frontier, where he had more facilities for gratifying his tastes than at Madrid. In that city, it is true, he did not much constrain himself, but he was forced to do so to some extent by courtly usages. He was, then, quite at home on the frontier; there was nothing to do; for the Austrians, weakened by the departure of the English, were quite unable to attack; and Vendome, floating upon the delights of his new dignities, thought only of enjoying himself in the midst of profound idleness, under pretext that operations could not at once be commenced.

In order to be more at liberty he separated from the general officers, and established himself with his valets and two or three of his most familiar friends, cherished companions everywhere, at Vignarez, a little isolated hamlet, almost deserted, on the sea-shore and in the kingdom of Valencia. His object was to eat fish there to his heart's content. He carried out that object, and filled himself to repletion for nearly a month. He became unwell—his diet, as may be believed, was enough to cause this—but his illness increased so rapidly, and in so strange a manner, after having for a long time seemed nothing that the few around him suspected poison, and sent on all sides for assistance. But the malady would not wait; it augmented rapidly with strange symptoms. Vendome could not sign a will that was presented to him; nor a letter to the King, its which he asked that his brother might be permitted to return to Court. Everybody near flew from him and abandoned him, so that he remained in the hands of three or four of the meanest valets, whilst the rest robbed him of everything and decamped. He passed thus the last two or three days of his life, without a priest,—no mention even had been made of one,—without other help than that of a single surgeon. The three or four valets who remained near him, seeing him at his last extremity, seized hold of the few things he still possessed, and for want of better plunder, dragged off his bedclothes and the mattress from under him. He piteously cried to them at least not to leave him to die naked upon the bare bed. I know not whether they listened to him.

Thus died on Friday, the 10th of June, 1712, the haughtiest of men; and the happiest, except in the later years of his life. After having been obliged to speak of him so often, I get rid of him now, once and for ever. He was fifty-eight years old; but in spite of the blind and prodigious favour he had enjoyed, that favour had never been able to make ought but a cabal hero out of a captain who was a very bad general, and a man whose vices were the shame of humanity. His death restored life and joy to all Spain.

Aguilar, a friend of the Duc de Noailles, was accused of having poisoned him; but took little pains to defend himself, inasmuch as little pains were taken to substantiate the accusation. The Princesse des Ursins, who had so well profited by his life in order to increase her own greatness, did not profit less by his death. She felt her deliverance from a new Don Juan of Spain who had ceased to be supple in her hands, and who might have revived, in the course of time, all the power and authority he had formerly enjoyed in France. She was not shocked them by the joy which burst out without constraint; nor by the free talk of the Court, the city, the army, of all Spain. But in order to sustain what she had done, and cheaply pay her court to M. du Maine, Madame de Maintenon, and even to the King, she ordered that the corpse of this hideous monster of greatness and of fortune should be carried to the Escurial. This was crowning the glory of M. de Vendome in good earnest; for no private persons are buried in the Escurial, although several are to be found in Saint-Denis. But meanwhile, until I speak of the visit I made to the Escurial—I shall do so if I live long enough to carry these memoirs up to the death of M. d'Orleans,—let me say something of that illustrious sepulchre.

The Pantheon is the place where only the bodies of kings and queens who have had posterity are admitted. In a separate place, near, though not on the same floor, and resembling a library, the bodies of children, and of queens who have had no posterity, are ranged. A third place, a sort of antechamber to the last named, is rightly called "the rotting room;" whilst the other improperly bears the same name. In whilst third room, there is nothing to be seen but four bare walls and a table in the middle. The walls being very thick, openings are made in them in which the bodies are placed. Each body has an opening to itself, which is afterwards walled up, so that nothing is seen. When it is thought that the corpse has been closed up sufficiently long to be free from odour the wall is opened, the body taken out, and put in a coffin which allows a portion of it to be seen towards the feet. This coffin is covered with a rich stuff and carried into an adjoining room.

The body of the Duc de Vendome had been walled up nine years when I entered the Escurial. I was shown the place it occupied, smooth like every part of the four walls and without mark. I gently asked the monks who did me the honours of the place, when the body would be removed to the other chamber. They would not satisfy my curiosity, showed some indignation, and plainly intimated that this removal was not dreamt of, and that as M. de Vendome had been so carefully walled up he might remain so!

Harlay, formerly chief-president, of whom I have so often had occasion to speak, died a short time after M. de Vendome. I have already made him known. I will simply add an account of the humiliation to which this haughty cynic was reduced. He hired a house in the Rue de l'Universite with a partition wall between his garden and that of the Jacobins of the Faubourg Saint-Germain. The house did not belong to the Jacobins, like the houses of the Rue Saint-Dominique, and the Rue du Bac, which, in order that they might command higher rents, were put in connection with the convent garden. These mendicant Jacobins thus derive fifty thousand livres a-year. Harlay, accustomed to exercise authority, asked them for a door into their garden. He was refused. He insisted, had them spoken to, and succeeded no better. Nevertheless the Jacobins comprehended that although this magistrate, recently so powerful, was now nothing by himself, he had a son and a cousin, Councillors of State, whom they might some day have to do with, and who for pride's sake might make themselves very disagreeable. The argument of interest is the best of all with monks. The Jacobins changed their mind. The Prior, accompanied by some of the notabilities of the convent, went to Harlay with excuses, and said he was at liberty, if he liked, to make the door. Harlay, true to his character, looked at them askance, and replied, that he had changed his mind and would do without it. The monks, much troubled by his refusal, insisted; he interrupted them and said, "Look you, my fathers, I am grandson of Achille du Harlay, Chief-President of the Parliament, who so well served the State and the Kingdom, and who for his support of the public cause was dragged to the Bastille, where he expected to be hanged by those rascally Leaguers; it would ill become me, therefore, to enter the house, or pray to God there, of folks of the same stamp as that Jacques Clement." And he immediately turned his back upon them, leaving them confounded. This was his last act of vigour. He took it into his head afterwards to go out visiting a good deal, and as he preserved all his old unpleasant manners, he afflicted all he visited; he went even to persons who had often cooled their heels in his antechambers. By degrees, slight but frequent attacks of apoplexy troubled his speech, so that people had great difficulty in understanding him, and he in speaking. In this state he did not cease his visits and could not perceive that many doors were closed to him. He died in this misery, and this neglect, to the great relief of the few who by relationship were obliged to see him, above all of his son and his domestic.

On the 17th July, a truce between France and England was published in Flanders, at the head of the troops of the two crowns. The Emperor, however, was not yet inclined for peace and his forces under Prince Eugene continued to oppose us in Flanders, where, however, the tide at last turned in our favour. The King was so flattered by the overflow of joy that took place at Fontainebleau on account of our successes, that he thanked the country for it, for the first time in his life. Prince Eugene, in want of bread and of everything, raised the siege of Landrecies, which he had been conducting, and terrible desertion took place among his troops.

About this time, there was an irruption of wolves, which caused great disorders in the Orleannais; the King's wolf-hunters were sent there, and the people were authorised to take arms and make a number of grand battues.

CHAPTER LXII.

Peace was now all but concluded between France and England. There was, however, one great obstacle still in its way. Queen Anne and her Council were stopped by the consideration that the king of Spain would claim to succeed to the Crown of France, if the little Dauphin should die. Neither England nor any of the other powers at war would consent to see the two principal crowns of Europe upon the same head. It was necessary, then, above all things to get rid of this difficulty, and so arrange the order of succession to our throne, that the case to be provided against could never happen. Treaties, renunciations, and oaths, all of which the King had already broken, appeared feeble guarantees in the eyes of Europe. Something stronger was sought for. It could not be found; because there is nothing more sacred among men than engagements which they consider binding on each other. What was wanting then in mere forms it was now thought could be supplied by giving to those forms the greatest possible solemnity.

It was a long time before we could get over the difficulty. The King would accord nothing except promises in order to guarantee to Europe that the two crowns should never be united upon the same head. His authority was wounded at the idea of being called upon to admit, as it were, a rival near it. Absolute without reply, as he had become, he had extinguished and absorbed even the minutest trace, idea, and recollection of all other authority, all other power in France except that which emanated from himself alone. The English, little accustomed to such maxims, proposed that the States-General should assemble in order to give weight to the renunciations to be made. They said, and with reason, that it was not enough that the King of Spain should renounce France unless France renounced Spain; and that this formality was necessary in order to break the double bonds which attached Spain to France, as France was attached to Spain. Accustomed to their parliaments, which are in effect their States-General, they believed ours preserved the same authority, and they thought such authority the greatest to be obtained and the best capable of solidly supporting that of the King.

The effect of this upon the mind of a Prince almost deified in his own eyes, and habituated to the most unlimited despotism, cannot be expressed. To show him that the authority of his subjects was thought necessary in order to confirm his own, wounded him in his most delicate part. The English were made to understand the weakness and the uselessness of what they asked; for the powerlessness of our States- General was explained to them, and they saw at once how vain their help would be, even if accorded.

For a long time nothing was done; France saying that a treaty of renunciation and an express confirmatory declaration of the King, registered in the Parliament, were sufficient; the English replying by reference to the fate of past treaties. Peace meanwhile was arranged with the English, and much beyond our hopes remained undisturbed.

In due time matters were so far advanced in spite of obstacles thrown in the way by the allies, that the Duc d'Aumont was sent as ambassador into England; and the Duke of Hamilton was named as ambassador for France. This last, however, losing his life in a duel with Lord Mohun, the Duke of Shrewsbury was appointed in his stead.

At the commencement of the new year the Duke and Duchess of Shrewsbury arrived in Paris. The Duchess was a great fat masculine creature, more than past the meridian, who had been beautiful and who affected to be so still; bare bosomed; her hair behind her ears; covered with rouge and patches, and full of finicking ways. All her manners were that of a mad thing, but her play, her taste, her magnificence, even her general familiarity, made her the fashion. She soon declared the women's head-dresses ridiculous, as indeed they were. They were edifices of brass wire, ribbons, hair, and all sorts of tawdry rubbish more than two feet high, making women's faces seem in the middle of their bodies. The old ladies wore the same, but made of black gauze. If they moved ever so lightly the edifice trembled and the inconvenience was extreme. The King could not endure them, but master as he was of everything was unable to banish them. They lasted for ten years and more, despite all he could say and do. What this monarch had been unable to perform, the taste and example of a silly foreigner accomplished with the most surprising rapidity. From extreme height, the ladies descended to extreme lowness, and these head-dresses, more simple; more convenient, and more becoming, last even now. Reasonable people wait with impatience for some other mad stranger who will strip our dames of these immense baskets, thoroughly insupportable to themselves and to others.

Shortly after the Duke of Shrewsbury arrived in Paris, the Hotel de Powis in London, occupied by our ambassador the Duc d'Aumont, was burnt to the ground. A neighbouring house was pulled down to prevent others catching fire. The plate of M. d'Aumont was saved. He pretended to have lost everything else. He pretended also to have received several warnings that his house was to be burnt and himself assassinated, and that the Queen, to whom he had mentioned these warnings, offered to give him a guard. People judged otherwise in London and Paris, and felt persuaded he himself had been the incendiary in order to draw money from the King and also to conceal some monstrous smuggling operations, by which he gained enormously, and which the English had complained of ever since his arrival. This is at least what was publicly said in the two courts and cities, and nearly everybody believed it.

But to return to the peace. The renunciations were ready, towards the middle of March, and were agreed upon. The King was invited to sign them by his own most pressing interest; and the Court of England, to which we owed all, was not less interested in consummating this grand work, so as to enjoy, with the glory of having imposed it upon all the powers, that domestic repose which was unceasingly disturbed by the party opposed to the government, which party, excited by the enemies of peace abroad, could not cease to cause disquiet to the Queen's minister, while, by delay in signing, vain hopes of disturbing the peace or hindering its ratification existed in people's minds. The King of Spain had made his renunciations with all the solidity and solemnity which could be desired from the laws, customs, and usages of Spain. It only remained for France to imitate him.

For the ceremony that was to take place, all that could be obtained in order to render it more solemn was the presence of the peers. But the King was so jealous of his authority, and so little inclined to pay attention to that of others, that he wished to content himself with merely saying in a general way that he hoped to find all the peers at the Parliament when the renunciations were made. I told M. d'Orleans that if the King thought such an announcement as this was enough he might rely upon finding not a single peer at the Parliament. I added, that if the King did not himself invite each peer, the master of the ceremonies ought to do so for him, according to the custom always followed. This warning had its effect. We all received written invitations, immediately. Wednesday, the 18th of May, was fixed for the ceremony.

At six o'clock on the morning of that day I went to the apartments of M. le Duc de Berry, in parliamentary dress, and shortly afterwards M. d'Orleans came there also, with a grand suite. It had been arranged that the ceremony was to commence by a compliment from the Chief-President de Mesmes to M. le Duc de Berry, who was to reply to it. He was much troubled at this. Madame de Saint-Simon, to whom he unbosomed himself; found means, through a subaltern, to obtain the discourse of the Chief- President, and gave it to M. le Duc de Berry, to regulate his reply by. This, however, seemed too much for him; he admitted so to Madame de Saint-Simon, and that he knew not what to do. She proposed that I should take the work off his hands; and he was delighted with the expedient. I wrote, therefore, a page and a half full of common-sized paper in an ordinary handwriting. M. le Duc de Berry liked it, but thought it too long to be learnt. I abridged it; he wished it to be still shorter, so that at last there was not more than three-quarters of a page. He had learned it by heart, and repeated it in his cabinet the night before the ceremony to Madame de Saint-Simon, who encouraged him as much as she could.

At about half-past six o'clock we set out—M. le Duc d'Orleans, M. le Duc de Berry, myself, and M. le Duc de Saint-Aignan, in one coach, several other coaches following. M. le Duc de Berry was very silent all the journey, appearing to be much occupied with the speech he had learned by heart. M. d'Orleans, on the contrary, was full of gaiety, and related some of his youthful adventures, and his wild doings by night in the streets of Paris. We arrived gently at the Porte de la Conference, that is to say—for it is now pulled down—at the end of the terrace, and of the Quai of the Tuileries.

We found there the trumpeters and drummers of M. le Duc de Berry's guard, who made a great noise all the rest of our journey, which ended at the Palais de justice. Thence we went to the Sainte-Chapelle to hear mass. The Chapelle was filled with company, among which were many people of quality. The crowd of people from this building to the grand chamber was so great that a pin could not have fallen to the ground. On all sides, too, folks had climbed up to see what passed.

All the Princes of the blood, the bastards, the peers and the parliament, were assembled in the palace. When M. le Duc de Berry entered, everything was ready. Silence having with difficulty been obtained, the Chief-President paid his compliment to the Prince. When he had finished, it was for M. le Duc de Berry to reply. He half took off his hat, immediately put it back again, looked at the Chief-President, and said, "Monsieur;" after a moment's pause he repeated "Monsieur." Then he looked at the assembly, and again said, "Monsieur." Afterwards he turned towards M. d'Orleans, who, like himself, was as red as fire, next to the Chief-President, and finally stopped short, nothing else than "Monsieur" having been able to issue from his mouth.

I saw distinctly the confusion of M. le Duc de Berry, and sweated at it; but what could be done? The Duke turned again towards M. d'Orleans, who lowered his head. Both were dismayed. At last the Chief-President, seeing there was no other resource, finished this cruel scene by taking off his cap to M. le Duc de Berry, and inclining himself very low, as if the response was finished. Immediately afterwards he told the King's people to begin. The embarrassment of all the courtiers and the surprise of the magistracy may be imagined.

The renunciations were then read; and by these the King of Spain and his posterity gave up all claim to the throne of France, and M. le Duc d'Orleans, and M. le Duc de Berry to succeed to that of Spain. These and other forms occupied a long time. The chamber was all the while crowded to excess. There was not room for a single other person to enter. It was very late when all was over.

When everything was at an end M. de Saint-Aignan and I accompanied M. le Duc de Berry and M. le Duc d'Orleans in a coach to the Palais Royal. On the way the conversation was very quiet. M. le Duc de Berry appeared dispirited, embarrassed, and vexed. Even after we had partaken of a splendid and delicate dinner, to which an immense number of other guests sat down, he did not improve. We were conducted to the Porte Saint- Honore with the same pomp as that in the midst, of which we had entered Paris. During the rest of the journey to Versailles M. le Duc de Berry was as silent as ever.

To add to his vexation, as soon as he arrived at Versailles the Princesse de Montauban, without knowing a word of what had passed, set herself to exclaim, with her usual flattery, that she was charmed with the grace and the appropriate eloquence with which he had spoken at the Parliament, and paraphrased this theme with all the praises of which it was susceptible. M. le Duc de Berry blushed with vexation without saying a word; she recommenced extolling his modesty, he blushing the more, and saying nothing. When at last he had got rid of her, he went to his own apartments, said not, a word to the persons he found there, scarcely one to Madame his wife, but taking Madame de Saint-Simon with him, went into his library, and shut himself up alone there with her.

Throwing himself into an armchair he cried out that he was dishonoured, and wept scalding tears. Then he related to Madame de Saint-Simon, in the midst of sobs, how he had stuck fast at the Parliament, without being able to utter a word, said that he should everywhere be regarded as an ass and a blockhead, and repeated the compliments he had received from Madame de Montauban, who, he said, had laughed at and insulted him, knowing well what had happened; then, infuriated against her to the last degree, he called her by all sots of names. Madame de Saint-Simon spared no exertion in order to calm M. de Berry, assuring him that it was impossible Madame de Montauban could know what had taken place at the Parliament, the news not having then reached Versailles, and that she had had no other object than flattery in addressing him. Nothing availed. Complaints and silence succeeded each other in the midst of tears. Then, suddenly falling upon the Duc de Beauvilliers and the King, and accusing the defects of his education: "They thought only;" he exclaimed, "of making me stupid, and of stifling all my powers. I was a younger son. I coped with my brother. They feared the consequences; they annihilated me. I was taught only to play and to hunt, and they have succeeded in making me a fool and an ass, incapable of anything, the laughing-stock and disdain of everybody." Madame de Saint-Simon was overpowered with compassion, and did everything to calm M. de Berry. Their strange tete-a-tete lasted nearly two hours, and resumed the next day but with less violence. By degrees M. le Duc de Berry became consoled, but never afterwards did any one dare to speak to him of his misadventure at the peace ceremony.

Let me here say that, the ceremony over, peace was signed at Utrecht on the 20th April, 1713, at a late hour of the night. It was published in Paris with great solemnity on the 22nd. Monsieur and Madame du Maine, who wished to render themselves popular, came from Sceaux to see the ceremony in the Place Royale, showed themselves on a balcony to the people, to whom they threw some money—a liberality that the King would not have permitted in anybody else. At night fires were lighted before the houses, several of which were illuminated: On the 25th a Te Deum was sung at Notre Dame, and in the evening there was a grand display of fireworks at the Grave, which was followed by a superb banquet given at the Hotel de Ville by the Duc de Tresmes, the Governor of Paris, to a large number of distinguished persons of both sexes of the Court and the city, twenty-four violins playing during the repast.

I have omitted to mention the death of M. de Chevreise, which took place between seven and eight o'clock in the morning on Saturday, the 5th of November; of the previous year (1712). I have so often alluded to M. de Chevreuse in the course of these pages, that I will content myself with relating here two anecdotes of him, which serve to paint a part of his character.

He was very forgetful, and adventures often happened to him in consequence, which diverted us amazingly. Sometimes his horses were put to and kept waiting for him twelve or fifteen hours at a time. Upon one occasion in summer this happened at Vaucresson, whence he was going to dine at Dampierre. The coachman, first, then the postilion, grew tired of looking after the horses, and left them. Towards six o'clock at night the horses themselves were in their turn worn out, bolted, and a din was heard which shook the house. Everybody ran out, the coach was found smashed, the large door shivered in pieces; the garden railings, which enclosed both sides of the court, broken down; the gates in pieces; in short, damage was done that took a long time to repair. M. de Chevreuse, who had not been disturbed by this uproar even for an instant, was quite astonished when he heard of it. M. de Beauvilliers amused himself for a long time by reproaching him with it, and by asking the expense.

Another adventure happened to him also at Vaucresson, and covered him with real confusion, comical to see, every time it was mentioned. About ten o'clock one morning a M. Sconin, who had formerly been his steward, was announced. "Let him take a turn in the garden," said M. de Chevreuse, "and come back in half an hour." He continued what he was doing, and completely forgot his man. Towards seven o'clock in the evening Sconin was again announced. "In a moment," replied M. de Chevreuse, without disturbing himself. A quarter of an hour afterwards he called Sconin, and admitted him. "Ah, my poor Sconin!" said he, "I must offer you a thousand excuses for having caused you to lose your day."

"Not at all, Monseigneur," replied Sconin. "As I have had the honour of knowing you for many years, I comprehended this morning that the half- hour might be long, so I went to Paris, did some business there, before and after dinner, and here I am again."

M. de Chevreuse was confounded. Sconin did not keep silence, nor did the servants of the house. M. de Beauvilliers made merry with the adventure when he heard of it, and accustomed as M. de Chevreuse might be to his raillery, he could not bear to have this subject alluded to. I have selected two anecdotes out of a hundred others of the same kind, because they characterise the man.

The liberality of M. du Maine which we have related on the occasion of the proclamation of peace at Paris, and which was so popular, and so surprising when viewed in connection with the disposition of the King, soon took new development. The Jesuits, so skilful in detecting the foibles of monarchs, and so clever in seizing hold of everything which can protect themselves and answer their ends, showed to what extent they were masters of these arts. A new and assuredly a very original History of France, in three large folio volumes, appeared under the name of Father Daniel, who lived at Paris in the establishment of the Jesuits. The paper and the printing of the work were excellent; the style was admirable. Never was French so clear, so pure, so flowing, with such happy transitions; in a word, everything to charm and entice the reader; admirable preface, magnificent promises, short, learned dissertations, a pomp, an authority of the most seductive kind. As for the history, there was much romance in the first race, much in the second, and much. mistiness in the early times of the third. In a word, all the work evidently appeared composed in order to persuade people—under the simple air of a man who set aside prejudices with discernment, and who only seeks the truth—that the majority of the Kings of the first race, several of the second, some even of the third, were, bastards, whom this defect did not exclude from the throne, or affect in any way.

I say bluntly here what was very delicately veiled in the work, and yet plainly seen. The effect of the book was great; its vogue such, that everybody, even women, asked for it. The King spoke of it to several of his Court, asked if they had read it; the most sagacious early saw how much it was protected; it was the sole historical book the King and Madame de Maintenon had ever spoken of. Thus the work appeared at Versailles upon every table, nothing else was talked about, marvellous eulogies were lavished upon it, which were sometimes comical in the mouths of persons either very ignorant, or who, incapable of reading, pretended to read and relish this book.

But this surprising success did not last. People perceived that this history, which so cleverly unravelled the remote part, gave but a meagre account of modern days, except in so far as their military operations were concerned; of which even the minutest details were recorded. Of negotiations, cabals, Court intrigues, portraits, elevations, falls, and the main springs of events, there was not a word in all the work, except briefly, dryly, and with precision as in the gazettes, often more superficially. Upon legal matters, public ceremonies, fetes of different times, there was also silence at the best, the same laconism; and when we come to the affairs of Rome and of the League, it is a pleasure to see the author glide over that dangerous ice on his Jesuit skates!

In due time critics condemned the work which, after so much applause, was recognised as a very wretched history, which had very industriously and very fraudulently answered the purpose for which it was written. It fell to the ground then; learned men wrote against it; but the principal and delicate point of the work was scarcely touched in France with the pen, so great was the danger.

Father Daniel obtained two thousand francs' pension for his history,— a prodigious recompense,—with a title of Historiographer of France. He enjoyed the fruits of his falsehood, and laughed at those who attacked him. Foreign countries did not swallow quite so readily these stories that declared such a number of our early kings bastards; but great care was taken not to let France be infected by the disagreeable truths therein published.

CHAPTER LXIII

It is now time that I should say something of the infamous bull 'Unigenitus', which by the unsurpassed audacity and scheming of Father Le Tellier and his friends was forced upon the Pope and the world.

I need not enter into a very lengthy account of the celebrated Papal decree which has made so many martyrs, depopulated our schools, introduced ignorance, fanaticism, and misrule, rewarded vice, thrown the whole community into the greatest confusion, caused disorder everywhere, and established the most arbitrary and the most barbarous inquisition; evils which have doubled within the last thirty years. I will content myself with a word or two, and will not blacken further the pages of my Memoirs. Many pens have been occupied, and will be occupied, with this subject. It is not the apostleship of Jesus Christ that is in question, but that of the reverend fathers and their ambitious clients.

It is enough to say that the new bull condemned in set terms the doctrines of Saint-Paul (respected like oracles of the Holy Spirit ever since the time of our Saviour), and also those of Saint-Augustin, and of other fathers; doctrines which have always been adopted by the Popes, by the Councils, and by the Church itself. The bull, as soon as published, met with a violent opposition in Rome from the cardinals there, who went by sixes, by eights, and by tens, to complain of it to the Pope. They might well do so, for they had not been consulted in any way upon this new constitution. Father Tellier and his friends had had the art and the audacity to obtain the publication of it without submitting it to them. The Pope, as I have said, had been forced into acquiescence, and now, all confused, knew not what to say. He protested, however, that the publication had been made without his knowledge, and put off the cardinals with compliments, excuses, and tears, which last he could always command.

The constitution had the same fate in France as in Rome. The cry against it was universal. The cardinals protested that it would never be received. They were shocked by its condemnation of the doctrines of Saint-Augustin and of the other fathers; terrified at its condemnation of Saint-Paul. There were not two opinions upon this terrible constitution. The Court, the city, and the provinces, as soon as they knew the nature of it, rose against it like one man.

In addition to the articles of this constitution which I have already named, there was one which excited infinite alarm and indignation, for it rendered the Pope master of every crown! As is well known, there is a doctrine of the Church, which says:

"An unjust excommunication ought got to hinder [us] from doing our duty."

The new constitution condemned this doctrine, and consequently proclaimed that:

"An unjust excommunication ought to hinder [us] from doing our duty."

The enormity of this last is more striking than the simple truth of the proposition condemned. The second is a shadow which better throws up the light of the first. The results and the frightful consequences of the condemnation are as clear as day.

I think I have before said that Father Tellier, without any advances on my part, without, in fact, encouragement of any kind, insisted upon keeping up an intimacy with me, which I could not well repel, for it came from a man whom it would have been very dangerous indeed to have for an- enemy. As soon as this matter of the constitution was in the wind, he came to me to talk about it. I did not disguise my opinion from him, nor did he disguise in any way from me the unscrupulous means he meant to employ in order to get this bull accepted by the clergy. Indeed, he was so free with me, showed me so plainly his knavery and cunning, that I was, as it were, transformed with astonishment and fright. I never could comprehend this openness in a man so false, so artificial, so profound, or see in what manner it could be useful to him.

One day he came to me by appointment, with a copy of the constitution in his hand in order that we might thoroughly discuss it. I was at Versailles. In order to understand what I am going to relate, I must give some account of my apartments there. Let me say, then, that I had a little back cabinet, leading out of another cabinet, but so arranged that you would not have thought it was there. It received no light except from the outer cabinet, its own windows being boarded up. In this back cabinet I had a bureau, some chairs, books, and all I needed; my friends called it my "shop," and in truth it did not ill resemble one.

Father Tellier came at the hour he had fixed. As chance would have it, M. le Duc and Madame la Duchesse de Berry had invited themselves to a collation with Madame de Saint-Simon that morning. I knew that when they arrived I should no longer be master of my chamber or of my cabinet. I told Father Tellier this, and he was much vexed. He begged me so hard to find some place where we might be inaccessible to the company, that at last, pressed by him to excess, I said I knew of only one expedient by which we might become free: and I told him that he must dismiss his 'vatble' (as the brother who always accompanies a monk is called), and that then, furnished with candles, we would go and shut ourselves up in my back cabinet, where we could neither be seen nor heard, if we took care not to speak loud when anybody approached. He thought the expedient admirable, dismissed his companion, and we sat down opposite each other, the bureau between us, with two candles alight upon it.

He immediately began to sing the praises of the Constitution Unigenitus, a copy of which he placed on the table. I interrupted him so as to come at once to the excommunication proposition. We discussed it with much politeness, but with little accord. I shall not pretend to report our dispute. It was warm and long. I pointed out to Father Tellier, that supposing the King and the little Dauphin were both to die, and this was a misfortune which might happen, the crown of France would by right of birth belong to the King of Spain; but according to the renunciation just made, it would belong to M. le Duc de Berry and his branch, or in default to M. le Duc d'Orleans. "Now," said I, "if the two brothers dispute the crown, and the Pope favouring the one should excommunicate the other, it follows, according to our new constitution, that the excommunicated must abandon all his claims, all his partisans, all his forces, and go over to the other side. For you say, an unjust excommunication ought to hinder us from doing our duty. So that in one fashion or another the Pope is master of all the crowns in his communion, is at liberty to take them away or to give them as he pleases, a liberty so many Popes have claimed and so many have tried to put in action."

My argument was simple, applicable, natural, and pressing: it offered itself, of itself.

Wherefore, the confessor was amazed by it; he blushed, he beat about the bush, he could not collect himself. By degrees he did so, and replied to me in a manner that he doubtless thought would convince me at once. "If the case you suggest were to happen," he said, "and the Pope declaring for one disputant were to excommunicate the other and all his followers, such excommunication would not merely be unjust, it would be false; and it has never been decided that a false excommunication should hinder us from doing our duty."

"Ah! my father," I said, "your distinction is subtle and clever, I admit. I admit, too, I did not expect it, but permit me some few more objections, I beseech you. Will the Ultramontanes admit the nullity of the excommunication? Is it not null as soon as it is unjust? If the Pope has the power to excommunicate unjustly, and to enforce obedience to his excommunication, who can limit power so unlimited, and why should not his false (or nullified) excommunication be as much obeyed and respected as his unjust excommunication? Suppose the case I have imagined were to happen. Suppose the Pope were to excommunicate one of the two brothers. Do you think it would be easy to make your subtle distinction between a false and an unjust excommunication understood by the people, the soldiers, the bourgeois, the officers, the lords, the women, at the very moment when they would be preparing to act and to take up arms? You see I point out great inconveniences that may arise if the new doctrine be accepted, and if the Pope should claim the power of deposing kings, disposing of their crowns, and releasing their subjects from the oath of fidelity in opposition to the formal words of Jesus Christ and of all the Scripture."

My words transported the Jesuit, for I had touched the right spring in spite of his effort to hide it. He said nothing personal to me, but he fumed. The more he restrained himself for me the less he did so for the matter in hand. As though to indemnify himself for his moderation on my account, he launched out the more, upon the subject we were discussing. In his heat, no longer master of himself, many things escaped him, silence upon which I am sure he would afterwards have bought very dearly. He told me so many things of the violence that would be used to make his constitution accepted, things so monstrous, so atrocious, so terrible, and with such extreme passion that I fell into a veritable syncope. I saw him right in front of me between two candles, only the width of the table between us (I have described elsewhere his horrible physiognomy). My hearing and my sight became bewildered. I was seized, while he was speaking, with the full idea of what a Jesuit was. Here was a man who, by his state and his vows, could hope for nothing for his family or for himself; who could not expect an apple or a glass of wine more than his brethren; who was approaching an age when he would have to render account of all things to God, and who, with studied deliberation and mighty artifice, was going to throw the state and religion into the most terrible flames, and commence a most frightful persecution for questions which affected him in nothing, nor touched in any way the honour of the School of Molina!

His profundities, the violence he spoke of—all this together, threw me into such an ecstasy, that suddenly I interrupted him by saying:

"My father, how old are you?"

The extreme surprise which painted itself upon his face as I looked at him with all my eyes, fetched back my senses, and his reply brought me completely to myself. "Why do you ask?" he replied, smiling. The effort that I made over myself to escape such a unique 'proposito', the terrible value of which I fully appreciated, furnished me an issue. "Because," said I, "never have I looked at you so long as I have now, you in front of me, these two candles between us, and your face is so fresh and so healthy, with all your labours, that I am surprised at it."

He swallowed the answer, or so well pretended to do so, that he said nothing of it then nor since, never ceasing when he met me to speak to me as openly, and as frequently as before, I seeking him as little as ever. He replied at that time that he was seventy-four years old; that in truth he was very well; that he had accustomed himself, from his earliest years, to a hard life and to labour; and then went back to the point at which I had interrupted him. We were compelled, however, to be silent for a time, because people came into my cabinet, and Madame de Saint-Simon, who knew of our interview, had some difficulty to keep the coast clear.

For more than two hours we continued our discussion, he trying to put me off with his subtleties and authoritativeness, I offering but little opposition to him, feeling that opposition was of no use, all his plans being already decided. We separated without having persuaded each other, he with many flatteries upon my intelligence, praying me to reflect well upon the matter; I replying that my reflections were all made, and that my capacity could not go farther. I let him out by the little back door of my cabinet, so that nobody perceived him, and as soon as I had closed it, I threw myself into a chair like a man out of breath, and I remained there a long time alone, reflecting upon the strange kind of ecstasy I had been in, and the horror it had caused me.

The results of this constitution were, as I have said, terrible to the last degree; every artifice, every cruelty was used, in order to force it down the throats of the clergy; and hence the confusion and sore trouble which arose all over the realm. But it is time now for me to touch upon other matters.

Towards the close of this year, 1713, peace with the Emperor seemed so certain, that the King disbanded sixty Battalions and eighteen men per company of the regiment of the guards, and one hundred and six squadrons; of which squadrons twenty-seven were dragoons. At peace now with the rest of Europe he had no need of so many troops, even although the war Against the Empire had continued; fortunately, however it did not. Negotiations were set on foot, and on the 6th of March of the following year, 1714, after much debate, they ended successfully. On that day, in fact, peace was signed at Rastadt. It was shortly afterwards published at Paris, a Te Deum sung, and bonfires lighted at night; a grand collation was given at the Hotel de Ville by the Duc de Tresmes, who at midnight also gave, in his own house, a splendid banquet, at which were present many ladies, foreigners, and courtiers.

This winter was fertile in balls at the Court; there were several, fancy- dress and masked, given by M. le Duc de Berry, by Madame la Duchesse de Berry, M. le Duc, and others. There were some also at Paris, and at Sceaux, where Madame du Maine gave many fetes and played many comedies, everybody going there from Paris and the Court—M. du Maine doing the Honours. Madame la Duchesse de Berry was in the family way, and went to no dances out of her own house. The King permitted her, on account of her condition, to sup with him in a robe de chambre, as under similar circumstances he had permitted the two Dauphines to do.

At the opera, one night this winter, the Abbe Servien, not liking certain praises of the King contained in a Prologue, let slip a bitter joke in ridicule of them. The pit took it up, repeated it, and applauded it. Two days afterwards, the Abbe Servien was arrested and taken to Vincennes, forbidden to speak to anybody and allowed no servant to wait upon him. For form's sake seals were put upon his papers, but he was not a man likely to have any fit for aught else than to light the fire. Though more than sixty-five years old, he was strangely debauched.

The Duc de la Rochefoucauld died on Thursday, the 11th of January, at Versailles, seventy-nine years of age, and blind. I have spoken of him so frequently in the course of these memoirs, that I will do nothing more now than relate a few particulars respecting him, which will serve in some sort to form his portrait.

He had much honour, worth, and probity. He was noble, good, magnificent, ever willing to serve his friends; a little too much so, for he oftentimes wearied the King with importunities on their behalf. Without any intellect or discernment he was proud to excess, coarse and rough in his manners—disagreeable even, and embarrassed with all except his flatterers; like a man who does not know how to receive a visit, enter or leave a room. He scarcely went anywhere except to pay the indispensable compliments demanded by marriage, death, etc., and even then as little as he could. He lived in his own house so shut up that no, one went to see him except on these same occasions. He gave himself up almost entirely to his valets, who mixed themselves in the conversation; and you were obliged to treat them with all sorts of attentions if you wished to become a frequenter of the house.

I shall never forget what happened to us at the death of the Prince of Vaudemont's son, by which M. de la Rochefoucauld's family came in for a good inheritance. We were at Marly. The King had been stag-hunting. M. de Chevreuse, whom I found when the King was being unbooted, proposed that we should go and pay our compliments to M. de la Rochefoucauld. We went. Upon entering, what was our surprise, nay, our shame, to find M. de la Rochefoucauld playing at chess with one of his servants in livery, seated opposite to him! Speech failed us. M. de la Rochefoucauld perceived it, and remained confounded himself. He stammered, he grew confused, he tried to excuse what we had seen, saying that this lackey played very well, and that chess-players played with everybody. M. de Chevreuse had not come to contradict him; neither had I; we turned the conversation, therefore, and left as soon as possible. As soon as we were outside we opened our minds to each other, and said what we thought of this rare meeting, which, however, we did not make public.

M. de Rochefoucauld, towards the end of his career at Court, became so importunate, as I have said, for his friends, that the King was much relieved by his death. Such have been his sentiments at the death of nearly all those whom he had liked and favoured.

Of the courage of M. de la Rochefoucauld, courtier as he was, in speaking to the King, I will relate an instance. It was during one of the visits at Marly, in the gardens of which the King was amusing himself with a fountain that he set at work. I know not what led to it, but the King, usually so reserved, spoke with him of the bishop of Saint-Pons, then in disgrace on account of the affairs of Port Royal. M. de la Rochefoucauld let him speak on to the end, and then began to praise the bishop. The discouraging silence of the King warned him; he persisted, however, and related how the bishop, mounted upon a mule, and visiting one day his diocese, found himself in a path which grew narrower at every step; and which ended in a precipice. There were no means of getting out of it except by going back, but this was impossible, there not being enough space to turn round or to alight. The holy bishop (for such was his term as I well remarked) lifted his eyes to Heaven, let go the bridle, and abandoned himself to Providence. Immediately his mule rose up upon its hind legs, and thus upright, the bishop still astride, turned round until its head was where its tail had been. The beast thereupon returned along the path until it found an opening into a good road. Everybody around the King imitated his silence, which excited the Duke to comment upon what he had just related. This generosity charmed me, and surprised all who were witness of it.

The day after the death of M. de la Rochefoucauld, the Chancellor took part in a very tragic scene. A Vice-bailli of Alencon had just lost a trial, in which, apparently, his honour, or his property, was much interested. He came to Pontchartrain's, where the Chancellor was at the moment, and waited until he came out into the court to get into his carriage. The Vice-bailli then asked him for a revision of the verdict. The Chancellor, with much gentleness and goodness represented to the man that the law courts were open to him if he insisted to appeal, but that as to a revision of the verdict; it was contrary to usage; and turned to get into his coach. While he was getting in; the unhappy bailli said there was a shorter way of escaping from trouble, and stabbed himself twice with a poniard. At the dies of the domestics the Chancellor descended from the coach, had the man carried into a room, and sent for a doctor, and a confessor. The bailli made confession very peacefully, and died an hour afterwards.

I have spoken in its time of the exile of Charmel and its causes, of which the chief was his obstinate refusal to present himself before the King. The vexation of the King against people who withdrew from him was always very great. In this case, it never passed away, but hardened into a strange cruelty, to speak within limits. Charmel, attacked with the stone, asked permission to come to Paris to undergo an operation. The permission was positively refused. Time pressed. The operation was obliged to be done in the country. It was so severe, and perhaps so badly done, that Charmel died three days afterwards full of penitence and piety. He had led a life remarkable for its goodness, was without education, but had religious fervour that supplied the want of it. He was sixty-eight years of age.

The Marechale de la Ferme died at Paris, at the same time, more than eighty years old. She was sister of the Comtesse d'Olonne, very rich and a widow. The beauty of the two sisters, and the excesses of their lives, made a great stir. No women, not even those most stigmatized for their gallantry, dared to see them, or to be seen anywhere with them. That was the way then; the fashion has changed since. When they were old and nobody cared for them, they tried to become devout. They lodged together, and one Ash Wednesday went and heard a sermon. This sermon, which was upon fasting and penitence, terrified them.

"My sister," they said to each other on their return, "it was all true; there was no joke about it; we must do penance, or we are lost. But, my sister, what shall we do?" After having well turned it over: "My sister," said Madame d'Olonne, "this is what we must do; we must make our servants fast." Madame d'Olonne thought she had very well met the difficulty. However, at last she set herself to work in earnest, at piety and penitence, and died three months after her sister, the Marechale de la Ferme. It will not be forgotten, that it was under cover of the Marechale that a natural child was first legitimated without naming the mother, in order that by this example, the King's natural children might be similarly honoured, without naming Madame de Montespan, as I have related in its place.

CHAPTER LXIV

The Queen of Spain, for a long time violently attacked with the king's evil around the face and neck, was just now at the point of death. Obtaining no relief from the Spanish doctors, she wished to have Helvetius, and begged the King by an express command to send him to her. Helvetius, much inconvenienced, and knowing besides the condition of the Princess, did not wish to go, but the King expressly commanded him. He set out then in a postchaise, followed by another in case his own should break down, and arrived thus at Madrid on the 11th of February, 1714. As soon as he had seen the Queen, he said there was nothing but a miracle could save her. The King of Spain did not discontinue sleeping with her until the 9th. On the 14th she died, with much courage, consciousness, and piety.

Despair was general in Spain, where this Queen was universally adored. There was not a family which did not lament her, not a person who has since been consoled. The King of Spain was extremely touched, but somewhat in a royal manner. Thus, when out shooting one day, he came close to the convoy by which the body of his queen was being conveyed to the Escurial; he looked at it, followed it with his eyes, and continued his sport! Are these princes made like other human beings?

The death of the Queen led to amazing changes, such as the most prophetic could not have foreseen. Let me here, then, relate the events that followed this misfortune.

I must commence by saying, that the principal cause which had so long and scandalously hindered us from making peace with the Emperor, was a condition, which Madame des Ursins wished to insert in the treaty, (and which the King of Spain supported through thick and thin) to the effect that she should be invested with a bona fide sovereignty. She had set her heart upon this, and the king of Spain was a long time before he would consent to any terms of peace that did not concede it to her. It was not until the King had uttered threats against him that he would give way. As for Madame des Ursins, she had counted upon this sovereignty with as much certainty as though it were already between her fingers. She had counted, too, with equal certainty upon exchanging it with our King, for the sovereignty of Touraine and the Amboise country; and had actually charged her faithful Aubigny to buy her some land near Amboise to build her there a vast palace, with courts and outbuildings; to furnish it with magnificence, to spare neither gilding nor paintings, and to surround the whole with the most beautiful gardens. She meant to live there as sovereign lady of the country. Aubigny had at once set about the work to the surprise of everybody: for no one could imagine for whom such a grand building could be designed. He kept the secret, pretended he was building a house for himself and pushed on the work so rapidly that just as peace was concluded without the stipulation respecting Madame des Ursins being inserted in the treaty, nearly all was finished. Her sovereignty scheme thoroughly failed; and to finish at once with that mad idea, I may as well state that, ashamed of her failure, she gave this palace to Aubigny, who lived there all the rest of his life: Chanteloup, for so it was called, has since passed into the hands of Madame d'Armantieres, his daughter. It is one of the most beautiful and most singular places in all France, and the most superbly furnished.

This sovereignty, coveted by Madame des Ursins, exceedingly offended Madame de Maintenon and wounded her pride. She felt, with jealousy, that the grand airs Madame des Ursins gave herself were solely the effect of the protection she had accorded her. She could not bear to be outstripped in importance by the woman she herself had elevated. The King, too, was much vexed with Madame des Ursins; vexed also to see peace delayed; and to be obliged to speak with authority and menace to the King of Spain, in order to compel him to give up the idea of this precious sovereignty. The King of Spain did not yield until he was threatened with abandonment by France. It may be imagined what was the rage of Madame des Ursins upon missing her mark after having, before the eyes of all Europe, fired at it with so much perseverance; nay, with such unmeasured obstinacy. From this time there was no longer the same concert between Madame de Maintenon and Madame des Ursins that had formerly existed. But the latter had reached such a point in Spain, that she thought this was of no consequence.

It has been seen with what art Madame des Ursins had unceasingly isolated the King of Spain; in what manner she had shut him up with the Queen, and rendered him inaccessible, not only to his Court but to his grand officers, his ministers, even his valets, so that he was served by only three or four attendants, all French, and entirely under her thumb. At the death of the Queen this solitude continued. Under the pretext that his grief demanded privacy, she persuaded the King to leave his palace and to instal himself in a quiet retreat, the Palace of Medina-Celi, near the Buen-Retiro, at the other end of the city. She preferred this because it was infinitely smaller than the Royal Palace, and because few people, in consequence, could approach the King. She herself took the Queen's place; and in order to have a sort of pretext for being near the King, in the same solitude, she caused herself to be named governess of his children. But in order to be always there, and so that nobody should know when they were together, she had a large wooden corridor made from the cabinet of the King to the apartment of his children, in which she lodged. By this means they could pass from one to the other without being perceived, and without traversing the long suite of rooms, filled with courtiers, that were between the two apartments. In this manner it was never known whether the King was alone or with Madame des Ursins; or which of the two was in the apartments of the other. When they were together or how long is equally unknown. This corridor, roofed and glazed, was proceeded with in so much haste, that the work went on, in spite of the King's devotion, on fete days and Sundays. The whole Court, which perfectly well knew for what use this corridor was intended, was much displeased. Those who directed the work were the same. Of this good proof was given. One day, the Comptroller of the royal buildings, who had been ordered to keep the men hard at it, Sundays and fete days, asked the Pere Robinet, the King's confessor, and the only good one he ever had; he asked, I say, in one of those rooms Madame des Ursins was so anxious to avoid, and in the presence of various courtiers, if the work was to be continued on the morrow, a Sunday, and the next day, the Fete of the Virgin. Robinet replied, that the King had said nothing to the contrary; and met a second appeal with the same answer. At the third, he added, that before saying anything he would wait till the King spoke on the subject. At the fourth appeal, he lost patience, and said that if for the purpose of destroying what had been commenced, he believed work might be done even on

Easter-day itself; but if for the purpose of continuing the corridor, he did not think a Sunday or a fete day was a fitting time. All the Court applauded; but Madame des Ursins, to whom this sally was soon carried, was much irritated.

It was suspected that she thought of becoming something more than the mere companion of the King. There were several princes. Reports were spread which appeared equivocal and which terrified. It was said that the King had no need of posterity, with all the children it had pleased God to bless him with; but now he only needed a wife who could take charge of those children. Not content with passing all her days with the King, and allowing him, like the deceased Queen, to work with his ministers only in her presence, the Princesse des Ursins felt that to render this habit lasting she must assure herself of him at all moments. He was accustomed to take the air, and he was in want of it all the more now because he had been much shut up during the last days of the Queen's illness, and the first which followed her death. Madame des Ursins chose four or five gentlemen to accompany him, to the exclusion of all others, even his chief officers, and people still more necessary. These gentlemen charged with the amusement of the King, were called recreadores. With so much circumspection, importunity, preparation, and rumour carefully circulated, it was not doubted that Madame des Ursins intended to marry him; and the opinion, as well as the fear, became general. The King (Louis XIV.), was infinitely alarmed; and Madame de Maintenon, who had twice tried to be proclaimed Queen and twice failed, was distracted with jealousy. However, if Madame des Ursins flattered herself then, it was not for long.

The King of Spain, always curious to learn the news from France, often demanded them of his confessor, the only man to whom he could speak who was not under the thumb of Madame des Ursins. The clever and courageous Robinet, as disturbed as others at the progress of the design, which nobody in the two Courts of France and Spain doubted was in execution, allowed himself to be pressed by questions—in an embrasure where the King had drawn him—played the reserved and the mysterious in order to excite curiosity more. When he saw it was sufficiently excited, he said that since he was forced to speak, his news from France was the same as that at Madrid, where no one doubted that the King would do the Princesse des Ursins the honour to espouse her. The King blushed and hastily replied, "Marry her! oh no! not that!" and quitted him.

Whether the Princesse des Ursins was informed of this sharp repartee, or whether she despaired already of success, she changed about; and judging that this interregnum in the Palace of Medina-Celi could not last for ever, resolved to assure herself of the King by a Queen who should owe to her such a grand marriage, and who, having no other support, would throw herself into her arms by gratitude and necessity. With this view she explained herself to Alberoni, who, since the death of the Duc de Vendome, had remained at Madrid charged with the affairs of Parma; and proposed to him the marriage of the Princess of Parma, daughter of the Duchess and of the late Duke of Parma, who had married the widow of his brother.

Alberoni could with difficulty believe his ears. An alliance so disproportioned appeared to him so much the more incredible, because he thought the Court of France would never consent to it, and that without its consent the marriage could not be concluded. The Princess in question was the issue of double illegitimacy; by her father descended from a pope, by her mother from a natural daughter of Charles Quint. She was daughter of a petty Duke of Parma, and of a mother, entirely Austrian, sister of the Dowager Empress and of the Dowager Queen of Spain (whose acts had excited such disapproval that she was sent from her exile at Toledo to Bayonne), sister too of the Queen of Portugal, who had induced the King, her husband, to receive the Archduke at Lisbon, and to carry the war into Spain. It did not seem reasonable, therefore, that such a Princess would be accepted as a wife for the King of Spain.

Nothing of all this, however, stopped the Princesse des Ursins; her own interest was the most pressing consideration with her; the will of the King of Spain was entirely subject to her; she felt all the change towards her of our King and of Madame de Maintenon; she no longer hoped for a return of their favour; she believed that she must look around for support against the very authority which had established her so powerfully, and which could destroy her; and occupied herself solely in pushing forward a marriage from which she expected everything by making the same use of the new queen as she had made of the one just dead. The King of Spain was devout, he absolutely wanted a wife, the Princesse des Ursins was of an age when her charms were but the charms, of art; in a word, she set Alberoni to work, and it may be believed she was not scrupulous as to her means as soon as they were persuaded at Parma that she was serious and not joking. Orry, always united with Madame des Ursins, and all-powerful, by her means, was her sole confidant in this important affair.

At that time the Marquis de Brancas was French ambassador at Madrid. He had flattered himself that Madame des Ursins would make him one of the grandees of Spain. Instead of doing so she simply bestowed upon him the order of the Golden Fleece. He had never pardoned her for this. Entirely devoted to Madame de Maintenon, he became on that very account an object of suspicion to Madame des Ursins, who did not doubt that he cherished a grudge against her, on account of the favour he had missed. She allowed him no access to her, and had her eyes open upon all he did. Brancas in like manner watched all her doings. The confessor, Robinet, confided to him his fears respecting Madame des Ursins, and the chiefs of a court universally discontented went and opened their hearts to him, thinking it was France alone which could set to rights the situation of Spain.

Brancas appreciated all the importance of what was told him, but warned by the fate of the Abbe d'Estrees, fearing even for his couriers, he took the precaution of sending word to the King that he had pressing business to acquaint him with, which he could not trust to paper, and that he wished to be allowed to come to Versailles for a fortnight. The reply was the permission asked for, accompanied, however, with an order to communicate en route with the Duc de Berwick, who was about to pass to Barcelona.

Madame des Ursins, who always found means to be informed of everything, immediately knew of Brancas's projected journey, and determined to get the start of him. At once she had sixteen relays of mules provided upon the Bayonne road, and suddenly sent off to France, on Holy Thursday, Cardinal del Giudice, grand inquisitor and minister of state, who had this mean complaisance for her. She thus struck two blows at once; she got rid, at least for a time, of a Cardinal minister who troubled her, and anticipated Brancas, which in our Court was no small point.

Brancas, who felt all the importance of arriving first, followed the Cardinal on Good Friday, and moved so well that he overtook him at Bayonne, at night while he was asleep; Brancas passed straight on, charging the Commandant to amuse and to delay the Cardinal as long as possible on the morrow; gained ground, and arrived at Bordeaux with twenty-eight post-horses that he had carried off with him from various stations, to keep them from the Cardinal. He arrived in Paris in this manner two days before the other, and went straight to Marly where the King was, to explain the business that had led him there. He had a long audience with the King, and received a lodging for the rest of the visit.

The Cardinal del Giudice rested four or five days at Paris, and then came to Marly, where he was introduced to the King. The Cardinal was somewhat embarrassed; he was charged with no business; all his mission was to praise Madame des Ursins, and complain of the Marquis de Brancas. These praises of Madame des Ursins were but vague; she had not sufficient confidence in the Cardinal to admit to him her real position in our Court, and to give him instructions accordingly, so that what he had to say was soon all said; against the Marquis de Brancas he had really no fact to allege, his sole crime that he was too sharp-sighted and not sufficiently devoted to the Princess.

The Cardinal was a courtier, a man of talent, of business, of intrigue, who felt, with annoyance, that for a person of his condition and weight, such a commission as he bore was very empty. He appeared exceedingly agreeable in conversation, of pleasant manners, and was much liked in good society. He was assiduous in his attentions to the King, without importuning him for audiences that were unnecessary; and by all his conduct, he gave reason for believing that he suspected Madame des Ursins' decadence in our Court, and sought to gain esteem and confidence, so as to become by the support of the King, prime minister in Spain; but as we shall soon see, his ultramontane hobbies hindered the accomplishment of his measures. All the success of his journey consisted in hindering Brancas from returning to Spain. This was no great punishment, for Brancas had nothing more to hope for from Madame des Ursins, and was not a man to lose his time for nothing.

Up to this period not a word had been said to the King (Louis XIV.) by the King of Spain upon the subject of his marriage; not a hint had been given that he meant to remarry, much less with a Parma princess. This proceeding, grafted upon the sovereignty claimed by the Princesse des Ursine, and all her conduct with the King of Spain since the death of the Queen, resolved our King to disgrace her without appeal.

A remark upon Madame des Ursins, accompanied by a smile, escaped from the King, generally so complete a master of himself, and appeared enigmatical to such an extent, although striking, that Torcy, to whom it was addressed, understood nothing. In his surprise, he related to Castries what the King had said; Castries told it to Madame la Duchesse d'Orleans, who reported it to M. d'Orleans and to me. We racked our brains to comprehend it, but in vain; nevertheless such an unintelligible remark upon a person like Madame des Ursins, who up to this time had been on such good terms with the King and Madame de Maintenon, did not appear to me to be favourable. I was confirmed in this view by what had just happened with regard to her sovereignty; but I was a thousand leagues from the thunderbolt which this lightning announced, and which only declared itself to us by its fall.

It wits not until the 27th of June that the King was made acquainted by the King of Spain with his approaching marriage. Of course, through other channels, he had not failed to hear of it long before. He passed in the lightest and gentlest manner in the world over this project, and the mystery so long and so complete! with which it had been kept from him, stranger, if possible, than the marriage itself. He could not hinder it; but from this moment he was sure of his vengeance against her who had arranged and brought it about in this manner. The disgrace of Madame des Ursine was in fact determined on between the King and Madame de Maintenon, but in a manner a secret before and since, that I know nobody who has found out by whom or how it was carried out. It is good to admit our ignorance, and not to give fictions and inventions in place of what we are unacquainted with.

I know not why, but a short time after this, the Princesse des Ursine conceived such strong suspicion of the lofty and enterprising spirit of the Princess of Parma that she repented having made this marriage; and wished to break it off. She brought forward; therefore, I know not what difficulties, and despatched a courier to Rome to Cardinal Acquaviva, who did the King of Spain's business there, ordering him to delay his journey to Parma, where he had been commanded to ask the hand of the Princess, and to see her provisionally espoused. But Madame des Ursins had changed her mind too late. The courier did not find Acquaviva at Rome. That Cardinal was already far away on the road to Parma, so that there were no means of retreat.

Acquaviva was received with great honour and much magnificence; he made his demand, but delayed the espousals as long as he could, and this caused much remark. The marriage, which was to have been celebrated on the 25th of August, did not take place until the 15th of September. Immediately after the ceremony the new Queen set out for Spain.

An envoy from Parma, with news of the marriage of the Princess, arrived at Fontainebleau on the 11th October, and had an audience with the King. This was rather late in the day: For dowry she had one hundred thousand pistoles, and three hundred thousand livres' worth of jewels. She had embarked for Alicante at Sestri di Levante. A violent tempest sickened her of the sea. She landed, therefore, at Monaco, in order to traverse by land Provence, Languedoc, and Guienne, so as to reach Bayonne, and see there the Queen Dowager of Spain; sister of her mother, and widow of Charles II. Desgranges, master of the ceremonies, was to meet her in Provence, with orders to follow her, and to command the governors, lieutenants-general, and intendants to follow her also, and serve her, though she travelled incognito.

The new Queen of Spain, on arriving at Pau, found the Queen Dowager, her aunt, had come expressly from Bayonne to meet her. As they approached each other, they both descended at the same time, and after saluting, mounted alone into a beautiful caleche that the Queen Dowager had brought with her, and that she presented to her niece. They supped together alone. The Queen Dowager conducted her to Saint-Jean Pied-de-Port (for in that country, as in Spain, the entrances to mountain passes are called ports). They separated there, the Queen Dowager making the Queen many presents, among others a garniture of diamonds. The Duc de Saint-Aignan joined the Queen of Spain at Pau, and accompanied her by command of the King to Madrid. She sent Grillo, a Genoese noble, whom she has since made grandee of Spain, to thank the King for sending her the Duc de Saint-Aignan, and for the present he brought with him. The officers of her household had been named by Madame des Ursins.

The Queen of Spain advanced towards Madrid with the attendants sent to accompany her. She was to be met by the King of Spain at Guadalaxara, which is about the same distance from Madrid as Paris is from Fontainebleau. He arrived there, accompanied by the attendants that the Princesse des Ursins had placed near him, to keep him company, and to allow no one else to approach him. She followed in her coach, so as to arrive at the same time, and immediately afterwards he shut himself up alone with her, and saw nobody until he went to bed. This was on the 22nd of December. The next day the Princesse des Ursins set out with a small suite for a little place, seven leagues further, called Quadraque, where the Queen was to sleep that night. Madame des Ursins counted upon enjoying all the gratitude that the queen would feel for the unhoped-for grandeur she had obtained by her means; counted upon passing the evening with her, and upon accompanying her next day to Guadalaxara. She found, upon arriving at Quadraque, that the Queen had already reached there. She at once entered into a lodging that had been prepared for her, opposite that of the Queen. She was in a full Court dress. After adjusting it in a hurried manner, she went to the Queen. The coldness and stiffness of her reception surprised her extremely. She attributed it in the first place to the embarrassment of the Queen, and tried to melt this ice. Everybody withdrew, in order to leave the two alone.

Then the conversation commenced. The Queen would not long allow Madame des Ursins to continue it; but burst out into reproaches against her for her manners, and for appearing there in a dress that showed want of respect for the company she was in. Madame des Ursins, whose dress was proper, and who, on account of her respectful manners and her discourse, calculated to win the Queen, believed herself to be far from meriting this treatment, was strangely surprised, and wished to excuse herself; but the Queen immediately began to utter offensive words, to cry out, to call aloud, to demand the officers of the guard, and sharply to; command Madame des Ursins to leave her presence. The latter wished to speak and defend herself against the reproaches she heard; but the Queen, increasing her fury and her menaces, cried out to her people to drive this mad woman from her presence and from the house; and absolutely had her turned out by the shoulders. Immediately afterwards, she called Amenzaga, lieutenant of the body-guard, and at the same time the ecuyer who had the control of her equipages. She ordered the first to arrest Madame des Ursins, and not quit her until he had placed her in a coach, with two sure officers of the guard and fifteen soldiers as sentinels over her; the second she commanded to provide instantly a coach and six, with two or three footmen, and send off in it the Princesse des Ursins towards Burgos and Bayonne, without once stopping on the road. Amenzago tried to represent to the Queen that the King of Spain alone had the power to give such commands; but she haughtily asked him if he had not received an order from the King of Spain to obey her in everything, without reserve and without comment. It was true he had received such an order, though nobody knew a word about it.

Madame des Ursins was then immediately arrested, and put into a coach with one of her waiting-women, without having had time to change her costume or her head-dress, to take any precaution against the cold, to provide herself with any money or other things, and without any kind of refreshment in the coach, or a chemise; nothing, in fact, to change or to sleep in! She was shipped off thus (with two officers of the guard; who were ready as soon as the coach), in full Court dress, just as she left the Queen. In the very short and tumultuous interval which elapsed, she sent a message to the Queen, who flew into a fresh passion upon not being obeyed, and made her set out immediately.

It was then nearly seven o'clock in the evening, two days before Christmas, the ground all covered with snow and ice, and the cold extreme and very sharp and bitter, as it always is in Spain. As soon as the Queen learned that the Princesse des Ursins was out of Quadraque, she wrote to the King of Spain, by an officer of the guards whom she despatched to Guadalaxara. The night was so dark that it was only by means of the snow that anything could be seen.

It is not easy to represent the state of Madame des Ursins in the coach. An excess of astonishment and bewilderment prevailed at first, and suspended all other sentiment; but grief, vexation, rage, and despair, soon followed. In their turn succeeded sad and profound reflections upon a step so violent, so unheard-of, and so unjustifiable as she thought. Then she hoped everything from the friendship of the King of Spain and his confidence in her; pictured his anger and surprise, and those of the group of attached servitors, by whom she had surrounded him, and who would be so interested in exciting the King in her favour. The long winter's night pissed thus; the cold was, terrible, there was nothing to ward it off; the coachman actually lost the use of one hand. The morning advanced; a halt was necessary in order to bait the horses; as for the travellers there is nothing for them ever in the Spanish inns. You are simply told where each thing you want is sold. The meat is ordinarily alive; the wine, thick, flat, and strong; the bread bad; the water is often worthless; as to beds, there are some, but only for the mule- drivers, so that you must carry everything with you, and neither Madame des Ursins nor those with her had anything whatever. Eggs, where they could find any, were their sole resource; and these, fresh or not, simply boiled, supported them during all the journey.

Until this halt for the horses, silence had been profound and uninterrupted; now it was broken. During all this long night the Princesse des Ursins had had leisure to think upon the course she should adopt, and to compose her face. She spoke of her extreme surprise, and of the little that had passed between her and the Queen. In like manner the two officers of the guard accustomed, as was all Spain, to fear and respect her more than their King, replied to her from the bottom of that abyss of astonishment from which they had not yet arisen. The horses being put to, the coach soon started again. Soon, too, the Princesse des Ursins found that the assistance she expected from the King did not arrive. No rest, no provisions, nothing to put on, until Saint-Jean de Luz was reached. As she went further on, as time passed and no news came, she felt she had nothing more to hope for. It may be imagined what rage succeeded in a woman so ambitious, so accustomed to publicly reign, so rapidly and shamefully precipitated from the summit of power by the hand that she herself had chosen as the most solid support of her grandeur. The Queen had not replied to the last two letters Madame des Ursins had written to her. This studied negligence was of bad augury, but who would have imagined treatment so strange and so unheard of?

Her nephews, Lanti and Chalais, who had permission to join her, completed her dejection. Yet she was faithful to herself. Neither tears nor regrets, neither reproaches nor the slightest weakness escaped her; not a complaint even of the excessive cold, of the deprivation of all things, or of the extreme fatigue of such a journey. The two officers who guarded her could not contain their admiration.

At Saint-Jean de Luz, where she arrived on the 14th of January, 1715, she found at last her corporeal ills at an end. She obtained a bed, change of dress, food, and her liberty. The guards, their officers, and the coach which had brought her, returned; she remained with her waiting-maid and her nephews. She had leisure to think what she might expect from Versailles. In spite of her mad sovereignty scheme so long maintained, and her hardihood in arranging the King of Spain's marriage without consulting our King, she flattered herself she should find resources in a Court she had so long governed. It was from Saint-Jean de Luz that she despatched a courier charged with letters for the King, for Madame de Maintenon, and for her friends. She briefly gave us an account in those letters of the thunderbolt which had fallen on her, and asked permission to come to the Court to explain herself more in detail. She waited for the return of her courier in this her first place of liberty and repose, which of itself is very agreeable. But this first courier despatched, she sent off Lanti with letters written less hastily, and with instructions. Lanti saw the King in his cabinet on the last of January, and remained there some moments. From him it was known that as soon as Madame des Ursins despatched her first courier, she had sent her compliments to the Queen Dowager of Spain at Bayonne, who would not receive them. What cruel mortifications attend a fall from a throne! Let us now return to Guadalaxara.

CHAPTER LXV

The officer of the guards, whom the Queen despatched with a letter for the King of Spain as soon as Madame des Ursins was out of Quadraque, found the King upon the point of going to bed. He appeared moved, sent a short reply to the Queen, and gave no orders. The officer returned immediately. What is singular is, that the secret was so well kept that it did not transpire until the next morning at ten o'clock. It may be imagined what emotion seized the whole Court, and what divers movements there were among all at Guadalaxara. However, nobody dared to speak to the King, and much expectation was built upon the reply he had sent to the Queen. The morning passed and nothing was said; the fate of Madame des Ursins then became pretty evident.

Chalais and Lanti made bold to ask the King for permission to go and join the Princess in her isolation. Not only he allowed them to do so, but charged them with a letter of simple civility, in which he told her he was very sorry for what had happened; that he had not been able to oppose the Queen's will; that he should continue to her her pensions, and see that they were punctually paid. He was as good as his word: as long as she lived she regularly received them.

The Queen arrived at Guadalaxara on the afternoon of the day before Christmas day, at the hour fixed, and as though nothing had occurred. The King received her in the same manner on the staircase, gave her his hand, and immediately led her to the chapel, where the marriage was at once celebrated; for in Spain the custom is to marry after dinner. After that he led her to her chamber, and straightway went to bed; it was before six o'clock in the evening, and both got up again for the midnight mass. What passed between them upon the event of the previous evening was entirely unknown, and has always remained so. The day after Christmas day the King and Queen alone together in a coach, and followed by all the Court, took the road for Madrid, where there was no more talk of Madame des Ursins than if the King had never known her. Our King showed not the least surprise at the news brought to him by a courier despatched from Guadalaxara by the Duc de Saint-Aignan, though all the Court was filled with emotion and affright after having seen Madame des Ursins so triumphant.

Let us now look about for some explanations that will enable us to pierce this mystery—that remark to Torcy which escaped the King, which Torcy could not comprehend, and which he related to Castries, who told it to Madame la Duchesse d'Orleans, from whom I learned it! Can we imagine that a Parma princess brought up in a garret by an imperious mother, would have dared to take upon herself, while six leagues from the King of Spain whom she had never seen, a step so bold and unheard-of, when we consider against whom directed, a person possessing the entire confidence of that King and reigning openly? The thing is explained by the order, so unusual and so secret, that Amenzago had from the King of Spain to obey the Queen in everything, without reserve and without comment; an order that became known only at the moment when she gave orders to arrest Madame des Ursins and take her away.

Let us remark, too, the tranquillity with which our King and the King of Spain received the first intelligence of this event; the inactivity of the latter, the coldness of his letters to Madame des Ursins, and his perfect indifference what became of a person who was so cherished the day before, and who yet was forced to travel deprived of everything, by roads full of ice and snow. We must recollect that when the King banished Madame des Ursins before, for opening the letter of the Abbe d'Estrees, and for the note she sent upon it, he did not dare to have his orders executed in the presence of the King of Spain. It was on the frontier of Portugal, where our King wished him to go for the express purpose, that the King of Spain signed the order by which the Princesse des Ursins was forced to withdraw from the country. Now we had a second edition of the same volume. Let me add what I learnt from the Marechal de Brancas, to whom Alberoni related, a long while after this disgrace, that one evening as the Queen was travelling from Parma to Spain, he found her pacing her chamber, with rapid step and in agitation muttering to herself, letting escape the name of the Princesse des Ursins, and then saying with heat, "I will drive her away, the first thing." He cried out to the Queen and sought to represent to her the danger, the madness, the inutility of the enterprise which overwhelmed him: "Keep all this quiet," said the Queen, "and never let what you have heard escape you. Not a word! I know what I am about."

All these things together threw much light upon a catastrophe equally astonishing in itself and in its execution, and clearly show our King to have been the author of it; the King of Spain a consenting party and assisting by the extraordinary order given to Amenzago; and the Queen the actress, charged in some mariner by the two Kings to bring it about. The sequel in France confirmed this opinion.

The fall of the Princesse des Ursins caused great changes in Spain. The Comtesse d'Altamire was named Camarera Mayor, in her place. She was one of the greatest ladies in all Spain, and was hereditary Duchess of Cardonne. Cellamare, nephew of Cardinal del Giudice, was named her grand ecuyer; and the Cardinal himself soon returned to Madrid and to consideration. As a natural consequence, Macanas was disgraced. He and Orry had orders to leave Spain, the latter without seeing the King. He carried with him the maledictions of the public. Pompadour, who had been named Ambassador in Spain only to amuse Madame des Ursins, was dismissed, and the Duc de Saint-Aignan invested with that character, just as he was about to return after having conducted the Queen to Madrid.

In due time the Princesse des Ursins arrived in Paris, and took up her quarters in the house of the Duc de Noirmoutiers, her brother, in the Rue Saint-Dominique, close to mine. This journey must have appeared to her very different from the last she had made in France, when she was Queen of the Court. Few people, except her former friends and those of her formal cabal, came to see her; yet, nevertheless, some curious folks appeared, so that for the first few days there was company enough; but after that, solitude followed when the ill-success of her journey to Versailles became known. M. d'Orleans, reunited now with the King of Spain, felt that it was due to his interest even more than to his vengeance to show in a striking manner, that it was solely owing to the hatred and artifice of Madame des Ursins that he had fallen into such disfavour on account of Spain, and had been in danger of losing his head. Times had changed. Monseigneur was dead, the Meudon cabal annihilated; Madame de Maintenon had turned her back upon Madame des Ursins; thus M. d'Orleans was free to act as he pleased. Incited by Madame la

Duchesse d'Orleans, and more still by Madame, he begged the King to prohibit Madame des Ursins from appearing anywhere (Versailles not even excepted) where she might meet Madame la Duchesse de Berry, Madame, Monsieur le Duc, and Madame la Duchesse d'Orleans, who at the same time strictly forbade their households to see her, and asked the persons to whom they were particularly attached to hold no intercourse with her. This made a great stir, openly showed that Madame des Ursins had utterly lost the support of Madame de Maintenon and the King, and much embarrassed her.

I could not feel that M. d'Orleans was acting wrong, in thus paying off his wrongs for the injuries she had heaped upon him, but I represented to him, that as I had always been an intimate friend of Madame des Ursins, putting aside her conduct towards him and making no comparison between my attachment for him and my friendship for her, I could not forget the marks of consideration she had always given me, particularly in her last triumphant journey (as I have already explained), and that it would be hard if I could not see her. We capitulated then, and M. le Duc and Madame la Duchesse d'Orleans permitted me to see her twice—once immediately; once when she left—giving my word that I would not see her three times, and that Madame de Saint-Simon should not see her at all; which latter clause we agreed to very unwillingly, but there was no remedy. As I wished at least to profit by my chance, I sent word to Madame des Ursins, explaining the fetters that bound me, and saying that as I wished to see her at all events at my ease since I should see her so little, I would let pass the first few days and her first journey to Court, before asking her for an audience.

My message was very well received; she had known for many years the terms on which I was with M. d'Orleans; she was not surprised with these fetters, and was grateful to me for what I had obtained. Some days after she had been to Versailles, I went to her at two o'clock in the day. She at once closed the door to all comers, and I was tete-a-tete with her until ten o'clock at night.

It may be imagined what a number of things were passed in review during this long discourse. Our eight hours of conversation appeared to me like eight moments. She related to me her catastrophe, without mixing up the King or the King of Spain, of whom she spoke well; but, without violently attacking the Queen, she predicted what since has occurred. We separated at supper time, with a thousand reciprocal protestations and regret that Madame de Saint-Simon could not see her. She promised to inform me of her departure early enough to allow us to pass another day together.

Her journey to Versailles did not pass off very pleasantly. She dined with the Duchesse de Luders, and then visited Madame de Maintenon; waited with her for the King, but when he came did not stop long, withdrawing to Madame Adam's, where she passed the night. The next day she dined with the Duchesse de Ventadour, and returned to Paris. She was allowed to give up the pension she received from the King, and in exchange to have her Hotel de Ville stock increased, so that it yielded forty thousand livres a-year. Her income, besides being doubled, was thus much more sure than would have been a pension from the King, which she doubted not M. d'Orleans, as soon as he became master, would take from her. She thought of retiring into Holland, but the States-General would have nothing to do with her, either at the Hague, or at Amsterdam. She had reckoned upon the Hague. She next thought of Utrecht, but was soon out of conceit with it, and turned her regards towards Italy.

The health of the King, meanwhile, visibly declining, Madame des Ursins feared lest she should entirely fall into the clutches of M. d'Orleans. She fully resolved, therefore, to make off, without knowing, however, where to fix herself; and asked permission of the King to come and take leave of him at Marly. She came there from Paris on Tuesday, the 6th of August, so as to arrive as he left dinner, that is, about ten o'clock. She was immediately admitted into the cabinet of the King, with whom she remained tete-a-tete full half an hour. She passed immediately to the apartments of Madame de Maintenon, with whom she remained an hour; and then got into her coach and returned to Paris. I only knew of this leave-taking by her arrival at Marly, where I had some trouble in meeting her. As chance would have it, I went in search of her coach to ask her people what had become of her, and was speaking to them when, to and behold! she herself arrived. She seemed very glad to see me, and made me mount with her into her coach, where for little less than an hour we discoursed very freely. She did not dissimulate from me her fears; the coldness the King and Madame de Maintenon had testified for her through all their politeness; the isolation she found herself in at the Court, even in Paris; and the uncertainty in which she was as to the choice of a retreat; all this in detail, and nevertheless without complaint, without regret, without weakness; always reassured and superior to events, as though some one else were in question. She touched lightly upon Spain, upon the ascendency the Queen was acquiring already over the King, giving me to understand that it could not be otherwise; running lightly and modestly over the Queen, and always praising the goodness of the King of Spain. Fear, on account of the passers-by, put an end to our conversation. She was very gracious to me; expressed regret that we must part; proceeded to tell me when she should start in time for us to have another day together; sent many compliments to Madame de Saint-Simon; and declared herself sensible of the mark of friendship I had given her, in spite of my engagement with M. d'Orleans. As soon as I had seen her off, I went to M. d'Orleans, to whom I related what I had just done; said I had not paid a visit, but had had simply a meeting; that it was true I could not hinder myself from seeking it, without prejudice to the final visit he had allowed me. Neither he nor Madame la Duchesse d'Orleans complained. They had fully triumphed over their enemy, and were on the point of seeing her leave France for ever, without hope in Spain.

Until now, Madame des Ursins amused by a residue of friends, increased by those of M. de Noirmoutiers with whom she lodged and who had money, had gently occupied herself with the arrangement of her affairs, changed as they were, and in withdrawing her effects from Spain. The fear lest she should find herself in the power of a Prince whom she had so cruelly offended, and who showed, since her arrival in France, that he felt it, hurried all her measures. Her terror augmented by the change in the King that she found at this last audience had taken place since her first. She no longer doubted that his end was very near; and all her attention was directed to the means by which she might anticipate it, and be well informed of his health; this she believed her sole security in France. Terrified anew by the accounts she received of it, she no longer gave herself time for anything, but precipitately set out on the 14th August, accompanied as far as

Essonne by her two nephews. She had no time to inform me, so that I have never seen her since the day of our conversation at Marly in her coach. She did not breathe until she arrived at Lyons.

She had abandoned the project of retiring into Holland, where the States- General would not have her. She herself, too, was disgusted with the equality of a republic, which counterbalanced in her mind the pleasure of the liberty enjoyed there. But she could not resolve to return to Rome, the theatre of her former reign, and appear there proscribed and old, as in an asylum. She feared, too, a bad reception, remembering the quarrels that had taken place between the Courts of Rome and Spain. She had lost many friends and acquaintances; in fifteen years of absence all had passed away, and she felt the trouble she might be subjected to by the ministers of the Emperor, and by those of the two Crowns, with their partisans. Turin was not a Court worthy of her; the King of Sardinia had not always been pleased with her, and they knew too much for each other. At Venice she would have been out of her element.

Whilst agitated in this manner, without being able to make up her mind, she learned that the King was in extreme danger, a danger exaggerated by rumour. Fear seized her lest he should die whilst she was in his realm. She set off immediately, therefore, without knowing where to go; and solely to leave France went to Chambery, as the nearest place of safety, arriving there out of breath, so to say.

Every place being well examined, she preferred Genoa; its liberty pleased her; there was intercourse there with a rich and numerous nobility; the climate and the city were beautiful; the place was in some sort a centre and halting-point between Madrid, Paris, and Rome, with which places she was always in communication, and always hungered after all that passed there. Genoa determined on, she went there. She was well received, hoped to fix her tabernacle there, and indeed stayed some years. But at last ennui seized her; perhaps vexation at not being made enough of. She could not exist without meddling, and what is there for a superannuated woman to meddle with at Genoa? She turned her thoughts, therefore, towards Rome. Then, on sounding, found her course clear, quitted Genoa, and returned to her nest.

She was not long there before she attached herself to the King and Queen of England (the Pretender and his wife), and soon governed them openly. What a poor resource! But it was courtly and had a flavour of occupation for a woman who could not exist without movement. She finished her life there remarkably healthy in mind and body, and in a prodigious opulence, which was not without its use in that deplorable Court. For the rest, Madame des Ursins was in mediocre estimation at Rome, was deserted by the Spanish, little visited by the French, but always faithfully paid by France and Spain, and unmolested by the Regent. She was always occupied with the world, and with what she had been, but was no longer; yet without meanness, nay, with courage and dignity.

The loss she experienced in January, 1720, of the Cardinal de la Tremoille, although there was no real friendship between them, did not fail, to create a void in her. She survived him three years, preserved all her health, her strength, her mind until death, and was carried off, more than eighty years of age, at Rome, on the 5th of December, 1722, after a very short illness.

She had the pleasure of seeing Madame de Maintenon forgotten and annihilated in Saint-Cyr, of surviving her, of seeing at Rome her two enemies, Giudice and Alberoni, as profoundly disgraced as she,—one falling from the same height, and of relishing the forgetfulness, not to say contempt, into which they both sank. Her death, which, a few years before, would have resounded throughout all Europe, made not the least sensation. The little English Court regretted her, and some private friends also, of whom I was one. I did not hide this, although,—on account of M. le Duc d'Orleans, I had kept up no intercourse with her; for the rest, nobody seemed to perceive she had disappeared. She was, nevertheless, so extraordinary a person, during all the course of her long life, everywhere, and had so grandly figured, although in various ways; had such rare intellect, courage, industry, and resources; reigned so publicly and so absolutely in Spain; and had a character so sustained and so unique, that her life deserves to be written, and would take a place among the most curious fragments of the history of the times in which she lived.

CHAPTER LVI

But I must return somewhat now, in order to make way for a crowd of events which have been pressing forward all this time, but which I have passed by, in going straightforward at once to the end of Madame des Ursins' history.

On Monday, the 30th April, 1714., the King took medicine, and worked after dinner with Pontchartrain. This was at Marly. About six o'clock, he went to M. le Duc de Berry, who had had fever all night. M. le Duc de Berry had risen without saying anything, had been with the King at the medicine-hour, and intended to go stag-hunting; but on leaving the King's chamber shivering seized him, and forced him to go back again. He was bled while the King was in his chamber, and the blood was found very bad; when the King went to bed the doctors told him the illness was of a nature to make them hope that it might be a case of contagion. M. le Duc de Berry had vomited a good deal—a black vomit. Fagon said, confidently, that it was from the blood; the other doctors fastened upon some chocolate he had taken on the Sunday. From this day forward I knew what was the matter. Boulduc, apothecary of the King, and extremely attached to Madame de Saint-Simon and to me, whispered in my ear that M. le Duc de Berry would not recover, and that, with some little difference, his malady was the same as that of which the Dauphin and Dauphine died. He repeated this the next day, and never once varied afterwards; saying to me on the third day, that none of the doctors who attended the Prince were of a different opinion, or hid from him what they thought.

On Tuesday, the 1st of May, the Prince was bled in the foot at seven o'clock in the morning, after a very bad night; took emetics twice, which had a good effect; then some manna; but still there were two accesses. The King went to the sick-room afterwards, held a finance council, would not go shooting, as he had arranged, but walked in his gardens. The doctors, contrary to their custom, never reassured him. The night was cruel. On Wednesday; the 2nd of May, the King went, after mass, to M. le Duc de Berry, who had been again bled in the foot. The King held the Council of State, as usual, dined in Madame de Maintenon's rooms, and afterwards reviewed his Guards. Coettenfao, chevalier d'honneur of Madame la Duchesse de Berry, came during the morning to beg the King, in her name, that Chirac, a famous doctor of M. d'Orleans, should be allowed to see M. le Duc de Berry. The King refused, on the ground that all the other doctors were in accord, and that Chirac, who might differ with them, would embarrass them. After dinner Mesdames de Pompadour and La Vieuville arrived, on the part of Madame la Duchesse de Berry, to beg the King that she might be allowed to come and see her husband, saying that she would come on foot rather than stay away. It would have been better, surely, for her to come in a coach, if she so much wished, and, before alighting, to send to the King for permission so to do. But the fact is, she had no more desire to come than M. de Berry had to see her. He never once mentioned her name, or spoke of her, even indirectly. The King replied to those ladies by saying that he would not close the door against Madame la Duchesse de Berry, but, considering the state she was in, he thought it would be very imprudent on her part to come. He afterwards told M. le Duc and Madame la Duchesse d'Orleans to go to Versailles and hinder her from coming. Upon returning from the review the King went again to see M. le Duc de Berry. He had been once more bled in the arm, had vomited all day much blood too—and had taken some Robel water three times, in order to stop his sickness. This vomiting put off the communion. Pere de la Rue had been by his side ever since Tuesday morning, and found him very patient and resigned.

On Thursday, the 3rd, after a night worse than ever, the doctors said they did not doubt that a vein had been broken in the stomach. It was reported that this accident had happened by an effort M. de Berry made when out hunting on the previous Thursday, the day the Elector of Bavaria arrived. His horse slipped; in drawing the animal up, his body struck against the pommel of the saddle, so it was said, and ever since he had spit blood every day. The vomiting ceased at nine o'clock in the morning, but the patient was no better. The King, who was going stag-hunting, put it off. At six o'clock at night M. de Berry was so choked that he could no longer remain in bed; about eight o'clock he found himself so relieved that he said to Madame, he hoped he should not die; but soon after, the malady increased so much that Pere de la Rue said it was no longer time to think of anything but God, and of receiving the sacrament. The poor Prince himself seemed to desire it.

A little after ten o'clock at night the King went to the chapel, where a consecrated Host had been kept prepared ever since the commencement of the illness. M. le Duc de Berry received it, with extreme unction, in presence of the King, with much devotion and respect. The King remained nearly an hour in the chamber, supped alone in his own, did not receive the Princesses afterwards, but went to bed. M. le Duc d'Orleans, at ten o'clock in the morning, went again to Versailles, as Madame la Duchesse de Berry wished still to come to Marly. M. le Duc de Berry related to Pere de la Rue, who at least said so, the accident just spoken of; but, it was added, "his head was then beginning to wander." After losing the power of speech, he took the crucifix Pere de la Rue held, kissed it, and placed it upon his heart. He expired on Friday, the 4th of May, 1714, at four o'clock in the morning, in his twenty-eighth year, having been born at Versailles, the last day of August, 1686.

M. le Duc de Berry was of ordinary height, rather fat, of a beautiful blonde complexion, with a fresh, handsome face, indicating excellent health. He was made for society, and for pleasure, which he loved; the best, gentlest, most compassionate and accessible of men, without pride, and without vanity, but not without dignity or self-appreciation. He was of medium intellect, without ambition or desire, but had very good sense, and was capable of listening, of understanding, and of always taking the right side in preference to the wrong, however speciously put. He loved truth, justice, and reason; all that was contrary to religion pained him to excess, although he was not of marked piety. He was not without firmness, and hated constraint. This caused it to be feared that he was not supple enough for a younger son, and, indeed, in his early youth he could not understand that there was any difference between him and his eldest brother, and his boyish quarrels often caused alarm.

He was the most gay, the most frank, and consequently the most loved of the three brothers; in his youth nothing was spoken of but his smart replies to Madame and M. de la Rochefoucauld.

He laughed at preceptors and at masters—often at punishment. He scarcely knew anything except how to read and write; and learned nothing after being freed from the necessity of learning. This ignorance so intimidated him, that he could scarcely open his mouth before strangers, or perform the most ordinary duties of his rank; he had persuaded himself that he was an ass and a fool; fit for nothing. He was so afraid of the King that he dared not approach him, and was so confused if the King looked hard at him, or spoke of other things than hunting, or gaming, that he scarcely understood a word, or could collect his thoughts. As may be imagined, such fear does not go hand in hand with deep affection.

He commenced life with Madame la Duchesse de Berry as do almost all those who marry very young and green. He became extremely amorous of her; this, joined to his gentleness and natural complaisance, had the usual effect, which was to thoroughly spoil her. He was not long in perceiving it; but love was too strong for him. He found a woman proud, haughty, passionate, incapable of forgiveness, who despised him, and who allowed him to see it, because he had infinitely less head than she; and because, moreover, she was supremely false and strongly determined. She piqued herself upon both these qualities, and on her contempt for religion, ridiculing M. le Duc de Berry for being devout; and all these things became insupportable to him. Her gallantries were so prompt, so rapid, so unmeasured, that he could not help seeing them. Her endless private interviews with M. le Duc d'Orleans, in which everything languished if he was present, made him furious. Violent scenes frequently took place between them; the last, which occurred at Rambouillet, went so far that Madame la Duchesse de Berry received a kick * * * * , and a menace that she should be shut up in a convent for the rest of her life; and when M. le Duc de Berry fell ill, he was thumbing his hat, like a child, before the King, relating all his grievances, and asking to be delivered from Madame la Duchesse de Berry. Hitherto I have only alluded to Madame la Duchesse de Berry, but, as will be seen, she became so singular a person when her father was Regent, that I will here make her known more completely than I have yet done.

She was tall, handsome, well made, with, however, but little grace, and had something in her, eyes which made you fear what she was. Like her father and mother, she spoke well and with facility. Timid in trifles, yet in other things terrifyingly bold,—foolishly haughty sometimes, and sometimes mean to the lowest degree,—it may be said that she was a model of all the vices, avarice excepted; and was all the more dangerous because she had art and talent. I am not accustomed to over-colour the picture I am obliged to present to render things understood, and it will easily be perceived how strictly I am reserved upon the ladies, and upon all gallantries, not intimately associated with what may be called important matters. I should be so here, more than in any other case, from self-love, if not from respect for the sex and dignity of the person. The considerable part I played in bringing about Madame la Duchesse de Berry's marriage, and the place that Madame de Saint-Simon, in spite of herself and of me, occupied in connection with her, would be for me reasons more than enough for silence, if I did not feel that silence would throw obscurity over all the sequel of this history. It is then to the truth that I sacrifice my self-love, and with the same truthfulness I will say that if I had known or merely suspected, that the

Princess was so bad as she showed herself directly after her marriage, and always more and more since, she would never have become Duchesse de Berry.

I have already told how she annoyed M. le Duc de Berry by ridiculing his devotion. In other ways she put his patience to severe trials, and more than once was in danger of public exposure. She partook of few meals in private, at which she did not get so drunk as to lose consciousness, and to bring up all she had taken on every side. The presence of M. le Duc de Berry, of M. le Duc and Madame la Duchesse d'Orleans, of ladies with whom she was not on familiar terms, in no way restrained her. She complained even of M. le Duc de Berry for not doing as she did. She often treated her father with a haughtiness which was terrifying on all accounts.

In her gallantries she was as unrestrained as in other things. After having had several favourites, she fixed herself upon La Haye, who from King's page had become private ecuyer of M. le Duc de Berry. The oglings in the Salon of Marly were perceived by everybody; nothing restrained them. At last, it must be said, for this fact encloses all the rest, she wished La Haye to run away with her from Versailles to the Low Countries, whilst M. le Duc de Berry and the King were both living. La Haye almost died with fright at this proposition, which she herself made to him. His refusal made her furious. From the most pressing entreaties she came to all the invectives that rage could suggest, and that torrents of tears allowed her to pronounce. La Haye had to suffer her attacks—now tender, now furious; he was in the most mortal embarrassment. It was a long time before she could be cured of her mad idea, and in the meanwhile she subjected the poor fellow to the most frightful persecution. Her passion for La Haye continued until the death of M. le Duc de Berry, and some time after.

M. le Duc de Berry was buried at Saint-Denis on Wednesday, the 16th of May; M. le Duc d'Orleans was to have headed the procession, but the same odious reports against him that had circulated at the death of the Dauphin had again appeared, and he begged to be let off. M. le Duc filled his place. Madame la Duchesse de Berry, who was in the family way, kept her bed; and in order that she should not be seen there when people came to pay her the usual visits of condolence, the room was kept quite dark. Many ridiculous scenes and much indecent laughter, that could not be restrained, thus arose. Persons accustomed to the room could see their way, but those unaccustomed stumbled at every step, and had need of guidance. For want of this, Pere du Trevoux, and Pere Tellier after him, both addressed their compliments to the wall; others to the foot of the bed. This became a secret amusement, but happily did not last long.

As may be imagined, the death of M. le Duc de Berry was a deliverance for Madame la Duchesse de Berry. She was, as I have said, in the family way; she hoped for a boy, and counted upon enjoying as a widow more liberty than she had been able to take as a wife. She had a miscarriage, however, on Saturday, the 16th of June, and was delivered of a daughter which lived only twelve hours. The little corpse was buried at Saint- Denis, Madame de Saint-Simon at the head of the procession. Madame la Duchesse de Berry, shortly before this event, received two hundred thousand livres income of pension; but the establishment she would have had if the child had been a boy was not allowed her.

CHAPTER LXVII.

It is time now that I should say something about an event that caused an immense stir throughout the land, and was much talked of even in foreign parts. I must first introduce, however, a sort of a personage whose intimacy was forced upon me at this period; for the two incidents are in a certain degree associated together.

M. d'Orleans for some little time had continually represented to me, how desirous one of his acquaintances was to secure my friendship. This acquaintance was Maisons, president in the parliament, grandson of that superintendent of the finances who built the superb chateau of Maisons, and son of the man who had presided so unworthily at the judgment of our trial with M. de Luxembourg, which I have related in its place. Maisons was a person of much ambition, exceedingly anxious to make a name, gracious and flattering in manners to gain his ends, and amazingly fond of grand society.

The position of Maisons, where he lived, close to Marly, afforded him many opportunities of drawing there the principal people of the Court. It became quite the fashion to go from Marly to his chateau. The King grew accustomed to hear the place spoken of, and was in no way displeased. Maisons had managed to become very intimate with M. le Duc and M. le Prince de Conti. These two princes being dead, he turned his thoughts towards M, d'Orleans. He addressed himself to Canillac, who had always been an intimate friend of M. d'Orleans, and by him soon gained the intimacy of that prince. But he was not yet satisfied. He wished to circumvent M. d'Orleans more completely than he could by means of Canillac. He cast his eye, therefore, upon me. I think he was afraid of me on account of what I have related concerning his father. He had an only son about the same age as my children. For a long time he had made all kinds of advances, and visited them often. The son's intimacy did not, however, assist the father; so that at last Maisons made M. le Duc d'Orleans speak to me himself.

I was cold; tried to get out of the matter with compliments and excuses. M. d'Orleans, who believed he had found a treasure in his new acquaintance, returned to the charge; but I was not more docile. A few days after, I was surprised by an attack of the same kind from M. de Beauvilliers. How or when he had formed an intimacy with Maisons, I have never been able to unravel; but formed it, he had; and he importuned me so much, nay exerted his authority over me, that at last I found I must give way. Not to offend M. d'Orleans by yielding to another after having refused to yield to him, I waited until he should again speak to me on the subject, so that he might give himself the credit of vanquishing me. I did not wait long. The Prince attacked me anew, maintained that nothing would be more useful to him than an intimacy between myself and Maisons, who scarcely dared to see him, except in secret, and with whom he had not the same leisure or liberty for discussing many things that might present themselves. I had replied to all this before; but as I had resolved to surrender to the Prince (after the authority of the Duc de Beauvilliers had vanquished me), I complied with his wish.

Maisons was soon informed of it, and did not let my resolution grow, cold. M. le Duc d'Orleans urged me to go and sleep a night in Paris. Upon arriving there, I found a note from

Maisons, who had already sent an ocean of compliments to me by the Prince and the Duke. This note, for reasons to be told me afterwards, appointed a meeting at eleven o'clock this night, in the plain behind the Invalides, in a very mysterious manner. I went there with an old coachman of my mother's and a lackey to put my people off the scent. There was a little moonlight. Maisons in a small carriage awaited me. We soon met. He mounted into my coach. I never could comprehend the mystery of this meeting. There was nothing on his part but advances, compliments, protestations, allusions to the former interview of our fathers; only such things, in fact, as a man of cleverness and breeding says when he wishes to form a close intimacy with any one. Not a word that he said was of importance or of a private nature.

I replied in the civillest manner possible to the abundance he bestowed upon me. I expected afterwards something that would justify the hour, the place, the mystery, in a word, of our interview. What was my surprise to hear no syllable upon these points. The only reason Maisons gave for our secret interview was that from that time he should be able to come and see me at Versailles with less inconvenience, and gradually increase the number and the length of his visits until people grew accustomed to see him there! He then begged me not to visit him in Paris, because his house was always too full of people. This interview lasted little less than half an hour. It was long indeed, considering what passed. We separated with much politeness, and the first time he went to Versailles he called upon me towards the middle of the day.

In a short time he visited me every Sunday. Our conversation by degrees became more serious. I did not fail to be on my guard, but drew him out upon various subjects; he being very willing.

We were on this footing when, returning to my room at Marly about midday- on Sunday, the 29th of July, I found a lackey of Maisons with a note from him, in which he conjured me to quit all business and come immediately to his house at Paris, where he would wait for me alone, and where I should find that something was in question, that could not suffer the slightest delay, that could not even be named in writing, and which was of the most extreme importance. This lackey had long since arrived, and had sent my people everywhere in search of me. I was engaged that day to dine with M. and Madame de Lauzun. To have broken my engagement would have been to set the curiosity and the malignity of M. de Lauzun at work. I dared not disappear; therefore I gave orders to my coachman, and as soon as I had dined I vanished. Nobody saw me get into my chaise; and I quickly arrived at Paris, and immediately hastened to Maisons' with eagerness easy to imagine.

I found him alone with the Duc de Noailles. At the first glance I saw two dismayed men, who said to me in an exhausted manner, but after a heated though short preface, that the King had declared his two bastards and their male posterity to all eternity, real princes of the blood, with full liberty to assume all their dignities, honours, and rank, and capacity to succeed to the throne in default of the others.

At this news, which I did not expect, and the secret of which had hitherto been preserved, without a particle of it transpiring, my arms fell. I lowered my head and remained profoundly silent, absorbed in my reflections. They were soon disturbed by cries which aroused me. These two men commenced pacing the chamber; stamped with their feet; pushed and struck the furniture; raged as though each wished to be louder than the other, and made the house echo with their noise. I avow that so much hubbub seemed suspicious to me on the part of two men, one so sage and so measured, and to whom this rank was of no consequence; the other always so tranquil, so crafty, so master of himself. I knew not why this sudden fury succeeded to such dejected oppression; and I was not without suspicion that their passion was put on merely to excite mine. If this was their design, it succeeded ill. I remained in my chair, and coldly asked them what was the matter. My tranquillity sharpened their fury. Never in my life have I seen anything so surprising.

I asked them if they had gone mad, and if instead of this tempest it would not be better to reason, and see whether something could not be done. They declared it was precisely because nothing could be done against a thing not only resolved on, but executed, declared, and sent to the Parliament, that they were so furious; that M. le Duc d'Orleans, on the terms he was with the King, would not dare even to whisper objections; that the Princes of the blood, mere children as they were, could only tremble; that the Dukes had no means of opposition, and that the Parliament was reduced to silence and slavery. Thereupon they set to work to see who could cry the louder and reviled again, sparing neither things nor persons.

I, also, was in anger, but this racket kept me cool and made me smile. I argued with them and said, that after all I preferred to see the bastards princes of the blood, capable of succeeding to the throne, than to see them in the intermediary rank they occupied. And it is true that as soon as I had cooled myself, I felt thus.

At last the storm grew calm, and they told me that the Chief-President and the Attorney-General—who, I knew, had been at Marly very early in the morning at the Chancellor's—had seen the King in his cabinet soon after he rose, and had brought back the declaration, all prepared. Maisons must, however, have known this earlier; because when the lackey he sent to me set out from Paris, those gentlemen could not have returned there. Our talk led to nothing, and I regained Marly in all haste, in order that my absence might not be remarked.

Nevertheless it was towards the King's supper hour when I arrived. I went straight to the salon, and found it very dejected. People looked, but scarcely dared to approach each other; at the most, a sign or a whisper in the ear, as the courtiers brushed by one another, was ventured out. I saw the King sit down to table; he seemed to me more haughty than usual, and continually looked all around. The news had only been known one hour; everybody was still congealed and upon his guard.

As soon as the King was seated (he had looked very hard at me in passing) I went straight to M. du Maine's. Although the hour was unusual, the doors fell before me; I saw a man, who received me with joyful surprise, and who, as it were, moved through the air towards me, all lame that he was. I said that I came to offer him a sincere compliment, that we (the Dukes) claimed no precedence over the Princes of the blood; but what we claimed was, that there should be nobody between the Princes of the blood and us; that as this intermediary rank no longer existed, we had nothing more to say, but to rejoice that we had no longer to support what was insupportable. The joy of M. du Maine burst forth at my compliments, and he startled me with a politeness inspired by the transport of triumph.

But if he was delighted at the declaration of the King, it was far otherwise with the world. Foreign dukes and princes fumed, but uselessly. The Court uttered dull murmurs more than could have been expected. Paris and the provinces broke out; the Parliament did not keep silent. Madame de Maintenon, delighted with her work, received the adoration of her familiars.

As for me, I will content myself with but few reflections upon this most monstrous, astounding, and frightful determination of the King. I will simply say, that it is impossible not to see in it an attack upon the Crown; contempt for the entire nation, whose rights are trodden under foot by it; insult to all the Princes of the blood; in fact the crime of high treason in its most rash and most criminal extent. Yes! however venerable God may have rendered in the eyes of men the majesty of Kings and their sacred persons, which are his anointed; however execrable may be the crime known as high treason, of attempting their lives; however terrible and singular may be the punishments justly invented to prevent that crime, and to remove by their horror the most infamous from the infernal resolution of committing it, we cannot help finding in the crime in question a plenitude not in the other, however abominable it may be: Yes! to overthrow the most holy laws, that have existed ever since the establishment of monarchy; to extinguish a right the most sacred—the most important—the most inherent in the nation: to make succession to the throne, purely, supremely, and despotically arbitrary; in a word, to make of a bastard a crown prince, is a crime more black, more vast, more terrible, than that of high treason against the chief of the State.

CHAPTER LXVIII

But let me now explain by what means the King was induced to arrive at, and publish this terrible determination.

He was growing old, and though no external change in him was visible, those near him had for some time begun to fear that he could not live long. This is not the place to descant upon a health hitherto so good and so even: suffice it to mention, that it silently began to give way. Overwhelmed by the most violent reverses of fortune after being so long accustomed to success, the King was even more overwhelmed by domestic misfortunes. All his children had disappeared before him, and left him abandoned to the most fatal reflections. At every moment he himself expected the same kind of death. Instead of finding relief from his anguish among those who surrounded him, and whom he saw most frequently, he met with nothing but fresh trouble there. Excepting Marechal, his chief surgeon, who laboured unceasingly to cure him of his suspicions, Madame de Maintenon, M. du Maine, Fagon, Bloin, the other principal valets sold to the bastard and his former governors,—all sought to augment these suspicions; and in truth it was not difficult to do so. Nobody doubted that poison had been used, nobody could seriously doubt it; and Marechal, who was as persuaded as the rest, held a different opinion before the King only to deliver him from a useless torment which could not but do him injury. But M. du Maine, and Madame de Maintenon also, had too much interest to maintain him in this fear, and by their art filled him with horror against M. d'Orleans, whom they named as the author of these crimes, so that the King with this prince before his eyes every day, was in a perpetual state of alarm.

With his children the King had lost, and by the same way, a princess, who in addition to being the soul and ornament of his court, was, moreover, all his amusement, all his joy, all his affection, in the hours when he was not in public. Never, since he entered the world, had he become really familiar with any one but her; it has been seen elsewhere to what extent. Nothing could fill up this great void: The bitterness of being deprived of her augmented, because he could find no diversion. This unfortunate state made him seek relief everywhere in abandoning himself more and more to Madame de Maintenon and M. du Maine.

They soon managed to obtain possession of him, as it were, entirely; leaving no art unexhausted in order to flatter, to amuse, to please, and to interest him. He was made to believe that M. du Maine was utterly without ambition; like a good father of a family, solely occupied with his children, touched with the grandeur of his nearness to the King, simple, frank, upright, and one who after working at his duties all day, and after giving himself time for prayer and piety, amused himself in hunting, and drew upon his natural gaiety and cheerfulness, without knowing anything of the Court, or of what was passing! Compare this portrait with his real character, and we shall feel with terror what a rattlesnake was introduced into the King's privacy.

Established thus in the mind and heart of the King, the opportunity seemed ripe for profiting by precious time that could not last long. Everybody smiled upon the project of M. du Maine and Madame de Maintenon. They had rendered M. d'Orleans odious in the eyes of the King and of the whole country, by the most execrable calumnies. How could he defend himself? shut up as the King was, how oppose them? how interfere with their dark designs? M. du Maine wished not only to be made prince of the blood, but to be made guardian of the heir to the throne, so as to dwarf the power of the Regent as much as possible. He flattered himself that the feeling he had excited against M. d'Orleans in the Court, in Paris, and in the provinces would be powerfully strengthened by dispositions so dishonourable; that he should find himself received as the guardian and protector of the life of the royal infant, to whom was attached the salvation of France, of which he would then become the idol; that the independent possession of the young King, and of his military and civil households, would strengthen with the public applause the power with which he would be invested in the state by this testament; that the Regent, reviled and stripped in this manner, not only would be in no condition to dispute anything, but would be unable to defend himself from any attempts the bastard might afterwards make against him. M. du Maine wished in fact to take from M. d'Orleans everything, except the name of Regent, and to divide all the power between himself and his brother. Such was his scheme, that the King by incredible art was induced to sanction and approve.

But the schemers had tough work before they obtained this success. They found that the King would not consent to their wishes without much opposition. They hit upon a devilish plan to overpower his resistance. Hitherto, they had only been occupied in pleasing him, in amusing him, in anticipating his wishes, in praising him—let me say the word— in adoring him. They had redoubled their attention, since, by the Dauphine's death, they had become his sole resource.

Not being able now to lead him as they wished, but determined to do so at all cost, they adopted another system, certain as they were that they could do so with impunity. Both became serious, often times dejected, silent, furnishing nothing to the conversation, letting pass what the King forced himself to say, sometimes not even replying, if it was not a direct interrogation. In this manner all the leisure hours of the King were rendered dull and empty; his amusements and diversions were made fatiguing and sad and a weight was cast upon him, which he was the more unable to bear because it was quite new to him, and he was utterly without means to remove it. The few ladies who were admitted to the intimacy of the King knew not what to make of the change they saw in Madame de Maintenon. They were duped at first by the plea of illness; but seeing at last that its duration passed all bounds, that it had no intermission, that her face announced no malady, that her daily life was in no way deranged, that the King became as serious and as sad as she, they sounded each other to find out the cause. Fear, lest it should be something in which they, unknowingly, were concerned, troubled them; so that they became even worse company to the King than Madame de Maintenon.

There was no relief for the King. All his resource was in the commonplace talk of the Comte de Toulouse, who was not amusing, although ignorant of the plot, and the stories of his valets, who lost tongue as soon as they perceived that they were not seconded by the Duc du Maine in his usual manner. Marechal and all the rest, astonished at the mysterious dejection of the Duc du Maine, looked at each other without being able to divine the cause. They saw that the King was sad and bored; they trembled for his health, but not one of them dared to do anything. Time ran on, and the dejection of M. du Maine and Madame de Maintenon increased. This is as far as the most instructed have ever been able to penetrate. To describe the interior scenes that doubtless passed during the long time this state of things lasted, would be to write romance. Truth demands that we should relate what we know, and admit what we are ignorant of. I cannot go farther, therefore, or pierce deeper into the density of these dark mysteries.

What is certain is, that cheerfulness came back all at once, with the same surprise to the witnesses of it, as the long-continued dejection had caused them, simply because they understood no more of the end than of the commencement. The double knowledge did not come to them until they heard the frightful crash of the thunderbolt which fell upon France, and astonished all Europe.

To give some idea of the opposition from the King, M. du Maine and Madame de Maintenon had to overcome, and to show how reluctantly he consented to their wishes, more than one incident may be brought forward. Some days before the news transpired, the King, full of the enormity of what he had just done for his bastards, looked at them in his cabinet, in presence of the valets, and of D'Antin and D'O, and in a sharp manner, that told of vexation, and with a severe glance, suddenly thus addressed himself to M. du Maine:

"You have wished it; but know that however great I may make you, and you may be in my lifetime, you are nothing after me; and it will be for you then to avail yourself of what I have done for you, if you can."

Everybody present trembled at a thunder-clap so sudden, so little expected, so entirely removed from the character and custom of the King, and which showed so clearly the extreme ambition of the Duc du Maine, and the violence he had done to the weakness of the King, who seemed to reproach himself for it, and to reproach the bastard for his ambition and tyranny. The consternation of M. du Maine seemed extreme at this rough sally, which no previous remark had led to. The King had made a clean breast of it. Everybody fixed his eyes upon the floor and held his breath. The silence was profound for a considerable time: it finished only when the King passed into his wardrobe. In his absence everybody breathed again. The King's heart was full to bursting with what he had just been made to do; but like a woman who gives birth to two children, he had at present brought but one into the world, and bore a second of which he must be delivered, and of which he felt all the pangs without any relief from the suffering the first had caused him.

Again, on Sunday, the 27th August, the Chief-President and the Attorney- General were sent for by the King. He was at Versailles. As soon as they were alone with him, he took from a drawer, which he unlocked, a large and thick packet, sealed with seven seals (I know not if by this M. du Maine wished to imitate the mysterious book with Seven Seals, of the Apocalypse, and so sanctify the packet). In handing it to them, the King said: "Gentlemen, this is my will. No one but myself knows its contents. I commit it to you to keep in the Parliament, to which I cannot give a greater testimony of my esteem and confidence than by rendering it the depository of it. The example of the Kings my predecessors, and that of the will of the King, my father, do not allow me to be ignorant of what may become of this; but they would have it; they have tormented me; they have left me no repose, whatever I might say. Very well! I have bought my repose. Here is the will; take it away: come what may of it, at least, I shall have rest, and shall hear no more about it."

At this last word, that he finished with a dry nod, he turned his back upon them, passed into another cabinet, and left them both nearly turned into statues. They looked at each other frozen by what they had just heard, and still more by what they had just seen in the eyes and the countenance of the King; and as soon as they had collected their senses, they retired, and went to Paris. It was not known until after dinner that the King had made a will and given it to them. In proportion as the news spread, consternation filled the Court, while the flatterers, at bottom as much alarmed as the rest, and as Paris was afterwards, exhausted themselves in praises and eulogies.

The next day, Monday, the 28th, the Queen of England came from Chaillot, where she almost always was, to Madame de Maintenon's. As soon as the King perceived her, "Madame," said he to her, like a man full of something and angry, "I have made my will; I have been tormented to do it;" then casting his eyes upon Madame de Maintenon, "I have bought repose; I know the powerlessness and inutility of it. We can do all we wish while we live; afterwards we are less than the meanest. You have only to see what became of my father's will immediately after his death, and the wills of so many other Kings. I know it well; but nevertheless they have wished it; they gave me no rest nor repose, no calm until it was done; ah, well! then, Madame, it is done; come what may of it, I shall be no longer tormented."

Words such as these so expressive of the extreme violence suffered by the King, of his long and obstinate battle before surrendering, of his vexation, and uneasiness, demand the clearest proofs. I had them from people who heard them, and would not advance them unless I were perfectly persuaded of their exactness.

As soon as the Chief-President and the Attorney-General returned to Paris, they sent for some workmen, whom they led into a tower of the Palace of justice, behind the Buvette, or drinking-place of the grand chamber and the cabinet of the Chief-President. They had a big hole made in the wall of this tower, which is very thick, deposited the testament there, closed up the opening with an iron door, put an iron grating by way of second door, and then walled all up together. The door and the grating each had three locks, the same for both; and a different key for each of the three, which consequently opened each of the two locks, the one in the door and the one in the grating. The Chief-President kept one key, the Attorney-General another, and the Chief-Greffier of the Parliament the third. The Parliament was assembled and the Chief-President flattered the members as best he might upon the confidence shown them in entrusting them with this deposit.

At the same time was presented to the Parliament an edict that the Chief-President and the Attorney-General had received from the hand of the Chancellor at Versailles the same morning the King had given them his will, and the edict was registered. It was very short. It declared that the packet committed to the Chief-President and to the Attorney-General contained the will of the King, by which he had provided for the protection and guardianship of the young King, and had chosen a Regency council, the dispositions of which—for good reasons he had not wished to publish; that he wished this deposit should be preserved during his life in the registry of the Parliament, and that at the moment when it should please God to call him from the world, all the chambers of the Parliament, all the princes of the royal house, and all the peers who might be there, should assemble and open the will; and that after it was read, all its dispositions should be made public and executed, nobody to be permitted to oppose them in any way.

Notwithstanding all this secrecy, the terms of the will were pretty generally guessed, and as I have said, the consternation was general. It was the fate of M. du Maine to obtain what he wished; but always with the maledictions of the public. This fate did not abandon him now, and as soon as he felt it, he was overwhelmed, and Madame de Maintenon exasperated, and their attentions and their care redoubled, to shut up the King, so that the murmurs of the world should not reach him. They occupied themselves more than ever to amuse and to please him, and to fill the air around him with praises, joy, and public adoring at an act so generous and so grand, and at the same time so wise and so necessary to the maintenance of good order and tranquillity, which would cause him to reign so gloriously even after his reign.

This consternation was very natural, and is precisely why the Duc du Maine found himself deceived and troubled by it. He believed he had prepared everything, smoothed everything, in rendering M. d'Orleans so suspected and so odious; he had succeeded, but not so much as he imagined. His desires and his emissaries had exaggerated everything; and he found himself overwhelmed with astonishment, when instead of the public acclamations with which he had flattered himself the will would be accompanied, it was precisely the opposite.

It was seen very clearly that the will assuredly could not have been made in favour of M. d'Orleans, and although public feeling against him had in no way changed, no one was so blind as not to see that he must be Regent by the incontestable right of his birth; that the dispositions of the testament could not weaken that right, except by establishing a power that should balance his; and that thus two parties would be formed in the state the chief of each of which would be interested in vanquishing the other, everybody being necessitated to join one side or other, thereby running a thousand risks without any advantage. The rights of the two disputants were compared. In the one they were found sacred, in the other they could not be found at all. The two persons were compared. Both were found odious, but M. d'Orleans was deemed superior to M. du Maine. I speak only of the mass of uninstructed people, and of what presented itself naturally and of itself. The better informed had even more cause to arrive at the same decision.

M. d'Orleans was stunned by the blow; he felt that it fell directly upon him, but during the lifetime of the King he saw no remedy for it. Silence respectful and profound appeared to him the sole course open; any other would only have led to an increase of precautions. The King avoided all discourse with him upon this matter; M. du Maine the same. M. d'Orleans was contented with a simple approving monosyllable to both, like a courtier who ought not to meddle with anything; and he avoided conversation upon this subject, even with Madame la Duchesse d'Orleans, and with anybody else. I was the sole person to whom he dared to unbosom himself; with the rest of the world he had an open, an ordinary manner, was on his guard against any discontented sign, and against the curiosity of all eyes. The inexpressible abandonment in which he was, in the midst of the Court, guaranteed him at least from all remarks upon the will. It was not until the health of the King grew more menacing that he began to speak and be spoken to thereon.

As for M. du Maine, despite his good fortune, he was not to be envied At Sceaux, where he lived, the Duchesse du Maine, his wife, ruined him by her extravagance. Sceaux was more than ever the theatre of her follies, and of the shame and embarrassment of her husband, by the crowd from the Court and the town, which abounded there and laughed at them. She herself played there Athalie (assisted by actors and actresses) and other pieces several times a week. Whole nights were passed in coteries, games, fetes, illuminations, fireworks, in a word, fancies and fripperies of every kind and every day. She revelled in the joy of her new greatness—redoubled her follies; and the Duc du Maine, who always trembled before her, and who, moreover, feared that the slightest contradiction would entirely turn her brain, suffered all this, even piteously doing the honours as often as he could without ceasing in his conduct to the King.

However great might be his joy, whatever the unimaginable greatness to which he had arrived, he was not tranquil. Like those tyrants who have usurped by their crimes the sovereign power, and who fear as so many conspiring enemies all their fallen citizens they have enslaved—he felt as though seated under that sword that Dionysius, tyrant of Syracuse, suspended by a hair over his table, above the head of a man whom he placed there because he believed him happy, and in this manner wished to make him feel what passed unceasingly in himself. M. du Maine, who willingly expressed in pleasantry the most serious things, frankly said to his familiars, that he was "like a louse between two fingernails" (the Princes of the blood and the peers), by which he could not fail to be cracked if he did not take care! This reflection troubled the excess of his pleasure, and that of the greatness and the power to which so many artifices had elevated him. He feared the Princes of the blood as soon as they should be of age to feel the infamy and the danger of the wound he had given them; he feared the Parliament, which even under his eyes had not been able to dissimulate its indignation at the violence he had committed against the most holy and the most inviolable laws; he even feared the Dukes so timid are injustice and tyranny!

CHAPTER LXIX

Let me return to Maisons. Five days after the King's will had been walled up, in the manner I have described, he came to me and made a pathetic discourse upon the injustice done to M. le Duc d'Orleans by this testament, and did all he could to excite me by railing in good set terms against dispositions intended to add to the power and grandeur of the bastards.

When he had well harangued, I said he had told me nothing new; that I saw the same truths as he with the same evidence; that the worst thing I found was that there was no remedy.

"No remedy!" he exclaimed, interrupting me, with his sly and cunning laugh; "courage and ability can always find one for everything, and I am astonished that you, who have both, should have nothing to suggest while everybody is going to confusion."

I asked him how it was possible to suppress a will registered by edict; a document solemn and public deposited with ceremony in the very depths of the palace, with precautions known to everybody—nature and art combining to keep it in safety?

"You are at a loss to know!" replied Maisons to me. "Have ready at the instant of the King's death sure troops and sensible officers, all ready and well instructed; and with them, masons and lock-smiths—march to the palace, break open the doors and the wall, carry off the will, and let it never be seen."

In my extreme surprise I asked him, what he expected would be the fruit of such violence? I pointed out that to seize by force of arms a public and solemn document, in the midst of the capital, in despite of all—all law and order, would be to put weapons into the hands of the enemies of M. le Duc d'Orleans, who assuredly would be justified in crying out against this outrage, and who would find the whole country disposed to echo their cries. I said too, that if in the execution of such an odious scheme a sedition occurred, and blood were shed, universal hatred and opprobrium would fall upon the head of M, le Duc d'Orleans, and deservedly so.

We carried on our discussion a long time, but Maisons would in no way give up his scheme. After leaving me he went to M. le Duc d'Orleans and communicated it to him. Happily it met with no success with the Duke, indeed, he was extremely astonished at it; but what astonished us more was, that Maisons persisted in it up to his death, which preceded by some few days that of the King, and pressed it upon M. le Duc d'Orleans and myself till his importunity became persecution.

It was certainly not his fault that I over and over again refused to go to the Grand Chamber of the Parliament to examine the place, as Maisons wished me to do; I who never went to the Parliament except for the reception of the peers or when the King was there. Not being able to vanquish what he called my obstinacy, Maisons begged me at the least to go and fix myself upon the Quai de la Megisserie, where so much old iron is sold, and examine from that spot the tower where the will was; he pointed it out to me; it looked out upon the Quai des Morforidus, but was behind the buildings on the quai. What information could be obtained from such a point of view may be imagined. I promised to go there, not to stop, and thus awake the attention of the passers-by, but to pass along and see what was to be seen; adding, that it as simply out of complaisance to him, and not because I meant to agree in any way to his enterprise. What is incomprehensible is, that for a whole year Maisons pressed his charming project upon us. The worst enemy of M. le Duc d'Orleans could not have devised a more rash and ridiculous undertaking. I doubt whether many people would have been found in all Paris sufficiently deprived of sense to fall in with it. What are we to think then of a Parliamentary President of such consideration as Maisons had acquired at the Palace of justice, at the Court, in the town, where he had always passed for a man of intellect, prudent, circumspect, intelligent, capable, measured? Was he vile enough, in concert with M. du Maine, to open this gulf beneath our feet, to push us to our ruin, and by the fall of M. le Duc d'Orleans—the sole prince of the blood old enough to be Regent—to put M. le Duc du Maine in his place, from which to the crown there was only one step, as none are ignorant, left to be taken? It seems by no means impossible: M. du Maine, that son of darkness, was, judging him by what he had already done, quite capable of adding this new crime to his long list.

The mystery was, however, never explained. Maisons died before its darkness could be penetrated. His end was terrible. He had no religion; his father had had none. He married a sister of the Marechal de Villars, who was in the same case. Their only son they specially educated in unbelief. Nevertheless, everything seemed to smile upon them. They had wealth, consideration, distinguished friends. But mark the end.

Maisons is slightly unwell. He takes rhubarb twice or thrice, unseasonably; more unseasonably comes Cardinal de Bissy to him, to talk upon the constitution, and thus hinder the operation of the rhubarb; his inside seems on fire, but he will not believe himself ill; the progress of his disease is great in a few hours; the doctors, though soon at their wits' ends, dare not say so; the malady visibly increases; his whole household is in confusion; he dies, forty-eight years of age, midst of a crowd of friends, of clients, without the power or leisure to think for a moment what is going to happen to his soul!

His wife survives him ten or twelve years, opulent, and in consideration, when suddenly she has an attack of apoplexy in her garden. Instead of thinking of her state, and profiting by leisure, she makes light of her illness, has another attack a few days after, and is carried off on the 5th of May, 1727, in her forty-sixth year, without having had a moment free.

Her son, for a long time much afflicted, seeks to distinguish himself and acquire friends. Taking no warning from what has occurred, he thinks only of running after the fortune of this world, and is surprised at Paris by the small-pox. He believes himself dead, thinks of what he has neglected all his life, but fear suddenly seizes him, and he dies in the midst of it, on the 13th of September, 1731, leaving an only son, who dies a year after him, eighteen months old, all the great wealth of the family going to collateral relatives.

These Memoirs are not essays on morality, therefore I have contented myself with the most simple and the most naked recital of facts; but I may, perhaps, be permitted to apply here those two verses of the 37th Psalm, which appear so expressly made for the purpose: "I have seen the impious exalted like the cedars of Lebanon: Yea, he passed away, and, lo, he was not; yea, I sought him, but he could not be found."

But let me leave this subject now, to treat of other matters. On Friday, the last day of August, I lost one of the best and most revered of friends, the Duc de Beavilliers. He died at Vaucresson after an illness of about two months, his intellect clear to the last, aged sixty-six years, having been born on the 24th of Oct 1648.

He was the son of M. de Saint-Aignan, who with honour and valour was truly romantic in gallantry, in belles-lettres, and in arms. He was Captain of the Guards of Gaston, and at the end of 1649 bought of the Duc de Liancourt the post of first-gentleman of the King's chamber. He commanded afterwards in Berry against the party of M. le Prince, and served elsewhere subsequently. In 1661 he was made Chevalier of the Order, and in 1661 Duke and Peer. His first wife he lost in 1679. At the end of a year he married one of her chambermaids, who had been first of all engaged to take care of her dogs. She was so modest, and he so shamefaced, that in despite of repeated pressing on the part of the King, she could not be induced to take her tabouret. She lived in much retirement, and had so many virtues that she made herself respected all her life, which was long. M. de Beauvilliers was one of the children of the first marriage. I know not what care M. and Madame de Saint-Aignan took of the others, but they left him, until he was six or seven years of age, to the mercy of their lodge-keeper. Then he was confided to the care of a canon of Notre Dame de Clery. The household of the canon consisted of one maid-servant, with whom the little boy slept; and they continued to sleep together until he was fourteen or fifteen years old, without either of them thinking of evil, or the canon remarking that the lad was growing into a man. The death of his eldest brother called M. de Beauvilliers home. He entered the army, served with distinction at the head of is regiment of cavalry, and was brigadier.

He was tall, thin, had a long and ruddy face, a large aquiline nose, a sunken mouth, expressive, piercing eyes, an agreeable smile, a very gentle manner but ordinarily retiring, serious, and concentrated. B disposition he was hasty, hot, passionate, fond of pleasure. Ever since God had touched him, which happened early in his life, he had become gentle, mildest, humble, kind, enlightened, charitable, and always full of real piety and goodness. In private, where he was free, he was gay, joked, and bantered pleasantly, and laughed with good heart. He liked to be made fun of there was only the story of his sleeping with the canon's servant that wounded his modesty, and I have seen him embarrassed when Madame de Beauvilliers has related it,— smiling, however, but praying her sometimes not to tell it. His piety, which, as I have said, commenced early in life, separated him from companions of his own age. At the army one day, during a promenade of the King, he walked alone, a little in front. Some one remarked it, and observed, sneeringly, that "he was meditating." The King, who heard this, turned towards the speaker, and, looking at him, said, "Yes, 'tis M. de Beauvilliers, one of the best men of the Court, and of my realm." This sudden and short apology caused silence, and food for reflection, so that the fault-finders remained in respect before his merit.

The King must have entertained a high regard for him, to give him, in 1670, the very delicate commission he entrusted to him. Madame had just been so openly poisoned, the conviction was so complete and so general that it was very difficult to palliate it. Our King and the King of England, between whom she had just become a stronger bond, by the journey she had made into

England, were penetrated by grief and indignation, and the English could not contain themselves. The King chose the Duc de Beauvilliers to carry his compliments of condolence to the King of England, and under this pretext to try to prevent this misfortune interfering with their friendship and their union, and to calm the fury of London and the nation. The King was not deceived: the prudent dexterity of the Duc de Beauvilliers brought round the King of England, and even appeased London and the nation.

M. de Beauvilliers had expressed a wish to be buried at Montargis, in the Benedictine monastery, where eight of his daughters had become nuns. Madame de Beauvilliers went there, and by an act of religion, terrible to think of, insisted upon being present at the interment. She retired to her house at Paris, where during the rest of her life she lived in complete solitude, without company or amusement of any kind. For nearly twenty years she remained there, and died in 1733, seventy-five years of age, infinitely rich in alms and all sorts of good works.

The King taxed the infantry regiments, which had risen to an excessive price. This venality of the only path by which the superior grades can be reached is a great blot upon the military system, and stops the career of many a man who would become an excellent soldier. It is a gangrene which for a long time has eaten into all the orders and all the parties of the state, and under which it will be odd if all do not succumb. Happily it is unknown, or little known, in all the other countries of Europe!

Towards the end of this year Cardinal d'Estrees died in Paris at his abbey of Saint-Germain-des-Pres, nearly eighty-seven years of age, having always enjoyed perfect health of body and mind until this illness, which was very short, and which left his intellect clear to the last. It is proper and curious to pause for a moment upon a personage, all his life of importance, and who at his death was Cardinal, Bishop of Albano, Abbe of Longpont, of Mount Saint-Eloi, of Saint-Nichoas-aux-Bois, of La Staffarde in Piedmont (where Catinat gained a celebrated battle before being Marechal of France), of Saint-Claude in Franche-Comte, of Anchin in Flanders, and of Saint-Germain-des-Pres in Paris. He was also Commander of the Order of the promotion of 1688.

Merit, aided by the chances of fortune, made out of an obscure family of the Boulonais country, a singularly illustrious race in the fourth generation, of which Mademoiselle de Tourbes alone remains. The Cardinal, brother of the last Marechal d'Estrees, their uncle, used to say; that he knew his fathers as far as the one who had been page of Queen Anne, Duchess of Brittany; but beyond that he knew nothing, and it was not worth while searching. Gabrielle d'Estrees, mistress of Henry IV., whose beauty made her father's fortune, and whose history is too well known to be here alluded to, was sister of the Cardinal's father, but died thirty years before he was born. It was through her that the family became elevated. The father of Cardinal d'Estrees was distinguished all his life by his merit, his capacity, and the authority and elevated posts he held. He was made Marshal of France in 1626, and it is a thing unique that he, his son, and his grandson were not only Marshals of France, but all three were in succession seniors of that corps for a long time.

The Cardinal d'Estrees was born in 1627, and for forty years lived with his father, profiting by his lessons and his consideration. He was of the most agreeable manners, handsome, well made, full of humour, wit, and ability; in society the pleasantest person in the world, and yet well instructed; indeed, of rare erudition, generous, obliging, dignified, incapable of meanness, he was with so much talent and so many great and amiable qualities generally loved and respected, and deserved to be. He was made Cardinal in 1671, but was not declared until after many delays had occurred. These delays much disturbed him. It was customary, then, to pay more visits. One evening the Abbe de la Victoire, one of his friends, and very witty, arrived very late at a supper, in a house where he was expected. The company inopportunely asked him where he had been, and what had delayed him.

"Alas!" replied the Abbe, in a tone of sadness, "where have I been? I have been all day accompanying the body of poor M. de Laon." [The Cardinal d'Estrees was then Bishop and Duke of Laon.]

"M. de Laon!" cried everybody, "M. de Laon dead! Why, he was quite well yesterday. 'Tis dreadful. Tell us what has happened."

"What has happened?" replied the Abbe, still with the same tone. "Why, he took me with him when he paid his visits, and though his body was with me, his spirit was at Rome, so that I quitted him very wearied." At this recital grief changed into merriment.

That grand dinner at Fontainebleau for the Prince of Tuscany, at which the Prince was to be the only guest, and yet never received his invitation from the Cardinal, I have already mentioned. He was oftentimes thus absent, but never when business or serious matters were concerned, so that his forgetfulness was amusing. He never could bear to hear of his domestic affairs. Pressed and tormented by his steward and his maitre d'hotel to overlook their accounts, that he had not seen for many years, he appointed a day to be devoted to them. The two financiers demanded that he should close his door so as not to be interrupted; he consented with difficulty, then changed his mind, and said that if Cardinal Bonzi came he must be admitted, but that it was not likely he would come on that particular day. Directly afterwards he sent a trusty servant to Cardinal Bonzi, entreating him to come on such and such a day, between three and four o'clock, conjuring him not to fail, and begging him above all to come as of his own accord, the reason to be explained afterwards. On the appointed day Cardinal d'Estrees told his porter to let no one enter in the afternoon except Cardinal Bonzi, who assuredly was not likely to come, but who was not to be sent away if he did. His people, delighted at having their master to themselves all day without interruption, arrived about three o'clock; the Cardinal quitted his family and the few friends who had that day dined with him, and passed into a cabinet where his business people laid out their papers. He said a thousand absurdities to them upon his expenditure, of which he understood nothing, and unceasingly looked towards the window, without appearing to do so, secretly sighing for a prompt deliverance. A little before four o'clock, a coach arrived in the court-yard; his business people, enraged with the porter, exclaimed that there will then be no more opportunity for working. The Cardinal in delight referred to the orders he had given. "You will see," he added, "that it is Cardinal Bonzi, the only man I excepted, and who, of all days in the world, comes to-day."

Immediately afterwards, the Cardinal was announced, and the intendant and maitre d'hotel were forced to make off with their papers and their table. As soon as he was alone with Bonzi, he explained why he had requested this visit, and both laughed heartily. Since then his business people have never caught him again, never during the rest of his life would he hear speak of them.

He must have had honest people about him; for every day his table was magnificent, and filled at Paris and at the Court with the best company. His equipages were so, also; he had numberless domestics, many gentlemen, chaplains, and secretaries. He gave freely to the poor, and to his brother the Marechal and his children (who were not well off), and yet died without owing a crown to a living soul.

His death, for which he had been long prepared, was fine-edifying and very Christian-like. He was universally regretted. A joke of his with the King is still remembered. One day, at dinner, where he always paid much attention to the Cardinal, the King complained of the inconvenience he felt in no longer having teeth.

"Teeth, sire!" replied the Cardinal; "why, who has any teeth?"

The joke is that the Cardinal, though old, still had very white and very beautiful teeth, and that his mouth, large, but agreeable, was so shaped that it showed them plainly in speaking. Therefore the King burst out laughing at this reply, and all present also, including the Cardinal, who was not in the slightest degree embarrassed. I might go on forever telling about him, but enough, perhaps, has been already said.

The commencement of the new year, 1715, was marked by the death of Fenelon, at Cambrai, where he had lived in disgrace so many years. I have already said something about him, so that I have now but little to add. His life at Cambrai was remarkable for the assiduity with which he attended to the spiritual and temporal wants of his flock. He was indefatigable in the discharge of his functions, and in endeavouring to gain all hearts. Cambrai is a place much frequented; through which many people pass. During the war the number of wounded soldiers he had received into his house or attended to in the hospitals passes all belief. He spared nothing for them, neither physical comforts nor spiritual consolations. Thus it is incredible to what an extent he became the idol of the whole army. His manners, to high and low, were most affable, yet everywhere he was the prelate, the gentleman, the author of "Telemachus." He ruled his diocese with a gentle hand, in no way meddled with the Jansenists; he left all untouched. Take him for all in all, he had a bright genius and was a great man. His admiration true or feigned for Madame Guyon remained to the last, yet always without suspicion of impropriety. He had so exactly arranged his affairs that he died without money, and yet without owing a sou to anybody.

VOLUME 10.: CHAPTER LXX

The reign of Louis XIV. was approaching its conclusion, so that there is now nothing more to relate but what passed during the last month of his life, and scarcely so much. These events, indeed, so curious and so important, are so mixed up with those that immediately followed the King's death, that they cannot be separated from them. It will be interesting and is necessary to describe the projects, the thoughts, the difficulties, the different resolutions, which occupied the brain of the Prince, who, despite the efforts of Madame de Maintenon and M. du Maine, was of necessity about to be called to the head of affairs during the minority of the young King. This is the place, therefore, to explain all these things, after which we will resume the narrative of the last month of the King's life, and go on to the events which followed his death.

But, as I have said, before entering upon this thorny path, it will be as well to make known, if possible, the chief personage of the story, the impediments interior and exterior in his path, and all that personally belonged to him.

M. le Duc d'Orleans was, at the most, of mediocre stature, full-bodied without being fat; his manner and his deportment were easy and very noble; his face was broad and very agreeable, high in colour; his hair black, and wig the same. Although he danced very badly, and had but ill succeeded at the riding-school, he had in his face, in his gestures, in all his movements, infinite grace, and so natural that it adorned even his most ordinary commonplace actions. With much ease when nothing constrained him, he was gentle, affable, open, of facile and charming access; the tone of his voice was agreeable, and he had a surprisingly easy flow of words upon all subjects which nothing ever disturbed, and which never failed to surprise; his eloquence was natural and extended even to his most familiar discourse, while it equally entered into his observations upon the most abstract sciences, on which he talked most perspicuously; the affairs of government, politics, finance, justice, war, the court, ordinary conversation, the arts, and mechanics. He could speak as well too upon history and memoirs, and was well acquainted with pedigrees. The personages of former days were familiar to him; and the intrigues of the ancient courts were to him as those of his own time. To hear him, you would have thought him a great reader. Not so. He skimmed; but his memory was so singular that he never forgot things, names, or dates, cherishing remembrance of things with precision; and his apprehension was so good, that in skimming thus it was, with him, precisely as though he had read very laboriously. He excelled in unpremeditated discourse, which, whether in the shape of repartee or jest, was always appropriate and vivacious. He often reproached me, and others more than he, with "not spoiling him;" but I often gave him praise merited by few, and which belonged to nobody so justly as to him; it was, that besides having infinite ability and of various kinds, the singular perspicuity of his mind was joined to so much exactness, that he would never have made a mistake in anything if he had allowed the first suggestions of his judgment. He oftentimes took this my eulogy as a reproach, and he was not always wrong, but it was not the less true. With all this he had no presumption, no trace of superiority natural or acquired; he reasoned with you as with his equal, and struck the most able with surprise. Although he never forgot his own position, nor allowed others to forget it, he carried no constraint with him, but put everybody at his ease, and placed himself upon the level of all others.

He had the weakness to believe that he resembled Henry IV. in everything, and strove to affect the manners, the gestures, the bearing, of that monarch. Like Henry IV. he was naturally good, humane, compassionate; and, indeed, this man, who has been so cruelly accused of the blackest and most inhuman crimes, was more opposed to the destruction of others than any one I have ever known, and had such a singular dislike to causing anybody pain that it may be said, his gentleness, his humanity, his easiness, had become faults; and I do not hesitate to affirm that that supreme virtue which teaches us to pardon our enemies he turned into vice, by the indiscriminate prodigality with which he applied it; thereby causing himself many sad embarrassments and misfortunes, examples and proofs of which will be seen in the sequel.

I remember that about a year, perhaps, before the death of the King, having gone up early after dinner into the apartments of Madame la Duchesse d'Orleans at Marly, I found her in bed with the megrims, and M. d'Orleans alone in the room, seated in an armchair at her pillow. Scarcely had I sat down than Madame la Duchesse began to talk of some of those execrable imputations concerning M. d'Orleans unceasingly circulated by Madame de Maintenon and M. du Maine; and of an incident arising therefrom, in which the Prince and the Cardinal de Rohan had played a part against M. d'Orleans. I sympathised with her all the more because the Duke, I knew not why, had always distinguished and courted those two brothers, and thought he could count upon them. "And what will you say of M. d'Orleans," added the Duchesse, "when I tell you that since he has known this, known it beyond doubt, he treats them exactly the same as before?"

I looked at M. d'Orleans, who had uttered only a few words to confirm the story, as it was being told, and who was negligently lolling in his chair, and I said to him with warmth:

"Oh, as to that, Monsieur, the truth must be told; since Louis the Debonnaire, never has there been such a Debonnaire as you."

At these words he rose in his chair, red with anger to the very whites of his eyes, and blurted out his vexation against me for abusing him, as he pretended, and against Madame la Duchesse d'Orleans for encouraging me and laughing at him.

"Go on," said I, "treat your enemies well, and rail at your friends. I am delighted to see you angry. It is a sign that I have touched the sore point, when you press the finger on it the patient cries. I should like to squeeze out all the matter, and after that you would be quite another man, and differently esteemed."

He grumbled a little more, and then calmed down. This was one of two occasions only, on which he was ever really angry with me.

Two or three years after the death of the King, I was chatting in one of the grand rooms of the Tuileries, where the Council of the Regency was, according to custom, soon to be held, and M. d'Orleans at the other end was talking to some one in a window recess. I heard myself called from mouth to mouth, and was told that M. d'Orleans wished to speak to me. This often happened before the Council. I went therefore to the window where he was standing. I found a serious bearing, a concentrated manner, an angry face, and was much surprised.

"Monsieur," said he to me at once, "I have a serious complaint against you; you, whom I have always regarded as my best of friends."

"Against me! Monsieur!" said I, still more surprised. "What is the matter, then, may I ask?"

"The matter!" he replied with a mien still more angry; "something you cannot deny; verses you have made against me."

"I—verses!" was my reply. "Why, who the devil has been telling you such nonsense? You have been acquainted with me nearly forty years, and do you not know, that never in my life have I been able to make a single verse—much less verses?"

"No, no, by Heaven," replied he, "you cannot deny these;" and forthwith he began to sing to me a street song in his praise, the chorus of which was: 'Our Regent is debonnaire, la la, he is debonnaire,' with a burst of laughter.

"What!" said I, "you remember it still!" and smiling, I added also, "since you are revenged for it, remember it in good earnest." He kept on laughing a long time before going to the Council, and could not hinder himself. I have not been afraid to write this trifle, because it seems to me that it paints the man.

M. d'Orleans loved liberty, and as much for others as for himself. He extolled England to me one day on this account, as a country where there are no banishments, no lettres de cachet, and where the King may close the door of his palace to anybody, but can keep no one in prison; and thereupon related to me with enjoyment, that besides the Duchess of Portsmouth, Charles the Second had many subordinate mistresses; that the Grand Prieur, young and amiable in those days, driven out of France for some folly, had gone to England to pass his exile and had been well received by the King. By way of thanks, he seduced one of those mistresses, by whom the King was then so smitten, that he sued for mercy, offered money to the Grand Prieur, and undertook to obtain his reconciliation in France. The Grand Prieur held firm. Charles prohibited him the palace. He laughed at this, and went every day to the theatre, with his conquest, and placed himself opposite the King. At last, Charles, not knowing what to do to deliver himself from his tormentor, begged our King to recall him, and this was done. But the Grand Prieur said he was very comfortable in England and continued his game. Charles, outraged, confided to the King (Louis XIV.) the state he was thrown into by the Grand Prieur, and obtained a command so absolute and so prompt, that his tormentor was afterwards obliged to go back into France.

M. d'Orleans admired this; and I know not if he would not have wished to be the Grand Prieur. He always related this story with delight. Thus, of ambition for reigning or governing, he had none. If he made a false move in Spain it was because he had been misdirected. What he would have liked best would have been to command armies while war lasted, and divert himself the rest of the time without constraint to himself or to others. He was, in fact, very fit for this. With much valour, he had also much foresight, judgment, coolness, and vast capacity. It may be said that he was captain, engineer, and army purveyor; that he knew the strength of his troops, the names and the company of the officers, and the most distinguished of each corps; that he knew how to make himself adored, at the same time keeping up discipline, and could execute the most difficult things, while unprovided with everything. Unfortunately there is another side of this picture, which it will be as well now to describe.

M. d'Orleans, by disposition so adapted to become the honour and the master-piece of an education, was not fortunate in his teachers. Saint-Laurent, to whom he was first confided, was, it is true, the man in all Europe best fitted to act as the instructor of kings, but he died before his pupil was beyond the birch, and the young Prince, as I have related, fell entirely into the hands of the Abbe Dubois. This person has played such an important part in the state since the death of the King, that it is fit that he should be made known. The Abbe Dubois was a little, pitiful, wizened, herring-gutted man, in a flaxen wig, with a weazel's face, brightened by some intellect. In familiar terms, he was a regular scamp. All the vices unceasingly fought within him for supremacy, so that a continual uproar filled his mind. Avarice, debauchery, ambition; were his gods; perfidy, flattery, foot-licking his means of action; complete impiety was his repose; and he held the opinion as a great principle, that probity and honesty are chimeras, with which people deck themselves, but which have no existence. In consequence, all means were good to him. He excelled in low intrigues; he lived in them, and could not do without them; but they always had an aim, and he followed them with a patience terminated only by success, or by firm conviction that he could not reach what he aimed at, or unless, as he wandered thus in deep darkness, a glimmer of light came to him from some other cranny. He passed thus his days in sapping and counter-sapping. The most impudent deceit had become natural to him, and was concealed under an air that was simple, upright, sincere, often bashful. He would have spoken with grace and forcibly, if, fearful of saying more than he wished, he had not accustomed himself to a fictitious hesitation, a stuttering—which disfigured his speech, and which, redoubled when important things were in question, became insupportable and sometimes unintelligible. He had wit, learning, knowledge of the world; much desire to please and insinuate himself, but all was spoiled by an odour of falsehood which escaped in spite of him through every pore of his body— even in the midst of his gaiety, which made whoever beheld it sad. Wicked besides, with reflection, both by nature and by argument, treacherous and ungrateful, expert in the blackest villainies, terribly brazen when detected; he desired everything, envied everything, and wished to seize everything. It was known afterwards, when he no longer could restrain himself, to what an extent he was selfish, debauched, inconsistent, ignorant of everything, passionate, headstrong, blasphemous and mad, and to what an extent he publicly despised his master, the state, and all the world, never hesitating to sacrifice everybody and everything to his credit, his power, his absolute authority, his greatness, his avarice, his fears, and his vengeance.

Such was the sage to whom M. le Duc d'Orleans was confided in early youth!

Such a good master did not lose his pains with his new disciple, in whom the excellent principles of Saint-Laurent had not had time to take deep root, whatever esteem and affection he may have preserved through life for that worthy man. I will admit here, with bitterness, for everything should be sacrificed to the truth, that M. le Duc d'Orleans brought into the world a failing—let us call things by their names—a weakness, which unceasingly spoiled all his talents, and which were of marvellous use to his preceptor all his life. Dubois led him into debauchery, made him despise all duty and all decency, and persuaded him that he had too much mind to be the dupe of religion, which he said was a politic invention to frighten ordinary, intellects, and keep the people in subjection. He filled him too with his favourite principle, that probity in man and virtue in woman, are mere chimeras, without existence in anybody except a few poor slaves of early training. This was the basis of the good ecclesiatic's doctrines, whence arose the license of falsehood, deceit, artifice, infidelity, perfidy; in a word, every villainy, every crime, was turned into policy, capacity, greatness, liberty and depth of intellect, enlightenment, good conduct, if it could be hidden, and if suspicions and common prejudices could be avoided.

Unfortunately all conspired in M. d'Orleans to open his heart and his mind to this execrable poison: a fresh and early youth, much strength and health, joy at escaping from the yoke as well as vexation at his marriage, the wearisomeness produced by idleness, the impulse of his passions, the example of other young men, whose vanity and whose interest it was to make him live like them. Thus he grew accustomed to debauchery, above all to the uproar of it, so that he could not do without it, and could only divert himself by dint of noise, tumult, and excess. It is this which led him often into such strange and such scandalous debauches, and as he wished to surpass all his companions, to mix up with his parties of pleasure the most impious discourses, and as a precious refinement, to hold the most outrageous orgies on the most holy days, as he did several times during his Regency on Good Friday, by choice, and on other similar days. The more debauched a man was, the more he esteemed him; and I have unceasingly seen him in admiration, that reached almost to veneration for the Grand Prieur,—because for forty years he had always gone to bed drunk, and had never ceased to keep mistresses in the most public manner, and to hold the most impious and irreligious discourses. With these principles, and the conduct that resulted from them, it is not surprising that M. le Duc d'Orleans was false to such an extent, that he boasted of his falsehood, and plumed himself upon being the most skilful deceiver in the world. He and Madame la Duchesse de Berry sometimes disputed which was the cleverer of the two; and this in public before M. le Duc de Berry, Madame de Saint-Simon, and others!

M. le Duc d'Orleans, following out the traditions of the Palais Royal, had acquired the detestable taste and habit of embroiling people one with the other, so as to profit by their divisions. This was one of his principal occupations during all the time he was at the head of affairs, and one that he liked the best; but which, as soon as discovered, rendered him odious, and caused him a thousand annoyances. He was not wicked, far from it; but he could not quit the habits of impiety, debauchery, and deceit into which Dubois had led him. A remarkable feature in his character is, that he was suspicious and full of confidence at the same time with reference to the very same people.

It is surprising that with all his talents he was totally without honest resources for amusing himself. He was born bored; and he was so accustomed to live out of himself, that it was insufferable to him to return, incapable as he was of trying even to occupy himself. He could only live in the midst of the movement and torrent of business; at the head of an army for instance, or in the cares that arose out of the execution of campaign projects, or in the excitement and uproar of debauchery. He began to languish as soon as he was without noise, excess, and tumult, the time painfully hanging upon his hands. He cast himself upon painting, when his great fancy for chemistry had passed or grown deadened, in consequence of what had been said upon it. He painted nearly all the afternoon at Versailles and at Marly. He was a good judge of pictures, liked them, and made a collection, which in number and excellence was not surpassed by those of the Crown. He amused himself afterwards in making composition stones and seals over charcoal, the fumes of which often drove me away; and the strongest perfumes, which he was fond of all his life, but from which I turned him because the King was very much afraid of them, and soon sniffed them. In fact, never was man born with so many talents of all kinds, so much readiness and facility in making use of them, and yet never was man so idle, so given up to vacuity and weariness. Thus Madame painted him very happily by an illustration from fairy tales, of which she was full.

She said, that all the fairies had been invited to his birth; that all came, and that each gave him some talent, so that he had them all. But, unfortunately, an old fairy, who had disappeared so many years ago that she was no longer remembered, had been omitted from the invitation lists. Piqued at this neglect, she came supported upon her little wand, just at the moment when all the rest had endowed the child with their gifts. More and more vexed, she revenged herself by rendering useless all the talents he had received from the other fairies, not one of which, though possessing them all, in consequence of her malediction, was he able to make use of. It must be admitted, that on the whole this is a speaking portrait.

One of the misfortunes of this Prince was being incapable of following up anything, and an inability to comprehend, even, how any one else could do so. Another, was a sort of insensibility which rendered him indifferent to the most mortal and the most dangerous offences; and as the nerve and principle of hatred and friendship, of gratitude and vengeance, are the same, and as they were wanting in him, the consequences were infinite and pernicious. He was timid to excess, knew it, and was so ashamed that he affected to be exactly the reverse, and plumed himself upon his daring. But the truth is, as was afterwards seen, nothing could be obtained from him, neither grace, nor justice, except by working upon his fears, to which he was very susceptible; or by extreme importunity. He tried to put people off by words, then by promises, of which he was monstrously prodigal, but which he only kept when made to people who had good firm claws. In this manner he broke so many engagements that the most positive became counted as nothing; and he promised moreover to so many different people, what could only be given to one, that he thus opened out a copious source of discredit to himself and caused much discontent. Nothing deceived or injured him more than the opinion he had formed, that he could deceive all the world. He was no longer believed, even when he spoke with the best faith, and his facility much diminished the value of everything he did. To conclude, the obscure, and for the most part blackguard company, which he ordinarily frequented in his debauches, and which he did not scruple publicly to call his roues, drove away all decent people, and did him infinite harm.

His constant mistrust of everything and everybody was disgusting, above all when he was at the head of affairs. The fault sprang from his timidity, which made him fear his most certain enemies, and treat them with more distinction than his friends; from his natural easiness, from a false imitation of Henry IV., in whom this quality was by no means the finest; and from the unfortunate opinion which he held, that probity was a sham. He was, nevertheless, persuaded of my probity; and would often reproach me with it as a fault and prejudice of education which had cramped my mind and obscured my understanding, and he said as much of Madame de Saint-Simon, because he believed her virtuous.

I had given him so many proofs of my attachment that he could not very well suspect me; and yet, this is what happened two or three years after the establishment of the Regency. I give it as one of the most striking of the touches that paint his portrait.

It was autumn. M. d'Orleans had dismissed the councils for a fortnight. I profited by this to go and spend the time at La Ferme. I had just passed an hour alone with the Duke, and had taken my leave of him and gone home, where in order to be in repose I had closed my door to everybody. In about an hour at most, I was told that Biron, with a message from M. le Duc d'Orleans, was at the door, with orders to see me, and that he would not go away without. I allowed Biron to enter, all the more surprised because I had just quitted M. le Duc d'Orleans, and eagerly asked him the news. Biron was embarrassed, and in his turn asked where was the Marquis de Ruffec (my son). At this my surprise increased, and I demanded what he meant. Biron, more and more confused, admitted that M. le Duc d'Orleans wanted information on this point, and had sent him for it. I replied, that my son was with his regiment at Besancon, lodging with M. de Levi, who commanded in Franche-Comte.

"Oh," said Biron, "I know that very well; but have you any letter from him?"

"What for?" I asked.

"Because, frankly, since I must tell you all," said he, "M. le Duc d'Orleans wishes to see his handwriting."

He added, that soon after I had quitted M. le Duc d'Orleans, whilst he was walking at Montmartre ma garden with his 'roues' and his harlots, some letters had been brought to him by a post-office clerk, to whom he had spoken in private; that afterwards he, Biron, had been called by the Duke, who showed him a letter from the Marquis de Ruffec to his master, dated "Madrid," and charged him, thereupon, with this present commission.

At this recital I felt a mixture of anger and compassion, and I did not constrain myself with Biron. I had no letters from my son, because I used to burn them, as I did all useless papers. I charged Biron to say to M. le Duc d'Orleans a part of what I felt; that I had not the slightest acquaintance with anybody in Spain; that I begged him at once to despatch a courier there in order to satisfy himself that my son was at Besancon.

Biron, shrugging his shoulders, said all that was very good, but that if I could find a letter from the Marquis de Ruffec it would be much better; adding, that if one turned up and I sent it to him, he would take care that it reached M. le Duc d'Orleans, at table, in spite of the privacy of his suppers. I did not wish to return to the Palais Royal to make a scene there, and dismissed Biron. Fortunately, Madame de Saint-Simon came in some time after. I related to her this adventure. She found the last letter of the Marquis de Ruffec, and we sent it to Biron. It reached the table as he had promised. M. le Duc d'Orleans seized it with eagerness. The joke is that he did not know the handwriting. Not only did he look at the letter, but he read it; and as he found it diverting, regaled his company with it; it became the topic of their discourse, and entirely removed his suspicions. Upon my return from La Ferme, I found him ashamed of himself, and I rendered him still more so by what I said to him on the subject.

I learnt afterwards that this Madrid letter, and others that followed, came from a sham Marquis de Ruffec, that is to say, from the son of one of Madame's porters, who passed himself off as my son. He pretended that he had quarrelled with me, and wrote to Madame de Saint-Simon, begging her to intercede for him; and all this that his letters might be seen, and that he might reap substantial benefits from his imposture in the shape of money and consideration. He was a well-made fellow, had much address and effrontery, knew the Court very well, and had taken care to learn all about our family, so as to speak within limits. He was arrested at Bayonne, at the table of Dadoncourt, who commanded there, and who suddenly formed the resolution, suspecting him not to be a gentleman, upon seeing him eat olives with a fork! When in gaol he confessed who he was. He was not new at the trade and was confined some little time.

CHAPTER LXXI: But to return to M. le Duc d'Orleans.

His curiosity, joined to a false idea of firmness and courage, had early led him to try and raise the devil and make him speak. He left nothing untried, even the wildest reading, to persuade himself there was no God; and yet believed meanwhile in the devil, and hoped to see him and converse with him! This inconsistency is hard to understand, and yet is extremely common. He worked with all sorts of obscure people; and above all with Mirepoix, sublieutenant of the Black Musketeers, to find out Satan. They passed whole nights in the quarries of Vanvres and of Vaugirard uttering invocations. M. le Duc d'Orleans, however, admitted to me that he had never succeeded in hearing or seeing anything, and at last had given up this folly.

At first it was only to please Madame d'Argenton, but afterwards from curiosity, that he tried to see the present and the future in a glass of water; so he said, and he was no liar. To be false and to be a liar are not one and the same thing, though they closely resemble each other, and if he told a lie it was only when hard pressed upon some promise or some business, and in spite of himself, so as to escape from a dilemma.

Although we often spoke upon religion, to which I tried to lead him so long as I had hope of success, I never could unravel the system he had formed for himself, and I ended by becoming persuaded that he wavered unceasingly without forming any religion at all.

His passionate desire, like that of his companions in morals, was this, that it would turn out that there is no God; but he had too much enlightenment to be an atheist; who is a particular kind of fool much more rare than is thought. This enlightenment importuned him; he tried to extinguish it and could not. A mortal soul would have been to him a resource; but he could not convince himself of its existence. A God and an immortal soul, threw him into sad straits, and yet he could not blind himself to the truth of both the one and the other. I can say then this, I know of what religion he was not; nothing more. I am sure, however, that he was very ill at ease upon this point, and that if a dangerous illness had overtaken him, and he had had the time, he would have thrown himself into the hands of all the priests and all the Capuchins of the town. His great foible was to pride himself upon his impiety and to wish to surpass in that everybody else.

I recollect that one Christmas-time, at Versailles, when he accompanied the King to morning prayers and to the three midnight masses, he surprised the Court by his continued application in reading a volume he had brought with him, and which appeared to be, a prayer book. The chief femme de chambre of Madame la Duchesse d'Orleans, much attached to the family, and very free as all good old domestics are, transfixed with joy at M. le Duc d'Orleans's application to his book, complimented him upon it the next day, in the presence of others. M. le Duc d'Orleans allowed her to go on some time, and then said, "You are very silly, Madame Imbert. Do you know what I was reading? It was 'Rabelais,' that I brought with me for fear of being bored."

The effect of this reply may be imagined. The thing was too true, and was pure braggadocio; for, without comparison of the places, or of the things, the music of the chapel was much superior to that of the opera, and to all the music of Europe; and at Christmas it surpassed itself. There was nothing so magnificent as the decoration of the chapel, or the manner in which it was lighted. It was full of people; the arches of the tribune were crowded with the Court ladies, in undress, but ready for conquest. There was nothing so surprising as the beauty of the spectacle. The ears were charmed also. M. le Duc d'Orleans loved music extremely; he could compose, and had amused himself by composing a kind of little opera, La Fare writing the words, which was performed before the King. This music of the chapel, therefore, might well have occupied him in the most agreeable manner, to say nothing of the brilliant scene, without his having recourse to Rabelais. But he must needs play the impious, and the wag.

Madame la Duchesse d'Orleans was another kind of person. She was tall, and in every way majestic; her complexion, her throat, her arms, were admirable; she had a tolerable mouth, with beautiful teeth, somewhat long; and cheeks too broad, and too hanging, which interfered with, but did not spoil, her beauty. What disfigured her most was her eyebrows, which were, as it were, peeled and red, with very little hair; she had, however, fine eyelashes, and well-set chestnut-coloured hair. Without being hump-backed or deformed, she had one side larger than the other, and walked awry. This defect in her figure indicated another, which was more troublesome in society, and which inconvenienced herself. She had a good deal of intellect, and spoke with much ability. She said all she wished, and often conveyed her meaning to you without directly expressing it; saying, as it were, what she did not say. Her utterance was, however, slow and embarrassed, so that unaccustomed ears with difficulty followed her.

Every kind of decency and decorum centred themselves in her, and the most exquisite pride was there upon its throne. Astonishment will be felt at what I am going to say, and yet, however, nothing is more strictly true: it is, that at the bottom of her soul she believed that she, bastard of the King, had much honoured M. d'Orleans in marrying him! M. le Duc d'Orleans often laughed at her pride, called her Madame Lucifer, in speaking to her, and she admitted that the name did not displease her. She always received his advances with coldness, and a sort of superiority of greatness. She was a princess to the backbone, at all hours, and in all places. Yet, at the same time, her timidity was extreme. The King could have made her feel ill with a single severe look; and Madame de Maintenon could have done likewise, perhaps. At all events, Madame la Duchesse d'Orleans trembled before her; and upon the most commonplace matters never replied to either him or her without hesitation, fear printed on her face.

M. le Duc and Madame la Duchesse d'Orleans lived an idle, languishing, shameful, indecent, and despised life, abandoned by all the Court. This, I felt, was one of the first things that must be remedied. Accordingly, I induced Madame la Duchesse d'Orleans to make an effort to attract people to her table. She did so, persevering against the coldness and aversion she met with, and in time succeeded in drawing a tolerably numerous company to her dinners. They were of exquisite quality, and people soon got over their first hesitation, when they found everything orderly, free, and unobjectionable. At these dinners, M. d'Orleans kept within bounds, not only in his discourse, but in his behaviour. But oftentimes his ennui led him to Paris, to join in supper parties and debauchery. Madame la Duchesse d'Orleans tried to draw him from these pleasures by arranging small parties at her pretty little villa, l'Etoile (in the park of Versailles), which the King had given to her, and which she had furnished in the most delightful manner. She loved good cheer, the guests loved it also, and at table she was altogether another person —free, gay, exciting, charming. M. le Duc d'Orleans cared for nothing but noise, and as he threw off all restraint at these parties, there was much difficulty in selecting guests, for the ears of many people would have been much confused at his loose talk, and their eyes much astonished to see him get drunk at the very commencement of the repast, in the midst of those who thought only of amusing and recreating themselves in a decent manner, and who never approached intoxication.

As the King became weaker in health, and evidently drew near his end, I had continued interviews with Madame d'Orleans upon the subject of the Regency, the plan of government to be adopted, and the policy she should follow. Hundreds of times before we had reasoned together upon the faults of the Government, and the misfortunes that resulted from them. What we had to do was to avoid those faults, educate the young King in good and rational maxims, so that when he succeeded to power he might continue what the Regency had not had time to finish. This, at least, was my idea; and I laboured hard to make it the idea of M. le Duc d'Orleans. As the health of the King diminished I entered more into details; as I will explain.

What I considered the most important thing to be done, was to overthrow entirely the system of government in which Cardinal Mazarin had imprisoned the King and the realm. A foreigner, risen from the dregs of the people, who thinks of nothing but his own power and his own greatness, cares nothing for the state, except in its relation to himself. He despises its laws, its genius, its advantages: he is ignorant of its rules and its forms; he thinks only of subjugating all, of confounding all, of bringing all down to one level. Richelieu and his successor, Mazarin, succeeded so well in this policy that the nobility, by degrees, became annihilated, as we now see them. The pen and the robe people, on the other hand, were exalted; so that now things have reached such a pretty pass that the greatest lord is without power, and in a thousand different manners is dependent upon the meanest plebeian. It is in this manner that things hasten from one extreme to the other.

My design was to commence by introducing the nobility into the ministry, with the dignity and authority due to them, and by degrees to dismiss the pen and robe people from all employ not purely judicial. In this manner the administration of public affairs would be entirely in the hands of the aristocracy. I proposed to abolish the two offices of secretary of state for the war department, and for foreign affairs, and to supply their place by councils; also, that the offices of the navy should be managed by a council. I insisted upon the distinct and perfect separation of these councils, so that their authority should never be confounded, and the public should never have the slightest trouble in finding out where to address itself for any kind of business.

M. le Duc d'Orleans exceedingly relished my project, which we much discussed. This point arrived at, it became necessary to debate upon the persons who were to form these councils. I suggested names, which were accepted or set aside, according as they met his approval or disapprobation. "But," said M. le Duc d'Orleans, after we had been a long time at this work, "you propose everybody and never say a word of yourself. What do you wish to be?"

I replied, that it was not for me to propose, still less to choose any office, but for him to see if he wished to employ me, believing me capable, and in that case to determine the place he wished me to occupy. This was at Marly, in his chamber, and I shall never forget it.

After some little debate, that between equals would have been called complimentary, he proposed to me the Presidency of the Council of Finance. But I had good reasons for shrinking from this office. I saw that disordered as the finances had become there was only one remedy by which improvement could be effected; and this was National Bankruptcy. Had I occupied the office, I should have been too strongly tempted to urge this view, and carry it out, but it was a responsibility I did not wish to take upon myself before God and man. Yet, I felt as I said, that to declare the State bankrupt would be the wisest course, and I am bold enough to think, that there is not a man, having no personal interest in the continuance of imposts, who of two evils, viz., vastly increased taxation, and national failure, would not prefer the latter. We were in the condition of a man who unfortunately must choose between passing twelve or fifteen years in his bed, in continual pain, or having his leg cut off. Who can doubt this? he would prefer the loss of his leg by a painful operation, in order to find himself two months after quite well, free from suffering and in the enjoyment of all his faculties.

I shrunk accordingly from the finances for the reason I have above given, and made M. le Duc d'Orleans so angry by my refusal to accept the office he had proposed to me, that for three weeks he sulked and would not speak to me, except upon unimportant matters.

At the end of that time, in the midst of a languishing conversation, he exclaimed, "Very well, then. You stick to your text, you won't have the finances?"

I respectfully lowered my eyes and replied, in a gentle tone, that I thought that question was settled. He could not restrain some complaints, but they were not bitter, nor was he angry, and then rising and taking a few turns in the room, without saying a word, and his head bent, as was his custom when embarrassed, he suddenly spun round upon me, and exclaimed, "But whom shall we put there?"

I suggested the Duc de Noailles, and although the suggestion at first met with much warm opposition from M. le Duc d'Orleans, it was ultimately accepted by him.

The moment after we had settled this point he said to me, "And you! what will you be?" and he pressed me so much to explain myself that I said at last if he would put me in the council of affairs of the interior, I thought I should do better there than elsewhere.

"Chief, then," replied he with vivacity.

"No, no! not that," said I; "simply a place in the council."

We both insisted, he for, I against. "A place in that council," he said, "would be ridiculous, and cannot be thought of. Since you will not be chief, there is only one post which suits you, and which suits me also. You must be in the council I shall be in the Supreme Council."

I accepted the post, and thanked him. From that moment this distinction remained fixed.

I will not enter into all the suggestions I offered to M. le Duc d'Orleans respecting the Regency, or give the details of all the projects I submitted to him. Many of those projects and suggestions were either acted upon only partially, or not acted upon at all, although nearly every one met with his approval. But he was variable as the winds, and as difficult to hold. In my dealings with him I had to do with a person very different from that estimable Dauphin who was so rudely taken away from us.

But let me, before going further, describe the last days of the King, his illness, and death, adding to the narrative a review of his life and character.

CHAPTER LXXII

LOUIS XIV. began, as I have before remarked, sensibly to decline, and his appetite, which had always been good and uniform, very considerably diminished. Even foreign countries became aware of this. Bets were laid in London that his life would not last beyond the first of September, that is to say, about three months, and although the King wished to know everything, it may be imagined that nobody was very eager to make him acquainted with the news. He used to have the Dutch papers read to him in private by Torcy, often after the Council of State. One day as Torcy was reading, coming unexpectedly—for he had not examined the paper—upon the account of these bets, he stopped, stammered, and skipped it. The King, who easily perceived this, asked him the cause of his embarrassment; what he was passing over, and why? Torcy blushed to the very whites of his eyes, and said it was a piece of impertinence unworthy of being read. The King insisted; Torcy also: but at last thoroughly confused, he could not resist the reiterated command he received, and read the whole account of the bets. The King pretended not to be touched by it, but he was, and profoundly, so that sitting down to table immediately afterwards, he could not keep himself from speaking of it, though without mentioning the gazette.

This was at Marly, and by chance I was there that day. The King looked at me as at the others, but as though asking for a reply. I took good care not to open my mouth, and lowered my eyes. Cheverny, (a discreet man,) too, was not so prudent, but made a long and ill-timed rhapsody upon similar reports that had come to Copenhagen from Vienna while he was ambassador at the former place seventeen or eighteen years before. The King allowed him to say on, but did not take the bait. He appeared touched, but like a man who does not wish to seem so. It could be seen that he did all he could to eat, and to show that he ate with appetite. But it was also seen that the mouthfuls loitered on their way. This trifle did not fail to augment the circumspection of the Court, above all of those who by their position had reason to be more attentive than the rest. It was reported that an aide-decamp of Lord Stair, who was then English ambassador to our Court, and very much disliked for his insolent bearing and his troublesome ways, had caused these bets by what he had said in England respecting the health of the King. Stair, when told this, was much grieved, and said 'twas a scoundrel he had dismissed.

As the King sensibly declined I noticed that although terror of him kept people as much away from M. d'Orleans as ever, I was approached even by the most considerable. I had often amused myself at the expense of these prompt friends; I did so now, and diverted M. d'Orleans by warning him beforehand what he had to expect.

On Friday, the 9th of August, 1715, the King hunted the stag after dinner in his caleche, that he drove himself as usual. 'Twas for the last time. Upon his return he appeared much knocked up. There was a grand concert in the evening in Madame de Maintenon's apartment.

On Saturday, the 10th of August, he walked before dinner in his gardens at Marly; he returned to Versailles about six o'clock in the evening, and never again saw that strange work of his hands. In the evening he worked with the Chancellor in Madame de Maintenon's rooms, and appeared to everybody very ill. On Sunday, the eleventh of August, he held the Council of State, walked, after dinner to Trianon, never more to go out again during life.

On the morrow, the 12th of August, he took medicine as usual, and lived as usual the following days. It was known that he complained of sciatica in the leg and thigh. He had never before had sciatica, or rheumatism, or a cold; and for a long time no touch of gout. In the evening there was a little concert in Madame de Maintenon's rooms. This was the last time in his life that he walked alone.

On Tuesday, the 13th of August, he made a violent effort, and gave a farewell audience to a sham Persian ambassador, whom Pontchartrain had imposed upon him; this was the last public action of his life. The audience, which was long, fatigued the King. He resisted the desire for sleep which came over him, held the Finance Council, dined, had himself carried to Madame de Maintenon's, where a little concert was given, and on leaving his cabinet stopped for the Duchesse de la Rochefoucauld, who presented to him the Duchesse de la Rocheguyon, her daughter-in-law, who was the last lady presented to him. She took her tabouret that evening at the King's grand supper, which was the last he ever gave. On the morrow he sent some precious stones to the Persian ambassador just alluded to. It was on this day that the Princesse des Ursins set off for Lyons, terrified at the state of the King as I have already related.

For more than a year the health of the King had diminished. His valets noticed this first, and followed the progress of the malady, without one of them daring to open his mouth. The bastards, or to speak exactly, M, du Maine saw it; Madame de Maintenon also; but they did nothing. Fagon, the chief physician, much fallen off in mind and body, was the only one of the King's intimates who saw nothing. Marechal, also chief physician, spoke to him (Fagon) several times, but was always harshly repulsed. Pressed at last by his duty and his attachment, he made bold one morning towards Whitsuntide to go to Madame de Maintenon. He told her what he saw and how grossly Fagon was mistaken. He assured her that the King, whose pulse he had often felt, had had for some time a slow internal fever; that his constitution was so good that with remedies and attention all would go well, but that if the malady were allowed to grow there would no longer be any resource. Madame de Maintenon grew angry, and all he obtained for his zeal was her anger. She said that only the personal enemies of Fagon could find fault with his opinion upon the King's health, concerning which the capacity, the application, the experience of the chief physician could not be deceived. The best of it is that Marechal, who had formerly operated upon Fagon for stone, had been appointed chief surgeon by him, and they had always lived on the best of terms. Marechal, annoyed as he related to me, could do nothing more, and began from that time to lament the death of his master. Fagon was in fact the first physician in Europe, but for a long time his health had not permitted him to maintain his experience; and the high point of authority to which his capacity and his favour had carried him, had at last spoiled him. He would not hear reason, or submit to reply, and continued to treat the King as he had treated him in early years; and killed him by his obstinacy.

The gout of which the King had had long attacks, induced Fagon to swaddle him, so to say, every evening in a heap of feather pillows, which made him sweat all night to such an extent that it was necessary in the morning to rub him down and change his linen before the grand chamberlain and the first gentleman of the chamber could enter. For many years he had drunk nothing but Burgundy wine, half mixed with water, and so old that it was used up instead of the best champagne which he had used all his life. He would pleasantly say sometimes that foreign lords who were anxious to taste the wine he used, were often mightily deceived. At no time had he ever drunk pure wine, or made use in any way of spirits, or even tea, coffee, or chocolate. Upon rising, instead of a little bread and wine and water, he had taken for a long time two glasses of sage and veronica; often between his meals, and always on going to bed, glasses of water with a little orange-flower water in them, and always iced. Even on the days when he had medicine he drank this, and always also at his meals, between which he never ate anything except some cinnamon lozenges that he put into his pocket at his dessert, with a good many cracknels for the bitches he kept in his cabinet.

As during the last year of his life the King became more and more costive, Fagon made him eat at the commencement of his repasts many iced fruits, that is to say, mulberries, melons, and figs rotten from ripeness; and at his dessert many other fruits, finishing with a surprising quantity of sweetmeats. All the year round he ate at supper a prodigious quantity of salad. His soups, several of which he partook of morning and evening, were full of gravy, and were of exceeding strength, and everything that was served to him was full of spice, to double the usual extent, and very strong also. This regimen and the sweetmeats together Fagon did not like, and sometimes while seeing the King eat, he would make most amusing grimaces, without daring however to say anything except now and then to Livry and Benoist, who replied that it was their business to feed the King, and his to doctor him. The King never ate any kind of venison or water-fowl, but otherwise partook of everything, fete days and fast days alike, except that during the last twenty years of his life he observed some few days of Lent.

This summer he redoubled his regime of fruits and drinks. At last the former clogged his stomach, taken after soup, weakened the digestive organs and took away his appetite, which until then had never failed him all his life, though however late dinner might be delayed he never was hungry or wanted to eat. But after the first spoonfuls of soup, his appetite came, as I have several times heard him say, and he ate so prodigiously and so solidly morning and evening that no one could get accustomed to see it. So much water and so much fruit unconnected by anything spirituous, turned his blood into gangrene; while those forced night sweats diminished its strength and impoverished it; and thus his death was caused, as was seen by the opening of his body. The organs were found in such good and healthy condition that there is reason to believe he would have lived beyond his hundredth year. His stomach above all astonished, and also his bowels by their volume and extent, double that of the ordinary, whence it came that he was such a great yet uniform eater. Remedies were not thought of until it was no longer time, because Fagon would never believe him ill, or Madame de Maintenon either; though at the same time she had taken good care to provide for her own retreat in the case of his death. Amidst all this, the King felt his state before they felt it, and said so sometimes to his valets: Fagon always reassured him, but did nothing. The King was contented with what was said to him without being persuaded: but his friendship for Fagon restrained him, and Madame de Maintenon still more.

On Wednesday, the 14th of August, the King was carried to hear mass for the last time; held the Council of State, ate a meat dinner, and had music in Madame de Maintenon's rooms. He supped in his chamber, where the Court saw him as at his dinner; was with his family a short time in his cabinet, and went to bed a little after ten.

On Thursday, the Festival of the Assumption, he heard mass in his bed. The night had been disturbed and bad. He dined in his bed, the courtiers being present, rose at five and was carried to Madame de Maintenon's, where music was played. He supped and went to bed as on the previous evening. As long as he could sit up he did the same.

On Friday, the 16th of August, the night had been no better; much thirst and drink. The King ordered no one to enter until ten. Mass and dinner in his bed as before; then he was carried to Madame de Maintenon's; he played with the ladies there, and afterwards there was a grand concert.

On Saturday, the 17th of August, the night as the preceding. He held the Finance Council, he being in bed; saw people at his dinner, rose immediately after; gave audience in his cabinet to the General of the order of Sainte-Croix de la Bretonnerie; passed to Madame de Maintenon's, where he worked with the Chancellor. At night, Fagon slept for the first time in his chamber.

Sunday, the 18th of August, passed like the preceding days, Fagon pretended there had been no fever. The King held a Council of State before and after his dinner; worked afterwards upon the fortifications with Pelletier; then passed to Madame de Maintenon's, where there was music.

Monday, the 19th, and Tuesday, the 20th of August, passed much as the previous days, excepting that on the latter the King supped in his dressing-gown, seated in an armchair; and that after this evening he never left his room or dressed himself again. That same day Madame de Saint-Simon, whom I had pressed to return, came back from the waters of Forges. The king, entering after supper into his cabinet, perceived her. He ordered his chair to be stopped; spoke to her very kindly upon her journey and her return; then had himself wheeled on by Bloin into the other cabinet. She was the last Court lady to whom he spoke. I don't count those who were always near him, and who came to him when he could no longer leave his room. Madame de Saint-Simon said to me in the evening that she should not have recognised the King if she had met him anywhere else. Yet she had left Marly for Forges only on the 6th of July.

On Wednesday, the 21st of August, four physicians saw the King, but took care to do nothing except praise Fagon, who gave him cassia. For some days it had been perceived that he ate meat and even bread with difficulty, (though all his life he had eaten but little of the latter, and for some time only the crumb, because he had no teeth). Soup in larger quantity, hash very light, and eggs compensated him; but he ate very sparingly.

On Thursday, the 22nd of August, the King was still worse. He saw four other physicians, who, like the first four, did nothing but admire the learned and admirable treatment of Fagon, who made him take towards evening some Jesuit bark and water and intended to give him at night, ass's milk. This same day, the King ordered the Duc de la Rochefoucauld to bring him his clothes on the morrow, in order that he might choose which he would wear upon leaving off the mourning he wore for a son of Madame la Duchesse de Lorraine. He had not been able to quit his chamber for some days; he could scarcely eat anything solid; his physician slept in his chamber, and yet he reckoned upon being cured, upon dressing himself again, and wished to choose his dress! In like manner there was the same round of councils, of work, of amusements. So true it is, that men do not wish to die, and dissimulate from themselves the approach of death as long as possible. Meanwhile, let me say, that the state of the King, which nobody was ignorant of, had already changed M. d'Orleans' desert into a crowded city.

Friday, the 23rd of August, the night was as usual, the morning also. The King worked with Pere Tellier, who tried, but in vain, to make him fill up several benefices that were vacant; that is to say, Pere Tellier wished to dispose of them himself, instead of leaving them to M. le Duc d'Orleans. Let me state at once, that the feebler the King grew the more Pere Tellier worried him; so as not to lose such a rich prey, or miss the opportunity of securing fresh creatures for his service. But he could not succeed. The King declared to him that he had enough to render account of to God, without charging himself with this nomination, and forbade him to speak again upon the subject.

On Saturday evening, the 24th of August, he supped in his dressing-gown, in presence of the courtiers, for the last time. I noticed that he could only swallow liquids, and that he was troubled if looked at. He could not finish his supper, and begged the courtiers to pass on, that is to say, go away. He went to bed, where his leg, on which were several black marks, was examined. It had grown worse lately and had given him much pain. He sent for Pere Tellier and made confession. Confusion spread among the doctors at this. Milk, and Jesuit bark and water had been tried and abandoned in turns; now, nobody knew what to try. The doctors admitted that they believed he had had a slow fever ever since Whitsuntide; and excused themselves for doing nothing on the ground that he did not wish for remedies.

On Sunday, the 25th of August, no more mystery was made of the King's danger. Nevertheless, he expressly commanded that nothing should be changed in the usual order of this day (the fete of St. Louis), that is to say, that the drums and the hautboys, assembled beneath his windows, should play their accustomed music as soon as he awoke, and that the twenty-four violins should play in the ante-chamber during his dinner. He worked afterwards with the Chancellor, who wrote, under his dictation, a codicil to his will, Madame de Maintenon being present. She and M. du Maine, who thought incessantly of themselves, did not consider the King had done enough for them by his will; they wished to remedy this by a codicil, which equally showed how enormously they abused the King's weakness in this extremity, and to what an excess ambition may carry us. By this codicil the King submitted all the civil and military household of the young King to the Duc du Maine, and under his orders to Marechal de Villeroy, who, by this disposition became the sole masters of the person and the dwelling place of the King, and of Paris, by the troops placed in their hands; so that the Regent had not the slightest shadow of authority and was at their mercy; certainly liable to be arrested or worse, any time it should please M. du Maine.

Soon after the Chancellor left the King, Madame de Maintenon, who remained, sent for the ladies; and the musicians came at seven o'clock in the evening. But the King fell asleep during the conversation of the ladies. He awoke; his brain confused, which frightened them and made them call the doctors. They found his pulse so bad that they did not hesitate to propose to him, his senses having returned, to take the sacrament without delay. Pere Tellier was sent for; the musicians who had just prepared their books and their instruments, were dismissed, the ladies also; and in a quarter of an hour from that time, the King made confession to Pere Tellier, the Cardinal de Rohan, meanwhile, bringing the Holy Sacrament from the chapel, and sending for the Cure and holy oils. Two of the King's chaplains, summoned by the Cardinal, came, and seven or eight candlesticks were carried by valets. The Cardinal said a word or two to the King upon this great and last action, during which the King appeared very firm, but very penetrated with what he was doing. As soon as he had received Our Saviour and the holy oils, everybody left the chamber except Madame de Maintenon and the Chancellor. Immediately afterwards, and this was rather strange, a kind of book or little tablet was placed upon the bed, the codicil was presented to the King, and at the bottom of it he wrote four or five lines, and restored the document to the Chancellor.

After this, the King sent for M. le Duc d'Orleans, showed him much esteem, friendship, and confidence; but what is terrible with Jesus Christ still upon his lips—the Sacrament he had just received—he assured him, he would find nothing in his will with which he would not feel pleased. Then he recommended to him the state and the person of the future King.

On Monday, the 26th of August, the King called to him the Cardinals de Rohan and de Bissy, protested that he died in the faith, and in submission to the Church, then added, looking at them, that he was sorry to leave the affairs of the Church as they were; that they knew he had done nothing except what they wished; that it was therefore for them to answer before God for what he had done; that his own conscience was clear, and that he was as an ignorant man who had abandoned himself entirely to them. What a frightful thunderbolt was this to the two Cardinals; for this was an allusion to the terrible constitution they had assisted Pere Tellier in forcing upon him. But their calm was superior to all trial. They praised him and said he had done well, and that he might be at ease as to the result.

This same Monday, 26th of August, after the two Cardinals had left the room, the King dined in his bed in the presence of those who were privileged to enter. As the things were being cleared away, he made them approach and addressed to them these words, which were stored up in their memory:—"Gentlemen, I ask your pardon for the bad example I have given you. I have much to thank you for the manner in which you have served me, and for the attachment and fidelity you have always shown for me. I am very sorry I have not done for you all I should have wished to do; bad times have been the cause. I ask for my grandson the same application and the same fidelity you have had for me. He is a child who may experience many reverses. Let your example be one for all my other subjects. Follow the orders my nephew will give you; he is to govern the realm; I hope he will govern it well; I hope also that you will all contribute to keep up union, and that if any one falls away you will aid in bringing him back. I feel that I am moved, and that I move you also. I ask your pardon. Adieu, gentlemen, I hope you will sometimes remember me."

A short time after he called the Marechal de Villeroy to him, and said he had made him governor of the Dauphin. He then called to him M. le Duc and M. le Prince de Conti, and recommended to them the advantage of union among princes. Then, hearing women in the cabinet, questioned who were there, and immediately sent word they might enter. Madame la Duchesse de Berry, Madame la Duchesse d'Orleans, and the Princesses of the blood forthwith appeared, crying. The King told them they must not cry thus, and said a few friendly words to them, and dismissed them. They retired by the cabinet, weeping and crying very loudly, which caused people to believe outside that the King was dead; and, indeed, the rumour spread to Paris, and even to the provinces.

Some time after the King requested the Duchesse de Ventadour to bring the little Dauphin to him. He made the child approach, and then said to him, before Madame de Maintenon and the few privileged people present, "My child, you are going to be a great king; do not imitate me in the taste I have had for building, or in that I have had for war; try, on the contrary, to be at peace with your neighbours. Render to God what you owe Him; recognise the obligations you are under to Him; make Him honoured by your subjects. Always follow good counsels; try to comfort your people, which I unhappily have not done. Never forget the obligation you owe to Madame de Ventadour. Madame (addressing her), let me embrace him (and while embracing him), my dear child, I give you my benediction with my whole heart."

As the little Prince was about to be taken off the bed, the King redemanded him, embraced him again, and raising hands and eyes to Heaven, blessed him once more. This spectacle was extremely touching.

On Tuesday, the 27th of August, the King said to Madame de Maintenon, that he had always heard, it was hard to resolve to die; but that as for him, seeing himself upon the point of death, he did not find this resolution so difficult to form. She replied that it was very hard when we had attachments to creatures, hatred in our hearts, or restitutions to make. "Ah," rejoined the King, "as for restitutions, to nobody in particular do I owe any; but as for those I owe to the realm, I hope in the mercy of God."

The night which followed was very agitated. The King was seen at all moments joining his hands, striking his breast, and was heard repeating the prayers he ordinarily employed.

On Wednesday morning, the 28th of August, he paid a compliment to Madame de Maintenon, which pleased her but little, and to which she replied not one word. He said, that what consoled him in quitting her was that, considering the age she had reached, they must soon meet again!

About seven o'clock in the morning, he saw in the mirror two of his valets at the foot of the bed weeping, and said to them, "Why do you weep? Is it because you thought me immortal? As for me, I have not thought myself so, and you ought, considering my age, to have been prepared to lose me."

A very clownish Provencal rustic heard of the extremity of the King, while on his way from Marseilles to Paris, and came this morning to Versailles with a remedy, which he said would cure the gangrene. The King was so ill, and the doctors so at their wits' ends, that they consented to receive him. Fagon tried to say something, but this rustic, who was named Le Brun, abused him very coarsely, and Fagon, accustomed to abuse others, was confounded. Ten drops of Le Brun's mixture in Alicante wine were therefore given to the King about eleven o'clock in the morning. Some time after he became stronger, but the pulse falling again and becoming bad, another dose was given to him about four o'clock, to recall him to life, they told him. He replied, taking the mixture, "To life or to death as it shall please God."

Le Brun's remedy was continued. Some one proposed that the King should take some broth. The King replied that it was not broth he wanted, but a confessor, and sent for him. One day, recovering from loss of consciousness, he asked Pere Tellier to give him absolution for all his sins. Pere Tellier asked him if he suffered much. "No," replied the King, "that's what troubles me: I should like to suffer more for the expiation of my sins."

On Thursday, the 29th of August, he grew a little better; he even ate two little biscuits steeped in wine, with a certain appetite. The news immediately spread abroad that the King was recovering. I went that day to the apartments of M. le Duc d'Orleans, where, during the previous eight days, there had been such a crowd that, speaking exactly, a pin would not have fallen to the ground. Not a soul was there! As soon as the Duke saw me he burst out laughing, and said, I was the first person who had been to see him all the day! And until the evening he was entirely deserted. Such is the world!

In the evening it was known that the King had only recovered for the moment. In giving orders during the day, he called the young Dauphin "the young King." He saw a movement amongst those around him. "Why not?" said he, "that does not trouble me." Towards eight o'clock he took the elixir of the rustic. His brain appeared confused; he himself said he felt very ill. Towards eleven o'clock his leg was examined. The gangrene was found to be in the foot and the knee; the thigh much inflamed. He swooned during this examination. He had perceived with much pain that Madame de Maintenon was no longer near him. She had in fact gone off on the previous day with very dry eyes to Saint-Cyr, not intending to return. He asked for her several times during the day. Her departure could not be hidden. He sent for her to Saint-Cyr, and she came back in the evening.

Friday, August the 30th, was a bad day preceded by a bad night. The King continually lost his reason. About five o'clock in the evening Madame de Maintenon left him, gave away her furniture to the domestics, and went to Saint-Cyr never to leave it.

On Saturday, the 31st of August, everything went from bad to worse. The gangrene had reached the knee and all the thigh. Towards eleven o'clock at night the King was found to be so ill that the prayers for the dying were said. This restored him to himself. He repeated the prayers in a voice so strong that it rose above all the other voices. At the end he recognised Cardinal de Rohan, and said to him, "These are the last favours of the Church." This was the last man to whom he spoke. He repeated several times, "Nunc et in hora mortis", then said, "Oh, my God, come to my aid: hasten to succour me."

These were his last words. All the night he was without consciousness and in a long agony, which finished on Sunday, the 1st September, 1715, at a quarter past eight in the morning, three days before he had accomplished his seventy-seventh year, and in the seventy-second of his reign. He had survived all his sons and grandsons, except the King of Spain. Europe never saw so long a reign or France a King so old.

CHAPTER LXXIII

I shall pass over the stormy period of Louis XIV.'s minority. At twenty- three years of age he entered the great world as King, under the most favourable auspices. His ministers were the most skilful in all Europe; his generals the best; his Court was filled with illustrious and clever men, formed during the troubles which had followed the death of Louis XIII.

Louis XIV. was made for a brilliant Court. In the midst of other men, his figure, his courage, his grace, his beauty, his grand mien, even the tone of his voice and the majestic and natural charm of all his person, distinguished him till his death as the King Bee, and showed that if he had only been born a simple private gentlemen, he would equally have excelled in fetes, pleasures, and gallantry, and would have had the greatest success in love. The intrigues and adventures which early in life he had been engaged in—when the Comtesse de Soissons lodged at the Tuileries, as superintendent of the Queen's household, and was the centre figure of the Court group—had exercised an unfortunate influence upon him: he received those impressions with which he could never after successfully struggle. From this time, intellect, education, nobility of sentiment, and high principle, in others, became objects of suspicion to him, and soon of hatred. The more he advanced in years the more this sentiment was confirmed in him. He wished to reign by himself. His jealousy on this point unceasingly became weakness. He reigned, indeed, in little things; the great he could never reach: even in the former, too, he was often governed. The superior ability of his early ministers and his early generals soon wearied him. He liked nobody to be in any way superior to him. Thus he chose his ministers, not for their knowledge, but for their ignorance; not for their capacity, but for their want of it. He liked to form them, as he said; liked to teach them even the most trifling things. It was the same with his generals. He took credit to himself for instructing them; wished it to be thought that from his cabinet he commanded and directed all his armies. Naturally fond of trifles, he unceasingly occupied himself with the most petty details of his troops, his household, his mansions; would even instruct his cooks, who received, like novices, lessons they had known by heart for years. This vanity, this unmeasured and unreasonable love of admiration, was his ruin. His ministers, his generals, his mistresses, his courtiers, soon perceived his weakness. They praised him with emulation and spoiled him. Praises, or to say truth, flattery, pleased him to such an extent, that the coarsest was well received, the vilest even better relished. It was the sole means by which you could approach him. Those whom he liked owed his affection for them to their untiring flatteries. This is what gave his ministers so much authority, and the opportunities they had for adulating him, of attributing everything to him, and of pretending to learn everything from him. Suppleness, meanness, an admiring, dependent, cringing manner—above all, an air of nothingness—were the sole means of pleasing him.

This poison spread. It spread, too, to an incredible extent, in a prince who, although of intellect beneath mediocrity, was not utterly without sense, and who had had some experience. Without voice or musical knowledge, he used to sing, in private, the passages of the opera prologues that were fullest of his praises.

He was drowned in vanity; and so deeply, that at his public suppers—all the Court present, musicians also—he would hum these self-same praises between his teeth, when the music they were set to was played!

And yet, it must be admitted, he might have done better. Though his intellect, as I have said, was beneath mediocrity, it was capable of being formed. He loved glory, was fond of order and regularity; was by disposition prudent, moderate, discreet, master of his movements and his tongue. Will it be believed? He was also by disposition good and just! God had sufficiently gifted him to enable him to be a good King; perhaps even a tolerably great King! All the evil came to him from elsewhere. His early education was so neglected that nobody dared approach his apartment. He has often been heard to speak of those times with bitterness, and even to relate that, one evening he was found in the basin of the Palais Royal garden fountain, into which he had fallen! He was scarcely taught how to read or write, and remained so ignorant, that the most familiar historical and other facts were utterly unknown to him! He fell, accordingly, and sometimes even in public, into the grossest absurdities.

It was his vanity, his desire for glory, that led him, soon after the death of the King of Spain, to make that event the pretext for war; in spite of the renunciations so recently made, so carefully stipulated, in the marriage contract. He marched into Flanders; his conquests there were rapid; the passage of the Rhine was admirable; the triple alliance of England, Sweden, and Holland only animated him. In the midst of winter he took Franche-Comte, by restoring which at the peace of Aix-la- Chapelle, he preserved his conquests in Flanders. All was flourishing then in the state. Riches everywhere. Colbert had placed the finances, the navy, commerce, manufactures, letters even, upon the highest point; and this age, like that of Augustus, produced in abundance illustrious men of all kinds,-even those illustrious only in pleasures.

Le Tellier and Louvois, his son, who had the war department, trembled at the success and at the credit of Colbert, and had no difficulty in putting into the head of the King a new war, the success of which caused such fear to all Europe that France never recovered from it, and after having been upon the point of succumbing to this war, for a long time felt the weight and misfortune of it. Such was the real cause of that famous Dutch war, to which the King allowed himself to be pushed, and which his love for Madame de Montespan rendered so unfortunate for his glory and for his kingdom. Everything being conquered, everything taken, and Amsterdam ready to give up her keys, the King yields to his impatience, quits the army, flies to Versailles, and destroys in an instant all the success of his arms! He repaired this disgrace by a second conquest, in person, of Franche-Comte, which this time was preserved by France.

In 1676, the King having returned into Flanders, took Conde; whilst Monsieur took Bouchain. The armies of the King and of the Prince of Orange approached each other so suddenly and so closely, that they found themselves front to front near Heurtebise. According even to the admission of the enemy, our forces were so superior to those of the Prince of Orange, that we must have gained the victory if we had attacked. But the King, after listening to the opinions of his generals, some for, and some against giving battle, decided for the latter, turned tail, and the engagement was talked of no more. The army was much discontented. Everybody wished for battle. The fault therefore of the King made much impression upon the troops, and excited cruel railleries against us at home and in the foreign courts. The King stopped but little longer afterwards in the army, although we were only in the month of May. He returned to his mistress.

The following year he returned to Flanders, and took Cambrai; and Monsieur besieged Saint-Omer. Monsieur got the start of the Prince of Orange, who was about to assist the place, gave him battle near Corsel, obtained a complete victory, immediately took Saint-Omer, and then joined the King. This contrast so affected the monarch that never afterwards did he give Monsieur command of an army! External appearances were perfectly kept up, but from that moment the resolution was taken and always well sustained.

The year afterwards the King led in person the siege of Ghent. The peace of Nimeguen ended this year the war with Holland, Spain, &c.; and on the commencement of the following year, that with the Emperor and the Empire. America, Africa, the Archipelago, Sicily, acutely felt the power of France, and in 1684 Luxembourg was the price of the delay of the Spaniards in fulfilling all the conditions of the peace. Genoa, bombarded, was forced to come in the persons of its doge and four of its senators, to sue for peace at the commencement of the following year. From this date, until 1688, the time passed in the cabinet less in fetes than in devotion and constraint. Here finishes the apogeum of this reign, and the fulness of glory and prosperity. The great captains, the great ministers, were no more, but their pupils remained. The second epoch of the reign was very different from the first; but the third was even more sadly dissimilar.

I have related the adventure which led to the wars of this period; how an ill-made window-frame was noticed at the Trianon, then building; how Louvois was blamed for it; his alarm lest his disgrace should follow; his determination to engage the King in a war which should turn him from his building fancies. He carried out his resolve: with what result I have already shown. France was ruined at home; and abroad, despite the success of her arms, gained nothing. On the contrary, the withdrawal of the King from Gembloux, when he might have utterly defeated the Prince of Orange, did us infinite harm, as I have shown in its place. The peace which followed this war was disgraceful. The King was obliged to acknowledge the Prince of Orange as King of England, after having so long shown hatred and contempt for him. Our precipitation, too, cost us Luxembourg; and the ignorance of our plenipotentiaries gave our enemies great advantages in forming their frontier. Such was the peace of Ryswick, concluded in September, 1697.

This peace seemed as though it would allow France some breathing time. The King was sixty years of age, and had, in his own opinion, acquired all sorts of glory. But scarcely were we at peace, without having had time to taste it, than the pride of the King made him wish to astonish all Europe by the display of a power that it believed prostrated. And truly he did astonish Europe. But at what a cost! The famous camp of Compiegne—for 'tis to that I allude—was one of the most magnificent spectacles ever seen; but its immense and misplaced prodigality was soon regretted. Twenty years afterwards, some of the regiments who took part in it were still in difficulties from this cause.

Shortly afterwards,—by one of the most surprising and unheard-of pieces of good fortune, the crown of Spain fell into the hands of the Duc d'Anjou, grandson of the King. It seemed as though golden days had come back again to France. Only for a little time, however, did it seem so. Nearly all Europe, as it has been seen, banded against France, to dispute the Spanish crown. The King had lost all his good ministers, all his able generals, and had taken good pains they should leave no successors. When war came, then, we were utterly unable to prosecute it with success or honour. We were driven out of Germany, of Italy, of the Low Countries. We could not sustain the war, or resolve to make peace. Every day led us nearer and nearer the brink of the precipice, the terrible depths of which were for ever staring us in the face. A misunderstanding amongst our enemies, whereby England became detached from the grand alliance; the undue contempt of Prince Eugene for our generals, out of which arose the battle of Denain; saved us from the gulf. Peace came, and a peace, too, infinitely better than that we should have ardently embraced if our enemies had agreed amongst themselves beforehand. Nevertheless, this peace cost dear to France, and cost Spain half its territory—Spain, of which the King had said not even a windmill would he yield! But this was another piece of folly he soon repented of.

Thus, we see this monarch, grand, rich, conquering, the arbiter of Europe; feared and admired as long as the ministers and captains existed who really deserved the name. When they were no more, the machine kept moving some time by impulsion, and from their influence. But soon afterwards we saw beneath the surface; faults and errors were multiplied, and decay came on with giant strides; without, however, opening the eyes of that despotic master, so anxious to do everything and direct everything himself, and who seemed to indemnify himself for disdain abroad by increasing fear and trembling at home.

So much for the reign of this vain-glorious monarch.

Let me touch now upon some other incidents in his career, and upon some points in his character.

He early showed a disinclination for Paris. The troubles that had taken place there during his minority made him regard the place as dangerous; he wished, too, to render himself venerable by hiding himself from the eyes of the multitude; all these considerations fixed him at Saint-Germain soon after the death of the Queen, his mother. It was to that place he began to attract the world by fetes and gallantries, and by making it felt that he wished to be often seen.

His love for Madame de la Valliere, which was at first kept secret, occasioned frequent excursions to Versailles, then a little card castle, which had been built by Louis XIII.—annoyed, and his suite still more so, at being frequently obliged to sleep in a wretched inn there, after he had been out hunting in the forest of Saint Leger. That monarch rarely slept at Versailles more than one night, and then from necessity; the King, his son, slept there, so that he might be more in private with his mistress, pleasures unknown to the hero and just man, worthy son of Saint-Louis, who built the little chateau.

These excursions of Louis XIV. by degrees gave birth to those immense buildings he erected at Versailles; and their convenience for a numerous court, so different from the apartments at Saint-Germain, led him to take up his abode there entirely shortly after the death of the Queen. He built an infinite number of apartments, which were asked for by those who wished to pay their court to him; whereas at Saint-Germain nearly everybody was obliged to lodge in the town, and the few who found accommodation at the chateau were strangely inconvenienced.

The frequent fetes, the private promenades at Versailles, the journeys, were means on which the King seized in order to distinguish or mortify the courtiers, and thus render them more assiduous in pleasing him.

He felt that of real favours he had not enough to bestow; in order to keep up the spirit of devotion, he therefore unceasingly invented all sorts of ideal ones, little preferences and petty distinctions, which answered his purpose as well.

He was exceedingly jealous of the attention paid him. Not only did he notice the presence of the most distinguished courtiers, but those of inferior degree also. He looked to the right and to the left, not only upon rising but upon going to bed, at his meals, in passing through his apartments, or his gardens of Versailles, where alone the courtiers were allowed to follow him; he saw and noticed everybody; not one escaped him, not even those who hoped to remain unnoticed. He marked well all absentees from the Court, found out the reason of their absence, and never lost an opportunity of acting towards them as the occasion might seem to justify. With some of the courtiers (the most distinguished), it was a demerit not to make the Court their ordinary abode; with others 'twas a fault to come but rarely; for those who never or scarcely ever came it was certain disgrace. When their names were in any way mentioned, "I do not know them," the King would reply haughtily. Those who presented themselves but seldom were thus Characterise: "They are people I never see;" these decrees were irrevocable. He could not bear people who liked Paris.

Louis XIV. took great pains to be well informed of all that passed everywhere; in the public places, in the private houses, in society and familiar intercourse. His spies and tell-tales were infinite. He had them of all species; many who were ignorant that their information reached him; others who knew it; others who wrote to him direct, sending their letters through channels he indicated; and all these letters were seen by him alone, and always before everything else; others who sometimes spoke to him secretly in his cabinet, entering by the back stairs. These unknown means ruined an infinite number of people of all classes, who never could discover the cause; often ruined them very unjustly; for the King, once prejudiced, never altered his opinion, or so rarely, that nothing was more rare. He had, too, another fault, very dangerous for others and often for himself, since it deprived him of good subjects. He had an excellent memory; in this way, that if he saw a man who, twenty years before, perhaps, had in some manner offended him, he did not forget the man, though he might forget the offence. This was enough, however, to exclude the person from all favour. The representations of a minister, of a general, of his confessor even, could not move the King. He would not yield.

The most cruel means by which the King was informed of what was passing— for many years before anybody knew it—was that of opening letters. The promptitude and dexterity with which they were opened passes understanding. He saw extracts from all the letters in which there were passages that the chiefs of the post-office, and then the minister who governed it, thought ought to go before him; entire letters, too, were sent to him, when their contents seemed to justify the sending. Thus the chiefs of the post, nay, the principal clerks were in a position to suppose what they pleased and against whom they pleased. A word of contempt against the King or the government, a joke, a detached phrase, was enough. It is incredible how many people, justly or unjustly, were more or less ruined, always without resource, without trial, and without knowing why. The secret was impenetrable; for nothing ever cost the King less than profound silence and dissimulation.

This last talent he pushed almost to falsehood, but never to deceit, pluming himself upon keeping his word,—therefore he scarcely ever gave it. The secrets of others he kept as religiously as his own. He was even flattered by certain confessions and certain confidences; and there was no mistress, minister, or favourite, who could have wormed them out, even though the secret regarded themselves.

We know, amongst many others, the famous story of a woman of quality, who, after having been separated a year from her husband, found herself in the family way just as he was on the point of returning from the army, and who, not knowing what else to do, in the most urgent manner begged a private interview of the King. She obtained it, and confined to him her position, as to the worthiest man in his realm, as she said. The King counselled her to profit by her distress, and live more wisely for the future, and immediately promised to retain her husband on the frontier as long as was necessary, and to forbid his return under any pretext, and in fact he gave orders the same day to Louvois, and prohibited the husband not only all leave of absence, but forbade him to quit for a single day the post he was to command all the winter. The officer, who was distinguished, and who had neither wished nor asked to be employed all the winter upon the frontier, and Louvois, who had in no way thought of it, were equally surprised and vexed. They were obliged, however, to obey to the letter, and without asking why; and the King never mentioned the circumstance until many years afterwards, when he was quite sure nobody could find out either husband or wife, as in fact they never could, or even obtain the most vague or the most uncertain suspicion.

CHAPTER LXXIV

Never did man give with better grace than Louis XIV., or augmented so much, in this way, the price of his benefits. Never did man sell to better profit his words, even his smiles,—nay, his looks. Never did disobliging words escape him; and if he had to blame, to reprimand, or correct, which was very rare, it was nearly always with goodness, never, except on one occasion (the admonition of Courtenvaux, related in its place), with anger or severity. Never was man so naturally polite, or of a politeness so measured, so graduated, so adapted to person, time, and place. Towards women his politeness was without parallel. Never did he pass the humblest petticoat without raising his hat; even to chamber- maids, that he knew to be such, as often happened at Marly. For ladies he took his hat off completely, but to a greater or less extent; for titled people, half off, holding it in his hand or against his ear some instants, more or less marked. For the nobility he contented himself by putting his hand to his hat. He took it off for the Princes of the blood, as for the ladies. If he accosted ladies he did not cover himself until he had quitted them. All this was out of doors, for in the house he was never covered. His reverences, more or less marked, but always light, were incomparable for their grace and manner; even his mode of half raising himself at supper for each lady who arrived at table. Though at last this fatigued him, yet he never ceased it; the ladies who were to sit down, however, took care not to enter after supper had commenced.

If he was made to wait for anything while dressing, it was always with patience. He was exact to the hours that he gave for all his day, with a precision clear and brief in his orders. If in the bad weather of winter, when he could not go out, he went to Madame de Maintenon's a quarter of an hour earlier than he had arranged (which seldom happened), and the captain of the guards was not on duty, he did not fail afterwards to say that it was his own fault for anticipating the hour, not that of the captain of the guards for being absent. Thus, with this regularity which he never deviated from, he was served with the utmost exactitude.

He treated his valets well, above all those of the household. It was amongst them that he felt most at ease, and that he unbosomed himself the most familiarly, especially to the chiefs. Their friendship and their aversion have often had grand results. They were unceasingly in a position to render good and bad offices: thus they recalled those powerful enfranchised slaves of the Roman emperors, to whom the senate and the great people paid court and basely truckled. These valets during Louis XIV.'s reign were not less courted. The ministers, even the most powerful, openly studied their caprices; and the Princes of the blood, nay, the bastards,—not to mention people of lower grade, did the same. The majority were accordingly insolent enough; and if you could not avoid their insolence, you were forced to put up with it.

The King loved air and exercise very much, as long as he could make use of them. He had excelled in dancing, and at tennis and mall. On horseback he was admirable, even at a late age. He liked to see everything done with grace and address. To acquit yourself well or ill before him was a merit or a fault. He said that with things not necessary it was best not to meddle, unless they were done well. He was very fond of shooting, and there was not a better or more graceful shot than he. He had always, in his cabinet seven or eight pointer bitches, and was fond of feeding them, to make himself known to them. He was very fond, too, of stag hunting; but in a caleche, since he broke his arm, while hunting at Fontainebleau, immediately after the death of the Queen. He rode alone in a species of "box," drawn by four little horses—with five or six relays, and drove himself with an address and accuracy unknown to the best coachmen. His postilions were children from ten to fifteen years of age, and he directed them.

He liked splendour, magnificence, and profusion in everything: you pleased him if you shone through the brilliancy of your houses, your clothes, your table, your equipages. Thus a taste for extravagance and luxury was disseminated through all classes of society; causing infinite harm, and leading to general confusion of rank and to ruin.

As for the King himself, nobody ever approached his magnificence. His buildings, who could number them? At the same time, who was there who did not deplore the pride, the caprice, the bad taste seen in them? He built nothing useful or ornamental in Paris, except the Pont Royal, and that simply by necessity; so that despite its incomparable extent, Paris is inferior to many cities of Europe. Saint-Germain, a lovely spot, with a marvellous view, rich forest, terraces, gardens, and water he abandoned for Versailles; the dullest and most ungrateful of all places, without prospect, without wood, without water, without soil; for the ground is all shifting sand or swamp, the air accordingly bad.

But he liked to subjugate nature by art and treasure.

He built at Versailles, on, on, without any general design, the beautiful and the ugly, the vast and the mean, all jumbled together. His own apartments and those of the Queen, are inconvenient to the last degree, dull, close, stinking. The gardens astonish by their magnificence, but cause regret by their bad taste. You are introduced to the freshness of the shade only by a vast torrid zone, at the end of which there is nothing for you but to mount or descend; and with the hill, which is very short, terminate the gardens. The violence everywhere done to nature repels and wearies us despite ourselves. The abundance of water, forced up and gathered together from all parts, is rendered green, thick, muddy; it disseminates humidity, unhealthy and evident; and an odour still more so. I might never finish upon the monstrous defects of a palace so immense and so immensely dear, with its accompaniments, which are still more so.

But the supply of water for the fountains was all defective at all moments, in spite of those seas of reservoirs which had cost so many millions to establish and to form upon the shifting sand and marsh. Who could have believed it? This defect became the ruin of the infantry which was turned out to do the work. Madame de Maintenon reigned. M. de Louvois was well with her, then. We were at peace. He conceived the idea of turning the river Eure between Chartres and Maintenon, and of making it come to Versailles. Who can say what gold and men this obstinate attempt cost during several years, until it was prohibited by the heaviest penalties, in the camp established there, and for a long time kept up; not to speak of the sick,—above all, of the dead,— that the hard labour and still more the much disturbed earth, caused? How many men were years in recovering from the effects of the contagion! How many never regained their health at all! And not only the sub-officers, but the colonels, the brigadiers and general officers, were compelled to be upon the spot, and were not at liberty to absent themselves a quarter of an hour from the works. The war at last interrupted them in 1688, and they have never since been undertaken; only unfinished portions of them exist which will immortalise this cruel folly.

At last, the King, tired of the cost and bustle, persuaded himself that he should like something little and solitary. He searched all around Versailles for some place to satisfy this new taste. He examined several neighbourhoods, he traversed the hills near Saint-Germain, and the vast plain which is at the bottom, where the Seine winds and bathes the feet of so many towns, and so many treasures in quitting Paris. He was pressed to fix himself at Lucienne, where Cavoye afterwards had a house, the view from which is enchanting; but he replied that, that fine situation would ruin him, and that as he wished to go to no expense, so he also wished a situation which would not urge him into any. He found behind Lucienne a deep narrow valley, completely shut in, inaccessible from its swamps, and with a wretched village called Marly upon the slope of one of its hills. This closeness, without drain or the means of having any, was the sole merit of the valley. The King was overjoyed at his discovery. It was a great work, that of draining this sewer of all the environs, which threw there their garbage, and of bringing soil thither! The hermitage was made. At first, it was only for sleeping in three nights, from Wednesday to Saturday, two or three times a-year, with a dozen at the outside of courtiers, to fill the most indispensable posts.

By degrees, the hermitage was augmented, the hills were pared and cut down, to give at least the semblance of a prospect; in fine, what with buildings, gardens, waters, aqueducts, the curious and well known machine, statues, precious furniture, the park, the ornamental enclosed forest,— Marly has become what it is to-day, though it has been stripped since the death of the King. Great trees were unceasingly brought from Compiegne or farther, three-fourths of which died and were immediately after replaced; vast spaces covered with thick wood, or obscure alleys, were suddenly changed into immense pieces of water, on which people were rowed in gondolas; then they were changed again into forest (I speak of what I have seen in six weeks); basins were changed a hundred times; cascades the same; carp ponds adorned with the most exquisite painting, scarcely finished, were changed and differently arranged by the same hands; and this an infinite number of times; then there was that prodigious machine just alluded to, with its immense aqueducts, the conduit, its monstrous resources solely devoted to Marly, and no longer to Versailles; so that I am under the mark in saying that Versailles, even, did not cost so much as Marly.

Such was the fate of a place the abode of serpents, and of carrion, of toads and frogs, solely chosen to avoid expense. Such was the bad taste of the King in all things, and his proud haughty pleasure in forcing nature; which neither the most mighty war, nor devotion could subdue!

CHAPTER LXXV

Let me now speak of the amours of the King in which were even more fatal to the state than his building mania. Their scandal filled all Europe; stupefied France, shook the state, and without doubt drew upon the King those maledictions under the weight of which he was pushed so near the very edge of the precipice, and had the misfortune of seeing his legitimate posterity within an ace of extinction in France. These are evils which became veritable catastrophes and which will be long felt.

Louis XIV., in his youth more made for love than any of his subjects— being tired of gathering passing sweets, fixed himself at last upon La Valliere. The progress and the result of his love are well known.

Madame de Montespan was she whose rare beauty touched him next, even during the reign of Madame de La Valliere. She soon perceived it, and vainly pressed her husband to carry her away into Guienne. With foolish confidence he refused to listen to her. She spoke to him more in earnest. In vain. At last the King was listened to, and carried her off from her husband, with that frightful hubbub which resounded with horror among all nations, and which gave to the world the new spectacle of two mistresses at once! The King took them to the frontiers, to the camps, to the armies, both of them in the Queen's coach. The people ran from all parts to look at the three queens; and asked one another in their simplicity if they had seen them. In the end, Madame de Montespan triumphed, and disposed of the master and his Court with an eclat that knew no veil; and in order that nothing should be wanting to complete the licence of this life, M. de Montespan was sent to the Bastille; then banished to Guienne, and his wife was appointed superintendent of the Queen's household.

The accouchements of Madame de Montespan were public. Her circle became the centre of the Court, of the amusements, of the hopes and of the fears of ministers and the generals, and the humiliation of all France. It was also the centre of wit, and of a kind so peculiar, so delicate, and so subtle, but always so natural and so agreeable, that it made itself distinguished by its special character.

Madame de Montespan was cross, capricious, ill-tempered, and of a haughtiness in everything which, readied to the clouds, and from the effects of which nobody, not even the King, was exempt. The courtiers avoided passing under her windows, above all when the King was with her. They used to say it was equivalent to being put to the sword, and this phrase became proverbial at the Court. It is true that she spared nobody, often without other design than to divert the King; and as she had infinite wit and sharp pleasantry, nothing was more dangerous than the ridicule she, better than anybody, could cast on all. With that she loved her family and her relatives, and did not fail to serve people for whom she conceived friendship. The Queen endured with difficulty her haughtiness—very different from the respect and measure with which she had been treated by the Duchesse de la Valliere, whom she always loved; whereas of Madame de Montespan she would say, "That strumpet will cause my death." The retirement, the austere penitence, and the pious end of Madame de Montespan have been already described.

During her reign she did not fail to have causes for jealousy. There was Mademoiselle de Fontange, who pleased the King sufficiently to become his mistress. But she had no intellect, and without that it was impossible to maintain supremacy over the King. Her early death quickly put an end to this amour. Then there was Madame de Soubise, who, by the infamous connivance of her husband, prostituted herself to the King, and thus secured all sorts of advantages for that husband, for herself, and for her children. The love of the King for her continued until her death, although for many years before that he had ceased to see her in private. Then there was the beautiful Ludre, demoiselle of Lorraine, and maid of honour to Madame, who was openly loved for a moment. But this amour was a flash of lightning, and Madame de Montespan remained triumphant.

Let us now pass to another kind of amour which astonished all the world as much as the other had scandalised it, and which the King carried with him to the tomb. Who does not already recognise the celebrated Francoise d'Aubigne, Marquise de Maintenon, whose permanent reign did not last less than thirty-two years?

Born in the American islands, where her father, perhaps a gentleman, had gone to seek his bread, and where he was stifled by obscurity, she returned alone and at haphazard into France. She landed at La Rochelle, and was received in pity by Madame de Neuillant, mother of the Marechale Duchesse de Navailles, and was reduced by that avaricious old woman to keep the keys of her granary, and to see the hay measured out to her horses, as I have already related elsewhere. She came afterwards to Paris, young, clever, witty, and beautiful, without friends and without money; and by lucky chance made acquaintance with the famous Scarron. He found her amiable; his friends perhaps still more so. Marriage with this joyous and learned cripple appeared to her the greatest and most unlooked-for good fortune; and folks who were, perhaps, more in want of a wife than he, persuaded him to marry her, and thus raise this charming unfortunate from her misery.

The marriage being brought about, the new spouse pleased the company which went to Scarron's house. It was the fashion to go there: people of the Court and of the city, the best and most distinguished went. Scarron was not in a state to leave his house, but the charm of his genius, of his knowledge, of his imagination, of that incomparable and ever fresh gaiety which he showed in the midst of his afflictions, that rare fecundity, and that humour, tempered by so much good taste that is still admired in his writings, drew everybody there.

Madame Scarron made at home all sorts of acquaintances, which, however, at the death of her husband, did not keep her from being reduced to the charity of the parish of Saint-Eustace. She took a chamber for herself and for a servant, where she lived in a very pinched manner. Her personal charms by degrees improved her condition. Villars, father of the Marechal; Beuvron, father of D'Harcourt; the three Villarceaux, and many others kept her.

This set her afloat again, and, step by step, introduced her to the Hotel d'Albret, and thence to the Hotel de Richelieu, and elsewhere; so she passed from one house to the other. In these houses Madame Scarron was far from being on the footing of the rest of the company. She was more like a servant than a guest. She was completely at the beck and call of her hosts; now to ask for firewood; now if a meal was nearly ready; another time if the coach of so-and-so or such a one had returned; and so on, with a thousand little commissions which the use of bells, introduced a long time after, differently disposes of.

It was in these houses, principally in the Hotel de Richelieu, much more still in the Hotel d'Albret, where the Marechal d'Albret lived in great state, that Madame Scarron made the majority of her acquaintances. The Marechal was cousin-german of M. de Montespan, very intimate with him, and with Madame de Montespan. When she became the King's mistress he became her counsellor, and abandoned her husband.

To the intimacy between the Marechal d'Albret and Madame de Montespan, Madame de Maintenon owed the good fortune she met with fourteen or fifteen years later. Madame de Montespan continually visited the Hotel d'Albret, and was much impressed with Madame Scarron. She conceived a friendship for the obliging widow, and when she had her first children by the King—M. du Maine and Madame la Duchesse, whom the King wished to conceal—she proposed that they should be confided to Madame Scarron. A house in the Marais was accordingly given to her, to lodge in with them, and the means to bring them up, but in the utmost secrecy. Afterwards, these children were taken to Madame de Montespan, then shown to the King, and then by degrees drawn from secrecy and avowed. Their governess, being established with them at the Court, more and more pleased Madame de Montespan, who several times made the King give presents to her. He, on the other hand, could not endure her; what he gave to her, always little, was by excess of complaisance and with a regret that he did not hide.

The estate of Maintenon being for sale, Madame de Montespan did not let the King rest until she had drawn from him enough to buy it for Madame Scarron, who thenceforth assumed its name. She obtained enough also for the repair of the chateau, and then attacked the King for means to arrange the garden, which the former owners had allowed to go to ruin.

It was at the toilette of Madame de Montespan that these demands were made. The captain of the guards alone followed the King there. M. le Marechal de Lorges, the truest man that ever lived, held that post then, and he has often related to me the scene he witnessed. The King at first turned a deaf ear to the request of Madame de Montespan, and then refused. Annoyed that she still insisted, he said he had already done more than enough for this creature; that he could not understand the fancy of Madame de Montespan for her, and her obstinacy in keeping her after he had begged her so many times to dismiss her; that he admitted Madame Scarron was insupportable to him, and provided he never saw her more and never heard speak of her, he would open his purse again; though, to say truth, he had already given too much to a creature of this kind! Never did M. le Marechel de Lorges forget these words; and he has always repeated them to me and others precisely as they are given here, so struck was he with them, and much more after all that he saw since, so astonishing and so contradictory. Madame de Montespan stopped short, very much troubled by having too far pressed the King.

M. du Maine was extremely lame; this was caused, it was said, by a fall he had from his nurse's arms. Nothing done for him succeeded; the resolution was then taken to send him to various practicians in Flanders, and elsewhere in the realm, then to the waters, among others to Bareges.

The letters that the governess wrote to Madame de Montespan, giving an account of these journeys, were shown to the King. He thought them well written, relished them, and the last ones made his aversion for the writer diminish.

The ill-humour of Madame de Montespan finished the work. She had a good deal of that quality, and had become accustomed to give it full swing. The King was the object of it more frequently than anybody; he was still amorous; but her ill-humour pained him. Madame de Maintenon reproached Madame de Montespan for this, and thus advanced herself in the King's favour. The King, by degrees, grew accustomed to speak sometimes to Madame de Maintenon; to unbosom to her what he wished her to say to Madame de Montespan; at last to relate to her the chagrin this latter caused him, and to consult her thereupon.

Admitted thus into the intimate confidence of the lover and the mistress, and this by the King's own doing, the adroit waiting-woman knew how to cultivate it, and profited so well by her industry that by degrees she supplanted Madame de Montespan, who perceived, too late, that her friend had become necessary to the King. Arrived at this point, Madame de Maintenon made, in her turn, complaints to the King of all she had to suffer, from a mistress who spared even him so little; and by dint of these mutual complaints about Madame de Montespan, Madame de Maintenon at last took her place, and knew well how to keep it.

Fortune, I dare not say Providence, which was preparing for the haughtiest of kings, humiliation the most profound, the most-public, the most durable, the most unheard-of, strengthened more and more his taste for this woman, so adroit and expert at her trade; while the continued ill-humour and jealousy of Madame de Montespan rendered the new union still more solid. It was this that Madame de Sevigne so prettily paints, enigmatically, in her letters to Madame de Grignan, in which she sometimes talks of these Court movements; for Madame de Maintenon had been in Paris in the society of Madame de Sevigne, of Madame de Coulange, of Madame de La Fayette, and had begun to make them feel her importance. Charming touches are to be seen in the same style upon the favour, veiled but brilliant enjoyed by Madame de Soubise.

It was while the King was in the midst of his partiality for Madame de Maintenon that the Queen died. It was at the same time, too, that the ill-humour of Madame de Montespan became more and more insupportable. This imperious beauty, accustomed to domineer and to be adored, could not struggle against the despair, which the prospect of her fall caused her. What carried her beyond all bounds, was that she could no longer disguise from herself, that she had an abject rival whom she had supported, who owed everything to her; whom she had so much liked that she had several times refused to dismiss her when pressed to do so by the King; a rival, too, so beneath her in beauty, and older by several years; to feel that it was this lady's-maid, not to say this servant, that the King most frequently went to see; that he sought only her; that he could not dissimulate his uneasiness if he did not find her; that he quitted all for her; in fine, that at all moments she (Madame de Montespan) needed the intervention of Madame de Maintenon, in order to attract the King to reconcile her with him, or to obtain the favours she asked for. It was then, in times so propitious to the enchantress, that the King became free by the death of the Queen.

He passed the first few days at Saint-Cloud, at Monsieur's, whence he went to Fontainebleau, where he spent all the autumn. It was there that his liking, stimulated by absence, made him find that absence insupportable. Upon his return it is pretended—for we must distinguish the certain from that which is not so—it is pretended, I say, that the King spoke more freely to Madame de Maintenon, and that she; venturing to put forth her strength, intrenched herself behind devotion and prudery; that the King did not cease, that she preached to him and made him afraid of the devil, and that she balanced his love against his conscience with so much art, that she succeeded in becoming what our eyes have seen her, but what posterity will never believe she was.

But what is very certain and very true, is, that some time after the return of the King from Fontainebleau, and in the midst of the winter that followed the death of the Queen (posterity will with difficulty believe it, although perfectly true and proved), Pere de la Chaise, confessor of the King, said mass at the dead of night in one of the King's cabinets at Versailles. Bontems, governor of Versailles, chief valet on duty, and the most confidential of the four, was present at this mass, at which the monarch and La Maintenon were married in presence of Harlay, Archbishop of Paris, as diocesan, of Louvois (both of whom drew from the King a promise that he would never declare this marriage), and of Montchevreuil. This last was a relative and friend of Villarceaux, to whom during the summer he lent his house at Montchevreuil, remaining there himself, however, with his wife; and in that house Villarceaux kept Madame Scarron, paying all the expenses because his relative was poor, and because he (Villarceaux) was ashamed to take her to his own home, to live in concubinage with her in the presence of his wife whose patience and virtue he respected.

The satiety of the honeymoon, usually so fatal, and especially the honeymoon of such marriages, only consolidated the favour of Madame de Maintenon. Soon after, she astonished everybody by the apartments given to her at Versailles, at the top of the grand staircase facing those of the King and on the same floor. From that moment the King always passed some hours with her every day of his life; wherever she might be she was always lodged near him, and on the same floor if possible.

What manner of person she was,—this incredible enchantress,—and how she governed all-powerfully for more than thirty years, it behoves me now to explain!

CHAPTER LXXVI

Madame de Maintenon was a woman of much wit, which the good company, in which she had at first been merely suffered, but in which she soon shone, had much polished; and ornamented with knowledge of the world, and which gallantry had rendered of the most agreeable kind. The various positions she had held had rendered her flattering, insinuating, complaisant, always seeking to please. The need she had of intrigues, those she had seen of all kinds, and been mixed up in for herself and for others, had given her the taste, the ability, and the habit of them. Incomparable grace, an easy manner, and yet measured and respectful, which, in consequence of her long obscurity, had become natural to her, marvellously aided her talents; with language gentle, exact, well expressed, and naturally eloquent and brief. Her best time, for she was three or four years older than the King, had been the dainty phrase period;—the superfine gallantry days,—in a word, the time of the "ruelles," as it was called; and it had so influenced her that she always retained evidences of it. She put on afterwards an air of importance, but this gradually gave place to one of devoutness that she wore admirably. She was not absolutely false by disposition, but necessity had made her so, and her natural flightiness made her appear twice as false as she was.

The distress and poverty in which she had so long lived had narrowed her mind, and abased her heart and her sentiments. Her feelings and her thoughts were so circumscribed, that she was in truth always less even than Madame Scarron, and in everything and everywhere she found herself such. Nothing was more repelling than this meanness, joined to a situation so radiant.

Her flightiness or inconstancy was of the most dangerous kind. With the exception of some of her old friends, to whom she had good reasons for remaining faithful, she favoured people one moment only to cast them off the next. You were admitted to an audience with her for instance, you pleased her in some manner, and forthwith she unbosomed herself to you as though you had known her from childhood. At the second audience you found her dry, laconic, cold. You racked your brains to discover the cause of this change. Mere loss of time!—Flightiness was the sole reason of it.

Devoutness was her strong point; by that she governed and held her place. She found a King who believed himself an apostle, because he had all his life persecuted Jansenism, or what was presented to him as such. This indicated to her with what grain she could sow the field most profitably.

The profound ignorance in which the King had been educated and kept all his life, rendered him from the first an easy prey to the Jesuits. He became even more so with years, when he grew devout, for he was devout with the grossest ignorance. Religion became his weak point. In this state it was easy to persuade him that a decisive and tremendous blow struck against the Protestants would give his name more grandeur than any of his ancestors had acquired, besides strengthening his power and increasing his authority. Madame de Maintenon was one of those who did most to make him believe this.

The revocation of the edict of Nantes, without the slightest pretext or necessity, and the various proscriptions that followed it, were the fruits of a frightful plot, in which the new spouse was one of the chief conspirators, and which depopulated a quarter of the realm, ruined its commerce, weakened it in every direction, gave it up for a long time to the public and avowed pillage of the dragoons, authorised torments and punishments by which so many innocent people of both sexes were killed by thousands; ruined a numerous class; tore in pieces a world of families; armed relatives against relatives, so as to seize their property and leave them to die of hunger; banished our manufactures to foreign lands, made those lands flourish and overflow at the expense of France, and enabled them to build new cities; gave to the world the spectacle of a prodigious population proscribed, stripped, fugitive, wandering, without crime, and seeking shelter far from its country; sent to the galleys, nobles, rich old men, people much esteemed for their piety, learning, and virtue, people well off, weak, delicate, and solely on account of religion; in fact, to heap up the measure of horror, filled all the realm with perjury and sacrilege, in the midst of the echoed cries of these unfortunate victims of error, while so many others sacrificed their conscience to their wealth and their repose, and purchased both by simulated abjuration, from which without pause they were dragged to adore what they did not believe in, and to receive the divine body of the Saint of Saints whilst remaining persuaded that they were only eating bread which they ought to abhor! Such was the general abomination born of flattery and cruelty. From torture to abjuration, and from that to the communion, there was often only twenty-four hours' distance; and executioners were the conductors of the converts and their witnesses. Those who in the end appeared to have been reconciled, more at leisure did not fail by their flight, or their behaviour, to contradict their pretended conversion.

The Edict of Nantes--painted by Jules Girardet

The King received from all sides news and details of these persecutions and of these conversions. It was by thousands that those who had abjured and taken the communion were counted; ten thousand in one place; six thousand in another—all at once and instantly. The King congratulated himself on his power and his piety. He believed himself to have renewed the days of the preaching of the Apostles, and attributed to himself all the honour. The bishops wrote panegyrics of him, the Jesuits made the pulpit resound with his praises. All France was filled with horror and confusion; and yet there never was so much triumph and joy—never such profusion of laudations! The monarch doubted not of the sincerity of this crowd of conversions; the converters took good care to persuade him of it and to beatify him beforehand. He swallowed their poison in long. draughts. He had never yet believed himself so great in the eyes of man, or so advanced in the eyes of God, in the reparation of his sins and of the scandals of his life. He heard nothing but eulogies, while the good and true Catholics and the true bishops, groaned in spirit to see the orthodox act towards error and heretics as heretical tyrants and heathens had acted against the truth, the confessors, and the martyrs. They could not, above all, endure this immensity of perjury and sacrilege. They bitterly lamented the durable and irremediable odium that detestable measure cast upon the true religion, whilst our neighbours, exulting to see us thus weaken and destroy ourselves, profited by our madness, and built designs upon the hatred we should draw upon ourselves from all the Protestant powers.

But to these spearing truths, the King was inaccessible. Even the conduct of Rome in this matter, could not open his eyes. That Court which formerly had not been ashamed to extol the Saint-Bartholomew, to thank God for it by public processions, to employ the greatest masters to paint this execrable action in the Vatican; Rome, I say, would not give the slightest approbation to this onslaught on the Huguenots.

The magnificent establishment of Saint-Cyr, followed closely upon the revocation of the edict of Nantes. Madame de Montespan had founded at Paris an establishment for the instruction of young girls in all sorts of fine and ornamental work. Emulation gave Madame de Maintenon higher and vaster views which, whilst gratifying the poor nobility, would cause her to be regarded as protectress in whom all the nobility would feel interested. She hoped to smooth the way for a declaration of her marriage, by rendering herself illustrious by a monument with which she could amuse both the King and herself, and which might serve her as a retreat if she had the misfortune to lose him, as in fact it happened.

This declaration of her marriage was always her most ardent desire. She wished above all things to be proclaimed Queen; and never lost sight of the idea. Once she was near indeed upon seeing it gratified. The King had actually given her his word, that she should be declared; and the ceremony was forthwith about to take place. But it was postponed, and for ever, by the representations of Louvois to the King. To this interference that minister owed his fall, and under circumstances so surprising and so strange, that I cannot do better, I think, than introduce an account of them here, by way of episode. They are all the more interesting because they show what an unlimited power Madame de Maintenon exercised by subterranean means, and with what patient perseverance she undermined her enemies when once she had resolved to destroy them.

Lauvois had gained the confidence of the King to such an extent, that he was, as I have said, one of the two witnesses of the frightful marriage of his Majesty with Madame de Maintenon. He had the courage to show he was worthy of this confidence, by representing to the King the ignominy of declaring that marriage, and drew from him his word, that never in his life would he do so.

Several years afterwards, Louvois, who took care to be well informed of all that passed in the palace, found out that Madame de Maintenon had been again scheming in order to be declared Queen; that the King had had the weakness to promise she should be, and that the declaration was about to be made. He put some papers in his hand, and at once went straight to the King, who was in a very private room. Seeing Louvois at an unexpected hour, he asked him what brought him there. "Something pressing and important," replied Louvois, with a sad manner that astonished the King, and induced him to command the valets present to quit the room. They went away in fact, but left the door open, so that they could hear all, and see all, too, by the glass. This was the great danger of the cabinets.

The valets being gone, Louvois did not dissimulate from the King his mission. The monarch was often false, but incapable of rising above his own falsehood. Surprised at being discovered, he tried to shuffle out of the matter, and pressed by his minister, began to move so as to gain the other cabinet where the valets were, and thus deliver himself from this hobble. But Louvois, who perceived what he was about, threw himself on his knees and stopped him, drew from his side a little sword he wore, presented the handle to the King, and prayed him to kill him on the spot, if he would persist in declaring his marriage, in breaking his word, and covering himself in the eyes of Europe with infamy. The King stamped, fumed, told Louvois to let him go. But Louvois squeezed him tighter by the legs for fear he should escape; represented to him the shame of what he had decided on doing; in a word, succeeded so well, that he drew for the second time from the King, a promise that the marriage should never be declared.

Madame de Maintenon meanwhile expected every moment to be proclaimed Queen. At the end of some days disturbed by the silence of the King, she ventured to touch upon the subject. The embarrassment she caused the King much troubled her. He softened the affair as much as he could, but finished by begging her to think no more of being declared, and never to speak of it to him again! After the first shock that the loss of her hopes caused her, she sought to find out to whom she was beholden for it. She soon learned the truth; and it is not surprising that she swore to obtain Louvois's disgrace, and never ceased to work at it until successful. She waited her opportunity, and undermined her enemy at leisure, availing herself of every occasion to make him odious to the King.

Time passed. At length it happened that Louvois, not content with the terrible executions in the Palatinate, which he had counselled, wished to burn Treves. He proposed it to the King. A dispute arose between them, but the King would not or could not be persuaded. It may be imagined that Madame de Maintenon did not do much to convince him.

Some days afterwards Louvois, who had the fault of obstinacy, came as usual to work with the King in Madame de Maintenon's rooms. At the end of the sitting he said, that he felt convinced that it was scrupulousness alone which had hindered the King from consenting to so necessary an act as the burning, of Treves, and that he had, therefore, taken the responsibility on himself by sending a courier with orders to set fire to the place at once.

The King was immediately, and contrary to his nature, so transported with anger that he seized the tongs, and was about to make a run at Louvois, when Madame de Maintenon placed herself between them, crying, "Oh, Sire, what are you going to do?" and took the tongs from his hands.

Louvois, meanwhile, gained the door. The King cried after him to recall him, and said, with flashing eyes: "Despatch a courier instantly with a counter order, and let him arrive in time; for, know this: if a single house is burned your head shall answer for it." Louvois, more dead than alive, hastened away at once.

Of course, he had sent off no courier. He said he had, believing that by this trick the King, though he might be angry, would be led to give way. He had reckoned wrongly, however, as we have seen.

From this time forward Louvois became day by day more distasteful to the King. In the winter of 1690, he proposed that, in order to save expense, the ladies should not accompany the King to the siege of Mons. Madame de Maintenon, we may be sure, did not grow more kindly disposed towards him after this. But as it is always the last drop of water that makes the glass overflow, so a trifle that happened at this siege, completed the disgrace of Louvois.

The King, who plumed himself upon knowing better than anybody the minutest military details, walking one day about the camp, found an ordinary cavalry guard ill-posted, and placed it differently. Later the same day he again visited by chance the spot, and found the guard replaced as at first. He was surprised and shocked. He asked the captain who had done this, and was told it was Louvois.

"But," replied the King, "did you not tell him 'twas I who had placed you?"

"Yes, Sire," replied the captain. The King piqued, turned towards his suite, and said: "That's Louvois's trade, is it not? He thinks himself a great captain, and that he knows everything," and forthwith he replaced the guard as he had put it in the morning. It was, indeed, foolishness and insolence on the part of Louvois, and the King had spoken truly of him. The King was so wounded that he could not pardon him. After Louvois's death, he related this incident to Pomponne, still annoyed at it, as I knew by means of the Abbe de Pomponne.

After the return from Mons the dislike of the King for Louvois augmented to such an extent, that this minister, who was so presumptuous, and who thought himself so necessary, began to tremble. The Marechale de Rochefort having gone with her daughter, Madame de Blansac, to dine with him at Meudon, he took them out for a ride in a little 'calache', which he himself drove. They heard him repeatedly say to himself, musing profoundly, "Will he? Will he be made to? No—and yet—no, he will not dare."

During this monologue Louvois was so absorbed that he was within an ace of driving them all into the water, and would have done so, had they not seized the reins, and cried out that he was going to drown them. At their cries and movement, Louvois awoke as from a deep sleep, drew up, and turned, saying that, indeed, he was musing, and not thinking of the vehicle.

I was at Versailles at that time, and happened to call upon Louvois about some business of my father's.

The same day I met him after dinner as he was going to work with the King. About four o'clock in the afternoon I learned that he had been taken rather unwell at Madame de Maintenon's, that the King had forced him to go home, that he had done so on foot, that some trifling remedy was administered to him there, and that during the operation of it he died!

The surprise of all the Court may be imagined. Although I was little more than fifteen years of age, I wished to see the countenance of the King after the occurrence of an event of this kind. I went and waited for him, and followed him during all his promenade. He appeared to me with his accustomed majesty, but had a nimble manner, as though he felt more free than usual. I remarked that, instead of going to see his fountains, and diversifying his walk as usual, he did nothing but walk up and down by the balustrade of the orangery, whence he could see, in returning towards the chateau, the lodging in which Louvois had just died, and towards which he unceasingly looked.

The name of Louvois was never afterwards pronounced; not a word was said upon this death so surprising, and so sudden, until the arrival of an officer, sent by the King of England from Saint-Germain, who came to the King upon this terrace, and paid him a compliment of condolence upon the loss he had received.

"Monsieur," replied the King, in a tone and with a manner more than easy, "give my compliments and my thanks to the King and Queen of England, and say to them in my name, that my affairs and theirs will go on none the worse for what has happened."

The officer made a bow and retired, astonishment painted upon his face, and expressed in all his bearing. I anxiously observed all this, and also remarked, that all the principal people around the King looked at each other, but said no word. The fact was, as I afterwards learned, that Louvois, when he died, was so deeply in disgrace, that the very next day he was to have been arrested and sent to the Bastille! The King told Chamillart so, and Chamillart related it to me. This explains, I fancy, the joy of the King at the death of his minister; for it saved him from executing the plan he had resolved on.

The suddenness of the disease and death of Louvois caused much talk, especially when, on the opening of the body, it was discovered that he had been poisoned. A servant was arrested on the charge; but before the trial took place he was liberated, at the express command of the King, and the whole affair was hushed up. Five or six months afterwards Seron, private physician of Louvois, barricaded himself in his apartment at Versailles, and uttered dreadful cries. People came but he refused to open; and as the door could not be forced, he went on shrieking all day, without succour, spiritual or temporal, saying at last that he had got what he deserved for what he had done to his master; that he was a wretch unworthy of help; and so he died despairing, in eight or ten hours, without having spoken of any ones or uttered a single name!

CHAPTER LXXVII

It must not be imagined that in order to maintain her position Madame de Maintenon had need of no address. Her reign, on the contrary, was only one continual intrigue; and that of the King a perpetual dupery.

Her mornings, which she commenced very early, were occupied with obscure audiences for charitable or spiritual affairs. Pretty often, at eight o'clock in the morning, or earlier, she went to some minister; the ministers of war, above all those of finance, were those with whom she had most business.

Ordinarily as soon as she rose, she went to Saint-Cyr, dined in her apartment there alone, or with some favourite of the house, gave as few audiences as possible, ruled over the arrangements of the establishment, meddled with the affairs of convents, read and replied to letters, directed the affairs of the house, received information and letters from her spies, and returned to Versailles just as the King was ready to enter her rooms. When older and more infirm, she would lie down in bed on arriving between seven and eight o'clock in the morning at Saint-Cyr, or take some remedy.

Towards nine o'clock in the evening two waiting-women came to undress her. Immediately afterwards, her maitre d'hotel, or a valet de chambre brought her her supper—soup, or something light. As soon as she had finished her meal, her women put her to bed, and all this in the presence of the King and his minister, who did not cease working or speak lower. This done, ten o'clock had arrived; the curtains of Madame de Maintenon were drawn, and the King went to supper, after saying good night to her.

When with the King in her own room, they each occupied an armchair, with a table between them, at either side of the fireplace, hers towards the bed, the King's with the back to the wall, where was the door of the ante-chamber; two stools were before the table, one for the minister who came to work, the other for his papers.

During the work Madame de Maintenon read or worked at tapestry. She heard all that passed between the King and his minister, for they spoke out loud. Rarely did she say anything, or, if so, it was of no moment. The King often asked her opinion; then she replied with great discretion. Never did she appear to lay stress on anything, still less to interest herself for anybody, but she had an understanding with the minister, who did not dare to oppose her in private, still less to trip in her presence. When some favour or some post was to be granted, the matter was arranged between them beforehand; and this it was that sometimes delayed her, without the King or anybody knowing the cause.

She would send word to the minister that she wished to speak to him. He did not dare to bring anything forward until he had received her orders; until the revolving mechanism of each day had given them the leisure to confer together. That done, the minister proposed and showed a list. If by chance the King stopped at the name Madame de Maintenon wished, the minister stopped too, and went no further. If the King stopped at some other, the minister proposed that he should look at those which were also fitting, allowed the King leisure to make his observations, and profited by them, to exclude the people who were not wanted. Rarely did he propose expressly the name to which he wished to come, but always suggested several that he tried to balance against each other, so as to embarrass the King in his choice. Then the King asked his opinion, and the minister, after touching upon other names, fixed upon the one he had selected.

The King nearly always hesitated, and asked Madame de Maintenon what she thought. She smiled, shammed incapacity, said a word upon some other name, then returned, if she had not fixed herself there at first, to that which the minister had proposed; so that three-fourths of the favours and opportunities which passed through the hands of the ministers in her rooms—and three-fourths even of the remaining fourth-were disposed of by her. Sometimes when she had nobody for whom she cared, it was the minister, with her consent and her help, who decided, without the King having the least suspicion. He thought he disposed of everything by himself; whilst, in fact, he disposed only of the smallest part, and always then by chance, except on the rare occasions when he specially wished to favour some one.

As for state matters, if Madame de Maintenon wished to make them succeed, fail, or turn in some particular fashion (which happened much less often than where favours and appointments were in the wind), the same intelligence and the same intrigue were carried on between herself and the minister. By these particulars it will be seen that this clever woman did nearly all she wished, but not when or how she wished.

There was another scheme if the King stood out; it was to avoid decision by confusing and spinning out the matter in hand, or by substituting another as though arising, opportunely out of it, and by which it was turned aside, or by proposing that some explanations should be obtained. The first ideas of the King were thus weakened, and the charge was afterwards returned to, with the same address, oftentimes with success.

It is this which made the ministers so necessary to Madame de Maintenon, and her so necessary to them: She rendered them, in fact, continual services by means of the King, in return for the services they rendered her. The mutual concerns, therefore, between her and them were infinite; the King, all the while, not having the slightest suspicion of what was going on!

The power of Madame de Maintenon was, as may be imagined, immense. She had everybody in her hands, from the highest and most favoured minister to the meanest subject of the realm. Many people have been ruined by her, without having been able to discover the author of their ruin, search as they might. All attempts to find a remedy were equally unsuccessful.

Yet the King was constantly on his guard, not only against Madame de Maintenon, but against his ministers also. Many a time it happened that when sufficient care had not been taken, and he perceived that a minister or a general wished to favour a relative or protege of Madame de Maintenon, he firmly opposed the appointment on that account alone, and the remarks he uttered thereupon made Madame de Maintenon very timid and very measured when she wished openly to ask a favour.

Le Tellier, long before he was made Chancellor, well knew the mood of the King. One of his friends asked him for some place that he much desired. Le Tellier replied that he would do what he could. The friend did not like this reply, and frankly said that it was not such as he expected from a man with such authority. "You do not know the ground," replied Le Tellier; "of twenty matters that we bring before the King, we are sure he will pass nineteen according to our wishes; we are equally certain that the twentieth will be decided against them. But which of the twenty will be decided contrary to our desire we never know, although it may be the one we have most at heart. The King reserves to himself this caprice, to make us feel that he is the master, and that he governs; and if, by chance, something is presented upon which he is obstinate, and which is sufficiently important for us to be obstinate about also, either on account of the thing itself, or for the desire we have that it should succeed as we wish, we very often get a dressing; but, in truth, the dressing over, and the affair fallen through, the King, content with having showed that we can do nothing, and pained by having vexed us, becomes afterwards supple and flexible, so that then is the time at which we can do all we wish."

This is, in truth, how the King conducted himself with his ministers, always completely governed by them, even by the youngest and most mediocre, even by the least accredited and the least respected—yet always on his guard against being governed, and always persuaded that he succeeded fully in avoiding it.

He adopted the same conduct towards Madame de Maintenon, whom at times he scolded terribly, and applauded himself for so doing. Sometimes she threw herself on her knees before him, and for several days was really upon thorns. When she had appointed Fagon physician of the King in place of Daquin, whom she dismissed, she had a doctor upon whom she could certainly rely, and she played the sick woman accordingly, after those scenes with the King, and in this manner turned them to her own advantage.

It was not that this artifice had any power in constraining the King, or that a real illness would have had any. He was a man solely personal, and who counted others only as they stood in relation to himself. His hard-heartedness, therefore, was extreme. At the time when he was most inclined towards his mistresses, whatever indisposition they might labour under, even the most opposed to travelling and to appearing in full court dress, could not save them from either. When enceinte, or ill, or just risen from child birth, they must needs be squeezed into full dress, go to Flanders or further, dance; sit up, attend fetes, eat, be merry and good company; go from place to place; appear neither to fear, nor to be inconvenienced by heat, cold, wind, or dust; and all this precisely to the hour and day, without a minute's grace.

His daughters he treated in the same manner. It has been seen, in its place, that he had no more consideration for Madame la Duchesse de Berry, nor even for Madame la Duchesse de Bourgogne—whatever Fagon, Madame de Maintenon, and others might do or say. Yet he loved Madame la Duchesse de Bourgogne as tenderly as he was capable of loving anybody: but both she and Madame la Duchesse de Berry had miscarriages, which relieved him, he said, though they then had no children.

When he travelled, his coach was always full of women; his mistresses, afterwards his bastards, his daughters-in-law, sometimes Madame, and other ladies when there was room. In the coach, during his journeys, there were always all sorts of things to eat, as meat, pastry, fruit. A quarter of a league was not passed over before the King asked if somebody would not eat. He never ate anything between meals himself, not even fruit; but he amused himself by seeing others do so, aye, and to bursting. You were obliged to be hungry, merry, and to eat with appetite, otherwise he was displeased, and even showed it. And yet after this, if you supped with him at table the same day, you were compelled to eat with as good a countenance as though you had tasted nothing since the previous night. He was as inconsiderate in other and more delicate matters; and ladies, in his long drives and stations, had often occasion to curse him. The Duchesse de Chevreuse once rode all the way from Versailles to Fontainebleau in such extremity, that several times she was well-nigh losing consciousness.

The King, who was fond of air, liked all the windows to be lowered; he would have been much displeased had any lady drawn a curtain for protection against sun, wind, or cold. No inconvenience or incommodity was allowed to be even perceived; and the King always went very quickly, most frequently with relays. To faint was a fault past hope of pardon.

Madame de Maintenon, who feared the air and many other inconveniences, could gain no privilege over the others. All she obtained, under pretence of modesty and other reasons, was permission to journey apart; but whatever condition she might be in, she was obliged to follow the King, and be ready to receive him in her rooms by the time he was ready to enter them. She made many journeys to Marly in a state such as would have saved a servant from movement. She made one to Fontainebleau when it seemed not unlikely that she would die on the road! In whatever condition she might be, the King went to her at his ordinary hour and did what he had projected; though several times she was in bed, profusely sweating away a fever. The King, who as I have said, was fond of air, and feared warm rooms, was astonished upon arriving to find everything close shut, and ordered the windows to be opened; would not spare them an inch; and up to ten o'clock, when he went to supper, kept them open, utterly regardless of the cool night air, although he knew well what a state she was in. If there was to be music, fever or headache availed not; a hundred wax candles flashed all the same in her eyes. The King, in fact, always followed his own inclination, without ever asking whether she was inconvenienced.

The tranquillity and pious resignation of the King during the last days of his illness, was a matter of some surprise to many people, as, indeed, it deserved to be. By way of explanation, the doctors said that the malady he died of, while it deadens and destroys all bodily pain, calms and annihilates all heart pangs and agitation of the mind.

They who were in the sick-chamber, during the last days of his illness, gave another reason.

The Jesuits constantly admit the laity, even married, into their company. This fact is certain. There is no doubt that Des Noyers, Secretary of State under Louis XIII., was of this number, or that many others have been so too. These licentiates make the same vow as the Jesuits, as far as their condition admits: that is, unrestricted obedience to the General, and to the superiors of the company. They are obliged to supply the place of the vows of poverty and chastity, by promising to give all the service and all the protection in their power to the Company, above all, to be entirely submissive to the superiors and to their confessor. They are obliged to perform, with exactitude, such light exercises of piety as their confessor may think adapted to the circumstances of their lives, and that he simplifies as much as he likes. It answers the purpose of the Company to ensure to itself those hidden auxiliaries whom it lets off cheaply. But nothing must pass through their minds, nothing must come to their knowledge that they do not reveal to their confessor; and that which is not a secret of the conscience, to the superiors, if the confessor thinks fit. In everything, too, they must obey without comment, the superior and the confessors.

It has been pretended that Pere Tellier had inspired the King, long before his death, with the desire to be admitted, on this footing, into the Company; that he had vaunted to him the privileges and plenary indulgences attached to it; that he had persuaded him that whatever crimes had been committed, and whatever difficulty there might be in making amends for them, this secret profession washed out all, and infallibly assured salvation, provided that the vows were faithfully kept; that the General of the Company was admitted into the secret with the consent of the King; that the King pronounced the vows before Pere Tellier; that in the last days of his life they were heard, the one fortifying, the other resposing upon these promises; that, at last, the King received from Pere Tellier the final benediction of the Company, as one of its members; that Pere Tellier made the King offer up prayers, partly heard, of a kind to leave no doubt of the matter; and that he had given him the robe, or the almost imperceptible sign, as it were, a sort of scapulary, which was found upon him. To conclude, the majority of those who approached the King in his last moments attributed his penitence to the artifices and persuasions of the Jesuits, who, for temporal interests, deceive sinners even up to the edge of the tomb, and conduct them to it in profound peace by a path strewn with flowers.

However it is but fair to say, that Marechal, who was very trustful, assured me he had never perceived anything which justified this idea, and that he was persuaded there was not the least truth in it; and I think, that although he was not always in the chamber or near the bed, and although Pere Tellier might mistrust and try to deceive him, still if the King had been made a Jesuit as stated, Marechal must have had sore knowledge or some suspicion of the circumstance.

VOLUME 11.: CHAPTER LXXVIII

After having thus described with truth and the most exact fidelity all that has come to my knowledge through my own experience, or others qualified to speak of Louis XIV. during the last twenty-two years of his life: and after having shown him such as he was, without prejudice (although I have permitted myself to use the arguments naturally resulting from things), nothing remains but to describe the outside life of this monarch, during my residence at the Court.

However insipid and perhaps superfluous details so well known may appear after what has been already given, lessons will be found therein for kings who may wish to make themselves respected, and who may wish to respect themselves. What determines me still more is, that details wearying, nay annoying, to instructed readers, who had been witnesses of what I relate, soon escape the knowledge of posterity; and that experience shows us how much we regret that no one takes upon himself a labour, in his own time so ungrateful, but in future years so interesting, and by which princes, who have made quite as much stir as the one in question, are characterise. Although it may be difficult to steer clear of repetitions, I will do my best to avoid them.

I will not speak much of the King's manner of living when with the army. His hours were determined by what was to be done, though he held his councils regularly; I will simply say, that morning and evening he ate with people privileged to have that honour. When any one wished to claim it, the first gentleman of the chamber on duty was appealed to. He gave the answer, and if favourable you presented yourself the next day to the King, who said to you, "Monsieur, seat yourself at table." That being done, all was done. Ever afterwards you were at liberty to take a place at the King's table, but with discretion. The number of the persons from whom a choice was made was, however, very limited. Even very high military rank did not suffice. M. de Vauban, at the siege of Namur, was overwhelmed by the distinction. The King did the same honour at Namur to the Abbe de Grancey, who exposed himself everywhere to confess the wounded and encourage the troops. No other Abbe was ever so distinguished. All the clergy were excluded save the cardinals, and the bishops, piers, or the ecclesiastics who held the rank of foreign princes.

At these repasts everybody was covered; it would have been a want of respect, of which you would have been immediately informed, if you had not kept your hat on your head. The King alone was uncovered. When the King wished to speak to you, or you had occasion to speak to him, you uncovered. You uncovered, also, when Monseigneur or Monsieur spoke to you, or you to them. For Princes of the blood you merely put your hand to your hat. The King alone had an armchair. All the rest of the company, Monseigneur included, had seats, with backs of black morocco leather, which could be folded up to be carried, and which were called "parrots." Except at the army, the King never ate with any man, under whatever circumstances; not even with the Princes of the Blood, save sometimes at their wedding feasts.

Let us return now to the Court.

At eight o'clock the chief valet de chambre on duty, who alone had slept in the royal chamber, and who had dressed himself, awoke the King. The chief physician, the chief surgeon, and the nurse (as long as she lived), entered at the same time; the latter kissed the King; the others rubbed and often changed his shirt, because he was in the habit of sweating a great deal. At the quarter, the grand chamberlain was called (or, in his absence, the first gentleman of the chamber), and those who had what was called the 'grandes entrees'. The chamberlain (or chief gentleman) drew back the curtains which had been closed again; and presented the holy- water from the vase, at the head of the bed. These gentlemen stayed but a moment, and that was the time to speak to the King, if any one had anything to ask of him; in which case the rest stood aside. When, contrary to custom, nobody had ought to say, they were there but for a few moments. He who had opened the curtains and presented the holy- water, presented also a prayer-book. Then all passed into the cabinet of the council. A very short religious service being over, the King called, they re-entered, The same officer gave him his dressing-gown; immediately after, other privileged courtiers entered, and then everybody, in time to find the King putting on his shoes and stockings, for he did almost everything himself and with address and grace. Every other day we saw him shave himself; and he had a little short wig in which he always appeared, even in bed, and on medicine days. He often spoke of the chase, and sometimes said a-word to somebody. No toilette table was near him; he had simply a mirror held before him.

As soon as he was dressed, he prayed to God, at the side of his bed, where all the clergy present knelt, the cardinals without cushions, all the laity remaining standing; and the captain of the guards came to the balustrade during the prayer, after which the King passed into his cabinet.

He found there, or was followed by all who had the entree, a very numerous company, for it included everybody in any office. He gave orders to each for the day; thus within a half a quarter of an hour it was known what he meant to do; and then all this crowd left directly. The bastards, a few favourites; and the valets alone were left. It was then a good opportunity for talking with the King; for example, about plans of gardens and buildings; and conversation lasted more or less according to the person engaged in it.

All the Court meantime waited for the King in the gallery, the captain of the guard being alone in the chamber seated at the door of the cabinet. At morning the Court awaited in the saloon; at Trianon in the front rooms as at Meudon; at Fontainebleau in the chamber and ante-chamber. During this pause the King gave audiences when he wished to accord any; spoke with whoever he might wish to speak secretly to, and gave secret interviews to foreign ministers in presence of Torcy. They were called "secret" simply to distinguish them from the uncommon ones by the bedsides.

The King went to mass, where his musicians always sang an anthem. He did not go below— except on grand fetes or at ceremonies. Whilst he was going to and returning from mass, everybody spoke to him who wished, after apprising the captain of the guard, if they were not distinguished; and he came and went by the door of the cabinet into the gallery. During the mass the ministers assembled in the King's chamber, where distinguished people could go and speak or chat with them. The King amused himself a little upon returning from mass and asked almost immediately for the council. Then the morning was finished.

On Sunday, and often on Monday, there was a council of state; on Tuesday a finance council; on Wednesday council of state; on Saturday finance council: rarely were two held in one day or any on Thursday or Friday. Once or twice a month there was a council of despatches on Monday morning; but the order that the Secretaries of State took every morning between the King's rising and his mass, much abridged this kind of business. All the ministers were seated accordingly to rank, except at the council of despatches, where all stood except the sons of France, the Chancellor, and the Duc de Beauvilliers.

Thursday morning was almost always blank. It was the day for audiences that the King wished to give—often unknown to any—back-stair audiences. It was also the grand day taken advantage of by the bastards, the valets, etc., because the King had nothing to do. On Friday after the mass the King was with his confessor, and the length of their audiences was limited by nothing, and might last until dinner. At Fontainebleau on the mornings when there was no council, the King usually passed from mass to Madame de Maintenon's, and so at Trianon and Marly. It was the time for their tete-a-tete without interruption. Often on the days when there was no council the dinner hour was advanced, more or less for the chase or the promenade. The ordinary hour was one o'clock; if the council still lasted, then the dinner waited and nothing was said to the King.

The dinner was always 'au petit couvert', that is, the King ate by himself in his chamber upon a square table in front of the middle window. It was more or less abundant, for he ordered in the morning whether it was to be "a little," or "very little" service. But even at this last, there were always many dishes, and three courses without counting the fruit. The dinner being ready, the principal courtiers entered; then all who were known; and the gentleman of the chamber on duty informed the King.

I have seen, but very rarely, Monseigneur and his sons standing at their dinners, the King not offering them a seat. I have continually seen there the Princes of the blood and the cardinals. I have often seen there also Monsieur, either on arriving from Saint-Cloud to see the King, or arriving from the council of despatches (the only one he entered), give the King his napkin and remain standing. A little while afterwards, the King, seeing that he did not go away, asked him if he would not sit down; he bowed, and the King ordered a seat to be brought for him. A stool was put behind him. Some moments after the King said, "Nay then, sit down, my brother." Monsieur bowed and seated himself until the end of the dinner, when he presented the napkin.

At other times when he came from Saint-Cloud, the King, on arriving at the table, asked for a plate for Monsieur, or asked him if he would dine. If he refused, he went away a moment after, and there was no mention of a seat; if he accepted, the King asked for a plate for him. The table was square, he placed himself at one end, his back to the cabinet. Then the Grand Chamberlain (or the first gentleman of the chamber) gave him drink and plates, taking them from him as he finished with them, exactly as he served the King; but Monsieur received all this attention with strongly marked politeness. When he dined thus with the King he much enlivened the conversation. The King ordinarily spoke little at table unless some family favourite was near. It was the same at hid rising. Ladies scarcely ever were seen at these little dinners.

I have, however, seen the Marechale de la Mothe, who came in because she had been used to do so as governess to the children of France, and who received a seat, because she was a Duchess. Grand dinners were very rare, and only took place on grand occasions, and then ladies were present.

Upon leaving the table the King immediately entered his cabinet. That was the time for distinguished people to speak to him. He stopped at the door a moment to listen, then entered; very rarely did any one follow him, never without asking him for permission to do so; and for this few had the courage. If followed he placed himself in the embrasure of the window nearest to the door of the cabinet, which immediately closed of itself, and which you were obliged to open yourself on quitting the King. This also was the time for the bastards and the valets.

The King amused himself by feeding his dogs, and remained with them more or less time, then asked for his wardrobe, changed before the very few distinguished people it pleased the first gentleman of the chamber to admit there, and immediately went out by the back stairs into the court of marble to get into his coach. From the bottom of that staircase to the coach, any one spoke to him who wished.

The King was fond of air, and when deprived of it his health suffered; he had headaches and vapours caused by the undue use he had formerly made of perfumes, so that for many years he could not endure any, except the odour of orange flowers; therefore if you had to approach anywhere near him you did well not to carry them.

As he was but little sensitive to heat or cold, or even to rain, the weather was seldom sufficiently bad to prevent his going abroad. He went out for three objects: stag-hunting, once or more each week; shooting in his parks (and no man handled a gun with more grace or skill), once or twice each week; and walking in his gardens for exercise, and to see his workmen. Sometimes he made picnics with ladies, in the forest at Marly or at Fontainebleau, and in this last place, promenades with all the Court around the canal, which was a magnificent spectacle. Nobody followed him in his other promenades but those who held principal offices, except at Versailles or in the gardens of Trianon. Marly had a privilege unknown to the other places. On going out from the chateau, the King said aloud, "Your hats, gentlemen," and immediately courtiers, officers of the guard, everybody, in fact, covered their heads, as he would have been much displeased had they not done so; and this lasted all the promenade, that is four or five hours in summer, or in other seasons, when he dined early at Versailles to go and walk at Marly, and not sleep there.

The stag-hunting parties were on an extensive scale. At Fontainebleau every one went who wished; elsewhere only those were allowed to go who had obtained the permission once for all, and those who had obtained leave to wear the justau-corps, which was a blue uniform with silver and gold lace, lined with red. The King did not like too many people at these parties. He did not care for you to go if you were not fond of the chase. He thought that ridiculous, and never bore ill-will to those who stopped away altogether.

It was the same with the play-table, which he liked to see always well frequented—with high stakes—in the saloon at Marly, for lansquenet and other games. He amused himself at

Fontainebleau during bad weather by seeing good players at tennis, in which he had formerly excelled; and at Marly by seeing mall played, in which he had also been skilful. Sometimes when there was no council, he would make presents of stuff, or of silverware, or jewels, to the ladies, by means of a lottery, for the tickets of which they paid nothing. Madame de Maintenon drew lots with the others, and almost always gave at once what she gained. The King took no ticket.

Upon returning home from walks or drives, anybody, as I have said, might speak to the King from the moment he left his coach till he reached the foot of his staircase. He changed his dress again, and rested in his cabinet an hour or more, then went to Madame de Maintenon's, and on the way any one who wished might speak to him.

At ten o'clock his supper was served. The captain of the guard announced this to him. A quarter of an hour after the King came to supper, and from the antechamber of Madame de Maintenon to the table—again, any one spoke to him who wished. This supper was always on a grand scale, the royal household (that is, the sons and daughters of France) at table, and a large number of courtiers and ladies present, sitting or standing, and on the evening before the journey to Marly all those ladies who wished to take part in it. That was called presenting yourself for Marly. Men asked in the morning, simply saying to the King, "Sire, Marly." In later years the King grew tired of this, and a valet wrote up in the gallery the names of those who asked. The ladies continued to present themselves.

After supper the King stood some moments, his back to the balustrade of the foot of his bed, encircled by all his Court; then, with bows to the ladies, passed into his cabinet, where, on arriving, he gave his orders.

He passed a little less than an hour there, seated in an armchair, with his legitimate children and bastards, his grandchildren, legitimate and otherwise, and their husbands or wives. Monsieur in another armchair; the Princesses upon stools, Monseigneur and all the other Princes standing.

The King, wishing to retire, went and fed his dogs; then said good night, passed into his chamber to the 'ruelle' of his bed, where he said his prayers, as in the morning, then undressed. He said good night with an inclination of the head, and whilst everybody was leaving the room stood at the corner of the mantelpiece, where he gave the order to the colonel of the guards alone. Then commenced what was called the 'petit coucher', at which only the specially privileged remained. That was short. They did not leave until be got into bed. It was a moment to speak to him. Then all left if they saw any one buckle to the King. For ten or twelve years before he died the 'petit coucher' ceased, in consequence of a long attack of gout be had had; so that the Court was finished at the rising from supper.

On medicine days, which occurred about once a month, the King remained in bed, then heard mass. The royal household came to see him for a moment, and Madame de Maintenon seated herself in the armchair at the head of his bed. The King dined in bed about three o'clock, everybody being allowed to enter the room, then rose, and the privileged alone remained. He passed afterwards into his cabinet, where he held a council, and afterwards went, as usual, to Madame de Maintenon's and supped at ten o'clock, according to custom.

During all his life, the King failed only once in his attendance at mass, It was with the army, during a forced march; he missed no fast day, unless really indisposed. Some days before Lent, he publicly declared that he should be very much displeased if any one ate meat or gave it to others, under any pretext. He ordered the grand prevot to look to this, and report all cases of disobedience. But no one dared to disobey his commands, for they would soon have found out the cost. They extended even to Paris, where the lieutenant of police kept watch and reported. For twelve or fifteen years he had himself not observed Lent, however. At church he was very respectful. During his mass everybody was obliged to kneel at the Sanctus, and to remain so until after the communion of the priest; and if he heard the least noise, or saw anybody talking during the mass, he was much displeased. He took the communion five times a year, in the collar of the Order, band, and cloak. On Holy Thursday, he served the poor at dinner; at the mass he said his chaplet (he knew no more), always kneeling, except at the Gospel.

He was always clad in dresses more or less brown, lightly embroidered, but never at the edges, sometimes with nothing but a gold button, sometimes black velvet. He wore always a vest of cloth, or of red, blue, or green satin, much embroidered. He used no ring; and no jewels, except in the buckles of his shoes, garters, and hat, the latter always trimmed with Spanish point, with a white feather. He had always the cordon bleu outside, except at fetes, when he wore it inside, with eight or ten millions of precious stones attached.

Rarely a fortnight passed that the King did not go to Saint-Germain, even after the death of King James the Second. The Court of Saint-Germain came also to Versailles, but oftener to Marly, and frequently to sup there; and no fete or ceremony took place to which they were not invited, and at which they were not received with all honours. Nothing could compare with the politeness of the King for this Court, or with the air of gallantry and of majesty with which he received it at any time. Birth days, or the fete days of the King and his family, so observed in the courts of Europe, were always unknown in that of the King; so that there never was the slightest mention of them, or any difference made on their account.

The King was but little regretted. His valets and a few other people felt his loss, scarcely anybody else. His successor was not yet old enough to feel anything. Madame entertained for him only fear and considerate respect. Madame la Duchesse de Berry did not like him, and counted now upon reigning undisturbed. M. le Duc d'Orleans could scarcely be expected to feel much grief for him. And those who may have been expected did not consider it necessary to do their duty. Madame de Maintenon was wearied with him ever since the death of the Dauphine; she knew not what to do, or with what to amuse him; her constraint was tripled because he was much more with her than before. She had often, too, experienced much ill-humour from him. She had attained all she wished, so whatever she might lose in losing him, she felt herself relieved, and was capable of no other sentiment at first. The ennui and emptiness of her life afterwards made her feel regret. As for M. du Maine, the barbarous indecency of his joy need not be dwelt upon. The icy tranquillity of his brother, the Comte de Toulouse, neither increased nor diminished. Madame la Duchesse d'Orleans surprised me. I had expected some grief, I perceived only a few tears, which upon all occasions flowed very readily from her eyes, and which were soon dried up. Her bed, which she was very fond of, supplied what was wanting during several days, amidst obscurity which she by no means disliked.

But the window curtains were soon withdrawn and grief disappeared.

As for the Court, it was divided into two grand parties, the men hoping to figure, to obtain employ, to introduce themselves: and they were ravished to see the end of a reign under which they had nothing to hope for; the others; fatigued with a heavy yoke, always overwhelming, and of the ministers much more than of the King, were charmed to find themselves at liberty. Thus all, generally speaking, were glad to be delivered from continual restraint, and were eager for change.

Paris, tired of a dependence which had enslaved everything, breathed again in the hope of liberty, and with joy at seeing at an end the authority of so many people who abused it. The provinces in despair at their ruin and their annihilation breathed again and leaped for joy; and the Parliament and the robe destroyed by edicts and by revolutions, flattered themselves the first that they should figure, the other that they should find themselves free. The people ruined, overwhelmed, desperate, gave thanks to God, with a scandalous eclat, for a deliverance, their most ardent desires had not anticipated.

Foreigners delighted to be at last, after so many years, quit of a monarch who had so long imposed his law upon them, and who had escaped from them by a species of miracle at the very moment in which they counted upon having subjugated him, contained themselves with much more decency than the French. The marvels of the first three quarters of this reign of more than seventy years, and the personal magnanimity of this King until then so successful, and so abandoned afterwards by fortune during the last quarter of his reign—had justly dazzled them. They made it a point of honour to render to him after his death what they had constantly refused him during life. No foreign Court exulted: all plumed themselves upon praising and honouring his memory. The Emperor wore mourning as for a father, and although four or five months elapsed between the death of the King and the Carnival, all kinds of amusements were prohibited at Vienna during the Carnival, and the prohibition was strictly observed. A monstrous fact was, that towards the end of this period there was a single ball and a kind of fete that the Comte du Luc our own ambassador, was not ashamed to give to the ladies, who seduced him by the ennui of so dull a Carnival. This complaisance did not raise him in estimation at Vienna or elsewhere. In France people were contented with ignoring it.

As for our ministry and the intendants of the provinces, the financiers and what may be called the canaille, they felt all the extent of their loss. We shall see if the realm was right or wrong in the sentiments it held, and whether it found soon after that it had gained or lost.

To finish at once all that regards the King, let me here say, that his entrails were taken to Notre Dame, on the 4th of September, without any ceremony, by two almoners of the King, without accompaniment. On Friday, the 6th of September, the Cardinal de Rohan carried the heart to the Grand Jesuits, with very little accompaniment or pomp. Except the persons necessary for the ceremony, not half a dozen courtiers were present. It is not for me to comment upon this prompt ingratitude, I, who for fifty-two years have never once missed going to Saint-Denis on the anniversary of the death of Louis XIII., and have never seen a single person there on the same errand. On the 9th of September, the body of the late King was buried at Saint-Denis. The Bishop of Aleth pronounced the oration. Very little expense was gone to; and nobody was found who cared sufficiently for the late King to murmur at the economy. On Friday, the 25th of October, his solemn obsequies took place at Saint- Denis in a confusion, as to rank and precedence, without example. On Thursday, the 28th of November, the solemn obsequies were again performed, this time at Notre Dame, and with the usual ceremonies.

CHAPTER LXXIX

The death of the King surprised M. le Duc d'Orleans in the midst of his idleness as though it had not been foreseen. He had made no progress in numberless arrangements, which I had suggested he should carry out; accordingly he was overwhelmed with orders to give, with things to settle, each more petty than the other, but all so provisional and so urgent that it happened as I had predicted, he had no time to think of anything important.

I learnt the death of the King upon awaking. Immediately after, I went to pay my respects to the new monarch. The first blood had already passed. I found myself almost alone. I went thence to M. le Duc d'Orleans, whom I found shut in, but all his apartments so full that a pin could not have fallen to the ground. I talked of the Convocation of the States-General, and reminded him of a promise he had given me, that he would allow the Dukes to keep their hats on when their votes were asked for; and I also mentioned various other promises he had made. All I could obtain from him was another promise, that when the public affairs of pressing moment awaiting attention were disposed of, we should have all we required. Several of the Dukes who had been witnesses of the engagement M. le Duc d'Orleans had made, were much vexed at this; but ultimately it was agreed that for the moment we would sacrifice our own particular interests to those of the State.

Between five and six the next morning a number of us met at the house of the Archbishop of Rheims at the end of the Pont Royal, behind the Hotel de Mailly, and there, in accordance with a resolution previously agreed upon, it was arranged that I should make a protest to the Parliament before the opening of the King's will there, against certain other usurpations, and state that it was solely because M. le Duc d'Orleans had given us his word that our complaints should be attended to as soon as the public affairs of the government were settled, that we postponed further measures upon this subject. It was past seven before our debate ended, and then we went straight to the Parliament.

We found it already assembled, and a few Dukes who had not attended our meeting, but had promised to be guided by us, were also present; and then a quarter of an hour after we were seated the bastards arrived. M. du Maine was bursting with joy; the term is strange, but his bearing cannot otherwise be described. The smiling and satisfied air prevailed over that of audacity and of confidence, which shone, nevertheless, and over politeness which seemed to struggle with them. He saluted right and left, and pierced everybody with his looks. His salutation to the Presidents had an air of rejoicing. To the peers he was serious, nay, respectful; the slowness, the lowness of his inclination, was eloquent. His head remained lowered even when he rose, so heavy is the weight of crime, even at the moment when nothing but triumph is expected. I rigidly followed him everywhere with my eyes, and I remarked that his salute was returned by the peers in a very dry and cold manner.

Scarcely were we re-seated than M. le Duc arrived, and the instant after M. le Duc d'Orleans. I allowed the stir that accompanied his appearance to subside a little, and then, seeing that the Chief-President was about to speak, I forestalled him, uncovered my head, and then covered it, and made my speech in the terms agreed upon. I concluded by appealing to M. le Duc d'Orleans to verify the truth of what I had said, in so far as it affected him.

The profound silence with which I was listened to showed the surprise of all present. M. le Duc d'Orleans uncovered himself, and in a low tone, and with an embarrassed manner, confirmed what I had said, then covered himself again.

Immediately afterwards I looked at M. du Maine, who appeared, to be well content at being let off so easily, and who, my neighbours said to me, appeared much troubled at my commencement.

A very short silence followed my protest, after which I saw the Chief- President say something in a low tone to M. le Duc d'Orleans, then arrange a deputation of the Parliament to go in search of the King's will, and its codicil, which had been put in the same place. Silence continued during this great and short period of expectation; every one looked at his neighbour without stirring. We were all upon the lower seats, the doors were supposed to be closed, but the grand chamber was filled with a large and inquisitive crowd. The regiment of guards had secretly occupied all the avenues, commanded by the Duc de Guiche, who got six hundred thousand francs out of the Duc d'Orleans for this service, which was quite unnecessary.

The deputation was not long in returning. It placed the will and the codicil in the hands of the Chief-President, who presented them, without parting with them, to M. le Duc d'Orleans, then passed them from hand to hand to Dreux, 'conseiller' of the Parliament, and father of the grand master of the ceremonies, saying that he read well, and in a loud voice that would he well heard by everybody. It may be imagined with what silence he was listened to, and how all eyes? and ears were turned towards him. Through all his; joy the Duc du Maine showed that his soul was, troubled, as though about to undergo an operation that he must submit to. M. le Duc d'Orleans showed only a tranquil attention.

I will not dwell upon these two documents, in which nothing is provided but the grandeur and the power of the bastards, Madame de Maintenon and Saint-Cyr, the choice of the King's education and of the council of the regency, by which M. le Duc d'Orleans was to be shorn of all authority to the advantage of M. le Duc du Maine.

I remarked a sadness and a kind of indignation which were painted upon all cheeks, as the reading advanced, and which turned into a sort of tranquil fermentation at the reading of the codicil, which was entrusted to the Abbe Menguy, another conseiller. The Duc du Maine felt it and grew pale, for he was solely occupied in looking at every face, and I in following his looks, and in glancing occasionally at M. le Duc d'Orleans.

The reading being finished, that prince spoke, casting his eyes upon all the assembly, uncovering himself, and then covering himself again, and commencing by a word of praise and of regret for the late King; afterwards raising his voice, he declared that he had only to approve everything just read respecting the education of the King, and everything respecting an establishment so fine and so useful as that of Saint-Cyr; that with respect to the dispositions concerning the government of the state, he would speak separately of those in the will and those in the codicil; that he could with difficulty harmonise them with the assurances the King, during the last days of his life, had given him; that the King could not have understood the importance of what he had been made to do for the Duc du Maine since the council of the regency was chosen, and M. du Maine's authority so established by the will, that the Regent remained almost without power; that this injury done to the rights of his birth, to his attachment to the person of the King, to his love and fidelity for the state, could not be endured if he was to preserve his honour; and that he hoped sufficiently from the esteem of all present, to persuade himself that his regency would be declared as it ought to be, that is to say, complete, independent, and that he should be allowed to choose his own council, with the members of which he would not discuss public affairs, unless they were persons who, being approved by the public, might also have his confidence. This short speech appeared to make a great impression.

The Duc du Maine wished to speak. As he was about to do so, M. le Duc d'Orleans put his head in front of M. le Duc and said, in a dry tone, "Monsieur, you will speak in your turn." In one moment the affair turned according to the desires of M. le Duc d'Orleans. The power of the council of the regency and its composition fell. The choice of the council was awarded to M. le Duc d'Orleans, with all the authority of the regency, and to the plurality of the votes of the council, the decision of affairs, the vote of the Regent to be counted as two in the event of an equal division. Thus all favours and all punishments remained in the hands of M. le Duc d'Orleans alone. The acclamation was such that the Duc du Maine did not dare to say a word. He reserved himself for the codicil, which, if adopted, would have annulled all that M. le Duc d'Orleans had just obtained.

After some few moments of silence, M. le Duc d'Orleans spoke again. He testified fresh surprise that the dispositions of the will had not been sufficient for those who had suggested them, and that, not content with having established themselves as masters of the state, they themselves should have thought those dispositions so strange that in order to reassure them, it had been thought necessary to make them masters of the person of the King, of the Regent, of the Court, and of Paris. He added, that if his honour and all law and rule had been wounded by the dispositions of the will, still more violated were they by those of the codicil, which left neither his life nor his liberty in safety, and placed the person of the King in the absolute dependence of those who had dared to profit by the feeble state of a dying monarch, to draw from him conditions he did not understand. He concluded by declaring that the regency was impossible under such conditions, and that he doubted not the wisdom of the assembly would annul a codicil which could not be sustained, and the regulations of which would plunge France into the greatest and most troublesome misfortune. Whilst this prince spoke a profound and sad silence applauded him without explaining itself.

The Duc du Maine became of all colours, and began to speak, this time being allowed to do so. He said that the education of the King, and consequently his person, being confided to him, as a natural result, entire authority over his civil and military household followed, without which he could not properly serve him or answer for his person. Then he vaunted his well-known attachment to the deceased King, who had put all confidence in him.

M. le Duc d'Orleans interrupted him at this word, and commented upon it. M. du Maine wished to calm him by praising the Marechal de Villeroy, who was to assist him in his charge. M. le Duc d'Orleans replied that it would be strange if the chief and most complete confidence were not placed in the Regent, and stranger still if he were obliged to live under the protection and authority of those who had rendered themselves the absolute masters within and without, and of Paris even, by the regiment of guards.

The dispute grew warm, broken phrases were thrown from one to the other, when, troubled about the end of an altercation which became indecent and yielding to the proposal that the Duc de la Force had just made me in front of the Duc de la Rochefoucauld, who sat between us, I made a sign with my hand to M. le Duc d'Orleans to go out and finish this discussion in another room leading out of the grand chamber and where there was nobody. What led me to this action was that I perceived M. du Maine grew stronger, that confused murmurs for a division were heard, and that M. le Duc d'Orleans did not shine to the best advantage since he descended to plead his cause, so to speak, against that of the Duc du Maine.

M. le Duc d'Orleans was short-sighted. He was entirely absorbed in attacking and repelling; so that he did not see the sign I made. Some moments after I increased it, and meeting with no more success, rose, advanced some steps, and said to him, though rather distant, "Monsieur, if you passed into the fourth chamber with M. du Maine you could speak there more easily," and advancing nearer at the same time I pressed him by a sign of the head and the eyes that he could distinguish. He replied to me with another sign, and scarcely was I reseated than I saw him advance in front of M. le Duc to the Duc du Maine, and immediately after both rose and went into the chamber I had indicated. I could not see who of the scattered group around followed them, for all present rose at their departure, and seated themselves again directly in complete silence. Some time after, M. le Comte de Toulouse left his place and went into the Chamber. M. le Duc followed him in a little while soon again the Duc de la Force did the same.

He did not stay long. Returning to the assembly; he passed the Duc de la Rochefoucauld and me, put his head between that of the Duc de Sully and mine, because he did not wish to be heard by La Rochefoucauld, and said to me, "In the name of God go there; things are getting on badly. M. le Duc d'Orleans gives way; stop the dispute; make M. le Duc d'Orleans come back; and, as soon as he is in his place, let him say that it is too late to finish, that the company had better go to dinner, and return to finish afterwards, and during this interval," added La Force, "send the King's people to the Palais Royal, and let doubtful peers be spoken to, and the chiefs among other magistrates."

The advice appeared to me good and important. I left the assembly and went to the chamber. I found a large circle of spectators. M. le Duc d'Orleans and the Duc du Maine stood before the fireplace, looking both very excited. I looked at this spectacle some moments; then approached the mantelpiece like a man who wishes to speak. "What is this, Monsieur?" said M. le Duc d'Orleans to me, with an impatient manner. "A pressing word, Monsieur, that I have to say to you," said I. He continued speaking to the Duc du Maine, I being close by. I redoubled my instances; he lent me his ear. "No, no," said I, "not like that, come here," and I took him into a corner by the chimney. The Comte de Toulouse, who was there, drew completely back, and all the circle on that side. The Duc du Maine drew back also from where he was.

I said to M. le Duc d'Orleans, in his ear, that he could not hope to gain anything from M. du Maine, who would not sacrifice the codicil to his reasonings; that the length of their conference became indecent, useless, dangerous; that he was making a sight of himself to all who entered; that the only thing to be done was to return to the assembly, and, when there, dissolve it. "You are right," said he, "I will do it."—"But," said I, "do it immediately, and do not allow yourself to be amused. It is to M. de la Force you owe this advice: he sent me to give it you." He quitted me without another word, went to M. du Maine, told him in two words that it was too late, and that the matter must be finished after dinner.

I had remained where he left me. I saw the Duc du Maine bow to him immediately, and the two separated, and retired at the same moment into the assembly.

The noise which always accompanies these entrances being appeased, M. le Duc d'Orleans said it was too late to abuse the patience of the company any longer; that dinner must be eaten, and the work finished afterwards. He immediately added, he believed it fitting that M. le Duc should enter the council of the regency as its chief; and that since the company had rendered the justice due to his birth and his position as Regent, he would explain what he thought upon the form to be given to the government, and that meanwhile he profited by the power he had to avail himself of the knowledge and the wisdom of the company, and restored to them from that time their former liberty of remonstrance. These words were followed by striking and general applause, and the assembly was immediately adjourned.

I was invited this day to dine with the Cardinal de Noailles, but I felt the importance of employing the time so precious and so short, of the interval of dinner, and of not quitting M. le Duc d'Orleans, according to a suggestion of M. le Duc de la Force. I approached M. le Duc d'Orleans, and said in his ear, "The moments are precious: I will follow you to the Palais Royal," and went back to my place among the peers. Jumping into my coach, I sent a gentleman with my excuses to the Cardinal de Noailles, saying, I would tell him the reason of my absence afterwards. Then I went to the Palais Royal, where curiosity had gathered together all who were not at the palace, and even some who had been there. All the acquaintances I met asked me the news with eagerness. I contented myself with replying that everything went well, and according to rule, but that all was not yet finished.

M. le Duc d'Orleans had passed into a cabinet, where I found him alone with Canillac, who had waited for him. We took our measures there, and M. le Duc d'Orleans sent for the Attorney-General, D'Aguesseau, afterwards Chancellor, and the chief Advocate-General, Joly de Fleury, since Attorney-General. It was nearly two o'clock. A little dinner was served, of which Canillac, Conflans, M. le Duc d'Orleans, and myself partook; and I will say this, by the way, I never dined with him but once since, namely, at Bagnolet.

We returned to the Parliament a little before four o'clock. I arrived there alone in my carriage, a moment before M. le Duc d'Orleans, and found everybody assembled. I was looked at with much curiosity, as it seemed to me. I am not aware if it was known whence I came. I took care that my bearing should say nothing. I simply said to the Duc de la Force that his advice had been salutary, that I had reason to hope all success from it, and that I had told M. le Duc d'Orleans whence it came. That Prince arrived, and (the hubbub inseparable from such a numerous suite being appeased) he said that matters must be recommenced from the point where they had been broken off in the morning; that it was his duty to say to the Court that in nothing had he agreed with M. du Maine and to bring again before all eyes the monstrous clauses of a codicil, drawn from a dying prince; clauses much more strange than the dispositions of the testament that the Court had not deemed fit to be put in execution, and that the Court could not allow M. du Maine to be master of the person of the King, of the camp, of Paris, consequently of the State, of the person, life, and liberty of the Regent, whom he would be in a position to arrest at any moment as soon as he became the absolute and independent master of the civil and military household of the King; that the Court saw what must inevitably result from an unheard-of novelty, which placed everything in the hands of M. du Maine; and that he left it to the enlightenment, to the prudence, to the wisdom, to the equity of the company, and its love for the State, to declare what they thought on this subject.

M. du Maine appeared then as contemptible in the broad open daylight as he had appeared redoubtable in the obscurity of the cabinets. He had the look of one condemned, and his face, generally so fresh-coloured, was now as pale as death. He replied in a very low and scarcely intelligible voice, and with an air as respectful and as humble as it had been audacious in the morning.

People opined without listening to him; and tumultuously, but with one voice, the entire abrogation of the codicil was passed. This was premature, as the abrogation of the testament had been in the morning— both caused by sudden indignation. D'Aguesseau and Fleury both spoke, the first in a few words, the other at greater length, making a very good speech. As it exists, in the libraries, I will only say that the conclusions of both orators were in everything favourable to M. le Duc d'Orleans.

After they had spoken, the Duc du Maine, seeing himself totally shorn, tried a last resource. He represented, with more force than could have been expected from his demeanour at this second sitting, but yet with measure, that since he had been stripped of the authority confided to him by the codicil, he asked to be discharged from the responsibility of answering for the person of the King, and to be allowed simply to preserve the superintendence of his education. M, le Duc d'Orleans replied, "With all my heart, Monsieur; nothing more is wanted." Thereupon the Chief. President formally put the question to the vote. A decree was passed by which all power was taken from the hands of M. du Maine and placed in those of the Regent, with the right of placing whom he pleased in the council; of dismissing anybody as it should seem good to him; and of doing all he might think fit respecting the form to be given to the government; authority over public affairs, nevertheless, to remain with the council, and decision to be taken by the plurality of votes, the vote of the Regent to count double in case of equal division; M. le Duc to be chief of the council under him, with the right to enter it at once and opine there.

During all this time, and until the end of the sitting, M. du Maine had his eyes always cast down, looked more dead than alive, and appeared motionless. His son and his brother gave no sign of taking interest in anything.

The decree was followed by loud acclamations of the crowd scattered outside, and that which filled the rest of the palace replied as soon as they learnt what had been decided.

This noise, which lasted some time, being appeased, the Regent thanked the company in brief, polished, and majestic terms; declared with what care he would employ for the good of the state, the authority with which he was invested; then said it was time he should inform them what he judged ought to be established in order to aid him in the administration of affairs. He added that he did so with the more confidence, because what he proposed was exactly what M. le Duc de Bourgogne ('twas thus he named him) had resolved, as shown by papers found in his bureau. He passed a short and graceful eulogy upon the enlightenment and intentions of that prince; then declared that, besides the council of the regency, which would be the supreme centre from which all the affairs of the government would spring, he proposed to establish a council for foreign affairs, one for war, one for the navy, one for finance, one for ecclesiastical matters, and one for home affairs and to choose some of the magistrates of the company to enter these last two councils, and aid them by their knowledge upon the police of the realm, the jurisprudence, and what related to the liberties of the Gallican church.

The applause of the magistrates burst out at this, and all the crowd replied to it. The Chief-President concluded the sitting by a very short compliment to the Regent, who rose, and at the same time all the assembly, which then broke up.

On Friday, the 6th of September, 1715, the Regent performed an action of most exquisite merit, if it had been actuated by the love of God, but which was of the utmost meanness, religion having no connection with it. He went at eight o'clock in the morning to see Madame de Maintenon at Saint-Cyr. He was nearly an hour with this enemy, who had wished to cut off his head, and who quite recently had sought to deliver him, tied hand and foot, to M. du Maine, by the monstrous dispositions of the King's will and codicil.

The Regent assured her during this visit that the four thousand livres the King had given her every month should be continued, and should be brought to her the first day of every month by the Duc de Noailles, who had apparently induced the Prince to pay this visit, and promise this present. He said to Madame de Maintenon that if she wished for more she had only to speak, and assured her he would protect Saint-Cyr. In leaving he was shown the young girls, all together in classes.

It must be remembered, that besides the estate of Maintenon, and the other property of this famous and fatal witch, the establishment of Saint-Cyr, which had more than four hundred thousand livres yearly income, and much money in reserve, was obliged by the rules which founded it, to receive Madame de Maintenon, if she wished to retire there; to obey her in all things, as the absolute and sole superior; to keep her and everybody connected with her, her domestics, her equipages, as she wished, her table, etc., at the expense of the house, all of which was very punctually done until her death. Thus she needed not this generous liberality, by which her pension of forty-eight thousand livres was continued to her. It would have been quite enough if M. le Duc d'Orleans had forgotten that she was in existence, and had simply left her untroubled in Saint-Cyr.

The Regent took good care not to inform me of his visit, before or after; and I took good care not to reproach him with it, or make him ashamed of it. It made much noise, and was not approved of. The Spanish affair was not yet forgotten, and the will and codicil furnished other matter for all conversations.

CHAPTER LXXX

Saturday, the 7th of September, was the day fixed for the first Bed of Justice of the King (Louis XV.); but he caught a cold during the night, and suffered a good deal. The Regent came alone to Paris. The Parliament had assembled, and I went to a door of the palace, where I was informed of the countermand which had just arrived. The Chief-President and the King's people were at once sent for to the Palais Royal, and the Parliament, which was about to adjourn, was continued for all the rest of the month for general business. On the morrow, the Regent, who was wearied with Versailles,—for he liked to live in Paris, where all his pleasures were within easy reach,—and who met with opposition from the Court doctors, all comfortably lodged at Versailles, to the removal of the person of the King to Vincennes, under pretext of a slight cold, fetched other doctors from Paris, who had been sent for to see the deceased King. These practitioners, who had nothing to gain by recommending Versailles, laughed at the Court doctors, and upon their opinion it was resolved to take the King to Vincennes, where all was ready for him on the morrow.

He set out, then, that day from Versailles, at about two o'clock in the day, in company with the Regent, the Duchesse de Ventadour, the Duc du Maine, and the Marechal de Villeroy, passed round the ramparts of Paris, without entering the city, and arrived at Vincennes about five o'clock, many people and carriages having come out along the road to see him.

On the day after the arrival of the King at Vincennes, the Regent worked all the morning with all the Secretaries of State separately, whom he had charged to bring him the list of all the 'lettres de cachet' issued from their bureaux, and a statement of the reasons for which they were delivered, as such oftentimes were slight. The majority of the 'lettres de cachet' of exile and of imprisonment had been drawn up against Jansenists, and people who had opposed the constitution; numbers the reasons of which were known only to the deceased King, and to those who had induced him to grant them; others were of the time of previous ministers, and among them were many which had been long forgotten and unknown. The Regent restored everybody to liberty, exiles and prisoners, except those whom he knew to have been arrested for grave crimes, or affairs of State; and brought down infinite benedictions upon himself by this act of justice and humanity.

Many very singular and strange stories were then circulated, which showed the tyranny of the last reign, and of its ministers, and caused the misfortunes of the prisoners to be deplored. Among those in the Bastille was a man who had been imprisoned thirty-five years. Arrested the day he arrived in Paris, on a journey from Italy, to which country he belonged. It has never been known why he was arrested, and he had never been examined, as was the case with the majority of the others: people were persuaded a mistake had been made. When his liberty was announced to him, he sadly asked what it was expected he could do with it. He said he had not a farthing; that he did not know a soul in Paris, not even a single street, or a person in all France; that his relatives in Italy had, doubtless, died since he left; that his property, doubtless, had been divided, so many years having elapsed during which no news had been received from him; that he knew not what to do. He asked to be allowed to remain in the Bastille for the rest of his days, with food and lodging. This was granted, with as much liberty as he wished.

As for those who were taken from the dungeons where the hatred of the ministers; of the Jesuits; and of the Constitution chiefs, had cast them, the horrible state they appeared in terrified everybody, and rendered credible all the cruel stories which, as soon as they were fully at liberty, they revealed.

The same day on which this merciful decision was come to, died Madame de la Vieuville, not old, of a cancer in the breast, the existence of which she had concealed until two days before her death, and thus deprived herself of help.

A few days after, the finances being in such a bad state, the Regent made Crosat treasurer of the order, in return for which he obtained from him a loan of a million, in bars of silver, and the promise of another two million. Previous to this, the hunting establishments of the King had been much reduced. Now another retrenchment was made. There were seven intendants of the finances, who, for six hundred thousand livres, which their places had cost them, enjoyed eighty thousand livres each per annum. They were all suppressed, and simply the interest of their purchase-money paid to them; that is to say, thirty thousand livres each, until that purchase-money could be paid. It was found that there were sixteen hundred thousand francs owing to our ambassadors, and to our agents in foreign countries, the majority of whom literally had not enough to pay the postage of their letters, having spent all they possessed. This was a cruel discredit to us, all over Europe. I might fill a volume in treating upon the state and the arrangements of our finances. But this labour is above my strength, and contrary to my taste. I will simply say that as soon as money could be spared it was sent to our ambassadors abroad. They were dying of hunger, were over head and ears in debt, had fallen into utter contempt, and our affairs were suffering accordingly.

The council of the regency, let me say here, was composed of the following persons: M. le Duc d'Orleans, M. le Duc, the Duc du Maine, the Comte de Toulouse, Voysin the Chancellor, myself—since I must name myself,—Marechal de Villeroy, Marechal d'Harcourt, Marechal de Besons, the Late Bishop of Troyes, and Torcy, with a right to vote; with La Vrilliere, who kept the register, and Pontchartrain, both without the right to vote.

I have already alluded to the presence of Lord Stair at this time in our Court, as ambassador from England. By means of intrigues he had succeeded in ingratiating himself into the favour of the Regent, and in convincing him that the interests of France and England were identical. One of the reasons—the main one—which he brought forward to show this, was that King George was an usurper; and that if anything happened to our King, M. le Duc d'Orleans would become, in mounting the throne of France, an usurper also, the King of Spain being the real heir to the French monarchy; that, in consequence of this, France and England ought to march together, protect each other; France assisting England against the Pretender, and England assisting France, if need be, against the King of Spain. M. le Duc d'Orleans had too much penetration not to see this snare; but, marvellous as it may seem, the crookedness of this policy, and not the desire of reigning, seduced him. I am quite prepared, if ever these memoirs see the day, to find that this statement will be laughed at; that it will throw discredit on others, and cause me to be regarded as a great ass, if I think to make my readers, believe it; or for an idiot, if I have believed it myself. Nevertheless, such is the pure truth, to which I sacrifice all, in despite of what my readers may think of me. However incredible it may be, it is, as I say, the exact verity; and I do not hesitate to advance, that there are many such facts, unknown to history, which would much surprise if known; and which are unknown, only because scarcely any history has been written at first hand.

Stair wished, above all, to hinder the Regent from giving any assistance to the Pretender, and to prevent him passing through the realm in order to reach a seaport. Now the Regent was between two stools, for he had promised the Pretender to wink at his doings, and to favour his passage through France, if it were made secretly, and at the same time he had assented to the demand of Stair. Things had arrived at this pass when the troubles increased in England, and the Earl of Mar obtained some success in Scotland. Soon after news came that the Pretender had departed from Bar, and was making his way to the coast. Thereupon Stair ran in hot haste to M. le Duc d'Orleans to ask him to keep his promise, and hinder the Pretender's journey. The Regent immediately sent off Contade, major in the guards, very intelligent, and in whom he could trust, with his brother, a lieutenant in the same regiment, and two sergeants of their choice, to go to Chateau-Thierry, and wait for the Pretender, Stair having sure information that he would pass there. Contade set out at night on the 9th of November, well resolved and instructed to miss the person he was to seek. Stair, who expected as much, took also his measures, which were within an inch of succeeding; for this is what happened.

The Pretender set out disguised from Bar, accompanied by only three or four persons, and came to Chaillot, where M. de Lauzun had a little house, which he never visited, and which he had kept for mere fancy, although he had a house at Passy, of which he made much use. It was in this, Chaillot's house, that the Pretender put up, and where he saw the Queen, his mother, who often stopped at the Convent of the Filles de Sainte Marie-Therese. Thence he set out in a post-chaise of Torcy's, by way of Alencon, for Brittany, where he meant to embark.

Stair discovered this scheme, and resolved to leave nothing undone in order to deliver his party of this, the last of the Stuarts. He quietly despatched different people by different roads, especially by that from Paris to Alencon. He charged with this duty Colonel Douglas (who belonged to the Irish (regiments) in the pay of France), who, under the protection of his name, and by his wit and his intrigues, had insinuated himself into many places in Paris since the commencement of the regency; had placed himself on a footing of consideration and of familiarity with the Regent; and often came to my house. He was good company; had married upon the frontier of Metz; was very poor; had politeness and much experience of the world; the reputation of distinguished valour; and nothing which could render him suspected of being capable of a crime.

Douglas got into a post-chaise, accompanied by two horsemen; all three were well armed, and posted leisurely along this road. Nonancourt is a kind of little village upon this route, at nineteen leagues from Paris; between Dreux, three leagues further, and Verneuil au Perche, four leagues this side. It was at Nonancourt that he alighted, ate a morsel at the post-house, inquired with extreme solicitude after a post-chaise which he described, as well as the manner in which it would be accompanied, expressed fear lest it had already passed, and lest he had not been answered truly. After infinite inquiries, he left a third horseman, who had just reached him, on guard, with orders to inform him when the chaise he was in search of appeared; and added menaces and promises of recompense to the post people, so as not to be deceived by their negligence.

The post-master was named L'Hospital; he was absent, but his wife was in the house, and she fortunately was a very honest woman, who had wit, sense, and courage. Nonancourt is only five leagues from La Ferme, and when, to save distance, you do not pass there, they send you relays upon the road. Thus I knew very well this post-mistress, who mixed herself more in the business than her husband, and who has herself related to me this adventure more than once. She did all she could, uselessly, to obtain some explanation upon these alarms. All that she could unravel was that the strangers were Englishmen, and in a violent excitement about something, that something very important was at stake,—and that they meditated mischief. She fancied thereupon that the Pretender was in question; resolved to save him; mentally arranged her plans, and fortunately enough executed them.

In order to succeed she devoted herself to the service of these gentlemen, refused them nothing, appeared quite satisfied, and promised that they should infallibly be informed. She persuaded them of this so thoroughly, that Douglas went away without saying where, except to this third horseman just arrived, but it was close at hand; so that he might be warned in time. He took one of his valets with him; the other remained with the horseman to wait and watch.

Another man much embarrassed the post-mistress; nevertheless, she laid her plans. She proposed to the horseman to drink something, because when he arrived Douglas had left the table. She served him in her best manner, and with her best wine, and kept him at table as long as she could, anticipating all his orders. She had placed a valet, in whom she could trust, as guard, with orders simply to appear, without a word, if he saw a chaise; and her resolution was to lock up the Englishman and his servant, and to give their horses to the chaise if it came. But it came not, and the Englishman grew tired of stopping at table. Then she manoeuvred so well that she persuaded him to go and lie down, and to count upon her, her people, and upon the valet Douglas had left. The Englishman told this valet not to quit the threshold of the house, and to inform him as soon as the chaise appeared. He then suffered himself to be led to the back of the house, in order to lie down. The post- mistress, immediately after, goes to one of her friends in a by-street, relates her adventure and her suspicions, makes the friend agree to receive and secrete in her dwelling the person she expected, sends for an ecclesiastic, a relative of them both, and in whom she could repose confidence, who came and lent an Abbe's dress and wig to match. This done, Madame L'Hospital returns to her home, finds the English valet at the door, talks with him, pities his ennui, says he is a good fellow to be so particular, says that from the door to the house there is but one step, promises him that he shall be as well informed as by his own eyes, presses him to drink something, and tips the wink to a trusty postilion, who makes him drink until he rolls dead drunk under the table. During this performance, the wary mistress listens at the door of the English gentleman's room, gently turns the key and locks him in, and then establishes herself upon the threshold of her door.

Half an hour after comes the trusty valet whom she had put on guard: it was the expected chaise, which, as well as the three men who accompanied it, were made, without knowing why, to slacken speed. It was King James. Madame L'Hospital accosts him, says he is expected, and lost if he does not take care; but that he may trust in her and follow her. At once they both go to her friends. There he learns all that has happened, and they hide him, and the three men of his suite as well as they could. Madame L'Hospital returns home, sends for the officers of justice, and in consequence of her suspicions she causes the English gentleman and the English valet, the one drunk, the other asleep, locked in the room where she had left him, to be arrested, and immediately after despatches a postilion to Torcy. The officers of justice act, and send their deposition to the Court.

The rage of the English gentleman on finding himself arrested, and unable to execute the duty which led him there, and his fury against the valet who had allowed himself to be intoxicated, cannot be expressed. As for Madame L'Hospital he would have strangled her if he could; and she for a long time was afraid of her life.

The Englishman could not be induced to confess what brought him there, or where was Douglas, whom he named in order to show his importance. He declared he had been sent by the English ambassador, though Stair had not yet officially assumed that title, and exclaimed that that minister would never suffer the affront he had received. They civilly replied to him, that there were no proofs he came from the English ambassador,—none that he was connected with the minister: that very suspicious designs against public safety on the highway alone were visible; that no harm or annoyance should be caused him, but that he must remain in safety until orders came, and there upon he was civilly led to prison, as well as the intoxicated valet.

What became of Douglas at that time was never known, except that he was recognised in various places, running, inquiring, crying out with despair that he had escaped, without mentioning any name. Apparently news came to him, or he sought it, being tired of receiving none. The report of what had occurred in such a little place as Nonancourt would easily have reached him, close as he was to it; and perhaps it made him set out anew to try and catch his prey.

But he journeyed in vain. King James had remained hidden at Nonancourt, where, charmed with the attentions of his generous post-mistress, who had saved him from his assassins, he admitted to her who he was, and gave her a letter for the Queen, his mother. He remained there three days, to allow the hubbub to pass, and rob those who sought him of all hope; then, disguised as an Abbe, he jumped into a post-chaise that Madame L'Hospital had borrowed in the neighbourhood—to confound all identity—and continued his journey, during which he was always pursued, but happily was never recognised, and embarked in Brittany for Scotland.

Douglas, tired of useless searches, returned to Paris, where Stair kicked up a fine dust about the Nonancourt adventure. This he denominated nothing less than an infraction of the law of nations, with an extreme audacity and impudence, and Douglas, who could not be ignorant of what was said about him, had the hardihood to go about everywhere as usual; to show himself at the theatre; and to present himself before M. le Duc d'Orleans.

This Prince ignored as much as he could a plot so cowardly and so barbarous, and in respect to him so insolent. He kept silence, said to Stair what he judged fitting to make him be silent likewise, but gave liberty to his English assassins. Douglas, however, fell much in the favour of the Regent, and many considerable people closed their doors to him. He vainly tried to force mine. But as for me I was a perfect Jacobite, and quite persuaded that it was the interest of France to give England domestic occupation, which would long hinder her from thinking of foreign matters. I then, as may be supposed, could not look upon the odious enterprise with a favourable eye, or pardon its authors. Douglas complained to me of my disregard for him, but to no purpose. Soon after he disappeared from Paris. I know not what became of him afterwards. His wife and his children remained there living by charity. A long time after his death beyond the seas, the Abbe de Saint-Simon passed from Noyan to Metz, where he found his widow in great misery.

The Queen of England sent for Madame L'Hospital to Saint-Germain, thanked her, caressed her, as she deserved, and gave her her portrait. This was all; the Regent gave her nothing; a long while after King James wrote to her, and sent her also his portrait. Conclusion: she remained post- mistress of Nonancourt as before, twenty or twenty-five years after, to her death; and her son and her daughter-in-law keep the post now. She was a true woman; estimated in her neighbourhood; not a single word that she uttered concerning this history has been contradicted by any one. What it cost her can never be said, but she never received a farthing. She never complained, but spoke as she found things, with modesty, and without seeking to speak. Such is the indigence of dethroned Kings, and their complete forgetfulness of the greatest perils and the most signal services.

Many honest people avoided Stair, whose insolent airs made others avoid him. He filled the cup by the insupportable manner in which he spoke upon that affair, never daring to admit he had directed it, or deigning to disculpate himself. The only annoyance he showed was about his ill-success.

CHAPTER LXXXI

I must say a few words now of Madame la Duchesse de Berry, who, as may be imagined, began to hold her head very high indeed directly the regency of Monsieur her father was established. Despite the representations of Madame de Saint-Simon, she usurped all the honours of a queen; she went through Paris with kettle-drums beating, and all along the quay of the Tuileries where the King was. The Marechal de Villeroy complained of this next day to M. le Duc d'Orleans, who promised him that while the King remained in Paris no kettle-drums should be heard but his. Never afterwards did Madame la Duchesse de Berry have any, yet when she went to the theatre she sat upon a raised dais in her box, had four of her guards upon the stage, and others in the pit; the house was better lighted than usual, and before the commencement of the performance she was harangued by the players. This made a strange stir in Paris, and as she did not dare to continue it she gave up her usual place, and took at the opera a little box where she could scarcely be seen, and where she was almost incognito. As the comedy was played then upon the opera stage for Madame, this little box served for both entertainments.

The Duchess desired apparently to pass the summer nights in all liberty in the garden of the Luxembourg. She accordingly had all the gates walled up but one, by which the Faubourg Saint-Germain, which had always enjoyed the privilege of walking there, were much deprived. M. le Duc thereupon opened the Conti garden to make up to the public for their loss. As may be imagined, strange things were said about the motives which led to the walling up of the garden.

As the Princess found new lovers to replace the old ones, she tried to pension off the latter at the expense of the public. She had a place created expressly for La Haye. She bought, or rather the King for her, a little house at the entry of the Bois de Boulogne, which was pretty, with all the wood in front, and a fine garden behind. It was called La Muette.

After many amours she had become smitten with Rion, a younger son of the house of Aydic. He was a fat, chubby, pale little fellow, who had so many pimples that he did not ill resemble an abscess. He had good teeth, but had no idea he should cause a passion which in less than no time became ungovernable, and which lasted a long while without however interfering with temporary and passing amours. He was not worth a penny, but had many brothers and sisters who had no more than he. He was a lieutenant of dragoons, relative of Madame Pons, dame d'atours of Madame la Duchesse de Berry, who sent for him to try and do something for him. Scarcely had he arrived than the passion of the Duchess declared itself, and he became the master of the Luxembourg where she dwelt. M. de Lauzun, who was a distant relative, was delighted, and chuckled inwardly. He thought he saw a repetition of the old times, when Mademoiselle was in her glory; he vouchsafed his advice to Rion.

Rion was gentle and naturally polished and respectful, a good and honest fellow. He soon felt the power of his charms, which could only have captivated the incomprehensible and depraved fantasy of such a princess. He did not abuse this power; made himself liked by everybody; but he treated Madame la Duchesse de Berry as M. de Lauzun had treated Mademoiselle. He was soon decorated with the most beautiful lace and the richest clothes covered with silver, loaded with snuffboxes, jewels, and precious stones. He took pleasure in making the Princess long after him, and be jealous; affecting to be still more jealous of her. He often made her cry. Little by little, he obtained such authority over her that she did not dare to do anything without his permission, not even the most indifferent things. If she were ready to go to the opera, he made her stay away; at other times he made her go thither in spite of herself. He made her treat well many ladies she did not like, or of whom she was jealous, and treat ill persons who pleased her, but of whom he pretended to be jealous. Even in her finery she had not the slightest liberty. He amused himself by making her disarrange her head-dress, or change her clothes, when she was quite dressed; and that so often and so publicly, that he accustomed her at last to take over night his orders for her morning's dress and occupation, and on the morrow he would change everything, and the Princess wept as much as she could, and more. At last she actually sent messages to him by trusty valets,—for he lived close to the Luxembourg,—several times during her toilet, to know what ribbons she should wear; the same with her gown and other things; and nearly always he made her wear what she did not wish for. If ever she dared to do the least thing without his permission, he treated her like a serving-wench, and her tears lasted sometimes several days. This princess, so haughty, and so fond of showing and exercising the most unmeasured pride, disgraced herself by joining in repasts with him and obscure people; she, with whom no man could lawfully eat if he were not a prince of the blood!

A Jesuit, named Pere Riglet, whom she had known as a child, and whose intimacy she had always cultivated since, was admitted to these private repasts, without being ashamed thereof, and without Madame la Duchesse de Berry being embarrassed. Madame de Mouchy was the confidante of all these strange parties she and Rion invited the guests, and chose the days. La Mouchy often reconciled the Princess to her lover, and was better treated by him than she, without her daring to take notice of it, for fear of an eclat which would have caused her to lose so dear a lover, and a confidante so necessary. This life was public; everybody at the Luxembourg paid court to M. de Rion, who, on his side, took care to be on good terms with all the world, nay, with an air of respect that he refused, even in public, to his princess. He often gave sharp replies to her in society, which made people lower their eyes, and brought blushes to the cheek of Madame la Duchesse de Berry, who, nevertheless, did not attempt to conceal her submission and passionate manners, even before others. A remarkable fact is, that in the midst of this life, she took an apartment at the Convent of the Carmelites of the Faubourg Saint- Germain, where she sometimes went in the afternoon, always slept there on grand religious fete days, and often remained there several days running. She took with her two ladies, rarely three, scarcely a single domestic; she ate with her ladies what the convent could supply for her table; attended the services, was sometimes long in prayer, and rigidly fasted on the appointed days.

Two Carmelites, of much talent, and who knew the world, were charged to receive her, and to be near her. One was very beautiful: the other had been so. They were rather young, especially the handsomer; but were very religious and holy, and performed the office entrusted to them much against their inclination. When they became more familiar they spoke freely to the Princess, and said to her that if they knew nothing of her but what they saw, they should admire her as a saint, but, elsewhere, they learnt that she led a strange life, and so public, that they could not comprehend why she came to their convent. Madame la Duchesse de Berry laughed at this, and was not angry. Sometimes they lectured her, called people and things by their names, and exhorted her to change so scandalous a life; but it was all in vain. She lived as before, both at the Luxembourg and at the Carmelites, and caused wonderment by this surprising conduct.

Madame la Duchesse de Berry returned with usury to her father, the severity and the domination she suffered at the hands of Rion—yet this prince, in his weakness, was not less submissive to her, attentive to her, or afraid of her. He was afflicted with the public reign of Rion, and the scandal of his daughter; but he did not dare to breathe a word, or if he did (after some scene, as ridiculous as it was violent, had passed between the lover and the Princess, and become public), he was treated like a negro, pouted at several days, and did not know how to make his peace.

But it is time now to speak of the public and private occupations of the Regent himself, of his conduct, his pleasure parties, and the employment of his days.

Up to five o'clock in the evening he devoted himself exclusively to public business, reception of ministers, councils, etc., never dining during the day, but taking chocolate between two and three o'clock, when everybody was allowed to enter his room. After the council of the day, that is to say, at about five o'clock, there was no more talk of business. It was now the time of the Opera or the Luxembourg (if he had not been to the latter place before his chocolate), or he went to Madame la Duchesse d'Orleans' apartments, or supped, or went out privately, or received company privately; or, in the fine season, he went to Saint- Cloud, or elsewhere out of town, now supping there, or at the Luxembourg, or at home. When Madame was at Paris, he spoke to her for a moment before his mass; and when she was at Saint-Cloud he went to see her there, and always paid her much attention and respect.

His suppers were always in very strange company. His mistresses, sometimes an opera girl, often Madame la Duchesse de Berry, and a dozen men whom he called his rows, formed the party. The requisite cheer was prepared in places made expressly, on the same floor, all the utensils were of silver; the company often lent a hand to the cooks. It was at these parties that the character of every one was passed in review, ministers and favourites like the rest, with a liberty which was unbridled license. The gallantries past and present of the Court and of the town; all old stories, disputes, jokes, absurdities were raked up; nobody was spared; M. le Duc d'Orleans had his say like the rest, but very rarely did these discourses make the slightest impression upon him. The company drank as much as they could, inflamed themselves, said the filthiest things without stint, uttered impieties with emulation, and when they had made a good deal of noise and were very drunk, they went to bed to recommence the same game the next day. From the moment when supper was ready, business, no matter of, what importance, no matter whether private or national, was entirely banished from view. Until the next morning everybody and everything were compelled to wait.

The Regent lost then an infinite amount of time in private, in amusements, and debauchery. He lost much also in audiences too long, too extended, too easily granted, and drowned himself in those same details which during the lifetime of the late King we had both so often reproached him with. Questions he might have decided in half an hour he prolonged, sometimes from weakness, sometimes from that miserable desire to set people at loggerheads, and that poisonous maxim which occasionally escaped him or his favourite, 'divide et impera'; often from his general mistrust of everybody and everything; nothings became hydras with which he himself afterwards was much embarrassed. His familiarity and his readiness of access extremely pleased people, but were much abused. Folks sometimes were even wanting in respect to him, which at last was an inconvenience all the more dangerous because he could not, when he wished, reprimand those who embarrassed him; insomuch as they themselves did not feel embarrassed.

What is extraordinary is, neither his mistress nor Madame la Duchesse de Berry, nor his 'roues', could ever draw anything from him, even when drunk, concerning the affairs of the government, however important. He publicly lived with Madame de Parabere; he lived at the same time with others; he amused himself with the jealousy and vexation of these women; he was not the less on good terms with them all; and the scandal of this public seraglio, and that of the daily filthiness and impiety at his suppers, were extreme and spread everywhere.

Towards the end of the year (1715) the Chevalier de Bouillon, who since the death of the son of the Comte d'Auvergne had taken the name of the Prince d'Auvergne, proposed to the Regent that there should be a public ball, masked and unmasked, in the opera three times a week, people to pay upon entering, and the boxes to be thrown open to those who did not care to dance. It was believed that a public ball, guarded as is the opera on days of performance, would prevent those adventures which happened so often at the little obscure balls scattered throughout Paris; and indeed close them altogether. The opera balls were established on a grand scale, and with all possible effect. The proposer of the idea had for it six thousand livres pension; and a machine admirably invented and of easy and instantaneous application, was made to cover the orchestra, and put the stage and the pit on the same level. The misfortune was, that the opera was at the Palais Royal, and that M. le Duc d'Orleans had only one step to take to reach it after his suppers and show himself there, often in a state but little becoming. The Duc de Noailles, who strove to pay court to him, went there from the commencement so drunk that there was no indecency he did not commit.

CHAPTER LXXXII: Let me speak now of another matter.

A Scotchman, I do not know of what family, a great player and combiner, who had gained much in various countries he had been in, had come to Paris during the last days of the deceased King. His name was Law; but when he became more known, people grew so accustomed to call him Las, that his name of Law disappeared. He was spoken of to M. le Duc d'Orleans as a man deep in banking and commercial matters, in the movements of the precious metals, in monies and finance: the Regent, from this description, was desirous to see him. He conversed with Law some time, and was so pleased with him, that he spoke of him to Desmarets as a man from whom information was to be drawn. I recollect that the Prince spoke of him to me at the same time. Desmarets sent for Law, and was a long while with him several times; I know nothing of what passed between them or its results, except that Desmarets was pleased with Law, and formed some esteem for him.

M. le Duc d'Orleans, after that, only saw him from time to time; but after the first rush of affairs, which followed the death of the King, Law, who had formed some subaltern acquaintances at the Palais Royal, and an intimacy with the Abbe Dubois, presented himself anew before M. le Duc d'Orleans, soon after conversed with him in private, and proposed some finance plans to him. The Regent made him work with the Duc de Noailles, with Rouille, with Amelot—this last for commercial matters. The first two were afraid of an intruder, favoured by the Regent, in their administration; so that Law was a long time tossed about, but was always backed by the Duc d'Orleans. At last, the bank project pleased that Prince so much that he wished to carry it out. He spoke in private to the heads of finance, in whom he found great opposition. He had often spoken to me of it, and I had contented myself with listening to him upon a matter I never liked, and which, consequently, I never well understood; and the carrying out of which appeared to me distant. When he had entirely formed his resolution, he summoned a financial and commercial assembly, in which Law explained the whole plan of the bank he wished to establish (this was on the 24th of October, 1715). He was listened to as long as he liked to talk. Some, who saw that the Regent was almost decided, acquiesced; but the majority opposed.

Law was not disheartened. The majority were spoken to privately in very good French. Nearly the same assembly was called, in which, the Regent being present, Law again explained his project. This time few opposed and feebly. The Duc de Noailles was obliged to give in. The bank being approved of in this manner, it had next to be proposed to the regency council.

M. le Duc d'Orleans took the trouble to speak in private to each member of the council, and gently to make them understand that he wished the bank to meet with no opposition. He spoke his mind to me thoroughly: therefore a reply was necessary. I said to him that I did not hide my ignorance or my disgust for all finance matters; that, nevertheless, what he had just explained to me appeared good in itself, that without any new tax, without expense, and without wronging or embarrassing anybody, money should double itself at once by means of the notes of this bank, and become transferable with the greatest facility. But along with this advantage I found two inconveniences, the first, how to govern the bank with sufficient foresight and wisdom, so as not to issue more notes than could be paid whenever presented: the second, that what is excellent in a republic, or in a monarchy where the finance is entirely popular, as in England, is of pernicious use in an absolute monarchy, such as France, where the necessities of a war badly undertaken and ill sustained, the avarice of a first minister, favourite, or mistress, the luxury, the wild expenses, the prodigality of a King, might soon exhaust a bank, and ruin all the holders of notes, that is to say, overthrow the realm. M. le Duc d'Orleans agreed to this; but at the same time maintained that a King would have so much interest in never meddling or allowing minister, mistress, or favourite to meddle with the bank, that this capital inconvenience was never to be feared. Upon that we for a long time disputed without convincing each other, so that when, some few days afterwards, he proposed the bank to the regency council, I gave my opinion as I have just explained it, but with more force and at length: and my conclusion was to reject the bank, as a bait the most fatal, in an absolute country, while in a free country it would be a very good and very wise establishment.

Few dared to be of this opinion: the bank passed. Duc d'Orleans cast upon me some little reproaches, but gentle, for having spoken at such length. I based my excuses upon my belief that by duty, honour, and conscience, I ought to speak according to my persuasion, after having well thought over the matter, and explained myself sufficiently to make my opinion well understood, and the reason I had for forming it. Immediately after, the edict was registered without difficulty at the Parliament. This assembly sometimes knew how to please the Regent with good grace in order to turn the cold shoulder to him afterwards with more efficacy.

Some time after, to relate all at once, M. le Duc d'Orleans wished me to see Law in order that he might explain to me his plans, and asked me to do so as a favour. I represented to him my unskilfulness in all finance matters; that Law would in vain speak a language to me of which I understood nothing, that we should both lose our time very uselessly. I tried to back out thus, as well as I could. The Regent several times reverted to the charge, and at last demanded my submission. Law came then to my house. Though there was much of the foreigner in his bearing, in his expressions, and in his accent, he expressed himself in very good terms, with much clearness and precision. He conversed with me a long while upon his bank, which, indeed, was an excellent thing in itself, but for another country rather than for France, and with a prince less easy than the Regent. Law had no other solutions to give me, of my two objections, than those the Regent himself had given, which did not satisfy me. But as the affair had passed, and there was nothing now to do but well direct it, principally upon that did our conversation turn. I made him feel as much as I could the importance of not showing such facility, that it might be abused, with a Regent so good, so easy, so open, so surrounded. I masked as well as I could what I wished to make him understand thereupon; and I dwelt especially upon the necessity of being prepared to satisfy instantly all bearers of notes, who should demand payment: for upon this depended the credit or the overthrow of the bank. Law, on going out, begged me to permit him to come sometimes and talk with me; we separated mutually satisfied, at which the Regent was still more so.

Law came several other times to my house, and showed much desire to grow intimate with me. I kept to civilities, because finance entered not into my head, and I regarded as lost time all these conversations. Some time after, the Regent, who spoke to me tolerably often of Law with great prepossession, said that he had to ask of me, nay to demand of me, a favour; it was, to receive a visit from Law regularly every week. I represented to him the perfect inutility of these conversations, in which I was incapable of learning anything, and still more so of enlightening Law upon subjects he possessed, and of which I knew naught. It was in vain; the Regent wished it; obedience was necessary. Law, informed of this by the Regent, came then to my house. He admitted to me with good grace, that it was he who had asked the Regent to ask me, not daring to do so himself. Many compliments followed on both sides, and we agreed that he should come to my house every Tuesday morning about ten o'clock, and that my door should be closed to everybody while he remained. This first visit was not given to business. On the following Tuesday morning he came to keep his appointment, and punctually came until his discomfiture. An hour-and-a-half, very often two hours, was the ordinary time for our conversations. He always took care to inform me of the favour his bank was obtaining in France and foreign countries, of its products, of his views, of his conduct, of the opposition he met with from the heads of finance and the magistracy, of his reasons, and especially of his balance sheet, to convince me that he was more than prepared to face all holders of notes whatever sums they had to ask for.

I soon knew that if Law had desired these regular visits at my house, it was not because he expected to make me a skilful financier; but because, like a man of sense—and he had a good deal—he wished to draw near a servitor of the Regent who had the best post in his confidence, and who long since had been in a position to speak to him of everything and of everybody with the greatest freedom and the most complete liberty; to try by this frequent intercourse to gain my friendship; inform himself by me of the intrinsic qualities of those of whom he only saw the outside; and by degrees to come to the Council, through me, to represent the annoyances he experienced, the people with whom he had to do; and lastly, to profit by my dislike to the Duc de Noailles, who, whilst embracing him every day, was dying of jealousy and vexation, and raised in his path, under-hand, all the obstacles and embarrassments possible, and would have liked to stifle him. The bank being in action and flourishing, I believed it my duty to sustain it. I lent myself, therefore, to the instructions Law proposed, and soon we spoke to each other with a confidence I never have had reason to repent. I will not enter into the details of this bank, the other schemes which followed it, or the operations made in consequence. This subject of finance would fill several volumes. I will speak of it only as it affects the history of the time, or what concerns me in particular. It is the history of my time I have wished to write; I should have been too much turned from it had I entered into the immense details respecting finance. I might add here what Law was. I defer it to a time when this curiosity will be more in place.

Arouet, son of a notary, who was employed by my father and me until his death, was exiled and sent to Tulle at this time (the early part of 1716), for some verses very satirical and very impudent.

I should not amuse myself by writing down such a trifle, if this same Arouet, having become a great poet and academician under the name of Voltaire, had not also become—after many tragical adventures—a manner of personage in the republic of letters, and even achieved a sort of importance among certain people.

CHAPTER LXXXIII

I have elsewhere alluded to Alberoni, and shown what filthy baseness he stooped to in order to curry favour with the infamous Duc de Vendome. I have also shown that he accompanied the new Queen of Spain from Parma to Madrid, after she had been married, by procuration, to Philip V. He arrived at the Court of Spain at a most opportune moment for his fortune. Madame des Ursins had just been disgraced; there was no one to take her place. Alberoni saw his opportunity and was not slow to avail himself of it. During the journey with the new Queen, he had contrived to ingratiate himself so completely into her favour, that she was, in a measure, prepared to see only with his eyes. The King had grown so accustomed to be shut out from all the world, and to be ruled by others, that he easily adapted himself to his new chains. The Queen and Alberoni, then, in a short time had him as completely under their thumb, as he had before been under that of Madame des Ursins.

Alberoni, unscrupulous and ambitious, stopped at nothing in order to consolidate his power and pave the way for his future greatness. Having become prime minister, he kept the King as completely inaccessible to the courtiers as to the world; would allow no one to approach him whose influence he had in any way feared. He had Philip completely in his own hands by means of the Queen, and was always on his guard to keep him there.

Ever since the Regent's accession to power an intimacy had gradually been growing up between the two governments of France and England. This was mainly owing to the intrigues of the Abbe Dubois, who had sold himself to the English Court, from which he secretly received an enormous pension. He was, therefore, devoted heart and soul—if such a despicable personage can be said to have the one or the other—to the interests of King George, and tried to serve them in every way. He had but little difficulty—comparatively speaking—in inducing M. le Duc d'Orleans to fall into his nets, and to declare himself in favour of an English alliance. Negotiations with this end in view were, in fact, set on foot, had been for some time; and about the month of September of this year (1716), assumed a more smiling face than they had yet displayed.

Both France and England, from different motives, wished to draw Spain into this alliance. The Regent, therefore, in order to further this desire, obtained from England a promise that she would give up Gibraltar to its former owners, the Spaniards. The King of England consented to do so, but on one condition: it was, that in order not to expose himself to the cries of the party opposed to him, this arrangement should be kept profoundly secret until executed. In order that this secrecy might be secured, he stipulated that the negotiation should not in any way pass through the hands of Alberoni, or any Spanish minister, but be treated directly between the Regent and the King of Spain, through a confidential agent chosen by the former.

This confidential agent was to take a letter respecting the treaty to the King of Spain, a letter full of insignificant trifles, and at the same time a positive order from the King of England, written and signed by his hand, to the Governor of Gibraltar, commanding him to surrender the place to the King of Spain the very moment he received this order, and to retire with his garrison, etc., to Tangiers. In order to execute this a Spanish general was suddenly to march to Gibraltar, under pretence of repressing the incursions of its garrison,—summon the Governor to appear, deliver to him the King of England's order, and enter into possession of the place. All this was very weakly contrived; but this concerned the King of England, not us.

I must not be proud; and must admit that I knew nothing of all this, save at second-hand. If I had, without pretending to be very clever, I must say that I should have mistrusted this fine scheme. The King of England could not be ignorant with what care and with what jealousy the Queen and Alberoni kept the King of Spain locked up, inaccessible to everybody—and that the certain way to fail, was to try to speak to him without their knowledge, in spite of them, or unaided by them. However, my opinion upon this point was not asked, and accordingly was not given.

Louville was the secret agent whom the Regent determined to send. He had already been in Spain, had gained the confidence of the King, and knew him better than any other person who could have been chosen. Precisely because of all these reasons, I thought him the most unfit person to be charged with this commission. The more intimate he had been with the King of Spain, the more firm in his confidence, the more would he be feared by the Queen and Alberoni; and the more would they do to cover his embassy with failure, so as to guard their credit and their authority. I represented my views on this subject to Louville, who acknowledged there was truth in them, but contented himself with saying, that he had not in his surprise dared to refuse the mission offered to him; and that if he succeeded in it, the restitution to Spain of such an important place as Gibraltar, would doubtless be the means of securing to him large arrears of pensions due to him from Philip the First: an object of no small importance in his eyes. Louville, therefore, in due time departed to Madrid, on his strange and secret embassy.

Upon arriving he went straight to the house of the Duc de Saint-Aignan, our ambassador, and took up his quarters there. Saint-Aignan who had received not the slightest information of his arriving, was surprised beyond measure at it. Alberoni was something more than surprised. As fortune would have it, Louville when at some distance from Madrid was seen by a courier, who straightway told Alberoni of the circumstance. As may be imagined, tormented as Alberoni was by jealousy and suspicion, this caused him infinite alarm. He was quite aware who Louville was; the credit he had attained with the King of Spain; the trouble Madame des Ursins and the deceased Queen had had to get him out of their way; the fear, therefore, that he conceived on account of this unexpected arrival, was so great that he passed all bounds, in order to free himself from it.

He instantly despatched a courier to meet Louville with an order prohibiting him to approach any nearer to Madrid. The courier missed Louville, but a quarter of an hour after this latter had alighted at Saint-Aignan's, he received a note from Grimaldo inclosing an order from the King of Spain, commanding him to leave the city that instant! Louville replied that he was charged with a confidential letter from the King of France, and with another from M. le Duc d'Orleans, for the King of Spain; and with a commission for his Catholic Majesty which would not permit him to leave until he had executed it. In consequence of this reply, a courier was at once despatched to the Prince de Cellamare, Spanish ambassador at Paris, ordering him to ask for the recall of Louville, and to declare that the King of Spain so disliked his person that he would neither see him, nor allow him to treat with any of the ministers!

Meanwhile the fatigue of the journey followed by such a reception so affected Louville, that during the night he had an attack of a disease to which he was subject, so that he had a bath prepared for him, into which he got towards the end of the morning.

Alberoni, not satisfied with what he had already done, came himself to the Duc de Saint-Aignan's, in order to persuade Louville to depart at once. Despite the representations made to him, he insisted upon penetrating to the sick-chamber. There he saw Louville in his bath. Nothing could be more civil than the words of Alberoni, but nothing could be more dry, more negative, or more absolute than their signification. He pitied the other's illness and the fatigue of his journey; would have wished to have known of this journey beforehand, so as to have prevented it; and had hoped to be able to overcome the repugnance of the King of Spain to see him, or at least to obtain permission for him to remain some days in Madrid. He added that he had been unable to shake his Majesty in any way, or to avoid obeying the very express order he had received from him, to see that he (Louville) departed at once.

Louville, however, was in a condition which rendered his departure impossible. Alberoni admitted this, but warned him that his stay must only last as long as his illness, and that the attack once over, he must away. Louville insisted upon the confidential letters, of which he was the bearer, and which gave him an official character, instructed as he was to execute an important commission from the King of France, nephew of the King of Spain, such as his Majesty could not refuse to hear direct from his mouth, and such as he would regret not having listened to. The dispute was long and warm, despite the illness of Louville, who could gain nothing. He did not fail to remain five or six days with the Duc de Saint-Aignan, and to make him act as ambassador in order to obtain an audience of the King, although Saint-Aignan was hurt at being kept ignorant of the object of the other's mission.

Louville did not dare to call upon a soul, for fear of committing himself, and nobody dared to call upon him. He hazarded, however, for curiosity, to go and see the King of Spain pass through a street, and ascertain if, on espying him, he would not be tempted to hear him, in case his arrival, as was very possible, had been kept a secret. But Alberoni had anticipated everything. Louville saw the King pass, certainly, but found it was impossible to make himself perceived by his Majesty. Grimaldo came afterwards to intimate to Louville an absolute order to depart, and to inform the Duc de Saint-Aignan that the King of Spain was so angry with the obstinacy of this delay, that he would not say what might happen if the stay of Louville was protracted; but that he feared the respect due to a representative minister, and above all an ambassador of France, would be disregarded.

Both Louville and Saint-Aignan clearly saw that all audience was impossible, and that in consequence a longer stay could only lead to disturbances which might embroil the two crowns; so that, at the end of seven or eight days, Louville departed, returning as he came. Alberoni began then to breathe again after the extreme fear he had had. He was consoled by this proof of his power, which showed he need no longer fear that any one could approach the King without his aid, or that any business could be conducted without him. Thus Spain lost Gibraltar, and she has never been able to recover it since.

Such is the utility of prime ministers!

Alberoni spread the report in Spain and in France, that Philip V. had taken a mortal aversion against Louville, since he had driven him out of the country for his insolence and his scheming; that he would never see him, and was offended because he had passed the Pyrenees; that Louville had no proposition to make, or commission to execute; that he had deceived the Regent, in making him believe that if once he found a pretext for appearing before the King of Spain, knowing him so well as he did, that prince would be ravished by the memory of his former affection, would reinstate him in his former credit, and thus France would be able to make Spain do all she wished. In a word, Alberoni declared that Louville had only come into the country to try and obtain some of the pensions he had been promised on quitting the King of Spain, but that he had not gone the right way to work to be so soon paid.

Nothing short of the effrontery of Alberoni would have been enough for the purpose of spreading these impostures. No one had forgotten in Spain what Madame des Ursins had done to get rid of Louville, how the King of Spain had resisted; that she was not able to succeed without the aid of France and her intrigues with Madame de Maintenon; and that the King, afflicted to the utmost, yielding to the orders given by France to Louville, had doubled the pensions which had for a long time been paid to him, given him a sum of money in addition, and the government of Courtray, which he lost only by the misfortune of the war that followed the loss of the battle of Ramillies. With respect to the commission, to deny it was an extreme piece of impudence, a man being concerned so well known as Louville, who descends at the house of the ambassador of France, says he has letters of trust from the King and the Regent, and an important mission which he can only confide to the King of Spain, the self-same ambassador striving to obtain an audience for him. Nothing was so easy as to cover Louville with confusion, if he had spoken falsely, by making him show his letters; if he had none he would have been struck dumb, and having no official character, Alberoni would have been free to punish him. Even if with confidential letters, he had only a complaint to utter in order to introduce himself and to solicit his pay, Alberoni would very easily have been able to dishonour him, because he had no commission after having roundly asserted that he was charged with one of great importance. But omnipotence says and does with impunity whatever it pleases.

Louville having returned, it was necessary to send word to the King of England of all he had done in Spain; and this business came to nothing, except that it set Alberoni against the Regent for trying to execute a secret commission without his knowledge; and that it set the Regent against Alberoni for frustrating a project so openly, and for showing the full force of his power. Neither of the two ever forgot this matter; and the dislike of Alberoni to the Regent led, as will be seen, to some strange results.

I will add here, that the treaty of alliance between France and England was signed a short time after this event. I did my utmost to prevent it, representing to the Regent that his best policy was to favour the cause of the Pretender, and thus by keeping the attention of Great Britain continually fixed upon her domestic concerns, he would effectually prevent her from influencing the affairs of the continent, and long were the conversations I had with him, insisting upon this point. But although, while he was with me, my arguments might appear to have some weight with him, they were forgotten, clean swept from his mind, directly the Abbe Dubois, who had begun to obtain a most complete and pernicious influence over him, brought his persuasiveness to bear. Dubois' palm had been so well greased by the English that he was afraid of nothing. He succeeded then in inducing the Regent to sign a treaty with England, in every way, it may safely be said, advantageous to that power, and in no way advantageous to France. Amongst other conditions, the Regent agreed to send the so-called Pretender out of the realm, and to force him to seek an asylum in Italy. This was, in fact, executed to the letter. King James, who for some time had retired to Avignon, crossed the Alps and settled in Rome, where he lived ever afterwards. I could not but deplore the adoption of a policy so contrary to the true interests of France; but the business being done I held my peace, and let matters take their course. It was the only course of conduct open to me.

CHAPTER LXXXIV

I have already shown in these memoirs, that the late King had made of the lieutenant of police a species of secret and confidential minister; a sort of inquisitor, with important powers that brought him in constant relation with the King. The Regent, with less authority than the deceased monarch, and with more reasons than he to be well informed of everything passing, intrigues included, found occupying this office of lieutenant of police, Argenson, who had gained his good graces chiefly, I fancy, when the affair of the cordelier was on the carpet, as shown in its place. Argenson, who had much intelligence, and who had desired this post as the entry, the basis, and the road of his fortune, filled it in a very superior manner, and the Regent made use of him with much liberty. The Parliament, very ready to show the extent of its authority everywhere, at the least as though in competition with that of the Regent, suffered impatiently what it called the encroachments of the Court. It wished to indemnify itself for the silence it had been compelled to keep thereon under the last reign, and to re-obtain at the expense of the Regent all it had lost of its authority over the police, of which it is the head. The lieutenant of police is answerable to this body—even receives his orders from it, and its reprimands (in public audiences, standing uncovered at the bar of the Parliament) from the mouth of the Chief-President, or of him who presides, and who calls him neither Master nor Monsieur, but nakedly by his name, although the lieutenant of police might have claimed these titles, being then Councillor of State.

The Parliament wished, then, to humiliate Argenson (whom it hated during the time of the deceased King); to give a disagreeable lesson to the Regent; to prepare worse treatment still for his lieutenant of police; to make parade of its power, to terrify thus the public, and arrogate to itself the right of limiting the authority of the Regent.

Argenson had often during the late reign, and sometimes since, made use of an intelligent and clever fellow, just suited to him, and named Pomereu, to make discoveries, arrest people, and occasionally keep them a short time in his own house. The Parliament believed, and rightly, that in arresting this man under other pretexts, it would find the thread of many curious and secret tortuosities, which would aid its design, and that it might plume itself upon protecting the public safety against the tyranny of secret arrests and private imprisonments. To carry out its aim it made use of the Chamber of justice, so as to appear as little as possible in the matter. This Chamber hastened on so well the proceedings, for fear of being stopped on the road, that the first hint people had of them was on learning that Pomereu was, by decree of this Chamber, in the prisons of the Conciergerie, which are those of the Parliament. Argenson, who was informed of this imprisonment immediately it took place, instantly went to the Regent, who that very moment sent a 'lettre de cachet', ordering Pomereu to be taken from prison by force if the gaoler made the slightest difficulty in giving him up to the bearers of the 'lettre de cachet'; but that gentleman did not dare to make any. The execution was so prompt that this man was not an hour in prison, and they who had sent him there had not time to seize upon a box of papers which had been transported with him to the Conciergerie, and which was very carefully carried away with him. At the same time, everything in any way bearing upon Pomereu, or upon the things in which he had been employed, was carefully removed and secreted.

The vexation of the Parliament upon seeing its prey, which it had reckoned upon making such a grand use of, carried off before its eyes, may be imagined. It left nothing undone in order to move the public by its complaints, and by its cries against such an attack upon law. The Chamber of justice sent a deputation to the Regent, who made, fun of it, by gravely giving permission to the deputies to re-take their prisoner, but without saying a single word to them upon his escape from gaol. He was in Paris, in a place where he feared nobody. The Chamber of justice felt the derisiveness of the Regent's permission, and ceased to transact business. It thought to embarrass the Regent thus, but 'twould have been at its own expense. This lasted only a day or two. The Duc de Noailles spoke to the Chamber; the members felt they could gain nothing by their strike, and that if they were obstinate they would be dispensed with, and others found to perform their duties. They recommenced their labours then, and the Parliament gained nothing by its attack, but only showed its ill-will, and at the same time its powerlessness.

I have forgotten something which, from its singularity, deserves recollection, and I will relate it now lest it should escape me again.

One afternoon, as we were about to take our places at the regency council, the Marechal de Villars drew me aside and asked me if I knew that Marly was going to be destroyed. I replied, "No;" indeed, I had not heard speak of it; and I added that I could not believe it. "You do not approve of it?" said the Marechal. I assured him I was far from doing so. He repeated that the destruction was resolved on, that he knew it beyond all doubt, and that if I wished to hinder it, I had not a moment to lose. I replied that when we took our places I would speak to M. le Duc d'Orleans. "Immediately," quickly replied the Marechal; "speak to him this instant, for the order is perhaps already given."

As all the council were already seated I went behind to M. le Duc d'Orleans, and whispered in his ear what I had just learnt without naming from whom, and begged him, if my information was right, to suspend execution of his project until I had spoken to him, adding that I would join him at the Palais Royal after the council. He stammered a little, as if sorry at being discovered, but nevertheless agreed to wait for me: I said so in leaving to the Marechal de Villars, and went to the Palais Royal, where M. le Duc d'Orleans admitted the truth of the news I had heard. I said I would not ask who had given such a pernicious counsel. He tried to show it was good by pointing to the saving in keeping up that would be obtained; to the gain that would accrue from the sale of so many water-conduits and materials; to the unpleasant situation of a place to which the King would not be able to go for several years; and to the expense the King was put to in keeping up so many other beautiful houses, not one of which admitted of pulling down.

I replied to him, that these were the reasons of the guardian of a private gentleman that had been presented to him, the conduct of whom could in no way resemble that of the guardian of a King of France; that the expenses incurred in keeping up Marly were necessary, and that, compared with the total of those of the King, they were but as drops in the ocean. I begged him to get rid of the idea that the sale of the materials would yield any profit,—all the receipts would go in gifts and pillage, I said; and also that it was not these petty objects he ought to regard, but that he should consider how many millions had been buried in this ancient sewer, to transform it into a fairy palace, unique as to form in all Europe—unique by the beauty of its fountains, unique also by the reputation that the deceased King had given to it; and that it was an object of curiosity to strangers of every rank who came to France; that its destruction would resound throughout Europe with censure; that these mean reasons of petty economy would not prevent all France from being indignant at seeing so distinguished an ornament swept away; that although neither he nor I might be very delicate upon what had been the taste and the favourite work of the late King, the Regent ought to avoid wounding his memory,—which by such a long reign, so many brilliant years, so many grand reverses so heroically sustained, and escaped from in so unhoped-for a manner—had left the entire world in veneration of his person: in fine, that he might reckon all the discontented, all the neutral even, would join in chorus with the Ancient Court, and cry murder; that the Duc du Maine, Madame de Ventadour, the Marechal de Villeroy would not hesitate to look upon the destruction of Marly as a crime against the King,—a crime they would not fail to make the best of for their own purposes during all the regency, and even after it was at an end. I clearly saw that M. le Duc d'Orleans had not in the least reflected upon all this. He agreed that I was right: promised that Marly should not be touched, that it should continue to be kept up, and thanked me for preserving him from this fault.

When I was well assured of him, "Admit," said I, "that the King, in the other world, would be much astonished if he could know that the Duc de Noailles had made you order the destruction of Marly, and that it was who hindered it."

"Oh! as to that," he quickly replied, "it is true he could not believe it." In effect Marly was preserved and kept up; and it is the Cardinal Fleury, with his collegiate proctor's avarice, who has stripped it of its river, which was its most superb charm.

I hastened to relate this good resolve to the Marechal de Villars. The Duc de Noailles, who, for his own private reasons, had wished the destruction of Marly, was furious when he saw his proposal fail. To indemnify himself in some degree for his vexation, he made the Regent agree, in the utmost secrecy, for fear of another failure, that all the furniture, linen, etc., should be sold. He persuaded M. le Duc d'Orleans that all these things would be spoiled and lost by the time the King was old enough to use them; that in selling them a large sum would be gained to relieve expenses; and that in future years the King could furnish Marly as he pleased. There was an immense quantity of things sold, but owing to favour and pillage they brought very little; and to replace them afterwards, millions were spent. I did not know of this sale, at which anybody bought who wished, and at very low prices, until it had commenced; therefore I was unable to hinder this very damaging parsimoniousness.

The Regent just about this time was bestowing his favours right and left with a very prodigal hand; I thought, therefore, I was fully entitled to ask him for one, which, during the previous reign, had been so rare, so useful, and accordingly so difficult to obtain; I mean the right of entering the King's room—the 'grandes entrees'—as it was called, and I attained it at once.

Since the occasion offers, I may as well explain what are the different sorts of entrees. The most precious are called the "grand," which give the right to enter into all the retired places of the

King's apartments, whenever the grand chamberlain and the chief gentlemen of the chamber enter. The importance of this privilege under a King who grants audiences with difficulty, need not be insisted on. Enjoying it, you can speak with him, tete-a-tete, whenever you please, without asking his permission, and without the knowledge of others; you obtain a familiarity, too, with him by being able to see him thus in private.

The offices which give this right are, those of grand chamberlain, of first gentleman of the chamber, and of grand master of the wardrobe on annual duty; the children, legitimate and illegitimate, of the King, and the wives and husbands of the latter enjoy the same right. As for Monsieur and M. le Duc d'Orleans they always had these entrees, and as sons of France, were at liberty to enter and see the King at all hours, but they did not abuse this privilege. The Duc du Maine and the Comte de Toulouse had the same, which they availed themselves of unceasingly, but by the back stairs.

The second entrees, simply called entrees, were purely personal; no appointment or change gave them. They conferred the right to see the King at his rising, after the grandes, and also to see him, but under difficulties, during all the day and evening.

The last entrees are those called chamber entrees. They also give the right to see the King at his rising, before the distinguished courtiers; but no other privilege except to be present at the booting of the King. This was the name employed when the King changed his coat, in going or returning from hunting or a walk. At Marly, all who were staying there by invitation, entered to see this ceremony without asking; elsewhere, those who had not the entree were excluded. The first gentleman of the chamber had the right, and used it sometimes, to admit four or five persons at the most, to the "booting," if they asked, and provided they were people of quality, or of some distinction.

Lastly, there were the entrees of the cabinet which gave you the right to wait for the King there when he entered after rising, until he had given orders for the day, and to pay your court to him, and to enter there when he entered to change his coat. Beyond this, the privilege attached to these admissions did not extend. The Cardinals and the Princes of the blood had the entrees of the chamber and those of the cabinet, so had all the chief officials.

I was the first who had the 'grandes entrees' from the Regent. D'Antin asked for them next. Soon after, upon this example, they were accorded to D'O. M. le Prince de Conti, the sole prince of the blood who had them not, because he was the sole prince of the blood who did not come from Madame de Montespan, received them next, and little by little the privilege was completely prostituted as so many others were.

By extremely rare good fortune a servant employed in the diamond mines of the Great Mogul found means to secrete about his person a diamond of prodigious size, and what is more marvellous, to gain the seashore and embark without being subjected to the rigid and not very delicate ordeal, that all persons not above suspicion by their name or their occupation, are compelled to submit to, ere leaving the country. He played his cards so well, apparently, that he was not suspected of having been near the mines, or of having had anything to do with the jewel trade. To complete his good fortune he safely arrived in Europe with his diamond. He showed it to several princes, none of whom were rich enough to buy, and carried it at last to England, where the King admired it, but could not resolve to purchase it. A model of it in crystal was made in England, and the man, the diamond, and the model (perfectly resembling the original) were introduced to Law, who proposed to the Regent that he should purchase the jewel for the King. The price dismayed the Regent, who refused to buy.

Law, who had in many things much grandour of sentiment, came dispirited to me, bringing the model. I thought, with him, that it was not consistent with the greatness of a King of France to be repelled from the purchase of an inestimable jewel, unique of its kind in the world, by the mere consideration of price, and that the greater the number of potentates who had not dared to think of it, the greater ought to be his care not to let it escape him. Law, ravished to find me think in this manner, begged me to speak to M. le Duc d'Orleans. The state of the finances was an obstacle upon which the Regent much insisted. He feared blame for making so considerable a purchase, while the most pressing necessities could only be provided for with much trouble, and so many people were of necessity kept in distress. I praised this sentiment, but I said that he ought not to regard the greatest King of Europe as he would a private gentleman, who would be very reprehensible if he threw away 100,000 livres upon a fine diamond, while he owed many debts which he could not pay: that he must consider the honour of the crown, and not lose the occasion of obtaining, a priceless diamond which would efface the lustre of all others in Europe: that it was a glory for his regency which would last for ever; that whatever might be the state of the finances the saving obtained by a refusal of the jewel would not much relieve them, for it would be scarcely perceptible; in fact I did not quit M. le Duc d'Orleans until he had promised that the diamond should be bought.

Law, before speaking to me, had so strongly represented to the dealer the impossibility of selling his diamond at the price he hoped for, and the loss he would suffer in cutting it into different pieces, that at last he made him reduce the price to two millions, with the scrapings, which must necessarily be made in polishing, given in. The bargain was concluded on these terms. The interest upon the two millions was paid to the dealer until the principal could be given to him, and in the meanwhile two millions' worth of jewels were handed to him as security.

M. le Duc d'Orleans was agreeably deceived by the applause that the public gave to an acquisition so beautiful and so unique. This diamond was called the "Regent." It is of the size of a greengage plum, nearly round, of a thickness which corresponds with its volume, perfectly white, free from all spot, speck, or blemish, of admirable water, and weighs more than 500 grains. I much applauded myself for having induced the Regent to make so illustrious a purchase.

CHAPTER LXXXV

In 1716 the Duchesse de Lesdiguieres died at Paris in her fine hotel. She was not old, but had been long a widow, and had lost her only son. She was the last relic of the Gondi who were brought into France by Catherine de' Medici, and who made so prodigious a fortune. She left great wealth. She was a sort of fairy, who, though endowed with much wit, would see scarcely anybody, still less give dinners to the few people she did see. She never went to Court, and seldom went out of her house. The door of her house was always thrown back, disclosing a grating, through which could be perceived a true fairy palace, such as is sometimes described in romances. Inside it was nearly desert, but of consummate magnificence, and all this confirmed the first impression, assisted by the singularity of everything, her followers, her livery, the yellow hangings of her carriage, and the two great Moors who always followed her. She left much to her servants, and for pious purposes, but nothing to her daughter-in-law, though poor and respectful to her. Others got magnificent legacies.

Cavoye died about the same time. I have said enough about him and his wife to have nothing to add. Cavoye, away from Court, was like a fish out of water; and he could not stand it long. If romances have rarely produced conduct like that of his wife towards him, they would with still greater difficulty describe the courage with which her lasting love for her husband sustained her in her attendance on his last illness, and the entombment to which she condemned herself afterwards. She preserved her first mourning all her life, never slept away from the house where he died, or went out, except to go twice a day to Saint-Sulpice to pray in the chapel where he was buried. She would never see any other persons besides those she had seen during the last moments of her husband, and occupied herself with good works also, consuming herself thus in a few years without a single sign of hesitation. A vehemence so equal and so maintained is perhaps an example, great, unique, and assuredly very respectable.

Peter I., Czar of Muscovy, has made for himself, and justly, such a great name, in his own country, in all Europe, and in Asia, that I will not undertake to describe so grand, so illustrious a prince—comparable to the greatest men of antiquity—who has been the admiration of his age, who will be that of years to come, and whom all Europe has been so much occupied in studying. The singularity of the journey into France of so extraordinary a prince, has appeared to me to deserve a complete description in an unbroken narrative. It is for this reason that I place my account of it here a little late, according to the order of time, but with dates that will rectify this fault.

Various things relating to this monarch have been seen in their place; his various journeys to Holland, Germany, Vienna, England, and to several parts of the North; the object of those journeys, with some account of his military actions, his policy, his family. It has been shown that he wished to come into France during the time of the late King, who civilly refused to receive him. There being no longer this obstacle, he wished to satisfy his curiosity, and he informed the Regent through Prince Kourakin, his ambassador at Paris, that he was going to quit the Low Countries, and come and see the King.

There was nothing for it but to appear very pleased, although the Regent would gladly have dispensed with this visit. The expenses to be defrayed were great; the trouble would be not less great with a prince so powerful and so clear-sighted, but full of whims, with a remnant of barbarous manners, and a grand suite of people, of behaviour very different from that common in these countries, full of caprices and of strange fashions, and both they and their master very touchy and very positive upon what they claimed to be due or permitted to them.

Moreover the Czar was at daggers drawn with the King of England, the enmity between them passing all decent limits, and being the more bitter because personal. This troubled not a little the Regent, whose intimacy with the King of England was public, the private interest of Dubois carrying it even to dependence. The dominant passion of the Czar was to render his territories flourishing by commerce; he had made a number of canals in order to facilitate it; there was one for which he needed the concurrence of the King of England, because it traversed a little corner of his German dominions. From jealousy George would not consent to it. Peter, engaged in the war with Poland, then in that of the North, in which George was also engaged, negotiated in vain. He was all the more irritated, because he was in no condition to employ force; and this canal, much advanced, could not be continued. Such was the source of that hatred which lasted all the lives of these monarchs, and with the utmost bitterness.

Kourakin was of a branch of that ancient family of the Jagellons, which had long worn the crowns of Poland, Denmark, Norway, and Sweden. He was a tall, well-made man, who felt all the grandeur of his origin; had much intelligence, knowledge of the way of managing men, and instruction. He spoke French and several languages very fairly; he had travelled much, served in war, then been employed in different courts. He was Russian to the backbone, and his extreme avarice much damaged his talents. The Czar and he had married two sisters, and each had a son. The Czarina had been repudiated and put into a convent near Moscow; Kourakin in no way suffered from this disgrace; he perfectly knew his master, with whom he kept on very free terms, and by whom he was treated with confidence and consideration. His last mission had been to Rome, where he remained three years; thence he came as ambassador to Paris. At Rome he was without official character, and without business except a secret one, with which the Czar had entrusted him, as to a sure and enlightened man.

This monarch, who wished to raise himself and his country from barbarism, and extend his power by conquests and treaties, had felt the necessity of marriages, in order to ally himself with the chief potentates of Europe. But to form such marriages he must be of the Catholic religion, from which the Greeks were separated by such a little distance, that he thought his project would easily be received in his dominions, if he allowed liberty of conscience there. But this prince was sufficiently sagacious to seek enlightenment beforehand upon Romish pretensions. He had sent for that purpose to Rome a man of no mark, but capable of well fulfilling his mission, who remained there five or six months, and who brought back no very satisfactory report. Later he opened his heart in Holland to King William, who dissuaded him from his design, and who counselled him even to imitate England, and to make himself the chief of his religion, without which he would never be really master in his own country. This counsel pleased the Czar all the more, because it was by the wealth and by the authority of the patriarchs of Moscow, his grandfathers, and great-grandfathers, that his father had attained the crown, although only of ordinary rank among the Russian nobility.

These patriarchs were dependent upon those of the Greek rite of Constantinople but very slightly. They had obtained such great power, and such prodigious rank, that at their entry into Moscow the Czar held their stirrups, and, on foot, led their horse by the bridle: Since the grandfather of Peter, there had been no patriarch at Moscow. Peter I., who had reigned some time with his elder brother, incapable of affairs, long since dead, leaving no son, had, like his father, never consented to have a patriarch there. The archbishops of Novgorod supplied their place in certain things, as occupying the chief see after that of Moscow, but with scarcely any authority that the Czar did not entirely usurp, and more carefully still after King William had given him the counsel before alluded to; so that by degrees he had become the real religious chief of his vast dominions.

Nevertheless, the passionate desire he had to give to his posterity the privilege of marrying with Catholic princes, the wish he had, above all, for the honour of alliances with the house of France, and that of Austria, made him return to his first project. He tried to persuade himself that the man whom he had secretly sent to Rome had not been well informed, or had ill understood; he resolved, therefore, to fathom his doubts, so that he should no longer have any as to the course he ought to adopt.

It was with this design that he chose Prince Kourakin, whose knowledge and intelligence were known to him, and sent him to Rome under pretence of curiosity, feeling that a nobleman of his rank would find the best, the most important, and the most distinguished society there ready to receive him; and that by remaining there, under pretext of liking the life he led, and of wishing to see and admire at his ease all the marvels of so many different kinds collected there, he should have leisure and means to return perfectly instructed upon everything he wished to know. Kourakin, in fact, remained in Rome three years, associating with the savans on the one hand and the best company on the other, whence by degrees he obtained all he wished to know; all the more readily because this Court boasts of its temporal pretensions and of its conquests of this kind, instead of keeping them secret. In consequence of the long and faithful report that Kourakin made to the Czar, that prince heaved a sigh, saying that he must be master in his own country, and could not place there anybody greater than himself; and never afterwards did he think of turning Catholic.

This fact respecting the Czars and Rome, Prince Kourakin did not hide. Everybody who knew him has heard him relate it. I have eaten with him and he with me, and I have talked a good deal with him, and heard him talk, with pleasure, upon many things.

The Regent, informed by him of the forthcoming arrival in France of the Czar by sea, sent the King's equipages; horses, coaches, vehicles, waggons, and tables and chambers with Du Libois, one of the King's gentlemen in ordinary, to go and wait for the Czar at Dunkerque, pay the expenses incurred by him and his suite on the way to Paris, and everywhere render him the same honour as to the King. The Czar proposed to allot a hundred days to his journey. The apartment of the Queen- mother at the Louvre was furnished for him, the councils usually held there taking place in the houses of the chiefs of these councils.

M. le Duc d'Orleans discussing with me as to the nobleman best fitted to be appointed to wait upon the Czar during his stay, I recommended the Marechal de Tesse, as a man without occupation, who well knew the language and usages of society, who was accustomed to foreigners by his journeys and negotiations in Spain, Turin, Rome, and in other courts of Italy, and who, gentle and polite, was sure to perform his duties well. M. le Duc d'Orleans agreed with me, and the next day sent for him and gave him his orders.

When it was known that the Czar was near Dunkerque, the Regent sent the Marquis de Neelle to receive him at Calais, and accompany him until they met the Marechal de Tesse, who was not to go beyond Beaumont to wait for him. At the same time the Hotel de Lesdiguieres was prepared for the Czar and his suite, under the idea that he might prefer a private house, with all his people around him, to the Louvre. The Hotel de Lesdiguieres was large and handsome, as I have said at the commencement of this chapter, adjoined the arsenal, and belonged by succession to the Marechal de Villeroy, who lodged at the Tuileries. Thus the house was empty, because the Duc de Villeroy, who was not a man fond of display, had found it too distant to live in. It was entirely refurnished, and very magnificently, with the furniture of the King.

The Czar arrived at Beaumont on Friday, the 7th of May, 1717, about mid- day. Tesse made his reverences to him as he descended from his coach, had the honour of dining with him, and of escorting him that very day to Paris.

The Czar entered the city in one of Tesse's coaches, with three of his suite with him, but not Tesse himself. The Marechal followed in another coach. The Czar alighted at nine o'clock in the evening at the Louvre, and walked all through the apartments of the Queen-mother. He considered them to be too magnificently hung and lighted, jumped into his coach again, and went to the Hotel de Lesdiguieres, where he wished to lodge. He thought the apartment destined for him too fine also, and had his camp-bed immediately spread out in a wardrobe. The Marechal de Tesse, who was to do the honours of his house and of his table, to accompany him everywhere, and not quit the place where he might be, lodged in an apartment of the Hotel de Lesdiguieres, and had enough to do in following and sometimes running after him. Verton, one of the King's maitres d'hotel, was charged with serving him and all the tables of the Czar and his suite. The suite consisted of forty persons of all sorts, twelve or fifteen of whom were considerable people in themselves, or by their appointments; they all ate with the Czar.

Verton was a clever lad, strong in certain company, fond of good cheer and of gaming, and served the Czar with so much order, and conducted himself so well, that this monarch and all the suite conceived a singular friendship for him.

The Czar excited admiration by his extreme curiosity, always bearing upon his views of government, trade, instruction, police, and this curiosity embraced everything, disdained nothing in the smallest degree useful; it was marked and enlightened, esteeming only what merited to be esteemed, and exhibited in a clear light the intelligence, justness, ready appreciation of his mind. Everything showed in the Czar the vast extent of his knowledge, and a sort of logical harmony of ideas. He allied in the most surprising manner the highest, the proudest, the most delicate, the most sustained, and at the same time the least embarrassing majesty, when he had established it in all its safety with a marked politeness. Yet he was always and with everybody the master everywhere, but with gradations, according to the persons he was with. He had a kind of familiarity which sprang from liberty, but he was not without a strong dash of that ancient barbarism of his country, which rendered all his actions rapid; nay, precipitous, his will uncertain, and not to be constrained or contradicted in anything. Often his table was but little decent, much less so were the attendants who served, often too with an openness of kingly audacity everywhere. What he proposed to see or do was entirely independent of means; they were to be bent to his pleasure and command. His desire for liberty, his dislike to be made a show of, his free and easy habits, often made him prefer hired coaches, common cabs even; nay, the first which he could lay his hands on, though belonging to people below him of whom he knew nothing. He jumped in, and had himself driven all over the city, and outside it. On one occasion he seized hold of the coach of Madame de Mattignon, who had come to gape at him, drove off with it to Boulogne and other country places near Paris. The owner was much astonished to find she must journey back on foot. On such occasions the Marechal de Tesse and his suite had often hard work to find the Czar, who had thus escaped them.

CHAPTER LXXXVI

The Czar was a very tall man, exceedingly well made; rather thin, his face somewhat round, a high forehead, good eyebrows, a rather short nose, but not too short, and large at the end, rather thick lips, complexion reddish brown, good black eyes, large, bright, piercing, and well open; his look majestic and gracious when he liked, but when otherwise, severe and stern, with a twitching of the face, not often occurring, but which appeared to contort his eyes and all his physiognomy, and was frightful to see; it lasted a moment, gave him a wild and terrible air, and passed away. All his bearing showed his intellect, his reflectiveness, and his greatness, and was not devoid of a certain grace. He wore a linen collar, a round-brown wig, as though without powder, and which did not reach to his shoulders; a brown coat tight to the body, even, and with gold buttons; vest, breeches, stockings, no gloves or ruffles, the star of his order over his coat, and the cordon under it, the coat itself being frequently quite unbuttoned, his hat upon the table, but never upon his head, even out of doors. With this simplicity ill-accompanied or ill mounted as he might be, the air of greatness natural to him could not be mistaken.

What he ate and drank at his two regular meals is inconceivable, without reckoning the beer, lemonade, and other drinks he swallowed between these repasts, his suite following his example; a bottle or two of beer, as many more of wine, and occasionally, liqueurs afterwards; at the end of the meal strong drinks, such as brandy, as much sometimes as a quart. This was about the usual quantity at each meal. His suite at his table drank more and ate in proportion, at eleven o'clock in the morning and at eight at night. There was a chaplain who ate at the table of the Czar, who consumed half as much again as the rest, and with whom the monarch, who was fond of him, much amused himself. Prince Kourakin went every day to the Hotel de Lesdiguieres, but lodged elsewhere.

The Czar well understood French, and I think could have spoken it, if he had wished, but for greatness' sake he always had an interpreter. Latin and many other languages he spoke very well. There was a detachment of guards in his house, but he would scarcely ever allow himself to be followed by them. He would not set foot outside the Hotel de Lesdiguieres, whatever curiosity he might feel, or give any signs of life, until he had received a visit from the King.

On Saturday, the day after his arrival, the Regent went in the morning to see the Czar. This monarch left his cabinet, advanced a few paces, embraced Monsieur d'Orleans with an air of great superiority, pointed to the door of the cabinet, and instantly turning on his heel, without the slightest compliment, entered there. The Regent followed, and Prince Kourakin after him to serve as interpreter. They found two armchairs facing each other, the Czar seated himself in the upper, the Regent in the other. The conversation lasted nearly an hour without public affairs being mentioned, after which the Czar left his cabinet; the Regent followed him, made him a profound reverence, but slightly returned, and left him in the same place as he had found him on entering.

On Monday, the 10th of May, the King went to see the Czar, who received him at the door, saw him alight from his coach, walked with him at his left into his chamber, where they found two armchairs equally placed. The King sat down in the right-hand one, the Czar in the other, Prince Kourakin served as interpreter. It was astonishing to see the Czar take the King under both arms, hoist him up to his level, embrace him thus in the air; and the King, young as he was, show no fear, although he could not possibly have been prepared for such a reception. It was striking, too, to see the grace which the Czar displayed before the King, the air of tenderness he assumed towards him, the politeness which flowed as it were naturally, and which nevertheless was mixed with greatness, with equality of rank, and slightly with superiority of age: for all these things made themselves felt. He praised the King, appeared charmed with him, and persuaded everybody he was. He embraced him again and again. The King paid his brief compliment very prettily; and M. du Maine, the Marechal de Villeroy, and the distinguished people present, filled up the conversation. The meeting lasted a short quarter of an hour. The Czar accompanied the King as he had received him, and saw him to his coach.

On Tuesday, the 11th of May, between four and five o'clock, the Czar went to see the King. He was received by the King at his carriage door, took up a position on his right, and was conducted within. All these ceremonies had been agreed on before the King went to see him. The Czar showed the same affection and the same attentions to the King as before; and his visit was not longer than the one he had received, but the crowd much surprised him.

He had been at eight o'clock in the morning to see the Place Royal, the Place des Victoires, and the Place de Vendome, and the next day he went to the Observatoire, the Gobelins, and the King's Garden of Simples. Everywhere he amused himself in examining everything, and in asking many questions.

On Thursday, the 13th of May, he took medicine, but did not refrain after dinner from calling upon several celebrated artificers. On Friday, the 14th, he went at six o'clock in the morning into the grand gallery of the Louvre, to see the plans in relief of all the King's fortified places, Hasfield, with his engineers, doing the honours. The Czar examined all these plans for a long time; visited many other parts of the Louvre, and descended afterwards into the Tuileries garden, from which everybody had been excluded. They were working then upon the Pont Tournant. The Czar industriously examined this work, and remained there a long time. In the afternoon he went to see, at the Palais Royal, Madame, who had sent her compliments to him by her officer. The armchair excepted, she received him as she would have received the King. M. le Duc d'Orleans came afterwards and took him to the Opera, into his grand box, where they sat upon the front seat upon a splendid carpet. Sometime after, the Czar asked if there was no beer to be had. Immediately a large goblet of it was brought to him, on a salver. The Regent rose, took it, and presented it to the Czar, who with a smile and an inclination of politeness, received the goblet without any ceremony, drank, and put it back on the salver which the Regent still held. In handing it back, the Regent took a plate, in which was a napkin, presented it to the Czar, who without rising made use of it, at which the house appeared rather astonished. At the fourth act the Czar went away to supper, but did not wish the Regent to leave the box. The next morning he jumped into a hired coach, and went to see a number of curiosities among the workmen.

On the 16th of May, Whit Sunday, he went to the Invalides, where he wished to see and examine everything. At the refectory he tasted the soldiers' soup and their wine, drank to their healths, struck them on the shoulders, and called them comrades. He much admired the church, the dispensary, and the infirmary, and appeared much pleased with the order of the establishment. The Marechal de Villars did the honours; the Marechale went there to look on. The Czar was very civil to her.

On Monday, the 17th, he dined early with Prince Ragotzi, who had invited him, and afterwards went to Meudon, where he found some of the King's horses to enable him to see the gardens and the park at his ease. Prince Ragotzi accompanied him.

On Tuesday, the 18th, the Marechal d'Estrees took him, at eight o'clock in the morning, to his house at Issy, gave him a dinner, and much amused him during the day with many things shown to him relating to the navy.

On Monday, the 24th, he went out early to the Tuileries, before the King was up. He entered the rooms of the Marechal de Villeroy, who showed him the crown jewels. They were more beautiful and more numerous than he suspected, but he said he was not much of a judge of such things. He stated that he cared but little for the beauties purely of wealth and imagination, above all for those he could not attain. Thence he wished to go and see the King, who spared him the trouble by coming. It had been expressly arranged thus, so that his visit should appear one of chance. They met each other in a cabinet, and remained there The King, who held a roll of paper in his hand, gave it to him, and said it was the map of his territories. This compliment much pleased the Czar, whose politeness and friendly affectionate bearing were the same as before, with much grace and majesty.

In the afternoon he went to Versailles, where the Marechal de Tesse left him to the Duc d'Antin. The apartment of Madame la Dauphine was prepared for him, and he slept in the room of Monseigneur le Dauphin (the King's father), now made into a cabinet for the Queen.

On Tuesday, the 25th, he had traversed the gardens, and had been upon the canal early in the morning, before the hour of his appointment with D'Antin. He saw all Versailles, Trianon, and the menagerie. His principal suite was lodged at the chateau. They took ladies with them, and slept in the apartments Madame de Maintenon had occupied, quite close to that in which the Czar slept. Bloin, governor of Versailles, was extremely scandalised to see this temple of prudery thus profaned. Its goddess and he formerly would have been less shocked. The Czar and his people were not accustomed to restraint.

The expenses of this Prince amounted to six hundred crowns a day, though he had much diminished his table since the commencement.

On Sunday, the 30th of May, he set out with Bellegarde, and many relays, to dine at Petit Bourg, with D'Antin, who received him there, and took him in the afternoon to see Fontainebleau, where he slept, and the morrow there was a stag-hunt, at which the Comte de Toulouse did the honours. Fontainebleau did not much please the Czar, and the hunt did not please him at all; for he nearly fell off his horse, not being accustomed to this exercise, and finding it too violent. When he returned to Petit Bourg, the appearance of his carriage showed that he had eaten and drunk a good deal in it.

On Friday, the 11th of June, he went from Versailles to Saint-Cyr, where he saw all the household, and the girls in their classes. He was received there like the King. He wished to see Madame de Maintenon, who, expecting his curiosity, had buried herself in her bed, all the curtains closed, except one, which was half-open. The Czar entered her chamber, pulled back the window-curtains upon arriving, then the bed-curtains, took a good long stare at her, said not a word to her,—nor did she open her lips,—and, without making her any kind of reverence, went his way. I knew afterwards that she was much astonished, and still more mortified at this; but the King was no more. The Czar returned on Saturday, the 12th of June, to Paris.

On Tuesday, the 15th of June, he went early to D'Antin's Paris house. Working this day with M. le Duc d'Orleans, I finished in half an hour; he was surprised, and wished to detain me. I said, I could always have the honour of finding him, but not the Czar, who was going away; that I had not yet seen him, and was going to D'Antin's to stare at my ease. Nobody entered except those invited, and some ladies with Madame la Duchesse and the Princesses, her daughters, who wished to stare also. I entered the garden, where the Czar was walking. The Marechal de Tesse, seeing me at a distance, came up, wishing to present me to the Czar. I begged him to do nothing of the kind, not even to perceive me, but to let me gape at my ease, which I could not do if made known. I begged him also to tell this to D'Antin, and with these precautions I was enabled to satisfy my curiosity without interruption. I found that the Czar conversed tolerably freely, but always as the master everywhere. He retired into a cabinet, where D'Antin showed him various plans and several curiosities, upon which he asked several questions. It was there I saw the convulsion which I have noticed. I asked Tesse if it often happened; he replied, "several times a day, especially when he is not on his guard to prevent it." Returning afterwards into the garden, D'Antin made the Czar pass through the lower apartments, and informed him that Madame la Duchesse was there with some ladies, who had a great desire to see him. He made no reply, but allowed himself to be conducted. He walked more gently, turned his head towards the apartment where all the ladies were under arms to receive him; looked well at them all, made a slight inclination of the head to the whole company at once, and passed on haughtily. I think, by the manner in which he received other ladies, that he would have shown more politeness to these if Madame la Duchesse had not been there, making her visit too pretentious. He affected even not to inquire which she was, or to ask the name of any of the others. I was nearly an hour without quitting him, and unceasingly regarding him. At last I saw he remarked it. This rendered me more discreet, lest he should ask who I was. As he was returning, I walked away to the room where the table was laid. D'Antin, always the same, had found means to have a very good portrait of the Czarina placed upon the chimney-piece of this room, with verses in her praise, which much pleased and surprised the Czar. He and his suite thought the portrait very like.

The King gave the Czar two magnificent pieces of Gobelins tapestry. He wished to give him also a beautiful sword, ornamented with diamonds, but he excused himself from accepting it. The Czar, on his side, distributed 60,000 livres to the King's domestics, who had waited upon him; gave to D'Antin, Marechal d'Estrees, and Marechal Tesse, his portrait, adorned with diamonds, and five gold and eleven silver medals, representing the principal actions of his life.

He made a friendly present to Verton, whom he begged the Regent to send to him as charge d'affaires of the King, which the Regent promised.

On Wednesday, the 16th of June, he attended on horseback a review of the two regiments of the guards; gendarmes, light horse, and mousquetaires. There was only M. le Duc d'Orleans with him; the Czar scarcely looked at these troops, and they perceived it. He partook of a dinner-supper at Saint Ouen, at the Duc de Tresmes, where he said that the excessive heat and dust, together with the crowd on horseback and on foot, had made him quit the review sooner than he wished. The meal was magnificent; the Czar learnt that the Marquise de Bethune, who was looking on, was the daughter of the Duc de Tresriles; he begged her to sit at table; she was the only lady who did so, among a crowd of noblemen. Several other ladies came to look on, and to these he was very civil when he knew who they were.

On Thursday, the 17th, he went for the second time to the Observatoire, and there supped with the Marechal de Villars.

On Friday, the 18th of June, the Regent went early to the Hotel de Lesdiguieres, to say adieu to the Czar, remaining some time with him, with Prince Kourakin present. After this visit the Czar went to say goodbye to the King at the Tuileries. It had been agreed that there should be no more ceremonies between them. It was impossible to display more intelligence, grace, and tenderness towards the King than the Czar displayed on all these occasions; and again on the morrow, when the King came to the Hotel de Lesdiguieres to wish him a pleasant journey, no ceremony being observed.

On Sunday, the 20th of June, the Czar departed, and slept at Ivry, bound straight for Spa, where he was expected by the Czarina. He would be accompanied by nobody, not even on leaving Paris. The luxury he remarked much surprised him; he was moved in speaking upon the King and upon France, saying, he saw with sorrow that this luxury would soon ruin the country. He departed, charmed by the manner in which he had been received, by all he had seen, by the liberty that had been left to him, and extremely desirous to closely unite himself with the King; but the interests of the Abbe Dubois, and of England, were obstacles which have been much deplored since.

The Czar had an extreme desire to unite himself to France. Nothing would have been more advantageous to our commerce, to our importance in the north, in Germany, in all Europe. The Czar kept England in restraint as to her commerce, and King George in fear for his German states. He kept Holland respectful, and the Emperor measured. It cannot be denied that he made a grand figure in Europe and in Asia, or that France would have infinitely profited by close union with him. He did not like the Emperor; he wished to sever us from England, and it was England which rendered us deaf to his invitations, unbecomingly so, though they lasted after his departure. Often I vainly pressed the Regent upon this subject, and gave him reasons of which he felt all the force, and to which he could not reply. He was bewitched by Dubois, who panted to become Cardinal, and who built all his hopes of success upon England. The English saw his ambition, and took advantage of it for their own interests. Dubois' aim was to make use of the intimacy between the King of England and the Emperor, in order that the latter might be induced by the former to obtain a Cardinalship from the Pope, over whom he had great power. It will be seen, in due time, what success has attended the intrigues of the scheming and unscrupulous Abbe.

CHAPTER LXXXVII

Courson, Intendant, or rather King of Languedoc, exercised his authority there so tyrannically that the people suffered the most cruel oppressions at his hands. He had been Intendant of Rouen, and was so hated that more than once he thought himself in danger of having his brains beaten out with stones. He became at last so odious that he was removed; but the credit of his father saved him, and he was sent as Intendant to Bordeaux. He was internally and externally a very animal, extremely brutal, extremely insolent, his hands by no means clean, as was also the case with those of his secretaries, who did all his work for him, he being very idle and quite unfit for his post.

Amongst other tyrannic acts he levied very violent and heavy taxes in Perigueux, of his own good will and pleasure, without any edict or decree of the Council; and seeing that people were not eager to satisfy his demands, augmented them, multiplied the expenses, and at last threw into dungeons some sheriffs and other rich citizens. He became so tyrannical that they sent a deputation to Paris to complain of him. But the deputies went in vain the round of all the members of the council of the regency, after having for two months kicked their heels in the ante- chamber of the Duc de Noailles, the minister who ought to have attended to their representations.

The Comte de Toulouse, who was a very just man, and who had listened to them, was annoyed that they could obtain no hearing of the Duc de, Noailles, and spoke to me on the subject. I was as indignant as he. I spoke to M. le Duc d'Orleans, who only knew the matter superficially. I showed him the necessity of thoroughly examining into complaints of this nature; the injustice of allowing these deputies to wear out hope, patience, and life, in the streets of Paris, without giving some audience; the cruelty of suffering honest citizens to languish in dungeons, without knowing why or by what authority they were there. He agreed with me, and promised to speak to the Duc de Noailles. At the first finance council after this, I apprised the Comte de Toulouse, and we both asked the Duc de Noailles when he meant to bring forward the affair of these Perigueux people.

He was utterly unprepared for this question, and wished to put us off. I said to him that for a long time some of these people had been in prison, and others had wandered the streets of Paris; that this was shameful, and could not be longer endured. The Comte de Toulouse spoke very firmly, in the same sense. M. le Duc d'Orleans arrived and took his place.

As the Duc de Noailles opened his bag, I said very loudly to M. le Duc d'Orleans that M. le Comte de Toulouse and I had just asked M. de Noailles when he would bring forward the Perigueux affair; that these people, innocent or guilty, begged only to be heard and tried; and that it appeared to me the council was in honour bound to keep them in misery no longer. On finishing, I looked at the Comte de Toulouse, who also said something short but rather strong. M. le Duc d'Orleans replied that we could not have done better. The Duc de Noailles began muttering something about the press of business; that he had not time, and so forth. I interrupted him by saying that he must find time, and that he ought to have found it long before; that nothing was so important as to keep people from ruin, or to extricate others from dungeons they were remaining in without knowing why. M. le Duc d'Orleans said a word to the same effect, and ordered the Duc de Noailles to get himself ready to bring forward the case in a week.

From excuse to excuse, three weeks passed over. At last I said openly to M. le Duc d'Orleans that he was being laughed at, and that justice was being trodden under foot. At the next council it appeared that M. le Duc d'Orleans had already told the Duc de Noailles he would wait no longer. M. le Comte de Toulouse and I continued to ask him if at last he would bring forward the Perigueux affair. We doubted not that it would in the end be brought forward, but artifice was not yet at an end.

It was on a Tuesday afternoon, when M. le Duc d'Orleans often abridged the council to go to the opera. Knowing this, the Duc de Noailles kept all the council occupied with different matters. I was between him and the Comte de Toulouse. At the end of each matter I said to him, "And the Perigueux affair?"—"Directly," he replied, and at once commenced something else. At last I perceived his project, and whispered so to the Comte de Toulouse, who had already suspected it, and resolved not to be its dupe. When the Duc de Noailles had exhausted his bag, it was five o'clock. After putting back his papers he closed his bag, and said to M. le Duc d'Orleans that there was still the Perigueux affair which he had ordered him to bring forward, but that it would be long and detailed; that he doubtless wished to go to the opera; that it could be attended to next week; and at once, without waiting for a reply, he rises, pushes back his stool, and turns to go away. I took him by the arm.

"Gently," said I. "You must learn his highness's pleasure. Monsieur," said I to M. le Duc d'Orleans, still firmly holding the sleeve of the Duc de Noailles, "do you care much to-day for the opera?"

"No, no," replied he; "let us turn to the Perigueux affair."

"But without strangling it," replied I.

"Yes," said M. le Duc d'Orleans: then looking at M. le Duc, who smiled; "you don't care to go there?"

"No, Monsieur, let us see this business," replied M. le Duc.

"Oh, sit down again then, Monsieur," said I to the Duc de Noailles in a very firm tone, pulling him sharply; "take your rest, and re-open your bag."

Without saying a word he drew forward his stool with a great noise, and threw himself upon it as though he would smash it. Rage beamed from his eyes. The Comte de Toulouse smiled; he had said his word, too, upon the opera, and all the company looked at us; nearly every one smiling, but astounded also.

The Duc de Noailles displayed his papers, and began reading them. As various documents were referred to, I turned them over, and now and then took him up and corrected him. He did not dare to show anger in his replies, yet he was foaming. He passed an eulogy upon Basville (father of the Intendant), talked of the consideration he merited; excused Courson, and babbled thereupon as much as he could to extenuate everything, and lose sight of the principal points at issue. Seeing that he did not finish, and that he wished to tire us, and to manage the affair in his own way, I interrupted him, saying that the father and the son were two people; that the case in point respected the son alone, and that he had to determine whether an Intendant was authorised or not, by his office, to tax people at will; to raise imposts in the towns and country places of his department, without edicts ordering them, without even a decree of council, solely by his own particular ordonnances, and to keep people in prison four or five months, without form or shadow of trial, because they refused to pay these heavy taxes, rendered still more heavy by expenses. Then, turning round so as to look hard at him, "It is upon that, Monsieur," added I, "that we must decide, since your report is over, and not amuse ourselves with a panegyric upon M. de Basville, who is not mixed up in the case."

The Duc de Noailles, all the more beside himself because he saw the Regent smile, and M. le Duc, who looked at me do the same, but more openly, began to speak, or rather to stammer. He did not dare, however, to decide against the release of the prisoners.

"And the expenses, and the ordonnance respecting these taxes, what do you do with them?"

"By setting the prisoners at liberty," he said, "the ordonnance falls to the ground."

I did not wish to push things further just then. The liberation of the prisoners, and the quashing of the ordonnance, were determined on: some voices were for the reimbursement of the charges at the expense of the Intendant, and for preventing him to do the like again.

When it was my turn to speak, I expressed the same opinions, but I added that it was not enough to recompense people so unjustly ill-treated; that I thought a sum of money, such as it should please the council to name, ought to be adjudged to them; and that as to an Intendant who abused the authority of his office so much as to usurp that of the King and impose taxes, such as pleased him by his own ordinances, and who threw people into dungeons as he thought fit by his private authority, pillaging thus a province, I was of opinion that his Royal Highness should be asked to make such an example of him that all the other Intendants might profit by it.

The majority of those who had spoken before me made signs that I was right, but did not speak again. Others were against me. M. le Duc d'Orleans promised the liberation of the prisoners, broke Courson's ordonnance, and all which had followed it; said that as for the rest, he would take care these people should be well recompensed, and Courson well blamed; that he merited worse, and, but for his father, would have received it. As we were about to rise, I said it would be as well to draw up the decree at once, and M. le Duc d'Orleans approved. Noailles pounced, like a bird of prey, upon paper and ink, and commenced writing. I bent down and read as he wrote. He stopped and boggled at the annulling of the ordonnance, and the prohibition against issuing one again without authorisation by edict or decree of council. I dictated the clause to him; he looked at the company as though questioning all eyes.

"Yes," said I, "it was passed like that—you have only to ask again." M. le Duc d Orleans said, "Yes." Noailles wrote. I took the paper, and read what he had written. He received it back in fury, cast it among the papers pell-mell into his bag, then shoved his stool almost to the other end of the room, and went out, bristling like a wild boar, without looking at or saluting anybody—we all laughing. M. le Duc and several others came to me, and with M. le Comte de Toulouse, were much diverted. M. de Noailles had, in fact, so little command over himself, that, in turning to go out, he struck the table, swearing, and saying he could endure it no longer.

I learnt afterwards, by frequenters of the Hotel de Noailles, who told it to my friends, that when he reached home he went to bed: and would not see a soul; that fever seized him, that the next day he was of a frightful temper, and, that he had been heard to say he could no longer endure the annoyances I caused him. It may be imagined whether or not this softened me. The Duc de Noailles had, in fact, behaved towards me with such infamous treachery, and such unmasked impudence, that I took pleasure at all times and at all places in making him feel, and others see, the sovereign disdain I entertained for him. I did not allow my private feelings to sway my judgment when public interests were at stake, for when I thought the Duc de Noailles right, and this often occurred, I supported him; but when I knew him to be wrong, or when I caught him neglecting his duties, conniving at injustice, shirking inquiry, or evading the truth, I in no way spared him. The incident just related is an illustration of the treatment he often received at my hands. Fret, fume, stamp, storm, as he might, I cared nothing for him. His anger to me was as indifferent as his friendship. I despised both equally. Occasionally he would imagine, after there had been no storm between us for some time, that I had become reconciled to him, and would make advances to me. But the stern and terrible manner in which I met them, —or rather refused to meet them, taking no more notice of his politeness and his compliments, than as if they made no appeal whatever to my eyes or ears,—soon convinced him of the permanent nature of our quarrel, and drove him to the most violent rage and despair.

The history of the affair was, apparently, revealed by somebody to the deputies of Perigueux (for this very evening it was talked of in Paris), who came and offered me many thanks. Noailles was so afraid of me, that he did not keep their business unsettled more than two days.

A few months afterwards Courson was recalled, amid the bonfires of his province. This did not improve him, or hinder him from obtaining afterwards one of the two places of councillor at the Royal Council of Finance, for he was already Councillor of State at the time of this affair of Perigueux.

An amusement, suited to the King's age, caused a serious quarrel. A sort of tent had been erected for him on the terrace of the Tuileries, before his apartments, and on the same level. The diversions of kings always have to do with distinction. He invented some medals to give to the courtiers of his own age, whom he wished to distinguish, and those medals, which were intended to be worn, conferred the right of entering this tent without being invited; thus was created the Order of the Pavilion. The Marechal de Villeroy gave orders to Lefevre to have the medals made. He obeyed, and brought them to the Marechal, who presented them to the King. Lefevre was silversmith to the King's household, and as such under the orders of the first gentleman of the chamber. The Duc de Mortemart, who had previously had some tiff with the Marechal de Villeroy, declared that it devolved upon him to order these medals and present them to the King. He flew into a passion because everything had been done without his knowledge; and complained to the Duc d'Orleans. It was a trifle not worth discussing, and in which the three other gentlemen of the chamber took no part. Thus the Duc de Mortemart, opposed alone to the Marechal de Villeroy, stood no chance. M. le Duc d'Orleans, with his usual love for mezzo termine, said that Lefevre had not made these medals, or brought them to the Marechal as silversmith, but as having received through the Marechal the King's order, and that nothing more must be said. The Duc de Mortemart was indignant, and did not spare the Marechal.

VOLUME 12.: CHAPTER LXXXVIII

The Abbe Alberoni, having risen by the means I have described, and acquired power by following in the track of the Princesse des Ursins, governed Spain like a master. He had the most ambitious projects. One of his ideas was to drive all strangers, especially the French, out of the West Indies; and he hoped to make use of the Dutch to attain this end. But Holland was too much in the dependence of England.

At home Alberoni proposed many useful reforms, and endeavoured to diminish the expenses of the royal household. He thought, with reason, that a strong navy was the necessary basis of the power of Spain; and to create one he endeavoured to economise the public money. He flattered the King with the idea that next year he would arm forty vessels to protect the commerce of the Spanish Indies. He had the address to boast of his disinterestedness, in that whilst working at all manner of business he had never received any grace from the King, and lived only on fifty pistoles, which the Duke of Parma, his master, gave him every month; and therefore he made gently some complaints against the ingratitude of princes.

Alberoni had persuaded the Queen of Spain to keep her husband shut up, as had the Princesse des Ursins. This was a certain means of governing a prince whose temperament and whose conscience equally attached him to his spouse. He was soon completely governed once more— under lock and key, as it were, night and day. By this means the Queen was jailoress and prisoner at the same time. As she was constantly with the King nobody could come to her. Thus Alberoni kept them both shut up, with the key of their prison in his pocket.

One of the chief objects of his ambition was the Cardinal's hat. It would be too long to relate the schemes he set on foot to attain his end. He was opposed by a violent party at Rome; but at last his inflexible will and extreme cunning gained the day. The Pope, no longer able to resist the menaces of the King of Spain, and dreading the vengeance of the all-powerful minister, consented to grant the favour that minister had so pertinaciously demanded. Alberoni was made Cardinal on the 12th of July, 1717. Not a soul approved this promotion when it was announced at the consistory. Not a single cardinal uttered a word in praise of the new confrere, but many openly disapproved his nomination. Alberoni's good fortune did not stop here. At the death, some little time after, of the Bishop of Malaga, that rich see, worth thirty thousand ecus a year, was given to him. He received it as the mere introduction to the grandest and richest sees of Spain, when they should become vacant. The King of Spain gave him also twenty thousand ducats, to be levied upon property confiscated for political reasons. Shortly after, Cardinal Arias, Archbishop of Seville, having died, Alberoni was named to this rich archbishopric.

In the middle of his grandeur and good luck he met with an adventure that must have strangely disconcerted him.

I have before explained how Madame des Ursins and the deceased Queen had kept the King of Spain screened from all eyes, inaccessible to all his Court, a very palace-hermit. Alberoni, as I have said, followed their example. He kept the King even more closely imprisoned than before, and allowed no one, except a few indispensable attendants, to approach him. These attendants were a small number of valets and doctors, two gentlemen of the chamber, one or two ladies, and the majordomo-major of the King. This last post was filled by the Duc d'Escalone, always called Marquis de Villena, in every way one of the greatest noblemen in Spain, and most respected and revered of all, and justly so, for his virtue, his appointment, and his services.

Now the King's doctors are entirely under the authority of the majordomo-major. He ought to be present at all their consultations; the King should take no remedy that he is not told of, or that he does not approve, or that he does not see taken; an account of all the medicines should be rendered to him. Just at this time the King was ill. Villena wished to discharge the duties attached to his post of majordomo-major. Alberoni caused it to be insinuated to him, that the King wished to be at liberty, and that he would be better liked if he kept at home; or had the discretion and civility not to enter the royal chamber, but to ask at the door for news. This was language the Marquis would not understand.

At the end of the grand cabinet of the mirrors was placed a bed, in which the King was laid, in front of the door; and as the room is vast and long, it is a good distance from the door (which leads to the interior) to the place where the bed was. Alberoni again caused the Marquis to be informed that his attentions were troublesome, but the Marquis did not fail to enter as before. At last, in concert with the Queen, the Cardinal resolved to refuse him admission. The Marquis, presenting himself one afternoon, a valet partly opened the door and said, with much confusion, that he was forbidden to let him enter.

"Insolent fellow," replied the Marquis, "stand aside," and he pushed the door against the valet and entered. In front of him was the Queen, seated at the King's pillow; the Cardinal standing by her side, and the privileged few, and not all of them, far away from the bed. The Marquis, who, though full of pride, was but weak upon his legs, leisurely advanced, supported upon his little stick. The Queen and the Cardinal saw him and looked at each other. The King was too ill to notice anything, and his curtains were closed except at the side where the Queen was. Seeing the Marquis approach, the Cardinal made signs, with impatience, to one of the valets to tell him to go away, and immediately after, observing that the Marquis, without replying, still advanced, he went to him, explained to him that the King wished to be alone, and begged him to leave.

"That is not true," said the Marquis; "I have watched you; you have not approached the bed, and the King has said nothing to you."

The Cardinal insisting, and without success, took him by the arm to make him go. The Marquis said he was very insolent to wish to hinder him from seeing the King, and perform his duties. The Cardinal, stronger than his adversary, turned the Marquis round, hurried him towards the door, both talking the while, the Cardinal with measure, the Marquis in no way mincing his words. Tired of being hauled out in this manner, the Marquis struggled, called Alberoni a "little scoundrel," to whom he would teach manners; and in this heat and dust the Marquis, who was weak, fortunately fell into an armchair hard by. Angry at his fall, he raised his little stick and let it fall with all his force upon the ears and the shoulders of the Cardinal, calling him a little scoundrel—a little rascal— a little blackguard, deserving a horsewhipping.

The Cardinal, whom he held with one hand, escaped as well as he could, the Marquis continuing to abuse him, and shaking the stick at him. One of the valets came and assisted him to rise from his armchair, and gain the door; for after this accident his only thought was to leave the room.

The Queen looked on from her chair during all this scene, without stirring or saying a word; and the privileged few in the chamber did not dare to move. I learned all this from every one in Spain; and moreover I asked the Marquis de Villena himself to give me the full details; and he, who was all uprightness and truth, and who had conceived some little friendship for me, related with pleasure all I have written. The two gentlemen of the chamber present also did the same, laughing in their sleeves. One had refused to tell the Marquis to leave the room, and the other had accompanied him to the door. The most singular thing is, that the Cardinal, furious, but surprised beyond measure at the blows he had received, thought only of getting out of reach. The Marquis cried to him from a distance, that but for the respect he owed to the King, and to the state in which he was, he would give him a hundred kicks in the stomach, and haul him out by the ears. I was going to forget this. The King was so ill that he saw nothing.

A quarter of an hour after the Marquis had returned home, he received an order to retire to one of his estates at thirty leagues from Madrid. The rest of the day his house was filled with the most considerable people of Madrid, arriving as they learned the news, which made a furious sensation through the city. He departed the next day with his children. The Cardinal, nevertheless, remained so terrified, that, content with the exile of the Marquis, and with having got rid of him, he did not dare to pass any censure upon him for the blows he had received. Five or six months afterwards he sent him an order of recall, though the Marquis had not taken the slightest steps to obtain it. What is incredible is, that the adventure, the exile, the return, remained unknown to the King until the fall of the Cardinal! The Marquis would never consent to see him, or to hear him talked of, on any account, after returning, though the Cardinal was the absolute master. His pride was much humiliated by this worthy and just haughtiness; and he was all the more piqued because he left nothing undone in order to bring about a reconciliation, without any other success than that of obtaining fresh disdain, which much increased the public estimation in which this wise and virtuous nobleman was held.

CHAPTER LXXXIX

I must not omit to mention an incident which occurred during the early part of the year 1718, and which will give some idea of the character of M. le Duc d'Orleans, already pretty amply described by me.

One day (when Madame la Duchesse d'Orleans had gone to Montmartre, which she quitted soon after) I was walking alone with M. le Duc d'Orleans in the little garden of the Palais Royal, chatting upon various affairs, when he suddenly interrupted me, and turning towards me; said, "I am going to tell you something that will please you."

Thereupon he related to me that he was tired of the life he led, which was no longer in harmony with his age or his desires, and many similar things; that he was resolved to give up his gay parties, pass his evenings more soberly and decently, sometimes at home, often with Madame la Duchesse d'Orleans; that his health would gain thereby, and he should have more time for business; that in a little while I might rely upon it —there would be no more suppers of "roues and harlots" (these were his own terms), and that he was going to lead a prudent and reasonable life adapted to his age and state.

I admit that in my extreme surprise ' was ravished, so great was the interest I took in him. I testified this to him with overflowing heart, thanking him for his confidence. I said to him that he knew I for a long time had not spoken to him of the indecency of his life, or of the time he lost, because I saw that in so doing I lost my own; that I had long since despaired of his conduct changing; that this had much grieved me; that he could not be ignorant from all that had passed between us at various times, how much I desired a change, and that he might judge of the surprise and joy his announcement gave me. He assured me more and more that his resolution was fixed, and thereupon I took leave of him, the hour for his soiree having arrived.

The next day I learned from people to whom the roues had just related it, that M. le Duc d'Orleans was no sooner at table than he burst out laughing, and applauded his cleverness, saying that he had just laid a trap for me into which I had fallen full length. He recited to them our conversation, at which the joy and applause were marvellous. It is the only time he ever diverted himself at my expense (not to say at his own) in a matter in which the fib he told me, and which I was foolish enough to swallow, surprised by a sudden joy that took from me reflection, did honour to me, though but little to him. I would not gratify him by telling him I knew of his joke, or call to his mind what he had said to me; accordingly he never dared to speak of it.

I never could unravel what fantasy had seized him to lead him to hoax me in this manner, since for many years I had never opened my mouth concerning the life he led, whilst he, on his side, had said not a word to me relating to it. Yet it is true that sometimes being alone with confidential valets, some complaints have escaped him (but never before others) that I ill-treated him, and spoke hastily to him, but all was said in two words, without bitterness, and without accusing me of treating him wrongfully. He spoke truly also; sometimes, when I was exasperated with stupidity or error in important matters which affected him or the State, or when he had agreed (having been persuaded and convinced by good reasons) to do or not to do some essential thing, and was completely turned from it by his feebleness, his easy-going nature (which he appreciated as well as I)—cruelly did I let out against him. But the trick he most frequently played me before others, one of which my warmth was always dupe, was suddenly to interrupt an important argument by a 'sproposito' of buffoonery. I could not stand it; sometimes being so angry that I wished to leave the room. I used to say to him that if he wished to joke I would joke as much as he liked, but to mix the most serious matters with tomfoolery was insupportable. He laughed heartily, and all the more because, as the thing often happened, I ought to have been on my guard; but never was, and was vexed both at the joke and at being surprised; then he returned to business. But princes must sometimes banter and amuse themselves with those whom they treat as friends. Nevertheless, in spite of his occasional banter, he entertained really sincere esteem and friendship for me.

By chance I learnt one day what he really thought of me. I will say it now, so as to leave at once all these trifles. M. le Duc d'Orleans returning one afternoon from the Regency Council at the Tuileries to the Palais Royal with M. le Duc de Chartres (his son) and the Bailli de Conflans (then first gentleman of his chamber) began to talk of me, passing an eulogium upon me I hardly dare to repeat. I know not what had occurred at the Council to occasion it. All that I can say is that he insisted upon his happiness in having a friend so faithful, so unchanging at all times, so useful to him as I was, and always had been; so sure, so true, so disinterested, so firm, such as he could meet with in no one else, and upon whom he could always count. This eulogy lasted from the Tuileries to the Palais Royal, the Regent saying to his son that he wished to teach him how to make my acquaintance, as a support and a source of happiness (all that I relate here is in his own words); such as he had always found in my friendship and counsel. The Bailli de Conflans, astonished at this abundant eloquence, repeated it to me two days after, and I admit that I never have forgotten it. And here I will say that whatever others might do, whatever I myself (from disgust and vexation at what I saw ill done) might do, the Regent always sought reconciliation with me with shame, confidence, confusion, and he has never found himself in any perplexity that he has not opened his heart to me, and consulted me, without however always following my advice, for he was frequently turned from it by others.

He would never content himself with one mistress. He needed a variety in order to stimulate his taste. I had no more intercourse with them than with his roues. He never spoke of them to me, nor I to him. I scarcely ever knew anything of their adventures. His roues and valets were always eager to present fresh mistresses to him, from which he generally selected one. Amongst these was Madame de Sabran, who had married a man of high rank, but without wealth or merit, in order to be at liberty. There never was a woman so beautiful as she, or of a beauty more regular, more agreeable, more touching, or of a grander or nobler bearing, and yet without affectation. Her air and her manners were simple and natural, making you think she was ignorant of her beauty and of her figure (this last the finest in the world), and when it pleased her she was deceitfully modest. With much intellect she was insinuating, merry, overflowing, dissipated, not bad-hearted, charming, especially at table. In a word, she was all M. le Duc d'Orleans wanted, and soon became his mistress without prejudice to the rest.

As neither she nor her husband had a rap, they were ready for anything, and yet they did not make a large fortune. One of the chamberlains of the Regent, with an annual salary of six thousand livres, having received another appointment, Madame de Sabran thought six thousand livres a year too good to be lost, and asked for the post for her husband. She cared so little for him, by the way, that she called him her "mastiff." It was she, who, supping with M. le Duc d'Orleans and his roues, wittily said, that princes and lackeys had been made of one material, separated by Providence at the creation from that out of which all other men had been made.

All the Regent's mistresses had one by one their turn. Fortunately they had little power, were not initiated into any state secrets, and received but little money.

The Regent amused himself with them, and treated them in other respects exactly as they deserved to be treated.

CHAPTER XC

It is time now that I should speak of matters of very great importance, which led to changes that filled my heart with excessive joy, such as it had never known before.

For a long time past the Parliament had made many encroachments upon the privileges belonging to the Dukes. Even under the late King it had begun these impudent enterprises, and no word was said against it; for nothing gave the King greater pleasure than to mix all ranks together in a caldron of confusion. He hated and feared the nobility, was jealous of their power, which in former reigns had often so successfully balanced that of the crown; he was glad therefore of any opportunity which presented itself that enabled him to see our order weakened and robbed of its dignity.

The Parliament grew bolder as its encroachments one by one succeeded. It began to fancy itself armed with powers of the highest kind. It began to imagine that it possessed all the authority of the English Parliament, forgetting that that assembly is charged with the legislative administration of the country, that it has the right to make laws and repeat laws, and that the monarch can do but little, comparatively speaking, without the support and sanction of this representative chamber; whereas, our own Parliament is but a tribunal of justice, with no control or influence over the royal authority or state affairs.

But, as I have said, success gave it new impudence. Now that the King was dead, at whose name alone it trembled, this assembly thought that a fine opportunity had come to give its power the rein. It had to do with a Regent, notorious for his easy-going disposition, his indifference to form and rule, his dislike to all vigorous measures. It fancied that victory over such an opponent would be easy; that it could successfully overcome all the opposition he could put in action, and in due time make his authority secondary to its own. The Chief-President of the Parliament, I should observe, was the principal promoter of these sentiments. He was the bosom friend of M. and Madame du Maine, and by them was encouraged in his views. Incited by his encouragement, he seized an opportunity which presented itself now, to throw down the glove to M. le Duc d'Orleans, in the name of the Parliament, and to prepare for something like a struggle. The Parliament of Brittany had recently manifested a very turbulent spirit, and this was an additional encouragement to that of Paris.

At first the Parliament men scarcely knew what to lay hold of and bring forward, as an excuse for the battle. They wished of course to gain the applause of the people as protectors of their interests—likewise those who for their private ends try to trouble and embroil the State—but could not at first see their way clear. They sent for Trudaine, Prevot des Marchand, Councillor of State, to give an account to them of the state of the Hotel de Ville funds. He declared that they had never been so well paid, and that there was no cause of complaint against the government. Baffled upon this point, they fastened upon a edict, recently rendered, respecting the money of the realm. They deliberated thereon, deputed a commission to examine the matter, made a great fuss, and came to the conclusion that the edict would, if acted upon, be very prejudicial to the country.

Thus much done, the Parliament assembled anew on Friday morning, the 17th of June, 1718, and again in the afternoon. At the end they decided upon sending a deputation to the Regent, asking him to suspend the operation of the edict, introduce into it the changes suggested by their body, and then send it to them to be registered. The deputation was sent, and said all it had to say.

On the morrow the Parliament again assembled, morning and afternoon, and sent a message to the Regent, saying, it would not separate until it had received his reply. That reply was very short and simple. The Regent sent word that he was tired of the meddling interference of the Parliament (this was not the first time, let me add, that he experienced it), that he had ordered all the troops in Paris, and round about, to hold themselves ready to march, and that the King must be obeyed. Such was in fact true. He had really ordered the soldiers to keep under arms and to be supplied with powder and shot.

The message did not intimidate the Parliament. The next day, Sunday, the Chief-President, accompanied by all the other presidents, and by several councillors, came to the Palais Royal. Although, as I have said, the leader of his company, and the right-hand man of M. and Madame du Maine, he wished for his own sake to keep on good terms with the Regent, and at the same time to preserve all authority over his brethren, so as to have them under his thumb. His discourse then to the Regent commenced with many praises and much flattery, in order to smooth the way for the three fine requests he wound up with. The first of these was that the edict should be sent to the Parliament to be examined, and to suffer such changes as the members should think fit to introduce, and then be registered; the second, that the King should pay attention to their remonstrances in an affair of this importance, which they believed prejudicial to the State; the third, that the works recently undertaken at the mint for recasting the specie should be suspended!

To these modest requests the Regent replied that the edict had been registered at the Cour des Monnaies, which is a superior court, and consequently sufficient for such registration; that there was only a single instance of an edict respecting the money of the realm having been sent before the Parliament, and then out of pure civility; that the matter had been well sifted, and all its inconveniences weighed; that it was to the advantage of the State to put in force this edict; that the works of the Mint could not be interfered with in any way; finally, that the King must be obeyed! It was quite true that the edict had been sent to the Parliament out of courtesy, but at the suggestion of the Regent's false and treacherous confidants, valets of the Parliament, such as the Marechals de Villeroy, and Huxelles, and Besons, Canillac, Effiat, and Noailles.

Notwithstanding the decisive answer they had received, the Parliament met the very next day, and passed a decree against the edict. The council of the regency, at its sitting on the afternoon of the same day, abrogated this decree. Thus, since war was in a measure declared between the Regent's authority and that of the Parliament, the orders emanating from the one were disputed by the other, and vice versa. A nice game of shuttlecock this, which it was scarce likely could last long!

The Regent was determined to be obeyed. He prohibited, therefore, the printing and posting up of the decree of the Parliament. Soldiers of the guards, too, were placed in the markets to hinder the refusal of the new money which had been issued. The fact is, by the edict which had been passed, the Louis worth thirty livres was taken at thirty-six livres, and the crown piece, worth a hundred sous, at six livres instead of five. By this edict also government notes were made legal tender until the new money should be ready. The finances were thus relieved, and the King gained largely from the recasting of the coin. But private people lost by this increase, which much exceeded the intrinsic value of the metal used, and which caused everything to rise in price. Thus the Parliament had a fine opportunity for trumpeting forth its solicitude for the public interest, and did not fail to avail itself of it.

During the night a councillor of the Parliament was surprised on horseback in the streets tearing down and disfiguring the decree of the Regency Council, which abrogated that of the Parliament. He was taken to prison.

On Monday, the 27th of June, the Chief-President, at the head of all the other presidents, and of forty councillors, went to the Tuileries, and in the presence of the Regent read the wire-drawn remonstrance of the Parliament upon this famous edict. The Keeper of the Seals said that in a few days the King would reply. Accordingly on Saturday, the 2nd of July, the same deputation came again to the Tuileries to hear the reply. The Regent and all the Princes of the blood were there, the bastards also. Argenson, who from lieutenant of police had been made keeper of the seals, and who in his former capacity had often been ill-used—nay, even attacked by the Parliament—took good care to show his superiority over that assembly. He answered that deputation in the name of the King, and concluded by saying that the edict would in no way be altered, but would receive complete application. The parliamentary gentlemen did not expect so firm a reply, and withdrew, much mortified.

They were not, however, vanquished. They reassembled on the 11th and 12th of August, and spat forth all their venom in another decree specially aimed at the authority of the Regent. By this decree the administration of the finances was henceforth entirely to be at the mercy of the Parliament. Law, the Scotchman, who, under the favour of M. le Duc d'Orleans, had been allowed some influence over the State money matters, was to possess that influence no longer; in fact, all power on the part of the Regent over the finances was to be taken from him.

After this the Parliament had to take but one step in order to become the guardian of the King and the master of the realm (as in fact it madly claimed to be), the Regent more at its mercy than the King, and perhaps as exposed as King Charles I. of England. Our parliamentary gentlemen began as humbly as those of England, and though, as I have said, their assembly was but a simple court of justice, limited in its jurisdiction like the other courts of the realm, to judge disputes between private people, yet by dint of hammering upon the word parliament they believed themselves not less important than their English brethren, who form the legislative assembly, and represent all the nation.

M. and Madame du Maine had done not a little to bring about these fancies, and they continued in secret to do more. Madame du Maine, it may be recollected, had said that she would throw the whole country into combustion, in order not to lose her husband's prerogative. She was as good as her word. Encouraged doubtless by the support they received from this precious pair, the Parliament continued on its mad career of impudent presumption, pride, and arrogance. It assembled on the 22nd of August, and ordered inquiry to be made of the Regent as to what had become of all the state notes that had been passed at the Chamber of justice; those which had been given for the lotteries that were held every month; those which had been given for the Mississippi or Western Company; finally, those which had been taken to the Mint since the change in the specie.

These questions were communicated to the Regent by the King's officers. In reply he turned his back upon them, and went away into his cabinet, leaving these people slightly bewildered. Immediately after this occurrence it was rumoured that a Bed of justice would soon be held. The Regent had not then thought of summoning such an important assembly, and his weakness and vacillation were such that no one thought he would dare to do so.

The memoirs of Cardinal de Retz, of Joly, of Madame Motteville, had turned all heads. These books had become so fashionable, that in no class was the man or woman who did not have them continually in hand. Ambition, the desire for novelty, the skill of those who circulated these books, made the majority of people hope to cut a figure or make a fortune, and persuaded them there was as little lack of personages as in the last minority. People looked upon Law as the Mazarin of the day— (they were both foreign)—upon M. and Madame du Maine, as the chiefs of the Fronde; the weakness of M. le Duc d'Orleans was compared to that of the Queen-mother, and so on.

To say the truth, all tended towards whatever was extreme—moderation seemed forgotten— and it was high time the Regent aroused himself from a supineness which rendered him contemptible, and which emboldened his enemies and those of the State to brave all and undertake all. This lethargy, too, disheartened his servants, and made all healthy activity on their part impossible. It had at last led him to the very verge of the precipice, and the realm he governed to within an inch of the greatest confusion. He had need, indeed, to be up and doing!

The Regent, without having the horrible vice or the favourites of Henry III., had even more than that monarch become notorious for his daily debauches, his indecency, and his impiety. Like Henry III., too, he was betrayed by his most intimate councillors and domestics. This treachery pleased him (as it had pleased that King) because it induced him to keep idle, now from fear, now from interest, now from disdain, and now from policy. This torpor was agreeable to him because it was in conformity with his humour and his tastes, and because he regarded those who counselled it as good, wise, and enlightened people, not blinded by their private interests, but seeing clearly things as they were; while he was importuned with opinions and explanations which would have disclosed the true state of affairs and suggested remedies.

He looked upon such people as offered these opinions and explanations as impetuous counsellors, who hurried everything and suggested everything, who wished to discount the future in order to satisfy their ambition, their aversion, their different passions. He kept on his guard against them; he applauded himself for not being their dupe. Now, he laughed at them; often he allowed them to believe he appreciated their reasoning, that he was going to act and rouse from his lethargy. He amused them thus, gained time, and diverted himself afterwards with the others. Sometimes he replied coldly to them, and when they pressed him too much he allowed his suspicions to peep out.

Long since I had perceived M. le Duc d'Orleans' mode of action. At the first movements of the Parliament, of the bastards, and of those who had usurped the name of nobility, I had warned him. I had done so again as soon as I saw the cadence and the harmony of the designs in progress. I had pointed out to him their inevitable sequel; how easy it was to hinder them at the commencement; how difficult after, especially for a person of his character and disposition. But I was not the man for such work as this. I was the oldest, the most attached, the freest spoken of all his servitors; I had given him the best proofs of this in the most critical times of his life, and in the midst of his universal abandonment; the counsels I had offered him in these sad days he had always found for his good; he was accustomed to repose in me the most complete confidence; but, whatever opinion he might have of me, and of my truth and probity, he was on his guard against what he called my warmth, and against the love I had for my dignity, so attacked by the usurpations of the bastards, the designs of the Parliament, and the modern fancies of a sham nobility. As soon as I perceived his suspicions I told him so, and I added that, content with having done my duty as citizen and as his servitor, I would say no more on the subject. I kept my word. For more than a year I had not of myself opened my mouth thereon. If he was sometimes spoken to before me, and I could not keep quite silent without being suspected of sulking or pique, I carelessly said something indefinite, with as little meaning in it as possible, and calculated to make us drop the subject.

Judge of my surprise, therefore, when as I was working as usual one afternoon with the Regent, he interrupted me to speak with bitterness of the Parliament. I replied with my accustomed coldness and pretended negligence, and continued my business. He stopped me, and said that he saw very well that I would not reply to him concerning the Parliament. I admitted it was true, and added that he must long since have perceived this. Pressed and pressed beyond measure, I coldly remarked that he could not but remember what I had said to him of the Parliament both before and after his accession to the regency, that other counsels had prevailed over mine, and that finding my opinions were misinterpreted by him, I had resolved to hold my tongue, and had done so. As the subject was now reopened I reminded him of a prophecy I had uttered long before, that he had missed the opportunity of governing the Parliament when he might have done so with a frown, and that step by step he would allow himself to be conducted by his easy-going disposition, until he found himself on the very verge of the abyss; that if he wished to recover his position he must begin at once to retrace his steps, or lose his footing for ever!

Such strong words (from my mouth they had been rare of late), pronounced with a slow, firm coldness, as though I were indifferent to the course he might adopt, made him feel how little capable I believed him of vigorous and sustained action, and what trifling trouble I took to make him adopt my views. Dubois, Argenson, and Law had also spoken to him, urging him to take strong measures against the Parliament; the effect of my speech was therefore marvellous.

It was indeed high time to do something, as I have before remarked. The Parliament, we found, after passing its last decree, had named a commission to inquire into the financial edict; this commission was working in the utmost secrecy; a number of witnesses had already been examined, and preparations were quietly making to arrest Law some fine morning, and hang him three hours after within the enclosure of the Palais de justice.

Immediately this fact became known, the Duc de la Force and Fagon (Councillor of State) went to the Regent—'twas on the 19th of August, 1718—and spoke to him with such effect, that he ordered them to assemble with Law that very day at my house in order to see what was to be done. They came, in fact, and this was the first intimation I had that the Regent had begun to feel the gravity of his position, and that he was ready to do something. In this conference at my house the firmness of Law, hitherto so great, was shaken so that tears escaped him. Arguments did not satisfy us at first, because the question could only be decided by force, and we could not rely upon that of the Regent. The safe- conduct with which Law was supplied would not have stopped the Parliament an instant. On every side we were embarrassed. Law, more dead than alive, knew not what to say; much less what to do. His safety appeared to us the most pressing matter to ensure. If he had been taken it would have been all over with him before the ordinary machinery of negotiation (delayed as it was likely to be by the weakness of the Regent) could have been set in motion; certainly, before there would have been leisure to think of better, or to send a regiment of guards to force open the Palais de justice; a critical remedy at all times, and grievous to the last degree, even when it succeeds; frightful, if instead of Law, only his suspended corpse had been found!

I advised Law, therefore, to retire to the Palais Royal, and occupy the chamber of Nancre, his friend, then away in Spain. Law breathed again at this suggestion (approved by de la Force and Fagon), and put it in execution the moment he left my house. He might have been kept in safety at the Bank, but I thought the Palais Royal would be better: that his retirement there would create more effect, and induce the Regent to hold firm to his purpose, besides allowing his Royal Highness to see the financier whenever he pleased.

CHAPTER XCI

This done I proposed, and the others approved my proposition, that a Bed of Justice should be held as the only means left by which the abrogation of the parliamentary decrees could be registered. But while our arguments were moving, I stopped them all short by a reflection which came into my mind. I represented to my guests that the Duc du Maine was in secret the principal leader of the Parliament, and was closely allied with Marechal de Villeroy; that both would oppose might and main the assembling of a Bed of justice, so contrary to their views, to their schemes, to their projects; that to hinder it they, as guardians of the young King, would plead on his behalf, the heat, which was in fact extreme, the fear of the crowd, of the fatigue, of the bad air; that they would assume a pathetic tone in speaking of the King's health, calculated to embarrass the Regent; that if he persisted they would protest against everything which might happen to His Majesty; declare, perhaps, that in order not to share the blame, they would not accompany him; that the King, prepared by them, would grow frightened, perhaps, and would not go to the Parliament without them; that then all would be lost, and the powerlessness of the Regent, so clearly manifested, might rapidly lead to the most disastrous results.

These remarks stopped short our arguments, but I had not started objections without being prepared with a remedy for them. I said, "Let the Bed of justice be held at the Tuileries; let it be kept a profound secret until the very morning it is to take place; and let those who are to attend it be told so only a few hours before they are to assemble. By these means no time will be allowed for anybody to object to the proceeding, to plead the health of the King, the heat of the weather, or to interfere with the arrangement of the troops which it will be necessary to make."

We stopped at this: Law went away, and I dictated to Fagon the full details of my scheme, by which secrecy was to be ensured and all obstacles provided against. We finished about nine o'clock in the evening, and I counselled Fagon to carry what he had written to the Abbe Dubois, who had just returned from England with new credit over the mind of his master.

The next day I repaired to the Palais Royal about four o'clock. A moment after La Vrilliere came and relieved me of the company of Grancey and Broglio, two roues, whom I had found in the grand cabinet, in the cool, familiarly, without wigs. When M. le Duc d'Orleans was free he led me into the cabinet, behind the grand salon, by the Rue de Richelieu, and on entering said he was at the crisis of his regency, and that everything was needed in order to sustain him on this occasion. He added that he was resolved to strike a heavy blow at the Parliament; that he much approved my proposition respecting the Bed of justice at the Tuileries, and that it would be held exactly as I had suggested.

I was delighted at his animation, and at the firmness he appeared to possess, and after having well discussed with him all the inconveniences of my plan, and their remedy, we came at last to a very important matter, the mechanical means, so to speak, by which that plan was to be put in force. There was one thing to be provided for, which may appear an exceedingly insignificant matter, but which in truth was of no light importance. When a Bed of justice is held, seats one above another must be provided for those who take part in it. No room in the Tuileries possessed such seats and how erect them without noise, without exciting remarks, without causing inquiries and suspicions, which must inevitably lead to the discovery and perhaps thereby to the failure of our project? I had not forgotten this difficulty, however, and I said to the Regent I would go in secret to Fontanieu, who controlled the crown furniture, explain all to him, and arrange matters with him so that these seats should be erected at the very last moment, in time for our purpose, but too late to supply information that could be made use of by our enemies. I hurried off accordingly, as soon as I could get away, in search of Fontanieu.

I had already had some relations with him, for he had married his daughter to the son of the sister of my brother-in-law, M. de Lauzun. I had done him some little service, and had therefore every reason to expect he would serve me on this occasion. Judge of my annoyance when upon reaching his house I learned that he had gone almost to the other end of the town, to the Marais, to conduct a suit at law, in which Monsieur and Madame de Lauzun were concerned, respecting an estate at Rondon they claimed!

The porter seeing me so vexed at being obliged to journey so far in search of Fontanieu, said, that if I would go and speak to Madame Fontanieu, he would see if his master was not still in the neighbourhood, at a place he intended to visit before going to the Marais. I acted upon this suggestion and went to Madame Fontanieu, whom I found alone. I was forced to talk to her of the suit of Monsieur and Madame de Lauzun, which I pretended was the business I came upon, and cruelly did I rack my brains to say enough to keep up the conversation. When Fontanieu arrived, for he was soon found, fortunately, I was thrown into another embarrassment, for I had all the pains in the world to get away from Madame Fontanieu, who, aided by her husband, begged me not to take the trouble to descend but to discuss the subject where I was as she was as well informed upon the case as he, I thought once or twice I should never escape her. At last, however, I led away Fontanieu, by dint of compliments to his wife, in which I expressed my unwillingness to weary her with this affair.

When Fontanieu and I were alone down in his cabinet, I remained some moments talking to him upon the same subject, to allow the valets who had opened the doors for us time to retire. Then, to his great astonishment, I went outside to see if there were no listeners, and carefully closed the doors. After this I said to Fontanieu that I had not come concerning the affair of Madame de Lauzun, but upon another very different, which demanded all his industry, a secrecy proof against every trial, and which M. le Duc d'Orleans had charged me to communicate to him; but that before explaining myself he must know whether his Royal Highness could certainly count upon him.

It is strange what an impression the wildest absurdities leave if they are spread abroad with art. The first thing Fontanieu did was to tremble violently all over and become whiter than his shirt. With difficulty he stammered out a few words to the effect that he would do for M. le Duc d'Orleans as much as his duty would permit him to do. I smiled, looking fixedly at him, and this smile warned him apparently that he owed me an excuse for not being quite at ease upon any affair that passed through my hands; he directly made me one, at all events, and with the confusion of a man who sees that his first view has dazzled the second, and who, full of this first view, does not show anything, yet lets all be seen.

I reassured him as well as I could, and said that I had answered for him to M. le Duc d'Orleans, and afterwards that a Bed of justice was wanted, for the construction of which we had need of him.

Scarcely had I explained this, than the poor fellow began to take breath, as though escaping from stifling oppression, or a painful operation for the stone, and asked me if that was what I wanted?

He promised everything, so glad was he to be let off thus cheaply, and in truth he kept to his word, both as to the secret and the work. He had never seen a Bed of justice, and had not the slightest notion what it was like. I sat down on his bureau, and drew out the design of one. I dictated to him the explanations in the margin, because I did not wish them to be in my handwriting. I talked more than an hour with him; I disarranged his furniture, the better to show to him the order of the assembly, and explained to him what was to be done, so that all might be carried to the Tuileries and erected in a very, few moments. When I found I had made everything sufficiently clear, and he had understood me, I returned to the Palais Royal as though recollecting something, being already in the streets, to deceive my people.

A servant awaited me at the top of the staircase, and the concierge of the Palais Royal at the door of M. le Duc d'Orleans' room, with orders to beg me to write. It was the sacred hour of the roues and the supper, at which all idea of business was banished. I wrote, therefore, to the Regent in his winter cabinet what I had just done, not without some little indignation that he could not give up his pleasure for an affair of this importance. I was obliged to beg the concierge not to give my note to M. le Duc d'Orleans unless he were in a state to read it and to burn it afterwards.

Our preparations for the Bed of justice continued to be actively but silently made during the next few days. In the course of the numberless discussions which arose upon the subject, it was agreed, after much opposition on my part, to strike a blow, not only at the Parliament, but at M. du Maine, who had fomented its discontent. M. le Duc, who had been admitted to our councils, and who was heart and soul against the bastards, proposed that at the Bed of justice the education of the young King should be taken out of the control of M. du Maine and placed in his hands. He proposed also that the title of Prince of the Blood should be taken from him, with all the privileges it conferred, and that he should be reduced to the rank of a simple Duke and Peer, taking his place among the rest according to the date of his erection; thus, at a bound, going down to the bottom of the peerage!

Should these memoirs ever see the light, every one who reads them will be able to judge how such a proposition as this harmonised with my personal wishes. I had seen the bastards grow in rank and importance with an indignation and disgust I could scarcely contain. I had seen favour after favour heaped upon them by the late King, until he crowned all by elevating them to the rank of Princes of the Blood in defiance of all law, of all precedent, of all decency, if I must say the word. What I felt at this accumulation of honours I have more than once expressed; what I did to oppose such monstrous innovations has also been said. No man could be more against M. du Maine than I, and yet I opposed this proposition of M. le Duc because I thought one blow was enough at a time, and that it might be dangerous to attempt the two at once. M. du Maine had supporters, nay; he was at the head of a sort of party; strip him of the important post he held, and what might not his rake, his disappointment, and his wounded ambition lead him to attempt? Civil war, perhaps, would be the result of his disgrace.

Again and again I urged these views, not only upon M. le Duc d'Orleans, but upon M. le Duc. Nay, with this latter I had two long stolen interviews in the Tuileries Gardens, where we spoke without constraint, and exhausted all our arguments. But M. le Duc was not to be shaken, and as I could do no more than I had done to move him, I was obliged at last to give in. It was resolved, however, that disgrace should fall upon M. du Maine alone; that his brother, the Comte de Toulouse, an account of the devotion to the State he had ever exhibited, and his excellent conduct since the death of the late King, should, when stripped of his title like the other, receive it back again the moment after, in acknowledgment of the services he had rendered to the Regent as Councillor of State, and as an expression of personal good feeling towards him, which his excellent qualities so justly merited.

I returned home from my last interview with M. le Duc, and went to mass at the Jacobins, to which I entered from my garden. It was not without a distracted mind. But I prayed to God sincerely and earnestly to guide my steps, so that I might labour for His glory and the good of the State without private ends. My prayer was heard, and in the sequel I had nothing to reproach myself with. I followed the straight road without turning to the right or to the left.

Fontanieu was waiting for me in my house as I returned home from mass, and I was obliged to listen to his questions and to reply to them, as though I had nothing on my mind. I arranged my chamber like a Bed of Justice, I made him understand several things; connected with the ceremonial that he had not under stood before, and that it was essential he should in no way omit. Thus everything went on satisfactorily, and I began to count the hours, by day as well as by night, until the great day was to arrive on which the arrogant pride of the Parliament was to receive a check, and the false plumage which adorned the bastards was to be plucked from them.

In the midst of the sweet joy that I felt, no bitterness entered. I was satisfied with the part I had played in this affair, satisfied that I had acted sincerely, honestly, that I had not allowed my own private motives to sway me; that in the interests of the State, as opposed to my own interests, I had done all in my power to save the Duc du Maine. And yet I did not dare to give myself up to the rosy thoughts suggested by the great event, now so rapidly approaching. I toyed with them instead of allowing myself to embrace them. I shrunk from them as it were like a cold lover who fears the too ardent caresses of his mistress. I could not believe that the supreme happiness I had so long pined for was at last so near. Might not M. le Duc d'Orleans falter at the last moment? Might not all our preparations, so carefully conducted, so cleverly planned, weigh upon his feebleness until they fell to the ground? It was not improbable. He was often firm in promises. How often was he firm in carrying them out? All these questions, all these restless doubts— natural as it appears to me under the circumstances—winged their way through my mind, and kept me excited and feverish as though life and death were hanging on one thread.

In the midst of my reflections, a messenger from M. le Duc d'Orleans, Millain by name, arrived at my house. It was on the afternoon of Thursday, the 25th of August, 1718. His message was simple. M. le Duc d'Orleans was in the same mood as ever, and I was to join him at the Palais Royal, according to previous agreement, at eight o'clock in the evening. The Bed of justice was to be held on the morrow.

Never was kiss given to a beautiful mistress sweeter than that which I imprinted upon the fat old face of this charming messenger! A close embrace, eagerly repeated, was my first reply, followed afterwards by an overflow of feeling for M. le Duc, and for Millain even, who had worthily served in this great undertaking.

The rest of the day I passed at home with the Abbe Dubois, Fagon, and the Duc de la Force, one after the other finishing up our work. We provided against everything: If the Parliament refused to come to the Tuileries, its interdiction was determined on: if any of the members attempted to leave Paris they were to be arrested; troops were to be assembled in order to carry out the Regent's orders; we left no accident without its remedy.

The Abbe Dubois arranged a little code of signals, such as crossing the legs, shaking a handkerchief, or other simple gestures, to be given the first thing in the morning to the officers of the body-guards chosen to be in attendance in the room where the Bed of Justice was to be held. They were to fix their eyes upon the Regent, and when he made any of the above signals, immediately to act upon it according to their written instructions. The Abbe Dubois also drew out a sort of programme for M. le Duc d'Orleans, of the different orders he was to give during the night, fixing the hour for each, so that they might not arrive a minute too soon or a minute too late, and secrecy thus be maintained to the very latest moment.

Towards eight o'clock in the evening I went to they Palais Royal. I was horror-struck to find M. le Duc d'Orleans in bed with fever, as he said; I felt his pulse. Fever, he had, sure enough; perhaps from excitement caused by the business in hand. I said to him it was only fatigue of body and mind, of which he would be quit in twenty-four hours; he, on his side, protested that whatever it might be, he would hold the Bed of justice on the morrow. M. le Duc, who had just entered, was at his pillow; the chamber lighted by a single wax candle. We sat down, M. le Duc and I, and passed in review the orders given and to give, not without much apprehension on account of this fever, come so strangely out of season to the healthiest man in the world, and who had never had it before.

I exhorted the Regent to take as much repose as he could, so that he might be fully able to execute the great work of the morrow, the safety of the Regency itself being at stake. After this I felt his pulse again, not without fear. I assured him, however, his illness would be nothing; without, it is true, being too sure of it myself. I took my leave about ten o'clock, and went out of the room with Millain. When I found myself alone with him in the cabinet, through which we passed, I embraced him with an extreme pleasure. We had entered by the backstairs; we descended by the same, so as not to be observed. It was dark, so that on both occasions we were obliged to grope our way. Upon arriving at the bottom I could not refrain from again embracing Millain, so great was my pleasure, and we separated each to his home.

The arrangements respecting the troops and for summoning the Parliament, etc., were all carried out to the letter during the night and early morning. At the hours agreed upon M. le Duc d'Orleans gave the various orders. About four o'clock in the morning the Duc du Maine, as colonel- general of the Swiss guards, was aroused. He had not been in bed above an hour, having just returned from a fete given at the arsenal by Madame du Maine. He was doubtless much astonished, but contained himself, hid his fear, and sent at once to instruct his companies of Swiss guards of the orders they were to execute. I don't think he slept very well after this, uncertain as he must have been what was going to happen. But I never knew what he or Madame du Maine did after being thus rudely disturbed.

Towards five o'clock in the morning drums began to be heard throughout the town, and soon soldiers were seen in movement. At six o'clock a message was sent to the Parliament requesting it to attend at the Tuileries. The reply was that the request should be obeyed. The members thereupon debated whether they should go to the Tuileries in coaches or on foot. The last mode was adopted as being the most ordinary, and in the hope of stirring the people and arriving at the Tuileries with a yelling crowd. What happened will be related in its place.

At the same time, horsemen went to all the Peers and officers of the Crown, and to all the chevaliers of the order, the governors and lieutenant-governors of the provinces (who were to accompany the King), informing them of the Bed of Justice. The Comte de Toulouse had been to supper at the house of M. de Nevers, near Saint-Denis, and did not return until late into the night. The French and Swiss guards were under arms in various quarters; the watch, the light horse, and the two companies of musketeers all ready in their barracks; the usual guard at the Tuileries.

If I had slept but little during the last eight days, I slept still less that night, so near to the most considerable events. I rose before six o'clock, and shortly after received my summons to the Bed of justice, on the back of which was a note that I was not to be awakened, a piece of politeness due to the knowledge of the bearer, who was aware that this summons would teach me nothing I did not know. All the others had been awakened, surprised thereby to an extent that may be imagined.

Towards eight o'clock in the morning a messenger from M. le Duc d'Orleans came to remind me of the Regency Council at eight o'clock, and to attend it in my mantle. I dressed myself in black, because I had only that suit with a mantle, and another, a magnificent one in cloth of gold, which I did not wish to wear lest it should cause the remark to be made, though much out of season, that I wished to insult the Parliament and M. du Maine. I took two gentlemen with me in my coach, and I went in order to witness all that was to take place. I was at the same time full of fear, hope, joy, reflection, and mistrust of M. le Duc d'Orleans' weakness, and all that might result from it. I was also firmly resolved to do my best, whatever might happen, but without appearing to know anything, and without eagerness, and I resolved to show presence of mind, attention, circumspection, modesty, and much moderation.

Upon leaving my house I went to Valincourt, who lived behind the hotel of the Comte de Toulouse. He was a very honourable man, of much intellect, moving among the best company, secretary-general of the navy, devoted to the Comte de Toulouse ever since his early youth, and possessing all his confidence. I did not wish to leave the Comte de Toulouse in any personal fear, or expose him to be led away by his brother. I sent therefore for Valincourt, whom I knew intimately, to come and speak to me. He came half-dressed, terrified at the rumours flying over the town, and eagerly asked me what they all meant. I drew him close to me and said, "Listen attentively to me, and lose not a word. Go immediately to M. le Comte de Toulouse, tell him he may trust in my word, tell him to be discreet, and that things are about to happen to others which may displease him, but that not a hair of his head shall be touched. I hope he will not have a moment's uneasiness. Go! and lose not an instant."

Valincourt held me in a tight embrace. "Ah, Monsieur," said he, "we foresaw that at last there would be a storm. It is well merited, but not by M. le Comte, who will be eternally obliged to you." And, he went immediately with my message to the Comte de Toulouse, who never forgot that I saved him from the fall of his brother.

CHAPTER XCII

Arrived at the grand court of the Tuileries about eight o'clock without having remarked anything extraordinary on the way. The coaches of the Duc de Noailles, of Marechal de Villars, of Marechal d'Huxelles, and of some others were already there. I ascended without finding many people about, and directed the two doors of the Salle des Gardes, which were closed, to be opened. The Bed of justice was prepared in the grand ante- chamber, where the King was accustomed to eat. I stopped a short time to see if everything was in proper order, and felicitated Fontanieu in a low voice. He said to me in the same manner that he had arrived at the Tuileries with his workmen and materials at six o'clock in the morning; that everything was so well constructed and put up that the King had not heard a sound; that his chief valet de chambre, having left the room for some commission about seven o'clock in the morning, had been much astonished upon seeing this apparatus; that the Marechal de Villeroy had only heard of it through him, and that the seats had been erected with such little noise that nobody had heard anything. After having well examined everything with my eyes I advanced to the throne, then being finished; wishing to enter the second ante-chamber, some servants came to me, saying that I could not go in, all being locked up. I asked where I was to await the assembling of the Council, and was admitted to a room upstairs, where I found a good number of people already congregated.

After chatting some time with the Keeper of the Seals, the arrival of M. le Duc d'Orleans was announced. We finished what we had to say, and went downstairs separately, not wishing to be seen together.

The Council was held in a room which ever since the very hot weather the King had slept in. The hangings of his bed, and of the Marechal de Villeroy's were drawn back. The Council table was placed at the foot of one of the beds. Upon entering the adjoining chamber I found many people whom the first rumours of such an unexpected occurrence had no doubt led there, and among the rest some of the Council. M. le Duc d'Orleans was in the midst of a crowd at the end of the room, and, as I afterwards learned, had just seen the Duc du Maine without speaking to him, or being spoken to.

After a passing glance upon this crowd I entered the Council chamber. I found scattered there the majority of those who composed the Council with serious and troubled looks, which increased my seriousness. Scarcely anybody spoke; and each, standing or seated here and there, kept himself in his place. The better to examine all, I joined nobody. A moment after M. le Duc d'Orleans entered with a gay, easy, untroubled air, and looked smilingly upon the company. I considered this of good augury. Immediately afterwards I asked him his news. He replied aloud that he was tolerably well; then approaching my ear, added that, except when aroused to give his orders, he had slept very well, and that he was determined to hold firm. This infinitely pleased me, for it seemed to me by his manner that he was in earnest, and I briefly exhorted him to remain so.

Came, afterwards, M. le Duc, who pretty soon approached me, and asked if I augured well from the Regent, and if he would remain firm. M. le Duc had an air of exceeding gaiety, which was perceptible to those behind the scenes. The Duc de Noailles devoured everything with his eyes, which sparkled with anger because he had not been initiated into the secret of this great day.

In due time M. du Maine appeared in his mantle, entering by the King's little door. Never before had he made so many or such profound reverences as he did now—though he was not usually very stingy of them— then standing alone, resting upon his stick near the Council table, he looked around at everybody. Then and there, being in front of him, with the table between us, I made him the most smiling bow I had ever given him, and did it with extreme volupty. He repaid me in the same coin, and continued to fix his eyes upon everybody in turn; his face agitated, and nearly always speaking to himself.

A few minutes after M. le Duc came to me, begging me to exhort M. le Duc d'Orleans to firmness: then the Keeper of the Seals came forth for the same purpose. M. le Duc d'Orleans himself approached me to say something a moment afterwards, and he had no sooner quitted my side than M. le Duc, impatient and troubled, came to know in what frame of mind was the Regent. I told him good in a monosyllable, and sent him away.

I know not if these movements, upon which all eyes were fixed, began to frighten the Duc du Maine, but no sooner had M. le Duc joined the Regent, after quitting me, than the Duc du Maine went to speak to the Marechal de Villeroy and to D'Effiat, both seated at the end of the room towards the King's little door, their backs to the wall. They did not rise for the Duc du Maine, who remained standing opposite, and quite near them, all three holding long discourses, like people who deliberate with embarrassment and surprise, as it appeared to me by the faces of the two I saw, and which I tried not to lose sight of.

During this time M. le Duc d'Orleans and M. le Duc spoke to each other near the window and the ordinary entrance door; the Keeper of the Seals, who was near, joined them. At this moment M. le Duc turned round a little, which gave me the opportunity to make signs to him of the other conference, which he immediately saw. I was alone, near the Council table, very attentive to everything, and the others scattered about began to become more so. A little while after the Duc du Maine placed himself where he had been previously: the two he quitted remained as before. M. du Maine was thus again in front of me, the table between us: I observed that he had a bewildered look, and that he spoke to himself more than ever.

The Comte de Toulouse arrived as the Regent had just quitted the two persons with whom he had been talking. The Comte de Toulouse was in his mantle, and saluted the company with a grave and meditative manner, neither accosting nor accosted: M. le Duc d'Orleans found himself in front of him and turned towards me, although at some distance, as though to testify his trouble. I bent my head a little while looking fixedly at him, as though to say, "Well, what then?"

A short time afterwards the Comte de Toulouse had a conversation with his brother, both speaking with agitation and without appearing to agree very well. Then the Count approached M. le Duc d'Orleans, who was talking again to M. le Duc, and they spoke at some length to each other. As their faces were towards the wall, nothing but their backs could be seen, no emotion and scarcely a gesture was visible.

The Duc du Maine had remained where he had spoken to his brother. He seemed half dead, looked askance upon the company with wandering eyes, and the troubled agitated manner of a criminal, or a man condemned to death. Shortly afterwards he became pale as a corpse, and appeared to me to have been taken ill.

He crawled to the end of the table, during which the Comte de Toulouse came and said a word to the Regent, and began to walk out of the room.

All these movements took place in a trice. The Regent, who was near the King's armchair, said aloud, "Now, gentlemen, let us take our places." Each approached to do so, and as I looked behind mine I saw the two brothers at the door as though about to leave the room. I leaped, so to speak, between the King's armchair and M. le Duc d'Orleans, and whispered in the Regent's ear so as not to be heard by the Prince de Conti:

"Monsieur, look at them. They are going."

"I know it," he replied tranquilly.

"Yes," I exclaimed with animation, "but do you know what they will do when they are outside."

"Nothing at all," said he: "the Comte de Toulouse has asked me for permission to go out with his brother; he has assured me that they will be discreet."

"And if they are not?" I asked.

"They will be. But if they are not, they will be well looked after."

"But if they commit some absurdity, or leave Paris?"

"They will be arrested. Orders have been given, and I will answer for their execution."

Therefore, more tranquil, I sat down in my place. Scarcely had I got there than the Regent called me back, and said that since they had left the room, he should like to tell the Council what was going to be done with respect to them. I replied that the only objection to this, their presence, being now removed—I thought it would be wrong not to do so. He asked M. le Duc in a whisper, across the table, afterwards called to the Keeper of the Seals; both agreed, and then we really seated ourselves.

These movements had augmented the trouble and curiosity of every one. The eyes of all, occupied with the Regent, had been removed from the door, so that the absence of the bastards was by no means generally remarked. As soon as it was perceived, everybody looked inquiringly around, and remained standing in expectation. I sat down in the seat of the Comte de Toulouse. The Duc de Guiche, who sat on the other side of me, left a seat between us, and still waited for the bastards. He told me to approach nearer to him, saying I had mistaken my place. I replied not a word, looking on at the company, which was a sight to see. At the second or third summons, I replied that he, on the contrary, must approach me.

"And M. le Comte de Toulouse?" replied he.

"Approach," said I, and seeing him motionless with astonishment, looking towards the Duc du Maine's seat, which had been taken by the Keeper of the Seals, I pulled him by his coat (I was seated), saying to him, "Come here and sit down."

I pulled him so hard that he seated himself near me without understanding aught.

"But what is the meaning of all this?" he demanded; "where are these gentlemen?"

"I don't know," replied I, impatiently; "but they are not here."

At the same time, the Duc de Noailles, who sat next to the Duc de Guiche, and who, enraged at counting for nothing in preparations for such a great day, had apparently divined that I was in the plot, vanquished by his curiosity, stretched over the table in front of the Duc de Guiche, and said to me:

"In the name of Heaven, M. le Duc, do me the favour to say what all this means?"

I was at daggers-drawn with him, as I have explained, and had no mercy for him. I turned, therefore, towards him with a cold and disdainful air, and, after having heard him out, and looked at him, I turned away again. That was all my reply. The Duc de Guiche pressed me to say something, even if it was only that I knew all. I denied it, and yet each seated himself slowly, because intent only upon looking around, and divining what all this could mean, and because it was a long time before any one could comprehend that we must proceed to business without the bastards, although nobody opened his mouth.

When everybody was in his place M. le Duc d'Orleans after having far a moment looked all around, every eye fixed upon him, said that he had assembled this Regency Council to hear read the resolutions adopted at the last; that he had come to the conclusion that there was no other means of obtaining the registration of the finance edict recently passed than that of holding a Bed of justice; that the heat rendering it unadvisable to jeopardise the King's health in the midst of the crowd of the Palais de justice, he had thought it best to follow the example of the late King, who had sometimes sent for the Parliament to the Tuileries; that, as it had become necessary to hold this Bed of justice, he had thought it right to profit by the occasion, and register the 'lettres de provision' of the Keeper of the Seals at the commencement of the sitting; and he ordered the Keeper of the Seals to read them.

During this reading, which had no other importance than to seize an occasion of forcing the Parliament to recognize the Keeper of the Seals, whose person and whose commission they hated, I occupied myself in examining the faces.

I saw M. le Duc d'Orleans with an air of authority and of attention, so new that I was struck with it. M. le Duc, gay and brilliant, appeared quite at his ease, and confident. The Prince de Conti, astonished, absent, meditative, seemed to see nothing and to take part in nothing. The Keeper of the Seals, grave and pensive, appeared to have too many things in his head; nevertheless, with bag, wax, and seals near him, he looked very decided and very firm. The Duc de la Force hung his head, but examined on the sly the faces of us all. Marechal Villeroy and Marechal de Villars spoke to each other now and then; both had irritated eyes and long faces. Nobody was more composed than the Marechal de Tallard; but he could not hide an internal agitation which often peeped out. The Marechal d'Estrees had a stupefied air, as though he saw nothing but a mist before him. The Marechal de Besons, enveloped more than ordinarily in his big wig, appeared deeply meditative, his look cast down and angry. Pelletier, very buoyant, simple, curious, looking at everything. Torcy, three times more starched than usual, seemed to look at everything by stealth. Effiat, meddlesome, piqued, outraged, ready to boil over, fuming at everybody, his look haggard, as it passed precipitously, and by fits and starts, from side to side. Those on my side I could not well examine; I saw them only by moments as they changed their postures or I mine; and then not well or for long. I have already spoken of the astonishment of the Duc de Guiche, and of the vexation and curiosity of the Duc de Noailles. D'Antin, usually of such easy carriage, appeared to me as though in fetters, and quite scared. The Marechal d'Huxelles tried to put a good face on the matter, but could not hide the despair which pierced him. Old Troyes, all abroad, showed nothing but surprise and embarrassment, and did not appear to know where he was.

From the first moment of this reading and the departure of the bastards, everybody saw that something was in preparation against them. What that something was to be, kept every mind in suspense. A Bed of justice, too, prepared in secret, ready as soon as announced, indicated a strong resolution taken against the Parliament, and indicated also so much firmness and measure in a Prince, usually supposed to be entirely incapable of any, that every one was at sea. All, according as they were allied to the Parliament or to the bastards, seemed to wait in fear what was to be proposed. Many others appeared deeply wounded because the Regent had not admitted them behind the scenes, and because they were compelled to share the common surprise. Never were faces so universally elongated; never was embarrassment more general or more marked. In these first moments of trouble I fancy few people lent an ear to the letters the Keeper of the Seals was reading. When they were finished, M. le Duc d'Orleans said he did not think it was worth while to take the votes one by one, either upon the contents of these letters or their registration; but that all would be in favour of commencing the Bed of justice at once.

After a short but marked pause, the Regent developed, in few words, the reasons which had induced the Council at its last sitting, to abrogate the decree of the Parliament. He added, that judging by the conduct of that assembly, it would have been to jeopardise anew the King's authority, to send for registration this act of abrogation to the Parliament, which would assuredly have given in public a proof of formal disobedience, in refusing to register; that there being no other remedy than a Bed of justice, he had thought it best to assemble one, but in secret, so as not to give time or opportunity to the ill-disposed to prepare for disobedience; that he believed, with the Keeper of the Seals, the frequency and the manner of the parliamentary remonstrances were such that the Parliament must be made to keep within the limits of its duty, which, long since, it seemed to have lost sight of; that the Keeper of the Seals would now read to the Council the act of abrogation, and the rules that were to be observed in future. Then, looking at the Keeper of the Seals, "Monsieur," said he, "you will explain this better than I. Have the goodness to do so before reading the decree."

The Keeper of the Seals then spoke, and paraphrased what his Royal Highness had said more briefly; he explained in what manner the Parliament had the right to remonstrate, showed the distinction between its power and that of the Crown; the incompetence of the tribunals in all matters of state and finance; and the necessity of repressing the remonstrances of Parliament by passing a code (that was the term used), which was to serve as their inviolable guide. All this explained without lengthiness, with grace and clearness, he began to read the decree, as it has since been printed and circulated everywhere, some trifling alteration excepted.

The reading finished, the Regent, contrary to his custom, showed his opinion by the praises he gave to this document: and then, assuming the Regent's tone and air he had never before put on, and which completed the astonishment of the company, he added, "To-day, gentlemen, I shall deviate from the usual rule in taking your votes, and I think it will be well to do so during all this Council."

Then after a slight glance upon both sides of the table, during which you might have heard a worm crawl, he turned towards M. le Duc and asked him his opinion. M. le Duc declared for the decree, alleging several short but strong reasons. The Prince de Conti spoke in the same sense. I spoke after, for the Keeper of the Seals had done so directly his reading was finished. My opinion was given in more general terms so as not to fall too heavily upon the Parliament, or to show that I arrogated to myself the right to support his Royal Highness in the same manner as a prince of the blood. The Duc de la Force was longer. All spoke, but the majority said but little, and some allowed their vexation to be seen, but did not dare to oppose, feeling that it would be of no use. Dejection was painted upon their faces; it was evident this affair, of the Parliament was not what they expected or wished. Tallard was the only one whose face did not betray him; but the suffocated monosyllable of the Marechal d'Huxelles tore off the rest of the mask. The Duc de Noailles could scarcely contain himself, and spoke more than he wished, with anguish worthy of Fresnes. M. le Duc d'Orleans spoke last, and with unusual force; then made a pause, piercing all the company with his eyes.

At this moment the Marechal de Villeroy, full of his own thoughts, muttered between his teeth, "But will the Parliament come?" This was gently taken up. M. le Duc d'Orleans replied that he did not doubt it; and immediately afterwards, that it would be as well to know when they set out. The Keeper of the Seals said he should be informed. M. le Duc d'Orleans replied that the door-keepers must be told. Thereupon up jumps M. de Troyes.

I was seized with such a sudden fear lest he should go and chatter at the door with some one that I jumped up also, and got the start of him. As I returned, D'Antin, who had turned round to lay wait for me, begged me for mercy's sake to tell him what all this meant. I sped on saying that I knew nothing. "Tell that to others! Ho, ho!" replied he. When he had resumed his seat, M. le Duc d'Orleans said something, I don't know what, M. de Troyes still standing, I also. In passing La Vrilliere, I asked him to go to the door every time anything was wanted, for fear of the babbling of M. de Troyes; adding, that distant as I was from the door, going there looked too peculiar. La Vrilliere did as I begged him all the rest of the sitting.

As I was returning to my place, D'Antin, still in ambush, begged me in the name of heaven, his hands joined, to tell him something. I kept firm, however, saying, "You will see." The Duc de Guiche pressed me as resolutely, even saying, it was evident I was in the plot. I remained deaf.

These little movements over, M. le Duc d'Orleans, rising a little in his seat, said to the company, in a tone more firm, and more like that of a master than before, that there was another matter now to attend to, much more important than the one just heard. This prelude increased the general astonishment, and rendered everybody motionless. After a moment of silence the Regent said, that the peers had had for some time good grounds of complaint against certain persons, who by unaccustomed favour, had been allowed to assume rank and dignity to which their birth did not entitle them; that it was time this irregularity should be stopped short, and that with this view, an instrument had been drawn up, which the Keeper of the Seals would read to them.

A profound silence followed this discourse, so unexpected, and which began to explain the absence of the bastards. Upon many visages a sombre hue was painted. As for me I had enough to do to compose my own visage, upon which all eyes successively passed; I had put upon it an extra coat of gravity and of modesty; I steered my eyes with care, and only looked horizontally at most, not an inch higher. As soon as the Regent opened his mouth on this business, M. le Duc cast upon me a triumphant look which almost routed my seriousness, and which warned me to increase it, and no longer expose myself to meet his glance. Contained in this manner, attentive in devouring the aspect of all, alive to everything and to myself, motionless, glued to my chair, all my body fixed, penetrated with the most acute and most sensible pleasure that joy could impart, with the most charming anxiety, with an enjoyment, so perseveringly and so immoderately hoped for, I sweated with agony at the captivity of my transport, and this agony was of a voluptuousness such as I had never felt before, such as I have never felt since. How inferior are the pleasures of the senses to those of the mind! and how true it is that the balance-weight of misfortunes, is the good fortune that finishes them!

A moment after the Regent had ceased speaking, he told the Keeper of the Seals to read the declaration. During the reading, which was more than music to my ears, my attention was again fixed on the company. I saw by the alteration of the faces what an immense effect this document, which embodied the resolutions I have already explained, produced upon some of our friends. The whole of the reading was listened to with the utmost attention, and the utmost emotion.

When it was finished, M. le Duc d'Orleans said he was very sorry for this necessity, but that justice must be done to the peers as well as to the princes of the blood: then turning to the Keeper of the Seals asked him for his opinion.

This latter spoke briefly and well; but was like a dog running over hot ashes. He declared for the declaration. His Royal Highness then called upon M. le Duc for his opinion. It was short, but nervous, and polite to the peers. M. le Prince de Conti the same. Then the Regent asked me my opinion. I made, contrary to my custom, a profound inclination, but without rising, and said, that having the honour to find myself the eldest of the peers of the Council, I offered to his Royal Highness my very humble thanks and those of all the peers of France, for the justice so ardently desired, and touching so closely our dignity and our persons, that he had resolved to render us; that I begged him to be persuaded of our gratitude, and to count upon our utmost attachment to his person for an act of equity so longed for, and so complete; that in this sincere expression of our sentiments consisted all our opinion, because, being pleaders, we could not be judges also. I terminated these few words with a profound inclination, without rising, imitated by the Duc de la Force at the same moment; all the rest of the Council briefly gave their opinions, approving what the majority of them evidently did not approve at all.

I had tried to modulate my voice, so that it should be just heard and no more, preferring to be indistinct rather than speak too loudly; and confined all my person to express as much as possible, gravity, modesty, and simple gratitude. M. le Duc maliciously made signs to me in smiling, that I had spoken well. But I kept my seriousness, and turned round to examine all the rest.

It would be impossible to describe the aspect of the company. Nothing was seen but people, oppressed with surprise that overwhelmed them, meditative, agitated, some irritated, some but ill at ease, like La Force and Guiche, who freely admitted so to me.

The opinions taken almost as soon as demanded, M. le Duc d'Orleans said, "Gentlemen, it is finished, then justice is done, and the rights of Messieurs the Peers are in safety. I have now an act of grace to propose to you, and I do so with all the more confidence, because I have taken care to consult the parties interested, who support me; and because, I have drawn up the document in a manner to wound no one. What I am going to explain to you, regards the Comte de Toulouse alone.

"Nobody is ignorant how he has disapproved all that has been done in favour of him and his brother, and that he has sustained it since the regency only out of respect for the wishes of the late King. Everybody knows also his virtue, his merit, his application, his probity, his disinterestedness. Nevertheless, I could not avoid including him in the declaration you have just heard. Justice furnishes no exception in his favour, and the rights of the Peers must be assured. Now that they are no longer attacked, I have thought fitly to render to merit what from equity I have taken from birth; and to make an exception of M. le Comte de Toulouse, which (while confirming the rule), will leave him in full possession of all the honours he enjoys to the exclusion of every other. Those honours are not to pass to his children, should he marry and have any, or their restitution be considered as a precedent to be made use of at any future time.

"I have the pleasure to announce that the Princes of the Blood consent to this, and that such of the Peers to whom I have been able to explain myself, share my sentiments. I doubt not that the esteem he has acquired here will render this proposition agreeable to you." And then turning to the Keeper of the Seals, "Monsieur, will you read the declaration?"

It was read at once.

I had, during the discourse of his Royal Highness, thrown all my attention into an examination of the impression it made upon the assembly. The astonishment it caused was general; it was such, that to judge of those addressed, it seemed that they understood nothing; and they did not recover themselves during all the reading. I inwardly rejoiced at success so pleasingly demonstrated and did not receive too well the Duc de Guiche, who testified to me his disapprobation. Villeroy confounded, Villars raging, Effiat rolling his eyes, Estrees beside himself with surprise, were the most marked. Tallard, with his head stretched forward, sucked in, so to speak, all the Regent's words as they were proffered, and those of the declaration, as the Keeper of the Seals read them. Noailles, inwardly distracted, could not hide his distraction; Huxelles, entirely occupied in smoothing himself, forgot to frown. I divided my attention between the declaration and these persons.

The document read, M. le Duc d'Orleans praised it in two words, and called upon the Keeper of the Seals to give his opinion. He did so briefly, in favour of the Comte de Toulouse. M. le Duc the same; M. le Prince de Conti the same. After him, I testified to his Royal Highness my joy at seeing him conciliate the justice and the safety of the peers with the unheard-of favour he had just rendered to the virtue of M. le Comte de Toulouse, who merited it by his moderation, his truthfulness, his attachment to the State; thus the more he had recognised the injustice of his elevation to the rank to which he was raised, the more he had rendered himself worthy of it, and the more it was advantageous to the peers to yield to merit, (when this exception was confined solely to his person, with formal and legal precautions, so abundantly supplied by the declaration) and voluntarily contribute thus to an elevation without example, (so much the more flattering because its only foundation was virtue), so as to incite that virtue more and more to the service and utility of the state; that I declared therefore with joy for the declaration, and did not fear to add the very humble thanks of the peers, since I had the honour to be the oldest present.

As I closed my mouth I cast my eyes in front of some, and plainly saw that my applause did not please, and, perhaps, my thanks still less. The others gave their opinion with heavy heart, as it were, to so terrible a blow, some few muttered I know not what between their teeth, but the thunderbolt upon the Duc du Maine's cabal was more and more felt, and as reflection succeeded to the first feeling of surprise, so a bitter and sharp grief manifested itself upon their faces in so marked a manner, that it was easy to see it had become high time to strike.

All opinions having been expressed, M. le Duc cast a brilliant leer at me, and prepared to speak; but the Keeper of the Seals, who, from his side of the table did not see this movement, wishing also to say something, M. le Duc d'Orleans intimated to him that M. le Duc had the start of him. Raising himself majestically from his seat, the Regent then said: "Gentlemen, M. le Duc has a proposition to make to you. I have found it just and reasonable; I doubt not, you will find it so too." Then turning towards M. le Duc, he added, "Monsieur, will you explain it?"

The movement these few words made among the company is inexpressible. 'Twas as though I saw before me people deprived of all power, and surprised by a new assembly rising up from the midst of them in an asylum they had breathlessly reached.

"Monsieur," said M. le Duc, addressing himself to the Regent, as usual; "since you have rendered justice to the Dukes, I think I am justified in asking for it myself. The deceased King gave the education of his Majesty to M. le Duc du Maine. I was a minor then, and according to the idea of the deceased King, M. du Maine was prince of the blood, capable of succeeding to the crown. Now I am of age, and not only M. du Maine is no longer prince of the blood, but he is reduced to the rank of his peerage. M. le Marechal de Villeroy is now his senior, and precedes him everywhere; M. le Marechal can therefore no longer remain governor of the King, under the superintendence of M. du Maine. I ask you, then, for M. du Maine's post, that I think my age, my rank, my attachment to the King and the State, qualify me for. I hope," he added, turning towards his left, "that I shall profit by the lessons of M. le Marechal de Villeroy, acquit myself of my duties with distinction, and merit his friendship."

At this discourse the Marechal de Villeroy almost slipped off his chair. As soon, at least, as he heard the Words, "Superintendence of the King's education," he rested his forehead upon his stick, and remained several moments in that posture. He appeared even to understand nothing of the rest of the speech. Villars and D'Effiat bent their backs like people who had received the last blow. I could see nobody on my own side except the Duc de Guiche, who approved through all his prodigious astonishment. Estrees became master of himself the first, shook himself, brightened up, and looked at the company like a man who returns from the other world.

As soon as M. le Duc had finished, M. le Duc d'Orleans reviewed all the company with his eyes, and then said, that the request of M. le Duc was just; that he did not think it could be refused; that M. le Marechal de Villeroy could not be allowed to remain under a person whom he preceded in rank; that the superintendence of the King's education could not be more worthily filled than by M. le Duc; and that he was persuaded all would be of one voice in this matter. Immediately afterwards, he asked M. le Prince de Conti to give his opinion, who did so in two words; then he asked the Keeper of the Seals, whose reply was equally brief; then he asked me.

I simply said, looking at M. le Duc, that I was for the change with all my heart. The rest, M. de la Force excepted (who said a single word), voted without speaking, simply bowing; the Marshals and D'Effiat scarcely moved their eyes, and those of Villars glistened with fury.

The opinions taken, the Regent turning towards M. le Duc, said, "Monsieur, I think you would like to read what you intend to say to the King at the Bed of Justice."

Therefore M. le Duc read it as it has been printed. Some moments of sad and profound silence succeeded this reading, during which the Marechal de Villeroy, pale and agitated, muttered to himself. At last, like a man who has made up his mind, he turned with bended head, expiring eyes, and feeble voice, towards the Regent, and said, "I will simply say these two words; here are all the dispositions of the late king overturned, I cannot see it without grief. M. du Maine is very unfortunate."

"Monsieur," replied the Regent, in a loud and animated tone, "M. du Maine is my brother-in-law, but I prefer an open enemy to a hidden one."

At this great declaration several lowered their heads. The Marechal de Villeroy nearly swooned; sighs began to make themselves heard near me, as though by stealth; everybody felt by this that the scabbard was thrown away.

The Keeper of the Seals, to make a diversion; proposed to read the speech he had prepared to serve as preface to the decree to be read at the Bed of justice, abrogating the Parliament decrees; as he was finishing it, some one entered to say he was asked for at the door.

He went out, returning immediately afterwards, not to his place, but to M. le Duc d'Orleans, whom he took into a window, meditative silence reigning around. The Regent having returned back to his place, said to the company, he had received information that the Chief-President of the Parliament, notwithstanding the reply previously made, had proposed that the Parliament should not go to the Tuileries, asking, "What it was to do in a place where it would not be free?" that he had proposed to send a message to the King, stating that "his Parliament would hear his wishes in their ordinary place of meeting, whenever it should please him to come or to send." The Regent added that these propositions had made considerable sensation, and that the

Parliament were at that moment debating upon them. The Council appeared much astounded at this news, but M. le Duc d'Orleans said, in a very composed manner, that he did not expect a refusal; he ordered the Keeper of the Seals, nevertheless, to propose such measures as it would be best to take, supposing the motion of the Chief-President should be carried.

The Keeper of the Seals declared that he could not believe the Parliament would be guilty of this disobedience, contrary to all law and usage. He showed at some length that nothing was so pernicious as to expose the King's authority to a formal opposition, and decided in favour of the immediate interdiction of the Parliament if it fell into this fault. M. le Duc d'Orleans added that there was no other course open, and took the opinion of M. le Duc, which was strongly in his favour. M. le Prince de Conti the same, mine also, that of M. de la Force and of M. de Guiche still more so. The Marechal de Villeroy, in a broken voice, seeking big words, which would not come in time to him, deplored this extremity, and did all he could to avoid giving a precise opinion. Forced at last by the Regent to explain himself, he did not dare to oppose, but added that he assented with regret, and wished to explain the grievous results of the proposed measure. But the Regent, interrupting him, said he need not take the trouble: everything had been foreseen; that it would be much more grievous to be disobeyed by the Parliament than to force it into obedience; and immediately after asked the Duc de Noailles his opinion, who replied that it would be very sad to act thus, but that he was for it. Villars wished to paraphrase, but contained himself, and said he hoped the Parliament would obey. Pressed by the Regent, he proposed to wait for fresh news before deciding; but, pressed more closely, he declared for the interdiction, with an air of warmth and vexation, extremely marked. Nobody after this dared to hesitate, and the majority voted by an inclination of the head.

A short time afterwards it was announced to M. le Duc d'Orleans that the Parliament had set out on foot, and had begun to defile through the palace. This news much cooled the blood of the company, M. le Duc d'Orleans more than that of any one else.

After this the Regent, in a cheerful manner, called upon the Presidents of the Councils to bring forward any business they might have on hand, but not one had any. The Marechal de Villars said, however, that he had a matter to produce, and he produced it accordingly, but with a clearness which, under the circumstances, was extraordinary. I fancy, however, that very few knew what he was talking about. We were all too much occupied with more interesting matters, and each voted without speaking. Bad luck to those who had had business to bring forward this day; they who conducted it would have known but little what they said: they who listened, still less.

The Council finished thus, from lack of matter, and a movement was made to adjourn it as usual. I stepped in front of M. le Prince de Conti to M. le Duc d'Orleans, who understood me, and who begged the company to keep their seats. La Vrilliere went out by order for news, but there was nothing fresh.

It was now a little after ten. We remained a good half-hour in our places, talking a little with each other, but on the whole rather silent. At the end some grew fidgety and anxious, rose and went to the windows. M. le Duc d'Orleans restrained them as well as he could; but at length Desgranges entered to say that the Chief-President had already arrived, in his coach, and that the Parliament was near. So soon as he had retired, the Council rose by groups, and could no longer be kept seated. M. le Duc d'Orleans himself at last rose, and all he could do was to prohibit everybody from leaving the room under any pretext, and this prohibition he repeated two or three times.

Scarcely had we risen when M. le Duc came to me, rejoiced at the success that had hitherto been had, and much relieved by the absence of the bastards. Soon after I quitted him the Duc d'Orleans came to me, overpowered with the same sentiment. I said what I thought of the consternation of every one; and painted the expression of M. d'Effiat, at which he was not surprised. He was more so about Besons. I asked if he was not afraid the bastards would come to the Bed of justice; but he was certain they would not. I was resolved, however, to prepare his mind against that contingency.

I walked about, slowly and incessantly without fixing myself on any one, in order that nothing should escape me, principally attending to the doors. I took advantage of the opportunity to say a word here and a word there, to pass continually near those who were suspected, to skim and interrupt all conversations. D'Antin was often joined by the Duc de Noailles, who had resumed his habit of the morning, and continually followed me with his eyes. He had an air of consternation, was agitated and embarrassed in countenance—he commonly so free and easy! D'Antin took me aside to see whether he could not, considering his position, be excused from attending the Bed of Justice. He received permission from the Regent on certain conditions.

I went then to break in upon the colloquy of D'Effiat and his friends, and taking them by surprise, caused D'Effiat to say that he had just heard strange resolutions, that he did not know who had advised them, that he prayed that M. d'Orleans would find them advantageous. I replied, agreeing with him. The Marechal de Villeroy sighed, muttered, and shook his wig, Villars spoke more at length, and blamed sharply what had been done. I assented to everything, being there not to persuade but to watch.

Nevertheless we grew weary of the slowness of the Parliament, and often sent out for news. Several of the Council tried to leave the room, perhaps to blab, but the Regent would allow no one but La Vrilliere to go out, and seeing that the desire to leave increased, stood at the door himself. I suggested to him that Madame d'Orleans would be in a great state of uneasiness, and suggested that he should write to her; but he could not be persuaded to do it, though he promised.

At last the Parliament arrived, and behold us! like children, all at the windows. The members came in red robes, two by two, by the grand door of the court, which they passed in order to reach the Hall of the Ambassadors, where the Chief-President, who had come in his carriage with the president Haligre, awaited them.

The Parliament being in its place, the peers having arrived, and the presidents having put on their furs behind the screens arranged for that purpose in an adjoining room, a messenger came to inform us that all was ready. The question had been agitated, whether the King should dine meanwhile, and I had it carried in the negative, fearing lest coming immediately after to the Bed of justice, and having eaten before his usual hour, he might be ill, which would have been a grievous inconvenience. As soon as it was announced to the Regent that we could set out, his Royal Highness sent word to the Parliament, to prepare the deputation to receive the King; and then said aloud to the company, that it was time to go in search of his Majesty.

At these words I felt a storm of joy sweep over me, at the thought of the grand spectacle that was going to pass in my presence, which warned me to be doubly on my guard. I tried to furnish myself with the strongest dose of seriousness, gravity, and modesty. I followed M. le Duc d'Orleans, who entered the King's room by the little door, and who found the King in his cabinet. On the way the Duc d'Albret made me some very marked compliments, with evident desire to discover something. I put him off with politeness, complaints of the crowd, of the annoyance of my dress, and gained thus the King's cabinet.

The King was dressed as usual. When the Duc d'Orleans had been a few moments with him, he asked him if he would be pleased to go: and the way was instantly' cleared, a procession formed, and the King moved towards the Hall of the Swiss Guard.

I now hastened to the chamber, where the Bed of justice was to be held. The passage to it was tolerably, free. The officers of the body-guard made place for me and for the Duc de la Force, and Marechal de Villars, who followed me, one by one. I stopped a moment in the passage at the entrance to the room, seized with joy upon seeing this grand spectacle, and at the thought of the grand movement that was drawing nigh, I needed a pause in order to recover myself sufficiently to see distinctly what I looked at, and to put on a new coat of seriousness and of modesty. I fully expected I should be well examined by a company which had been carefully taught not to like me, and by the curious spectators waiting to see what was to be hatched out of so profound a secret, in such an important assembly, summoned so hastily. Moreover, nobody was ignorant that I knew all, at least from the Council of the Regency I had just left.

I did not deceive myself. As soon as I appeared, all eyes were fixed upon me. I slowly advanced towards the chief greffier, and introducing myself between the two seats, I traversed the length of the room, in front of the King's people, who saluted me with a smiling air, and I ascended over three rows of high seats, where all the peers were in their places, and who rose as I approached the steps. I respectfully saluted them from the third row.

Seated in my elevated place, and with nothing before me, I was able to glance over the whole assembly. I did so at once, piercing everybody with my eyes. One thing alone restrained me; it was that I did not dare to fix my eyes upon certain objects. I feared the fire and brilliant significance of my looks at that moment so appreciated by everybody: and the more I saw I attracted attention, the more anxious was I to wean curiosity by my discreetness. I cast, nevertheless, a glittering glance upon the Chief-President and his friends, for the examination of whom I was admirably placed. I carried my looks over all the Parliament, and saw there an astonishment, a silence, a consternation, such as I had not expected, and which was of good augury to me. The Chief-President, insolently crest-fallen, the other presidents disconcerted, and attentive to all, furnished me the most agreeable spectacle. The simply curious (among which I rank those who had no vote) appeared to me not less surprised (but without the bewilderment of the others), calmly surprised; in a word, everybody showed much expectation and desire to divine what had passed at the Council.

I had but little leisure for this examination, for the King immediately arrived. The hubbub which followed his entrance, and which lasted until his Majesty and all who accompanied him were in their places, was another singularity. Everybody sought to penetrate the Regent, the Keeper of the Seals, and the principal personages. The departure of the bastards from the cabinet of the Council had redoubled attention, but everybody did not know of that departure; now everybody perceived their absence. The consternation of the Marechals—of their senior—(the governor of the King) was evident. It augmented the dejection of the Chief-President, who not seeing his master the Duc du Maine, cast a terrible glance upon M. de Sully and me, who exactly occupied the places of the two brothers. In an instant all the eyes of the assembly were cast, at the same time, upon us; and I remarked that the meditativeness and expectation increased in every face. That of the Regent had an air of gentle but resolute majesty completely new to it, his eyes attentive, his deportment grave, but easy. M. le Duc, sage, measured, but encircled by I know not what brilliancy, which adorned all his person and which was evidently kept down. M. le Prince de Conti appeared dull, pensive, his mind far away perhaps. I was not able during the sitting to see them except now and then, and under pretext of looking at the King, who was serious, majestic, and at the same time as pretty as can be imagined; grave, with grace in all his bearing, his air attentive, and not at all wearied, playing his part very well and without embarrassment.

When all was ready, Argenson, the Keeper of the Seals, remained some minutes at his desk motionless, looking down, and the fire which sprang from his eyes seemed to burn every breast. An extreme silence eloquently announced the fear, the attention, the trouble, and the curiosity of all the expectants. The Parliament, which under the deceased King had often summoned this same Argenson, and as lieutenant of police had often given him its orders, he standing uncovered at the bar of the house; the Parliament, which since the regency had displayed its ill-will towards him so far as to excite public remark, and which still detained prisoners and papers to vex him; this Chief President so superior to him, so haughty, so proud of his Duc du Maine; this Lamoignon, who had boasted he would have him hanged at his Chamber of justice, where he had so completely dishonoured himself: this Parliament and all saw him clad in the ornaments of the chief office of the robe, presiding over them, effacing them, and entering upon his functions to teach them their duty, to read them a public lesson the first time he found himself at their head! These vain presidents were seen turning their looks from a man who imposed so strongly upon their pride, and who annihilated their arrogance in the place even whence they drew it, and rendered them stupid by regards they could not sustain.

After the Keeper of the Seals (according to the manner of the preachers) had accustomed himself to this august audience, he uncovered himself, rose, mounted to the King, knelt before the steps of the throne, by the side of the middle of the steps, where the grand chamberlain was lying upon cushions, and took the King's orders, descended, placed himself in his chair and covered himself. Let us say it once for all, he performed the same ceremony at the commencement of each business, and likewise before and after taking the opinion upon each; at the bar of justice neither he nor the chamberlain ever speaks otherwise to the King; and every time he went to the King on this occasion the Regent rose and approached him to hear and suggest the orders. Having returned back into his place, he opened, after some moments of silence, this great scene by a discourse. The report of the Bed of justice, made by the Parliament and printed, which is in the hands of everybody, renders it unnecessary for me to give the discourse of the Keeper of the Seals, that of the Chief-President, those of the King's people, and the different papers that were read and registered. I will simply content myself with some observations. This first discourse, the reading of the letters of the Keeper of the Seals, and the speech of the Advocate-General Blancmesnil which followed, the opinions taken, the order given, sometimes reiterated to keep the two double doors open, did not surprise anybody; served only as the preface to all the rest; to sharpen curiosity more and more as the moment approached in which it was to be satisfied.

This first act finished, the second was announced by the discourse of the Keeper of the Seals, the force of which penetrated all the Parliament. General consternation spread itself over their faces. Scarcely one of the members dared to speak to his neighbour. I remarked that the Abbe Pucelle, who, although only counsellor-clerk, was upon the forms in front of me, stood, so that he might hear better every time the Keeper of the Seals spoke. Bitter grief, obviously full of vexation, obscured the visage of the Chief-President. Shame and confusion were painted there.

After the vote, and when the Keeper of the Seals had pronounced, I saw the principal members of the Parliament in commotion. The Chief- President was about to speak. He did so by uttering the remonstrance of the Parliament, full of the most subtle and impudent malice against the Regent, and of insolence against the King. The villain trembled, nevertheless, in pronouncing it. His voice broken, his eyes constrained, his flurry and confusion, contradicted the venomous words he uttered; libations he could not abstain from offering to himself and his company. This was the moment when I relished, with delight utterly impossible to express, the sight of these haughty lawyers (who had dared to refuse us the salutation), prostrated upon their knees, and rendering, at our feet, homage to the throne, whilst we sat covered upon elevated seats, at the side of that same throne. These situations and these postures, so widely disproportioned, plead of themselves with all the force of evidence, the cause of those who are really and truly 'laterales regis' against this 'vas electum' of the third estate. My eyes fixed, glued, upon these haughty bourgeois, with their uncovered heads humiliated to the level of our feet, traversed the chief members kneeling or standing, and the ample folds of those fur robes of rabbit-skin that would imitate ermine, which waved at each long and redoubled genuflexion; genuflexions which only finished by command of the King.

The remonstrance being finished, the Keeper of the Seals mentioned to the King their wishes, asking further opinions; took his place again; cast his eyes on the Chief-President, and said: The King wishes to be obeyed, and obeyed immediately.

This grand speech was a thunder-bolt which overturned councillors and presidents in the most marked manner. All of them lowered their heads, and the majority kept them lowered for a long time. The rest of the spectators, except the marshals of France, appeared little affected by this desolation.

But this—an ordinary triumph—was nothing to that which was to follow. After an interval of some few minutes, the Keeper of the Seals went up again to the King, returned to his place, and remained there in silence some little time. Then everybody clearly saw that the Parliamentary affair being finished, something else must be in the wind. Some thought that a dispute which the Dukes had had with the Parliament, concerning one of its usurpations, was now to be settled in our favour. Others who had noticed the absence of the bastards, guessed it was something that affected them; but nobody divined what, much less its extent.

At last the Keeper of the Seals opened his mouth, and in his first sentence announced the fall of one brother and the preservation of the other. The effect of this upon every one was inexpressible. However occupied I might be in containing mine, I lost nothing. Astonishment prevailed over every other sentiment. Many appeared glad, either from hatred to the Duc du Maine, or from affection for the Comte de Toulouse; several were in consternation. The Chief-President lost all countenance; his visage, so self-sufficient and so audacious, was seized with a convulsive movement; the excess alone of his rage kept him from swooning. It was even worse at the reading of the declaration. Each word was legislative and decreed a fresh fall. The attention was general; every one was motionless, so as not to lose a word; all eyes were fixed upon the 'greffier' who was reading. A third of this reading over, the Chief- President, gnashing the few teeth left in his head, rested his forehead upon his stick that he held in both hands, and in this singular and marked position finished listening to the declaration, so overwhelming for him, so resurrectionary for us.

Yet, as for me, I was dying with joy. I was so oppressed that I feared I should swoon; my heart dilated to excess, and no longer found room to beat. The violence I did myself, in order to let nothing escape me, was infinite; and, nevertheless, this torment was delicious. I compared the years and the time of servitude; the grievous days, when dragged at the tail of the Parliamentary car as a victim, I had served as a triumph for the bastards; the various steps by which they had mounted to the summit above our heads; I compared them, I say, to this court of justice and of rule, to this frightful fall which, at the same time, raised us by the force of the shock. I thanked myself that it was through me this had been brought about. I had triumphed, I was revenged; I swam in my vengeance; I enjoyed the full accomplishment of desires the most vehement and the most continuous of all my life. I was tempted to fling away all thought and care. Nevertheless, I did not fail to listen to this vivifying reading (every note of which sounded upon my heart as the bow upon an instrument), or to examine, at the same time, the impressions it made upon every one.

At the first word the Keeper of the Seals said of this affair, the eyes of the two bishop-peers met mine. Never did I see surprise equal to theirs, or so marked a transport of joy. I had not been able to speak to them on account of the distance of our places; and they could not resist the movement which suddenly seized them. I swallowed through my eyes a delicious draught of their joy, and turned away my glance from theirs, lest I should succumb beneath this increase of delight. I no longer dared to look at them.

The reading finished, the other declaration in favour of the Comte de Toulouse was immediately commenced by the 'greffier', according to the command of the Keeper of the Seals, who had given them to him both together. It seemed to complete the confusion of the Chief-President and the friends of the Duc du Maine, by the contrast between the treatment of the two brothers.

After the Advocate-General had spoken, the Keeper of the Seals mounted to the King, with the opinions of the Princes of the Blood; then came to the Duc de Sully and me. Fortunately I had more memory than he had, or wished to have; therefore it was exactly my affair. I presented to him my hat with a bunch of feathers in the front, in an express manner very marked, saying to him loudly enough: "No, Monsieur, we cannot be judges; we are parties to the cause, and we have only to thank the King for the justice he renders us."

He smiled and made an excuse. I pushed him away before the Duc de Sully had time to open his mouth; and looking round I saw with pleasure that my refusal had been marked by everybody. The Keeper of the Seals retired as he came, and without taking the opinions of the peers, or of the bishop- peers, went to the marshals of France; thence descended to the Chief-President and to the 'presidents a mortier', and so to the rest of the lower seats; after which, having been to the King and returned to his place, he pronounced the decree of registration, and thus put the finishing touch to my joy.

Immediately after M. le Duc rose, and having made his reverences to the King forgot to sit down and cover himself to speak, according to the uninterrupted right and usage of the peers of France; therefore not one of us rose. He made, then, slowly and uncovered, the speech which has been printed at the end of the preceding ones, and read it not very intelligibly because his organ was not favourable. As soon as he had finished, M. le Duc d'Orleans rose, and committed the same fault. He said, also standing and uncovered, that the request of M. le Duc appeared to him just; and after some praises added, that M. le Duc du Maine was now reduced to the rank given to him by his peerage, M. le Marechal de Villeroy, his senior, could no longer remain under him, which was a new and very strong reason in addition to those M. le Duc had alleged. This request had carried to the highest point the astonishment of the assembly and the despair of the Chief-President, and the handful of people who appeared by their embarrassment to be interested in the Duc du Maine. The Marechal de Villeroy, without knitting his brow, had a disturbed look, and the eyes of the chief accuser oftener were inundated with tears. I was not able to distinguish well his cousin and intimate friend the Marechal d'Huxelles, who screened himself beneath the vast brim of his hat, thrust over his eyes, and who did not stir. The Chief- President, stunned by this last thunder-bolt, elongated his face so surprisingly, that I thought for a moment his chin had fallen upon his knees.

However, the Keeper of the Seals having called upon the King's people to speak, they replied that they had not heard the proposition of M. le Duc, therefore his paper was passed to them from hand to hand, during which the Keeper of the Seals repeated very kindly what the Regent had added upon the seniority of the Marechal de Villeroy over the Duc du Maine. Blancmesnil merely threw his eyes upon the paper of M. le Duc, and spoke, after which the Keeper of the Seals put it to the vote. I gave mine loud enough, and said, "As for this affair I vote with all my heart for giving the superintendence of the King's education to M. le Duc."

The votes being taken, the Keeper, of the Seals called the chief 'greffier', ordered him to bring his paper and his little bureau near his, so as to do all at once; and in presence of the King register everything that had been read and resolved, and signed also. This was done without any difficulty, according to forms, under the eyes of the Keeper of the Seals, who never raised them: but as there were five or six documents to register they took up a long time.

I had well observed the King when his education was in question, and I remarked in him no sort of alteration, change, or constraint. This was the last act of the drama: he was quite lively now the registrations commenced. However, as there were no more speeches to occupy him, he laughed with those near, amused himself with everything, even remarking that the Duc de Louvigny had on a velvet coat, and laughed at the heat he must feel, and all this with grace. This indifference for M. du Maine struck everybody, and publicly contradicted what his partisans tried to publish, viz., that his eyes had been red, but that neither at the Bed of justice, nor since, he had dared to show his trouble. The truth is he had his eyes dry and serene the whole time, and pronounced the name of the Duc du Maine only once since, which was after dinner the same day, when he asked where he had gone, with a very indifferent air, without saying a word more, then or since, or naming his children, who took little trouble to see him; and when they went it was in order to have even in his presence their little court apart, and to divert themselves among themselves. As for the Duc du Maine, either from policy or because he thought it not yet time, he only, saw the King in the morning, sometimes in his bed, and not at all during the rest of the day, except when obliged by his functions.

During the registration I gently passed my eyes over the whole assembly., and though I constantly constrained them, I could not resist the temptation to indemnify myself upon the Chief-President; I perseveringly overwhelmed him, therefore, a hundred different times during the sitting, with my hard-hitting regards. Insult, contempt, disdain, triumph, were darted at him from my eyes,—and pierced him to the very marrow often he lowered his eyes when he caught my gaze once or twice he raised his upon me, and I took pleasure in annoying him by sly but malicious smiles which completed his vexation. I bathed myself in his rage, and amused myself by making him feel it. I sometimes played with him by pointing him out to my two neighbours when he could perceive this movement; in a word, I pressed upon him without mercy, as heavily as I could.

At last the registration finished, the King descended the throne, and was followed by the Regent, the two Princes of the Blood, and the necessary gentlemen of the suite. At the same time the Marshals of France descended, and while the King traversed the room, accompanied by the deputation which had received him, they passed between the seats of the councillors opposite us, to follow him to the door by which his Majesty departed; and at the same time the two bishop-peers, passing before the throne, came to put themselves at our head, and squeezed my hands and my head (in passing before me) with warm gratification.

We followed them two by two according to seniority, and went straight forward to the door. The Parliament began to move directly afterwards. Place was made for us to the steps. The crowd, the people, the display contrasted our conversation and our joy. I was sorry for it.

I immediately gained my coach, which I found near, and which took me skilfully out of the court, so that I met with no check, and in a quarter of an hour after leaving the sitting, I was at home.

I had need of a little rest, for pleasure even is fatigue, and happiness, pure and untroubled as it may be, wearies the spirit. I entered my house, then, at about two o'clock in the afternoon, intending to repose myself, and in order to do so in security, I closed my door to everybody.

Alas! I had not been many minutes at home when I was called away to perform one of the most painful and annoying commissions it was ever my ill fortune to be charged with.

CHAPTER XCIV.

A little while before leaving the Cabinet of the Council for the Bed of Justice, M. le Duc d'Orleans had begged me to go to the Palais Royal with the Keeper of the Seals immediately after the ceremony had ended. As I saw that nothing had been undertaken, I thought myself free of this conference, and was glad to avoid a new proof that I had been in a secret which had excited envy. I went, therefore, straight home, arriving between two and three. I found at the foot of the steps the Duc d'Humieres, Louville, and all my family, even my mother, whom curiosity had drawn from her chamber, which she had not left since the commencement of the winter. We remained below in my apartment, where, while changing my coat and my shirt, I replied to their eager questions; when, lo! M. de Biron, who had forced my door which I had closed against everybody, in order to obtain a little repose, was announced.

Biron put his head in at my door, and begged to be allowed to say a word to me. I passed, half-dressed, into my chamber with him. He said that M. le Duc d'Orleans had expected me at the Palais Royal immediately after the Bed of justice, and was surprised I had not appeared. He added that there was no great harm done; and that the Regent wished to see me now, in order that I might execute a commission for him. I asked Biron what it was? He replied that it was to go to Saint-Clerc to announce what had taken place to Madame la Duchesse d'Orleans!

This was a thunder-bolt for me. I disputed with Biron, who exhorted me to lose no time, but to go at once to the Palais Royal, where I was expected with impatience. I returned into my cabinet with him, so changed in aspect that Madame de Saint-Simon was alarmed. I explained what was the matter, and after Biron had chatted a moment, and again pressed me to set out at once, he went away to eat his dinner. Ours was served. I waited a little time in order to recover myself, determined not to vex M. le Duc d'Orleans by dawdling, took some soup and an egg, and went off to the Palais Royal.

It was in vain that, using all the eloquence I could command and all the liberty I dared employ, I protested against being employed for this duty. I represented to the Regent what an ill-chosen messenger I should be to carry to Madame la Duchesse d'Orleans news of the disgrace of her brother the Duc du Maine; I, who had always been such an open and declared enemy to the bastards! I represented to him that people would say I went on purpose to triumph over her at what had been done, and that she herself would look upon my presence as a kind of insult. In vain! in vain! were my arguments, my entreaties, my instances. M. le Duc d'Orleans had determined that I should go on this errand, and go I must.

As I left his house to execute my luckless commission, I found one of Madame la Duchesse d'Orleans' pages, booted and spurred, who had just arrived from Saint-Cloud. I begged him to return at once, at a gallop, and say, on arriving, to the Duchesse Sforze (one of Madame la Duchesse d'Orleans' ladies) that I should be there soon with a message from M. le Duc d'Orleans, and to ask her to meet me as I descended from my coach. My object was to charge her with the message I had to deliver, and not to see Madame la Duchesse d'Orleans at all. But my poor prudence was confounded by that of the page, who had not less than I. He took good care not to be the bearer of such ill news as he had just learned at the Palais Royal, and which was now everywhere public. He contented himself with saying that I was coming, sent by M. le Duc d'Orleans, spoke not a word to the Duchesse Sforze, and disappeared at once. This is what I afterwards learned, and what I saw clearly enough on arriving at Saint- Cloud.

I went there at a gentle trot, in order to give time to the page to arrive before me, and to the Duchesse Sforze to receive me. During the journey I applauded myself for my address, but feared lest I should be obliged to see Madame la Duchesse d'Orleans after Madame Sforze. I could not imagine that Saint-Cloud was in ignorance of what had occurred, and, nevertheless, I was in an agony that cannot be expressed, and this increased as I approached the end of my journey. If it is disagreeable to announce unpleasant news to the indifferent, how much more is it to announce them to the deeply interested!

Penetrated with this dolorous sentiment I arrived in the grand court of Saint-Cloud, and saw everybody at the windows, running from all parts. I alighted, and asked the first comer to lead me to the Duchesse Sforze, the position of whose apartments I am unacquainted with. I was told that Madame Sforze was in the chapel with Madame la Duchesse d'Orleans. Then I asked for the Marechale de Rochefort, and after a time she arrived, hobbling along with her stick. I disputed with her, wishing to see Madame Sforze, who was not to be found. I was anxious at all events to go to her room and wait, but the inexorable Marechale pulled me by the arm, asking what news I brought. Worn out at last, I said, "News? news that you are acquainted with."

"How, acquainted with?" she asked. "We know nothing, except that a Bed of justice has been held, and we are expiring to know why, and what has passed there."

My astonishment at this ignorance was extreme, and I made her swear and repeat four times over that nothing was known at Saint-Cloud. I told her thereupon what had happened, and she, in her turn, astonished, almost fell backwards! But where was Madame Sforze? she came not, and do what I must, say what I might, I was forced to carry, my message to Madame la Duchesse d'Orleans. I was sorely loth to do so, but was dragged by the hand almost as a sheep is led to the slaughter.

I stood before Madame la Duchesse d'Orleans after having passed through an apartment filled with her people, fear painted upon all their faces. I saluted her; but, oh! how differently from my usual manner! She did not perceive this at first, and begged me, with a cheerful natural air, to approach her; but seeing my trouble, she exclaimed, "Good Heavens, Monsieur, what a face you wear! What news bring you?"

Seeing that I remained silent and motionless, she became more moved, and repeated her questions. I advanced a few steps towards her, and at her third appeal, I said: "Madame, you know nothing then?"

"No, Monsieur; I simply know that there has been a Bed of justice: what has passed there I am quite ignorant of."

"Ah, Madame," I replied, half turning away; "I am more unhappy, then, than I thought to be."

"What is the matter?" exclaimed she; "what has happened?" (rising and sitting bolt upright on the sofa she was stretched upon.) "Come near and sit down!"

I approached; stated that I was in despair. She, more and more moved, said to me, "But speak; better to learn bad news from one's friend than from others."

This remark pierced me to the heart, and made me sensible of the grief I was going to inflict upon her. I summoned up courage, and I told her all.

The tears of Madame la Duchesse d'Orleans flowed abundantly at my recital. She did not answer a word, uttered no cry, but wept bitterly. She pointed to a seat and I sat down upon it, my eyes during several instants fixed upon the floor. Afterwards I said that M. le Duc d'Orleans, who had rather forced upon me this commission, than charged me with it, had expressly commanded me to tell her that he had very strong proofs in his hands against M. du Maine; that he had kept them back a long time, but could no longer do so now. She gently replied to me that her brother was very unfortunate and shortly afterwards asked if I knew what his crime was. I said that M. le Duc d'Orleans had not told me; and that I had not dared to question him upon a subject of this nature, seeing that he was not inclined to talk of it.

More tears shortly afterwards filled her eyes. Her brother must be very criminal, she said, to be so treated.

I remained some time upon my seat, not daring to raise my eyes, in the most painful state possible, and not knowing whether to remain or go away. At last I acquainted her with my difficulty; said I fancied she would like to be alone some little time before giving me her orders, but that respect kept me equally in suspense as to whether I should go or stay. After a short silence, she said she should like to see her women. I rose, sent them to her, and said to them, if her Royal Highness asked for me, I should be with the Duchesse Sforze, or the Marechale Rochefort; but I could find neither of these two ladies, so I went up to Madame.

She rose as soon as I appeared, and said to me, with eagerness, "Well, Monsieur, what news?" At the same time her ladies retired, and I was left alone with her.

I commenced by an excuse for not coming to see her first, as was my duty, on the ground that M. le Duc d'Orleans had assured me she would not object to my commencing with Madame la Duchesse d'Orleans. She did not object, in fact, but asked me for my news with much eagerness. I told her what had happened. Joy spread over her face. She replied with a mighty, "At last!" which she repeated, saying, her son long since ought to have struck this blow, but that he was too good. I mentioned to her that she was standing, but for politeness she remained so. After some further talk she begged me to state all the details of this celebrated morning.

I again recalled to her mind that she was standing, and represented that what she desired to learn would take a long time to relate; but her ardor to know it was extreme. I began then my story, commencing with the very morning. At the end of a quarter of an hour, Madame seated herself, but with the greatest politeness. I was nearly an hour with her, continually telling and sometimes replying to her questions. She was delighted at the humiliation of the Parliament, and of the bastards, and that her son had at last displayed some firmness.

At this point the Marechale de Rochefort entered, and summoned me back to Madame la Duchesse d'Orleans. I found that princess extended upon the sofa where I had left her, an inkstand upon her knees and a pen in her hand. She had commenced a reply to M. le Duc d'Orleans, but had not been able to finish it. Looking at me with an air of gentleness and of friendship, she observed, "Tears escape me; I have begged you to descend in order to render me a service; my hand is unsteady, I pray you finish my writing for me;" and she handed to me the inkstand and her letter. I took them, and she dictated to me the rest of the epistle, that I at once added to what she had written.

I was infinitely amazed at the conciseness and appropriateness of the expressions she readily found, in the midst of her violent emotion, her sobs, and her tears. She finished by saying that she was going to Montmartre to mourn the misfortunes of her brother, and pray God for his prosperity. I shall regret all my life I did not transcribe this letter. All its expressions were so worthy, so fitting, so measured, everything being according to truth and duty; and the letter, in fact, being so perfectly well written, that although I remember it roughly, I dare not give it, for fear of spoiling it. What a pity that a mind capable of such self-possession, at such a moment, should have become valueless from its leaning towards illegitimacy.

After this I had another interview with Madame, and a long talk with my sure and trusty friend Madame Sforze. Then I set out for Paris, went straight to the Palais Royal, and found M. le Duc d'Orleans with Madame la Duchesse de Berry. He was delighted when he heard what Madame had said respecting him; but he was not particularly pleased when he found that Madame la Duchesse d'Orleans (who after telling me she would go to Montmartre, had changed her mind), was coming to the Palais Royal.

I learned afterwards that she came about half an hour after I left. At first she was all humility and sorrow, hoping to soften the Regent by this conduct. Then she passed to tears, sobs, cries, reproaches, expecting to make him by these means undo what he had done, and reinstate M. du Maine in the position he had lost. But all her efforts proving vain, she adopted another course: her sorrow turned to rage,—her tears to looks of anger. Still in vain. She could gain nothing; vex and annoy M. le Duc d'Orleans as she might by her conduct. At last, finding there was no remedy to be had, she was obliged to endure her sorrow as best she might.

As for me, I was erased entirely from her books. She looked upon me as the chief cause of what had occurred, and would not see me. I remained ever afterwards at variance with her. I had nothing to reproach myself with, however, so that her enmity did not very deeply penetrate me.

CHAPTER XCV

It was scarcely to be expected, perhaps, that M. du Maine would remain altogether quiet under the disgrace which had been heaped upon him by the proceedings at the Bed of Justice. Soon indeed we found that he had been secretly working out the most perfidious and horrible schemes for a long time before that assembly; and that after his fall, he gave himself up with redoubled energy to his devilish devices.

Towards the end of this memorable year, 1718, it was discovered that Alberoni, by means of Cellamare, Spanish Ambassador at our Court, was preparing a plot against the Regent. The scheme was nothing less than to throw all the realm into revolt against the government of M. le Duc d'Orleans; to put the King of Spain at the head of the affairs of France, with a council and ministers named by him, and a lieutenant, who would in fact have been regent; this self-same lieutenant to be no other than the Duc du Maine!

This precious plot was, fortunately, discovered before it had come to maturity. Had such not happened, the consequences might have been very serious, although they could scarcely have been fatal. The conspirators counted upon the Parliaments of Paris and of Brittany, upon all the old Court accustomed to the yoke of the bastards, and to that of Madame de Maintenon; and they flung about promises with an unsparing hand to all who supported them. After all, it must be admitted, however, that the measures they took and the men they secured, were strangely unequal to the circumstances of the case, when the details became known; in fact, there was a general murmur of surprise among the public, at the contemptible nature of the whole affair.

But let me relate the circumstances accompanying the discovery of M. du Maine's pitiable treachery.

Cellamare, as I have said, was Spanish Ambassador at our Court. He had been one of the chief movers in the plot. He had excited, as much as lay in his power, discontent against the Regent's government; he had done his best to embroil France with Spain; he had worked heart and soul with M. du Maine, to carry out the common end they had in view. So much preparation had been made; so much of the treason train laid, that at last it became necessary to send to Alberoni a full and clear account of all that had been done, so as to paint exactly the position of affairs, and determine the measures that remained to be taken. But how to send such an account as this? To trust it to the ordinary channels of communication would have been to run a great risk of exposure and detection. To send it by private hand would have been suspicious, if the hand were known, and dangerous if it were not: Cellamare had long since provided for this difficulty.

He had caused a young ecclesiastic to be sent from Spain, who came to Paris as though for his pleasure. There he was introduced to young Monteleon, son of a former ambassador at our Court, who had been much liked. The young ecclesiastic was called the Abbe Portocarrero, a name regarded with favour in France. Monteleon came from the Hague, and was going to Madrid. Portocarrero came from Madrid, and was going back there. What more natural than that the two young men should travel in company? What less natural than that the two young men, meeting each other by pure accident in Paris, should be charged by the ambassador with any packet of consequence, he having his own couriers, and the use, for the return journey, of those sent to him from Spain? In fact, it may be believed that these young people themselves were perfectly ignorant of what they were charged with, and simply believed that, as they were going to Spain, the ambassador merely seized the occasion to entrust them with some packet of no special importance.

They set out, then, at the commencement of December, furnished with passports from the King—(for Alberoni had openly caused almost a rupture between the two Courts)—with a Spanish banker, who had been established in England, where he had become bankrupt for a large amount, so that the English government had obtained permission from the Regent to arrest him, if they could, anywhere in France. It will sometimes be perceived that I am ill-instructed in this affair; but I can only tell what I know: and as for the rest, I give my conjectures. In fact, the Abbe Dubois kept everybody so much in the dark, that even M. le Duc d'Orleans was not informed of all.

Whether the arrival of the Abbe Portocarrero in Paris, and his short stay there, seemed suspicious to the Abbe Dubois and his emissaries, or whether he had corrupted some of the principal people of the Spanish Ambassador and this Court, and learned that these young men were charged with a packet of importance; whether there was no other mystery than the bad company of the bankrupt banker, and that the anxiety of Dubois to oblige his friends the English, induced him to arrest the three travellers and seize their papers, lest the banker should have confided his to the young men, I know not: but however it may have been, it is certain that the Abbe Dubois arrested the three travellers at Poitiers, and carried off their papers, a courier bringing these papers to him immediately afterwards.

Great things sometimes spring from chance. The courier from Poitiers entered the house of the Abbe Dubois just as the Regent entered the opera. Dubois glanced over the papers, and went and related the news of this capture to M. le Duc Orleans, as he left his box. This prince, who was accustomed to shut himself up with his roues at that hour, did so with a carelessness to which everything yielded, under pretext that Dubois had not had sufficient time to examine all the papers. The first few hours of the morning he was not himself. His head, still confused by the fumes of the wine and by the undigested supper of the previous night, was not in a state to understand anything, and the secretaries of state have often told me that was the time they could make him sign anything. This was the moment taken by Dubois to acquaint the Regent with as much or as little of the contents of the papers as he thought fit. The upshot of their interview was, that the Abbe was allowed by the Duc d'Orleans to have the control of this matter entirely in his own hands.

The day after the arrival of the courier from Poitiers, Cellamare, informed of what had occurred, but who flattered himself that the presence of the banker had caused the arrest of the young men, and the seizure of their papers, hid his fears under a very tranquil bearing, and went, at one o'clock in the day, to M. le Blanc, to ask for a packet of letters he had entrusted to Portocarrero and Monteleon on their return to Spain. Le Blanc (who had had his lesson prepared beforehand by the Abbe Dubois) replied that the packet had been seen; that it contained important things, and that, far from being restored to him, he himself must go back to his hotel under escort, to meet there M. l'Abbe Dubois. The ambassador, who felt that such a compliment would not be attempted with out means having been prepared to put it in execution, made no difficulty, and did not lose for a moment his address or his tranquillity.

During the three hours, at least, passed in his house, in the examination of all his bureaux and his boxes, and his papers, Cellamare, like a man who fears nothing, and who is sure of his game, treated M. le Blanc very civilly; as for the Abbe Dubois, with whom he felt he had no measure to keep (all the plot being discovered), he affected to treat him with the utmost disdain. Thus Le Blanc, taking hold of a little casket, Cellamare cried, "M. le Blanc, M. le Blanc, leave that alone; that is not for you; that is for the Abbe Dubois" (who was then present). Then looking at him, he added, "He has been a pander all his life, and there are nothing but women's letters there."

Search of the Spanish Ambassador--painted by Maurice Leloir

The Abbe Dubois burst out laughing, not daring to grow angry.

When all was examined, the King's seal, and that of the ambassador, were put upon all the bureaux and the caskets which contained papers. The Abbe Dubois and Le Blanc went off together to give an account of their proceedings to the Regent, leaving a company of musketeers to guard the ambassador and his household.

I heard of the capture effected at Poitiers, at home, the morning after it occurred, without knowing anything of those arrested. As I was at table, a servant came to me from M. le Duc d'Orleans, summoning me to a council of the regency, at four o'clock that day. As it was not the usual day for the council, I asked what was the matter. The messenger was surprised at my ignorance and informed me that the Spanish ambassador was arrested. As soon as I had eaten a morsel, I quitted my company, and hastened to the Palais Royal, where I learnt from M. le Duc d'Orleans all that I have just related. Our conversation took up time, and, when it was over, I went away to the Tuileries. I found there astonishment painted upon several faces; little groups of two, three, and four people together; and the majority struck by the importance of the arrest, and little disposed to approve it.

M. le Duc d'Orleans arrived shortly after. He had, better than any man I have ever known, the gift of speech, and without needing any preparation he said exactly what he wanted to say, neither more nor less; his expressions were just and precise, a natural grace accompanied them with an air of proper dignity, always mixed with an air of politeness. He opened the council with a discourse upon the people and the papers seized at Poitiers, the latter proving that a very dangerous conspiracy against the state was on the eve of bursting, and of which the Ambassador of Spain was the principal promoter. His Royal Highness alleged the pressing reasons which had induced him to secure the person of this ambassador, to examine his papers, and to place them under guard. He showed that the protection afforded by the law of nations did not extend to conspiracies, that ambassadors rendered themselves unworthy of that protection when they took part in them, still more when they excited people against the state where they dwelt. He cited several examples of ambassadors arrested for less. He explained the orders he had given so as to inform all the foreign ministers in Paris of what had occurred, and had ordered Dubois to render an account to the council of what he had done at the ambassador's, and offered to read the letters from Cellamare to Cardinal Alberoni, found among the papers brought from Poitiers.

The Abbe Dubois stammered out a short and ill-arranged recital of what he had done at the ambassador's house, and dwelt upon the importance of the discovery and upon that of the conspiracy as far as already known. The two letters he read left me no doubt that Cellamare was at the head of this affair, and that Alberoni had entered into it as far as he. We were much scandalised with the expressions in these letters against M. le Duc d'Orleans, who was in no way spared.

This prince spoke again, to say he did not suspect the King or Queen of Spain to be mixed up in this affair, but that he attributed it all to the passion of Alberoni, and that of his ambassador to please him, and that he would ask for justice from their Catholic Majesties. He showed the importance of neglecting no means in order to clear up an affair so capital to the repose and tranquillity of the kingdom, and finished by saying, that until he knew more he would name nobody who was mixed up in the matter. All this speech was much applauded, and I believe there were some among the company who felt greatly relieved when they heard the Regent say he would name nobody nor would he allow suspicions to be circulated until all was unravelled.

Nevertheless the next day, Saturday, the 10th of December, more than one arrest was made. Others took place a few days afterwards.

On Tuesday, the 13th of December, all the foreign ministers went to the Palais Royal, according to custom; not one made any complaint of what had happened. A copy of the two letters read at the council was given to them. In the afternoon, Cellamare was placed in a coach with a captain of cavalry and a captain of dragoons, chosen to conduct him: to Blois, until Saint-Aignan, our ambassador in Spain, should arrive in France.

The position of our ambassador, Saint-Aignan, at Madrid, was, as may be imagined, by no means agreeable. The two courts were just upon the point of an open rupture, thanks to the hatred Alberoni had made it a principle to keep up in Spain against M. le Duc d'Orleans, by crying down his actions, his government, his personal conduct, his most innocent acts, and by rendering suspicious even his favourable proceedings with regard to Spain. Alberoni for a long time had ceased to keep on even decent terms with Saint-Aignan, scandalising thus even the most unfavourably disposed towards France. Saint-Aignan only maintained his position by the sagacity of his conduct, and he was delighted when he received orders to return to France. He asked for his parting audience, and meanwhile bade adieu to all his friends and to all the Court. Alberoni, who every moment expected decisive news from Cellamare respecting the conspiracy, wished to remain master of our ambassador, so as, in case of accident, to have a useful hostage in his hands as security for his own ambassador. He put off therefore this parting audience under various pretexts. At last, Saint-Aignan, pressed by his reiterated orders (orders all the more positive because suspicion had already begun to foresee a disturbance ever alarming), spoke firmly to the Cardinal, and declared that if this audience were not at once accorded to him, he would do without it! Therefore the Cardinal, in anger, replied with a menace, that he knew well enough how to hinder, him, from acting thus.

Saint-Aignan wisely contained himself; but seeing to what sort of a man he was exposed, and judging rightly why he was detained at Madrid, took his measures so secretly and so well, that he set out the same night, with his most necessary equipage, gained ground and arrived at the foot of the Pyrenees without being overtaken and arrested; two occurrences which he expected at every moment, knowing that Alberoni was a man who would stick at nothing.

Saint-Aignan, already so far advanced, did not deem it advisable to expose himself any longer, bothered as he would be among the mountains by his carriages. He and the Duchess, his wife, followed by a waiting-woman and three valets, with a very trusty guide, mounted upon mules and rode straight for Saint-Jean-Pied-de-Port without stopping a moment more on the road than was necessary. He sent on his equipages to Pampeluna at a gentle pace, and placed in his carriage an intelligent valet de chambre and a waiting-woman, with orders to pass themselves off as the ambassador and ambassadress of France, and in case they were arrested to cry out a good deal. The arrest did not fail to happen. The people despatched by Alberoni soon came up with the carriage. The pretended ambassador and ambassadress played their parts very well, and they who had arrested them did not doubt for a moment they had made a fine capture, sending news of it to Madrid, and keeping the prisoners in Pampeluna, to which the party returned.

This device saved M. and Madame de Saint-Aignan, and gave them means to reach Saint-Jean-Pied-de-Port; as soon as they arrived there they sent for assistance and carriages to Bayonne, which they gained in safety, and reposed after their fatigue. The Duc de Saint-Aignan sent word of all this to M. le Duc d'Orleans by a courier, and, at this arrival in Bayonne, despatched a message to the Governor of Pampeluna, begging him to send on his equipages. Alberoni's people were very much ashamed of having been duped, but Alberoni when he heard of it flew into a furious rage, and cruelly punished the mistake. The equipages were sent on to Bayonne.

CHAPTER XCVI: To return now to what took place at Paris.

On Sunday, the 25th of December, Christmas Day, M. le Duc d'Orleans sent for me to come and see him at the Palais Royal, about four o'clock in the afternoon. I went accordingly, and after despatching some business with him, other people being present, I followed him into his little winter cabinet at the end of the little gallery, M. le Duc being present.

After a moment of silence, the Regent told me to see if no one was outside in the gallery, and if the door at the end was closed. I went out, found the door shut, and no one near.

This being ascertained, M. le Duc d'Orleans said that we should not be surprised to learn that M. and Madame du Maine had been mixed up all along with this affair of the Spanish Ambassador Cellamare; that he had written proofs of this, and that the project was exactly that which I have already described. He added, that he had strictly forbidden the Keeper of the Seals, the Abbe Dubois, and Le Blanc, who alone knew of this project, to give the slightest sign of their knowledge, recommended to me the same secrecy, and the same precaution; and finished by saying that he wished, above all things, to consult M. le Duc and me upon the course he ought to adopt.

M. le Duc at once went to the point and said M. and Madame du Maine must at once be arrested and put where they could cause no apprehension. I supported this opinion, and showed the perilous annoyances that might arise if this step were not instantly taken; as much for the purpose of striking terror into the conspirators, as for disconcerting their schemes. I added that there was not a moment to lose, and that it was better to incur uncertain danger than to wait for that which was certain.

Our advice was accepted by M. le Duc d'Orleans, after some little debate. But now the question arose, where are the prisoners to be put? The Bastille and Vincennes both seemed to me too near to Paris. Several places were named without one appearing to suit. At lasts M. le Duc d'Orleans mentioned Dourlens. I stopped him short at the name, and recommended it warmly. I knew the governor, Charost, and his son to be men of probity, faithful, virtuous, and much attached to the state. Upon this it was agreed to send M. du Maine to Dourlens.

Then we had to fix upon a place for his wife, and this was more difficult; there were her sex, her fiery temper, her courage; her daring,—all to be considered; whereas, her husband, we knew, so dangerous as a hidden enemy, was contemptible without his mask, and would fall into the lowest state of dejection in prison, trembling all over with fear of the scaffold, and attempting nothing; his wife, on the contrary, being capable of attempting anything:

Various places discussed, M. le Duc d'Orleans smiled, and proposed the chateau of Dijon! Now, the joke of this suggestion was, that Dijon belonged to M. le Duc, and that he was nephew of Madame du Maine, whom the Regent proposed to lock up there! M. le Duc smiled also, and said it was a little too bad to make him the gaoler of his aunt! But all things considered, it was found that a better choice than Dijon could not be made, so M. le Duc gave way. I fancy he had held out more for form's sake than for any other reason. These points settled, we separated, to meet another time, in order to make the final arrangements for the arrest.

We met accordingly, the Monday and Tuesday following, and deliberated with the same secrecy as before. On Wednesday we assembled again to put the final touch to our work. Our conference was long, and the result of it was, that M. and Madame du Maine were to be arrested on the morrow; all the necessary arrangements were made, and, as we thought, with the utmost secrecy. Nevertheless, the orders given to the regiment of the guards, and to the musketeers somehow or other transpired during the evening, and gave people reason to believe that something considerable was in contemplation. On leaving the conference, I arranged with Le Blanc that, when the blow was struck, he should inform me by simply sending a servant to inquire after my health.

The morrow, about ten o'clock in the morning, having noiselessly and without show placed the body-guard around Sceaux, La Billardiere, lieutenant of the regiment, entered there, and arrested the Duc du Maine as he was leaving his chapel after hearing mass, and very respectfully begged him not to re-enter the house, but to mount immediately into a coach which he had brought. M. du Maine, who had expected this arrest, and who had had time to put his papers in order, mad not the slightest resistance. He replied that he had anticipated this compliment for some days, and at once moved into the coach. La Billardiere placed himself by his side, and in front was an exempt of the bodyguards, and Favancourt, brigadier in the first company of musketeers, destined to guard him in his prison.

As these two latter persons did not appear before the Duc du Maine until the moment he entered the coach, be appeared surprised and moved to see Favancourt.

He would not have been at the exempt, but the sight of the other depressed him. He asked La Billardiere what this meant. Billardiere could not dissimulate that Favancourt had orders to accompany him, and to remain with him in the place to which they were going. Favancourt himself took this moment to pay his compliments as best he might to the Duc du Maine, to which the Duke replied but little, and that in a civil and apprehensive manner. These proceedings conducted them to the end of the avenue of Sceaux, where the bodyguards appeared. The sight of them made the Duc du Maine change colour.

Silence was but little interrupted in the coach. Now and then M. du Maine would say that he was very innocent of the accusation which had been formed against him; that he was much attached to the King, and not less so to M. le Duc d'Orleans, who could not but recognise it; and that it was very unfortunate his Royal Highness should put faith in his enemies (he never named anybody). All this was said in a broken manner, and amid many sighs; from time to time signs of the cross; low mumblings as of prayers; and plunges at each church or each cross they passed. He took his meals in the coach, ate very little, was alone at night, but with good precautions taken. He did not know until the morrow that he was going to Dourlens. He showed no emotion thereupon. All these details I learnt from Favancourt, whom I knew very well, and who was in the Musketeers when I served in that corps.

At the moment of the arrest of M. du Maine, Ancenis, captain of the body- guard, arrested the Duchesse du Maine in her house in the Rue St. Honore. A lieutenant, and an exempt of the foot body-guards, with other troops, took possession of the house at the same time, and guarded the doors. The compliment of the Duc d'Ancenis was sharply received. Madame du Maine wished to take away some caskets. Ancenis objected. She demanded, at the least, her jewels; altercations very strong on one side, very modest on the other: but she was obliged to yield. She raged at the violence done to a person of her rank, without saying anything too disobliging to M. d'Ancenis, and without naming anybody. She delayed her departure as long as she could, despite the instances of d'Ancenis, who at last presented his hand to her, and politely, but firmly, said she must go. She found at her door two six-horse coaches, the sight of which much shocked her. She was obliged, however, to mount. Ancenis placed himself by her side, the lieutenant and the exempt of the guard in front, two chambermaids whom she had chosen were in the other coach, with her apparel, which had been examined. The ramparts were followed, the principal streets avoided; there was no stir, and at this she could not restrain her surprise and vexation, or check a tear, declaiming by fits and starts against the violence done her. She complained of the rough coach, the indignity it cast upon her, and from time to time asked where she was being led to. She was simply told that she would sleep at Essonne, nothing more. Her three guardians maintained profound silence. At night all possible precautions were taken. When she set out the next day, the Duc d'Ancenis took leave of her, and left her to the lieutenant and to the exempt of the body-guards, with troops to conduct her. She asked where they were leading her to: he simply replied, "To Fontainebleau." The disquietude of Madame du Maine augmented as she left Paris farther behind, but when she found herself in Burgundy, and knew at last she was to go to Dijon, she stormed at a fine rate.

It was worse when she was forced to enter the castle, and found herself the prisoner of M. le Duc. Fury suffocated her. She raged against her nephew, and the horrible place chosen for her. Nevertheless, after her first transports, she returned to herself, and began to comprehend that she was in no place and no condition to play the fury. Her extreme rage she kept to herself, affected nothing but indifference for all, and disdainful security. The King's lieutenant of the castle, absolutely devoted to M. le Duc, kept her fast, and closely watched her and her chambermaids. The Prince de Dombes and the Comte d'Eu (her sons) were at the same time exiled to Eu, where a gentleman in ordinary always was near them; Mademoiselle du Maine was sent to Maubuisson.

Several other people were successively arrested and placed either in the Bastille or Vincennes. The commotion caused by the arrest and imprisonment of M. and Madame du Maine was great; many faces, already elongated by the Bed of justice, were still further pulled out by these events. The Chief-President, D'Effiat, the Marechal de Villeroy, the Marechal de Villars, the Marechal d'Huxelles, and other devoted friends of M. du Maine, were completely terrified; they did not dare to say a word; they kept out of the way; did not leave their houses except from necessity; fear was painted upon their faces. All their pride was put aside; they became polite, caressing, would have eaten out of your hand; and by this sudden change and their visible embarrassment betrayed themselves.

As for the Comte de Toulouse he remained as upright and loyal as ever. The very day of the double arrest he came to M. le Duc d'Orleans and said that he regarded the King, the Regent, and the State as one and the same thing; that he should never be wanting in his duty or in his fidelity towards them; that he was very sorry at what had happened to his brother, but that he was in no way answerable for him. The Regent stated this to me the same day, and appeared, with reason, to be charmed with such straightforward honesty.

This arrest of M. and Madame du Maine had another effect. For some time past, a large quantity of illicit salt had been sold throughout the country. The people by whom this trade was conducted, 'faux sauniers', as they were called, travelled over the provinces in bands well armed and well organized. So powerful had they become that troops were necessary in order to capture them. There were more than five thousand faux saumers, who openly carried on their traffic in Champagne and Picardy. They had become political instruments in the hands of others, being secretly encouraged and commanded by those who wished to sow trouble in the land. It could not be hidden that these 'faux sauniers' were redoubtable by their valour and their arrangements; that the people were favourable to them, buying as they did from them salt at a low price, and irritated as they were against the gabelle and other imposts; that these 'faux sauniers' spread over all the realm, and often marching in large bands, which beat all opposed to them, were dangerous people, who incited the population by their examples to opposition against the government.

I had proposed on one occasion the abolition of the salt tax to the Regent, as a remedy for these evils; but my suggestion shared the fate of many others. It was favourably listened to, and nothing more. And meanwhile the 'faux sauniers' had gone on increasing. I had no difficulty in discovering by whom they were encouraged, and the event showed I was right. Directly after the arrest of M. and Madame du Maine, the 'faux sauniers' laid down their arms, asked, and obtained pardon. This prompt submission showed dearly enough by whom they had been employed, and for what reason. I had uselessly told M. le Duc d'Orleans so long before, who admitted that I was right, but did nothing. It was his usual plan.

Let me finish at once with all I shall have to say respecting M. and Madame du Maine.

They remained in their prisons during the whole of the year 1719, supplied with all the comforts and attentions befitting their state, and much less rigorously watched than at first, thanks to the easy disposition of M. le Duc d'Orleans, whose firmness yielded even more rapidly than beauty to the effects of time. The consequence of his indulgence towards the two conspirators was, that at about the commencement of the following year, 1720, they began to play a very ridiculous comedy, of which not a soul was the dupe; not even the public, nor the principal actors, nor the Regent.

The Duc and Duchesse du Maine, thanks to the perfidy of the Abbe Dubois, had had time to hide away all their papers, and to arrange together the different parts they should play. Madame du Maine, supported by her sex and birth, muffled herself up in her dignity, when replying to the questions addressed to her, of which just as many, and no more, were read to the replying counsel as pleased the Abbe Dubois; and strongly accusing Cellamare and others; protected as much as possible her friends, her husband above all, by charging herself with all; by declaring that what she had done M. du Maine had no knowledge of; and that its object went no farther than to obtain from the Regent such reforms in his administration as were wanted.

The Duc du Maine, shorn of his rank and of his title of prince of the blood, trembled for his life. His crimes against the state, against the blood royal, against the person of the Regent, so long, so artfully, and so cruelly offended, troubled him all the more because he felt they deserved severe punishment. He soon, therefore, conceived the idea of screening himself beneath his wife's petticoats. His replies, and all his observations were to the same tune; perfect ignorance of everything. Therefore when the Duchess had made her confessions, and they were communicated to him, he cried out against his wife,—her madness, her felony,—his misfortune in having a wife capable of conspiring, and daring enough to implicate him in everything without having spoken to him; making him thus a criminal without being so the least in the world; and keeping him so ignorant of her doings, that it was out of his power to stop them, to chide her, or inform M. le Duc d'Orleans if things had been pushed so far that he ought to have done so!

From that time the Duc du Maine would no longer hear talk of a woman who, without his knowledge, had cast him and his children into this abyss; and when at their release from prison, they were permitted to write and send messages to each other, he would receive nothing from her, or give any signs of life. Madame du Maine, on her side, pretended to be afflicted at this treatment; admitting, nevertheless, that she had acted wrongfully towards her husband in implicating him without his knowledge in her schemes. They were at this point when they were allowed to come near Paris. M. du Maine went to live at Clagny, a chateau near Versailles, built for Madame de Montespan. Madame du Maine went to Sceaux. They came separately to see M. le Duc d'Orleans at Paris, without sleeping there; both played their parts, and as the Abbe Dubois judged the time had come to take credit to himself in their eyes for finishing their disgrace, he easily persuaded M. le Duc d'Orleans to, appear convinced of the innocence of M. du Maine.

During their stay in the two country-houses above named, where they saw but little company, Madame du Maine made many attempts at reconciliation with her husband, which he repelled. This farce lasted from the month of January (when they arrived at Sceaux and at Clagny) to the end of July. Then they thought the game had lasted long enough to be put an end to. They had found themselves quit of all danger so cheaply, and counted so much upon the Abbe Dubois, that they were already thinking of returning to their former considerations; and to work at this usefully, they must be in a position to see each other, and commence by establishing themselves in Paris, where they would of necessity live together.

The sham rupture had been carried to this extent, that the two sons of the Duc du Maine returned from Eu to Clagny a few days after him, did not for a long time go and see Madame du Maine, and subsequently saw her but rarely, and without sleeping under her roof.

At last a resolution being taken to put an end to the comedy, this is how it was terminated by another.

Madame la Princesse made an appointment with the Duc du Maine, at Vaugirard on the last of July, and in the house of Landais, treasurer of the artillery. She arrived there a little after him with the Duchesse du Maine, whom she left in her carriage. She said to M. du Maine she had brought a lady with her who much desired to see him. The thing was not difficult to understand; the piece had been well studied. The Duchesse du Maine was sent for. The apparent reconcilement took place. The three were a long time together. To play out the comedy, M. and

Madame du Maine still kept apart, but saw and approached each other by degrees, until at last the former returned to Sceaux, and lived with his wife as before.

VOLUME 13.: CHAPTER XCVII: To go back, now, to the remaining events of the year 1719.

The Marquise de Charlus, sister of Mezieres, and mother of the Marquis de Levi, who has since become a duke and a peer, died rich and old. She was the exact picture of an "old clothes" woman and was thus subject to many insults from those who did not know her, which she by no means relished. To relieve a little the seriousness of these memoirs, I will here relate an amusing adventure of which she was heroine.

She was very avaricious, and a great gambler. She would have passed the night up to her knees in water in order to play. Heavy gambling at lansquenet was carried on at Paris in the evening, at Madame la Princesse de Conti's. Madame de Charlus supped there one Friday, between the games, much company being present. She was no better clad than at other times, and wore a head-dress, in vogue at that day, called commode, not fastened, but put on or taken off like a wig or a night-cap. It was fashionable, then, to wear these headdresses very high.

Madame de Charlus was near the Archbishop of Rheims, Le Tellier. She took a boiled egg, that she cracked, and in reaching for some salt, set her head dress on fire, at a candle near, without perceiving it. The Archbishop, who saw her all in flames, seized the head-dress and flung it upon the ground. Madame de Charlus, in her surprise, and indignant at seeing her self thus uncovered, without knowing why, threw her egg in the Archbishop's face, and made him a fine mess.

Nothing but laughter was heard; and all the company were in convulsions of mirth at the grey, dirty, and hoary head of Madame de Charlus, and the Archbishop's omelette; above all, at the fury and abuse of Madame de Charlus, who thought she had been affronted, and who was a long time before she would understand the cause, irritated at finding herself thus treated before everybody. The head-dress was burnt, Madame la Princesse de Conti gave her another, but before it was on her head everybody had time to contemplate her charms, and she to grow in fury. Her, husband died three months after her. M. de Levi expected to find treasures; there had been such; but they had taken wing and flown away.

About this time appeared some verses under the title of Philippiques, which were distributed with extraordinary promptitude and abundance. La Grange, formerly page of Madame la Princesse de Conti, was the author, and did not deny it. All that hell could vomit forth, true and false, was expressed in the most beautiful verses, most poetic in style, and with all the art and talent imaginable. M. le Duc d'Orleans knew it, and wished to see the poem, but he could not succeed in getting it, for no one dared to show it to him.

He spoke of it several times to me, and at last demanded with such earnestness that I should bring it to him, that I could not refuse. I brought it to him accordingly, but read it to him I declared I never would. He took it, therefore, and read it in a low tone, standing in the window of his little cabinet, where we were. He judged it in reading much as it was, for he stopped from time to time to speak to me, and without appearing much moved. But all on a sudden I saw him change countenance, and turn towards me, tears in his eyes, and himself ready to drop.

"Ah," said he, "this is too much, this horrible poem beats me completely."

He was at the part where the scoundrel shows M. le Duc d'Orleans having the design to poison the King, and quite ready to execute his crime. It is the part where the author redoubles his energy, his poetry, his invocations, his terrible and startling beauties, his invectives, his hideous pictures, his touching portraits of the youth and innocence of the King, and of the hopes he has, adjuring the nation to save so dear a victim from the barbarity of a murderer; in a word, all that is most delicate, most tender, stringent, and blackest, most pompous, and most moving, is there.

I wished to profit by the dejected silence into which the reading of this poem had thrown M. le Duc d'Orleans, to take from him the execrable paper, but I could not succeed; he broke out into just complaints against such horrible wickedness, and into tenderness for the King; then finished his reading, that he interrupted more than once to speak to me. I never saw a man so penetrated, so deeply touched, so overwhelmed with injustice so enormous and sustained. As for me, I could not contain myself. To see him, the most prejudiced, if of good faith, would have been convinced he was innocent of the come imputed to him, by the horror he displayed at it. I have said all, when I state that I recovered myself with difficulty, and that I had all the pains in the world to compose him a little.

This La Grange, who was of no personal value, yet a good poet—only that, and never anything else—had, by his poetry, insinuated himself into Sceaux, where he had become one of the great favourites of Madame du Maine. She and her husband knew his life, his habits, and his mercenary villainy. They knew, too, haw to profit by it. He was arrested shortly afterwards, and sent to the Isle de Sainte Marguerite, which he obtained permission to leave before the end of the Regency. He had the audacity to show himself everywhere in Paris, and while he was appearing at the theatres and in all public places, people had the impudence to spread the report that M. le Duc d'Orleans had had him killed! M. le Duc d'Orleans and his enemies have been equally indefatigable; the latter in the blackest villainies, the Prince in the most unfruitful clemency, to call it by no more expressive name.

Before the Regent was called to the head of public affairs, I recommended him to banish Pere Tellier when he had the power to do so. He did not act upon my advice, or only partially; nevertheless, Tellier was disgraced, and after wandering hither and thither, a very firebrand wherever he went, he was confined by his superiors in La Fleche.

This tyrant of the Church, furious that he could no longer move, which had been his sole consolation during the end of his reign and his terrible domination, found himself at La Fleche, reduced to a position as insupportable as it was new to him.

The Jesuits, spies of each other, and jealous and envious of those who have the superior authority, are marvellously ungrateful towards those who, having occupied high posts, or served the company with much labour and success, become useless to it, by their age or their infirmities. They regard them with disdain, and instead of bestowing upon them the attention merited by their age, their services, and their merit, leave them in the dreariest solitude, and begrudge them even their food!

I have with my own eyes seen three examples of this in these Jesuits, men of much piety and honour, who hid filled positions of confidence and of talent, and with whom I was very intimate.

The first had been rector of their establishment at Paris, was distinguished by excellent works of piety, and was for several years assistant of the general at Rome, at the death of whom he returned to Paris; because the rule is, that the new general has new assistants. Upon his return to the Paris establishment he was put into a garret, at the very top of the house, amid solitude, contempt, and want.

The direction of the royal conscience had been the principal occupation of the two others, one of whom had even been proposed as confessor to Madame la Dauphine. One was long ill of a malady he died of. He was not properly nourished, and I sent him his dinner every day, for more than five months, because I had seen his pittance. I sent him even remedies, for he could not refrain from admitting to me that he suffered from the treatment he was subjected to.

The third, very old and very infirm, had not a better fate. At last, being no longer able to hold out, he asked to be allowed to pay a visit to my Versailles house (after having explained himself to me), under pretext of fresh air. He remained there several months, and died at the noviciate in Paris. Such is the fate of all the Jesuits, without excepting the most famous, putting aside a few who having shone at the Court and in the world by their sermons and their merit, and having made many friends—as Peres Bordaloue, La Rue, Gaillard—have been guaranteed from the general disgrace, because, often visited by the principal persons of the Court and the town, policy did not permit them to be treated like the rest, for fear of making so many considerable people notice what they would not have suffered without disturbance and scandal.

It was, then, in this abandonment and this contempt that Pere Tellier remained at La Fleche, although he had from the Regent four thousand livres pension. He had ill-treated everybody. When he was confessor of the King, not one of his brethren approached him without trembling, although most of them were the "big-wigs" of the company. Even the general of the company was forced to bend beneath the despotism he exercised upon all. There was not a Jesuit who did not disapprove the violence of his conduct, or who did not fear it would injure the society. All hated him, as a minister is hated who is coarse, harsh, inaccessible, egotistical, and who takes pleasure in showing his power and his disdain.

His exile, and the conduct that drew it upon him, were fresh motives for hatred against him, unveiling, as they did, a number of secret intrigues he had been concerned in, and which he had great interest in hiding. All these things together did not render agreeable to Tellier his forced retirement at La Fleche. He found there sharp superiors and equals, instead of the general terror his presence had formerly caused among the Jesuits. All now showed nothing but contempt for him, and took pleasure in making him sensible of it. This King of the Church, in part of the State, and in private of his society, became a common Jesuit like the rest, and under superiors; it may be imagined what a hell this was to a man so impetuous and so accustomed to a domination without reply, and without bounds, and abused in every fashion. Thus he did not endure it long. Nothing more was heard of him, and he died after having been only six months at La Fleche.

There was another death, which I may as well mention here, as it occurred about the same time.

On Saturday evening, the 15th of April, 1719, the celebrated and fatal Madame de Maintenon died at Saint-Cyr. What a stir this event would have made in Europe, had it happened a few years earlier. It was scarcely mentioned in Paris!

I have already said so much respecting this woman, so unfortunately famous, that I will say but little more now. Her life at Saint-Cyr was divided between her spiritual duties, the letters she received, from her religious correspondents, and the answers she gave to them. She took the communion twice a-week, ordinarily between seven and eight o'clock in the morning; not, as Dangeau says in his Memoires, at midnight or every day. She was very rich, having four thousand livres pension per month from the Regent, besides other emoluments. She had, too, her estate at Maintenon, and some other property. With all this wealth, too, she had not a farthing of expense at Saint-Cyr. Everything was provided for herself and servants and their horses, even wood, coals, and candles. She had nothing to buy, except dress for herself and for her people. She kept a steward, a valet, people for the horses and the kitchen, a coach, seven or eight horses, one or two others for the saddle, besides having the young ladies of Saint-Cyr, chambermaids, and Mademoiselle d'Aumale to wait upon her.

The fall of the Duc du Maine at the Bed of justice struck the first blow at her. It is not too much to presume that she was well informed of the measures and the designs of this darling, and that this hope had sustained her; but when she saw him arrested she succumbed; continuous fever seized her, and she died at eighty-three years of age, in the full possession of all her intellect.

Regret for her loss, which was not even universal in Saint-Cyr, scarcely passed the walls of that community. Aubigny, Archbishop of Rouen, her pretended cousin, was the only man I ever heard of, who was fool enough to die of grief on account of it. But he was so afflicted by this loss, that he fell ill, and soon followed her.

CHAPTER XCVII.

Madame la Duchesse de Berry was living as usual, amid the loftiest pride, and the vilest servitude; amid penitence the most austere at the Carmelite convent of the Faubourg Saint-Germain, and suppers the most profaned by vile company, filthiness, and impiety; amid the most shameless debauchery, and the most horrible fear of the devil and death; when lo! she fell ill at the Luxembourg.

I must disguise nothing more, especially as what I am relating belongs to history; and never in these memoirs have I introduced details upon gallantry except such as were necessary to the proper comprehension of important or interesting matters to which they related. Madame la Duchesse de Berry would constrain herself in nothing; she was indignant that people would dare to speak of what she did not take the trouble to hide from them; and nevertheless she was grieved to death that her conduct was known.

She was in the family way by Rion, but hid—it as much as she could. Madame de Mouchy was their go-between, although her conduct was as clear as day. Rion and Mouchy, in fact, were in love with each other, and had innumerable facilities for indulging their passion. They laughed at the Princess, who was their dupe, and from whom they drew in council all they could. In one word, they were the masters of her and of her household, and so insolently, that M. le Duc and Madame la Duchesse d'Orleans, who knew them and hated them, feared them also and temporised with them. Madame de Saint-Simon, sheltered from all that, extremely loved and respected by all the household, and respected even by this couple who made themselves so much dreaded and courted, only saw Madame la Duchesse de Berry during the moments of presentation at the Luxembourg, whence she returned as soon as all was finished, entirely ignorant of what was passing, though she might have been perfectly instructed.

The illness of Madame la Duchesse de Berry came on, and this illness, ill prepared for by suppers washed down by wine and strong liquors, became stormy and dangerous. Madame de Saint-Simon could not avoid becoming assiduous in her attendance as soon as the peril appeared, but she never would yield to the instances of M. le Duc and Madame la Duchesse d'Orleans, who, with all the household; wished her to sleep in the chamber allotted to her, and which she never put foot in, not even during the day. She found Madame la Duchesse de Berry shut up in a little chamber, which had private entrances—very useful just then, with no one near her but La Mouchy and Rion, and a few trusty waiting-women. All in attendance had free entrance to this room. M. le Duc and Madame la Duchesse d'Orleans were not allowed to enter when they liked; of course it was the same with the lady of honour, the other ladies, the chief femme de chambre, and the doctors. All entered from time to time, but ringing for an instant. A bad headache or want of sleep caused them often to be asked to stay away, or, if they entered, to leave directly afterwards. They did not press their presence upon the sick woman, knowing only too well the nature of her malady; but contented themselves by asking after her through Madame de Mouchy, who opened the door to reply to them, keeping it scarcely ajar: This ridiculous proceeding passed before the crowd of the Luxembourg, of the Palais Royal, and of many other people who, for form's sake or for curiosity, came to inquire the news, and became common town-talk.

The danger increasing, Languet, a celebrated cure of Saint-Sulpice, who had always rendered himself assiduous, spoke of the sacraments to M. le Duc d'Orleans. The difficulty was how to enter and propose them to Madame la Duchesse de Berry. But another and greater difficulty soon appeared. It was this: the cure, like a man knowing his duty, refused to administer the sacrament, or to suffer it to be administered, while Rion or Madame de Mouchy remained in the chamber, or even in the Luxembourg! He declared this aloud before everybody, expressly in presence of M. le Duc d'Orleans, who was less shocked than embarrassed. He took the cure aside, and for a long time tried to make him give way. Seeing him inflexible, he proposed reference to the Cardinal de Noailles. The cure immediately agreed, and promised to defer to his orders, Noailles being his bishop, provided he was allowed to explain his reasons. The affair passed, and Madame la Duchesse de Berry made confession to a Cordelier, her confessor. M. le Duc d'Orleans flattered himself, no doubt, he would find the diocesan more flexible than the cure. If he hoped so he deceived himself.

The Cardinal de Noailles arrived; M. le Duc d'Orleans took him aside with the cure, and their conversation lasted more than half an hour. As the declaration of the cure had been public, the Cardinal Archbishop of Paris judged it fitting that his should be so also. As all three approached the door of the chamber, filled with company, the Cardinal de Noailles said aloud to the cure, that he had very worthily done his duty, that he expected nothing less from such a good, experienced, and enlightened man as he was; that he praised him for what he had demanded before administering the sacrament to Madame la Duchesse de Berry; that he exhorted him not to give in, or to suffer himself to be deceived upon so important a thing; and that if he wanted further authorisation he, as his bishop, diocesan, and superior, prohibited him from administering the sacraments, or allowing them to be administered, to Madame la Duchesse de Berry while Rion and Madame de Mouchy were in the chamber, or even in the Luxembourg.

It may be imagined what a stir such inevitable scandal as this made in a room so full of company; what embarrassment it caused M. le Duc d'Orleans, and what a noise it immediately made everywhere. Nobody, even the chiefs of the constitution, the mass without, enemies of the Cardinal de Noailles, the most fashionable bishops, the most distinguished women, the libertines even—not one blamed the cure or his archbishop: some because they knew the rules of the Church, and did not dare to impugn them; others, the majority, from horror of the conduct of Madame la Duchesse de Berry, and hatred drawn upon her by her pride.

Now came the question between the Regent, the Cardinal, and the cure, which should announce this determination to Madame la Duchesse de Berry, who in no way expected it, and who, having confessed, expected every moment to see the Holy Sacrament enter, and to take it. After a short colloquy urged on by the state of the patient, the Cardinal and the cure withdrew a little, while M. le Duc d'Orleans slightly opened the door and called Madame de Mouchy. Then, the door ajar, she within, he without, he told her what was in debate. La Mouchy, much astonished, still more annoyed, rode the high horse, talked of her merit, and of the affront that bigots wished to cast upon her and Madame la Duchesse de Berry, who would never suffer it or consent to it, and that she would die—in the state she was—if they had the impudence and the cruelty to tell it to her.

The conclusion was that La Mouchy undertook to announce to Madame la Duchesse de Berry the resolution that had been taken respecting the sacraments—what she added of her own may be imagined. A negative response did not fail to be quickly delivered to M. le Duc d'Orleans through the half-opened door. Coming through such a messenger, it was just the reply he might have expected. Immediately after, he repeated it to the Cardinal, and to the cure; the cure, being supported by his archbishop, contented himself with shrugging his shoulders. But the Cardinal said to M. le Duc d'Orleans that Madame de Mouchy, one of the two who ought to be sent away, was not a fit person to bring Madame la Duchesse to reason; that it was his duty to carry this message to her, and to exhort her to do her duty as a Christian shortly about to appear before God; and the Archbishop pressed the Regent to go and say so to her. It will be believed, without difficulty, that his eloquence gained nothing. This Prince feared too much his daughter, and would have been but a feeble apostle with her.

Reiterated refusals determined the Cardinal to go and speak to Madame la Duchesse de Berry, accompanied by the cure, and as he wished to set about it at once, M. le Duc d'Orleans, who did not dare to hinder him, but who feared some sudden and dangerous revolution in his daughter at the sight and at the discourses of the two pastors, conjured him to wait until preparations could be made to receive him. He went, therefore, and held another colloquy through the door with Madame de Mouchy, the success of which was equal to the other. Madame la Duchesse de Berry flew into fury, railed in unruly terms against these hypocritical humbugs, who took advantage of her state and their calling to dishonour her by an unheard- of scandal, not in the least sparing her father for his stupidity and feebleness in allowing it. To have heard her, you would have thought that the cure and the Cardinal ought to be kicked downstairs.

M. le Duc d'Orleans returned to the ecclesiastics, looking very small, and not knowing what to do between his daughter and them. However, he said to them that she was so weak and suffering that they must put off their visit, persuading them as well as he could. The attention and anxiety of the large company which filled the room were extreme: everything was known afterwards, bit by bit, during the day.

The Cardinal de Noailles remained more than two hours with M. le Duc d'Orleans, round whom people gathered at last. The Cardinal, seeing that he could not enter the chamber without a sort of violence, much opposed to persuasion, thought it indecent and useless to wait any longer. In going away, he reiterated his orders to the cure, and begged him to watch so as not to be deceived respecting the sacraments, lest attempts were made to administer them clandestinely. He afterwards approached Madame de Saint-Simon, took her aside, related to her what had passed, and deplored with her a scandal that he had not been able to avoid. M. le Duc d'Orleans hastened to announce to his daughter the departure of the Cardinal, at which he himself was much relieved. But on leaving the chamber he was astonished to find the cure glued against the door, and still more so to hear he had taken up his post there, and meant to remain, happen what might, because he did not wish to be deceived respecting the sacraments. And, indeed, he remained there four days and four nights, except during short intervals for food and repose that he took at home, quite close to the Luxembourg, and during which his place was filled by two priests whom he left there. At last, the danger being passed, he raised the siege.

Madame la Duchesse de Berry, safely delivered of a daughter, had nothing to do but to re-establish herself; but she remained firm against the cure and the Cardinal de Noailles, neither of whom she ever pardoned. She became more and more bewitched by the two lovers, who laughed at her, and who were attached to her only for their fortune and their interest. She remained shut up without seeing M. and Madame la Duchesse d'Orleans, except for a few moments; no one, commencing with Madame de Saint-Simon, showed any eagerness to see her, for everybody knew what kept the door shut.

Madame la Duchesse de Berry, infinitely pained by the manner in which everybody, even the people, looked upon her malady, thought to gain a little lost ground by throwing open the gardens of the Luxembourg to the public, after having long since closed them. People were glad: they profited by the act; that was all. She made a vow that she would give herself up to religion, and dress in white—that is, devote herself to the service of the Virgin—for six months. This vow made people laugh a little.

Her illness had begun on the 26th of March, 1719, and Easter-day fell on the 9th of April. She was then quite well, but would not see a soul. A new cause of annoyance had arisen to trouble her. Rion, who saw himself so successful as the lover of Madame la Duchesse de Berry, wished to improve his position by becoming her husband. He was encouraged in this desire by his uncle, M. de Lauzun, who had also advised him to treat her with the rigour, harshness—nay, brutality, which I have already described. The maxim of M. de Lauzun was, that the Bourbons must be ill-used and treated with a high hand in order to maintain empire over them. Madame de Mouchy was as strongly in favour of this marriage as Rion. She knew she was sure of her lover, and that when he became the husband of Madame la Duchesse de Berry, all the doors which shut intimacy would be thrown down. A secret marriage accordingly took place.

This marriage gave rise to violent quarrels, and much weeping. In order to deliver herself from these annoyances, and at the same time steer clear of Easter, the Duchess resolved to go away to Meudon on Easter Monday. It was in vain that the danger was represented to her, of the air, of the movement of the coach, and of the change of place at the end of a fortnight. Nothing could make her endure Paris any longer. She set out, therefore, followed by Rion and the majority of her ladies and her household.

M. le Duc d'Orleans informed me then of the fixed design of Madame la Duchesse de Berry to declare the secret marriage she had just made with Rion. Madame la Duchesse d'Orleans was at Montmartre for a few days, and we were walking in the little garden of her apartments. The marriage did not surprise me much, knowing the strength of her passion, her fear of the devil, and the scandal which had just happened. But I was astonished, to the last degree, at this furious desire to declare the marriage, in a person so superbly proud.

M. le Duc d'Orleans dilated upon his troubles, his anger, that of Madame (who wished to proceed to the most violent extremities), and the great resolve of Madame la Duchesse d'Orleans.

Fortunately the majority of the officers destined to serve against Spain, (war with that country had just been declared) were leaving every day, and Rion had remained solely on account of the illness of Madame la Duchesse de Berry, M. le Duc d'Orleans thought the shortest plan would be to encourage hope by delay, in forcing Rion to depart, flattering himself that the declaration would be put off much more easily in his absence than in his presence. I strongly approved this idea, and on the morrow, Rion received at Meudon a curt and positive order to depart at once and join his regiment in the army of the Duc de Berwick. Madame la Duchesse de Berry was all the more outraged, because she knew the cause of this order, and consequently felt her inability to hinder its execution. Rion on his side did not dare to disobey it. He set out, therefore; and M. le Duc d'Orleans, who had not yet been to Meudon, remained several days without going there.

Father and daughter feared each other, and this departure had not put them on better terms. She had told him, and repeated it, that she was a rich widow, mistress of her own actions, independent of him; had flown into a fury, and terribly abused M. le Duc d'Orleans when he tried to remonstrate with her. He had received much rough handling from her at the Luxembourg when she was better; it was the same at Meudon during the few visits he paid her there. She wished to declare her marriage; and all the art, intellect, gentleness, anger, menace, prayers, and interest of M. le Duc d'Orleans barely sufficed to make her consent to a brief delay.

If Madame had been listened to, the affair would have been finished before the journey to Meudon; for M. le Duc d'Orleans would have thrown Rion out of the windows of the Luxembourg!

The premature journey to Meudon, and quarrels so warm, were not calculated to re-establish a person just returned from the gates of death. The extreme desire she had to hide her state from the public, and to conceal the terms on which she was with her father (for the rarity of his visits to her began to be remarked), induced her to give a supper to him on the terrace of Meudon about eight o'clock one evening. In vain the danger was represented to her of the cool evening air so soon after an illness such as she had just suffered from, and which had left her health still tottering. It was specially on this account that she stuck more obstinately to her supper on the terrace, thinking that it would take away all suspicion she had been confined, and induce the belief that she was on the same terms as ever with M. le Duc d'Orleans, though the uncommon rarity of his visits to her had been remarked.

This supper in the open air did not succeed. The same night she was taken ill. She was attacked by accidents, caused by the state in which she still was, and by an irregular fever, that the opposition she met with respecting the declaration of her marriage did not contribute to diminish. She grew disgusted with Meudon, like people ill in body and mind, who in their grief attribute everything to the air and the place. She was annoyed at the few visits she received from M. le Duc and Madame la Duchesse d'Orleans,-her pride, however, suffering more than her tenderness.

In despite of all reason, nothing could hinder her from changing her abode. She was transferred from Meudon to the Muette, wrapped up in sheets, and in a large coach, on Sunday, the 14th of May, 1719. Arrived so near Paris, she hoped M. le Duc and Madame la Duchesse d'Orleans would come and see her more frequently, if only for form's sake.

This journey was painful by the sufferings it caused her, added to those she already had, which no remedies could appease, except for short intervals, and which became very violent. Her illness augmented; but hopes and fears sustained her until the commencement of July. During all this time her desire to declare her marriage weakened, and M. le Duc and Madame la Duchesse d'Orleans, as well as Madame, who passed the summer at Saint-Cloud, came more frequently to see her. The month of July became more menacing because of the augmentation of pain and fever. These ills increased so much, in fact, that, by the 14th of July, fears for her life began to be felt.

The night of the 14th was so stormy, that M. le Duc d'Orleans was sent to at the Palais Royal, and awakened. At the same time Madame de Pons wrote to Madame de Saint-Simon, pressing her to come and establish herself at La Muette. Madame de Saint-Simon, although she made a point of scarcely ever sleeping under the same roof as Madame la Duchesse de Berry (for reasons which need no further explanation than those already given), complied at once with this request, and took up her quarters from this time at La Muette.

Upon arriving, she found the danger great. Madame la Duchesse de Berry had been bled in the arm and in the foot on the 10th, and her confessor had been sent for. But the malady still went on increasing. As the pain which had so long afflicted her could not induce her to follow a regimen necessary for her condition, or to think of a future state, relations and doctors were at last obliged to speak a language to her, not used towards princesses, except at the most urgent extremity. This, at last, had its effect. She submitted to the medical treatment prescribed for her, and received the sacrament with open doors, speaking to those present upon her life and upon her state, but like a queen in both instances. After this sight was over, alone with her familiars, she applauded herself for the firmness she had displayed, asked them if she had not spoken well, and if she was not dying with greatness and courage.

A day or two after, she wished to receive Our Lord once more. She received, accordingly, and as it appeared, with much piety, quite differently from the first time.

At the extremity to which she had arrived, the doctors knew not what to do; everybody was tried. An elixir was spoken of, discovered by a certain Garus, which made much stir just then, and the secret of which the King has since bought. Garus was sent for and soon arrived. He found Madame la Duchesse de Berry so ill that he would answer for nothing. His remedy was given, and succeeded beyond all hopes. Nothing remained but to continue it. Above all things, Garus had begged that nothing should, on any account, be given to Madame la Duchesse de Berry except by him, and this had been most expressly commanded by M. le Duc and Madame la Duchesse d'Orleans. Madame la Duchesse de Berry continued to be more and more relieved and so restored, that Chirac, her regular doctor, began to fear for his reputation, and taking the opportunity when Garus was asleep upon a sofa, presented, with impetuosity, a purgative to Madame la Duchesse de Berry, and made her swallow it without saying a word to anybody, the two nurses standing by, the only persons present, not daring to oppose him.

The audacity of this was as complete as its villainy, for M. le Duc and Madame la Duchesse d'Orleans were close at hand in the salon. From this moment to that in which the patient fell into a state worse than that from which the elixir had drawn her, there was scarcely an interval. Garus was awaked and called. Seeing this disorder, he cried that a purgative had been given, and whatever it might be, it was poison in the state to which the princess was now reduced. He wished to depart, he was detained, he was taken to Madame la Duchesse d'Orleans. Then followed a great uproar, cries from Garus, impudence and unequalled hardihood of Chirac, in defending what he had done.

He could not deny it, for the two nurses had been questioned, and had told all. Madame la Duchesse de Berry drew near her end during this debate, and neither Chirac nor Garus could prevent it. She lasted, however, the rest of the day, and did not die until about midnight. Chirac, seeing the death-agony advance, traversed the chamber, made an insulting reverence at the foot of the bed, which was open, and wished her "a pleasant journey" (in equivalent terms), and thereupon went off to Paris. The marvel is that nothing came of this, and that he remained the doctor of M. le Duc d'Orleans as before!

While the end was yet approaching, Madame de Saint-Simon, seeing that there was no one to bear M. le Duc d'Orleans company, sent for me to stand by him in these sad moments. It appeared to me that my arrival pleased him, and that I was not altogether useless to him in relieving his grief. The rest of the day was passed in entering for a moment at a time into the sick-chamber. In the evening I was nearly always alone with him.

He wished that I should charge myself with all the funeral arrangements, and in case Madame la Duchesse de Berry, when opened, should be found to be enceinte, to see that the secret was kept. I proposed that the funeral should be of the simplest, without show or ceremonial. I explained my reasons, he thanked me, and left all the orders in my hands. Getting rid of these gloomy matters as quickly as possible, I walked with him from time to time in the reception rooms, and in the garden, keeping him from the chamber of the dying as much as possible.

The night was well advanced, and Madame la Duchesse de Berry grew worse and worse, and without consciousness since Chirac had poisoned her. M. le Duc d'Orleans returned into the chamber, approached the head of the bed—all the curtains being pulled back; I allowed him to remain there but a few moments, and hurried him into the cabinet, which was deserted just then. The windows were open, he leaned upon the iron balustrade, and his tears increased so much that I feared lest they should suffocate him. When this attack had a little subsided, he began to talk of the misfortunes of this world, and of the short duration of its most agreeable pleasures. I urged the occasion to say to him everything God gave me the power to say, with all the gentleness, emotion, and tenderness, I could command. Not only he received well what I said to him, but he replied to it and prolonged the conversation.

After we had been there more than an hour, Madame de Saint-Simon gently warned me that it was time to try and lead M. le Duc d'Orleans away, especially as there was no exit from the cabinet, except through the sick-chamber. His coach, that Madame de Saint-Simon had sent for, was ready. It was without difficulty that I succeeded in gently moving away M. le Duc d'Orleans, plunged as he was in the most bitter grief. I made him traverse the chamber at once, and supplicated him to return to Paris. At last he consented. He wished me to remain and give orders, and begged, with much positiveness, Madame de Saint-Simon to be present when seals were put upon the effects, after which I led him to his coach, and he went away. I immediately repeated to Madame de Saint-Simon the orders he had given me respecting the opening of the body, in order that she might have them executed, and I hindered her from remaining in the chamber, where there was nothing now but horror to be seen.

At last, about midnight, on the 21st of July, 1819, Madame la Duchesse de Berry died, ten days after Chirac had consummated his crime. M. le Duc d'Orleans was the only person touched. Some people grieved; but not one of them who had enough to live upon appeared ever to regret her loss. Madame la Duchesse d'Orleans felt her deliverance, but paid every attention to decorum. Madame constrained herself but little. However affected M. le Duc d'Orleans might be, consolation soon came. The yoke to which he had submitted himself, and which he afterwards found heavy, was severed. Above all, he was free from all annoyance on the score of Rion's marriage, and its results, annoyance that would have been all the greater, inasmuch as at the opening of the poor princess she was found to be again enceinte; it was also found that her brain was deranged. These circumstances were for the time carefully hidden. It may be imagined what a state Rion fell into in learning at the army the death of Madame la Duchesse de Berry. All his romantic notions of ambition being overturned, he was more than once on the point of killing himself, and for a long time was always kept in sight by his friends. He sold out at the end of the campaign. As he had been gentle and polite to his friends, they did not desert him. But he ever afterwards remained in obscurity.

On account of this death the theatres were closed for eight days.

On Saturday, the 22nd of July, the heart of Madame la Duchesse de Berry was taken to the Val-de-Grace.

On Sunday, the 23rd of July, her body was carried in an eight-horse coach to Saint-Denis. There was very little display; only about forty torches were carried by pages and guards.

The funeral service was performed at Saint-Denis in the early part of September. There was no funeral oration.

Madame de Saint-Simon had been forced, as I have shown, to accept the post of lady of honour to Madame la Duchesse de Berry, and had never been able to quit it. She had been treated with all sorts of consideration, had been allowed every liberty, but this did not console her for the post she occupied; so that she felt all the pleasure, not to say the satisfaction, of a deliverance she did not expect, from a princess twenty-four years of age. But the extreme fatigue of the last days of the illness, and of those which followed death, caused her a malignant fever, which left her at death's portal during six weeks in a house at Passy. She was two months recovering herself.

This accident, which almost turned my head, sequestered me from anything for two months, during which I never left the house, scarcely left the sick-chamber, attended to nothing, and saw only a few relatives or indispensable friends.

When my wife began to be re-established, I asked M. le Duc d'Orleans for a lodging at the new chateau at Meudon. He lent me the whole chateau; completely furnished. We passed there the rest of this summer, and several other summers afterwards. It is a charming place for rides or drives. We counted upon seeing only our friends there, but the proximity to Paris overwhelmed us with people, so that all the new chateau was sometimes completely filled, without reckoning the people of passage.

I have little need to say anything more of Madame la Duchesse de Berry. These pages have already painted her. She was a strange mixture of pride and shamelessness. Drunkenness, filthy conversation, debauchery of the vilest kind, and impiety, were her diversions, varied, as has been seen, by occasional religious fits. Her indecency in everything, language, acts, behaviour, passed all bounds; and yet her pride was so sublime that she could not endure that people should dare to speak of her amid her depravity, so universal and so public; she had the hardihood to declare that nobody had the right to speak of persons of her rank, or blame their most notorious actions!

Yet she had by nature a superior intellect, and, when she wished, could be agreeable and amiable. Her face was commanding, though somewhat spoiled at last by fat. She had much eloquence, speaking with an ease and precision that charmed and overpowered. What might she not have become, with the talents she possessed! But her pride, her violent temper, her irreligion, and her falsehood, spoiled all, and made her what we have seen her.

CHAPTER XCIX

Law had established his Mississippi Company, and now began to do marvels with it. A sort of language had been invented, to talk of this scheme, language which, however, I shall no more undertake to explain than the other finance operations. Everybody was mad upon Mississippi Stock. Immense fortunes were made, almost in a breath; Law, besieged in his house by eager applicants, saw people force open his door, enter by the windows from the garden, drop into his cabinet down the chimney! People talked only of millions.

Law, who, as I have said, came to my house every Tuesday, between eleven and twelve, often pressed me to receive some shares for nothing, offering to manage them without any trouble to me, so that I must gain to the amount of several millions! So many people had already gained enormously by their own exertions that it was not doubtful Law could gain for me even more rapidly. But I never would lend myself to it. Law addressed himself to Madame de Saint-Simon, whom he found as inflexible. He would have much preferred to enrich me than many others; so as to attach me to him by interest, intimate as he saw me with the Regent. He spoke to M. le Duc d'Orleans, even, so as to vanquish me by his authority. The Regent attacked me more than once, but I always eluded him.

At last, one day when we were together by appointment, at Saint-Cloud, seated upon the balustrade of the orangery, which covers the descent into the wood of the goulottes, the Regent spoke again to me of the Mississippi, and pressed me to receive some shares from Law.

The more I resisted, the more he pressed me, and argued; at last he grew angry, and said that I was too conceited, thus to refuse what the King wished to give me (for everything was done in the King's name), while so many of my equals in rank and dignity were running after these shares. I replied that such conduct would be that of a fool, the conduct of impertinence, rather than of conceit; that it was not mine, and that since he pressed me so much I would tell him my reasons. They were, that since the fable of Midas, I had nowhere read, still less seen, that anybody had the faculty of converting into gold all he touched; that I did not believe this virtue was given to Law, but thought that all his knowledge was a learned trick, a new and skilful juggle, which put the wealth of Peter into the pockets of Paul, and which enriched one at the expense of the other; that sooner or later the game would be played out, that an infinity of people would be ruined; finally, that I abhorred to gain at the expense of others, and would in no way mix myself up with the Mississippi scheme.

M. le Duc d'Orleans knew only too well how to reply to me, always returning to his idea that I was refusing the bounties of the King. I said that I was so removed from such madness, that I would make a proposition to him, of which assuredly I should never have spoken, but for his accusation.

I related to him the expense to which my father had been put in defending Blaye against the party of M. le Prince in years gone by. How he had paid the garrison, furnished provisions, cast cannon, stocked the place, during a blockade of eighteen months, and kept up, at his own expense, within the town, five hundred gentlemen, whom he had collected together. How he had been almost ruined by the undertaking, and had never received a sou, except in warrants to the amount of five hundred thousand livres, of which not one had ever been paid, and that he had been compelled to pay yearly the interest of the debts he had contracted, debts that still hung like a mill-stone upon me. My proposition was that M. le Duc d'Orleans should indemnify me for this loss, I giving up the warrants, to be burnt before him.

This he at once agreed to. He spoke of it the very next day to Law: my warrants were burnt by degrees in the cabinet of M. le Duc d'Orleans, and it was by this means I paid for what I had done at La Ferme.

Meanwhile the Mississippi scheme went on more swimmingly than ever. It was established in the Rue Quincampoix, from which horses and coaches were banished. About the end of October of this year, 1817, its business so much increased, that the office was thronged all day long, and it was found necessary to place clocks and guards with drums at each end of the street, to inform people, at seven o'clock in the morning, of the opening of business, and of its close at night: fresh announcements were issued, too, prohibiting people from going there on Sundays and fete days.

Never had excitement or madness been heard of which approached this.

M. le Duc d'Orleans distributed a large number of the Company's shares to all the general officers and others employed in the war against Spain. A month after, the value of the specie was diminished; then the whole of the coin was re-cast.

Money was in such abundance—that is to say, the notes of Law, preferred then to the metallic currency—that four millions were paid to Bavaria, and three millions to Sweden, in settlement of old debts. Shortly after, M. le Duc d'Orleans gave 80,000 livres to Meuse; and 80,000 livres to Madame de Chateauthiers, dame d'atours of Madame. The Abbe Alari, too, obtained 2000 livres pension. Various other people had augmentation of income given to them at this time.

Day by day Law's bank and his Mississippi increased in favour. The confidence in them was complete. People could not change their lands and their houses into paper fast enough, and the result of this paper was, that everything became dear beyond all previous experience. All heads were turned, Foreigners envied our good fortune, and left nothing undone to have a share in it. The English, even, so clear and so learned in banks, in companies, in commerce, allowed themselves to be caught, and bitterly repented it afterwards. Law, although cold and discreet, felt his modesty giving way. He grew tired of being a subaltern. He hankered after greatness in the midst of this splendour; the Abbe Dubois and M. le Duc d'Orleans desired it for him more than he; nevertheless, two formidable obstacles were in the way: Law was a foreigner and a heretic, and he could not be naturalised without a preliminary act of abjuration. To perform that, somebody must be found to convert him, somebody upon whom good reliance could be placed. The Abbe Dubois had such a person all ready in his pocket, so to speak. The Abbe Tencin was the name of this ecclesiastic, a fellow of debauched habits and shameless life, whom the devil has since pushed into the most astonishing good fortune; so true it is that he sometimes departs from his ordinary rules, in order to recompense his servitors, and by these striking examples dazzle others, and so secure them.

As may be imagined, Law did not feel very proud of the Abbe who had converted him: more especially as that same Abbe was just about this time publicly convicted of simony, of deliberate fraud, of right-down lying (proved by his own handwriting), and was condemned by the Parliament to pay a fine, which branded him with infamy, and which was the scandal of the whole town. Law, however, was converted, and this was a subject which supplied all conversation.

Soon after, he bought, for one million livres, the Hotel Mazarin for his bank, which until then had been established in a house he hired of the Chief-President, who had not need of it, being very magnificently lodged in the Palace of the Parliament by virtue of his office. Law bought, at the same time, for 550,000 livres, the house of the Comte de Tesse.

Yet it was not all sunshine with this famous foreigner, for the sky above him was heavy with threatening clouds. In the midst of the flourishing success of his Mississippi, it was discovered that there was a plot to kill him. Thereupon sixteen soldiers of the regiment of the Guards were given to him as a protection to his house, and eight to his brother, who had come to Paris some little time before.

Law had other enemies besides those who were hidden. He could not get on well with Argenson, who, as comptroller of the finances, was continually thrown into connection with him. The disorder of the finances increased in consequence every day, as well as the quarrels between Law and Argenson, who each laid the blame upon the other. The Scotchman was the best supported, for his manners were pleasing, and his willingness to oblige infinite. He had, as it were, a finance tap in his hand, and he turned it on for every one who helped him. M. le Duc, Madame la Duchesse, Tesse, Madame de Verue, had drawn many millions through this tap, and drew still. The Abbe Dubois turned it on as he pleased. These were grand supports, besides that of M. le Duc d'Orleans, who could not part with his favourite.

Argenson, on the contrary, was not much liked. He had been at the head of the police so long that he could not shake off the habits he had acquired in that position: He had been accustomed to give audiences upon all sorts of police matters at dead of night, or at the small hours of the morning, and he appeared to see no reason why he should not do the same now that he was Keeper of the Seals. He irritated people beyond all bearing, by making appointments with them at these unreasonable hours, and threw into despair all who worked under him, or who had business with him. The difficulty of the finances, and his struggles with Law, had thrown him into ill-humour, which extended through all his refusals. Things, in fact, had come to such a pass, that it was evident one or the other must give up an administration which their rivalry threw into confusion.

Argenson saw the storm coming, and feeling the insecurity of his position, wished to save himself. He had too much sense and too much knowledge of the world not to feel that if he obstinately clung to the finances he should not only lose them but the seals also. He yielded therefore to Law, who was at last declared comptroller-general of the finances, and who, elevated to this (for him) surprising point, continued to visit me as usual every Tuesday morning, always trying to persuade me into belief of his past miracles, and of those to come.

Argenson remained Keeper of the Seals, and skilfully turned to account the sacrifice he had made by obtaining through it the permission to surrender his appointment of Chancellor of the Order of Saint-Louis to his eldest son, and the title, effectively, to his younger son. His place of Conseiller d'Etat, that he had retained,—he also gave to his eldest son, and made the other lieutenant of police. The murmur was great upon seeing a foreigner comptroller-general, and all abandoned to a finance system which already had begun to be mistrusted. But Frenchmen grow accustomed to everything, and the majority were consoled by being no longer exposed to the sharp humour of Argenson, or his strange hours of business.

But Law's annoyances were not over when this change had been made. M. le Prince de Conti began to be troublesome. He was more grasping than any of his relatives, and that is not saying a little. He accosted Law now, pistol in hand, so to speak, and with a perfect "money or your life" manner. He had already amassed mountains of gold by the easy humour of M. le Duc d'Orleans; he had drawn, too, a good deal from Law, in private. Not content with this, he wished to draw more. M. le Duc d'Orleans grew tired, and was not over-pleased with him. The Parliament just then was at its tricks again; its plots began to peep out, and the Prince de Conti joined in its intrigues in order to try and play a part indecent, considering his birth; little fitting his age; shameful, after the monstrous favours unceasingly heaped upon him.

Repelled by the Regent, he turned, as I have said, towards Law, hoping for more success. His expectations were deceived; prayers, cringing meanness (for he stopped at nothing to get money) being of no effect, he tried main strength, and spared Law neither abuse nor menaces. In fact, not knowing what else to do to injure his bank, he sent three waggons there, and drove them away full of money, which he made Law give him for paper he held. Law did not dare to refuse, and thus show the poverty of his metallic funds, but fearing to accustom so insatiable a prince to such tyranny as this, he went, directly the waggons left, to M. le Duc d'Orleans, and complained of what had occurred. The Regent was much annoyed; he saw the dangerous results, and the pernicious example of so violent a proceeding, directed against an unsupported foreigner, whom rather lightly he had just made comptroller-general. He flew into a violent rage, sent for the Prince de Conti, and, contrary to his nature, reprimanded him so severely, that he was silenced and cried for mercy. But annoyed at having failed, and still more at the sharp scolding he had received, the Prince de Conti consoled himself, like a woman, by spreading all sorts of reports against Law, which caused him but little fear, and did him still less harm, but which did slight honour to M. le Prince de Conti, because the cause of these reports, and also the large sums he had drawn from the financier, were not unknown to the public; blame upon him was general, and all the more heavy, because Law had fallen out of public favour, which a mere trifle had changed into spite and indignation.

This is the trifle. The Marechal de Villeroy, incapable of inspiring the King with any solid ideas, adoring even to worship the deceased King, full of wind, and lightness, and frivolity, and of sweet recollections of his early years, his grace at fetes and ballets, his splendid gallantries, wished that the King, in imitation of the deceased monarch, should dance in a ballet. It was a little too early to think of this. This pleasure seemed a trifle too much of pain to so young a King; his timidity should have been vanquished by degrees, in order to accustom him to society which he feared, before engaging him to show himself off in public, and dance upon a stage.

The deceased King,—educated in a brilliant Court, where rule and grandeur were kept up with much distinction, and where continual intercourse with ladies, the Queen-mother, and others of the Court, had early fashioned and emboldened him, had relished and excelled in these sorts of fetes and amusements, amid a crowd of young people of both sexes, who all rightfully bore the names of nobility, and amongst whom scarcely any of humble birth were mixed, for we cannot call thus some three or four of coarser stuff, who were admitted simply for the purpose of adding strength and beauty to the ballet, by the grace of their faces and the elegance of their movements, with a few dancing-masters to regulate and give the tone to the whole. Between this time and that I am now speaking of was an abyss. The education of those days instructed every one in grace, address, exercise, respect for bearing, graduated and delicate politeness, polished and decent gallantry. The difference, then, between the two periods is seen at a glance, without time lost in pointing it out.

Reflection was not the principal virtue of the Marechal de Villeroy. He thought of no obstacle either on the part of the King or elsewhere, and declared that his Majesty would dance in a ballet. Everything was soon ready for the execution. It was not so with the action. It became necessary to search for young people who could dance: soon, whether they danced ill or well, they were gladly received; at last the only question was, "Whom can we get?" consequently a sorry lot was obtained. Several, who ought never to have been admitted, were, and so easily, that from one to the other Law had the temerity to ask M. le Duc d'Orleans to allow his son, who danced very well, to join the ballet company! The Regent, always easy, still enamoured of Law, and, to speak truth, purposely contributing as much as possible to confusion of rank, immediately accorded the demand, and undertook to say so to the Marechal de Villeroy.

The Marechal, who hated and crossed Law with might and main, reddened with anger, and represented to the Regent what, in fact, deserved to be said: the Regent, in reply, named several young people, who, although of superior rank, were not so well fitted for the ballet as young Law; and although the answer to this was close at hand, the Marechal could not find it, and exhausted himself in vain exclamations. He could not, therefore, resist the Regent; and having no support from M. le Duc, superintendent of the King's education and a great protector of Law and of confusion, he gave in, and the financier's son was named for the ballet.

It is impossible to express the public revolt excited by this bagatelle, at which every one was offended. Nothing else was spoken of for some days; tongues wagged freely, too; and a good deal of dirty water was thrown upon other dancers in the ballet.

At last the public was satisfied. The small-pox seized Law's son, and (on account of its keeping him from the ballet) caused universal joy. The ballet was danced several times, its success answering in no way to the Marechal de Villeroy. The King was so wearied, so fatigued, with learning, with rehearsing, and with dancing this ballet, that he took an aversion for these fetes and for everything offering display, which has never quitted him since, and which does not fail to leave a void in the Court; so that this ballet ceased sooner than was intended, and the Marechal de Villeroy never dared to propose another.

M. le Duc d'Orleans, either by his usual facility, or to smooth down the new elevation of Law to the post of comptroller-general, bestowed a number of pecuniary favours; he gave 600,000 livres to La Fare, captain of his guard; 200,000 livres to Castries, chevalier d'honneur to Madame la Duchesse d'Orleans; 200,000 livres to the old Prince de Courtenay, who much needed them; 20,000 livres pension to the Prince de Talmont; 6000 livres to the Marquise de Bellefonds, who already had a similar sum; and moved by cries on the part of M. le Prince de Conti, 60,000 livres to the Comte de la Marche his son, scarcely three years old; he gave, also, smaller amounts to various others. Seeing so much depredation, and no recovery to hope for, I asked M. le Duc d'Orleans to attach 12,000 livres, by way of increase, to my government of Senlis, which was worth only 1000 livres, and of which my second son had the reversion. I obtained it at once.

CHAPTER C

About the commencement of the new year, 1720, the system of Law approached its end. If he had been content with his bank his bank within wise and proper limits—the money of the realm might have been doubled, and an extreme facility afforded to commerce and to private enterprise, because, the establishment always being prepared to meet its liabilities, the notes it issued would have been as good as ready money, and sometimes even preferable, on account of the facility of transport. It must be admitted, however, as I declared to M. le Duc d'Orleans in his cabinet, and as I openly said in the Council of the Regency when the bank passed there, that good as this establishment might be in itself, it could only be so in a republic, or in a monarchy, like that of England, where the finances are absolutely governed by those who furnish them, and who simply furnish as much or as little as they please; but in a trivial, changing, and more than absolute state like France solidity necessarily is wanting, consequently confidence (at least of a discreet and proper kind): since a king, and under his name, a mistress, a minister, favourites; still more, extreme necessities, such as the deceased King experienced in the years 1707-8-9 and 10,—a hundred things, in fact, could overthrow the bank, the allurements of which were, at once, too great and too easy. But to add to the reality of this bank, the chimera of the Mississippi, with its shares, its special jargon, its science (a continual juggle for drawing money from one person to give it to another), was to almost guarantee that these shares should at last end in smoke (since we had neither mines, nor quarries of the philosopher's stone), and that the few would be enriched at the expense of the many, as in fact happened.

What hastened the fall of the bank, and of the system, was the inconceivable prodigality of M. le Duc d'Orleans, who, without bounds, and worse still, if it can be, without choice, could not resist the importunities even of those whom he knew, beyond all doubt, to have been the most opposed to him, and who were completely despicable, but gave with open hands; and more frequently allowed money to be drawn from him by people who laughed at him, and who were grateful only to their effrontery. People with difficulty believe what they have seen; and posterity will consider as a fable what we ourselves look upon as a dream. At last, so much was given to a greedy and prodigal nation, always covetous and in want on account of its luxury, its disorder, and its confusion of ranks, that paper became scarce, and the mills could not furnish enough.

It may be imagined by this, what abuse had been made of a bank, established as a resource always ready, but which could not exist as such without being always delicately adjusted; and above all, kept in a state to meet the obligations it had contracted. I obtained information on this point from Law, when he came to me on Tuesday mornings; for a long time he played with me before admitting his embarrassments, and complained modestly and timidly, that the Regent was ruining everything by his extravagance. I knew from outsiders more than he thought, and it was this that induced me to press him upon his balance-sheet. In admitting to me, at last, although faintly, what he could no longer hide, he assured me he should not be wanting in resources provided M. le Duc d'Orleans left him free. That did not persuade me. Soon after, the notes began to lose favour; then to fall into discredit, and the discredit to become public. Then came the necessity to sustain them by force, since they could no longer be sustained by industry; and the moment force showed itself every one felt that all was over. Coercive authority was resorted to; the use of gold, silver, and jewels was suppressed (I speak of coined money); it was pretended that since the time of Abraham,—Abraham, who paid ready money for the sepulchre of Sarah,— all the civilised nations in the world had been in the greatest error and under the grossest delusion, respecting money and the metals it is made of; that paper alone was useful and necessary; that we could not do greater harm to our neighbours—jealous of our greatness and of our advantages—than to send to them all our money and all our jewels; and this idea was in no way concealed, for the Indian Company was allowed to visit every house, even Royal houses, confiscate all the louis d'or, and the coins it could find there; and to leave only pieces of twenty sous and under (to the amount of not more than 200 francs), for the odd money of bills, and in order to purchase necessary provisions of a minor kind, with prohibitions, strengthened by heavy punishment, against keeping more; so that everybody was obliged to take all the ready money he possessed to the bank, for fear of its being discovered by a valet. But nobody, as may be imagined, was persuaded of the justice of the power accorded to the Company, and accordingly authority was more and more exerted; all private houses were searched, informations were laid against people in order that no money might be kept back, or if it were, that the guilty parties might be severely punished.

Never before had sovereign power been so violently exercised, never had it attacked in such a manner the temporal interests of the community. Therefore was it by a prodigy, rather than by any effort or act of the government, that these terribly new ordonnances failed to produce the saddest and most complete revolutions; but there was not even talk of them; and although there were so many millions of people, either absolutely ruined or dying of hunger, and of the direst want, without means to procure their daily subsistence, nothing more than complaints and groans was heard.

This violence was, however, too excessive, and in every respect too indefensible to last long; new paper and new juggling tricks were of necessity resorted to; the latter were known to be such—people felt them to be such—but they submitted to them rather than not have twenty crowns in safety in their houses; and a greater violence made people suffer the smaller. Hence so many projects, so many different faces in finance, and all tending to establish one issue of paper upon another; that is to say, always causing loss to the holders of the different paper (everybody being obliged to hold it), and the universal multitude. This is what occupied all the rest of the government, and of the life of M. le Duc d'Orleans; which drove Law out of the realm; which increased six-fold the price of all merchandise, all food even the commonest; which ruinously augmented every kind of wages, and ruined public and private commerce; which gave, at the expense of the public, sudden riches to a few noblemen who dissipated it, and were all the poorer in a short time; which enabled many financiers' clerks, and the lowest dregs of the people, profiting by the general confusion, to take advantage of the Mississippi, and make enormous fortunes; which occupied the government several years after the death of M. le Duc d'Orleans; and which, to conclude, France never will recover from, although it may be true that the value of land is considerably augmented. As a last affliction, the all-powerful, especially the princes and princesses of the blood, who had been mixed up, in the Mississippi, and who had used all their authority to escape from it without loss, re-established it upon what they called the Great Western Company, which with the same juggles and exclusive trade with the Indies, is completing the annihilation of the trade of the realm, sacrificed to the enormous interest of a small number of private individuals, whose hatred and vengeance the government has not dared to draw upon itself by attacking their delicate privileges.

Several violent executions, and confiscations of considerable sums found in the houses searched, took place. A certain Adine, employed at the bank, had 10,000 crowns confiscated, was fined 10,000 francs, and lost his appointment. Many people hid their money with so much secrecy, that, dying without being able to say where they had put it, these little treasures remained buried and lost to the heirs.

In the midst of the embarrassments of the finances, and in spite of them, M. le Duc d'Orleans continued his prodigal gifts. He attached pensions of 6000 livres and 4000 livres to the grades of lieutenant-general and camp-marshal. He gave a pension of 20,000 livres to old Montauban; one of 6000 livres to M. de Montauban (younger brother of the Prince de Guemene); and one of 6000 livres to the Duchesse de Brissac. To several other people he gave pensions of 4000 livres; to eight or ten others, 3000 or 2000 livres. I obtained one of 8000 livres for Madame Marechal de Lorges; and one of 6000 livres was given to the Marechal de Chamilly, whose affairs were much deranged by the Mississippi. M. de Soubise and the Marquis Noailles had each upwards of 200,000 livres. Even Saint- Genies, just out of the Bastille, and banished to Beauvais, had a pension of 1000. Everybody in truth wanted an augmentation of income, on account of the extreme high price to which the commonest, almost necessary things had risen, and even all other things; which, although at last diminished by degrees, remain to this day much dearer than they were before the Mississippi.

The pensions being given away, M. le Duc d'Orleans began to think how he could reduce the public expenditure. Persuaded by those in whose financial knowledge he had most confidence, he resolved to reduce to two per cent. the interest upon all the funds. This much relieved those who paid, but terribly cut down the income of those who received, that is to say, the creditors of the state, who had lent their money at five per cent., according to the loan—and, public faith and usage, and who had hitherto peacefully enjoyed that interest. M. le Duc d'Orleans assembled at the Palais Royal several financiers of different rank, and resolved with them to pass this edict. It made much stir among the Parliament men, who refused to register it. But M. le Duc d'Orleans would not change his determination, and maintained his decree in spite of them.

By dint of turning and turning around the Mississippi, not to say of juggling with it, the desire came to establish, according to the example of the English, colonies in the vast countries beyond the seas. In order to people these colonies, persons without means of livelihood, sturdy beggars, female and male, and a quantity of public creatures were carried off. If this had been executed with discretion and discernment, with the necessary measures and precautions, it would have ensured the object proposed, and relieved Paris and the provinces of a heavy, useless, and often dangerous burthen; but in Paris and elsewhere so much violence, and even more roguery, were mixed up with it, that great murmuring was excited. Not the slightest care had been taken to provide for the subsistence of so many unfortunate people, either while in the place they were to embark from, or while on the road to reach it; by night they were shut up, with nothing to eat, in barns, or in the dry ditches of the towns they stopped in, all means of egress being forbidden them. They uttered cries which excited pity and indignation; but the alms collected for them not being sufficient, still less the little their conductors gave them, they everywhere died in frightful numbers.

Mississippi Colonization--painted by C. E. Delort

This inhumanity, joined to the barbarity of the conductors, to violence of a kind unknown until this, and to the rascality of carrying off people who were not of the prescribed quality, but whom others thus got rid of by whispering a word in the ear of the conductors and greasing their palms; all these things, I say, caused so much stir, so much excitement, that the system, it was found, could not be kept up. Some troops had been embarked, and during the voyage were not treated much better than the others. The persons already collected were set at liberty, allowed to do what they pleased, and no more were seized. Law, regarded as the author of these seizures, became much detested, and M. le Duc d'Orleans repented having ever fallen in with the scheme.

The 22nd of May of this year, 1720, became celebrated by the publication of a decree of the Council of State, concerning the shares of the Company of the Indies (the same as that known under the name of Mississippi) and the notes of Law's bank. This decree diminished by degrees, and from month to month, the value of the shares and the notes, so that, by the end of the year, that value would have been reduced one-half.

This, in the language of finance and of bankruptcy, was to turn tail with a vengeance: and its effect, while remedying nothing, was to make people believe that things were in a worse state than was actually the case. Argenson, who, as we have seen, had been turned out of the finances to make room for Law, was generally accused of suggesting this decree out of malice, already foreseeing all the evils that must arise from it. The uproar was general and frightful. There was not a rich person who did not believe himself lost without resource; not a poor one who did not see himself reduced to beggary. The Parliament, so opposed to the new money system, did not let slip this fine opportunity. It rendered itself the protector of the public by refusing to register the decree, and by promptly uttering the strongest remonstrance against it. The public even believed that to the Parliament was due the sudden revocation of the edict, which, however, was simply caused by the universal complaining, and the tardy discovery of the fault committed in passing it. The little confidence in Law remaining was now radically extinguished; not an atom of it could ever be set afloat again. Seditious writings and analytical and reasonable pamphlets rained on all sides, and the consternation was general.

The Parliament assembled on Monday, the 27th of May, in the morning, and named certain of its members to go to M. le Duc d'Orleans, with remonstrances against the decree. About noon of the same day, M. le Duc d'Orleans sent La Vrilliere to say to the Parliament that he revoked that decree, and that the notes would remain as before. La Vrilliere, finding that the Parliament had adjourned, went to the Chief-President, to say with what he was charged. After dinner the Parliamentary deputies came to the Palais Royal, where they were well received; M. le Duc d'Orleans confirmed what they had already heard from La Vrilliere, and said to them that he would re-establish the funds of the Hotel de Ville at two-and-a- half percent. The deputies expected that in justice and in goodness he ought to raise them to at least three per cent. M. le Duc d'Orleans answered, that he should like not only to raise them to three, but to four, nay, five per cent.; but that the state of affairs would not permit him to go beyond two-and-a-half. On the next day was published the counter-decree, which placed the shares and actions as they were before the 22nd of May. The decree of that date was therefore revoked in six days, after having caused such a strange effect.

On Wednesday, the 29th, a pretty little comedy was played. Le Blanc, Secretary of State, went to Law, told him that M. le Duc d'Orleans discharged him from his office as comptroller-general of the finances, thanked him for the attention he had given to it, and announced that as many people in Paris did not like him, a meritorious officer should keep guard in his house to prevent any accident that might happen to him. At the same time, Benzualde, major of the regiment of Swiss guards, arrived with sixteen of his men to remain night and day in Law's house.

The Scotchman did not in the least expect this dismissal or this guard, but he appeared very tranquil respecting both, and maintained his usual coolness. The next day he was taken by the Duc de la Force to the Palais Royal. Then comedy number two was played. M. le Duc d'Orleans refused to see the financier, who went away without an interview. On the day after, however, Law was admitted by the back stairs, closeted with the Regent, and was treated by him as well as ever. The comedies were over.

On Sunday, the 2nd of June, Benzualde and his Swiss withdrew from Law's house. Stock-jobbing was banished at the same time from the Rue Quincampoix, and established in the Place Vendome. In this latter place there was more room for it. The passers-by were not incommoded. Yet some people did not find it as convenient as the other. At this time the King gave up to the bank one hundred million of shares he had in it.

On the 5th July, a decree of the Council was issued, prohibiting people from possessing jewels, from keeping them locked up, or from selling them to foreigners. It may be imagined what a commotion ensued. This decree was grafted upon a number of others, the object of all, too visibly, being to seize upon all coin, in favour of the discredited paper, in which nobody could any longer have the slightest confidence. In vain M. le Duc d'Orleans, M. le Duc, and his mother, tried to persuade others, by getting rid of their immense stores of jewels, that is to say, by sending them abroad on a journey—nothing more: not a person was duped by this example; not a person omitted to conceal his jewels very carefully: a thing much more easy to accomplish than the concealment of gold or silver coin, on account of the smaller value of precious stones. This jewellery eclipse was not of long duration.

CHAPTER CI

Immediately after the issue of this decree an edict was drawn up for the establishment of an Indian commercial company, which was to undertake to reimburse in a year six, hundred millions of bank notes, by paying fifty thousand dollars per month. Such was the last resource of Law and his system. For the juggling tricks of the Mississippi, it was found necessary to substitute something real; especially since the edict of the 22nd of May, so celebrated and so disastrous for the paper. Chimeras were replaced by realities—by a true India Company; and it was this name and this thing which succeeded, which took the place of the undertaking previously known as the Mississippi. It was in vain that the tobacco monopoly and a number of other immense monopolies were given to the new company; they could not enable it to meet the proper claims spread among the public, no matter what trouble might be taken to diminish them at all hazard and at all loss.

It was now necessary to seek other expedients. None could be found except that of rendering this company a commercial one; this was, under a gentler name, a name vague and unpretending, to hand over to it the entire and exclusive commerce of the country. It may be imagined how such a resolution was received by the public, exasperated by the severe decree, prohibiting people, under heavy penalties, from having more than five-hundred livres, in coin, in their possession, subjecting them to visits of inspection, and leaving them nothing but bank notes to, pay for the commonest necessaries of daily life. Two things resulted; first, fury, which day by day was so embittered by the difficulty of obtaining money for daily subsistence, that it was a marvel all Paris did not revolt at once, and that the emeute was appeased; second, the Parliament, taking its stand upon this public emotion, held firm to the end in refusing to register the edict instituting the new company.

On the 15th of July, the Chancellor showed in his own house the draught of the edict to deputies from the Parliament, who remained with him until nine o'clock at night, without being persuaded. On the morrow, the 16th, the edict was brought forward in the Regency Council. M. le Duc d'Orleans, sustained by M. le Duc, spoke well upon it, because he could not speak ill, however bad his theme. Nobody said a word, and all bowed their necks. It was resolved, in this manner, to send the edict to the Parliament on the morrow, the 17th of July.

That same 17th of July, there was such a crowd in the morning, at the bank and in the neighbouring streets, for the purpose of obtaining enough money to go to market with, that ten or twelve people were stifled. Three of the bodies were tumultuously carried to the Palais Royal, which the people, with loud cries, wished to enter. A detachment of the King's guards at the Tuileries was promptly sent there. La Vrilliere and Le Blanc separately harangued the people. The lieutenant of police came; brigades of the watch were sent for. The dead bodies were afterwards carried away, and by gentleness and cajoleries the people were at length dispersed. The detachment of the King's guards returned to the Tuileries. By about ten o'clock in the morning, all being over, Law took it into his head to go to the Palais Royal. He received many imprecations as he passed through the streets. M. le Duc d'Orleans thought it would be well not to let him leave the Palais Royal, and gave him a lodging there. He sent back Law's carriage, however, the windows of which were smashed on the way by the stones thrown at them. Law's house, too, was attacked, amid much breaking of windows. All this was known so late in our quarter of the Jacobins of the Saint-Dominique, that when I arrived at the Palais Royal there was not a vestige visible of any disturbance. M. le Duc d'Orleans, in the midst of a very small company, was very tranquil, and showed that you would not please him unless you were so also. I did not stop long, having nothing to do or say.

This same morning the edict was carried to the Parliament, which refused to register it, and sent a deputation to M. le Duc d'Orleans with its reasons for this, at which the Regent was much vexed. The next morning an ordonnance of the King was pasted all over the town, prohibiting the people, under heavy penalties, to assemble, and announcing that in consequence of the disturbances which had taken place the previous day at the bank, that establishment would remain closed until further notice, and no more money would be paid by it. Luck supplied the place of prudence; for people knew not how they were to live in the meanwhile, yet no fresh disturbance occurred fact which shows the goodness and obedience of the people, subjected to so many and to such strange trials. Troops, however, were collected at Charenton, who were at work upon the canal of Montargis: some regiments of cavalry and of dragoons were stationed at Saint-Denis, and the King's regiment was posted upon the heights of Chaillot. Money was sent to Gonesse to induce the bakers to come as usual, and for fear they should refuse bank notes, like the Paris workmen and shopkeepers, nearly all of whom would no longer receive any paper, the regiment of the guards had orders to hold itself ready, and the musketeers to keep within their quarters, their horses saddled and bridled.

As for the Parliament, M. le Duc d'Orleans determined to punish its disobedience by sending it to Blois. This resolution was carried in full council. The Regent hoped that the Parliamentary men, accustomed to the comfort of their Paris homes, and to the society there of their wives; children, and friends, would soon grow tired of being separated from them, and of the extra expense they would be put to, and would give in. I agreed to the project, although I saw, alas! that by this exile the Parliament would be punished, but would be neither conciliated nor tamed into submission. To make matters worse, Blois was given up, and Pontoise was substituted for it! This latter town being close to Paris, the chastisement became ridiculous, showed the vacillating weakness of the Regent, and encouraged the Parliament to laugh at him. One thing was, however, well done. The resolution taken to banish the Parliament was kept so secret that that assembly had not the slightest knowledge of it.

On Sunday, the 21st of July, squadrons of the guards, with officers at their head, took possession, at four o'clock in the morning, of all the doors of the Palais de justice. The musketeers seized at the same time upon the doors of the Grand Chamber, whilst others invaded the house of the Chief-President, who was in much fear during the first hour. Other musketeers went in parties of four to all the officers of the Parliament, and served them with the King's order, commanding them to repair to Pontoise within twice twenty-four hours. All passed off very politely on both sides, so that there was not the slightest complaint: several members obeyed the same day and went to Pontoise.

Rather late in the evening M. le Duc d'Orleans sent to the Attorney- General 200,000 livres in coin, and as much in bank notes of 100 livres, and of 10 livres to be given to those who should need them for the journey, but not as gifts. The Chief-President was more brazen and more fortunate; he made so many promises, showed so much meanness, employed so much roguery, that abusing by these means the feebleness and easiness of the Regent, whom he laughed at, he obtained more than 100,000 ecus for his expenses. The poor prince gave him the money, under the rose, in two or three different payments, and permitted the Duc de Bouillon to lend him his house at Pontoise, completely furnished, and the garden of which, on the banks of the river, is admirable and immense, a masterpiece of its kind, and had been the delight of Cardinal Bouillon, being perhaps the only thing in France he regretted. With such fine assistance the Chief-President—on bad terms with his companions, who had openly despised him for some time— perfectly made it up with them. He kept at Pontoise open table for the Parliament; all were every day at liberty to use it if they liked, so that there were always several tables, all equally, delicately, and splendidly served. He sent, too, to those who asked for them, liquors, etc., as they could desire. Cooling drinks and fruits of all kinds were abundantly served every afternoon, and there were a number of little one and two-horse vehicles always ready for the ladies and old men who liked a drive, besides play-tables in the apartments until supper time. The result of all this magnificence was, as I have said, that the Chief-President completely reinstated himself in the good graces of his companions; but it was at the expense of the Regent, who was laughed at for his pains. A large number of the members of the Parliament did not go to Pontoise at all, but took advantage of the occasion to recreate themselves in the country. Only a few of the younger members mounted guard in the assembly, where nothing but the most trivial and make- believe business was conducted. Everything important was deliberately neglected. Woe! to those, therefore, who had any trial on hand. The Parliament, in a word, did nothing but divert itself, leave all business untouched, and laugh at the Regent and the government. Banishment to Pontoise was a fine punishment!

This banishment of the Parliament to Pontoise was followed by various financial operations and by several changes in the administrations. Des Forts had the general control of the finances and all authority, but without the name. The disordered state of the exchequer did not hinder M. le Duc d'Orleans from indulging in his strange liberalities to people without merit and without need, and not one of whom he could possibly care a straw for. He gave to Madame la Grande Duchesse an augmentation of her pension of 50,000 livres; one of 8,000 livres to Trudaine: one of 9,000 livres to Chateauneuf; one of 8,000 livres to Bontems, chief valet de chambre of the King; one of 6,000 livres to the Marechal de Montesquieu; one of 3,000 livres to Faucault; and one of 9,000 livres to the widow of the Duc d'Albemarle, secretly remarried to the son of Mahoni.

All this time the public stock-jobbing still continued on the Place Vendome. The Mississippi had tempted everybody. It was who should fill his pockets first with millions, through M. le Duc d'Orleans and Law. The crowd was very great. One day the Marechal de Villars traversed the

Place Vendome in a fine coach, loaded with pages and lackeys, to make way for which the mob of stock-jobbers had some difficulty. The Marechal upon this harangued the people in his braggart manner from the carriage window, crying out against the iniquity of stock-jobbing, and the shame it cast upon all. Until this point he had been allowed to say on, but when he thought fit to add that his own hands were clean, and that he had never dabbled in shares, a voice uttered a cutting sarcasm, and all the crowd took up the word, at which the Marechal, ashamed and confounded, despite his ordinary authority, buried himself in his carriage and finished his journey across the Place Vendome at a gentle trot in the midst of a hue and cry, which followed him even beyond, and which diverted Paris at his expense for several days, nobody pitying him.

At last it was found that this stock-jobbing too much embarrassed the Place Vendome and the public way; it was transferred, therefore, to the vast garden of the Hotel de Soissons. This was, in fact, its proper place. Law, who had remained at the Palais Royal some time, had returned to his own house, where he received many visits. The King several times went to see the troops that had been stationed near Paris; after this they were sent away again. Those which had formed a little camp at Charenton, returned to Montargis to work at the canal making there.

Law, for commercial reasons, had some time ago caused Marseilles to be made a free port. The consequence of this was that an abundance of vessels came there, especially vessels from the Levant, and from want of precautions the plague came also, lasted a long while, desolated the town, province; and the neighbouring provinces. The care and precautions afterwards taken restrained it as much as possible, but did not hinder it from lasting a long time, or from creating frightful disorders. These details are so well known that they can be dispensed with here.

I have a few more words to say of Law and his Mississippi. The bubble finally burst at the end of the year (1720). Law, who had no more resources, being obliged secretly to depart from the realm, was sacrificed to the public. His flight was known only through the eldest son of Argenson, intendant at Mainbeuge, who had the stupidity to arrest him. The courier he despatched with the news was immediately sent back, with a strong reprimand for not having deferred to the passport with which Law had been furnished by the Regent. The financier was with his son, and they both went to Brussels where the Marquis de Prie, Governor of the Imperial Low Countries, received them very well, and entertained them. Law did not stop long, gained Liege and Germany, where he offered his talents to several princes, who all thanked him; nothing more. After having thus roamed, he passed through the Tyrol, visited several Italian courts, not one of which would have him, and at last retired to Venice. This republic, however, did not employ him. His wife and daughter followed him some time after. I don't know what became of them or of the son.

Law was a Scotchman; of very doubtful birth; tall and well made; of agreeable face and aspect; gallant, and on very good terms with the ladies of all the countries he had travelled in. His wife was not his wife; she was of a good English family and well connected; had followed Law for love; had had a son and a daughter by him, passed for his wife, and bore his name without being married to him. This was suspected towards the end; after his departure it became certain. She had one eye and the top of one cheek covered by an ugly stain as of wine; otherwise she was well made, proud, impertinent in her conversation and in her manners, receiving compliments, giving next to none, paying but few visits, these rare and selected, and exercising authority in her household. I know not whether her credit over her husband was great; but he appeared full of regard, of care, and of respect for her; at the time of their departure they were each about fifty and fifty-five years old. Law had made many acquisitions of all kinds and still more debts, so that this tangle is not yet unravelled by the committee of the council appointed to arrange his affairs with his creditors. I have said elsewhere, and I repeat it here, that there was neither avarice nor roguery in his composition. He was a gentle, good, respectable man, whom excess of credit and fortune had not spoiled, and whose deportment, equipages, table, and furniture could not scandalise any one. He suffered with singular patience and constancy all the vexations excited by his operations, until towards the last, when, finding himself short of means and wishing to meet his difficulty, he became quick and bad-tempered, and his replies were often ill-measured. He was a man of system, of calculation, of comparison, well and profoundly instructed in these things, and, without ever cheating, had everywhere gained at play by dint of understanding—which seems to me incredible—the combinations of cards.

His bank, as I have elsewhere said, was an excellent thing for a republic, or for a country like England, where finance is as in a republic. His Mississippi he was the dupe of, and believed with good faith he should make great and rich establishments in America. He reasoned like an Englishman, and did not know how opposed to commerce and to such establishments are the frivolity of the (French) nation, its inexperience, its avidity to enrich itself at once, the inconvenience of a despotic government, which meddles with everything, which has little or no consistency, and in which what one minister does is always destroyed by his successor.

Law's proscription of specie, then of jewels, so as to have only paper in France, is a system I have never comprehended, nor has anybody, I fancy, during all the ages which have elapsed since that in which Abraham, after losing Sarah, bought, for ready-money, a sepulchre for her and for her children. But Law was a man of system, and of system so deep, that nobody ever could get to the bottom of it, though he spoke easily, well and clearly, but with a good deal of English in his French.

He remained several years at Venice, upon very scanty means, and died there a Catholic, having lived decently, but very humbly, wisely, and modestly, and received with piety the last sacraments of the Church.

Thus terminates all I have to say of Law. But a painful truth remains. I have to speak of the woful disorder in the finances which his system led to, disorder which was not fully known until after his departure from France. Then people saw, at last, where all the golden schemes that had flooded upon popular credulity had borne us;—not to the smiling and fertile shores of Prosperity and Confidence, as may be imagined; but to the bleak rocks and dangerous sands of Ruin and Mistrust, where dull clouds obscure the sky, and where there is no protection against the storm.

CHAPTER CII

Not long after the flight of Law, that is to say, on Sunday, the 24th of January, of the new year, 1721, a council was held at the Tuileries, at four o'clock in the afternoon, principally for the purpose of examining the state of the finances and of Law's Bank and India Company. It was, in fact, high time to do something to diminish the overgrown disorder and confusion everywhere reigning. For some time there had been complete stagnation in all financial matters; the credit of the King had step by step diminished, private fortune had become more and more uncertain. The bag was at last empty, the cards were cast aside, the last trick was played: The administration of the finances had passed into the hands of La Houssaye, and his first act was to call the attention of the Regency Council to the position of the bank and the company. We were prepared to hear that things were in a very bad state, but we were scarcely prepared to find that they so closely resembled utter ruin and bankruptcy.

I need not relate all that passed at this council; the substance of it is enough. From the statement there of M. le Duc d'Orleans, it appeared that Law had issued 1,200,000,000 livres of bank notes more than he ought to have issued. The first 600,00,000 livres had not done much harm, because they had been kept locked up in the bank; but after the 22nd of May, another issue of 600,000,000 had taken place, and been circulated among the public, without the knowledge of the Regent, without the authorisation of any decree. "For this," said M. le Duc d'Orleans, "Law deserved to be hanged, but under the circumstances of the case, I drew him from his embarrassment, by an ante-dated decree, ordering the issue of this quantity of notes."

Thereupon M. le Duc said to the Regent, "But, Monsieur, why, knowing this, did you allow him to leave the realm?"

"It was you who furnished him with the means to do so," replied M. le Duc d'Orleans.

"I never asked you to allow him to quit the country," rejoined M. le Duc.

"But," insisted the Regent, "it was you yourself who sent him his passports."

"That's true," replied M. le Duc, "but it was you who gave them to me to send to him; but I never asked you for them, or to let him leave the realm. I know that I have the credit for it amongst the public, and I am glad of this opportunity to explain here the facts of the case. I was against the proposition for sending M. Law to the Bastille, or to any other prison, because I believed that it was not to your interest to sanction this, after having made use of him as you had; but I never asked you to let him leave the realm, and I beg you, Monsieur, in presence of the King, and before all these gentlemen, to say if I ever did."

"'Tis true," replied the Regent, "you never asked me; I allowed him to go, because I thought his presence in France would injure public credit, and the operations of the public."

"So far was I from asking you," said M. le Duc, "that if you had done me the honour to demand my opinion, I should have advised you to take good care not to let him depart from the country."

This strange conversation, which roused our astonishment to an incredible point, and which was sustained with so much out-spoken freedom by M. le Duc, demands a word or two of explanation.

M. le Duc was one of those who, without spending a farthing, had drawn millions from Law's notes and shares. He had had large allotments of the latter, and now that they had become utterly valueless, he had been obliged to make the best of a bad bargain, by voluntarily giving them up, in order to lighten the real responsibilities of the Company. This he had done at the commencement of the Council, M. le Prince de Conti also. But let me explain at greater length.

The 22nd of May, the day of the decree, was the period at which commenced the final decay of the Company, and of the bank, and the extinction of all confidence by the sad discovery that there was no longer any money wherewith to pay the bank notes, they being so prodigiously in excess of the coin. After this, each step had been but a stumble: each operation a very feeble palliation. Days and weeks had been gained, obscurity had been allowed to give more chance, solely from fear of disclosing the true and terrible state of affairs, and the extent of the public ruin. Law could not wash his hands of all this before the world; he could not avoid passing for the inventor and instrument, and he would have run great risk at the moment when all was unveiled. M. le Duc d'Orleans, who, to satisfy his own prodigality, and the prodigious avidity of his friends, had compelled Law to issue so many millions of livres of notes more than he had any means of paying, and who had thus precipitated him into the abyss, could not let him run the chance of perishing, still less to save him, could he proclaim himself the real criminal. It was to extricate himself from this embarrassment that he made Law leave the country, when he saw that the monstrous deceit could no longer be hidden.

This manifestation, which so strongly interested the shareholders, and the holders of bank notes, especially those who had received shares or notes as favours due to their authority, and who could show no other title to them, threw every one into despair. The most important holders, such as the Princes of the Blood, and others, whose profits had been immense, had by force or industry delayed this manifestation as long as possible. As they knew the real state of affairs, they felt that the moment all the world knew it also, their gains would cease, and their paper become worthless, that paper from which they had drawn so much, and which had not cost them a farthing! This is what induced M. le Duc d'Orleans to hide from them the day of this manifestation, so as to avoid being importuned by them; and by a surprise, to take from them the power of preparing any opposition to the measures it was proposed to carry out. M. le Duc, when he learned this, flew into a fury, and hence the strange scene between him and M. le Duc d'Orleans, which scandalised and terrified everybody in the Council.

M. le Duc d'Orleans, who, from taste, and afterwards from necessity, lived upon schemes and trickery, thought he had done marvels in saddling M. le Duc with the passport of Law. He wished to lay the blame of Law's departure upon M. le Duc; but as I have shown, he was defeated by his own weapons. He had to do with a man as sharp as himself. M. le Duc, who knew he had nothing to fear, would not allow it to be supposed that he had sanctioned the flight of the financier. That was why he pressed M. le Duc d'Orleans so pitilessly, and forced him to admit that he had never asked him to allow Law to leave the country.

The great and terrible fact brought out by this Council was, that Law, without the knowledge or authority of the Regent, had issued and disseminated among the public 600,000,000 livres of notes; and not only without being authorised by any edict, but contrary to express prohibition. But when the Regent announced this, who did he suppose would credit it? Who could believe that Law would have had the hardihood to issue notes at this rate without the sanction and approbation of his master?

However, to leave once and for all these unpleasant matters, let me say what was resolved upon by way of remedy to the embarrassments discovered to exist. The junction of the India Company with the bank, which had taken place during the previous February, had led to transactions which made the former debtor to the latter to an immense amount. But the bank being a governmental establishment, the King became thus the creditor of the Company. It was decreed, in fact, that the Company should be considered as debtor to the King. It was decided, however, that other debtors should receive first attention. Many private people had invested their money in the shares of the Company. It was not thought just that by the debt of the Company to the King, these people should be ruined; or, on the other hand, that those who had left the Company in good time, who had converted their shares into notes, or who had bought them at a low price in the market, should profit by the misfortune of the bona fide shareholders. Accordingly, commissioners, it was decided, were to be named, to liquidate all these papers and parchments, and annul those which did not proceed from real purchases.

M. le Duc said, upon this, "There are at least eighty thousand families, the whole of whose wealth consists of these effects; how are they to live during this liquidation?"

La Houssaye replied, that so many commissioners could be named, that the work would soon be done.

And so the Council ended.

But I must, perforce, retrace my steps at this point to many other matters, which I have left far behind me in going on at once to the end of this financial labyrinth. And first let me tell what happened to that monstrous personage, Alberoni, how he fell from the lofty pinnacle of dower on which he had placed himself, and lost all consideration and all importance in the fall. The story is mightily curious and instructive.

CHAPTER CIII

Alberoni had made himself detested by all Europe,—for all Europe, in one way or another, was the victim of his crimes. He was detested as the absolute master of Spain, whose guides were perfidy, ambition, personal interest, views always oblique, often caprice, sometimes madness; and whose selfish desires, varied and diversified according to the fantasy of the moment, were hidden under schemes always uncertain and oftentimes impossible of execution. Accustomed to keep the King and Queen of Spain in chains, and in the narrowest and obscurest prison, where he allowed them to communicate with no one, and made them see, feel, and breathe through him, and blindly obey his every wish; he caused all Spain to tremble, and had annihilated all power there, except his own, by the most violent acts, constraining himself in no way, despising his master and his mistress, whose will and whose authority he had utterly absorbed. He braved successively all the powers of Europe, and aspired to nothing less than to deceive them all, then to govern them, making them serve all his ends; and seeing at last his cunning exhausted, tried to execute alone, and without allies, the plan he had formed.

This plan was nothing less than to take away from the Emperor all that the peace of Utrecht had left him in Italy; all that the Spanish house of Austria had possessed there; to dominate the Pope and the King of Sicily; to deprive the Emperor of the help of France and England, by exciting the first against the Regent through the schemes of the ambassador Cellamare and the Duc du Maine; and by sending King James to England, by the aid of the North, so as to keep King George occupied with a civil war. In the end he wished to profit by all these disorders, by transporting into Italy (which his cardinalship made him regard as a safe asylum against all reverses) the immense treasures he had pillaged and collected m Spain, under pretext of sending the sums necessary to sustain the war, and the conquests he intended to make; and this last project was, perhaps, the motive power of all the rest. The madness of these schemes, and his obstinacy in clinging to them, were not discovered until afterwards. The astonishment then was great indeed, upon discovering the poverty of the resources with which he thought himself capable of carrying out these wild projects. Yet he had made such prodigious preparations for war, that he had entirely exhausted the country without rendering it able for a moment to oppose the powers of Europe.

Alberoni, abhorred in Spain as a cruel tyrant, in France, in England, in Rome, and by the Emperor as an implacable and personal enemy, did not seem to have the slightest uneasiness. Yet he might have had some, and with good cause, at the very moment when he fancied himself most powerful and most secure.

The Regent and the Abbe Dubois, who for a long time had only too many reasons to regard Alberoni as their personal enemy, were unceasingly occupied in silently plotting his fall; they believed the present moment favourable, and did not fail to profit by it. How they did so is a curious fact, which, to my great regret, has never reached me. M. le Duc d'Orleans survived Dubois such a few months that many things I should have liked to have gained information upon, I had not the time to ask him about; and this was one.

All I know is, that what Alberoni always dreaded, at last happened to him. He trembled, at every one, no matter of how little importance, who arrived from Parma (the Queen of Spain, it has not been forgotten, was of that Duchy); he omitted nothing by the aid of the Duke of Parma, and by other means, to hinder the Parmesans from coming to Madrid; and was in terror of the few of those whose journey he could not hinder, and whose dismissal he could not obtain.

Among these few people there was nobody he feared so much as the Queen's nurse, whom he drew up with a round turn occasionally, so to speak, but less from policy than ill-temper. This nurse, who was a rough country- woman of Parma, was named Donna Piscatori Laura. She had arrived in Spain some years after the Queen, who had always liked her, and who made her, shortly after her arrival, her 'assofeta', that is to say, her chief 'femme de chambre'; an office more considerable in Spain than with us. Laura had brought her husband with her, a peasant in every way, seen and known by nobody; but Laura had intelligence, shrewdness, cleverness, and ambitious views, in spite of the external vulgarity of her manners, which she had preserved either from habit, or from policy, for make herself less suspected. Like all persons of this extraction, she was thoroughly selfish. She was not unaware how impatiently Alberoni endured her presence, and feared her favour with the Queen, whom he wished to possess alone; and, more sensible to the gentle taps she from time to time received from him, than to his ordinary attentions, she looked upon him simply as a very formidable enemy, who kept her within very narrow limits, who hindered her from profiting by the favour of the Queen, and whose design was to send her back to Parma, and to leave nothing undone until he had carried it out.

This is all the information I have ever been able to obtain. The probability is, that Donna Laura was gained by the money of the Regent and the intrigues gained Dubois; and that she succeeded in convincing the Queen of Spain that Alberoni was a minister who had ruined the country, who was the sole obstacle in the way of peace, and who had sacrificed everything and everybody to his personal views, their Catholic Majesties included. However, as I relate only what I know, I shall be very brief upon this interesting event.

Laura succeeded. Alberoni, at the moment he least expected it, received a note from the King of Spain ordering him to withdraw at once, without attempting to see him or the Queen, or to write to them; and to leave Spain in twice twenty-four hours! An officer of the guards was to accompany him until his departure: How this overruling order was received, and what the Cardinal did, I know not; I only know that he obeyed it, and took the road for Arragon. So few precautions had been taken, that he carried off an immense number of papers, money, and jewels; and it was not until a few days had elapsed, that the King of Spain was informed that the original will of Charles the Second could not be found. It was at once supposed that Alberoni had carried away this precious document (by which Charles the Second named Philippe V. King of Spain), in order to offer it, perhaps, to the Emperor, so as to gain his favour and good graces. Alberoni was stopped. It was not without trouble, the most terrible menaces, and loud cries from him, that he surrendered the testament, and some other important papers which it was perceived were missing. The terror he had inspired was so profound, that, until this moment, no one had dared to show his joy, or to speak, though the tyrant was gone. But this event reassured every one against his return, and the result was an unexampled overflow of delight, of imprecations, and of reports against him, to the King and Queen, of the most public occurrences (which they alone were ignorant of) and of. private misdeeds, which it was no longer thought necessary to hide.

M. le Duc d'Orleans did not restrain his joy, still less the Abbe Dubois; it was their work which had overthrown their personal enemy; with him fell the wall of separation, so firmly erected by Alberoni between the Regent and the King of Spain; and (at the same time) the sole obstacle against peace. This last reason caused joy to burst out in Italy, in Vienna, in London; and peace between France, and Spain soon resulted.

The allied princes felicitated themselves on what had happened; even the Dutch were ravished to be delivered of a minister so double-dealing, so impetuous, so powerful. M. le Duc d'Orleans dispatched the Chevalier de Morcieu, a very skilful and intelligent man, and certainly in the hands of the Abbe Dubois, to the extreme confines of the frontiers to wait for Alberoni, accompanying him until the moment of his embarkation in Provence for Italy; with orders never to lose sight of him, to make him avoid the large towns and principal places as much as possible; suffer no honours to be rendered to him; above all, to hinder him from communicating with anybody, or anybody with him; in a word, to conduct him civilly, like a prisoner under guard.

Morcieu executed to the letter this disagreeable commission; all the more necessary, because, entirely disgraced as was Alberoni, everything was to be forced from him while traversing a great part of France, where all who were adverse to the Regent might have recourse to him. Therefore it was not without good reason that every kind of liberty was denied him.

It may be imagined what was suffered by a man so impetuous, and so accustomed to unlimited power; but he succeeded in accommodating himself to such a great and sudden change of condition; in maintaining his self- possession; in subjecting himself to no refusals; in being sage and measured in his manners; very reserved in speech, with an air as though he cared for nothing; and in adapting himself to everything without questions, without pretension, without complaining, dissimulating everything, and untiringly pretending to regard Morcieu as an accompaniment of honour. He received, then, no sort of civility on the part of the Regent, of Dubois, or of anybody; and performed the day's journeys, arranged by Morcieu, without stopping, almost without suite, until he arrived on the shores of the Mediterranean, where he immediately embarked and passed to the Genoa coast.

Alberoni, delivered of his Argus, and arrived in Italy, found himself in another trouble by the anger of the Emperor, who would suffer him nowhere, and by the indignation of the Court of Rome, which prevailed, on this occasion, over respect for the purple. Alberoni for a long time was forced to keep out of the way, hidden and a fugitive, and was not able to approach Rome until the death of the Pope. The remainder of the life of this most extraordinary man is not a subject for these memoirs. But what ought not to be forgotten is the last mark of rage, despair, and madness that he gave in traversing France. He wrote to M. le Duc d'Orleans, offering to supply him with the means of making a most dangerous war against Spain; and at Marseilles, ready to embark, he again wrote to reiterate the same offers, and press them on the Regent.

I cannot refrain from commenting here upon the blindness of allowing ecclesiastics to meddle with public affairs; above all, cardinals, whose special privilege is immunity from everything most infamous and most degrading. Ingratitude, infidelity, revolt, felony, independence, are the chief characteristics of these eminent criminals.

Of Alberoni's latter days I will say but a few words.

At the death of Clement XI., legal proceedings that had been taken to deprive Alberoni of his cardinalship, came to an end. Wandering and hidden in Italy, he was summoned to attend a conclave for the purpose of electing a new Pope. Alberoni was the opprobrium of the sacred college; proceedings, as I have said, were in progress to deprive him of his cardinalship. The King and Queen of Spain evidently stimulated those proceedings: the Pope just dead had opposed him; but the cardinals would not agree to his disgrace; they would not consent to strip him of his dignity. The example would have been too dangerous. That a cardinal, prince, or great nobleman, should surrender his hat in order to marry, the store of his house demands it; well and good; but to see a cardinal deprive himself of his hat by way of penitence, is what his brethren will not endure. A cardinal may be poisoned, stabbed, got rid of altogether, but lose his dignity he never can. Rome must be infallible, or she is nothing.

It was decided, that if, at the election of the new Pope, Alberoni were not admitted to take part in the proceedings, he always might protest against them, and declare them irregular. Therefore he was, as I have said, admitted to the conclave. He arrived in Rome, without display, in his own coach, and was received in the conclave with the same honours as all the other cardinals, and performed all the duties of his position.

A few days after the election, he absented himself from Rome, as though to see whether proceedings would be continued against him. But they fell of themselves. The new Pope had no interest in them. The cardinals wished only for silence. Spain felt at last the inutility of her cries. Dubois was in favour of throwing a veil over his former crimes, so that, after a short absence, Alberoni hired in Rome a magnificent palace, and returned there for good, with the attendance, expense, and display his Spanish spoils supplied. He found himself face to face with the Cardinal Giudice, and with Madame des Ursins. The three formed a rare triangle, which caused many a singular scene in home. After seeing them both die, Alberoni became legate at Ferrara, continued there a long time, little esteemed at Rome, where he is now living, sound in mind and body, and eighty-six years of age.

The King attended the Royal Council for the first time on Sunday, the 18th of February, 1720. He said nothing while there, or on going away, excepting that when M. le Duc d'Orleans, who feared he might grow weary of the proceedings, proposed to him to leave, he said he would stop to the end. After this he did not come always, but often, invariably remaining to the last, without moving or speaking. His presence changed nothing in the order of our arrangements, because his armchair was always there, alone, at the end of the table, and M. le Duc d'Orleans, whether his Majesty came or not, had but a "stool" similar to those we all sat upon. Step by step this council had been so much increased, that now, by the entry of the Duc de Berwick, it numbered sixteen members! To say truth, we were far too many, and we had several among us who would have been much better away. I had tried, but in vain, to make the Regent see this. He did see at last, but it was too late; and meanwhile we were, as I have stated, sixteen in the council. I remember that one day, when the King came, a kitten followed him, and some time after jumped upon him, and thence upon the table, where it began to walk; the Duc de Noailles immediately crying out, because he did not like cats. M. le Duc d'Orleans wished to drive the animal away. I smiled, and said, "Oh, leave the kitten alone, it will make the seventeenth."

M. le Duc d'Orleans burst out laughing at this, and looked at the company, who laughed also, the King as well. His Majesty briefly spoke of it to me on the morrow, as though appreciating the joke, which, by the way, immediately ran over all Paris.

The Abbe Dubois still maintained his pernicious influence over the Regent, and still looked forward to a cardinalship as the reward of his scheming, his baseness, and his perfidy. In the meantime, the Archbishopric of Cambrai became vacant (by the death, at Rome, of the Cardinal Tremoille). That is to say, the richest archbishopric, and one of the best posts in the Church. The Abbe Dubois was only tonsured; 150,000 livres, a year tempted him, and perhaps this position, from which he could more easily elevate himself to the cardinalship. Impudent as he might be, powerful as might be the empire he had acquired over his master, he was much embarrassed, and masked his effrontery under a trick. He said to M. le Duc d'Orleans, he had a pleasant dream; and related to him that he had dreamt he was Archbishop of Cambrai! The Regent, who smelt the rat, turned on his heel, and said nothing. Dubois, more and more embarrassed, stammered, and paraphrased his dream; then, re-assuring himself by an effort, asked, in an offhand manner, why he should not obtain it, His Royal Highness, by his will alone, being able thus to make his fortune.

M. le Duc d'Orleans was indignant, even terrified, little scrupulous as he might be as to the choice of bishops, and in a tone of contempt replied to Dubois, "What, you Archbishop of Cambrai!" making him thus feel his low origin, and still more the debauchery and scandal of his life. Dubois was, however, too far advanced to stop on the road, and cited examples; unfortunately these were only too many.

M. le Duc d'Orleans, less touched by such bad reasoning than embarrassed how to resist the ardor of a man whom for a long time he had not dated to contradict, tried to get out of the difficulty, by saying, "But you being such a scoundrel, where will you find another to consecrate you?"

"Oh, if it's only that!" exclaimed Dubois, "the thing is done. I know very well who will consecrate me; he is not far from here."

"And who the devil is he who will dare to do so?" asked the Regent.

"Would you like to know?" replied the Abbe, "and does the matter rest only upon that?"

"Well, who?" said the Regent.

"Your chief chaplain," replied Dubois, "who is close at hand. Nothing will please him better; I will run and speak to him."

And thereupon he embraces the knees of M. le Duc d'Orleans (who, caught thus in his own trap, had not the strength to refuse), runs to the Bishop of Nantes, says that he is to have Cambrai, begs the Bishop to consecrate him, and receives his promise to do so, returns, wheels round, tells M. le Duc d'Orleans that his chief chaplain has agreed to the consecration; thanks, praises, admires the Regent, fixes more and more firmly the office by regarding it as settled, and by persuading M. le Duc d'Orleans, who dares not say no; and in this manner was Dubois made Archbishop of Cambrai!

The extreme scandal of this nomination caused a strange, stir. Impudent as was the Abbe Dubois, he was extremely embarrassed; and M. le Duc d'Orleans so much ashamed, that it was soon remarked he was humbled if you spoke to him upon the subject. The next question was, from whom Dubois was to receive holy orders? The Cardinal de Noailles was applied to, but he stoutly refused to assist in any way. It may be imagined what an affront this was to Dubois. He never in his life pardoned the Cardinal, who was nevertheless universally applauded for his refusal. But the Abbe Dubois was not a man to be daunted by an ordinary obstacle; he turned his glances elsewhere, and soon went through all the formalities necessary.

The very day he took orders there was a Regency Council at the old Louvre, because the measles, which were then very prevalent, even in the Palais Royal, hindered us from meeting as usual in the Tuileries. A Regency Council without the Abbe Dubois present was a thing to marvel at, and yet his arrival to-day caused even more surprise than his absence would have caused. But he was not a man to waste his time in thanksgiving for what had just happened to him. This was a new scandal, which revived and aggravated the first. Everybody had arrived in the cabinet of the council, M. le Duc d'Orleans also; we were scattered about and standing. I was in a corner of the lower end, when I saw Dubois enter in a stout coat, with his ordinary bearing. We did not expect him on such a day, and naturally enough cried out surprised. M. le Prince de Conti, with his father's sneering manner, spoke to the Abbe Dubois, on his appearance among us on the very day of taking orders, and expressed his surprise at it with the most pathetic malignity imaginable.

Dubois, who had not had time to reply one word, let him say to the end; then coldly observed, that if he had been a little more familiar with ancient history, he would not have found what astonished him very strange, since he (the Abbe) had only followed the example of Saint-Ambrose, whose ordination he began to relate. I did not wait for his recital; at the mere mention of Saint-Ambrose I flew to the other end of the cabinet, horror-struck at the comparison Dubois had just made, and fearing lest I should be tempted to say to him, that the ordination of Saint-Ambrose had been forced upon him in spite of his resistance. This impious citation of Saint-Ambrose ran all over the town with the effect that may be imagined. The nomination and this ordination took place towards the end of February.

I will finish at once all that relates to this matter, so as not to separate it, or have to return to it. Dubois had his bulls at the commencement of May, and the consecration was fixed for Sunday the 9th of June. All Paris and the Court were invited to it, myself excepted. I was on bad terms with Dubois, because I in no way spared him when with M. le Duc d'Orleans. He on his side, fearing the power I had over the Regent, the liberty I enjoyed with him, and the freedom with which I spoke to him, did as much as he could to injure me, and to weaken the confidence of M. le Duc d'Orleans in me. Dubois and I continued, nevertheless, to be on good terms with each other in appearance, but it was in appearance only.

This consecration was to be magnificent, and M. le Duc d'Orleans was to be present at it. If the nomination and the ordination of the Abbe Dubois had caused much stir, scandal, and horror, the superb preparations for the consecration caused even more: Great was the indignation against M. le Duc d'Orleans. I went, therefore, to him the evening before this strange ceremony was to take place, to beg him not to attend it. I represented to him that the nomination and ordination of the Abbe Dubois had created frightful effect upon the public, and that the consecration of a man of such low extraction, and whose manners and mode of life were so notorious; would create more. I added, that if he attended this ceremony, people would say it was simply for the purpose of mocking God, and insulting His Church; that the effect of this would be terrible, and always much to be feared; and that people would say the Abbe Dubois abused the mastery he had over him, and that this was evidence of dependence would draw down upon him hatred, disdain, and shame, the results of which were to be dreaded. I concluded by saying, that I spoke to him as his disinterested servitor; that his absence or his presence at this consecration would change in, nothing the fortune of the Abbe Dubois, who would be Archbishop of Cambrai all the same without prostituting his master in the eyes of all France, and of all Europe, by compelling him to be guilty of a measure to which it would be seen he had been urged by force. I conjured him not to go; and to show him on what terms I was with the Abbe Dubois, I explained to him I was the sole man of rank he had not invited to his consecration; but that, notwithstanding this circumstance, if he would give me his word that he would not go, I on my side would agree to go, though my horror at doing so would be very great.

My discourse, pronounced with warmth and developed with freedom, was listened to from beginning to end. I was surprised to hear the Regent say I was right, but I opened my eyes very wide when he embraced me, said that I spoke like a true friend, and that he would give me his word, and stick to it, he would not go. We parted upon this, I strengthening him in his resolution, promising anew I would go, and he thanking me for this effort. He showed no impatience, no desire that I should go; for I knew him well, and I examined him to the very bottom of his soul, and quitted him much pleased at having turned him from a measure so disgraceful and so extraordinary. Who could have guessed that he would not keep his word? But so it happened.

Although as I have said I felt sure of him, yet the extreme weakness of this prince, and the empire the Abbe Dubois had acquired over him; induced me to be quite certain of him before going to the consecration. I sent therefore the next morning to the Palais Royal to inquire after M. le Duc d'Orleans; keeping my carriage all ready for a start. But I was much confused, accustomed as I might be to his miserable vacillation, to hear from the person I had sent, that he had just seen the Regent jump into his coach, surrounded by all the pomp usual on grand occasions, and set out for the consecration. I had my horses put up at once, and locked myself into my cabinet.

A day or two after I learnt from a friend of Madame de Parabere, then the reigning Sultana, but not a faithful one, that M. le Duc d'Orleans had been with her the previous night, and had spoken to her in praise of me, saying he would not go to the ceremony, and that he was very grateful to me for having dissuaded him from going. La Parabere praised me, admitted I was right, but her conclusion was that he would go.

M. le Duc d'Orleans, surprised, said to her she was then mad.

"Be it so," replied she, "but you will go."

"But I tell you I will not go," he rejoined.

"Yes, yes, I tell you," said she; "you will go."

"But," replied he, "this is admirable. You say M. de Saint-Simon is quite right, why then should I go?"

"Because I wish it," said she.

"Very good," replied he, "and why do you wish I should go—what madness is this?"

"I wish it because—," said she.

"Oh, because," replied he, "that's no reason; say why you wish it."

(After some dispute) "You obstinately desire then to know? Are you not aware that the Abbe Dubois and I quarreled four days ago, and that we have not yet made it up. He mixes in everything. He will know that you have been with me to-night. If to-morrow you do not go to his consecration, he will not fail to believe it is I who have hindered you; nothing will take this idea out of his head; he will never pardon me; he will undermine in a hundred ways my credit with you, and finish by embroiling us. But I don't wish such a thing to happen, and for that reason you must go to his consecration, although M. de Saint-Simon is right."

Thereupon ensued a feeble debate, then resolution and promise to go, which was very faithfully kept.

As for me I could only deplore the feebleness of the Regent, to whom I never afterwards spoke of this consecration, or he to me; but he was very much ashamed of himself, and much embarrassed with me afterwards. I do not know whether he carried his weakness so far as to tell Dubois what I had said to hinder him from going to the ceremony or whether the Abbe was told by La Parabere, who thought thus to take credit to herself for having changed the determination of M. le Duc d'Orleans, and to show her credit over him. But Dubois was perfectly informed of it, and never pardoned me.

The Val de Grace was chosen for the consecration as being a royal monastery, the most magnificent of Paris, and the most singular church. It was superbly decorated; all France was invited, and nobody dared to stop away or to be out of sight during the whole ceremony.

There were tribunes with blinds prepared for the ambassadors and Protestant ministers. There was another more magnificent for M. le Duc d'Orleans and M. le Duc de Chartres, whom he took there. There were places for the ladies, and as M. le Duc d'Orleans entered by the monastery, and his tribune was within, it was open to all comers, so that outside and inside were filled with refreshments of all kinds, which officers distributed in profusion. This disorder continued all day, on account of the large number of tables that were served without and within for the subordinate people of the fete and all who liked to thrust themselves in. The chief gentlemen of the chamber of M. le Duc d'Orleans, and his chief officers did the business of the ceremony; placed distinguished people in their seats, received them, conducted them, and other of his officers paid similar attentions to less considerable people, while, all the watch and all the police were occupied in looking after the arrival and departure of the carriages in proper and regular order.

During the consecration, which was but little decent as far as the consecrated and the spectators were concerned, above all when leaving the building, M. le Duc d'Orleans evinced his satisfaction at finding so many considerable people present, and then went away to Asnieres to dine with Madame Parabere—very glad that a ceremony was over upon which he had bestowed only indirect attention, from the commencement to the end. All the prelates, the distinguished Abbes, and a considerable number of the laity, were invited during the consecration by the chief officers of M. le Duc d'Orleans to dine at the Palais Royal. The same officers did the honours of the feast, which was served with the most splendid abundance and delicacy. There were two services of thirty covers each, in a large room of the grand suite of apartments, filled with the most considerable people of Paris, and several other tables equally well served in adjoining rooms for people less distinguished. M. le Duc d'Orleans gave to the new Archbishop a diamond of great price to serve him as ring.

All this day was given up to that sort of triumph which draws down neither the approbation of man nor the blessing of God. I saw nothing of it all, however, and M. le Duc d'Orleans and I never spoke of it.

The Comte de Horn had been in Paris for the last two months, leading an obscure life of gaming and debauchery. He was a man of two-and-twenty, tall and well made, of that ancient and grand family of Horn, known in the eleventh century among the little dynasties of the Low Countries, and afterwards by a long series of illustrious generations. The Comte de Horn in question had been made captain in the Austrian army, less on account of his youth than because he was such an ill-behaved dog, causing vast trouble to his mother and brother. They heard so much of the disorderly life he was leading in Paris, that they sent there a confidential gentleman with money to pay his debts, to try and persuade him to return, and failing in this, to implore the authority of the Regent (to whom, through Madame, the Horns were related), in order to compel him to do so. As ill-luck would have it, this gentleman arrived the day after the Comte had committed the crime I am about to relate.

On Friday, the 22nd of March, 1720, he went to the Rue Quincampoix, wishing, he said, to buy 100,000 ecus worth of shares, and for that purpose made an appointment with a stockbroker in a cabaret. The stock-broker came there with his pocket-book and his shares; the Comte de Horn came also, accompanied, as he said, by two of his friends; a moment after, they all three threw themselves upon this unfortunate stock-broker; the Comte de Horn stabbed him several times with a poniard, and seized his pocket-book; one of his pretended friends (a Piedmontese named Mille), seeing that the stock-broker was not dead, finished the work. At the noise they made the people of the house came, not sufficiently quick to prevent the murder, but in time to render themselves masters of the assassins, and to arrest them. In the midst of the scuffle, the other cut-throat escaped, but the Comte de Horn and Mille were not so fortunate. The cabaret people sent for the officers of justice, who conducted the criminals to the Conciergerie. This horrible crime, committed in broad daylight, immediately made an immense stir, and several kinsmen of this illustrious family at once went to M. le Duc d'Orleans to beg for mercy; but the Regent avoided speaking to them as much as possible, and very rightly ordered full and prompt justice to be done.

At last, the relatives of Horn penetrated to the Regent: they tried to make the Count pass for mad, saying even that he had an uncle confined in an asylum, and begging that he might be confined also. But the reply was, that madmen who carried their madness to fury could not be got rid of too quickly. Repulsed in this manner, they represented what an infamy it would be to their illustrious family, related to nearly all the sovereigns of Europe, to have one of its members tried and condemned. M. le Duc d'Orleans replied that the infamy was in the crime, and not in the punishment. They pressed him upon the honour the family had in being related to him. "Very well, gentlemen," said he, "I will divide the shame with you."

The trial was neither long nor difficult. Law and the Abbe Dubois, so interested in the safety of the stock-jobbers (without whom the paper must have fallen at once), supported M. le Duc d'Orleans might and main, in order to render him inexorable, and he, to avoid the persecutions he unceasingly experienced on the other side, left nothing undone in order to hurry the Parliament into a decision; the affair, therefore; went full speed, and it seemed likely that the Comte de Horn would be broken on the wheel.

The relatives, no longer hoping to save the criminal, thought only of obtaining a commutation of the sentence. Some of them came to me, asking me to save them: though I was not related to the Horn family, they explained to me, that death on the wheel would throw into despair all that family, and everybody connected with it in the Low Countries, and in Germany, because in those parts there was a great and important difference between the punishments of persons of quality who had committed crimes; that decapitation in no way influenced the family of the decapitated, but that death on the wheel threw such infamy upon it, that the uncles, aunts, brothers, and sisters, and the three next generations, were excluded from entering into any noble chapter, which, in addition to the shame, was a very injurious deprivation, annihilating the family's chance of ecclesiastic preferment; this reason touched me, and I promised to do my best with M. le Duc d'Orleans to obtain a commutation of the sentence.

I was going off to La Ferme to profit by the leisure of Holy Week. I went therefore to M. le Duc d'Orleans, and explained to him what I had just learnt. I said that after the detestable crime the Comte de Horn had committed, every one must feel that he was worthy of death; but that every one could not admit it was necessary to break him on the wheel, in order to satisfy the ends of justice. I showed him how the family would suffer if this sentence were carried out, and I concluded by proposing to the Regent a 'mezzo termine', such as he was so fond of.

I suggested that the decree ordering death by the wheel should be pronounced. That another decree should at the same time be prepared and kept ready signed and sealed, with only a date to fill in, revoking the first, and changing the punishment into decapitation. That at the last moment this second decree should be produced, and immediately afterwards the head of the Comte de Horn be cut off. M. le Duc d'Orleans offered no objection, but consented at once to my plan. I said to him, by way of conclusion, that I was going to set out the next day, and that I begged him not to be shaken in the determination he had just formed, by the entreaties of Dubois or Law, both of whom were strongly in favour of punishment by the wheel. He assured me he would keep firm; reiterated the assurance; I took leave of him; and the next day went to La Ferme.

He was firm, however, in his usual manner. Dubois and Law besieged him, and led the attack so well that he gave in, and the first thing I learnt at La Ferme was that the Comte de Horn had been broken alive on the wheel at the Greve, on Holy Friday; the 26th March, 1720, about 4 o'clock in the afternoon, and the scoundrel Mille with him on the same scaffold, after having both suffered torture.

The result of this was as I anticipated. The Horn family and all the grand nobility of the Low Countries, many of Germany, were outraged, and contained themselves neither in words nor in writings. Some of them even talked of strange vengeance, and a long time after the death of M. le Duc d'Orleans, I met with certain of the gentlemen upon whose hearts the memory of this punishment still weighed heavily.

VOLUME 14: CHAPTER CV

For a long time a species of war had been declared between the King of England and his son, the Prince of Wales, which had caused much scandal; and which had enlisted the Court on one side, and made much stir in the Parliament. George had more than once broken out with indecency against his son; he had long since driven him from the palace, and would not see him. He had so cut down his income that he could scarcely subsist. The father never could endure this son, because he did not believe him to be his own. He had more than suspected the Duchess, his wife, to be in relations with Count Konigsmarck. He surprised him one morning leaving her chamber; threw him into a hot oven, and shut up his wife in a chateau for the rest of her days. The Prince of Wales, who found himself ill- treated for a cause of which he was personally innocent, had always borne with impatience the presence of his mother and the aversion of his father. The Princess of Wales, who had much sense, intelligence, grace, and art, had softened things as much as possible; and the King was unable to refuse her his esteem, or avoid loving her. She had conciliated all England; and her Court, always large, boasted of the presence of the most accredited and the most distinguished persons. The Prince of Wales feeling his strength, no longer studied his father, and blamed the ministers with words that at least alarmed them. They feared the credit of the Princess of Wales; feared lest they should be attacked by the Parliament, which often indulges in this pleasure. These considerations became more and more pressing as they discovered what was brewing against them; plans such as would necessarily have rebounded upon the King. They communicated their fears to him, and indeed tried to make it up with his son, on certain conditions, through the medium of the Princess of Wales, who, on her side, felt all the consciousness of sustaining a party against the King, and who always had sincerely desired peace in the royal family. She profited by this conjuncture; made use of the ascendency she had over her husband, and the reconciliation was concluded. The King gave a large sum to the Prince of Wales, and consented to see him. The ministers were saved, and all appeared forgotten.

The excess to which things had been carried between father and son had not only kept the entire nation attentive to the intestine disorders ready to arise, but had made a great stir all over Europe; each power tried to blow this fire into a blaze, or to stifle it according as interest suggested. The Archbishop of Cambrai, whom I shall continue to call the Abbe Dubois, was just then very anxiously looking out for his cardinal's hat, which he was to obtain through the favour of England, acting upon that of the Emperor with the Court of Rome. Dubois, overjoyed at the reconciliation which had taken place, wished to show this in a striking manner, in order to pay his court to the King of England. He named, therefore, the Duc de la Force to go to England, and compliment King George on the happy event that had occurred.

The demonstration of joy that had been resolved on in France was soon known in England. George, annoyed by the stir that his domestic squabbles had made throughout all Europe, did not wish to see it prolonged by the sensation that this solemn envoy would cause. He begged the Regent, therefore, not to send him one. As the scheme had been determined on only order to please him, the journey of the Duc de la Force was abandoned almost as soon as declared. Dubois had the double credit, with the King of England, of having arranged this demonstration of joy, and of giving it up; in both cases solely for the purpose of pleasing his Britannic Majesty.

Towards the end of this year, 1720, the Duc de Brissac married Mlle. Pecoil, a very rich heiress, whose father was a 'maitre des requetes', and whose mother was daughter of Le Gendre, a very wealthy merchant of Rouen. The father of Mlle. Pecoil was a citizen of Lyons, a wholesale dealer, and extremely avaricious. He had a large iron safe, or strong- box, filled with money, in a cellar, shut in by an iron door, with a secret lock, and to arrive at which other doors had to be passed through. He disappeared so long one day, that his wife and two or three valets or servants that he had sought him everywhere. They well knew that he had a hiding-place, because they had sometimes seen him descending into his cellar, flat-candlestick in hand, but no one had ever dared to follow him.

Wondering what had become of him, they descended to the cellar, broke open the doors, and found at last the iron one. They were obliged to send for workmen to break it open, by attacking the wall in which it was fixed. After much labour they entered, and found the old miser dead in his strong-box, the secret spring of which he had apparently not been able to find, after having locked himself in; a horrible end in every respect.

The Brissacs have not been very particular in their alliances for some time, and yet appear no richer. The gold flies away; the dross remains.

I had almost forgotten to say that in the last day of this year, 1720, a Prince of Wales was born at Rome.

The Prince was immediately baptised by the Bishop; of Montefiascone, and named Charles. The event caused a great stir in the Holy City. The Pope sent his compliments to their Britannic Majesties, and forwarded to the King of England (the Pretender) 10,000 Roman crowns, gave him, for his life, a country house at Albano, which until then, he had only lent him, and 2000 crowns to furnish it. A Te Deum was sung in the chapel of the Pope, in his presence, and there were rejoicings at Rome. When the Queen of England was able to see company, Cardinal Tanora came in state, as representative of the Sacred College, to congratulate her.

The birth of the Prince also made much stir at the Court of England, and among the priests and Jacobites of that country. For very different reasons, not only the Catholics and Protestants, enemies of the government, were ravished at it, but nearly all the three realms showed as much joy as they dared; not from any attachment to the dethroned house, but for the satisfaction of seeing a line continue with which they could always menace and oppose their kings and the royal family.

Jacobites Drinking to the Pretender--painted by F. Willems

In France we were afraid to show any public feeling upon the event. We were too much in the hands of England; the Regent and Dubois too much the humble servants of the house of Hanover; Dubois especially, waiting, as he was, so anxiously for his cardinal's hat. He did not, as will be seen, have to wait much longer.

The new Pope had given, in writing, a promise to Dubois, that if elected to the chair of St.

Peter he would make him cardinal. Time had flown, and the promise was not yet fulfilled. The impatience of Dubois increased with his hopes, and gave him no repose. He was much bewildered when he learnt that, on the 16th of June, 1721, the Pope had elevated to the cardinalship; his brother, who for ten years had been Bishop of Terracine and Benedictine monk of Mount Cassini. Dubois had expected that no promotion would be made in which he was not included. But here was a promotion of a single person only. He was furious; this fury did not last long, however; a month after, that is to say, on the 16th of July, the Pope made him cardinal with Dion Alexander Alboni, nephew of the deceased Pope, and brother of the Cardinal Camarlingue.

Dubois received the news and the compliment that followed with extreme joy, but managed to contain himself with some little decency, and to give all the honour of his nomination to M. le Duc d'Orleans, who, sooth to say, had had scarcely anything to do with it. But he could not prevent himself from saying to everybody that what honoured him more than the Roman purple was the unanimous eagerness of all the European powers to procure him this distinction; to press the Pope to award it; to desire that his promotion would be hastened without waiting for their nominations. He incessantly blew these reports about everywhere without ever being out of breath; but nobody was the dupe of them.

Shortly after this, that is, on the last day of July, the King, who had until then been in perfect health, woke with headache and pain in the throat; shivering followed, and towards afternoon, the pains in the head and throat being augmented, he went to bed. I repaired the next day about twelve to inquire after him. I found he had passed a bad night, and that within the last two hours he had grown worse. I saw everywhere consternation. I had the grandes entrees, therefore I went into his chamber. I found it very empty. M. le Duc d'Orleans, seated in the chimney corner, looked exceedingly downcast and solitary. I approached him for a moment, then I went to the King's bed. At this moment Boulduc, one of the apothecaries, gave him something to take. The Duchesse de la Ferme, who, through the Duchesse de Ventadour, her sister, had all the entrees as godmother to the King, was at the heels of Boulduc, and turning round to see who was approaching, saw me, and immediately said in a tone neither high nor low, "He is poisoned! he is poisoned!"

"Hold your tongue, Madame," said I. "This is terrible."

But she kept on, and spoke so loudly that I feared the King would hear her. Boulduc and I looked at each other, and I immediately withdrew from the bed and from this mad woman, with whom I was in no way familiar. During this illness, which lasted only five days (but of which the first three were violent) I was much troubled, but at the same time I was exceedingly glad that I had refused to be the King's governor, though the Regent had over and over again pressed me to accept the office. There were too many evil reports in circulation against M. le Duc d'Orleans for me to dream of filling this position. For was I not his bosom friend known to have been on the most intimate terms with him ever since his child hood—and if anything had happened to excite new suspicions against him, what would not have been said? The thought of this so troubled me during the King's illness, that I used to wake in the night with a start, and, oh, what joy was mine when I remembered that I had not this duty on my head!

The malady, as I have said, was not long, and the convalescence was prompt, which restored tranquillity and joy, and caused an overflow of Te Deums and rejoicing. Helvetius had all the honour of the cure; the doctors had lost their heads, he preserved his, and obstinately proposed bleeding at the foot, at a consultation at which M. le Duc d'Orleans was present; his advice prevailed, change for the better immediately took place, cure soon after.

The Marechal de Villeroy (the King's governor) did not let slip this occasion for showing all his venom and his baseness; he forgot nothing, left nothing undone in order to fix suspicion upon M. le Duc d'Orleans, and thus pay his court to the robe. No magistrate, however unimportant, could come to the Tuileries whom he did not himself go to with the news of the King and caresses; whilst to the first nobles he was inaccessible. The magistrates of higher standing he allowed to enter at all times into the King's chamber, even to stand by his bed in order to see him, while they who had the 'grandes entrees' with difficulty enjoyed a similar privilege.

He did the same during the first days of convalescence, which he prolonged as much as possible, in order to give the same distinction to the magistrates, come at what time they might, and privately to the great people of the Court and the ambassadors. He fancied himself a tribune of the people, and aspired to their favour and their dangerous power. From this he turned to other affectations which had the same aim against M. le Duc d'Orleans. He multiplied the Te Deums that he induced the various ranks of petty officers of the King to have sung on different days and in different churches; he attended all, took with him as many people as he could, and for six weeks continued this game. A Te Deum was sung in every church in Paris. He spoke of nothing else, and above the real joy he felt at the King's recovery, he put on a false one which had a party smell about it, and which avowed designs not to be mistaken.

The King went in state to Notre Dame and Saint Genevieve to thank God. These mummeries, thus prolonged, extended to the end of August and the fete Saint-Louis. Each year there, is on that day a concert in the garden. The Marechal de Villeroy took care that on this occasion, the concert should become a species of fete, to which he added a display of fireworks. Less than this would have been enough to draw the crowd. It was so great that a pin could not have fallen to the ground through the mass of people wedged against each other in the garden. The windows of the Tuileries were ornamented, and were filled with people. All the roofs of the Carrousel, as well as the Place, were covered with spectators.

The Marechal de Villeroy was in; his element, and importuned the King, who tried to hide himself in the corners at every moment. The Marechal took him by the arm, and led him, now to the windows where he could see the Carrousel, and the houses covered with people; now to those which looked upon the garden, full of the innumerable crowd waiting for the fete. Everybody cried 'Vive le Roi!' when he appeared, but had not the Marechal detained him, he would have run away and hid himself.

"Look, my master," the Marechal would say, "all that crowd, all these people are yours, all belong to you; you are the master of them: look at them a little therefore, to please them, for they are all yours, they are all devoted to you."

A nice lesson this for a governor to give to a young King, repeating it every time he leads him to the windows, so fearful is he lest the boy- sovereign shall forget it! I do not know whether he received similar lessons from those who had the charge of his education. At last the Marechal led him upon the terrace, where, beneath a dais, he heard the end of the concert, and afterwards saw the fireworks. The lesson of the Marechal de Villeroy, so often and so publicly repeated, made much stir, and threw but little honour upon him. He himself experienced the first effect of is fine instruction.

M. le Duc d'Orleans conducted himself in a manner simple, so prudent, that he infinitely gained by it. His cares and his reasonable anxiety were measured; there was much reserve in his conversation, an exact and sustained attention in his language, and in his countenance, which allowed nothing to escape him, and which showed as little as possible that he was the successor to the crown; above all, he never gave cause for people to believe that he thought the King's illness more or less serious than it was, or that his hopes were stronger than his fears.

He could not but feel that in a conjuncture so critical, all eyes were fixed upon him, and as in truth he never wished for the crown (however unlikely the statement may seem), he had no need to constrain himself in any way, but simply to be measured in his bearing. His conduct was, in fact, much remarked, and the cabal opposed to him entirely reduced to silence. Nobody spoke to him upon the event that might happen, not even his most familiar friends and acquaintances, myself included; and at this he was much pleased. He acted entirely upon the suggestions of his own good sense.

This was not the first time, let me add, that the Marechal de Villeroy, in his capacity of governor of the King, had tacitly insulted M. le Duc d'Orleans. He always, in fact, affected, in the discharge of his duties, a degree of care, vigilance, and scrutiny, the object of which was evident. He was particularly watchful of the food of the King, taking it up with his own hands, and making a great show of this precaution; as though the King could not have been poisoned a thousand times over in spite of such ridiculous care. 'Twas because M. le Duc d'Orleans was vexed with this childish behaviour, so calculated to do him great injury, that he wished me to supersede the Marechal de Villeroy as governor of the King. This, as before said, I would never consent to. As for the Marechal, his absurdities met with their just reward, but at a date I have not yet come to.

CHAPTER CVI

Before this illness of the King, that is to say, at the commencement of June, I went one day to work with M, le Duc d'Orleans, and found him alone, walking up and down the grand apartment.

"Holloa! there," said he, as soon as he saw me; then, taking me by the hand, "I cannot leave you in ignorance of a thing which I desire above all others, which is of the utmost importance to me, and which will cause you as much joy as me; but you must keep it profoundly secret." Then bursting out laughing, "If M. de Cambrai knew that I had told it to you, he would never pardon me." And he proceeded to state that perfect reconciliation had been established between himself and the King and Queen of Spain; that arrangements had been made by which our young King was to marry the Infanta of Spain, as soon as he should be old enough; and the Prince of the Asturias (the heir to the Spanish throne) was to marry Mademoiselle de Chartres, the Regent's daughter.

If my joy at this was great, my astonishment was even greater; M. le Duc d'Orleans embraced me, and the first surprise over, I asked him how he had contrived to bring about these marriages; above all, that of his daughter. He replied that it had all been done in a trice by the Abbe Dubois, who was a regular devil when once he had set his mind upon anything; that the King of Spain had been transported at the idea of the King of France marrying the Infanta; and that the marriage of the Prince of the Asturias had been the 'sine qua non' of the other.

After we had well talked over the matter and rejoiced thereon, I said to the Regent that the proposed marriage of his daughter must be kept profoundly secret until the moment of her departure for Spain; and that of the King also, until the time for their execution arrived; so as to prevent the jealousy of all Europe. At this union, so grand and so intimate, of the two branches of the royal family, such a union having always been the terror of Europe and disunion the object of all its policy—this policy having only too well succeeded—I urged that the sovereigns must be left as long as possible in the confidence they had acquired, the Infanta above all, being but three years old (she was born at Madrid on the morning of the 30th of March, 1718), by which means the fears of Europe upon the marriage of Mademoiselle de Chartres with the Prince of the Asturias would be coloured—the Prince could wait, he having been born in August, 1707, and being accordingly only fourteen years of age. "You are quite right," replied M. le Duc d'Orleans, "but this can't be, because in Spain they wish to make public the declarations of marriage at once, indeed, as soon as the demand is made and the declaration can be signed."

"What madness!" cried I; "what end can this tocsin have except to arouse all Europe and put it in movement! They must be made to understand this, and we must stick to it; nothing is so important."

"All this is true," said M. le Duc d'Orleans. "I think exactly like you, but they are obstinate in Spain; they have wished matters to be arranged thus, and their wishes have been agreed to. Everything is arranged, fixed, finished. I am so much interested in the matter that you surely would not have advised me to break off for this condition."

I said of course not, shrugging my shoulders at his unseasonable impatience.

During the discussion which followed, I did not forget to think of myself, the occasion being so opportune for making the fortunes of my second son. I remembered then, that as matters were advanced to this point, a special ambassador must be sent to Spain, to ask the hand of the Infanta for the King, and to sign the compact of marriage; that the ambassador must be a nobleman of mark and title, and thus I begged the Duke to give me this commission, with a recommendation to the King of Spain, so as to make my second son, the Marquis of Ruffec, grandee of Spain.

M. le Duc d'Orleans scarcely allowed me to finish, immediately accorded me what I had asked, promised me the recommendation with many expressions of friendship, and asked me to keep the whole matter secret, and make no preparation that would disclose it.

I knew well enough why he enjoined me to secrecy. He wished to have the time to make Dubois swallow this pill. My thanks expressed, I asked him two favours; first, not to pay me as an ambassador, but to give me a round sum sufficient to provide for all my expenses without ruining myself; second, not to entrust any business to me which might necessitate a long stay in Spain, inasmuch as I did not wish to quit him, and wanted to go to Spain simply for the purpose of obtaining the honour above alluded to for my second son. The fact is, I feared that Dubois, not being able to hinder my embassy, might keep me in Spain in a sort of exile, under pretence of business, in order to get rid of me altogether. Events proved that my precaution was not altogether useless.

M. le Duc d'Orleans accorded both the favours I asked, with many obliging remarks, and a hope that my absence would not be long. I thought I had then done great things for my family, and went home much pleased. But, mon Dieu! what are the projects and the successes of men!

Dubois, as I expected, was vexed beyond measure at my embassy, and resolved to ruin me and throw me into disgrace. I was prepared for this, and I soon saw it was so. At first, I received from him nothing but professions of friendship and of attachment for me, congratulations that M. le Duc d'Orleans had accorded to me an embassy my merit deserved, and which would be productive of such useful results for my children. He took care, however, in the midst of these fine phrases, to introduce not one word upon my arrangements, so that he might be able to drive me into a corner at the last moment, and cause me all the inconvenience possible. He slipped through my hands like an eel until the moment for my departure drew near. As he saw it approach, he began to preach to me of magnificence, and wished to enter into details respecting my suite. I described it to him, and everybody else would have been satisfied, but as his design was to ruin me, he cried out against it, and augmented it by a third. I represented to him the excessive expense this augmentation would cause, the state of the finances, the loss upon the exchange: his sole reply was that the dignity of the King necessitated this expense and show; and that his Majesty would bear the charge. I spoke to M. le Duc d'Orleans, who listened to me with attention, but being persuaded by the Cardinal, held the same language.

This point settled, the Cardinal must needs know how many coats I should take, and how many I should give to my sons.—in a word, there was not a single detail of table or stable that he did not enter into, and that he did not double. My friends exhorted me not to be obstinate with a man so impetuous, so dangerous, so completely in possession of M. le Duc d'Orleans, pointing out to me that when once I was away he might profit by my absence, and that, meanwhile, everything relating to my embassy must pass through his hands. All this was only too true. I was obliged, therefore, to yield, although I felt that, once embarked, the King's purse would be spared at the expense of mine.

As soon as the marriages were declared, I asked to be declared as ambassador, so that I might openly make my preparations, which, it will be remembered, I had been forbidden to do. Now that there was no secret about the marriage, I fancied there need be no secret as to the ambassador by whom they were to be conducted. I was deceived: Whatever I might allege, the prohibition remained. The Cardinal wished to put me to double the necessary expense, by compelling me to have my liveries, dresses, etc., made in the utmost precipitation; and this happened. He thought, too, I should not be able to provide myself with everything in time; and that he might represent this to M. le Duc d'Orleans, and in Spain, as a fault, and excite envious cries against me.

Nevertheless, I did not choose to press him: to announce my embassy, at the same time trying to obtain from him the instructions I was to receive, and which, passing through him and the Regent done, told nothing to the public, as my preparations would have done. But I could not obtain them. Dubois carelessly replied to me, that in one or two conversations the matter would be exhausted. He wished me to know nothing, except vaguely; to leave no time for reflection, for questions, for explanations; and to throw me thus into embarrassments, and to cause me to commit blunders which he intended to make the most of.

At last, tired of so many and such dangerous postponements, I went on Tuesday, the 23rd of September, to M. le Duc d'Orleans, arranging my visit so that it took place when he was in his apartments at the Tuileries; there I spoke with such effect, that he said I had only to show myself to the King. He led me to his Majesty at once, and there and then my embassy was announced. Upon leaving the King's cabinet, M. le Duc d'Orleans made me jump into his coach, which was waiting for him, and took me to the Palais Royal, where we began to speak seriously upon the affairs of my embassy.

I fancy that Cardinal Dubois was much annoyed at what had been done, and that he would have liked to postpone the declaration yet a little longer. But this now was impossible. The next day people were sent to work upon my equipments, the Cardinal showing as much eagerness and impatience respecting them, as he had before shown apathy and indifference. He urged on the workmen; must needs see each livery and each coat as it was finished; increased the magnificence of each; and had all my coats and those of my children sent to him. At last, the hurry to make me set out was so great, that such of the things as were ready he sent on by rapid conveyance to Bayonne, at a cost by no means trifling to me.

The Cardinal next examined the list of persons I intended to have with me, and approved it. To my extreme surprise he said, however, that I must add forty officers of cavalry and infantry, from the regiments of my sons. I cried out against the madness and the expense of such a numerous military accompaniment. I represented that it was not usual for ambassadors, with a peaceful mission, to take with them such an imposing force by way of escort; I showed that these officers, being necessarily gay men, might be led away into indiscreet gallantries, which would give me more trouble than all the business of my embassy. Nothing could be more evident, true, and reasonable than my representations, nothing more useless or worse received.

The Cardinal had resolved to ruin me, and to leave me in Spain with all the embarrassment, business, and annoyances he could. He rightly thought that nothing was more likely to make him succeed than to charge me with forty officers. Not finding them, I took only twenty-nine, and if the Cardinal succeeded as far as concerned my purse, I was so fortunate, and these gentlemen were so discreet, that he succeeded in no other way.

Let me add here, before I give the details of my journey to Spain, in what manner the announcement of these two marriages was received by the King and the public.

His Majesty was by no means gratified when he heard that a wife had been provided for him. At the first mention of marriage he burst out crying. The Regent, M. le Duc, and M. de Frejus, had all the trouble in the world to extract a "yes" from him, and to induce him to attend the Regency Council, in which it was necessary that he should announce his consent to the proposed union, or be present while it was announced for him. The council was held, and the King came to it, his eyes swollen and red, and his look very serious.

Some moments of silence passed, during which M. le Duc d'Orleans threw his eyes over all the company (who appeared deeply expectant), and then fixed them on the King, and asked if he might announce to the council the marriage of his Majesty. The King replied by a dry "yes," and in a rather low tone, but which was heard by the four or five people on each side of him, and the Regent immediately announced the marriage. Then, after taking the opinions of the council, which were for the most part favorable, he turned towards the King with a smiling air, as though inviting him to assume the same, and said, "There, then, Sire, your marriage is approved and passed, and a grand and fortunate matter finished." The council then broke up.

The news of what had taken place immediately ran over all Paris. The Tuileries and the Palais Royal were soon filled with people who came to present themselves before the King to compliment him and the Regent on the conclusion of this grand marriage, and the crowd continued the following days. The King had much difficulty in assuming some little gaiety the first day, but on the morrow he was less sombre, and by degrees he quite recovered himself.

M. le Duc d'Orleans took care not to announce the marriage of his daughter with the Prince of the Asturias at the same time that the other marriage was announced. He declared it, however, the next day, and the news was received with the utmost internal vexation by the cabal opposed to him. Men, women, people of all conditions who belonged to that cabal, lost all countenance. It was a pleasure to me, I admit, to look upon them. They were utterly disconcerted. Nevertheless, after the first few days of overthrow, they regained courage, and set to work in order to break off both the marriages.

CHAPTER CVII

I have already said that Dubois looked most unfavourably upon my embassy to Spain, and that I saw he was determined to do all in his power to throw obstacles in its way. I had fresh proofs of this. First, before my departure: when he gave me my written instructions, he told me that in Spain I must take precedence of everybody during the signing of the King's contract of marriage, and at the chapel, at the two ceremonies of the marriage of the Prince of the Asturias, allowing no one to be before me!

I represented to him that the Pope's nuncio would be present, and that to him the ambassadors of France gave place everywhere, and even the ambassadors of the Emperor also, who, without opposition, preceded those of the King. He replied that that was true, except in special cases like the present, and that his instructions must be obeyed: My surprise was great at so strange an order. I tried to move him by appealing to his pride; asking him how I should manage with a cardinal, if one happened to be present, and with the majordomo-major, who corresponds, but in a very superior degree, with our grand master of France. He flew in a rage, and declared that I must precede the majordomo-major also; that there would be no difficulty in doing so; and that, as to the cardinals, I should find none. I shrugged my shoulders, and begged him to think of the matter. Instead of replying, to me, he said he had forgotten to acquaint me with a most essential particular: it was, that I must take care not to visit anybody until I had been first visited.

I replied that the visiting question had not been forgotten in my instructions, and that those instructions were to the effect that I should act in this respect as the Duc de Saint-Aignan had acted, and that the usage he had followed was to pay the first visit to the Minister of Foreign Affairs, and to the Councillors of State (when there were any), who are the same as are known here under the name of ministers. Thereupon he broke out afresh, prated, talked about the dignity of the King, and did not allow me the opportunity of saying another word. I abridged my visit, therefore, and went away.

However strange might appear to me these verbal orders of such a new kind, I thought it best to speak to the Duc de Saint-Aignan and Amelot on the subject, so as to convince myself of their novelty. Both these ambassadors, as well as those who had preceded them, had visited in an exactly opposite manner; and they thought it extravagant that I should precede the nuncio, no matter where. Amelot told me, moreover, that I should suffer all sorts of annoyances, and succeed in nothing, if I refused the first visit to the Minister of Foreign Affairs; that as for the Councillors of State, they existed only in name, the office having fallen into desuetude; and that I must pay other visits to certain officers he named (three in number), who would be justly offended and piqued if I refused them what every one who had preceded me had rendered them. He added that I had better take good care to do so, unless I wished to remain alone in my house, and have the cold shoulder turned upon me by every principal person of the Court.

By this explanation of Amelot I easily comprehended the reason of these singular verbal orders. The Cardinal wished to secure my failure in Spain, and my disgrace in France: in Spain by making me offend at the outset all the greatest people and the minister through whose hands all my business would pass; draw upon myself thus complaints here, which, as I had no written orders to justify my conduct, he (Dubois) would completely admit the justice of, and then disavow me, declaring he had given me exactly opposite orders. If I did not execute what he had told me, I felt that he would accuse me of sacrificing the King's honour and the dignity of the Crown, in order to please in Spain, and obtain thus honours for myself and my sons, and that he would prohibit the latter to. accept them. There would have been less uproar respecting the nuncio; but if I preceded him, Dubois felt persuaded that the Court of Rome would demand justice; and this justice in his hands would have been a shameful recall.

My position appeared so difficult, that I resolved to leave nothing undone in order to change it. I thought M. le Duc d'Orleans would not resist the evidence I should bring forward, in order to show the extraordinary nature of Dubois' verbal instructions: I deceived myself. It was in vain that I spoke to M. le Duc d'Orleans. I found nothing but feebleness under the yoke of a master; by which I judged how much I could hope for during my absence. Several times I argued with him and the Cardinal; but in vain. They both declared that if preceding ambassadors had paid the first visits, that was no example for me, in an embassy so solemn and distinguished as that I was about to execute. I represented that, however solemn and however distinguished might be my embassy, it gave me no rank superior to that of extraordinary ambassadors, and that I could claim none. Useless! useless! To my arguments there was no reply, but obstinacy prevailed; and I clearly saw the extreme malignity of the valet, and the unspeakable weakness of the master. It was for me to manage as I could.

The Cardinal now began ardently to press my departure; and, in fact, there was no more time to lose. He unceasingly hurried on the workmen who were making all that I required,—vexed, perhaps, that being in such prodigious number, he could not augment them. There was nothing more for him to do but to give me the letters with which I was to be charged. He delayed writing them until the last moment previous to my departure, that is to say; the very evening before I started; the reason will soon be seen. The letters were for their Catholic Majesties, for the Queen Dowager at Bayonne, and for the Prince of the Asturias; letters from the King and from the Duc d'Orleans. But before giving them to me, the Regent said he would write two letters to the Prince of the Asturias, both alike, except in this respect, that in the one he would address the Prince as "nephew," and in the other as "brother and nephew," and that I was to try and deliver the latter, which he passionately wished; but that if I found too much difficulty in doing so, I must not persevere but deliver the former instead.

I had reason to believe that here was another plot of Dubois, to cause me trouble by embroiling me with M. le Duc d'Orleans. The Regent was the last man in the world to care for these formalities. The Prince of the Asturias was son of the King and heir to the Crown, and, in consequence, of the rank of a son of France. In whatever way regarded, M. le Duc d'Orleans was extremely inferior in rank to him; and it was something new and adventurous to treat him on terms of equality. This, however, is what I was charged with, and I believe, in the firm hope of Cardinal Dubois that I should fail, and that he might profit by my failure.

Finally, on the morning of the day before my departure, all the papers with which I was to be charged were brought to me. I will not give the list of them. But among these letters there was none from the King to the Infanta! I thought they had forgotten to put it with the others. I said so to the persons who brought them to me. What was my surprise when they told me that the letter was not written, but that I would have it in the course of the day.

This appeared so strange to me, that my mind was filled with suspicion. I spoke of the letter to the Cardinal and to M. le Duc d'Orleans, who assured me that I should have it in the evening. At midnight it had not arrived. I wrote to the Cardinal. Finally I set out without it. He wrote to me, saying I should receive it before arriving at Bayonne; but nothing less. I wrote him anew. He replied to me, saying that I should have it before I arrived at Madrid. A letter from the King to the Infanta was not difficult to write; I could not doubt, therefore, that there was some design in this delay. Whatever it might be, I could not understand it, unless the intention was to send the letter afterwards, and make me pass for a heedless fellow who had lost the first.

Dubois served me another most impudent turn, seven or eight days before my departure. He sent word to me, by his two devoted slaves, Le Blanc and Belleisle, that as he had the foreign affairs under his charge, he must have the post, which he would not and could not any longer do without; that he knew I was the intimate friend of Torcy (who had the post in his department), whose resignation he desired; that he begged me to write to Torcy, and send my letter to him by an express courier to Sable (where he had gone on an excursion); that he should see by my conduct on this occasion, and its success, in what manner he could count upon me, and that he should act towards me accordingly. To this his two slaves added all they could to persuade me to comply, assuring me that Dubois would break off my embassy if I did not do as he wished. I did not for a moment doubt, after what I had seen of the inconceivable feebleness of M. le Duc d'Orleans, that Dubois was really capable of thus affronting and thwarting me, or that I should have no aid from the Regent. At the same time I resolved to run all hazards rather than lend myself to an act of violence against a friend, so sure; so sage, and so virtuous, and who had served the state with such reputation, and deserved so well of it.

I replied therefore to these gentlemen that I thought the commission very strange, and much more so their reasoning of it; that Torcy was not a man from whom an office of this importance could be taken unless he wished to give it up; that all I could do was to ask him if he wished to resign, and if so, on what conditions; that as to exhorting him to resign, I could do nothing of the kind, although I was not ignorant of what this refusal might cost me and my embassy. They tried in vain to reason with me; all they could obtain was this firm resolution.

Castries and his brother, the Archbishop, were intimate friends of Torcy and of myself. I sent for them to come to me in the midst of the tumult of my departure. They immediately came, and I related to them what had just happened. They were more indignant at the manner and the moment, than at the thing itself; for Torcy knew that sooner or later the Cardinal would strip him of the post for his own benefit. They extremely praised my reply, exhorted me to send word to Torcy, who was on the point of departing from Sable, or had departed, and who would make his own terms with M. le Duc d'Orleans much more advantageously, present, than absent. I read to them the letter I had written to Torcy, while waiting for them, which they much approved, and which I at once despatched.

Torcy of himself, had hastened his return. My courier found him with his wife in the Parc of Versailles, having passed by the Chartres route. He read my letter, charged the courier with many compliments for me (his wife did likewise), and told me to say he would see me the next day. I informed M. Castries of his arrival. We all four met the next day. Torcy warmly appreciated my conduct, and, to his death, we lived on terms of the greatest intimacy, as may be imagined when I say that he committed to me his memoirs (these he did not write until long after the death of M. le Duc d'Orleans), with which I have connected mine. He did not seem to care for the post, if assured of an honourable pension.

I announced then his return to Dubois, saying it would be for him and M. le Duc d'Orleans to make their own terms with him, and get out of the matter in this way. Dubois, content at seeing by this that Torcy consented to resign the post, cared not how, so that the latter made his own arrangements, and all passed off with the best grace on both sides. Torcy had some money and 60,000 livres pension during life, and 20,000 for his wife after him. This was arranged before my departure and was very well carried out afterwards.

A little while after the declaration of the marriage, the Duchesse de Ventadour and Madame de Soubise, her granddaughter, had been named, the one governess of the Infanta, the other successor to the office; and they were both to go and meet her at the frontier, and bring her to Paris to the Louvre, where she was to be lodged a little while after the declaration of my embassy: the Prince de Rohan, her son-in-law, had orders to go and make the exchange of the Princesses upon the frontier, with the people sent by the King of Spain to perform the same function. I had never had any intimacy with them, though we were not on bad terms. But these Spanish commissions caused us to visit each other with proper politeness. I forgot to say so earlier and in the proper place.

At last, viz., on the 23rd of October, 1721, I set out, having with me the Comte de Lorge, my children, the Abbe de Saint-Simon, and his brother, and many others. The rest of the company joined me at Blaye. We slept at Orleans, at Montrichard; and at Poictiers. On arriving at Conte my berline broke down. This caused a delay of three hours, and I did not arrive at Ruffec until nearly midnight. Many noblemen of the neighbourhood were waiting for me there, and I entertained them at dinner and supper during the two days I stayed. I experienced real pleasure in embracing Puy-Robert, who was lieutenant-colonel of the Royal Roussillon Regiment when I was captain.

From Ruffec I went in two days to La Cassine, a small house at four leagues from Blaye, which my father had built on the borders of his marshes of Blaye, and which I felt much pleasure in visiting; I stopped there during All Saints' Day and the evening before, and the next day I early betook myself to Blaye again, where I sojourned two days. I found several persons of quality there, many of the nobility of the country and of the adjoining provinces, and Boucher, Intendant of Bordeaux, brother- in-law of Le Blanc, who was waiting for me, and whom I entertained with good cheer morning and evening during this short stay.

We crossed to Bordeaux in the midst of such bad weather that everybody pressed me to delay the trip; but I had so few, days at my command that I did not accede to their representations. Boucher had brought his brigantine magnificently equipped, and boats enough to carry over all my company, most of whom went with us. The view of the port and the town of Bordeaux surprised me, with more than three hundred ships of all nations ranged in two lines upon my passage, decked out in all their finery, and with a great noise from their cannons and those of the Chateau Trompette.

Bordeaux is too well known to need description at my hands: I will simply say that after Constantinople it presents the finest view of any other port. Upon landing we received many compliments, and found many carriages, which conducted us to the Intendant's house, where the Jurats came to compliment me in state dress. I invited them to supper with. me, a politeness they did not expect, and which they appeared to highly appreciate. I insisted upon going to see the Hotel de Ville, which is amazingly ugly, saying to the Jurats that it was not to satisfy my curiosity, but in order to pay a visit to them, that I went. This extremely pleased.

After thanking M. and Madame Boucher for their attention, we set out again, traversed the great Landes, and reached in due time Bayonne. The day after my arrival there, I had an audience with the Queen Dowager of Spain. I was astonished upon arriving at her house. It had only two windows in front, looked upon a little court, and had but trifling depth. The room I entered was very plainly furnished. I found the Queen, who was waiting for me, accompanied by the Duchesse de Linorez and very few other persons. I complimented her in the name of the King, and presented to her his letter. Nothing could be more polite than her bearing towards me.

Passing the Pyrenees, I quitted with France, rain and bad weather, and found a clear sky, a charming temperature, with views and perspectives which changed at each moment, and which were not less charming. We were all mounted upon mules, the pace of which is good but easy. I turned a little out of my way to visit Loyola, famous by the birth of Saint Ignatius, and situated all alone in a narrow valley. We found there four or five Jesuits, very polite and instructed, who took care of the prodigious building erected there for more than a hundred Jesuits and numberless scholars. A church was there nearly finished, of rotunda shape, of a grandeur and size which surprised me. Gold, painting, sculpture, the richest ornaments of all kinds, are distributed everywhere with prodigality but taste. The architecture is correct and admirable, the marble is most exquisite; jasper, porphyry, lapis, polished, wreathed, and fluted columns, with their capitals and their ornaments of gilded bronze, a row of balconies between each altar with little steps of marble to ascend them, and the cage encrusted; the altars and that which accompanied them admirable. In a word, the church was one of the most superb edifices in Europe, the best kept up, and the most magnificently adorned. We took there the best chocolate I ever tasted, and, after some hours of curiosity and admiration, we regained our road.

On the 15th, we arrived at Vittoria, where I found a deputation of the province, whom I invited to supper, and the next day to breakfast. They spoke French and I was surprised to see Spaniards so gay and such good company at table. Joy on account of my journey burst out in every place through which I passed in France and Spain, and obtained for me a good reception. At Salinas, among other towns which I passed through without stopping, ladies, who, to judge by their houses and by themselves, appeared to me to be quality folks, asked me with such good grace to let them see the man who was bringing happiness to Spain, that I thought it would only be proper gallantry to enter their dwellings. They appeared ravished, and I had all the trouble in the world to get rid of them, and to continue my road.

I arrived on the 18th at Burgos, where I meant to stay at least one day, to see what turn would take a rather strong fever which had seized my eldest son; but I was so pressed to hasten on that I was obliged to leave my son behind with nearly all his attendants.

I left Burgos therefore on the 19th. We found but few relays, and those ill-established. We travelled night and day without going to bed, until we reached Madrid, using such vehicles as we could obtain. I performed the last twelve leagues on a posthorse, which cost twice as much as in France. In this manner we arrived in Madrid on Friday, the 21st, at eleven o'clock at night.

We found at the entrance of the town (which has neither gates nor walls, neither barriers nor faubourgs,) people on guard, who asked us who we were, and whence we came. They had been placed there expressly so as to know the moment of my arrival. As I was much fatigued by travelling incessantly from Burgos without stopping, I replied that we were the people of the Ambassador of France, who would arrive the next day.

I learnt afterwards, that the minister had calculated that I could not reach Madrid before the 22d.

CHAPTER CVIII

Early the next morning I received a visit from Grimaldo, Minister of Foreign Affairs, who, overjoyed at my arrival, had announced it to their Catholic Majesties before coming to me. Upon his example, apparently, the three other ministers, whom, according to usage, I ought to have visited first, came also; so that one infamous difficulty which Cardinal Dubois had placed in my path was happily overcome without effort on my part.

Grimaldo at once conducted me to the palace, and introduced me to the King. I made a profound reverence to him; he testified to me his joy at my arrival, and asked me for news of the King, of M. le Duc d'Orleans, of my journey, and of my eldest son, whom, as he knew, I had left behind at Burgos. He then entered alone into the Cabinet of the Mirrors. I was instantly surrounded by all the Court with compliments and indications of joy at the marriages and union of the crowns. Nearly all the seigneurs spoke French, and I had great difficulty in replying to their numberless compliments.

A half quarter of an hour after the King had entered his cabinet, he sent for me. I entered alone into the Hall of Mirrors, which is very vast, but much less wide than long. The King, with the Queen on his left, was nearly at the bottom of the salon, both their Majesties standing and touching each other. I approached with three profound reverences, and I will remark, once for all, that the King never covers himself except at public audiences, and when he goes to and comes from his mass. The audience lasted half an hour, and was principally occupied, on the part of the King and Queen, with compliments and expressions of joy at the marriages that were to take place. At its close, the Queen asked me if I would like to see the children, and conducted me to them.

I never saw prettier boys than Don Carlos and Don Ferdinand, nor a prettier babe than Don Philip. The King and Queen took pleasure in making me look at them, and in making them turn and walk before me with very good grace. Their Majesties entered afterwards into the Infanta's chamber, where I tried to exhibit as much gallantry as possible. In fact, the Infanta was charming-like a little woman—and not at all embarrassed. The Queen said to me that she already had begun to learn French, and the King that she would soon forget Spain.

"Oh!" cried the Queen, "not only Spain, but the King and me, so as to attach herself to the King, her husband, alone." Upon this I tried not to remain dumb, and to say what was appropriate. Their Majesties dismissed me with much goodness, and I was again encircled by the crowd with many compliments.

A few moments after the King recalled me, in order to see the Prince of the Asturias, who was with their Majesties in the same Hall of Mirrors. I found him tall, and really made to be painted; fine light-brown hair, light fresh-coloured complexion, long face, but agreeable; good eyes, but too near the nose. I found in him also much grace and politeness. He particularly asked after the King, M. le Duc d'Orleans, and Mademoiselle de Montpensier, to whom he was to be betrothed.

Their Catholic Majesties testified much satisfaction to me at the diligence I had used; said that a single day would be sufficient for the ceremonies that had to be gone through (demanding the hand of the Infanta, according it, and signing the marriage contract). Afterwards they asked me when all would be ready. I replied it would be any day they pleased; because, as they wished to go into the country, I thought it would be best to throw no delay in their path. They appeared much pleased at this reply, but would not fix the day, upon which I proposed the following Tuesday. Overjoyed at this promptness, they fixed the Thursday for their departure, and left me with the best possible grace.

I had got over one difficulty, as I have shown, that connected with the first visits, but I had others yet to grapple with. And first, there was my embarrassment at finding no letter for the Infanta. I confided this fact to Grimaldo, who burst out laughing, was to have my first audience with the Infanta the next day, and it was then that the letter ought to be produced. Grimaldo said he would arrange so that when I—went, the governess should come into the antechamber, and say that the Infanta was asleep, and upon offering to awake her, I should refuse to allow her, take my leave, and wait until the letter from the King arrived before I visited her again. Everything happened just as it had been planned, and thus the second obstacle which the crafty and malicious Cardinal had put in my path, for the sake of overturning me, was quietly got over. Grimaldo's kindness encouraged me to open my heart under its influence. I found that the Spanish minister knew, quite as, well as I did, what manner of person Dubois was.

On Sunday, the 23rd, I had in the morning my first private audience of the King and Queen, together, in the Hall of Mirrors, which is the place where they usually give it. I was accompanied by Maulevrier, our ambassador. I presented to their Catholic Majesties the Comte de Lorge, the Comte de Cereste, my second son, and the Abbe de Saint-Simon and his bother. I received many marks of goodness from the Queen in this audience.

On Tuesday, the 25th of November, I had my solemn audience. I went to the palace in a magnificent coach, belonging to the King, drawn by eight grey horses, admirably dappled. There were no postillions, and the coachman drove me, his hat under his arm. Five of my coaches filled with my suite followed, and about twenty others (belonging to noblemen of the Court, and sent by them in order to do me honour), with gentlemen in each. The King's coach was surrounded by my musicians, liveried servants on foot, and by officers of my household. On arriving at the open place in front of the palace, I thought myself at the Tuileries. The regiments of Spanish guards, clad, officers and soldiers, like the French guards, and the regiment of the Walloon guards, clad, officers and, soldiers, like the Swiss guards, were under arms; the flags waved, the drums beat, and the officers saluted with the half-pike. On the way, the streets were filled with people, the shops with dealers and artisans, all the windows were crowded. Joy showed itself on every face, and we heard nothing but benedictions.

The audience passed off admirably. I asked the hand of the Infanta in marriage on the part of the King; my request was graciously complied with, compliments passed on both sides, and I returned to my house, well pleased with the reception I had met with from both their Catholic Majesties.

There was still the marriage contract to be signed, and this was to take place in the afternoon. Here was to be my great trial, for the majordomo-major and the nuncio of the Pope were to be present at the ceremony, and, according to the infamous and extraordinary instructions I had received from Dubois, I was to precede them! How was this to be done? I had to bring all my ingenuity to bear upon the subject in order to determine. In the embarrassment I felt upon this position, I was careful to affect the most marked attention to the nuncio and the majordomo-major every time I met them and visited them; so as to take from them all idea that I wished to precede them, when I should in reality do so.

The place the majordomo-major was to occupy at this ceremony was behind the King's armchair, a little to the right, so as to allow room for the captain of the guards on duty; to put myself there would be to take his place, and push the captain of the guards away, and those near him. The place of the nuncio was at the side of the King, his face to the armchair; to take it would have been to push him beyond the arm of the chair, which assuredly he would no more have submitted to than the majordomo-major on the other side. I resolved, therefore, to hazard a middle term; to try and introduce myself at the top of the right arm of the chair, a little sideways, so as to take the place of neither, entirely; but, nevertheless, to drive them out, and to cover this with an air of ignorance and of simplicity; and, at the same time, of eagerness, of joy, of curiosity, of courtier-like desire to speak to the King as much as possible: and all this I exactly executed, in appearance stupidly, and in reality very successfully!

When the time for the audience arrived, I took up my position, accordingly, in the manner I have indicated. The majordomo-major and the nuncio entered, and finding me thus placed, and speaking to the King, appeared much surprised. I heard Signor and Sefor repeated right and left of me, and addressed to me—for both expressed themselves with difficulty in French—and I replied with bows to one and to the other with the smiling air of a man entirely absorbed in joy at his functions, and who understands nothing of what is meant; then I recommenced my conversation with the King, with a sort of liberty and enthusiasm, so that the nuncio and majordomo-major: soon grew tired of appealing to a man whose spirit was so transported that he no longer knew where he was, or what was said to him. In this manner I defeated the craft, cunning, and maliciousness of Dubois. At the conclusion of the ceremony, I accompanied the King and Queen to the door of the Hall of Mirrors, taking good care then to show every deference to the majordomo-major and the nuncio, and yielding place to them, in order to remove any impression from their minds that I had just acted in a contrary manner from design. As soon as their Catholic Majesties had departed, and the door of the salon was closed upon them, I was encircled and, so to speak, almost stifled by the company present, who, one after the other, pressed upon me with the greatest demonstrations of joy and a thousand compliments. I returned home after the ceremony, which had lasted a long time. While I occupied my stolen position I was obliged, in order to maintain it, to keep up an incessant conversation with the King, and at last, no longer knowing what to talk about, I asked him for an audience the next day, which he readily accorded me. But this direct request was contrary to the usage of the Court, where the ambassadors, the other foreign ministers, and the subjects of the country of, whatever rank, address their requests to an officer who is appointed to receive them, who communicates with the King, and names the day and the hour when his Majesty will grant the interview.

Grimaldo, a little after the end of ceremony, had gone to work with the King and Queen, as was customary.—I was surprised, an hour after returning home, to receive a letter from this minister, asking me if I had anything to say to the King I did not wish the Queen to hear, referring to the audience I had asked of the King for the morrow, and begging me to tell him what it was for. I replied to him instantly, that having found the opportunity good I had asked for this audience; but if I had not mentioned the Queen, it was because I had imagined she was so accustomed to be present that there was no necessity to allude to her: but as to the rest, I had my thanks to offer to the King upon what had just passed, and nothing to say to him that I should not wish to say to the Queen, and that I should be very sorry if she were not present.

As I was writing this reply, Don Gaspard Giron invited me to go and see the illuminations of the Place Mayor. I quickly finished my letter; we jumped into a coach, and the principal people of my suite jumped into others. We were conducted by detours to avoid the light of the illuminations in approaching them, and we arrived at a fine house which looks upon the middle of the Place, and which is that where the King and Queen go to see the fetes that take place. We perceived no light in descending or in ascending the staircase. Everything had been closed, but on entering into the chamber which looks upon the Place, we were dazzled, and immediately we entered the balcony speech failed me, from surprise, for more than seven or eight minutes.

This Place is superficially much vaster than any I had ever seen in Paris or elsewhere, and of greater length than breadth. The five stories of the houses which surround it are all of the same level; each has windows at equal distance, and of equal size, with balconies as deep as they are long, guarded by iron balustrades, exactly alike in every case. Upon each of these balconies two torches of white wax were placed, one at each end of the balcony, supported upon the balustrade, slightly leaning outwards, and attached to nothing. The light that this—gives is incredible; it has a splendour and a majesty about it that astonish you and impress you. The smallest type can be read in the middle of the Place, and all about, though the ground-floor is not illuminated.

As soon as I appeared upon the balcony, all the people beneath gathered round and began to cry, Senor! tauro! tauro! The people were asking me to obtain for them a bull-fight, which is what they like best in the world, and what the King had not permitted for several years from conscientious principles. Therefore I contented myself the next day with simply telling him of these cries, without asking any questions thereon, while expressing to him my astonishment at an illumination so surprising and so admirable.

Don Gaspard Giron and the Spaniards who were with me in the house from which I saw the illumination, charmed with the astonishment I had displayed at this spectacle, published it abroad with all the more pleasure because they were not accustomed to the admiration of the French, and many noblemen spoke of it to me with great pleasure. Scarcely had I time to return home and sup after this fine illumination than I was obliged to go to the palace for the ball that the King had prepared there, and which lasted until past two in the morning.

The salon was very vast and splendid;'the dresses of the company were sumptuous; the appearance of our finest fancy-dress balls did not approach the appearance of this.

What seemed strange to me was to see three bishops in lawn sleeves and cloaks in the ball-room, remaining, too, all the evening, and to see the accoutrement of the camerara-mayor, who held exposed in her hand a great chaplet, and who, while talking and criticising the ball and the dancers, muttered her prayers, and continued to do so while the ball lasted. What I found very strange was, that none of the men present (except six special officers and Maulevrier and myself) were allowed to sit, not even the dancers; in fact, there was not a single seat in the whole salon, not even at the back, except those I have specified.

In Spain, men and women of all ages wear all sorts of colours, and dance if they like, even when more than sixty years old, without exciting the slightest ridicule or astonishment. I saw several examples of this among men and women.

Amongst the company present was Madame Robecque, a Frenchwoman, one of the Queen's ladies, whom I had known before she went to Spain. In former days we had danced together at the Court. Apparently she said so to the Queen, for after having danced with one of the children, she traversed the whole length of the salon, made a fine curtsey to their Catholic Majesties, and came to dislodge me from my retreat, asking me with a curtsey and a smile to dance. I replied to her by saying she was laughing at me; dispute, gallantries; finally, she went to the Queen, who called me and told me that the King and she wished me to dance.

I took the liberty to represent to her that she wished to divert herself at my expense; that this order could not be serious; I alleged my age, my position, the number of years since I had danced; in a word, I did all I could to back out. But all was useless. The King mixed himself in the matter; both he and the Queen begged me to comply, tried to persuade me I danced very well; at last commanded me, and in such a manner that I was obliged to obey. I acquitted myself, therefore, as well as I could.

The ball being finished, the Marquis de Villagarcias, one of the majordomos, and one of the most honest and most gracious of men I ever saw (since appointed Viceroy of Peru), would not let me leave until I had rested in the refreshment-room, where he made me drink a glass of excellent neat wine, because I was all in a sweat from the minuets and quadrilles I had gone through, under a very heavy coat.

This same evening and the next I illuminated my house within and without, not having a moment's leisure to give any fete in the midst of the many functions I had been so precipitately called upon to fulfil.

CHAPTER CIX

On Thursday, the 27th of November, the King and Queen were to depart from Madrid to Lerma, a pretty hamlet six leagues from Burgos, where they had a palace. On the same day, very early in the morning, our ambassador, Maulevrier, came to me with despatches from Cardinal Dubois, announcing that the Regent's daughter, Mademoiselle de Montpensier, had departed on the 18th of November for Spain, and giving information as to the places she would stop at, the people she would be accompanied by, the day she would arrive at the frontier, and the persons charged with the exchange of the Princesses.

Maulevrier and I thought this news so important that we felt there was no time to lose, and at once hastened away to the palace to communicate it to their Majesties, who we knew were waiting for it most impatiently. We arrived at such an early hour that all was deserted in the palace, and when we reached the door of the Hall of Mirrors, we were obliged to knock loudly in order to be heard. A French valet opened the door, and told us that their Catholic Majesties were still in bed. We did not doubt it, and begged him to apprise them that we wished to have the honour of speaking to them. Such an honour was unheard of, except under extraordinary circumstances; nevertheless the valet quickly returned, saying that their Majesties would receive us, though it was against all rule and usage to do so while they were in bed.

We traversed therefore the long and grand Hall of Mirrors, turned to the left at the end into a large and fine room, then short off to the left again into a very little chamber, portioned off from the other, and lighted by the door and by two little windows at the top of the partition wall. There was a bed of four feet and a half at most, of crimson damask, with gold fringe, four posts, the curtains open at the foot and at the side the King occupied. The King was almost stretched out upon pillows with a little bed-gown of white satin; the Queen sitting upright, a piece of tapestry in her hand, at the left of the King, some skeins of thread near her, papers scattered upon the rest of the bed and upon an armchair at the side of it. She was quite close to the King, who was in his night-cap, she also, and in her bed-gown, both between the sheets, which were only very imperfectly hidden by the papers.

They made us abridge our reverences, and the King, raising himself a little impatiently, asked us our business. We were alone, the valet having retired after showing us the door.

"Good news, Sire," replied I. "Mademoiselle de Montpensier set out on the 18th; the courier has this instant brought us the news, and we have at once come to present ourselves to you and apprise your Majesties of it."

Joy instantly painted itself on their faces, and immediately they began to question us at great length upon the details the courier had brought us. After an animated conversation, in which Maulevrier took but little part, their Catholic Majesties dismissed us, testifying to us the great pleasure we had caused them by not losing a minute in acquainting them with the departure of Mademoiselle de Montpensier, above all in not having been stopped by the hour, and by the fact that they were in bed.

We went back to my house to dine and returned to the palace in order to see the King and

Queen depart. I again received from them a thousand marks of favour. Both the King and Queen, but especially the latter, several times insisted that I must not lose any time in following them to Lerma; upon which I assured them they would find me there as they alighted from their coach.

I set out, in fact, on the 2nd of December, from Madrid, to join the Court, and was to sleep at the Escurial, with the Comtes de Lorges and de Cereste, my second son, the Abbe de Saint-Simon and his brother, Pacquet, and two principal officers of the King's troops, who remained with me as long as I stayed in Spain. In addition to the orders of the King of Spain and the letters of the Marquis de Grimaldo, I was also furnished with those of the nuncio for the Prior of the Escurial, who is, at the same time, governor, in order that I might he shown the marvels of this superb and prodigious monastery, and that everything might be opened for me that I wished to visit; for I had been warned that, without the recommendation of the nuncio, neither that of the King and his minister, nor any official character, would have much served me. It will be seen that, after all, I did not fail to suffer from the churlishness and the superstition of these coarse Jeronimites.

They are black and white monks, whose dress resembles that of the Celestins; very idle, ignorant, and without austerity, who, by the number of their monasteries and their riches, are in Spain much about what the Benedictines are in France, and like them are a congregation. They elect also, like the Benedictines, their superiors, local and general, except the Prior of the Escurial, who is nominated by the King, remains in office as long as the King likes and no more, and who is yet better lodged at the Escurial than his Catholic Majesty. 'Tis a prodigy, this building, of extent, of structure, of every kind of magnificence, and contains an immense heap of riches, in pictures, in ornaments, in vases of all kinds, in precious stones, everywhere strewn about, and the description of which I will not undertake, since it does not belong to my subject. Suffice it to say that a curious connoisseur of all these different beauties might occupy himself there for three months without cessation, and then would not have examined all. The gridiron (its form, at least) has regulated all the ordonnance of this sumptuous edifice in honour of Saint-Laurent, and of the battle of Saint-Quentin, gained by Philippe II., who, seeing the action from a height, vowed he would erect this monastery if his troops obtained the victory, and asked his courtiers, if such were the pleasures of the Emperor, his father, who in fact did not go so far for them as that.

There is not a door, a lock, or utensil of any kind, or a piece of plate, that is not marked with a gridiron.

The distance from Madrid to the Escurial is much about the same as that from Paris to Fontainebleau. The country is very flat and becomes a wilderness on approaching the Escurial, which takes its name from a large village you pass, a league off. It is upon an eminence which you ascend imperceptibly, and upon which you see endless deserts on three sides; but it is backed, as it were, by the mountain of Guadarama, which encircles Madrid on three sides, at a distance of several leagues, more or less. There is no village at the Escurial; the lodging of their Catholic Majesties forms the handle of the gridiron. The principal grand officers, and those most necessary, are lodged, as well as the Queen's ladies, in the monastery; on the side by which you arrive all is very badly built.

The church, the grand staircase, and the grand cloister, surprised me. I admired the elegance of the surgery, and the pleasantness of the gardens, which, however, are only a long and wide terrace. The Pantheon frightened me by a sort of horror and majesty. The grand-altar and the sacristy wearied my eyes, by their immense opulence. The library did not satisfy me, and the librarians still less: I was received with much civility, and invited to a good supper in the Spanish style, at which the Prior and another monk did the honours. After this fast repast my people prepared my meals, but this fat monk always supplied one or two things that it would not have been civil to refuse, and always ate with me; for, in order that he might conduct us everywhere, he never quitted our sides. Bad Latin supplied the place of French, which he did not understand; nor even Spanish.

In the sanctuary at the grand altar, there are windows behind the seats of the priest and his assistants, who celebrate the grand mass. These windows, which are nearly on a level with the sanctuary (very high), belong to the apartment that Philippe II. had built for himself, and in which he died. He heard service through these windows. I wished to see this apartment, which was entered from behind. I was refused. It was in vain that I insisted on the orders of the King and of the nuncio, authorising me to see all I wished. I disputed uselessly. They told me this apartment had been closed ever since the death of Philippe II., and that nobody had entered it. I maintained that King Philippe V. and his suite had seen it. They admitted the fact, but at the same time told me that he had entered by force as a master, threatening to break in the doors, that he was the only King who had entered since Philippe II., and that they would not open the apartment to anybody. I understood nothing of all this superstition, but I was forced to rest content in my ignorance. Louville, who had entered with the King, had told me that the place contained only five or six dark chambers, and some holes and corners with wainscots plastered with mud; without tapestry, when he saw it, or any kind of furniture; thus I did not lose much by not entering.

In the Rotting-Room, which I have elsewhere described, we read the inscriptions near us, and the monk read others as we asked him. We walked thus, all round, talking and discoursing thereon. Passing to the bottom of the room, the coffin of the unhappy Don Carlos offered itself to our sight.

"As for him," said I, "it is well known why, and of what he died." At this remark, the fat monk turned rusty, maintained he had died a natural death, and began to declaim against the stories which he said had been spread abroad about him. I smiled, saying, I admitted it was not true that his veins had been opened. This observation completed the irritation of the monk, who began to babble in a sort of fury. I diverted myself with it at first in silence; then I said to him, that the King, shortly after arriving in Spain; had had the curiosity to open the coffin of Don Carlos, and that I knew from a man who was present ('twas Louville), that his head had been found between his legs; that Philippe II., his father, had had it cut off before him in the prison.

"Very well!" cried the monk in fury, "apparently he had well deserved it; for Philippe II., had permission from the Pope to do so!" and, thereupon, he began to cry with all his might about the marvels of piety and of justice of Philippe II., and about the boundless power of the Pope, and to cry heresy against any one who doubted that he could not order, decide, and dispose of all.

Such is the fanaticism of the countries of the Inquisition, where science is a crime, ignorance and superstition the first of virtues. Though my official character protected me, I did not care to dispute, and cause a ridiculous scene with this bigot of a monk. I contented myself with smiling, and by making a sign of silence as I did so to those who were with me. The monk, therefore, had full swing, and preached a long time without giving over. He perceived, perhaps, by our faces, that we were laughing at him, although without gestures or words. At last he showed us the rest of the chamber, still fuming; then we descended to the Pantheon. They did me the singular favour to light about two-thirds of the immense and admirable chandelier, suspended from the middle of the roof, the lights of which dazzled us, and enabled us to distinguish in every part of the Rotting-Room; not only the smallest details of the smallest letter, but the minutest features of the place.

I passed three days in the Escurial, lodged in a large and fine apartment, and all that were with me well lodged also. Our monk, who had always been in an ill-humour since the day of the Rotting-Room, did not recover himself until the parting breakfast came. We quitted him without regret, but not the Escurial, which would pleasantly occupy a curious connoisseur during more than a three months' stay. On the road we met the Marquis de Montalegre, who invited, us to dinner with him. The meal was so good that we little regretted the dinner my people had prepared for us.

At last we arrived on the 9th, at our village of Villahalmanzo, where I found most comfortable quarters for myself and all who were with me. I found there, also, my eldest son, still merely, convalescent, with the Abbe de Monthon, who came from Burgos. We supped very gaily, and I reckoned upon taking a good excursion the next day, and upon amusing myself in reconnoitring the village and the environs; but fever seized me during the night, augmented during the day, became violent the following night, so that there was no more talk of going on the 11th to meet the King and Queen at Lerma, as they alighted from their coach, according to arrangement.

The malady increased with such rapidity that I was found to be in great danger, and immediately after, on the point of death. I was bled shortly after. The small-pox, with which the whole country was filled, appeared. The climate was such this year that it froze hard twelve or fourteen hours every day, while from eleven o'clock in 'the morning till nearly four, the sun shone as brightly as possible, and it was too hot about mid-day for walking! Yet in the shade it did not thaw for an instant. This cold weather was all the more sharp because the air was purer and clearer, and the sky continually of the most perfect serenity.

The King of Spain, who was dreadfully afraid of the small-pox, and who with reason had confidence only in his chief doctor, sent him to me as soon as he was informed of my illness, with orders not to quit me until I was cured. I had, therefore, five or six persons continually around me, in addition to the domestics who served me, one of the best and most skilful physicians in Europe, who, moreover, was capital company, and who did not quit me night or day, and three very good surgeons. The small- pox came out very abundantly all over me; it was of a good kind, and I had no dangerous accident. Every one who waited upon me, master or man, was cut off from all intercourse with the rest of the world; even those who cooked for us, from those who did not.

The chief physician nearly every day provided new remedies in case of need, and yet administered none to me, except in giving me, as my sole beverage, water, in which, according to its quantity, oranges were thrown, cut in two with their skins on, and which gently simmered before my fire; occasionally some spoonful of a gentle and agreeable cordial during the height of the suppuration, and afterwards a little Rota wine, and some broth, made of beef and partridge.

Nothing was wanting, then, on the part of those who had charge of me. I was their only patient, and they had orders not to quit me, and nothing was wanting for my amusement, when I was in a condition to take any, so much good company being around me, and that at a time when convalescents of this malady experience all the weariness and fretfulness of it. At the end of my illness I was bled and purged once, after which I lived as usual, but in a species of solitude.

During the long interval in which this illness shut me out from all intercourse with the world, the Abbe de Saint-Simon corresponded for me with Cardinal Dubois, Grimaldo, Sartine, and some others.

The King and Queen, not content with having sent me their chief physician, M. Hyghens, to be with me night and day, wished to hear how I was twice a day, and when I was better, unceasingly showed to me a thousand favours, in which they were imitated by all the Court.

But I was six weeks ill in all.

CHAPTER CX

Here I think will be the fitting place to introduce an account of the daily life of the King and Queen of Spain, which in many respects was entitled to be regarded as singular. During my stay at the Court I had plenty of opportunity to mark it well, so that what I relate may be said to have passed under my own eyes. This, then, was their daily life wherever they were, and in all times and seasons.

The King and Queen never had more than one apartment, and one bed between them, the latter exactly as I have described it when relating my visit with Maulevrier to their Catholic Majesties to carry to them the news of the departure from Paris of the future Princess of the Asturias. During fevers, illness, no matter of what kind, or on whose side, childbirth even,—never were they a single night apart, and even when the deceased Queen was eaten up with the scrofula, the King continued to sleep with her until a few nights before her death!

About nine o'clock in the morning the curtains were drawn by the Asafeta, followed by a single valet carrying a basin full of caudle. Hyghens, during my convalescence, explained to me how this caudle was made, and in fact concocted some for me to taste. It is a light mixture of broth, milk, wine (which is in the largest quantity), one or two yolks of eggs, sugar, cinnamon, and a few cloves. It is white; has a very strong taste, not unmixed with softness. I should not like to take it habitually, nevertheless it is not disagreeable. You put in it, if you like, crusts of bread, or, at times, toast, and then it becomes a species of soup; otherwise it is drunk as broth; and, ordinarily, it was in this last fashion the King took it. It is unctuous, but very warm, a restorative singularly good for retrieving the past night, and, for preparing you for the next.

While the King partook of this brief breakfast, the Asafeta brought the Queen some tapestry to work at, passed bed-gowns to their Majesties, and put upon the bed some of the papers she found upon the adjoining seats, then withdrew with the valet and what he had brought. Their Majesties then said their morning prayers. Grimaldo afterwards entered. Sometimes they signalled to him to wait, as he came in, and called him when their prayer was over, for there was nobody else, and the bedroom was very small. Then Grimaldo displayed his papers, drew from his pocket an inkstand, and worked with the King; the Queen not being hindered by her tapestry from giving her opinion.

This work lasted more or less according to the business, or to the conversation. Grimaldo, upon leaving with his papers, found the adjoining room empty, and a valet in that beyond, who, seeing him pass, entered into the empty room, crossed it, and summoned the Asafeta, who immediately came and presented to the King his slippers and his dressing- gown; he at once passed across the empty room and entered into a cabinet, where he dressed himself, followed by three valets (never changed) and by the Duc del Arco, or the Marquis de Santa Cruz, and after by both, nobody else ever being present at the ceremony.

The Queen, as soon as the King had passed into his cabinet, put on her stockings and shoes alone with the Asafeta, who gave her her dressing- gown. It was the only moment in which this person could speak to the Queen, or the Queen to her; but this moment did not stretch at the most to more than half a quarter of an hour. Had they been longer together the King would have known it, and would have wanted to hear what kept them. The Queen passed through the empty chamber and entered into a fine large cabinet, where her toilette awaited her. When the King had dressed in his cabinet—where he often spoke to his confessor—he went to the Queen's toilette, followed by the two seigneurs just named. A few of the specially—privileged were also admitted there. This toilette lasted about three-quarters of an hour, the King and all the rest of the company standing.

When it was over, the King half opened the door of the Hall of Mirrors, which leads into the salon where the Court assembled, and gave his orders; then rejoined the Queen in that room which I have so often called the empty room. There and then took place the private audiences of the foreign ministers, and of, the seigneurs, or other subjects who obtained them. Once a week, on Monday, there was a public audience, a practice which cannot be too much praised where it is not abused. The King, instead of half opening the door, threw it wide open, and admitted whoever liked to enter. People spoke to the King as much as they liked, how they liked, and gave him in writing what they liked. But the Spaniards resemble in nothing the French; they are measured, discreet, respectful, brief.

After the audiences, or after amusing himself with the Queen—if there are none, the King went to dress. The Queen accompanied him, and they took the communion together (never separately) about once a week, and then they heard a second mass. The confession of the King was said after he rose, and before he went to the Queen's toilette.

Upon returning from mass, or very shortly after, the dinner was served. It was always in the Queen's apartment, as well as the supper, but the King and Queen had each their dishes; the former, few, the latter, many, for she liked eating, and ate of everything; the King always kept to the same things—soup, capon, pigeons, boiled and roast, and always a roast loin of veal—no fruit; or salad, or cheese; pastry, rarely, never maigre; eggs, often cooked in various fashion; and he drank nothing but champagne; the Queen the same. When the dinner was finished, they prayed to God together. If anything pressing happened, Grimaldo came and gave them a brief account of it.

About an hour after dinner, they left the apartment by a short passage accessible to the court, and descended by a little staircase to their coach, returning by the same way. The seigneurs who frequented the court pretty constantly assembled, now one, now another, in this passage, or followed their Majesties to their coaches. Very often I saw them in this passage as they went or returned. The Queen always said something pleasant to whoever was there. I will speak elsewhere of the hunting- party their Majesties daily made.

Upon returning, the King gave his orders. If they had not partaken of a collation in the coach, they partook of one upon arriving. It was for the King, a morsel of bread, a big biscuit, some water and wine; and for the Queen, pastry and fruit in season, sometimes cheese. The Prince and the Princess of the Asturias, and the children, followed and waited for them in the inner apartment. This company withdrew in less than half a quarter of an hour. Grimaldo came and worked ordinarily for a long time; it was the time for the real work of the day. When the Queen went to confession this also was the time she selected. Except what related to the confession, she and her confessor had no time to say anything to each other. The cabinet in which she confessed to him was contiguous to the room occupied by the King, and when the latter thought the confession too long, he opened the door and called her. Grimaldo being gone, they prayed together, or sometimes occupied themselves with spiritual reading until supper. It was served like the dinner. At both meals there were more dishes in the French style than in the Spanish, or even the Italian.

After supper, conversation or prayers conducted them to the hour for bed, when nearly the same observances took place as in the morning. Finally, their Catholic Majesties everywhere had but one wardrobe between them, and were never in private one from another.

These uniform days were the same in all places, and even during the journeys taken by their Majesties, who were thus never separated, except for a few minutes at a time. They passed their lives in one long tete-a-tete. When they travelled it was at the merest snail's pace, and they slept on the road, night after night, in houses prepared for them. In their coach they were always alone; when in the palace it was the same.

The King had been accustomed to this monotonous life by his first queen, and he did not care for any other. The new Queen, upon arriving, soon found this out, and found also that if she wished to rule him, she must keep him in the same room, confined as he had been kept by her predecessor. Alberoni was the only person admitted to their privacy. This second marriage of the King of Spain, entirely brought about by Madame des Ursins, was very distasteful to the Spaniards, who detested that personage most warmly, and were in consequence predisposed to look unfavourably upon anyone she favoured. It is true, the new Queen, on arriving, drove out Madame des Ursins, but this showed her to be possessed of as much power as the woman she displaced, and when she began to exercise that power in other directions the popular dislike to her was increased. She made no effort to mitigate it—hating the Spaniards as much as they hated her—and it is incredible to what an extent this reciprocal aversion stretched.

When the Queen went out with the King to the chase or to the atocha, the people unceasingly cried, as well as the citizens in their shops, "Viva el Re y la Savoyana, y la Savoyana," and incessantly repeated, with all their lungs, "la Savoyana," which is the deceased Queen (I say this to prevent mistake), no voice ever crying "Viva la Reina." The Queen pretended to despise this, but inwardly raged (as people saw), she could not habituate herself to it. She has said to me very frequently and more than once: "The Spaniards do not like me, and in return I hate them," with an air of anger and of pique.

These long details upon the daily life of the King and Queen may appear trivial, but they will not be judged so by those who know, as I do, what valuable information is to be gained from similar particulars. I will simply say in passing, that an experience of twenty years has convinced me that the knowledge of such details is the key to many others, and that it is always wanting in histories, often in memoirs the most interesting and instructive, but which would be much more so if they had not neglected this chapter, regarded by those who do not know its price, as a bagatelle unworthy of entering into a serious recital. Nevertheless, I am quite certain, that there is not a minister of state, a favourite, or a single person of whatever rank, initiated by his office into the domestic life of sovereigns, who will not echo my sentiments.

And now let me give a more distinct account of the King of Spain than I have yet written.

Philip V. was not gifted with superior understanding or with any stock of what is called imagination. He was cold, silent, sad, sober, fond of no pleasure except the chase, fearing society, fearing himself, unexpansive, a recluse by taste and habits, rarely touched by others, of good sense nevertheless, and upright, with a tolerably good knowledge of things, obstinate when he liked, and often then not to be moved; nevertheless, easy at other times to govern and influence.

He was cold. In his campaigns he allowed himself to be led into any position, even under a brisk fire, without budging in the slightest; nay, amusing himself by seeing whether anybody was afraid. Secured and removed from danger he was the same, without thinking that his glory could suffer by it. He liked to make war, but was indifferent whether he went there or not; and present or absent, left everything to the generals without doing anything himself.

He was extremely vain; could bear no opposition in any of his enterprises; and what made me judge he liked praise, was that the Queen invariably praised him—even his face; and asked me one day, at the end of an audience which had led us into conversation, if I did not think him very handsome, and more so than any one I knew?—His piety was only custom, scruples, fears, little observances, without knowing anything of religion: the Pope a divinity when not opposed to him; in fact he had the outside religion of the Jesuits, of whom he was passionately fond.

Although his health was very good, he always feared for it; he was always looking after it. A physician, such as the one Louis XI. enriched so much at the end of his life; a Maitre Coythier would have become a rich and powerful personage by his side; fortunately his physician was a thoroughly good and honourable man, and he who succeeded him devoted to the Queen. Philip V. could speak well—very well, but was often hindered by idleness and self-mistrust. To the audiences I had with him, however, he astonished me by the precision, the grace, the easiness of his words. He was good, easy to serve, familiar with a few. His love of France showed itself in everything. He preserved much gratitude and veneration for the deceased King, and tenderness for the late Monsieur; above all for the Dauphin, his brother, for whose loss he was never consoled. I noticed nothing in him towards any other of the royal family, except the King; and he never asked me concerning anybody in the Court, except, and then in a friendly manner, the Duchesse de Beauvilliers.

He had scruples respecting his crown, that can with difficulty be reconciled with the desire he had to return, in case of misfortune, to the throne of his fathers, which he had more than once so solemnly renounced. He believed himself an usurper! and in this idea nourished his desire to return to France, and abandon Spain and his scruples at one and the same time. It cannot be disguised that all this was very ill- arranged in his head, but there it was, and he would have abandoned Spain had it been possible, because he felt compelled by duty to do so. It was this feeling which principally induced him, after meditating upon it long before I arrived in Spain, to abdicate his throne in favour of his son. It was the same usurpation in his eyes, but not being able to obey his scruples, he contented himself by doing all he could in abdicating. It was still this feeling which, at the death of his son, troubled him so much, when he saw himself compelled to reascend the throne; though, during his abdication, that son had caused him not a little vexation. As may well be imagined, Philip V. never spoke of these delicate matters to me, but I was not less well informed of them elsewhere.

The Queen desired not less to abandon Spain, which she hated, and to return into France and reign, where she hoped to lead a life of less seclusion, and much more agreeable.

Notwithstanding all I have said, it is perfectly true that Philip V. was but little troubled by the wars he made, that he was fond of enterprises, and that his passion was to be respected and dreaded, and to figure grandly in Europe.

But let me now more particularly describe the Queen.

This princess had much intellect and natural graces, which she knew how to put to account. Her sense, her reflection, and her conduct, were guided by that intellect, from which she drew all the charms and, all the advantages possible. Whoever knew her was astonished to find how her intelligence and natural capacity supplied the place of her want of knowledge of the world, of persons, of affairs, upon all of which subjects, her garret life in Parma, and afterwards her secluded life with the King of Spain, hindered her from obtaining any real instruction. The perspicuity she possessed, which enabled her to see the right side of everything that came under her inspection, was undeniable, and this singular gift would have become developed in her to perfection if its growth had not been interrupted by the ill-humour she possessed; which it must be admitted the life she led was more than enough to give her. She felt her talent and her strength, but did not feel the fatuity and pride which weakened them and rendered them ridiculous. The current of her life was simple, smooth, with a natural gaiety even, which sparkled through the eternal restraint of her existence; and despite the ill- temper and the sharpness which this restraint without rest gave her, she was a woman ordinarily without pretension, and really charming.

When she arrived in Spain she was sure, in the first place, of driving away Madame des Ursins, and of filling-her place in the government at once. She seized that place, and took possession also of the King's mind, which she soon entirely ruled. As to public business, nothing could be hidden from her. The King always worked in her presence, never otherwise; all that he saw alone she read and discussed with him. She was always present at all the private audiences that he gave, whether to his subjects or to the foreign ministers; so that, as I have before remarked, nothing possibly could escape her.

As for the King, the eternal night and day tete-a-tete she had with him enabled her to sound him thoroughly, to know him by heart, so to speak. She knew perfectly the time for preparatory insinuations, their success; the resistance, when there was any, its course and how to overcome it; the moments for yielding, in order to return afterwards to the charge, and those for holding firm and carrying everything by force. She stood in need of all these intrigues, notwithstanding her credit with the King. If I may dare to say it, his temperament was her strong point, and she sometimes had recourse to it. Then her coldness excited tempests. The King cried and menaced;

now and then went further; she held firm, wept, and sometimes defended herself. In the morning all was stormy. The immediate attendants acted towards King and Queen often without penetrating the cause of their quarrel. Peace was concluded at the first opportunity, rarely to the disadvantage of the Queen, who mostly had her own way.

A quarrel of this sort arose when I was at Madrid; and I was advised, after hearing details I will not repeat, to mix myself up in it, but I burst out laughing and took good care not to follow this counsel.

CHAPTER CXI.

The chase was every day the amusement of the King, and the Queen was obliged to make it hers. But it was always the same. Their Catholic Majesties did me the singular honour to invite me to it once, and I went in my coach. Thus I saw this pleasure well, and to see it once is to see it always. Animals to shoot are not met with in the plains. They must be sought for among the mountains,—and there the ground is too rugged for hunting the stag, the wild boar, and other beasts as we hunt the hare,—and elsewhere. The plains even are so dry, so hard, so full of deep crevices (that are not perceived until their brink is reached), that the best hounds or harriers would soon be knocked up, and would have their feet blistered, nay lamed, for a long time. Besides, the ground is so thickly covered with sturdy vegetation that the hounds could not derive much help from their noses. Mere shooting on the wing the King had long since quitted, and he had ceased to mount his horse; thus the chase simply resolved itself into a battue.

The Duc del Orco, who, by his post of grand ecuyer, had the superintendence of all the hunting arrangements, chose the place where the King and Queen were to go. Two large arbours were erected there, the one against the other, entirely shut in, except where two large openings, like windows, were made, of breast-height. The King, the Queen, the captain of the guards, and the grand ecuyer were in the first arbour with about twenty guns and the wherewithal to load them. In the other arbour, the day I was present, were the Prince of the Asturias, who came in his coach with the Duc de Ponoli and the Marquis del Surco, the Marquis de Santa Cruz, the Duc Giovenazzo, majordomo, major and grand ecuyer to the Queen, Valouse, two or three officers of the body-guard, and I myself. We had a number of guns, and some men to load them. A single lady of the palace followed the Queen all alone, in another coach, which she did not quit; she carried with her, for her consolation, a book or some work, for no one approached her. Their Majesties and their suite went to the chase in hot haste with relays of guards and of coach horses, for the distance was at least three or four leagues; at the least double that from Paris to Versailles. The party alighted at the arbours, and immediately the carriages, the poor lady of the palace, and all the horses were led away far out of sight, lest they should frighten the beasts.

Two, three, four hundred peasants had early in the morning beaten the country round, with hue and cry, after having enclosed it and driven all the animals together as near these arbours as possible. When in the arbour you were not allowed to stir, or to make the slightest remarks, or to wear attractive colours; and everybody stood up in silence.

This period of expectation lasted an hour and a half, and did not appear to me very amusing. At last we heard loud cries from afar, and soon after we saw troops of animals pass and repass within shot and within half-shot of us; and then the King and the Queen banged away in good earnest. This diversion, or rather species of butchery, lasted more than half an hour, during which stags, hinds, roebucks, boars, hares, wolves, badgers, foxes, and numberless pole-cats passed; and were killed or lamed.

We were obliged to let the King and Queen fire first, although pretty often they permitted the grand ecuyer and the captain of the guard to fire also; and as we did not know from whom came the report, we were obliged to wait until the King's arbour was perfectly silent; then let the Prince shoot, who very often had nothing to shoot at, and we still less. Nevertheless, I killed a fox, but a little before I ought to have done so, at which, somewhat ashamed, I made my excuses to the Prince of the Asturias, who burst out laughing, and the company also, I following their example and all passing very politely.

In proportion as the peasants approach and draw nearer each other, the sport advances, and it finishes when they all come close to the arbours, still shouting, and with nothing more behind them. Then the coaches return, the company quits the arbours, the beasts killed are laid before the King. They are placed afterwards behind the coaches. During all this, conversation respecting the sport rolls on. We carried away this day about a dozen or more beasts, some hares, foxes, and polecats. The night overtook us soon after we quitted the arbours.

And this is the daily diversion of their Catholic Majesties.

It is time now, however, to resume the thread of my narrative, from which these curious and little-known details have led me.

I have shown in its place the motive which made me desire my embassy; it was to obtain the 'grandesse' for my second son, and thus to "branch" my house. I also desired to obtain the Toison d'Or for my eldest son, that he might derive from this journey an ornament which, at his age, was a decoration. I had left Paris with full liberty to employ every aid, in order to obtain these things; I had, too, from M. le Duc d'Orleans, the promise that he would expressly ask the King of Spain for the former favour, employing the name of the King, and letters of the strongest kind from Cardinal Dubois to Grimaldo and Father Aubenton. In the midst of the turmoil of affairs I spoke to both of these persons, and was favourably attended to.

Grimaldo was upright and truthful. He conceived a real friendship for me, and gave me, during my stay at Madrid, all sorts of proofs of it. He said that this union of the two Courts by the two marriages might influence the ministers. His sole point of support, in order to maintain himself in the post he occupied, so brilliant and so envied, was the King of Spain. The Queen, he found, could never be a solid foundation on which to repose. He wished, then, to support himself upon France, or at least to have no opposition from it, and he perfectly well knew the duplicity and caprices of Cardinal Dubois. The Court of Spain, at all times so watchful over M. le Duc d'Orleans, in consequence of what had passed in the time of the Princesse des Ursins, and during the Regency, was not ignorant of the intimate and uninterrupted confidence of this prince in me, or of the terms on which I was with him. These sort of things appear larger than they are, when seen from afar, and the choice that had been made of me for this singular embassy confirmed it still more! Grimaldo, then, might have thought to assure my friendship in his behalf, and my influence with M. le Duc d'Orleans, occasion demanding it; and I don't think I am deceiving myself in attributing to him this policy while he aided me to obtain a favour, at bottom quite natural, and which could cause him no inconvenience.

I regarded the moment at which the marriage would be celebrated as that at which I stood most chance of obtaining what I desired, and I considered that if it passed over without result to me, all would grow cold, and become uncertain, and very disagreeable. I had forgotten nothing during this first stay in Madrid, in order to please everybody, and I make bold to say that I had all the better succeeded because I had tried to give weight and merit to my politeness, measuring it according to the persons I addressed, without prostitution and without avarice, and that's what made me hasten to learn all I could of the birth, of the dignities, of the posts, of the alliances, of the reputation of each, so as to play my cards well, and secure the game.

But still I needed the letters of M. le Duc d'Orleans, and of Cardinal Dubois. I did not doubt the willingness of the Regent, but I did doubt, and very much too, that of his minister. It has been seen what reason I had for this.

These letters ought to have arrived at Madrid at the same time that I did, but they had not come, and there seemed no prospect of their arriving. What redoubled my impatience was that I read them beforehand, and that I wished to have the time to reflect, and to turn round, in order to draw from them, in spite of them, all the help I could. I reckoned that these letters would be in a feeble spirit, and this opinion made me more desirous to fortify my batteries in Spain in order to render myself agreeable to the King and Queen, and to inspire them with the desire to grant me the favours I wished.

A few days before going to Lerma I received letters from Cardinal Dubois upon my affair. Nobody could be more eager or more earnest than the Cardinal, for he gave me advice how to arrive at my aim, and pressed me to look out for everything which could aid me; assuring me that his letters, and those of M. le Duc d'Orleans, would arrive in time. In the midst of the perfume of so many flowers, the odour of falsehood could nevertheless be smelt. I had reckoned upon this. I had done all in my power to supply the place of these letters. I received therefore not as gospel, all the marvels Dubois sent me, and I set out for Lerma fully resolved to more and more cultivate my affair without reckoning upon the letters promised me; but determined to draw as much advantage from them as I could.

Upon arriving at Lerma I fell ill as I have described, and the small-pox kept me confined forty days: The letters so long promised and so long expected did not arrive until the end of my quarantine. They were just what I expected. Cardinal Dubois explained himself to Grimaldo in turns and circumlocution, and if one phrase displayed eagerness and desire, the next destroyed it by an air of respect and of discretion, protesting he wished simply what the King of Spain would himself wish, with all the seasoning necessary for the annihilation of his good offices under the pretence that he did not wish to press his Majesty to anything or to importune him.

This written stammering savoured of the bombast of a man who had no desire to serve me, but who, not daring to break his word, used all his wits to twist and overrate the little he could not hinder himself from saying. This letter was simply for Grimaldo, as the letter of M. le Duc d'Orleans was simply for the King of Spain. The last was even weaker than the first. It was like a design in pencil nearly effaced by the rain, and in which nothing, connected appeared. It scarcely touched upon the real point, but lost itself in respects, in reservations, in deference, and would propose nothing that was not according to the taste of the King! In a word, the letter withdrew rather than advanced, and was a sort of ease-conscience which could not be refused, and which did not promise much success.

It is easy to understand that these letters much displeased me. Although I had anticipated all the malice of Cardinal Dubois, I found it exceeded my calculations, and that it was more undisguised than I imagined it would be.

Such as the letters were I was obliged to make use of them. The Abbe de Saint-Simon wrote to Grimaldo and to Sartine, enclosing these letter, for I myself did not yet dare to write on account of the precautions I was obliged to use against the bad air. Sartine and Grimaldo, to whom I had not confided my suspicions that these recommendations would be in a very weak tone, were thrown into the utmost surprise on reading them.

They argued together, they were indignant, they searched for a bias to strengthen that which had so much need of strength, but this bias could not be found; they consulted together, and Grimaldo formed a bold resolution, which astonished me to the last degree, and much troubled me also.

He came to the conclusion that these letters would assuredly do me more harm than good; that they must be suppressed, never spoken of to the King, who must be confirmed without them in the belief that in according me these favours he would confer upon M. le Duc d'Orleans a pleasure, all the greater, because he saw to what point extended all his reserve in not speaking to him about this matter, and mine in not asking for these favours through his Royal Highness, as there was every reason to believe I should do. Grimaldo proposed to draw from these circumstances all the benefit he proposed to have drawn from the letters had they been written in a fitting spirit, and he said he would answer for it; I should have the 'grandesse' and the 'Toison d'Or' without making the slightest allusion to the cold recommendations of M. le Duc d'Orleans to the King of Spain, and of Dubois to him.

Sartine, by his order, made this known to the Abbe de Saint-Simon, who communicated it to me, and after having discussed together with Hyghens, who knew the ground as well as they, and who had really devoted himself to me, I blindly abandoned myself to the guidance and friendship of Grimaldo, with full success, as will be seen.

In relating here the very singular fashion by which my affair succeeded, I am far indeed from abstracting from M. le Duc d'Orleans all gratitude. If he had not confided to me the double marriage, without the knowledge of Dubois, and in spite of the secrecy that had been asked for, precisely on my account, I should not have been led to beg of him the embassy.

I instantly asked for it, declaring that my sole aim was the grandesse for my second son, and he certainly accorded it to me with this aim, and promised to aid me with his recommendation in order to arrive at it, but with the utmost secrecy on account of the vexation Dubois would feel, and in order to give himself time to arrange with the minister and induce him to swallow the pill.

If I had not had the embassy in this manner, it would certainly have escaped me; and thus would have been lost all hope of the grandesse, to obtain which there would have been no longer occasion, reason, or means.

The friendship and the confidence of this prince prevailed then over the witchery which his miserable preceptor had cast upon him, and if he afterwards yielded to the roguery, to the schemes, to the folly which Dubois employed in the course of this embassy to ruin and disgrace me, and to bring about the failure of the sole object which had made me desire it, we must only blame his villainy and the deplorable feebleness of M. le Duc d'Orleans, which caused me many sad embarrassments, and did so much harm, but which even did more harm to the state and to the prince himself.

It is with this sad but only too true reflection that I finish the year 1721.

CHAPTER CXII

The Regent's daughter arrived in Spain at the commencement of the year 1722, and it was arranged that her marriage with the Prince of the Asturias should be celebrated on the 30th of January at Lerma, where their Catholic Majesties were then staying. It was some little distance from my house. I was obliged therefore to start early in the morning in order to arrive in time. On the way I paid a visit of ceremony to the Princess, at Cogollos, ate a mouthful of something, and turned off to Lerma.

As soon as I arrived there, I went to the Marquis of Grimaldo's apartments. His chamber was at the end of a vast room, a piece of which had been portioned off, in order to serve as a chapel. Once again I had to meet the nuncio, and I feared lest he should remember what had passed on a former occasion, and that I should give Dubois a handle for complaint. I saw, therefore, but very imperfectly, the reception of the Princess; to meet whom the King and Queen (who lodged below) and the Prince precipitated themselves, so to speak, almost to the steps of the coach. I quietly went up again to the chapel.

The prie-dieu of the King was placed in front of the altar, a short distance from the steps, precisely as the King's prie-dieu is placed at Versailles, but closer to the altar, and with a cushion on each side of it. The chapel was void of courtiers. I placed myself to the right of the King's cushion just beyond the edge of the carpet, and amused myself there better than I had expected. Cardinal Borgia, pontifically clad, was in the corner, his face turned towards me, learning his lesson between two chaplains in surplices, who held a large book open in front of him. The good prelate did not know how to read; he tried, however, and read aloud, but inaccurately. The chaplains took him up, he grew angry, scolded them, recommenced, was again corrected, again grew angry, and to such an extent that he turned round upon them and shook them by their surplices. I laughed as much as I could; for he perceived nothing, so occupied and entangled was he with his lesson.

Marriages in Spain are performed in the afternoon, and commence at the door of the church, like baptisms. The King, the Queen, the Prince, and the Princess arrived with all the Court, and the King was announced. "Let them wait," said the Cardinal in choler, "I am not ready." They waited, in fact, and the Cardinal continued his lesson, redder than his hat, and still furious. At last he went to the door, at which a ceremony took place that lasted some time. Had I not been obliged to continue at my post, curiosity would have made me follow him. That I lost some amusement is certain, for I saw the King and Queen laughing and looking at their prie-dieu, and all the Court laughing also. The nuncio arriving and seeing by the position I had taken up that I was preceding him, again indicated his surprise to me by gestures, repeating, "Signor, signor;" but I had resolved to understand nothing, and laughingly pointed out the Cardinal to him, and reproached him for not having better instructed the worthy prelate for the honour of the Sacred College. The nuncio understood French very well, but spoke it very badly. This banter and the innocent air with which I gave it, without appearing to notice his demonstrations, created such a fortunate diversion, that nobody else was thought of; more especially as the poor cardinal more and more caused amusement while continuing the ceremony, during which he neither knew where he was nor what he was doing, being taken up and corrected every moment by his chaplains, and fuming against them so that neither the King nor the Queen could; contain themselves. It was the same with everybody else who witnessed the scene.

I could see nothing more than the back of the Prince and the Princess as they knelt each upon a cushion between the prie-dieu and the altar, the Cardinal in front making grimaces indicative of the utmost confusion. Happily all I had to think of was the nuncio, the King's majordomo-major having placed himself by the side of his son, captain of the guards. The grandees were crowded around with the most considerable people: the rest filled all the chapel so that there was no stirring.

Amidst the amusement supplied to us by the poor Cardinal, I remarked extreme satisfaction in the King and Queen at seeing this grand marriage accomplished. The ceremony finished, as it was not long, only the King, the Queen, and, when necessary, the Prince and Princess kneeling, their Catholic Majesties rose and withdrew towards the left corner of their footcloth, talked together for a short time, after which the Queen remained where she was, and the King advanced to me, I being where I had been during all the ceremony.

The King did me the honour to say to me, "Monsieur, in every respect I am so pleased with you, and particularly for the manner in which you have acquitted yourself of your embassy, that I wish to give you some marks of my esteem, of my satisfaction; of my friendship. I make you Grandee of Spain of the first class; you, and, at the same time, whichever of your sons you may wish to have the same distinction; and your eldest son I will make chevalier of the Toison d'Or."

I immediately embraced his knees, and I tried to testify to him my gratitude and my extreme desire to render myself worthy of the favour he deigned to spread upon me, by my attachment, my very humble services, and my most profound respect. Then I kissed his hand, turned and sent for my children, employing the moments which had elapsed before they came in uttering fresh thanks. As soon as my sons appeared, I called the younger and told him, to embrace the knees of the King who overwhelmed us with favours, and made him grandee of Spain with me. He kissed the King's hand in rising, the King saying he was very glad of what he had just done. I presented the elder to him afterwards, to thank him for the Toison. He simply bent very low and kissed the King's hand. As soon as this was at an end, the King went towards the Queen, and I followed him with my children. I bent very low before the Queen, thanked her, then presented to her my children, the younger first, the elder afterwards. The Queen received us with much goodness, said a thousand civil things, then walked away with the King, followed by the Prince, having upon his arm the Princess, whom we saluted in passing; and they returned to their apartments. I wished to follow them, but was carried away, as it were, by the crowd which pressed eagerly around me to compliment me. I was very careful to reply in a fitting manner to each, and with the utmost politeness, and though I but little expected these favours at this moment, I found afterwards that all this numerous court was pleased with me.

A short time after the celebration of the marriage between the Regent's daughter and the Prince of the Asturias, the day came on which my eldest son was to receive the Toison d'Or. The Duc de

Liria was to be his, godfather, and it was he who conducted us to the place of ceremony. His carriage was drawn by four perfectly beautiful Neapolitan horses; but these animals, which are often extremely fantastical, would not stir. The whip was vigorously applied; results—rearing, snorting, fury, the carriage in danger of being upset. Time was flying; I begged the Duc de Liria, therefore, to get into my carriage, so that we might not keep the King and the company waiting for us. It was in vain I represented to him that this function of godfather would in no way be affected by changing his own coach for mine, since it would be by necessity. He would not listen to me. The horses continued their game for a good half hour before they consented to start.

All my cortege followed us, for I wished by this display to show the King of Spain how highly I appreciated the honours of his Court. On the way the horses again commenced their pranks. I again pressed the Duc de Liria to change his coach, and he again refused. Fortunately the pause this time was much shorter than at first; but before we reached the end of our journey there came a message to say that the King was waiting for us. At last we arrived, and as soon as the King was informed of it he entered the room where the chapter of the order was assembled. He straightway sat himself down in an armchair, and while the rest of the company were placing themselves in position; the Queen, the Princess of the Asturias, and their suite, seated themselves as simple spectators at the end of the room.

All the chapter having arranged themselves in order, the door in front of the King, by which we had entered, was closed, my son remaining outside with a number of the courtiers. Then the King covered himself, and all the chevaliers at the same time, in the midst of a silence, without sign, which lasted as long as a little prayer. After this, the King very briefly proposed that the Vidame de Chartres should be received into the order. All the chevaliers uncovered themselves, made an inclination, without rising, and covered themselves again. After another silence, the King called the Duc de Liria, who uncovered himself, and with a reverence approached the King; by whom he was thus addressed: "Go and see if the Vidame de Chartres is not somewhere about here."

The Duc de Liria made another reverence to the King, but none to the chevaliers (who, nevertheless, were uncovered at the same time as he), went away, the door was closed upon him, and the chevaliers covered themselves again. The reverences just made, and those I shall have occasion to speak of in the course of my description, were the same as are seen at the receptions of the chevaliers of the Saint-Esprit, and in all grand ceremonies.

The Duc de Liria remained outside nearly a quarter of an hour, because it is assumed that the new chevalier is ignorant of the proposition made for him, and that it is only by chance he is found in the palace, time being needed in order to look for him. The Duc de Liria returned, and immediately after the door was again closed, and he advanced to the King, as before, saying that the Vidame de Chartres was in the other room.

Upon this the King ordered him to go and ask the Vidame if he wished to accept the Order of the Toison d'Or, and be received into it, and undertake to observe its statutes, its duties, its ceremonies, take its oaths, promise to fulfil all the conditions submitted: to every one who is admitted into it, and agree to conduct himself in everything like a good, loyal, brave, and virtuous chevalier. The Duc de Liria withdrew as he had before withdrawn. The door was again closed. He returned after having been absent a shorter time than at first. The door was again closed, and he approached the King as before, and announced to him the consent and the thanks of the Vidame. "Very well," replied the King. "Go seek him, and bring him here."

The Duc de Liria withdrew, as on the previous occasions, and immediately returned, having my son on his left. The door being open, anybody was at liberty to enter, and see the ceremony.

The Duc de Liria conducted my son to the feet of the King, and then seated himself in his place. My son, in advancing, had lightly inclined himself to the chevaliers, right and left; and, after having made in the middle of the room a profound bow, knelt before the King, without quitting his sword, and having his hat under his arm, and no gloves on. The chevaliers, who had uncovered themselves at the entry of the Duc de Liria, covered themselves when he sat down; and the Prince of the Asturias acted precisely as they acted.

The King repeated to my son the same things, a little more lengthily, that had been said to him by the Duc de Liria, and received his promise upon each in succession. Afterwards, an attendant, who was standing in waiting behind the table, presented to the King, from between the table and the chair, a large book, open, and in which was a long oath, that my son repeated to the King, who had the book upon his knees, the oath in French, and on loose paper; being in it. This ceremony lasted rather a long time: Afterwards, my son kissed the King's hand, and the King made him rise and pass, without reverence; directly before the table, towards the middle of which he knelt, his back to the Prince of the Asturias, his face to the attendant, who showed him (the table being between them) what to do. There was upon this table a great crucifix of enamel upon a stand, with a missal open at the Canon, the Gospel of Saint-John, and forms, in French, of promises and oaths to be made, whilst putting the hand now upon the Canon, now upon the Gospel. The oath-making took up some time; after which my son came back and knelt before the King again as before.

Then, the Duc del Orco, grand ecuyer, and Valouse, premier ecuyer, who have had the Toison since, and who were near me, went away, the Duke first, Valouse behind him, carrying in his two hands, with marked care and respect, the sword of the Grand Captain, Don Gonzalvo de Cordova, who is never called otherwise. They walked, with measured step, outside the right-hand seats of the chevaliers, then entered the chapter, where the Duc de Liria had entered with my son, marched inside the left-hand seats of the chevaliers, without reverence, but the Duke inclining himself; Valouse not doing so on account of the respect due to the sword; the grandees did not incline themselves.

The Duke on arriving between the Prince of the Asturias and the King, knelt, and Valouse knelt behind him. Some moments after, the King made a sign to them; Valouse drew the sword from its sheath which he put under his arm, held the naked weapon by the middle of the blade, kissed the hilt, and presented it to the King, who, without uncovering himself, kissed the pommel, took the sword in both hands by the handle, held it upright some moments; then held it with one hand, but almost immediately with the other as well, and struck it three times upon each shoulder of my son, alternately, saying to him, "By Saint-George and Saint-Andrew I make you Chevalier." And the weight of the sword was so great that the blows did not fall lightly. While the King was striking them, the grand ecuyer and the premier remained in their places kneeling. The sword was returned as it had been presented, and kissed in the same manner. Valouse put it back into its sheath, after which the grand ecuyer and the premier ecuyer returned as they came.

This sword, handle included, was more than four feet long; the blade four good digits wide, thick in proportion, insensibly diminishing in thickness and width to the point, which was very small. The handle appeared to me of worked enamel, long and very large; as well as the pommel; the crossed piece long, and the two ends wide, even, worked, without branch. I examined it well, and I could not hold it in the air with one-hand, still less handle it with both hands except with much difficulty. It is pretended that this is the sword the Great Captain made use of, and with which he obtained so many victories.

I marvelled at the strength of the men in those days, with whom I believe early habits did much. I was touched by the grand honour rendered to the Great Captain's memory; his sword becoming the sword of the State, carried even by the King with great respect. I repeated, more than once, that if I were the Duc de Scose (who descends in a direct line from the Great Captain by the female branch, the male being extinct), I would leave nothing undone to obtain the Toison, in order to enjoy the honour and the sensible pleasure of being struck by this sword, and with such great respect for my ancestor. But to return to the ceremony from which this little digression has taken me.

The accolade being given by the King after the blows with the sword, fresh oaths being taken at his feet, then before the table as at first, and on this occasion at greater length, my son returned and knelt before the King, but without saying anything more. Then Grimaldo rose and, without reverence, left the chapter by the left, went behind the right- hand seats of the chevaliers, and took the collar of the Toison which was extended at the end of the table. At this moment the King told my son to rise, and so remain standing in the same place. The Prince of the Asturias, and the Marquis de Villena then rose also, end approached my son, both covered, all the other chevaliers remaining seated and covered. Then Grimaldo, passing between the table and the empty seat of the Prince of the Asturias, presented; standing, the collar to the King, who took it with both hands, and meanwhile Grimaldo, passing behind the Prince of the Asturias, went and placed himself behind my son. As soon as he was there, the King told my son to bend very low, but without kneeling, and then leaning forward, but without rising, placed the collar upon him, and made him immediately after stand upright. The King then took hold of the collar, simply holding the end of it in his hand. At the same time, the collar was attached to the left shoulder by the Prince of the Asturias, to the right shoulder by the Marquis de Villena, and behind by Grimaldo; the King still holding the end.

When the collar was attached, the Prince of the Asturias, the Marquis de Villena, and Grimaldo, without making a reverence and no chevalier uncovering himself, went back to their places, and sat down; at, the same moment my son knelt before the King, and bared, his head. Then the Duc de Liria, without reverence, and uncovered (no chevalier uncovering himself), placed himself before the King at the left, by the side of my son, and both made their reverences to the King; turned round to the Prince of the Asturias, did the same to him, he rising and doing my son the honour to embrace him, and as soon as he was reseated they made a reverence to him; then, turning to the King, made him one; afterwards they did the same to the Marquis de Villena, who rose and embraced my son. Then he reseated himself; upon which they made a reverence to him, then turning again towards the King, made another to him; and so an from right to left until every chevalier had been bowed to in a similar manner. Then my son sat down, and the Duc de Liria returned to his place.

After this long series of bows, so bewildering for those who play the chief part in it, the King remained a short time in his armchair, them rose, uncovered himself, and retired into his apartment as he came. I had instructed my son to hurry forward and arrive before him at the door of his inner apartment. He was in time, and I also, to kiss the hand of the King, and to express our thanks, which were well received. The Queen arrived and overwhelmed us with compliments. I must observe that the ceremony of the sword and the accolade are not performed at the reception of those who, having already another order, are supposed to have received them; like the chevaliers of the Saint-Esprit and of Saint-Michel, and the chevaliers of Saint-Louis.

Their Catholic Majesties being gone, we withdrew to my house, where a very grand dinner was prepared. The usage is, before the reception, to visit all the chevaliers of the Toison, and when the day is fixed, to visit all those invited to dinner on the day of the ceremony; the godfather, with the other chevalier by whom he is accompanied, also invites them at the palace before they enter the chapter, and aids the new chevalier to do the honours of the repast. I had led my son with me to pay these visits. Nearly all the chevaliers came to dine with us, and many other nobles. The Duc d'Albuquerque, whom I met pretty often, and who had excused himself from attending a dinner I had previously given, on account of his stomach (ruined as he said in the Indies), said he, would not refuse me twice, on condition that I permitted him to take nothing but soup, because meat was too solid for him. He came, and partook of six sorts of soup, moderately of all; he afterwards lightly soaked his bread in such ragouts as were near him, eating only the end, and finding everything very good. He drank nothing but wine and water. The dinner was gay, in spite of the great number of guests. The Spaniards eat as much as, nay more than, we, and with taste, choice, and pleasure: as to drink, they are very modest.

On the 13th of March, 1722, their Catholic Majesties returned from their excursion to the Retiro. The hurried journey I had just made to the former place, immediately after the arrival of a courier, and in spite of most open prohibitions forbidding every one to go there, joined to the fashion, full of favour and goodness, with which I had been distinguished by their Majesties ever since my arrival in Spain, caused a most ridiculous rumour to obtain circulation, and which, to my great surprise, at once gained much belief.

It was reported there that I was going to quit my position of ambassador from France, and be declared prime minister of Spain! The people who had been pleased, apparently, with the expense I had kept up, and to whom not one of my suite had given the slightest cause of complaint, set to crying after me in the streets; announcing my promotion, displaying joy at it, and talking of it even in the shops. A number of persons even assembled round my house to testify to me their pleasure. I dispersed them as civilly and as quickly as possible, assuring them the report was not true, and that I was forthwith about to return to France.

This was nothing more than the truth. I had finished all my business. It was time to think about setting out. As soon, however, as I talked about going, there was nothing which the King and the Queen did not do to detain me. All the Court, too, did me the favour to express much friendship for me, and regret at my departure. I admit even that I could not easily make up my mind to quit a country where I had found nothing but fruits and flowers, and to which I was attached, as I shall ever be, by esteem and gratitude. I made at once a number of farewell visits among the friends I had been once acquainted with; and on the 21st of March I had my parting state audiences of the King and Queen separately. I was surprised with the dignity, the precision, and the measure of the King's expressions, as I had been surprised at my first audience. I received many marks of personal goodness, and of regret at my departure from his Catholic Majesty, and from the Queen even more; from the Prince of the Asturias a good many also. But in another direction I met with very different treatment, which I cannot refrain from describing, however ridiculous it may appear.

I went, of course, to say my adieux to the Princess of the Asturias, and I was accompanied by all my suite. I found the young lady standing under a dais, the ladies on one side, the grandees on the other; and I made my three reverences, then uttered my compliments. I waited in silence her reply, but 'twas in vain. She answered not one word.

After some moments of silence, I thought I would furnish her with matter for an answer; so I asked her what orders she had for the King; for the Infanta, for Madame, and for M. and Madame la Duchesse d'Orleans. By way of reply, she looked at me and belched so loudly in my face, that the noise echoed throughout the chamber. My surprise was such that I was stupefied. A second belch followed as noisy as the first.

I lost countenance at this, and all power of hindering myself from laughing. Turning round, therefore, I saw everybody with their hands upon their mouths, and their shoulders in motion. At last a third belch, still louder than the two others, threw all present into confusion, and forced me to take flight, followed by all my suite, amid shouts of laughter, all the louder because they had previously been kept in. But all barriers of restraint were now thrown down; Spanish gravity was entirely disconcerted; all was deranged; no reverences; each person, bursting with laughter, escaped as he could, the Princess all the while maintaining her countenance. Her belches were the only answers she made me. In the adjoining room we all stopped to laugh at our ease, and express our astonishment afterwards more freely.

The King and Queen were soon informed of the success of this audience, and spoke of it to me after dinner at the Racket Court. They were the first to laugh at it, so as to leave others at liberty to do so too; a privilege that was largely made use of without pressing. I received and I paid numberless visits; and as it is easy to flatter one's self, I fancied I might flatter myself that I was regretted.

I left Madrid on the 24th of March, after having had the honour of paying my court to their Catholic Majesties all the afternoon at the Racket Court, they overwhelming me with civilities, and begging me to take a final adieu of them in their apartments. I had devoted the last few days to the friends whom, during my short stay of six months, I had made. Whatever might be the joy and eagerness I felt at the prospect of seeing Madame de Saint-Simon and my Paris friends again, I could not quit Spain without feeling my heart moved, or without regretting persons from whom I had received so many marks of goodness, and for whom, all I had seen of the nation, had made me conceive esteem, respect, and gratitude. I kept up, for many years, a correspondence with Grimaldo, while he lived, in fact, and after his fall and disgrace, which occurred long after my departure, with more care and attention than formerly. My attachment, full of respect and gratitude for the King and Queen of Spain, induced me to do myself the honour of writing to them on all occasions. They often did me the honour to reply to me; and always charged their new ministers in France and the persons of consideration who came there, to convey to me the expression of their good feeling for me.

After a journey without particular incident, I embarked early one morning upon the Garonne, and soon arrived at Bordeaux. The jurats did me the honour to ask, through Segur, the under-mayor, at what time they might come and salute me. I invited them to supper, and said to Segur that compliments would be best uttered glass in hand. They came, therefore, to supper, and appeared to me much pleased with this civility: On the morrow, the tide early carried me to Blaye, the weather being most delightful. I slept only one night there, and to save time did not go to Ruffec.

On the 13th of April, I arrived, about five o'clock in the afternoon, at Loches. I slept there because I wished to write a volume of details to the Duchesse de Beauvilliers, who was six leagues off, at one of her estates. I sent my packet by an express, and in this manner I was able to say what I liked to her without fearing that the letter would be opened.

On the morrow, the 14th, I arrived at Etampes, where I slept, and the 15th, at ten o'clock in the morning, I reached Chartres, where Madame de Saint-Simon was to meet me, dine, and sleep, so that we might have the pleasure of opening our hearts to each other, and of finding ourselves together again in solitude and in liberty, greater than could be looked for in Paris during the first few days of my return. The Duc d'Humieres and Louville came with her. She arrived an hour after me, fixing herself in the little chateau of the Marquis d'Arpajan, who had lent it to her, and where the day appeared to us very short as well as the next morning, the 16th of April.

To conclude the account of my journey, let me say that I arrived in Paris shortly after, and at once made the best of my way to the Palais Royal, where M. le Duc d'Orleans gave me a sincere and friendly welcome.

VOLUME 15.: CHAPTER CXIII

Few events of importance had taken place during my absence in Spain. Shortly after my return, however, a circumstance occurred which may fairly claim description from me. Let me, therefore, at once relate it.

Cardinal Dubois, every day more and more firmly established in the favour of M. le Duc d'Orleans, pined for nothing less than to be declared prime minister. He was already virtually in that position, but was not publicly or officially recognised as being so. He wished, therefore, to be declared.

One great obstacle in his path was the Marechal de Villeroy, with whom he was on very bad terms, and whom he was afraid of transforming into an open and declared enemy, owing to the influence the Marechal exerted over others. Tormented with agitating thoughts, every day that delayed his nomination seemed to him a year. Dubois became doubly ill-tempered and capricious, more and more inaccessible, and accordingly the most pressing and most important business was utterly neglected. At last he resolved to make a last effort at reconciliation with the Marechal, but mistrusting his own powers, decided upon asking Cardinal Bissy to be the mediator between them.

Bissy with great willingness undertook the peaceful commission; spoke to Villeroy, who appeared quite ready to make friends with Dubois, and even consented to go and see him. As chance would have it, he went, accompanied by Bissy, on Tuesday morning. I at the same time went, as was my custom, to Versailles to speak to M. le Duc d'Orleans upon some subject, I forget now what.

It was the day on which the foreign ministers had their audience of Cardinal Dubois, and when Bissy and Villeroy arrived, they found these ministers waiting in the chamber adjoining the Cardinal's cabinet.

The established usage is that they have their audience according to the order in which they arrive, so as to avoid all disputes among them as to rank and precedence. Thus Bissy and Villeroy found Dubois closeted with the Russian minister. It was proposed to inform the Cardinal at once, of a this, so rare as a visit from the Marechal de Villeroy; but the Marechal would not permit it, and sat down upon a sofa with Bissy to wait like the rest.

The audience being over, Dubois came from his cabinet, conducting the Russian minister, and immediately saw his sofa so well ornamented. He saw nothing but that in fact; on the instant he ran there, paid a thousand compliments to the Marechal for anticipating him, when he was only waiting for permission to call upon him, and begged him and Bissy to step into the cabinet. While they were going there, Dubois made his excuses to the ambassadors for attending to Villeroy before them, saying that his functions and his assiduity as governor of the King did not permit him to be long absent from the presence of his Majesty; and with this compliment he quitted them and returned into his cabinet.

At first nothing passed but reciprocal compliments and observations from Cardinal Bissy, appropriate to the subject. Then followed protestations from Dubois and replies from the

Marechal. Thus far, the sea was very smooth. But absorbed in his song, the Marechal began to forget its tune; then to plume himself upon his frankness and upon his plain speaking; then by degrees, growing hot in his honours, he gave utterance to divers naked truths, closely akin to insults.

Dubois, much astonished, pretended not to feel the force of these observations, but as they increased every moment, Bissy tried to call back the Marechal, explain things to him, and give a more pleasant tone to the conversation. But the mental tide had begun to rise, and now it was entirely carrying away the brains of Villeroy. From bad to worse was easy. The Marechal began now to utter unmistakable insults and the most bitter reproaches. In vain Bissy tried to silence him; representing to him how far he was wandering from the subject they came to talk upon; how indecent it was to insult a man in his own house, especially, after arriving on purpose to conclude a reconciliation with him. All Bissy could say simply had the effect of exasperating the Marechal, and of making him vomit forth the most extravagant insults that insolence and disdain could suggest.

Dubois, stupefied and beside himself, was deprived of his tongue, could not utter a word; while Bissy, justly inflamed with anger, uselessly tried to interrupt his friend. In the midst of the sudden fire which had seized the Marechal, he had placed himself in such a manner that he barred the passage to the door, and he continued his invectives without restraint. Tired of insults, he passed to menaces and derision, saying to Dubois that since he had now thrown off all disguise, they no longer were on terms to pardon each other, and then he assured Dubois that, sooner or later, he would do him all the injury possible, and gave him what he called good counsel.

"You are all powerful," said he; "everybody bends before you; nobody resists you; what are the greatest people in the land compared with you? Believe me, you have only one thing to do; employ all your power, put yourself at ease, and arrest me, if you dare. Who can hinder you? Arrest me, I say, you have only that course open."

Thereupon, he redoubled his challenges and his insults, like a man who is thoroughly persuaded that between arresting him and scaling Heaven there is no difference. As may well be imagined, such astounding remarks were not uttered without interruption, and warm altercations from the Cardinal de Bissy, who, nevertheless, could not stop the torrent. At last, carried away by anger and vexation, Bissy seized the Marechal by the arm and the shoulder, and hurried him to the door, which he opened, and then pushed him out, and followed at his heels. Dubois, more dead than alive, followed also, as well as he could—he was obliged to be on his guard against the foreign ministers who were waiting. But the three disputants vainly tried to appear composed; there was not one of the ministers who did not perceive that some violent scene must have passed in the cabinet, and forthwith Versailles was filled with this news; which was soon explained by the bragging, the explanations, the challenges, and the derisive speeches of the Marechal de Villeroy.

I had worked and chatted for a long time with M. le Duc d'Orleans. He had passed into his wardrobe, and I was standing behind his bureau arranging his papers when I saw Cardinal

Dubois enter like a whirlwind, his eyes starting out of his head. Seeing me alone, he screamed rather than asked, "Where is M. le Duc d'Orleans?" I replied that he had gone into his wardrobe, and seeing him so overturned, I asked him what was the matter.

"I am lost, I am lost!" he replied, running to the wardrobe. His reply was so loud and so sharp that M. le Duc d'Orleans, who heard it, also ran forward, so that they met each other in the doorway. They returned towards me, and the Regent asked what was the matter.

Dubois, who always stammered, could scarcely speak, so great was his rage and fear; but he succeeded at last in acquainting us with the details I have just given, although at greater length. He concluded by saying that after the insults he had received so treacherously, and in a manner so basely premeditated, the Regent must choose between him and the Marechal de Villeroy, for that after what had passed he could not transact any business or remain at the Court in safety and honour, while the Marechal de Villeroy remained there!

I cannot express the astonishment into which M. le Duc d'Orleans and I were thrown. We could not believe what we had heard, but fancied we were dreaming. M. le Duc d'Orleans put several questions to Dubois, I took the liberty to do the same, in order to sift the affair to the bottom. But there was no variation in the replies of the Cardinal, furious as he was. Every moment he presented the same option to the Regent; every moment he proposed that the Cardinal de Bissy should be sent for as having witnessed everything. It may be imagined that this second scene, which I would gladly have escaped, was tolerably exciting.

The Cardinal still insisting that the Regent must choose which of the two be sent away, M. le Duc d'Orleans asked me what I thought. I replied that I was so bewildered and so moved by this astounding occurrence that I must collect myself before speaking. The Cardinal, without addressing himself to me but to M. le Duc d'Orleans, who he saw was plunged Memoirs in embarrassment, strongly insisted that he must come to some resolution. Upon this M. le Duc d'Orleans beckoned me over, and I said to him that hitherto I had always regarded the dismissal of the Marechal de Villeroy as a very dangerous enterprise, for reasons I had several times alleged to his Royal Highness: but that now whatever peril there might be in undertaking it, the frightful scene that had just been enacted persuaded me that it would be much more dangerous to leave him near the King than to get rid of him altogether. I added that this was my opinion, since his Royal Highness wished to know it without giving me the time to reflect upon it with more coolness; but as for the execution, that must be well discussed before being attempted.

Whilst I spoke, the Cardinal pricked up his ears, turned his eyes upon me, sucked in all my words, and changed colour like a man who hears his doom pronounced. My opinion relieved him as much as the rage with which he was filled permitted. M. le Duc d'Orleans approved what I had just said, and the Cardinal, casting a glance upon me as of thanks, said he was the master, and must choose, but that he must choose at once, because things could not remain as they were. Finally, it was agreed that the rest of the day (it was now about twelve) and the following morning should be given to reflection upon the matter, and that the next day, at three o'clock in the afternoon, I should meet M. le Duc d'Orleans.

The next day accordingly I went to M. le Prince, whom I found with the Cardinal Dubois. M.

le Duc entered a moment after, quite full of the adventure. Cardinal Dubois did not fail, though, to give him an abridged recital of it, loaded with comments and reflections. He was more his own master than on the preceding day, having had time to recover himself, we cherishing hopes that the Marechal would be sent to the right about. It was here that I heard of the brag of the Marechal de Villeroy concerning the struggle he had had with Dubois, and of the challenges and insults he had uttered with a confidence which rendered his arrest more and more necessary.

After we had chatted awhile, standing, Dubois went away. M. le Duc d'Orleans sat down at his bureau, and M. le Duc and I sat in front of him. There we deliberated upon what ought to be done. After a few words of explanation from the Regent, he called upon me to give my opinion. I did so as briefly as possible, repeating what I had said on the previous day. M. le Duc d'Orleans, during my short speech, was very attentive, but with the countenance of a man much embarrassed.

As soon as I had finished, he asked M. le Duc what he thought. M. le Duc said his opinion was mine, and that if the Marechal de Villeroy remained in his office there was nothing for it but to put the key outside the door; that was his expression. He reproduced some of the principal reasons I had alleged, supported them, and concluded by saying there was not a moment to lose. M. le Duc d'Orleans summed up a part of what had been said, and agreed that the Marechal de Villeroy must be got rid of. M. le Duc again remarked that it must be done at once. Then we set about thinking how we could do it.

M. le Duc d'Orleans asked me my advice thereon. I said there were two things to discuss, the pretext and the execution. That a pretext was necessary, such as would convince the impartial, and be unopposed even by the friends of the Marechal de Villeroy; that above all things we had to take care to give no one ground for believing that the disgrace of Villeroy was the fruit of the insults he had heaped upon Cardinal Dubois; that outrageous as those insults might be, addressed to a cardinal, to a minister in possession of entire confidence, and at the head of affairs, the public, who envied him and did not like him, well remembering whence he had sprung, would consider the victim too illustrious; that the chastisement would overbalance the offence, and would be complained of; that violent resolutions, although necessary, should always have reason and appearances in their favour; that therefore I was against allowing punishment to follow too quickly upon the real offence, inasmuch as M. le Duc d'Orleans had one of the best pretexts in the world for disgracing the Marechal, a pretext known by everybody, and which would be admitted by everybody.

I begged the Regent then to remember that he had told me several times he never had been able to speak to the King in private, or even in a whisper before others; that when he had tried, the Marechal de Villeroy had at once come forward poking his nose between them, and declaring that while he was governor he would never suffer any one, not even his Royal Highness, to address his Majesty in a low tone, much lest to speak to him in private. I said that this conduct towards the Regent, a grandson of France, and the nearest relative the King had, was insolence enough to disgust every one, and apparent as such at half a glance. I counselled M. le Duc d'Orleans to make use of this circumstance, and by its means to lay a trap for the Marechal into which there was not the slightest doubt he would fall. The trap was to be thus arranged. M. le Duc d'Orleans was to insist upon his right to speak to the King in private, and upon the refusal of the Marechal to recognise it, was to adopt a new tone and make Villeroy feel he was the master. I added, in conclusion, that this snare must not be laid until everything was ready to secure its success.

When I had ceased speaking, "You have robbed me," said the Regent; "I was going to propose the same thing if you had not. What do you think of it, Monsieur?" regarding M. le Duc. That Prince strongly approved the proposition I had just made, briefly praised every part of it, and added that he saw nothing better to be done than to execute this plan very punctually.

It was agreed afterwards that no other plan could be adopted than that of arresting the Marechal and sending him right off at once to Villeroy, and then, after having allowed him to repose there a day or two, on account of his age, but well watched, to see if he should be sent on to Lyons or elsewhere. The manner in which he was to be arrested was to be decided at Cardinal Dubois' apartments, where the Regent begged me to go at once. I rose accordingly, and went there.

I found Dubois with one or two friends, all of whom were in the secret of this affair, as he, at once told me, to put me at my ease. We soon therefore entered upon business, but it would be superfluous to relate here all that passed in this little assembly. What we resolved on was very well executed, as will be seen. I arranged with Le Blanc, who was one of the conclave, that the instant the arrest had taken place, he should send to Meudon, and simply inquire after me; nothing more, and that by this apparently meaningless compliment, I should know that the Marechal had been packed off.

I returned towards evening to Meudon, where several friends of Madame de Saint-Simon and of myself often slept, and where others, following the fashion established at Versailles and Paris, came to dine or sup, so that the company was always very numerous. The scene between Dubois and Villeroy was much talked about, and the latter universally blamed. Neither then nor during the ten days which elapsed before his arrest, did it enter into the head of anybody to suppose that anything worse would happen to him than general blame for his unmeasured violence, so accustomed were people to his freaks, and to the feebleness of M. le Duc d'Orleans. I was now delighted, however, to find such general confidence, which augmented that of the Marechal, and rendered more easy the execution of our project against him; punishment he more and more deserved by the indecency and affectation of his discourses, and the audacity of his continual challenges.

Three or four days after, I went to Versailles, to see M. le Duc d'Orleans. He said that, for want of a better, and in consequence of what I had said to him on more than one occasion of the Duc de Charost, it was to him he intended to give the office of governor of the King: that he had secretly seen him that Charost had accepted with willingness the post, and was now safely shut up in his apartment at Versailles, seeing no one, and seen by no one, ready to be led to the King the moment the time should arrive. The Regent went over with me all the measures to be taken, and I returned to Meudon, resolved not to budge from it until they were executed, there being nothing more to arrange.

On Sunday, the 12th of August, 1722, M. le Duc d'Orleans went, towards the end of the afternoon, to work with the King, as he was accustomed to do several times each week; and as it was summer time now, he went after his airing, which he always took early. This work was to show the King by whom were to be filled up vacant places in the church, among the magistrates and intendants, &c., and to briefly explain to him the reasons which suggested the selection, and sometimes the distribution of the finances. The Regent informed him, too, of the foreign news, which was within his comprehension, before it was made public. At the conclusion of this labour, at which the Marechal de Villeroy was always present, and sometimes M. de Frejus (when he made bold to stop), M. le Duc d'Orleans begged the King to step into a little back cabinet, where he would say a word to him alone.

The Marechal de Villeroy at once opposed. M. le Duc d'Orleans, who had laid this snare far him, saw him fall into it with satisfaction. He represented to the Marechal that the King was approaching the age when he would govern by himself, that it was time for him, who was meanwhile the depository of all his authority, to inform him of things which he could understand, and which could only be explained to him alone, whatever confidence might merit any third person. The Regent concluded by begging the Marechal to cease to place any obstacles in the way of a thing so necessary and so important, saying that he had, perhaps, to reproach himself for,—solely out of complaisance to him, not having coerced before.

The Marechal, arising and stroking his wig, replied that he knew the respect he owed, him, and knew also quite as well the respect he owed to the King, and to his place, charged as he was with the person of his Majesty, and being responsible for it. But he said he would not suffer his Royal Highness to speak to the King in private (because he ought to know everything said to his Majesty), still less would he suffer him to lead the King into a cabinet, out of his sight, for 'twas his (the Marechal's) duty never to lose sight of his charge, and in everything to answer for it.

Upon this, M. le Duc d'Orleans looked fixedly at the Marechal and said, in the tone of a master, that he mistook himself and forgot himself; that he ought to remember to whom he was speaking, and take care what words he used; that the respect he (the Regent) owed to the presence of the King, hindered him from replying as he ought to reply, and from continuing this conversation. Therefore he made a profound reverence to the King, and went away.

The Marechal, thoroughly angry, conducted him some steps, mumbling and gesticulating; M. le Duc d'Orleans pretending to neither see nor hear him, the King astonished, and M. de Frejus laughing in his sleeve. The bait so well swallowed,—no one doubted that the Marechal, audacious as he was, but nevertheless a servile and timid courtier, would feel all the difference between braving, bearding, and insulting Cardinal Dubois (odious to everybody, and always smelling of the vile egg from which he had been hatched) and wrestling with the Regent in the presence of the King, claiming to annihilate M. le Duc d'Orleans' rights and authority, by appealing to his own pretended rights and authority as governor of the King. People were not mistaken; less than two hours after what had occurred, it was known that the Marechal, bragging of what he had just done, had added that he should consider himself very unhappy if M. le Duc d'Orleans thought he had been wanting in respect to him, when his only idea was to fulfil his precious duty; and that he would go the next day to have an explanation with his Royal Highness, which he doubted not would be satisfactory to him.

At every hazard, all necessary measures had been taken as soon as the day was fixed on which the snare was to be laid for the Marechal. Nothing remained but to give form to them directly it was known that on the morrow the Marechal would come and throw himself into the lion's mouth.

Beyond the bed-room of M. le Duc d'Orleans was a large and fine cabinet, with four big windows looking upon the garden, and on the same floor, two paces distant, two other windows; and two at the side in front of the chimney, and all these windows opened like doors. This cabinet occupied the corner where the courtiers awaited, and behind was an adjoining cabinet, where M. le Duc d'Orleans worked and received distinguished persons or favourites who wished to talk with him.

The word was given. Artagnan, captain of the grey musketeers, was in the room (knowing what was going to happen), with many trusty officers of his company whom he had sent for, and former musketeers to be made use of at a pinch, and who clearly saw by these preparations that something important was in the wind, but without divining what. There were also some light horse posted outside these windows in the same ignorance, and many principal officers and others in the Regent's bed-room, and in the grand cabinet.

All things being well arranged, the Marechal de Villeroy arrived about mid-day, with his accustomed hubbub, but alone, his chair and porters remaining outside, beyond the Salle des Gardes. He enters like a comedian, stops, looks round, advances some steps. Under pretext of civility, he is environed, surrounded. He asks in an authoritative tone, what M. le Duc d'Orleans is doing: the reply is, he is in his private room within.

The Marechal elevates his tone, says that nevertheless he must see the Regent; that he is going to enter; when lo! La Fare, captain of M. le Duc d'Orleans' guards, presents himself before him, arrests him, and demands his sword. The Marechal becomes furious, all present are in commotion. At this instant Le Blanc presents himself. His sedan chair, that had been hidden, is planted before the Marechal. He cries aloud, he is shaking on his lower limbs; but he is thrust into the chair, which is closed upon him and carried away in the twinkling of an eye through one of the side windows into the garden, La Fare and Artagnan each on one side of the chair, the light horse and musketeers behind, judging only by the result what was in the wind. The march is hastened; the party descend the steps of the orangery by the side of the thicket; the grand gate is found open and a coach and six before it. The chair is put down; the Marechal storms as he will; he is cast into the coach; Artagnan mounts by his side; an officer of the musketeers is in front; and one of the gentlemen in ordinary of the King by the side of the officer; twenty musketeers, with mounted officers, surround the vehicle, and away they go.

This side of the garden is beneath the window of the Queen's apartments (when occupied by the Infanta). This scene under the blazing noon-day sun was seen by no one, and although the large number of persons in M. le Duc d'Orleans' rooms soon dispersed, it is astonishing that an affair of this kind remained unknown more than ten hours in the chateau of Versailles. The servants of the Marechal de Villeroy (to whom nobody had dared to say a word) still waited with their master's chair near the Salle des Gardes. They were, told, after M. le Duc d'Orleans had seen the King, that the Marechal had gone to Villeroy, and that they could carry to him what was necessary.

I received at Meudon the message arranged. I was sitting down to table, and it was only towards the supper that people came from Versailles to tell us all the news, which was making much sensation there, but a sensation very measured on account of the surprise and fear paused by the manner in which the arrest had been executed.

It was no agreeable task, that which had to be performed soon after by the Regent; I mean when he carried the news of the arrest to the King. He entered into his Majesty's cabinet, which he cleared of all the company it contained, except those people whose post gave them aright to enter, but of them there were not many present. At the first word, the King reddened; his eyes moistened; he hid his face against the back of an armchair, without saying a word; would neither go out nor play. He ate but a few mouthfuls at supper, wept, and did not sleep all night. The morning and the dinner of the next day, the 14th, passed off but little better.

CHAPTER CXIV

That same 14th, as I rose from dinner at Meudon, with much company, the valet de chambre who served me said that a courier from Cardinal Dubois had a letter for me, which he had not thought good to bring me before all my guests. I opened the letter. The Cardinal conjured me to go instantly and see him at Versailles, bringing with me a trusty servant, ready to be despatched to La Trappe, as soon as I had spoken with him, and not to rack my brains to divine what this might mean, because it would be impossible to divine it, and that he was waiting with the utmost impatience to tell it to me. I at once ordered my coach, which I thought a long time in coming from the stables. They are a considerable distance from the new chateau I occupied.

This courier to be taken to the Cardinal, in order to be despatched to La Trappe, turned my head. I could not imagine what had happened to occupy the Cardinal so thoroughly so soon after the arrest of Villeroy. The constitution, or some important and unknown fugitive discovered at La Trappe, and a thousand other thoughts, agitated me until I arrived at Versailles.

Upon reaching the chateau, I saw Dubois at a window awaiting me, and making many signs to me, and upon reaching the staircase, I found him there at the bottom, as I was about to mount. His first word was to ask me if I had brought with me a man who could post to La Trappe. I showed him my valet de chambre, who knew the road well, having travelled over it with me very often, and who was well known to the Cardinal, who, when simple Abbe Dubois, used very frequently to chat with him while waiting for me.

The Cardinal explained to me, as we ascended the stairs, the cause of his message. Immediately after the departure of the Marechal de Villeroy, M. le Frejus, the King's instructor, had been missed. He had disappeared. He had not slept at Versailles. No one knew what had become of him! The grief of the King had so much increased upon receiving this fresh blow— both his familiar friends taken from him at once—that no one knew what to do with him. He was in the most violent despair, wept bitterly, and could not be pacified. The Cardinal concluded by saying that no stone must be left unturned in order to find M. de Frejus. That unless he had gone to Villeroy, it was probable he had hid himself in La Trappe, and that we must send and see. With this he led me to M. le Duc d'Orleans. He was alone, much troubled, walking up and down his chamber, and he said to me that he knew not what would become of the King, or what to do with him; that he was crying for M. de Frejus, and—would listen to nothing; and the Regent began himself to cry out against this strange flight.

After some further consideration, Dubois pressed me to go and write to La Trappe. All was in disorder where we were; everybody spoke at once in the cabinet; it was impossible, in the midst of all this noise, to write upon the bureau, as I often did when I was alone with the King. My apartment was in the new wing, and perhaps shut up, for I was not expected that day. I went therefore, instead, into the chamber of Peze, close at hand, and wrote my letter there. The letter finished, and I about to descend, Peze, who had left me, returned, crying, "He is found! he is found! your letter is useless; return to M. le Duc d'Orleans."

He then related to me that just before, one of M. le Duc d'Orleans' people, who knew that

Frejus was a friend of the Lamoignons, had met Courson in the grand court, and had asked him if he knew what had become of Frejus; that Courson had replied, "Certainly: he went last night to sleep at Basville, where the President Lamoignon is;" and that upon this, the man hurried Courson to M. le Duc d'Orleans to relate this to him.

Peze and I arrived at M. le Duc d'Orleans' room just after Courson left it. Serenity had returned. Frejus was well belaboured. After a moment of cheerfulness, Cardinal Dubois advised M. le Duc d'Orleans to go and carry this good news to the King, and to say that a courier should at once be despatched to Basville, to make his preceptor return. M. le Duc d'Orleans acted upon the suggestion, saying he would return directly. I remained with Dubois awaiting him.

After having discussed a little this mysterious flight of Frejus, Dubois told me he had news of Villeroy. He said that the Marechal had not ceased to cry out against the outrage committed upon his person, the audacity of the Regent, the insolence of Dubois, or to hector Artagnan all the way for having lent himself to such criminal violence; then he invoked the Manes of the deceased King, bragged of his confidence in him, the importance of the place he held, and for which he had been preferred above all others; talked of the rising that so impudent an enterprise would cause in Paris, throughout the realm, and in foreign countries; deplored the fate of the young King and of all the kingdom; the officers selected by the late King for the most precious of charges, driven away, the Duc du Maine first, himself afterwards; then he burst out into exclamations and invectives; then into praises of his services, of his fidelity, of his firmness, of his inviolable attachment to his duty. In fact, he was so astonished, so troubled, so full of vexation and of rage, that he was thoroughly beside himself. The Duc de Villeroy, the Marechal de Tallard and Biron had permission to go and see him at Villeroy: scarcely anybody else asked for it.

M. le Duc d'Orleans having returned from the King, saying that the news he had carried had much appeased his Majesty, we agreed we must so arrange matters that Frejus should return the next morning, that M. le Duc d'Orleans should receive him well, as though nothing had happened, and give him to understand that it was simply to avoid embarrassing him, that he had not been made aware of the secret of the arrest (explaining this to him with all the more liberty, because Frejus hated the Marechal, his haughtiness, his jealousy, his capriciousness, and in his heart must be delighted at his removal, and at being able to have entire possession of the—King), then beg him to explain to the King the necessity of Villeroy's dismissal: then communicate to Frejus the selection of the Duc de Charost as governor of the King; promise him all the concert and the attention from this latter he could desire; ask him to counsel and guide Charost; finally, seize the moment of the King's joy at the return of Frejus to inform his Majesty of the new governor chosen, and to present Charost to him. All this was arranged and very well, executed next day.

When the Marechal heard of it at Villeroy, he flew into a strange passion against Charost (of whom he spoke with the utmost contempt for having accepted his place), but above all against Frejus, whom he called a traitor and a villain! His first moments of passion, of fury, and of transport, were all the more violent, because he saw by the tranquillity reigning everywhere that his pride had deceived him in inducing him to believe that the Parliament, the markets, all Paris would rise if the Regent dared to touch a person so important and so well beloved as he imagined himself to be. This truth, which he could no longer hide from himself, and which succeeded so rapidly to the chimeras that had been his food and his life, threw him into despair, and turned his head. He fell foul of the Regent, of his minister, of those employed to arrest him, of those who had failed to defend him, of all who had not risen in revolt to bring him back in triumph, of Charost, who had dared to succeed him, and especially of Frejus, who had deceived him in such an unworthy manner. Frejus was the person against whom he was the most irritated. Reproaches of ingratitude and of treachery rained unceasingly upon him; all that the Marechal had done for him with the deceased King was recollected; how he had protected, aided, lodged, and fed him; how without him (Villeroy) he (Frejus) would never have been preceptor of the King; and all this was exactly true.

The treachery to which he alluded he afterwards explained. He said that he and Frejus had agreed at the very commencement of the regency to act in union; and that if by troubles or events impossible to foresee, but which were only too common in regencies, one of them should be dismissed from office, the other not being able to hinder the dismissal, though not touched himself, should at once withdraw and never return to his post, until the first was reinstated in his. And after these explanations, new cries broke out against the perfidy of this miserable wretch— (for the most odious terms ran glibly from the end of his tongue)—who thought like a fool to cover his perfidy with a veil of gauze, in slipping off to Basville, so as to be instantly sought and brought back, in fear lest he should lose his place by the slightest resistance or the slightest delay, and who expected to acquit himself thus of his word, and of the reciprocal engagement both had taken; and then he returned to fresh insults and fury against this serpent, as he said, whom he had warmed and nourished so many years in his bosom.

The account of these transports and insults, promptly came from Villeroy to Versailles, brought, not only by the people whom the Regent had placed as guards over the Marechal, and to give an exact account of all he said and did, day by day, but by all the domestics who came and went, and before whom Villeroy launched out his speeches, at table, while passing through his ante-chambers, or while taking a turn in his gardens.

All this weighed heavily upon Frejus by the rebound. Despite the apparent tranquillity of his visage, he appeared confounded. He replied by a silence of respect and commiseration in which he enveloped himself; nevertheless, he could not do so to the Duc de Villeroy, the Marechal de Tallard, and a few others. He tranquilly said to them, that he had done all he could to fulfil an engagement which he did not deny, but that after having thus satisfied the call of honour, he did not think he could refuse to obey orders so express from the King and the Regent, or abandon the former in order to bring about the return of the Marechal de Villeroy, which was the object of their reciprocal engagement, and which he was certain he could not effect by absence, however prolonged. But amidst these very sober excuses could be seen the joy which peeped forth from him, in spite of himself, at being freed from so inconvenient a superior, at having to do with a new governor whom he could easily manage, at being able when he chose to guide himself in all liberty towards the grand object he had always desired, which was to attach himself to the King without reserve, and to make out of this attachment, obtained by all sorts of means, the means of a greatness which he did not yet dare to figure to himself, but which time and opportunity would teach him how to avail himself of in the best manner, marching to it meanwhile in perfect security.

The Marechal was allowed to refresh himself, and exhale his anger five or six days at Villeroy; and as he was not dangerous away from the King, he was sent to Lyons, with liberty to exercise his functions of governor of the town and province, measures being taken to keep a watch upon him, and Des Libois being left with him to diminish his authority by this manifestation of precaution and surveillance, which took from him all appearance of credit. He would receive no honours on arriving there. A large quantity of his first fire was extinguished; this wide separation from Paris and the Court, where not even the slightest movement had taken place, everybody being stupefied and in terror at an arrest of this importance; took from him all remaining hope, curbed his impetuosity, and finally induced him to conduct himself with sagacity in order to avoid worse treatment.

Such was the catastrophe of a man, so incapable of all the posts he had occupied, who displayed chimeras and audacity in the place of prudence and sagacity, who everywhere appeared a trifler and a comedian, and whose universal and profound ignorance (except of the meanest arts of the courtier) made plainly visible the thin covering of probity and of virtue with which he tried to hide his ingratitude, his mad ambition, his desire to overturn all in order to make himself the chief of all, in the midst of his weakness and his fears, and to hold a helm he was radically incapable of managing. I speak here only of his conduct since the establishment of the regency. Elsewhere, in more than one place, the little or nothing he was worth has been shown; how his ignorance and his jealousy lost us Flanders, and nearly ruined the State; how his felicity was pushed to the extreme, and what deplorable reverses followed his return. Sufficient to say that he never recovered from the state into which this last madness threw him, and that the rest of his life was only bitterness, regret, contempt! He had persuaded the King that it was he, alone, who by vigilance and precaution had preserved his life from poison that others wished to administer to him. This was the source of those tears shed by the King when Villeroy was carried off, and of his despair when Frejus disappeared. He did not doubt that both had been removed in order that this crime might be more easily committed.

The prompt return of Frejus dissipated the half, of his fear, the continuance of his good health delivered him by degrees from the other. The preceptor, who had a great interest in preserving the King, and who felt much relieved by the absence of Villeroy, left nothing undone in order to extinguish these gloomy ideas; and consequently to let blame fall upon him who had inspired them. He feared the return of the Marechal when the King, who was approaching his majority, should be the master; once delivered of the yoke he did not wish it to be reimposed upon him. He well knew that the grand airs, the ironies, the authoritative fussiness in public of the Marechal were insupportable to his Majesty, and that they held together only by those frightful ideas of poison. To destroy them was to show the Marechal uncovered, and worse than that to show to the King, without appearing to make a charge against the Marechal, the criminal interest he had in exciting these alarms, and the falsehood and atrocity of such a venomous invention. These reflections; which the health of the King each day confirmed, sapped all esteem, all gratitude, and left his Majesty in full liberty of conscience to prohibit, when he should be the master, all approach to his person on the part of so vile and so interested an impostor.

Frejus made use of these means to shelter himself against the possibility of the Marechal's return, and to attach himself to the King without reserve. The prodigious success of his schemes has been only too well felt since.

The banishment of Villeroy, flight and return of Frejus, and installation of Charost as governor of the King, were followed by the confirmation of his Majesty by the Cardinal de Rohan, and by his first communion, administered to him by this self-same Cardinal, his grand almoner.

Villeroy being banished, the last remaining obstacle in Dubois' path was removed. There was nothing: now, to hinder him from being proclaimed prime minister. I had opposed it as stoutly as I could; but my words were lost upon M. le Duc d'Orleans. Accordingly, about two o'clock in the afternoon of the 23rd of August, 1722, Dubois was declared prime minister by the Regent, and by the Regent at once conducted to the King as such.

After this event I began insensibly to withdraw from public affairs. Before the end of the year the King was consecrated at Rheims. The disorder at the ceremony was inexpressible. All precedent was forgotten. Rank was hustled and jostled, so to speak, by the crowd. The desire to exclude the nobility from all office and all dignity was obvious, at half a glance. My spirit was ulcerated at this; I saw approaching the complete re-establishment of the bastards; my heart was cleft in twain, to see the Regent at the heels of his unworthy minister. He was a prey to the interest, the avarice, the folly, of this miserable wretch, and no remedy possible. Whatever experience I might have had of the astonishing weakness of M. le Duc d'Orleans, it had passed all bounds when I saw him with my own eyes make Dubois prime minister, after all I had said to him on the subject,—after all he had said to me. The year 1723 commenced, and found me in this spirit. It is at the end of this year I have determined to end those memoirs, and the details of it will not be so full or so abundant as of preceding years. I was hopelessly wearied with M. le Duc d'Orleans; I no longer approached this poor prince (with so many great and useless talents buried in him)—except with repugnance. I could not help feeling for him what the poor, Israelites said to themselves in the desert about the manna: "Nauseat anima mea suffer cibum istum tevissimum." I no longer deigned to speak to him. He perceived this: I felt he was pained at it; he strove to reconcile me to him, without daring, however, to speak of affairs, except briefly, and with constraint, and yet he could not hinder himself from speaking of them. I scarcely took the trouble to reply to him, and I cut his conversation as short as possible. I abridged and curtailed my audiences with him; I listened to his reproaches with coldness. In fact, what had I to discuss with a Regent who was no longer one, not even over himself, still less over a realm plunged in disorder?

Cardinal Dubois, when he met me, almost courted me. He knew not how to catch me. The bonds which united me to M. le Duc d'Orleans had always been so strong that the prime minister, who knew their strength, did not dare to flatter himself he could break them. His resource was to try to disgust me by inducing his master to treat me with a reserve which was completely new to him, and which cost him more than it cost me; for, in fact, he had often found my confidence very useful to him, and had grown accustomed to it. As for me, I dispensed with his friendship more than willingly, vexed at being no longer able to gather any fruit from it for the advantage of the State or himself, wholly abandoned as he was to his Paris pleasures and to his minister. The conviction of my complete inutility more and more kept me in the background, without the slightest suspicion that different conduct could be dangerous to me, or that, weak and abandoned to Dubois as was the Regent, the former could ever exile me, like the Duc de Roailles, and

Cariillac, or disgust me into exiling myself. I followed, then, my accustomed life. That is to say, never saw M. le Duc d'Orleans except tete-a-tete, and then very seldom at intervals that each time grew longer, coldly, briefly, never talking to him of business, or, if he did to me, returning the conversation, and replying it! a manner to make it drop. Acting thus, it is easy to see that I was mixed up in nothing, and what I shall have to relate now will have less of the singularity and instructiveness of good and faithful memoirs, than of the dryness and sterility of the gazettes.

First of all I will finish my account of Cardinal Dubois. I have very little more to say of him; for he had scarcely begun to enjoy his high honours when Death came to laugh at him for the sweating labour he had taken to acquire them.

On the 11th of June, 1723, the King went to reside at Meudon, ostensibly in order that the chateau of Versailles might be cleared—in reality, to accommodate Cardinal Dubois. He had just presided over the assembly of the day, and flattered to the last degree at this, wished to repose upon the honour. He desired, also, to be present sometimes at the assembling of the Company of the Indies. Meudon brought him half-way to Paris, and saved him a journey. His debauchery had so shattered his health that the movement of a coach gave him pains which he very carefully hid.

The King held at Meudon a review of his household, which in his pride the Cardinal must needs attend. It cost him dear. He mounted on horseback the better, to enjoy his triumph; he suffered cruelly, and became so violently ill that he was obliged to have assistance. The most celebrated doctors and physicians were called in, with great secrecy. They shook their heads, and came so often that news of the illness began to transpire. Dubois was unable to go to Paris again more than once or twice, and then with much trouble, and solely to conceal his malady, which gave him no repose.

He left nothing undone, in fact, to hide it from the world; he went as often as he could to the council; apprised the ambassadors he would go to Paris, and did not go; kept himself invisible at home, and bestowed the most frightful abuse upon everybody who dared to intrude upon him. On Saturday, the 7th of August, he was so ill that the doctors declared he must submit to an operation, which was very urgent, and without which he could hope to live but a few days; because the abscess he had having burst the day he mounted on horseback, gangrene had commenced, with an overflow of pus, and he must be transported, they added, to Versailles, in order to undergo this operation. The trouble this terrible announcement caused him, so overthrew him that he could not be moved the next day, Sunday, the 8th; but on Monday he was transported in a litter, at five o'clock in the morning.

After having allowed him to repose himself a little, the doctors and surgeons proposed that he should receive the sacrament, and submit to the operation immediately after. This was not heard very peacefully; he had scarcely ever been free from fury since the day of the review; he had grown worse on Saturday, when the operation was first announced to him. Nevertheless, some little time after, he sent for a priest from Versailles, with whom he remained alone about a quarter of an hour. Such a great and good man, so well prepared for death, did not need more: Prime ministers, too, have privileged confessions. As his chamber again filled, it was proposed that he should take the viaticum; he cried out that that was soon said, but there was a ceremonial for the cardinals, of which he was ignorant, and Cardinal Bissy must be sent to, at Paris, for information upon it. Everybody looked at his neighbour, and felt that Dubois merely wished to gain time; but as the operation was urgent, they proposed it to him without further delay. He furiously sent them away, and would no longer hear talk of it.

The faculty, who saw the imminent danger of the slightest delay, sent to Meudon for M. le Duc d'Orleans, who instantly came in the first conveyance he could lay his hands on. He exhorted the Cardinal to suffer the operation; then asked the faculty, if it could be performed in safety. They replied that they could say nothing for certain, but that assuredly the Cardinal had not two hours to live if he did not instantly agree to it. M. le Duc d'Orleans returned to the sick man, and begged him so earnestly to do so, that he consented.

The operation was accordingly performed about five o'clock, and in five minutes, by La Peyronie, chief surgeon of the King, and successor to Marechal, who was present with Chirac and others of the most celebrated surgeons and doctors. The Cardinal cried and stormed strongly. M. le Duc d'Orleans returned into the chamber directly after the operation was performed, and the faculty did not dissimulate from him that, judging by the nature of the wound, and what had issued from it, the Cardinal had not long to live. He died, in fact, twenty-four hours afterwards, on the 10th, of August, at five o'clock in the morning, grinding his teeth against his surgeons and against Chirac, whom he had never ceased to abuse.

Extreme unction was, however, brought to him. Of the communion, nothing more was said—or of any priest for him—and he finished his life thus, in the utmost despair, and enraged at quitting it. Fortune had nicely played with him; slid made him dearly and slowly buy her favours by all sorts of trouble, care, projects, intrigues, fears, labour, torment; and at last showered down upon him torrents of greater power, unmeasured riches, to let him enjoy them only four years (dating from the time when he was made Secretary of State, and only two years dating from the time when he was made Cardinal and Prime Minister), and then snatched them from him, in the smiling moment when he was most enjoying them, at sixty- six years of age.

He died thus, absolute master of his master, less a prime minister than an all-powerful minister, exercising in full and undisturbed liberty the authority and the power of the King; he was superintendent of the post, Cardinal, Archbishop of Cambrai, had seven abbeys, with respect to which he was insatiable to the last; and he had set on foot overtures in order to seize upon those of Citeaux, Premonte, and others, and it was averred that he received a pension from England of 40,000 livres sterling! I had the curiosity to ascertain his revenue, and I have thought what I found curious enough to be inserted here, diminishing some of the benefices to avoid all exaggeration. I have made a reduction, too, upon what he drew from his place of prime minister, and that of the post. I believe, also, that he had 20,000 livres from the clergy, as Cardinal, but I do not know it as certain. What he drew from Law was immense. He had made use of a good deal of it at Rome, in order to obtain his Cardinalship; but a prodigious sum of ready cash was left in his hands. He had an extreme quantity of the most beautiful plate in silver and enamel, most admirably worked; the richest furniture, the rarest jewels of all kinds, the finest and rarest horses of all countries, and the most superb equipages. His table was in every way exquisite and superb, and he did the honours of it very well, although extremely sober by nature and by regime.

The place of preceptor of M. le Duc d'Orleans had procured for him the Abbey of Nogent-sous-Coucy; the marriage of the Prince that of Saint- Just; his first journeys to Hanover and England, those of Airvause and of Bourgueil: three other journeys, his omnipotence. What a monster of Fortune! With what a commencement, and with what an end!

ACCOUNT OF HIS RICHES:

On Wednesday evening, the day after his death, Dubois was carried from Versailles to the church of the chapter of Saint-Honore, in Paris, where he was interred some days after. Each of the academies of which he was a member had a service performed for him (at which they were present), the assembly of the clergy had another (he being their president); and as prime minister he had one at Notre Dame, at which the Cardinal de Noailles officiated, and at which the superior courts were present. There was no funeral oration at any of them. It could not be hazarded. His brother, more modest than he, and an honest man, kept the office of secretary of the cabinet, which he had, and which the Cardinal had given him. This brother found an immense heritage. He had but one son, canon of Saint-Honore, who had never desired places or livings, and who led a good life. He would touch scarcely anything of this rich succession. He employed a part of it in building for his uncle a sort of mausoleum (fine, but very modest, against the wall, at the end of the church, where the Cardinal is interred, with a Christian-like inscription), and distributed the rest to the poor, fearing lest this money should bring a curse upon him.

It was found some time after his death that the Cardinal had been long married, but very obscurely! He paid his wife to keep silent when he received his benefices; but when he dawned into greatness became much embarrassed with her. He was always in agony lest she should come forward and ruin him. His marriage had been made in Limousin, and celebrated in a village church. When he was named Archbishop of Cambrai he resolved to destroy the proofs of this marriage, and employed Breteuil, Intendant of Limoges, to whom he committed the secret, to do this for him skilfully and quietly.

Breteuil saw the heavens open before him if he could but succeed in this enterprise, so delicate and so important. He had intelligence, and knew how to make use of it. He goes to this village where the marriage had been celebrated, accompanied by only two or three valets, and arranges his journey so as to arrive at night, stops at the cure's house, in default of an inn, familiarly claims hospitality like a man surprised by the night, dying of hunger and thirst, and unable to go a step further.

The good cure; transported with gladness to lodge M. l'Intendant, hastily prepared all there was in the house, and had the honour of supping with him, whilst his servant regaled the two valets in another room, Breteuil having sent them all away in order to be alone with his host. Breteuil liked his glass and knew how to empty it. He pretended to find the supper good and the wine better. The cure, charmed with his guest, thought only of egging him on, as they say in the provinces. The tankard was on the table, and was drained again and again with a familiarity which transported the worthy priest. Breteuil; who had laid his project, succeeded in it, and made the good man so drunk that he could not keep upright, or see, or utter a word. When Breteuil had brought him to this state, and had finished him off with a few more draughts of wine, he profited by the information he had extracted from him during the first quarter of an hour of supper. He had asked if his registers were in good order, and how far they extended, and under pretext of safety against thieves, asked him where he kept them, and the keys of them, so that the moment Breteuil was certain the cure could no longer make use of his senses, he took his keys, opened the cupboard, took from it the register of the marriage of the year he wanted, very neatly detached the page he sought (and woe unto that marriage registered upon the same page), put it in his pocket, replaced the registers where he had found them, locked up the cupboard, and put back the keys in the place he had taken them from. His only thought after this was to steal off as soon as the dawn appeared, leaving the good cure snoring away the effects of the wine, and giving, some pistoles to the servant.

He went thence to the notary, who had succeeded to the business and the papers of the one who had made the contract of marriage; liked himself up with him, and by force and authority made him give up the minutes of the marriage contract. He sent afterwards for the wife of Dubois (from whose hands the wily Cardinal had already obtained the copy of the contract she possessed), threatened her with dreadful dungeons if she ever dared to breathe a word of her marriage, and promised marvels to her if she kept silent.

He assured her, moreover, that all she could say or do would be thrown away, because everything had been so arranged that she could prove nothing, and that if she dared to speak, preparations were made for condemning her as a calumniator and impostor, to rot with a shaven head in the prison of a convent! Breteuil placed these two important documents in the hands of Dubois, and was (to the surprise and scandal of all the world) recompensed, some time after, with the post of war secretary, which, apparently; he had done nothing to deserve, and for which he was utterly unqualified. The secret reason of his appointment was not discovered until long after.

Dubois' wife did not dare to utter a whisper. She came to Paris after the death of her husband. A good proportion was given to her of what was left. She lived obscure, but in easy circumstances, and died at Paris more than twenty years after the Cardinal Dubois, by whom she had had no children. The brother lived on very good terms with her. He was a village doctor when Dubois sent for him to Paris: In the end this history was known, and has been neither contradicted nor disavowed by anybody.

We have many examples of prodigious fortune acquired by insignificant people, but there is no example of a person so destitute of all talent (excepting that of low intrigue), as was Cardinal Dubois, being thus fortunate. His intellect was of the most ordinary kind; his knowledge the most common-place; his capacity nil; his exterior that of a ferret, of a pedant; his conversation disagreeable, broken, always uncertain; his falsehood written upon his forehead; his habits too measureless to be hidden; his fits of impetuosity resembling fits of madness; his head incapable of containing more than one thing at a time, and he incapable of following anything but his personal interest; nothing was sacred with him; he had no sort of worthy intimacy with any one; had a declared contempt for faith, promises, honour, probity, truth; took pleasure at laughing at all these things; was equally voluptuous and ambitious, wishing to be all in all in everything; counting himself alone as everything, and whatever was not connected with him as nothing; and regarding it as the height of madness to think or act otherwise. With all this he was soft, cringing, supple, a flatterer, and false admirer, taking all shapes with the greatest facility, and playing the most opposite parts in order to arrive at the different ends he proposed to himself; and nevertheless was but little capable of seducing. His judgment acted by fits and starts, was involuntarily crooked, with little sense or clearness; he was disagreeable in spite of himself. Nevertheless, he could be funnily vivacious when he wished, but nothing more, could tell a good story, spoiled, however, to some extent by his stuttering, which his falsehood had turned into a habit from the hesitation he always had in replying and in speaking. With such defects it is surprising that the only man he was able to seduce was M. le Duc d'Orleans, who had so much intelligence, such a well-balanced mind, and so much clear and rapid perception of character. Dubois gained upon him as a child while his preceptor; he seized upon him as a young man by favouring his liking for liberty, sham fashionable manners and debauchery, and his disdain of all rule. He ruined his heart, his mind, and his habits, by instilling into him the principles of libertines, which this poor prince could no more deliver himself from than from those ideas of reason, truth, and conscience which he always took care to stifle.

Dubois having insinuated himself into the favour of his master in this manner, was incessantly engaged in studying how to preserve his position. He never lost sight of his prince, whose great talents and great defects he had learnt how to profit by. The Regent's feebleness was the main rock upon which he built. As for Dubois' talent and capacity, as I have before said, they were worth nothing. All his success was due to his servile pliancy and base intrigues.

When he became the real master of the State he was just as incompetent as before. All his application was directed towards his master, and it had for sole aim that that master should not escape him. He wearied himself in watching all the movements of the prince, what he did, whom he saw, and for how long; his humour, his visage, his remarks at the issue of every audience and of every party; who took part in them, what was said and by whom, combining all these things; above all, he strove to frighten everybody from approaching the Regent, and kept no bounds with any one who had the temerity to do so without his knowledge and permission. This watching occupied all his days, and by it he regulated all his movements. This application, and the orders he was obliged to give for appearance sake, occupied all his time, so that he became inaccessible except for a few public audiences, or for others to the foreign ministers. Yet the majority of those ministers never could catch him, and were obliged to lie in wait for him upon staircases or in passages, where he did not expect to meet them. Once he threw into the fire a prodigious quantity of unopened letters, and then congratulated himself upon having got rid of all his business at once. At his death thousands of letters were found unopened.

Thus everything was in arrear, and nobody, not even the foreign ministers, dared to complain to M. le Duc d'Orleans, who, entirely abandoned to his pleasures, and always on the road from

Versailles to Paris, never thought of business, only too satisfied to find himself so free, and attending to nothing except the few trifles he submitted to the King under the pretence of working with his Majesty. Thus, nothing could be settled, and all was in chaos. To govern in this manner there is no need for capacity. Two words to each minister charged with a department, and some care in garnishing the councils attended by the King, with the least important despatches (settling the others with M. le Duc d'Orleans) constituted all the labour of the prime minister; and spying, scheming, parade, flatteries, defence, occupied all his time. His fits of passion, full of insults and blackguardism, from which neither man nor woman, no matter of what rank, was sheltered, relieved him from an infinite number of audiences, because people preferred going to subalterns, or neglecting their business altogether, to exposing themselves to this fury and these affronts.

The mad freaks of Dubois, especially when he had become master, and thrown off all restraint, would fill a volume. I will relate only one or two as samples. His frenzy was such that he would sometimes run all round the chamber, upon the tables and chairs, without touching the floor! M. le Duc d'Orleans told me that he had often witnessed this.

Another sample:

The Cardinal de Gesvres came over to-day to complain to M. le Duc d'Orleans that the Cardinal Dubois had dismissed him in the most filthy terms. On a former occasion, Dubois had treated the Princesse de Montauban in a similar manner, and M. le Duc d'Orleans had replied to her complaints as he now replied to those of the Cardinal de Gesvres. He told the Cardinal, who was a man of good manners, of gravity, and of dignity (whereas the Princess deserved what she got) that he had always found the counsel of the Cardinal Dubois good, and that he thought he (Gesvres) would do well to follow the advice just given him! Apparently it was to free himself from similar complaints that he spoke thus; and, in fact, he had no more afterwards.

Another sample:

Madame de Cheverny, become a widow, had retired to the Incurables. Her place of governess of the daughters of M. le Duc d'Orleans had been given to Madame de Conflans. A little while after Dubois was consecrated, Madame la Duchesse d'Orleans asked Madame de Conflans if she had called upon him. Thereupon Madame de Conflans replied negatively and that she saw no reason for going, the place she held being so little mixed up in State affairs. Madame la Duchesse d'Orleans pointed out how intimate the Cardinal was with M. le Duc d'Orleans. Madame de Conflans still tried to back out, saying that he was a madman, who insulted everybody, and to whom she would not expose herself. She had wit and a tongue, and was supremely vain, although very polite. Madame la Duchesse d'Orleans burst out laughing at her fear, and said, that having nothing to ask of the Cardinal, but simply to render an account to him of the office M. le Duc d'Orleans had given her, it was an act of politeness which could only please him, and obtain for her his regard, far from having anything disagreeable, or to be feared about it; and finished by saying to her that it was proper, and that she wished her to go.

She went, therefore, for it was at Versailles, and arrived in a large cabinet, where there were eight or ten persons waiting to speak to the Cardinal, who was larking with one of his favourites, by the mantelpiece. Fear seized upon Madame de Conflans, who was little, and who appeared less. Nevertheless, she approached as this woman retired. The Cardinal, seeing her advance, sharply asked her what she wanted.

"Monseigneur," said she,—"Oh, Monseigneur—"

"Monseigneur," interrupted the Cardinal, "I can't now."

"But, Monseigneur," replied she—

"Now, devil take me, I tell you again," interrupted the Cardinal, "when I say I can't, I can't."

"Monseigneur," Madame de Conflans again said, in order to explain that she wanted nothing; but at this word the Cardinal seized her by the shoulders; and pushed her out, saying, "Go to the devil, and let me alone."

She nearly fell over, flew away in fury, weeping hot tears, and reached, in this state, Madame la Duchesse d'Orleans, to whom, through her sobs, she related the adventure.

People were so accustomed to the insults of the Cardinal, and this was thought so singular and so amusing, that the recital of it caused shouts of laughter, which finished off poor Madame de Conflans, who swore that, never in her life, would she put foot in the house of this madman.

The Easter Sunday after he was made Cardinal, Dubois woke about eight o'clock, rang his bells as though he would break them, called for his people with the most horrible blasphemies, vomited forth a thousand filthy expressions and insults, raved at everybody because he had not been awakened, said that he wanted to say mass, but knew not how to find time, occupied as he was. After this very beautiful preparation, he very wisely abstained from saying mass, and I don't know whether he ever did say it after his consecration.

He had taken for private secretary one Verrier, whom he had unfrocked from the Abbey of Saint-Germain-des-Pres, the business of which he had conducted for twenty years, with much cleverness and intelligence. He soon accommodated himself to the humours of the Cardinal, and said to him all he pleased.

One morning he was with the Cardinal, who asked for something that could not at once be found. Thereupon Dubois began to blaspheme, to storm against his clerks, saying that if he had not enough he would engage twenty, thirty, fifty, a hundred, and making the most frightful din. Verrier tranquilly listened to him. The Cardinal asked him if it was not a terrible thing to be so ill-served, considering the expense he was put to; then broke out again, and pressed him to reply.

"Monseigneur," said Verrier, "engage one more clerk, and give him, for sole occupation, to swear and storm for you, and all will go well; you will have much more time to yourself and will be better served."

The Cardinal burst out laughing, and was appeased.

Every evening he ate an entire chicken for his supper. I know not by whose carelessness, but this chicken was forgotten one evening by his people. As he was about to go to bed he bethought him of his bird, rang, cried out, stormed against his servants, who ran and coolly listened to him. Upon this he cried the more, and complained of not having been served. He was astonished when they replied to him that he had eaten his chicken, but that if he pleased they would put another down to the spit.

"What!" said he, "I have eaten my chicken!"

The bold and cool assertion of his people persuaded him, and they laughed at him.

I will say no more, because, I repeat it, volumes might be filled with these details. I have said enough to show what was this monstrous personage, whose death was a relief to great and little, to all Europe, even to his brother, whom he treated like a negro. He wanted to dismiss a groom on one occasion for having lent one of his coaches to this same brother, to go somewhere in Paris.

The most relieved of all was M. le Duc d'Orleans. For a long time he had groaned in secret beneath the weight of a domination so harsh, and of chains he had forged for himself. Not only he could no longer dispose or decide upon anything, but he could get the Cardinal to do nothing, great or small, he desired done. He was obliged, in everything, to follow the will of the Cardinal, who became furious, reproached him, and stormed at him when too much contradicted. The poor Prince felt thus the abandonment into which he had cast himself, and, by this abandonment, the power of the Cardinal, and the eclipse of his own power. He feared him; Dubois had become insupportable to him; he was dying with desire, as was shown in a thousand things, to get rid of him, but he dared not—he did not know how to set about it; and, isolated and unceasingly wretched as he was, there was nobody to whom he could unbosom himself; and the Cardinal, well informed of this, increased his freaks, so as to retain by fear what he had usurped by artifice, and what he no longer hoped to preserve in any other way.

As soon as Dubois was dead, M. le Duc d'Orleans returned to Meudon, to inform the King of the event. The King immediately begged him to charge himself with the management of public affairs, declared him prime minister, and received, the next day, his oath, the patent of which was immediately sent to the Parliament, and verified. This prompt declaration was caused by the fear Frejus had to see a private person prime minister. The King liked M. le Duc d'Orleans, as we have already seen by the respect he received from him, and by his manner of working with him. The Regent, without danger of being taken at his word, always left him master of all favours, and of the choice of persons he proposed to him; and, besides, never bothered him, or allowed business to interfere with his amusements. In spite of all the care and all the suppleness Dubois had employed in order to gain the spirit of the King, he never could succeed, and people remarked, without having wonderful eyes, a very decided repugnance of the King for him. The Cardinal was afflicted, but redoubled his efforts, in the hope at last of success. But, in addition to his own disagreeable manners, heightened by the visible efforts he made to please, he had two enemies near the King, very watchful to keep him away from the young prince—the Marechal de Villeroy, while he was there, and Frejus, who was much more dangerous, and who was resolved to overthrow him. Death, as we have seen, spared him the trouble.

The Court returned from Meudon to Paris on the 13th of August. Soon after I met M. le Duc d'Orleans there.

As soon as he saw me enter his cabinet he ran to me, and eagerly asked me if I meant to abandon him. I replied that while his Cardinal lived I felt I should be useless to him, but that now this obstacle was removed, I should always be very humbly at his service. He promised to live with me on the same terms as before, and, without a word upon the Cardinal, began to talk about home and foreign affairs. If I flattered myself that I was to be again of use to him for any length of time, events soon came to change the prospect. But I will not anticipate my story.

CHAPTER CXVI

The Duc de Lauzun died on the 19th of November, at the age of ninety years and six months. The intimate union of the two sisters I and he had espoused, and our continual intercourse at the Court (at Marly, we had a pavilion especially for us four), caused me to be constantly with him, and after the King's death we saw each other nearly every day at Paris, and unceasingly frequented each other's table. He was so extraordinary a personage, in every way so singular, that La Bruyere, with much justice, says of him in his "Characters," that others were not allowed to dream as he had lived. For those who saw him in his old age, this description seems even more just. That is what induces me to dwell upon him here. He was of the House of Caumont, the branch of which represented by the Ducs de la Force has always passed for the eldest, although that of Lauzun has tried to dispute with it.

The mother of M. de Lauzun was daughter of the Duc de la Force, son of the second Marechal Duc de la Force, and brother of the Marechale de Turenne, but by another marriage; the Marechale was by a first marriage. The father of M. de Lauzun was the Comte de Lauzun, cousin-german of the first Marechal Duc de Grammont, and of the old Comte de Grammont.

M. de Lauzun was a little fair man, of good figure, with a noble and expressively commanding face, but which was without charm, as I have heard people say who knew him when he was young. He was full of ambition, of caprice, of fancies; jealous of all; wishing always to go too far; never content with anything; had no reading, a mind in no way cultivated, and without charm; naturally sorrowful, fond of solitude, uncivilised; very noble in his dealings, disagreeable and malicious by nature, still more so by jealousy and by ambition; nevertheless, a good friend when a friend at all, which was rare; a good relative; enemy even of the indifferent; hard upon faults, and upon what was ridiculous, which he soon discovered; extremely brave, and as dangerously bold. As a courtier he was equally insolent and satirical, and as cringing as a valet; full of foresight, perseverance, intrigue, and meanness, in order to arrive at his ends; with this, dangerous to the ministers; at the Court feared by all, and full of witty and sharp remarks which spared nobody.

He came very young to the Court without any fortune, a cadet of Gascony, under the name of the Marquis de Puyguilhem. The Marechal de Grammont, cousin-german of his brother, lodged him: Grammont was then in high consideration at the Court, enjoyed the confidence of the Queen-mother, and of Cardinal Mazarin, and had the regiment of the guards and the reversion of it for the Comte de Guiche, his eldest son, who, the prince of brave fellows, was on his side in great favour with the ladies, and far advanced in the good graces of the King and of the Comtesse de Soissons, niece of the Cardinal, whom the King never quitted, and who was the Queen of the Court. This Comte de Guiche introduced to the Comtesse de Soissons the Marquis de Puyguilhem, who in a very little time became the King's favourite. The King, in fact, gave him his regiment of dragoons on forming it, and soon after made him Marechal de Camp, and created for him the post of colonel-general of dragoons.

The Duc de Mazarin, who in 1669 had already retired from the Court, wished to get rid of his post of grand master of the artillery; Puyguilhem had scent of his intention, and asked the King for this office. The King promised it to him, but on condition that he kept the matter secret some days. The day arrived on which the King had agreed to declare him. Puyguilhem, who had the entrees of the first gentleman of the chamber (which are also named the grandes entrees), went to wait for the King (who was holding a finance council), in a room that nobody entered during the council, between that in which all the Court waited, and that in which the council itself was held. He found there no one but Nyert, chief valet de chambre, who asked him how he happened to come there. Puyguilhem, sure of his affair, thought he should make a friend of this valet by confiding to him what was about to take place. Nyert expressed his joy; then drawing out his watch, said he should have time to go and execute a pressing commission the King had given him. He mounted four steps at a time the little staircase, at the head of which was the bureau where Louvois worked all day—for at Saint-Germain the lodgings were little and few—and the ministers and nearly all the Court lodged each at his own house in the town. Nyert entered the bureau of Louvois, and informed him that upon leaving the council (of which Louvois was not a member), the King was going to declare Puyguilhem grand master of the artillery, adding that he had just learned this news from Puyguilhem himself, and saying where he had left him.

Louvois hated Puyguilhem, friend of Colbert, his rival, and he feared his influence in a post which had so many intimate relations with his department of the war, the functions and authority of which he invaded as much as possible, a proceeding which he felt Puyguilhem was not the kind of man to suffer. He embraces Nyert, thanking him, dismisses him as quickly as possible, takes some papers to serve as an excuse, descends, and finds Puyguilhem and Nyert in the chamber, as above described. Nyert pretends to be surprised to see Louvois arrive, and says to him that the council has not broken up.

"No matter," replied Louvois, "I must enter, I have something important to say to the King;" and thereupon he enters. The King, surprised to see him, asks what brings him there, rises, and goes to him. Louvois draws him into the embrasure of a window, and says he knows that his Majesty is going to declare Puyguilhem grand master of the artillery; that he is waiting in the adjoining room for the breaking up of the council; that his Majesty is fully master of his favours and of his choice, but that he (Louvois) thinks it his duty to represent to him the incompatibility between Puyguilhem and him, his caprices, his pride; that he will wish to change everything in the artillery; that this post has such intimate relations with the war department, that continual quarrels will arise between the two, with which his Majesty will be importuned at every moment.

The King is piqued to see his secret known by him from whom, above all, he wished to hide it; he replies to Louvois, with a very serious air, that the appointment is not yet made, dismisses him, and reseats himself at the council. A moment after it breaks up. The King leaves to go to mass, sees Puyguilhem, and passes without saying anything to him. Puyguilhem, much astonished, waits all the rest of the day, and seeing that the promised declaration does not come, speaks of it to the King at night. The King replies to him that it cannot be yet, and that he will see; the ambiguity of the response, and the cold tone, alarm Puyguilhem; he is in favour with the ladies, and speaks the jargon of gallantry; he goes to Madame de Montespan, to whom he states his disquietude, and conjures her to put an end to it. She promises him wonders, and amuses him thus several days.

Tired of this, and not being able to divine whence comes his failure, he takes a resolution— incredible if it was not attested by all the Court of that time. The King was in the habit of visiting Madame de Montespan in the afternoon, and of remaining with her some time. Puyguilhem was on terms of tender intimacy with one of the chambermaids of Madame de Montespan. She privately introduced him into the room where the King visited Madame de Montespan, and he secreted himself under the bed. In this position he was able to hear all the conversation that took place between the King and his mistress above, and he learned by it that it was Louvois who had ousted him; that the King was very angry at the secret having got wind, and had changed his resolution to avoid quarrels between the artillery and the war department; and, finally, that Madame de Montespan, who had promised him her good offices, was doing him all the harm she could. A cough, the least movement, the slightest accident, might have betrayed the foolhardy Puyguilhem, and then what would have become of him? These are things the recital of which takes the breath away, and terrifies at the same time.

Puyguilhem was more fortunate than prudent, and was not discovered. The King and his mistress at last closed their conversation; the King dressed himself again, and went to his own rooms. Madame de Montespan went away to her toilette, in order to prepare for the rehearsal of a ballet to which the King, the Queen, and all the Court were going. The chambermaid drew Puyguilhem from under the bed, and he went and glued himself against the door of Madame de Montespan's chamber.

When Madame de Montespan came forth, in order to go to the rehearsal of the ballet, he presented his hand to her, and asked her, with an air of gentleness and of respect, if he might flatter himself that she had deigned to think of him when with the King. She assured him that she had not failed, and enumerated services she had; she said, just rendered him. Here and there he credulously interrupted her with questions, the better to entrap her; then, drawing near her, he told her she was a liar, a hussy, a harlot, and repeated to her, word for word, her conversation with the King!

Madame de Montespan was so amazed that she had not strength enough to reply one word; with difficulty she reached the place she was going to, and with difficulty overcame and hid the trembling of her legs and of her whole body; so that upon arriving at the room where the rehearsal was to take place, she fainted. All the Court was already there. The King, in great fright, came to her; it was not without much trouble she was restored to herself. The same evening she related to the King what had just happened, never doubting it was the devil who had so promptly and so precisely informed Puyguilhem of all that she had said to the King. The King was extremely irritated at the insult Madame de Montespan had received, and was much troubled to divine how Puyguilhem had been so exactly and so suddenly instructed.

Puyguilhem, on his side, was furious at losing the artillery, so that the King and he were under strange constraint together. This could last only a few days. Puyguilhem, with his grandes entrees, seized his opportunity and had a private audience with the King. He spoke to him of the artillery, and audaciously summoned him to keep his word. The King replied that he was not bound by it, since he had given it under secrecy, which he (Puyguilhem) had broken.

Upon this Puyguilhem retreats a few steps, turns his back upon the King, draws his sword, breaks the blade of it with his foot, and cries out in fury, that he will never in his life serve a prince who has so shamefully broken his word. The King, transported with anger, performed in that moment the finest action perhaps of his life. He instantly turned round, opened the window, threw his cane outside, said he should be sorry to strike a man of quality, and left the room.

The next morning, Puyguilhem, who had not dared to show himself since, was arrested in his chamber, and conducted to the Bastille. He was an intimate friend of Guitz, favourite of the King, for whom his Majesty had created the post of grand master of the wardrobe. Guitz had the courage to speak to the King in favour of Puyguilhem, and to try and reawaken the infinite liking he had conceived for the young Gascon. He succeeded so well in touching the King, by showing him that the refusal of such a grand post as the artillery had turned Puyguilhem's head, that his Majesty wished to make amends far this refusal. He offered the post of captain of the King's guards to Puyguilhem, who, seeing this incredible and prompt return of favour, re-assumed sufficient audacity to refuse it, flattering himself he should thus gain a better appointment. The King was not discouraged. Guitz went and preached to his friend in the Bastille, and with great trouble made him agree to have the goodness to accept the King's offer. As soon as he had accepted it he left the Bastille, went and saluted the King, and took the oaths of his new post, selling that which he occupied in the dragoons.

He had in 1665 the government of Berry, at the death of Marechal de Clerembault. I will not speak here of his adventures with Mademoiselle, which she herself so naively relates in her memoirs, or of his extreme folly in delaying his marriage with her (to which the King had consented), in order to have fine liveries, and get the marriage celebrated at the King's mass, which gave time to Monsieur (incited by M. le Prince) to make representations to the King, which induced him to retract his consent, breaking off thus the marriage. Mademoiselle made a terrible uproar, but Puyguilhem, who since the death of his father had taken the name of Comte de Lauzun, made this great sacrifice with good grace, and with more wisdom than belonged to him. He had the company of the hundred gentlemen, with battle-axes, of the King's household, which his father had had, and he had just been made lieutenant-general.

Lauzun was in love with Madame de Monaco, an intimate friend of Madame, and in all her Intrigues: He was very jealous of her, and was not pleased with her. One summer's afternoon he went to Saint-Cloud, and found Madame and her Court seated upon the ground, enjoying the air, and Madame de Monaco half lying down, one of her hands open and outstretched. Lauzun played the gallant with the ladies, and turned round so neatly that he placed his heel in the palm of Madame de Monaco, made a pirouette there, and departed. Madame de Monaco had strength enough to utter no cry, no word!

A short time after he did worse. He learnt that the King was on intimate terms with Madame de Monaco, learnt also the hour at which Bontems, the valet, conducted her, enveloped in a cloak, by a back staircase, upon the landing-place of which was a door leading into the King's cabinet, and in front of it a private cabinet. Lauzun anticipates the hour, and lies in ambush in the private cabinet, fastening it from within with a hook, and sees through the keyhole the King open the door of the cabinet, put the key outside (in the lock) and close the door again. Lauzun waits a little, comes out of his hiding-place, listens at the door in which the King had just placed the key, locks it, and takes out the key, which he throws into the private cabinet, in which he again shuts himself up.

Some time after Bontems and the lady arrive. Much astonished not to find the key in the door of the King's cabinet, Bontems gently taps at the door several times, but in vain; finally so loudly does he tap that the King hears the sound. Bontems says he is there, and asks his Majesty to open, because the key is not in the door. The King replies that he has just put it there. Bontems looks on the ground for it, the King meanwhile trying to open the door from the inside, and finding it double- locked. Of course all three are much astonished and much annoyed; the conversation is carried on through the door, and they cannot determine how this accident has happened. The King exhausts himself in efforts to force the door, in spite of its being double-locked. At last they are obliged to say good-bye through the door, and Lauzun, who hears every word they utter, and who sees them through the keyhole, laughs in his sleeve at their mishap with infinite enjoyment.

CHAPTER CXVII

In 1670 the King wished to make a triumphant journey with the ladies, under pretext of visiting his possessions in Flanders, accompanied by an army, and by all his household troops, so that the alarm was great in the Low Countries, which he took no pains to appease. He gave the command of all to Lauzun, with the patent of army-general. Lauzun performed the duties of his post with much intelligence, and with extreme gallantry and magnificence. This brilliancy, and this distinguished mark of favour, made Louvois, whom Lauzun in no way spared, think very seriously. He united with Madame de Montespan (who had not pardoned the discovery Lauzun had made, or the atrocious insults he had bestowed upon her), and the two worked so well that they reawakened in the King's mind recollections of the broken sword, the refusal in the Bastille of the post of captain of the guards, and made his Majesty look upon Lauzun as a man who no longer knew himself, who had suborned Mademoiselle until he had been within an inch of marrying her, and of assuring to himself immense wealth; finally, as a man, very dangerous on account of his audacity, and who had taken it into his head to gain the devotion of the troops by his magnificence, his services to the officers, and by the manner in which he had treated them during the Flanders journey, making himself adored. They made him out criminal for having remained the friend of, and on terms of great intimacy with, the Comtesse de Soissons, driven from the Court and suspected of crimes. They must have accused Lauzun also of crimes which I have never heard of, in order to procure for him the barbarous treatment they succeeded in subjecting him to.

Their intrigues lasted all the year, 1671, without Lauzun discovering anything by the visage of the King, or that of Madame de Montespan. Both the King and his mistress treated him with their ordinary distinction and familiarity. He was a good judge of jewels (knowing also how to set them well), and Madame de Montespan often employed him in this capacity. One evening, in the middle of November, 1671, he arrived from Paris, where Madame de Montespan had sent him in the morning for some precious stones, and as he was about to enter his chamber he was arrested by the Marechal de Rochefort, captain of the guards.

Lauzun, in the utmost surprise, wished to know why, to see the King or Madame de Montespan—at least, to write to them; everything was refused him. He was taken to the Bastille, and shortly afterwards to Pignerol, where he was shut up in a low-roofed dungeon. His post of captain of the body-guard was given to M. de Luxembourg, and the government of Berry to the Duc de la Rochefoucauld, who, at the death of Guitz, at the passage of the Rhine, 12th June, 1672, was made grand master of the wardrobe.

It may be imagined what was the state of a man like Lauzun, precipitated, in a twinkling, from such a height to a dungeon in the chateau of Pignerol, without seeing anybody, and ignorant of his crime. He bore up, however, pretty well, but at last fell so ill that he began to think about confession. I have heard him relate that he feared a fictitious priest, and that, consequently, he obstinately insisted upon a Capuchin; and as soon as he came he seized him by the beard, and tugged at it, as hard as he could, on all sides, in order to see that it was not a sham one! He was four or five years in his gaol. Prisoners find employment which necessity teaches them. There ware prisoners above him and at the side of him. They found means to speak to him. This intercourse led them to make a hole, well hidden, so as to talk more easily; then to increase it, and visit each other.

The superintendent Fouquet had been enclosed near them ever since December, 1664. He knew by his neighbours (who had found means of seeing him) that Lauzun was under them. Fouquet, who received no news, hoped for some from him, and had a great desire to see him. He, had left Lauzun a young man, dawning at the Court, introduced by the Marechal de Grammont, well received at the house of the Comtesse de Soissons, which the King never quitted, and already looked upon favourably. The prisoners, who had become intimate with Lauzun, persuaded him to allow himself to be drawn up through their hole, in order to see Fouquet in their dungeon. Lauzun was very willing. They met, and Lauzun began relating, accordingly, his fortunes and his misfortunes, to Fouquet. The unhappy superintendent opened wide his ears and eyes when he heard this young Gasepan (once only too happy to be welcomed and harboured by the Marechal de Grammont) talk of having been general of dragoons, captain of the guards, with the patent and functions of army-general! Fouquet no longer knew where he was, believed Lauzun mad, and that he was relating his visions, when he described how he had missed the artillery, and what had passed afterwards thereupon: but he was convinced that madness had reached its climax, and was afraid to be with Lauzun, when he heard him talk of his marriage with Mademoiselle, agreed to by the King, how broken, and the wealth she had assured to him. This much curbed their intercourse, as far as Fouquet was concerned, for he, believing the brain of Lauzun completely turned, took for fairy tales all the stories the Gascon told him of what had happened in the world, from the imprisonment of the one to the imprisonment of the other.

The confinement of Fouquet was a little relieved before that of Lauzun. His wife and some officers of the chateau of Pignerol had permission to see him, and to tell him the news of the day. One of the first things he did was to tell them of this poor Puyguilhem, whom he had left young, and on a tolerably good footing for his age, at the Court, and whose head was now completely turned, his madness hidden within the prison walls; but what was his astonishment when they all assured him that what he had heard was perfectly true! He did not return to the subject, and was tempted to believe them all mad together. It was some time before he was persuaded.

In his turn, Lauzun was taken from his dungeon, and had a chamber, and soon after had the same liberty that had been given to Fouquet; finally, they were allowed to see each other as much as they liked. I have never known what displeased Lauzun, but he left Pignerol the enemy of Fouquet, and did him afterwards all the harm he could, and after his death extended his animosity to his family.

During the long imprisonment of Lauzun, Madame de Nogent, one of his sisters, took such care of his revenues that he left Pignerol extremely rich.

Mademoiselle, meanwhile, was inconsolable at this long and harsh imprisonment, and took all possible measures to deliver Lauzun. The King at last resolved to turn this to the profit of the Duc du Maine, and to make Mademoiselle pay dear for the release of her lover. He caused a proposition to be made to her, which was nothing less than to assure to the Duc du Maine, and his posterity after her death, the countdom of Eu, the Duchy of Aumale, and the principality of Domfes! The gift was enormous, not only as regards the value, but the dignity and extent of these three slices. Moreover, she had given the first two to Lauzun, with the Duchy of Saint-Forgeon, and the fine estate of Thiers, in Auvergne, when their marriage was broken off, and she would have been obliged to make him renounce Eu and Aumale before she could have disposed of them in favour of the Duc du Maine. Mademoiselle could not, make up her mind to this yoke, or to strip Lauzun of such considerable benefits. She was importuned to the utmost, finally menaced by the ministers, now Louvois, now Colbert. With the latter she was better pleased, because he had always been on good terms with Lauzun, and because he handled her more gently than Louvois, who, an enemy of her lover, always spoke in the harshest terms. Mademoiselle unceasingly felt that the King did not like her, and that he had never pardoned her the Orleans journey, still less her doings at the Bastille, when she fired its cannons upon the King's troops, and saved thus M. le Prince and his people, at the combat of the Faubourg Saint-Antoine. Feeling, therefore, that the King, hopelessly estranged from her, and consenting to give liberty to Lauzun only from his passion for elevating and enriching his bastards, would not cease to persecute her until she had consented—despairing of better terms, she agreed to the gift, with the most bitter tears and complaints. But it was found that, in order to make valid the renunciation of Lauzun, he must be set at liberty, so that it was pretended he had need of the waters of Bourbon, and Madame de Montespan also, in order that they might confer together upon this affair.

Lauzun was taken guarded to Bourbon by a detachment of musketeers, commanded by Maupertuis. Lauzun saw Madame de Montespan at Bourbon; but he was so indignant at the terms proposed to him as the condition of his liberty, that after long disputes he would hear nothing more on the subject, and was reconducted to Pignerol as he had been brought.

This firmness did not suit the King, intent upon the fortune of his well- beloved bastard. He sent Madame de Nogent to Pignerol; then Borin (a friend of Lauzun, and who was mixed up in all his affairs), with menaces and promises. Borin, with great trouble, obtained the consent of Lauzun, and brought about a second journey to Bourbon for him and Madame de Montespan, with the same pretext of the waters. Lauzun was conducted there as before, and never pardoned Maupertuis the severe pedantry of his exactitude. This last journey was made in the autumn of 1680. Lauzun consented to everything. Madame de Montespan returned triumphant. Maupertuis and his musketeers took leave of Lauzun at Bourbon, whence he had permission to go and reside at Angers; and immediately after, this exile was enlarged, so that he had the liberty of all Anjou and Lorraine. The consummation of the affair was deferred until the commencement of February, 1681, in order to give him a greater air of liberty. Thus Lauzun had from Mademoiselle only Saint-Forgeon and Thiers, after having been on the point of marrying her, and of succeeding to all her immense wealth. The Duc du Maine was instructed to make his court to Mademoiselle, who always received him very coldly, and who saw him take her arms, with much vexation, as a mark of his gratitude, in reality for the Sake of the honour it brought him;

for the arms were those of Gaston, which the Comte de Toulouse afterwards took, not for the same reason, but under pretext of conformity with his brother; and they have handed them down to their children.

Lauzun, who had been led to expect much more gentle treatment, remained four years in these two provinces, of which he grew as weary as was Mademoiselle at his absence. She cried out in anger against Madame de Montespan and her son; complained loudly that after having been so pitilessly fleeced, Lauzun was still kept removed from her; and made such a stir that at last she obtained permission for him to return to Paris, with entire liberty; on condition, however, that he did not approach within two leagues of any place where the King might be.

Lauzun came, therefore, to Paris, and assiduously visited his benefactors. The weariness of this kind of exile, although so softened, led him into high play, at which he was extremely successful; always a good and sure player, and very straightforward, he gained largely. Monsieur, who sometimes made little visits to Paris, and who played very high, permitted him to join the gambling parties of the Palais Royal, then those of Saint-Cloud. Lauzun passed thus several years, gaining and lending much money very nobly; but the nearer he found himself to the Court, and to the great world, the more insupportable became to him the prohibition he had received.

Finally, being no longer able to bear it, he asked the King for permission to go to England, where high play was much in vogue. He obtained it, and took with him a good deal of money, which secured him an open-armed reception in London, where he was not less successful than in Paris.

James II., then reigning, received Lauzun with distinction. But the Revolution was already brewing. It burst after Lauzun had been in England eight or ten months. It seemed made expressly for him, by the success he derived from it, as everybody is aware. James II., no longer knowing what was to become of him—betrayed by his favourites and his ministers, abandoned by all his nation, the Prince of Orange master of all hearts, the troops, the navy, and ready to enter London—the unhappy monarch confided to Lauzun what he held most dear—the Queen and the Prince of Wales, whom Lauzun happily conducted to Calais. The Queen at once despatched a courier to the King, in the midst of the compliments of which she insinuated that by the side of her joy at finding herself and her son in security under his protection, was her grief at not daring to bring with her him to whom she owed her safety.

The reply of the King, after much generous and gallant sentiment, was, that he shared this obligation with her, and that he hastened to show it to her, by restoring the Comte de Lauzun to favour.

In effect, when the Queen presented Lauzun to the King, in the Palace of Saint-Germain (where the King, with all the family and all the Court, came to meet her), he treated him as of old, gave him the privilege of the grandes entrees, and promised him a lodging at Versailles, which he received immediately after. From that day he always went to Marly, and to Fontainebleau, and, in fact, never after quitted the Court. It may be imagined what was the delight of such an ambitious courtier, so completely re-established in such a sudden and brilliant manner. He had also a lodging in the chateau of Saint-Germain, chosen as the residence of this fugitive Court, at which King James soon arrived.

Lauzun, like a skilful courtier, made all possible use of the two Courts, and procured for himself many interviews with the King, in which he received minor commissions. Finally, he played his cards so well that the King permitted him to receive in Notre Dame, at Paris, the Order of the Garter, from the hands of the King of England, accorded to him at his second passage into Ireland the rank of lieutenant-general of his auxiliary army, and permitted at the same time that he should be of the staff of the King of England, who lost Ireland during the same campaign at the battle of the Boyne. He returned into France with the Comte de Lauzun, for whom he obtained letters of the Duke; which were verified at the Parliament in May, 1692. What a miraculous return of fortune! But what a fortune, in comparison with that of marrying Mademoiselle, with the donation of all her prodigious wealth, and the title and dignity of Duke and Peer of Montpensier. What a monstrous pedestal! And with children by this marriage, what a flight might not Lauzun have taken, and who can say where he might have arrived?

CHAPTER CXVIII

I have elsewhere related Lauzun's humours, his notable wanton tricks, and his rare singularity.

He enjoyed, during the rest of his long life, intimacy with the King, distinction at the Court, great consideration, extreme abundance, kept up the state of a great nobleman, with one of the most magnificent houses of the Court, and the best table, morning and evening, most honourably frequented, and at Paris the same, after the King's death: All this did not content him. He could only approach the King with outside familiarity; he felt that the mind and the heart of that monarch were on their guard against him, and in an estrangement that not all his art nor all his application could ever overcome. This is what made him marry my sister-in-law, hoping thus to re-establish himself in serious intercourse with the King by means of the army that M. le Marechal de Lorge commanded in Germany; but his project failed, as has been seen. This is what made him bring about the marriage of the Duc de Lorge with the daughter of Chamillart, in order to reinstate himself by means of that ministry; but without success. This is what made him undertake the journey to Aix- la-Chapelle, under the pretext of the waters, to obtain information which might lead to private interviews with the King, respecting the peace; but he was again unsuccessful. All his projects failed; in fact, he unceasingly sorrowed, and believed himself in profound disgrace—even saying so. He left nothing undone in order to pay his court, at bottom with meanness, but externally with dignity; and he every year celebrated a sort of anniversary of his disgrace, by extraordinary acts, of which ill-humour and solitude were oftentimes absurdly the fruit. He himself spoke of it, and used to say that he was not rational at the annual return of this epoch, which was stronger than he. He thought he pleased the King by this refinement of attention, without perceiving he was laughed at.

By nature he was extraordinary in everything, and took pleasure in affecting to be more so, even at home, and among his valets. He counterfeited the deaf and the blind, the better to see and hear without exciting suspicion, and diverted himself by laughing at fools, even the most elevated, by holding with them a language which had no sense. His manners were measured, reserved, gentle, even respectful; and from his low and honeyed tongue, came piercing remarks, overwhelming by their justice, their force, or their satire, composed of two or three words, perhaps, and sometimes uttered with an air of naivete or of distraction, as though he was not thinking of what he said. Thus he was feared, without exception, by everybody, and with many acquaintances he had few or no friends, although he merited them by his ardor in seeing everybody as much as he could, and by his readiness in opening his purse. He liked to gather together foreigners of any distinction, and perfectly did the honours of the Court. But devouring ambition poisoned his life; yet he was a very good and useful relative.

During the summer which followed the death of Louis XIV. there was a review of the King's household troops, led by M. le Duc d'Orleans, in the plain by the side of the Bois de Boulogne. Passy, where M. de Lauzun had a pretty house, is on the other side. Madame de Lauzun was there with company, and I slept there the evening before the review. Madame de Poitiers, a young widow, and one of our relatives, was there too, and was dying to see the review, like a young person who has seen nothing, but who dares not show herself in public in the first months of her mourning.

How she could be taken was discussed in the company, and it was decided that Madame de Lauzun could conduct her a little way, buried in her carriage. In the midst of the gaiety of this party, M. de Lauzun arrived from Paris, where he had gone in the morning. He was told what had just been decided. As soon as he learnt it he flew into a fury, was no longer master of himself, broke off the engagement, almost foaming at the mouth; said the most disagreeable things to his wife in the strongest, the harshest, the most insulting, and the most foolish terms. She gently wept; Madame de Poitiers sobbed outright, and all the company felt the utmost embarrassment. The evening appeared an age, and the saddest refectory repast a gay meal by the side of our supper. He was wild in the midst of the profoundest silence; scarcely a word was said. He quitted the table, as usual, at the fruit, and went to bed. An attempt was made to say something afterwards by way of relief, but Madame de Lauzun politely and wisely stopped the conversation, and brought out cards in order to turn the subject.

The next morning I went to M. de Lauzun, in order to tell him in plain language my opinion of the scene of the previous evening. I had not the time. As soon as he saw me enter he extended his arms, and cried that I saw a madman, who did not deserve my visit, but an asylum; passed the strongest eulogies upon his wife (which assuredly she merited), said he was not worthy of her, and that he ought to kiss the ground upon which she walked; overwhelmed himself with blame; then, with tears in his eyes, said he was more worthy of pity than of anger; that he must admit to me all his shame and misery; that he was more than eighty years of age; that he had neither children nor survivors; that he had been captain of the guards; that though he might be so again, he should be incapable of the function; that he unceasingly said this to himself, and that yet with all this he could not console himself for having been so no longer during the many years since he had lost his post; that he had never been able to draw the dagger from his heart; that everything which recalled the memory of the past made him beside himself, and that to hear that his wife was going to take Madame de Poitiers to see a review of the body-guards, in which he now counted for nothing, had turned his head, and had rendered him wild to the extent I had seen; that he no longer dared show himself before any one after this evidence of madness; that he was going to lock himself up in his chamber, and that he threw himself at my feet in order to conjure me to go and find his wife, and try to induce her to take pity on and pardon a senseless old man, who was dying with grief and shame. This admission, so sincere and so dolorous to make, penetrated me. I sought only to console him and compose him. The reconciliation was not difficult; we drew him from his chamber, not without trouble, and he evinced during several days as much disinclination to show himself, as I was told, for I went away in the evening, my occupations keeping me very busy.

I have often reflected, apropos of this, upon the extreme misfortune of allowing ourselves to be carried away by the intoxication of the world, and into the formidable state of an ambitious man, whom neither riches nor comfort, neither dignity acquired nor age, can satisfy, and who, instead of tranquilly enjoying what he possesses, and appreciating the happiness of it, exhausts himself in regrets, and in useless and continual bitterness. But we die as we have lived, and 'tis rare it happens otherwise. This madness respecting the captaincy of the guards so cruelly dominated M. de Lauzun, that he often dressed himself in a blue coat, with silver lace, which, without being exactly the uniform of the captain of, the body-guards, resembled it closely, and would have rendered him ridiculous if he had not accustomed people to it, made himself feared, and risen above all ridicule.

With all his scheming and cringing he fell foul of everybody, always saying some biting remark with dove-like gentleness. Ministers, generals, fortunate people and their families, were the most ill-treated. He had, as it were, usurped the right of saying and doing what he pleased; nobody daring to be angry with him. The Grammonts alone were excepted. He always remembered the hospitality and the protection he had received from them at the outset of his life. He liked them; he interested himself in them; he was in respect before them. Old Comte Grammont took advantage of this and revenged the Court by the sallies he constantly made against Lauzun, who never returned them or grew angry, but gently avoided him. He always did a good deal for the children of his sisters.

During the plague the Bishop of Marseilles had much signalised himself by wealth spent and danger incurred. When the plague had completely passed away, M. de Lauzun asked M. le Duc d'Orleans for an abbey for the Bishop. The Regent gave away some livings soon after, and forgot M. de Marseilles. Lauzun pretended to be ignorant of it, and asked M. le Duc d'Orleans if he had had the goodness to remember him. The Regent was embarrassed. The Duc de Lauzun, as though to relieve him from his embarrassment, said, in a gentle and respectful tone, "Monsieur, he will do better another time," and with this sarcasm rendered the Regent dumb, and went away smiling. The story got abroad, and M. le Duc d'Orleans repaired his forgetfulness by the bishopric of Laon, and upon the refusal of M. de Marseilles to change, gave him a fat abbey.

M. de Lauzun hindered also a promotion of Marshal of France by the ridicule he cast upon the candidates. He said to the Regent, with that gentle and respectful tone he knew so well how to assume, that in case any useless Marshals of France (as he said) were made, he begged his Royal Highness to remember that he was the oldest lieutenant-general of the realm, and that he had had the honour of commanding armies with the patent of general. I have elsewhere related other of his witty remarks. He could not keep them in; envy and jealousy urged him to utter them, and as his bon-mots always went straight to the point, they were always much repeated.

We were on terms of continual intimacy; he had rendered me real solid friendly services of himself, and I paid him all sorts of respectful attentions, and he paid me the same. Nevertheless, I did not always escape his tongue; and on one occasion, he was perhaps within an inch of doing me much injury by it.

The King (Louis XIV.) was declining; Lauzun felt it, and began to think of the future. Few people were in favour with M. le Duc d'Orleans; nevertheless, it was seen that his grandeur was approaching. All eyes were upon him, shining with malignity, consequently upon me, who for a long time had been the sole courtier who remained publicly attached to him, the sole in his confidence. M. de Lauzun came to dine at my house, and found us at table. The company he saw apparently displeased him; for he went away to Torcy, with whom I had no intimacy, and who was also at table, with many people opposed to M. le Duc d'Orleans, Tallard, among others, and Tesse.

"Monsieur," said Lauzun to Torcy, with a gentle and timid air, familiar to him, "take pity upon me, I have just tried to dine with M. de Saint- Simon. I found him at table, with company; I took care not to sit down with them, as I did not wish to be the 'zeste' of the cabal. I have come here to find one."

They all burst out laughing. The remark instantly ran over all Versailles. Madame de Maintenon and M. du Maine at once heard it, and nevertheless no sign was anywhere made. To have been angry would only have been to spread it wider: I took the matter as the scratch of an ill- natured cat, and did not allow Lauzun to perceive that I knew it.

Two or three years before his death he had an illness which reduced him to extremity. We were all very assiduous, but he would see none of us, except Madame de Saint-Simon, and her but once. Languet, cure of Saint- Sulpice, often went to him, and discoursed most admirably to him. One day, when he was there, the Duc de la Force glided into the chamber: M. de Lauzun did not like him at all, and often laughed at him. He received him tolerably well, and continued to talk aloud with the cure.

Suddenly he turned to the cure, complimented and thanked him, said he had nothing more valuable to give him than his blessing, drew his arm from the bed, pronounced the blessing, and gave it to him. Then turning to the Duc de la Force, Lauzun said he had always loved and respected him as the head of his house, and that as such he asked him for his blessing.

These two men, the cure and the Duc de la Force, were astonished, could not utter a word. The sick man redoubled his instances. M. de la Force, recovering himself, found the thing so amusing, that he gave his blessing; and in fear lest he should explode, left the room, and came to us in the adjoining chamber, bursting with laughter, and scarcely able to relate what had happened to him.

A moment after, the cure came also, all abroad, but smiling as much as possible, so as to put a good face on the matter. Lauzun knew that he was ardent and skilful in drawing money from people for the building of a church, and had often said he would never fall into his net; he suspected that the worthy cure's assiduities had an interested motive, and laughed at him in giving him only his blessing (which he ought to have received from him), and in perseveringly asking the Duc de la Force for his. The cure, who saw the point of the joke, was much mortified, but, like a sensible man, he was not less frequent in his visits to M. de Lauzun after this; but the patient cut short his visits, and would not understand the language he spoke.

Another day, while he was still very ill, Biron and his wife made bold to enter his room on tiptoe, and kept behind his curtains, out of sight, as they thought; but he perceived them by means of the glass on the chimney- piece. Lauzun liked Biron tolerably well, but Madame Biron not at all; she was, nevertheless, his niece, and his principal heiress; he thought her mercenary, and all her manners insupportable to him. In that he was like the rest of the world. He was shocked by this unscrupulous entrance into his chamber, and felt that, impatient for her inheritance, she came in order to make sure of it, if he should die directly. He wished to make her repent of this, and to divert himself at her expense. He begins, therefore; to utter aloud, as though believing himself alone, an ejaculatory orison, asking pardon of God for his past life, expressing himself as though persuaded his death was nigh, and saying that, grieved at his inability to do penance, he wishes at least to make use of all the wealth he possesses, in order to redeem his sins, and bequeath that wealth to the hospitals without any reserve; says it is the sole road to salvation left to him by God, after having passed a long life without thinking of the future; and thanks God for this sole resource left him, which he adopts with all his heart!

He accompanied this resolution with a tone so touched, so persuaded, so determined, that Biron and his wife did not doubt for a moment he was going to execute his design, or that they should be deprived of all the succession. They had no desire to spy any more, and went, confounded, to the Duchesse de Lauzun, to relate to her the cruel decree they had just heard pronounced, conjuring her to try and moderate it. Thereupon the patient sent for the notaries, and Madame Biron believed herself lost. It was exactly the design of the testator to produce this idea. He made the notaries wait; then allowed them to enter, and dictated his will, which was a death-blow to Madame de Biron. Nevertheless, he delayed signing it, and finding himself better and better, did not sign it at all. He was much diverted with this farce, and could not restrain his laughter at it, when reestablished. Despite his age, and the gravity of his illness, he was promptly cured and restored to his usual health.

He was internally as strong as a lion, though externally very delicate. He dined and supped very heartily every day of an excellent and very delicate cheer, always with good company, evening and morning; eating of everything, 'gras' and 'maigre', with no choice except that of his taste and no moderation. He took chocolate in the morning, and had always on the table the fruits in season, and biscuits; at other times beer, cider, lemonade, and other similar drinks iced; and as he passed to and fro, ate and drank at this table every afternoon, exhorting others to do the same. In this way he left table or the fruit, and immediately went to bed.

I recollect that once, among others, he ate at my house, after his illness, so much fish, vegetables, and all sorts of things (I having no power to hinder him), that in the evening we quietly sent to learn whether he had not felt the effects of them. He was found at table eating with good appetite.

His gallantry was long faithful to him. Mademoiselle was jealous of it, and that often controlled him. I have heard Madame de Fontenelles (a very enviable woman, of much intelligence, very truthful, and of singular virtue), I have heard her say, that being at Eu with Mademoiselle, M. de Lauzun came there and could not desist from running after the girls; Mademoiselle knew it, was angry, scratched him, and drove him from her presence. The Comtesse de Fiesque reconciled them. Mademoiselle appeared at the end of a long gallery; Lauzun was at the other end, and he traversed the whole length of it on his knees until he reached the feet of Mademoiselle. These scenes, more or less moving, often took place afterwards. Lauzun allowed himself to be beaten, and in his turn soundly beat Mademoiselle; and this happened several times, until at last, tired of each other, they quarrelled once for all and never saw each other again; he kept several portraits of her, however, in his house or upon him, and never spoke of her without much respect. Nobody doubted they had been secretly married. At her death he assumed a livery almost black, with silver lace; this he changed into white with a little blue upon gold, when silver was prohibited upon liveries.

His temper, naturally scornful and capricious, rendered more so by prison and solitude, had made him a recluse and dreamer; so that having in his house the best of company, he left them to Madame de Lauzun, and withdrew alone all the afternoon, several hours running, almost always without books, for he read only a few works of fancy—a very few—and without sequence; so that he knew nothing except what he had seen, and until the last was exclusively occupied with the Court and the news of the great world. I have a thousand times regretted his radical incapacity to write down what he had seen and done. It would have been a treasure of the most curious anecdotes, but he had no perseverance, no application. I have often tried to draw from him some morsels. Another misfortune. He began to relate; in the recital names occurred of people who had taken part in what he wished to relate. He instantly quitted the principal object of the story in order to hang on to one of these persons, and immediately after to some other person connected with the first, then to a third, in the manner of the romances; he threaded through a dozen histories at once, which made him lose ground and drove him from one to the other without ever finishing anything; and with this his words were very confused, so that it was impossible to learn anything from him or retain anything he said. For the rest, his conversation was always constrained by caprice or policy; and was amusing only by starts, and by the malicious witticisms which sprung out of it. A few months after his last illness, that is to say, when he was more than ninety years of age, he broke in his horses and made a hundred passades at the Bois de Boulogne (before the King, who was going to the Muette), upon a colt he had just trained, surprising the spectators by his address, his firmness, and his grace. These details about him might go on for ever.

His last illness came on without warning, almost in a moment, with the most horrible of all ills, a cancer in the mouth. He endured it to the last with incredible patience and firmness, without complaint, without spleen, without the slightest repining; he was insupportable to himself. When he saw his illness somewhat advanced, he withdrew into a little apartment (which he had hired with this object in the interior of the Convent of the Petits Augustins, into which there was an entrance from his house) to die in repose there, inaccessible to Madame de Biron and every other woman, except his wife, who had permission to go in at all hours, followed by one of her attendants.

Into this retreat Lauzun gave access only to his nephews and brothers-in- law, and to them as little as possible. He thought only of profiting by his terrible state, of giving all his time to the pious discourses of his confessor and of some of the pious people of the house, and to holy reading; to everything, in fact, which best could prepare him for death. When we saw him, no disorder, nothing lugubrious, no trace of suffering, politeness, tranquillity, conversation but little animated, indifference to what was passing in the world, speaking of it little and with difficulty; little or no morality, still less talk of his state; and this uniformity, so courageous and so peaceful, was sustained full four months until the end; but during the last ten or twelve days he would see neither brothers-in-law nor nephews, and as for his wife, promptly dismissed her. He received all the sacraments very edifyingly, and preserved his senses to the last moment: The morning of the day during the night of which he died, he sent for Biron, said he had done for him all that Madame de Lauzun had wished; that by his testament he gave him all his wealth, except a trifling legacy to the son of his other sister, and some recompenses to his domestics; that all he had done for him since his marriage, and what he did in dying, he (Biron) entirely owed to Madame de Lauzun; that he must never forget the gratitude he owed her; that he prohibited him, by the authority of uncle and testator, ever to cause her any trouble or annoyance, or to have any process against her, no matter of what kind. It was Biron himself who told me this the next day, in the terms I have given. M. de Lauzun said adieu to him in a firm tone, and dismissed him. He prohibited, and reasonably, all ceremony; he was buried at the Petits Augustins; he had nothing from the King but the ancient company of the battle-axes, which was suppressed two days after. A month before his death he had sent for Dillon (charged here with the affairs of King James, and a very distinguished officer general), to whom he surrendered his collar of the Order of the Garter, and a George of onyx, encircled with perfectly beautiful and large diamonds, to be sent back to the Prince.

I perceive at last, that I have been very prolix upon this man, but the extraordinary singularity of his life, and my close connexion with him, appear to me sufficient excuses for making him known, especially as he did not sufficiently figure in general affairs to expect much notice in the histories that will appear. Another sentiment has extended my recital. I am drawing near a term I fear to reach, because my desires cannot be in harmony with the truth; they are ardent, consequently gainful, because the other sentiment is terrible, and cannot in any way be palliated; the terror of arriving there has stopped me—nailed me where I was—frozen me.

It will easily be seen that I speak of the death (and what a death!) of M. le Duc d'Orleans; and this frightful recital, especially after such a long attachment (it lasted all his life, and will last all mine), penetrates me with terror and with grief for him. The Regent had said, when he died he should like to die suddenly: I shudder to my very marrow, with the horrible suspicion that God, in His anger, granted his desire.

CHAPTER CXIX

The new chateau of Meudon, completely furnished, had been restored to me since the return of the Court to Versailles, just as I had had it before the Court came to Meudon. The Duc and Duchesse d'Humieres were with us there, and good company. One morning towards the end of October, 1723, the Duc d'Humieres wished me to conduct him to Versailles, to thank M. le Duc d'Orleans.

We found the Regent dressing in the vault he used as his wardrobe. He was upon his chair among his valets, and one or two of his principal officers. His look terrified me. I saw a man with hanging head, a purple-red complexion, and a heavy stupid air. He did not even see me approach. His people told him. He slowly turned his head towards me, and asked me with a thick tongue what brought me. I told him. I had intended to pass him to come into the room where he dressed himself, so as not to keep the Duc d'Humieres waiting; but I was so astonished that I stood stock still.

I took Simiane, first gentleman of his chamber, into a window, and testified to him my surprise and my fear at the state in which I saw M. le Duc d'Orleans.

Simiane replied that for a long time he had been so in the morning; that to-day there was nothing extraordinary about him, and that I was surprised simply because I did not see him at those hours; that nothing would be seen when he had shaken himself a little in dressing. There was still, however, much to be seen when he came to dress himself. The Regent received the thanks of the Duc d'Humieres with an astonished and heavy air; he who always was so gracious and so polite to everybody, and who so well knew how to express himself, scarcely replied to him! A moment after, M. d'Humieres and I withdrew. We dined with the Duc de Gesvres, who led him to the King to thank his Majesty.

The condition of M. le Duc d'Orleans made me make many reflections. For a very long time the Secretaries of State had told me that during the first hours of the morning they could have made him pass anything they wished, or sign what might have been the most hurtful to him. It was the fruit of his suppers. Within the last year he himself had more than once told me that Chirac doctored him unceasingly, without effect; because he was so full that he sat down to table every evening without hunger, without any desire to eat, though he took nothing in the morning, and simply a cup of chocolate between one and two o'clock in the day (before everybody), it being then the time to see him in public. I had not kept dumb with him thereupon, but all my representations were perfectly useless. I knew moreover, that Chirac had continually told him that the habitual continuance of his suppers would lead him to apoplexy, or dropsy on the chest, because his respiration was interrupted at times; upon which he had cried out against this latter malady, which was a slow, suffocating, annoying preparation for death, saying that he preferred apoplexy, which surprised and which killed at once, without allowing time to think of it!

Another man, instead of crying out against this kind of death with which he was menaced, and of preferring another, allowing him no time for reflection, would have thought about leading a sober, healthy, and decent life, which, with the temperament he had, would have procured him a very long time, exceeding agreeable in the situation—very probably durable— in which he found himself; but such was the double blindness of this unhappy prince.

I was on terms of much intimacy with M. de Frejus, and since, in default of M. le Duc d'Orleans, there must be another master besides the King, until he could take command, I preferred this prelate to any other. I went to him, therefore, and told him what I had seen this morning of the state of M. le Duc d'Orleans. I predicted that his death must soon come, and that it would arrive suddenly, without warning. I counselled Frejus, therefore, to have all his arrangements ready with the King, in order to fill up the Regent's place of prime minister when it should become vacant. M. de Frejus appeared very grateful for the advice, but was measured and modest as though he thought the post much above him!

On the 22nd of December, 1723, I went from Meudon to Versailles to see M. le Duc d'Orleans; I was three-quarters of an hour with him in his cabinet, where I had found him alone. We walked to and fro there, talking of affairs of which he was going to give an account to the King that day. I found no difference in him, his state was, as usual, languid and heavy, as it had been for some time, but his judgment was clear as ever. I immediately returned to Meudon, and chatted there some time with Madame de Saint-Simon on arriving. On account of the season we had little company. I left Madame de Saint-Simon in her cabinet, and went into mine.

About an hour after, at most, I heard cries and a sudden uproar. I ran out and I found Madame de Saint-Simon quite terrified, bringing to me a groom of the Marquis de Ruffec, who wrote to me from Versailles, that M. le Duc d'Orleans was in a apoplectic fit. I was deeply moved, but not surprised; I had expected it, as I have shown, for a long time. I impatiently waited for my carriage, which was a long while coming, on account of the distance of the new chateau from the stables. I flung myself inside; and was driven as fast as possible.

At the park gate I met another courier from M. de Ruffec, who stopped me, and said it was all over. I remained there more than half an hour absorbed in grief and reflection. At the end I resolved to go to Versailles, and shut myself up in my rooms; I learnt there the particulars of the event.

M. le Duc d'Orleans had everything prepared to go and work with the King. While waiting the hour, he chatted with Madame Falari, one of his mistresses. They were close to each other, both seated in armchairs, when suddenly he fell against her, and never from that moment had the slightest glimmer of consciousness.

La Falari, frightened as much as may be imagined, cried with all her might for help, and redoubled her cries. Seeing that nobody replied, she supported as best she could this poor prince upon the contiguous arms of the two chairs, ran into the grand cabinet, into the chamber, into the ante-chambers, without finding a soul; finally, into the court and the lower gallery. It was the hour at which M. le Duc d'Orleans worked with the King, an hour when people were sure no one would come and see him, and that he had no need of them, because he ascended to the King's room by the little staircase from his vault, that is to say his wardrobe. At last La Falari found somebody, and sent the first who came to hand for help. Chance; or rather providence, had arranged this sad event at a time when everybody was ordinarily away upon business or visits, so that a full half-hour elapsed before doctor or surgeon appeared, and about as long before any domestics of M. le Duc d'Orleans could be found.

As soon as the faculty had examined the Regent; they judged his case hopeless. He was hastily extended upon the floor, and bled, but he gave not the slightest sign of life, do what they might to him. In an instant, after the first announcement, everybody flocked to the spot; the great and the little cabinet were full of people. In less than two hours all was over, and little by little the solitude became as great as the crowd had been. As soon as assistance came, La Falari flew away and gained Paris as quickly as possible.

La Vrilliere was one of the first who learnt of the attack of apoplexy. He instantly ran and informed the King and the Bishop of Frejus. Then M. le Duc, like a skilful courtier, resolved to make the best of his time; he at once ran home and drew up at all hazards the patent appointing M. le Duc prime minister, thinking it probable that that prince would be named. Nor was he deceived. At the first intelligence of apoplexy, Frejus proposed M. le Duc to the King, having probably made his arrangements in advance. M. le Duc arrived soon after, and entered the cabinet where he saw the King, looking very sad, his eyes red and tearful.

Scarcely had he entered than Frejus said aloud to the King, that in the loss he had sustained by the death of M. le Duc d'Orleans (whom he very briefly eulogised), his Majesty could not do better than beg M. le Duc, there present, to charge himself with everything, and accept the post of prime minister M. le Duc d'Orleans had filled. The King, without saying a word, looked at Frejus, and consented by a sign of the head, and M. le Duc uttered his thanks.

La Vrilliere, transported with joy at the prompt policy he had followed, had in his pocket the form of an oath taken by the prime minister, copied from that taken by M. le Duc d'Orleans, and proposed to Frejus to administer it immediately. Frejus proposed it to the King as a fitting thing, and M. le Duc instantly took it. Shortly after, M. le Duc went away; the crowd in the adjoining rooms augmented his suite, and in a moment nothing was talked of but M. le Duc.

M. le Duc de Chartres (the Regent's son), very awkward, but a libertine, was at Paris with an opera dancer he kept. He received the courier which brought him the news of the apoplexy, and on the road (to Versailles), another with the news of death. Upon descending from his coach, he found no crowd, but simply the Duc de Noailles, and De Guiche, who very 'apertement' offered him their services, and all they could do for him. He received them as though they were begging-messengers whom he was in a hurry to get rid of, bolted upstairs to his mother, to whom he said he had just met two men who wished to bamboozle him, but that he had not been such a fool as to let them. This remarkable evidence of intelligence, judgment, and policy, promised at once all that this prince has since performed. It was with much trouble he was made to comprehend that he had acted with gross stupidity; he continued, nevertheless, to act as before.

He was not less of a cub in the interview I shortly afterwards had with him. Feeling it my duty to pay a visit of condolence to Madame la Duchesse d'Orleans, although I had not been on terms of intimacy with her for a long while, I sent a message to her to learn whether my presence would be agreeable. I was told that Madame la Duchesse d'Orleans would be very glad to see me. I accordingly immediately went to her.

I found her in bed, with a few ladies and her chief officers around, and M. le Duc de Chartres making decorum do double duty for grief. As soon as I approached her she spoke to me of the grievous misfortune—not a word of our private differences. I had stipulated thus. M. le Duc de Chartres went away to his own rooms. Our dragging conversation I put an end to as soon as possible.

From Madame la Duchesse d'Orleans I went to M. le Duc de Chartres. He occupied the room his father had used before being Regent. They told me he was engaged. I went again three times during the same morning. At the last his valet de chambre was ashamed, and apprised him of my visit, in despite of me. He came across the threshold of the door of his cabinet, where he had been occupied with some very common people; they were just the sort of people suited to him.

I saw a man before me stupefied and dumfounded, not afflicted, but so embarrassed that he knew not where he was. I paid him the strongest, the clearest, the most energetic of compliments, in a loud voice. He took me, apparently, for some repetition of the Ducs de Guiche and de Noailles, and did not do me the honour to reply one word.

I waited some moments, and seeing that nothing would come out of the mouth of this image, I made my reverence and withdrew, he advancing not one step to conduct me, as he ought to have done, all along his apartment, but reburying himself in his cabinet. It is true that in retiring I cast my eyes upon the company, right and left, who appeared to me much surprised. I went home very weary of dancing attendance at the chateau.

The death of M. le Duc d'Orleans made a great sensation abroad and at home; but foreign countries rendered him incomparably more justice, and regretted him much more, than the French. Although foreigners knew his feebleness, and although the English had strangely abused it, their experience had not the less persuaded them of the range of his mind, of the greatness of his genius and of his views, of his singular penetration, of the sagacity and address of his policy, of the fertility of his expedients and of his resources, of the dexterity of his conduct under all changes of circumstances and events, of his clearness in considering objects and combining things; of his superiority over his ministers, and over those that various powers sent to him; of the exquisite discernment he displayed in investigating affairs; of his learned ability in immediately replying to everything when he wished. The majority of our Court did not regret him, however. The life he had led displeased the Church people; but more still, the treatment they had received from his hands.

The day after death, the corpse of M. le Duc d'Orleans was taken from Versailles to Saint-Cloud, and the next day the ceremonies commenced. His heart was carried from Saint-Cloud to the Val de Grace by the Archbishop of Rouen, chief almoner of the defunct Prince. The burial took place at Saint-Denis, the funeral procession passing through Paris, with the greatest pomp. The obsequies were delayed until the 12th of February. M. le Duc de Chartres became Duc d'Orleans.

After this event, I carried out a determination I had long resolved on. I appeared before the new masters of the realm as seldom as possible— only, in fact, upon such occasions where it would have been inconsistent with my position to stop away. My situation at the Court had totally changed. The loss of the dear Prince, the Duc de Bourgogne, was the first blow I had received. The loss of the Regent was the second. But what a wide gulf separated these two men!

Made in the USA
San Bernardino, CA
19 December 2016